**THOMSON**

**SOUTH-WESTERN**

**Fraud Examination, 2nd Edition**
W. Steve Albrecht, Conan C. Albrecht, Chad O. Albrecht

**VP/Editorial Director**
Jack W. Calhoun

**Publisher**
Rob Dewey

**Sr. Acquisitions Editor**
Sharon Oblinger

**Associate Developmental Editor**
Allison Haden Rolfes

**Marketing Manager**
Keith Chassé

**Sr. Production Editor**
Tim Bailey

**Technology Project Editor**
Kelly Reid

**Manufacturing Coordinator**
Doug Wilke

**Art Director**
Chris A. Miller

**Cover and Internal Designer**
Knapke Design

**Production**
Electro-Publishing

**Printer**
Transcontinental Printing
Louisville, Canada

Library of Congress Control Number:
2004114000

For more information about our products, contact us at:

Thomson Learning Academic Resource Center

1-800-423-0563

**Thomson Higher Education**
5191 Natorp Boulevard
Mason, OH 45040
USA

**Asia (including India)**
Thomson Learning
5 Shenton Way
#01-01 UIC Building
Singapore 068808

**Australia/New Zealand**
Thomson Learning Australia
102 Dodds Street
Southbank, Victoria 3006
Australia

**Canada**
Thomson Nelson
1120 Birchmount Road
Toronto, Ontario
M1K 5G4
Canada

**Latin America**
Thomson Learning
Seneca, 53
Colonia Polanco
11560 Mexico
D.F.Mexico

**UK/Europe/Middle East/Africa**
Thomson Learning
High Holborn House
50/51 Bedford Row
London WC1R 4LR
United Kingdom

**Spain (including Portugal)**
Thomson Paraninfo
Calle Magallanes, 25
28015 Madrid, Spain

# FRAUD EXAMINATION

## 2ND EDITION

**W. STEVE ALBRECHT**

Brigham Young University

**CONAN C. ALBRECHT**

Brigham Young University

**CHAD O. ALBRECHT**

**THOMSON**

™

**SOUTH-WESTERN**

Australia · Canada · Mexico · Singapore · Spain · United Kingdom · United States

*To*
*LeAnn, Laurel, and Jenny*

# ABOUT THE AUTHORS

W. Steve Albrecht is the Associate Dean of the Marriott School of Management and Arthur Andersen LLP Alumni Professor at Brigham Young University. His interest in fraud examination began about 25 years ago, when he was part of a research team that studied ways to better detect fraud. Since that time, he has written over 50 academic articles on fraud as well as several books and training courses for the AICPA and others.

Earlier in his career, Dr. Steve Albrecht decided that he needed to get some "hands-on" investigative experience, rather than just approach the topic from an academic perspective. For a period of approximately six years, he worked closely with a Fortune 500 corporation, helping them coordinate fraud investigations and participating in those investigations. Since then, he has consulted with many other corporations in the areas of fraud prevention, fraud detection, and fraud investigation. Some of his work in the fraud area has involved interviewing actual fraud perpetrators.

Dr. Steve Albrecht has been an expert witness in some of the largest fraud cases ever, including a current case totaling $3 billion. Dr. Steve Albrecht teaches frequently for the FBI and other governmental organizations, and he is a highly requested speaker on fraud-related topics all over the world. Steve was the first president of the Association of Certified Fraud Examiners (ACFE), was a member of COSO for four years, was on the AICPA task force that wrote SAS 82, and has served in several other fraud-related capacities with numerous organizations. In August 1998, he received the ACFE's Cressey Award the highest award given for achievement in fraud detection and deterrence. He has been named as one of the top 100 accountants in the U.S. in 1998, 1999, 2001, 2002, and 2003 by *Accounting Today*.

Dr. Steve Albrecht received his undergraduate degree in accounting from Brigham Young University, and his MBA and Ph.D. degrees from the University of Wisconsin at Madison. His writing also includes a financial accounting text and a principles of accounting text, both of which are in their ninth editions. With Robert Sack, he completed a major study (Accounting Education: Charting the Course through a Perilous Future) on the future of accounting education in the United States.

*Conan C. Albrecht* is a professor of Information Systems and eBusiness Fellow at Brigham Young University. He teaches classes in enterprise development, middleware, and network programming. Dr. Conan Albrecht actively researches fraud detection techniques and online group dynamics. Dr. Conan Albrecht previously held a faculty position as the Director of Programming for the Center for the Management of Information for the University of Arizona. He continues today as research associate with the UA.

Dr. Conan Albrecht has published articles on fraud detection and information theory in *The Journal of Forensic Accounting, The Journal of Accounting, The Communications of the ACM, Decision Support Systems, Information and Management*, and many other academic and professional outlets.

Dr. Conan Albrecht is an active programmer in the open source community. He has developed many open source applications and web sites, including EasyScout.org, AuctionSam.com, and Picalo.org. Dr. Conan Albrecht is actively developing two applications, Picalo and GroupMind. Picalo is a framework for the development of fraud-related analysis routines—free for use by fraud detectors anywhere. GroupMind is a groupware application that uses DHTML to create dynamic, interactive web interfaces for group meetings. Dr. Conan Albrecht teaches ACFE members how to detect fraud using technology at several seminars per year.

Chad O. Albrecht graduated from BYU in 2004 with his B.S. in accounting. For many years, he has had a strong interest in fraud prevention, detection and investigation. He has applied and been accepted into the Ph.D. Program in Management at one of the top European Universities. His goal is to teach international business and fraud-related courses from a management and behavioral perspective. As a former student of our fraud class at BYU, Chad made sure that the book was written in a student-friendly way.

In addition to coauthoring the first and second editions of this book, Chad has the following publications:

Albrecht, W. Steve, and Chad O. Albrecht, *Fraud Examination and Prevention*, Thomson South-Western, Cincinnati, Ohio, 2004.

Albrecht, W. Steve, Chad O. Albrecht, and Conan C. Albrecht, *Maximizing Options*, forthcoming in *Personal Excellence*.

Albrecht, Chad O., W. Steve Albrecht, Conan C. Albrecht, and Timothy Williams, *Conducting Ethical Investigations*, forthcoming in *Security Management*.

Albrecht, Conan C., W. Steve Albrecht, and Chad O. Albrecht, *Fraud and Corporate Executives: Agency, Stewardship and Broken Trust, Journal of Forensic Accounting*, Volume V, Number 1, January–June 2004, pp. 109–130.

Albrecht, Chad O., ORCA: Research and Creative Activities, *A Key Ingredient in Fraud Detection: The Net Worth Method*, Brigham Young University, 2001.

# BRIEF CONTENTS

# CONTENTS

## PART THREE: FRAUD DETECTION, 121

## PART SIX: OTHER TYPES OF FRAUD, 483

### CHAPTER 14  CONSUMER FRAUD, 485

# FORWARD

According to the Association of Certified Fraud Examiners' 2004 Report to the Nation on Occupational Fraud and Abuse, organizations lose, on average, about 6 percent of their revenues to dishonesty from within.

If multiplied by the U.S. Gross Domestic Product, the cost of occupational fraud and abuse may run a staggering $660 billion annually. By the breadth of the definition, it covers all corporate dishonesty—from the mailroom to the boardroom. While executives are "cooking" the company's earnings to show better profits, purchasing agents are getting kickbacks from suppliers, and employees are embezzling money to improve their lifestyles.

Knowing how much fraud actually costs is a difficult—if not impossible—task. The cases we know about only represent the tip of the iceberg; those discovered tend to be greedy or careless. Executives and employees who are neither may well commit fraud throughout their entire careers and get away with it.

The huge cost of occupational fraud begs an obvious question: Why does it occur? The answers aren't always easy. Although the simple answer is greed — it's a natural human trait — even greedy people don't always lie, cheat, and steal. A more complete answer for corporate dishonesty involves three factors: the individual, the workplace, and society.

Individuals likely to commit occupational fraud are often on the financial ropes. This can occur when people spend more money than they make or when there is a personal financial crisis demanding immediate resolution. Although many of us have had such difficult situations, dishonest employees are more likely to salve their consciences with rationalizations that justify fraud. In short, they lack the convictions of their own ethics.

Workplace environments also contribute to occupational fraud. Organizations that are viewed by employees as uncaring, stingy, or dishonest run a much higher risk of being victimized from within. Many workers—in an attempt to right what they consider to be corporate wrongs—address these perceived injustices in a variety of ways: goldbricking, excessive absences, pilferage, and dishonesty.

Moreover, some entities unwittingly contribute to the problem. By failing to establish reasonable safeguards and controls, companies make fraud too easy, and thus too tempting. Organizations have a duty to help keep the workforce honest. Societal conditions also influence the rate of occupational fraud. If dishonesty is easily accepted and goes largely unpunished, we can only expect it to thrive.

It was my own search for answers to occupational fraud over a decade ago that led me to W. Steve Albrecht. In the mid-1980s, after ten years with the FBI, I practiced as a fraud examiner. Increasingly, my corporate clients were referring me cases of embezzlement, corruption, and other misdeeds.

One client, certainly on the cutting-edge at the time, wanted help in developing an anti-fraud program. That request led me to the vast libraries of the University of Texas at Austin, where I discovered one of Dr. Albrecht's first published works on the subject, *Deterring Fraud: The Internal Auditor's Perspective.*

After reading this seminal research by Steve and his colleagues, I sought him out personally. Even though Steve had never heard my name, he graciously answered my questions and volunteered his valuable time to aid in further research on the topic of occupational fraud. After that, we stayed in touch.

Neither of us at that time could have imagined the paths our lives would take together. In 1988, Steve was a major influence in encouraging me to start the Association of Certified Fraud Examiners, and he served with distinction as its first president.

Since that time, the ACFE has grown to more than 30,000 members in over 120 countries. Steve's lifetime of contributions to the field of fraud detection and deterrence simply cannot be overstated. The ACFE recognized the enormity of Dr. Albrecht's body of work in 1998 when it honored him with its most valued prize: the Cressey Award.

However, the many awards Steve has received may not capture the kind of man he is. A devoted father and husband, Steve lives his life by high example. Regardless of his many accomplishments, you won't hear about them from him; humility is one of his most endearing traits. I am proud to call Steve Albrecht my friend.

Steve and I are of a common mind when it comes to fraud. First, the accounting community, which has the lion's share of responsibility to control occupational fraud, is ill-equipped for the job. Second, education is the cornerstone to preventing fraud. The more we know, the less likely we are to become victims.

The terms "fraud examination" and "forensic accounting" are often used interchangeably. However, they refer to different but overlapping concepts. The latter phrase, although highly popular as a euphemism for fraud investigation, actually refers to any kind of accounting work done for litigation purposes.

According to the *Fraud Examiners Manual*, fraud examination is a methodology for resolving allegations of fraud from inception to disposition. The process involves gathering evidence, taking statements, writing reports, and assisting in the detection and deterrence of fraud. Although many organizations employ fraud examiners, audit professionals and others also conduct fraud examinations on a limited, as-needed basis. The fraud examination field draws its common body of knowledge from four areas: accounting and auditing, fraud investigation techniques, the legal elements of fraud, and criminology and ethics.

For accountants, anti-fraud education has been practically non-existent for decades. One of the main reasons has been the lack of authoritative texts on the subject. Educators and students alike will find *Fraud Examination* to be a solution. Packed full of real examples, thought-provoking discussion issues and questions, this book is ideal for both undergraduate and graduate students.

Moreover, practitioners will find a great deal of guidance in resolving current cases. Managers and executives will benefit from understanding the myriad of issues that can assist them in deterring occupational fraud. And for all of us, *Fraud Examination* is a wonderfully engaging read.

Joseph T. Wells, CFE, CPA
Chairman of the Board of Directors
The Association of Certified Fraud Examiners
Austin, Texas
jwells@cfenet.com
http://www.cfenet.com/home.asp

# PREFACE

Fraud examination (sometimes called forensic accounting) is one of the most exciting careers for students studying accounting and business today. The AICPA has called forensic accounting one of the seven hot new "sizzling" career areas in accounting. It is estimated that there will be a shortage of between 25,000 and 50,000 security professionals in the next few years in the United States. Exciting opportunities for accounting and business students who become knowledgeable in fraud prevention, detection, and investigation abound in various federal agencies, such as the FBI and Postal Inspectors, major corporations, and professional service and consulting firms. Both the size and the number of frauds is increasing, which will result in an even greater demand for fraud-fighting professionals in the future.

You've probably heard about Enron, WorldCom and other major management frauds. But, there are many other types of frauds that occur every day. Fraud is an extremely costly business problem. For example, not long ago a Fortune 500 automaker experienced a $436 million fraud. Because the fraud reduced the company's net income by $436 million from what it would have been and because the company had a profit margin (net income divided by net sales) of approximately 10 percent, the company would have to generate an additional $4.36 billion (10 times the amount lost in the fraud) in revenues to restore net income to its pre-fraud level. And, if you assume that an average car sells for $20,000, this company would have to make and sell an additional 218,000 cars ($4.36 billion divided by $20,000 sales price) to recover the effect on net income. In other words, this company faced a major business problem: it could either make and sell 218,000 more cars, or it could work hard to prevent these types of frauds from occurring in the future. When faced with the choice of generating that much additional revenue, which would have been difficult if not impossible, the company decided that reducing and eliminating future frauds was the more effective way to spend its money. As a result, it hired additional fraud and control experts and implemented extensive fraud prevention procedures. Eliminating fraud is a problem that every organization faces, and you can help them deal with this growing problem.

Even if you decide not to become a fraud expert, the topics you will study in this course will help you be a better professional in whatever career path you choose. The technology, interviewing, document examination, public records, and other tools you will study will make you a better consultant, auditor, tax professional, or manager, as well as a better and more astute investor.

As you will discover in this book, there is also a very active professional organization that deals with fighting fraud called the Association of Certified Fraud Examiners (ACFE), which currently has about 30,000 members and is based in Austin, Texas. This organization, as well as others, can provide future fraud training. In addition, the ACFE will provide its educational materials free of charge to educators who teach fraud examination topics. These materials include 12 original videos of interviews with actual white-collar criminals. Most of the videos are in two 25-minute segments, for a total of 50 minutes in length. A complete listing of the ACFE's materials and other information can be found at the Association's Web site at http://www.cfenet.com/home.asp.

## New To This Edition

For our second edition, we have added enhancements and updates that will help you better understand the significance of fraud in the modern accounting world:

- Chapter 6 now contains a major new appendix concerning the use of data analysis to detect fraud. Chapter 7, with the topics of investigating theft and concealment, has been broken out into two chapters in order to greatly expand on both parts.
- Chapter 14 is a new chapter on consumer fraud, and Chapter 16 (formerly Chapter 14) contains information about tax fraud.

- We have also significantly enhanced the end-of-chapter materials by adding new extrended cases to each chapter, and we have updated the Financial Statement Fraud Standards Appendix at the end of the text to include information about SAS 99 and Sarbanes-Oxley.
- We have made many other significant changes throughout the book to make it more current and broader in scope.

## Featured Topics by Chapter

In this book, we cover seven different topics:

- Part 1, comprising Chapters 1, 2, and 3, provides an introduction to fraud and an overview of the fraud problem. Chapter 1 discusses the nature of fraud, Chapter 2 describes fraud perpetrators and their motivations for being dishonest, and Chapter 3 provides an overview of the different ways to fight and, hopefully, reduce fraud.
- The second and third parts of the book focus on fraud prevention (Chapter 4) and fraud detection (Chapters 5 and 6.) Chapter 5 provides an overview of and discusses traditional fraud detection methods, while Chapter 6 introduces you to the use of technology to proactively detect fraud.
- Part 4 covers the various elements of fraud investigation. In Chapter 7, we cover theft act investigation methods; in chapter 8, we cover concealment investigation methods; in Chapter 9, we discuss conversion investigative methods; and in Chapter 10, we cover various types of interviewing and other query approaches to investigating fraud. The interview techniques you learn in Chapter 10 will make you a more discerning husband or wife, parent, manager, employee, or friend.
- Parts 5 and 6 discuss various types of fraud. In Part 5, we include three chapters on management, or financial statement, fraud. In Chapter 11, we provide an overview of financial statement fraud and introduce a proactive model for detecting fraud in the financial statements. In Chapter 12 we discuss both revenue- and inventory-related frauds, the two most common ways to manipulate financial statements. In Chapter 13, we discuss three other types of financial statement frauds: understating liabilities and expenses, overstating assets, and inadequate disclosures. These chapters will help you better understand and critique the financial statements of any organization. In Part 6, we discuss four other types of fraud. Chapter 14 covers consumer fraud, a chapter that will have immediate relevance to you and will alert you to the fraud exposures you face everyday.
- Chapter 15 covers fraud committed against organizations by employees, vendors, and customers. Chapter 16 introduces divorce, tax and bankruptcy fraud, all of which are very common because people often try to hide assets from those who want to take them away—the government in the case of taxes and others in the cases of divorce and bankruptcy. Chapter 17 discusses e-Business frauds, a new and growing type of fraud problem because of the increasing use of the Internet to conduct business.
- The final part in the book includes only Chapter 18 and discusses options that victims have when deciding how to follow-up on frauds they experience. This chapter provides an overview of the criminal and civil statutes governing fraud legal proceedings and helps you understand the various ways organizations have to resolve dishonest acts.

We realize that there are many other fraud-related topics that we could have included. We have tried to strike a balance between brevity and topics of general interest and detailed investigation and specific knowledge that experienced professional fraud examiners would need. We also realize that, for most of you, this will be the only fraud-related course you will take in your college studies. We are certain, however, that it will be one of your most exciting and will spark an interest that will stimulate career-changing plans for some of you. At a minimum, after taking this course, you should be a much more careful investor and business decision maker. You will never view business transactions or reports the same way, and you will be a much more careful and skeptical observer and participant in future endeavors.

We are excited to share this exciting topic with you. We wish you success and enthusiasm as you study the pages of this book, and we welcome suggestions for improvement.

W. Steve Albrecht, Ph.D., CFE, CPA, CIA
Conan C. Albrecht, Ph.D.
Chad O. Albrecht

# ACKNOWLEDGMENTS

Several reviewers provided valuable comments on the manuscript for this book. They were:

Michael Blue
Bloomsburg University

Gayle Bolinger
Lebanon Valley College

Rich Brody
University of South Florida, St.
Petersburg

Thomas Buckoff
Buckoff, O-Halloran, and Eide
Bailly, LLP

John Byrd
St.Leo University

Kay Carnes
Gonzaga University

Russ Cheatham
Cumberland University

Freddie Choo
San Francisco State University

Gregory Claypool
Youngstown State University

Susann Cuperus
University of Mary

Todd DeZoort
University of Alabama

Bruce Dorris
Louisiana State University-
Shreveport

Danie du Plessis
University of Pretoria

Tom Frecka
University of Notre Dame

Ross Fuerman
Suffolk University

George Gardner
Bemidji State University

Lawrence Gramling
University of Connecticut

William Haslinger
Hilbert College

Steven R. Jackson
Loyola University of New
Orleans

Stanley Earl Jenne
The University of Montana

Kevan Jensen
University of Oklahoma

Tim Kizirian
Chico State University

Mark Lehman
Mississippi State University

Alan Lord
Bowling Green State University

Mark Morgan
Mississippi College and
Mississippi State Tax
Commission

Sherry Mills
New Mexico State University

Michael J. Palmiotto
Wichita State University

Deborah Pavelka
Roosevelt University

Bonita Peterson
Montana State University-
Bozeman

Barbara Reider
University of Montana

Gerald Smith
University of Northern Iowa

Leonard Stokes
Siena College

John Suroviak
Pacific University

Mark Taylor
University of South Carolina

Steve Teeter
Utah Valley State College

Bill Thomas
Baylor University

We are very grateful for the help of many other individuals who made this book possible. We appreciate the talented word processing help of Heather Hall, our secretary. We appreciate the able and talented editing of Sharon Oblinger, Ken Martin, Allison Rolfes, and Tim Bailey of South-Western. We also appreciate Brigham Young University for its support and for providing an environment of stimulation and challenge. Joseph T. Wells, Chairman of the Association of Certified Fraud Examiners (ACFE), has been inspiring and helpful in many ways. In this area of fraud examination, he has been our closest and most supportive friend. He and the ACFE have made their materials available to us in writing this book and, through their generous offer to support fraud education, will make their videos and other materials available to professors. Joseph Wells, through his work with the ACFE, has done more to fight fraud in the United States and the world than any other person we know. We also appreciate the help of valuable colleagues with whom we have collaborated previously. Gerald W. Wernz and Timothy L. Williams were co-authors on a previous book and several academic articles from which many ideas for this book were taken. Gregory J. Dunn has been a co-author on journal articles from which ideas have been taken as well. We are also grateful to the many law firms, professional service firms, corporations, and government organizations that have provided us with consulting and expert witnessing opportunities to enrich our fraud experience and background.

# PART ONE

## INTRODUCTION TO FRAUD

1

# CHAPTER 1

# THE NATURE OF FRAUD

## LEARNING OBJECTIVES

After studying this chapter, you should be able to:

1. Understand the seriousness of the fraud problem and how it affects individuals, consumers, and organizations.

2. Define fraud.

3. Classify frauds into various types.

4. Understand how expensive fraud is to a company, investors, and a nation.

5. Distinguish between criminal and civil fraud laws and how they relate to fraud.

6. Be familiar with the types of fraud-fighting careers available today.

*Enron is a multinational company that specializes in marketing electricity, natural gas, energy, and other physical commodities. Enron initiated the wholesale natural gas and electricity markets in the United States. It was officially formed in 1985 as a result of the merger of Houston Natural Gas and InterNorth of Omaha, Nebraska. In 2000, Enron reported revenues of $101 billion, making it the seventh largest U.S. company in terms of revenue. In 2000, Enron employed 21,000 employees and operated in more than 40 countries.*

*In October 2001, it was determined that a large financial statement fraud had been occurring at Enron and that revenues, income, and assets had been significantly overstated. Its stock price, which reached a high of $90 earlier in the year, dropped to less than $1 in a matter of days. Enron is still trying to struggle back after declaring one of the largest corporate bankruptcies in U.S. history. Since the scandal was discovered, numerous Enron officers have either plea bargained or pleaded guilty, and indictments have been issued against other corporate officers.[1] Arthur Andersen, Enron's auditor, has gone out of business, largely because of "destruction of evidence" charges brought against it by the U.S. government.*

*Enron, citing accounting errors, had to restate its financial statements, cutting profits for the three years 1999–2001 by about 20%, or approximately $586 million. Many of the lawsuits that have been filed against Enron and related parties allege that executives reaped personal gains from "off-the-book" partnerships, while the energy giant violated basic rules of accounting and ethics. As the accounting discrepancies became public knowledge, Enron investors lost billions of dollars, shattering their retirement plans.*

*In reacting to the Enron scandal, the American Institute of Certified Public Accountants (AICPA) released the following statement to all AICPA members:*

*Our profession enjoys a sacred public trust and for more than one hundred years has served the public interest. Yet, in a short period of time, the stain from Enron's collapse has eroded our most important asset: Public Confidence.[2]*

# Seriousness of the Fraud Problem

Enron is an example of a company whose management misrepresented the company and allegedly committed fraud. Financial statement fraud, like the Enron fraud, is just one of the many types of frauds that represent major problems for businesses throughout the world.

Although most people and even most researchers believe that fraud is increasing both in size and frequency, it is difficult to know for sure. First, it is impossible to know what percentage of fraud **perpetrators** are actually caught. Are perfect frauds perpetrated that are never detected, or are all frauds eventually discovered? In addition, many frauds that are detected are handled quietly by the victims and never made public. In many cases of employee fraud, for example, companies merely hide the frauds and quietly terminate or transfer perpetrators rather than make the frauds public.

Statistics on how much fraud is occurring, whether it is increasing or decreasing, and how much the average fraud costs come from four basic sources:

1. *Government agencies:* Agencies such as the Federal Bureau of Investigation (FBI), Federal Deposit Insurance Corporation (FDIC), Internal Revenue Service (IRS), or various health agencies publish fraud statistics from time to time, but only those statistics related to their **jurisdiction**. Generally, their statistics are not complete, are not collected randomly, and do not provide a total picture even of all the fraud in the areas for which they have responsibility.

2. *Researchers:* Researchers often conduct studies about particular types of fraud in particular industrial sectors. Unfortunately, data on actual frauds are difficult to get and, as a result, most research studies only provide small insights into the magnitude of the problem, even in the specific area being studied. Comprehensive research on the occurrence of fraud is rare and is not always based on sound scientific approaches.

3. *Insurance companies:* Insurance companies often provide fidelity bonding or other types of coverage against employee and other fraud. When fraud occurs, they undertake investigations and, as a result, have collected some fraud statistics. Generally, however, their statistics relate only to actual cases where they provided employee bonding or other insurance. At best, their analysis of the problem is incomplete.

4. *Victims of fraud:* Sometimes we learn about fraud from those who have been **victims**. Most industries do not have an organized way for victims to report fraud and, even if they did, many companies would choose not to make their fraud losses public.

The **Association of Certified Fraud Examiners (ACFE)** conducted one of the most comprehensive fraud studies ever undertaken in 1996 and then updated that study in 2002. The original study was based on voluntary reports of more than 2,600 frauds, while the 2002 update was based on 663 fraud cases reported by CFEs who investigated them. In its 1996 study, the ACFE estimated that fraud costs U.S. organizations more than $400 billion annually. It estimated that the average organization's fraud losses are more than $9 per day per employee, and that about 6 percent of a company's total annual revenue is lost to fraud of various types.[3]

In its 2002 study, the ACFE reaffirmed that 6 percent of revenues will be lost as a result of occupational fraud and abuse. Applied to the U.S. Gross Domestic Product (GDP), this percentage translates to losses of approximately $600 billion, or about $4,500 per employee. Even with the difficulties in measuring fraud, most people believe that fraud is a growing problem. Both the numbers of frauds committed and the total dollar amounts lost from fraud seem to be increasing. Because fraud affects how much we pay for goods and services, each of us pays not only a portion of the fraud bill but also for the detection and investigation of fraud. It is almost impossible to read a newspaper or business magazine without coming across multiple incidents of fraud. A recent issue of *The Wall Street Journal*, for example, contained five fraud-related stories (May 13, 2004) First was an article about the Securities and Exchange Commission (SEC) unveiling a settlement with Lucent detailing 10 instances of hidden side agreements, falsified documents, and lax internal controls, all part of a financial statement fraud at the company. Second, an article discussed a Pfizer unit that agreed to plead guilty to criminal wrongdoing with the parent company paying about $430 million in fines in a settlement over the marketing of its Neurontin drug to doctors for unapproved uses. The deal represents one of the largest-ever Medicaid-fraud settlements. The third article covered the restating of $5 billion in earnings at Freddie Mac and the ousting of its longtime chairman and CEO, Leland Brendsel, along with several other top executives. Fourth was an article about the Enron employees who lost money in their 40k(k) plans and how they will participate in an $85 million settlement of a class-action lawsuit following the fraud at Enron. Finally, an article about class-action lawyers told how they competed with gusto to get lead positions and cash in on the mutual fund scandals where leading U.S. mutual funds engaged in market timing and late trading frauds. And, in *The Wall Street Journal* the next day, an article appeared about a Philadelphia businessman who illegally moved $680 million through U.S. banks over nearly a decade, suggesting that the nation's financial system remains vulnerable to large-scale money laundering. The businessman, a Russian émigré named Michael Rakita, who officials say has ties to a suspected member of Russian organized crime, was indicted on illegal money-transmittal and money-laundering charges.

Many sources, including the FBI, have labeled fraud the fastest-growing crime. For years, the FBI's White-Collar Crime Program has been the largest and most diverse of all FBI criminal programs, which included organized crime/drugs, violent crimes, and civil rights. (Recent focus on national security and terrorism have probably changed the percentage of resources dedicated to various programs, although such statistics are not yet available.) The While-Collar Crime Program is a dynamic program and is changing at a rapid rate due to the globalization of communications, travel, business activities, and crime. During fiscal year 1998 (October 1, 1997 to September 30, 1998), for example, the White-Collar Crime Program used approximately 25 percent of FBI agent resources and achieved 36 percent of the FBI's total convictions (http://baltimore.fbi.gov/whitecol.htm, accessed on May 20, 2004).

Even more alarming than the increased number of fraud cases is the size of discovered frauds. In earlier times, if a thief wanted to steal from his or her employer, the perpetrator had to physically remove the assets from the business premise. Because of fear of being caught with the goods, frauds tended to be small. With the advent of computers, the Internet, and complex accounting systems, employees now need only make a telephone call, misdirect purchase invoices, bribe a supplier, manipulate a computer program, or simply push a key on the keyboard to misplace company assets. Because physical possession of stolen property is no longer required and because it is just as easy to program a computer to embezzle $1 million as it is $1,000, the size and number of frauds have increased tremendously.

In addition, as companies give in to the pressures to meet Wall Street's earnings expectations and as these pressures to "meet the numbers" intensifies, some large financial statement frauds are committed. Frauds totaling several hundred million or even billions of dollars are not unusual. In some cases, the decline in market value of the company's stock has been in the billions of dollars.

To understand how costly fraud is to organizations, consider what happens when fraud is committed against a company. Losses incurred from fraud reduce a firm's income on a dollar-for-dollar basis. This correlation means that for every $1 of fraud, **net income** is reduced by $1. Because fraud reduces net income, it takes significantly more **revenue** to recover the effect of the fraud on net income. To illustrate, consider the $436 million fraud loss that a U.S. automobile manufacturer experienced a few years ago.[4] If the automobile manufacturer's **profit margin** (net income divided by revenues) at the time was 10 percent, the company would have to generate up to $4.36 billion in additional revenue (or 10 times the amount of the fraud) to recover the effect on net income. If we assume an average selling price of $20,000 per car, the company must make and sell an additional 218,000 cars. Considered this way, fighting fraud is serious business. The automobile company can spend its efforts manufacturing and marketing additional new cars, or trying to reduce fraud, or a combination of both.

As another example, a large bank was the victim of frauds that totaled $100 million in one year. With a profit margin of 5 percent, and assuming that the bank made $100 per year per checking account, how many new checking accounts must the bank generate to compensate for the fraud losses? The answer, of course, is up to 20 million new checking accounts ($100 million fraud loss/0.05=$2 billion in additional revenues; $2 billion/$100 per account= 20 million new accounts).

Firms are not the only victims of fraud. In the aggregate, national economies also pick up the tab. Continuing the logic used previously, consider a fictitious economy comprised of only three firms. If Company A, whose profit margin is 10 percent, loses $500 million to fraud, it must generate $5 billion of additional revenue to offset the loss to net income. If Company B, whose profit margin is also 10 percent, loses $200 million to fraud, it must generate $2 billion. Finally, if Company C, whose profit margin is 5 percent, loses $100 million to fraud, it must also generate $2 billion. In all, an economy hit by $800 million of fraud must create $8 billion of additional revenue to recover the loss to aggregate income. The strain fraud imposes on the economy is tremendous. If just one fraud is prevented, billions of dollars of resources are saved; resources that can be invested in building the economy. Given this analysis, it is easy to see how difficult it is for countries with high amounts of corruption and fraud to ever compete with countries with low rates of corruption and fraud. Economists, lawmakers, and regulators can spend their efforts enhancing business and trade or trying to reduce fraud, all to the same end: growing their economies.

In today's global environment, economic performance has become a race against history, where national economies compete not only against each other but against their own previous performances. A growing economy is a healthy economy, and a stagnant economy is not only stagnant, it is also failing. Gross Domestic Product is the total dollar amount of all final goods and services produced in an economy; essentially, GDP represents aggregate income. As previously indicated, the Association of Certified Fraud Examiners estimates that U.S. organizations lose on average 6 percent of revenue to fraud, and that on the whole fraud in the United States is 6 percent of GDP. Thus, fraud, whether seen as decreasing revenue or increasing operating costs, adversely affects individual incomes and collective GDP.

Now assume that GDP in the fictitious economy described was $20 billion in the year prior to the frauds (year 1). If that economy were growing at 5 percent, its GDP in year 2 would have been $21 billion, but because the frauds reduce aggregate income by $800 million, GDP in year 2 is only $20.2 billion and the economy has grown by only 1 percent. If no frauds were committed in year 2 (and GDP had reached $21 billion), assuming a rate of growth of 5 percent in year 3, GDP in year 3 would have been $22.1 billion. However, reducing GDP by the amount of the frauds committed in year 2 before increasing it by 5 percent means that the economy only reaches a GDP of $21.2 billion in year 3 (setting it back by almost a full year's growth). In other words, the economy must grow at an unattainable 9 percent in year 3 to reach the original $22.1 billion mark. Moreover, if the economy in year 3 is plagued by the same dollar amount of frauds as in year 2 ($800 million), the economy will have to grow by almost 13 percent to reach $22.1 billion. Don't forget, in addition to a direct debit against year 2's GDP, year 2's frauds also indirectly push $9 billion of year 3's revenue toward recovering year 2's lost profits.

In addition to the actual reduction in GDP, the amount of fraud in an economy has a big impact on how willing investors are to invest in that economy. When companies commit fraud, investors lose confidence in the integrity of financial results and stock market valuations and are more hesitant to invest. For example, after the revelations of corporate wrongdoing in the United States, foreign investors' purchases of U.S. stocks in 2002 dropped to $49.5 billion, the lowest level since 1996's $12.5 billion. Whether these foreign investors' money moved to stocks in other economies that were deemed safer or whether investors decided to stand on the sidelines to see what happened because of the corporate scandals is not clear. What is clear is that the U.S economy was hurt significantly by the corporate frauds. The Brookings Institute estimated that the cost of the corporate scandals in the first year alone was $35 billion.[5] Figure 1-1 shows the rise and fall of the NASDAQ during the period 1996 to 2002. As seen in this exhibit, the drop in NASDAQ as a result of stock market scandals was much greater than the drop caused by the September 11th terrorist attacks.

Because of different cost/revenue structures, the amount of additional revenues a firm or economy must generate to recover fraud losses varies from firm to firm and from country to country. It is easy to see that in order to maximize profits or GDP, eliminating fraud should be a key goal of every business and economy. The best way to minimize fraud is to prevent it from occurring. In this book, we will cover fraud prevention, as well as fraud detection and investigation. ✳

## What Is Fraud?

Two principal methods are used to get something from others illegally. Either you physically force someone to give you what you want (using a gun, knife, other weapon, or brute force), or you trick them out of their assets. The first type of theft we call robbery, and the second type we call **fraud**. Robbery is

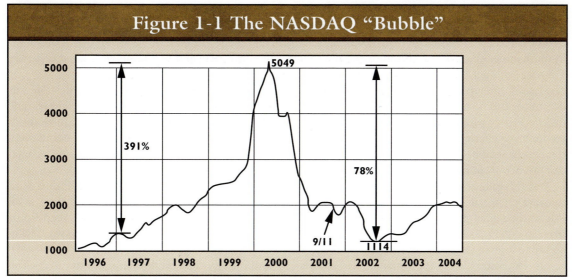

**Figure 1-1 The NASDAQ "Bubble"**

generally more violent and more traumatic than fraud and attracts much more media attention, but losses from fraud far exceed losses from robbery. Fraud always involves deception, confidence, and trickery.

Among the are many definitions of fraud, probably the most common is the following:

> Fraud *is a generic term, and embraces all the multifarious means which human ingenuity can devise, which are resorted to by one individual, to get an advantage over another by false representations. No definite and invariable rule can be laid down as a general proposition in defining fraud, as it includes surprise, trickery, cunning and unfair ways by which another is cheated. The only boundaries defining it are those which limit human knavery.*[6]

Fraud is deception that includes the following elements:

1. A *representation*
2. About a *material* point
3. Which is *false*
4. And *intentionally* or *recklessly* so
5. Which is *believed*
6. And *acted upon* by the victim
7. To the victim's *damage*

Fraud is different from unintentional errors. If, for example, someone mistakenly enters incorrect numbers on a **financial statement**, is this fraud? No, it is not fraud because it was not done with intent or for the purpose of gaining advantage over another through false pretense. But, if in the same situation, someone purposely enters incorrect numbers on a financial statement to trick investors, then it is fraud!

One of the most famous frauds of all time was Charles Ponzi's investment scam.[7] Carlo "Charles" Ponzi was born in Parma, Italy, in 1882, and then emigrated to the United States in November 1903. Over the next 14 years, Ponzi wandered from city to city and from job to job. He worked as a dishwasher, waiter, store clerk, and even as an Italian interpreter. In 1917, he settled back in Boston where he took a job typing and answering foreign mail. It was in Boston on that fateful day in August 1919 that Ponzi discovered the mechanism to make both him and his investors very wealthy.

At the time, Ponzi was considering issuing an export magazine. He had written a letter about the proposed publication to a gentleman in Spain, and when Ponzi received his reply, the man had included an international postal reply coupon. The idea behind this enclosure was quite simple. Ponzi was to take the coupon to his local post office and exchange it for American postage stamps. He would then use those American stamps to send the magazine to Spain.

Ponzi noticed that the postal coupon had been purchased in Spain for about one cent in American funds. Yet, when he cashed it in, he was able to get six American one-cent stamps. Just think of the possibilities. You could buy $100 worth of stamps in Spain and then cash them in for $600 worth of stamps in the United States. Then cash in or sell the stamps to a third party and you have, well, good old cash. You just can't get this kind of interest in the bank.

Ponzi's mind quickly went into overdrive and devised a clever scheme to capitalize on his idea. He was determined to be a rich man. His first step was to convert his American money into Italian lire (or any other currency where the exchange rate was favorable). Ponzi's foreign agents would then use these funds to purchase international postal coupons in countries with weak economies. The stamp coupons were then exchanged back into a favorable foreign currency and finally back into American funds. He claimed that his net profit on all these transactions was in excess of 400 percent.

Was he really able to carry out this scheme? The answer is a definite no. The red tape of dealing with the various postal organizations, coupled with the long delays in transferring currency, ate away at all Ponzi's imagined profits. Then things got just a bit out of hand. A failed scheme couldn't keep Ponzi from bragging about his great idea. Friends and family members easily understood what he was saying and they wanted in on the investment.

On December 26, 1919, Ponzi filed an application with the city clerk establishing his business as The Security Exchange Company. He promised 50 percent interest in 90 days and the world wanted in on it. Yet, he claimed to be able to deliver on his promise in just 45 days. This claim, of course, translates into being able to double your money in just 90 days.

Word spread quickly about Ponzi's great idea and within a few short months the lines outside the door of his School Street office began to grow. Thousands of people purchased Ponzi promissory notes at values ranging from $10 to $50,000. The average investment was estimated to be about $300, a large sum of money in those days.

Why would so many people invest in a scheme that didn't work? The real reason was that the early investors did see the great returns on their money. Ponzi used the money from later investors to pay off his earlier obligations. It was a new twist on the age-old pyramid scheme.

With an estimated income of $1,000,000 per week at the height of his scheme, his newly hired staff couldn't take the money in fast enough. They were literally filling all of the desk drawers, wastepaper baskets, and closets in the office with investor's cash. Branch offices opened and copycat schemes popped up across New England.

By the summer of 1920, Ponzi had taken in millions and started living the life of a rich man. Ponzi dressed in the finest of suits, had dozens of gold-handled canes, showered his wife with fine jewels, and purchased a 20-room Lexington mansion.

Any get-rich scheme is certain to attract the attention of the law, and Ponzi was no exception. From the start, federal, state, and local authorities investigated him. Yet, no one could pin Ponzi with a single charge of wrongdoing. Ponzi had managed to pay off all of his notes in the promised 45 days and, since everyone was happy to get their earnings, not a single complaint had ever been filed.

On July 26, 1920, Ponzi's house of cards began to collapse. *The Boston Post* headlined a story on the front page questioning the legitimacy of Ponzi's scheme. Later that day, the district attorney was somehow convinced to suspend allowing new investments until an auditor examined Ponzi's books. Within hours, crowds of people lined up outside Ponzi's door demanding that they get their investment back. Ponzi obliged and assured the public that his organization was financially stable and that he could meet all obligations. He returned the money to those who requested it. By the end of the first day, he had settled nearly 1,000 claims with the panicked crowd.

By continuing to meet all of his obligations, the angry masses began to dwindle and public support swelled. Crowds followed Ponzi's every move. He was urged by many to enter politics and was hailed as a hero. Loud cheers and applause were coupled with people eager to touch his hand and assure him of their confidence.

And Ponzi continued to dream. He had planned to establish a new type of bank where the profits would be split equally between the shareholders and the depositors. He also planned to reopen his company under a new name, the Charles Ponzi Company, whose main purpose was to invest in major industries around the world

The public continued to support him until August 10, 1920. On this date, the auditors, banks, and newspapers declared that Ponzi was definitely bankrupt. Two days later, Ponzi confessed that he had a criminal record, which just worsened his situation. In 1908, he had served 20 months in a Canadian prison on forgery charges related to a similar high-interest scheme that he had participated in there. This term was followed in 1910 by an additional two-year sentence in Atlanta, Georgia for smuggling five Italians over the Canadian border into the United States.

On August 13, Ponzi was finally arrested by federal authorities and released on $25,000 bond. Just moments later he was re-arrested by Massachusetts authorities and re-released on an additional $25,000 bond.

Following his arrest, events included federal and state civil and criminal trials, bankruptcy hearings, suits against Ponzi, suits filed by Ponzi, and the ultimate closing of five different banks. An estimated 40,000 people had entrusted an estimated $15 million (about $140 million in U.S. funds today) in Ponzi's scheme. A final audit of his books concluded that he had taken in enough funds to buy approximately 180,000,000 postal coupons, of which they could only actually confirm the purchase of two.

Ponzi's only legitimate source of income was $45 that he received as a dividend of five shares of telephone stock. His total assets came to $1,593,834.12, which didn't come close to paying off the outstanding debt. It took about eight years, but note holders were able to have an estimated 37 percent of their investment returned in installments.

Ultimately, Ponzi was sentenced to five years in federal prison for using the mails to defraud. After three and one-half years in prison, Ponzi was sentenced to an additional seven to nine years by Massachusetts authorities. He was released on $14,000 bond pending an appeal and disappeared about one month later.

He turned up a short time later in Florida. Under the assumed name of Charles Borelli, Ponzi was involved in a pyramid land scheme. He was purchasing land at $16 an acre, subdividing it into 23 lots, and selling each lot off at $10 a piece. He promised all investors that their initial $10 investment would translate into $5,300,000 in just two years. Unfortunately, much of the land was underwater and absolutely worthless.

Ponzi was indicted for fraud and sentenced to one year in a Florida prison. Once again, he jumped bail on June 3, 1926, and ended up in Texas. He hopped a freighter headed for Italy but was captured on June 28 in a New Orleans port. On June 30 he sent a telegram to President Calvin Coolidge asking to be deported. Ponzi's request was denied and he was sent back to Boston to complete his jail term. After seven years, Ponzi was released on good behavior and deported to Italy on October 7, 1934. Back in Rome, Ponzi became an English translator. Mussolini then offered him a position with Italy's new airline, and he served as the Rio de Janeiro branch manager from 1939 to 1942. Ponzi discovered that several airline officials were using the carrier to smuggle currency and Ponzi wanted a cut. When they refused to include him, he tipped off the Brazilian government. The Second World War brought about the airline's failure and Ponzi found himself unemployed.

Ponzi died in January 1949 in the charity ward of a Rio de Janeiro hospital. He left behind an unfinished manuscript appropriately titled "The Fall of Mister Ponzi" (http://home.nycap.rr.com/useless/ponzi/).

Ponzi's scam is extremely helpful in understanding fraud. Certainly, the scheme involved deception. It also involved greed—greed by the perpetrator and the *investors,* who wanted higher-than-sensible returns. Finally, Ponzi's scheme involved the element of *confidence*. If he had not paid returns to original investors, no one would have invested additional money. By paying early "returns," Ponzi gained investors' confidence and convinced them that he had a legitimate business. In fact, confidence is the single most critical element for a fraud to be successful. (The word *con*, which means to deceive, comes from *confidence*.) It is difficult to con anyone out of anything unless the deceived has confidence in the deceiver. We cannot be conned unless we trust the person trying to deceive us. Similarly, employers cannot con employees if they do not have their employees' trust and confidence. And, without investor confidence, fraudulent companies cannot con unsuspecting investors.

The following example illustrates the role that confidence plays in committing fraud: Two men enter a bank. One is dressed in a business suit and is well groomed. The second has scraggly hair, tattoos up and down both arms, is wearing tattered jeans, and is carrying a motorcycle helmet under his arm. Based on the probably unfounded categorization of these two individuals by most people in society, which one do you think is in the best position to successfully con a teller?

Most of us would agree that the man in the business suit is in a better position to defraud the bank. He is, simply put, much more likely to be trusted, stereotypes being what they are. Most people would argue that the scraggly fellow is unlikely to pull off a successful fraud because the bank employees are less likely to trust him initially.

One common response of fraud victims is disbelief: "I can't believe she would do this. She was my most trusted employee... Or my best customer... Or my best friend." Someone who understands fraud will sadly tell you, "What else could they be? They wouldn't have succeeded *without* your trust!" Indeed, fraud perpetrators are often the least suspected and the most trusted of all the people with whom victims associate.

One company's research revealed that its largest group of fraud perpetrators are people between the ages of 36 and 45.[8] The statistics don't tell us why this characteristic is common, but one reason may be that this age group includes managers who have worked themselves into positions of trust. In addition, they are probably the group with the highest financial pressures. When young people graduate from college, they look ahead and think, "By the time I'm 40, I'll have my house and cars paid off and have savings to pay for my children's college." But, when many people reach 40, their houses and cars are mortgaged to the hilt and they have no savings to pay for their children's college. During this same time frame (ages 36–45), people are also better positioned in their careers to commit fraud. Alas, any time opportunity and life pressures are present together, the number of cases of fraud climbs steeply, and the result for companies can be financial implosion.

## Types of Fraud

A common way to classify fraud is to divide frauds into those committed *against* organizations and those committed *on behalf* of organizations.

In employee fraud, the victim of the fraud is the employee's organization. On the other hand, with financial statement fraud, for example, executives usually commit fraud "on behalf" of an organization, often to make its reported financial results look better than they actually were. In this case, the executives of a company are usually indirect winners because a company's stock price increases or remains artificially high and the victims are investors in the company's stock. Sometimes, executives misstate earnings in order to ensure a larger year-end bonus. Financial statement fraud often occurs in companies that are experiencing net losses or have profits much less than expectations.

Another way to classify frauds is to use the ACFE's definition of *occupational fraud*: "The use of one's occupation for personnel enrichment through the deliberate misuse or misapplication of the employing organization's resources or assets."[9] Occupational fraud results from the misconduct of employees, managers, or executives. Occupational fraud can be anything from lunch break abuses to high-tech schemes. *The Report to the Nation on Occupation Fraud and Abuse* by the Association of Certified Fraud Examiners states that, "The key to occupational fraud is that the activity (1) is clandestine, (2) violates the employee's fiduciary duties to the organization, (3) is committed for the purpose of direct or indirect financial benefit to the employee, and (4) costs the employing organization assets, revenues, or reserves."[10]

The ACFE includes three major categories of occupational fraud: (1) asset misappropriations, which involve the theft or misuse of an organization's assets, (2) corruption, in which fraudsters wrongfully use their influence in a business transaction in order to procure some benefit for themselves or another person, contrary to their duty to their employer or the rights of another, and (3) fraudulent statements, which generally involve falsification of an organization's financial statements.

A more inclusive classification scheme divides fraud into the following six types:

1. Employee embezzlement
2. Management fraud
3. Investment scams
4. Vendor fraud

5. Customer fraud
6. Miscellaneous fraud

Fraud that doesn't fall into one of the first five types and may have been committed for reasons other than financial gain is simply labeled **miscellaneous fraud**. The other five types of fraud are summarized in Table 1-1 and are discussed in the following paragraphs.

## Employee Embezzlement

**Employee embezzlement** is the most common type of occupational fraud. As stated previously, in this type of fraud, employees deceive their employers by taking company assets. Embezzlement can be either direct or indirect. Direct fraud occurs when an employee steals company cash, inventory, tools, supplies, or other assets. It also occurs when employees establish dummy companies and have their employers pay for goods that are not actually delivered. With direct fraud, company assets go directly into the perpetrator's pockets without the involvement of third parties. Indirect employee fraud, on the other hand, occurs when employees take bribes or kickbacks from vendors, customers, or others outside the company to allow for lower sales prices, higher purchase prices, nondelivery of goods, or the delivery of inferior goods. In these cases, payment to employees is usually made by organizations that deal with the perpetrator's employer, not by the employer itself.

One example of direct employee fraud is the fraud perpetrated against Liahona Construction, a home repair business. What management did not know was that one of its employees was in the same business. The employee used $25,000 of the company's supplies and equipment to do his own remodeling jobs, pocketing the profits himself.

Here is an example of indirect employee fraud: Mark worked for "Big D" Advertising. In his role as purchase agent, Mark paid a company in New York City nearly $100,000 for contracted work that should have cost about $50,000. The contractor then paid Mark a kickback of nearly $30,000. Only after someone noticed that the quality of work performed by the New York contractor decreased substantially was the fraud suspected and detected.

The ACFE's 2002 fraud study revealed that more than 80 percent of all occupational frauds (using their definition) involved asset misappropriation. Most of this fraud is committed by employees. Of all assets misappropriated, cash was the most targeted asset, being taken 90 percent of the time.

## Table 1-1 Types of Fraud

| Fraud | Victim | Perpetrator | Explanation |
|---|---|---|---|
| 1. Employee embezzlement | Employers | Employees | Employees directly or indirectly steal from their employers. |
| 2. Management fraud | Stockholders, lenders, and others who rely on financial statements | Top management | Top management provides misrepresentation, usually in financial information. |
| 3. Investment scams | Investors | Individuals | Individuals trick investors into putting money into fraudulent investments. |
| 4. Vendor fraud | Organizations that buy goods or services | Organizations or individuals that sell goods or services | Organizations overcharge for goods or services or nonshipment of goods, even though payment is made. |
| 5. Customer fraud | Organizations that sell goods or services | Customers | Customers deceive sellers into giving customers something they should not have or charging them less than they should. |

## Management Fraud

As stated previously, **management fraud** is distinguished from other types of fraud both by the nature of the perpetrators and by the method of deception. In its most common form, management fraud involves top management's deceptive manipulation of financial statements. Well-known examples of alleged management fraud in recent years include WorldCom, Waste Management, Sunbeam, Rite-Aid, Enron, PharMor, Crazy Eddie, Inc., ZZZZ Best, ESM Government Securities, Regina Vacuum Company, and MiniScribe Corporation, among others.[11]

To illustrate management fraud, consider John Blue, the CEO for a fast-growing music store chain. The company was opening new stores almost monthly. The fast-growing music chain had lots of business and was famous for its low prices. When the company went public, shares of the stock soared. Here is what the shareholders didn't know: The chain was selling the music below cost—it was *losing* money on each item sold. Blue and his CFO hid the losses by inflating inventories and recording fictitious revenues. The scam eventually unraveled when a top accountant reported the fraud. When word leaked out, shares of the company's stock became worthless overnight.

## Investment Scams

Closely related to management fraud are **investment scams**. In these scams, fraudulent and usually worthless investments are sold to unsuspecting investors. Telemarketing fraud usually falls into this category, as does the selling of worthless partnership interests and other investment opportunities. Charles Ponzi is regarded as the father of investment scams. Unfortunately, he has not lacked for imitators. His form of deception is extremely common today, with one estimate being that one of every three Americans will fall prey to this type of fraud sometime during his or her lifetime.

The National Fraud Information Center states that in 2000 alone more than $5 billion was lost from telemarketing fraud. Table 1-2 shows a list of the top 10 types of telemarketing frauds in 1999 and 2000.[12]

### Table 1-2 Top 10 Investment Scams

| 1999 | | 2000 | |
| --- | --- | --- | --- |
| Work-at-home schemes | 20% | Prizes/sweepstakes | 18% |
| Prizes/sweepstakes | 19% | Magazine sales | 14% |
| Credit card issuing | 17% | Credit card offers | 13% |
| Advance-fee loans | 9% | Work-at-home schemes | 10% |
| Magazine sales | 7% | Advance-fee loans | 7% |
| Telephone slamming | 4% | Telephone slamming | 7% |
| Buyer's club | 3% | Credit card loss protection | 4% |
| Credit card loss protection | 2% | Buyers' clubs | 3% |
| Nigerian money offers | 2% | Telephone cramming | 2% |
| Telephone pay-per-call services | 2% | Travel/vacations | 2% |

Consider Brian, a hard-working college student, who was victimized by an investment scam. During the day, Brian attended school, and at night, to support himself, he was a waiter at a downtown diner. On a good night, Brian brought home about $90 in tips. During a period of three years, Brian saved almost $1,200. One day at lunch, Brian's friend, Lance, told him about a startup company in Canada. "If you get in now," Lance said, "you'll be in on the bottom floor. You'll make *at least* three times your money in only a couple of weeks." That same night, Brian accompanied Lance to a meeting describing the investment opportunity. The following day they each invested $1,000. Lance and Brian had never been so excited. They thought the opportunity was almost too good to be true—and unfortunately, they were right! The investment *was* too good to be true. The whole venture was a scam, and Brian and Lance never saw their $1,000 again, let alone any of the exorbitant earnings they were promised.

Although some people may not include recent mutual fund frauds as investment scams, that's exactly what they were. Since the beginning of the mutual fund industry in the 1920s, mutual funds have been thought of as a relatively safe investment vehicle. Mutual funds were sold as a limited risk investment which were, in the words of the great poet Bob Dylan, "always safe" and, thus, represented as a "shelter from the storm."[13] However, revelations in 2003 showed that America's $7 trillion mutual fund industry was rife with illegality and impropriety. Not only were funds preferentially allowing select investors to unlawfully trade in exchange for higher fees and other forms of profit, but fund insiders, including the most senior executives and founders of certain funds, engaged in the same unlawful trading conduct for their own personal gains.

Most of the mutual fund frauds involved basic schemes in which mutual fund companies allowed certain preferred clients to make illegal trades, including rapid in-and-out trades and well as trades based upon information not yet reflected in the price of the mutual fund's assets. The unlawful trading schemes engaged in by mutual funds involved two practices known as *market timing* and *late trading*." These manipulative practices were possible because of the way in which mutual funds are valued. Specifically, mutual funds in the United States are valued once a day, at 4:00 p.m. Eastern Time (ET) following the close of the financial markets in New York. The price, known as the net asset value (NAV), reflects the closing prices of the securities that comprise a particular fund's portfolio plus the value of any uninvested cash that the fund manager maintains for the fund. Thus, although the shares of a mutual fund are bought and sold all day long, the price at which the shares trade does not change during the course of the day. Orders placed any time up to 4:00 p.m. are priced at that day's NAV, and orders placed after 4:01 p.m. are priced at the next day's NAV. This practice, known as forward pricing, has been required by law since 1968.

Illegal market timing is an investment technique that involves short-term in-and-out trading of mutual fund shares. According to a Stanford University study[14], market timing may have caused losses to long-term mutual fund investors of approximately $5 billion each year. Rapid trading is antithetical to the premise that mutual funds are long-term investments meant for buy-and-hold investors. In-and-out trading capitalizes on the fact that a mutual fund's price does not reflect the fair value of the assets held by the fund. A typical example of market timing involves a U.S. mutual fund that holds Japanese shares. Because of the time zone difference, the Japanese market may close at 2:00 a.m. ET in the United States. If the U.S. mutual fund manager uses the closing prices of the Japanese shares in his or her fund to arrive at an NAV at 4:00 p.m. in New York, the manager is relying on market information that is 14 hours old. Any positive market moves during the New York trading day, which are a reliable indicator that the Japanese market will rise when it later opens, mean that the fund's stale NAV will not reflect the expected price change and, thus, will be artificially low. The NAV does not reflect the time-current market value of the stocks held by the mutual fund. Thus, a trader who buys the Japanese fund at the stale price is virtually assured of a profit that can be realized the next day by selling at the higher NAV. Because the artificial difference between the NAV and fair value has long been recognized, mutual funds represented to their investors that they imposed policies to prevent investors from profiting from the stale pricing by rapidly trading in and out of the funds. Most mutual fund prospectuses represent to investors that the funds monitor, prohibit, and prevent rapid trading because it is detrimental to long-term investors. Despite their representations to the contrary, mutual funds as well as their investment advisers, permitted such trading for their own profit. The resulting harm caused by the transfer of wealth from long-term investors to market timers, known as *dilution*, came dollar-for-dollar at the expense of long-term investors' profits.

Late trading was a fraudulent practice that was even worse. Late trading allowed selected investors to purchase mutual funds after 4:00 p.m., using that day's NAV, rather than the next day's NAV, as required under the law. It has been likened to betting today on yesterday's horse races. Because a fund's NAV is calculated after the markets close at 4:00 p.m. ET, orders to buy, sell, or exchange mutual fund shares placed before 4:00 p.m. Eastern Time on a given day receive that day's NAV. Orders placed after 4:00 p.m. ET are supposed to be priced at the following day's NAV. This pricing mechanism was legislated in order to place all investors on a level playing field whereby no investor can benefit from after-hours information in making investment decisions. Certain mutual funds, however, allowed select customers to capitalize on positive earnings news by agreeing to sell them mutual fund shares at the prior trading day's NAV. In essence, these select investors were allowed to immediately reap the benefit of the stock's upward movement the following day due to information learned after 4:00 p.m. ET. In contrast, all other investors who purchased after 4:00 p.m. ET were required to pay the next day's NAV. Again, any money made in this manner comes out of the value of the mutual fund and, therefore, on a dollar-for-dollar basis, out of the pockets of its investors. Mutual funds presumably allowed this late trading to happen in exchange for the hedge funds' business in other areas. This egregious practice was not limited to a few isolated cases but rather was rampant throughout the industry. *↳ OUTRAGEOUSLY BAD; BLATANT*

Examples of violators were Putnam Investments and Pilgrim, Baxter & Associates. Putnam was the fifth largest fund firm in the United States with $263 billion in assets. In Putnam's case, four investment fund managers engaged in market timing trades and personally made large windfalls. Two other fund managers made market timing trades in funds they didn't manage and also made huge windfalls. It turns out that Putnam discovered the problem as early as 2000, but took no disciplinary action. As a result, the SEC charged Putnam and the managers with civil securities fraud. Putnam also faces 16 class-action lawsuits, and when the problems were discovered, Putnam's investors withdrew more than 10 percent of the funds' assets. Harold Baxter of Pilgrim supposedly gave nonpublic portfolio information to a friend, who in turn gave that information to clients who conducted rapid trades in Pilgrim's PBHG family of funds. Supposedly, Gary Pilgram made millions in profits from short-term trading. Based on allegations of illegal market timing and late trading, the following mutual funds now have investigations or civil suits against them: Massachusetts Financial Services Co. (MFS), Strong Financial, Invesco Funds Group, Federated Investors, Securities Trust Co., Pilgrim, Baxter & Associates, Putnam Investments, Fred Alger Management, Bank One, Prudential Securities, Alliance Capital Management, Bank of America, Janus Capital Group, and Canary Capital Partners.

## Vendor Fraud

**Vendor fraud** has been in the news repeatedly over the years because of significant overcharges by major vendors on defense and other government contracts. Vendor fraud, which is extremely common in the United States, comes in two main varieties: (1) fraud perpetrated by vendors acting alone, and (2) fraud perpetrated through collusion between buyers and vendors. Vendor fraud usually results in either an overcharge for purchased goods, the shipment of inferior goods, or the nonshipment of goods even though payment is made.

A recent Department of Defense case is a typical vendor fraud. As a result of a joint FBI/Department of Defense investigation, an Illinois-based corporation pleaded guilty to false claims and conspiracy charges pertaining to cost overruns and executive personnel expenses charged to the Department of Defense. The corporation agreed to make restitution of $115 million to the government. The corporation later agreed to an additional payment of $71.3 million to resolve pending administrative and non-criminal issues and to dismiss certain officers proven criminally culpable through investigation.[15]

At the time this text was going to press, large, potential vendor fraud claims were being investigated involving Halliburton's contracts in helping to rebuild Iraq. It has been alleged that the Pentagon secretly awarded billions of dollars of Iraq oil field work to Halliburton without any other contractors given a chance to bid on the work. Allegations of overcharging the government by Halliburton have also been made.

## Customer Fraud

In **customer fraud**, customers either do not pay the full price for goods purchased, or they get something for nothing, or they deceive organizations into giving them something they should not have. For example, consider the bank customer who walked into a branch of a large bank one Saturday morning and convinced the branch manager to give her a $525,000 cashier's check, even though she had only $13,000 in her bank account. The manager believed she was a very wealthy customer and didn't want to lose her business. Unfortunately for the bank, she was a white-collar thief, and she proceeded to defraud the bank of more than $500,000. In another customer fraud, six individuals sitting in a downtown Chicago hotel room pretended to be representatives of large corporate customers, made three calls to a Chicago bank, and had the bank transfer nearly $70 million to their accounts in another financial institution in New Jersey. Once the money was transferred to New Jersey, it was quickly transferred to Switzerland, withdrawn, and used to purchase Russian diamonds.

# Criminal and Civil Prosecution of Fraud

When people commit fraud, they can be prosecuted criminally and civilly. To succeed in a criminal or civil prosecution, it is usually necessary to show that the perpetrator acted with *intent* to defraud the victim. Showing intent on the part of the perpetrator is best accomplished by gathering evidential matter. **Evidential matter** consists of the underlying data and all corroborating information available. In a later chapter, we discuss types of evidence and the role evidence plays in successful prosecution or litigation.

## Criminal Law

**Criminal law** is that branch of law that deals with offenses of a public nature, or those offenses against society as a whole. They are prosecuted either federally or by a state for violating a **statute** that prohibits some type of activity. Every state and the federal government have statutes prohibiting a wide variety of fraudulent and corrupt practices. Some of the principal federal statutes are presented in Table 1-3.

### Table 1-3 Principal Federal Fraud Statutes

| Statute | Title and Code | Description |
|---|---|---|
| Bribery of Public Officials and Witnesses | Title 18, U.S. Code § 201 | Bribery is punishable by up to 15 years in prison, a fine of up to three times the thing of value given or received, and disqualification of officer. |
| Anti-Kickback Act of 1986 | Title 41, U.S . Code § 51 to 58 | This act outlaws the giving or receiving of any thing of value by a subcontractor to a prime contractor in U.S. government contracts. Willful violations are punished by a fine and up to 10 years in prison. |
| Mail Fraud | Title 18, U.S. Code §1341 | "Whoever, having devised or intending to devise any scheme or artifice to defraud, or for obtaining money or property by means of false or fraudulent pretenses, representations, or promises, … for the purpose of executing such scheme or artifice or attempting so to do, places in any post office or authorized deposits or causes to be deposited any matter or thing whatever to be sent or delivered by an private or commercial interstate carrier, … shall be fined under this title… or imprisoned." |
| Bank Fraud | Title 18, U.S. Code §1344 | Any scheme to defraud federally insured financial institutions by customers, officers, employees, and owners. Covers banks, savings and loans, credit unions, and other financial institutions insured by government agencies. |
| Racketeer Influenced and Corrupt Organizations (RICO) Statute | Title 18, U.S. Code §1961 | This statute makes it an offense for any person associated with an "enterprise" engaged in interstate commerce to conduct the affairs of the enterprise through a "pattern of racketeering activity." A pattern is defined as two or more enumerated criminal violations. |

## Table 1-3 Principal Federal Fraud Statutes (continued)

| Statute | Title and Code | Description |
|---|---|---|
| Computer Frauds | Title 18, U.S. Code §1030 | Section 1030 punishes any intentional, unauthorized access to a "protected computer" for the purpose of obtaining restricted data regarding national security, obtaining confidential financial information, using a computer which is intended for use by the U.S. government, committing a fraud, or damaging or destroying information contained in the computer. |
| Securities Fraud | Rule10(b)5 Securities Act of 1934, §17(a) | It is unlawful for an insider who has material inside information to purchase or sell the company's securities, irrespective of whether the insider deals directly or through an exchange. The antifraud provisions impose civil liability on those who perpetrate or who aid and abet any fraud in connection with any offer and sale of securities. |
| Foreign Corrupt Practices Act (FCPA) | Title 15, U.S. Code §78m, 78a(b), 78dd-1, 78dd-2, 78ff | This law outlaws bribery of foreign officials by U.S. companies for business purposes. The FCPA also requires that SEC-regulated companies keep accurate books and records, and have sufficient internal controls to assure that "access to assets is permitted only in accordance with management's ... authorization," to prevent slush funds and bribe payments. |
| Tax Evasion | Title 26, U.S. Code §7201 | Failure to report income from fraud or bribes may be prosecuted as tax evasion, or for filing a false return. Also, bribes may not lawfully be deducted as business expenses. |

A variety of statutes cover fraudulent activity. Usually, when perpetrators are credibly convicted, they serve jail sentences and/or pay fines. Before perpetrators are convicted, they must be proven guilty "beyond a reasonable doubt." Juries must rule unanimously on guilt for the perpetrator to be convicted. Recent cases of people who were convicted criminally include the CEO of Financial News Network, who was sentenced to five years in prison for spinning companies he controlled into a plot that inflated FNN's sales; the CEO of Towers Financial, who was sentenced to 20 years for a Ponzi-like scheme that defrauded investors of $450 million; and Donald Ferrarini, who was convicted in February 1999 and sentenced to 12 years and one month in prison for reporting nonexistent revenues that made his income-losing company look like a profit maker.[16]

Sometimes fraud perpetrators and other criminals plead guilty without being tried in order to seek more lenient sentences. These guilty pleas usually are accompanied by a willingness to help prosecutors in their investigations of other perpetrators. For example, in the Enron case, former Enron executive Michael Kopper pleaded guilty to charges of money laundering and wire fraud. Subsequent to Kopper, numerous other Enron executives, who now knew the government had a knowledgeable conspirator on its side, also pleaded guilty.

As part of his plea deal, Kopper will cooperate with prosecutors and will pay back $12 million of assets.

## Civil Law

**Civil law** is the body of law that provides remedies for violations of private rights. Civil law deals with rights and duties between individuals. Civil claims begin when one party files a complaint against another, usually for the purpose of gaining financial restitution. The purpose of a civil lawsuit is to compensate for harm done to another individual. Unlike criminal cases, juries in civil cases need not consist of 12 jurors but may have as few as 6 jurors. The verdict of the jury need not be unanimous. Civil cases are often heard by judges instead of juries. To be successful, plaintiffs in civil cases must only prove their case by the "preponderance of the evidence." In other words, only slightly more evidence supporting the plaintiff than supporting the defendant is needed. In both civil and criminal proceedings, the parties often call expert witnesses to give their opinion on matters thought to be too technical for the jurors or judge to understand. Fraud examiners and accountants are often used as experts in fraud cases to compute and testify to the amount of damages. When fraud is committed, criminal prosecution usually proceeds first.

Table 1-4 identifies the major differences between a civil and a criminal case.

## Table 1-4 Distinctions Between Civil and Criminal Cases

| | Criminal Case | Civil Case |
|---|---|---|
| Purpose | To right a wrong | To obtain a remedy |
| Consequences | Jail and/or fines | Restitution and damage payments |
| Burden of Proof | "Beyond a reasonable doubt" | "Preponderance of evidence" *↑ SUPERIORITY, OF WEIGHT, , POWER OR IMPORTANCE* |
| Jury | Jury must have 12 people | May consist of fewer than 12 persons |
| Initiation | Determination by a grand jury that sufficient evidence exists to indict | Filing of a claim by a plaintiff – *PARTY THAT INSTITUTES A SUIT* |
| Verdict | Unanimous verdict | Parties may stipulate to a less than unanimous verdict |
| Claims | Only one claim at a time | Various claims may be joined in one action |

As an example of civil litigation, after the WorldCom fraud was disclosed, several organizations, including some of the banks that loaned money to WorldCom and allegedly participated in the financial fraud, were sued by investors. In 2004, one of those banks, Citigroup, agreed to settle investors' civil claims by agreeing to pay $2.65 billion to investors. These kinds of out-of-court settlements often occur before civil cases can go to trial.

## How to Prepare to Be a Fraud-Fighting Professional

Few universities have a major called "Fraud Prevention, Detection, and Investigation." Rather, students who want to prepare for fraud-fighting careers must usually choose majors and courses that will teach the skills needed by a successful fraud fighter. The following are the three most important skills for a fraud-fighting professional:

1. *Analytical skills:* Fraud detection and investigation are analytical processes in which investigators identify the kinds of fraud that could occur, the kinds of symptoms and indicators those frauds would generate, and ways in which to examine and follow up on symptoms that are found. Being a fraud investigator is much like being a physician: it requires significant amounts of diagnostic and exploratory work to discover what is really happening. It is impossible to be a good fraud examiner without having good analytical skills.
2. *Communication skills:* Fraud examiners spend considerable amounts of time interviewing witnesses and suspects and communicating those findings to witnesses, to courts, and to others. A good communicator will know how hard to push for evidence and confessions, how to structure questions and interviews to make them most productive, and how to write reports that are valued by courts, lawyers, and others. It is impossible to be a good fraud examiner without good communication skills.
3. *Technology skills:* Fraud detection used to involve more luck than anything else. However, with the technological advances of the last few years, we can now proactively search for fraud symptoms, and fraud perpetrators, and build both fraud-free and fraudulent profiles. Technology allows fraud examiners to analyze huge databases quickly. Real-time and even post hoc fraud detection and investigation in the future will involve the use of technology.

Although these three skills are critical and most important, other skills will also be useful for future fraud examiners:

- *Some understanding of accounting and business:* One of the major differences between fraud and other crimes is the attempts to hide the fraud. Usually concealment attempts involve altering accounting records and documents. Those fraud examiners who understand accounting and business will be highly valued in the future. For example, the FBI has a large number of agents who are CPAs. The expertise of those agents is highly valued by the FBI.
- *A knowledge of civil and criminal laws, criminology, privacy issues, employee rights, fraud statutes, and other legal fraud-related issues:* Investigating and resolving frauds always involves legal questions such as "Should this case be pursued in the criminal or civil courts?" "Are certain evidence-gathering techniques legal?" and "When do I need to involve law enforcement?"
- *The ability to speak and write in a foreign language:* With developments in travel, communications, and technology, many frauds today involve individuals in multiple countries. Cross-border investigations are not uncommon and the ability to speak and write a foreign language, such as Spanish, will be valued.
- *A knowledge of human behavior:* Knowing why and how people rationalize dishonesty, how they react when caught, and what is the most effective way to deter individuals from committing fraud is a skill usually learned in psychology, social psychology, or sociology courses.

About now, you are probably wondering which major on your campus will provide you with these skills. The answer is probably none. However, majors such as information systems, accounting, and law can provide a basic understanding that is helpful. Regardless of the major you choose, you should fill your elective requirements with courses in these topics. For example, if you are an accounting major, you should probably take as many technology and behavioral classes as you can. No candidate will possess all of the skills identified. However, the more of these skills you possess, the better your qualifications to be a successful fraud examiner in the future.

## Fraud-Fighting Careers

As the number of frauds and the amounts of fraud losses increase, so do the opportunities for successful careers in fraud-fighting. In fact, *U.S. News and World Report* identified fraud examination as one of the fastest-growing and most financially rewarding careers.[17] The American Institute of Certified Public Accountants and the Department of Labor has stated that the demand for forensic accountants will grow in the future.[18] Although numerous opportunities exist for fraud-fighting professionals, careers in forensic work can be broadly classified according to employer, as shown in Table 1-5.

Taken together, the costs of fighting fraud are high. In high-profile civil cases, it is not uncommon for defendants and plaintiffs to spend tens or even hundreds of millions of dollars defending and prosecuting alleged frauds. Many large fraud cases involve multiple law firms, multiple lawyers from each firm, multiple investigators, and expert witnesses and large support staffs. Often, after spending large sums of money defending or prosecuting a fraud case, a pretrial settlement is reached with no public announcement of the terms of the settlement.

You will find your study of fraud examination to be helpful, regardless of whether you become a professional fraud-fighter. As a businessperson, understanding the tremendous costs of fraud losses and learning to recognize fraud warning signs may someday mean the difference between your business surviving or failing. If you become a financial consultant, you will be better equipped to help your clients avoid high-risk and fraudulent investments. As an investor, you will learn skills that help you distinguish

## Table 1-5 Careers in Fraud Fighting

| Employer | Types of Work |
|---|---|
| Government | FBI, Postal Inspectors, Criminal Investigation Division of the IRS, U.S. Marshals, inspector generals of various governmental agencies, state investigators, and law enforcement officials |
| CPA firms, forensic accounting firms, litigations support firms, and law firms | Conduct investigations, support firms in litigations, do bankruptcy-related fraud work, serve as expert witnesses, consult in fraud prevention and detection, and provide other fee-based work |
| Corporations | Prevent, detect, and investigate fraud within a company, includes internal auditors, corporate security officers, and in-house legal counsels |
| Organizations involved in civil cases | Lawyers to defend and/or prosecute cases |
| Universities, hospitals, technology corporations, etc. | Consult, serve as expert witnesses, extract evidence from computers and servers, investigate public records, and serve on grand or trial juries |

between fraudulent and profitable investments. If you become an auditor, you will find the document examination and evidence-gathering skills you learn here invaluable. If you work with taxes, you will be alert to when information from clients is questionable. And, the interviewing skills you will learn will stand you in good stead in numerous endeavors.

You may find, to your surprise, that fraud examination and forensic accounting are not only rewarding and challenging, they are also intriguing (what good mystery isn't?) and endlessly interesting. We hope you enjoy the adventure.

## KEY TERMS

**Association of Certified Fraud Examiners (ACFE):** An international organization, based in Austin, Texas, dedicated to fighting fraud and white-collar crime.

**Civil law:** The body of law that provides remedies for violations of private rights.

**Criminal law:** The branch of law that deals with offenses of a public nature.

**Customer fraud:** Customers not paying for goods purchased, getting something for nothing, or deceiving organizations into giving them something they should not have.

**Employee embezzlement:** Employees deceiving their employers by taking company assets.

**Evidential matter:** The underlying data and all corroborating information available about a fraud.

**Financial statements:** Reports such as the balance sheet, income statement, and statement of cash flows, that summarize the financial status and results of operations of a business entity.

**Fraud:** "A generic term that embraces all the multifarious means which human ingenuity can devise, which are resorted to by one individual, to get an advantage over another by false representations. No definite and invariable rule can be laid down as a general proposition in defining fraud, as it includes surprise, trickery, cunning and unfair ways by which another is cheated. The only boundaries defining it are those which limit human knavery."

**Investment scams:** The selling of fraudulent and worthless investments to unsuspecting investors.

**Jurisdiction:** The limit or territory over which an organization has authority.

**Management fraud:** Deception perpetrated by an organization's top management through the manipulation of financial statement amounts or disclosures.

**Miscellaneous fraud:** Deception that doesn't fall into any of the other five categories of fraud.

**Net income:** An overall measure of the performance of a company; equal to revenues minus expenses for the period.

**Perpetrator:** A person who has committed a fraud.

**Profit margin:** Net income divided by total revenues. Also known as return on sales, profit margin percentage, profit margin ratio, operating performance ratio.

**Revenue:** Increases in a company's resources from the sale of goods or services.

**Statute:** A law or regulation; a law enacted by the legislative branch of a government.

**Vendor fraud:** An overcharge for purchased goods, the shipment of inferior goods, or the nonshipment of goods even though payment is made.

**Victim:** The person or organization deceived by the perpetrator.

## QUESTIONS AND CASES

### DISCUSSION QUESTIONS

1. What is fraud?

2. How does fraud affect individuals, consumers, and organizations?

3. List and describe the five different types of frauds.

4. How did fraudulent mutual funds engage in illegal behavior?

5. In what ways did fraudulent mutual funds benefit from committing fraud?

6. What is the difference between civil and criminal laws?

7. For each of the following, indicate whether it is a characteristic of a civil or a criminal case:
   a. Jury may consist of fewer than 12 jurors.
   b. Verdict must be unanimous.
   c. Multiple claims may be joined in one action.
   d. "Beyond a reasonable doubt."
   e. Purpose is to right a public wrong.
   f. Purpose is to obtain remedy.
   g. Consequences include jail and/or fines.
   h. Juries may have a less-than-unanimous verdict.

8. Why was Charles Ponzi so successful with his fraud scheme?

9. What are some of the different types of fraud-fighting careers?

10. How do employee fraud and management fraud differ?

11. Do you think the demand for careers in fraud prevention and detection is increasing or decreasing? Why?

12. Why are accurate fraud statistics hard to find?

## TRUE/FALSE

1. All frauds that are detected are made public.

2. Perpetrators use trickery, confidence, and deception to commit fraud.

3. One of the most common responses to fraud is disbelief.

4. Manufacturing companies with a profit margin of 10 percent must usually generate about 10 times as much revenue as the dollar amount from the fraud in order to restore net income to its prefraud level.

5. Fraud involves using physical force to take something from someone.

6. Telemarketing fraud is an example of employee embezzlement.

7. When perpetrators are convicted of fraud, they often serve jail sentences and/or pay fines.

8. Management fraud is deception perpetrated by an organization's top management.

9. Mutual fund frauds could be considered to be a type of investment scam.

10. Most people agree that fraud-related careers will be in demand in the future.

11. In civil cases, fraud experts are rarely used as expert witnesses.

12. Many companies hide their losses from fraud rather than make them public.

13. The only group/business that must report employee embezzlement is the federal government.

14. Advances in technology have had no effect on the size or frequency of frauds committed.

15. Fraud losses generally reduce a firm's income on a dollar-for-dollar basis.

16. The single most critical element for a fraud to be successful is opportunity.

17. Fraud perpetrators are often those who are least suspected and most trusted.

18. Unintentional errors in financial statements are a form of fraud.

19. Occupational fraud is usually fraud committed on behalf of an organization.

20. Companies that commit financial statement fraud are often experiencing net losses or have profits less than expectations.

21. Indirect fraud occurs when a company's assets go directly into the perpetrator's pockets without the involvement of third parties.

22. In vendor fraud, customers don't pay for goods purchased.

23. A negative outcome in a civil lawsuit usually results in jail time for the perpetrator.

24. When fraud is committed, criminal prosecution usually proceeds first.

## MULTIPLE CHOICE                5/21/06        12:30 AM

1. Why does fraud seem to be increasing at such an alarming rate?
   page 5 *
   a. Computers, the Internet, and technology make fraud easier to commit and cover up.
   b. Most frauds today are detected, whereas in the past many were not.
   c. A new law requires that fraud be reported within 24 hours.
   d. People don't understand the consequences of fraud to organizations and businesses.

2. Which of the following is *not* an important element of fraud?
   a. Confidence        PAGE 7
   b. Deception
   c. Trickery
   d. Intelligence

3. Fraud is considered to be:   pg. 5
   a. A serious problem that continues to grow.
   b. A problem felt by a few individuals, but not by most people.
   c. A mild problem that most businesses need not worry about.
   d. A problem under control.

4. People who commit fraud are usually:
   a. New employees.
   b. Not well-groomed, and have long hair and tattoos.
   c. People with strong personalities.
   d. Trusted individuals.

*pg. 10*

5. "The use of one's occupation for personal enrichment through the deliberate misuse or misapplication of the employing organization's resources or assets" is the definition of which of the following types of fraud?
   a. Employee embezzlement or occupational fraud
   b. Investment scams
   c. Management fraud
   d. Vendor fraud

*pg. 10*

6. Corporate employee fraud-fighters:
   a. Work as postal inspectors and law enforcement officials.
   b. Prevent, detect, and investigate fraud within a company.
   c. Are lawyers who defend or prosecute fraud cases.
   d. None of the above.

*pg. 19*

7. Investment scams most often include:
   a. An action by top management against employees.
   b. Worthless investments or assets sold to unsuspecting investors.
   c. An overcharge for purchased goods.
   d. Nonpayment of invoices for goods purchased by customers.

*pg. 12*

8. Which of the following is *not* true of civil fraud?
   a. Usually begins when one party files a complaint.
   b. The purpose is to compensate for harm done to another.
   c. Must be heard by 12 jurors.
   d. Only "the preponderance of the evidence" is needed for plaintiff to be successful.

*pg. 17*

9. Future careers in fraud will most likely be:
   a. In low demand.
   b. In about the same demand as now.
   c. Low paying.
   d. In higher demand and financially rewarding.

*pg. 18*

10. Studying fraud will help you to:
    a. Learn evidence-gathering skills.
    b. Avoid high-risk and fraudulent activities.
    c. Learn valuable interviewing skills.
    d. All of the above.

*pg. 18-19*

11. Which of the following is not a reliable resource for fraud statistics?
    a. FBI agencies
    b. Health agencies
    c. Insurance organizations
    d. Fraud perpetrators

*page 4*

12. Which of the following statements is true?
    a. Bank robberies are more costly than frauds.
    b. Fraud is often labeled the fastest-growing crime.
    c. FBI agencies are spending approximately 35 percent of their time on fraudulent activities.

*pg. 5*

13. Which of the following is not an element of fraud?
    a. False representation
    b. Accidental behavior
    c. Damage to a victim
    d. Intentional or reckless behavior

*pg. 7*

14. What is the best way to minimize fraud within an organization?
    a. Detection of fraud
    b. Investigation of fraudulent behavior
    c. Prevention activities
    d. Research company activities

*pg. 4*

15. What is the most important element in successful fraud schemes?
    a. Promised benefits
    b. Confidence in the perpetrator
    c. Profitable activities
    d. Complexity

*pg. 9*

16. Which of the following characters is least likely to be involved in a fraud?
    a. Middle-aged person who has a middle management position
    b. A long-haired teenager wearing leather pants
    c. Recent college graduate
    d. Senior executives who have obtained stock options

*pg. 10*

17. Which of the following is *not* a fraud type?
    a. Direct employee embezzlement
    b. Indirect employee embezzlement
    c. Supervisor fraud
    d. Investment scams

*11*

18. Which of the following is not a form of vendor fraud?
    a. Overcharge for purchased goods
    b. Shipment of inferior goods
    c. Nonshipment of goods even though payment is made
    d. Not paying for goods purchased

*pg. 14*

19. Civil law performs which of the following functions?
    a. Remedy for violation of private rights
    b. Remedy for violations against society as a whole
    c. Punishment for guilt "beyond reasonable doubt"
    d. Monetary reimbursement for federal damages

*pg. 16*

20. Fraud-fighting includes what type of careers?
    a. Professors
    b. Lawyers
    c. CPA firms
    d. All of the above

*pg. 9*

## SHORT CASES

**Case 1.** Clever, Inc., is a car manufacturer. Its 2005 income statement is as follows:

Clever, Inc.
Income Statement
For the year ended Dec. 31, 2005

| | |
|---|---|
| Sales revenue | $20,000 |
| Less cost of goods sold | $10,000 |
| Gross margin | $10,000 |
| Expenses | $ 8,000 |
| Net income | $ 2,000 |

Alexander, Inc., is a car rental agency based in Florida. Its 2005 income statement is as follows:

Alexander, Inc.
Income Statement
For the year ended December 31, 2005

| | |
|---|---|
| Sales revenue | $20,000 |
| Expenses | $15,000 |
| Net income | $ 5,000 |

During 2005, both Clever, Inc., and Alexander, Inc., incurred a $1,000 fraud loss. How much additional revenue must each company generate to recover the losses from the fraud? Why are these amounts different? Which company will probably have to generate less revenue to recover the losses?

**Case 2.** You are having lunch with another graduate student. During the course of your conversation, you tell your friend about your exciting fraud examination class. After you explain the seriousness of fraud in the business world, she asks you two questions:

1. What is the difference between fraud and an unintentional error?

2. With all the advances in technology, why is fraud a growing problem? With advanced technology, shouldn't companies, police, the FBI, and others be able to prevent and detect fraud much more easily?

**Case 3.** For each of the following examples, identify whether it is employee embezzlement, management fraud, investment scam, vendor fraud, customer fraud, or miscellaneous fraud.

1. Marcus bought a $70 basketball for only $30, simply by exchanging the price tags before purchasing the ball.

2. Craig lost $500 by investing in a multilevel marketing scam.

3. The Bank of San Felipe lost more than $20,000 in 2005. One of its employees took money from a wealthy customer's account and put it into his own account. By the time the fraud was detected, the employee had spent the money and the bank was held responsible.

4. The CEO of Los Andes Real Estate was fined and sentenced to six months in prison for deceiving investors into believing the company made a profit in 2005, when it actually lost more than $150 million.

5. The government lost more than $50 million in 2005 because many of its contractors and subcontractors charged for fictitious hours and equipment on a project in the Middle East.

6. A student broke into the school's computer system and changed his grades in order to be accepted into graduate school.

**Case 4.** Fellow students in your fraud examination class are having a hard time understanding why statistics on fraud are so difficult to obtain. What would you say to enlighten them?

**Case 5.** You're telling your husband about your classes for the new semester. He's intrigued by the idea of your becoming a fraud detective, but he wants to know whether you will have job security and what kinds of jobs you might get. How would you respond to his questions?

**Case 6.** A bookkeeper in a $3 million retail company had earned the trust of her supervisor, so various functions normally reserved for management were assigned to her, including the authority to issue and authorize customer refunds. She proceeded to issue refunds to nonexistent customers and created documents with false names and addresses. She adjusted the accounting records and stole about $15,000 cash. She was caught when internal audit sent routine confirmations to customers on a mailing list and received excessive return-to-sender replies. The investigation disclosed a telling pattern. The bookkeeper initially denied accusations but admitted the crime upon presentation of the evidence.

You are a lawyer for the retail company. Now that the fraud has been detected, would you prosecute her criminally or civilly, or both? What process would you use to try to recover the $15,000?

**Case 7.** You are a new summer intern working for a major professional services firm. During your lunch break each day, you and a fellow intern, Bob, eat at a local sandwich shop. One day, Bob's girlfriend joins you for lunch. When the bill arrives, Bob pays with a company credit card and writes the meal off as a business expense. Bob and his girlfriend continue to be "treated" to lunch for a number of days. You know Bob is well aware of a recent memo that came down from management stating casual lunches are not valid business expenses. When you ask Bob about the charges, he replies, "Hey, we're interns. Those memos don't apply to us. We can expense anything we want."

1. Is fraud being committed against the firm?

2. What responsibility, if any, do you have to report the activity?

**Case 8.** After receiving an anonymous note indicating fraudulent activities in the company, XYZ Company officials discover that an employee has embezzled a total of $50,000 over the past year. Unfortunately, this employee used an assumed identity and has vanished without a trace. The CFO at XYZ wants to know how badly this fraud has hurt the company. If XYZ has a profit margin of 7%, how much additional revenue will XYZ most likely have to generate to cover the loss?

**Case 9.** Your friend John works for an insurance company. John holds a business degree and has been involved in the insurance business for many years. John shares some recent company gossip with you. He has heard that the internal auditors estimate the company has lost about $2,500,000 because of fraud in the last few years. Because you are a Certified Fraud Examiner, John asks you how this will affect the company's profitability. John doesn't have access to the company's financial information.

Compute the additional revenues needed to make up for the lost money, assuming that the company has a profit margin of 5 percent, 10 percent, and 15 percent. Give examples of three types of fraud that could affect the insurance company. Who are the victims and who are the perpetrators?

**Case 10.** You are an accounting student at the local university pursuing your master's degree. One of your friends has been intrigued by the numerous frauds that have recently been reported in the news. This friend knows you are training for a job as an auditor with a large

public accounting firm, but your friend does not understand the difference between what you will be doing and what fraud examiners do. Write a paragraph that explains the difference between auditing and fraud examination.

**Case 11.** You own a local pizza delivery store. Cesar Rodriquez has been working for you as a manager for two years and has been a close friend. Cesar has the reputation of being a hard worker and has not taken time off the entire time he has worked for you. Last week, Cesar left town to attend a family funeral. While he was gone you received several phone calls that seemed suspicious. The calls occurred in the following manner. A potential customer would call and ask for the manager. When you answered the phone (representing the manager) the customer would ask for the "manager's special." When informed that there was not a "manager's special" offered this weekend the caller would quickly hang up. This type of call occurred several times. When Cesar returned you decided to spend an evening observing the order-taking process. It became apparent that Cesar was skimming cash from the business. Cesar would take the order for the "manager's special" without entering the sale into the computer. Cesar would then deliver the pizza and pocket the money.

1. Write a paragraph explaining why Cesar should be terminated from employment.

2. Write a paragraph explaining why it is important that Cesar is prosecuted for his crime.

**Case 12.** Bob, who works as a credit manager for a large bank, has a reputation for being a hard worker. His convenient downtown apartment is located near the bank, which allows him to work undisturbed late into the night. Everyone knows that Bob loves his job because he has been with the bank for many years and hardly ever takes a vacation. He is a strict credit manager and has the reputation for asking difficult questions to loan applicants before approving any credit.

Nancy, Bob's director, noticed that Bob has not taken a mandatory week long vacation for a number of years. Given Bob's history of being tough on approving credit for the bank, should Nancy be concerned?

## EXTENSIVE CASES

**Extensive Case 1.** A recent newspaper contained the following story:

### Sweepstakes Company Agrees to Pay Up

*Publishers Clearing House agreed to pay $34 million in a deal with 26 states to settle allegations the sweepstakes company employed deceptive marketing practices. The $34 million will cover customer refunds, legal expenses, and administrative cost to the states. Each state's share has yet to*

*be determined. In the lawsuits, state attorneys general accused Publishers Clearing House of deceptive marketing for its sweepstakes promotions. The suit alleged that the company was misleading consumers by making them believe they had won prizes or would win if they bought magazines from Publishers Clearing House.*

*As part of the settlement, the company will no longer use phrases like "guaranteed winner." "This will in fact revolutionize the sweepstakes industry," Michigan Attorney*

*General Jennifer Granholm stated. "We listened to the states' concerns and have agreed to responsive and significant changes that will make our promotions the clearest, most reliable and trustworthy in the industry," said Robin Smith, chairman and CEO of the Port Washington, N.Y.–based company.*

*Publishers Clearing House reached a $34 million settlement last August with 26 states and the District of Columbia. The states involved in the latest settlement are: Arizona, Arkansas, Colorado, Connecticut, Delaware, Florida, Indiana, Iowa, Kansas, Kentucky, Maine, Maryland, Massachusetts, Michigan, Minnesota, Missouri, New Jersey, North Carolina, Oregon, Pennsylvania, Rhode Island, Tennessee, Texas, Vermont, West Virginia, and Wisconsin.[19]*

Based on this information do you believe Publishers Clearing House committed fraud? Why or why not?

**Extensive Case 2.** The credit card industry is all too familiar with the high cost and pervasive problem of fraud. In fact, it is estimated that between 9 percent and 12 percent of all U.S. credit card transactions are fraudulent. A large percentage of the costs to issue and service credit cards involves the detection and prevention of fraud. VISA, MasterCard, American Express, and institutions that facilitate the use of debit and credit cards have gone to great lengths to learn the behavior of fraudsters so they can recognize patterns and predict behavior. These organizations keep databases of all fraudulent transactions in order to analyze data and devise new strategies to combat this persistent problem. Many banks use expensive fraud-detection software to try to stop fraudsters before their scams become too big. For instance, patterns suggest that people who have stolen credit cards will often go to gas stations to see whether the credit card will authorize at unattended gas pumps. If the gas purchase is authorized, the thieves then go directly to jewelry stores, electronics stores, or footwear stores and spend as much money as they can as fast as they can. Computer software can detect this pattern and then decline subsequent transactions.

One type of fraud that the credit card industry faces is the protection of bank identification numbers, or BINs. A BIN identifies the member bank that issues credit cards and is used in the account number of cardholders. Fraudsters have become very sophisticated at either creating their own credit cards with valid BINs or stealing cards and changing the numbers of an active account. Through this method fraudsters steal large amounts of money. For example, if certain protections are not put in place by new start-up credit card institutions and its BIN first becomes valid in the network of bankcard authorizing systems, fraudsters can authorize credit cards even though the institution may not have any valid credit cards. However, because its BIN is active, valid credit card numbers that include the BIN could potentially be authorized. This type of credit card fraud usually involves $1 million or more.

These problems are not the only ones that credit card companies face; "identity theft" is increasing dramatically. Identity theft occurs when someone uses your name and personal information to do such things as open up credit card accounts. Identity thieves find information in garbage dumps or anywhere they can gather information. One common scheme is for a fraudster to call people on the phone, posing as an employee of their bank. Through this method fraudsters are able to learn all kinds of information about people, such as social security numbers, place of birth, and personal identification numbers (PIN) without much effort. Another scheme occurs in restaurants with dishonest waiters. Dishonest waiters often have a device on their belt that looks like a pager. In reality it is a reader that can store information from the magnetic strip on the back of your credit card. They swipe your card just before they charge you for the meal, and they have enough information to make a fake credit card. These examples describe just a few of the common fraudulent credit card schemes.

**Questions**

1. Is this problem just a concern for the institutions that issue credit cards? How are you affected?

2. How can you protect yourself from identity fraud?

**Extensive Case 3.** Gus Jackson was hired from a Big Four public accounting firm to start a new internal audit function for ABC Company, a newly acquired subsidiary of a large organization. His first tasks involved getting to know ABC management and supporting the public accountants in their year-end audit work.

Once the year-end work was wrapped up, Gus started an audit of the accounts payable function. He was supported in that audit activity by Jane Ramon, who had worked on the parent company's internal audit staff for about four years.

The accounts payable audit went smoothly, although many employees made no effort to conceal their hostility and resentment toward anyone associated with the new parent company. One exception was Hank Duckworth, the accounts payable manager. Hank was extremely helpful and complimentary of the professional approach used by the auditors. Gus had actually met Hank four years earlier, when Hank had been an accounting supervisor for an audit client where Gus was the junior accountant.

As the audit neared completion, Gus reviewed an audit comment Jane had written, a statement concerning some accounts payable checks that lacked complete endorsement by the payees. Both Gus and Jane recognized that in some situations and in some organizations less-than-perfect endorsements were not a critical concern; but these checks were payable to dual payees, and the endorsement of each payee was required. Gus asked Jane to make some photocopies of the examples so the evidence would be available for the audit close-out meeting with management.

Jane returned 20 minutes later with a puzzled expression. "I pulled the examples," she said, "but look at these!" Jane placed five checks on the desk in front of Gus. "What do you make of these?" she asked.

"Make of what?" asked Gus.

"Don't you see it? The handwriting on all the endorsements looks the same, even though the names are different! And these are manual checks, which in this system usually means they were walked through the system as rush payments."

"They do look similar," Gus replied, "but a lot of people have similar handwriting."

It hit Jane and Gus at the same time. All five checks had been cashed at the same convenience store less than five miles from the home office, even though the mailing address of the payee on one of the checks was over 200 miles away!

Jane decided to pull the supporting documentation for the payments but found there was none! She then identified other payments to the same payees and retrieved the paid checks. The endorsements did not look at all like the endorsements on the suspicious checks. To determine which of the endorsements were authentic, Jane located other examples of the payees' signatures in the lease, correspondence, and personnel files. The checks with supporting documentation matched other signatures on file for the payees.

Gus and Jane decided to assess the extent of the problem while investigating quietly. They wanted to avoid prematurely alerting perpetrators or management that an investigation was underway. With the help of other internal auditors from the parent company, they worked after normal business hours and reviewed endorsements on 60,000 paid checks in three nights. Ninety-five checks that had been cashed at the convenience store were identified.

Still, all Gus and Jane had were suspicions—no proof. They decided to alert executive management at the subsidiary and get their help for the next steps.

### The Follow-Through

Since the subsidiary had little experience with dishonest and fraudulent activity, they had no formalized approach or written fraud policy. Gus and Jane, therefore, maintained control of the investigation all the way to conclusion. With the help of operating management, the auditors contacted carefully selected payees. As is often the case involving fictitious payments to real payees, the real

payees had no knowledge of the payments and had no money due them. The auditors obtained affidavits of forgery.

In order to identify the perpetrator, the auditors documented the processing in more detail than had been done in the original preliminary survey for the routine audit. There were seven people who had access, opportunity, and knowledge to commit the fraud. The auditors then prepared a Personnel Spreadsheet detailing information about every employee in the department. The spreadsheet revealed that one employee had evidence of severe financial problems in his personnel file. It also showed that Hank Duckworth's former residence was three blocks from the convenience store.

Armed with the affidavits of forgery, the auditors advised management that the case was no longer merely based on suspicions. Along with members of operating management, the auditors confronted the convenience store owners to learn why they had cashed the checks, and who had cashed them.

The convenience store manager had a ready answer. "We cash those for Hank Duckworth. He brings in several checks a month to be cashed. He used to live down the street. Never had one of those checks come back!"

The rest is history. Hank was confronted, and he confessed. The fully documented case was turned over to law enforcement. Hank pled guilty and received a probated sentence in return for full restitution, which he paid.[20]

### Questions

1. What clues caused Jane to suspect that fraud was involved?

2. Why is it important for fraud examiners to follow up on even the smallest inconsistencies?

3. In an attempt to identify possible suspects, the auditors researched the personal files of every employee in the department. What things might they have been looking for to help them identify possible suspects?

**Extensive Case 4.** In December 2003, Prudential Securities was charged with fraud for late trading. It was the first major brokerage house to be charged with the illegal practice of buying mutual funds after hours.

The regulators who accused Prudential Securities charged them with carrying out a large-scale, late trading scheme that involved more than 1,212 trades valued at a remarkable $162.4 million. These trades were placed after hours in order to benefit favored hedge funds. The complaint did not contain information regarding any profits that were protected by the scandal.

The regulators who accused Prudential stated that Prudential should have noticed the considerable number of trades being placed after 4 p.m. and should have begun an internal inquiry. However, the complaint said that Prudential possessed "no internal supervisory procedures" to detect trades placed after hours.

Market timing, often done in conjunction with late trading, involves rapid in-and-out trading of a mutual fund designed to take advantage of delays in marking up prices of securities in the funds. By buying before the markups and selling quickly after them, Prudential traders realized quick profits for the firm's clients at the expense of others, the state alleges. A group of managers and top-producing brokers were charged last month by the SEC or the state in separate civil actions related to market timing. The firm denies all wrongdoing.

Normally, orders to buy funds after 4 p.m. should be filled at the price set the next day. In late trading, which is illegal, orders instead get the same day's 4 p.m. price, enabling an investor to react to news one trading day ahead of other investors.

In order to accomplish late trading, the complaint gave this account: Prudential clients would submit a list of potential trades to brokers before the 4 p.m. deadline by fax, e-mail, or telephone. After 4 p.m, clients notified Prudential which of the long list of trades it wished to execute. Prudential brokers would take the original order, cross out the trades the client didn't want to execute, then forward the order to the firm's New York trading desk. The time stamp on the fax would often deceptively reflect the time it was received originally, but not the time that the client confirmed the order, according to the complaint.

For example, on October 19, 2001, at 4:58 p.m., Prudential's New York office executed more than 65 mutual fund trades, for a total of $12.98 million, according to the complaint.

Prudential did nothing to substantiate that orders were received before 4 p.m., according to the complaint. In early 2003, the brokerage firm issued a policy change requiring branch managers to initial a cover sheet for trades before faxing them to New York. Lists of trades could be received at Prudential's New York trading desk as late as 4:45 p.m., the state alleges. "The orders were never rejected" and they were executed at same-day prices, the complaint says.

Prudential also allowed the brokers involved in the market timing and late trading scheme to have dedicated wire-room personnel to execute trades, according to the complaint. The brokers compensated the wire-room employees for their efforts, by sharing year-end bonuses, according to exhibits. The state alleges that Prudential also authorized one broker to obtain special software that gave the employee "electronic capacity to enter bulk mutual fund exchanges after 4 p.m.," the complaint says.[21]

**Questions**

1. Determine whether this case would be prosecuted as criminal or civil offense and state reasons to support your conclusion.

2. Who are the victims that will be hurt because of this late trading scheme and how will they be hurt?

## INTERNET ASSIGNMENT

Your best friend wants to know why on earth you are taking a fraud examination class. He is curious about what careers this class prepares you for. Go to the Internet and find information about two different careers that you could pursue in the field of fraud examination. Write two or three brief paragraphs about what you found. Remember to include the Web sites where you found the information so that your friend can do some investigating of his own.

## DEBATE

For the past year, you've been working as a secretary/processor for a local construction company, XYZ Homes, which specializes in the building of low-cost, limited-option homes. You left a comfortable, good-paying job to work for XYZ because it was family-owned and operated by some long-time friends.

Soon after you began working for XYZ, you noticed questionable behavior on the part of Mr. and Mrs. XYZ's two sons, who are company salesmen. In fact, you are positive that they are falsifying documents to increase their commissions and to trick local banks into approving mortgages to customers who don't meet credit standards.

You are trying to decide how to handle the situation when one of the sons approaches you and asks you to produce and sign a memo to a bank, falsely stating that a certain potential home buyer is creditworthy. You refuse to do so and, after much consideration, approach Mr. XYZ about the situation. To your surprise, he simply brushes off your comments as unimportant and laughingly states that "boys will be boys."

What would you do in this situation? Is the fact that you correctly refused to produce and sign a false memo enough, or are you obligated to report these crimes to the banks and proper authorities? Discuss the options, responsibilities, and implications you are facing.

## END NOTES

1. Laura Goldberg and Ralph Bivins, "Enron's Former Chief Financial Officer Surfaces," *Wall Street City* (December 13, 2001).

2. "Letter to Members," transcript of Barry Melancon (January 24, 2002), http://www.aicpa.org/info/letter_02_01.htm, accessed on Sept. 9, 2004.

3. The Association of Certified Fraud Examiners, *The Report to the Nation on Occupation Fraud and Abuse* (Austin, TX: ACFE, 1996), p. 4.

4. "McNamara's Money Game," *Newsday: The Long Island Newspaper,* (April 16, 1992), pp. 4–5.

5. http://www.brookings.edu/comm/policybriefs/pb106.htm, accessed May 21, 2004.

6. *Webster's New World Dictionary, College Edition,* Cleveland and New York: World, (1964), p. 380.

7. Charles K. Ponzi Web site, http://www.mark-knutson.com.

8. This statistic is the proprietary information of a major financial institution for which the author was a consultant.

9. The Association of Certified Fraud Examiners, *The Report to the National on Occupational Fraud and Abuse* (Austin, TX, ACFE, 1996), p. 4.

10. The Association of Certified Fraud Examiners, *The Report to the National on Occupational Fraud and Abuse* (Austin, TX, ACFE, 1996), p. 4.

11. U.S. Securities and Exchange Commission, Litigation Release No. 17039, June 19, 2001. http://www.sec.gov, accesses on June 19, 2001.

12. http://www.fraud.org/telemarketing/teleset.htm, accessed on June 19, 2001. The National Fraud Information Center.

13. Much of this discussion was taken from Berstein Litowitz Berger & Grossman LLP, Institutional Investor Advocate, Volume 5, Fourth Quarter 2003.

14. http://www.fool.com/News/mft/2003/mft03091208.htm, accessed on May 1, 2004.

15. Federal Bureau of Investigation, *White Collar Crime: A Report to the Nation,* (Washington, DC: Department of Justice, 1989), p. 6.

16. Securities and Exchange Commission, Litigation Release No. 16489, March 29, 2000; Release No. 38765, June 24, 1997, http://codesign.scu.edu/505/set02/005/webproject/page6.htm.

17. "Careers to Count On," *U.S. News and World Report,* February 18, 2002.

18. http://stats.bls.gove/oco/ocos001.htm, accessed on Sept. 9, 2004.

19. News Release, Iowa Department of Justice, Attorney General Tom Miller (June 26, 2001), http://www.state.ia.us/government/ag/PCH_settlement_release_IA.htm.

20. *Courtenay Thompson,* **The Internal Auditor**, vol. 52, (August 1995), no. 4; p. 68, 3 pgs *Copyright Institute of Internal Auditors, Incorporated, August 1995.*

21. The Wall Street Journal, "Fraud Charges Widen Scope of Scandal Facing Mutual Funds," December 12 , 2003, p. C-1.

# CHAPTER 2

# WHO COMMITS FRAUD AND WHY

## LEARNING OBJECTIVES

After studying this chapter, you should be able to:

1. Recognize who commits fraud.

2. Understand why people commit fraud.

3. Become familiar with the fraud triangle.

4. Understand how pressure contributes to fraud.

5. Know why opportunities must be present in order for fraud to be committed.

6. Identify controls that prevent or detect fraudulent behavior.

7. Identify noncontrol factors that provide opportunities for fraud.

8. Understand why people rationalize.

*I, Dennis Greer, am making this statement on my own, without threat or promises, as to my activities in regard to the activity of kiting between Bank A and Bank B. As of May 19XX, I was having extreme emotional and financial difficulties. For religious reasons, I was required without notice to move out of where I was living, and I had no place to go. Also, my grandmother— the only family member I was close to—was dying. I had to live out of my car for three and a half weeks. At the end of this time, my grandmother died. She lived in Ohio. I went to the funeral and I returned with a $1,000 inheritance. I used this money to secure an apartment. The entire sum was used up for the first month's rent, deposit, and the application fee. From that time, mid-June, until the first part of August, I was supporting myself on my minimum-wage job at the nursery. I had no furniture or a bed. I was barely making it. I was feeling distraught over the loss of my grandmother and problems my parents and brother were having. I felt all alone. The first part of August arrived and my rent was due. I did not have the full amount to pay it. This same week, I opened a checking account at Bank B. I intended to close my Bank A account because of a lack of ATMs, branches, and mis-understanding. As I said, my rent was due and I did not know how to meet it. On an impulse, I wrote the apartment manager a check for the amount due. I did not have the funds to cover it. I thought I could borrow it, but I could not. During the time I was trying to come up with the money, I wrote a check from my Bank B account to cover the rent check and put it into Bank*

*A. I did not know it was illegal. I knew it was unethical, but I thought since the checks were made out to me that it wasn't illegal. This went on for about a week— back and forth between banks. I thought I could get the money to cover this debt but I never did. My grandmother's estate had been quite large, and I expected more money, but it was not to happen. After a week of nothing being said to me by the banks, I began to make other purchases via this method. I needed something to sleep on and a blanket and other items for the apartment. I bought a sleeper sofa, a desk, a modular shelf/bookcase, dishes, and also paid off my other outstanding debts—college loans, dentist bill, and credit. I was acting foolishly. No one had questioned me at the banks about any of this. I usually made deposits at different branches to try to avoid suspicion, but when I was in my own branches, no one said a thing. I thought maybe what I was doing wasn't wrong after all. So I decided to purchase a new car, stereo, and a new computer to use at home for work. Still, I did not have a problem making deposits at the banks. But, I was feeling very guilty. I knew I needed to start downsizing the "debt" and clear it up. I began to look for a better-paying job. Finally, last week I got a call from Bank B while I was at work: They had discovered a problem with my account. I realized then that the banks had found out. Later that day, I got another call from Bank A. They told me that what I had been doing was illegal and a felony. I was in shock. I didn't know it was that bad. I realize now how wrong what I did was. From the start, I knew it was unethical, but I didn't know it was*

*indeed a crime until now. I have had to do a lot of thinking, praying, and talking to those close to me about this. I am truly sorry for what I have done, and I don't EVER plan to do it again. All I want now is to make amends with the banks. I do not have the money to pay back either bank right now. I realize this hurts them. I want to try to set this right, whether I go to prison or not. I am prepared to work however long it takes to pay the banks back in full with reasonable interest from a garnishment of my wages from now until the full amount is paid and settled. I committed this act because I was feeling desperate. I was emotionally a wreck and physically tired. I felt I didn't have a* *choice but to do what I did or return to living in my car. I know now that what I did was wrong, and I am very sorry for it. I am attempting to seek psychological counseling to help me deal with and resolve why I did this. I feel I have a lot to offer society, once I am able to clean up my own life and get it straightened out. I pray the bank employees and officers will forgive me on a personal level for the hardship my actions have caused them, and I want to make full restitution. I have done wrong, and I must now face the consequences. This statement has been made in my own words, by myself, without threat or promise, and written by my own hand.*
*Dennis Greer*

Obviously, the names of the perpetrator and the banks are fictional. However, this true confession was written by a person who was involved in the fraud of kiting—using the float time between banks to give the impression that he had money in his accounts. This example shows a fraud perpetrated by a customer.

In Chapter 1, we talked about what fraud is, the seriousness of the fraud problem, different types of frauds, including customer frauds such as Dennis Greer's, how much fraud costs organizations, and the difference between civil and criminal law. In this chapter, we discuss who commits frauds and why they commit fraud. To prevent, detect, and investigate fraud, you must understand what motivates fraudulent behavior or why otherwise honest people behave unethically.

## Who Commits Fraud

Research shows that anyone can commit fraud. Fraud perpetrators usually can't be distinguished from other people on the basis of demographic or psychological characteristics. Most fraud perpetrators have profiles that look like those of other honest people.

In one study of the characteristics of fraud perpetrators, the perpetrators, were compared with (1) prisoners incarcerated for property offenses and (2) a noncriminal sample of college students. The personal backgrounds and psychological profiles of the three groups were compared. The results indicated that incarcerated fraud perpetrators were different from other incarcerated prisoners. When compared to other criminals, they were less likely to be caught, turned in, arrested, convicted, and incarcerated. They were also less likely to serve long sentences. In addition, fraud perpetrators were considerably older. Although only 2 percent of the property offenders were female, 30 percent of fraud perpetrators were women. Fraud perpetrators were better educated, more religious, less likely to have criminal records, less likely to have abused alcohol, and considerably less likely to have used drugs. They were also in better psychological health. They enjoyed more optimism, self-esteem, self-sufficiency, achievement, motivation, and family harmony than other property offenders. Fraud perpetrators also seemed to express more social conformity, self-control, kindness, and empathy than other property offenders.[1]

When fraud perpetrators were compared with college students, they differed only slightly. Fraud perpetrators suffered more psychic pain and were more dishonest, more independent, more sexually mature, more socially deviant, and more empathetic than college students. However, fraud perpetrators were much more similar to college students than they were to property offenders. The diagram In Figure 2-1 illustrates the differences among the three groups:

It is important to understand the characteristics of fraud perpetrators because they appear to be much like people who have traits that organizations look for in hiring employees, seeking out customers and clients, and selecting vendors. This knowledge helps us to understand that (1) most employees, customers, vendors, and business associates and partners fit the profile of fraud perpetrators and are probably capable of committing fraud; and (2) it is impossible to predict in advance which employees, vendors,

## Figure 2-1 Profiles of Fraud Perpetrators

College Students        Fraud Perpetrators        Other Property Offenders

clients, customers, and others will become dishonest. In fact, when fraud does occur, the most common reaction by those around the fraud is denial. Victims can't believe that individuals who look much like them and who are usually those most trusted can behave dishonestly.

# Why People Commit Fraud

Of the thousands of ways to perpetrate fraud, Dennis Greer's example illustrates the three key elements common to all of them. His fraud included (1) a perceived pressure, (2) a perceived opportunity, and (3) some way to rationalize the fraud as acceptable. These three elements make up what we call the fraud triangle, as shown in Figure 2-2.

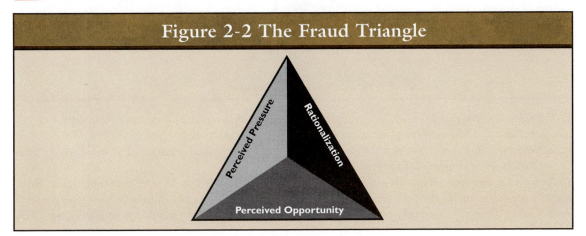

## Figure 2-2 The Fraud Triangle

Perceived Pressure

Rationalization

Perceived Opportunity

After moving into an apartment, Dennis Greer could not pay the second month's rent. Faced with a choice between being dishonest or going back to living in his car, Dennis chose to be dishonest. Every fraud perpetrator faces some kind of *perceived pressure*. Most pressures involve a financial need, although nonfinancial pressures, such as the need to report results better than actual performance, frustration with work, or even a challenge to beat the system, can also motivate fraud. In Dennis Greer's case, he had an actual pressure. You may look at a fraud perpetrator and say "you didn't have a real pressure." But it doesn't matter what you think—it is only what is in the fraud perpetrator's mind that matters. Later in this chapter we will discuss the different kinds of pressures experienced by fraud perpetrators.

Dennis found a way to commit fraud by repeatedly writing bad checks to give the impression that he was depositing real money in his accounts. He didn't need access to cash, to use force, or to even confront his victims physically. Rather, he simply wrote checks to himself in the privacy of his own apartment and deposited them in two different banks. His weapons of crime were a pen and checks from the financial institutions. Whether Dennis could actually get away with his crime didn't matter. What mattered was that Dennis believed he could conceal the fraud—in other words, he had a *perceived opportunity*.

Fraud perpetrators need a way to ***rationalize*** their actions as acceptable. Dennis's rationalizations were twofold: (1) he didn't believe what he was doing was "illegal," although he recognized it might be unethical; and (2) he believed he would get an inheritance and be able to pay the money back. In his mind, he was only *borrowing*, and, even though his method of borrowing was perhaps unethical, he would repay the debt. After all, almost everyone borrows money.

Perceived pressure, perceived opportunity, and rationalization are common to every fraud. Whether the fraud is one that benefits the perpetrators directly, such as employee fraud, or one that benefits the perpetrator's organization, such as management fraud, the three elements are always present. In the case of management fraud, for example, the pressure could be the need to make earnings look better to meet debt covenants, the opportunity could be a weak audit committee, and the rationalization could be that we'll only "cook the books" until we can get over this temporary hump.

In many ways, fraud is like fire. In order for a fire to occur, three elements are necessary: (1) oxygen, (2) fuel, and (3) heat. These three elements make up the "fire triangle" in Figure 2-3. When all three elements come together, fire results.

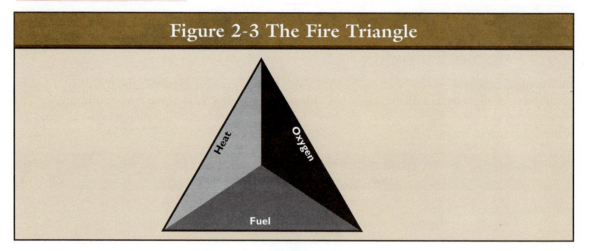

## Figure 2-3 The Fire Triangle

Firefighters know that a fire can be extinguished by eliminating any one of the three elements. Oxygen is often eliminated by smothering, by using chemicals, or by causing explosions, as is the case in oil well fires. Heat is most commonly eliminated by pouring water on fires. Fuel is removed by building fire lines or fire breaks or by shutting off the source of the fuel.

As with the elements in the fire triangle, the three elements in the fraud triangle are interactive. With fire, the more flammable the fuel, the less oxygen and heat it takes to ignite. Similarly, the purer the oxygen, the less flammable the fuel needs to be to ignite. With fraud, the greater the perceived opportunity or the more intense the pressure, the less rationalization it takes to motivate someone to commit fraud. Likewise, the more dishonest a perpetrator is, the less opportunity or pressure it takes to motivate fraud. The scale in Figure 2-4 illustrates the relationship between the three elements.

As we will show in later chapters, people who try to prevent fraud usually work on only one of the three elements of the fraud triangle: opportunity. Because fraud fighters generally believe that opportunities can be eliminated by having good internal controls, they focus all or most of their preventive efforts on implementing controls and ensuring adherence to them. Rarely do they focus on the pressures motivating fraud or on the rationalizations of perpetrators.

It is interesting to note that almost every study of honesty performed in advanced countries reveals that levels of honesty are decreasing. Given the interactive nature of the elements in the fraud triangle, the decreasing levels of honesty present a scary future concerning fraud. Less honesty makes it easier to rationalize, thus requiring less perceived opportunity or pressure for fraud to occur.

Rationalizations and related honesty levels, as well as fraud opportunities, will be discussed later in this chapter. We now turn our attention to a discussion of the pressures motivating individuals to commit fraud.

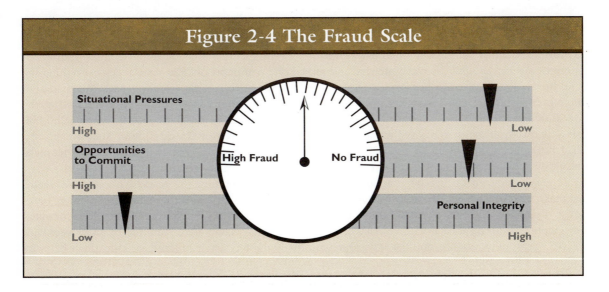

**Figure 2-4 The Fraud Scale**

## The First Element of the Fraud Triangle: Pressure

Fraud can be perpetrated to benefit oneself or to benefit an organization. Employee fraud, in which an individual embezzles from his or her employer, usually benefits the perpetrator. Management fraud, in which an organization's officers deceive investors and creditors usually by manipulating financial statements, is most often perpetrated to benefit an organization, and indirectly, its officers. In this section we discuss the different pressures that motivate individuals to perpetrate fraud on their own behalf. Most fraud experts divide pressures into four types: (1) financial pressures, (2) vices, (3) work-related pressures, and (4) other pressures.

### Financial Pressures

Studies show that approximately 95 percent of all frauds involve either financial or vice-related pressures. Dennis Greer's financial pressures were that he was living in his car, didn't have furniture or other living necessities, and was broke. Common financial pressures associated with fraud that benefits perpetrators directly include the following:

1. Greed
2. Living beyond one's means
3. High bills or personal debt
4. Poor credit
5. Personal financial losses
6. Unexpected financial needs

This list is not exhaustive, and these pressures are not mutually exclusive. However, each pressure in this list has been associated with numerous frauds. We know of individuals, for example who have committed fraud because they were destitute. We know of other fraud perpetrators who were living lifestyles far beyond that of their peers. When one perpetrator was caught embezzling more than $1.3 million from his employer, for example, investigators discovered that he spent the money on monogrammed shirts and gold cuff links, two Mercedes Benz cars, an expensive suburban home, a beachfront condominium, furs, rings, and other jewelry for his wife, a new car for his father-in-law, and a country club membership. Most people would say he really didn't have financial pressures. But to him, the pressures to possess these luxuries were enough to motivate him to commit fraud.

Financial pressures can occur suddenly or can be long term. Unfortunately, few fraud perpetrators inform others when they are having financial problems. As an example, consider Susan Jones. She worked at the same company for more than 32 years. Her integrity had never been questioned. At age 63, she became a grandmother. Almost immediately, she became a spendaholic. She bought everything she could get her hands on for her two grandchildren. She even became addicted to the Home Shopping Network, a cable TV channel. During the three years prior to her retirement, Susan stole about $650,000 from her employer. When caught, she was sentenced and served one year in prison. She also deeded everything she and her husband owned to her former employer in an attempt to pay the employer back. By giving her employer her home, her retirement account, and her cars, she repaid approximately $400,000 of the $650,000 she stole. She also entered into a restitution agreement to pay back the remaining $250,000 she still owed, although in reality she wasn't even paying the interest on the $250,000. And, because she had not paid income taxes on the $250,000 of fraudulent "income," the IRS required her to make monthly tax payments after she got out of prison.

The fact that someone has been an "honest" employee for a long time (32 years in this example) seems to make no difference when severe financial pressures occur or an individual perceives that such pressures exist. Recent studies found that although approximately 30 percent of employee frauds are perpetrated by employees during their first three years of employment, 70 percent are committed by employees with 4 to 35 years of experience, and the age group with the highest evidence of fraud are individuals between 35 and 44 years old.

Financial pressure is the most common type of pressure to commit fraud. Usually when management fraud occurs, companies overstate assets on the balance sheet and net income on the income statement. They usually have pressure to do so because of a poor cash position, receivables that aren't collectible, a loss of customers, obsolete inventory, a declining market, or restrictive loan covenants that are being violated. For example, Regina Vacuum was a company whose management committed massive financial statement fraud. Their major pressure was that the vacuum cleaners they were selling were defective and had melting parts, and thousands were being returned. The large number of sales returns reduced revenues significantly and created such income pressures that management intentionally understated sales returns and overstated sales.

## Vice Pressures

Closely related to financial pressures are motivations created by vices such as gambling, drugs, alcohol, and expensive extramarital relationships. As an example of how these vices motivate a person to commit fraud, consider one individual's confession of how gambling led to his dishonest acts:

> As I sat on the stool in front of the blackjack table I knew I was in trouble. I had just gambled away my children's college fund. I stumbled to my hotel room, hoping to wake up and realize this evening was nothing more than a nightmare. While driving back to San Jose from Reno Sunday morning, I could not face the embarrassment of telling my wife. I had to come up with the money. I was sure that if I had only $500, I could win the money back. But how could I get $500? A short time later at work, an accounts payable clerk came to my office seeking assistance with a problem. The clerk was matching invoices with purchase orders. He had found an invoice for $3,200 that did not match the purchase order. Immediately, I realized how I could get the $500 "loan." My company was a fast-growing microchip producer whose internal controls were quite good on paper but were often not followed. The company had a policy of paying, without secondary approval, any invoice of $500 or less. I decided to set up a dummy company that would issue invoices to my employer for amounts up to $500. I was confident my winnings from these "borrowings" would not only allow me to replace the college fund, but would also allow repayment of the "loan." I couldn't believe how easy it was to "borrow" the money. The first check showed up in a PO box I had opened a few days earlier. I called my wife with the bad news. Together with the controller, I would have to fly to Los Angeles over the weekend to meet with lawyers over a company matter. Within minutes, I was on my way to Reno. Upon arrival, I went straight to the craps tables. By 4:00 A.M., I was not only out of money but was in the hole over $600. I was concerned about the losses, but not as worried as before. I would just submit more fictitious bills to the company. Over the next few months, my fraud progressed to the point where I had set up two more dummy companies and insisted that accounts payable clerks not verify any invoice of less than $750. No one questioned my changing the policy because I had

> *worked for the company for over 14 years and was a "trusted" employee. After one year, I had replaced the college fund and purchased a new automobile; I had stolen over $75,000. I was caught when the internal auditors matched addresses of vendors and found that my three dummy vendors all had the same PO box.*

Vices are the worst kind of pressures to commit fraud. We are aware of female employees who embezzled because their children were on drugs and they couldn't stand to see them go through withdrawal pains. We are also aware of "successful" managers who, in addition to embezzling from their companies, burglarized homes and engaged in other types of theft to support their drug habits. To understand how addictive vices can be, consider the following confessions from reformed gamblers.

- "Gambling was the ultimate experience for me—better than sex, better than any drug. I had withdrawal tortures just like a heroin junkie."
- "I degraded myself in every way possible. I embezzled from my own company; I conned my six-year-old out of his allowance."
- "Once I was hooked, any wager would do. I would take odds on how many cars would pass over a bridge in the space of 10 minutes."
- "I stole vacation money from the family sugar jar. I spent every waking hour thinking about getting to the track."
- "After I woke up from an appendectomy, I sneaked out of the hospital, cashed a bogus check, and headed for my bookie. I was still bleeding from the operation."
- "I'll never forget coming home from work at night, looking through the window at my family waiting for me, and then leaving to place a couple more bets. I was crying the whole time, but I had simply lost all control."

Someone who will steal from a six-year-old child or sneak out of a hospital still bleeding from an operation, will certainly steal from an employer or commit other types of fraud. The number of embezzlers who trace their motivation for embezzlement to alcohol, gambling, and expensive extramarital relationships is high. However, the motivation to steal for drugs may even be higher. Consider these confessions of former addicted drug users.

- "I began living with a man who was a heavy drug user. We had a child, but the relationship didn't last. By the time it ended, I was high on drugs and alcohol so much of the time I could barely manage to make it to work every day."
- "I was the branch manager of a large bank. But secretly I was shooting up in my office all day and stealing money from my employer to finance it."
- "One day my daughter stretched out her little arms in front of me. She had made dots with a red pen on each of the creases in her arms. 'I want to be just like my Daddy,' she said proudly."
- "My wife and I literally whooped for joy at the sight of our newborn son: a 7-pound baby with big eyes and rosy cheeks—normal and healthy looking. But we both knew the moment we had been dreading was now just hours away. The baby would be going through withdrawal. We didn't want him to suffer because of our awful habit. And we had to keep the doctors from finding out he had drugs in his system, or he would be taken from us and placed in foster care. We felt we had no choice. When the nurses left the room, I cradled our baby in my arms and clipped a thin piece of heroin under his tongue."
- " I lost my job. I was robbing and stealing every day to support my habit, which cost $500 per day."

Someone who will clip a piece of heroin under a newborn baby's tongue or burglarize homes to support a habit will surely look for ways to embezzle from employers or commit other types of fraud.

## Work-Related Pressures

Financial pressures and vices may motivate most frauds, but some people commit fraud to get even with their employer or others. Factors such as getting little recognition for job performance, having a feeling of job dissatisfaction, fearing losing one's job, being overlooked for a promotion, and feeling underpaid have motivated many frauds. An example is shown on the next page.

*I began my career at the XYZ Company as a staff accountant. I am a religious person. In fact, I spent a year volunteering with a nonprofit agency that provided relief to people in need of food and shelter. Because of this experience and because of my six years with the company, I was considered a person of impeccable character and a very trusted employee. The president of XYZ is a workaholic and considers an eight-hour day to be something a part-time employee works. As a result, I spent six years working in my finance position, putting in between 12 and 14 hours per day. During this period, I was paid a salary, with no overtime compensation. Early in my career, the extra hours didn't bother me; I considered them an investment in my future. Soon, I was named manager of the purchasing department. After two years in that position, I realized that the 12- to 14-hour days were still an expected way of life at the company. I was becoming bitter about the expectation of overtime and felt that the company "owed me" for the time I had worked for "nothing." I decided to get my "pay" from the company. Working with a favored vendor, I accepted kickbacks to allow over $1.5 million in overcharges to the company. I figured the $80,000 I received in kickbacks was compensation that I deserved.[2]*

## Other Pressures

Once in a while, fraud is motivated by other pressures, such as a spouse who insists on an improved lifestyle or a challenge to beat the system. One perpetrator, for example, embezzled more than $450,000 so her husband could drive a new car, enjoy a higher lifestyle, and eat steak instead of hamburger. One famous computer consultant who is now retained by major companies to help them deter and detect computer fraud, once felt personally challenged to "commit the perfect crime." After purchasing and taking delivery of more than $1.5 million in inventory that was paid for by accessing a large company's computer records, he was caught when one of his inventory managers turned him in.

Most of us face pressures in our lives: We have legitimate financial needs; we make foolish or speculative investments; we are possessed by addictive vices; we feel overworked and underpaid; or we are greedy and want more. We sometimes have a difficult time distinguishing between wants and needs. Indeed, the objective of most people in a capitalistic society is to obtain wealth. We often measure success by how much money or wealth a person has. If you say you have a very successful relative, you probably mean that he or she lives in a big house, has a cabin or a condominium, drives expensive automobiles, and has money to do whatever he or she wants.

To some people, being successful is more important than being honest. If they were to rank the personal characteristics they value most in their lives, being successful would rank higher than having integrity. Psychologists tell us that most people have a price at which they will be dishonest. Individuals with high integrity and low opportunity need high pressure to be dishonest.

Most of us can think of scenarios in which we, too, might commit fraud. If for example, we were starving, and we worked in an environment where cash was abundant and not accounted for, and we really believed that we would repay the money taken to feed ourselves, we might commit fraud. The U.S. president most famous for his honesty, Abraham Lincoln, once threw a man out of his office, angrily turning down a substantial bribe. When someone asked why he was so angry, he said, "Every man has his price, and he was getting close to mine." One thing is for certain—eliminating pressures in the fraud triangle has an effect similar to the removal of heat from the fire triangle. Without some kind of pressure, fraud rarely occurs.

## The Second Element of the Fraud Triangle: Opportunity

A perceived opportunity to commit fraud, to conceal it, or to avoid being punished is the second element of the fraud triangle. In this section we discuss fraud opportunities. First, we will discuss controls that increase opportunities for individuals to commit fraud within an organization. Then, we will provide a number of settings to illustrate noncontrol issues that should be considered when deciding whether a fraud opportunity is present.

At least six major factors increase opportunities for individuals to commit fraud within an organization. The following list of these factors is not exhaustive, but it does provide a sufficient number of settings to illustrate the role of opportunities in the fraud triangle.

1. Lack of or circumvention of controls that prevent or detect fraudulent behavior
2. Inability to judge quality of performance
3. Failure to discipline fraud perpetrators
4. Lack of access to information
5. Ignorance, apathy, and incapacity
6. Lack of an audit trail

## Control Factor: Controls That Prevent or Detect Fraudulent Behavior

Having an effective control framework is probably the most important step an organization can take to prevent and detect employee fraud. The organization that established the common internal control framework that most businesses subscribe to is (Committee of Sponsoring Organizations (COSO)). COSO identifies five elements of an organization's internal control framework, here we will only discuss three of them.

## Table 2-1 An Organization's Internal Control Framework

| | |
|---|---|
| **Control Environment** | The control environment sets the tone of an organization, influencing the control consciousness of its people. It is the foundation for all other components of internal control, providing discipline and structure. Control environment factors include the integrity, ethical values, and competence of the entity's people; management's philosophy and operating style; the way management assigns authority and responsibility, and organizes and develops its people; and the attention and direction provided by the board of directors. |
| **Risk Assessment** | Risk assessment is the identification and analysis of relevant risks to achievement of the entity's established objectives, forming a basis for determining how the risks should be managed. Because economic, industry, regulatory and operating conditions will continue to change, |
| **Control Activities** | Control activities are the policies and procedures that help ensure management directives are carried out and necessary actions are taken to address risks. Control activities occur throughout the organization, at all levels and in all functions. They include a range of activities as diverse as approvals, authorizations, verifications, reconciliations, reviews of operating performance, security of assets and segregation of duties. |
| **Information and Communication** | Pertinent information must be identified, captured, and communicated in a form and time frame that enable people to carry out their responsibilities. Information systems produce reports, containing operational, financial and compliance-related information, that make it possible to run and control the business. They deal not only with internally generated data, but also information about external events, activities and conditions necessary to informed business decision making and external reporting. Effective communication also must occur in a broader sense, flowing down, across and up the organization. There also needs to be effective communication with external parties, such as customers, suppliers, regulators and shareholders. |
| **Monitoring** | The monitoring of the internal control systems assesses the quality of the system's performance over time through ongoing monitoring activities, separate evaluations, or a combination of the two. Ongoing monitoring occurs in the course of operations and includes regular management and supervisory activities, and other actions personnel take in performing their duties. The scope and frequency of separate evaluations will depend primarily on an assessment of risks and the effectiveness of ongoing monitoring procedures. |

## THE CONTROL ENVIRONMENT

The *control environment* is the work atmosphere that an organization establishes for its employees. The most important element in establishing an appropriate environment is *management's role and example*. In numerous instances, management's dishonest or inappropriate behavior may be learned and modeled by employees. In the famous Equity Funding case, management was writing insurance policies on individuals who didn't exist and selling them to other insurance companies. Seeing this dishonest behavior, one employee said to himself, "It doesn't make sense to have all these fictitious people live forever. I'll knock a few of them off and collect death proceeds. My actions won't be any different from those of the management of this company." In another case, employees realized top management was overstating revenues. In response, the employees began overstating expenses on their travel reimbursement forms, billing for hours not worked, and perpetrating other types of fraud.

> Proper **modeling** *(being an example) and proper* **labeling** *(communication) are some of the most important elements in the control environment. When management models unacceptable behavior, the control environment is contaminated. Similarly, if management models a behavior that is inconsistent with good control procedures, the effectiveness of the control system is eroded. Managers who say, "Don't loan keys or share passwords with others," and then share their password or keys, send mixed signals and inappropriate behavior will be followed by other employees. In other words, "actions speak louder than words." Management's example or model is the most critical element of the control environment when it comes to preventing fraud. Inappropriate behavior by management allows others to justify overriding and ignoring control procedures. As an example of how a manager's lack of proper modeling can lead to fraud consider the following case: A branch manager stole $36,357 from the bank by cashing in seven customer CDs. She used the passwords of two other employees to execute six of the transactions and her own password to execute the seventh. She was caught when a customer complained. Why would this manager have the other employees passwords? Most likely, she had set a tone through her modeling that the security of passwords was not important.*

The importance of tone at the top was emphasized in the Sarbanes-Oxley legislation that was passed in 2002. One of its requirements is that every public company have a code of ethics or conduct to help deter wrongdoing and to promote the following:

1. "Honest and ethical conduct, including the ethical handling of actual or apparent conflicts of interest between personal and professional relationships"
2. Avoidance of conflicts of interest, including disclosure to an appropriate person or persons identified in the code of any material transaction or relationship that reasonably could be expected to give rise to such a conflict
3. "Full, fair, accurate, timely, and understandable disclosure" in reports and documents that a company files with, or submits to, the Securities and Exchange Commission and in other public communications made by the company
4. "Compliance with applicable governmental laws, rules and regulations"
5. The prompt internal reporting of code violations to an appropriate person or persons identified in the code
6. Accountability for adherence to the code

Under this new requirement, a company would be required to disclose in its annual report whether it has a code of ethics. Companies are also required to disclose either on Form 8-K or on their Internet Web sites any changes to, or waivers of, such code of ethics.

The second critical element in the control environment is *management's communication*. Communicating what is and is not appropriate is critical. Just as parents who are trying to teach their children to be honest must communicate often and openly with them, organizations that want employees to behave in a certain way must clearly label what is and is not acceptable. Codes of conduct, orientation meetings, training, supervisor/employee discussions, and other types of communication that distinguish between acceptable and unacceptable behavior are critical.

To be an effective deterrent to fraud, communication must be consistent. Messages that change based on circumstances and situations serve not only to confuse employees but also to encourage rationalizations. One of the reasons so many frauds occur in crash or rush projects is that typical control procedures are not followed. Inconsistent messages relating to procedures and controls are often conveyed. Strikes, mergers, bankruptcies, and other dramatic events usually result in inconsistent communication and allow for increased fraud.

Just as good communication between managers and employees is critical, accurate and consistent communication between organizations and their customers, vendors, and shareholders is also critical. Consider the following example of a fraud and lawsuit that occurred between a bank and its customer because of failed communication:

> *A financial institution was sending out new credit cards to customers whose credit cards were about to expire. However, the financial institution sent a credit card belonging to one customer to a different customer with the same name but with a different address and social security number. The unintended recipient immediately used the card to withdraw a cash advance of approximately $1,300. Then he used the credit card to buy several items, totaling approximately $5,000. The bank sent him the credit card bill (because it now had the incorrect address for the card). The man, however, didn't pay. After several months of nonpayment, the financial institution called the true owner of the card. When the owner insisted that he had never received the card, the bank researched the problem and discovered that the person using the card was someone different from the owner. The financial institution turned this information over to law enforcement who put out an all points bulletin (APB) on the thief. The man was caught and arrested in a nearby state. He spent three days in jail before being transported back to the state where the financial institution was located. Because he had been incarcerated, he sued the financial institution for $3 million for unlawful imprisonment. Before the case was settled, the financial institution had spent nearly $300,000 defending itself. Making sure they were communicating with the proper customer would have prevented the entire mess.*

The third critical element in creating the proper control structure is *appropriate hiring*. Research has shown that nearly 30 percent of all people in the United State are dishonest, another 30 percent are situationally honest (honest where it pays to be honest and dishonest where it pays to be dishonest), and 40 percent are honest all the time.[3] Even though most organizations are convinced that their employees, customers, and vendors are among the 40 percent who are honest, it usually isn't the case.

When dishonest individuals are hired, even the best controls will not prevent fraud. For example, a bank has tellers, managers, loan officers, and others who have daily access to cash and can steal. Because it is impossible to deter all bank fraud, banks hope that personal integrity, together with preventive and detective controls and the fear of punishment will deter theft.

As an example of the consequences of poor hiring, consider the case of a famous country singer who was raped a few years ago. The singer checked into a well-known hotel. A few hours after her arrival, a knock on her door was accompanied by the words "Room service." She hadn't ordered anything but thought that maybe, because she was famous, the hotel was bringing her a basket of fruit or some complimentary wine. When she opened the door, three hotel custodians burst into her room and raped her. She later sued the hotel for $4 million and won. The basis of her lawsuit was that the hotel had inadequate hiring procedures because all three custodians had previous arrest records and had been fired from previous jobs because of rape.

If an organization does not carefully screen job applicants and hires dishonest individuals, it will have fraud, regardless of how good its other controls are. To understand how good hiring practices can help prevent fraud and other problems, consider a company that decided to take extra precautions in its hiring practices. Their approach was first to train all persons associated with hiring decisions to be expert interviewers and, second, to check three background references for each prospective employee thoroughly. Because of these extra precautions, more than 800 applicants (13 percent of all individuals) who would have been hired were disqualified. These applicants had undisclosed problems, such as falsified employment information, previous arrest records, uncontrollable tempers, alcoholism, drug addiction, and a pattern of being fired from previous jobs.

The effects of poor hiring practices are illustrated in the following excerpt from an article in *Business Week Online*:

> *These days, it's tempting to hire the first person who seems capable of doing a job. But do you know what lurks behind that spiffy resume? The Association of Certified Fraud Examiners estimates that employee fraud costs small companies an average of $120,000 per incident. It's a good idea to check the backgrounds of all applicants. At the very least, you'll be certain the person has the credentials they claim… Three years ago managers hired a security expert to conduct background checks on employees and potential hires, examining credit and criminal backgrounds and verifying education and experience. Good thing they did— the company was on the verge of hiring a director of finance who turned out to have neither the MBA nor any of the experience he said he had. [4]*

The fourth fraud-deterring element of the control environment is a *clear organizational structure*. When everyone in an organization knows exactly who has responsibility for each business activity, fraud is less likely to be committed. In such situations, it is easier to track missing assets and harder to embezzle without being caught. Strict accountability for job performance is critical for a good control environment.

As an example of how failure to assign proper custody resulted in a fraud, consider the case of Jane D:

> *I was one of eight tellers in a medium-sized bank. Because we all had access to money orders and bank checks, I stole 16 money orders. I didn't use them for two weeks to see whether anyone would notice them missing. Then, I used one for $300. After nothing being said during the next two weeks, I used seven more.*

In this case, someone independent from the teller should have had the organizational responsibility to reconcile money orders on a daily basis.

The fifth element of the control environment is an *effective internal audit department,* combined with security or loss prevention programs. Most studies find that internal auditors detect only about 20 percent of all employee frauds (others are detected through tips, by alert employees, or accidentally), but the mere presence of internal auditors provides a significant deterrent effect. Internal auditors provide independent checks and cause perpetrators to question whether they can act and not be caught. A visible and effective security function, in conjunction with an appropriate loss prevention program, can help ensure that fraud is properly investigated and that control weaknesses and violations are appropriately punished.

Taken together, the five control environment elements—(1) proper management modeling, (2) good communication or labeling, (3) effective hiring procedures, (4) clear organizational structure and assigned responsibilities, and (5) an effective internal audit department and security function—can create an atmosphere in which fraud opportunities are decreased because employees see that fraud is not acceptable and not tolerated. Relaxing any one of these five elements increases fraud opportunities.

## THE ACCOUNTING SYSTEM

The second component of the control structure is a good ***accounting system***. Every fraud is comprised of three elements: (1) the theft act, in which assets are taken, (2) concealment, which is the attempt to hide the fraud from others, and (3) conversion, in which the perpetrator spends the money or converts the stolen assets to cash and then spends the money. An effective accounting system provides an ***audit trail*** that allows frauds to be discovered and makes concealment difficult. Unlike bank robbery, in which the perpetrator usually makes no effort to conceal the theft act, concealment is one of the major distinguishing elements of fraud.

Frauds are often concealed in the accounting records. Accounting records are based on transaction documents, either paper or electronic. To cover up a fraud, paper or electronic documentation must be altered, misplaced, or made fraudulent. Frauds can be discovered in the accounting records by examining transaction entries that have no support or by probing financial statement amounts that are not reasonable. Without a good accounting system, distinguishing between actual fraud and unintentional errors is often difficult. A good accounting system should ensure that recorded transactions are (1) valid, (2) properly authorized, (3) complete, (4) properly classified, (5) reported in the proper period, (6) properly valued, and (7) summarized correctly.

## CONTROL ACTIVITIES (PROCEDURES)

The third component of the control structure is good ***control activities (or procedures)***. An individual who owns his or her own business and is the sole employee probably does not need many control procedures. Although such people may have ample opportunity to defraud their companies, they have no incentive to do so. They wouldn't steal from themselves, and they would never want to treat customers poorly. However, organizations that involve many employees must have control procedures so that the actions of employees will be congruent with the goals of management or the owners. In addition, with control procedures, opportunities to commit or conceal frauds are eliminated or minimized. No matter what the business is, whether it is the business of raising children; the business of operating a financial institution, a grocery store, or a *Fortune* 500 company; or the business of investing personal assets, five primary control procedures are needed:

1. Segregation of duties, or dual custody
2. System of authorizations
3. Independent checks
4. Physical safeguards
5. Documents and records

Businesses may follow thousands of control procedures, but they are all variations of each of these five basic procedures. Good fraud detection and prevention efforts involve matching the most effective control procedures with the various risks of fraud. As an illustration of how control procedures can be used to achieve goal congruence and prevent fraud, consider the following situation:

> *Mark was a seventh grader. At the parent-teacher conference, Mark's parents discovered that he was getting straight As in all of his classes except one—a German class in which he was getting an F. When Mark's parents later asked him about the class, he said, "I hate the teacher. She is a jerk and I refuse to work for her." After discussions with the teacher and Mark, Mark's parents decided to implement three controls so that his actions would be consistent with the desires of his parents. First, Mark's parents printed up some simple forms (documents) for the teacher to check off each day. These pieces of paper contained two simple statements: (1) Mark (was) (was not) prepared for class today, and (2) Mark (was) (was not) responsible in class today. The teacher would circle the appropriate response to each phrase, initial the paper, and send it home with Mark. By insisting on reading the note each night, Mark's parents were performing an independent check on his performance. In addition, his roller blades were taken away until his grade improved. Taking away his right to play street hockey on his roller blades was a variation of an authorization control. (He lost his authorized use.) When Mark's parents invoked the three controls of (1) documents, (2) independent checks, and (3) taking away an authorized activity, his behavior performance in German changed to become more in line with the goals of his parents. By the end of the term, his grade in German changed from an F to a B.*

**Segregation of Duties and Dual Custody.** Activities can usually be better controlled by invoking either *segregation of duties* or dual-custody control. Segregation of duties involves dividing a task into two parts, so that one person does not have complete control of the task. Dual custody requires two individuals to work together at the same task. Either way, it takes two people to do one job. This form of control, like most preventive controls, is most often used when cash is involved. For example, the opening of incoming cash in a business is usually done by two people or by segregating duties. The accounting for and the handling of cash are separated so that one person does not have access to both. An example of the ease with which fraud can be perpetrated when accounting for and custody of assets are not separated is the fraud of Fred R.

> *Fred R. worked for a medium-size homebuilder. He was in charge of writing checks as well as reconciling bank statements. Over a period of time, Fred stole more than $400,000 by manipulating the check register and forcing the bank reconciliation to balance. If, for example, his employer owed a subcontractor $15,000, Fred would write the check for $15,000 and write $20,000 on the check stub. Then, using the next check, he would write himself a check for $5,000 and mark the check stub "voided." When the bank statement was returned, he would destroy the checks written to himself and force the reconciliation.*

Fred's fraud could easily have been caught, if not prevented, if someone besides Fred had either reconciled the bank statements or written checks. Even small business owners should either set up as segregated duties or always do themselves the following three critical functions: (1) writing checks, (2) making bank deposits, and (3) reconciling bank statements.

Because two individuals are involved, dual custody or segregation of duties is usually the most expensive of all controls. Labor costs are high, and hiring two people to complete one job is a luxury that most businesses don't believe they can afford. This control always involves a trade-off between higher labor cost and less opportunity for error and fraud. Besides being expensive, good dual custody is often difficult to enforce. When two individuals are working on the same task, they shouldn't take their eyes or their minds off the task to answer telephones, use the restroom, respond to a question, or even sneeze. An example of a fraud that was perpetrated in a supposed dual-custody environment is the case of Roger M., who made the following confession:

> *On January 20xx, I took the amount of $3,062 in cash, which was contained in a disposable night drop bag. I concealed my actions by putting it inside a night drop envelope that I processed on the same day. I have no real excuse for taking money. I saw an easy way of taking the money, and I took advantage of it. Circumstances that made it seem easy to take the money without being caught or observed were that I was situated on the customer side of the merchant vault, which obscured the view of my dual-custody partner. I have reimbursed the bank today (January 27, 20xx) the amount of $3,062.*

**System of Authorizations.** The second internal control procedure is a proper *system of authorizations*. Authorization control procedures take many forms. Passwords authorize individuals to use computers and to access certain databases. Signature cards authorize individuals to enter safe deposit boxes, to cash checks, and to perform other functions at financial institutions. Spending limits authorize individuals to spend only what is in their budget or approved level.

When people are not authorized to perform an activity, the opportunity to commit fraud is reduced. For example, when individuals are not authorized to enter safe deposit boxes, they cannot enter and steal someone else's contents. When individuals are not authorized to approve purchases, they cannot order items for personal use and have their companies pay for the goods. As the following fraud case shows, the failure to enforce authorization controls makes the perpetration of fraud quite simple.

> *Mary and Ron had been customers of a certain bank for many years. Because Ron owned a jewelry store, they maintained a safe deposit box at the bank to store certain inventory. Most employees of the bank knew them well because of their frequent visits to make deposits and conduct other business. What was unknown to the bank employees was that Mary and Ron were having marital difficulties, which ended in a bitter divorce. After the divorce, they canceled their joint safe deposit box. Ron came in to the bank a short time later and opened a new safe deposit box, with his daughter as cosigner. Because Mary was bitter about the divorce settlement, she entered the bank one day and told the safe deposit custodian (who had been away on vacation when she and Ron closed their box) that she had lost her key and needed to have the box drilled. Because the custodian knew Mary and didn't know the old box had been closed and a new one opened, Mary arranged to force open the box. Without any problems, the box was drilled*

*and Mary emptied the contents. When Ron tried to open the box a few days later, he discovered what had happened. Because Mary was not a signer on the account at the time the box was forced open, the bank was completely liable and settled out of court with the jeweler for $200,000. This fraud was allowed to be perpetrated because the authorization control of matching signatures to a signature card was not performed.*

**Independent Checks.** The theory behind ***independent checks*** is that if people know their work or activities will be monitored by others, the opportunity to commit and conceal a fraud will be reduced. For example, the Office of the Controller of the Currency (OCC) requires that every bank employee in the United States take one week's vacation (five consecutive days) each year. While employees are gone, others are supposed to perform their work. If an employee's work piles up while he or she is out for the week, this "mandatory vacation" control is not working as it should and the opportunity to commit fraud is not eliminated.

Periodic job rotations, cash counts or certifications, supervisor reviews, employee hot lines, and the use of auditors are other forms of independent checks. One large department store in Europe has a complete extra staff of employees for its chain of department stores. This staff goes to a store and works while everyone who is employed there goes on vacation for a month. While they are gone, the transient staff operates the store. One of the purposes of this program is to provide complete, independent checks on the activities of store employees. If someone who is committing fraud is forced to leave for a month, the illegal activity is often discovered.

As an illustration of the creative use of independent checks, consider the case of a Baskin-Robbins ice cream store in Washington, D.C.

*Upon entering this 31-flavors establishment, the customer is greeted by a smiling cashier. Two large signs hang on the wall behind the cashier. One sign reads, "If you have problems with service, please call the manager at this telephone number." The other reads, "If you get a star on your sales receipt, you receive a free sundae."*

In an ice cream store or any other retail establishment, one of the easiest way to perpetrate fraud is to accept cash from customers and either not ring it into the cash register or ring it in as a lesser amount. If the store happens to sell ice cream, cones can be made a little smaller during the day so that the extra ice cream used in the cones that are not entered into the cash register is not noticeable. The purpose of the Baskin-Robbins signs is to encourage customers to receive and examine their sales receipts. In order for customers to be able to look for a star, sales receipts must be issued. If the cashier charges $2 for an ice cream cone and rings only $1 into the cash register, sooner or later a customer will report the embezzlement.

**Physical Safeguards.** Physical safeguards are often used to protect assets from theft by fraud or other means. ***Physical safeguards***, such as vaults, safes, fences, locks, and keys, take away opportunities to commit fraud by making it difficult for people to access assets. Money locked in a vault, for example, cannot be stolen unless someone gains unauthorized access or unless someone who has access violates the trust. Physical controls are often used to protect inventory by storing it in locked cages or warehouses, small assets such as tools or supplies by locking them in cabinets, and cash by locking it in vaults or safes.

**Documents and Records.** The fifth control procedure involves using ***documents or records*** to create a record of transactions and an audit trail. Documents rarely serve as preventive controls but provide excellent detective controls. Banks, for example, prepare kiting suspect reports as well as reports of employee bank account activity to detect abuse by employees or customers. Most companies require a customer order to initiate a sales transaction. In a sense, the entire accounting system serves as a documentary control. Without documents, no accountability exists. Without accountability, it is much easier to perpetrate fraud and not get caught.

Sometimes an organization can have good documents and records but not use them appropriately. For example, most banks maintain safe deposit boxes for their customers. To enter the safe deposit box area, banks require customers to sign a signature card and provide proof of box ownership. In one case, however, the bank employee looked at the signature and document but opened the wrong box for a customer. Instead of opening the customer's box, he mistakenly opened a box that the bank was storing its excess cash in. Once the teller had left the room, the customer put the bank's excess cash (approximately $110,000) in his briefcase and exited the bank. He hadn't entered the bank intending to steal, but the bank teller, by not examining the document containing his box number carefully, made it too easy for him not to take the money.

## Summary of the Controls That Prevent or Detect Fraud

The control environment, the accounting system, and the many variations of the five control activities or procedures work together to eliminate or reduce the opportunity for employees and others to commit fraud. A good control environment establishes an atmosphere in which proper behavior is modeled and labeled, honest employees are hired, and all employees understand their job responsibilities. The accounting system provides records that make it difficult for perpetrators to gain access to assets, to conceal frauds, and to convert stolen assets without being discovered. Together, these three components make up the control structure of an organization. Table 2-2 summarizes these components and their elements:

## Table 2-2 Internal Control Structure

| Control Environment | Accounting System | Control Activities or Procedures |
|---|---|---|
| • Management philosophy and operating style, modeling | • Valid transactions | • Segregation of duties |
| • Effective hiring procedures | • Properly authorized | • Proper procedures for authorization |
| • Clear organizational structure of proper modeling and labeling | • Completness | • Adequate documents and records |
| • Effective internal audit department | • Proper classification | • Physical control over assets and records |
| | • Proper timing | • Independent checks on performance |
| | • Proper valuation | |
| | • Correct summarization | |

Unfortunately, many frauds are perpetrated in environments in which controls are supposed to be in place but are not being followed. Indeed, it is the overriding and ignoring of existing controls, not the lack of controls, that allow most frauds to be perpetrated.

## Noncontrol Factor: Inability to Judge the Quality of Performance

If you pay someone to construct a fence, you can probably examine the completed job and determine whether the quality of work meets your specifications and is consistent with the agreed-upon contract. If, however, you hire a lawyer, a doctor, a dentist, an accountant, an engineer, or an auto mechanic, it is often difficult to know whether you are paying an excessive amount or receiving inferior service or products. With these kinds of contracts, it is easy to overcharge, perform work not needed, provide inferior service, or charge for work not performed. As an example of fraud perpetrated by a professional whose work quality could not be assessed, consider the following excerpt from a *Los Angeles Times* article.

> *A dermatologist who was struck and killed after walking into freeway traffic last week had been under investigation by the state medical board for allegedly faking diagnoses of skin cancer to collect higher fees. Dr. Orville Stone, who once headed the dermatology department at UC Irvine Medical Center, was accused by five former employees of using cancerous patients' skin tissue to fake diagnoses for hundreds of other patients.... Last Friday, the day after the board served a search warrant at his Huntington Beach practice.... Stone, 61, walked in front of traffic on the San Bernardino Freeway near Indio, the California Highway Patrol said. "He basically parked his car, walked down to the embankment and walked in front of the path of a truck and was struck by four other cars." The Highway Patrol listed the death as suicide. Former employees accused Stone of hoarding cancerous moles or skin tissue he removed from at least 3 patients. He then would take healthy tissue from patients, diagnose them as having cancer and switch tissues, sending the diseased tissue to a laboratory for analysis. Stone normally charged about $50 to remove noncancerous skin tissue and about $150 to remove cancerous ones.[5]*

Another example of this noncontrol factor is the case of Sears Automotive in California:

> *Prompted by an increasing number of consumer complaints, the California Department of Consumer Affairs completed a one-year investigation into allegations that Sears Tire and Auto Centers overcharged their customers for auto repair services. The undercover investigation was conducted in two phases. In the first phase, agents took 38 cars known to have defects in the brakes and no other mechanical faults to 27 different Sears Automotive Centers in California during 19xx. In 34 of the 38 cases, or 89 percent of the time, agents were told that additional work was necessary, involving additional costs. Their average amount of the overcharge was $223, but in the worst case, which occurred in San Francisco, agents were overcharged $585 to have the front brake pads, front and rear springs, and control-arm bushings replaced. Although a spokesman for Sears denies the allegations and says that Sears will fight any attempt to deprive them of their license to do auto repair work in California, the evidence of fraud is substantial. In one case, Ruth Hernandez, a citizen of Stockton, California, went to Sears to have new tires put on her car. While she was there, the mechanic informed her that she also needed new struts, which would cost an additional $419.95. When Mrs. Hernandez sought a second opinion, she was told her struts were fine. The Sears mechanic later admitted to having made an incorrect diagnosis.[6]*

In trying to understand why a well-established, well-reputed company such as Sears might commit such a fraud, it is important to know that Sears had established a quota for parts, services, and repair sales for each eight-hour shift. Allegedly, mechanics who consistently did not meet their quotas either had their hours reduced or were transferred out of the parts and service department. Apparently, faced with the pressure to cheat or fail, and believing that customers would not know for themselves whether the parts and services were actually needed, many service center employees decided to commit fraud.

## Noncontrol Factor: Failure to Discipline Fraud Perpetrators

Criminologists generally agree that rapists have the highest rate of repeat offenses (recidivism) of all criminals. The next highest rate of repeat offenders is probably fraud perpetrators who are not prosecuted or disciplined. An individual who commits fraud and is not punished or is merely terminated suffers no significant penalty and often resumes the fraudulent behavior.

Fraud perpetrators are usually individuals who command respect in their jobs, communities, churches, and families. If they are marginally sanctioned or terminated, they rarely inform their families and others of the real reason for their termination or punishment. On the other hand, if they are prosecuted, they usually suffer significant embarrassment from having family, friends, and business associates know about their offenses. Indeed, it is usually suffering humiliation, more than any other factor, that deters future fraud activity by fraud perpetrators.

Because of the expense and time involved in prosecuting, many organizations merely dismiss dishonest employees, hoping to rid themselves of the problem. What these organizations fail to realize is that such action is rather shortsighted. Although they may rid themselves of one fraud perpetrator, they have sent a signal to others in the organizations that fraud perpetrators do not suffer significant consequences for their actions. Indeed, lack of prosecution can give others "perceived opportunity" that, when combined with pressure and rationalization, can result in additional frauds in the organization. Perceived opportunity is removed when organizations maintain a high probability that perpetrators will be punished, not just discovered.

In a society in which workers are mobile and often move from job to job, mere termination often helps perpetrators build an attractive resume but does not eliminate fraud opportunities. A man, John Doe, is a classic example of someone whose termination without being punished for fraud allowed him to get increasingly attractive jobs at increased salary levels. His employment and fraud history for 14 years is presented in Table 2-3.

## Table 2-3 John Doe's Employment and Fraud History

| Occupation | Job Length | Amount Embezzled |
|---|---|---|
| Insurance sales | 10 months | $200 |
| Office manager | 2 years | 1,000 |
| Bookkeeper | 1 year | 30,000 |
| Accountant | 2 years | 20,000 |
| Accountant | 2 years | 30,000 |
| Controller and CFO | 6 years | 1,363,700 |
| Manager | Still employed | ? |

According to one reference who described the fraud, this man was never prosecuted. His victim organizations either felt sorry for him, thought prosecution would be too time-consuming and too expensive, or merely chose to pass the problem on to others. As a result, every succeeding job this perpetrator obtained was better than his previous one until he became a controller and chief financial officer (CFO) making $130,000 a year. By merely terminating the perpetrator, his victims helped him build a resume and secure increasingly attractive jobs.

## Noncontrol Factor: Lack of Access to Information

Many frauds are allowed to be perpetrated because victims don't have access to information possessed by the perpetrators. This factor is especially prevalent in many of the large management frauds that have been perpetrated against stockholders, investors, and debt holders. In the famous ESM[7] fraud case, for example, the same securities had been sold to investors several times. Yet, because those investment records were only in the possession of ESM, victims didn't know of the fraudulent sales.

A classic example of a fraud in which lack of information allowed the fraud to be perpetrated is the Lincoln Savings and Loan case. On January 6, 1992, Charles Keating and his son, Charles Keating III, were convicted on 73 and 64 counts, respectively, of racketeering and fraud. Charles Keating had created sham transactions to make Lincoln Savings look more profitable than it really was in order to please auditors and regulators. He was able to perpetrate the fraudulent schemes because auditors and regulators were not given complete access to transactions. For example, one transaction, known as the *RA Homes sale*, was structured as follows:

> *On September 30, 1986, defendants Keating and others caused a subsidiary of Lincoln Savings to engage in a fraudulent sale of approximately 1,300 acres of undeveloped land northwest of Tucson, Arizona, to RA Homes, Inc., at a price of approximately $25 million, consisting of a $5 million cash down payment and a $20 million promissory note, secured only by the undeveloped land. Defendants Keating and others caused Lincoln to record a sham profit of approximately $8.4 million on the sale. RA Homes agreed to purchase the land only after Keating orally (1) promised that Lincoln would reimburse RA Homes for the down payment on the purchase, (2) agreed that the Lincoln subsidiary would retain responsibility for developing and marketing the property, and (3) guaranteed that RA Homes would be able to sell the land at a profit within a year following the purchase.[8]*

Auditors didn't know about any of the oral commitments, all of which violated accounting standards for recording a real estate sale. Subsequent to these oral agreements, in supposedly separate transactions, Keating loaned RA Homes $5 million (to cover the down payment) and then continued to manage, market, and develop the "sold" property. When the real estate agent, who supposedly had an exclusive selling arrangement, discovered that the 1,300 acres had supposedly been sold by Charles Keating himself, he contacted Charles Keating for commissions on the sale and was told that no real estate commission was due because the land had just been "parked' with RA Homes. With the higher reported profits of his company, Lincoln Savings and Loan was able to appear profitable and further perpetrate its fraud on investors and others.[9]

Most investment scams and management frauds are dependent on the ability to withhold information from victims. Individuals can attempt to protect themselves against such scams by insisting on full disclosure, including audited financial statements, a business history, and other information that could reveal the fraudulent nature of such organizations.

Certain employee frauds are also allowed to be perpetrated because only offenders have access to information. One small business employee, for example, stole $452,000 from her employer by writing checks to herself. Because she both wrote checks and reconciled the bank statement, no one caught her illegal activity. If, for example, a vendor was owed $10,000, she would write a check to that vendor for $10,000 but enter $20,000 in the check register. Then, after writing a $10,000 check to herself, she would write the word "VOID" in the check register next to the $10,000 check number. Her very simple fraud continued undetected because she was the only employee who had access to the checking account, the check register, and the bank statement.

Lack of information or asymmetrical information has in several cases led to lawsuits. For example, a company had a controller who embezzled more than $5 million from the company. He committed the fraud by writing company checks to himself. Even though the company had poor internal controls, especially a lack of segregation of duties, it sued the financial institution for negligence to recover the stolen funds. The basis of its lawsuit was that the bank had superior information to detect the fraud because both the perpetrator and the company had accounts at the same bank. And, since the perpetrator embezzled money by writing company checks from an account in the bank and depositing the checks in his personal account at the bank, the plaintiff company believed the bank had the best information to detect the fraud.

## Noncontrol Factor: Ignorance, Apathy, and Incapacity

Older people, individuals with language difficulty, and other "vulnerable" citizens are often fraud victims because perpetrators know that such individuals may not have the capacity or the knowledge to detect their illegal acts. Such vulnerable people as these are easier to deceive. For example, consider the following:

> *A nurse with purple hands was charged with embezzling money from patients' rooms at a local hospital. The nurse's hands were purple because invisible dye had been put on money planted in a purse used to trap the embezzler. The nurse was on loan from a temporary help agency. Two sisters reported to hospital security that money had been taken from their purses, which had been left unattended in their father's room. A check of the*

*staff roster showed that the nurse had been alone in the room just before the money was discovered missing. Hospital security put a purse containing dye-covered bills in a room. Later that day, a supervisor reported that the nurse had dye on her hands. When confronted, the nurse first said she had accidentally knocked the purse to the floor and her hands had been stained while she was replacing the items. After further questioning, however, the nurse admitted to taking the money from the women's purses.*

The nurse had found that elderly patients were an easy target for theft. In a hospital room, where patients are often under the influence of sedating drugs, victims may not have the ability to recognize that they have been robbed.

Frauds called **pigeon drops** are specifically designed to take advantage of elderly victims. In such thefts, perpetrators often pose as bank examiners trying to catch dishonest bankers, or they may use some other scheme to get elderly or non-English-speaking customers to withdraw money from banks. When these customers leave the bank with their money, the perpetrators grab the money and flee instead of examining it as promised, knowing the elderly person has no chance to catch them.

Many investment scams are also designed to take advantage of elderly victims. In the AFCO Fraud case, a real estate investment scam, elderly victims were convinced to take out mortgages on their homes. They were persuaded by questions and statements such as the following:

- Do you know you have a sleeping giant in your home that you are not using?
- Your home is worth $100,000, is completely paid off, and you could get $80,000 out of it with no debt to you.
- If you are willing to borrow and invest $80,000, we'll make the mortgage payments, pay you interest of 10% on the money you're making nothing on now, and buy you a new luxury car to drive.

A financially prudent person would recognize that the perpetrators could not possibly pay the 60 percent interest they were promising on the loan, 10 percent interest, plus the new car, but many elderly victims found the offer too good to refuse. As a result, several hundred elderly, retired citizens invested more than $39 million in the AFCO scam.

Many scams prey on elderly or uneducated victims. White-collar crimes such as prime bank fraud, pyramid scams, Internet fraud, phone scams, chain letters, modeling agency, telemarketing fraud, and Nigerian scams are all crimes of persuasion that try to get victims to unknowingly invest money.

Consider Nigerian investment scams, for example. Few of us have not received a letter inviting us to share in huge wealth if only we will make a small investment or share bank account information. Estimates put the losses from these "Nigerian Advance Fee" operations at more than $1 million every single day in the United States alone. The multistage fraud starts when you receive a scam fax, e-mail, or letter such as the one in Figure 2-5.

## Noncontrol Factor: Lack of an Audit Trail

Organizations go to great lengths to create documents that will provide an audit trail so that transactions can be reconstructed and understood. Many frauds, however, involve cash payments or manipulation of records that cannot be followed. Smart employee fraud perpetrators understand that their frauds must be concealed. They also know that such concealment must usually involve manipulation of financial records. When faced with a decision about which financial record to manipulate, perpetrators almost always manipulate the income statement, because they understand that the audit trail will quickly be erased. Here is an example:

*Joan Rivera was the controller for a small bank. Over a period of four years, she stole more than $100,000 by having an upstream bank pay her credit card bills. She covered her fraud by creating an accounting entry like the following:*

*Advertising Expense . . . . . . . . . . . . . . . . . . . . . .1,000*
*Cash . . . . . . . . . . . . . . . . . . . . . . . . . . . . . . . . . .1,000*

## Figure 2-5 Nigerian Scam Letter

Lagos, Nigeria.

Dear Sir,

Confidential Business Proposal

Having consulted with my colleagues and based on the information gathered from the Nigerian Chambers of Commerce and Industry, I have the privilege to request your assistance to transfer the sum of $47,500,000.00 (forty seven million, five hundred thousand United States dollars) into your accounts. The above sum resulted from an over-invoiced contract, executed, commissioned and paid for about five years (5) ago by a foreign contractor. This action was however intentional and since then the fund has been in a suspense account at the Central Bank of Nigeria Apex Bank.

We are now ready to transfer the fund overseas and that is where you come in. It is important to inform you that as civil servants, we are forbidden to operate a foreign account; that is why we require your assistance. The total sum will be shared as follows: 70% for us, 25% for you and 5% for local and international expenses incidental to the transfer.

The transfer is risk free on both sides. I am an accountant with the Nigerian National Petroleum Corporation (NNPC). If you find this proposal acceptable, we shall require the following documents:

(a) your banker's name, telephone, account and fax numbers.

(b) your private telephone and fax numbers — for confidentiality and easy communication.

(c) your letter-headed paper stamped and signed.

Alternatively we will furnish you with the text of what to type into your letter-headed paper, along with a breakdown explaining, comprehensively what we require of you. The business will take us thirty (30) working days to accomplish.

Please reply urgently.

Best regards

*Joan used this approach because she knew that at year-end all expense accounts, including advertising expense, would be closed and brought to zero balances. If bank auditors and officials didn't catch the fraud before year-end, the audit trail would be erased and the fraud would be difficult to detect. On the other hand, she knew that if she covered the cash shortage by overstating outstanding checks on the bank reconciliation, the cash shortage would be carried from month to month, creating a "permanent" concealment problem. She also knew for example, that if she manipulated the inventory, an asset, that inventory shortage would carry over into the next period.*

In the preceding example, Joan was not caught until she got greedy and started using other fraud methods that were not as easily concealed.

## The Third Element of the Fraud Triangle: Rationalization

So far, we discussed the first two elements of the fraud triangle: perceived pressure and perceived opportunity. The third element is *rationalization*. An example of how rationalization contributes to fraud is the case of Jim Bakker and Richard Dortch. These men were convicted on 23 counts of wire and mail fraud and one count of conspiracy to commit wire and mail fraud. As a result of their conviction, the perpetrators of one of the largest and most bizarre frauds in the history of the United States were sent to jail. In his remarks to the court prior to Jim Bakker's sentencing, prosecutor Jerry Miller summarized this PTL (Praise-the-Lord) fraud with the comments on the following page.

> *The biggest con man to come through this courtroom, a man corrupted by power and money and the man who would be God at PTL, is a common criminal. The only thing uncommon about him was the method he chose and the vehicle he used to perpetrate his fraud. He was motivated by greed, selfishness, and a lust for power. He is going to be right back at it as soon as he gets the chance. Mr. Bakker was a con man who in the beginning loved people and used things, but he evolved into a man, a ruthless man, who loved things and used people.*

How did Jim Bakker, the beloved TV minister of the PTL network, rationalize the committing of such a massive fraud? Here is his story.

> *PTL had a modest beginning in 1973 when it began operating out of a furniture show-room in Charlotte, North Carolina. By October 1975, it had purchased a 25-acre estate in Charlotte, North Carolina, and had constructed Heritage Village, a broadcast network of approximately 70 television stations in the United States, Canada, and Mexico on which the PTL ministry's show was aired. PTL's corporate charter stated that the religious purposes of the organization were (1) establishing and maintaining a church and engaging in all types of religious activity, including evangelism, religious instruction, and publishing and distributing Bibles; (2) engaging in other religious publication; (3) missionary work, both domestic and foreign; and (4) establishing and operating Bible schools and Bible training centers. Over the following 11 years, PTL built a multimillion-dollar empire that consisted of PTL and a 2,300-acre Heritage USA tourist center valued at $172 million. Specific activities of the organization included Heritage Church with a weekly attendance of more than 3,000; Upper Room prayer services where counselors ministered to people; Prison Ministry, with a volunteer staff of 4,000; Fort Hope, a missionary outreach house for homeless men; Passion Play, a portrayal of the life of Christ in an outdoor amphitheater; a dinner theater; a day care center; Heritage Academy; a summer day camp; the Billy Graham Home; workshops; and a Christmas nativity scene that had been visited by more than 500,000 people.*

> *PTL also had a wide range of activities that were ultimately deemed by the IRS to be commercial. In one such venture, PTL viewers were given an opportunity to become lifetime partners in a hotel for $1,000 each. Bakker promised that only 25,000 lifetime partnership interest would be sold and that partners could use the hotel free each year for 4 days and 3 nights. In the end, however, 68,412 such partnerships were sold. Through this and similar solicitations, Jim Bakker's PTL had amassed gross receipts of over $600 million, much of which had been used to support the extravagant lifestyle of Bakker and other officers of PTL. Time and time again, Bakker misled worshippers, investors, and his faithful followers by misusing contributions, overselling investments, evading taxes, and living an extravagant lifestyle.[10]*

How could a minister perpetrate such a large and vicious fraud in the name of religion? Most people believe that Jim Bakker's ministry was initially sincere, inspired by a real desire to help others and to teach the word of God. He believed that what he was doing was for a good purpose and rationalized that any money he received would directly or indirectly help others. He even recognized at one time that money might be corrupting him and his empire. In 1985 he said, "I was going to say to listeners, 'Please stop giving.' But, I just couldn't say that." What started out as a sincere ministry was corrupted by money until Jim Bakker rationalized on a television program, "I have never asked for a penny for myself… God has always taken care of me." His rationalizations increased to the point that one of the trial attorneys, in her closing argument, stated, "You can't lie to people to send you money—it's that simple. What unfolded before you over the past month was a tale of corruption—immense corruption… What was revealed here was that Mr. Bakker was a world-class master of lies and half-truths."

Jim Bakker rationalized his dishonest acts by convincing himself that the PTL network had a good purpose and that he was helping others. In a similar way, folklore has it that Robin Hood rationalized his dishonest acts by arguing that he was "stealing from the rich and giving to the poor."

Nearly every fraud involves the element of rationalization. Most fraud perpetrators are first-time offenders who would not commit other crimes. In some way, they must rationalize away the dishonesty of their acts. Common rationalizations used by fraud perpetrators include the following:

- The organization owes it to me.
- I am only borrowing the money and will pay it back.
- Nobody will get hurt.
- I deserve more.
- It's for a good purpose.
- We'll fix the books as soon as we get over this financial difficulty.
- Something has to be sacrificed—my integrity or my reputation. (If I don't embezzle to cover my inability to pay, people will know I can't meet my obligations and that will be embarrassing because I'm a professional.)

Among countless other rationalizations, the preceding examples serve as an adequate basis to discuss the role of rationalization in the perpetration of fraud.

It is important to recognize that very few, if any, people do not rationalize. We rationalize being overweight. We rationalize not exercising enough. We rationalize spending more than we should. Most of us rationalize being dishonest. Here are two examples of rationalization of dishonesty.

> *A wife works hard, saves her money, and buys a new dress. When she puts it on for the first time, she asks her husband, "How do you like my new dress?" Realizing that the wife worked hard for the money and that she must really like the dress or she wouldn't have purchased it, the husband says, "Oh, it is beautiful," although he really doesn't like it. Why did the husband lie? He probably rationalized in his mind that the consequence of telling the truth was more severe than the consequence of lying. "After all, if she likes it, I'd better like it, too," he reasons. Unfortunately, the rationalization of not wanting to hurt his wife's feelings results in lying, which is dishonest. In fact, the husband will pay for his dishonesty. His wife will continue to wear the dress because she believes her husband likes it. What the husband could have said is, "Honey, you are a beautiful woman and that is one reason I married you. I like most of the clothes you buy and wear, but this dress is not my favorite."*

> *You go to your mother-in-law's for dinner. For dessert, she bakes a cherry pie. Even though you don't like pie, you lie and say, " This pie is delicious." Why did you lie? Because you rationalized that you didn't want to hurt your mother-in-law's feelings and that, in fact, it would make her feel good if you complimented her cooking. As in the dress example, you will pay for your dishonesty because your mother-in-law, believing you like her cherry pie, will serve it again the next time you visit. Dishonesty could have been avoided by remaining silent or by saying, "Mom, you are an excellent cook, and I really like most of the food you cook. However, cherry pie is not my favorite."*

These two examples of rationalization involve the dishonesty of lying. Dishonesty is rationalized by the desire to make other people feel good. The same sort of rationalization often allows the perpetration of fraud. Sometimes it's lying to oneself. Sometimes it's lying to others. The following example of rationalization allows one to be dishonest by breaking the law:

> *You get in your car and start down the freeway. You see a sign that says, "65 miles per hour." What do you do? Most likely you will go faster than 65, justifying your speeding by using one or more of the following rationalizations.*

- Nobody drives 65. Everyone else speeds.
- My car was made to go faster.
- Sixty-five miles per hour is a stupid law. Going faster is still safe.
- I must keep up with the traffic or I'll cause an accident.
- It's all right to get one or two speeding tickets.
- I'm late.
- The speed limit is really 72 or 73.

Is it okay to break the law and speed just because everyone else is doing it? What if everyone else were committing fraud? If so, would that make it right for you to commit fraud?

An example of rationalization more closely related to fraud involves income tax evasion. Many people rationalize underpaying taxes by using the following rationalizations:

- I pay more than my fair share of taxes.
- The rich don't pay enough taxes.
- The government wastes money.
- I "work" for my money.

To understand the extent of income tax fraud, consider that, in 1988, for the first time, the IRS required taxpayers who claimed dependents to list the social security numbers for their dependents. In 1987, seventy-seven million dependents were claimed on federal tax returns. In 1988, the number of dependents claimed dropped to 70 million. Fully one-tenth of the dependents claimed, or 7 million dependents, disappeared. Where did they go? Had they never existed? Or had they simply existed in backyards, run around on four legs, and had names like Fido and Felix? The IRS determined that in 1987 and probably in previous years, more than 60,000 households claimed four or more dependents who didn't exist, and several million claimed one or more who didn't exist.

Claiming dependents who don't exist is one of the most blatant and easiest-to-catch income tax frauds. Yet, rationalizations were strong enough to allow millions of citizens to blatantly cheat on their tax returns.

When interviewed, most fraud perpetrators say things like, "I intended to pay the money back. I really did." They are sincere. In their minds, they intended to (or rationalized that they would) repay the money, and because they judge themselves by their intentions, they do not see themselves as criminals. On the other hand, victims judge perpetrators by their actions and say, "You dirty rotten crook! You stole money from me and my organization."

One of the first white-collar criminals to be convicted and incarcerated during the major fraud scandals of 2002–2003 was Dr. Sam Waksal, CEO of ImClone. Waksal was convicted in the same insider trading scandal involving Martha Stewart. In 2000, Waksal was one of Wall Street's men of the moment. As the CEO of ImClone, he had just sold an interest in a new cancer drug called Erbitux to Bristol Myers for $2 billion. Everyone expected that the Food and Drug Administration would soon approve the drug. Shortly thereafter, however, Waksal learned from a Bristol Myers executive that the drug wouldn't be approved. The FDA was refusing to consider the Erbitux application—not because the drug didn't work, but because the data were insufficient. New clinical trials would have to be conducted, and the price of ImClone stock was going to plummet. What happened was that Sam Waksal did something stupid. He told his daughter to sell her shares, thinking that the price was about to go down. He also tried to sell 79,000 of his own shares (he owned millions of shares)—about $5 million worth. He transferred the 79,000 shares to his daughter thinking that if she sold them that was okay. He rationalized that he wasn't doing the selling.

Later on, when explaining his actions, Waksal said the following: "I could sit there at the same time thinking I was the most honest CEO that ever lived. And, at the same time, I could glibly do something and rationalize it because I cut a corner, because I didn't think I was going to get caught. And who cared? Look at me. I'm doing X, so what difference does it make that I do a couple of things that aren't exactly kosher?" In fact, Waksal's rationalization had allowed him to have a long history of ethical lapses, reckless behavior, and embellishing the truth. He had been dismissed from a number of academic and research positions for questionable conduct. One former colleague said "cutting corners for Sam was like substance abuse. He did it in every aspect of his life, throughout his entire life.[11]

## SUMMARY OF THE FRAUD TRIANGLE

I n concluding this chapter, consider one last example of fraud. Jerry Schneider, at age 21, was the model West Coast Business executive, bright and well educated. He was different from others in only one respect. He embezzled more than $1 million from Pacific Telephone Company. Here is the story of his fraud.

*Jerry Schneider's fraud had its genesis at a warm, open-air evening party where he and some friends had gathered for drinks, socializing, and small talk. Schneider was the young president of his own electronics corporation. This night, the talk was of organized crime and whether or not it could be profitable. "All these press stories of the big-time killings, and the crooks who build palaces down in Florida and out here on the coast, aagh...." Said a cynical male voice, "They're cooked up for the movies."*

*Schneider recognized the speaker as a young scriptwriter whose last outline—a crime story set among the Jewish mafia—had been turned down. "Not so," he said. "Some of them clean up. Some of them walk away clean, with a huge pot. You only hear of the ones that don't. The others become respectable millionaires."*

*A lawyer asked, "You believe in the perfect crime, do you?"*

*"Yes, if what you mean is the crime that doesn't get detected. I don't say nobody knows it has been done—though there must be some of those, too. But I'm sure there are crooks clever enough to figure ways to beat the system."*

*Long after everyone had left the party, Jerry Schneider was still thinking about whether or not there was a perfect crime. He had a great knowledge of computers and he thought maybe he could use his knowledge to perpetrate the perfect crime. Finally, about 2:00 A.M. he felt sick about the whole idea.*

*No one knows why Schneider later changed his mind. An investigator with the district attorney's office in Los Angeles believes it was because Jerry got possession of a stolen computer code book from Pacific Telephone Company. Schneider accessed the company's computer from the outside. Exactly how he did it was not fully revealed at his trial. He used a touch-tone telephone to place large orders with Pacific's supply division, inserting the orders into the company's computer. He then programmed Pacific Telephone's computers to pay for the merchandise. After he received the merchandise, he sold it on the open market.*

*Schneider was caught when an embittered employee noticed that much of the stuff Schneider was selling was Pacific's. The employee leaked to the police a hint about how Schneider had acquired the material. An investigation revealed that huge amounts of equipment were missing from Pacific's dispatch warehouse. Invoices showed that the equipment had been ordered and authorized for dispatch. The goods had then been packaged and put out on the loading bays ready for collection. Schneider had collected the goods himself, always early in the morning. To avoid the scrutiny of a gate guard and a tally clerk, who would have required bills of lading, Schneider left home at two and three in the morning night after night, in a pickup truck painted to look like a company transport.*

*Schneider merely drove in among the assorted wagons and freight piles. He had somehow acquired keys, and documents issued by the computer gave him access to the yard. The inexperienced night security guards not only let him through but even offered him cups of coffee and cigarettes as he and his men loaded the equipment.*

*Schneider started to have fears about what he was doing: the morality of it and the cheating it involved. He had intended the theft to be just a brilliant near-scientific feat. Jerry began to realize that the effort of the crime was greater than the reward. In Schneider's words, "It got so that I was afraid of my ex-employees, men I knew were aware of what I was up to because they'd seen the stuff come in, day after day, and go out again as our stuff. I began to feel hunted. Scared." The crime left him short of sleep, exhausted, and feeling guilty. In addition, the value of the stolen material passing into his possession was rising dramatically.[12]*

Schneider claims to have "robbed" the company of nearly $1 million worth of equipment. His crime is interesting because his rationalization was "to see if the perfect crime could be committed." In fact, he probably couldn't have rationalized committing a crime for any other reason. When he was asked whether he considered himself an honest man, Schneider responded with a firm "yes." When he was asked whether, if he saw a wallet on the sidewalk, he would pocket it or try to return it to the owner, his answer was that he was like everyone else—he'd try to return it if it was at all possible. However, when he was asked whether, if he saw $10,000 lying in an open cash box in a supermarket and nobody was watching him, if he would take the money, he answered, "Sure, I would. If the company was careless enough to leave the money there, it deserved to have the money taken."

Schneider's pressures were greed, retaliation (it was revealed at his trial that he hated Pacific Telephone Company), and a compulsion to prove his superiority. Schneider is a man of inner disciplines. He is a strict vegetarian who does a lot of physical exercise to keep fit. He works hard, brilliantly, and successfully at whatever he undertakes. Undoubtedly, he could be a valued and even trusted executive at most corporations. Schneider's opportunity was his tremendous knowledge of computers and ability to get keys and passwords.

Jerry Schneider's "perfect crime" failed. It would have never happened, however, if he hadn't acted on a personal challenge and rationalized that he was only playing a game—a game of intellectual chess with a faceless company.

## KEY TERMS

**Accounting system:** Policies and procedures for recording an organization's economic transactions.

**Audit trail:** Documents and records that can be used to trace transactions.

**Control environment:** A set of characteristics that defines good management control features other than accounting policies and control activities.

**Control procedures or activities:** Specific error checking routines performed by company personnel.

**Documents and records:** Documentary of all transactions that create an audit trail.

**Independent checks:** Periodically monitoring the work or activities of others.

**Labeling:** Teaching and training.

**Modeling:** Setting an example.

**Perceived opportunity:** A situation where someone believes he or she has a favorable or promising combination of circumstances to commit fraud and not be detected.

**Perceived pressure:** A situation where someone perceives he or she has a need to commit fraud; a constraining influence on the will or mind, as a moral force.

**Physical safeguards:** Vaults, fences, locks, and similar barriers that physically protect assets from theft.

**Rationalization:** To devise self-satisfying but incorrect reasons for one's behavior.

**Segregation of duties:** Dividing a task into two parts, so one person does not have complete control of the task.

**System of authorizations:** Specified limits on who can and cannot perform certain functions.

## QUESTIONS AND CASES

### DISCUSSION QUESTIONS

1. What types of people commit fraud?

2. What motivates people to commit fraud?

3. What is the fraud triangle, and why is it important?

4. What is the fraud scale, and how does it relate to pressure, opportunity, and integrity?

5. What are some different types of pressures?

6. What are some of the controls that prevent or detect fraudulent behavior?

7. What are some common noncontrol factors that provide opportunities for fraud?

8. How does rationalization contribute to fraud?

9. What were Jim Bakker's pressures, opportunities, and rationalizations to commit fraud?

10. In what ways did Sam Waksal rationalize his illegal and unethical actions?

### TRUE/FALSE

1. When hiring, it is usually difficult to know which employees are capable of committing fraud, especially without performing background checks.

2. The three elements of the fraud triangle are a perceived pressure, a perceived opportunity, and rationalization.

3. Management's example or model is of little importance to the control environment.

4. Good controls will often increase opportunities for individuals to commit fraud within an organization.

5. Effective fraud fighters usually put most of their time and effort into minimizing the pressures for fraud perpetrators to commit fraud.

6. The greater the perceived opportunity or more intense the pressure, the less rationalization it takes for someone to commit fraud.

7. Fraud can be perpetrated to benefit oneself or to benefit one's organization.

8. Fraud perpetrators who are prosecuted, incarcerated, or severely punished usually commit fraud again.

9. Many organizations merely dismiss dishonest employees because of the expense and time involved in prosecuting them.

10. Appropriate hiring will not decrease an organization's risk of fraud.

11. An individual who owns his or her own business and is the sole employee needs many control procedures.

12. A proper system of authorization will help ensure good internal controls.

13. Good documents and records are some of the best preventive controls.

14. Many frauds are allowed to be perpetrated because victims don't have access to information possessed by the perpetrators.

## MULTIPLE CHOICE

1. Fraud perpetrators:
   a. Look like other criminals.
   b. Have profiles that look like most honest people.
   c. Are usually very young.
   d. None of the above.

2. Which of the following is not one of the three elements of fraud?
   a. Perceived pressure
   b. Perceived opportunity
   c. Rationalization
   d. Intelligence

3. Which of the following is a common perceived pressure?
   a. The ability to outsmart others
   b. Opportunity to cheat others
   c. A financial need
   d. The ability to "borrow" money by committing fraud

4. If pressures and opportunities are high and personal integrity is low, the chance of fraud is:
   a. High
   b. Medium
   c. Low
   d. Very Low

5. Which of the following is not a common type of fraud pressure?
   a. Vices
   b. Work-related pressures
   c. Financial pressures
   d. Pressure to outsmart peers

6. Opportunity involves:
   a. Opportunity to conceal fraud.
   b. Opportunity to avoid being punished for fraud.
   c. Opportunity to commit fraud.
   d. All of the above.
   e. None of the above.

7. Which of the following is not one of the three elements of the control system of an organization?
   a. The control environment
   b. The accounting system
   c. Management
   d. Control activities or procedures

8. Which of the following noncontrol factors provide opportunities for fraud?
   a. Inability to judge the quality of performance
   b. Lack of access to information
   c. Failure to discipline fraud perpetrators
   d. Lack of an audit trail
   e. All of the above

9. Who generally has the highest risk of becoming a fraud victim?
   a. Businessperson
   b. Older, less educated people
   c. College students
   d. None of the above

10. How frequently do most people rationalize?
    a. Often
    b. Sometimes
    c. Rarely
    d. Never

11. Which of the following kinds of pressures is most often associated with fraud?
    a. Work-related pressures
    b. Financial pressures
    c. Vice pressures
    d. All of the above

12. Which of the following is *not* a primary control procedure?
    a. Use of documents and records to create an audit trail
    b. Independent checks
    c. Decreasing work-related pressure
    d. Physical safeguards

13. It is the _____ and _____ of existing controls, not the _____ of controls, that allow most frauds to be perpetrated.
    a. Existence, Use, Lack
    b. Lack, Ignoring, Existence
    c. Overriding, Ignoring, Lack
    d. Overriding, Lack, Use

14. On what element of the fraud triangle do most fraud fighters usually focus all or most of their preventive efforts?
    a. Perceived pressure
    b. Perceived opportunity
    c. Perceived weak internal controls
    d. Rationalization

15. Which of the following is **not** a control activity (procedure)?
    a. System of authorizations
    b. Appropriate hiring procedures
    c. Independent checks
    d. Documents and records

16. Which of the following common vices motivates people to commit fraud?
    a. Gambling
    b. Drugs
    c. Expensive extramarital relationships
    d. Alcohol
    e. All of the above

17. Which of the following is a way that management can establish a good control environment?
    a. Having a clear organizational structure
    b. Proper training
    c. Communicating openly
    d. Appropriate hiring procedures
    e. All of the above

18. Which of the following is *not* an element of most frauds?
    a. Taking the assets
    b. Concealment
    c. Breaking and entering
    d. Conversion

## SHORT CASES

**Case 1.** As an auditor, you have discovered the following problems with the accounting system of Jefferson Retailers. For each of the following occurrences, tell which of the five internal control procedures was lacking. Also, recommend how the company should change its procedures to avoid the problem in the future.

a. Jefferson Retailers' losses due to bad debts have increased dramatically over the past year. In an effort to increase sales, the managers of certain stores have allowed large credit sales to occur without review or approval of the customers.

b. An accountant hid his theft of $200 from the company's bank account by overstating outstanding checks on monthly reconciliation. He believed the manipulation would not be discovered.

c. Michael Meyer works in a storeroom. He maintains the inventory records, counts the inventory, and has unlimited access to the storeroom. He occasionally steals items of inventory and hides his thefts by including overstating the physical inventory accounts.

d. Receiving reports are sometimes filled out days after shipments have arrived.

**Case 2.** A few years ago, the top executive of a large oil refining company (based in New York) was convicted of financial statement fraud. One of the issues in the case involved the way the company accounted for its oil inventories. In particular, the company would purchase crude oil from exploration companies and then process the oil into finished oil products, such as jet fuel, diesel fuel, and so forth. Because of the ready market for these finished products, the company would record its oil inventory at the selling prices of the finished products less the cost to refine the oil (instead of at cost) as soon as it purchased or discovered the crude oil. In addition to the fraud in the case, this type of accounting was questioned because it allowed the company to recognize profit before the actual sale (and even refining) of the oil. This method was even attested to by one of the large CPA firms. If you were the judge in this case, would you be critical of this accounting practice? Do you believe this "aggressive" accounting was a warning signal that fraud might be occurring?

**Case 3.** Helen Weeks worked for Bonne Consulting Group (BCG) as the executive secretary in the administrative department for nearly 10 years. Her apparent integrity and dedication to her work earned her a reputation as an outstanding employee and resulted in increased responsibilities. Her present responsibilities include making arrangements for outside feasibility studies, maintaining client files, working with outside marketing consultants, initiating the payment process, and notifying the accounting department of all openings or closings of vendor accounts.

During Helen's first five years of employment, BCG subcontracted all of its feasibility and marketing studies through Jackson & Co. This relationship was subsequently terminated because Jackson & Co. merged with a larger, more expensive consulting group. At the time of termination, Helen and her supervisor were forced to select a new firm to conduct BCG's market research. However, Helen never informed the accounting department that the Jackson & Co. account had been closed.

Because her supervisor allowed Helen to sign the payment voucher for services rendered, Helen was able to continue to process checks made payable to Jackson's account. Because her supervisor completely trusted her, he allowed her to sign for all voucher payments less than $10,000. The accounting department continued to process the payments, and Helen would take responsibility for distributing the payments. Helen opened a bank account in a nearby city under the name of Jackson and Co., where she would make the deposit. She paid all of her personal expenses out of this account.

Assume that you have been hired by Bonne Consulting Group to help detect and prevent fraud.

1. What internal controls are missing in Helen's company?

2. What opportunities gave Helen the opportunity to perpetrate the fraud?

3. How could this fraud have been detected?

**Case 4.** The following describes an actual fraud that occurred in a communications company:

What Ruth Mishkin did in her spare time didn't concern the Boca Raton, Florida, public relations firm where she worked very much. "We thought she was just playing cards with the girls," says Ray Biagiotti, the president of the Communications Group, the firm that had employed her for nine years.

She had become such a trusted employee that her bosses put her in charge of paying bills, balancing bank accounts, and handling other cash management chores. They didn't realize their mistake until Mrs. Mishkin took a sick leave and they discovered she had been pocketing company funds for years. The money had helped stoke a gambling habit that took the 60-year-old widow on junkets to casinos in the Bahamas, Monte Carlo, and Las Vegas. In all, the company claims she stole about $320,000.

Mrs. Mishkin pleaded guilty to one count of grand theft and four counts of check forgery. She was placed on 10 years' probation and ordered to attend meetings of a chapter of Gamblers Anonymous, the national self-help group.

1. What were Ruth's perceived opportunities?

2. What pressure did Ruth have to commit fraud?

3. How did the fact that Ruth was a trusted employee give her more opportunity to commit fraud?

4. How do vices such as gambling motivate people to commit fraud?

**Case 5.** Full-of-Nature is a vitamin supplement company in New York that makes different herbal pills for gaining muscular strength, losing weight, and living a healthier life. You have been hired to audit Full-of-Nature and you soon realize that the company has many problems. You notice the following frauds being committed and are writing a report to the Board of Directors about what should be done to fix the problems. For each fraud, list one control procedure that was not followed and suggest how the company should eliminate the fraud and deal with the perpetrator.

1. Journal entries for consulting expenses, when traced back, show five companies using the same post office box for receiving consulting fees from Full-of-Nature. You discover that the accountant has been embezzling money and recording it as consulting expenses.

2. The warehouse manager has been stealing pills to help his son get stronger (he wants his son to play football). To cover the losses, he issued credit memos to customers, showing that they returned bad goods that were replaced with new pills.

3. The CEO decided he did not like paying payroll taxes anymore, so he fired all of his employees and rehired them as contractors. However, he still withholds payroll taxes and keeps the money for himself.

4. The accounts payable clerk likes to go shopping with the company checkbook and always buys herself a little something when she orders office supplies. However, because she is the one who handles office supplies, no one knows what was purchased for the company and what was ordered for her living room.

**Case 6.** Alexia Jones is a worker at a local 24-hour pharmacy. Alexia works the night shift and is the only worker. Because management is cost conscious and business is slow at night, Alexia has been given the responsibility to do the accounting from the previous day. Alexia has two children, and her husband does not work. Alexia has strong pressure to provide well for her family.

1. Is the pharmacy at risk for fraud? Why or why not?

2. How does the fraud scale help us to determine whether risk for fraud is high or low in this situation?

3. Assuming that you were recently hired by the pharmacy as a business consultant, what information would you provide to the owner of the pharmacy concerning fraud?

**Case 7.** Bob's Country Kitchen, a small family-owned restaurant in northern New York, has seen a drop in profitability over the past 3 years and the owners want to know why. Bob's has been a local favorite for the past 20 years. Two brothers opened it in the early 1980s because they couldn't find a burger they liked. Bob's initially served only hamburgers, but has rapidly expanded to almost all types of American food. Bob's became so popular in the late 1980s that Tom and Bob (the owners) hired several people to help manage the day-to-day activities of the restaurant. Until this point, Tom and Bob had managed the place themselves.

Bob and Tom felt that their new management was doing a good job and so they gradually became less and less involved. In 2000, Bob and Tom gave up all management duties to Joel, a friend of the family who had been employed by Bob's for 15 years. Bob's has no computer system in place for customer orders, each order is written on a pad with a duplicate carbon, one copy is taken to the kitchen, and the other is given to the customer. All customers pay at the old cash register at the front of the restaurant, after which their receipts are pegged on a tack and are totaled at day's end to determine total sales. Bob and Tom have noticed a gradual decline in profits over the past three years and, up until now, figured it was just because of increased restaurant competition in the area.

However, it seemed odd to Bob and Tom that revenues had increased substantially but profits had not. When asked about the change in relationships between revenues and profits, Joel said it was because of a large increase in the cost of food and that he had to pay his employees more with the increased competition. Bob and Tom have no reason to disbelieve Joel, since he is a trusted family friend. Joel's responsibilities at Bob's include preparing the nightly deposits, managing accounts payable, handling payroll, and performing the bank reconciliations. He also has the power to write and sign checks. No one checks his work.

1. What possible opportunities does Joel have to commit fraud?

2. What signs could signal a possible fraud?

3. How likely is it that a few internal controls could reduce the opportunities for fraud?

4. Which internal controls would you suggest be implemented?

**Case 8.** In October 2001, the following case was heard in New Jersey.

A former optometrist was sentenced to seven years in State prison for conspiracy, theft by deception, falsifying records, and falsification of records relating to medical care, as part of a massive health insurance fraud. In addition to his prison sentence, the optometrist was ordered to pay a criminal insurance fraud fine of $100,000 and

restitution of $97,975. The state is also in the process of seeking an additional $810,000 in civil insurance fraud penalties.

The optometrist was found guilty of false insurance billing for providing eyeglasses and routine eye exams at no cost or at reduced cost, and making up the difference by billing insurance carriers for services not rendered to patients. The optometrist also had his office staff create approximately 997 false patient records and charts and falsely bill insurance carriers for prescribed optometric services that were not rendered to his patients. He would also bill insurance companies for optometric treatments and tests for ocular conditions that patients did not actually suffer. The optometrist was also changed for falsifying patient records and charts.

What noncontrol factors provided the optometrist with an opportunity to commit fraud?

**Case 9.** FCS Fund Management is an investment marketing business with sales of more than $10 million and with offices in Norwich, Connecticut, Dubai, and Hong Kong. It sold high-yield investment schemes, offering returns of up to 20 percent. FCS has clients in the United Kingdom, Europe, and the Middle East, many of whom are U.S. expatriates. FCS sold its investment products through salespeople operating in these locations. The CEO of FCS Fund Management, James Hammond, knew that many of the accounts were, or might be, misleading, false, or deceptive in that they purported to confirm the existence of genuine investments.

Describe how the rationalization element of the fraud triangle is present in this case.

**Case 10.** Len Haxton is the owner of a local CPA firm with four separate offices in a medium-size town. He and his wife started the firm 20 years ago, and they now have more than 50 full-time employees. Recently, he discovered that one of his employees had stolen $20,000 from the business during the past six months because of lax internal controls. Len was furious about the situation, but was uncertain about whether he should initiate a criminal investigation or just fire the employee.

1. List four reasons why Len should have the employee prosecuted.

2. List three reasons why Len might not want to seek prosecution of his employee.

3. If you were Len, what would you do?

**Case 11.** As a new staff member in a large, national company, you are excited about your career opportunities. You hope to learn from senior employees in the company that you are perceived as being one of the "rising stars." During your first week of training, you are assigned a mentor. The mentor's role is to help you learn your way around the company and to answer questions you may have about the work you are expected to complete. As it turns out, your mentor is another "rising star" whom you respect. One day, she takes you out to lunch. While you are eating, you begin discussing company policies. She explains to you the expense reimbursement policy. Company policy dictates that expenses such as lunch are the responsibility of the employee and are not reimbursable. The exception to this policy is for lunches with clients and potential recruits, or for other work-related circumstances. She tells you "off the record" that nobody really follows this policy, and that you can always find a "business purpose" to justify your lunch expenses with fellow employees, as long as you don't do it every day. Besides, your supervisor won't really scrutinize any expense reimbursement requests that are below $25, so why worry about it?

1. Is it a fraud to charge the company for personal lunches that you submit as business expenses?

2. What elements of fraud, if any, are present in this situation?

3. How would you respond to your mentor or to other employees who may encourage you to pick up the tab for lunch with the understanding that you will charge the company for the lunch?

**Case 12.** You are the owner of a local department store in a small town. Many of your employees have worked for your company for years, and you know them and their families well. Because your business is relatively small, and because you know your employees so well, you haven't worried about establishing many internal controls. You do set a good example for how you wish your employees to work, you are actively involved in the business, and you provide adequate training to new employees. One day you become suspicious about an employee at a checkout desk. You fear that he may be stealing from the company by altering the day's totals at his register. He has worked for you for 15 years, and he has always been honest and reliable. After several weeks of investigation, you discover that your fears are correct—he is stealing from the company. You confront him with the evidence, and he admits to stealing $25,000 over several years. He explains that, at first, he stole mainly to pay for small gifts for his wife and young children. But then last year his wife lost her job, they had another child, and he wasn't sure how to pay all of the bills.

1. What elements of fraud are present in this case?

2. How might you have detected this fraud earlier or prevented it from happening?

3. How will you approach your employee interaction and relationships in the future?

4. Do you feel a better system of internal controls, such as surveillance cameras and an improved computer system, are necessary or justified to prevent future frauds?

**Case 13.** A prominent New York fertility doctor was recently sentenced to more than seven years in prison for his insurance fraud conviction. Dr. Niels Lauersen received the seven-year, three-month sentence and was ordered to pay $3.2 million in restitution and an additional $17,500 in fines.

Lauersen was convicted of pocketing $2.5 million during a 10-year period. Prosecutors say he stole from insurance companies by falsely billing fertility surgeries that were not covered by insurance as gynecological surgeries. Tearful former patients called out to Lauersen and wished him well as he was led away. He is now in prison.

At his sentencing, the judge said, "You were a medical doctor at the top of your profession and a public figure at the apex of New York society. Your fall from prestige has been Faustian in its dimensions." A probation report recommended that Lauersen be sentenced to 14 years imprisonment. Lauersen, 64, has lived in the United States since 1967, when he left Denmark. His lawyer, Gerald Shargel, argued for leniency, saying Lauersen had an honorable purpose: to make it affordable for women with fertility problems to have children.

"This is a very tough sentence. This is a very unusual case," Shargel said. Shargel said his client had treated 14,000 women, delivering 3,000 children in a single year.

1. What pressure might have motivated Lauersen to commit fraud?

2. What opportunity might have allowed Lauersen to commit fraud?

3. How did Lauersen rationalize his fraudulent activities?

4. How could Lauersen have both helped his patients and not lied or stolen from the insurance company?

**Case 14.** Nancy is the receptionist and office manager at a local doctor's office where you are working as a doctor's assistant. The doctor leaves Nancy to handle all office duties including collecting cash receipts, billing patients, depositing checks, and reconciling the monthly bank statement. The doctor doesn't have any training in accounting or collecting insurance payments and wants to be able to focus on treating his patients. Because the work in the office doesn't require an additional employee, Nancy assumed all office managing responsibility. The receptionist could share the office managing duties but she is too busy greeting patients, pulling charts, and answering phone calls. Nancy is also a single mother of four. She likes to give her children the best possible care and enjoys having the finer things of life to the extent that she can afford them. Nancy also works a second job because her job as office manager "just never seems to pay the bills."

Most patients visiting the doctor have insurance and are only required to pay a copayment for the services that they receive. As you are filling out some patient information during a routine visit you overhear the patient say to her husband, "Honey, do you have any cash with you today? This office prefers the copayment be paid in cash and I forgot to stop by the ATM this morning." You thought that this comment was interesting because you had never heard of the office having a cash copayment preference. In addition, you haven't seen a written sign

nor have ever heard the doctor preferring cash copayments be made. You are aware that in addition to a copayment, Nancy bills the entire remaining cost of service. The remaining amount is then billed directly to the patent. While you filed patient records you often heard Nancy complain that "full payment cannot be collected from yet another patient." You are aware that several accounts are written off each month due to the high amount of uncollectible accounts. A high percentage of bad debts seems to be a common and expected occurrence in the physician/patient business. You are currently taking a fraud class and realize that several opportunities for fraud exist.

1. Consider the fraud triangle. What opportunities and motivation exist for Nancy to commit fraud?

2. What should be done to improve internal controls and reduce the risk of fraud as it relates to the segregation of duties?

## EXTENSIVE CASES

**Extensive Case 1.** GreenGrass is a small, family-operated company whose core service is in horticultural care and lawn care for customers in the local city. The owner of the company is the father of the family. He has used the company to cover the costs of his children's college education. At the same time, he has been able to give his children some work experience and an opportunity to earn their own money to pay for school. The company has grown steadily over the last few years, and the manager has hired many employees outside of the family to be able to keep up with the demand of the increasing number of customers. The company is run from a small office building, with only one employee running the operations in the company office. The father had usually been in charge of this aspect of the company, but now leaves the responsibility to his trusted friend, who has experience in accounting and information systems. This employee is in charge of scheduling the routes of all the employees and is responsible for payments, receipts, and balancing the books.

The company performs two major operations. First, it provides lawn care using insecticides, fertilizer, and weed killers. Eight employees are responsible for this activity. They each drive a truck and are responsible for collecting money from the customers they serve. They are also responsible for loading and mixing chemicals in the tanks they use during the day. The second part of the operation is the lawn mowing care. Usually, a four-person crew is responsible for all the machines used, and crew members are responsible for taking care of the lawns on their daily schedule. The manager has hired his children to work on this crew, and the whole team is usually made

up of workers younger than the team that works with the chemicals.

Over the years, GreenGrass experienced small growth and success. Profits increased steadily as the company picked up new clients. However, the manager noticed that last year's accounts were different. The revenues increased a marginal amount, while the expenses for the company increased more than they should have. The manager noticed that his interactions with his friend in the office have been fewer. Also, his employees have been finishing their routes later in the day than in previous years.

### Questions

1. What are some of the fraud opportunities within GreenGrass?

2. What symptoms of fraud exist, and what symptoms should the manager look for if he believes fraud may be occurring?

3. What steps should be taken to make sure fraud does not occur, and what are the costs associated with these steps?

**Extensive Case 2.** James Watkins, an ambitious 22-year-old, started an entertainment business called Best Club after he graduated from California State University. Best Club initially was a business failure because James ignored day-to-day operations and cost controls. One year later, James was heavily in debt. Despite his debt, James decided to open another location of Best Club. He was confident that Best Club would bring him financial success.

However, as his expenses increased, Watkins could not meet his debts. He turned to insurance fraud to save his business. He would stage a break-in at a Best Club location and then claim a loss. In addition, Watkins reported fictitious equipment to secure loans, falsified work order contracts to secure loans, stole money orders for cash, and added zeros to customers bills who paid with credit cards. Watkins was living the "good life," with an expensive house and a new sports car.

Two years later, Watkins decided to make Best Club a public corporation. He falsified financial statements to greatly improve the reported financial position of Best Club. In order to avoid the SEC's scrutiny of his financial statements, Watkins merged Best Club with Red House, an inactive New York computer firm, and acquired Red House's publicly owned shares in exchange for stock in the newly formed corporation. Watkins personally received 79 percent of the shares. He was now worth $24 million on paper. Watkins was continually raising money from new investors to pay off debts. A few months later, Best Club's stock was selling for $21 a share, and the company's book value was $310 million. Watkins was worth $190 million on paper. A short time later, Watkins met John Gagne, president of AM Firm, an advertising service. Gagne agreed to raise $100 million, via junk bonds, for Best Club to buy out Sun Society, a travel service.

Afterward, with television appearances, Watkins became a "hot figure" and developed a reputation as an entrepreneurial genius. However, this reputation changed after an investigative report was published in a major newspaper. The report chronicled some of Watkins early credit card frauds. Within two weeks, Best Club's stock plummeted from $21 to $5.

After an investigation, Watkins was charged with insurance, bank, stock, and mail fraud, money laundering, and tax evasion, and Best Club's shares were selling for just pennies. A company once supposedly worth hundreds of millions of dollars dropped in value to only $48,000.

From this case, identify the following:

1. The pressures, opportunities, and rationalizations that led Watkins to commit his fraud

2. The signs that could signal a possible fraud

3. Controls or actions that could detect Watkins's behavior

**Extensive Case 3.** Johnson Manufacturing, a diversified manufacturer, has seven divisions that operate in the United States, Mexico, and Canada. Johnson Manufacturing historically allowed its divisions to operate independently. Corporate intervention occurs only when planned results were not obtained. Corporate management has high integrity, although the board of directors is not especially active. Johnson has a policy of performing employee screenings on all employees before hiring them. Johnson feels its employees are all well educated and honest.

The company has a code of conduct, but employees are not closely monitored. Employee compensation is highly dependent on the performance of the company.

During the past year, a new competitor entered one of the Johnson's highly successful markets and undercut Johnson's prices. Johnson's manager of this unit, Harris, responded by matching price cuts in hopes of maintaining market share. Harris is concerned because she cannot see any other areas where costs can be reduced so that the division's growth and profitability can be maintained. If profitability is not maintained, the division managers' salaries and bonuses will be reduced.

Harris decides that one way to make the division more profitable is to overstate inventory, because it represents a large amount of the division's balance sheet. She also knows that controls over inventory are weak. She views this overstatement as a short-run solution to the profit decline due to the competitor's price cutting. The manager is certain that once the competitor stops cutting prices or goes bankrupt, the misstatements in inventory can be corrected with little impact on the bottom line.

**Questions**

1. What factors in Johnson's control environment led to and facilitated the manager's manipulation of inventory?

2. What pressures did Harris feel in deciding to overstate inventory?

3. What rationalization did Harris use to justify her fraud?

**Extensive Case 4.** The following describes an actual investment fraud that occurred:

Armstrong stands accused in a federal indictment for committing one of the most common frauds in the history of finance: making big promises to investors that he couldn't deliver. Armstrong allegedly tried to cover up millions of dollars in bets on the yen and other markets that went horribly wrong.

It is probably not the ending that the 49-year-old Armstrong envisioned when he fell in love with business as a boy. It was a love that turned him into an active stamp dealer at just 13 years old, only to be kicked out of the stamp world's most elite fraternity as a young man in 1972, amid accusations of selling extremely rare stamps that he didn't own and couldn't deliver.

Undaunted, he fought back and became a stamp authority and eventually an authority on the far-more-sophisticated financial markets on which he was widely quoted. His self-confident forecasting style made him a hit in

Japan, where Armstrong is now accused of bilking investors out of $950 million.

Documents he used to sell his investments show that he promised buyers of his securities that a yield of 4 percent was guaranteed on the fixed-rate instrument, a strong selling point in a country where interest rates on government bonds are less than half that amount. Moreover, the securities were designed to offer further returns as high as 25 percent, depending on market conditions.

Armstrong's bets on the markets increasingly began turning against him. The Securities and Exchange Commission says that from late 1997, Armstrong began to rack up increasingly big losses on large investments he made in currencies and options. Between November 1997 and August 1999, for example, SEC officials say Armstrong lost $295 million in trading the yen alone—all money that belonged to clients. "In the wake of the discovery of the fraud," the SEC said in its civil complaint that was filed, "Armstrong has transferred millions of dollars from Princeton Global accounts into foreign-bank accounts he controls." SEC officials declined to disclose how much money Armstrong allegedly transferred overseas, or to what countries.

On two previous instances, Armstrong faced commodities trading scrutiny. In 1985, the agency overseeing commodities trading in the United States lodged a complaint against him for allegedly not registering and maintaining proper investment records. Then in June 1987, the same agency fined Armstrong $10,000 and suspended his trading privileges for a year for improper risk disclosure and misrepresentation of his trading returns. Part of the complaint was related to advertising in a Princeton newsletter.

### Questions

1. How does trust or confidence contribute to Armstrong's fraud?

2. In the chapter, lack of access to information was discussed as one of the noncontrol factors that provides opportunities for fraud. If investors would have known of Armstrong's background and had access to other information about him, how would it have affected the fraud? Why?

**Extensive Case 5** "But I intended to pay it all back, I really did." Joseph Swankie said as he talked to his manager. How did I ever get into this situation, he thought?

Two years ago Joe received the promotion he had been working for. His new manager told him he had a promising future. Joe and his wife quickly purchased a new home. Not long after, Joe and his wife Janae had their fourth child, and life was great. After having their fourth child, Janae quit work to spend more time with her kids.

Suddenly, things started to turn upside down. The economy took a downturn and had a negative impact on Joe's company. His pay, which was based on commission, was reduced nearly 50 percent. Joe still worked hard but thought he should be paid more. Unable to find another job, Joe resentfully decided he would stay with the company even with the lower pay.

Not long after he started receiving lower commissions, Joe noticed the controls over the petty cash fund weren't very strong. The records were not reviewed often, and any small shortages were usually written off. One week Joe took $50. When questioned by his wife, Joe said he had found a few odd jobs after work. Joe continued this habit of taking small amounts for a couple of weeks. After realizing that no one had noticed the shortage, he started to take up to $100 a week.

One day another employee noticed Joe take some cash from the fund and put it in his wallet. When questioned, he simply stated that it was a reimbursement the company owed him for supplies. An investigation began and Joe's fraud was discovered.

### Questions

1. Identify the opportunities, pressures, and rationalizations that led Joe to commit this fraud.

2. What simple procedures could the company have implemented to prevent the fraud from occurring?

## INTERNET ASSIGNMENTS

1. Visit the Association of Certified Fraud Examiners Web site at http://www.cfenet.com/home.asp. Once you log onto the site, explore the pages of the site and then answer the following questions:
   a. How many professionals make up the Association of Certified Fraud Examiners?
   b. What are the requirements to become a Certified Fraud Examiner?
   c. What is the overall mission of the Association of Certified Fraud Examiners?

   d. What does a Certified Fraud Examiner (CFE) do? What are some of the professions they originate from?
   e. Take the CFE Practice Quiz. Do you have what it takes to be a Certified Fraud Examiner?
   f. List a few of the products offered on the Web site for educating those interested in fraud examination. Which materials would be most beneficial to you in your profession? Why?

g.  What service does the association provide to allow individuals to anonymously report allegations of ethical violations, fraud, waste, and abuse? How does this service work?

h.  Visit the Media Center. Click on Fraud Statistics and list a couple fraud statistics that surprise you the most. Click on Fraud Follies and read a humorous story about fraud.

2.  The Serious Fraud Office (SFO) is a government agency in the United Kingdom that investigates and prosecutes serious frauds. Its Web site contains press releases of recently settled cases. These cases provide excellent examples of the fraud triangle at work. Visit the Web site of the SFO at http://www.sfo.gov.uk, and click on Press Releases. Choose a case that interests you and describe the fraud in terms of the fraud triangle. Clearly identify the elements of perceived pressure, rationalization, and perceived opportunity.

## END NOTES

1.  Marshall B. Romney, W. Steve Albrecht, and David J. Cherrington, "Red-Flagging the White-Collar Criminal," *Management Accounting* (March 1980), pp. 51–57.

2.  This case was relayed to us by a former student who asked that we not identify the source.

3.  Richard C. Hollinger, *Dishonesty in the Workplace: A Manager's Guide to Preventing Employee Theft* (Park Ridge, IL: London House Press, 1989), pp. 1–5.

4.  Alison Stein Wellner, "Background Checks," *Business Week Online*, August 14, 2000.

5.  "Doctor Listed as Suicide Was Target of Fraud Investigation," *Los Angeles Times,* (December 10, 1992), p. A3.

6.  ESM was a $400 million fraud that occurred in Ohio and Florida. The company's officers were selling the same investments several times. When one of the perpetrators died suddenly of a heart attack, the fraud was exposed. Because Ohio's largest Saving and Loan had invested heavily in ESM's government securities and went bankrupt, there was a run by deposits on financial institution deposits. Then Govern Celeste of Ohio declared a banking holiday (closed all financial institutions for a day), the first time this had happened since the great depression. Author Steve Albrecht was an expert witness in this case.

7.  Kevin Kelly, "How Did Sears Blow the Gasket? Some Say the Retailer's Push for Profits Sparked Its Auto-Repair Woes," *Business Week,* (June 29, 1992) p. 38; and Tung Yin, "Sears Is Accused of Billing Fraud at Auto Centers," *The Wall Street Journal* (June 12, 1992) p. B1.

8.  Expert witness testimony, June 1990 grand jury indictment, U.S. District Court for the Central District of California.

9.  The information on Lincoln Savings and Loan was taken from the June 1990 grand jury indictment, U.S. District Court for the Central District of California.

10. Facts about the PTL case were taken from "PTL: Where Were the Auditors?" a working paper by Gary L. Tidwell, Associate Professor of Business Administration, School of Business and Economics, College of Charleston, Charleston, SC.

11. CBSNews.com, "Sam Waksal: I Was Arrogant, (October 6, 2003), http://www.cbsnews.com/stores/2003/10/02/60_minutes/main576328.shtml, accessed on May 22, 2004.

12. Information about this fraud was acquired from Donn Parker's computer fraud files at the Stanford Research Institute. Donn Parker personally interviewed Jerry Schneider.

# CHAPTER 3

# FIGHTING FRAUD: AN OVERVIEW

## LEARNING OBJECTIVES

After studying this chapter, you should be able to:

1. Understand the importance of fraud prevention.
2. Recognize the importance of early fraud detection.
3. Describe different approaches to fraud investigation.
4. Be familiar with the different options for legal action that can be taken once fraud has occurred.

During the past two years, Mark-X Corporation experienced three major frauds. The first involved a division manager overstating division profits by reporting fictitious revenues. Faced with declining sales and being fearful of not receiving an annual bonus or even being terminated, the manager inflated the amounts of service contracts to overstate revenues by $22 million. The second fraud was committed by the manager of the purchasing department. In his responsibility to secure uniforms for company employees, he provided favored treatment to a certain vendor. In return for allowing the vendor to charge higher prices and provide inferior service, the vendor hired the purchasing manager's daughter as an "employee" and paid her more than $400,000 for essentially rendering no service. In fact, when investigated, the daughter didn't even know the location of the vendor's offices or telephone number where she supposedly worked. The daughter then funneled the "bribes" to her father, the purchasing agent. As a result of this kickback scheme, Mark-X purchased $11 million of uniforms at inflated prices. The third fraud involved two warehouse managers stealing approximately $300,000 in inventory. The fraud was perpetrated by issuing credit memos to customers who supposedly returned defective merchandise and were given product replacements. In fact, the merchandise was never returned. Instead, the credit memos were used to conceal the theft of high-value merchandise from the warehouse.

All three of these frauds were reported in newspapers and brought significant embarrassment to the company's management and board of directors. The frauds also cost the company a tremendous amount of money to investigate. In a Board of Directors meeting, the chairman of the board made the following comment to the CEO: "I am sick and tired of these fraud surprises hitting the newspapers. If there is one more high-profile fraud in this company, three of us will be resigning from the board and recommending that you be replaced as CEO."

Following the board meeting, the CEO called a meeting with the CFO, the internal audit director, in-house legal counsel, and the director of corporate security. In the meeting, he told them that unless the company successfully developed a proactive fraud program, all of them were going to lose their jobs. He reviewed the three major frauds that occurred and told them what the chairman of the board had said. His final words were, "I don't care how much you spend, but I want the best proactive fraud-mitigating program possible. Hire whatever consultants you need, but get me a proactive fraud program that I can report to the Board."

What advice would a consultant give this company? A consultant would probably start by listing four activities on which money can be spent to mitigate the occurrence of fraud: (1) fraud prevention, (2) early fraud detection, (3) fraud investigation, and (4) follow-up legal action or resolution. A comprehensive fraud program focuses on all four. Mark-X probably now focuses its fraud efforts on only the last two: fraud investigation and follow-up legal action. These activities are probably the least effective and most expensive fraud-fighting efforts.

In this book, we cover all the activities that can mitigate fraud occurrences. Chapter 4 discusses the prevention of fraud. Chapters 5 and 6 cover fraud detections. Chapters 7 through 10 cover fraud investigation. Chapters 11 through 17 discuss various kinds of fraud and unique e-business frauds. Chapter 18 discusses ways to follow up once a fraud has been investigated.

In this chapter, we provide an overview of the four elements of a comprehensive fraud program. You will then have a structure to help you understand the kinds of fraud-fighting efforts that are possible.

## Fraud Prevention

Preventing fraud is generally the most cost-effective way to reduce losses from fraud. The commission of a fraud leaves no winners. Perpetrators lose because they suffer humiliation and embarrassment as well as legal consequences. They usually must make tax and restitution payments, along with other financial penalties and consequences. Victims lose because assets are stolen. They also incur legal fees, lost time, negative publicity, and other adverse consequences. Organizations and individuals that have proactive fraud prevention measures usually find that those measures pay big dividends. On the other hand, the investigation of fraud can be expensive.

As we explained in Chapter 2, people commit fraud because of a combination of three factors: (1) perceived pressure, (2) perceived opportunity, and (3) some way to rationalize the fraud as acceptable. In Chapter 2, we also introduced a scale showing that these factors differ in intensity from fraud to fraud. When perceived pressures and opportunities are high, a person needs less rationalization to commit fraud. When perceived pressures and opportunities are low, a person needs more rationalization to commit fraud. Unfortunately, sometimes pressures or the ability to rationalize are so high that, no matter how hard an organization tries to prevent fraud, some theft still occurs. Indeed, fraud is generally impossible to prevent, especially in a cost-effective way. The best an organization can hope for is to manage the costs of fraud effectively.

Some organizations have significantly higher levels of employee fraud and are more susceptible to fraudulent financial reporting than are other organizations. Research consistently shows that almost all organizations have fraud of one type or another. Only those organizations that explicitly consider fraud risks and take proactive steps to create the right kind of environment and reduce its occurrence are successful in preventing fraud.

*Fraud prevention* involves two fundamental activities: (1) taking steps to create and maintain a culture of honesty and high ethics, and (2) assessing the risk of fraud and developing concrete responses to mitigate the risks and eliminate the opportunities for fraud. We discuss these activities next.

## Creating a Culture of Honesty and High Ethics

Companies may use several methods to create a culture of honesty and high ethics. Five critical elements are (1) having top management model appropriate behavior, (2) hiring the right kind of employees, (3) communicating expectations throughout the organization and requiring periodic written confirmation of acceptance of those expectations, (4) creating a positive work environment, and (5) developing and maintaining an effective policy for handling fraud once it occurs.

Research in moral development strongly suggests that honesty can be best reinforced when a proper example (model) is set—sometimes referred to as "the tone at the top." The management of an organization cannot act one way and expect others in the organization to behave differently. Management must reinforce to its employees through its actions that dishonest, questionable, or unethical behavior will not be tolerated.

*Research into why people lie (or are dishonest) indicates four major reasons. The first is fear. Fear is the most common reason that people may lie, and they are taking shelter from a perceived punishment. It may be because they know they have done something wrong. If they are always in fear of being punished, it may become a habit, which is a second reason for lying. Even when confronted by the truth, they insist the lie is the truth in this case. A third reason is because they have learned to lie through modeling. When a people see others lie, especially when they get away with it, they may become more prone to lying. Finally, people lie because they feel if they tell the truth they won't get what they want.[1]*

The second element is hiring the right employees. Not all people are equally honest or have equally well-developed personal codes of ethics. In fact, research results indicate that many people, when faced with significant pressure and opportunity, will behave dishonestly rather than face the "negative consequences" of honest behavior (e.g., losing reputation or esteem, failing to meet quotas or expectations, having inadequate performance be exposed, inability to pay debts, etc.). If an organization is to be successful in preventing fraud, it must have effective hiring policies that discriminate between marginal and highly ethical individuals, especially when recruiting for high-risk positions. Proactive hiring procedures include such things as conducting background investigations on prospective employees, thoroughly checking references and learning how to interpret responses to inquiries asked about candidates, and testing for honesty and other attributes.

Consider the following case of how poor hiring allowed fraud to occur in an organization:

*Philip Crosby was a former president of ITT. While president, he wrote a book advocating that producing error-free products was possible, and could be very profitable. He left ITT to form Philip Crosby Associates, Inc. (PCA), a consulting firm based on his book's principles. The new company worked so well that it began to attract Fortune 500 executives, who paid as much as $1,800 each to spend a few days at the PCA college with Crosby. PCA was a unique reflection of its founder's values. Crosby argued that to produce error-free products, you have to have an environment of mutual respect. If employees have pride in working for their company, and feel that their company is open and honest, they will perform to the best of their abilities and will not steal from the company. PCA had an international division, created in 1984, that posted $2 million in sales its first year and had expectations to double that figure in 1985. In February 1985, PCA opened an office in Brussels, and had more offices in the planning stages. PCA decided they needed a director of finance who could work with each new country's reporting rules and translate foreign currencies into their U.S. equivalents. After a reasonable search, the eight senior PCA executives agreed to hire John C. Nelson. Nelson had an MBA, and seemed to have an impressive understanding of the technical aspects of the international marketplace. He also had an impressive reference provided to PCA by his previous company. Steve Balash, vice president of human resources, said, "He seemed like the kind of honest individual we'd want to hire." Unfortunately, John C. Nelson was not an honest individual. In fact, he wasn't even John C. Nelson. Rather, his real name was Robert W. Liszewski. When hired, Liszewski decorated his office with an Illinois CPA license; the CPA certificate had been created on his home computer. The background reference that was provided to PCA had been written by Liszewski's wife, who was a part-time worker with "John's former employer." Liszewski's job at PCA was to develop financial information for PCA's fast-growing international operations. Liszewski's work did not go very smoothly, even from the start. He was terribly slow at converting numbers from foreign currencies to U.S. dollars, which should not have been a tough task for a CPA. In addition, his monthly reports were always late. After about a year on the job, Liszewski faced his first big test. The company's third-quarter report deadline had passed and Liszewski was far from completing it. His excuses ranged from "The outside bookkeepers...haven't yet computed the final receipts" to "the computer crashed." PCA executives decided to let Liszewski continue because he seemed to be catching on and was doing better on other projects. In*

*December 1986 Liszewski's bookkeeper quit, leaving him completely in charge of all the money that flowed through that division (approximately $12 million that year). Liszewski quickly became hopelessly behind in keeping the books, and was finally called in to explain his problems to the chief financial officer. In the interview, Liszewski started crying, saying that he had cancer and had only three months to live. The chief financial officer believed Liszewski's lie and he was allowed to keep his job. PCA's business began to get worse. In 1986, the company's stock fell to $12 from $20 the year before. On March 12, the chief financial officer tried to move $500,000 from one bank account to another. He was informed by the controller that the account did not have a sufficient balance for the transfer. The CFO knew that the account was supposed to have at least $1 million in it. To see where the money went, the controller scanned the ledgers of wire transfers from the questionable account. She found an unposted transfer that did not appear to be legitimate: $82,353 had been transferred to a U.S. company called Allied Exports, supposedly to pay for shipping products to Brussels. The materials were being sent from South Bend, Indiana, to Brussels. The controller knew that South Bend was Liszewski's hometown, but did not think anything of it. Subsequent searches found several more wire transfers to South Bend totaling more than $425,000. The company called the Indiana secretary of state's office to check on Allied Export's incorporation records. They were informed that the president of Allied Export was a woman named Patricia Fox. Management recognized Fox as Liszewski's wife. With help from his wife, Liszewski had created a dummy company in South Bend, Indiana. To satisfy his bookkeeper, PCA's only check on Liszewski, he had photocopied the CFO's signature and affixed it to the contracts he created. For more than eight months, Liszewski funneled more than $961,000 to the dummy company by charging the expenditures to a number of different expense accounts. Liszewski's wife was arrested in South Bend when she tried to withdraw $230,000 from the account. In their home, detectives found PCA's ledgers that Liszewski had stolen, and a lockbox containing all of Allied Export's monthly statements, canceled checks, and incorporation papers. While searching the house, the police spotted Liszewski driving by in a white Porsche, but they were unable to catch him. Two weeks later, police computers showed a new driver's license had been issued to a John C. Nelson. When they checked out the address, police found an elderly man. The man was the real John C. Nelson, who identified Liszewski's picture as his old boss, Bruce Fox, who had been fired from a bank in Indiana when the bank discovered that he had previously served an 18-month sentence for embezzling $400,000.*

The third critical element—communicating expectations—includes (1) identifying appropriate values and ethics, (2) fraud awareness training that helps employees understand potential problems they may encounter and how to resolve or report them, and (3) communicating consistent expectations about punishment of violators. For codes of conduct to be effective, they must be written and communicated to employees, vendors, and customers. They must also be developed in a manner that will encourage management and employees to take ownership of them. Requiring employees to confirm in writing that they understand the organization's expectations is an effective element of communication in creating a culture of honesty. In fact, many successful organizations find that annual written confirmation is effective in both preventing fraud and detecting frauds before they become large. Expectations about punishment must be clearly communicated from top management throughout the organization. For example, a strong statement from management that dishonest actions will not be tolerated and that violators will be terminated and prosecuted to the fullest extent of the law is helpful as part of a fraud prevention program.

The reason Codes of Conduct are required under the Sarbanes-Oxley legislation is to convey expectations about what is and is not appropriate in an organization. As an example, Figure 3-1 contains the **Code of Conduct** developed by American Express Corporation for its board of directors[2].

This code educates (clarifies expectations) directors about what is and what is not acceptable. Every public company today must have such a code for its directors and officers.

## Figure 3-1 American Express's Code of Conduct

The Board of Directors of American Express Company hereby adopts the following Code of Business Conduct for directors of the Company. This code is intended to focus each director on areas of conflicts of interest, provide guidance relating to the recognition and handling of ethical issues, provide mechanisms to report potential conflicts or unethical conduct, and help foster a culture of openness and accountability.

Since no code or policy can anticipate every situation that may arise, this Code is intended to provide guidance for handling unforeseen situations which may arise. Directors are encouraged to bring questions about particular situations to the attention of the Chairman of the Nominating and Governance Committee, who may consult with the Secretary, the General Counsel or outside legal counsel as appropriate.

Directors who also serve as employees of the Company should read this Code in conjunction with the American Express Company Code of Conduct for employees.

### 1. Conflicts of Interest.

Directors shall avoid conflicts of interest between the director and the Company. Any situation that involves, or may reasonably be expected to involve, a conflict of interest with the Company, should be disclosed promptly to the Chairman of the Nominating and Governance Committee or the Secretary.

A "conflict of interest" occurs when a director's personal interest is adverse to—or may appear to be adverse to—the interests of the Company. Conflicts of interest may also arise when a director, or a member of his or her immediate family[1], receives personal benefits as a result of his or her position as a director of the Company beyond normal directors fees or compensation.

Some of the more common conflicts which directors should avoid are set out below.
- *Relationships with third parties.* Directors should not receive a personal benefit from any person or firm which is seeking to do business or to retain business with the Company. A director shall recuse him or herself from any Company Board decision involving another firm or company with which the director is affiliated.
- *Gifts.* Directors and members of their families should not accept gifts from persons or firms which deal with the Company where any such gift has a value beyond what is a normal and customary business courtesy.
- *Personal use of Company assets.* Directors should not use Company aircraft, assets, resources or information except in connection with Company business.

### 2. Pre-notification of Outside Positions.

- *Acceptance of corporate directorships.* Directors should inform the Secretary of the Company prior to accepting a directorship or officership position with another business corporation, whether or not they are public companies. This will permit the Company to review the line(s) of business of the other company to assure that no conflict exists between the companies and to evaluate the Company's business relationship, if any, with the other Company.
- *Acceptance of directorships of charitable or non-profit organizations.* Directors should contact the Secretary of the Company prior to accepting a position with a charitable organization. Directors should also inform the Secretary when any members of their immediate family accept such positions. This notification will allow the Company to monitor the level of contributions, if any, that the Company makes to the charitable organization.
- *Acceptance of other positions.* Directors should inform the Secretary prior to affiliating with a law firm or Audit firm that provides services to the Company. Directors should also notify the Company when any members of their immediate family accept such positions.

[1]New York Stock Exchange Rule 303A(2)(b) defines "immediate family" to include a person's spouse, parents, children, siblings, fathers and mothers-in-law, sons and daughters-in-law, brothers and sisters-in-law, and anyone (other than employees) who share such person's home.

*Continued*

## Figure 3-1 American Express's Code of Conduct (cont.)

**3. Corporate Opportunities.**

Directors are prohibited from: (a) taking for themselves or for their companies opportunities related to the Company's business; (b) using the Company's property or information for personal gain; or (c) competing with the Company for business opportunities; however, if the Company's disinterested directors determine that the Company will not pursue an opportunity that relates to the Company's business, a director may then do so.

**4. Confidentiality.**

Directors shall maintain the confidentiality of information entrusted to them by the Company and any other confidential information about the Company that comes to them, from whatever source, in their capacity as a director, except when disclosure is authorized or legally mandated.

**5. Compliance with laws, rules and regulations; fair dealing**

Directors shall comply with all applicable laws, rules and regulations applicable to the Company, including insider trading laws. Transactions in Company securities shall be pre-cleared with the Secretary or General Counsel and are governed by the Company's policies on trading in Company securities.

   Directors shall assure that the Company has current policies in place that require fair dealing by employees with the company's customers, suppliers and competitors.

**6. Encouraging the reporting of any illegal or unethical behavior.**

Directors should promote ethical behavior and take steps to ensure that the Company: (a) encourages employees to report violations of laws, rules, regulations or the Company's Code of Conduct to appropriate personnel; (b) encourages employees to talk to supervisors, managers and other appropriate personnel when in doubt about the best course of action in a particular situation and (c) has a "whistle blower" policy that assures employees that the Company will not retaliate for reports made in good faith.

**7. Handling News about American Express.**

Confidential information about the Company, including information that can be expected to have an impact on the market for the Company's stock such as forward-looking information such as projections of revenue or earnings, may be released only in accordance with Company guidelines and United States securities laws. Contacts with news organizations should be handled through the Company's Corporate Affairs & Communications personnel.

**8. Compliance with the Code.**

Directors should communicate any suspected violations of this Code promptly to the Chairman of the Nominating and Governance Committee or the Secretary. Violations will be investigated by the Board or by persons designated by the Board, and appropriate action will be taken in the event of any violations.

    The fourth element in creating a culture of honesty involves developing a positive work environment. Research results indicate that fraud occurs less frequently when employees have positive feelings of ownership about an organization than when they feel abused, threatened, or ignored. Factors associated with high levels of fraud and that detract from a positive work environment include the following:

1. Top management that does not care about or pay attention to appropriate behavior
2. Negative feedback and lack of recognition of job performance
3. Perceived inequities in an organization
4. Autocratic rather than participative management

5. Low organizational loyalty
6. Unreasonable budget expectations
7. Unrealistically low pay
8. Poor training and promotion opportunities
9. High turnover and absenteeism
10. Lack of clear organizational responsibilities
11. Poor communication practices within the organization

The last critical element is an organization's policy for handling fraud once it occurs. No matter how well an organization develops a culture of honesty and high ethics it will likely still have some fraud. The way an organization reacts to these incidents sends a strong signal that affects the number of future incidents. An effective policy for handling fraud should assure that the facts are investigated thoroughly, firm and consistent actions are taken against perpetrators, risks and controls are assessed and improved, and communication and training are ongoing.

## Assessing and Mitigating the Risk of Fraud

Neither fraud committed by top management on behalf of an organization nor fraud committed against an organization can occur without opportunity. Organizations can proactively eliminate fraud opportunities by (1) accurately identifying sources and measuring risks, (2) implementing appropriate preventative and detective controls, (3) creating widespread monitoring by employees, and (4) having the right kinds of independent checks, including an effective audit function.

Identifying, sourcing, and measuring the risk of fraud means that an organization should have a process in place that both defines where the greatest risks are and evaluates and tests controls that mitigate those risks. In identifying fraud risks, organizations should consider organizational, industry, and country-specific characteristics that influence the risk of fraud.

Some risks are inherent in the environment of an organization, but need to be addressed with an appropriate system of control. Once fraud risk assessment has taken place, the organization can identify the processes, controls, and other procedures that are needed to mitigate the identified risks. An appropriate internal control system will include a well-developed control environment, an effective accounting system, and appropriate control procedures.

Research shows that it is employees and managers, not auditors, who detect most frauds. To effectively prevent and detect fraud, employees and managers must be taught how to watch for and recognize fraud. The most effective way to involve employees in the monitoring process is to provide a protocol for communication that informs employees and others where to report suspected fraud and what form that communication should take. The protocol should assure confidentiality and stress that retribution will not be tolerated. Organizations that are serious about fraud prevention must make it easy for employees and others to come forward and must reward and not punish them for doing so.

The *Sarbanes-Oxley* legislation recognized the value of having a system for employees and others to report wrongdoing, including fraud. Section 307 of that law requires every public company to have a whistle-blower system in place, and Section 806 prohibits retaliation against any employee or other person who reports questionable activities using the whistle-blower system. One of the events that prompted this legislation was a letter former Enron chairman Kenneth Lay received from a senior executive in August 2001, warning that the company—once a pillar of the U.S. energy industry—could "implode in a wave of financial scandals." Apparently, the letter pointed out the questionable nature of some partnerships involving company executives.

The letter was unsigned, but its author was later identified as Sherron Watkins, a vice president for corporate development at Enron. If Enron directors had seen Sherron Watkins's whistle-blowing letter, Enron might still be a going concern, but, unfortunately, she sent her letter to the CEO, not the board…and the rest is now history. Congress's response to Enron and other corporate scandal is to place responsibility on a company's audit committee (a subcommittee of the board of directors) to implement and oversee a whistle-blowing process for soliciting, evaluating, and acting on complaints about how the company handles financial reporting and securities law compliance.

# Fraud Detection

In a fraud perpetrated by a bank teller, the following amounts were taken on the following dates:

| | | | | | | | |
|------|-------|------|-------|------|-------|------|-------|
| 4-1  | $10   | 5-8  | $20   | 6-5  | $50   | 7-16 | $600  |
| 4-4  | $20   | 5-9  | $30   | 6-9  | $30   | 7-23 | $600  |
| 4-7  | $20   | 5-12 | $30   | 6-10 | $40   | 8-4  | $20   |
| 4-9  | $20   | 5-13 | $30   | 6-11 | $30   | 8-8  | $20   |
| 4-10 | $20   | 5-14 | $30   | 6-12 | $50   | 8-11 | $30   |
| 4-14 | $40   | 5-15 | $30   | 6-13 | $50   | 8-14 | $30   |
| 4-16 | $30   | 5-16 | $40   | 6-16 | $50   | 8-19 | $20   |
| 4-22 | $30   | 5-19 | $40   | 6-17 | $50   | 8-22 | $40   |
| 4-23 | $30   | 5-20 | $40   | 6-18 | $30   | 8-26 | $400  |
| 4-24 | $30   | 5-21 | $40   | 6-20 | $70   | 8-27 | $600  |
| 4-25 | $30   | 5-22 | $20   | 6-23 | $100  | 8-28 | $400  |
| 4-28 | $30   | 5-27 | $30   | 6-24 | $200  | 9-2  | $400  |
| 4-29 | $30   | 5-28 | $40   | 6-25 | $400  | 9-5  | $100  |
| 4-30 | $30   | 5-29 | $40   | 6-26 | $600  | 9-12 | $100  |
| 5-1  | $20   | 5-30 | $50   | 7-8  | $400  | 9-15 | $200  |
| 5-5  | $30   | 6-2  | $40   | 7-9  | $700  | 9-16 | $400  |
| 5-6  | $30   | 6-3  | $50   | 7-14 | $400  |      |       |
| 5-7  | $20   | 6-4  | $50   | 7-15 | $600  |      |       |

When caught, the teller made the following statement: "I can't believe this fraud went on this long without anyone ever suspecting a thing, especially given the larger and larger amounts."

As you can see, this fraud started small, with the perpetrator stealing larger and larger amounts as it continued. Not being caught, the perpetrator's confidence in the fraud scheme increased, and the perpetrator became greedier and greedier. In fact, you will note that, on July 23, fraudulent behavior stopped for a two-week period. The reason for this pause in the perpetrator's dishonest behavior was that auditors came to that particular branch of the bank. You will also notice that once the auditors left, the perpetrator resumed fraudulent behavior but only stole small amounts. After a short time of testing the system to make sure the auditors hadn't detected the fraud or put processes in place that would reveal the dishonest activity, the perpetrator once again had confidence and quickly escalated the amounts stolen into hundreds of dollars per day.

Although the amounts involved in this fraud are small, the pattern is typical. Like most frauds, it started small and, because it was not detected, continued to get larger and larger. Events that scare or threaten the perpetrator result in discontinuance of the fraud, only to be resumed when the threats pass. Because perpetrators increase the amounts they steal, in most cases, amounts taken during the last few days or months of a fraud far exceed those taken during earlier periods. In one case, for example, the amounts taken quadrupled every month during the period the fraud continued. Indeed, there are no small frauds—just large ones that are detected early. And, in cases where it is top management or business owners who are perpetrating the fraud, fraud prevention is difficult and early detection is critical. Consider the following fraud:

> *The president of a New Hampshire temporary service company intentionally misclassified employees as independent contractors rather than as employees of his company. The misclassification allowed him to avoid paying $211,201 in payroll taxes over a three-year period. In addition, he provided an insurance company with false information on the number of people he actually employed, thereby avoiding $426,463 in workers' compensation premiums.*

When fraud is committed by the president or owner of an organization, as it was in this case, prevention is not relevant. Maybe the president's company could have had a higher code of ethics, but if the president wants to commit fraud, no one is likely to be able to stop him. Rather, the emphasis on these types of fraud must be on fraud detection.

Because most frauds increase dramatically over time, it is extremely important that when fraud cannot be prevented, it be detected early.

As a third example of how frauds increase over time, consider the case of a Japanese copper trader who was making rogue trades. Over a period of nine years, his rogue trading resulted in a fraud totaling $2.6 billion. The following theft amounts show how much the fraud grew by not being detected early:

| Year of Fraud | Cumulative Amount of the Fraud |
|---|---|
| Year 1 | $600,000 |
| Year 3 | $4 million |
| Year 5 | $80 million |
| Year 7 | $600 million |
| Year 9 | $2.6 billion |

In years 8 and 9, four of the world's largest banks became involved and lost more than $500 million.

The detection of fraud includes those steps or actions taken to discover a fraud that has been committed. Detection does not include investigative procedures taken to determine motives, extent, method of embezzlement, or other elements of the dishonest act. As you will discover in the next chapter, fraud is unlike other crimes in which the occurrence of the crime is easily recognized. Because fraud is rarely obvious, one of the most difficult tasks is determining whether a fraud has actually occurred.

Detection of fraud usually begins by identifying symptoms, indicators, or red flags that tend to be associated with fraud. Unfortunately, these red flags can often be associated with nonfraud factors as well. The two primary ways to detect fraud include: (1) by chance, and (2) by proactively searching for or encouraging the early recognition of symptoms. In the past, most frauds were detected by accident. Unfortunately, by the time detection occurred, the frauds were usually large and had been going on for some time. In most cases, individuals in the victim organizations suspected that fraud was occurring but did not come forward, either because they weren't sure, didn't want to wrongly accuse someone, didn't know how to report the fraud, or were fearful of the consequences of becoming a whistle-blower.

In recent years, organizations have implemented a number of initiatives to better detect fraud. Probably the most common proactive fraud detection approach has been to install reporting hotlines (*whistle-blowing systems*) whereby employees, coworkers, and others can call in using a telephone or submit (using a Web page) an anonymous tip of a suspicion of fraud. Some of these hotlines are maintained within the company, and others are outsourced to independent organizations to provide hotline services for them. (The Association of Certified Fraud Examiners and a company called SilentWhistle, for example, provide fee-based hotline service.) Organizations that have installed hotlines have detected many frauds that would have remained undetected, but they have often paid a fairly high price for doing so. Not surprisingly, many of the calls do not involve fraud at all. Some represent hoaxes, some are motivated by grudges, anger, or a desire to do harm to an organization or individual, and some represent honest recognition of fraud symptoms that are caused by nonfraud factors.

Except for hotlines, only recently have serious proactive fraud detection efforts been taken by organizations. Developments in technology allow organizations to analyze and mine databases to proactively look for fraud symptoms. Banks, for example, install programs to identify suspected kiting. These programs draw the bank's attention to customers with a high volume of bank transactions within a short period of time. Insurance companies implement programs that examine claims within a short time after purchasing insurance. Some organizations even implement comprehensive fraud detection programs by systematically identifying the kinds of frauds that could be occurring, cataloging the various symptoms those frauds would generate, and then building real-time queries into their computer systems to search for these symptoms. Fraud-detection research, mostly using technology-based search techniques, is now being conducted by academics and other investigators. Anyone who is seriously interested in understanding and fighting fraud should be following this research. In the next two chapters, we will discuss proactive fraud detection.

As an example of proactive *fraud detection*, a large U.S. bank installed a backroom function that used computer programs to scan customer transactions looking for unusual activity. Customers who make rapid deposit and withdrawal transactions, especially depositing checks written on the same account, for example, are often committing the fraud of kiting. Once kiting is suspected, the branch where the suspect's account is domiciled is contacted and told to look into possible fraud. In one instance, the branch was warned that a particular three-year customer had account activity that looked as if he were kiting. Unfortunately, the branch manager knew the customer and felt that he was trustworthy. A few days later, the branch was again notified that this same customer's deposit and withdrawal activity looked suspicious. Finally, after the third warning, the branch manager decided to investigate. In the meantime, the other bank the dishonest customer was using had discovered the kiting and this bank was left to cover a loss that had grown from $70,000 to more than $600,000 between the first and third notification by the back office. As this real account illustrates, proactive fraud detection can be valuable, but only when the symptoms generated are not ignored.

## Fraud Investigation

> *Mark and Jane were husband and wife. Mark was the CEO of McDonald's Incorporated, and Jane was a partner in the CPA firm of Watkiss and McCloy. After a hard day at work, they met at a local restaurant for dinner. Mark told Jane about an incident that happened at work. He showed her an anonymous note that stated: "You had better look into the relationship between John Beasley (the manager of the purchasing department) and the Brigadeer Company (a supplier) because something fishy is going on." He told Jane that he had no idea who sent him the note and that he wasn't even sure how or what to do about it. He told her that he was concerned about possible collusion and should probably pursue the "lead." Jane couldn't believe what she was hearing. "What a coincidence," she stated. "Today, something very similar happened to me." She said that a junior auditor had approached her, confiding in her that he was concerned that the client's sales were overstated. He said that he had found some sales contracts without support (there was usually significant documentation supporting the contracts), all signed at the end of the accounting period. He told Jane that he was concerned that the client was artificially inflating revenues to improve the company's financial performance.*

Both of these situations involve matters that need to be investigated. If Mark does not investigate the anonymous tip, he may never uncover a possible kickback fraud and inflated purchasing costs for the company. Likewise, Jane needs to perform some follow-up investigation on the revenue problem brought to her attention by the junior auditor.

For at least three reasons, the auditors must determine whether the client is really overstating revenues. First, the company's shareholders could face significant losses. Second, the auditors' failure to discover the overstatement could expose them to legal action (and consequent losses). Finally, and perhaps most important, an overstatement of revenues may expose management's integrity to such serious doubt as to make the firm "unauditable."

Both of these situations create a *predication of fraud*. **Predication** refers to the circumstances, taken as a whole, that would lead a reasonable, prudent professional to believe a fraud has occurred, is occurring, or will occur. Fraud investigations should not be conducted without predication. A specific allegation of fraud against another party is not necessary, but some reasonable basis for concern that fraud may be occurring is certainly necessary. Once predication is present, as in these cases, an investigation is usually undertaken to determine whether fraud is actually occurring, as well as the who, why, how, when, and where elements of the fraud. The purpose of an investigation is to find the truth—to determine whether the symptoms actually represent fraud or whether they represent unintentional errors or other factors. Fraud investigation is a complex and sensitive matter. If investigations are not properly conducted, the reputations of innocent individuals can be irreparably injured, guilty parties can go undetected and be free to repeat the act, and the offended entity may not have information to use in preventing and detecting similar incidents or in recovering damages.

## Approaches to Fraud Investigation

The investigation of fraud symptoms within an organization must have management's approval. Investigations can be quite expensive, and thus should be pursued only when sufficient reason exists to believe that fraud has occurred (when predication is present).

The approaches to fraud investigation vary, although most investigators rely heavily on interviews.

Fraud investigations can be classified according to the types of evidence produced or according to the elements of fraud. Using the first approach, the evidence square in Figure 3-2 shows the four classifications of investigation techniques.

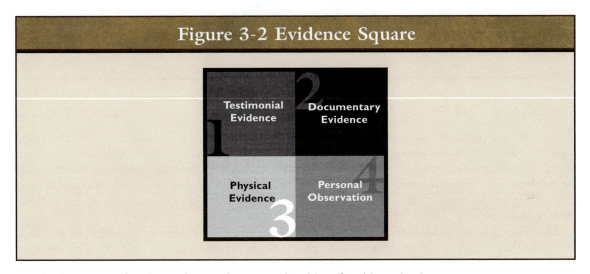

### Figure 3-2 Evidence Square

The four types of evidence that can be accumulated in a fraud investigation are:

1. *Testimonial evidence, which is gathered from individuals.* Specific investigative techniques used to gather testimonial evidence are interviewing, interrogation, and honesty tests.
2. *Documentary evidence, gathered from paper, computers, and other written or printed sources.* Some of the most common investigative techniques for gathering this evidence include document examination, public records searches, audits, computer searches, net worth calculations, and financial statement analysis. Corporate databases and e-mail servers often prove to be useful sources of documentary evidence.
3. *Physical evidence.* Fingerprints, tire marks, weapons, stolen property, identification numbers or marks on stolen objects, and other tangible evidence can be associated with dishonest acts. The gathering of physical evidence often involves forensic analysis by experts.
4. *Personal observation.* involves evidence is sensed (seen, heard, felt, etc.) by the investigators themselves. Personal observation investigative techniques involve invigilation, surveillance, and covert operations, among others.

The three elements of fraud are a preferable way to classify investigative approaches. These elements include the theft act, concealment, and conversion, as illustrated in Figure 3-3.

Theft act investigative methods involve efforts to catch the perpetrator(s) in the embezzlement act or to gather information about the actual theft acts. Concealment investigative methods involve focusing on records, documents, computer programs and servers, and other places where perpetrators might try to conceal or hide their dishonest acts. Conversion investigative methods involve searching for ways in which perpetrators spent their stolen assets. A fourth set of investigative techniques represents an overall approach to all these elements. It is labeled *inquiry methods.* Thus, this approach to classifying investigative techniques is called the *fraud triangle plus inquiry approach.* In the next chapter we discuss the investigation methods that fall in each of these four categories.

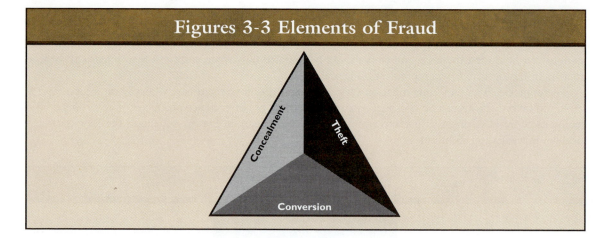

## Figures 3-3 Elements of Fraud

## Conducting a Fraud Investigation

For now, it is important to know that a fraud investigator needs some way to coordinate the fraud investigation. Some investigations are quite large and conducting the various investigative steps in the wrong order or doing them inappropriately can lead to a failed investigation and other problems. For example, an incorrectly calculated checksum hash on hard drive evidence or an improperly seized computer can make evidence impermissible in court. In fact, it is important that you understand the significant risks investigators face.

You must also remember that investigating a fraud is a traumatic experience for everyone involved, including the perpetrators. As stated previously, most fraud perpetrators are first-time offenders who have positive reputations in their work, community, family, and church environments. Sometimes, admitting that they are being investigated for fraud or have committed fraud is more than they can take. Consider the following obituary, for example:

> *Memorial services for John Jones will be held Thursday, May 5, 2001, at the Springer-Wilson funeral home. John was 35 at the time of his death. He was preceded in death by his mother, Jane Jones, and a younger brother, Tom Jones. John is survived by his wife, Rebecca, and four children ages 9, 7, 6, and 4. He is also survived by three brothers, a sister, and his father. In lieu of flowers, please make contributions to the Improvement Memorial Fund for Children.*

This obituary, which has been modified slightly, is for a person who embezzled $650,000 from his employer's company. Over a seven-year period, he embezzled nearly half of all cash received from customers. He did not steal money paid by customers who used checks or credit cards to pay their bills. When the company finally determined that he was stealing, they called him on the telephone at night and asked him to meet with the company's lawyers the next morning. John did two things that night after receiving the telephone call. First, he called an attorney and told her that he had been stealing from his employer for seven years and would like her to represent him at a meeting with the company's attorneys the next morning. Then, a couple of hours later, he drove into some nearby mountains and committed suicide.

This actual case illustrates one reason why investigations must be conducted carefully. Maintaining high ethics in conducting investigations is also important. At a minimum, investigations of fraud must proceed as follows:

1. They must be undertaken only to "establish the truth of a matter under question."
2. The individuals charged with the responsibility for conducting the investigation must be experienced and objective. If individuals charged with investigations do not exercise care in choosing words to describe the incident or fail to maintain a neutral perspective, their objectivity can immediately become suspect in the eyes of management and employees. Investigators should never jump to conclusions.

3.  Any hypothesis investigators have about whether someone committed fraud should be closely guarded when discussing the progress of an investigation with others. Although good investigators may form preliminary opinions or impressions at the start of an investigation, they must objectively weigh every bit of information against known facts and evidence and must always protect the confidentiality of the investigation.

4.  Investigators must ensure that those who have a need to know (e.g., management) are kept apprised of investigation activities and agree to the investigation and techniques employed.

5.  Good investigators must ensure that all information collected during an inquiry is independently corroborated and determined to be factually correct. Failure to corroborate evidence is often a key mistake made by inexperienced investigators.

6.  Investigators must exercise care to avoid questionable investigative techniques. Experienced investigators make sure that any technique used is scientifically and legally sound and fair. Usually, thoroughness and dogged tenacity rather than questionable techniques lead to a successful investigation.

7.  Investigators must report all facts fairly and objectively. Communications throughout the term of an investigation, from preliminary stage to final report, should be carefully controlled to avoid obscuring facts and opinions. Communication, including investigative reports, must not only include information obtained that points to guilt, but must also include facts and information that may exonerate. Ignoring and failing to document information is a serious investigative flaw, with potential for serious consequences.

## Legal Action

One of the major decisions a company, stockholders, or others have to make when fraud is committed is what kind of follow-up action should be taken. Why the fraud occurred should always be determined, and controls or other measures to prevent or deter its reoccurrence should be implemented. The bigger question that must be addressed is what legal action should be taken with respect to the perpetrators.

Most organizations and other fraud victims usually make one of three choices: (1) take no legal action; (2) pursue civil remedies; or (3) pursue criminal action against the perpetrators, which is sometimes done for them by law enforcement agencies. We addressed civil and criminal law in Chapter 1 and will discuss follow-up action in future chapters. Here we will briefly review some of the pros and cons of each alternative.

Descriptive fraud research consistently shows that legal action is taken against perpetrators who commit fraud against organizations in fewer than half of all fraud cases. Management often only wants to get the fraud behind it as quickly as possible. It understands that pursuing legal action is expensive, time consuming, sometimes embarrassing, and is often considered an unproductive use of time. Most often, management terminates fraud perpetrators, but sometimes it does not even do that. Unfortunately, when organizations do not pursue legal action, the word spreads quickly throughout the organization that "nothing serious will happen if you steal from the company." Employees who understand this message are more likely to steal than are employees of organizations who expect strict punishment for dishonest acts. When one *Fortune* 500 company changed its stance on fraud from "the CEO is to be informed when someone is prosecuted for fraud" to "the CEO is to be informed when someone who commits fraud is not prosecuted," the number of frauds in the company decreased significantly.

## Civil Action

As you learned in Chapter 1, the purpose of a civil action is to recover money or other assets from the fraud perpetrators and others associated with the fraud. Civil actions are quite rare in cases of employee fraud (because perpetrators usually spend the money they steal), but are much more common when frauds involve other organizations. Vendors who pay kickbacks to company employees are often the target of civil actions by victim companies, especially if the losses to the company are high. Likewise, stockholders and creditors who suffer losses when management fraud occurs almost always sue not only the perpetrators, but usually the auditors and others associated with the company as well. The plaintiff's lawyers are usually more than willing to represent shareholders in a class action, contingent fee lawsuit.[3]

## Criminal Action

Criminal action can only be brought by law enforcement or statutory agencies. Organizations that want to pursue criminal action against perpetrators must work with local, state, or federal agencies to get their employees or other perpetrators prosecuted. As you learned in Chapter 1, criminal penalties usually involve fines, prison terms, or both. They can also involve the perpetrators entering into restitution agreements to pay back stolen funds over a period of time. Pursuing criminal penalties is becoming more and more common in cases of fraud. Corporate executives who commit fraud are often sentenced for up to 10 years in jail and ordered to pay fines equal to the amounts they embezzled. Remember, however, that it is much more difficult to get a criminal conviction than it is to get a judgment in a civil case. Whereas only a preponderance of the evidence (more than 50 percent) is necessary to win a civil case, convictions are only successful if proof "beyond a reasonable doubt" is presented to indicate that the perpetrator "intentionally" stole money or other assets.

## SUMMARY OF FRAUD-FIGHTING ACTIVITIES

Most organizations spend most of their fraud-fighting dollars investigating frauds once predication is present. Investigation is only one of four major activities related to fraud. Organizations that do not work proactively at fraud prevention and fraud detection usually have fraud more frequently and at a greater cost than organizations that adopt a proactive approach. In addition, even when organizations successfully investigate fraud, they often merely terminate perpetrators rather than seek legal action because termination is "the easy way out." Unfortunately, organizations that merely terminate or do not sanction perpetrators usually have more fraud than organizations who have strict prosecution policies. Perpetrators have not usually committed a crime before and are respected employees, clients, vendors, or customers. If they are terminated, they usually do not tell even their families the reason for their termination. Without suffering the embarrassment of having friends, family members, and other loved ones become aware of the dishonest activity, fraud perpetrators often undertake fraudulent activities again in the future.

Organizations must decide how much fraud they are willing to tolerate. Although it is difficult to get accurate statistics, money spent on proactive prevention and detection and rigorous, legal follow-up tends to reduce future occurrences of fraud. One *Fortune* 500 company that had approximately $25 million in known fraud per year, for example, decided to take proactive steps to reduce fraud. The company worked hard on fraud prevention, including making a video that was shown periodically to provide every employee with fraud awareness training (and awareness training in other undesirable activities, such as substance abuse, safety violations, and discrimination). The company also provided every employee with cards that specified who they should contact if they saw any of these problems. It created a proactive code of conduct that every employee signed each year. Not only did it focus on fraud prevention, but it also employed several proactive fraud detection methods, including computer search techniques and a fraud hotline. Finally, it developed a comprehensive fraud policy specifying who and how potential frauds would be investigated and what actions would be taken against fraud perpetrators. Its efforts paid large dividends, especially given the multiplier effect discussed in Chapter 1. In only a couple of years, known frauds in the organization totaled less than $1 million.

## KEY TERMS

**Fraud prevention:** Eliminating the occurrence of fraud by taking steps to create and maintain a culture of honesty and high ethics and assessing the risk of fraud and developing responses to mitigate the risks and eliminate the opportunities for fraud.

**Code of conduct:** A written statement that conveys expectations about what is and is not appropriate in an organization.

**Sarbanes-Oxley:** U.S. legislation passed in 2002 whose goal is to minimize the occurrence of fraud and increase the penalties for perpetrators when it occurs.

**Whistle-blower system:** A response mechanism that makes it easy for employees and others to report questionable activities. (Also called hotlines.)

**Fraud detection:** The activity of searching for or finding indicators that suggest that fraud may be occurring, finding predication of fraud.

**Predication:** Circumstances taken as a whole that would lead a reasonable, prudent professional to believe that a fraud has occurred, is occurring or will occur.

**Testimonial evidence:** Evidence conveyed by individual, either orally or in writing.

**Documentary evidence:** evidence comprised of written records, either electronic or paper.

**Physical evidence:** Any tangible evidence except documentary evidence.

**Personal observation:** Evidence observed personally by fraud investigators.

**Fraud investigation:** Following up on fraud predication to determine if fraud is or has occurred and, if so, by whom, for how much, in what ways, and where. The process of gathering evidence to either confirm or reject the fraud predication.

**Theft act:** The commission of a fraud.

**Concealment:** Efforts taken to hide a fraud from being discovered.

**Conversion:** The spending of stolen assets by perpetrators.

## QUESTIONS AND CASES

### DISCUSSION QUESTIONS

1. Why is fraud prevention so important?

2. How does building a culture of honesty and high ethics help to reduce the possibility of fraud?

3. How does a company assess and mitigate the risk of fraud within the organization?

4. Why is it important to detect fraud early?

5. Why is it important to recognize fraud symptoms early?

6. Why is it important to conduct a thorough fraud investigation when fraud is suspected?

7. Describe the evidence square.

8. How is the evidence square useful in thinking about fraud investigation?

9. For each of the following, identify whether the evidence would be classified as testimonial evidence,

documentary evidence, physical evidence, or personal observation.
   a. Surveillance
   b. Tire marks
   c. Honesty test
   d. Interview
   e. A computer hard drive
   f. A financial statement analysis
   g. Invigilation
   h. A paper report
   i. Identification numbers on vehicles
   j. Audit of financial statements
   k. Check stubs
   l. Fingerprints
   m. Background checks
   n. Forensic analysis

10. What are some of the legal actions that can occur after a fraud has occurred?

### TRUE/FALSE

1. Once fraud has been committed, everyone loses.

2. Fraud prevention involves two fundamental activities: (1) a hotline for tips and (2) assessing the risk of fraud and developing concrete responses to mitigate the risks and eliminate opportunities for fraud.

3. Developing a positive work environment is of little importance when creating a culture of honesty.

4. No matter how well an organization has developed a culture of honesty and high ethics, most organizations will still have some fraud.

5. Research has shown that it is employees and managers, not auditors, who detect most frauds.

6. Organizations that want to prevent fraud must make it easy for employees and others to report suspicious activities.

7. Perpetrators who are not caught lose confidence in the scheme and become less and less greedy.

8. Once predication is present, an investigation is usually undertaken to determine whether fraud is actually occurring.

9. Most investigators rely heavily on interviews to obtain the truth.

10. Physical evidence includes evidence gathered from paper, computers, and other written documents.

11. The fraud triangle plus inquiry approach is an effective way to categorize investigative techniques.

12. Legal action taken by an organization can affect the probability of whether fraud will reoccur.

13. Investigating fraud is the most cost-effective way to reduce losses from fraud.

14. Fraud prevention includes taking steps to create and maintain a culture of honesty and high ethics.

15. Effective hiring policies that discriminate between marginal and highly ethical individuals contribute to an organization's success in preventing fraud.

16. Expectations about punishment must be communicated randomly among work groups if fraud is to be prevented.

17. Frauds typically start large and get smaller as the perpetrator tries to conceal dishonest acts.

18. Fraud is difficult to detect because some fraud symptoms often cannot be differentiated from nonfraud factors that appear to be symptoms.

19. The three elements of the fraud triangle by which the investigative techniques are often classified are (1) the theft act, (2) concealment efforts, and (3) conversion methods.

20. Organizations often want to avoid embarrassment and expense, so they terminate fraudulent employees without having them prosecuted further.

21. Criminal conviction is much more difficult to achieve than a civil judgment because it requires proof "beyond a reasonable doubt" that the perpetrator intentionally stole assets.

## MULTIPLE CHOICE

1. The most effective way to reduce losses from fraud is:
   a. Detecting fraud early.
   b. Implementing proactive fraud detection programs.
   c. Preventing fraud from occurring.
   d. Severely punishing fraud perpetrators.

2. To successfully prevent fraud, an organization must:
   a. Identify internal control weaknesses
   b. Explicitly consider fraud risks.
   c. Take proactive steps to create the right kind of environment.
   d. All of the above.

3. The best way for management to model appropriate behavior is to:
   a. Enforce a strict code of ethics.
   b. Set an example of appropriate behavior.
   c. Train employees about appropriate behavior.
   d. Make employees read and sign a code of conduct.

4. Which of the following is not a proactive way for a company to eliminate fraud opportunities?
   a. Severely punishing fraud perpetrators
   b. Assessing risks
   c. Implementing appropriate preventive and detective controls
   d. Creating widespread monitoring of employees

5. Most frauds start small and:
   a. If not detected, continue to get larger.
   b. Usually decrease in amount.

   c. Remain steady and consistent.
   d. None of the above.

6. It is most difficult to prevent which type of fraud?
   a. Investment scams
   b. Fraud committed by a company president
   c. Employee fraud
   d. Customer fraud

7. _____ refers to the circumstances, taken as a whole, that would lead a reasonable prudent professional to believe fraud has occurred, is occurring, or will occur.
   a. Evidential circumstance
   b. Investigation
   c. Service of process
   d. Predication

8. An investigative approach that includes testimonial evidence, documentary evidence, physical evidence, and personal observations is referred to as the:
   a. Investigative square of evidence.
   b. Investigation square.
   c. Evidence square.
   d. Fraud triangle plus.

9. An investigative approach that includes the theft act, concealment, conversion, and inquiry methods is referred to as:
   a. Investigative square.
   b. Evidence square.
   c. Fraud triangle plus inquiry approach.
   d. Investigative square of evidence.

10. Usually, for everyone involved—especially victims—the investigation of fraud is very:
    a. Pleasant and relaxing.
    b. Educational.
    c. Exciting.
    d. Traumatic and difficult.

11. To prevent fraud from reoccurring, most organizations and other fraud victims should:
    a. Take no legal action.
    b. Pursue civil remedies.
    c. Pursue criminal remedies.
    d. Pursue either civil or criminal action.

12. All of the following are ways to create a culture of honesty and high ethics except:
    a. Creating a positive work environment.
    b. Hiring the right kind of employees.
    c. Having top management model appropriate behavior.
    d. Eliminating opportunities for fraud.

13. The "Tone at the Top" when related to fraud usually refers to management's attitude about:
    a. Office parties.
    b. Fraud prosecution.
    c. Employee absenteeism.
    d. How it models and labels appropriate behavior.

14. Research shows that fraud occurs less frequently when employees feel:
    a. Abused by management.
    b. Threatened.
    c. Challenged with unreasonable performance goals.
    d. Ownership in the organization.

15. Opportunities to commit fraud can be eliminated by identifying sources of fraud, implementing controls, and through independent checks. One other effective way of eliminating opportunities is:
    a. Teaching employees to monitor and report fraud.
    b. Terminating and punishing employees who commit fraud.
    c. Failing to terminate or punish employees who commit fraud.
    d. Identifying indicators of fraud or red flags.

16. Drawbacks to establishing a hotline for employees to report fraud include all of the following except:
    a. Expense.
    b. Many incidents reported are hoaxes motivated by grudges.
    c. Fraud symptoms reported are caused by non-fraud factors.
    d. This method for finding fraud is outdated.

17. "Predication of fraud" is defined as:
    a. Reasonable belief that fraud has occurred.
    b. Irrefutable evidence that fraud has been committed.
    c. Motivation for committing fraud.
    d. Punishment of fraud perpetrators.

18. Which of the four types of evidence includes interrogation and honesty testing?
    a. Testimonial
    b. Documentary
    c. Physical
    d. Personal observation

19. The three elements of fraud are:
    a. Theft act, rationalization, and opportunity.
    b. Pressure, opportunity, and conversion.
    c. Theft act, concealment, and conversion.
    d. Theft act, pressure, and opportunity.

20. Most often victims of fraud do not take legal action against perpetrators because legal action can be:
    a. Unproductive.
    b. Embarrassing.
    c. Expensive.
    d. All of the above.

21. Arguments for taking legal action against perpetrators of fraud include:
    a. Huge cash settlements from prosecuting fraud are an excellent source of revenue.
    b. Legal action usually results in positive publicity for the company.
    c. Prosecution keeps lawyers busy.
    d. Prosecution discourages reoccurrence of fraud.

## SHORT CASES

**Case 1.** Assume that you are the consultant for Long Range Builders, a company that specializes in the mass production of wood trusses. The trusses are used in the building of houses throughout the United States, Canada, and Mexico. While implementing a fraud prevention program, you realize the importance of creating a culture of honesty and high ethics within the company.

1. What critical elements are key factors in creating an atmosphere of honesty and high ethics?

2. How would you implement these elements in your company?

**Case 2.** The chapter stressed that preventing fraud is the most cost-effective way to reduce losses from fraud. Why is fraud prevention more cost-effective than fraud detection or investigation?

**Case 3.** Fraud detection is an important element of minimizing losses due to fraud, especially if frauds can be detected early. Explain why it is important that frauds be detected early.

**Case 4.** Assume that you are the fraud expert for a large *Fortune* 500 company located in Miami, Florida. In a recent meeting with the executive committee, one of the officers explains that the fraud prevention program, which teaches managers and employees how to detect and report fraud, costs the company $150,000 a year. The officer then explains that it is a waste of time and money for the company to educate employees and managers about fraud. "Is it not the responsibility of the auditors to detect fraud?" he questions. As the fraud expert of the company, the president asks you to explain why managers and employees should be educated in the detection of fraud.

1. What would you tell the committee about why it is important to train managers and employees in fraud detection?

2. After explaining to the committee why it is important to train management and employees, the president asks you about effective ways to involve employees and managers in the prevention and detection of fraud. What would you tell the president?

**Case 5.** You recently graduated from college with an MBA. Upon graduation, you start working for Roosevelt Power Plant. Upon arrival, the boss describes to you a large fraud that recently took place in the company. The boss then asks you what actions should be taken to ensure that fraud does not occur again. After analyzing the company, you compile a list of actions and present this list of necessary steps and controls to be taken. The boss notices "Create a culture of honesty and create a positive work environment for employees" on the list and is enraged and wants to know what a positive work environment has to do with the prevention and detection of fraud.

1. What would you tell the boss about why a positive work environment will help prevent fraud?

2. What factors would you tell the boss contribute to a negative work environment?

**Case 6.** The text pointed out that it is important to hire employees who are honest and have a well-developed personal code of ethics. Derek Bok, former law professor and president of Harvard University, suggested that colleges and universities have a special obligation to train students to be more thoughtful and perceptive about moral and ethical issues. Other individuals conclude that it is not possible to "teach" ethics. What do you think? Can ethics be taught? If you agree that colleges and universities can teach ethics, how might the ethical dimensions of business be taught to students?

**Case 7.** Predication refers to circumstances that would lead a reasonable professional to believe that fraud has occurred. Why should you not conduct a fraud investigation without predication?

**Case 8.** When a fraud has occurred within an organization, management must decide what follow-up action to take. Briefly describe the three follow-up alternatives available to organizations.

**Case 9.** In 2001, the country of Peru was thrown into political turmoil as its president, Alberto Fujimori, was accused of conspiring with the head of the national army to accept bribes and steal money from the government. As a result, Fujimori fled the country to avoid impeachment and prosecution. Fujimori was elected 10 years earlier based on his promises to lower inflation and combat terrorism. He was not, however, elected for his honesty. At the time he was elected, many people expressed the thought, "All of our presidents steal from us, but he steals the least." Although he was successful as a president, what could the Peruvian people have done to avoid the frauds committed by President Fujimori?

## EXTENSIVE CASES

**Extensive Case 1.** Plutonium was an Internet start-up company founded in 1988 at the beginning of the technology boom. One of the largest problems for Plutonium was developing the technological systems necessary to support the rapidly expanding user base. Furthermore, due to rapid expansion in the recent years, many of their systems had been added hastily, resulting in poor integration and eroding data integrity. As a result, the CEO of Plutonium announced an initiative to integrate all systems and increase the quality of internal data. In compliance with this initiative, Plutonium purchased an expensive and complex billing system called Gateway, which would automate the billing for thousands of Internet accounts via credit cards. During the integration, Gateway, in collaboration with Visa, created a phony credit card number that could be used by developers and programmers to test the functionality and integration of the Gateway system. Moreover, this credit card number was fully functional in "live" environments so that testers and developers could ensure functionality without being required to use actual personal or company credit card numbers. (The activity on this card was not monitored.) The integration went smoothly; however, it created thousands of corrupt accounts that required fixing.

Jonathan, the manager of the operations department, was responsible for the resolution of all data integrity issues. His team was tasked with fixing all corrupt accounts created by the launch and integration of the Gateway system. As a result, Jonathan was given the phony credit card number, which was kept on a Post-it note in his drawer.

One of the top performers on the operations team was a 29-year-old man named Chris. Chris worked in operations for more than a year, making $15 per hour, the same salary at which he was hired. He was an introvert working to support a family and put himself through school. Chris was the most technologically savvy individual on the team and his overall systems knowledge even exceeded that of his manager, Jonathan. Chris was brilliant in creating more efficient tools and methods to repair corrupted accounts. Therefore, Chris was tasked with conducting training for new employees and updating team members on new processes and tools that he had created. As a result, Chris quickly became a trusted and valuable team member; thus, Jonathan gave him and other team members the phony credit card number in order to further increase the productivity of the team.

However, after six months of working at Plutonium, Chris received an official reprimand from the company for using the company system to access Web sites containing pirated software and music. The FBI attended the investigation and determined that Chris had not been a major player in the piracy. Therefore, Chris was quietly warned and placed on a short-term probation. Jonathan was asked to write a warning letter for the action; however, after a brief conversation with Chris, Jonathan determined that Chris's intentions were good and never officially submitted the letter because Chris was a trusted employee and elevated the overall performance of the team. A few months after the piracy incident, Jonathan noticed some changes in Chris's behavior such as: his computer monitor was repositioned so that his screen was not visible to other coworkers; he had almost all the latest technological innovations; new Palm Pilot, MP3 Player, Play Station, a new laptop, and a new car stereo system; he was going out to lunch more frequently; and he had multiple fake user names and passwords that he frequently used for testing purposes.

### Questions

1. Evaluate this case using the three elements of the fraud triangle to identify:
   a. Potential pressures for Chris to commit fraud.
   b. Potential opportunities for Chris to commit fraud.
   c. Potential rationalizations that Chris could use to commit fraud.

2. What are some of the symptoms that fraud potentially exists in this situation?

3. What could Jonathan have done to eliminate some of the opportunities for fraud?

**Extensive Case 2.** Diana worked for a reputable global consulting firm. Her firm specialized in helping companies analyze their people, processes, systems, and strategy. Diana was hired into the San Francisco office and was put through weeks of training to help her understand the firm methodology, technology, and culture. The firm looked for people with the right aptitude who had demonstrated a record of success in previous school, work, or extracurricular activities. They found that this type of person worked out best for the type of work the firm was paid to do.

Diana was flattered to be considered the right type of person for this company. She was excited to be assigned to a project and begin work. Even though Diana was trained in certain technologies, she was assigned a project for which she had no training. The project was implementing SAP—a multimillion-dollar enterprise resource planning software package. The client was a mid-sized manufacturer located in Topeka, Kansas.

Diana was not trained in SAP and found out that she was replacing two managers who were just removed from the project. The project was running over budget so the firm looked for ways to get the work done less expensively. Diana, who billed out at the lower consultant rate (instead of the manager rate) was a cheap solution although it would be a tough sell to the client. The client liked the previous managers and felt comfortable with their skill level. Because of the demand for the SAP experts, Diana's firm could charge Diana's time at a billing rate of $200 per hour—expensive but less than the client was paying for the managers.

During the first day on the job, Diana's manager took her out to lunch to give her "the scoop" on what was happening at the project and what she would be expecting from Diana. "Diana, this is going to be a very difficult assignment. You've replaced two skilled managers the client likes. I know you haven't been trained or actually even seen SAP before, but you're smart and can come up to speed quickly. I had to tell the client you were an expert in the software in order for them to agree to bring you on. If you have any questions, don't hesitate to ask me but definitely don't look stupid or seem like you don't know what you're doing in front of the client. The client will be skeptical of you at first but be confident and you'll win them over. I think the transition will smooth out quickly. See me if you have any questions."

Diana was scared to death—but what was she to do? Was this standard procedure to throw employees into this situation? Either way, she had to get to work. Her immediate tasks were to map out the processes for the client's Order-to-Cash, Purchase-to-Pay, and Capital Acquisition business scenarios. This process mapping involved interviewing managers and looking around most of the functional departments in the company. Here are some interesting things she found as she did his work.

The head of purchasing, Mike, was so different from any other employee Diana encountered while at the client. He wore expensive suits to work and liked to talk about his clothes with colleagues. He also drove the latest model BMW and would take the other consultants on the project for rides during lunch. Diana thought this behavior was odd because she didn't think a purchasing manager at this company made enough money to have these luxuries. Mike also took his relationships with "his" vendors very seriously. He would spend lots of time "understanding who they were." Some days Mike was supportive of Diana and other days seemed completely different and almost hostile and combative. When Diana informally inquired about the purchasing manager's clothes and car and his Dr. Jekyll/Mr. Hyde syndrome, she heard the following justification: "He probably has a lot of money because he's worked here for over 20 years. Plus, he never takes vacations. Come to think of it, the vacation part probably explains why he seems hostile to you some of the time." Diana couldn't figure this guy out but proceeded to do his work with the purchasing department.

Internal sales was run by a stressed-out single mom named Kathy. You could tell at first glance she had probably lived a rough life. Kathy was probably not college educated but had an ample amount of "street smarts." Kathy was cooperative with Diana. During the course of their interaction, Diana noticed how periodically huge returns were stacked nearly to the ceiling in the shipping department. When Diana inquired about these periodic huge returns, Kathy told her that sometimes they would ship orders to customers based on past purchasing habits even though the customer had not recently placed an order. As it turns out, when the customers saw a delivery at their door someone would just assumed they had placed an order and would keep it. However, other customers would quickly return the supplies. "Was that a good business practice?" Diana inquired. "Well, we have

to make our numbers at quarter's end—you have to do what you have to do, " Kathy replied. On one of Diana's weekly flights home, she picked up a newspaper and began to read about all the current frauds. "Man, it seems like every company is doing fraud these days," Diana thought to herself after seeing multiple fraud-related articles. Diana hadn't had any fraud training but began to wonder whether her firm or the client she was working for could be committing fraud.

Based on the case data, comment on the following issues as they relate to possible fraud.

1. Diana's firm "selling" Diana to the client as an "SAP expert" even though she hadn't seen the software before

2. The unpredictable well-dressed purchasing manager

3. The sales practices revealed in the internal sales department

**Extensive Case 3.** Peter Jones, a senior accountant, and Mary Miller, a junior accountant, were the only accountants for XYZ Company, a medium-sized business. Peter Jones had been with the company for more than four years and was responsible for the purchasing department. Mary Miller had been working at the company for a little over five years and had neither applied for a vacation nor taken any days off in the last three years. She was responsible for cash receipts and disbursements. She also collected the cash from the cash register, counted it and matched it with cash register receipts, made a record of daily receipts, and then put the money in the safe. Once a week she would take the paperwork to her supervisor, Susan Lowe, one of the managers, who would check it. Mary Miller later resigned from the company. At the time of her resignation, Peter was asked to handle Mary's responsibilities while the company looked for a person to replace her. Peter soon realized some manipulation of accounting records and embezzlement of funds had occurred. Investigations revealed that approximately $30,000 had been stolen.

**Questions**

1. What circumstances do you think might have allowed this fraud?

2. How could this fraud have been avoided?

## INTERNET ASSIGNMENTS

1. Visit the Web site of the National White Collar Crime Center at http://www.nw3c.com. This site is funded through a grant from the Department of Justice. Its purpose is to assist federal law enforcement agencies in the investigation and prevention of white-collar crime. The Center also has a college internship program. Find the research topics on their Web page, read the study on health care fraud, and answer the following questions:

   a. What organization or type of professional is the largest perpetrator of health care fraud?

   b. What is health care fraud?

   c. What are the current losses and why are they expected to double?

   d. Why is Medicare the largest target of fraudulent acts?

2. Go to http://www.fraud.org/ and learn about the National Fraud Information Center (NFIC). What do they do, and specifically, how do they make it easy for people to report fraud?

## DEBATE

Fred is a friend of yours and works with you at the same company. He is a well-respected and trusted employee. He has five young children and is a leader in his community. You discover that Fred embezzled $3,000 over a period of several years. Even though this amount is not much money for such a large company, you suspect that if you don't report him, the problem may get worse. On the other hand, he has young children and has done so much good in the company and the community. If you report him, he may go to prison because your company has an aggressive fraud-prosecution policy. Should you report him for such a small amount of money?

## END NOTES

1. http://www.mental-health-matters.com/articles/article.php?artID=153, accessed on May 22, 2004.

2. http://www.corporate-ir.net/ireye/ir_site.zhtml?ticker=axp&script=11960&item_id='CG_custom.htm, accessed on May 22, 2004.

3. Class action lawsuits are permitted under federal and some state rules of court procedure in the United States. In a class action suit, a relatively small number of aggrieved plaintiffs with small individual claims can bring suit for large damages in the name of an extended class. After a fraud, for example, 40 bondholders who lost $40,000 might decide to sue, and they can sue on behalf of the entire class of bondholders for all their alleged losses (say, $50 million). Lawyers are more than happy to take such suits on a contingency fee basis (a percentage of the judgment, if any).

# PART TWO

# FRAUD PREVENTION

**Chapter 4    Preventing Fraud**

# CHAPTER 4

# PREVENTING FRAUD

## LEARNING OBJECTIVES

After studying this chapter, you should be able to:

1.  Understand how to create a culture of honesty, openness, and assistance.
2.  Know how to eliminate opportunities for fraud.
3.  Identify the importance of good internal controls.
4.  Discourage collusion between employees and outside parties.
5.  Inform outside vendors of company policies.
6.  Recognize how to monitor employees.
7.  Set up a response line for anonymous tips.
8.  Conduct proactive fraud auditing.
9.  Create an effective organization to minimize fraud.

*Margaret worked for First National Bank. For 34 years, she was an honest and trusted employee. In the three years prior to her retirement, she embezzled more than $600,000. The fraud was discovered after she retired. Once the fraud was known, Margaret suffered tremendous adverse consequences. The bank took possession of her home and her retirement account. Her husband, who supposedly had no knowledge of the fraud, contributed the proceeds of his retirement account from another company to the bank. The bank took possession of virtually every asset the couple owned. In addition, Margaret still owes the bank more than $200,000 and has entered into a restitution agreement to make regular payments toward meeting the agreement. Margaret was prosecuted and incarcerated for one year. All of her friends and family members, including her children and grandchildren, now know that their grandmother is a convicted felon. When Margaret was released from prison, she was ordered by the judge to seek active employment so she could start making restitution pay-ments. If she fails to make regular payments, she violates her parole agreement and must go back to jail.*

*When Margaret's fraud was discovered, it was written up in a local newspaper, and many of her longtime friends called the bank to find out what happened. The bank was required to submit a criminal referral form to the Office of the Controller of the Currency (OCC). By law, the OCC was required to turn over a copy of the referral form to the FBI and the IRS. The FBI investigated Margaret, and the IRS came after her. The IRS levied fines, penalties, interest, and back taxes on Margaret because she had more than $600,000 in income that she had failed to report on her tax returns. (Although in subsequent negotiations, that portion she paid back by giving the bank her assets was determined to be a nontaxable loan.) Margaret will always have difficulty getting a job, buying life or car insurance, or doing many other things without informing people that she is a convicted felon. In many ways, Margaret's life and reputation have been ruined.*

As you can see from this example, no one wins when fraud occurs. At best, a person who commits fraud may enjoy a higher lifestyle or keep a company going for a while. In the end, however, the dishonesty usually costs perpetrators much more than they embezzled.

Even in management fraud cases, both the perpetrators and the company usually end up losing. Take the case of Bernie Ebbers, the CEO of WorldCom, for example. As of the writing of this book, federal grand juries had filed nine criminal charges against him. Ebbers, now 62 years old, faces one count of conspiracy, one count of securities fraud, and seven counts of making false filings to the SEC. Each count carries a maximum sentence of 10 years and a fine of $1 million or twice the gain or loss resulting from the crime, which could mean 85 years in prison. Not only does he face criminal prosecution, but Ebbers was also ousted by WorldCom's board when the frauds were discovered and faces civil fraud cases related to loans he received and profits he made on trading in WorldCom's stock. Not only did Bernie Ebbers lose personally, but the fraud and bankruptcy at WorldCom wiped out shares with a market capitalization of about $185 billion at their peak in 1999. The company went into Chapter 11 bankruptcy protection in July 2002 and only emerged as a new company named MCI in April 2004. Even Ebbers's most trusted ally at WorldCom, chief financial officer Scott Sullivan, who was facing a potential prison sentence of 165 years himself, agreed to plead guilty to securities fraud and cooperate with prosecutors in building a case against Ebbers.[1]

Organizations or individuals from whom funds are stolen are also losers. In Margaret's case, the bank's name was splashed across the front pages of the local newspapers. Some customers terminated business relationships with the bank for fear that "if the bank can't safeguard funds, then my money is not safe there." The bank also lost the money that Margaret hasn't yet paid (more than $200,000), plus interest on the $600,000 that she embezzled. Margaret will probably never be able to pay back the entire sum she stole because the kinds of jobs available to her upon release from prison don't pay much. In addition, bank employees spent hundreds of hours investigating, preparing legal defenses, and testifying in the case.

Clearly, fraud prevention is where the big savings occur. Fraud that is prevented eliminates detection and investigation costs. The organization doesn't have to make tough termination and prosecution decisions. Valuable work time is not lost to unproductive activities and dealing with crises.

## Just About Everyone Can Be Dishonest

It would be nice to believe that most individuals and most employees are so honest that they would never commit fraud and, therefore, the kind of culture an organization creates and the fraud opportunities that exist aren't important. Unfortunately, such is not the case. Most people are capable of committing fraud, and many people adapt to their environment. When placed in an environment of low integrity, poor controls, loose accountability, or high pressure, people tend to become increasingly dishonest. In numerous examples, top management's dishonest practices were adopted by a company's workers after seeing the bad modeling by top executives. In the Equity Funding case, for example, management created fictitious policyholders and wrote insurance policies on them. The fraudulent policies were then sold to other insurance companies or reinsurers. An employee of the company, who observed the dishonest behavior, thought to himself, "I might as well get in on the action. It doesn't make sense that all these fake insurance policies are written and no one ever dies." Therefore, he started causing a few of the fictitious people to "die" and personally collected the death proceeds.

Organizations can create either a low-fraud or a high-fraud environment. In this chapter, we identify two essential factors involved in a low-fraud environment that are important in preventing fraud. The first involves creating a culture of honesty, openness, and assistance—attributes of a low-fraud environment. The second involves eliminating opportunities to commit fraud and creating expectations that fraud will be punished. At the end of the chapter, we show how fraud prevention, detection, and investigation efforts should be combined to provide a comprehensive fraud-fighting program for a company.

## Creating a Culture of Honesty, Openness, and Assistance

Three major factors in fraud prevention relate to creating a culture of honesty, openness, and assistance. These three factors are (1) hiring honest people and providing fraud awareness training; (2) creating a positive work environment, which means having a well-defined code of conduct, having an open-door policy, not operating on a crisis basis, and having a low-fraud atmosphere; and (3) providing an employee assistance program (EAP) that helps employees deal with personal pressures.

## Hiring Honest People and Providing Fraud Awareness Training

Effectively screening applicants so that only "honest" employees are hired is important. As stated earlier in this book, studies indicate that nearly 31 percent of Americans are dishonest, 40 percent are situationally honest, and only about 30 percent are honest all the time. Nonpublic studies conducted at other firms also show that 25 percent of all frauds are committed by employees who have worked three years or less. Individuals with gambling, financial, drug, or past criminal problems should not be hired, or, at least, if they are hired, the adverse information about their backgrounds or characters should be known.

As an example of how prevalent lying is by potential recruits, consider the following article about executives who lied about their educational backgrounds.

> *Research analysts do it. Even poets laureate do it. It's the edu-fib. An edu-fib is a lie on a resume about one's educational history, usually used early in a career to enhance professional opportunities. But if that lie is still there when an executive hits the heights of success, an edu-fib can make for some mighty embarrassing (and expensive) retractions, especially in today's low-tolerance climate for dishonesty.*

> *According to Joseph Daniel McCool, editor of Executive Recruiter News, between 5 percent and 15 percent of executive resumes contain a falsification, embellishment, or omission. A raft of them have been outed in the past two months, including Ken Lonchar, CFO of Veritas Software; Ronald Zarrella, chairman and CEO of Bausch & Lomb; Bryan J. Mitchell, chairman and CEO of MCG Capital; Ram Kumar, director of U.S. research for Institutional Shareholder Services; Quincy Troupe, poet laureate of California (who knew poets needed resumes?); and analyst Jack Grubman.*

> *All the edu-fibbers admitted, eventually, that they fabricated parts of their resumes. Lonchar and Troupe lost their jobs, but Zarrella and Mitchell were both allowed to stay on, though they were docked bonus payments (Zarrella lost $1.1 million; Mitchell forfeited $350,000, his chairmanship, and had his severance package cut). All the companies affected reaffirmed their faith in the accuracy of their financials—despite their truth-challenged executives.*

> *"We had just gone through the due diligence for the certification process when this came out," said a spokesperson for Veritas. "We are confident in the numbers." Bausch & Lomb's board is also buying Zarrella's "unqualified representation that there are no other issues of trust or veracity about which we need to be concerned," according to a company statement. This is remarkable, since Zarrella first claimed the fib was a "proof-reading" error.[2]*

With today's stringent privacy laws, it is essential that companies have good employee screening policies. Even in a highly controlled environment, dishonest employees with severe pressures often commit fraud. No employer is immune from negligent hiring claims, but resume verification and certification are two tactics that employers can use to prevent such claims. One of the most important responsibilities of an employer is the hiring and retention of its employees. In today's market, turnover tends to be high and employee loyalty may be low. An employer's efforts to hire and retain competent employees not only results in increased productivity and profits, but also in a reduction in the employer's liability exposure in claims for negligent hiring or retention.

Poor hiring decisions can lead not only to hiring employees who are dishonest, but under a negligent hiring or retention claim, an employer may be liable for acts or omissions of the employee, either within or outside the scope of the employee's employment. The injured party must show that the injury resulted from the employer's negligent hiring or retention of the individual causing injury, and not solely the individual's own acts or omissions, to be successful in a claim of negligence.

Most negligent hiring or retention claims arise from violence or abuse of the employee. An example of negligent hiring or retention claims include a trucking company liable for a wrongful death resulting from one of its truckers driving drunk on the wrong side of the road and colliding with an oncoming car, killing the driver. The trucking company failed to verify the trucker's claimed perfect driving record, which would have shown numerous prior drunk driving violations.

Another example is a church member who is raped during counseling sessions with the church employee. In his lawsuit, the church member claims that the church should not have had the church employee in a counseling position, especially in light of his prior record of sexual offenses during such sessions.

No employer can totally immunize itself from hiring fraudulent employees or from liability for claims asserting negligent hiring or negligent retention. However, the employer who follows the following recommendations as part of its hiring and retention policies and practices will be as successful as possible in avoiding frauds and negligent hiring claims.

First, before hiring an applicant for any position, especially key management positions, the employer should verify all information on the applicant's resume and application. The verification should be complete and conducted by an employee who is thorough and persistent in this important procedure, which is unquestionably a resource-consuming process. (In the case of a top executive, you should make sure that a search firm that is hired verifies all information of candidates' resumes. The benefits of such precautions include increased knowledge of the applicant and any propensity to be truthful, as well as significant reduction in hiring and retaining dangerous, unfit, or dishonest employees.)

An important part of the employer's verification of all information on the applicant's resume and application is checking of the applicant's references. Due to statutory restrictions on the dissemination of such information and the applicant's reasonable expectation of privacy, employers should always obtain a written authorization from the applicant to obtain information from references. Moreover, prior to checking with references, the prudent employer will secure a "hold harmless" agreement from the applicant to release the employer from any liability resulting from the verification process (e.g., slander, libel).

Second, the employer should require all applicants to certify that all information on their application and resume is accurate. A requirement that all applicants must affirm the truth of the matters set forth in their application and resume will act as deterrent against false or misleading statements or omissions. The application should provide in writing, acknowledged and agreed to by the applicant, that in the event false information, in the form of statement or omission discovered on the application or resume, such discovery is grounds for immediate termination.

Third, the employer should train management to conduct thorough and skillful interviews. One of the primary purposes of these interviews is to screen out dishonest or unqualified applicants. Many prudent employers require interviewers to ask a standard set of questions designed to elicit certain information from the application. The interviewer is then left to his or her own discretion to follow up or ask additional questions during the course of the interview. Regardless of whether the employer uses standard questions, the interviewer should be aware of and strive to attain the exact goals of the interview.[3]

Other creative ways to determine applicants' honesty can be used in hiring processes. Many financial institutions, for example, now use systems to determine whether prospective employees and customers have had past credit problems. Banks are also fingerprinting new employees and customers and comparing the fingerprints with law enforcement records. Other organizations are hiring private investigators or using publicly available databases to search information about people's backgrounds. Some organizations are administering drug tests. Pen-and-pencil honesty tests are also being used as a screening tool.

One company, for example, extensively trained several interviewers to know which questions were legal to ask and which were illegal, to recognize deception and lying, and to probe legally into applicants' backgrounds. It also adopted a policy of calling three previous references instead of one. It developed a rule that if no gratuitously positive information was received in any of the three background checks, these checks would be viewed as negative. (The interviewers tried to call references who personally knew the applicants, rather than personnel officers who didn't know them.) Over a three-year period, this company found that 851 prospective employees, or 14 percent of all applicants, had undisclosed problems, such as previous unsatisfactory employment, false education or military information, criminal records, poor credit ratings, physical or mental illness, alcoholism, or uncontrolled tempers. People with these types of problems generally find it easier to rationalize dishonest acts, and preventing such people from being hired can reduce fraud.

As an example of poor screening, consider the following actual fraud:

> *A controller defrauded his company of several million dollars. When the fraud was investigated, it was discovered that he had been fired from three of his previous five jobs, all in the last eight years. He was discovered when the CEO came to the office one night and found a stranger working in the accounting area. The nocturnal stranger was a phantom controller who was actually doing the work of the hired "corporate controller," who wasn't even trained in accounting.*

Once people have been hired, it is important to have employees participate in an employee awareness program that educates them about what is acceptable and unacceptable, how they are hurt when someone is dishonest, and what actions they should take if they see someone being dishonest. A comprehensive awareness program should educate employees about how costly fraud and other types of business abuses are. Employees must know that fraud takes a bite out of their benefits, and that no dishonest acts of any kind will be tolerated. Most companies with successful fraud awareness programs have packaged fraud training with other sensitive issues that are important to employees, such as employee safety, discrimination, substance abuse, and the availability of employee assistance programs.

One company, for example, educates all employees about abuses and gives them small cards to carry in their wallets. The cards list four possible actions employees can take if they suspect that abuses are taking place. They can (1) talk to management, (2) call corporate security, (3) call internal audit, or (4) call an 800 hotline number. Employees are told that they can either provide information anonymously or disclose their identities. This company also made a video about company abuses, including fraud, that is shown to all new employees. New posters relating to the awareness program are posted conspicuously throughout the organization on a regular basis. Because of these awareness programs, fraud and other abuses decreased substantially.

## Creating a Positive Work Environment

The second factor important in a culture of honesty, openness, and assistance is creating a positive work environment. Positive work environments do not happen automatically; rather, they must be cultivated. It is a fact that employee fraud and other dishonest acts are more prevalent in some organizations than in others. Organizations that are highly vulnerable to fraud can be distinguished from those that are less vulnerable by comparing their corporate climates. Three elements that contribute to the creation of a positive work environment, thus making the organization less vulnerable to fraud, are (1) creating expectations about honesty through having a good corporate code of conduct and conveying those expecations throughout the organization, (2) having open-door policies, and (3) having positive personnel and operating procedures.

Setting proper expectations is a powerful tool in motivating employees to behave honestly. Consider the following story about expecations:

> *Imagine Miss Periwinkle, a fourth-grade teacher, arriving for class on the first day of school. Before she enters her classroom, the principal stops her in the hall.*
>
> *"Miss Periwinkle, there's something you should know about this class. We've placed all the bright and talented children on the right side of the room. On the left, we've seated the ones we know are slower and lack motivation. We thought the seating arrangement would help you in your teaching."*
>
> *Armed with this information, she begins a semester of instruction. But there's a catch. There are no divisions of intelligence or motivation in this classroom; those on both sides of the room were randomly selected from a group of equally able and motivated students. They are part of an experiment to determine whether the teacher's expectations will affect the children's learning and testing.*
>
> *This hypothetical recasting of various psychological experiments has been done many times over the last 30 years. The results are invariably the same. Students the teacher thinks are "smart" score well on tests; the "dull" ones don't do as well. The difference is not a result of biased grading; the "dull" ones really have learned less. Why?*

The explanation is often described as the *Pygmalion effect*. Sterling Livingston, writing in the *Harvard Business Review* (September 1988) extended the phenomenon into management with a simple thesis: People generally perform according to a leader's expectations. If expectations are low, actual performance is likely to be "substandard." If, however, expectations are high, performance is usually high as well. "It is as though there were a law that caused subordinates' performance to rise or fall to meet managers expectations," Livingston wrote.

The power of expectations is nothing new to physicians. Numerous research studies have linked attitude with a patient's ability to recover from disease or trauma. Physicians, as managers of treatment, have a discernible effect on reinforcing (or eroding) patients' attitudes. Understanding this correlation in medicine can be a powerful tool in the hands of skilled managers.

In newsrooms and other workplaces, people tend to do what they believe they are expected to do. Faced with "grunt work," a willing hand will get it done, but the nature of the assignment itself is interpreted as a signal of the boss's low evaluation, and therefore, expectation: *"If that's all he thinks I can do…" usually leads to "…that's all I'll do for him."*

Livingston and others also found that expectations must be genuine and accepted by leaders. The studies concluded that people know when they are being conned. If expectations are unrealistically high or if workers are not being taken seriously by leaders, people know it. Conversely, if a manager pretends to have confidence and high expectations when in reality the manager has doubts, people will know that, too. The lesson about expectations is clear: People have keen senses about expectations. You can't fool them; expectations must be genuine. Trying to create expectations, especially about integrity and ethics, when top management isn't serious about the expectations, only erodes management's credibility. According to the researchers, "A good axiom to remember is, 'What you expect is probably what you'll get'."[4]

One way to create and communicate clear expectations about what is and is not acceptable in an organization is to have an articulated Code of Conduct. Section 406 of the Sarbanes-Oxley Act of 2002, "Code of Ethics for Senior Financial Officers," requires that every public company have a Code of Ethics for management and its board of directors. Shortly after Congress passed the Sarbanes-Oxley Act, mandating companies to hold senior financial officers to a code of conduct, the Securities and Exchange Commission (SEC) revised its listing standards to require public companies to create and distribute a code of conduct to all employees. Merely having a code of conduct, however, is not sufficient. It must be visible and communicated frequently. Some companies have found it helpful to even have employees read and sign their code annually and certify that they have not violated the code or seen others who have. As an example of a good code of ethics for all employees, consider Hormel Foods' code in Figure 4-1.

Hormel's code not only clarifies what is and is not acceptable, but it also specifies the disciplinary action that will be applied to violators and provides contact (whistle-blower) information for reporting violations. If Hormel is successful in keeping this code in front of its employees, just the mere fact that everyone knows that others know what is expected, what expected punishments are, and how to report information about violations will reduce the number of dishonest incidents in the company.

Literature on moral development suggests that if you want someone to behave honestly, you must both label and model honest behavior. As we have discussed, a clearly defined code of conduct labels for employees what is acceptable and unacceptable. Having employees periodically read and sign a company code of ethics reinforces their understanding of what constitutes appropriate and inappropriate behavior. A clearly specified code inhibits rationalizations, such as "It's really not that serious," "You would understand if you knew how badly I needed it," "I'm really not hurting anyone," "Everyone is a little dishonest," or "I'm only temporarily borrowing it." When a company specifies what is acceptable and what is unacceptable and requires employees to acknowledge that they understand the organization's expectations, they realize that fraud hurts the organization, that not everyone is a little dishonest, that the organization won't tolerate dishonest acts, that dishonest behavior is serious, and that unauthorized borrowing is not acceptable.

# Figure 4-1 Hormel Foods Code of Ethical Business Conduct

All employees should avoid any personal activity or participation in any venture which may create a conflict with the employee's responsibility to protect and promote the best interests of our Company. Employees should assure that their spouses and dependents avoid any activity which would constitute a conflict of interest if engaged in by the employee. For example, any activity which would allow you, or a member of your immediate family, to enjoy personal gain or benefit as a result of your employment relationship with the Company would be considered a conflict of interest.

## Gifts

No gift, loan or favor will be made to or accepted by employees or their immediate families involving any supplier, customer, or others with whom our Company does business if it is intended to influence a business decision. This will not prohibit casual entertainment, business entertainment consistent with the Company's usual practices, or gifts which are reasonably viewed under the circumstances in which they are given or received to be of nominal value. For this purpose, any gift in kind of less than $100 would be considered of nominal value. Acceptance of cash or cash equivalents is not acceptable under any circumstances. By way of example, attendance at a professional sporting event as a guest of a supplier or customer would constitute business entertainment consistent with the Company's usual practices; however, the receipt of tickets to the same event from a supplier or customer without the attendance of the supplier or customer would be viewed as a gift which must be of nominal value.

## Illegal Payments

Any payments by our Company to United States or foreign persons or companies are prohibited if the payments would be illegal under the Foreign Corrupt Practices Act of 1977 or other United States or foreign laws. This prohibition includes any payments to government officials or their agents, domestic or foreign, unless Company counsel has advised the payment is legal and acceptable. It is never acceptable to pay any third party anywhere an undisclosed commission, kickback or bribe to obtain business.

## Illegal Political Contributions

No corporate funds or assets will be used for any illegal political contribution. This prohibition includes any political contribution unless otherwise advised by Company counsel. Employees are encouraged to make personal contributions to candidates and political parties of their choice.

## Improper Use of Company Assets

The use of any funds or other assets of, or the providing of any services by, our Company for any purpose which is unlawful under applicable laws of the United States, any state thereof, or any foreign jurisdiction, is prohibited. Employees may not use employees, materials, equipment or other assets of our Company for any unauthorized purpose.

## Proper Accounting

Employees will comply with prescribed accounting, internal accounting, and auditing procedures and controls at all times. All records must accurately reflect and properly describe the transactions they record. All assets, liabilities, revenues and expenses shall be properly recorded on a timely basis in the books of our Company.

## Insider Information

Employees will not buy or sell Company stock or make recommendations regarding it based upon insider information. Insider information is material information that is not generally known by those outside our Company that could significantly affect the value of our Company's stock.

## Confidential Information

Employees will not directly or indirectly use or disclose any secret or confidential knowledge or data of our Company. Any notes, memoranda, notebooks, drawings or other documents made, compiled or delivered to employees during the period of their employment are the exclusive property of our Company and will be turned over to it at the time of termination of their employment or at any other time upon our Company's request. Additionally, while it is appropriate to gather information about our markets, including publicly available information regarding our competitors, employees will not seek to acquire proprietary and confidential information of competitors by unlawful or unethical means, including information resulting in the breach of nondisclosure obligations by competitors' employees or other third parties.

## Inventions, Developments, Improvements

Any inventions, developments or improvements which are conceived by employees during the period of employment by our Company will be promptly disclosed to our Company in writing, and will in most cases be our Company's exclusive property. Inventions which were developed on their own time and are not related to our Company's business or research would not be our Company's property.

## Figure 4-1 (continued)

**Antitrust Compliance**

Employees must observe the highest ethical standards in relationships with competitors, suppliers and customers. Activity which violates the antitrust laws of the United States, any state thereof, or comparable laws of foreign jurisdictions, is prohibited. Areas in which employees must be sensitive to antitrust problems include pricing, termination of existing relationships with customers or suppliers, the establishment of either exclusive customers or suppliers, tie-in sales, boycotts and reciprocity.

**Harassment**

All employees have a right to work in an environment free of harassment, and our Company prohibits harassment of its employees in any form—by supervisors, co-workers, customers, or suppliers.

**Safety**

All employees have a right to work in an environment which is as safe as possible, and all safety rules as well as common safety practices must be followed. Conduct which is unsafe, including possession or being under the influence of a controlled substance on Company premises or Company time, is prohibited.

**Government Reporting**

Employees must assure that any reports to any listing agency, or any governmental unit or agency in the United States or abroad, including the Securities and Exchange Commission, and the Internal Revenue Service, made by them or under their supervision, are honest, accurate and complete.

**Environmental Responsibility**

All employees are required to comply with all applicable federal, state and local laws and regulations relating to the protection of the environment, as well as any requirements which pertain to our Company's operations outside the United States. Additionally, practices having adverse effects on the environment should be avoided.

**Product Integrity**

Our Company's products and their labeling must reflect the integrity of our Company and its employees. All Company products will be produced, labeled and handled in keeping with our Company's high standards of sanitation, and in compliance with all Company specifications and governmental requirements for content and process, to produce safe and wholesome, high quality and accurately labeled products.

**Diversity**

The Company welcomes diversity in its employees, suppliers, customers, and others with whom the Company does business. The Company is affirmatively committed to providing the same opportunities for success to all individuals, regardless of race, religion, national origin, age, sex, or disability. All employees are expected to share in and support that commitment.

**Fair Employment Practices**

In addition to prohibiting harassment and providing a safe workplace, our Company and its employees will comply with all applicable laws governing employment. Discrimination on account of race, religion, national origin, sex, age, disability, or status as a veteran will not be tolerated.

**Foreign Trade**

Employees involved in foreign trade operations will be expected to maintain an awareness of, and comply with, the requirements of the U.S. Antiboycott Laws, the U.S. Trade Embargo Regulations, and any other U.S. or foreign laws applicable to the Company's foreign trading operations. The U.S. Antiboycott Laws prohibit U.S. companies and their foreign subsidiaries from entering into agreements in support of any foreign boycott which has not been sanctioned by the U.S. government. The U.S. Trade Embargo Regulations prohibit U.S. companies and their foreign subsidiaries from entering into transactions with countries with whom the U.S. government maintains a trade embargo, as well as with entities that are owned or controlled by those countries.

**Responsible Delegation**

Discretionary authority will not be delegated to anyone, within or on behalf of the Company, where there is reason to believe that individual might engage in illegal activities.

---

## Figure 4-1 (continued)

**Disciplinary Action**

While the Company relies on each employee's voluntary compliance with this Code as a matter of personal integrity, disciplinary action will be taken in appropriate instances. These include: actions which violate this Code; withholding information regarding violations; supervision which is inadequate to the point of evidencing a negligent or willful disregard for this Code in connection with a violation; and any form of retaliation against an employee reporting a violation. Disciplinary action may include suspension, termination, recovery of damages, or criminal prosecution.

**Reporting Violations of the Code**

With the exception of concerns or complaints regarding questionable accounting or auditing matters, or internal accounting controls which must be promptly forwarded directly to the Audit Committee of the Board of Directors, any employee who observes or otherwise becomes aware of any violation of the Code of Ethical Business Conduct shall report the violation to supervision, or, if the employee prefers, to the General Counsel, or the Director of Internal Audit, or he or she may report the matter to any member of the Audit Committee of the Board of Directors. Additionally, employees may report any violation, or suspected violation, of the Code of Ethical Business Conduct, including concerns regarding questionable accounting or auditing matters, by using the anonymous "Hot Line" established for this purpose. The telephone number for this Hot Line is: 1-800-750-4972.

*Source: http://www.hormel.com/templates/corporate.asp?catitemid=71&id=634, accessed on May 26, 2004.*

A second way to create a positive work environment, thus making the organization less vulnerable to fraud, is having open-door policies. Open-door policies prevent fraud in two ways. First, many people commit fraud because they feel they have no one to talk to. Sometimes, when people keep their problems to themselves, they lose perspective about the appropriateness of actions and about the consequences of wrongdoing. This loss of perspective can lead to making decisions to be dishonest. Second, open-door policies allow managers and others to become aware of employees' pressures, problems, and rationalizations. This awareness enables managers to take fraud prevention steps. Studies have shown that most frauds (71 percent in one study) are committed by someone acting alone. Having people to talk to can prevent this type of fraud. One person who embezzled said, in retrospect, "Talk to someone. Tell someone what you are thinking and what your pressures are. It's definitely not worth it… It's not worth the consequences."

As an example of a person who committed fraud that probably could have been prevented had the organization had an open-door policy, consider Micky:

> *Micky was the controller for a small fruit-packing company. In that position, he embezzled more than $212,000 from the company. When asked why, he said, "Nobody at the company, especially the owners, ever talked to me. They treated me unfairly. They talked down to me. They were rude to me. They deserve everything they got."*

A third way to create a positive work environment, thus making the organization less vulnerable to fraud, is having positive personnel and operating policies. Research indicates that positive personnel and operating policies are important factors in contributing to high- or low-fraud environments. Uncertainty about job security, for example, has been associated with high-fraud environments. Other personnel and operating conditions and procedures that appear to contribute to high-fraud environments include the following:

- Managers who don't care about or pay attention to honesty (who model apathetic or inappropriate behavior)
- Inadequate pay
- Lack of recognition for job performance
- Imposition of unreasonable budget expectations
- Expectations that employees live a certain lifestyle (e.g., belong to a country club)
- Perceived inequalities in the organization
- Inadequate expense accounts
- Autocratic or dictatorial management
- Low company loyalty

- Short-term business focus
- Management by crisis
- Rigid rules
- Negative feedback and reinforcement
- Repression of differences
- Poor promotion opportunities
- Hostile work environments
- High turnover and absenteeism
- Cash flow problems or other financial problems
- Reactive rather than proactive management
- Managers who model wheeler-dealer, impulsive, insensitive, emotional, or dominant personalities
- Rivalrous rather than supportive relationships
- Poor training
- Lack of clear organizational responsibilities
- Poor communication practices

Each of these conditions or procedures contributes to creating a high-fraud environment. For example, crisis or rush jobs contribute to additional opportunities to commit fraud. When a special project is being hurried toward completion, the normal controls are often set aside or ignored. Signatures are obtained to authorize uncertain purchases. Reimbursements are made rapidly, with little documentation. Record keeping falls behind and cannot be reconstructed. Inventory and supplies come and go rapidly and can easily be manipulated or misplaced. Job lines and responsibilities are not as well defined. In a recent interview, the controller of a *Fortune* 500 company indicated that the company experienced three large frauds in the past year. Two of them, both in the millions of dollars, occurred while the company was rushing to complete crash projects.

It would be easy to include many examples of fraud that have been facilitated by each of these high-fraud environmental factors, but we include only two. The first is an example of fraud associated with inadequate pay. The second is an example of fraud associated with the imposition of unreasonable expectations.

A long-time employee of a company believed that he had performed well, but was passed over for a raise he felt he had earned. He was earning $30,000 a year and decided that he was entitled to a 10 percent raise. He stole $250 a month, which was exactly 10 percent of his salary. His moral standards permitted him to steal that much because he felt it was "owed to him," but he could not embezzle one cent more, because that would have been "dishonest."

A division manager of a large conglomerate was told he would increase his division's segment margin by 20 percent during the coming year. When he realized he would not meet budget, he decided to fabricate his reports and overstate assets rather than fail. He concluded that it was better to be dishonest than not to meet his assigned budget.

## Implementing Employee Assistance Programs

The third factor in creating a culture of honesty, openness, and assistance is having formal *employee assistance programs (EAPs)*. One of the three elements of the fraud triangle is perceived pressure. Often, fraud-motivating pressures are ones that perpetrators consider to be unsharable or pressures that they believe have no possible legal solutions. Companies that provide employees with effective avenues for dealing with personal pressures eliminate many potential frauds. The most common method of assisting employees with pressures is by implementing formal EAPs. EAPs help employees deal with substance abuse (alcohol and drugs), gambling, money management, and health, family, and personal problems.

An EAP that is successfully integrated into an organization's other employee support systems with programs and services that include wellness, team building, coaching, conflict resolution, critical incident response, assessment, counseling, and referral can and does help reduce fraud and other forms of dishonesty. Employees welcome this benefit, they use it, and they report consistently in impact surveys that the EAP made a difference in their lives, and in the quality of their work.

Most successful organizations view EAP as an important contributor to the success of their business and a valuable benefit for their employees. Employers are convinced that EAP makes a difference. Why? Organizations recognize that having the ability to provide a troubled employee with timely and appropriate services results in reducing the financial and human costs associated with an employee who is not fully functioning. Valuable employees have been assisted in dealing successfully with issues that threatened their health, relationships, energy, and ability to contribute strongly in the workplace.

Return on investment (ROI) for employee assistance programs has been studied repeatedly, yet definitive proof of their benefits remains difficult to demonstrate. Companies do make claims of positive return on investment, McDonnell Douglas Corporation reported the following in February 1993:

> *We have data for the cost of troubled employees, based upon productivity, health care use, disability and workers' compensation costs, and we have data for their impact on the bottom line. We factor in the cost of the (EAP) program and the cost of treatment. We subtract the cost savings revealed by people who have used EAR (their internal EAP). We've tracked the cost of the (EAP) program and we know that we have saved money.*[5]

The return on investment has been identified as varying between $2 to (as high as) $64 for every dollar spent.

A study of *Fortune* 500 companies found that 67 percent of companies surveyed had formal EAPs.[6] Most respondents felt that fewer than 10 percent of their company's employees had ever used their EAPs, and only 50 percent of the respondents felt that the EAPs returned less than $1 for every $1 spent. Other research showed, however, that when used effectively, EAPs can return between $3 and $6 for every $1 spent. When asked what type of problems their EAPs assisted with, 67 percent of the respondents in the previously cited study stated alcohol and drug problems, 63 percent identified emotional problems, 57 percent identified family and marital problems, 38 percent covered gambling problems, 37 percent covered personal financial problems, and 32 percent provided legal assistance. In addition, 11 percent provided some form of investment counseling. Ninety-two percent of all respondents felt that assisting employees with personal financial pressures would help to prevent employee fraud.

As examples of frauds that might have been prevented with EAPs, consider the following two cases:

1. An unmarried woman became pregnant. She didn't want her parents or anyone else to know. Needing money desperately, she stole $300 from her company. Then, realizing how easy the theft had been, she stole another $16,000 before being detected.
2. An employee of a large bank embezzled more than $35,000. When she was caught and asked why, she stated that her son was "hooked on heroin at a cost of nearly $500 per day." Because she could not stand to see him go through withdrawal pains, she embezzled to support his habit.

## Eliminating Opportunities for Fraud

Earlier in this text, the fraud triangle—perceived pressure, perceived opportunity, and rationalization—was introduced to explain why fraud occurs. When pressure, opportunity, and rationalization come together, the likelihood of a fraud being perpetrated increases dramatically. If one of the three elements is missing, fraud is unlikely. In this section, we discuss eliminating opportunities to commit dishonest acts as a second key element in preventing fraud.

We will cover seven methods of eliminating fraud opportunities:

1. Having good internal controls,
2. Discouraging collusion between employees and customers or vendors,
3. Clearly informing vendors and other outside contacts of the company's policies against fraud,
4. Monitoring employees,
5. Providing a hotline (whistle-blowing system) for anonymous tips,
6. Creating an expectation of punishment,
7. Conducting proactive auditing.

Each of these methods reduces either the actual or perceived opportunity to commit fraud, and all of them together combine with the culture factors described earlier to provide a comprehensive fraud prevention program.

## Having a Good System of Internal Controls

The most widely recognized way to deter or prevent fraud is by having a good system of controls. The Institute of Internal Auditors' standard on fraud, for example, states the following:

> *Deterrence consists of those actions taken to discourage the perpetration of fraud and limit the exposure if fraud does occur. The principal mechanism for deterring fraud is control. Primary responsibility for establishing and maintaining control rests with management.*
>
> *Internal auditing is responsible for assisting in the deterrence of fraud by examining and evaluating the adequacy and the effectiveness of control, commensurate with the extent of the potential exposure/risk in the various segments of the entity's operations. In carrying out this responsibility, internal auditing should, for example, determine whether:*
>
> *a. The organizational environment fosters control consciousness.*
>
> *b. Realistic organizational goals and objectives are set.*
>
> *c. Written corporate policies (e.g., codes of conduct) exist that describe prohibited activities and the action required whenever violations are discovered.*
>
> *d. Appropriate authorization policies for transactions are established and maintained.*
>
> *e. Policies, practices, procedures, reports and other mechanisms are developed to monitor activities and safeguard assets, particularly in high-risk areas.*
>
> *f. Communication channels provide management with adequate and reliable information.*
>
> *g. Recommendations need to be made for the establishment or enhancement of cost-effective controls to help deter fraud. (See SIAS No. 1, Control: Concepts and Responsibilities.)*[7]

As stated previously in this text, the Committee of Sponsoring Organizations (COSO) definition of an internal control framework of an organization should include (1) a good control environment, (2) a good accounting system, (3) good control procedures (activities), (4) monitoring, and (5) good communication and information. The *control environment* is the tone that management establishes through its modeling and labeling. As stated in a COSO report, the control environment sets the tone of an organization, influencing the control consciousness of its people.[8] It is the foundation for all other components of internal control, providing discipline and structure. Control environment factors include the integrity, ethical values, and competence of the entity's people, management's philosophy and operating style, the way management assigns authority and responsibility and organizes and develops its people, and the attention and direction provided by the board of directors. The control environment also includes well-defined hiring practices, clear organization, and a good internal audit department.

A good *accounting system* is important so that the information provided is valid, complete, and timely. The system should also provide information that is properly valued, classified, authorized, and summarized.

Good *control procedures* (activities) involve policies and practices that provide physical control of assets, proper authorizations, segregation of duties, independent checks, and proper documentation. (Physical control, proper authorization, and segregation of duties are controls that usually prevent fraud, while independent checks and documents and records are usually detective controls that provide early fraud detection opportunities.) A control system that meets these requirements provides reasonable assurance that the goals and objectives of the organization will be met and that fraud will be reduced.

Obviously, if a person owns his or her own company and is that company's only employee, not many controls are needed. The owner would not likely steal from the company or serve customers poorly. In organizations with hundred or thousands of employees or even two or three, controls are needed to ensure that employees behave the way the owners would want them to.

No internal control structure can ever be completely effective, regardless of the care followed in its design and implementation. Even when an ideal control system is designed, its effectiveness depends on the competency and dependability of the people enforcing it. Consider, for example, an organization that has a policy requiring the dual counting of all incoming cash receipts. If either of the two employees involved in the task fails to understand the instructions, or if either is careless in opening and counting incoming cash, money can easily be stolen or miscounted. One of the employees might decide to understate the count intentionally to cover up a theft of cash. Dual custody can be maintained only if both employees pay full attention to the task and completely understand how it is to be performed.

Because of the inherent limitations of controls, a control system by itself can never provide absolute assurance that all fraud will be prevented. Trying to prevent fraud by only having a good control system is like fighting a skyscraper fire with a garden hose. In combination with other methods, however, controls are an extremely important part of any fraud prevention program.

In determining what kind of control procedures (activities) an organization should have, it is important to identify the nature of risks involved and the types of abuses that could result from these risks. Based on the assessment of risks, controls that would eliminate or mitigate the risks should be identified. Once identified and put into place, *monitoring* of the controls are necessary to ensure that they are effective and are being followed.

In determining what kinds of controls to implement, it is important to assess their costs and benefits. For example, while the most appropriate control from a risk perspective might involve segregation of duties, this control is usually quite expensive. In small businesses with only a few employees, segregation of duties may be too expensive or even impossible. In such cases, it is important to identify less expensive or "compensating" controls that can provide some fraud prevention assurance. For example, in a small service business with eight employees, the owner might personally sign all checks and reconcile all bank statements to control cash.

Often the problem when fraud is committed is not a lack of controls, but the overriding of existing controls by management or others. Consider the role of controls in the theft of $3.2 million from a small bank—a case discussed previously.

> *Marjorie, head of accounting and bookkeeping in a small bank, was responsible for all proof reconciliations and activities. Over a seven-year period, she embezzled $3.2 million, or approximately 10 percent of the bank's assets. Auditors and management recognized the lack of segregation of duties in her department, but believed they had compensating controls in place that would prohibit such a theft—that would provide "reasonable assurance" that no fraud was possible in the bank. Some of the compensating controls and the ways they were overridden to allow her fraud were as follows:*
>
> 1. *All deposits and transfers of funds were to be made through tellers. Yet, proof employees were making transfers for bank officers and for themselves directly through proof. Most people in the bank were aware of this practice, but because it was being done at the president's request, they didn't think it was wrong.*
>
> 2. *All documents were to be accessible to external auditors. Yet, Marjorie kept a locked cabinet next to her desk, and only she had a key. A customer whose statement had been altered by Marjorie complained, but was told that he would have to wait until Marjorie returned from vacation, because the documentation relating to his account was in Marjorie's locked cabinet.*
>
> 3. *Auditors were supposed to have access to all employees, but Marjorie told her employees not to talk to auditors. Thus, all questions were referred to her during audits.*
>
> 4. *Every employee and every officer of the bank was required to take a two-week consecutive vacation. At Marjorie's request, management allowed this control to be*

*overridden. Based on her memos, that "proof would get behind if she took a two-week vacation," Marjorie was allowed to take her vacation one day at a time. In addition, no one was allowed to perform Marjorie's most sensitive duties while she was away.*

5. *General ledger tickets were supposed to be approved by an individual other than the person who completed the ticket. To override this control, Marjorie had her employees presign 10 or 12 general ledger tickets, so she wouldn't have to "bother" them when they were busy.*

6. *Opening and closing procedures were supposed to be in place to protect the bank, but many employees had all the necessary keys and could enter the bank at will.*

7. *An effective internal audit function was supposed to be in place. For a period of two years, however, no internal audit reports were issued. Even when the reports were issued, internal audit did not check employee accounts or perform critical control tests, such as surprise openings of the bank's incoming and outgoing cash letters to and from the Federal Reserve.*

8. *Incoming and outgoing cash letters were supposed to be microfilmed immediately. This compensating control was violated in three ways. First, letters were not usually filmed immediately. Second, for a time, letters were not filmed at all. Third, Marjorie regularly removed items from the cash letters before they were filmed.*

9. *Employees' accounts were not regularly reviewed by internal audit or by management. On the rare occasions when accounts were reviewed, numerous deposits to and checks drawn on Marjorie's account that exceeded her annual salary were not questioned.*

10. *Loans were supposed to be made only to employees who met all lending requirements, as if they were normal customers. At one point, a $170,000 mortgage loan was made by the bank to Marjorie, without any explanation as to how the loan would be repaid or how she could afford such a house.*

11. *Employees in proof and bookkeeping were not supposed to handle their own bank statements. Yet, employees regularly pulled out their own checks and deposit slips before the statements were mailed.*

12. *Managers were supposed to be reviewing key daily documents, such as the daily statement of condition, the significant items and major fluctuation report, and the overdraft report. Either managers didn't review these reports, or they didn't pay close attention to them when they did review them. There were daily fluctuations in the statement of conditions of more than $3 million. The significant items and major fluctuation report revealed huge deposits to and checks drawn on Marjorie's account. In addition, Marjorie appeared on the overdraft report 97 times during the first four years she was employed by the bank she defrauded.*

If these controls had been in place and effective, Marjorie's fraud would have been prevented or at least detected in its early stages. Because management and internal auditors were overriding controls, the bank's "reasonable assurance" became no assurance at all.

Having a good system of internal control is the single most effective tool in preventing and detecting fraud. Control procedures such as authorizations, physical safeguards, and segregation of duties help prevent fraud. Control procedures such as document and record verification and independent checks can assist in the early detection of fraud. Unfortunately, in practice, control procedures are rarely followed the way they are designed or intended. Sometimes, a lack of compliance occurs because employees emulate management's apathetic attitude toward controls. Other times, managers properly model and label good control procedures, but employees do not comply because of disinterest, lack of reward for following or punishment for not following controls, lack of focus, or other reasons. Because control procedures can provide only reasonable assurance at best, controls are only one element of a comprehensive fraud prevention plan.

## Discouraging Collusion Between Employees and Others

As stated previously, approximately 71 percent of all frauds are committed by individuals acting alone. The remaining 29 percent of frauds that involve collusion are usually the most difficult to detect and often involve the largest amounts. Because collusive fraud is usually slower to develop (it takes time to get to know others well enough to collude and to "trust" that they will cooperate rather than blow the whistle), many collusive frauds can be prevented by requiring mandatory vacations or job transfers. When an organization leaves an employee in close contact with the same vendors or customers for long periods of time, the risk of individuals deciding to profit personally are increased dramatically. An example is the case discussed earlier where an accounts receivable employee "managed" a customer's receivables to benefit both himself and the customer at the expense of the company.

Unfortunately, two developments in business may increase the number of collusive frauds. The first is the increasingly complex nature of business. In complex environments, trusted employees are more likely to operate in isolated or specialized surroundings in which they are separated from other individuals. The second is the increasing prominence of supplier alliances, where oral agreements replace paper trails and closer relationships exist between buyers and suppliers. Certainly, increased cost savings and increased productivity come from using these new management methods. How much fraud will increase is still unknown, although fraud seems to be increasing every year. Generally, it is the people we "trust" and "have confidence in" who can and do commit most frauds. The reaction of one manager to a recent fraud involving a trusted vendor was, "I just couldn't believe he would do it. It's like realizing your brother is an ax murderer."

The problem with trusting people too much is that opportunity and temptation increase. A helpful analogy is that of a company nearly a century ago that was looking for someone to drive its wagons over a rugged mountain.

> *In interviewing prospective drivers, the interviewer asked the first driver, "How close to the edge of the cliff can you get without going over?" "Why, I can maneuver within six inches without any problems," was the response. When asked the same question, the second interviewee responded, "I can drive within three inches of the edge without going over the cliff." When the third and final applicant was asked, he responded, "I will drive as far away from the edge as I possibly can, because it is foolish to place yourself in a risky position." Guess which one got the job!*

Fraud is similar. When the risk is higher, problems are more likely. Especially in environments where preventive and detective controls are minimal or absent, employees should be regularly reviewed, periodically transferred or rotated, or required to take prolonged periods of vacation. If any of these procedures had been in place, Robert probably would not have been able to commit the following fraud:

> *Robert was the chief teller in a large New York bank. Over a period of three years, he embezzled more than $1.5 million. When the fraud was discovered, it was learned that Robert had a compulsive gambling habit. He had taken money by manipulating dormant accounts. When a customer complained about his account, Robert would always be the one to explain the discrepancy. He usually used the excuse, "It's a computer error." He later said that the bank had placed far too much trust and supervisory authority in him. He stated that had there been one other supervisor with the same responsibility, or a one-week mandatory vacation requirement combined with periodic rotations, Robert would not have been able to defraud the bank.*

When employees are solely responsible for large contracts, bribes and kickbacks often occur. In some cases, employees can double or triple their salaries by allowing increases in costs of purchased goods of less than 1 percent. Purchase and sales frauds are the most common types of fraud. When the opportunity is too high, even individuals whose professional lives are guided by codes of conduct will sometimes commit fraud. Consider the ESM fraud as an example.

> *In the ESM fraud case, the CPA firm partner accepted under-the-table payments from his client, in return for staying quiet about fraudulent financial transactions. The*

*fraud being perpetrated by the client exceeded $300 million. The CPA had been the partner-in-charge of the engagement for more than eight years. For not disclosing the fraud, the client paid him $150,000. If the CPA firm had not allowed him to be managing partner of the job for such a long time, his participation in the fraud and erosion of integrity probably would not have been impossible.*

## Alerting Vendors and Contractors to Company Policies

Sometimes otherwise innocent vendors and customers are drawn into fraud by an organization's employees because they fear that if they don't participate, the business relationship will be lost. In most cases, such customers or vendors have only one or two contacts with the firm. They are often intimidated by the person who requests illegal gratuities or suggests other types of fraudulent behavior. A periodic letter to vendors that explains an organization's policy of not allowing employees to accept gifts or gratuities helps vendors understand whether buyers and sellers are acting in accordance with the organization's rules. Such letters clarify expectations, which is important in preventing fraud. Many frauds have been uncovered when, after such a letter was sent, vendors expressed concern about their buying or selling relationships.

*A large chicken fast-food restaurant discovered a $200,000 fraud involving kickbacks from suppliers. After investigating the fraud, the restaurant management decided to write letters to all vendors explaining that it was against company policy for buyers to accept any form of gratuities from suppliers. The result of the letters was the discovery of two additional buyer-related frauds.*

A related precaution that is often effective in discouraging kickback-type frauds is printing a right-to-audit clause on the back of all purchase invoices. Such a clause alerts vendors that the company reserves the right to audit their books at any time. Vendors who know that their records are subject to audit are generally more reluctant to make bribery payments than are those who believe their records are confidential or will never be examined. A right-to-audit clause is also a valuable tool in fraud investigations.

## Monitoring Employees

Individuals who commit fraud and hoard stolen proceeds are virtually nonexistent. Almost always, perpetrators use their stolen money to support expensive habits or to pay for expenses already incurred. When managers and fellow employees pay close attention to lifestyle symptoms resulting from these expenditures, fraud is often detected early. Most stolen funds are spent in conspicuous ways. Fraud perpetrators usually buy automobiles, expensive clothes, and new homes, take extravagant vacations, purchase expensive recreational toys, such as boats, condominiums, motor homes, or airplanes, or support extramarital relationships or outside business interests. Consider again the case of Marjorie:

*Marjorie first started working for the bank in 1980. During her first four years of employment, she took out a debt consolidation loan of approximately $12,000 and had 97 personal overdrafts. During the next seven years, while she was committing the fraud, her salary never exceeded $22,000 per year. Yet, fellow employees and officers of the bank knew that she had done the following:*

- *Taken several expensive cruises.*
- *Built a home on a golf course, costing $600,000.*
- *Purchased a Rolls Royce, Jeep Cherokee, Audi, and Maserati.*
- *Purchased expensive jewelry, including 16 diamonds and sapphires; computers, stereos, VCRs, and electronic gear; snowmobiles and a golf cart; expensive gifts for fellow employees and relatives, a fur coat, and a suntanning machine; and expensive clothes.*
- *Taken limousines many times.*
- *Held extravagant parties for employees and others.*

- *Bought a condominium for her mother-in-law.*
- *Purchased a glass art collection costing more than $1.5 million.*
- *Taken many domestic trips to buy glass art.*
- *Had her home decorated.*

Anyone paying attention would have realized that her lifestyle was inconsistent with her level of income. When someone did finally ask how she could afford everything, she explained her expensive lifestyle by saying that her husband had received one-third of an inheritance of $250,000. The story wasn't true, but even if it had been, the $83,333 that her husband had supposedly inherited wouldn't have paid for the Maserati, let alone all the other luxuries that managers knew she had purchased.

Close monitoring facilitates early detection. It also deters frauds because potential perpetrators realize that "others are watching."

## Providing Whistle-Blowing Mechanisms

As stated previously, Section 307 of the Sarbanes-Oxley Act requires that every company have a whistle-blowing system in place, and Section 806 requires that whistle-blowers be protected when they disclose information about illegal acts or violations of a company's code of conduct or otherwise assist criminal investigators, federal regulators, Congress, supervisors (or other proper people within a corporation), or parties in a judicial proceeding in detecting and stopping fraud. Congress passed the Sarbanes-Oxley Act and the SEC implemented the whistle-blowing provisions because they believed that having an easy way for employees and others to report misdeeds would go a long way toward disclosing potential dishonest activities. In most studies of fraud, one or more individuals actually suspected or knew that fraud was occurring but were either afraid to come forward with information or didn't know how to reveal the information. The new whistle-blowing laws should help in these cases.

Even with advances in technology, the most common way in which fraud is detected is through tips. In one company, for example, 33 percent of all frauds were detected through tips, while only 18 percent were detected by auditors. In another company that experienced more than 1,000 frauds in one year, 42 percent were discovered through tips and complaints from employees and customers. A good whistle-blowing program is one of the most effective fraud prevention tools. When employees know that colleagues have an easy, nonobligatory way to report suspected fraud, they are more reluctant to become involved in dishonest acts.

Unfortunately, prior to Sarbanes-Oxley, too few organizations had effective tip programs. In an earlier study of *Fortune* 500 companies, only 52 percent of the respondents indicated that their companies had formal whistle-blowing systems. Of the companies that did provide a way for employees to report suspicious acts by their co-workers, 16 percent had toll-free hot- lines, 17 percent directed employees to discuss the matter with their managers, and 29 percent told them to contact corporate security directly.

Deloitte & Touche, a consultant in implementing whistle-blowing systems, states that several reasons explain why whistle-blowing systems fail in their attempts to help detect misconduct:

1. *Lack of anonymity:* One of the biggest impediments for whistleblowers to report misconduct is the fear of retribution. If employees have to report misconduct through an internal channel that doesn't guarantee anonymity then they are less likely to blow the whistle. They want to alert their organization to misconduct but not at a personal expense.

2. *Culture:* An organization's culture is set by the tone at the top. If management sets a poor example in relation to misconduct, then employees are less likely to speak out for two reasons: firstly, fear of being chastised by management; and secondly if management has a culture of misconduct then they are unlikely to act on a whistleblower's report, especially if it relates to the management team.

3. *Policies:* If policies in relation to acceptable behavior and ethics are not abundantly clear within an organization then employees will be uncertain about what constitutes misconduct and whether to make a report.

4. *Lack of awareness:* If the existence of the whistleblowing system is not communicated effectively or continually reinforced then employees are less likely to use it or know how to access it.[9]

On the other hand, for a whistle-blowing system to work effectively to help identify misconduct in the workplace, it must have the following elements:

1. *Anonymous:* Employees must be assured that they can report suspected incidents of misconduct without fear of retribution. An effective system must conceal the identity of a whistleblower. While this may lead to a proportion of mischievous reports, these can be easily verified through a follow up investigation of the incident.
2. *Independent:* Employees feel more comfortable about reporting misconduct to an independent party who is not in any way related to the organization or the party or parties involved in the misconduct.
3. *Accessible:* Employees need to have several different channels through which they can report misconduct, i.e. via the telephone, email, online or via mail. This ensures all employees—blue collar, white collar, office bound or remote—can anonymously make a report using the channel that suits them.
4. *Follow up:* Incidents reported through to the whistleblowing system must be followed up and corrective action taken where necessary. This will demonstrate the benefit of the system and encourage further reporting of misconduct.

An example of one company's whistle-blower system is the following:

> *XYZ's core values and culture create an atmosphere of open communication and trust between employees and management. Though the Company has always encouraged employees to communicate freely and directly with their supervisors and/or managers, the Company is also committed to ensuring that employees feel comfortable reporting unethical or illegal behavior. The Company has therefore implemented a worldwide, toll-free hotline to allow its employees to anonymously report suspected wrongdoing without fear of reprisal.*
>
> *Under the Sarbanes-Oxley Act of 2002, the Company is required to provide a means by which employees may anonymously report concerns regarding questionable accounting or auditing matters to the Audit Committee of the Board of Directors. The Company also encourages employees to report any concerns regarding suspected fraud, noncompliance with the Company's accepted business practices; the Company's established policies; or federal, state, and local laws.*
>
> *The anonymity of the hotline caller is absolutely assured. The calls are answered by a live third-party (non-company) answering service, there are no recording devices used, and there is no caller identification on the hotline. The caller will not be asked to identify himself, but will be asked to provide sufficient details about the allegations so that they may be appropriately investigated.*
>
> *All complaints received by the hotline will be taken seriously. The Legal Department will work with the Audit Committee of the Board of Directors to ensure the complaints are resolved in a timely and appropriate manner.*
>
> *The Company prefers that employees communicate openly and freely with their supervisors and managers. However, employees may also take advantage of the hotline if they wish to remain anonymous.*

## Creating an Expectation of Punishment

The sixth factor in eliminating fraud opportunities is creating an expectation that dishonesty will be punished. As stated several times, probably the greatest deterrent to dishonesty is fear of punishment. In today's business and social environment, merely being terminated is not meaningful punishment. Real punishment involves having to tell family members and friends about the dishonest behavior. Fraud perpetrators are usually first-time offenders who suffer tremendous embarrassment when they are forced to inform their loved ones that they have committed fraud. When fraud perpetrators are merely terminated, they usually give those close to them a morally acceptable, but false, reason for the termination, such as, "The company laid me off."

A strong prosecution policy that lets employees know that dishonest acts will be harshly punished, that not everyone is dishonest, and that unauthorized borrowing from the company will not be tolerated, is essential in reducing fraud. Even though prosecution is often expensive and time consuming, and even though it stimulates concerns about unfavorable press coverage, not prosecuting is a cost-effective strategy only in the short run. In the long run, failure to seek prosecution sends a message to other employees that fraud is tolerated and that the worst thing that happens to perpetrators is termination. Because of today's privacy laws and high job turnover rates, termination alone is not a strong fraud deterrent. Like a good code of ethics, a strong policy of punishment helps eliminate rationalizations.

Concerning the value of prosecution, an article in the *New York Times* confirmed that prosecution can make a difference. Here are some excerpts from that article:

> *In the last two years, prosecutors and juries have repeatedly sent corporate America the message that white-collar crime is a crime after all, starting with the prosecution of the accounting firm Arthur Andersen, which resulted in its conviction and demise in 2002. Since then, dozens of executives at Enron, Tyco International and other big public companies have been charged with fraud, obstruction of justice and other crimes. Many have pleaded guilty; others are being tried or awaiting trial. Now the prosecutions may have reached a critical mass that will make executives think twice before lying to shareholders and federal officials, experts on white-collar crime say.*

> *"The pressures on executives to cut corners and shade the truth is very strong, and there's a lot of rationalization that goes on," said Donald C. Langevoort, a professor at the Georgetown University Law Center, and a former lawyer for the Securities and Exchange Commission. Often, executives tell themselves that questionable decisions are for the good of their companies, not personal gain, Mr. Langevoort said.*

> *Now they will have to think about how a prosecutor or jury might view their actions, he said. The convictions are "going to hit home for a lot of executives."*

> *Kirby D. Behre, a former federal prosecutor who is a white-collar defense lawyer at Paul, Hastings, said senior executives had already become warier of pushing legal boundaries. "I think the effect is already incredibly profound," Mr. Behre said. "The wake-up call was sent and received in a huge way."*

> *"The current wave of cases has shown executives that they can face long prison terms for the sort of accounting gimmickry that during the 1990's often led to little more than minor civil charges from the S.E.C. Just as federal prosecutors used aggressive prosecutions in the 1980's to force Wall Street to change its view toward insider trading, which was long considered a minor offense, the new cases have compelled some executives to rethink their attitude toward fraud."[10]*

## Conducting Proactive Fraud Auditing

Few organizations actively audit for fraud. Rather, their auditors are content to conduct financial, operational, and other audits, and to investigate fraud only if it is suspected. Organizations that proactively audit for fraud create an awareness among employees that their actions are subject to review at any time. By increasing the fear of getting caught, proactive auditing reduces fraudulent behavior.

Good fraud auditing involves four steps: (1) identifying risk exposures, (2) identifying the fraud symptoms of each exposure, (3) building audit programs to proactively look for symptoms and exposures, and (4) investigating any fraud symptoms identified. (These steps will be discussed further in Chapter 6.) One company, for example, decided to use proactive computer auditing techniques to compare employees' telephone numbers with vendors' telephone numbers. The search revealed 1,117 instances in which telephone numbers matched, indicating that the company was purchasing goods and services from employees—a direct conflict of interest.

Even CPA firms have become very serious about proactively auditing for fraud. Part of this motivation comes because of a new auditing standard, which became effective in December 2002. Statement on Auditing Standards (SAS) No. 99, *Consideration of Fraud in a Financial Statement Audit,* carries the same title as its predecessor, SAS 82, but is clearly more far-reaching than SAS No. 82. The new provisions of SAS No. 99 include sections dealing with brainstorming the risks of fraud while emphasizing increased professional skepticism; discussions with management and others as to whether they are aware of fraud; the use of unpredictable audit tests; and responding to management override of controls by requiring on every audit certain procedures responsive to detecting management override.

The new standard was issued because the Auditing Standards Board believed that the requirements and guidance provided in the statement will result in a substantial change in auditor's performance and thereby improve the likelihood that auditors will detect material misstatements due to fraud in a financial statement audit. This standard seems to be making a difference in the seriousness with which auditors consider the possibility of fraud by their clients.

In addition to be more skeptical in their auditing of financial statements, large CPA and other firms have developed dedicated units to proactively detect fraud. With advances in technology, the proactive detection of fraud is now possible more than ever before. This topic will be addressed in a future chapter. For now, you only need know that proactive fraud detection not only can catch frauds that are occurring early, but can also serve as a powerful deterrent when employees and others know that an organization is always searching for fraud that may be going on.

## Preventing Fraud—A Summary

So far in this chapter, we stated that fraud is reduced and prevented by (1) creating a culture of honesty, openness, and assistance, and (2) eliminating fraud opportunities. These two fraud prevention activities, together with their subelements, are shown in Figure 4-2.

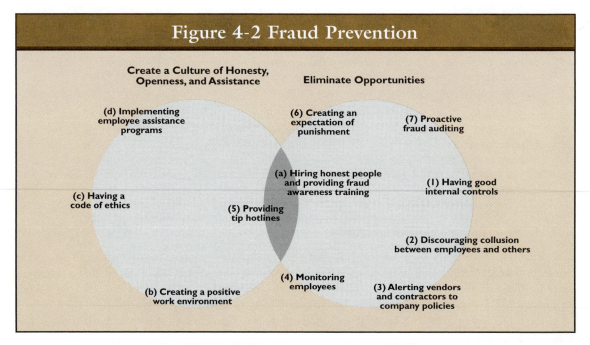

**Figure 4-2 Fraud Prevention**

**Create a Culture of Honesty, Openness, and Assistance**

**Eliminate Opportunities**

(d) Implementing employee assistance programs

(6) Creating an expectation of punishment

(7) Proactive fraud auditing

(a) Hiring honest people and providing fraud awareness training

(1) Having good internal controls

(c) Having a code of ethics

(5) Providing tip hotlines

(2) Discouraging collusion between employees and others

(4) Monitoring employees

(b) Creating a positive work environment

(3) Alerting vendors and contractors to company policies

Organizations that employ these steps and techniques have significantly fewer fraud problems than those that don't. One company that worked hard at implementing these steps reduced known fraud from an average of more than $20 million per year to less than $1 million per year.

# A Comprehensive Approach To Fighting Fraud

Thus far, this chapter has focused only on preventing fraud. We now combine prevention with detection, investigation, and follow-up to consider a comprehensive approach to fighting fraud. In a study mentioned earlier, that involved *Fortune* 500 companies, questionnaires were sent to each of the 500 companies, with instructions that the individual in the company who was most responsible for fraud prevention should respond. Of the 242 responses, 62 percent (150 responses) came from directors of internal audit, 28 percent (67 responses) from directors of corporate security, and 10 percent (25 responses) from personnel or human resource directors. Many respondents wrote that their organization had no one person who was "most responsible for fraud prevention," but that they personally were taking responsibility for completing the questionnaire.

The diversity in the job titles of respondents, combined with comments that no one in the organization was primarily responsible for preventing fraud, is a discouraging commentary on the status of fraud prevention in the United States. Fraud is an extremely costly problem for organizations. Yet, responsibility for fraud in an organization is often seen as belonging to "someone else." Independent auditors maintain they can't detect fraud because it isn't their responsibility and because their materiality levels are too high.[11] Internal auditors usually stress that their functions are to evaluate controls and to improve operational efficiency. If they happen to find fraud, they pursue or report it, but fraud isn't their primary responsibility. Corporate security officers, in most organizations, believe that theirs is an investigative role and that they will pursue reported frauds. They don't envision their role as including prevention or detection. Managers usually perceive running the business as their responsibility and seldom even acknowledge the possibility that fraud could occur in their organization. Fraud, to them, is something that happens in "other organizations." Further, they don't know how to handle fraud situations that do occur. Employees who are usually in the best position to prevent and detect fraud often don't know what to do or to whom to talk when they have suspicions, and they also often feel that it is unethical or unwise to blow the whistle or report fellow employees.

Because this nonownership attitude regarding fraud is prevalent in most businesses, frauds like the one described that follows will continue to occur.

> *Jerry Watkins had been working for Ackroyd Airlines for 17 years. During this time, he held several positions in accounting, finance, and purchasing. Jerry was the father of three children, two boys and one girl. Over the years, Jerry and his family had been active in the community and in their church. Jerry coached both Little League baseball and football. He and his wife, Jill, both had college degrees, both worked full time, and both had a long-term goal of sending their children to college. Despite their plans for college, each year the Watkins spent most of what they made and saved very little for college tuition and other expenses.*
>
> *After Jerry had been working at Ackroyd for 15 years, Steve (Jerry and Jill's oldest son) attended college at a well-known Ivy League university. He performed well, and both Jerry and Jill were proud of his and their other children's accomplishments. Approximately a year later, Jerry, who handled all the family finances, realized they could no longer pay Steve's college expenses, let alone pay future college expenses for their other two children. Jerry, a proud man, could not bring himself to admit his financial inadequacy to his family. He already had a large mortgage and several credit card and other debts, and he knew he could not borrow the money needed for college.*
>
> *Because of his financial predicament, Jerry decided to embezzle money from Ackroyd Airlines. He had heard of several other thefts in the company, and none of the perpetrators had been prosecuted. In fact, the frauds that he knew about had resulted in the company merely transferring the employees. In addition, Jerry rationalized that he would pay the money back in the future. In his current position as purchasing manager, he found it easy to take kickbacks from a vendor who had previously approached him with favors to get business. At first, Jerry took only small amounts. As the kickbacks proceeded, however, he found that he increasingly relied on the extra money to meet all kinds of financial "needs" in addition to college expenses. He felt guilty about the*

*kickbacks but knew that the company auditors never thought about fraud as a possibility. Anyway, he felt the company would understand if they knew how badly he needed the money. Significant good was coming from his "borrowing." His children were getting an education they could otherwise not have afforded, and Ackroyd didn't really miss the money. Because of his pressure, his opportunity, his rationalization, and Ackroyd's inattention to fraud prevention and detection, the company's honest employee of 17 years stole several hundred thousand dollars.*

What is alarming is that Jerry's case is not unusual. Jerry had never signed a code of conduct. Ackroyd's auditors had never proactively searched for fraud. The company didn't have an EAP to help employees with financial and other needs. Furthermore, as Jerry was well aware, the company had never taken actions harsher than terminating previous fraud offenders.

## Organizations And Fraud—The Current Model

Like Ackroyd Airlines, many organizations do not have a proactive approach to dealing with fraud and reducing fraudulent behavior. Because fraud prevention is not emphasized in many companies, employees may experience significant confusion about who has responsibility for the detection, prevention, and investigation of fraud. The current model that most organizations typically use for dealing with fraud, often by default, is shown in Figure 4-3.

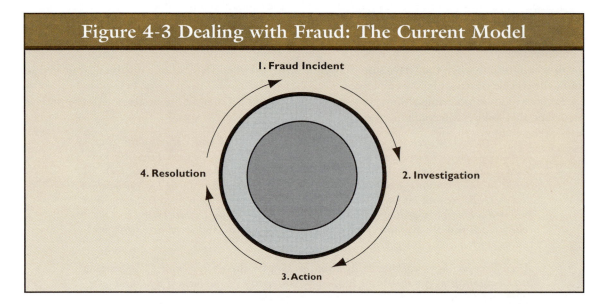

**Figure 4-3 Dealing with Fraud: The Current Model**

1. Fraud Incident
2. Investigation
3. Action
4. Resolution

This model is characterized by four stages.[12] In stage 1, a fraud incident occurs in an organization. This fraud incident is not preceded by formal awareness training or other prevention measures. Once the incident occurs, the firm shifts into a crisis mode, because it (a) needs to identify the perpetrator, (b) wants to avoid publicity, (c) wants to attempt to recover the losses, (d) wants to minimize the overall impact of the occurrence on the organization, and (e) is caught up in the emotion of the crisis.

Stage 2 is investigation. Here security and internal audit usually become involved. Most of the investigative work involves interviewing and document examination. Investigation may or may not lead to resolution, can take extensive time, and may be relatively costly.

In stage 3, after the investigation has been completed, the company must decide what actions to take regarding the perpetrator(s). The choices are: (a) take no action, (b) terminate or transfer only, or (c) terminate and seek prosecution.

Stage 4 involves closing the file, tying together loose ends, replacing the employee (obviously incurring additional costs), perhaps implementing some new controls, and otherwise resolving the problem.

Once these four stages are completed, no further action is taken—until another fraud occurs. Unfortunately, with this model, fraud never decreases. Instead, it becomes a recurring problem. A much better approach to fighting fraud is described in Figure 4-4.

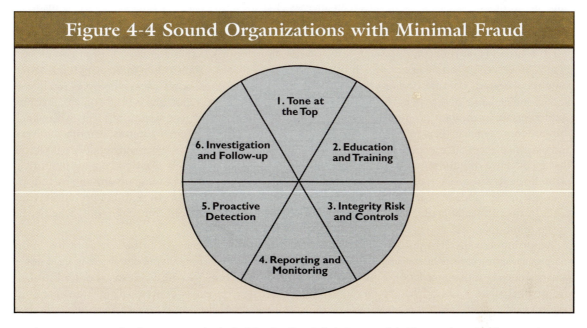

## Figure 4-4 Sound Organizations with Minimal Fraud

As you can see, six elements are included in the fraud-fighting model. First and probably most important is having management, the board of directors, and others at the top of an organization set a positive "tone at the top." Creating a positive tone involves two steps: (1) caring enough about having a positive organization that effective fraud awareness training is conducted throughout the organization, and a well-defined corporate code of conduct is promoted, and (2) setting a proper example or modeling appropriate management behavior.

When the management of one company changed its attitude from "we want to know when someone who commits fraud is prosecuted" to "we want to know when someone who commits fraud *isn't* prosecuted" and made fraud against the company, along with safety, discrimination, and substance abuse, significant issues in the organization, the number and size of frauds decreased substantially. Likewise, top management cannot accept expensive perks and gifts from vendors and others and not expect employees to do the same.

The second element in this fraud-fighting model is educating employees and others about the seriousness of fraud and informing them what to do if fraud is suspected. As we have repeatedly said, it is fraud prevention, not detection or investigation, that results in big savings. Therefore, significant attention should be given to instituting proactive fraud education initiatives, rather than to dealing with losses that have already occurred.

Fraud awareness training helps to prevent fraud and ensure that any frauds that do occur are detected at early stages, thus limiting the financial exposure of the corporation and minimizing the negative impact on the work environment. Education includes instructing vendors and other outsiders, not just employees, about the organization's expectations.

The third fraud-fighting element involves integrity risk assessment and having a good internal control system. We already discussed internal controls in this chapter. It is important to note that a good system of controls includes an explicit study of all frauds and why they occurred, together with implementation of control activities necessary to prevent future occurrences of the same types of frauds.

Analysis of frauds involves determinations by people in management, audit, security, human resources, control, and finance of why and how the fraud occurred. The focus is on the individuals who were involved, the controls that were compromised or absent, the environment that facilitated the fraud, and related factors. This step is important in understanding the kinds of preventive measures that are needed within the environment in which the fraud occurred. An appropriate preventive solution does not take long to be developed, once all the parties work together to resolve the problems. Obviously, additional or new controls must meet the cost-effectiveness test and may not be implemented. The decision not to implement, however, should be based on an analysis of costs and benefits. They should not be made by default because the proper analysis was not conducted.

The fourth element consists of a system of reporting and monitoring. Fraud reporting must be facilitated. Murder, bank robbery, or assault, leave no question about whether a crime has been committed. Fraud, however, is a subtle crime, which usually entails no obvious signs. Only fraud symptoms or red flags are observed. Because hotlines or other reporting systems often don't exist, employees rarely volunteer information about possible fraud symptoms. This lack of reporting is unfortunate, because employees are in the best position to recognize dishonest behavior or to question red flags with which they are more familiar than anyone else. Monitoring involves having internal auditors, external auditors, and even management watching and performing audits and reviews. Employees and vendors who know that an effective monitoring and reporting system is in place are much less likely to commit fraud than are individuals who work in high fraud environments. Effective prevention of fraud usually involves efforts to create in the minds of potential perpetrators that their activities will be uncovered. For prevention purposes, it doesn't really matter whether a perpetrator actually will be caught, but rather only whether he or she thinks they will.

Reporting also involves publishing facts about the fraud to those who can benefit from the information. Publication does not mean making sure the case and all its accompanying details are in local newspapers. Indeed, until a conviction is obtained, such publication is ill-advised, because it can lead to slander or libel suits. Rather, what "publication" means in this context is depersonalizing the case (i.e., disguising the identities of the perpetrators and other people involved) and publishing it internally in a security newsletter or a memo that is distributed to auditors, security personnel, and appropriate management and employees. Even generic publication of fraud has a tremendous impact, because it helps readers understand that fraud happens in their own organization and is not just a horrible nightmare that occurs elsewhere.

The fifth element of a good fraud-fighting system puts proactive fraud detection methods in place. No matter how good fraud prevention efforts are, some frauds will still be committed. And because frauds grow geometrically over time, it is important to detect frauds early. Proactive fraud detection methods, such as those discussed in Chapter 6, are not only effective in detecting fraud, but knowledge of their use is a good fraud deterrent.

The final element requires effective investigations and follow-up when fraud occurs. Effective investigation means an organization will have prespecified formal fraud policies stating who will carry out all elements of an investigation. The investigation procedures must be well established, including (a) who will conduct the investigation, (b) how the matter will be communicated to management, (c) whether and when law enforcement officials will be contacted, (d) who will determine the scope of investigation, (e) who will determine the investigation methods, (f) who will follow up on tips of suspected fraud, (g) who will conduct interviews, review documents, and perform other investigation steps, and (h) who will ultimately determine the corporate response to fraud in the form of, disciplines, control, and other activities. This stage also involves having preset policies regarding follow-up actions against perpetrators.

Taking no action should not even be a possibility; rather, whenever possible, fraud perpetrators should be prosecuted. A strong prosecution policy must have the support of top managers, and they must be informed if someone commits fraud and is not prosecuted. Gone are the days when prosecution resulted in bad publicity. Most people now realize that fraud exists in every organization. They also realize that organizations that take a tough prosecution stance will reduce the number of future frauds significantly and will ultimately be more profitable because of the deterrent effect of prosecution.

As stated previously, the single greatest factor in deterring dishonest acts is the fear of punishment. Companies with successful prosecution policies have developed their own internal investigation experts. They recognize that in order to obtain cooperation from law enforcement officers and the justice system, it is almost always necessary to conduct a thorough and complete investigation (usually including obtaining a signed confession) before the overworked law enforcement agencies and criminal justice systems can accommodate the prosecution.

# KEY TERM

**Employee assistance programs (EAP):**
Employee assistance programs are programs that help employees deal with problems such as substance abuse, gambling, money management and debt, health, family, and other pressures.

# QUESTIONS AND CASES

## DISCUSSION QUESTIONS

1. How do organizations create a culture of honesty, openness, and assistance?

2. What are different ways in which companies can eliminate opportunities for fraud?

3. What is the purpose of adopting a code of ethics throughout a company?

4. Why are good internal controls important?

5. In what ways can organizations discourage collusive fraud?

6. Why is it important to inform outside vendors of company policies concerning payments to buyers?

7. How can organizations monitor their employees?

8. In what ways can organizations conduct proactive fraud auditing?

9. How does a response hotline for anonymous tips help to prevent fraud?

10. Why is it important for companies to create an effective organizational structure?

## TRUE/FALSE

1. Even with the right opportunity or significant pressure, most people would probably not steal or embezzle.

2. Studies show that a positive and honest work culture in a company does little to prevent fraud.

3. An important factor in creating a culture of honesty, openness, and assistance in the workplace is maintaining an employee assistance program.

4. A good internal control system within a company can ensure the absence of fraud.

5. When fraud is committed, the problem often is not a lack of controls, but the overriding of existing controls by management and others.

6. The two elements in creating a positive work environment are (1) having an open-door policy, and (2) having positive personnel and operating procedures.

7. Not prosecuting fraud perpetrators is cost-effective both in the short run and the long run.

8. Even a good system of internal controls will often not be completely effective because of fallibilities of the people applying and enforcing the controls.

9. The increasingly complex nature of business helps to decrease the number of collusive frauds.

10. Tips and complaints are the most common way fraud is detected.

## MULTIPLE CHOICE

1. People will often be dishonest if they are placed in an environment of:
   a. Poor controls.
   b. High pressure.
   c. Low integrity.
   d. Loose accountability.
   e. All of the above.

2. _____ is/are factor(s) contributing to creating a corporate culture of honesty and openness.
   a. Hiring honest people
   b. Performing criminal background checks
   c. Not having an open-door policy
   d. Having a well-understood and respected code of ethics
   e. Both a and d
   f. All of the above

3. Personnel and operating policies that contribute to high-fraud environment(s) include:
   a. Management by crisis.
   b. Rigid rules.
   c. High employee lifestyle expectations.
   d. Poor promotion opportunities.
   e. All of the above.

4. _____ is usually the single most effective tool in preventing and detecting fraud.
   a. Monitoring employees
   b. Having a good system of internal controls
   c. Having a well-written company code of ethics
   d. Strict hiring procedures

5. A company's control environment includes:
   a. The tone that management establishes toward what is honest and acceptable behavior.
   b. Corporate hiring practices.
   c. Having an internal audit department.
   d. All of the above.

6. Which of the following factors generally results in a high-fraud environment?
   a. Hiring honest people
   b. Providing an EAP
   c. Autocratic management
   d. Both a and b

7. Which of the following aspects of fighting fraud usually results in the largest savings?
   a. Fraud prevention
   b. Fraud detection
   c. Fraud investigation
   d. It is impossible to tell

8. Which of the following is usually the most effective tool in preventing and detecting fraud?
   a. Discouraging collusion between employees and customers or vendors
   b. Effective investigations of fraud symptoms
   c. Having a good system of internal controls
   d. Creating an expectation of punishment in the company

9. Which of the following is the typical fraud model that describes most firms?
   a. Fraud incident, assessing risk, investigation, reporting
   b. Fraud incident, investigation, action, resolution
   c. Assessing risk, fraud incident, investigation, resolution
   d. Assessing risk, investigation, implementing a fraud program, reporting

10. The "tone at the top" is an important element in fighting fraud. This tone at the top involves:
    a. Doing a good job of integrity risk assessment.
    b. Having a positive organization where effective fraud teaching and training is conducted.
    c. Setting a proper example or modeling appropriate management behavior.
    d. Both b and c.

## SHORT CASES

**Case 1.** Karen, a friend of yours, recently started her own business, The Bike and Boulder Company (B&B). B&B specializes in the sale of mountain bikes and rock climbing equipment. Karen is putting the finishing touches on her company policies and procedures. She knows you are taking a fraud class and asks you to review what she has completed thus far. You quickly notice that Karen neglected to address fraud and fraud prevention in her policies and procedures.

What policies and procedures would you suggest Karen implement to prevent and detect fraud at B&B?

**Case 2.** Because ABC Company suffered large losses from fraud last year, senior management decided to be more proactive in implementing a fraud prevention environment. In interviewing employees, they found that many employees were unclear about which behaviors were ethical and which were not.

What could management do to better educate employees about ethical behavior?

**Case 3.** Jason works at a new software development company. The company has been in existence for only two years. Because the company is new, everybody is working extra hours and spending all of their time developing new products that can be sold to customers. Everybody is busy, leaving little time for manager-employee interviews. The culture of the company is trusting and fun. When Jason started with the company, the only agreement he had to sign was an agreement to not transfer company software secrets to other organizations. Earlier in the year, Jason learned of an instance where another employee in accounting was fired. The reason was rumored to be fraudulent behavior, but nobody really knew the reason.

What about this organization's operating procedures encourages fraudulent behavior?

**Case 4.** Nellie works for a large *Fortune* 500 company. She heads the information systems department and works closely with the accounting department. The company works with many associates. They have many buyer and supplier companies they work with. Nellie knows a lot about the database systems and accounting practices in the company. She even works closely with buyers and suppliers to create data communication lines. Recently, Nellie has become concerned about the integrity and reliability of the accounting and information systems. The company has grown to a point where she cannot manage or supervise all the activities performed in these areas.

What proactive steps can Nellie take to ensure systems and accounting integrity and prevent fraudulent behavior?

**Case 5.** While performing an audit of TCC Corporation, the audit team noticed something that didn't look right. The company's receivables aging report showed that bank loan eligible receivables were approximately $91 million. The audit team calculated the bank loan eligible receivables to be approximately $50 million. The client didn't identify specific accounts in writing off bad debts, credit memo processing was extremely slow, and management had not focused on items that remained uncollectible and ineligible for financing. In addition, over the last two years, the company's credit department experienced unusually high turnover—four different people had held the credit manager position under an intimidating CFO. The current credit manager was a friend of the CFO and had worked with him at a previous company. After looking at some invoices and asking about customer information to confirm, the credit manager admitted to creating false documents and arranging fictitious sales with clients—all with the knowledge of the CFO.

1. What are some of the red flags that point to the possibility of fraud?

2. What would you say was the main problem in this case that allowed the fraud to occur?

**Case 6.** Joseph Gonzales recently bought a new business that included a small 20-room motel and coffee shop. He hired a young couple to run the business and plans to pay them a monthly salary. The couple will live for free in a small apartment behind the motel office and will be in charge of the daily operations of the motel and coffee shop. They will also be responsible for hiring and supervising the four or five part-time employees who will help with cleaning the rooms, cooking, and waiting on customers in the restaurant. The couple will also maintain records of rooms rented, meals served, and payments received (which can be in the form of cash, checks, or credit cards). They will make weekly deposits of the business's proceeds at the local bank. Joseph lives about six hours away and will only be able to visit periodically.

What are your two biggest concerns regarding possible fraud on the part of the couple? For each concern, identify a possible control that could reduce the risk of fraud.

**Case 7.** Danny has been working at Gant Chevrolet for two years. He feels fortunate to have held his job for so long, considering his past, which involved being fired for fraudulent activities in two different cases. His boss, Mr. Gant, is generally a pretty cold person and only talks to Danny upon arriving and leaving work each day. All of the guys at work tend to slack a little here and there. They don't mind eating lunch at the company's expense, and the place shows a general lack of order. Danny has been feeling tight on cash lately, having just moved into a home that is perhaps a little too expensive. With this internal pressure and no one on whom to unload his troubles or with whom to talk, Danny decides to steal parts from the parts garage and sell them on the street for cash.

What could Gant Chevrolet have done to prevent Danny's fraud?

**Case 8.** Mary S. is the owner of a small flower shop. With only 12 employees, the environment is one of trust. Mary personally knows each employee, and most have worked at the shop since its opening. Although few controls exist, Mary is the only person allowed to sign checks. Mary's good friend, Steve, is important to the business. Not only is he the head accountant, but he also helps maintain relationships with vendors. Steve is the proud father of three children, two sons and one daughter. Steve's son was soon to start college at an Ivy League school. Although immensely proud, Steve was worried about making tuition payments as well as providing for the rest of his family. After his son's freshman year, things began to get really tight. Not wanting his son to know that the family was hurting financially, he decided to talk to a vendor who was interested in doing business with the company. After accepting the first kickback, the second was easier. Soon Steve was able to pay for his son's tuition and more. He began buying expensive jewelry for his wife and taking extravagant trips. Because Mary was a personal friend, she inquired where the money was coming from. Steve told Mary that his wife had received an inheritance from an aunt. Because Mary trusted him, she believed his story. She did not become suspicious until one day she tried to contact a vendor directly. Steve would not allow her to do so and insisted that she talk to the vendor through him. Soon Mary discovered that Steve had taken a substantial amount of money and had taken advantage of their trusting relationship.

How could this fraud have been prevented?

**Case 9.** Robert was the chief teller in a large New York bank. Over a period of three years, he embezzled $1.5 million. He took the money by manipulating dormant accounts. When a customer would complain about his

account, Robert was always the one to explain the discrepancy. He usually used the excuse that "it's a computer error."

What internal control weaknesses allowed this fraud to occur?

**Case 10.** A controller of a small fruit-packing company in California stole $212,000 from the company. When asked why, he said "Nobody at the company (especially the owners) ever talked to me. They treated me unfairly, they talked down to me, and they were rude to me. They deserve everything they got."

What could the company have done to prevent this fraud?

## EXTENSIVE CASES

**Extensive Case 1.** Friday, May 13, 1988, will be remembered by a major Chicago bank. Embezzlers nearly escaped with $69 million! Armand Moore, who was released after serving four years of his eleven-year sentence for a $180,000 fraud, decided it was time to put his fingers in something a little bigger and better. He instigated a $68.7 million fraud plan. Naming himself as "Chairman," he assembled Herschel Bailey, Otis Wilson, Neal Jackson, Leonard Strickland, and Ronald Carson to complete the formation of his "Board." Most importantly, the Board was able to convince an employee of the Chicago Bank to provide their "in." The caper required one month of planning in a small hotel in Chicago, and took all of 64 minutes to complete.

The bank employee had worked for the Chicago Bank for eight years, and he was employed in the bank's wire-transfer section, which dispatches multimillion-dollar sums around the world via computers and phone lines. Some of the bank's largest customers send funds from their accounts directly to creditors and suppliers. For electronic transfers, most banks require that a bank employee call back another executive at the customer's offices to reconfirm the order, using various code numbers. All such calls are automatically taped. The crooked employee participated in these deposits and confirmations, and he had access to all the code numbers and names of appropriate executives with whom to communicate.

The Board's targets were Merrill Lynch, United Airlines, and Brown-Forman distillers. A few members of the gang set up phony bank accounts in Vienna under the false names of Lord Investments, Walter Newman, and GTL Industries. At 8:30 a.m., a gang member posing as a Merrill Lynch executive called the bank to arrange a transfer of $24 million to the account of Lord Investments, and was assisted by one of the crooked employee's unsuspecting coworkers. In accordance with

the bank's practice of confirming the transfers with a second executive of the company, the employee stepped in and called another supposed Merrill Lynch executive who was actually Bailey, his partner in crime. Bailey's unfaltering, convincing voice was recorded automatically on the tape machine, and the crooked employee wired the funds to Vienna via the New York City Bank. The same procedure followed at 9:02 and 9:34 a.m. with phony calls on behalf of United Airlines and Brown-Forman. The funds were initially sent to Citibank and Chase Manhattan Bank, respectively.

On Monday, May 16, the plot was uncovered. The Chairman and his Board were discovered due to no effort on the part of the Chicago Bank nor any investigative authority. Although bank leaders do not like to admit just how close the culprits came to getting away with it, investigators were amazed at how far the scheme proceeded before being exposed. Had the men been a little less greedy, say possibly $40 million, or if they had chosen accounts that were a little less active, they may have been touring the world today! The plot was discovered because the transfers overdrew the balances in two of the accounts, and when the companies were contacted to explain the NSF transactions, they knew nothing about the transfers.

### Question

How could this fraud have been prevented? Why is this fraud difficult to prevent?

**Extensive Case 2.** During the Christmas holiday season diamonds are a hot buy throughout the United States. Sales have been growing dramatically at International Jewelers, a regional diamond retailer in Washington and Oregon. International Jewelers positions itself as a high-quality diamond retailer with stores just across the street from malls to provide a convenient location without the added markup. Over the past three years, the Bellevue store experienced a dramatic sales increase, almost 38 percent (see Exhibit A). John Pastella, president and owner of International Jewelers, praised the efforts of Wade Sullivan, manager, of the Bellevue store for his tenacity in pushing sales growth. John said, "He hasn't missed a day of work in three years." Sales representatives are paid by commission and are pushed to meet daily sales goals that are progressively higher each day between Thanksgiving and Christmas. Cash bonuses are distributed to individuals each day as sales goals are achieved. Sullivan, disburses the cash on a daily basis and performs all duties of store management including books. Sullivan reports to Pastella on a quarterly basis.

Over the past three years a few sales representatives saw Sullivan take cash from the register during the holiday season and leave the building. He was approached about the matter and said he was only borrowing the money to refurbish his 1954 Chevy and that he would repay the money. Sales representatives also noted that during the past year Wade had purchased a Bentley that he drove to work on occasion. He also bought a new home on Lake Washington. His explanation about these new luxuries was that he inherited a large sum of money from his grandfather who passed away a few years ago. Management first questioned the low profitability of the Bellevue store when the financial statements of the past three years were reviewed. Pastella couldn't understand why net income was so flat despite the fact that sales had grown almost 38 percent in the past three years. After a few days of frustration and no solutions, Pastella hired a local Certified Fraud Examiner who solved the problem. Sullivan had embezzled up to $277,500 from the company by falsely recording receivables.

**Questions**

1. What should the sales representatives have done after discovering Sullivan's habit of taking cash from the register?

2. What controls could Pastella have put in place to prevent the fraud from occurring?

3. What clues hinted that fraud was taking place?

## Exhibit A

| | 2004 | 2003 | 2002 |
|---|---|---|---|
| **Sales** | $1,365,060 | $1,099,700 | $992,159 |
| **COGS** | 530,800 | 501,690 | 456,080 |
| **Gross Margin** | 834,260 | 598,010 | 536,079 |
| **Operating Expenses** | 360,600 | 357,005 | 360,009 |
| **EBT** | 473,660 | 241,005 | 176,070 |
| **Taxes** | 189,464 | 96,402 | 70,428 |
| **True Net Income** | $ 284,196 | $144,603 | $105,642 |
| **Fraud** | 197,500 | 60,000 | 20,000 |
| **Net Income** | $ 86,000 | $ 84,603 | $ 85,642 |

**Extensive Case 3.** Nu Skin Enterprises developed the following code of ethics:

> *Corporate Governance*
> *Code of Ethics for Financial Professionals*
>
> *This Code of Ethics for Financial Professionals (the "Code of Ethics") applies to the Chief Executive Officer, Chief Financial Officer and all professionals worldwide serving in a finance, accounting, treasury, tax or investor relations role at Nu Skin Enterprises, Inc. ("NSE"). NSE expects all of its employees to act in accordance with the highest standards of personal and professional integrity in all aspects of their activities. NSE therefore has existing Codes of Ethics and Business Conduct applicable to all directors, officers and employees of NSE. In addition to the Codes of Ethics and*

> *Business Conduct, the CEO, CFO and all other financial professionals are subject to the following additional specific policies:*
>
> *As the Chief Executive Officer, Chief Financial Officer, or other financial professional, I agree to:*
>
> *a. Engage in and promote honest and ethical conduct, including the ethical handling of actual or apparent conflicts of interest between personal and professional relationships;*
>
> *b. Avoid conflicts of interest and to disclose to the General Counsel any material transaction or relationship that reasonably could be expected to give rise to such a conflict;*
>
> *c. Take all reasonable measures to protect the confidentiality of nonpublic information about NSE or its subsidiaries and their customers*

*obtained or created in connection with my activities and to prevent the unauthorized disclosure of such information unless required by applicable law or regulation or legal or regulatory process;*

d. *Produce full, fair, accurate, timely, and understandable disclosure in reports and documents that NSE or its subsidiaries files with, or submits to, the Securities and Exchange Commission and other regulators and in other public communications made by NSE or its subsidiaries;*

e. *Comply in all material respects with applicable governmental laws, rules and regulations, as well as the rules and regulations of the New York Stock Exchange and other appropriate private and public regulatory agencies.*

f. *Promptly report any possible violation of this Code of Ethics to the General Counsel or any of the parties or through any of the channels described in NSE's Whistleblower Policy.*

*I understand that I am prohibited from directly or indirectly taking any action to fraudulently influence, coerce, manipulate or mislead NSE or its subsidiaries' independent public auditors for the purpose of rendering the financial statements of NSE or its subsidiaries misleading.*

*I understand that I will be held accountable for my adherence to this Code of Ethics. My failure to observe the terms of this Code of Ethics may result in disciplinary action, including termination of employment. Violations of this Code of Ethics may also constitute violations of law and may result in civil and criminal penalties against me, my supervisors and/or NSE.*

*Any questions regarding the best course of action on a particular situation should be directed to the General Counsel. Please be aware that NSE's Whistleblower Policy provides the option to remain anonymous in reporting any possible violation of the Code of Ethics.*

## Questions

1. Nu Skin Enterprises created multiple codes of conduct applicable to different groups of employees. Why wouldn't they create just one code of conduct, applicable to everyone in the company? Who, specifically, has agreed to follow the "Code of Ethics for Financial Professionals" shown in this case?

2. How is Nu Skin helping to prevent white-collar crime within its company by defining and clarifying appropriate and inappropriate behavior in its codes of conduct?

3. What actions are listed as possible punishments for violators of the Code of Ethics? How can creating an expectation of punishment help to deter fraudulent behavior?

**Extensive Case 4.** You are the owner of a private, moderate-sized company. The business was founded more than 20 years ago and has experienced impressive growth and profitability. The only frustrating thing, however, is that you know the company's profits would be significantly higher if you could rid it of its problems with fraud. Your accountants estimate that the company lost approximately 7 percent of its earnings to fraud over the past five years.

The company has adequate controls in place, and you try to ensure that people don't override them. Because you are the owner, however, you often bypass some controls. You know that you aren't out to rob the company, so you believe that the controls aren't applicable to you.

You try to keep a close eye on most aspects of the business, but with about 500 employees, it's difficult to know about everything that is going on. Employees have been caught in fraudulent activities in the past, but you have never bothered prosecuting them. You wish to avoid the negative publicity that would result, and you see no valid reason to publicly humiliate former employees—their shame won't bring back the money they've stolen.

What aspects of the company can you change in order to reduce the amount of fraud that is occurring? Use the five factors described in the chapter relating to creating a culture of honesty, openness, and assistance to explain your answer.

## INTERNET ASSIGNMENT

As mentioned in the chapter, the Committee of Sponsoring Organizations (COSO) produced a report on internal control. They also published a report on fraudulent financial reporting.

Visit the Web site at http://www.coso.org/ Publications/ NCFFR_Part_5.htm and read the chapter on recommendations for the public company. Report on any similarities/differences.

## DEBATES

1. You work for a small manufacturing firm, where it is clearly too expensive to have proper segregation of duties. Because of this lack of control, management knows that opportunities exist to perpetrate fraud within the company. Management is particularly concerned with possible collusion between purchasing agents and vendors because of the relatively small size of the company and the fact that a single purchasing agent is often solely responsible for a vendor's account. Management knows now that a lot of money can be saved by proactively preventing fraud and not just acting on a reactionary or crisis basis. They have started to establish an open-door policy where all employees are encouraged to talk about pressures and opportunities faced while on the job. Management also wants to establish a hotline where employees can report suspicious activity.

    a. Is an employee hotline necessary?

    b. Is this sort of whistle-blowing ethical?

    c. What can management do as they establish this hotline to encourage employees to actually use it?

2. During the past year, your company discovered three major frauds. The first was a $3.9 million theft of inventory that had been going on for six years. The second was a $2.8 million kickback scheme involving the most senior purchasing agent. She had been allowing certain customers to overcharge for products in return for personal payments and other financial favors. The third was an overstatement of receivables and inventories by a subsidiary manager to enhance reported earnings. Without the overstatement, his unit's profit would have fallen far short of budget. The amount of overstatement has yet to be determined. All three of these frauds were reported in the financial newspapers and have been embarrassing to the company.

    In response to these incidents, the Board of Directors demanded that management take "positive steps to eliminate future fraud occurrences." In their words, they are "sick and tired of significant hits to the bottom line and negative exposure in the press." The responsibility to develop a program to eradicate fraud has fallen on your shoulders. You are to outline a comprehensive plan to prevent future frauds. In devising your strategy, outline the roles the following groups will play in preventing fraud:

    1. Top management

    2. Middle management

    3. Internal audit

    4. Corporate security

    5. Audit committee

    6. Legal counsel

    Have six groups (or six students) assume these six positions and discuss what each group's responsibility is to prevent fraud. Debate the issues.

## END NOTES

1. Shawn Young "Ebbers Is Charged with Falsifying Filings to the SEC," *The Wall Street Journal*, (May 25, 2004), p. A3.

2. http://articles.findarticles.com/p/articles/mi_m3870/is_13_18/ai_95320230, accessed on May 25, 2004.

3. http://www.lawsight.com/jjart12.htm, accessed on May 25, 2004.

4. http://www.pnafoundation.org/Training/ColumnsByEdMiller/Power.htm, accessed on May 25, 2004.

5. http://www.familyserviceseap.com/employer/value_money_e.html, accessed on May 26, 2004.

6. W. Steve Albrecht and Jerry Wernz, "The Three Factors of Fraud," *Security Management* (July 1993), pp. 95-97.

7. *Deterrence, Detection, Investigation, and Reporting of Fraud* (Maitland, FL: Institute of Internal Auditors), pp. 3–4.

8. Committee of Sponsoring Organizations, *Internal Control—Integrated Framework*, Treadway Commission 1992.

9. http://www.deloitte.com/dtt/alert/0,2296,sid%253D5628%2526cid%253D42825,00.html, accessed on May 26, 2004.

10. Alex Berenson, "Are We Deterring Corporate Crime?" *New York Times* (March 8, 2004).

11. Independent auditors examine the consolidated financial statements of an organization. In that role, they are primarily concerned only with amounts significantly large enough to effect the financial statements. In some cases, amounts of several million dollars are considered "immaterial."

12. Part of the material that follows has been previously published in "How Companies Can Reduce the Cost of Fraud," W.S. Albrecht, E.A. McDermott, and T.L. Williams, *The Internal Auditor*.

# PART THREE

## FRAUD DETECTION

# CHAPTER 5

# RECOGNIZING THE SYMPTOMS OF FRAUD

## LEARNING OBJECTIVES

After studying this chapter, you should be able to:

1. Understand how symptoms help in the detection of fraud.
2. Recognize and understand accounting symptoms of fraud.
3. Identify internal controls that help detect fraud.
4. Identify and understand analytical symptoms of fraud.
5. Realize how lifestyle changes help detect fraud.
6. See how behavioral symptoms help detect fraud.
7. Recognize the importance of tips and complaints as fraud symptoms.

*Elgin Aircraft had claims processing and claims payment departments to administer its health care plans. The company was self-insured for claims under $50,000. Claims above this amount were forwarded to an independent insurance company. The claims processing department's responsibility was to verify the necessary documentation for payment and then to forward the documentation to the claims payment department. The claims payment department approved and signed the payment.*

*Elgin employees had a choice between two different types of insurance plans. The first was a health maintenance organization (HMO) plan in which employees went to an approved doctor. Elgin had a contract with a group of medical doctors who treated the employees for a set fee. The second plan allowed employees to go to doctors of their own choice rather than to the HMO, but only 80 percent of their medical bills were paid by Elgin.*

*Management believed that the company had an excellent internal control system. In addition, the company continually had various auditors on their premises: government contract auditors, defense auditors, outside auditors, and internal auditors. Health claims were processed from an extensive form filled out by the attending physician and a statement from his or her office verifying the nature of the dollar amount of the treatment. This form was given to the claims processing department, which would verify the following:*

- *That the patient was an employee of Elgin Aircraft.*
- *That treatments were covered by the plan.*
- *That amounts charged were within approved guidelines.*

- *That the amount of the claims per individual for the year were not over $50,000; if they were, a claim was submitted to the insurance company.*
- *Which plan the employee was on, and that the calculation for payment was correct.*

*After verification of these facts, the claims were forwarded to the claims payment department, which paid the doctor directly. No payments ever went to employees.*

*One day, a defense auditor observed the manager of the claims payment department taking her department employees to lunch in a chauffeured limousine. The auditor was curious about how the manager could afford such expensive occasions and was concerned that the cost of the lunch and the limousine were being paid for by the government. In speaking with the vice president of finance, he learned that the manager was "one of the company's best employees." He also learned that she had never missed a day of work in the last 10 years. She was indeed a very conscientious employee, and her department had one of the best efficiency ratings in the entire company.*

*Concerned about the limousine and other factors, the auditor began an investigation that revealed that the claims payment department manager had embezzled more than $12 million from Elgin Aircraft in four years. Her scheme involved setting up 22 dummy "doctors" who would submit medical bills on employees who had not had much medical work during the year. Her fictitious doctors would create claims forms and submit them to the claims processing department. The claims processing department would send the approved forms to the claims payment department, which would then send payment to the dummy doctors.*

Fraud is a crime that is seldom observed. The discovery of a body that is obviously the victim of murder, leaves no question about whether a crime has been committed. The dead body can be touched and seen. Likewise, if a bank is robbed, a crime has been committed. Everyone in the bank, including customers and employees, witnessed the robbery. In most cases, the entire episode is captured on video and can be replayed for doubters. With fraud, however, it is not usually obvious that a crime has been committed. Only fraud symptoms, red flags, or indicators are observed.

## Symptoms of Fraud

A person's lifestyle may change, a document may be missing, a general ledger may be out of balance, someone may act suspiciously, a change in an analytical relationship may not make sense, or someone may provide a tip that an embezzlement is taking place. Unlike videos in robbery or bodies in a murder, however, these factors are only symptoms rather than conclusive proof of fraud. Other explanations of the "fraud indicators" may exist. Lifestyle changes may have occurred because of inherited money. Documents may have been legitimately lost. The general ledger may be out of balance because of an unintentional accounting error. Suspicious actions may be caused by family dissension or personal problems. Unexplained analytical relationships may be the result of unrecognized changes in underlying economic factors. A tip may be motivated by an envious or disgruntled employee's grudge or by someone outside the company desiring to settle a score.

To detect fraud, managers, auditors, employees, and examiners must learn to recognize these indicators or symptoms (sometimes called *red flags*) and pursue them until sufficient evidence has been collected. Investigators must discover whether the symptoms resulted from actual fraud or were caused by other factors. Unfortunately, in many cases, many fraud symptoms go unnoticed, and even symptoms that are recognized are often not vigorously pursued. Many frauds could be detected earlier if fraud symptoms were pursued.

Symptoms of fraud can be separated into six groups: (1) accounting anomalies, (2) internal control weaknesses, (3) analytical anomalies, (4) extravagant lifestyle, (5) unusual behavior, and (6) tips and complaints. In this chapter we will discuss these six types of symptoms in detail. But first, we illustrate how these types of symptoms could have revealed to management, auditors, and others that fraud was occurring in the Elgin Aircraft case.

Several ***accounting anomalies*** at Elgin Aircraft could have alerted auditors to the fraud. The fraudulent claim forms from the 22 phony doctors originated from two locations. One was a post office box, and the other was a business located in a nearby city that was owned by the manager's husband. The checks being paid to the 22 doctors were sent to the same two common addresses. Checks were deposited in the same two bank accounts and contained handwritten rather than stamped endorsements.

The likely reasons that none of these accounting symptoms were recognized are that managers trusted the perpetrator completely and that auditors merely matched claim forms with canceled checks. The auditors did not ask such questions as:

- Are these payments reasonable? (For example, claims for hysterectomies for men were made.)
- Do the endorsements make sense?
- Why are the checks going to and the bills coming from the same two addresses?

A major difference between financial statement auditors and fraud examiners is that most financial statement auditors merely match documents to see whether support exists and is adequate. Auditors and examiners who detect fraud go beyond ascertaining the mere existence of documents to determine whether the documents are real or fraudulent, whether the expenditures make sense, and whether all aspects of the documentation are in order.

Significant ***internal control weaknesses*** were ignored by the Elgin Aircraft auditors. First, the manager of the claims payment department had not taken a vacation in 10 years. Second, employees of Elgin Aircraft never received confirmation of payments so they could determine whether the medical claims being paid on their behalf were incurred by them. Third, payments to new doctors were never investigated or cleared by the company.

Allowing employees to forgo vacations is a serious control weakness that must always be questioned. One of the most effective ways to deter fraud is to implement a system of independent checks. Employee transfers, audits, and mandatory vacations are all ways to provide independent checks on employees. As previously stated, the Office of the Controller of the Currency requires all bank employees in the United States to take at least one week of consecutive vacation days each year. Many frauds come to light when employees are on vacation and cannot cover their tracks. In Elgin's case, if another employee had made payments during the manager's absence, the common addresses or the payments being made to a business may have been recognized.

The lack of confirmation to employees of payments made is a serious control weakness. In Elgin's case, doctors were being paid for hysterectomies, tonsillectomies, gall bladder surgeries, and other procedures that were never performed. If employees had been aware that payments were being made for these fabricated services, they probably would have complained and the fraud scheme would have been discovered much sooner.

Another problem is that even if most auditors and managers had discovered the internal control weaknesses, they may still not have uncovered the fraud. Most likely, they would have recommended that the control weaknesses be fixed without giving thought to the possibility that the weaknesses might have already been exploited. A major difference between an auditor who uncovers fraud and one who does not is that the first auditor, upon discovering the weakness, immediately enlists procedures to determine whether the weakness has been exploited and takes measures to correct it. The second auditor ignores or minimizes the possibility of exploitation and merely fixes the control weakness.

Before doctors were cleared for payment, some kind of background check should have been conducted to determine whether they were legitimate doctors. Just as Dun & Bradstreet checks should be performed on companies with which business is conducted, the legitimacy of doctors should be verified by checking with state licensing boards, medical groups, or even telephone books.

*Analytical anomalies* are relationships, procedures, and events that do not make sense, such as a change in a volume, mix, or price that is not reasonable. In the case of Elgin Aircraft, several analytical symptoms should have alerted others to the fraud. The sheer volume of insurance work performed by the 22 fictitious doctors was quite high. Why would $12 million be paid to doctors over a period of four years? None of the phony doctors were licensed by the state. Yet payments to them exceeded payments to almost all other doctors. Another analytical symptom was that no other payments were made to any of the dummy doctors by outside insurance companies. In other words, none of the payments to these doctors were for employees who incurred more than $50,000 of medical expenses in any year. Finally, medical costs for the company increased significantly (29 percent) during the four years of the fraud.

Several lifestyle symptoms at Elgin Aircraft should have been recognized. How common is it for a manager to take employees to lunch in a limousine? An inquiry by the Defense Department auditor revealed that the manager was paying for the limousine from personal funds and that she was independently wealthy. She had told employees that she had inherited a large sum of money from her husband's parents. All her employees knew that she lived in a an expensive house, drove luxury cars, and wore expensive clothes and jewelry. If she had such wealth, someone should have wondered why she worked and especially why she never took a vacation. Even though wealthy people may be employed because of love of work, rarely is their love so great that they never take a vacation.

Several behavioral symptoms should have alerted others that something was wrong. Employees in the department regularly joked that their manager had a "Dr. Jekyll and Mrs. Hyde" personality. Sometimes she was the nicest person to be around, and other times she would have periods of unexplained anger. Interviews with employees revealed that her highs and lows had become more intense and more frequent in recent months.

With the Elgin Aircraft fraud, no tips or complaints were made. No employees who felt that something was wrong came forward, and other doctors were still getting all the legitimate business. They had no reason to complain. Indeed, the only party really being hurt was Elgin Aircraft.

The Elgin Aircraft fraud was discovered because an observant auditor noticed a fraud symptom. In this chapter we will discuss how understanding fraud symptoms helps us detect fraud much more effectively. The following sections look in detail at the six groups of fraud symptoms.

# Accounting Anomalies

Common accounting anomaly fraud symptoms involve problems with source documents, faulty journal entries, and inaccuracies in ledgers.

## Irregularities in Source Documents

Common fraud symptoms involving source documents (either electronic or paper—such as checks, sales invoices, purchase orders, purchase requisitions, and receiving reports—include the following:

- Missing documents
- Stale items on bank reconciliations
- Excessive voids or credits
- Common names or addresses of payees or customers
- Increased past due accounts
- Increased reconciling items
- Alterations on documents
- Duplicate payments
- Second endorsements on checks
- Document sequences that do not make sense
- Questionable handwriting on documents
- Photocopied documents

To illustrate how these document symptoms can signal that embezzlement is taking place, we describe three actual frauds. The first involves the use of photocopied documents; the second, the recognition of increased past due accounts receivable; and the third, excessive voids or credits. Although we discuss only three frauds, many frauds have been detected by using source documents.

The first example is a fraud that was detected by an alert internal auditor who was examining the authorization for the purchase of new equipment. Further investigation revealed a large, collusive fraud.

> *A thin line running through a photocopied letter in a vendor invoice file alerted the auditor to probe further. The photocopied letter was from a manufacturer to a vendor, which had suggested the repair of machinery parts as an alternative to the expensive option of replacement, which was also set forth in the letter. By cutting out the paragraph pertaining to the repair of existing machinery, the vendor had substantiated the need for replacing the equipment, thus ensuring a large commission on the sale of new machinery.*

In the second example, a fraud was detected by recognizing an increase in past due accounts from customers. This employee fraud was committed against one of the largest *Fortune* 500 companies in the United States.

> *Mark Rogers was the accounts receivable department manager at XYZ Foods. In this position, he developed a close relationship with one of the company's largest customers and used the relationship to defraud his employer. In return for a kickback, he offered to "manage" his company's receivable from the customer. By "managing" the large receivable, Rogers permitted the customer to pay later than would otherwise have been required. The customer's payable was not recognized as delinquent or past due. Because the receivable involved millions of dollars, paying 30 to 60 days later than was required cost Mark's employer $3 million in lost interest. The accounts receivable manager received kickbacks totaling $350,000 from the customer.*

Mark's fraud was discovered when an alert coworker realized that the company's accounts receivable turnover ratio was decreasing substantially. The coworker prepared an aging schedule of individual accounts receivable balances that identified the customer who was paying kickbacks to Mark as the source of the problem. A subsequent investigation revealed the kickback scheme.

The third example is a fraud that was discovered because of excessive credit memos. The case involved a fraud of more than $5,000 by a supervisor in the shipping department of a wholesale-retail distribution center warehouse facility.

> *The supervisor was responsible for the overall operations of the warehouse and had individual accountability for a cash fund that was used for collecting money (usually amounts of $25 to $500) from customers who came to the warehouse to pick up cash-on-delivery (COD) orders. The established procedures called for the supervisor to issue the customer a cash receipt, which was recorded in a will-call delivery log book. The file containing details on the customer order would eventually be matched with cash receipts by accounting personnel, and the transaction would be closed.*

> *Over a period of approximately one year, the supervisor defrauded the company by stealing small amounts of money. He attempted to conceal the fraud by submitting credit memos (with statements such as "billed to the wrong account," "to correct billing adjustment," or "miscellaneous") to clear the accounts receivable file. The accounts would be matched with the credit memo, and the transaction would be closed. A second signature was not needed on the credit memos, and accounting personnel asked no questions about credit memos originated by the supervisor of the warehouse.*

> *At first, the supervisor submitted only two to three fraudulent credit memos a week, totaling approximately $100. After a few months, however, he increased the amount of his theft to about $300 per week. To give the appearance of randomness—to keep the accounting personnel from becoming suspicious—the supervisor intermixed small credit memo amounts with large ones.*

> *The fraud surfaced when the supervisor accidentally credited the wrong customer's account for a cash transaction. By coincidence, the supervisor was on vacation when the error surfaced (and the customer complained) and was not available to cover his tracks when accounting personnel queried the transaction. Because of his absence, the accounts receivable clerk questioned the manager of the warehouse, who investigated the problem. The manager scrutinized cash receipts and determined that fraud had occurred.*

## Faulty Journal Entries

Accounting is a language, just as English and Japanese are languages. For example, consider the following journal entry:

```
Legal Expense . . . . . . . . . . . 5,000
        Cash . . . . . . . . . . . . . . . . . . 5,000
```

In the English language, this entry says "An attorney was paid $5,000 in cash." In the language of accounting, this entry says "Debit Legal Expense; credit Cash." A person who speaks both accounting and English will realize that these statements say exactly the same thing.

The problem with the language of accounting is that it can be manipulated to lie just as English or Japanese or any other language can. For example, with the preceding journal entry, how do you know that an attorney was actually paid $5,000? Instead, maybe an employee embezzled $5,000 in cash and attempted to conceal the fraud by labeling the theft as a legal expense. Smart embezzlers sometimes conceal their actions in exactly this way, realizing that the fraudulent legal expense will be closed to Retained Earnings at the end of the accounting period, making the audit trail difficult to follow. And, if the fraudulent employers routinely pays large amounts of legal expenses, this small fraud could easily go unnoticed. To understand whether journal entries represent truth or are fictitious, one must learn to recognize journal entry fraud symptoms.

An embezzler usually steals assets, such as cash or inventory. (No one steals liabilities!) To conceal the theft, the embezzler must find a way to decrease either the liabilities or the equities of the victim organization. Otherwise, the accounting records will not balance and the embezzler will be quickly detected. Smart embezzlers understand that decreasing liabilities is not a good concealment method. In reducing payables, amounts owed are eliminated from the books. This manipulation of the accounting records will be recognized when vendors do not receive payments for amounts owed to them. When the liability becomes delinquent, they will notify the company. Subsequent investigation will usually reveal the fraud.

Smart embezzlers also realize that most equity accounts should not be altered. The owners' equity balance is decreased by the payment of dividends and expenses and is increased by sales of stock and by revenues. Embezzlers rarely conceal their frauds by manipulating either dividends or stock accounts, because these accounts have relatively few transactions and alterations can be quickly noticed. In addition, transactions involving stock or dividends usually require approval by the board of director and go through a transfer agent and are monitored closely.

By the process of elimination, only revenues and expenses remain as possibilities for decreasing the right side of the accounting equation and making the accounting records balance when stealing an asset. Balancing the equation by manipulating revenues would require that individual revenue accounts be reduced. However, because revenues increase or are zero, but rarely decrease (except through adjusting entries at the end of an accounting period), a decrease in a revenue account would quickly draw attention. Therefore, embezzlers who manipulate accounting records to conceal their frauds usually attempt to balance the accounting equation by increasing expenses. Increasing expenses decreases net income, which decreases retained earnings and owners' equity, thus leaving the accounting equation in balance, as illustrated in Figure 5-1.

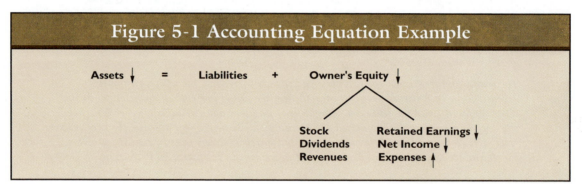

Figure 5-1 Accounting Equation Example

Recording an expense to conceal fraud involves making a fictitious journal entry. Fraud detectors must be able to recognize signals that a journal entry may not be legitimate and may be concealing a fraud. Manipulating expense accounts also has an advantage in that expenses are closed or brought to zero balances at year-end, thus obscuring the audit trail. The following are common journal entry fraud symptoms:

- Journal entries without documentary support
- Unexplained adjustments to receivables, payables, revenues, or expenses
- Journal entries that do not balance
- Journal entries made by individuals who would not normally make such entries
- Journal entries made near the end of an accounting period

To illustrate journal entry fraud symptoms, we will describe three actual embezzlements. The first, a $150,000 embezzlement by the controller of a bank, illustrates journal entries without support.

> *John Doe was the controller of a small bank. Over a period of several years, he embezzled approximately $150,000 from his employer by telephoning larger banks and having them pay his personal credit card bills. He concealed his fraud by creating fictitious journal entries to recognize the shortages as advertising expense. Because the total amount of advertising expense was large and the increase in expense resulting from his fraud was relatively small, no one ever questioned the legitimacy of his journal entries. Because he was the bank's controller and in charge of all accounting, he did not even forge fictitious documentation to support the entries. He was caught when he became more greedy and deposited in his own personal bank account a duplicate $10,000 payment from one of the bank's customers. When the customer realized he had paid twice, he asked for a refund, and the deposit was traced to John's account.*

If anyone had questioned the journal entries that were being made without documentary support, John's fraud would have been quickly discovered. In this case, however, if John had not become more greedy, his fraud might have continued indefinitely.

The second example of journal entry fraud symptoms is manipulation of income at Lincoln Savings and Loan. This example illustrates journal entries made at the ends of accounting periods to artificially inflate reported net income. For many successive quarters, large journal entries recorded fictitious revenues that took Lincoln Savings and Loan from a loss to a profit position.

The accounting firm that reviewed Lincoln's transactions (after the fraud was discovered) concluded that these 13 transactions overstated income by more than $100 million. The investigative auditors called the transactions the most egregious misapplication of accounting they had ever seen. If Lincoln's auditors and regulators had recognized the pattern of successive last-minute entries, Lincoln's massive fraud might have been ended much earlier and investors would have been spared millions of dollars of losses.

The third journal entry fraud was one that existed at Waste Management Corporation. In this case, the chief financial officer (CFO) who committed the fraud realized that the company's outside auditors only perform audits on the annual financial statements and that only a cursory (SAS 72) review was performed at the end of each quarter. Therefore, to overstate net income at the end of each quarter, he made a simple "topside" journal entry that debited or increased accounts receivable and credited or increased revenue. These entries, which cumulatively got larger each quarter during the year, were reversed at the start of each successive quarter. Then, at the end of the year, the fraud that had been committed with the topside entries was hidden in merger reserves by reversing into income excessive merger reserves and asset impairments that had been accrued. This type of fraud, where topside entries are made without any support, is quite egregious and was part of the financial statement fraud committed at several other companies as well.

## Inaccuracies in Ledgers

The definition of a ledger is "a book of accounts." In other words, all transactions related to specific accounts, such as cash or inventory, are summarized in the ledger. The accuracy of account balances in the ledger is often proved by ensuring that the total of all asset accounts equals the total of all liability and equity accounts or if revenues and expenses have not yet been closed out, that the total of all debit balances equals the total of all credit balances. Many frauds involve manipulating receivables from customers or payables to vendors. Most companies have master (control) receivable and payable accounts, the total of which should equal the sum of all the individual customer and vendor account balances. Two common fraud symptoms relate to ledgers:

1. A ledger that does not balance (i.e., the total of all debit balances does not equal the total of all credit balances)
2. Master (control) account balances that do not equal the sum of the individual customer or vendor balances

The first symptom is indicative of frauds in which a cover-up in the accounting records is not complete. For example, a perpetrator may embezzle inventory (an asset) but not record expenses or effect a decrease to the right-hand side of the accounting equation. In this case, the actual inventory balance, as determined by a physical count, is lower than the recorded amount of inventory, and the ledger does not balance. Another example of a ledger out of balance would be the theft of cash accompanied by the failure to record an expense. In this case, total assets would be less than total liabilities plus owners' equity.

The second ledger symptom is indicative of manipulation of an individual customer or vendor's balance without altering the master receivable or payable account in the ledger. In this case, the sum of the individual customer or vendor balances does not agree with the master account balance.

An example of fraud characterized by this second ledger symptom was perpetrated by the bookkeeper for a small bank. Using the following schemes, she embezzled more than $3 million from the bank, which had only $30 million in total assets.

*Note: The Federal Reserve is the "bankers' bank; that is, every bank has one or more accounts at the Federal Reserve. When a check drawn on one bank is sent to the Federal Reserve by a different bank, the Federal Reserve increases the account of the depositing bank and decreases the account of the bank on which the check was drawn. The Federal Reserve then accumulates all checks drawn on a given bank and sends them back to that bank in what's called the incoming cash letter. All checks drawn on different banks and sent to the Federal reserve for credit are sent to the Federal Reserve in what is called the outgoing cash letter.*

*Using two different schemes, Marjorie defrauded First National Bank of Atlanta of more than $3 million. Her first scheme involved writing personal checks on her bank account at First National to pay for expensive art, jewelry, automobiles, home furnishings, and other expensive acquisitions. Then, when her check would be sent from the Federal Reserve to the bank (in the incoming cash letter), she would allow the overall demand deposit account balance to be reduced but would pull her checks before they could be processed and deducted from her personal account. The result of this scheme was that the master demand deposit account balance was lower than the sum of the bank's individual customers' demand deposits. The second scheme involved making deposits into her account by using checks drawn on other banks and then pulling the checks before they were sent in the outgoing cash letter to the Federal Reserve. Thus, her checks were never deducted from her accounts at the other banks. In fact, her accounts at the banks did not contain sufficient funds to cover the checks if they had been processed. The result of this scheme was that the individual demand deposit balances increased, but the master demand deposit account balance did not.*

*Both of these schemes had the effect of making the master demand deposit account balances lower than the sum of the individual account balances. Over time, as Marjorie wrote checks and made fictitious deposits, the difference between the sum of the individual accounts and the master account balances became larger and larger.*

*At the end of each accounting period, to cover her tracks and prevent the auditors from discovering the fraud, Marjorie would pull some official bank checks (cashier's checks) that had previously been used and send them in the outgoing cash letter to the Federal Reserve. Because the Federal Reserve procedures were automated, no one there ever personally examined the checks or noticed that they had already been processed several times. (In fact, some of the checks were totally black from being processed so many times.) Her fraud was assisted by the Federal Reserve's policy of giving immediate credit to First National for the total amount supposedly contained in the outgoing cash letter. The next day, as the checks were processed using bank routing numbers, the Federal Reserve would realize that the official checks were not drawn on other banks but were really First National's own checks and would reverse the credit previously given to First National. The reduction would again throw First National's ledger accounts out of balance. But, for one day—the day the auditors examined the records—the bank's books would be balanced and the shortage would be "parked" at the Federal Reserve. Because the financial statements were prepared for that one day, the bank records balanced for the auditors and the Federal Reserve confirmed the illegitimate receivable from them as being real.*

This fraud could easily have been discovered if someone had noticed that, although the books balanced at month-end, they were out of balance during the rest of the month. Bank managers received daily statements of condition and other reports that showed demand deposit balances significantly different from the balances on the financial statements. They never questioned these unusual balances.

This fraud could also have been uncovered if someone had recognized many other symptoms and several control weaknesses. For example, Marjorie had significant personality conflicts with other employees, and she lived a lifestyle far beyond what her income would have supported. In addition, individual accounting records had been altered, and a previous fraud at the same bank had indicated a need for reports and procedures that, if implemented, would have made the fraud impossible. Surprisingly, the fraud was not discovered until a cashier's check that Marjorie had reused several times was kicked out of a Federal Reserve sorter because it could not be read.

# Internal Control Weaknesses

As discussed previously, fraud occurs when pressure, opportunity, and rationalization come together. Many individuals and organizations have pressures. Everyone rationalizes. When internal controls are absent or overridden, the fraud triangle is completed, increasing the risk of fraud.

As discussed in Chapter 2, internal control is comprised of the control environment, the accounting system, and control procedures. Common internal control fraud symptoms include the following:

- Lack of segregation of duties
- Lack of physical safeguards
- Lack of independent checks
- Lack of proper authorization
- Lack of proper documents and records
- Overriding of existing controls
- Inadequate accounting system

Many studies have found that the element most common in frauds is the overriding of existing internal controls. Three examples of control weaknesses that allowed fraud to occur are discussed next. In the first, a control weakness allowed a customer to defraud a bank of more than $500,000. In the second, a significant internal control weakness allowed a fraud to continue over several years.

> *Lorraine was a customer of Second National Bank. She opened her account 16 months previously, and she often made deposits and withdrawals in the hundreds of thousands of dollars. She claimed to be a member of a well-known wealthy family. She drove a Porsche, dressed nicely, and was able to earn the trust and confidence of the bank's branch manager. One day, she approached the manager and said that she needed a cashier's check in the amount of $525,000. The manager, realizing that she had only $13,000 in her account, first denied the request. Then, deciding that she was a valued customer, and based on her promise to cover the shortage the next day, gave her the cashier's check. It turned out that she was not who she claimed to be. In fact, she was an embezzler who had stolen more than $5 million from her employer; all the funds that had gone through her bank account were stolen. Her employer had caught her and promised not to seek prosecution if she would repay the company. She was stealing from Second National to repay the money.*

As it turned out, Second National had a control requiring two signatures on all cashier's checks exceeding $500,000. However, the bank manager, who was an imposing figure, had "ordered" his assistant to sign the cashier's check. Without making an independent decision and because the manager told him to sign, the assistant had merely followed the manager's order without questioning the appropriateness of the request. As a result, the control that required two independent signatures was compromised. Both the assistant and the manager, who are now unemployed, later wished the assistant had made an independent, informed decision.

The second example of an internal control weakness fraud is the famous Hochfelder case, which went all the way to the U.S. Supreme Court before it was decided that Ernst & Ernst (now Ernst and Young), a large public accounting firm, had not been negligent in performing the audit.

> *Lestor B. Nay, the president of First Securities Co. of Chicago, fraudulently convinced certain customers to invest funds in escrow accounts that he represented would yield a high return. Instead of actual escrow accounts, Nay converted the customers' funds to his own use.*
>
> *The transactions were not in the usual form of dealings between First Securities and its customers. First, all correspondence with customers was done solely by Nay. Because of a "mail rule" that Nay had imposed, such mail was opened only by him. Second, checks of the customers were made payable to Nay. Third, the escrow accounts were not reflected on the books of First Securities, nor in filings with the SEC, nor in connection with customers' other investment accounts. The fraud was uncovered only after Nay's suicide.*

*Respondent customers sued in district court for damages against Ernst & Ernst as aiders and abettors under Section 10b-5 of the 1933 SEC Act. They alleged that Ernst & Ernst had failed to conduct a proper audit, which would have led them to discover the mail rule and the fraud. The court reasoned that Ernst & Ernst had a common law and statutory duty of inquiry into the adequacy of First Securities' internal control system, because the firm had contracted to audit First Securities and to review the annual report filings with the SEC.*

*The U.S. Supreme Court reversed the decision of the court of appeals, concluding that the interpretation of Section 10b-5 required the "intent to deceive, manipulate or defraud." Justice Powell wrote, in the Supreme Court's opinion: "When a statute speaks so specifically in terms of manipulation and deception, and of implementing devices and contrivances—the commonly understood terminology of intentional wrongdoing—and when its history reflects no more expansive intent, we are quite unwilling to extend the scope of the statute to negligent conduct."*

*The Supreme Court pointed out that in certain areas of the law, recklessness is considered to be a form of intentional conduct for purposes of imposing liability.*

In this case, the mail rule that required that no one except Lester B. Nay open the mail was an internal control weakness. Had this weakness not been allowed, Nay's fraud would probably have been revealed much earlier and investors would not have lost nearly so much money.

The third case is a simple one. A few years ago, one of the authors of this text had a new home built by a building contractor. Shortly after the home was finished, the author received a call from the builder whom he had now come to know quite well. The building contractor told the author that his secretary/bookkeeper had stolen more than $10,000 and he had caught her. When asked how she did it, the builder replied, "She both wrote checks and reconciled the bank statement." To steal the money, she had simply written checks to herself and then listed the checks as "outstanding" on the bank reconciliation. The builder caught her when he had to submit bank statements to a lender for a loan and the amount shown on the bank statements was significantly different from what he had been told it was. After he discovered the theft, he called this book's author and asked what he should do. The author told him that people who embezzle and are not prosecuted have a high likelihood of committing fraud again and that he should probably fire her and have her prosecuted. He didn't and the second time, the secretary/bookkeeper stole more than $25,000.

Small business owners should follow three simple procedures when they can't afford sufficient numbers of employees to guarantee a segregation of duties. The first is that they should always open the bank statement themselves and, if possible, reconcile the bank statement. Second, they should pay everything by check to ensure a record. Third, they should sign every check themselves and not delegate the signing to anyone else. These simple procedures, if done on a timely basis, will prevent many frauds from occurring.

## Analytical Fraud Symptoms

Analytical fraud symptoms are procedures or relationships that are unusual or too unrealistic to be believable. They include transactions or events that happen at odd times or places; that are performed by or involve people who would not normally participate; or that include odd procedures, policies, or practices. They also include transactions and amounts that are too large or too small, that are performed or occur too often or too rarely, or that result in too much or too little of something. Basically, analytical symptoms represent anything out of the ordinary. They are the unexpected.

Common examples of analytical symptoms include:

- Unexplained inventory shortages or adjustments
- Deviations from specifications
- Increased scrap
- Excess purchases

- Too many debit or credit memos
- Significant increases or decreases in account balances, ratios, or relationships
- Physical abnormalities
- Cash shortages or overages
- Excessive late charges
- Unreasonable expenses or reimbursements
- Excessive turnover of executives
- Strange financial statement relationships, such as:
  - Increased revenues with decreased inventory
  - Increased revenues with decreased receivables
  - Increased revenues with decreased cash flows
  - Increased inventory with decreased payables
  - Increased volume with increased cost per unit
  - Increased volume with decreased scrap
  - Increased inventory with decreased warehousing costs

An example of fraud detected by considering analytical relationships was the Mayberry fraud.

> *The internal auditors for the Mayberry Corporation, a conglomerate with about $1 billion in sales, were auditing the company's sheet metal division. Every past audit had resulted in favorable outcomes with few audit findings. This year, however, something did not seem right. Their observation of inventory had revealed no serious shortages, and yet inventory seemed dramatically overstated. Why would inventory increase five-fold in one year? Suspecting something was wrong, the auditors performed some "midnight auditing." Their investigation revealed that the sheet metal inventory was grossly overstated. The auditors had almost been deceived. Local management had falsified the inventory by preparing fictitious records. The auditors had verified the amount of inventory shown on the tags and had deposited their verifications in a box in the conference room they used during the audit. A manager had added spurious tags to the box at night. However, since there was not enough time to fabricate a large number of reasonable tags, some were made to show very large rolls of sheet metal. The manger had also substituted new inventory reconciliation lists to conform with the total of the valid and spurious tags.*

The magnitude of the fraud was discovered when the auditors performed some analytical tests. First, they converted the purported $30 million of sheet metal inventory into cubic feet. Second, they determined the volume of the warehouse that was supposed to contain the inventory. At most, it could have contained only one-half the reported amounts; it was far too small to house the total. Third, they examined the inventory tags and found that some rolls of sheet metal would weigh 50,000 pounds. However, none of the forklifts that were used to move the inventory could possibly lift more than 3,000 pounds. Finally, the auditors verified the reported inventory purchases and found purchase orders supporting an inventory of about 30 million pounds. Yet, the reported amount was 60 million pounds.

Faced with this evidence, managers admitted that they had grossly overstated the value of the inventory to show increased profits. The budget for the sheet metal division called for increased earnings, and without the overstatement, the earnings would have fallen far short of target.

In this case, it was the relationship between amounts recorded and the weight and volume that the recorded amounts represented that did not make sense. Unfortunately, few managers or auditors ever think of examining physical characteristics of inventory.

Sometimes, it is not unusual relationships that signal fraud but transactions or events that do not make sense. Such was the case with the following fraud:

> *Don was the business manager of Regal Industries. In this position, he often arranged and paid for services performed by various vendors. An alert accountant caught Don committing a fraud. The first symptom observed by the accountant was payments being made to an Oldsmobile dealership, though the company only had a few company cars and all were Cadillacs. The accountant thought it strange that the company cars were being serviced at an Oldsmobile dealership rather than at a Cadillac dealership. He*

*knew that both cars were made by General Motors (GM), but still wondered about the transactions. Maybe the Oldsmobile dealership was closer, he reasoned. Upon checking, he discovered that it was not. Further investigation by the accountant revealed that although payments had also been made to the Oldsmobile dealership for body damage on company cars, no claims had been filed with insurance companies. The accountant also noticed that payments of exactly the same amount were being made to the Oldsmobile dealer every month. The combination of Oldsmobile dealer, body damage without corresponding insurance claims, expenditures every month, and expenditures of the same amount did not make sense. He concluded that the only legitimate explanation for all these anomalies would be a fixed-fee maintenance contract with the Oldsmobile dealer to service the company's Cadillacs. An investigation revealed that no such maintenance contract existed. Further investigation confirmed that Don had a girlfriend who worked at the Oldsmobile dealership, and that he was buying her a car by having the company make the monthly payments.*

In this case, an alert accountant saved his company approximately $15,000. Unfortunately, many accountants and auditors would have missed this fraud. They would probably have seen the check being paid to the Oldsmobile dealer, matched it with the invoice that Don's girlfriend supplied each month, and been satisfied. They would not have asked whether the expenditure made sense or why Cadillacs were being serviced at an Oldsmobile dealership.

Recognizing analytical symptoms has always been an excellent method of detecting fraud. A successful fraud investigator became interested in investigation when he discovered his first fraud. This discovery, which determined his lifelong career, is one of the best examples of the use of analytical symptoms. Here is the career-changing experience.

*It was the summer of 1956. That's what I remember, at least, though it was a long time ago and things get distorted when you look back. And, I have looked back quite a bit since then, for the entire episode was quite an eye-opener for an 18-year-old kid. I was a "numbers man" then and still am. Mathematics is an art to me. I find a beauty in pure numbers that I never see in the vulgar excesses that most of society chases after. I was working in a movie theater that summer because I needed employment. I'd just graduated from South High and was waiting to begin college. To earn money, I took a job as a ticket taker at the Classic Theater. As movie theaters go, the Classic was considered one of the best. It had a certain charm in the same way that drive-in hamburger joints of the decade did. But it was not the kind of job that a dedicated numbers man usually sought. As it turned out, my numbers did come in useful—for that's how I caught on to him.*

*Ticket taking is not the most exciting job there is, and I didn't find it a real intellectual challenge. My mind was free to wander, and I got in the habit of noting the number of each ticket that I tore: 57, 58, 59, 60. Sometimes I noticed the sequence would be off. A whole chunk of numbers would appear that should have come through earlier: 65, 66, 40, 41, 42. It would happen almost every time I worked. I thought it was odd and was curious about what could be disturbing the symmetry of my numbers. I came to realize that it always happened after my daily break. The manager, Mr. Smith, would relieve me while I was on break. I watched closer and noticed another fact: the numbers would always be off while the ticket seller, who had the break after mine, was being relieved. Mr. Smith filled in for the ticket seller too.*

*After more observation and thought, I solved Mr. Smith's scheme. When he relieved me as ticket taker during my break, he would pocket the tickets instead of tearing them in two. Then, when he relieved the ticket seller, he would resell the tickets he had just pocketed and keep the cash. Thus, the ticket numbers that I saw coming through out of sequence were really coming through for the second time.*

Although this small fraud took place in a little theater, it illustrates that when things do not look right, they probably are not right. If the ticket taker had not been fascinated with numbers, the manager probably would not have been detected. The manager was trusted more than other workers. The number of tickets he pocketed was small in relation to the total number of tickets sold in a day, and so management did not see a large drop in profits. Every night, the bookkeeper computed the total number of tickets sold, using the beginning and ending ticket numbers, and compared the total to the cash taken in. Unfortunately, the balance was not wrong. The theater hired separate people to sell and take tickets specifically to avoid this type of fraud. But Smith was the manager, and no one perceived a problem with letting him do both jobs while others were on break. Smith's fraud would not have been caught without the "numbers man" who saw relationships in the numbers that did not make sense.

This same kind of relationship between numbers is available in financial statements. To individuals who really understand accounting, financial statements tell a story. The elements of the story must be internally consistent. Many large financial statement frauds could have been discovered much earlier if financial statement preparers, auditors, analysts, and others better understood numbers in the financial statements.

One of the best examples of financial statement numbers that did not make sense was the numbers in MiniScribe Corporation's financial statements. MiniScribe was a Denver-based producer of computer disk drives. Here is a description of the MiniScribe fraud and an analysis of the numbers in the firm's financial statements that did not make sense.

*On May 18, 1989, MiniScribe Corporation announced that the financial statements issued for 1986, 1987, and the first three quarters of 1988 could not be relied upon because sales and net income had been grossly overstated.*

*In 1988, MiniScribe was voted the most "well-managed" personal computer (PC) disk drive company. The company had experienced an increase in sales from $113.9 million in 1985, a year in which it lost International Business Machines (IBM)—its largest customer—to a reported $603 million in 1988. In April 1985, Quentin Thomas Wiles was appointed CEO and director of the company, with the hope that he might lead the company, which was operating in the red, out of financial trouble. Under his management, the company's sales and profits seemed to increase, even though downturns in the market and severe price cutting were taking place within the industry. Unfortunately, the financial statement numbers were fraudulent.*

*Wiles had a reputation for using a strict, overbearing management style to reach his goal of turning failing companies into successes. At MiniScribe, he set stringent goals for each manager to increase sales and income and did not tolerate failure to reach these goals. In an effort to please Wiles, reports were forged and manipulated throughout the company. One marketing manager revealed that division managers were told to "force the numbers" if they needed to. Thus, the fraud began with managers simply touching up internal documents as they moved up the line. Wiles continued, however, to push for increases in sales, even during times of recession and price cutting within the industry. This pressure led managers to invent various schemes to make the company look better than it really was. Some of the schemes used were:*

- *Packaging bricks, shipping them, and recording them as sales of hard drives.*
- *Dramatically increasing shipments to warehouses and booking them as sales.*
- *Shipping defective merchandise repeatedly and booking the shipments as sales.*
- *Shipping excess merchandise that was not returned until after the financial statements had been released.*
- *Understating bad debts expense and the allowance for doubtful accounts.*
- *Changing shipping dates on shipments to overseas customers so that revenues were recognized before sales were made.*
- *Changing auditors' working papers.*

*The result of these and other schemes was a significant overstatement of net income and sales. Inventory records as of the end of 1987 revealed $12 million on hand; in reality, it was more like $4 million. In 1989, the company booked a $40 million charge to income to offset these overstatements. On January 1, 1990, the company filed for bankruptcy, listing liabilities of $257.7 million and only $86.1 million in assets.*

Several analytical symptoms indicated that things were not right at MiniScribe. First, MiniScribe's results were not consistent with industry performance. During the period of the fraud, severe price cutting was going on, sales were declining, and competition was stiff. MiniScribe Corporation reported increases in sales and profits, while other companies were reporting losses. MiniScribe had few large customers and had lost several major customers, including Apple Computer, IBM, and Digital Equipment Corporation (DEC). MiniScribe was also falling behind on its payments to suppliers. Returns to suppliers forced the bankruptcy of MiniScribe's major supplier of aluminum disks, Domain Technologies.

In addition, numbers that were reported at the end of each quarter were amazingly close to the projections made by Wiles. Financial results were the sole basis for management bonuses. Although receivable showed significant increases, the allowance for doubtful accounts was far less than the industry average. An aging of receivables revealed that many accounts were old and probably not collectable. A simple correlation of inventory with sales would have revealed that as reported sales were increasing, inventory failed to increase proportionately. Indeed, financial statement numbers did not make sense. Relationships within the statements, relationships with industry standards, and an examination of MiniScribe's customers provided analytical symptoms suggesting that something was seriously wrong. Unfortunately, by the time these symptoms were recognized, investors, auditors, lawyers, and others had been fooled, and many people had lost money in the scam

Several research papers focused on different kinds of analytical "symptoms" to determine whether they have predictive value. For example, one study examined the relationship between high management turnover and financial distress and accounting fraud. This paper, based on an analysis of SEC Accounting and Auditing Enforcement Releases between 1990 and 2000 found that fraud firms are more likely to be financially distressed and have higher management turnover (both analytical symptoms) than are non-fraud firms.[1]

Auditors often use analytical procedures (APs) to look for analytical fraud symptoms. Unfortunately, APs are not always effective because sometimes analytical relationships stay the same even when fraud is being perpetrated. Such was the case at WorldCom. In this case, significant decreases in the purchase of fixed assets were offset by improper capitalization of expenses, thus leaving the relative amount of increases in assets about the same from period to period. Here is what happened at WorldCom.

> *On July 8, 2002, Melvin Dick, Arthur Andersen's former senior global managing partner, technology, media, and communications practice, testified before the House Committee on Financial Services:*
>
> > *We performed numerous analytical procedures at various financial statement line items, including line costs, revenues in and plant and service, in order to determine if there were significant variations that required additional work. We also utilized sophisticated auditing software to study WorldCom's financial statement line items, which did not trigger any indication that there was a need for additional work.*
>
> *Dick's statement is an acknowledgment that APs failed to detect the greatest management fraud in history. Why?*
>
> *While the details of Andersen's APs have not been disclosed, it would not be unreasonable to assume that Andersen used sophisticated procedures. The nature of the problem the firm faced may be illustrated by comparing key financial statement ratios for WorldCom with those of seven other publicly held communications companies: Sprint, AT&T, Nextel, Castle Crown, AmTelSat, U.S. Cellular, and Western Wireless. Five ratios, all related to revenues, expenses, and (gross) plant and equipment are... information, taken from the companies' SEC filings.*
>
> *We know now that WorldCom's revenues, expenses, and property and equipment were materially misstated in 2000 and 2001. The first two ratios—cost of revenues to revenues, and the change in cost of revenues to the change in revenues showed declining trends for WorldCom, but nothing that would be characterized as unusual. By 2001, WorldCom was in the middle of the pack.*

> *The property, plant and equipment ratios revealed greater volatility in the WorldCom values, but normal values for the critical years 2000 and 2001. If anything, these ratios showed unusual changes in the years preceding the fraud (1996–1998).*
>
> *Each of these ratios, or some variation, might have been considered by Andersen. Because the ratios are presented at high levels of aggregation, they may not be sufficiently sensitive to display unusual behavior. One can only assume that Andersen's "sophisticated auditing software" disaggregated the data and analyzed them at a more refined level. Nevertheless, these ratios suggest why no unusual behavior was revealed to Andersen: Management had manipulated the data to conform to expectations. Writing in the Mississippi Business Journal (July 22, 2002), James R. Crockett, an accounting professor at the University of Southern Mississippi, noted that "WorldCom had previously invested heavily in capital equipment and had quit making as much investment. By shifting expenses to plant and equipment accounts, WorldCom was able to disguise the changing conditions by meeting expectations." In other words, the historical trend no longer applied, but management manipulated the data to make it appear as though that trend continued to be valid.[2]*

## Extravagant Lifestyles

Most people who commit fraud are under financial pressure. Sometimes the pressures are real; sometimes they represent mere greed. Once perpetrators meet their financial needs, they usually continue to steal, using the embezzled funds to improve their lifestyles. Often they buy new cars. They sometimes buy other expensive toys, take vacations, remodel their homes or move into more expensive houses, buy expensive jewelry or clothes, or just start spending more money on food and other day-to-day living expenses. Few perpetrators save what they steal. Indeed, most immediately spend everything that they steal. As they become more and more confident in their fraud schemes, they steal and spend increasingly larger amounts. Soon they are living lifestyles far beyond what they can reasonably afford. To illustrate how people's lifestyles change when they embezzle, consider the following two examples.

> *Kay embezzled nearly $3 million from her employer. She and her husband worked together to perfect the scheme over a period of seven years. Because they knew they might someday get caught, they decided explicitly not to have children. With their stolen funds, they purchased a new, expensive home (supposedly worth $500,000) and five luxury cars—a Maserati, a Rolls Royce, a Jeep Cherokee, and two Audis. They filled their home with expensive artwork and glass collections. They bought a boat and several expensive computers, and they paid cash to have their yard extensively landscaped. They frequently invited Kay's coworkers to parties at their home and served expensive foods, including lobster flown in from the East Coast. Yet none of the employees noticed the change in lifestyle. They did not note, for example, that Kay drove a different car to work every day of the week, and that all her cars were extremely expensive.*
>
> *Randy stole more than $600,000 from his friend's small company, for which he worked. The business constantly had cash flow problems, but Randy drove a Porsche, bought a cabin in the mountains, and took expensive vacations. At one point, he even loaned his friend $16,000 to keep the business going. Never once did the owner question where the money was coming from, even though Randy was being paid less than $25,000 per year.*

Embezzlers are people who take shortcuts to appear successful. Few crooks, at least those who are caught, save embezzled money. The same motivation for stealing seems to also compel them to seek immediate gratification. People who can delay gratification and spending are much less likely to possess the motivation to be dishonest.

Lifestyle changes are often the easiest of all symptoms to detect. They can be helpful in detecting fraud against organizations by employees and others but not as helpful in detecting fraud on behalf of a corporation, such as management fraud. If managers, coworkers, and others pay attention, they notice embezzlers living lifestyles that their incomes do not support. Although lifestyle symptoms provide only circumstantial evidence of fraud, such evidence is easy to corroborate. Bank records, investment records, and tax return information are difficult to access, but property records, Uniform Commercial Code (UCC) filings, and other records are easy to check to determine whether assets have been purchased or liens have been removed.

## Unusual Behaviors

Research in psychology reveals that when a person (especially a first-time offender, as many fraud perpetrators are) commits a crime, he or she becomes engulfed by emotions of fear and guilt. These emotions express themselves in an extremely unpleasant sensation called stress. The individual then exhibits unusual and, usually, recognizable behavior patterns to cope with the stress, as shown in Figure 5-2.

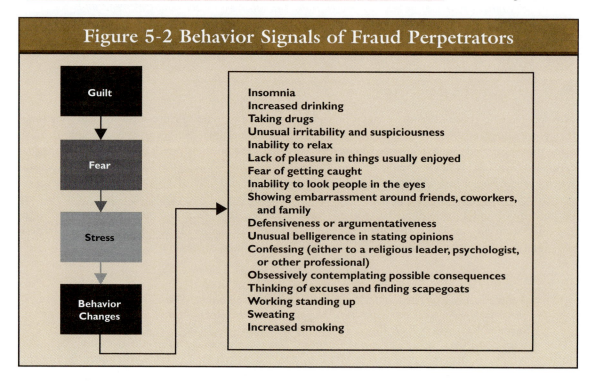

### Figure 5-2 Behavior Signals of Fraud Perpetrators

Guilt → Fear → Stress → Behavior Changes

Insomnia
Increased drinking
Taking drugs
Unusual irritability and suspiciousness
Inability to relax
Lack of pleasure in things usually enjoyed
Fear of getting caught
Inability to look people in the eyes
Showing embarrassment around friends, coworkers, and family
Defensiveness or argumentativeness
Unusual belligerence in stating opinions
Confessing (either to a religious leader, psychologist, or other professional)
Obsessively contemplating possible consequences
Thinking of excuses and finding scapegoats
Working standing up
Sweating
Increased smoking

No particular behavior signals fraud; rather, changes in behavior are signals. People who are normally nice may become intimidating and belligerent. People who are normally belligerent may suddenly become nice.

Even perpetrators recognize their behavioral changes. A woman who stole more than $400,000 said, "I had to be giving off signals. I could not look anyone in the eye." A man who embezzled $150,000 said, "Sometimes I would be so wound up I would work 12 or 14 hours a day, often standing up. Other times I would be so despondent I could not get off the couch for over a week at a time." Eddie Antar, mastermind of the Crazy Eddie fraud, became very intimidating and then finally vanished.

*Crazy Eddie, Inc., a 42-store retail company located in New York, New Jersey, Connecticut, and Pennsylvania, sold entertainment and consumer electronic products. Eddie hired his father, his brother, his uncle, his cousin, and his father's cousin as officers of the company. Allegedly, he overstated inventory by more than $65 million. As the fraud progressed, he was said to have become increasingly overbearing. Finally, overwhelmed by fears that he would be caught and prosecuted, he skipped the country and ended up in Israel. He has since been extradited back to the United States and is now facing charges for his fraud.*

Two other examples of changes in behavior motivated by the stress caused by committing fraud were the behaviors of both Donald Sheelen, CEO of Regina Vacuum Company, and Lester B. Nay, CEO of First National of Chicago. Although their actions were different, neither was able to cope with the stress. Although his fraud had not been discovered, Donald Sheelen went to his priest and confessed his entire scheme. Lester B. Nay's actions were even more dramatic. After penning a suicide note detailing how he had defrauded investors of millions of dollars, he took his life. However a perpetrator copes with the stress caused by guilt—by being intimidating, by confessing, or by committing suicide—stress always seems to be present.

The following fraud that occurred in a small company illustrates how stress can change the behavior of a perpetrator.

*Johnson Marine is an industrial diving company that services marine-related problems all over the eastern United States. The firm salvages downed aircraft in oceans, lays submarine pipelines, inspects dams, conducts insurance recoveries, and performs search-and-rescue missions. Johnson's part-time accountant, Rick Smith, uncovered a serious fraud that had been perpetrated by Joseph Simons, vice president of the company. After Rick was hired by the office manager, Joseph told Rick that he was to report only to him, to pay bills only when he asked, and to ask only him whenever he had a question. It was apparent to Rick that the office manager was intimidated by Joseph. Joseph not only treated the office manager like a slave but also continually reminded him that if he did not mind his own business, he would no longer be with the company.*

*Rick's first job was to update all the balances in accounts payable. Upon close inspection, he found very few of the 120 balances to be correct. He spent a week fixing them on the computer, only to be criticized by Joseph. Joseph said that Rick should spend his time on more productive work and not worry about trivial things. When Rick opened the petty cash box and tried to identify the petty cash system, he found none. He found that no petty cash reconciliation had been done in over five months, and that a negative difference of $13,600 existed between checks written to replenish the cash box and total receipts in the cash box. Rick immediately went to Joseph to tell him what he had found and was told to make an adjusting entry on the computer to fix the problem.*

*Rick's next discovery came when he reviewed the company's life insurance policies, two of which were for more than $1 million. Joseph was listed as the beneficiary. Next, Rick noticed that large balances were being accrued on the company's American Express card. Although overdue notices were being received, Joseph forbade Rick to pay the bill. When Rick asked the president about it, the president informed Rick that the company did not have an American Express card. Yet, the balance was over $5,500. A similar problem was occurring with the Phillips 66 bill. Again, Joseph told Rick not to pay the bill, even though final notices were being sent. Rick later learned that the company used only Chevron cards.*

*Looking back over the accounts payable balances, Rick noticed an account with TMC Consulting that had an outstanding balance more than 90 days old. He tried to find out more about the account, but there was nothing on file. By coincidence, while he was looking at the account information, Rick noticed that the address was 10 Windsor Circle, the same address to which Rick had sent a diving catalog that was addressed to Joseph two weeks previously. Upon printing out a history of the company's transactions with TMC Consulting, Rick found a series of five $2,000 payments on the account spread over a period of several months. He presented this information to the president, who confronted Joseph. Joseph stalled the president until the next day but never came back. Investigation revealed that he had moved to California, leaving no forwarding address.*

In this case, Joseph's intimidating personality had kept the office manager and others at a distance. Although the office manager seemed to know something was wrong, he had never been given the chance to find out. The office manager had always been blamed by Joseph when petty cash was out of balance, yet he had never been allowed to balance it. In fact, Joseph had constantly blamed others for problems.

In retrospect, employees understood that Joseph's intimidating behavior was his way of keeping the fraud from being discovered and of dealing with the stress he felt because he was committing the crime.

The largest fraud to ever be perpetrated in Australia was HIH, a fraud that was discovered in 2002. The HIH fraud was concealed for years by an executive who changed his behavior to intimidate others so that they did exactly what he wanted. By becoming almost totalitarian, he essentially was able to do anything he wanted. Here is the story.

> *HIH was one of Australia's biggest home-building market insurers. HIH was the underwriter for thousands of professional indemnity, public liability, home warranty, and travel insurance policies. HIH Investment Holdings Limited, a related company, invested proceeds from premium policies. The collapse of HIH resulted in losses of $3 billion to investors.[3]*
>
> *HIH was started in 1968 by Raymond Williams and Michael Payne. Michael Payne was chief executive of the U.K. operations until 1997 when health problems forced him to limit his activities in the company. He became chairman of the main U.K. entity in 1999. He was an executive director of the holding company from 1992 until June 1998 and a nonexecutive director from July 1998 until September 2000. Raymond Williams was the chief executive officer for HIH from its inception in 1968 until October 2000.*
>
> *Other key employees were George Sturesteps and Terrence Cassidy, who became members of senior management in 1969 and 1970, respectively. They both held their positions until September 2000 and March 2001, respectively.*
>
> *Williams was the dominant member of management at HIH. Although many close members of upper management team had been with him for over 25 years, they were reluctant to tell him how to run the business, give suggestions, question motives or Williams's business decisions. The Royal Commission report, which summarizes the Australian government's investigation into HIH, suggested that a lack of strategic direction and of questioning authority set the stage for the eventual downfall of the HIH Insurance group. If asked about the strategic goals or mission of HIH, the report states that neither Williams nor the Board of Directors would have been able to explain them. Although HIH was a public company that had grown quickly, the report states that Williams continued to run HIH much like the small company it had been when they first started. That is, he made most of the decisions, he used business accounts as personal accounts, he overrode internal controls and so forth. Within an environment dominated by a larger-than-life CEO, Ray Williams, the board presided over a string of ill-fated expansions—which cost HIH more than $3 billion—without ever analyzing the group's strategy or assessing its risks.*
>
> *Although the Royal Commission report points to many different ancillary reasons for the HIH downfall, they summed up the main problem as HIH did not provide properly for future claims and the failure of all involved to understand the degree of the short-fall. Apparently, HIH's financial statements were misstated because of inflated profits, overstated accounts, and understated liabilities. According to the report, all other problems were supportive in nature and helped to promote HIH's downfall.*
>
> *Like Enron and WorldCom, the investigation into HIH found breakdowns of governance and oversight structures at basically every level. HIH's board, management, auditors, and regulator were, it appears, incompetent and lacked diligence. It didn't help that almost everyone supposed to oversee management was misled. It has been argued that HIH didn't fail because of any systemic fraud but because of an inherent flaw in its business model—it consistently underprovided for its claims—and the dysfunctional nature of its governance structures, caused largely by the willingness of the board and senior management to allow themselves to be dominated by Williams. There was insufficient ability and independence of mind in and associated with the organization to see what had to be done and what had to be stopped or avoided. Risks were not properly identified and managed. Unpleasant information was hidden, filtered, or sanitized. And, there was a lack of skeptical questioning and analysis when and where it mattered.*

> *The external checks also failed, with the Royal Commission report stating that while the auditors had been misled and the quality of HIH's accounting and information systems was deficient, the auditors had failed to detect the "manifest deficiencies" in how the accounts were prepared and presented and had to accept some of the responsibility. [Arthur Andersen, the company's auditor, is now out of business.]*

> *The diligence of other organizations who had responsibility such as APRA's, the regulator, has been questioned seriously. Apparently, ARPA missed many warning signs, was slow to act and made misjudgments about vital matters. Virtually no one who had any involvement with HIH escaped unscathed. HIH experienced a near-total breakdown of governance and supervisory structures. None of the checks and balances within the systems functioned. The people involved failed to meet their responsibilities.*

Once in a while, someone commits a fraud or other crime and does not feel stress. Such people are called sociopaths or ***psychopaths***. They feel no guilt because they have no conscience. The following case is an example of a psychopathic individual.

> *Confessed killer Marvin Harris's ability to pass a lie detector test left two nationally known polygraph experts baffled and anxious to question the dealer in bogus documents on how he passed the test.*

> *Harris pleaded guilty to the bombing deaths of two people, which he said he had carried out to avoid exposure of his fraudulent documents dealings. He had been judged truthful during an earlier polygraph test and had denied his involvement with the slayings.*

> *What was most puzzling to the polygraph experts was that Harris did not just sneak by on the tests. On the plus-minus scale used to gauge truthfulness, a score of plus 6 would have been considered a clear indication that the subject was not lying; but Harris had scored twice that—plus 12. The experts were simply wrong. Apparently, Marvin Harris had no conscience and thus felt no guilt about creating bogus documents or killing people.*

## Tips and Complaints

Auditors are often criticized for not detecting more frauds. Yet, because of the nature of fraud, auditors are often in the worst position to detect its occurrence. The factors that make fraud possible were depicted in a triangle. These factors consist of pressure, opportunity, and rationalization. As we illustrated in previous chapters, the ***elements of fraud*** can also be illustrated as shown in Figure 5-3.

The *theft act* involves the actual taking of cash, inventory, information, or other assets. Theft can occur manually, by computer, or by telephone. *Concealment* involves the steps taken by the perpetrator to hide

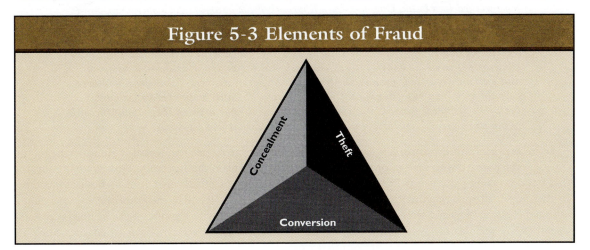

### Figure 5-3 Elements of Fraud

the fraud from others. Concealment can involve altering financial records, miscounting cash or inventory, or destroying evidence. *Conversion* involves selling stolen assets or transferring them into cash and then spending the cash. If the asset taken is cash, conversion means merely spending the stolen funds. As noted previously, virtually all perpetrators spend their stolen funds.

Fraud can be detected in all three elements. First, in the theft act, someone can witness the perpetrator taking cash or other assets. Second, in concealment, altered records or miscounts of cash or inventory can be recognized. Third, in conversion, the lifestyle changes that perpetrators almost inevitably make when they convert their embezzled funds are visible.

Who in an organization is in the best position to recognize fraud in each of these elements? Certainly, in the theft act, it is not the auditors. Auditors are rarely present when funds are stolen or fraud is committed. Rather, they spend one or two weeks on periodic audits, and thefts usually stop during the audit periods. Instead, coworkers, managers, and other employees are usually in the best position to detect fraud in the theft act stage.

In concealment, auditors do have a chance to detect fraud. If audit samples include altered documents, miscounts, or other concealment efforts, auditors may detect fraud. Similarly, they may see internal control weaknesses or analytical relationships that don't make sense. However, company accountants and even coworkers are probably in a better position to detect fraud in concealment.

At the conversion stage, the auditors are definitely not in the best position to detect fraud. For example, auditors could almost never recognize certain changes, such as an employee who used to drive a used Ford Focus now drives a new BMW or Lexus. Likewise, auditors will not recognize a perpetrator's unusual activities, such as wearing designer clothes, taking expensive vacations, buying expensive jewelry, or buying a new home with stolen funds. Auditors do not have a reference point from which to see these changes in lifestyle. Again, it is coworkers, friends, and managers who should detect fraud in conversion.

Although coworkers and managers are in the best position to detect fraud, they are usually the least trained to recognize fraud or even be aware that it can exist. Even so, many frauds are detected when an employee, a friend, a manager, a customer, or another untrained person provides a tip or complaint that something is wrong. One large company, for example, which uncovered more than 1,500 individual frauds, discovered 43 percent of the frauds on the basis of customer complaints or employee tips.

Complaints and tips are categorized as fraud symptoms rather than actual evidence of fraud because many tips and complaints turn out to be unjustified. It is often difficult to know what motivates a person to complain or provide a tip. Customers, for example, may complain because they feel they are being taken advantage of. Employee tips may be motivated by malice, personal problems, or jealousy. Tips from spouses and friends may be motivated by anger, divorce, or blackmail. Whenever tips or complaints are received, they must be treated with care and considered only as fraud symptoms. Individuals should always be considered innocent until proven guilty and should not be unjustly suspected or indicted. Tips can be spurious, as shown in the following example.

> *Joan worked in a bank. One day, Joan approached the bank branch's operations manager and informed her that two weeks ago she had seen Jean, a coworker, place a bundle of bills (currency) in her blouse. She said that for two weeks she had not been able to sleep, so she had finally decided to inform the bank. For several days, auditors and security people scoured the bank's records and cash vault. Employees cried, and suspicion and distrust abounded. Finally, the fraud investigators discovered that Jean had been sleeping with Joan's boyfriend, and Joan's tip was false and motivated by jealousy. Joan then resigned. Because of the nature of the event that aroused the jealousy, branch management could not inform all employees about what had happened.*

In most organizations, coworkers and others have knowledge or suspicions that fraud is occurring but do not come forward with their information. Several reasons explain this hesitancy. First, knowing for sure that fraud is taking place is usually impossible. Because fraud does not involve dead bodies or videotapes of the crime, all that potential informants see are symptoms. They may see someone experiencing a changed lifestyle, behaving strangely, or stashing company inventory in a garage. Because they recognize that they are seeing only symptoms, they do not want to wrongly accuse. Even when suspicions are strong, legitimate reasons for the symptom may exist.

Second, informants may be hesitant to come forward because they have often read or heard horror stories about what happens to whistle-blowers. Even though such reports are usually anomalies and are often exaggerated, people often fear that they will suffer or undergo some reprisal if they become informants. The new whistle-blower protection laws mandated by the Sarbanes-Oxley Act are attempts to eliminate this fear and provide protection for whistle-blowers.

Third, employees and others are often intimidated by perpetrators. Especially when perpetrators are superiors, subordinates are afraid to come forward with their suspicions. For example, one fraud continued for six years, even though seven coworkers knew about it. The perpetrator had such a dominant personality that he made others afraid of him, and he quickly fired people who questioned his integrity.

Fourth, many of us have been conditioned to believe that it is not good to squeal on others, even when they are doing something wrong. Technically, one who will not tell on another is an ethnological liar. Not squealing is the creed of the Mafia. As an illustration of people's general reluctance to become an informant, consider the following actual event.

> *Scott was a junior in high school, enrolled in a word processing class. He was informed that students' grades for the class would be mostly determined by how many processed projects they completed. The teacher informed the students that they must work alone, and, in fact, that working together constituted cheating and would result in an F for the course. One night, Scott informed his dad that the best grade he could get in word processing was a B unless he cheated, and then he could probably get an A.*

> *"What do you mean?" Scott's dad asked.*

> *"Well," said Scott, "our grades are mostly based on the number of jobs we complete. And while we have been told we must work alone, a number of student groups have formed in the class. Within these groups, each member completes a certain number of projects and then they all copy each other's disks as though they had completed the projects themselves. There is no way I can complete as many projects alone as a group of three or four students can. I have been invited to work in a group, but I do not know whether I should. What do you want me to do, Dad? Should I cheat and get an A or settle for a B?"*

> *Needless to say, Scott's dad was frustrated. Although he did not want Scott to cheat, he did not want him to be disadvantaged and earn a B either. His counsel to Scott was to do neither but to go to the teacher and inform her what was happening. Scott's quick reply was "I can't." When asked why, Scott said, "These are my friends," he said, "and it would not be right to squeal on them."*

A fifth reason most employees and others have not historically come forward with their suspicions or knowledge of fraud is that organizations have not made it easy for them to do so. In most organizations, employees do not know to whom they should talk if they suspect fraud, how the information should be conveyed, or what the consequences would be if they did come forward. In addition, they did not know whether their tips would remain anonymous or whether their squealing would be exposed.

The new whistle-blowing laws fixed this problem, especially for public companies, by mandating that every public company have a whistle-blower system in place and that it be promoted among employees and others.

These new whistle-blowing laws should be effective in helping reveal many frauds that would not have been discovered otherwise. Even before these laws were passed, some organizations found that effectively encouraging and dealing with tips could make a difference. They found that by giving employees easy avenues for whistle-blowing they did discover frauds. Domino's Pizza, for example, for years, made available a hotline for drivers to call if managers send them out with so little time that they would have to speed in order to deliver a pizza within the allotted 30 minutes. Complete anonymity is guaranteed. Another company included fraud in a list of such undesirable actions as drug use, safety violations, discrimination, and harassment. It trained all employees what to do if they saw any of these activities. In this company, the training took the form of seminars for new hires, posters and other periodic reminders, a billfold card listing alternative actions employees could take if they witnessed violations, and videos that were periodically shown. Employees were told, and the information was reinforced on the billfold card, that they had five options if they suspected problems in any of these areas: (1) they could talk to their manager or to their manager's manager; (2) they could call corporate security at a specified number; (3) they could call internal audit at a specified number; (4) they could call a companywide ombudsman, who forwarded the complaint or tip; or (5) they could call an 800-number hotline, which connected them to an independent monitoring service that screened the calls, guaranteed anonymity, and forwarded the information to relevant company individuals who dealt with the problem.

Whistle-blowing systems should not be considered substitutes for maintaining an open environment in which employees feel comfortable about reporting known or suspected fraudulent activities. Employees should be encouraged to first consider reporting such activities to someone in their management chain, to an internal auditor, to corporate security, or to legal counsel. They should, however, be kept aware of the hotline option and encouraged to use it if they are not comfortable with other options.

Companies that provide hotlines have detected numerous frauds that would not otherwise have been detected. These companies have also reported that the hotline use is somewhat erratic, with periods of considerable use and periods of very little use. What is important is to create a reporting option for employees who would not otherwise reveal suspected activities.

Many organizations have adopted whistle-blowing systems that are managed by third parties. Some organizations have even gone so far as to reward employees for legitimate tips. Even though research evidence suggests that hotlines are an excellent fraud detection tool, the evidence about rewarding employees for tips is mixed at best.

Three frauds that were detected by tips and complaints or that involved whistle-blowers are the GE fraud, the Revere Armored Car Company fraud, and Enron. A description of GE's fraud follows:

> *A few years ago, John Michael Gravitt, a machine foreman at GE, stood up at an assertiveness training session and told the class that GE was ripping off the government. He told approximately 30 colleagues that the time cards going into supervisor's offices were not the same ones coming out. Within a few minutes several other foremen stood up to confirm Gravitt's story. Even after his outburst in the assertiveness class, Gravitt's superiors still pressured him to coax his subordinates to cheat on their time cards. Gravitt was told that if his subordinates would not alter their own time cards, he was to do so. When Gravitt refused, his supervisors altered the cards for him. According to Gravitt, the process was hardly subtle. "With black or blue felt-tipped pens, they (the supervisors) altered the billing vouchers. Usually they scrawled the number of a project safely within cost constraints over the number of a job that was already running over budget. Foremen who refused to falsify vouchers had their vouchers sent to the unit manager, Robert Kelly. Kelly would then complete the blank vouchers himself. When Kelly died, his successor, Bill Wiggins, continued the falsification of time cards and billing vouchers. At one time, Wiggins told Gravitt that GE was like a great big pie and that everyone who participated (in cheating) got a piece; those who did not participate did not get a slice.*

> *Falsifying at GE had become a way of life. One foreman confessed to personally altering 50 to 60 percent of his subordinates' time cards during an eight-month period. Once, when Gravitt told his foreman that he could go to jail for altering cards, the foreman replied that he was only carrying out orders and that there was not any chance of getting caught. Finally, Gravitt decided he needed to alert someone who could do something about the problem. One weekend he slipped into a secretary's office and photocopied about 150 altered time cards and billing vouchers. He wrote an eight-page letter explaining what had been going on. The next week, he delivered the letter and the photocopies to Brian H. Rowe, the senior vice president in charge of the engine plant. The same day, Gravitt was dismissed from GE. A subsequent investigation by the FBI and the Defense Contract Audit Agency revealed that $7.2 million of idle time had been falsely billed to the U.S. government. They also found that 27 percent of the time-sheet vouchers in the shop where Gravitt worked had been falsified during the three years Gravitt worked at GE.*

In this case, John Gravitt's tips were the sole reason fraud was detected. Certainly GE did not make it easy for Gravitt to come forward. GE's fraud highlights many of the mistakes that companies make regarding informants. Even though Gravitt knew that fraud was occurring, the firm's punishment and intimidation of whistle-blowers and their not making it easy to come forward allowed the fraud to be concealed for a long time.

A second fraud revealed by tips was the Revere Armored Car case, in which the informants were competitors.

> *The revelation of fraud at Revere Armored Car began when some competitors, tired of losing customers to Revere's cutthroat prices, employed a video camera. In December 1992, the competitors taped a Revere delivery of $100 million to the New York Federal Reserve Bank's Buffalo branch. They were hoping for evidence of shoddy security. They got it. In the parking lot of a highway restaurant, the tape showed the driver and a guard leaving the truck locked but unguarded, its engine running, while they went inside to eat. The competitors presented their tape to Lloyd's of London, the underwriting group that had insured Revere for $100 million. The tape was aimed at demonstrating to Lloyd's the "ease with which someone could whack 'em." The video prompted Lloyd's to hire an investigator to check out Revere. Among other things, the investigation turned up evidence of past wrongdoings. Based on the evidence, federal authorities launched a pre-dawn raid on Revere headquarters and found what could be the biggest scandal ever in the armor-truck industry: millions of dollars missing, allegedly pilfered by Revere owners Robert and Susanna Scaretta. Of the $84.6 million that banks say they had in storage at Revere, only $45 million was discovered. Apparently the Scarettas had run up significant gambling debts. They may have been using Armored Car as a money-laundering operation for illegal gambling proceeds. Several banks lost considerable amounts of money in this fraud. Citicorp's Citibank lost more than $11 million, and Marine Midland Bank lost nearly $34.8 million.*

This fraud was allowed to continue because banks and Lloyd's of London did not perform adequate due diligence. Neither the banks nor Lloyd's were regularly monitoring Revere's operations. If it had not been for the tip from competitors, this fraud might still be going on today. Revere had been commingling funds of different banks rather than keeping each bank's funds separate. Even though large amounts had been stolen, it was always able to have enough money on hand to satisfy auditors of any one bank at a given time.

Enron is probably the most famous fraud in the history of the United States. Although it is famous for many reasons, one reason it will be forever known is the anonymous whistle-blower letter that was sent to its CEO, Kenneth Lay, by Sherron Watkins. Sensing that something was seriously wrong at Enron, Watkins wrote the letter shown in Figure 5-4.

## Figure 5-4 Watkins's Whistle-Blower Letter to Enron Chairman

Has Enron become a risky place to work? For those of us who didn't get rich over the last few years, can we afford to stay?

Skilling's abrupt departure will raise suspicions of accounting improprieties and valuation issues. Enron has been very aggressive in its accounting—most notably the Raptor transactions and the Condor vehicle. We do have valuation issues with our international assets and possibly some of our EES MTM positions.

The spotlight will be on us, the market just can't accept that Skilling is leaving his dream job. I think that the valuation issues can be fixed and reported with other good will write-downs to occur in 2002. How do we fix the Raptor and Condor deals? They unwind in 2002 and 2003, we will have to pony up Enron stock and that won't go unnoticed.

To the layman on the street, it will look like we recognized funds flow of $800 million from merchant asset sales in 1999 by selling to a vehicle (Condor) that we capitalized with a promise of Enron stock in later years. Is that really funds flow or is it cash from equity issuance?

*continued*

## Figure 5-4 Watkins's Whistle-Blower Letter to Enron Chairman (continued)

We have recognized over $550 million of fair value gains on stocks via our swaps with Raptor. Much of that stock has declined significantly—Avici by 98 percent from $178 million, to $5 million; the New Power Company by 80 percent from $40 a share, to $6 a share. The value in the swaps won't be there for Raptor, so once again Enron will issue stock to off-set these losses. Raptor is an LJM entity. It sure looks to the layman on the street that we are hiding losses in a related company and will compensate that company with Enron stock in the future.

I am incredibly nervous that we will implode in a wave of accounting scandals. My eight years of Enron work history will be worth nothing on my résumé, the business world will consider the past successes as nothing but an elaborate accounting hoax. Skilling is resigning now for "personal reasons" but I would think he wasn't having fun, looked down the road and knew this stuff was unfixable and would rather abandon ship now than resign in shame in two years.

Is there a way our accounting gurus can unwind these deals now? I have thought and thought about a way to do this, but I keep bumping into one big problem—we booked the Condor and Raptor deals in 1999 and 2000, we enjoyed wonder-fully high stock price, many executives sold stock, we then try and reverse or fix the deals in 2001, and it's a bit like rob-bing the bank in one year and trying to pay it back two years later. Nice try, but investors were hurt, they bought at $70 and $80 a share looking for $120 a share and now they're at $38 or worse. We are under too much scrutiny and there are probably one or two disgruntled "redeployed" employees who know enough about the "funny" accounting to get us in trouble.

What do we do? I know this question cannot be addressed in the all-employee meeting, but can you give some assur-ances that you and Causey will sit down and take a good hard objective look at what is going to happen to Condor and Raptor in 2002 and 2003?

Summary of Alleged Issues:

RAPTOR Entity was capitalized with LJM equity. That equity is at risk; however, the investment was completely offset by a cash fee paid to LJM. If the Raptor entities go bankrupt LJM is not affected, there is no commitment to contribute more equity.

The majority of the capitalization of the Raptor entities is some form of Enron N/P, restricted stock and stock rights.

Enron entered into several equity derivative transactions with the Raptor entities locking in our values for various equity investments we hold.

As disclosed in 2000, we recognized $500 million of revenue from the equity derivatives offset by market value changes in the underlying securities.

This year, with the value of our stock declining, the underlying capitalization of the Raptor entities is declining and credit is pushing for reserves against our MTM positions.

To avoid such a write-down or reserve in quarter one 2001, we "enhanced" the capital structure of the Raptor vehicles, committing more ENE shares.

My understanding of the third-quarter problem is that we must "enhance" the vehicles by $250 million.

I realize that we have had a lot of smart people looking at this and a lot of accountants including AA & Co. have blessed the accounting treatment. None of that will protect Enron if these transactions are ever disclosed in the bright light of day. (Please review the late 90's problems of Waste Management (news/quote)—where AA paid $130 million plus in litigation re questionable accounting practices.)

The overriding basic principle of accounting is that if you explain the "accounting treatment" to a man in the street, would you influence his investing decisions? Would he sell or buy the stock based on a thorough understanding of the facts? If so, you best present it correctly and/or change the accounting.

My concern is that the footnotes don't adequately explain the transactions. If adequately explained, the investor would know that the "entities" described in our related party footnote are thinly capitalized, the equity holders have no skin in the game, and all the value in the entities comes from the underlying value of the derivatives (unfortunately in this case, a big loss) AND Enron stock and N/P. Looking at the stock we swapped, I also don't believe any other company would have entered into the equity derivative transactions with us at the same prices or without substantial premiums from Enron. In other words, the $500 million in revenue in 2000 would have been much lower. How much lower?

Raptor looks to be a big bet if the underlying stocks did well, then no one would be the wiser. If Enron stock did well, the stock issuance to these entities would decline and the transactions would be less noticeable. All has gone against us. The stocks, most notably Hanover, the New Power Company and Avici are underwater to great or lesser degrees.

I firmly believe that executive management of the company must have a clear and precise knowledge of these transactions and they must have the transactions reviewed by objective experts in the fields of securities law and accounting. I believe

*continued*

# Figure 5-4 Watkins's Whistle-Blower Letter to Enron Chairman (continued)

Ken Lay deserves the right to judge for himself what he believes the probabilities of discovery to be and the estimated damages to the company from those discoveries and decide one of two courses of action:

1. The probability of discovery is low enough and the estimated damage too great; therefore we find a way to quietly and quickly reverse, unwind, write down these positions/transactions.

2. The probability of discovery is too great, the estimated damages to the company too great; therefore, we must quantify, develop damage containment plans and disclose.

I firmly believe that the probability of discovery significantly increased with Skilling's shocking departure. Too many people are looking for a smoking gun.

Summary of Raptor Oddities:

1. The accounting treatment looks questionable.

   a. Enron booked a $500 million gain from equity derivatives from a related party.

   b. That related party is thinly capitalized with no party at risk except Enron.

   c. It appears Enron has supported an income statement gain by a contribution of its own shares.

One basic question: The related party entity has lost $500 million in its equity derivative transactions with Enron. Who bears that loss? I can't find an equity or debt holder that bears that loss. Find out who will lose this money. Who will pay for this loss at the related party entity?

If it's Enron, from our shares, then I think we do not have a fact pattern that would look good to the S.E.C. or investors.

2. The equity derivative transactions do not appear to be at arms length.

   a. Enron hedged New Power, Hanover and Avici with the related party at what now appears to be the peak of the market. New Power and Avici have fallen away significantly since. The related party was unable to lay off this risk. This fact pattern is once again very negative for Enron.

   b. I don't think any other unrelated company would have entered into these transactions at these prices. What else is going on here? What was the compensation to the related party to induce it to enter into such transactions?

3. There is a veil of secrecy around LJM and Raptor. Employees question our accounting propriety consistently and constantly. This alone is cause for concern.

   a. Jeff McMahon was highly vexed over the inherent conflicts of LJM. He complained mightily to Jeff Skilling and laid out five steps he thought should be taken if he was to remain as treasurer. Three days later, Skilling offered him the C.E.O. spot at Enron Industrial Markets and never addressed the five steps with him.

   b. Cliff Baxter complained mightily to Skilling and all who would listen about the inappropriateness of our transactions with LJM.

   c. I have heard one manager-level employee from the principal investments group say, "I know it would be devastating to all of us, but I wish we would get caught. We're such a crooked company." The principal investments group hedged a large number of their investments with Raptor. These people know and see a lot. Many similar comments are made when you ask about these deals. Employees quote our C.F.O. as saying that he has a handshake deal with Skilling that LJM will never lose money.

4. Can the general counsel of Enron audit the deal trail and the money trail between Enron and LJM/Raptor and its principals? Can he look at LJM? At Raptor? If the C.F.O. says no, isn't that a problem?

Condor and Raptor Work:

1. Postpone decision on filling office of the chair, if the current decision includes C.F.O. and/or C.A.O.

2. Involve Jim Derrick and Rex Rogers to hire a law firm to investigate the Condor and Raptor transactions to give Enron attorney-client privilege on the work product. (Can't use V & E due to conflict—they provided some true sale opinions on some of the deals).

3. Law firm to hire one of the big 6, but not Arthur Andersen or PricewaterhouseCoopers due to their conflicts of interest: AA & Co. (Enron); PWC (LJM).

4. Investigate the transactions, our accounting treatment and our future commitments to these vehicles in the form of stock, NP, etc., For instance: In the third quarter we have a $250 million problem with Raptor 3 (NPW) if we don't "enhance" the capital structure of Raptor 3 to commit more ENE shares. By the way: in Q. 1 we enhanced the Raptor 3 deal, committing more ENE shares to avoid a write-down.

*continued*

## Figure 5-4 Watkins's Whistle-Blower Letter to Enron Chairman (continued)

5. Develop cleanup plan:

   a. Best case: Clean up quietly if possible.

   b. Worst case: Quantify, develop P.R. and I.R. campaigns, customer assurance plans (don't want to go the way of Salomon's trading shop), legal actions, severance actions, disclosure.

6.   Personnel to quiz confidentially to determine if I'm all wet:

   a. Jeff McMahon

   b. Mark Koenig

   c. Rick Buy

   d. Greg Walley

To put the accounting treatment in perspective I offer the following:

1. We've contributed contingent Enron equity to the Raptor entities. Since it's contingent, we have the consideration given and received at zero. We do, as Causey points out, include the shares in our fully diluted computations of shares outstanding if the current economics of the deal imply that Enron will have to issue the shares in the future. This impacts 2002–2004 earnings-per-share projections only.

2. We lost value in several equity investments in 2000, $500 million of lost value. These were fair-value investments; we wrote them down. However, we also booked gains from our price risk management transactions with Raptor, recording a corresponding PRM account receivable from the Raptor entities. That's a $500 million related party transaction—it's 20 percent of 2000 IBIT, 51 percent of NI pretax, 33 percent of NI after tax.

3. Credit reviews the underlying capitalization of Raptor, reviews the contingent shares and determines whether the Raptor entities will have enough capital to pay Enron its $500 million when the equity derivatives expire.

4. The Raptor entities are technically bankrupt; the value of the contingent Enron shares equals or is just below the PRM account payable that Raptor owes Enron. Raptor's inception-to-date income statement is a $500 million loss.

5. Where are the equity and debt investors that lost out? LJM is whole on a cash-on-cash basis. Where did the $500 million in value come from? It came from Enron shares. Why haven't we booked the transaction as $500 million in a promise of shares to the Raptor entity and $500 million of value in our "economic interests" in these entities? Then we would have a write-down of our value in the Raptor entities. We have not booked the latter, because we do not have to yet. Technically we can wait and face the music in 2002–2004.

6. The related party footnote tries to explain these transactions. Don't you think that several interested companies, be they stock analysts, journalists, hedge fund managers, etc., are busy trying to discover the reason Skilling left? Don't you think their smartest people are poring over that footnote disclosure right now? I can just hear the discussions - "it looks like they booked a $500 million gain from this related party company and I think, from all the undecipherable half-page on Enron's contingent contributions to this related party entity, I think the related party entity is capitalized with Enron stock."…"No, no, no, you must have it all wrong, it can't be that, that's just too bad, too fraudulent, surely AA & Co. wouldn't let them get away with that?" "Go back to the drawing board, it's got to be something else. But find it!"…"Hey, just in case you might be right, try and find some insiders or `redeployed' former employees to validate your theory."

*Source: http://news.bbc.co.uk/1/hi/business/1764308.stm, accessed on June 1, 2004.*

The Watkins letter, together with whistle-blowing acts by Colleen Rowley of the FBI and Cynthia Cooper of WorldCom, resulted in the three of them being named Time Magazine's 2002 "Persons of the Year." As Time Magazine stated, "These three did the right thing by just doing their jobs rightly."

## KEY TERMS

**Accounting anomalies:** Inaccuracies in source documents, journal entries, ledgers, or financial statements.

**Analytical anomalies:** Relationships, procedures, or events that do not make sense.

**Elements of fraud:** The theft act, concealment, and conversion that are present in every fraud.

**Internal control weakness:** Weakness in the control environment, accounting system, or the control activities or procedures.

**Psychopath:** A person having a personality disorder, especially one manifested in aggressively antisocial behavior. A psychopath feels no stress when being dishonest.

## QUESTIONS AND CASES

### DISCUSSION QUESTIONS

1. How do fraud symptoms help in detecting fraud?
2. How do internal control weaknesses contribute to fraud?
3. What are accounting symptoms?
4. What are analytical symptoms?
5. How can lifestyle changes help in detecting fraud?
6. How can behavioral symptoms help in detecting fraud?
7. How can tips and complaints help in detecting fraud?
8. What is the theft act of a fraud?
9. What is conversion?
10. What is concealment?

### TRUE/FALSE

1. Analytical anomalies are present in every fraud.
2. Recording an expense is a possible way to conceal the theft of cash.
3. A check is an example of a source document.
4. Internal control weaknesses give employees opportunities to commit fraud.
5. Internal control is composed of the control environment, the accounting system, and control procedures (activities).
6. Analytical fraud symptoms are the least effective way to detect fraud.
7. Most people who commit fraud use the embezzled funds to save for retirement.
8. As fraud perpetrators become more confident in their fraud schemes, they steal and spend increasingly larger amounts.
9. First-time offenders usually exhibit no psychological changes.
10. Psychopaths feel no guilt because they have no conscience.
11. Fraud can be detected in all three elements of fraud.
12. The fraud elements consist of concealment, conversion, and completion.
13. Auditors can best help detect fraud in conversion.
14. Some complaints and tips turn out to be unjustified.
15. Fraud is a crime that is seldom observed.
16. Because of the nature of fraud, auditors are often in the best position to detect its occurrence.
17. Most people who commit fraud are under financial pressure.
18. Studies generally find that the most common internal control problem when frauds occur is having a lack of proper authorizations.
19. Fraud perpetrators who manipulate accounting records to conceal embezzlements often attempt to balance the accounting equation by recording expenses.
20. Employee transfers, audits, and mandatory vacations are all ways to provide independent checks on employees.

## MULTIPLE CHOICE

1. Which of the following is true regarding fraud?
   a. It is easily identified.
   b. It is seldom observed.
   c. When a fraud occurs, there is no question whether a crime has been committed.
   d. Many witnesses are usually available when fraud occurs.

2. Which of the following is *not* a fraud symptom related to source documents?
   a. Duplicate payments
   b. Missing documents
   c. A tip from an employee
   d. Photocopied documents

3. Which of the following is a fraud symptom related to an internal control weakness?
   a. Lack of proper authorization
   b. Lack of independent checks
   c. Inadequate accounting system
   d. Lack of physical safeguards
   e. All of the above

4. In the three elements of fraud (theft act, concealment, and conversion), who is usually in the best position to detect the fraud?
   a. Coworkers and managers
   b. Customers
   c. Owners
   d. Vendors

5. When a person commits a crime:
   a. He or she usually becomes engulfed by emotions of fear and guilt.
   b. He or she will experience no changes in behavior.
   c. He or she usually becomes friendly and nice.
   d. He or she experiences a lower stress level.

6. Most people who commit fraud:
   a. Use the embezzled funds to build a savings account.
   b. Give the embezzled funds to charity.
   c. Experience no change in their lifestyle.
   d. Use the embezzled funds to improve their lifestyle.
   e. All of the above are reasons coworkers and others are hesitant to come forward with information about suspected fraud.

7. Which of the following is *not* a reason why coworkers and others are hesitant to come forward with information about suspected fraud?
   a. It is usually possible to know for sure that fraud is taking place.
   b. They have read or heard horror stories about what happens to whistle-blowers.
   c. Employees and others are sometimes intimidated by perpetrators.

d. Many people are conditioned to believe that it is not good to squeal on others, even when it appears that they are doing something wrong.

8. Which of the following is *not one* of the categories of employee fraud symptoms?
   a. Accounting anomalies
   b. Analytical anomalies
   c. Tips and complaints
   d. Firm structure

9. Embezzlement of assets reduces the left side of the accounting equation. To conceal the theft, the embezzler must find a way to reduce the right side of the accounting equation. A perpetrator would most likely reduce the right side of the equation by:
   a. Reducing accounts payable.
   b. Paying dividends.
   c. Increasing expenses.
   d. Altering stock accounts.

10. Which of the following is *not* a fraud symptom related to journal entries?
    a. Unexplained adjustments to receivables, payables, revenues, or expenses
    b. Journal entries that do not balance
    c. Journal entries without documentary support
    d. Journal entries made near the beginning of accounting periods

11. Which of the following is *not* a common internal control fraud symptom or problem?
    a. Lack of segregation of duties
    b. Unexplained adjustments to receivables, payables, revenues, or expenses
    c. Lack of independent checks
    d. Overriding of existing controls

12. Once in a while, someone commits fraud or another crime and does not feel stress. Such people are referred to as:
    a. Psychopathic.
    b. Altruistic.
    c. Philanthropic.
    d. Magnanimous.

13. Fraud is usually detected by recognizing and pursuing:
    a. Synonyms.
    b. Symptoms.
    c. Equity.
    d. Legends.

14. A letter is most likely to be fraudulent if:
    a. It is signed only by one person.
    b. It is addressed to an individual, rather than a department.
    c. It is a photocopy of an original letter.
    d. It is written on outdated company letterhead.

15. If a perpetrator has stolen assets, which of the following is the easiest method for concealing the theft?
    a. Reduce liabilities (such as payables)
    b. Manipulate dividend or stock accounts
    c. Increase other assets (such as receivables)
    d. Increase expenses

16. Which of the following indicate common fraud systems relating to ledgers?
    a. A ledger that does not balance
    b. A ledger that balances too perfectly
    c. Master account balances that do not equal the sum of the individual customer or vendor balances
    d. Both a and c

## SHORT CASES

**Case 1.** Cal Jr. is the night manager at a local doughnut shop that is doing well. The shop sells doughnuts 7 days a week, 24 hours a day. Cal runs the graveyard shift by himself, because none of the other employees want to work at night. Since opening six months ago, Cal has not been able to find anyone to work for him and therefore has never missed one day of work. Cal makes his deposit every morning before going home.

Cal feels that he is overworked and underpaid. The franchise owner, Kenny Count, has praised Cal for his hard work and dedication to the company. Kenny's only concern was that, once or twice a week, an entire batch of traditional glazed doughnuts is thrown away because of overbaking. Despite these problems, Cal maintains a clean work environment and is considered a valuable employee.

Recently, Cal yelled at people on shifts before and after him for seemingly insignificant reasons. He was hired as manager because he gets along with everyone and is usually easy going. His recent irritability could stem from the fact that business is slowing down and he does not have much interaction with anyone at night. He also has been complaining that he has not been getting very much sleep. One day Cal came to work in a new BMW M3, the car of his dreams. Cal said that his dad helped him buy the car.

1. What areas of the business are most at risk for fraud?

2. Identify any symptoms of fraud that appear to exist at the doughnut shop.

3. What steps could be taken to reduce opportunities for fraud?

**Case 2.** James Monte owns a small Internet service provider business. Recently, customers have been complaining that they are overcharged and are not receiving timely customer service. Billing rates seem to increase without notice.

Five years ago, James used funding from several different investors in order to start his Internet service. Currently, he has 17 outstanding bills to be paid, all with late charges. Five of the bills include notices stating that lawsuits are pending. Also, he has not paid dividends to investors in two years.

Everyday James drives either his Mercedes Benz or his new Lexus to work. Before starting the business, James drove only one car, a Suzuki Samurai. James now lives in a palatial home and owns expensive furniture. Employees constantly ask James for new equipment, but the "boss" refuses to update the old equipment. Two weeks ago, James was irate and fired one of his accounting clerks for not depositing some checks on time. James is known for losing his temper.

1. Discuss any fraud symptoms that are present in this case.

2. Why would complaints from customers be a fraud symptom?

**Case 3.** Joan Bakers, along with three of her best friends, started her own ranching operation in Hawaii. The business began with two bulls and 20 heifers. After their first year, the partners were turning profits and everything seemed to be going well. The heifers were bred each year by using a patented new technique, and the steer population grew to 100 in two years. Most heifers would produce twins, and 90% were male. This ratio allowed for future breading of the remaining 10%.

New investment was needed, so limited partners were invited to join the partnership with an initial investment of $20,000 each. The partnership interests were advertised as "hot in the hands" and "very exclusive." In interviews, Joan Bakers described the investments as a "double-your-money, sure thing." She stated that the best way to get in was to act within 10 days of the initial offering of the investment. The annual report of the company showed enormous growth, with the pro forma statements predicting phenomenal success. Because of the exorbitant food prices in Hawaii, Joan says she can demand a premium for all cattle sold.

Based on this scenario, what symptoms of fraud exist?

**Case 4.** The text points out that tips and complaints are not evidence of fraud but instead are fraud symptoms. Do you agree with this statement and why?

**Case 5.** You are a staff auditor on an important audit engagement. You are assigned to audit two parts of your client's purchasing department. After several days of studying purchase orders and sales invoices, you notice that three vendors have identical addresses. After further examination, you notice that the documents only have one of the two required signatures for purchases of those accounts. You decided to interview the purchasing manager in charge of those accounts, but you discover that he is "out to lunch." While you are waiting for him, you notice through his office window a very nice Bose™ stereo system. It's the same stereo system you have been wanting, but will only be able to afford after you make partner.

What symptoms of fraud exist?

**Case 6.** You have been hired by a small firm to analyze its accounts receivable department and assess how susceptible it is to fraud. The company operates a table manufacturing facility. The only employee in accounts receivable is Joanne, an employee of 10 years. Joanne opens all cash receipts, credits the clients' accounts, and deposits the money at the bank. What fraud-related risks does this company face, and what changes, if any, should be made?

**Case 7.** Many people feel that it is the job of auditors to detect fraud. What circumstances make it difficult for auditors to detect fraud? Who is more likely to be in a good position to detect fraud?

**Case 8.** According to the chapter, which groups (auditors, managers, coworkers, company accountants, or friends) are in the best position to observe fraud symptoms in each of the three elements of fraud? Which group is surprisingly absent in each element?

**Case 9.** Sally was aware of a fraud being committed by one of her coworkers, but she never reported it. What are some possible reasons for her hesitancy to come forward?

**Case 10.** John Parker is the manager at a local store. The store opened four years ago and has been doing well. With current business growing, Parker decided to hire James Peter to work as an accountant. When Peter started working at the store, he found several things that appeared to be unusual. For example, six receiving documents were lost, the general ledger was out of balance, one customer complained that he is continually overcharged, and another customer complained that she does not receive timely service. John Parker lives in an expensive house and has several beautiful sports cars.

As a class, discuss whether fraud could be occurring. Does fraud actually exist, or are only fraud symptoms present?

## EXTENSIVE CASES

**Extensive Case 1** The balance sheet and income statement for ABC Company for the years 2002 and 2003 are as follows.

Perform vertical and/or horizontal analysis of the statements and identify two things that appear to be unusual and could be possible symptoms of fraud.

**Balance Sheet**

| | 2003 | 2004 |
|---|---|---|
| Cash | $ 460 | $ 300 |
| Accounts receivable | 620 | 480 |
| Inventory | 1,000 | 730 |
| Total assets | $ 2,080 | $ 1,510 |
| Accounts payable | $ 580 | $ 310 |
| Notes payable | 500 | 100 |
| Common stock | 400 | 400 |
| Retained earnings | 600 | 700 |
| Total liabilities and stockholders' equity | $ 2,080 | $ 1,510 |

**Income Statement**

| | 2003 | 2004 |
|---|---|---|
| Net sales | $ 550 | $ 840 |
| Cost of goods sold | 120 | 160 |
| Gross margin | $ 430 | $ 680 |
| Expenses: | | |
| Salaries | $ 100 | $ 150 |
| Warehousing costs | 80 | 120 |
| Advertising | 60 | 90 |
| Taxes | 45 | 75 |
| Total expenses | $ 285 | $ 435 |
| Net income | $ 145 | $ 245 |

## Extensive Case 2. "The Dude"[4]

In his own words, Daniel Feussner was "The Dude." With his waist-long dreadlocks, part-time rock band, and well-paid job managing Microsoft's online search directory—he seemed to have it all. Originally from Germany, Feussner, now age 32, earned his doctorate and taught at the University of Munich before coming to the U.S. where he started his career in computers. In 1996, Fuessner started working with Microsoft as a director of operations for U.S.-Speech Engineering Service and Retrieval Technology—working on a new, closely guarded search engine tied to the company's .NET concept.

Microsoft allows employees to order an unlimited amount of software and hardware, at no cost, for business purposes. Between December 2001 and November 2002, Feussner ordered or used his assistant and other employees (including a high school intern) to order nearly 1,700 pieces of software. He then resold them on the street for reduced prices—reaping more than $9 million. When items with a cost of goods sold of more than $1,000 are ordered, an e-mail is sent to the employee's direct supervisor, who must click on an "Approve" button before the order is filled. In no individual order was the cost of goods more than $1,000—he made sure none of the orders required a supervisor's approval. The loosely controlled internal ordering system reflects the trust the company puts in its employees.

In June, FBI agents said they saw Feussner exchanging a large box of software for cash in a Fred Meyer parking lot in Bellevue. The FBI contacted Microsoft security and began monitoring Feussner's bank accounts. Previously, one account with Washington Mutual Bank had an average balance of $2,159. In a short time, however, the average balance ballooned to $129,775. Another account with Wells Fargo showed irregular deposits totaling $500,000 —none of which appeared to be from any legitimate income or other legitimate source.

Investigators also noted that Feussner purchased a $95,000 Ferrari F355 Berlinetta, a $36,000 Jaguar XJ6, and traded in lesser vehicles for a $37,000 black Hummer, a Mercedes 500SEL, and a $21,900 Harley-Davidson. He also bought an $8,000 platinum diamond ring, a $2,230 Rolex wristwatch, and a $4,000 bracelet. "You figured that I like big boy's toys by looking at some of my pictures," Fuessner wrote on his personal Web page. "I just can't resist." The Dude's Web page includes a camera for monitoring his cat, Mr. Mietze Lebowski, and his photos of his yacht, cars, and other treasures. For a relatively low-level manager it was an impressive collection. But at Microsoft, where teenage software engineers can earn more than company directors, no one batted an eyelid.

Steve Schnase, who lived across the street from Feussner, said his neighbor was clearly wealthy, but not flamboyant with his money. He described Feussner as an intelligent man who didn't flaunt his education, would loan neighbors tools and was always friendly. Schnase was surprised to hear the accusations against someone he called his friend. All he knew about Feussner was that he was a good neighbor who loved cars. "He was very, very helpful. The few times I had problems with my PC, he'd come and help straighten them out," Schnase said. "They are just ideal neighbors. I feel terrible for him and his wife." Feussner and his wife lived in a modest 1960s split-level home.

In 2001, he joined the Bellevue Breakfast Rotary Club where he seemed more outgoing and personable than the stereotype techie said Steve Goldfarb, a Bellevue jeweler and immediate past president of the club. "He seemed like what I would expect a genius computer software developer to be."

The Dude was fired from Microsoft in December 2002, shortly after the fraud was discovered. He has been charged with 15 counts of wire, mail, and computer fraud—with each count carrying a maximum of five years in prison. He is expected to remain in custody until a preliminary hearing.

### Questions

1. Describe the symptoms of fraud that might be evident to a fellow Microsoft employee.

2. Recently, Microsoft has been putting more emphasis on controlling cost. With the slowing of the overall technology spending, executives ordered managers to closely monitor expenses and gave vice presidents greater responsibility for balance sheets. What positive or negative consequences might these changes pose for Microsoft in future fraud prevention?

3. As discussed in Chapter 2, all frauds involve the following key elements: perceived pressure, perceived opportunity, and rationalization. Describe two of the key elements of the Feussner fraud: pressure and opportunity.

4. From the scenario, what can you determine are measures Microsoft has taken that have or will prevent future frauds? In what ways could Microsoft improve?

**Extensive Case 3.** ABC Corp., a retailer, had the following comparative balance sheets at December 31, 2004:

|  | 12/31/03 | 12/31/04 |
|---|---|---|
| Cash | $ 800,000 | $ 900,000 |
| Accounts receivable | 4,000,000 | 4,250,000 |
| Inventory | 9,000,000 | 8,500,000 |
| Warehouse (net) | 10,000,000 | 10,500,000 |
|  | $23,800,000 | $24,150,000 |
| Accounts payable | $ 1,490,000 | $ 1,400,000 |
| Notes payable | 12,000,000 | 13,200,000 |
| Stockholders' equity | 10,310,000 | 9,500,000 |
|  | $23,800,000 | $24,150,000 |

Interest expense was $1.7 million in 2003 and $1.5 million in 2004. Other companies with credit ratings comparable to ABC's can borrow at 9 percent.

## Question

Based on this information, do you have any reason to believe that ABC is underreporting its liabilities? Discuss symptoms you looked for and the results of your analysis. Estimate the extent to which liabilities may be underreported.

**Extensive Case 4.** In June of a recent year, allegations of fraud regarding repair contracts for work onboard U.S. Naval Ships (USNS) were reported to law enforcement agents. The allegations indicated that fraud was rampant and could possibly impact the seaworthiness of these vessels. Employees from Bay Ship Management (BSM), the entity in charge of getting contracts for USNS, were demanding that a high volume of contracts be processed, and they were also demanding faster processing time for these contracts. When some employees started quitting because of increased pressure, BSM made sure it did not get attention from the federal government. BSM had close relationships with some of the subcontractors, but had always kept totally independent from these subcontractors. A task force of agents from the FBI, Defense Criminal Investigative Service, and the Naval Criminal Investigative Service was quickly formed to investigate. The task force agreed that the most effective approach to investigating possible fraud was the use of an undercover operation utilizing a covert contracting business.

## Questions

1. What are some of the symptoms of fraud in this case?

2. What questions would you ask yourself about fraud symptoms that might help you investigate this fraud?

3. Why would an undercover operation be the most effective approach to investigation?

**Extensive Case 5.** MKK is a high-tech company that produces miniature computer processor chips. MKK is one of the most successful companies in its industry because it is always developing faster and more efficient processors in order to maintain a competitive advantage. Sales and earnings have increased significantly in recent quarters causing MKK's stock prices to rise.

Hal Parks was recently appointed as new CFO of MKK Corporation. Hal is 45 years old and has worked at MKK for more than 15 years. Hal was promoted to CFO because he has an excellent understanding of MKK and the high-tech industry. Hal is well respected and knows everyone well.

At the close of the third quarter, Mark Kip, CEO of MKK, asked Hal and management to meet with him to discuss year-end projections. During the meeting, Hal noticed that Mark and other members appeared to be stressed and nervous that the company might not meet analysts' expectations because it had lost a contract with one of its major vendors.

In the following weeks, Hal noticed Mark and other key employees begin to appear more stressed and worried than normal. In addition, Hal recognized that Mark and one of his internal auditors would work continually into the night. At the close of the fourth quarter, everyone cheered when the company managed to meet its earnings expectations. Hal was relieved to see that the company achieved its goal, but couldn't help wondering whether something suspicious was going on.

## Questions

1. List and briefly describe the six different types of fraud symptoms.

2. Describe the different fraud symptoms present at MKK Corporation.

3. Assume that Hal has access to the company's income statement and balance sheet. What types of analysis can Hal perform to determine whether fraud may be occurring at MKK?

## INTERNET ASSIGNMENTS

1. How many different Web sites can you find dealing with fraud auditing and detection? Try a few different search strings in a search engine and see what sites are available. Also, locate the Association of Certified Fraud Examiners Web site at http://www.cfenet.com. What services do they offer?

2. Locate the Web site of the American Society of Questioned Document Examiners (ASQDE) at http://www.asqde.org. What is the ASQDE? What is its purpose?

# END NOTES

1. http://207.36.165.114/NewOrleans/Papers/1401559.pdf

2. http://www.nysscpa.org/cpajournal/2004/204/essentials/p32.htm, accessed on June 1, 2004.

3. Much of this discussion came from the HIH Royal Commission Report and from articles written about the report, such as those found at http://www.smh.com.au/articles/2003/04/16/1050172655327.html.

4. Chris Ayres, "Microsoft and the Dude's Downfall," *The Times*, London (December 14, 2002)

# CHAPTER 6

# PROACTIVE APPROACHES TO DETECTING FRAUD

## LEARNING OBJECTIVES

After studying this chapter, you should be able to:

1. Explain the importance of proactive fraud detection.
2. Describe the role commercial data-mining software plays in detection.
3. List the advantages and disadvantages of data mining and digital analysis.
4. Recognize Benford's law.
5. Understand inductive fraud detection.
6. Identify how fraud is detected by analyzing financial statements.

*In 1996, Yasuo Hamanaka, a trader for Sumitomo Trading Company of Japan, was convicted of committing fraud totaling approximately $2. 6 billion. Hamanaka, widely thought to be a trading genius, supposedly controlled 5 percent of the world's copper market and 50 percent of the copper futures traded on the London Metals Exchange. Unfortunately, Hamanaka was not a genius at all but a rogue trader, and many of his trades were fictitious, causing tremendous losses for his company. His fictitious trading had been going on for several years, starting quite small in the late 1980s and eventually increasing to several hundred million dollars a year before he was caught in 1996.*

*Hamanaka was first employed in the copper trading division of Sumitomo Corporation in the mid-1980s. Copper trading had not been profitable, and another employee began creating some fictitious off-the-books transactions to make the division look profitable. Before retiring, this employee brought Hamanaka into the fraud.*

*Hamanaka was much more successful in "managing" the fraud so it wouldn't be detected by his colleagues. Most of his dishonest transactions were conducted through Sumitomo's Hong Kong affiliate, which didn't follow the controls established by the Tokyo headquarters. Through a series of complicated swap, hedge, and other types of derivatives and futures transactions, he was able to fool his superiors at Sumitomo into believing he was making huge profits for the company. In fact, in the early 1990s, Sumitomo featured Hamanaka in its annual report as its "star" trader. Before he was caught through an investigation of the Commodity Futures Trading Corporation (CFTC) in the United States, Hamanaka was widely known as "Mr. 5%." In subsequent civil litigation, a number of U. S. and international firms were sued by Sumitomo for complicity with Hamanaka. Most of these cases were settled out of court, so the world will never know whether Hamanaka acted alone or whether he had accomplices.*

Hamanaka's fraud is typical in that it started small and grew geometrically over time. Had it been detected early on, Sumitomo Corporation would have saved itself billions of dollars. Proactive fraud detection is one of the most effective ways to minimize a company's losses due to fraud.

In Chapter 5, we discussed the symptoms of fraud and how to recognize them. Most frauds are detected by management and fellow employees—by accident, through a tip or complaint of wrongdoing—rather than by proactive efforts of auditors and fraud examiners. Historically, the primary detection methods used were whistle-blower hotlines and statistical sampling. Because of developments in technology, however, new methods are now used to detect fraud and identify fraud perpetrators. In this chapter, we spend most of our time discussing ways to use technology to detect fraudulent transactions on financial statements. The high cost of fraud to business and its high growth rate make the use of these new methods critical to minimizing the occurrence of fraud.

## Proactive Fraud Detection

As we discussed in Chapter 5, detecting fraud is different from investigating it. Fraud detection involves identifying symptoms that often indicate fraud is being, or has been, committed. Fraud investigation, on the other hand, is about examining and studying the symptoms or red flags once identified. Fraud investigation involves determining who committed the fraud, the scheme(s) used, when it was committed, what motivated it, and how much money or other assets were taken. Obviously, an investigation cannot proceed until a fraud has been detected. Because symptoms can be caused by factors other than fraud, investigators must remain objective and neutral, assuming neither guilt nor innocence.

In this chapter, we address proactive ways that help us suspect fraud early on. We then examine two technology-based *inductive fraud detection* methods and one *deductive fraud detection* method. In the second section we demonstrate how financial statements can be analyzed to detect fraud. Finally, we will discuss how technology is used to detect or identify fraud perpetrators. This innovative technology being created by some forward-looking firms is an exciting new development in fraud detection.

## Inductive Method #1: Commercial Data-Mining Software

One of the most popular detection approaches uses *commercial data-mining software*, such as *Audit Command Language (ACL)* or CaseWare IDEA, to look for anomalies in databases. To illustrate the application of such software, let's consider the case of XYZ Corporation. Believing that a high-risk area for fraud indicated kickbacks from vendors to buyers, XYZ used a data-mining package to examine purchasing trends of various products. Sorting records by vendor and by volume (an enormous task before the advent of this software), the company observed that total purchases from one vendor were increasing, even though total purchases from all other vendors were decreasing. Upon further analysis, the company also found that the favored vendor's prices were increasing at a faster rate. These patterns were suspect, especially considering the number of complaints about this vendor's products. XYZ investigated further and discovered that its buyer was accepting kickbacks. The bribery caused XYZ to purchase more than $11 million of unneeded inventory and supplies.

Purchasing patterns frequently signal kickback fraud because, once a buyer starts accepting kickbacks, the control of transactions switches from buyer to vendor. Once the vendor takes control of the relationship, prices often increase, the volume for the favored vendor increases, purchases from other vendors decrease, and, sometimes, even the quality of the goods purchased decreases.

In this and other such database searches for fraud, suspicious patterns are symptoms of fraud, not evidence of it. The reasons why buyers are purchasing more from one vendor and less from others may, in fact, be legitimate, even if the favored vendor's prices are higher. Perhaps the favored vendor's quality is superior or their deliveries more timely.

The major advantage of commercial data-mining software is that it is easy to use. On small databases, it does an excellent job of identifying trends, anomalies, and other unusual activity. It is popular because it is so easy to use. Another advantage is the scripting capabilities of most data-mining packages. For example, ACLScript is the scripting portion of the ACL application. Unfortunately, many users do not explore and learn these advanced capabilities.

Although commercial data-mining software can be extremely helpful in detecting fraud, it does have disadvantages. The most obvious one is that the databases kept by large corporations are, by definition, large. Most auditors and fraud examiners run their analysis on personal laptops. Compared with corporate servers that often hold terabytes of data, personal computers or laptops simply do not have the power or capacity to analyze entire data sets. The result is many examiners work with a subset or summarized version of the entire data set, limiting their investigative power. A second disadvantage is commercial packages are often general-purpose tools that cannot be refined or focused enough for specific needs without resorting to their scripting abilities. Because few examiners learn how to script these applications, they often generate hundreds or thousands of leads that are too voluminous for detailed follow-up.

## Inductive Method #2: Digital Analysis of Company Databases

Data-mining software packages are one kind of inductive analysis. Another type searches company databases in a manner similar to analytical review procedures already familiar to most accountants. The idea behind these analysis is to use the company's own databases to search for accounting anomalies or unusual or unexpected relationships between numbers.

One common analysis applies *Benford's law* to various types of data sets. To understand Benford's law, suppose someone hands you a stack of 10,000 random invoices and asks you to estimate how many of the dollar amounts on them begin with the digit 1. You might guess that the answer is about 1 in 9, but the truth is that some integers show up as first digits in data sets much more often than others.

In 1881, the American astronomer Simon Newcomb noticed that the first pages of books of logarithms were much more soiled than the remaining pages. In 1938, Frank Benford applied Newcomb's observation to various types of data sets. According to Benford's law, the first digit of random data sets will begin with a 1 more often than with a 2, a 2 more often than with a 3, and so on. In fact, Benford's law accurately predicts for many kinds of financial data that the first digits of each group of numbers in a set of random numbers will conform to the distribution pattern shown in Figure 6-1. Note that Benford's law applies only to numbers that describe similar items; it does not apply to assigned numbers, such as personal identification (ID) numbers or lists where the numbers have built-in minimums or maximums or have preassigned patterns.

As Figure 6-1 indicates, the first digit is expected to be a 1 about 30 percent of the time, whereas a 9 is expected as the first digit only about 4. 6 percent of the time. Therefore, if you compare the

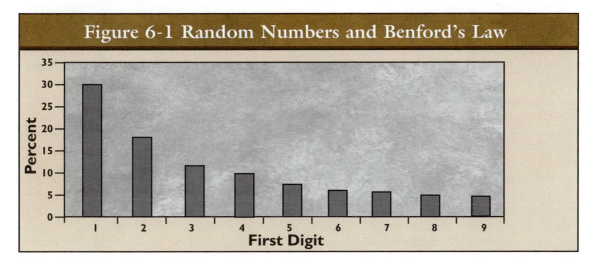

### Figure 6-1 Random Numbers and Benford's Law

distribution of the first numbers in a small set from your 10,000 invoices to Benford's distribution and find that for 70 percent of your invoice numbers the first digit is an 8 or a 9, you probably have a fraud.

One company, a multi-billion-dollar organization we will call "Company X," decided to test its data from supplier invoices against Benford's law. First, Company X analyzed the first digits of dollar amounts on its total population of 820,651 supplier invoices and plotted the results against the expectations of Benford's law and an upper and lower bound. Figure 6-2 shows the results.

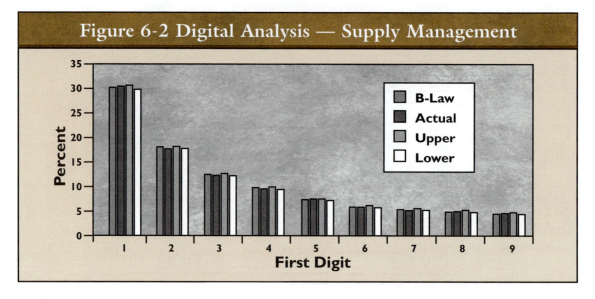

Figure 6-2 Digital Analysis — Supply Management

The company's results for its entire population of supplier invoices tracked Benford's predicted results closely. In fact, for all digits except 2, their actual results fell within Benford's upper and lower bounds. Such close tracking might cause many managers to decide that all is well in supply management and move on to other business. Fortunately, those in charge of this analysis knew that just because the entire population looked good did not rule out the possibility that specific populations would still deviate and thereby indicate fraud. So Company X compared the first digits of dollar amounts on invoices from *each* supplier against Benford's distribution. The following four charts in Figure 6-3 show the results for four suppliers.

Supplier 1 appears to be in good shape. Its actuals conform closely to Benford's predictions. Although no upper and lower bounds are shown, the actual distribution is obviously within bounds at all points.

Supplier 2 also follows the general slope, but the results are not so precise. Even though the results conform to the general shape of the distribution, the variances are still enough to convince most fraud examiners that a follow-up is in order.

Suppliers 3 and 4 have some major problems. Random distributions of first digits simply do not follow the predicted patterns. Fraud examiners should be highly suspicious of these results. Supplier 4 particularly looks rigged; someone has attempted to use numbers that would look random. In other words, someone tried to use every digit approximately the same number of times as every other digit.

One major advantage in using Benford's law to detect fraud is that it is the least expensive method to implement and use. Because you apply it to the company's own databases (i.e., you don't query data that are then analyzed by consultants or others), potential suspects are less likely to know you are trying to detect fraud. Fraud perpetrators are certainly easier to catch if they have not ceased their activities because they believe someone suspects them.

A major disadvantage of Benford's law is that using it is tantamount to hunting fraud with a shotgun: You pull the trigger and hope that a few pellets hit something important. To understand this concept, consider Company X again. What would have happened if the analysts had stopped after seeing that all vendor invoices taken together tracked Benford's predictions so closely? They might very well have concluded that their organization was free from fraud.

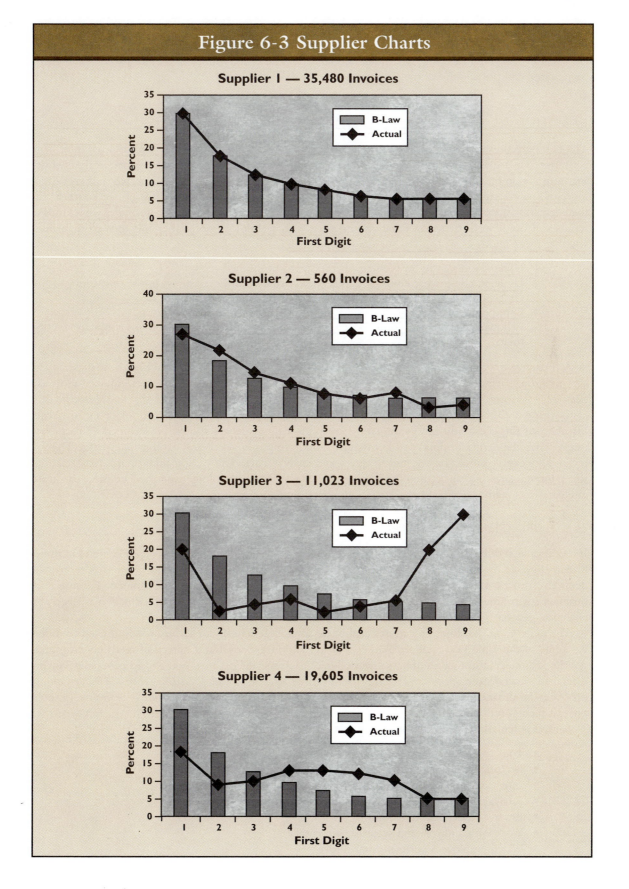

Figure 6-3 Supplier Charts

Another shortfall of relying solely on Benford's law is that it only broadly identifies the possible existence of fraud; it fails to narrow possibilities to a manageable field of promising leads. Once anomalies are identified by Benford's law, the fraud examiner must still determine the nature of the fraud being perpetrated and the identity of the perpetrator.

# Deductive Fraud Detection

The two detection methods just discussed are quite similar. They examine large databases (or infer from a sample to a larger population) in an effort to find anomalies that suggest the existence of fraud. Both methods are, in many ways, a shotgun approach. No particular type of fraud is suspected; rather, various types of analysis are performed on databases in the hope that something will show up. In contrast, the final detection method we discuss in this chapter uses an deductive approach. It determines what kinds of frauds can occur in a particular situation and then uses technology and other methods to determine whether those frauds exist. It follows a five-step process:

1. Understanding the business or operations to be studied
2. Understanding what kinds of frauds could occur (fraud exposures) in the operation
3. Determining the symptoms that the most likely frauds would generate
4. Using databases and information systems to search for those symptoms
5. Following up on symptoms to determine whether actual fraud or other factors are causing them

A proactive fraud detection team should include three primary individuals, although its makeup can vary by project. First, a domain expert should be selected who understands the target industry and business. This person will provide valuable insights into potential frauds and schemes that could not be otherwise gained. Often, the domain expert is a trusted employee, like an internal auditor or security team member, of the client you are investigating. Second, a fraud expert should be included. This person understands the nature of fraud and knows how fraud symptoms occur and exhibit themselves. Third, a technology expert should be selected to query and analyze data. This person understands data relationships, foreign keys, and structured query language (SQL). The technology expert will connect to corporate databases, gather data, and analyze it with scripts and applications.

## Step 1: Understand the Business

In traditional, inductive fraud detection, fraud examiners typically do not have any specific fraud in mind; rather, they see or learn of an event or anomaly that prompts the investigation. Quite differently, the deductive process starts with an understanding of the business or unit being examined. Because each business environment is different—even within the same industry or firm—fraud detection is largely an analytical process.

The same fraud detection procedures cannot be applied generically to all businesses or even to different units of the same organization. Rather than rely upon generic fraud detection methods or generic queries, examiners must gain intimate knowledge of each specific organization and its processes. Having a detailed understanding provides the basis for the entire strategic fraud detection process. Understanding processes in an organization or unit is similar to the activities undertaken when performing business process reengineering.

Several potential methods can be used to gather information about a business:

- Tour the business, department, or plant.
- Become familiar with competitor processes.
- Interview key personnel.
- Analyze financial statements and other information.
- Review process documentation.
- Work with auditors and security personnel.
- Watch employees perform their duties.

## Step 2: Identify What Kinds of Fraud Could Occur

Once the team is confident with their understanding of the business, the next step is to determine what possible frauds might exist or could occur in the operation being examined. This *risk assessment* step requires an understanding of the nature of different frauds, how they occur, and what symptoms they exhibit.

The fraud identification process begins by conceptually dividing the business unit into its individual functions. Most businesses or even subunits are simply too large and diverse for examiners to consider simultaneously. Dividing the business into its individual functions helps focus the detection process. For example, an examiner might decide to focus directly on the manufacturing plant, the collections department, or the purchasing function.

In this step, people involved in the business functions are interviewed. Fraud examiners should ask such questions as:

- Who are the key players in the business?
- What types of employees, vendors, or contractors are involved in the business transactions?
- How do insiders and outsiders interact with each another?
- What types of fraud have occurred or been suspected in the past?
- What types of fraud could be committed against the company or on behalf of the company?
- How could employees or management acting alone commit fraud?
- How could vendors or customers acting alone commit fraud?
- How could vendors or customers working in collusion with employees commit fraud?

Also during this stage, the fraud detection team should brainstorm potential frauds by type and player. The likely occurrence of the various frauds should be considered, and in the end, a laundry list of frauds that will be studied should be developed.

## Step 3: Determine Generated Symptoms

As you learned in earlier chapters, fraud itself is never seen; only its symptoms are observed. What appear to be a fraud symptom often ends up being explained by other, nonfraud factors, creating confusion, delay, and additional expense for the fraud team. For example, a company's accounts receivable balance might be increasing at a rate that appears to be unrealistically high. The increasing receivables balance could be the result of fraud, or it could just be the result of major customers having financial difficulties, or a change in credit terms. In addition, no empirical evidence indicates that the presence of more apparent red flags increases the probability of fraud (although more confirmed red flags generally mean a higher probability of fraud), or that certain red flags have greater predictive ability than other red flags.

Even with these weaknesses, however, identifying red flags or fraud symptoms is often the best, and often the only, practical method of proactive fraud detection. All auditing fraud standards, for example, recommend the red flag approach for detecting fraud. Although tips and reports account for the detection of most serious frauds, they usually occur too late, after the fraud has grown to the stage that the tipster overcomes his or her natural reluctance to report it. And for every fraud that is eventually reported, perhaps 10 or more are never detected or disclosed.

### TYPES OF FRAUD SYMPTOMS

As discussed in Chapter 5, fraud symptoms can be divided into the following groups:

- Accounting anomalies
- Internal control weakensses
- Analytical anomalies
- Extravagant lifestyles
- Unusual behaviors
- Tips and complaints

Note that up to and including this step (step 3), the deductive method of fraud detection is purely analytical. No data have been collected and results have not been analyzed. The first three steps are generic and can be applied in any type of organization or subunit. This strategic approach produces a comprehensive and zero-based analysis the specific types of fraud that might be found in various business entities.

In step 3 of the proactive fraud detection program, the fraud examiner should carefully consider what type of symptoms or red flags, could be present in the potential frauds identified in step 2. A matrix, tree diagram, or brainstorming map can be created that correlates specific symptoms with specific possible frauds.

For example, kickbacks from vendors to buyers might generate the symptoms shown in Figure 6-4.

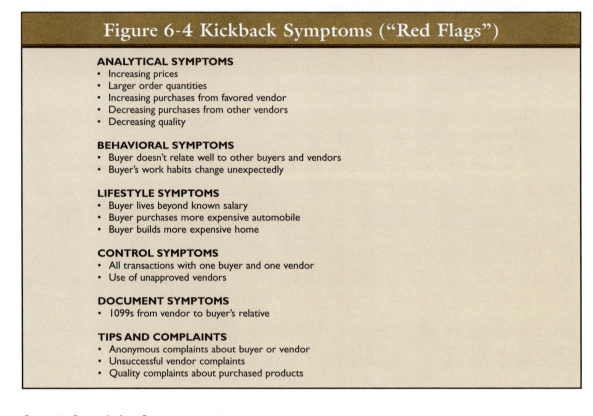

## Figure 6-4 Kickback Symptoms ("Red Flags")

**ANALYTICAL SYMPTOMS**
- Increasing prices
- Larger order quantities
- Increasing purchases from favored vendor
- Decreasing purchases from other vendors
- Decreasing quality

**BEHAVIORAL SYMPTOMS**
- Buyer doesn't relate well to other buyers and vendors
- Buyer's work habits change unexpectedly

**LIFESTYLE SYMPTOMS**
- Buyer lives beyond known salary
- Buyer purchases more expensive automobile
- Buyer builds more expensive home

**CONTROL SYMPTOMS**
- All transactions with one buyer and one vendor
- Use of unapproved vendors

**DOCUMENT SYMPTOMS**
- 1099s from vendor to buyer's relative

**TIPS AND COMPLAINTS**
- Anonymous complaints about buyer or vendor
- Unsuccessful vendor complaints
- Quality complaints about purchased products

## Step 4: Search for Symptoms

Once symptoms are defined and correlated with specific frauds, supporting data are extracted from corporate databases, online Web sites, and other sources. Although the technology expert performs this step, the fraud examiner should have working knowledge of how databases are organized so he or she can effectively direct the work of the technology expert. The appendix to this chapter discusses in detail how to convert data from databases and other sources into useful information. It contains introductory material for those wanting to learn advanced data analysis techniques.

Although the previous steps were general, analytical exercises, searching for symptoms is specific to each company. Searching can be done with standard applications, such as Microsoft Access, ACL, and IDEA, or it can be done using custom-built scripts that run on corporate servers. They can be more costly, but custom scripts often provide the most power because they are specific to your client.

The deliverable of this step is a set of data that matches the symptoms identified in the previous step. Because real-world data sources are *noisy* (meaning they contain errors from a variety of sources), searching for symptoms is often an iterative process. For example, in the oil company case described later in this chapter, thousands of matching records were found on the first search for symptoms. These records were quickly analyzed for nonfraudulent errors and the scripts or algorithms were modified to filter out these errors. After several iterations of this step, each symptom had only a few records, documents, or people to investigate.

## Step 5: Follow Up on Symptoms

Once anomalies are highlighted and determined by the examiners to be indications of fraud, they are investigated either using traditional or technology-based methods. As computer-based analysis is often the most efficient method of investigation, every effort should be made to screen results using computer algorithms. Investigation of leads should only be done on anomalies that cannot be explained through continued analysis. Examiners normally work with auditors and security personnel to identify reasons for anomalies. They talk with coworkers, investigate paper documents, and contact outside individuals.

One advantage of the deductive approach is its potential reuse. analysis can often can be automated and integrated directly into corporate systems in a way that provides real-time analysis and detection of fraud as well as prevention of known fraud types. Subsequent runs through the deductive steps reach economies of scale because many of the steps can be reused.

### BANK FRAUD CASE

One example of this detection approach involves a small bank with five branches. Realizing that controls were quite loose, especially those involving top management, the board of directors decided that a risk analysis would be cost effective. The risk assessment would determine major management fraud exposures, identify symptoms those frauds would generate, and then search 16 years of bank data for the symptoms. The tests revealed the following symptoms:

- Exception reports, reflecting fraudulent transactions, which exhibited unusual, atypical, and otherwise questionable patterns of supervisory overrides, transactions with no apparent business purpose, and transactions involving unusually large amounts. This symptom occurred at least 211 times.
- Journal vouchers containing only one signature, containing incorrect information, or reflecting transfers between different customers' accounts. This symptom occurred at least 20 times on exception reports.
- Deposit slips with missing information, incomplete names, or where the name of the depositor did not match the name on the passbook or the account name in the bank's records. This symptom occurred in at least 41 of 56 exception reports.
- Deposits and withdrawals exceeding $1,000 in one executive's passbook account. This symptom occurred in 39 of 85 exception reports.
- Deposits and withdrawals from the same account made on the same day or within a short period of time and appearing on the exception reports. This symptom occurred on every exception report.
- Bank checks reflecting transfers between different customers' accounts or checks with altered dates. All 11 exception reports contained this symptom.
- Withdrawal vouchers and checks containing purported customer signatures readily distinguishable upon comparison with the customers' signatures. This symptom occurred at least 73 times.
- Large negative available balances in slush accounts and other customer accounts. This symptom appeared 15 times.
- Deposit slips of customer funds between accounts of different customers or deposits of customer checks where cash was received back. This symptom occurred in 8 of 9 exception reports.
- CDs closed prematurely, with proceeds placed in lower interest-bearing passbook accounts, sometimes with large penalties. This symptom occurred in 36 of 42 exception reports.
- Customers not present when accounts were opened and closed or when transactions were effected in the account. This symptom occurred numerous times.
- Large withdrawals of cash by executives from customers' accounts. Out of 234 exception reports, withdrawals happened in 129 of them.
- The mailing of customer account statements to executives instead of to the customer, without written authorization, happened with at least 40 accounts.

Follow-up investigation of the symptoms found that one executive vice president had embezzled several million dollars through various schemes over several years.

## OIL COMPANY CASE

A second case involves a search for fraud in one of the world's largest oil refineries. The refinery's situation provided an excellent search laboratory because it involved tens of thousands of vendor and employee transactions. Its two databases gave the investigators a data-rich environment to explore. The databases contained detailed information on material acquisitions, project status, and vendor labor billings showing hours worked by individuals. During the period investigated, 41 vendors had transactions with the refinery totaling more than $1 million each, 242 vendors had transactions totaling moe than $100,000 each, 497 vendors had transactions totaling more than $25,000 each, for a total of 1,983 vendors. The period studied produced more than 47,000 vendor invoices and at least that many expense reimbursement, payroll, and other employee-driven transactions. In addition, because the refinery was heavily unionized and employed many second- and third-generation employees, the company believed that some employees might know about frauds but were reticent to come forward with information.

As part of the database search, the investigators developed customized queries that combined data in new and different ways. In addition, a *time engine* was developed that analyzed fraud symptoms by time period as well as by individual, invoice, product, purchase order, and other factors under consideration. Using this approach, a number of possible fraud symptoms were observed. Because of management's interest and the availability of the data, detection efforts focused primarily on various types of vendor and contractor fraud. Table 6-1 identifies the types of possible fraud, the symptoms associated with the various frauds, and some of the searches that were performed.

## Table 6-1 Database Search for Fraud

| Type of Fraud | Red Flags Identified | Red-Flag Searches |
|---|---|---|
| **Vendor(s) committing fraud** | Overcharging for goods purchased | Price increases greater than 30% for four consecutive years |
| | Providing poor quality goods | Work orders with cost overruns exceeding 50%<br>Dollar amount, number, and percentage of goods returned to vendor |
| | Billing more than once for the same purchase | Duplicate invoice numbers<br>Vendors with invoices for the same amount on the same day<br>Multiple invoices for the same item description by vendor |
| | Short shipping | Quantity paid for exceeds quantity received, ranked by dollar differences |
| | Billing for goods not ordered or shipped | Vendors with sequential invoices |
| **Employee(s) committing purchasing fraud** | Establishing dummy vendors | Two or more suppliers with same telephone number and/or address<br>Matching of vendors paid with company's master vendor list and with Dun & Bradstreet listings<br>Contractors with common names, first two letters match exactly, and 90% of the name is the same<br>Employee and vendor telephone numbers are the same<br>Contractors with only one buyer for all contracts |
| | Purchasing goods for personal use | Purchase orders with zero dollar amounts by buyer<br>Invoices exceeding purchase order dollar amount ranked by dollar difference<br>Invoices without valid purchase order |

## Table 6-1 Database Search for Fraud (continued)

| Type of Fraud | Red Flags Identified | Red-Flag Searches |
|---|---|---|
| **Vendor and company employee(s) committing fraud in collusion** | Kickbacks or other favors | Price increases greater than 30% for four consecutive years |
| | | Dollar amount, number, and percentage of items returned by vendor and buyer |
| | | Payments without receiving reports |
| | | Increased volume of purchases by vendor and buyer |
| | | Combination of increased prices and increased purchases from specific vendors |
| **Contractor(s) committing fraud** | Charging more hours than actually worked | Ranking of hours worked by contractor employee |
| | Working excessive overtime for higher per-hour rates | Ranking of overtime hours worked per two-week pay periods by contractor and contractor employee |
| | | Ranking of contractors with rising overtime charges |
| | Overbilling for equipment used | Trends in equipment rental rates by type of equipment by contractor |
| | | Differences between standard (allowed) rates and actual rates by contractor over time |
| | Billing for equipment not used | Equipment charges when no labor is charged |
| | Billing at the wrong rates | Licenses of workers for various crafts vs. licenses issued by states |
| | | Changes in craft designation for employees by contractor |
| | Charging higher labor rates than allowed | Contractor employees with significant jumps in labor rates |
| | | Ranking of labor rates by craft by contractor |
| | | Contractors with outrageous rates per hour |
| | Charging for fake employees | Contractor employee social security numbers arranged by ascending numbers |
| **Company employee(s) committing contractor-related fraud** | Charging for more hours than contractor actually worked and paying fictitious employees | Employees ranked by hours worked per pay period |
| | Working excessive overtime for higher rates | Employees with rising overtime charges |
| | | Employees with high overtime per time card |
| **Contractor and company employee(s) committing fraud in collusion** | Kickbacks for favors | Increased volume of work by vendor by buyer employee(s) committing: |
| | | Higher than normal rates for services |
| | | Excessive charges for equipment use |
| | | Contractors with rapidly rising invoice amounts |
| | | Increasing trend of equipment rental rates by contracting employee |
| | | Amounts contracted by contractor by buyer |
| | | Invoices with outrageous costs per hour |
| **All types of fraud** | Nonrandomness in invoice numbers and amounts | Benford's digits tests |

Although the actual instances of fraud at the oil refinery are still being investigated (or litigated), the detection effort led to both discoveries of fraud and data errors. In addition, several of the findings that did not involve fraud resulted in valuable information for management. Here are some of the red flags identified:

- The search for the dollar amount, number, and percentage of returned items by vendor uncovered three suspicious vendors. The refinery was rejecting more than 50 percent of goods received from these vendors, due to poor quality. Two of these were small suppliers, but one represented a relationship with one of the refinery's largest vendors.

- The search for multiple invoices for the same item description by vendor uncovered six invoices for the same amounts from the same vendor on the same day, all for $1,044,000. Three invoices from the same vendor, on the same day, for the same items, each for $900,000, were also found.

- Using various combinations of red flags, four companies that appeared to be committing large-scale contractor fraud were identified. The refinery no longer conducts business with two of these vendors and is pursuing recovery.

- The search for price increases greater than 30 percent per year for four consecutive years uncovered one company that had increased prices 581,700 percent and another that had increased prices by 331,879 percent. In total, 35 companies had raised prices more than 1,000 percent, and 202 companies had raised prices at least 100 percent.

- No incidences were found where employee and vendor telephone numbers were the same, but six employees had the same addresses as vendors.

- Of the 319 vendors with common names and addresses, all but two of these had reasonable explanations for the coincidence.

- The search for vendors not listed in the master file uncovered one unapproved vendor from whom the company had purchased $791,268 of services. Purchases from all other unapproved vendors totaled less than $10,000.

- In 20 purchases greater than $100,000, the quantity paid for was greater than the quantity received.

- The search for high-volume purchases by vendor uncovered only one vendor with unusually high transactions. The company paid $56,201 for items with unit prices of 19 cents and 12 cents each. The volume on these items far exceeded the refinery's needs.

- The search for contractor employees with excessive overtime was one of the most useful analysis. Four companies had employees who reported working 150+ hours over 20 consecutive two-week pay periods. Employees of one company submitted time cards from different locations for the same periods. Another company's employees averaged 2,046 hours of overtime for the year. In one year, ten companies had averages of more than 200 overtime hours per two-week period, 388 had some overtime, and hundreds had no overtime.

- Per-hour charges by craft and by company and employee ranged from $56. 11 per hour to $15. 43 for the same craft. Also, 40 companies had standard deviations for rates billed that were more than 40 percent of the average rates billed for the same craft.

- Invoices from seven companies exceeded purchase order amounts by $100,000 or more. The largest difference was $713,791 on an original invoice of $21,621.

- The search for vendors with sequential invoices revealed 19 vendors that submitted sequentially numbered invoices in more than 50 percent of all invoices. With one vendor, 83 percent of the invoices submitted were sequential.

- The search uncovered three companies with more than 100 zero-amount purchase orders.

- Nine contractors had cost overruns exceeding 50 percent and $100,000. The highest percentage overrun was 2,431 percent.

- Finally, only 65 companies could not be matched with Dun & Bradstreet listings. Except in a few instances, purchases from nonlisted companies were small.

# Which Transaction-Based Approach Is Best?

Each of the transaction-based approaches described has advantages and disadvantages. Using commercial data-mining software is usually the most inexpensive approach. However, its usefulness can be limited when databases are large. In addition, the generic searches that such software performs often lead to excessive listings of possible fraud symptoms. In one case, for example, applications using Microsoft's FoxPro in a generic way led to 26,000 possible symptoms. The major advantage of commercial data-mining software is that it is easy to use and can be quickly modified and applied.

*Statistical analysis*, such as using Benford's law, can be performed on databases of any size. They are most useful when a particular type of fraud, such as vendor kickbacks, is suspected. However, statistical analysis also tend to identify large numbers of symptoms.

The major disadvantage of the deductive approach is that it is more expensive. However, the data and output can be continuously modified and refined until most alternative explanations are eliminated.

In deciding which approach to use, consider the size of the databases to be analyzed and whether the search is a one-time or multiple-application activity. If the refined analysis of the deductive approach can be used repeatedly or be automated as a real-time fraud detection activity, it is both preferable and cost-effective. On the other hand, if the databases are small and the search a one-time-only application, commercial data-mining software is preferable.

All of these methods are proactive approaches in that they can detect fraud early and can pay large dividends. Early detection of fraud not only results in significant cost savings, but the idea that fraud detection activities are in place and used routinely can be a strong deterrent.

# Analyzing Financial Statements Reports

*Financial statements* are the end product of the *accounting cycle*. They can be viewed as summaries of all the transactions that occurred during a specific period of time. Fraud can be detected anywhere along the way—through transaction source documents, journal entries of the transactions based on those documents, ledger balances (which are summaries of journal entries)—and finally in the resulting financial statements (which summarize the ledger totals in prescribed formats). Unless a fraud is large, however, it may not affect summarized financial statements significantly enough to be detected. Large frauds, however, are a different "animal," and can often be detected through financial statements. Small frauds are usually detected by focusing on source documents or other symptoms.

To detect fraud through financial statements, investigators focus on unexplained changes. For example, in most companies, few customers pay cash at the time of purchase. Rather, their payments are made by check, based on monthly bills. As a result, revenues normally do not increase without a corresponding increase in accounts receivable. Similarly, an increase in revenues should be accompanied by an increase in cost of goods sold and in inventory purchased and accounts payable balances. Also, inventory levels don't usually increase while purchases and accounts payable remain constant. In all cases, unexplained changes must be the focus of attention.

To understand how financial statement changes can signal fraud, one must be familiar with the nature of the three primary financial statements. Most organizations publish periodic balance sheets, income statements, and statements of cash flow. The *balance sheet* is a position statement. It shows what an organization's asset, liability, and equity balances are at a *specific* point in time (like a snapshot). A balance sheet prepared as of December 31, 2004, for example, reveals what the organization owns and owes on that date only. A balance sheet prepared on January 3, 2005 (three days later), may show drastically different numbers. Because a balance sheet is a position statement as of a specific date, it must be converted to a change statement before it can be used to detect fraud. The changes can then be analyzed to determine whether they make sense or represent symptoms that should be investigated.

An *income statement* shows what an organization's revenues, expenses, and income were for a period of time. An income statement prepared for the year ending December 31, 2004, for example, would reveal revenues, expenses, and income for the 12 months January through December 2004. Although an income statement is for a period, rather than as of a specific date, it is not a change statement. Like a balance sheet, it must also be converted to a change statement before it can be used effectively as a fraud detection tool.

Balance sheets and income statements are converted from position and period statements to change statements in four ways:

1. Comparing account balances in the statements from one period to the next
2. Calculating key ratios and comparing them from period to period
3. Performing horizontal analysis
4. Performing vertical analysis

The first approach compares numbers in the statement from one period to the next. For example, the accounts receivable balance of one period is compared to the balance in a subsequent period to see whether the change is in the expected direction and whether the magnitude of change is reasonable, given changes in other numbers. Unfortunately, because financial statement numbers are often large and difficult to compare, assessing levels of change can be difficult.

In the second approach—converting balance sheets and income statements to change statements—key financial statement ratios are calculated and changes in these ratios from period to period are compared. The *quick ratio* (also called the *acid-test ratio*) and the *current ratio* assess a company's liquidity. *Accounts receivable turnover* and *inventory turnover ratios* assess a company's operational efficiency. *Debt-to-equity ratio* and times-interest-earned ratios assess a company's solvency. *Profit margin*, return on assets, *return on equity*, and earnings per share ratios assess profitability. By examining ratios, it is possible to see whether resulting changes in liquidity, efficiency, solvency, and profitability are as expected. Changes in ratios that do not make sense are often the result of fraudulent activity by managers.

Detecting fraud through financial statement ratios is much easier than assessing changes in the financial statement numbers themselves. Ratios usually involve small, easily understood numbers that are sensitive to changes in key variables. In addition, benchmarks for most ratios are well known. Common ratios that can be used to detect fraud are shown in the Table 6-2.

## Table 6-2 Common Ratios

| Common Ratios | | |
|---|---|---|
| 1. Current ratio | = | $\dfrac{\text{Current Assets}}{\text{Current Liabilities}}$ |
| 2. Quick ratio (acid-test) | = | $\dfrac{\text{Current Assets (minus Inventory)}}{\text{Current Liabilities}}$ |
| 3. Accounts receivable turnover | = | $\dfrac{\text{Sales}}{\text{Average Accounts Receivable}}$ |
| 4. Days in receivable | = | $\dfrac{365}{\text{Receivable Turnover}}$ |
| 5. Receivable percentage | = | $\dfrac{\text{Accounts Receivable}}{\text{Total Assets}}$ |
| 6. Bad debt percentage | = | $\dfrac{\text{Bad Debt Expense}}{\text{Average Accounts Receivable}}$ |
| | = | $\dfrac{\text{Bad Debt Expense}}{\text{Total Sales}}$ |
| 7. Inventory turnover | = | $\dfrac{\text{Cost of Goods Sold}}{\text{Average Inventory}}$ |
| 8. Days in inventory | = | $\dfrac{365}{\text{Inventory Turnover}}$ |
| 9. Cost of goods sold percentage | = | $\dfrac{\text{Cost of Goods Sold}}{\text{Sales}}$ |
| 10. Inventory percentage | = | $\dfrac{\text{Inventory}}{\text{Total Assets}}$ |

## Table 6-2 Common Ratios (continued)

| | Common Ratios | | |
|---|---|---|---|
| 11. | Property, plant, and equipment (PPE) turnover | = | $\dfrac{\text{Sales}}{\text{Average PPE}}$ |
| 12. | PPE percentage | = | $\dfrac{\text{PPE}}{\text{Total Assets}}$ |
| 13. | Sales return percentage | = | $\dfrac{\text{Sales Returns}}{\text{Total Sales}}$ |
| 14. | Debt to equity (leverage) | = | $\dfrac{\text{Total Liabilities}}{\text{Stockholders' Equity}}$ |
| 15. | Debt percentage | = | $\dfrac{\text{Total Liabilities}}{\text{Total Assets}}$ |
| 16. | Profit margin | = | $\dfrac{\text{Net Income}}{\text{Net Sales}}$ |
| 17. | Earnings per share | = | $\dfrac{\text{Net Income}}{\text{Number of Shares of Stock}}$ |

The third approach—converting balance sheets and income statements to change statements—uses vertical analysis, which converts financial statement numbers to percentages. For a balance sheet, total assets are set at 100 percent and all other balances are a percentage of total assets. A simple example of *vertical analysis* of a balance sheet is shown in Figure 6-5.

## Figure 6-5 Vertical Analysis of a Balance Sheet

**JOHN DOE COMPANY** Vertical Analysis of Balance Sheet December 31, 2004 and 2003

| | 2004 | | 2003 | |
|---|---|---|---|---|
| Cash | $ 64,000 | 8% | $ 50,000 | 5% |
| Accounts receivable | 96,000 | 12 | 100,000 | 10 |
| Inventory | 160,000 | 20 | 200,000 | 20 |
| Fixed assets | 480,000 | 60 | 650,000 | 65 |
| Total assets | $800,000 | 100% | $1,000,000 | 100% |
| | | | | |
| Accounts payable | $ 16,000 | 2% | $ 70,000 | 7% |
| Mortgage payable | 80,000 | 10 | 120,000 | 12 |
| Bonds payable | 160,000 | 20 | 200,000 | 20 |
| Common stock | 400,000 | 50 | 400,000 | 40 |
| Retained earnings | 144,000 | 18 | 210,000 | 21 |
| Total liabilities and equity | $800,000 | 100% | $1,000,000 | 100% |

Vertical analysis is a useful fraud detection technique, because percentages are easily understood. When we spend $1 or part of $1, we know what it means. If we spend it all, we know we have spent 100 percent. Similarly, all through school, we scored 70 or 80 or 90 percent on examinations. Everyone understands which of these scores is good, which is bad, and what the percentage represents. Changes in cumbersome financial statement balances can be readily assessed by converting the numbers to percentages. Understanding that sales increased 20 percent, for example, is much easier than understanding that sales increased from $862,000 to $1,034,400.

When vertical analysis is used to analyze changes in income statement balances, gross sales are set at 100 percent and all other amounts are converted to a percentage of sales. A simple example of an income statement converted to percentages by using vertical analysis is shown in Figure 6-6.

In this example, the cost of goods sold increased from 50 percent of sales in year 1 to 60 percent of sales in year 2. Does this change make sense? Why would the cost of sales increase twice as much as sales? Possible explanations include (1) inventory costs rose faster than sales prices, (2) inventory is being stolen,

# Figure 6-6 Vertical Analysis of an Income Statement

**JOHN DOE COMPANY** Vertical Analysis of Income Statement For the Period Ending December 31, 2004 and 2003

|  | 2004 |  | 2003 |  |
|---|---|---|---|---|
| Sales | $1,000,000 | 100% | $800,000 | 100% |
| Cost of goods sold | 600,000 | 60 | 400,000 | 50 |
| Gross margin | $ 400,000 | 40% | $400,000 | 50% |
| Expenses: |  |  |  |  |
| Selling expenses | $ 150,000 | 15% | $120,000 | 15% |
| Administrative expenses | 100,000 | 10 | 88,000 | 11 |
|  | $ 250,000 | 25% | $208,000 | 26 |
| Income before taxes | $ 150,000 | 15% | $192,000 | 24% |
| Income taxes | 60,000 | 6 | 80,000 | 10 |
| Net income | $ 90,000 | 9% | $112,000 | 14% |

and (3) the accounting records are not accurate. An analyst can easily determine which of these (or other) factors caused the unusual changes.

The fourth approach—converting balance sheets and income statements to change statements—uses horizontal analysis. Horizontal analysis resembles vertical analysis in that it converts financial statement balances to percentages. However, instead of computing financial statement amounts as percentages of total assets or gross sales, it converts the percentage change in balance sheet and income statement numbers from one period to the next. Simple examples of horizontal analysis of a balance sheet and horizontal analysis of an income statement are shown in Figure 6-7.

# Figure 6-7 Horizontal Analysis of a Balance Sheet and an Income Statement

**JOHN DOE COMPANY** Horizontal Analysis of Balance Sheet December 31, 2004 and 2003

|  | 2004 | 2003 | Change | % Change |
|---|---|---|---|---|
| Cash | $ 50,000 | $ 64,000 | $(14,000) | (22)% |
| Accounts receivable | 100,000 | 96,000 | 4,000 | 4 |
| Inventory | 200,000 | 160,000 | 40,000 | 25 |
| Fixed assets | 650,000 | 480,000 | 170,000 | 35 |
| Total assets | $1,000,000 | $800,000 | $200,000 | 25% |
|  |  |  |  |  |
| Accounts payable | $ 70,000 | $ 16,000 | $ 54,000 | 338% |
| Mortgage payable | 120,000 | 80,000 | 40,000 | 50 |
| Bonds payable | 200,000 | 160,000 | 40,000 | 25 |
| Common stock | 400,000 | 400,000 | -0- | -0- |
| Retained earnings | 210,000 | 144,000 | 66,000 | 46 |
| Total liabilities and equity | $1,000,000 | $800,000 | $200,000 | 25% |

**JOHN DOE COMPANY** Horizontal Analysis of Income Statements December 31, 2004 and 2003

|  | 2004 | 2003 | Change | % Change |
|---|---|---|---|---|
| Net sales | $1,000,000 | $800,000 | $200,000 | 25% |
| Cost of goods sold | 600,000 | 400,000 | 200,000 | 50 |
| Gross margin | $ 400,000 | $400,000 | 0 | 0 |
|  |  |  |  |  |
| Expenses: |  |  |  |  |
| Selling expenses | $ 150,000 | $120,000 | $ 30,000 | 25 |
| Administrative expenses | 100,000 | 88,000 | 12,000 | 14 |
|  | $ 250,000 | $208,000 | $ 42,000 | 20 |
| Income before taxes | $ 150,000 | $192,000 | $(42,000) | 22 |
| Income taxes | 60,000 | 80,000 | (20,000) | 25 |
| Net income | $ 90,000 | $112,000 | $ 22,000 | (20) |

Horizontal analysis is the most direct method of focusing on changes. With ratios and vertical analysis, statements are converted to numbers that are easier to understand, and then the numbers are compared from period to period. With horizontal analysis, the changes in amounts from period to period are converted to percentages (change / Year 1 amount = % change).

As an example of the usefulness of vertical and horizontal analysis, consider the ESM fraud as described by an expert witness in the case.

> *I received a call from an attorney asking me to be an expert witness in a major fraud case. The case was ESM Government, a securities dealer that had been in the news recently. The attorney indicated that the large accounting firm he was defending was being sued for some $300 million by the insurance commission for negligent auditing. The suit related to the firm's audit of a savings and loan that had invested in ESM. To defend the firm, the attorney was trying to understand the nature and extent of the fraud as well as to obtain an independent opinion on whether his client was negligent in performing the audit.*

## ESM Government

**Horizontal Analysis***

| Assets | Year 1 to Year 2 | Year 2 to Year 3 | Year 3 to Year 4 |
|---|---|---|---|
| Cash | 1,684% | (40%) | (67%) |
| Deposits | 0 | 0 | 0 |
| Receivables from brokers and dealers | (91) | 1,706 | 102 |
| Receivables from customers | 19.5 | (48) | (23) |

**Horizontal Analysis***

| | Year 1 to Year 2 | Year 2 to Year 3 | Year 3 to Year 4 |
|---|---|---|---|
| Securities purchased under agreement to resell | (3) | (44) | 205 |
| Accrued interest | 0 | 190 | 487 |
| Securities purchased not sold at market | 829 | 13 | 120 |
| Total assets | 7.5 | (38) | 183 |
| | | | |
| *Liabilities and Shareholder. Equity* | | | |
| Short-term bank loans | 898 | 40 | 14 |
| Payable to brokers and dealers | (72) | 658 | 33 |
| Payable to customer | 50 | (64) | 158 |
| Securities sold under agreement to repurchase | (3) | (44) | 232 |
| Accounts payable and accrued expenses | 192 | (100) | 55 |
| Accounts payable—parent and affiliates | 279 | (25) | (4) |
| Common stock | 0 | 0 | 0 |
| Additional contributed capital | 0 | 0 | 0 |
| Retained earnings | 127 | 113 | 21 |

*Dollar amounts are omitted to simplify the presentation.

*Note:* This horizontal analysis, based on ESM's actual financial statements, was prepared by Steve Albrecht.

## ESM Government

### Vertical Analysis

|  | $ (Year 1) | % | $ (Year 2) | % | $ (Year 3) | % | $ (Year 4) | % |
|---|---|---|---|---|---|---|---|---|
| **Assets** |  |  |  |  |  |  |  |  |
| Cash | $ 99,000 | 0.000 | $ 1,767,000 | 0.001 | $ 1,046,000 | 0.001 | $ 339,000 | 0.000 |
| Deposits | 25,000 | 0.000 | 25,000 | 0.000 | 25,000 | 0.000 | 25,000 | 0.000 |
| Receivables from brokers and dealers | 725,000 | 0.000 | 60,000 | 0.000 | 1,084,000 | 0.001 | 2,192,000 | 0.001 |
| Receivables from customers | 33,883,000 | 0.024 | 40,523,000 | 0.027 | 21,073,000 | 0.022 | 16,163,000 | 0.006 |
| Securities purchased under agreement to resell | 1,367,986,000 | 0.963 | 1,323,340,000 | 0.867 | 738,924,000 | 0.781 | 2,252,555,000 | 0.840 |
| Accrued interest | 433,000 | 0.000 | 433,000 | 0.000 | 1,257,000 | 0.001 | 7,375,000 | 0.003 |
| Securities purchased not sold at market | 17,380,000 | 0.010 | 161,484,000 | 0.106 | 182,674,000 | 0.193 | 402,004,000 | 0.150 |
| Total assets | $1,420,531,000 |  | $1,527,632,000 |  | $946,083,000 |  | $2,680,653,000 |  |
| **Liabilities and equity** |  |  |  |  |  |  |  |  |
| Short-term bank loans | $ 5,734,000 | 0.005 | $ 57,282,000 | 0.037 | $ 80,350,000 | 0.085 | $ 91,382,000 | 0.034 |
| Payable to brokers and dealers | 1,721,000 | 0.001 | 478,000 | 0.000 | 3,624,000 | 0.004 | 5,815,000 | 0.000 |
| Payable to customers | 2,703,000 | 0.002 | 4,047,000 | 0.003 | 1,426,000 | 0.002 | 3,683,000 | 0.000 |
| Securities sold under agreement to repurchase | 1,367,986,000 | 0.963 | 1,323,340,000 | 0.867 | 738,924,000 | 0.781 | 2,457,555,000 | 0.917 |
| Accounts payable and accrued expenses | 272,000 | 0.000 | 796,000 | 0.000 | 591,000 | 0.001 | 1,377,000 | 0.000 |
| Accounts payable— parent and affiliates | 33,588,000 | 0.020 | 127,604,000 | 0.084 | 95,861,000 | 0.101 | 92,183,000 | 0.014 |
| Common stock | 1,000 | 0.000 | 1,000 | 0.000 | 1,000 | 0.000 | 1,000 | 0.000 |
| Additional contributed capital | 4,160,000 | 0.040 | 4,160,000 | 0.003 | 4,160,000 | 0.004 | 4,160,000 | 0.000 |
| Retained earnings | 4,366,000 | 0.040 | 9,924,000 | 0.006 | 21,146,000 | 0.022 | 24,497,000 | 0.010 |
| Total liabilities and equity | $1,420,531,000 |  | $1,527,632,000 |  | $946,083,000 |  | $2,680,653,000 |  |

Note: This vertical analysis, based on ESM's actual journal, was prepared by Steve Albrecht.

*The attorney requested that I analyze the financial statements to determine whether fraud existed and, if so, in which accounts. In my analysis, I used both horizontal and vertical analysis. My converted financial statements are shown below here.*

*Based on my analysis, I drew three conclusions. First, if there were fraud, it had to be in either the "securities sold under agreement to repurchase (repo) account" or in the "securities purchased under agreement to resale (reverse repo)" account. I was not familiar with either of these accounts, but recognized them as being the only accounts large enough to hide massive fraud. Second, I wondered why these two accounts would have identical balances in three of the four years. After I realized that these accounts were really only payables and receivables for the company, my concern heightened. It did not make sense that a company's receivable balance should exactly equal its payable balance in even one year, let alone three in a row. Third, the numbers in the financial statements jumped around randomly. There were large changes from year to year, and often these changes were in opposite directions. In a stable company, only small, consistent changes from year to year are the norm.*

*I called the attorney with my conclusions, and stated that I wasn't sure whether the financial statements were fraudulent but that there were three very significant red flags. I also stated that if fraud were present, it would have to be in the repo and reverse repo accounts.*

Based on this analysis, I was retained as an expert witness in the case. I did not testify, however, because the case was settled out of court for less than $5 million.

Examples of financial statement fraud abound. Some of these frauds are missed by auditors, but they could be easily detected using horizontal or vertical analysis. In many cases, the unexplained changes are obvious; in other cases, they are subtle. Unfortunately, however, managers and even auditors generally use ratios, horizontal analysis, and vertical analysis only as tools for assessing an organization's performance. Rarely do they use these measures to detect fraud.

The third financial statement—the *statement of cash flows*—is already a change statement and doesn't need to be converted. The statement of cash flows shows the cash inflows and cash outflows during a period. A graphic description of this statement is shown in Figure 6-8.

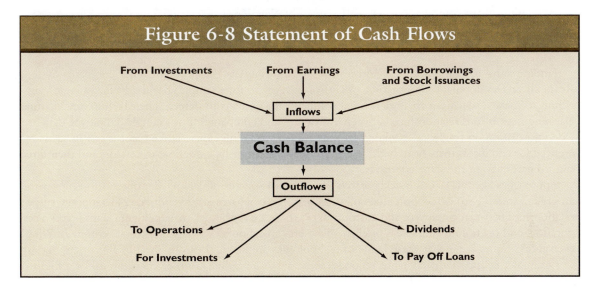

Figure 6-8 Statement of Cash Flows

Increases or decreases that do not make sense serve as red flags and should be investigated. Because the statement of cash flows focuses on changes, it can be used to answer such questions as:

- Is the increase in cash flow as expected?
- Why did receivables go up (down)?
- Why did inventory increase (decrease)?
- Why did payables increase (decrease)?
- Why was there an increase in payables when inventory decreased?
- Why were assets sold (bought)?
- Where did the cash come from to pay dividends?

## Detecting or Identifying Fraud Perpetrators

Thus far our discussion in this chapter has focused on identifying fraudulent transactions. In this last section of the chapter, we discuss the exciting developments in using technology to identify fraud perpetrators and other high-risk individuals. Every time an individual moves, applies for a job or loan, is married, applies for a driver's or other license, takes a certifying examination, is arrested, logs onto the Internet, or conducts any kind of business transaction, identifying data are captured. Like walking in the sand on the beach, we leave financial and other footprints almost anytime we do anything. Relevant information from these records, such as telephone number, address, name, affiliations, and criminal activity, are cross-referenced across databases to search for predictive matches and evaluations.

Although cross-correlations such as these might seem simple, they are actually complicated. The major problem is that personal data contain so many inconsistencies. For example, assume that your address is 925 South, 700 East, Jackson, New Jersey, 00035-4658. The following are ways in which you might write your address:

925 S. 700 East, Jackson, New Jersey, 00035-4658

925 So. 700 East, Jackson, New Jersey, 00035-4658

925 So. 700 E. , Jackson, New Jersey, 00035-4658

925 S. 700 E. Jackson, New Jersey, 00035-4658

925 South 700 E. Jackson, New Jersey, 00035-4658

All of these combinations with N. J. instead of New Jersey

All of these combinations with NJ instead of New Jersey

All of these combinations with 00035 instead of 00035-4658

Other variations

Finding ways to combine these non-obvious relationships is the problem. One company, Systems Research & Development Corporation (SRD) of Las Vegas, for example, has used "fuzzy logic" algorithms to make associations that are normally difficult for humans to detect. Their technology identifies alarming nonobvious relationships between individuals and companies. For example, employee data provide information on residence, banking, phone number, and affiliations. These records can be cross-referenced for criminal activity or to highlight questionable relationships, such as supervisors and their direct subordinates having the same addresses.

Approaches like SRD's can quickly search through vast sources of data to identify relationships within an organization (1) to detect potential collusion between employees and vendors, (2) to identify suspect relationships between employees and customers, (3) to locate repeat risk management claims across a corporation, and (4) to find employees or clients who are "in cahoots" with lists of known criminals. What's even more impressive is that these kinds of technologies are fast and can be used in almost any setting. For example, in approximately eight seconds, someone at an airline counter checking in for a flight or purchasing a ticket can be identified as someone appearing on a terrorist list, someone shopping at a store can be identified as a person who passes bad checks, someone betting at a blackjack table at a casino can be identified as a person who has previously been caught cheating, someone applying for a driver's license can be recognized as a person owing back child support, or someone proposing to your daughter could be identified as one having a criminal record.

Three case studies recently conducted by SRD, for example, found the following:

> *Case 1.* The data from a large consumer product distributor with more than 800,000 employees was analyzed. The analysis revealed 564 employees who had vendor or criminal relationships and 26 employees who were in fact vendors.
>
> *Case 2.* In collusion testing at a major Las Vegas resort, an analysis of more than 20,000 employees (current and terminated), all vendors, customers, in-house arrests and incidents, and their known list of problem people, they found 24 active players who were known criminals, 192 employees who had possible vendor relationships, and seven employees who were in fact vendors.
>
> *Case 3.* A government organization's 10,000 employees, 75,000 vendors, and more than 50,000 known problem people were analyzed. The analysis found 140 employee relationships with vendors, 1,451 vendor relationships to security concerns, 253 employee relationships to security concerns, two vendors who constituted a security concern, and some employees who were either a security concern or vendor.

As these types of technology-based programs become more refined, other nonobvious relationships will become capable of being examined. For example, individuals who have one or two pieces of identification in common but some elements that are different will be able to be analyzed to see if they have relationships.

Although these types of programs are useful in identifying fraud perpetrators or other troublemakers, the concern is that they could be used by individuals who want to cause harm, injury, or loss to others. Unfortunately, those risks are part of our new information economy. As one person recently observed, with developments such as those described here, "There is just no place to hide anymore."

## SUMMARY

Proactive fraud detection methods, especially the high-tech ones, are in their infancy. For years, the only detection method possible, other than hotlines, was discovery sampling, which we will cover in Chapter 7.

With respect to fraud, developments in technology have been both good news and bad news. Computers have given creative perpetrators many new opportunities to commit fraud. Some of these frauds have been much larger than we thought possible. Perpetrators understand that exploiting vulnerabilities in technology means they don't need to physically move the stolen assets. Rather, they merely make a telephone call, key in a transaction, or speak into voice recording instruments. "So if I'm going to steal," the reasoning goes, "I might as well add a few zeros and make life interesting. " However, just as technology has made some frauds easier to commit, it has also made detection much easier.

In this chapter, we discussed three transaction-based technology fraud detection approaches. We also discussed how financial statement analysis can detect fraud. We also discussed new developments that focus on perpetrators, rather than on transactions, to detect fraud. These methods are currently the most effective, but new approaches continue to be developed. Current applications of technology are one of the most exciting areas in fraud research.

When proactive approaches are used, remember that symptoms you observe are just that—only symptoms. Although they may indicate actual fraud, factors other than fraud can also create symptoms. Therefore, symptoms should be thoroughly investigated before you conclude that fraud exists.

## KEY TERMS

**Accounting cycle:** Procedures for analyzing, recording, classifying, summarizing, and reporting the transactions of a business.

**Accounts receivable turnover ratio:** The rate at which a company collects its receivables; computed by dividing sales by average accounts receivable.

**Audit Command Language (ACL):** Popular commercial data-mining software; helps investigators detect fraud.

**Balance sheet:** Financial statement that reports a company's assets, liabilities, and owners' equity as of a particular date.

**Benford's law:** Mathematical algorithm that accurately predicts that, for many data sets, the first digit of each group of numbers in a random sample will begin with a 1 more than a 2, a 2 more than a 3, a 3 more than a 4, and so on; predicts the percentage of time each digit will appear in a sequence of numbers.

**Commercial data-mining software:** Commercial software packages that use query techniques to detect patterns and anomalies in data that may suggest fraud.

**Current ratio:** Measure of the liquidity of a business; equal to current assets divided by current liabilities.

**Database:** Set of interrelated, centrally controlled data files that are stored with as little redundancy as possible.

A database consolidates many records previously stored in separate files into a common pool of data and serves a variety of users and data processing applications.

**Debt-to-equity ratio:** The number of dollars of borrowed funds for every dollar invested by owners; computed as total liabilities divided by total equity.

**Deductive fraud detection:** Determining the types of frauds that can occur and then using query techniques and other methods to determine whether those frauds may actually exist.

**Financial statements:** A document showing credits and debits.

**Horizontal analysis:** Tool that determines the percentage *change* in balance sheet and income statement numbers from one period to the next.

**Income statement:** Financial statement that reports the amount of net income earned by a company during a specified period.

**Inductive fraud detection:** Proactively searching for fraud by identifying anomalies or unusual or unexpected patterns or relationships, without determining in advance the kinds of fraud you are looking for.

**Inventory turnover ratio:** A measure of the efficiency with which inventory is managed; computed by dividing cost of goods sold by average inventory for a period.

**Profit margin:** Measure of the profit generated from each dollar of revenue; calculated by dividing net income by revenue.

**Quick (acid-test) ratio:** Measure of a firm's ability to meet current liabilities, computed by dividing net quick assets (all current assets, except inventories and prepaid expenses) by current liabilities.

**Return on equity:** Measure of the profit earned per dollar of investment; computed by dividing net income by equity.

**Risk assessment:** The identification, analysis, and management of risk, such as the risk associated with the possibility of fraud.

**Statement of cash flows:** Financial statement that reports an entity's cash inflows (receipts) and outflows (payments) during an accounting period.

**Statistical analysis:** The use of statistics and number patterns to discover relationships in certain data, such as Benford's law.

**Vertical analysis:** Tool that converts financial statement numbers to percentages so that they are easy to understand and analyze.

# QUESTIONS AND CASES

## DISCUSSION QUESTIONS

1. Why is it important to proactively detect fraud?

2. What is the purpose of commercial data-mining software?

3. What are the advantages of using commercial data-mining software to detect fraud?

4. What are the disadvantages of using commercial data-mining software?

5. What are the advantages of using statistical analysis to detect fraud?

6. What are the disadvantages of statistical analysis?

7. What is Benford's law?

8. What is deductive fraud detection?

9. How can fraud be detected by analyzing financial statements?

10. What is the significance of unexplained changes in financial statements in detecting fraud?

11. What are some of the difficulties in trying to correlate customers, vendors, or employees with known problem people?

## TRUE/FALSE

1. Unusual patterns always indicate the existence of fraud.

2. Transferring all corporate data in original form can involve the transfer of terabytes of information.

3. Statistical analysis uses the company's database to search for normal relationships between numbers.

4. According to Benford's law, the first digit of random sets of numbers will begin with a 9 more often than with an 8.

5. When using Benford's law, potential suspects are less likely to know you are trying to detect fraud than if you use more direct detection techniques.

6. Understanding the kinds of frauds that can occur is not important when using a deductive detection method.

7. Statistical analysis, such as Benford's law, can be performed on databases of any size.

8. Proactive fraud detection can pay large dividends and is an effective way to reduce the cost of fraud in any organization.

9. Unexplained changes are common in financial statements.

10. Balance sheets must be converted to change statements before they can be used in detecting fraud.

11. Vertical analysis is a more direct method than horizontal analysis in focusing on changes in financial statements from one period to another.

12. Vertical analysis is a useful detection technique because percentages are easily understood.

13. It is impossible to identify an employee who has a previous arrest record, but who changes his name and lives at the same address.

## MULTIPLE CHOICE

1. When detecting fraud, it is important that fraud investigators:
   a. Remain objective and neutral.
   b. Assume guilt.
   c. Assume innocence.
   d. None of the above.

2. Data mining:
   a. Determines the cost of fraud.
   b. Identifies possible fraud suspects.
   c. Looks for anomalies in databases.
   d. All of the above.

3. Once a buyer starts accepting kickbacks from a supplier:
   a. Prices often increase.
   b. Purchases from other vendors often decrease.
   c. The supplier usually takes control of the purchasing relationship.
   d. All of the above.

4. What is the most obvious disadvantage of data mining?
   a. Databases are very large and often cannot be analyzed using off-the-shelf products.
   b. High cost.
   c. The decrease in employee morale.
   d. None of the above.

5. Benford's law:
   a. Is usually unsuccessful as a fraud detection tool.
   b. Predicts that the first digit of random number sets will begin with a 1 more often than a 2, a 2 more often than a 3, and so on.
   c. Applies to personal ID numbers.
   d. All of the above.

6. A detection method that focuses on the kinds of frauds that can occur and then uses technology to determine whether those frauds actually exist is called:
   a. Fishing fraud detection.
   b. Data mining.
   c. Deductive fraud detection.
   d. Benford's law.

7. When deciding which detection method to use, it is important to:
   a. Determine the advantages and disadvantages of each approach.
   b. Identify the costs involved.
   c. Determine which method will meet the client's objectives.
   d. All of the above.

8. Fraud is best detected through financial statements by focusing on:
   a. Unexplained changes in financial statement balances.
   b. Consistencies.
   c. Intuition.
   d. Management's behavior when financial statements are released.

9. The most effective way to convert balance sheets and income statements from position and period statements to change statements is to:
   a. Compare balances in the statements from one period to the next.
   b. Calculate key ratios and compare them from period to period.
   c. Perform horizontal and vertical analysis.
   d. All of the above.

10. Profit margin, return on assets, and return on equity are all examples of:
    a. Vertical analysis.
    b. Key financial statement ratios.
    c. Horizontal analysis.
    d. None of the above.

11. When vertical analysis is performed:
    a. Ratios are used to detect fraud.
    b. Changes in significant balance totals are examined.
    c. Financial statement balances are converted to percentages.
    d. Total revenues are compared to total expenses.

12. Horizontal analysis is different from vertical analysis in that:
    a. Horizontal analysis is more important than vertical analysis.
    b. Horizontal analysis calculates the percentage change in balance sheet and income statement numbers from one period to the next, while vertical analysis converts balances in a single period to percentages.
    c. Horizontal analysis converts balances in a single period to percentages, while vertical analysis calculates the percentage change in balance sheet and income statement numbers from one period to the next.
    d. Key ratios are compared from one period to the next.

13. Which of the following is *not* a disadvantage of using commercial data-mining software to detect fraud?
   a. It is a static approach, and results cannot be recombined in different ways.
   b. Data-mining software can only be used to analyze small data sets.
   c. Commercial data-mining software often identifies thousands of possible fraud symptoms.
   d. Commercial data-mining software is easy to use in detecting fraud.

14. Benford's law is:
   a. The most expensive of all the digital analysis methods to implement and use.
   b. The most effective way to identify actual frauds.
   c. A method that uses vertical financial statement analysis.
   d. An effective way to identify anomalies in data sets.

15. If a search reveals that an employee and a vendor have the same telephone number, this result may indicate:
   a. Vendors are overcharging for goods purchased.
   b. Employees may be establishing dummy vendors.
   c. Contractors are billing at the wrong rates.
   d. A vendor is receiving kickbacks or other favors.

16. When conducting financial statement analysis, which ratio will be the most useful in determining whether a company has erroneously inflated accounts receivable?
   a. Current ratio.
   b. Profit margin.
   c. Accounts receivable turnover.
   d. Debt percentage.

## SHORT CASES

**Case 1.** Boxer Incorporated hired you as a consultant to implement a proactive fraud detection program in the company. One of the owners, Priscilla Boxer, asks you to give a presentation to several executives about the different approaches you are considering. After evaluating the company, you narrow the possibilities down to two choices: (a) commercial data-mining software, and (b) statistical analysis, such as Benford's law.

1. List the advantages and disadvantages of each approach.

2. What factors will you need to know to make your decision?

**Case 2.** A large manufacturing business hired you as a fraud detection specialist. The first day on the job, your boss asks you the following questions:

1. What is Benford's law?

2. In what situations is it appropriate to use Benford's law, and in what situations is Benford's law inappropriate?

**Case 3.** Dennis Jones, an old college friend, contacted you last week. Dennis owns several car washes and believes that financial statement fraud may be occurring. (He pays each car wash manager a bonus if a certain level of profits is earned and is worried that some managers are overstating profits to earn a higher bonus.) Dennis is coming over today to see whether you can help him determine whether his suspicions are valid. He is bringing along the financial statements for each car wash (income statements, balance sheets, and cash flow statements) for the last five years.

What kind of financial statement analysis could you perform to help Dennis detect possible fraud?

**Case 4.** Your boss knows you are taking a fraud examination course at a local university. He is interested in learning more about proactive fraud detection and asks you to prepare a short memo briefly explaining proactive fraud detection methods and approaches. List three proactive fraud detection approaches and briefly explain them.

**Case 5.**

> There once was a corporation from Nantucket,
> Its controls leaked like holes in a bucket.
> Smelling trouble with the buyer,
> And with the supplier,
> They determined to fix it or chuck it.

This limerick accurately depicts Bucket Corp., which manufactures wood furniture. Bucket has enjoyed several years of good profits, but now recently sees some alarming trends in its bottom line. Although not drastic, Bucket's profits first stagnated, and are now beginning to decline. After some cost analysis and investigation of financial records, the company determined that the problem may be coming from the procurement division of operations. On the next page is a small random sample of invoices from various vendors:

| Supplier | Product | Price/Ton | Quantity | Total |
|---|---|---|---|---|
| Woods 'R' Us | Oak | $157.00 | 2 | $314.00 |
| | Cherry | 75.00 | 3 | 225.00 |
| | Cedar | 125.00 | 1.5 | 187.50 |
| | Spruce | 42.00 | 3 | 126.00 |
| Harris Lumber | Oak | 215.00 | 4 | 860.00 |
| | Cherry | 115.00 | 8 | 920.00 |
| | Cedar | 140.00 | 6 | 840.00 |
| | Spruce | 80.00 | 9 | 720.00 |
| Lumber Jack's | Oak | 158.00 | 1 | 158.00 |
| | Cherry | 74.00 | 2 | 148.00 |
| | Cedar | 124.00 | 2 | 248.00 |
| | Spruce | 43.00 | 3 | 129.00 |
| Small's Lumber | Oak | 156.00 | 3 | 468.00 |
| | Cherry | 76.00 | 3 | 228.00 |
| | Cedar | 127.00 | 1 | 127.00 |
| | Spruce | 41.00 | 4 | 164.00 |

What could the CFO do to investigate the potential problems in the procurement department of Bucket Corp. Do you think fraud is involved? Why?

**Case 6.** By ordering unnecessary products at inflated prices, the purchasing manager of XYZ Company defrauded his employer of more than $40,000 over a two-year period.

How could you have detected this fraud?

**Case 8.**

| Check No. | Description | Amount |
|---|---|---|
| 2001 | Payment to US West for phone bill | $ 235.65 |
| 2002 | John's Heating and Cooling for fixing A/C in December | $ 654.36 |
| 2003 | Sharky's Used Car Dealership for Yugo truck | $4,987.36 |
| 2004 | Salt River Project for power in December | $ 339.13 |
| 2005 | Arizona Department of Internal Revenue for taxes | $ 475.98 |
| 2006 | Grainger Corp. for power tools | $ 254.14 |
| 2007 | Home Depot for outdoor carport | $ 504.17 |
| 2008 | Steelin's consulting for help with computer network | $ 171.54 |
| 2009 | Payment to US West for phone bill in January | $ 326.45 |
| 2010 | Bank of America for loan payment | $ 477.67 |

1. Compare the first-digit frequency in these transactions with Benford's law. What are the results?

2. Could fraud be occurring in this organization?

**Case 9.** As an internal auditor for CRA, Inc., you are assigned to a team working on an ongoing project to identify possible fraud. The project started as a data-mining exercise to analyze the company's databases and identify possible problems. The project was started last year, but because of budget problems, it was delayed until this year. Most of the data mining is complete, but the team is having problems sorting through all the information. Your manager is certain that this data-mining approach is the best method in a large company such as CRA.

**Case 7.** As CEO of your company, you go over your financial statements and notice something disturbing. You perform a horizontal analysis and find that sales have been increasing at a rate of 3 percent per year, while inventory has risen at a rate of 29 percent per year.

1. Could fraud be occurring? Why or why not?

2. Assuming that fraud is being committed, how would you investigate?

1. Discuss the strengths and possible weaknesses of the data-mining approach for CRA.

2. What other approaches should be considered?

**Case 10.** Large frauds can often be detected by performing financial statement analysis. Although such analysis can raise areas of concern, not all red flags are the result of fraudulent activities. Reasonable explanations often exist for anomalies in financial statements.

The statement of cash flows is one financial statement that is analyzed in order to identify possible fraud. The statement for Kelly Enterprises, Inc., for a three-year period follows.

**Kelly Enterprises, Inc.**
**Statement of Cash Flows**
**For the Period Ended December 31, 2004**

| In millions | 2004 | 2003 | 2002 |
|---|---|---|---|
| **Cash from Operations** | | | |
| Net income | $900 | $800 | $ 450 |
| Change in accounts receivable | (706) | (230) | 25 |
| Change in accounts payable | 150 | 45 | 90 |
| Change in inventory | 50 | (15) | 25 |
| Depreciation | 105 | 90 | 65 |
| Net cash from operations | 499 | 690 | 655 |
| | | | |
| **Cash from Investing** | | | |
| Additions to property, plant, and equipment | (950) | (690) | (790) |
| Proceeds from sale of securities | 25 | 56 | 15 |
| Net cash from investing | (925) | (634) | (775) |
| | | | |
| **Cash from Financing** | | | |
| Borrowings of long-term debt | 250 | 150 | 34 |
| Cash dividends | (140) | (85) | (45) |
| Net cash from financing | 110 | 65 | (11) |
| Increase (decrease) in cash | $(316) | $121 | $(131) |

1. Identify possible red flags.

2. Indicate any reasonable explanations that might exist for the areas of concern.

**Case 11.** By examining first digits, Company XYZ suspects fraud. You are asked to review the following sample of invoices to make sure they make sense. You are familiar with several fraud detection methods and are eager to try out Benford's law.

Do you suspect possible fraud? Why?

| | Invoice Amounts | |
|---|---|---|
| $149,200.00 | $ 19,489.00 | $1,134.00 |
| 1,444.00 | 12,485.00 | 446.00 |
| 1,756.00 | 26,995.00 | 678.00 |
| 91.59 | 235,535.00 | 456.00 |
| 2,250.00 | 59,155.00 | 341.00 |
| 38,005.00 | 109,995.00 | 890.00 |
| 45,465.00 | 212,536.00 | 402.00 |
| 112,495.00 | 685.00 | 467.00 |
| 137,500.00 | 765.00 | 465.00 |
| 37,300.00 | 234.00 | 1,516.00 |
| 36,231.00 | 435.00 | 375.00 |
| 26,695.00 | 1,045.00 | 679.00 |

# EXTENSIVE CASES

**Extensive Case 1.** You are in your first month as an internal auditor in the corporate offices of Cover-Up Fraud-Mart, a large regional variety store chain based in Los Angeles. Your manager has just given you a general overview of the company's problems with fraud. In fact, losses from fraud exceed losses from shoplifting by tenfold, and management wants your perspective on what it can do to proactively detect fraud. From your fraud auditing class, you know that the deductive approach is one of the most effective detection methods.

**Questions**

1. What is the difference between the two inductive fraud detection methods discussed in this chapter and this deductive method?

2. List the five steps involved in the deductive fraud detection method.

**Extensive Case 2.** Using the financial information provided here and on the following pages, compute the required ratios list on the ratio analysis sheet, and then complete the horizontal and vertical analysis worksheets.

**ABC Company**
**Balance Sheet**
As of December 31, 2002

| ASSETS | 2002 | 2001 | 2000 |
|---|---|---|---|
| Current assets | | | |
| Cash | $ 501,992 | $ 434,215 | $ 375,141 |
| Accounts receivable | 335,272 | 302,514 | 241,764 |
| Inventory | 515,174 | 505,321 | 310,885 |
| Prepaid expenses | 251,874 | 231,100 | 136,388 |
| Total current assets | $1,604,312 | $1,473,150 | $1,064,178 |
| Property, plant, and equipment | 765,215 | 735,531 | 705,132 |
| Accumulated depreciation | (218,284) | (196,842) | (175,400) |
| TOTAL ASSETS | $2,151,243 | $2,011,839 | $1,593,910 |
| LIABILITIES | | | |
| Current liabilities | | | |
| Accounts payable | $ 248,494 | $ 366,864 | $ 322,156 |
| Accrued liabilities | 122,192 | 216,533 | 215,474 |
| Income taxes payable | 10,645 | 25,698 | 22,349 |
| Current portion of long-term debt | 42,200 | 42,200 | 42,200 |
| Total current liabilities | $ 423,531 | $ 651,295 | $ 602,179 |
| Long-term liabilities | | | |
| Long-term debt | 425,311 | 400,311 | 375,100 |
| TOTAL LIABILITIES | $ 848,842 | $1,051,606 | $ 977,279 |
| | | | |
| STOCKHOLDERS' EQUITY | | | |
| Common stock | $ 370,124 | $ 356,758 | $ 320,841 |
| Additional paid-in capital | 29,546 | 24,881 | 21,910 |
| Retained earnings | 578,594 | 273,880 | 75,315 |
| Total stockholders' equity | $ 978,264 | $ 655,519 | $ 418,066 |
| TOTAL LIABILITIES AND STOCKHOLDERS' EQUITY | $1,827,106 | $1,707,125 | $1,395,345 |

**ABC Company**
**Income Statement**
For the Period Ended December 31, 2002

| | 2002 | 2001 | 2000 |
|---|---|---|---|
| Sales | $1,572,134 | $1,413,581 | $1,158,417 |
| Cost of goods sold | 601,215 | 556,721 | 500,702 |
| Gross profit | $ 970,919 | $ 856,860 | $ 657,715 |
| EXPENSES | | | |
| Advertising | $ 55,153 | $ 50,531 | $ 42,150 |
| Depreciation | 21,442 | 21,442 | 21,442 |
| Bad debts | 20,151 | 18,934 | 17,943 |
| Legal | 17,261 | 10,207 | 9,701 |
| Miscellaneous | 91,014 | 31,214 | 29,104 |
| Rent | 148,321 | 142,078 | 141,143 |
| Repairs and maintenance | 14,315 | 13,642 | 11,932 |
| Salaries and wages | 47,121 | 45,312 | 39,142 |
| Utilities | 15,912 | 15,643 | 14,217 |
| Total expenses | $ 430,690 | $ 349,003 | $ 326,774 |
| Net income before income tax | $ 540,229 | $ 507,857 | $ 330,941 |
| Income tax expense | 216,092 | 203,143 | 132,376 |
| NET INCOME | $ 324,137 | $ 304,714 | $ 198,565 |
| Number of shares of stock outstanding | 35,913 | 26,786 | 23,712 |

**ABC Company**
**Ratio Analysis**
December 31, 2002

| LIQUIDITY RATIOS: | 12/31/02 | 12/31/01 | Change | % Change |
|---|---|---|---|---|
| Current ratio | | | | |
|    Current assets / Current liabilities | _____ | _____ | _____ | _____ |
| Quick ratio | | | | |
|    (Current assets − Inventory) / Current liabilities | _____ | _____ | _____ | _____ |
| Accounts receivable turnover | | | | |
|    Sales / Average accounts receivable | _____ | _____ | _____ | _____ |
| Days sales in accounts receivable | | | | |
|    365 / Accounts receivable turnover | _____ | _____ | _____ | _____ |
| Inventory turnover | | | | |
|    Cost of goods sold / Average inventory | _____ | _____ | _____ | _____ |
| **PROFITABILITY/PERFORMANCE RATIOS:** | | | | |
| Profit margin | | | | |
|    Net income / Net sales | _____ | _____ | _____ | _____ |
| Gross profit margin (%) | | | | |
|    Gross profit / Sales | _____ | _____ | _____ | _____ |
| Earnings per share | | | | |
|    Net income / Number of shares of stock | _____ | _____ | _____ | _____ |
| Sales / Total assets | | | | |
|    Sales / Total assets | _____ | _____ | _____ | _____ |
| Sales / Working capital | | | | |
|    Sales / (Current assets − Current liabilities) | _____ | _____ | _____ | _____ |
| **EQUITY POSITION RATIOS:** | | | | |
| Owners' equity / Total assets | | | | |
|    Total stockholders' equity / Total assets | _____ | _____ | _____ | _____ |
| Current liabilities / Owners' equity | | | | |
|    Current liabilities / Total stockholders' equity | _____ | _____ | _____ | _____ |
| Total liabilities / Owners' equity | | | | |
|    Total liabilities / Total stockholders' equity | _____ | _____ | _____ | _____ |

**ABC Company**
**Income Statement**
For the Period Ended December 31, 2002

| | 2002 | 2001 | $ Change | % Change |
|---|---|---|---|---|
| Sales | $1,572,134 | $1,413,581 | | |
| Cost of goods sold | 601,215 | 556,721 | _____ | _____ |
| Gross profit | $ 970,919 | $ 856,860 | _____ | _____ |
| | | | | |
| EXPENSES | | | | |
|   Advertising | $ 55,153 | $ 50,531 | | |
|   Depreciation | 21,442 | 21,442 | | |
|   Bad debts | 20,151 | 18,934 | | |
|   Legal | 17,261 | 10,207 | | |
|   Miscellaneous | 91,014 | 31,214 | | |
|   Rent | 148,321 | 142,078 | | |
|   Repairs and maintenance | 14,315 | 13,642 | | |
|   Salaries and wages | 47,121 | 45,312 | | |
|   Utilities | 15,912 | 15,643 | _____ | _____ |
|   Total expenses | $ 430,690 | $ 349,003 | _____ | _____ |
| Net income before income tax | $ 540,229 | $ 507,857 | | |
|   Income tax expense | 216,092 | 203,143 | _____ | _____ |
| NET INCOME | $ 324,137 | $ 304,714 | _____ | _____ |

**ABC Company**
**Balance Sheet**
As of December 31, 2002

| | 2002 | % Total Assets | 2001 | % Total Assets | 2000 | % Total Assets |
|---|---|---|---|---|---|---|
| **ASSETS** | | | | | | |
| **Current assets** | | | | | | |
| Cash | $ 501,992 | | $ 434,215 | | $ 375,141 | |
| Accounts receivable | 335,272 | | 302,514 | | 241,764 | |
| Inventory | 515,174 | | 505,321 | | 310,885 | |
| Prepaid expenses | 251,874 | | 231,100 | | 136,388 | |
| Total current assets | $1,604,312 | | $1,473,150 | | $1,064,178 | |
| Property, plant, and equipment | 765,215 | | 735,531 | | 705,132 | |
| Accumulated depreciation | (218,284) | | (196,842) | | (175,400) | |
| **TOTAL ASSETS** | $2,151,243 | | $2,011,839 | | $1,593,910 | |
| **LIABILITIES** | | | | | | |
| **Current liabilities** | | | | | | |
| Accounts payable | $ 248,494 | | $ 366,864 | | $ 322,156 | |
| Accrued liabilities | 122,192 | | 216,533 | | 215,474 | |
| Income taxes payable | 10,645 | | 25,698 | | 22,349 | |
| Current portion of long-term debt | 42,200 | | 42,200 | | 42,200 | |
| Total current liabilities | $ 423,531 | | $ 651,295 | | $ 602,179 | |
| **Long-term liabilities** | | | | | | |
| Long-term debt | 425,311 | | 400,311 | | 375,100 | |
| **TOTAL LIABILITIES** | $ 848,842 | | $1,051,606 | | $ 977,279 | |
| **STOCKHOLDERS' EQUITY** | | | | | | |
| Common stock | $ 370,124 | | $ 356,758 | | $ 320,841 | |
| Additional paid-in capital | 29,546 | | 24,881 | | 21,910 | |
| Retained earnings | 578,594 | | 273,880 | | 75,315 | |
| Total stockholders' equity | $ 978,264 | | $ 655,519 | | $ 418,066 | |
| **TOTAL LIABILITIES AND STOCKHOLDERS' EQUITY** | $1,827,106 | | $1,707,125 | | $1,395,345 | |

## INTERNET ASSIGNMENTS

1. Read the article entitled "Following Benford's Law, or Looking Out for No. 1" found at http://256.com/gray/info/benfords.html. The article mentions that a statistics professor can easily discern if students flipped a coin 200 times or if they merely faked it. Of this exercise, the professor stated, "Most people do not know the real odds of such an exercise, so they cannot fake data convincingly. " How does that exercise relate to Benford's law and detecting fraud?

2. Go to http://technewsworld.com/story/ 31280.html and http://www.aaai.org/AITopics/ html/fraud.html and answer the following questions.

   a. What is a neural network?
   b. How can neural networks be used to detect fraud?
   c. Which industries will benefit most from neural network technology?
   d. Who is developing this technology?

3. Credit card companies are concerned with the growing problem of credit card fraud. They spend enormous amounts of money each year on detection. Go to the Web site of a large credit card company, such as Visa, MasterCard, or American Express. What are some of the proactive measures these institutions are taking to control fraud and to persuade the public that it is safe to use credit cards?

## DEBATE

You are the new controller of a major U. S. manufacturing firm. In your previous employment, you detected multiple varieties of fraud. The CFO of your new company informs you that top management is concerned about possible fraud in the organization and is interested in taking a proactive approach both to detecting fraud and deterring fraud. After noting that he has recommended you for the fraud detection assignment, the CFO tells you that he is a little nervous about how much these investigative approaches will cost and asks you to keep your choices simple and inexpensive. You and the CFO are good friends, and you've never had a problem suggesting ideas about upcoming projects in the past.

You know that to be most effective in completing your new assignment, you should do some extensive data analysis because of the large size of the company and its databases.

Have one person take the position of the CFO who wants to keep analysis simple and another the position of the controller who believes more extreme approaches are necessary. Debate the appropriateness of the various detection approaches, including the deductive approach, for your company. Explain why data mining using commercial software may not be sufficient.

# APPENDIX

## DATA ANALYSIS BASICS

In Chapter 6, we identified two methods of fraud detection: the inductive and deductive approaches. In both approaches, the analysis of data from transactions, corporate servers, and Web sites is often required. In recent years, data analysis has become an important part of fraud detection and investigation for many reasons. First, because most data created in the past few decades are stored as digital transactions on servers, they provide efficient and powerful access to large stores of information. Second, most fraud schemes are hidden in transactions; data analysis provides a primary means of locating these transactions. Finally, the rapidly increasing speed and capacity of corporate servers, personal computers, and laptops puts significant power in the hands of fraud investigators.

Data analysis is the process of systematically applying statistical and logical techniques to describe, summarize, and compare data. Fraud investigators use a variety of data analysis techniques to compare data against each other. Comparisons can be made on individual transactions, such as receiving reports, or on summarizations of transactions, such as monthly income statements.

The purpose of this appendix is to introduce you to the concepts required for data analysis. It is important to understand that data analysis is a complex and comprehensive topic. Indeed, students in fields such as statistics or information systems spend considerable time studying different methods of data representation and analysis. This Appendix offers the foundation for further study, should you choose to do so. If you can understand how data are organized, represented, and accessed, you will know how to study additional topics or direct members of your investigative teams appropriately.

## Fraud Investigators as Data Analysts

As a fraud examiner, you will always be an investigator in the traditional sense: you will collect facts, interview subjects, and gather other types of evidence. However, as the world becomes increasingly digital, you will find yourself wearing the hat of a *data analyst*. Today's evidence is often found in corporate transaction databases, e-mail servers, chat rooms, electronic spreadsheets, and other digital areas.

Data analysis provides an excellent source of fraud evidence for several reasons. First, data are objective. They represent facts about a transaction, communication, or event that can be related to one another objectively. Double-entry accounting (matching debits and credits on each entry) ensures that transactions always affect at least two accounts. Fraud is often found through discrepancies between accounts.

Second, data can be searched and analyzed without arousing suspicion. With most investigations, it is important to keep a low profile during the early stages. For example, you would normally want to interview your primary target only after all other parties have been interviewed. One advantage of data analysis comes from being able to perform it behind the scenes and without any contact with those involved in the case.

Third, data analysis can provide evidence that helps with other areas of your investigation. For example, you may find facts about transactions that direct your public database searches.

Finally, data analysis often provides facts needed to gain confessions during interviews. It helps you plan questions and strategies for successful interviews.

Auditors, investigators, and fraud examiners used to sort through thousands of paper documents. Boxes of paper documents were shipped to team member offices, where they were examined for bits of evidence that could be combined to make a case. This work was tedious, somewhat boring, and expensive. Even though paper documents will likely always be important, increasing amounts of data are stored electronically. The availability of electronic data presents both an advantage and a challenge to fraud investigators. The advantage of electronic evidence is the incredible power of computers at your disposal. It takes a computer script only seconds to analyze transactions that traditionally took days to examine. Using computers, you can be more efficient and more thorough; you can examine 100 percent of the available transactions. Once programmed, a program obeys your instructions tirelessly and exactly. Some may argue that it takes just as much time to write a script to do an analysis as it does to perform the analysis manually. Although this argument may be true at times, writing a short program to analyze data is generally preferred. First, you know the analysis is performed exactly without human error. Second, you have not only the results, but also a script that can be reused at a later date. Over time, you can develop a "toolbox" of general-purpose scripts to apply to new investigations. This toolbox will help you reach economies of scale on future projects. Most importantly, this approach gives you the satisfaction of knowing you spent your time doing something clever and interesting rather than relegating yourself to the mediocrity of repetitive work.

The challenge of electronic data is that it raises the bar for fraud investigators. In addition to knowing traditional skills such as investigating and interviewing, you need to know how data are organized, stored, accessed, and analyzed. As with most fields, the advent of computers presents new topics and methods for students to learn.

You may be wondering how skilled in analysis you need to become. Currently, many investigators rely upon IT departments to do their "heavy lifting" in data analysis. Other investigators simply hire an information systems or computer science graduate to work on their teams. You may choose these options, but keep in mind that relying upon others to do your analysis has several disadvantages:

- If you only use the applications designed by an IT department (such as a sales entry or journal entry application), you normally see only the reports that come out of the system. These reports typically show only 10–20 percent of the available data columns. You may miss columns that could be vital to your investigation.
- IT departments are normally busy and overworked. Ad hoc requests can sometimes take a long time (days or weeks) when employees generally must maintain their routine workload as well.
- Most importantly, forensic analysis is usually iterative in nature. Because real-world data are noisy, the first run of an analysis script or algorithm generally produces only marginal results. You need to run your analysis, evaluate the results, tweak the analysis, rerun, evaluate, tweak, rerun, evaluate, and so forth through many iterations. If you work through another person or IT department, this iterative process is often lengthened. If you run the analysis yourself, iterations can be done in a fraction of the time it would take otherwise.

In sum, when you know how to query and analyze data yourself, you are significantly more efficient and effective because you are able to get to all the data quickly. We recognize that it is not practical for all fraud detectives to become data analysis experts. However, we project that the common fraud investigator will be more and more tech-savvy in the future. To learn these skills, identify something new each year to learn about data analysis. You have a whole career to work toward mastery of all forensic topics. Be sure to include data analysis in your continuing education each year.

Fraud investigators need to decide how literate to become in the analysis of transactions. Understanding of data analysis occurs on several levels:

1. Total ignorance of data analysis possibilities
2. Understanding of what data are available
3. Understanding of what procedures and analysis routines can be done (and for what purpose)
4. Ability to generate reports out of preprogrammed systems
5. Ability to query underlying databases for data, then load into Excel or Access for analysis
6. Full scripting ability to analyze the underlying databases directly

If you decide to specialize in an area other than data analysis, you should at least know the basics of what is possible and what is available. This knowledge will help you work with IT departments and hired data analysis specialists effectively.

## Data and Information

It is important to understand the difference between *data* and *information*. In common use, the two terms are often used interchangeably. However, when used technically, the two terms are quite different. "A datum is a statement accepted at face value."[1] In other words, data are facts about a case. Examples of data are *30 brooms were ordered for $8.99 on June 3*; *Sally's brother is Dave*; and *Sally earns $13.50 per hour*. "Data on its own has little meaning; only when interpreted by some kind of data processing system does it take on meaning and become information."[2] Information is created when data are processed, compared, or analyzed. Examples of information are *30 brooms were ordered at 50% above regular cost*; *one* *of our purchaser's brothers is a vendor we pay high prices to*; and *Sally earned 100% percent more this year than last year*. It is the job of the forensic analyst to process data in ways that create useful information about a case. As evident in the stated examples, information is normally created for fraud detection by comparing data.

For example, suppose Joe purchases equipment for $18,900 from a given supplier. What does this statement tell us? On its own, this datum provides little knowledge about potential fraud. However, if through searching the database, we find out that the average price of this equipment across all suppliers is $11,000, we immediately question Joe's purchase. By comparing associated data, we generate information.

## Data Types

Each datum in a database or file is of a certain type. For example, a pay rate is typically represented with a *float* type, meaning it has an integer part and a decimal part. Data types are important because they allow the computer to know what operations can occur on values in a database. For example, division has meaning for two floats, but it has no meaning for character values such as a first name.

When preparing data for analysis, it is important to know the types of fields you will work with. Investigators who analyze data without understanding their types often produce unexpected results. The following list describes several basic data types:

- *String*: A string (also known as *text*, *char*, or *varchar*) can contain text (letters and numbers). String fields in databases normally specify a maximum size of 10 characters, 50 characters, and so on. Strings often contain names, cities, descriptions, and other textual data.
- *Integer*: An integer (also known as *int, long, bigint*, or *smallint*) is a whole number such as 3, 5, or 597. Integer fields support math operations, including calculations on groups in the form of sums, averages, and so on. Regular integer fields do not allow decimal points.
- *Float*: A floating-point field (also known as *double* or *money*) is a regular number comprised of an integer part and a decimal part like 3.14, 5.0, and 597.2. As with integers, floats support math operations. Although floats may seem to encompass the functionality of integers, they have important differences. First, floats take more memory per value. Second, because computers approximate the actual decimal value of a float, 1.0 + 1.0 might equal 1.9999998 rather than 2.0.
- *Date*: A date field (also known as *time* or *timestamp*) holds a date and/or a time of day.

While operations on most data types may be obvious to you, working with dates has several challenges. This complication is unfortunate because dates and periods (e.g., two weeks) are usually important to fraud investigators. First, the apparent nonlinear Gregorian calendar used in most of the modern world is challenging for most people to use. For example, Julius Ceasar originally made all odd months 31 days long. When Augustus had a month named after him, he moved a day from February to August so his month would also have 31 days. As another example, what are the rules for leap years? If you think every four years, you've only begun to explore the rules. The variety of days in months, weeks, and years progressing independently, time zones, and other variations cause confusion for fraud analysts.

Second, date representation from one country to the next (and one database to the next) is rarely consistent. Although ISO standards define standard formats for dates, many implementations use alternative formats. For example, does 01/02/03 refer to January 2, 2003; February 1, 2003; March 2, 2001; or some other date? The answer depends upon the country and database where the question is asked.

Fortunately, an easy solution has relieved a great deal of date confusion. If you think about time, it is a simple, linear line going into the past and into the future—like a single-axis number line counting forward and backward. Many operating systems simply pick a point in time to be the *epoch*, or zero point, and count seconds (or milliseconds) forward or backward from that point. The number of seconds from the epoch is called the *tick* value. For example, January 1, 1970 (the Unix epoch) is 0 ticks in the Unix operating system; December 25, 2006 is 1,167,116,400 ticks; and April 6, 1930 is -1,254,070,800 ticks.

If dates are converted to *ticks* during import, most date problems are solved. For example, date arithmetic becomes simple addition or subtraction between two numbers. Many analysis programs and scripting languages contain built-in functions that convert to and from ticks. Although ticks may be difficult for you to read, they work extremely well in analysis.

# Data Organization and Format

Often the most difficult data analysis step is gaining access to it, organizing it, and formatting it appropriately for your analysis. This section describes how data are stored, transferred, and formatted.

At their core, digital computers store data using bits: binary 1s and 0s. These bits may be located in computer memory or on disk, CD, or tape. The storage of data is always in bits, but the arrangement of the bits varies from application to application. This arrangement is similar to the way that many European languages use the same basic character set but arrange the characters differently. Fortunately, most corporate data are stored using one of two mechanisms: file-based storage and database-based storage.

## File Based Data

A file is a section of storage on a computer. You are probably familiar with many different types of files: word-processing documents, spreadsheets, MP3 music files, and pictures from a digital camera. File-based corporate data are most often stored in structured text files called *fixed format*, *delimited text*, or *eXtensible Markup Language (XML)* files. Even when data are stored in a format other than text, it is almost always converted text when transmitted. For example, suppose you request a set of electronic invoice records from a company. The company will most likely convert the data to fixed format or delimited text format before sending them to you. Text files can be read with a standard text editor such as Windows Notepad or WordPad. More advanced editors are available at shareware prices on the Internet.[3] Most often, you will import text files into a spreadsheet, database, or more advanced analysis package. For example, Microsoft Excel imports fixed format and delimited text files easily.

Fixed format is one of the oldest data formats still in use today. In these files, each row delineates a new record; the first row normally specifies the field (column) names. Each field is a specified number of characters. Consider the following example (the column numbers are not part of the file):

```
          10        20        30        40        50        60        70
12345678901234567890123456789012345678901234567890123456789012345678901234567890
ID    First     Last      Street        City           State   ZIP
1001 Ted        Wils, Jr. 132 Maple     Brooksville    AL      10232
1002 Sheena     Taylor    92 Roundy Way Dana           CA      83222
```

The first line of the file provides the field names (ID, First, Last, etc.). Ted's record is in line 2 and Sheena's record is in line 3. By looking at the file, we see that the fields start and end with the following character numbers:

| Field | Start | End | Length |
|-------|-------|-----|--------|
| ID    | 1     | 5   | 5 characters |
| First | 6     | 15  | 10 characters |
| Last  | 16    | 25  | 10 characters |
| Street | 26   | 39  | 14 characters |
| City  | 40    | 54  | 15 characters |
| State | 55    | 60  | 6 characters |
| ZIP   | 61    | 65  | 5 characters |

Delimited text files are similar to fixed format files, except they allow variable field length and use a special character to separate (delimit) fields. Two common implementations of delimited text are comma-separated values (CSV) and tab-separated values (TSV). Consider the following CSV example that uses a comma to separate the values:

```
ID,First,Last,Street,City,State,ZIP
1001,Ted,"Wils, Jr.",132 Maple,Brooksville,AL,10232
1002,Sheena,Taylor,92 Roundy Way,Dana,CA,83222
```

Note that while fixed format is easier to read, delimited text is more concise. Note also that quotes are required around Ted's last name—Wils, Jr.—because it contains a comma as part of the value of the field. Further rules specify what happens when both commas and quotes appear in field values. An Internet search can provide the exact rules of delimited text files. It is important for this discussion that you understand the basic layout of delimited text files.

One limitation of text files is they hold only the raw data; they do not contain information about field type. For example, neither the fixed format nor delimited text file specifies whether the ID field is a number or a character field. Field type becomes important when arithmetic or dates are needed.

Recently, XML has become a popular alternative for transferring data. XML is actually a simplified version of a much older technology called SGML. XML uses hierarchical start and end tags to delineate data fields and records, and it provides much more freedom and specificity than fixed format or delimited text files. Consider the following example:

```
<records>
  <person>
    <field name="ID" type="int">1001</field>
    <field name="First" type="char">Ted</field>
    <field name="Last" type="char">Wils, Jr.</field>
    <field name="Street" type="char">132 Maple</field>
    <field name="City" type="char">Brooksville</field>
    <field name="State" type="char">AL</field>
    <field name="ZIP" type="int">10232</field>
  </person>
  <person>
    <field name="ID" type="int">1002</field>
    <field name="First" type="char">Sheena</field>
    <field name="Last" type="char">Taylor</field>
    <field name="Street" type="char">92 Roundy Way</field>
    <field name="City" type="char">Dana</field>
    <field name="State" type="char">CA</field>
    <field name="ZIP" type="int">83222</field>
  </person>
</records>
```

The tag names in XML (records, person, field) are specific to each implementation. In other words, as long as those involved in writing and reading the data agree upon the names and attributes, it works. Some industries are standardizing tags to be used across their industries. For example, the eXtensible Business Reporting Language (XBRL) group has defined a hierarchy of tag names and attributes that represent financial statement data. Theoretically, if companies publish reports using the approved format, these standard tags will allow importing of financial statements from various companies into standard applications nearly effortlessly.

A final type of text file is an *electronic report*. Most computers can redirect a report to a file; that is, instead of printing a report to the printer, a program can "print" a report to a disk file. At times, printing to file is the only way to extract data from an application. Data that are meant for the printer usually contain extra characters, such as line feeds and formatting characters. Reports can contain master and detail entries on the same page. For example, an invoice report might contain the master information (invoice number, date, and customer) first with subsequent lines for invoice line items. Detail lines are noted only by their indentation on the report.

Electronic reports must be converted to more standard formats (such as delimited text) before their data can be imported into an analysis package. Programs such as Datawatch Monarch specialize in converting electronic reports into standard text formats. Another alternative is the use of *regular expressions*, a pattern matching library found in languages such as Perl and Python. Regular expressions require learning the pattern language and a small amount of scripting, but they provide a powerful mechanism for data retrieval.

## Databases

Most corporations store their data in large, server-based databases such as Oracle, Microsoft SQL Server, or MySQL. Although a variety of historical database types exist, most databases today are *relational*. A relational database is a collection of relations (tables of data). Common tables are an invoice table, a journal entry table, a customer table, and so forth. Tables are related to each other through common field values.

Databases should be your first choice for data access because they provide strong data typing, store the links between tables (e.g., an invoice is related to a customer and a set of purchased products), and provide efficient searching mechanisms. Even though gaining access to corporate databases is not always politically easy, databases provide significant power to a fraud investigator.

This section provides a short introduction to relational databases as they pertain to fraud detection and investigation. We encourage you to continue learning about databases beyond this introduction.

## Spreadsheet and Relational Layouts

You are probably familiar with spreadsheets like Microsoft Excel, so we introduce databases by comparing them to spreadsheets. At first glance, a database may seem like a set of related spreadsheets. Like spreadsheets, databases are organized using tables with records (rows) and fields (columns). Spreadsheets use a predefined number of rows and columns, but a database has only as many records as it has data, and it has only as many columns as it has fields. Fields in databases are named rather than lettered. A spreadsheet typically holds about 65,000 rows, whereas a database can hold virtually unlimited numbers of records.

Databases do not allow columns to be calculated from other cells in the same way spreadsheets do. In fact, duplicate data in a database is normally taboo. Queries, views, and scripts make necessary calculations on the fly. Databases hold only source data.

The primary difference between databases and spreadsheets is their underlying structure and layout.[4] Consider the representation of data in spreadsheet layout as shown in Figure 6A-1.

### Figure 6A-1 Data in Spreadsheet Layout

| ◇ | A | B | C | D | E |
|---|---|---|---|---|---|
| 1 | | Notebook | Desktop | Accessories | Support |
| 2 | Carl | $203,000 | $140,000 | $50,000 | $20,000 |
| 3 | Debbie | $505,000 | $602,000 | $40,315 | $30,252 |
| 4 | Lindsey | $306,212 | $311,233 | $31,525 | $21,223 |
| 5 | Daniel | $71,732 | $61,232 | $62,313 | $15,251 |
| 6 | Ryan | $8,200 | $13,222 | $52,555 | $62,313 |

The data being kept are the sales per person per product area. This example shows a primary limitation of spreadsheet layout: It models a maximum of two dimensions. How would you add the sales month to the spreadsheet? Common answers are to keep a separate sheet on the *z*-axis for each month or to duplicate the columns for every month required. These solutions often lead to complex formulas that involve multiple sheets and disparate spreadsheet cells. You may even have inherited a similarly complex spreadsheet before. Spreadsheets continue to become more and more complex as additional dimensions are added (such as geographic area, customer type, sales discounts, etc.) until they become what programmers call "spaghetti bowls."

Databases solve this problem by representing data differently. Instead of placing dimensions along the *x* and *y* axes, databases create a field for each dimension. This approach leads to the format shown in Figure 6A-2.

## Figure 6A-2 Database Format

| SalesPerson | Area | Amount |
|---|---|---|
| Carl | Notebook | $203,000 |
| Carl | Desktop | $140,000 |
| Carl | Accessories | $50,000 |
| Carl | Support | $20,000 |
| Debbie | Notebook | $505,000 |
| Debbie | Desktop | $602,000 |

Note that each record lists the amount for each salesperson and product area. Adding additional dimensions, such as month and geographic area involves simply adding an additional field to the database. In fact, most databases keep data in their most detailed representation as possible, such as a table of individual sales. Totals for area, salesperson, or geographic area are not part of the underlying data. Instead, totals are usually calculated on the fly using queries.

Spreadsheets also experience a problem called *null values*. Suppose the spreadsheet recorded $0 for Carl and Notebooks (cell B2). Does the $0 entry mean he had no notebook sales or does it mean he doesn't sell notebooks? Databases solve this problem by not listing a record if Carl doesn't sell notebooks or listing $0 if he sells them but had no success.

You may have used *pivot tables* or *crosstables* in your spreadsheet application before. Pivot tables are a conversion from database layout to spreadsheet layout. They reconcile the problem that arises when most corporate data are in database layout, but most people like to work with data in spreadsheet format. Pivot tables are extremely useful when analyzing data extracted from databases because they provide the link between the two layouts.

## Linking Tables

Most corporate databases contain a significant number of tables (usually in the tens, hundreds, or even thousands). The most important thing to understand when trying to understand a database is the links between tables—called *primary* and *foreign keys*. A primary key is a unique identifier for a record. It is synonymous with an invoice number, a social security number, or a product ID. A primary key is never repeated in a table; rather, it specifically and individually references a single record. Typically, the first field (or set of fields) in a table is its primary key.

A foreign key is the inclusion of another table's primary key in a record. For example, suppose the telephone company bills John for last month's cell phone service. When John signed up for cell service, he gave his name, address, and other information to the company. This information is stored as a record in the *Customer* table. John's primary key in the *Customer* table is assigned as 1002. Last month's bill creates a new record in the *Invoice* table containing the start and end dates, the amount of minutes used, and amount due. Rather than including all of John's information in the invoice record, the database simply inserts John's *Customer* primary key (1002) into the new record in the *Invoice* table. This primary key, when included in the *Invoice* table, is a foreign key linking the last month's invoice record to John's master customer record.

Because they link tables to one another, primary and foreign keys form the lattice work of a database. They are invaluable to fraud detection because fraud is most often found through the comparisons of data. Foreign keys allow queries that compare data in one table against related data in another table.

## Querying Data

One of the primary advantages of a database is the ability to link tables using queries. A *query* is a simple statement that pulls matching records from the underlying tables in a database. Simple queries are easy to write, especially when a visual tool such as Microsoft Access is used. We leave the instruction on how to write queries to other textbooks and program Help pages, but we encourage you to learn the basic technique of querying because it offers the primary benefit of using databases for fraud detection and investigation.

# Connecting to a Database

Some organizations will let you connect directly to their databases. Direct connections provide significant power because (1) you gain full access to the entire set of available data; (2) you can quickly run iterative analysis to refine your queries; and (3) your queries run directly on the database server rather than on your personal computer—harnessing the power inherent in the mainframe. It is not always possible to connect directly to databases because of security, efficiency, and stability concerns. You may be relegated to having an IT department query data and send text files to you. However, if you can gain direct access, you will be much more efficient and effective.

Almost all databases allow connections using a standard protocol called Open Database Connectivity (ODBC). Because it is standard across databases, clients using Microsoft Access, scripting languages, and other analysis packages can connect whether the database is Oracle, PostgreSQL, or Sybase. Simply put, ODBC is your friend.

The first step to gaining a connection is the installation of the appropriate ODBC driver on your personal computer. Ask your clients what databases they use and retrieve the corresponding drivers from the database vendor. For example, if you learn that the database you want to connect to is Oracle, search for "ODBC driver" on Oracle's Web site. The driver is a free download, and it installs easily.

Once the driver is installed on your system, configure an ODBC connection using the driver in the Windows Control Panel. The company's database administrator will provide you with the server name, your username, and password. An example of this process is given in Figure 6A-3.

You may now use your ODBC connection in any ODBC-compliant application. Most data analysis applications and client databases, such as Microsoft Access, are ODBC-compliant, and they make connections nearly seamless. Microsoft Access, in particular, makes you go through a roundabout process to link tables, but once they are linked, they act as if they were normal, local tables. Access' process for ODBC linking is described in Figure 6A-3.

In most applications, such as Access, data can be linked or imported. Linking allows the data tables to remain on the server. It is the best option for large databases with millions of records because it uses the corporate servers to run queries. By definition, the corporate servers should be able to handle the data they hold. Importing copies the data to your personal computer and discontinues the ODBC connection. Imported tables are local tables in every sense: They use your local processor and hard disk space. Importing provides the best option for smaller data sets or for instances when you don't want to burden corporate servers. Consult with the database administrator on which option he or she prefers and is best for your instance.

Figure 6A-3 Setting Up an ODBE Connection

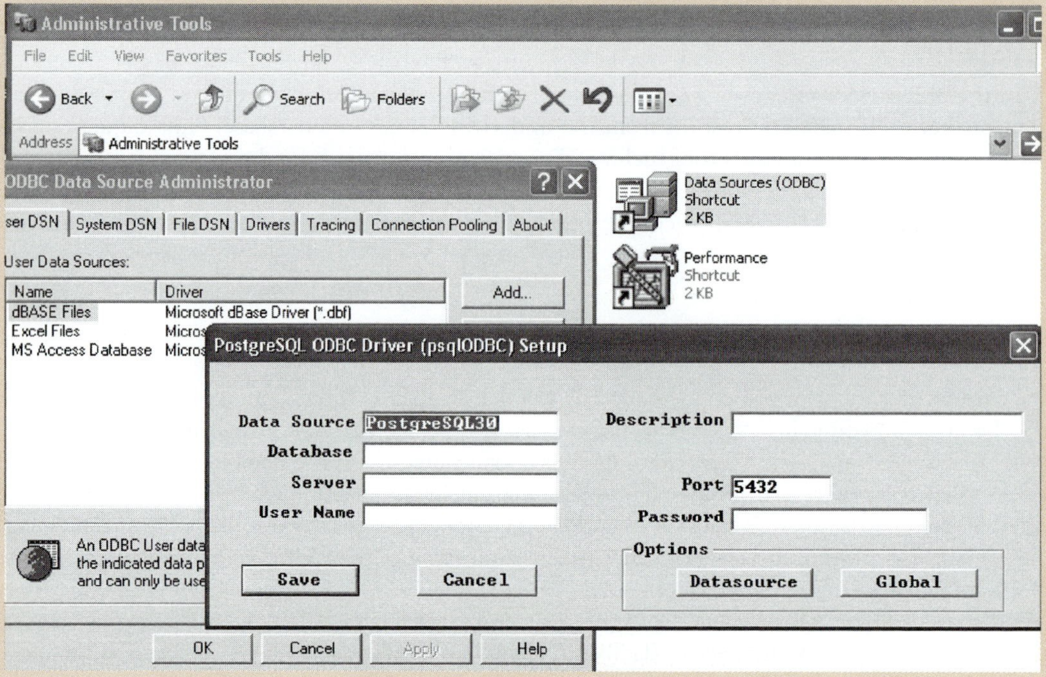

Suppose Mary wants to connect to a client's database and has been given permission to do so. A search of PostgreSQL's Web site yields the following URL: http://odbc.postrgres.org/. She downloads the free driver and installs it by double-clicking the downloaded file. The installation process requires her to restart her computer, which she does.

In Windows XP, Mary opens the Control Panel and switches to Classic View. She double-clicks Administrative Tools, then Data Sources (ODBC). She clicks Add… and selects the PostgreSQL driver from the list. She enters the information given her by the client's database administrator and clicks Save. A screen shot of these windows is shown here.

Mary now has an ODBC connection that she can use in any ODBC-compliant application. She decides to use Microsoft Access for her analysis, so she creates a new, blank database in Access. She links to the database tables by selecting File; then Get External Data; then Link Tables…. In the dialog box that comes up, she selects ODBC Databases in the Files of Type drop-down menu. The Link dialog box disappears and a new Select Data Source dialog box comes up. She clicks the Machine Data Source tab and finds her new PostgreSQL ODBC connection listed. She selects her ODBC connection and clicks OK. In the Link Tables dialog box she selects the tables of interest to her. Like magic, the linked tables now show up in her project as if they were local tables.

## Data Transfer

Data normally need to be transferred for analysis from a database server to your personal computer. The following list describes several popular options for transfer:

- **ODBC**: When you connect to a database via ODBC, query results are automatically transferred back to your personal computer. This approach is optimal because the searching is done on the server and the transfer is transparent. If you are able to get an ODBC connection, transfer is automatic.
- **Internet**: If you need to transfer text files like delimited text, several methods of direct transfer over the Internet exist. File Transfer Protocol (FTP) is one of the oldest methods of downloading files from a server. If your database server has an FTP server installed, simply type the URL into the Windows Explorer location: ftp://username@my.database.server

where username is given to you by the server administrator, and my.database.server is the server name. Other options include using a program such as WinSCP[5] to transfer your files. WinSCP connections are encrypted and compressed, resulting in more secure and efficient transmissions. Ask the administrator if WinSCP is available.

- **Disk**: If ODBC and direct Internet transfer are not available, transfer via disk may be required. Today's external, portable hard drives are relatively inexpensive, and they hold significant amounts of data. Most computers today can also read DVDs or CDs.

## Storing Data

Companies generally do not allow significant analysis work on their production servers. Instead, you need to move data to a temporary location for analysis. Some investigators simply keep data in files on their personal computers. Other investigators set up data warehouses to hold case data. However you decide to store your data, it is extremely important that the method be structured, defined, and organized.

Databases, run on your personal computer or firm server, provide excellent means for data storage. Many investigators have access to Oracle or Microsoft SQL Server and can utilize its power. In recent years, two open source databases have proved capable of handling immense volumes of data efficiently: PostgreSQL and MySQL. Although Microsoft Access is an excellent front end to SQL Server or another database, its Jet engine (the database part of Access) should only be used for small data sets.

Text files in fixed format, electronic reports, and delimited text are generally poor choices for data storage. These formats do not contain typing information, are slow to process, and take significant disk space. Rather, text files should be used for transfer of data from one system to another.

## Massage Therapy

Once data are queried, transferred, and stored appropriately, they normally need to be *massaged*: converted into a usable form. Source data are rarely useable immediately. For example, they contain noise: errors introduced into the system through versioning, buggy programming, unintentional data entry errors, and so forth. They may not be scaled or typed correctly for the analysis you wish to perform. Suppose you are looking for employees who charge too many hours per timecard. Timecard data normally contains a record for the clock-in time and another record for the clock-out time. In order to calculate the number of hours worked each day, you need to match the *in* record with its corresponding *out* record and calculate the time at work. This process of conversion is termed *massaging the data*.

A common massage action ensures that data types are correct. Although ODBC connections carry specified data types over from the source database, data types are missing from fixed format and delimited text files. Many applications allow you to specify each field's type upon import. Other applications import fields as strings and expect you to convert numeric and date fields manually. Types are important for mathematical calculations. For example, the string "1" plus the string "1" equals "11" rather than the expected "2." Because both fields are strings, most applications concatenate the fields! Only after conversion of the fields to numeric fields such as integers is the correct result of 2 achieved.

Another common massage action converts scales and formats. As discussed earlier, date formats and usage vary significantly between countries and database vendors. It is extremely important that dates are converted to a standard format with which you are comfortable. For example, the ticks method discussed earlier is a powerful way to work with date ranges. Fields containing monetary values are often in thousands or millions and can sabotage analysis if they go unseen. An extreme example of scale conversion was seen when NASA lost a $125 million Mars orbiter in 1999 because one of the engineering teams used English units of measurement instead of the more common metric system. After a 286-day journey, the spacecraft burned up in orbit around Mars. Fortunately, the orbiter was unmanned.

A final example of massaging data involves the calculation of new columns. One of the most important rules of databases is the exclusion of calculable data. In other words, only raw, detailed data are kept. analysis typically begin with the calculation of summarizations, groupings, or other computations.

## Outliers and Norms

Outliers are data points outside the normal range of values for a data set. These special data points are often extremely important for fraud analysis because investigations normally search for anomalies. In fact, many searches for symptoms—high prices, high volume purchases, line item bids too low, or high number of quality complaints—focus specifically on outliers.

Suppose you had a data set with the numbers 1, 2, 2, and 4. Is the last entry an outlier? It may be for some analysis and may not be for others. One of the most productive methods of identifying outliers is the z-score. A *z-score* is a statistical calculation that determines how many standard deviations a given point is away from the center of a normally distributed set of data. The z-score is calculated as follows:

$$z = \frac{Value - Mean}{Standard\ Deviation}$$

A positive z-score indicates that the value is greater than the data set mean (average); a negative score indicates it is less than the mean. Statistical theory states that 68% of the data will be between −1.0 and 1.0, 95% of the data will be between −2.0 and 2.0, and 99.7% of the data will be between −3.0 and 3.0. In many real-world data sets, it is not uncommon to find a few records with z-scores of 6, 8, or even 10. Given the statistical improbability, it is easy to flag these records as outliers.

The generation of norms is another method of finding values that may be indicative of fraud. Suppose you are evaluating the labor rate of painters on a project. The normal price for a painter is found by averaging the labor rate across all painters that have worked on the project. Even though this calculation may seem obvious, too many fraud examiners overlook the ability to generate norms directly from the data. Once the norm is generated, it is easy to find how each painter evaluates against the normal labor rate.

## Time Axis Standardization

Fraud is often found by analyzing changes over time. Most corporate databases store transactions as they occur rather than by time interval. This week might include 5 records, 50 next week, and none for the rest of the month. The lack of consistency in the time interval can adversely affect analysis if the time axis is not standardized. To illustrate this effect, consider the following record set of purchases of computer items as shown in Table 6A-1.

The data are graphed as shown in Figure 6A-4. Because the graph line is not rising, it does not appear at first glance to be indicative of fraud.

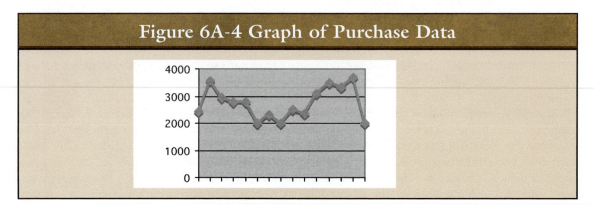

### Figure 6A-4 Graph of Purchase Data

More detailed inspection of the data set reveals that even though the amount of purchases is staying relatively constant, the number of purchases is increasing rapidly. A better representation of these data is found when the time (*x*) axis is standardized. For example, Table 6A-2 shows the data summarized for each 15 days.

## Table 6A-1 Record Set of Purchases

| Item Number | Item Name | Purchase Date | Amount |
|---|---|---|---|
| 135 | Computer Systems | 1/1/2005 | 2,450 |
| 135 | Computer Systems | 1/10/2005 | 3,550 |
| 135 | Computer Systems | 1/18/2005 | 2,935 |
| 135 | Computer Systems | 1/25/2005 | 2,799 |
| 135 | Computer Systems | 1/30/2005 | 2,799 |
| 135 | Computer Systems | 1/30/2005 | 1,999 |
| 135 | Computer Systems | 2/5/2005 | 2,300 |
| 135 | Computer Systems | 2/6/2005 | 1,999 |
| 135 | Computer Systems | 2/7/2005 | 2,500 |
| 135 | Computer Systems | 2/8/2005 | 2,350 |
| 135 | Computer Systems | 2/10/2005 | 3,100 |
| 135 | Computer Systems | 2/11/2005 | 3,499 |
| 135 | Computer Systems | 2/14/2005 | 3,330 |
| 135 | Computer Systems | 2/15/2005 | 3,700 |
| 135 | Computer Systems | 2/15/2005 | 2,019 |
| | | | |
| | | | |

## Table 6A-2 Time Axis Standardization of Data

| Item Number | Item Name | Date Range | Amount |
|---|---|---|---|
| 135 | Computer Systems | 1/1/2005 – 1/15/2005 | 6,000 |
| 135 | Computer Systems | 1/16/2005 – 1/31/2005 | 10,532 |
| 135 | Computer Systems | 2/1/2005 – 2/15/2005 | 24,797 |

The more appropriate graph looks like the one shown in Figure 6A-5. This graph is rising rapidly, and it is much more indicative of fraud.

## Figure 6A-5 Graph of Time Axis

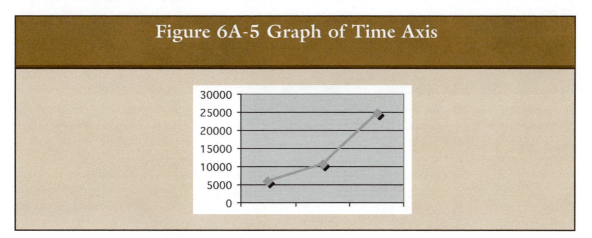

## Data Analysis Packages

A significant number of data analysis packages are available for download or purchase. Although it is impossible to list all of these packages here, we describe some of the popular packages. (In providing this list, we are not trying to advertise for any specific product.)

- **Microsoft Excel and Access:** Because Excel and Access come with Microsoft Office, they are installed on most personal computers today. Most readers are familiar with Microsoft Excel and spreadsheets. Access is an entry-level database application. It is sometimes seen as a "toy" database, but it is more than adequate for smaller data sets. Access's real strength is its ability to link to corporate servers via ODBC as described earlier in this appendix. When you connect to a corporate database, you get the simplicity of Access with the power of big iron. Access provides scripting via Visual Basic, easy movement of data to Excel for numerical analysis, and powerful reporting capabilities.
- **Audit Applications:** Audit Command Language (ACL) and IDEA are two applications commonly used for audit analysis. These applications specialize in data extraction, ODBC connections, sampling, and basic data analysis. They are not specifically designed for fraud detection, but many investigators are familiar with them because of related audit work.
- **Computer Forensics:** Guidance Software's EnCase is a popular application that clones hard drives and searches them for keywords and patterns. It is designed to help an investigator acquire evidence from a seized computer. The Forensic Toolkit from AccessData searches hard drive for files, text, and patterns. It boasts the ability to view and search hundreds of file formats without the need for additional programs. These two programs have increasingly overlapped in features in recent versions. Also worthy of note is the Linux operating system. Linux may not be as user-friendly as Windows, but self-booting CDs like *Knoppix*, *Security Tools Distribution*, and *the Penguin Sleuth* can read, search, and clone hard drives without modifying them.
- **Scripting Languages:** Scripting languages often provide the most flexibility in analysis and forensic work. The initial investment is somewhat costly and time intensive, but investigators who are skilled scripters often develop a "toolbelt" of scripts they use repetitively to achieve results not available with other methods. Common scripting languages are Visual Basic, Perl, and Python. For example, *Picalo*, a free, open source scripting application, is based upon Python and connects to corporate databases, analyzes data, and prints reports. Picalo is in early development, but its basic tools are in production use.

## CONCLUSION

The analysis of transactions and electronic evidence is one of the most effective methods of detecting and investigating fraud. Indeed, the use of electronic means for data collection and analysis has increased significantly in recent years. The foundation of data analysis includes an understanding of data and information, data types, relational tables and foreign keys, connections such as ODBC, transfer, and storage of data.

## END NOTES

[1] http://en.wikipedia.org/wiki/Datum

[2] http://en.wikipedia.org/wiki/Information

[3] For example, a Google search for "Windows Text Editor" brings up results for numerous editors with various feature sets.

[4] Note the focus here on spreadsheet and relational *layouts*. Both layouts could be created in a spreadsheet application, and both layouts could be created in a database. However, a spreadsheet layout is the common representation of data in a spreadsheet such as Microsoft Excel, and database layout is the common representation of data in a database such as Microsoft Access.

[5] http://winscp.sourceforge.net/.

# PART FOUR

## FRAUD INVESTIGATION

# CHAPTER 7

# INVESTIGATING THEFT ACTS

## LEARNING OBJECTIVES

After studying this chapter, you should be able to:

- Understand theft investigation methods and how they are used to investigate suspected fraud.
- Know how to coordinate an investigation, using a vulnerability chart.
- Describe the nature of surveillance and covert operations.
- Understand the effectiveness of invigilation to investigate fraud.
- Realize how physical evidence can be used in a fraud investigation.
- Recognize how to seize and analyze computers, including hard drive information and e-mail messages.
- Use trash and other social engineering methods to investigate fraud

*No single promotion lured more people to McDonald's than its popular Monopoly game—until August of 2001—when it was discovered that the Monopoly game was a large fraud. Simon Marketing, which ran the monopoly game on behalf of McDonald's, was responsible for the fraud. Simon Marketing allegedly defrauded McDonald's out of $13 million worth of game prizes.[1]*

*In a quiet, upper-class subdivision of brick and stucco mansions in Lawrenceville, Georgia, Jerome Jacobson spent the past six years masterminding one of the largest promotional contests ever held. As Simon's longtime manager of game security, Jacobson, 58, traveled the country and randomly placed winning peel-off contest stickers on things like soft-drink cups and French fry boxes in McDonald's restaurants and inserted instant-winner tickets in magazines and Sunday news-paper circulars. However, the FBI says, Jacobson devised his own cash-in scheme, embezzling winning game pieces and instant tickets. In turn, he would sell them to prearranged winners for kickbacks of $50,000 or more.*

*Jacobson pocketed at least $50,000 each from up to 13 separate $1 million prize winners. The government's lengthy complaint described Jacobson as a savvy manipulator and crime ringleader, willing to double-cross those who dared hold back payments. Jacobson recruited at least two accomplices who acted as recruiters themselves.*

*In exchange for negotiated payments, the "winners" were provided winning game pieces and instant prize tickets. They were also instructed at length on how to disguise their actual residences and what to tell McDonald's about where and how they had picked up game pieces and instant-winner tickets.*

*According to federal prosecutors, at least 17 recruits won ill-gotten prizes. Besides the 13 winners of the $1 million game, one recipient won a 1996 Dodge Viper valued at about $60,000. Others won cash prizes of $100,000 and $200,000.*

Without the informant who contacted the Jacksonville FBI office last year, the contest rip-offs allegedly orchestrated by Jacobson would likely have continued unabated. FBI agents obtained court permission for several telephone wiretaps and began tailing Jacobson and others. The FBI also got McDonald's to agree to delay issuing checks to winners, which helped the FBI secure evidence from wiretaps.

In the previous chapter, we provided an overview of fraud investigation. We identified two different approaches to fraud investigation: (1) the evidence square approach and (2) the fraud triangle plus inquiry approach. The fraud triangle plus inquiry approach, together with the various investigative techniques is shown in Figure 7-1.

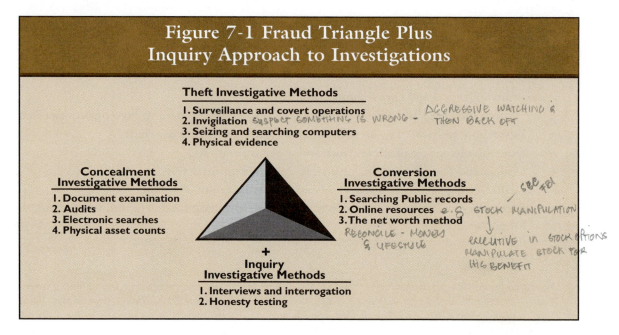

## Figure 7-1 Fraud Triangle Plus Inquiry Approach to Investigations

**Theft Investigative Methods**
1. Surveillance and covert operations
2. Invigilation
3. Seizing and searching computers
4. Physical evidence

**Concealment Investigative Methods**
1. Document examination
2. Audits
3. Electronic searches
4. Physical asset counts

**Conversion Investigative Methods**
1. Searching Public records
2. Online resources
3. The net worth method

**+ Inquiry Investigative Methods**
1. Interviews and interrogation
2. Honesty testing

In this chapter, we discuss the different methods of investigating the theft act. In the next chapter, we discuss the different concealment investigative methods. Because manipulating source documents conceals most frauds, we discuss the various techniques to gather the documents and evidence that have been manipulated in order to perpetrate fraud. We will discuss conversion investigative methods in Chapter 9.

Before discussing specific types of evidence, it is important to understand the considerations involved in deciding whether to investigate. As we discussed previously, investigation of a fraud only follows occasions of predication, meaning symptoms or indications (red flags) of a fraud may be occurring. That predication may have arisen because someone provided a tip or complaint or it may have come from proactively searching for fraud. Once predication is present, however, individuals must decide whether to investigate. That decision is often made by auditors, security personnel, human resource personnel, attorneys, or even law enforcement officials. Some of the factors that are considered in deciding whether to investigate are (1) perceived strength of the predication, (2) perceived cost of the investigation, (3) exposure or amount that could have been taken, (4) the signal that investigation or noninvestigation will send to others in the organization, (5) risks of investigating and not investigating, (6) public exposure or loss of reputation from investigating and not investigating, and (7) the nature of the possible fraud. For example, under recent changes in the laws, the risks would be much higher for not fully investigating a potential fraud perpetrated by the CEO of an organization than it would be to not investigate a fraud perpetrated by an assembly worker.

Generally, after predication, the best policy is to investigate the potential fraud to determine the who, why, how, and how much of the fraud. Sometimes what is observed or what resulted in predication is only the tip of the iceberg. Other times, the investigation of predication may lead to exonerating those who were suspected of wrongdoing. And, because most frauds grow geometrically over time, it is better to investigate them while they are still relatively small than to wait until they bankrupt or cause extreme embarrassment for the organization.

Once the decision has been made to investigate, the investigation methods that will be used must be determined. In deciding which methods to use, investigators should focus on the strongest type of evidence for the specific fraud. For example, because inventory frauds involve the transporting of stolen goods, such frauds are often investigated by using theft investigative techniques. On the other hand, payroll frauds, such as charging excess overtime or adding ghost employees to the payroll, can usually be most easily investigated by focusing on concealment efforts. Such frauds must be concealed in the records of an organization, and it is usually quite easy to gather documentary evidence. Collusive or kickback-type frauds, however, generally lack any direct documentary evidence. (Indirect documentary evidence, such as purchasing records, shows increasing prices or increasing work by a particular vendor.) As a result, concealment investigative techniques usually do not work well in kickback situations. With such frauds, investigators often use theft act investigative methods, such as tailing or wiretaps, which were used in the McDonald's case, or gather circumstantial conversion evidence from public records and other sources showing a lifestyle beyond what the perpetrator's known income could support. Inquiry investigative methods are usually helpful in investigating all types of frauds.

## Theft Act Investigative Methods

Theft act investigations should usually begin by using techniques that will not arouse suspicion and, most importantly, will not wrongly incriminate innocent people. Therefore, initially, as few people as possible should be involved, words such as *investigation* should be avoided (*audit* and *inquiry* are more acceptable), and the investigation should be started by using techniques that will not likely be recognized. As the inquiry proceeds, investigative methods will work inward toward the prime suspect, until finally he or she is confronted in an interview. The diagram In Figure 7-2 illustrates this pattern.

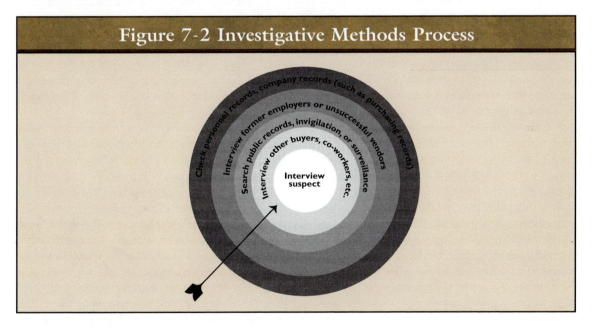

**Figure 7-2 Investigative Methods Process**

Check personnel records, company records (such as purchasing records)

Interview former employers or unsuccessful vendors

Search public records, invigilation, or surveillance

Interview other buyers, co-workers, etc.

**Interview suspect**

To illustrate, if a purchasing employee is suspected of taking kickbacks, the investigation might proceed through the following seven steps:

1. Check the employee's personnel records for evidence of liens or other financial difficulties, or for previous problems.
2. Perform a "special audit" of the purchasing function in order to examine trends and changes in prices and purchasing volume from various vendors.
3. Search public records and other sources to gather evidence about the suspect's lifestyle.
4. Perform surveillance or other covert operations.

5. Interview former buyers and unsuccessful vendors.
6. Interview current buyers, including the suspect's manager, only if no collusion with management is suspected.
7. Simultaneously interview the suspected buyer and the suspected vendor.

Several of these steps can be performed without arousing suspicion or without anyone being aware that an investigation is being conducted. For example, security personnel, auditors, and fraud examiners commonly examine personnel records during normal audits. Similarly, purchasing records and public records searches usually do not create suspicion, because they are normal audit procedures or because they can be performed offsite.

Surveillance, when properly performed, is done without the suspect's knowledge. Only when interviews begin is the suspect likely to become aware of the investigation. Even then, interviews should normally be conducted first with individuals who are objective and are not currently associated with the suspect, and should work inward until the suspect is finally interviewed. The purposes of starting tangentially and working inward are to avoid alerting suspects too early that they are under investigation and to avoid creating undue stress or suspicion among other employees. In addition, this process best protects the target of the investigation, especially if evidence later reveals that the individual was not, in fact, involved.

## Coordinating an Investigation

When beginning a fraud investigation, it is often useful to develop theories about what kind of fraud could have occurred, who the possible perpetrators could have been, what their motivations might have been, and how much could be taken. One way to develop such theories is to use a vulnerability chart as a tool for explicitly considering all aspects of the fraud and for establishing fraud theories. A vulnerability chart coordinates the various elements of the possible fraud, including (1) assets that were taken or are missing, (2) individuals who have theft opportunities, (3) theft investigative methods, (4) concealment possibilities, (5) conversion possibilities, (6) symptoms observed, (7) pressures of possible perpetrators, (8) rationalization of perpetrators, and (9) key internal controls that had to be compromised for the theft to occur. For example, assume that a bank customer complained that a deposit she made last month was not credited to her account. A vulnerability chart similar to the one in Table 7-1 would identify all the factors involved in the fraud.

As shown in the top section of this vulnerability chart, the assets that may have been taken included the customer's deposit. Theft opportunities may have been available to the teller who processed the transaction, to an operations officer who supervised the teller, or to the proof operator who processed the credit to the customer's account. Movement of the assets was easy and could have occurred by entering a credit into the wrong account, placing the checks (if the deposit involved checks) in the cash drawer and withdrawing cash, stealing cash, or falsely endorsing checks. Concealment was possible by destroying the customer's deposit slip, creating a new deposit slip, or forging a signature. Because the stolen funds involved cash, conversion opportunities were unlimited. Symptoms observed might include changed behavior, an improved lifestyle, or another customer complaint. Pressures motivating the fraud could have involved a tax lien against the teller's property, an expensive new home purchased by the proof operator, or a recent divorce by the operations officer. Rationalizations could have involved the perpetrator's feelings of being underpaid or treated poorly. Key internal controls that would have had to be overridden could have involved not allowing an employee to enter credits into his or her own account, use of processing jackets in the proof department, the teller omitting certification, or restricted access to the computer system.

Similar vulnerability charts can be prepared for any potential fraud. For example, frauds involving stolen inventory and overcharged goods are also shown in Table 7-1. The advantage of using a vulnerability chart is that it forces investigators to explicitly consider all aspects of a fraud.

We now discuss the different type of theft-act investigation methods.

## Table 7-1 Vulnerability Chart

| What was taken? | Who had opportunity? | How were assets moved? | How was theft concealed? | How are assets converted? | Red-flag symptoms? | Vulnerability Chart Possible Motive(s) | | Key Internal Controls |
|---|---|---|---|---|---|---|---|---|
| | | | | | | Pressures | Rationalization | |
| Customer deposit | Teller Operations officer Proof operator | Entering verified credits Stealing check; endorsing it | Destroying deposit slip Forged signature Entering credit in own account | Unlimited | Changed behavior Changed lifestyle Customer complaint | Tax lien New home Divorce | Feels underpaid or poorly treated | Use processing jacket Certification Teller counts customer receipts |
| Goods delivered | Receiving trucker | Not received Truck | Night Included with trash | Fenced Used personally | Control not followed Goods not counted | New car Spouse laid off | Passed over for promotion | Receiving report |
| Overcharged for goods | Purchasing agent | N/A | Kickback | Cash Hire spouse | Extravagant lifestyle Asset sold inexpensively | Maintain lifestyle | Greed | Bids |

# Surveillance and Covert Operations

Surveillance and covert or undercover operations are theft investigation techniques that rely on the senses, especially hearing and seeing. Surveillance or observation means watching and recording (on paper, film, or magnetic tape) the physical facts, acts, and movements, which form part of a fraud. Technically, the three types of surveillance are (1) stationary or fixed point, (2) moving or tailing, and (3) electronic surveillance. Some form of surveillance is used in investigating most frauds, including even financial statement frauds.

Simple fixed-point or stationary observations can be conducted by anyone. In conducting these observations, the investigator should locate the scene that should be observed, anticipate the action that is most likely to occur at the scene, and either keep detailed notes on all activities involving the suspect or record them on film or tape. The detailed records should include the date and day of observation, the name of the observer, the names of corroborating witnesses, the position from which the observation was made, its distance from the scene, and the time the observation began and ended, along with a detailed time log of all the movements and activities of the suspect. An example of a surveillance log is shown in Table 7-2. The person under surveillance was suspected of taking kickbacks from a vendor.

Mobile observation, or tailing, as was used in the McDonald's fraud, is much more risky than stationary surveillance. In one case, an internal auditor was shot at while tailing a suspect. Even though the potential rewards for this type of surveillance are high and may include identifying the receiver of stolen goods or the payer of bribes or kickbacks, the chances of failure are high. Tailing should be done only by professionals.

Electronic surveillance of employees, via video cameras is frequently used. Wire-tapping, another form of surveillance, can only be used by law enforcement officers. Electronic surveillance may have limited value in the investigation of employee frauds and many other white-collar crimes because of concerns regarding employees' privacy in the workplace. However, it is useful in kickback-type schemes, such as the McDonald's case, where law enforcement is involved. Several corporations have instituted strict controls over all forms of electronic surveillance, including video, electronic mail (e-mail) privacy, wire-tapping, and access to PCs.

Surveillance and covert operations are legal as long as they do not invade a person's reasonable expectation of privacy under the Fourth Amendment to the Constitution, which protects the right of a person against unreasonable searches. Legal counsel and human resources should always be consulted before any form of surveillance takes place. In addition, all corporations and institutions should implement strict protocols regarding the use of any form of surveillance in order to ensure that controls are in place and that a "reasonable person" test is given to any application. The net value of surveillance can be more than offset by employee problems caused by inappropriate or improper application of the techniques.

Undercover operations are both legal and valid, provided they are not used as fishing expeditions. Undercover operations can be extremely costly and time-consuming and should be used with extreme care. Undercover investigations should be used only when (1) large-scale collusive fraud or crime is likely, (2) other methods of fraud investigation fail, (3) the investigation can be closely monitored, (4) significant reason exists to believe the fraud is occurring or reoccurring, (5) the investigation is in strict compliance with the laws and ethics of the organization, (6) the investigation can remain secretive, and (7) law enforcement authorities are informed when appropriate evidence has been accumulated.

Three illustrations of actual undercover operations highlight some of the risks involved. In the first instance, which was successful, collusive fraud was suspected. The undercover agent was able to get valuable evidence that led to the conviction of several individuals. The other two undercover operations, which were unsuccessful, were concerned with suspected drug dealing at manufacturing facilities. (Drug dealing is an activity that no organization can tolerate, because if an employee purchases and uses drugs on the job and then is involved in an automobile accident on the way home from work, for example, the organization may be legally liable for damages.) In the second operation, the agent became fearful and quit. In the third operation, the agent became sympathetic to the suspects and was not helpful.

With developments in technology, companies in health care, finance, stocks, and retailing are using artificial intelligence systems to provide surveillance or filter huge amounts of data and identify suspicious transactions. Instead of tailing or following individuals, programs using artificial intelligence now tail or

## Table 7-2 Surveillance Log

| January 29, 2005 Date/Time | Event |
|---|---|
| 6:30 pm | Instituted surveillance at Flatirons Country Club, 457 W. Arapahoe, Boulder, CO |
| 6:40 pm | Alex Tong and unidentified white male seen leaving racquetball courts and entering locker rooms. |
| 7:00 pm | Both men seen leaving locker room. |
| 7:05 pm | Tong and white male enter club restaurant and order drinks. White male orders beer; Tong orders orange liquid drink. |
| 7:10 pm | Twosome order dinner. |
| 7:25 pm | Dinner arrives. Tong has white, cream-based soup and club sandwich. White male has steak and potatoes. |
| 7:30 pm | Break: Surveillance terminated. |
| 7:36 pm | Surveillance re-instituted. Twosome still eating at table. |
| 7:55 pm | Tong goes to restroom. White male remains at table. |
| 8:00 pm | Tong returns to table. |
| 8:15 pm | Twosome order two drinks. |
| 8:25 pm | White male requests check. |
| 8:30 pm | Check arrives and is presented to white male. White male hands credit card to waitress without examining check. |
| 8:35 pm | Waitress returns, gives bill to white male, who signs bill. Waitress gives yellow slip to white male. No indication of Tong attempting to pay check. |
| 8:40 pm | White male removes envelope from portfolio and gives it to Tong. Tong looks pleased and places envelope in his pocket. Twosome leave and are seen getting into a Mercedes Benz and a 2002 Lexus, respectively, and drive away. |
| 8:45 pm | Waitress is interviewed. She displays a copy of a Citibank Gold MasterCard charge slip in the name of Christopher D. Ballard, account number 5424-1803-1930-1493. Card expires 03/2006. The amount of the check is $78.65. Waitress is given $20 cash tip for information. |
| 9:00 pm | Surveillance terminated. |

monitor transactions to find transactions that are unusual or look suspicious. For example, credit card fraud costs the industry an estimate $1 billion each year, or 7 cents out of every $100 spent on plastic. That amount is down significantly from its peak about a decade ago due, in large part, to the use of powerful technology that works like a surveillance camera and can recognize unusual spending patterns. Many of us have been participants in this credit card surveillance activity. How many times have you been traveling to an unfamiliar destination, only to make a large charge purchase and have the credit card company call you on the telephone to make sure the purchase was made by you? It called you because its surveillance tracking system recognized a transaction that appeared unusual given your typical spending habits.

Driven by needs ranging from security to fraud protection to quality of service, applications for monitoring, surveillance, and recording are growing in importance and sophistication. In telecommunications systems, for example, signaling protocols provide access to databases and real-time call establishment requests containing highly detailed and useful information regarding locations, calling patterns, destinations, duration, and call frequency. These data are often mined for a variety of functions from traditional call setup to billing, while signaling traffic can also be monitored for quality of service, fraud prevention, legal intercept, and billing. These capabilities can greatly enhance service providers' efforts to reduce expenses, preserve capital, and retain customers. They can also provide telecommunications vendors with a vast source of information from which they can build new applications and revenues.

As a final example of electronic surveillance, consider the tracking system used by the National Association of Security Dealers (NASD). NASD is the largest securities industry self-regulatory organization in the United States. Through its subsidiaries, NASD Regulation, Inc., and the NASDAQ Stock Market, Inc., the NASD develops rules and regulations, conducts regulatory reviews of members' activities, and designs, operates, and regulates securities markets all for the benefit and protection of investors.

In order to maintain its leading position as a regulator of the securities industry for the benefit and protection of investors, NASD Regulation, Inc., implemented the most effective automated capability possible to provide continued surveillance of NASDAQ and other stock markets. The market regulation department is responsible for monitoring of all activity to ensure compliance with market rules in order to provide a level playing field for all market participants and investors. An automated system screens all trades and quotes according to approved, standardized criteria to identify potential violations for review and, if appropriate, regulatory action.

Fraud detection capabilities are provided through rule and sequence-matching algorithms, which are used to detect instances in the database that match patterns that could indicate fraud. The surveillance techniques provide customized visualizations for depicting the relevant relationships in the data, as well as capabilities for multiple users to review and manage the alerts that are generated and the patterns that are used.

Whether the surveillance is manual or electronic, observing someone's activities is a fraud detection tool that attempts to catch fraud and other types of crime at the theft act stage. Those who use such methods are not trying to understand the cover-up or concealment fraud or even how the money is being spent, unless, of course, the spending of the money is the actual theft act as it would be with credit card fraud.

## Invigilation

*Invigilation* is a theft act investigative technique that involves close supervision of suspects during an examination period. Such strict temporary controls are imposed on an activity that, during the period of invigilation, makes fraud virtually impossible to commit. As already indicated, opportunity is one of the three conditions that must exist before fraud can occur. When controls are made so strict that opportunities to commit fraud are nonexistent or limited, a fraud-free profile can be established. If detailed records are kept before, during, and after the invigilation period, evidence about whether fraud is occurring can be obtained. The diagram in Figure 7-3 outlines invigilation.

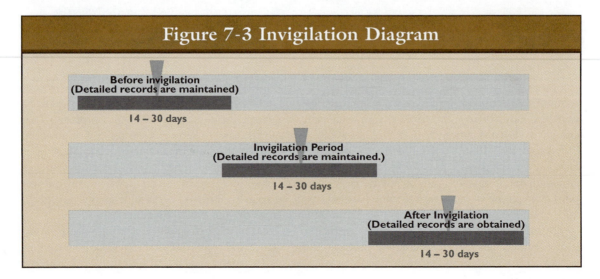

### Figure 7-3 Invigilation Diagram

**Before invigilation**
**(Detailed records are maintained)**
14 – 30 days

**Invigilation Period**
**(Detailed records are maintained.)**
14 – 30 days

**After Invigilation**
**(Detailed records are obtained)**
14 – 30 days

The following example describes invigilation in detecting a fraud that involved inventory losses:

> *An oil distributor was experiencing inventory losses of 0.23 percent of the inventory. The manager suspected that fraud was taking place but was not sure how or when. Observation and other investigative methods failed to produce evidence. For a 30-day period, the installation was saturated with security guards and auditors. Every movement of goods both in and out was checked, all documents were verified, and inventory and equipment were regularly reviewed. During the period of invigilation, losses ceased. After the invigilation, records kept at the plant were examined for absolute, proportional, and reasonableness changes during the invigilation period. Two service stations—which before the exercise had bought an average of only 2,000 gallons of gasoline a week—suddenly doubled their orders. During the 30 days, in fact, each received more than 19,000 gallons. In addition, a shift foreman, who in 23 years of service had taken no sick leave, was away from work on 19 of the 30 days. Two or three months were allowed to elapse, and during this time, covert observation was maintained on the service stations, whose orders by this time had reverted to 2,000 gallons per week. Using night vision equipment and cameras, unrecorded deliveries to the service stations were detected. The owners were interviewed, and their books were examined. They were subsequently charged with fraud extending back two years and involving 62,000 gallons of gasoline.*

This example of invigilation took place in a large company and involved losses in inventory. Invigilation can also be used as a fraud investigation tool in smaller organizations. The following example illustrates such a scenario:

> *Mark owned an auto tune-up shop. The company had 12 bays, 12 mechanics, and one accountant, John, who Mark trusted completely. John handled all accounting duties, including cash receipts, bank deposits, the writing of checks, payroll, and taxes. Each year, Mark's business serviced more cars, but each year cash flows became worse. Not knowing what to do, Mark consulted a friend, who was a CPA. The friend performed various cost, volume, and profit analysis and informed Mark that he should be profitable. He suggested to Mark that maybe someone was embezzling money. Mark's reply was that the only one that was in a position to embezzle was John. The CPA friend encouraged Mark to try an experiment. He suggested that Mark first make copies of all bank statements and other cash records for one month. Next, Mark should tell all employees, including John, that he was thinking about selling the shop and that the prospective buyer insisted on daily audited records for one month. During this month, an outside CPA would come daily to count cash receipts, make bank deposits, write all checks, and check on parts and inventory. After one month, Mark was to inform all employees that the sale had fallen through and that he was not going to sell the shop. Following the invigilation period, Mark was again to copy bank statements and other cash records for one month. To Mark's surprise, cash paid by customers as a percentage of total receipts, (customers either paid by check, credit card, or cash) was 7 percent before the invigilation period, 15 percent during the one-month invigilation period, and again approximately 7 percent in the month following the invigilation period. Faced with the evidence, John admitted that had been embezzling cash from Mark's business. A subsequent analysis revealed that the total amount he had stolen exceeded $600,000.*

Invigilation is an investigative technique that can be expensive. It should be used only with management's approval, and it should be restricted to a discrete and self-contained area of business. Most commonly, it is used in such high-risk areas as expensive inventory, areas with poor controls over the receipt and loading of goods, and areas with poor controls over accounting records.

When using invigilation, management must decide on the precise nature of the increased temporary controls necessary to remove fraud opportunities. Past records should be analyzed in order to establish an operating profile for the unit under review. This profile must include such things as normal losses, the number and nature of transactions per day, the number and type of exceptional transactions, and the number of vehicle movements in and out of the facility. To get an accurate reading, it is generally agreed that the invigilation period must be at least 14 days in length. In individual cases, however, the optimal duration will depend on the frequency and nature of transactions.

Once in a while, invigilation backfires. One company, for example, was suffering significant small tool losses from its manufacturing plant. To determine who was taking the tools, the company decided to check all workers' lunch boxes as they exited the facility. The practice so upset employees that they caused a work slowdown that was more expensive than the fraud losses.

## Physical Evidence

The final theft act investigation technique is the use of physical evidence. Until recently, physical evidence was more commonly associated with nonfraud types of crimes, such as property crimes, murder, rape, and robbery. However, it recent years, it is rare that the confiscating and searching of computers is not associated with a fraud investigation. In one famous financial statement fraud investigation, for example, computers of the CFO, CEO, controller, and other key management personnel were confiscated and searched by fraud examiners. The search of the computer hard drives revealed strong evidence that they had participated in perpetrating and covering up the financial statement fraud.

Gathing physical evidence involves analyzing objects such as inventory, assets, and broken locks; substances such as grease and fluids; traces such as paints and stains; and impressions such as cutting marks, tire tracks, and fingerprints or searching computers. For example, physical evidence was used to discover who was involved in the 1993 bombing of the World Trade Center in New York City. The vehicle identification number engraved on the axle of the rented van that contained the explosives made it possible to trace the van to a rental agency. When the perpetrator came back to the rental agency to recover his deposit and make a claim that the van had been stolen, the FBI arrested him.

Another example of the use of physical evidence involved the famed detective, William J. Burns, who once solved a counterfeit currency conspiracy by tracking down a single clue to its source. Here is how he used the clue to solve the case.

> *Burns used a four-digit number preceded by "xx," which was imprinted on a burlap covering to a sofa shipped from the United States to Costa Rica. In the sofa were hidden nearly 1 million counterfeit pesos. By tracing the clue to its source, Burns gained a great deal of evidence, blew the case wide open, and was instrumental in sending the counterfeiters to Sing Sing State Prison. Burns took the following steps during the investigation:*

1. *Located and called on burlap manufacturers.*
2. *Learned the significance of the imprinted number on the burlap covering, and how it might help in tracing the specific piece of burlap to its purchaser.*
3. *Dug for the precise four-digit order number in a pile of old, discarded order forms.*
4. *Located the retail dry goods store that had sold the particular piece of burlap.*
5. *Asked a retail clerk about the specific purchase and obtained a description of the person who had purchased the burlap: a little old lady dressed in black and wearing a shawl.*
6. *Located the purchaser. (Burns later learned that she had bought the burlap for her son-in-law.)*
7. *Invented a pretense to take the young retail clerk with him to call on the lady, so that the clerk would later be able to identify her.*
8. *Checked out a number of furniture moving companies to locate the one that had moved the old couch containing the pesos to the docks.*
9. *Questioned a succession of dockhands until he found one who remembered loading the sofa. The dockhand also remembered the undue concern of a dark, handsome man, who constantly urged the dock hands to handle the sofa with care. The dockhand said he was sure he could identify the man.*
10. *Located the man who had been so concerned for the safe shipment of the sofa.*

11. *Discovered that the man, whose name he now knew, had made a trip to Costa Rica shortly before the shipment of the peso-packed sofa. He had been accompanied by a beautiful woman who traveled under her real name.*

12. *Learned who had engraved the counterfeit plates used to print the pesos. The engraver turned out to be the son of a lithographer in a plant owned by the two people who had traveled to Costa Rica. The chief product of the plant was revolutionary literature that tied in with the plot to overthrow the Costa Rican government.*

The immense amount of electronic data available today provides new opportunities for physical evidence gathering. Information on computers, such as transaction databases, e-mail repositories, word processing and spreadsheet documents, graphics, Web activity logs, and other data can be found using tools like ACL, IDEA, EnCase, and the Forensic Toolkit. Applications that specialize in analysis and electronic evidence gathering were discussed in the Chapter 6 Appendix. This section describes the process of gathering electronic evidence regardless of the applications used.

## OBTAINING PHYSICAL ACCESS

The first step in any electronic data collection is physical access to the data. The data may be stored on in a corporate database, personal computer, or e-mail server. If the data are stored in a corporate database, you only need permission of the database administrator to access the data. As described in the Chapter 6 Appendix, ODBC connections directly to the data source are the best option. In some instances, you may have to work with IT personnel and transfer text files manually over the Internet or via disk. Analysis of data using databases is often done early in an investigation because it can be done silently; in other words, it does not alert subjects in a case that an investigation is underway.

Many times the data you seek are stored on an employee's personal computer or laptop. The first step in any seizure of electronic evidence is to ensure you have the legal right to seize the hardware. Counsel with attorneys to ensure that seizure is within your legal rights. When seizing a computer, it is important to exercise care in respect to chain of custody, evidence marking, and so forth. These topics are discussed in length in the next chapter.

Once you have verified your right to seize hardware, do so in the presence of at least one neutral witness. Contrary to what your IT representative may have told you, do *not* turn the computer off normally. Instead, cut power to the machine by unplugging it directly or removing its battery. When most operating systems shut down normally, they clear important disk caches that might contain evidence. Cutting power to a computer ensures the operating system does not have the opportunity to modify the disk further.

Once the disk is in your custody, calculate a checksum number and clone it to another drive. It is important in court that you show that you have not modified the disk since seizure. Checksums are calculations—based upon encryption technologies—of the contents of a file or disk. They are engineered such that even a minor change to the data will cause a significantly different checksum result. Checksums have been used in court cases to prove that data have not been adversely affected during analysis. Most forensic applications can calculate checksum numbers.

One widely accepted checksum method is the *secure hash* (SHA-1) algorithm from NIST. Table 7-3 shows the SHA-1 result for two source data strings. Note that a change in only two letters produces a significantly different result. The SHA-1 result is always the same length regardless of the length of the input data.

## Table 7-3 Secure Hash Algorithm

| Data | SHA-1 Hexadecimal Result |
|------|--------------------------|
| The fat cat sat | 919d1cb454e3225455fd41c402b9f89ba5a0b8c8 |
| The fat cat met | 4458151a5f69f0911c2bb745b98eb843db12481e |

Cloning a drive means performing a bit-for-bit copy of its data. A typical hard drive contains a significant amount of "empty" space that may contain valuable evidence. When a file is deleted on a disk, its space is marked as empty in the disk's index. The data are not actually removed from the disk because removal would take additional, unneeded time. The data actually remains accessible until another program saves new data to that location of the disk. This fact is extremely important for fraud examiners because subjects may delete important files in an attempt to hide their frauds. Applications such as EnCase and the Forensic Toolkit can search both active and "erased" space on a disk for key terms or phrases.

Common areas of the disk to search include the following:

- Computer logs such as web activity, recent files on the Start menu, Web favorites, the browser history
- The My Documents folder because most applications save data to this location
- The trash can or recycle bin
- USB keys, CDs, or disks found around the computer
- Recently loaded files listed in the File menu of many applications (such as Microsoft Word or Excel)
- Chat logs and e-mail client caches (e.g., most Instant Messenger clients save conversations in the background)

E-mail systems often prove an incredible repository of communications between subjects and other people. It is surprising how many people still believe e-mail to be a secure method of communicating. For example, in one case of bribery, a perpetrator sent an flaming e-mail to his partner stating, "Where is my money? Why haven't you paid me?" The e-mail then discussed the details of the fraud and why the perpetrator was owed money!

The first step in gaining access to a person's e-mail account is determining the type of e-mail they use. Looking at the client that is installed on the person's computer will reveal this information. The following are common e-mail types:

1. *Microsoft Outlook or Outlook Express*: These clients normally connect to Microsoft Exchange servers run by a company. The Exchange administrator can give you access to e-mail stored on the server.
2. *Eudora, Pegasus, Apple Mail, or another installed client*: These clients normally connect via POP or IMAP to an e-mail server. You can determine which protocol is used by opening their e-mail preferences in their client. If the method is POP, e-mail is downloaded from the sever to their personal computer. It will be located in a file or set of files on the subject's hard drive. If the method is IMAP, e-mail is located both on their personal computer and on their e-mail server. The easiest way to retrieve IMAP-based e-mail is to ask the e-mail administrator for their e-mail files.
3. *Web mail account such as Hotmail*: Although some mail may be stored in the web browser cache, web mail is stored entirely on the Web site the subject is signed up with. Unless the subject's password is stored by the browser (which happens quite often), you need a warrant to gain access to these accounts.

## A Comprehensive Example of Methods for Investigating Theft

To conclude this chapter and illustrate the value of theft act investigation methods, let's review excerpts from an article written by Thomas Buckhoff and James Clinton entitled "Exotic Embezzling: Investigating Off-Book Fraud Schemes." The investigators in this fraud case made extensive use of both surveillance and invigilation.

> *Northern Exposure [all names in this case study have been changed] was a gentleman's club featuring exotic dancers. Its primary revenue sources were cover charges and food, beer, and liquor sales. A recent local ordinance outlawed the type of entertainment offered by Northern Exposure. The club's manager, however, successfully petitioned the city council to obtain an exemption, and Northern Exposure was allowed to continue operations in a competition-free environment. The substantial effort by the manager on*

*the club's behalf earned her the owner's trust and loyalty. In the initial fraud investigation interview, the owner said that anyone could be a suspect—except the manager.*

*Because of the exemption, the club's profit potential was enormous. Northern Exposure generated huge amounts of incoming cash, because no credit cards or checks were accepted. However, a huge risk existed that employees would figure out a way to divert incoming cash into their own pockets.*

*Larry Swenson, Northern Exposure's owner, was not satisfied with the 10 percent margins being realized. He engaged two fraud examiners to determine why the club was not generating the 35 percent margins he had expected. They embarked upon a typical fraud examination, whose steps include understanding cash controls, generating fraud theories, collecting and evaluating evidence, estimating losses, assisting in filing claims or bringing charges, and making recommendations.*

*By interviewing Swenson and other personnel, the fraud investigators learned that cash flowed into the business as follows: Customers paid a $6 cover charge to enter the club. No receipt was given, nor was a head count made. Customers placed orders for food or beverages with the servers. The servers started out with $40 in a cash pouch. They paid the bartenders for their orders from this pouch and then collected payment from the customer. At their shift's end, the server gave the initial $40 back to the manager and kept the difference as tips. At the end of the night, the manager counted the cash and closed out the cash registers; the cash was deposited by the manager the next morning. Changes in beer and liquor inventory were not reconciled to the drinks rung into the cash register, nor were the register tapes reconciled to deposits listed on the bank statements.*

*The fraud examiners determined that it would be relatively easy for employees to steal and not be caught, based on the control levels they discovered. They developed the following fraud theories:*

- *Employees collecting the $6 cover charge could pocket some of the money or allow free admission to friends.*

- *Servers and bartenders could get drinks for customers, not ring them into the registers, and pocket the cash received from the customers.*

- *Anyone with access to the cash registers (i.e., servers, bartenders, and the manager) could simply take cash directly from the registers.*

- *The manager could perpetrate any of the schemes available to the employees, and could steal part of the deposit.*

*Off-book frauds such as the first two are called skimming and are essentially unrecorded sales. The second two would be considered on-book frauds. Because there was a transaction record, the fraud could be detected by reconciling the cash register tapes to the deposits. In Northern Exposure's case, however, cash register printing ribbons were not replaced on a timely basis, resulting in illegible tapes.*

### Collecting and Evaluating Evidence

*Indirect investigative methods were used to test the four possible fraud theories. Financial statement analysis is one such method that can be used to test all four fraud theories presented. If employees are indeed stealing cash from the club, then the actual sales markup-over-cost ratios are expected to be less than the budgeted ratios. Accordingly, the fraud investigators determined the actual markup-cost ratios for beer and food sales. Beer was purchased for $.60 per bottle, then sold to customers for $3 each, a markup of 500%. Food items costing $5 were sold to customers for $12.50, a 250% markup. One year's budgeted revenue was calculated, based on cost of sales and expected markup ratios, then compared to one year's actual revenue. The significant differences in ratios clearly supported the fraud theories—in fact, food sales were less than their cost* *of sales! Using this indirect investigative method, the total estimated annual fraud loss due to skimming or cash larceny was $379,974.*

*The investigators now knew that the club had a big problem with fraud; determining which employees were responsible came next. Undercover surveillance can be used effectively for identifying dishonest employees. Posing as customers, a team of six trained fraud investigators (with experience as bartenders and servers) spent a collective 40-hour week at the club observing the employees' activities and behavior. This surveillance revealed that 90% of them, including the manager, regularly stole cash from the club, with little regard to subtlety. The reason that employees never complained about salary levels, despite low base wages and a lack of raises, became clear. In fact, several servers and bartenders had been there for years, which is highly unusual for this type of club. The lead investigators communicated their findings to Swenson, who, though concerned, was reluctant to take action without more substantive evidence of employee theft.*

*To more firmly establish the fraud losses and estimate their amount, the fraud investigators conducted a week-long invigilation. In invigilation, the cash received and deposited during the invigilation period is compared to the periods before and after. As an indirect investigative method, invigilation can be effective in estimating fraud losses. The key to invigilation success is making the employees think that any theft during that period will be detected. Instilling the perception of detection in this case was accomplished by sending in the same team of six investigators to watch the employees for one week. The club's employees and manager were informed that the investigators were there to make sure that every dollar collected from customers made it into the bank at the end of the day and that changes in consumable inventories were properly accounted for. During the invigilation, the investigators conspicuously watched employees handling cash, conducted surprise cash counts, reconciled changes in inventory to cash register tapes, monitored end-of-night cash counts, and witnessed the daily cash deposits.*

*The first day brought an incident that greatly heightened the perception of detection. Meals were served downstairs, away from the live entertainment area. Suspecting the single server working downstairs of skimming money from food sales, one of the investigators conducted a surprise cash count and reconciled cash rung into the register to meals prepared by the cooks. The server had skimmed $25 in the first hour she worked. When confronted with the evidence, the server confessed and was immediately terminated. News quickly spread to the other employees, who realized that their activities were indeed under close surveillance. No other employees were caught skimming during the remainder of the invigilation.*

*During the invigilation's first night, a Friday, $8,300 in cash was deposited into the bank—the largest sum for one night in the entire 15-year history of the club. This deposit amount occurred on what was considered a "slow" night—unlike the previous week, which had seen near-record attendance. The manager and employees all soon realized that setting such a record on a slow night reflected poorly on them. This convinced Swenson that his employees were stealing from him, and he wanted to fire everyone on the spot. The investigators persuaded him to allow the invigilation to continue for the entire week as planned. The results of the week-long invigilation are summarized as follows:*

*Gross cash receipts during the invigilation were $30,960, compared with $25,775 the previous week and $22,006 for the annual weekly average. The revenue during the week of invigilation exceeded the average weekly revenue by $8,954 and the previous week's revenue by $5,185, despite being a slow week. The above differences implied that at least $259,250 and as much as $447,700 was skimmed per year. (After changes were implemented following the investigation, the remaining nine months' sales were $300,000 higher than for the same period in the prior year.)*

*Swenson no longer doubted that his employees were stealing from him. As noted earlier, Swenson had had difficulty believing his manager was stealing because of her efforts to exempt the club from the city ordinance. It became apparent that these efforts were motivated by a desire to protect her illicit cash flow.*

*Employee interviews were held during the week of the invigilation. Their purpose was twofold: to further enhance the perception of detection during the invigilation period, and to provide employees with an opportunity to report any fraudulent activities. Very specific questions were asked during the interviews, based upon information from the prior undercover surveillance and the ongoing invigilation. Although no one admitted to stealing, they did implicate fellow employees; many claimed that manager Betsy Smith was the primary thief.*

*During her interview, Betsy Smith was confronted with the evidence from the undercover surveillance, invigilation, and employee interviews. After 2 hours, she admitted to stealing almost $100,000 over three years. Her admission was converted to a written statement, which she ultimately signed. The statement detailed the amounts she had skimmed, when she had done so, and the various techniques (skimming from liquor sales, bank deposits, video sales, and food deliveries) she had used. An attached summary totaled the funds skimmed by source. Because evidence collected in resolving off-book fraud schemes is mostly indirect and circumstantial, obtaining a signed admission statement greatly facilitates the filing of employee dishonesty insurance claims or criminal charges. In this case, such a claim was filed by the fraud investigators on behalf of Northern Exposure.*

*The insurance company restituted Northern Exposure for the maximum coverage amount provided by their policy, $50,000. Clearly, the coverage amount was inadequate given the exposure to risk for such a cash-intensive business. As required by the insurance provider, evidence collected during the fraud examination was turned over to local law enforcement for prosecution.*

# KEY TERMS

**Theft Act Investigation:** Fraud investigation methods that focus on the fraudulent transfer of assets; includes surveillance, invigilation, seizing computers and examining physical evidence.

**Vulnerability Chart:** As investigative scheme used to coordinate the various elements of a possible fraud.

**Surveillance:** Watching and recoding suspects and their activities during a period of time. These types of surveillance are (1) stationary, (2) moving, and (3) electronic.

**Invigilation:** Imposing strict controls for a period of time during which fraud is impossible or difficult to perpetrate and contrasting the before, during, and post period results; purpose is to compare results for a fraud-free period with before and after fraud periods.

# QUESTIONS AND CASES

## DISCUSSION QUESTIONS

1. How are theft investigative methods used to investigate suspected fraud?

2. What factors should be considered when deciding whether to investigate a case of fraud?

3. How does a vulnerability chart help coordinate an investigation of suspected fraud?

4. What is a surveillance log?

5. What is invigilation?

6. How is physical evidence used to investigate fraud?

7. Why is it important to use investigation techniques that will not arouse suspicion among possible perpetrators?

8. Why is it important to consult legal counsel and human resources before any form of surveillance takes place?

9. What role does the Fourth Amendment to the Constitution play in cases of fraud investigation?

10. What aspects constitute the fraud triangle plus inquiry approach to investigations?

## TRUE/FALSE

1. The fraud triangle plus inquiry paradigm is an effective way to understand the various types of investigative methods.

2. One advantage of using a vulnerability chart is that it forces investigators to consider all aspects of a fraud.

3. Electronic surveillance is often of limited value in the investigation of employee fraud because of concerns regarding employees' privacy rights.

4. Surveillance is a theft investigation technique that relies on the examination of documents.

5. Mobile observation is usually much more risky than stationary surveillance.

6. During invigilation, no controls are imposed on any activities.

7. Surveillance logs should always be drafted before an investigation begins.

8. Not only are undercover operations both legal and valid, but they are also inexpensive.

9. Investigation of fraud only takes place when predication has first been established.

10. When using theft act investigation methods, interviewing the prime suspects should happen last.

11. Tailing includes the use of video, e-mail, wire-tapping, and access to PCs.

12. Invigilation is a theft act investigative technique that involves close supervision of suspects during an examination period.

13. To get an accurate reading, it is generally agreed that the invigilation period should be at least four days in length.

14. In determining which investigative method to use, investigators should focus on the costs of each possible method.

15. Seizing and searching computers is usually illegal because it infringes on the rights guaranteed by the Fourth Amendment to the Constitution.

## MULTIPLE CHOICE

1. Which of the following is *not* a category used in the fraud triangle plus inquiry paradigm?
   a. Theft investigative techniques
   b. Concealment investigative techniques
   c. Action investigative techniques
   d. Conversion investigative techniques

2. When beginning an investigation, fraud examiners should use techniques that will:
   a. Not arouse suspicion.
   b. Identify the perpetrator.
   c. Determine the amount of the fraud.
   d. Identify when the fraud occurred.

3. When conducting an investigation, which of the following words should usually be avoided when conducting interviews?
   a. Audit
   b. Inquiry
   c. Investigation
   d. Record examination

4. When beginning a fraud investigation, which of the following methods is most useful in identifying possible suspects?
   a. Preparing an identification chart
   b. Preparing a vulnerability chart
   c. Preparing a surveillance log
   d. None of the above

5. Invigilation:
   a. Is most commonly associated with crimes such as robbery, murder, and property offenses.
   b. Can create tremendous amounts of documentary evidence.
   c. Provides evidence to help determine whether fraud is occurring.
   d. All of the above are true.

6. Which of the following is not a theft act investigation method?
   a. Invigilation
   b. Honesty testing
   c. Seizing and searching computers
   d. Surveillance and covert operations

7. When deciding whether to investigate, which of the following factors should an organization not consider?
   a. Possible cost of the investigation
   b. Perceived strength of the predication
   c. Possible public exposure resulting because of investigation
   d. All of the above should be considered

8. Surveillance, when properly performed, is done
   a. Without the perpetrator's knowledge.
   b. During nonworking hours.
   c. By expert fraud examiners.
   d. None of the above.

9. Which of the following is not included in a vulnerability chart?
   a. Explanations of the fraud triangle in relation to suspects of fraud
   b. Breakdowns in key internal controls that may have created fraud opportunities
   c. Internal controls that a company plans to institute in the future
   d. Theft investigation methods

10. A vulnerability chart:
    a. Forces investigators to explicitly consider all aspects of a fraud.
    b. Shows the history of fraud in a company.
    c. Identifies weaknesses in every aspect of a company's internal control.
    d. Gives a detailed record of all the movements and activities of the suspect.

11. Fixed-point or stationary observations can be conducted by:
    a. Certified Fraud Examiners.
    b. Company personnel.
    c. Private investigators.
    d. Anyone.

12. Surveillance logs should include all of the following except:
    a. Time the observation began and ended.
    b. Cost of the surveillance equipment used.
    c. Movements and activities of the suspect.
    d. Distance the observer was from the scene.

13. Wire-tapping, a form of electronic surveillance, can be used by:
    a. Internal Auditors.
    b. Company controllers.
    c. CPAs.
    d. All of the above.
    e. None of the above.

14. Which theft investigative method is most limited in value during employee fraud investigations because of concerns regarding employees' privacy at work?
    a. Electronic surveillance
    b. Invigilation
    c. Forensic accounting
    d. Interviewing and interrogation

15. Who should be consulted before any form of surveillance takes place?
    a. Public Investors and the company's board of directors
    b. State attorney general
    c. Legal counsel and human resources
    d. All company executives

## SHORT CASES

**Case 1.** ABC Company is a relatively small dry-cleaning operation that has a steady level of business. Since the company hired a new employee, however, cash inflows have decreased and the amount of promotional coupon redemptions have increased dramatically. The owner of the company has been impressed with this new employee, but has suspicions regarding her cashiering practices. When comparing cash sales to check and credit card sales, the owner noted that the coupon redemption rate was dramatically higher for cash sales. The owner does not want to wrongly accuse the employee if she is innocent, but does want to find out whether fraud is occurring. The owner calls you as an expert on fraud and asks you to recommend a reliable way to gather evidence that could determine whether fraud is the issue.

What are some possible investigative methods you could suggest?

**Case 2.** You are a fraud examiner and have been hired by Bellevue Company to carry out an investigation. Bellevue is a beverage company that has experienced increased shipments of beverages but no increase in revenue. Management suspects that inventory is being shipped to unknown places or is being stolen.

How could you use invigilation to help you determine whether inventory is being stolen or shipped to unknown locations? Briefly explain how you would carry out this investigative procedure.

**Case 3.** A man in Los Amigos County was discovered committing workers' compensation fraud. He had been observed working while at the same time receiving disability benefits. Surveillance showed the man working at an automobile auction. The investigator interviewed the owner of the auction and found that the claimant was being paid $200 per week in cash for washing vehicles and performing other shop tasks. Surveillance video showed the man carrying 25-pound bags of pet food, loading boxes, and rummaging through a trash dumpster. Obviously, he was not still injured.

1. Was surveillance the proper method to use in this case? Why?

2. What are some of the restrictions you have to be careful about in conducting surveillance?

**Case 4.** This chapter included an example of a manufacturing firm that had problems with employee theft of tools. The company decided that it would search every employee's lunch box at the end of each shift. The results were that the employees were enraged and caused a work slowdown.

Give three alternative suggestions for how the company could have investigated this theft effectively without causing morale problems with employees.

**Case 5.** Assume that someone in your company is taking money from the petty cash fund. Complete a vulnerability chart similar to the one in the chapter in order to coordinate the various aspects of the fraud.

**Case 6.** Craig Ferguson, an internal auditor for HHG Freight Service, had been investigating a case of embezzlement fraud for nearly two months. After searching personnel and company records, visiting with former employees, employing invigilation tactics, and finally interviewing with several coworkers, Craig concluded that Lane Flemming, head of the shipping and receiving department, was involved in a large kickback scheme, costing the company hundreds of thousands of dollars. Finally, with evidence in hand, Craig met with Lane, presented his evidence, and steered Lane to confess that he was indeed the perpetrator.

1. Was the order of events, in which Craig conducted his investigation, in accordance with appropriate theft act investigative methods? Explain.

2. When investigating a case of fraud, why is it important to work inward toward the prime suspect, saving a confronting interview until the end of the investigation?

**Case 7.** A group of fraud examiners are coordinating an investigation at a local law firm. Several lawyers at the firm are suspected of overbilling clients and possibly creating fake client accounts and then charging the firm for services unperformed to these fake clients. The fraud examiners begin preparing for the investigation by creating a vulnerability chart. Explain what a vulnerability chart is and how it can direct the fraud examiners in their investigation.

**Case 8.** ABC Company instituted good internal controls and never, until last month, had a problem with fraud. However, several weeks ago someone with access to keys entered the controller's office and took two company checkbooks. Since then several checks have been forged totaling $5,670. You are a Certified Fraud Examiner and have been recruited to investigate the case. Which theft act investigative method(s) should you use in this investigation?

**Case 9.** In the Northern Exposure case discussed in this chapter, the fraud investigators conducted a week long invigilation. The results during this period were compared to the results taken during the weeks immediately before and immediately after the invigilation. Was invigilation an effective method to use in this case? Why?

**Case 10.** As lead accountant for a small company, you notice that inventory purchases from a certain vendor increased dramatically over the past few months, while purchases from all other vendors decreased. You suspect that something may not be right. Which method(s) would you use to investigate your suspicions?

**Case 11.** While auditing a client, the CEO asks you to look carefully at the cash flow. You notice that cash flows decreased every year. Upon learning of your findings, the CEO remarks, "I seem to bring in more customers every year, but the cash is not there." You tell him that fraud may be occurring, and he asks you to investigate. You agree that the most likely place for a fraud to be occurring is cash collections. Which investigative method(s) would be best for finding the fraud?

**Case 12.** Jim is the owner and president of ZZZ Company. He and his close friend, Dan, graduated with MBAs. They always dreamed about being successful and making lots of money. They have worked in the same company for years, working their way up to senior management and eventually senior executive roles. ZZZ Company has been a success the entire time that Jim and Dan worked for the company. Stock prices increased every year, and revenues grew by a compounded rate of 20 percent per year. Jim is becoming a little suspicious of the company's results because the earnings per share is always equal to Wall Street's projections. In the past couple of years, Jim noticed that his friend's personal life has become troubled. Dan got a divorce and continues to struggle financially, even though Jim knows that Dan is making plenty of money to cover his bills. One night Jim stopped by Dan's office to respond to some e-mails he could not get to during the day. He noticed that Dan was working late as well. Dan was the CEO, and Jim just assumed that he was working late because it was close to the end of the quarter. However, after reviewing the quarter's results, Jim is suspicious again because the results are exactly equal to Wall Street's forecasts. Jim decides he needs to begin an investigation into financial reporting practices.

What issues must Jim consider in deciding how to investigate the financial results of the company?

## EXTENSIVE CASES

**Extensive Case 1.** By the time the New York identity theft fraud case was solved, more than 30,000 people had suffered a total combined loss in excess of $2.7 million. This money had been stolen by a ring of New York residents who accessed the victims' credit information and exploited that information to steal the victims' identity.

The fraud began when Linus Baptiste approached Philip Cummings about a plan to steal and sell people's personal information. Philip Cummings had begun to work at Teledata Communications, Inc., a third party credit-reporting agency that facilitates the retrieval of credit history data. Teledata had outstanding contracts with more than 25,000 companies, allowing these companies to check on the creditworthiness of potential customers, thus creating a direct line past the three main credit bureaus. As a customer service representative, Cummings had obtained access to many confidential access codes. These access codes were used by the clients of Teledata to gain approval on credit requests. With access to these codes, Cummings had the opportunity to commit fraud.

In early 2000, Cummings and Baptiste began to steal credit reports. The two fraudsters had a buyer for the information in a group of Nigerian nationalists. The Nigerians would pay up to $60 for one person's information. After some time, the Nigerian nationalists began to provide the two fraudsters with names and social security numbers to help facilitate the process even further.

To convert the information into money, the Nigerians used the information to gain access to the victim's bank accounts and other financial information. The Nigerians would then:

- Deplete the bank accounts of the victims through wire transfers.

- Change the addresses of the accounts so the current information was not sent to the victims.

- Order new checks to be written off of the victim's bank accounts.

- Order new ATM cards so the money could be taken out in cash.

- Order new credit cards under the victim's names.

- Establish new lines of credit under the victim's name.

By using these techniques, the fraud ring was able to steal more than $2.7 million from consumers. This money was stolen over a period of about three years from late 1999 to late 2002. The most intriguing aspect of the fraud was that Cummings quit working at Teledata in early 2000, but was able to continue to steal the information for an additional two years. Cummings claimed that most of the access codes he stole while working at Teledata remained unchanged for the full two years after he left the company.

Finally, in early 2002, Cummings began to get greedy and his greed led to the detection of fraud. Perceiving that he needed to make more money, Cummings stole about 15,000 credit reports from Teledata by using the access codes of Ford Motor Company. Then from February 2002 to May 2002, Cummings again stole a large number of names. This time Cummings used the access codes of Washington Mutual Bank to steal 6,000 credit reports. Finally, in September 2002, Cummings made what would be his last big credit report theft. Using the access codes of Central Texas Energy Supply, Cummings was able to steal 4,500 credit reports.

After the theft using Ford's access codes, Equifax, one of the three large credit bureaus in the United States, began to see the request spikes in Ford's account. After the next two large batches of requests, Equifax decided to investigate further. Equifax found that almost all of the credit report requests came from one phone number, and that the request were done in large batches of about 100. The location of the phone number was found and a search by federal authorities turned up a computer and other equipment used in the fraud.[3]

As of today, Cummings is facing a possible 30 years in prison and large fines. The victims are facing the dreadful task of restoring their credit, a process that can take years to solve.

Assuming you are an agent with the Federal Bureau of Investigation, do the following:

1. Coordinate an investigation in a manner that would not cause suspicion from Cummings and Baptiste.

2. Create a vulnerability chart to coordinate the various elements of the possible fraud.

3. Assuming your investigation used surveillance and/or covert investigation techniques, what types of surveillance and/or covert operations would you use? How would technology play a role in this part of the investigation?

4. Finally, how would analysis of physical evidence help in this investigation? What types of physical evidence would be especially helpful?

**Extensive Case 2.** The following surveillance log was taken during two fixed-point surveillances of an employee suspected of stealing cash from the company while making nightly bank deposits.

Surveillance Log

| | |
|---|---|
| 10:47 pm | John Doe exits car carrying black deposit bag. Shuts car door and looks around him in every direction. |
| 10:49 pm | John approaches ATM, unzips deposit bag, and pulls out a white envelope. John places white envelope in coat pocket. |
| 10:50 pm | John deposits cash into ATM |
| 11:34 pm | John enters bar and sits at table with a white male. The two order drinks from waitress. |
| 11:37 pm | Waitress returns with drinks and bill. |
| 11:48 pm | Two men drink. John removes white envelope from pocket and hands it to white male. White male immediately places white envelope in his pocket. |
| 11:57 pm | Two men leave bar. |

**Questions**

1. What is wrong with this surveillance log?

2. Why is it important to take detailed notes during surveillance and covert operations?

*1) NO DATES? WHEN IT STARTED*
*WHICH BANK?*
*WHO PAID*
*2) PART OF EVIDENTIAL MATTER*

## INTERNET ASSIGNMENT

In August 2001, it was discovered that the McDonald's monopoly game was a fraud. Simon Marketing, which ran the game on behalf of McDonald's, was responsible for the fraud. During the investigation to uncover the fraud, the FBI used several different forms of surveillance. Using the Internet, find newspapers and other sources of information that describe these forms of surveillance and then answer the following questions:

1. How did the FBI use surveillance to gather evidence regarding Simon Marketing's illegal activities?

2. Was the surveillance methods used by the FBI effective?

3. If you were in charge of the McDonald's investigation what other methods of surveillance might you have used?

## DEBATE

The Discount Plus Company has been concerned for some time about its cash flows. Since the company began five years ago, Discount's business has increased steadily, yet cash flows have remained virtually the same every year. You have been hired by Discount Plus to detect possible fraud within the company. Discount's management is almost certain that one of its accountants is embezzling cash and has informed you that they have already begun installing surveillance cameras in possible "problem areas." In addition, management is considering some form of covert operation to detect the fraud.

What problems or dilemmas is Discount's management facing by installing cameras and implementing a covert (undercover) operation? What privacy issues to need to be addressed?

## END NOTES

1.  Gary Strauss, "Informant Key to Unlocking Scam Behind Golden Arches," *USA Today*, (Friday, August 24, 2001).

2.  Thomas Buckhoff and James Clifton, "Exotic Embezzling: Investigation Off-Book Fraud Schemes," *The CPA Journal* (September 2003), http://www.nysscpa.org/cpajournal/2003/0903/dept/d095603.htm, accessed September 2, 2004.

3.  Based on a true case from http://lawlibrary.rutgers.edu/fed/html/scarfo2.html-1.html.

# CHAPTER 8

# INVESTIGATING CONCEALMENT

## LEARNING OBJECTIVE

After studying this chapter, you should be able to:

1. Recognize concealment investigation methods and how they relate to fraud.
2. Understand the value of documents in a fraud investigation.
3. Explain the importance of obtaining documentary evidence.
4. Know how to perform discovery sampling to obtain documentary evidence.
5. Understand how to obtain hard-to-get documentary evidence.

*A number of years ago, the general partners in some limited real estate partnerships committed significant fraud by using millions of dollars of investments made by limited partners for their personal use. They had their own private real estate investments that were losing money and rather than lose those investments, they siphoned money from the partnerships for personal use. The limited partnerships used money from investors to purchase buildings for use by fast-food chains such as Denny's, KFC, and Sizzler steak houses. The buildings, which were fully paid for by limited partner investments, were then leased to owner-operators on a triple-net lease basis, which meant that the lessees were responsible for maintenance and for paying property taxes. To steal money from the limited partnerships, the general partners found banks in distant states that were willing to loan money against the equity in the properties and used the loan proceeds to support their personal investments.*

*As part of their audit procedures, the external accountants who audited the partnerships realized that a possible risk was that lessees might not be paying the property taxes on a timely basis, thus putting the properties at risk. As a result, they performed a lien search in each of the counties where the properties were located. To their surprise, they discovered liens on some properties located in Arizona and Texas, placed on the properties by banks*

*in Kansas and Nebraska, two states where the partnerships didn't own any properties. The auditors then did what all good auditors would do: they sent confirmations to the banks to see what the balances and terms were on any existing loans on the properties. Their confirmations revealed loans totaling several million dollars on the properties. Follow-up investigation revealed the fraud by the general partners.*

*Interestingly, one of the specific frauds that auditors discovered was stolen money supposedly being held in an escrow account by a title company in Alaska to build a new Sizzler Restaurant. The general partners had told the auditors that $3.2 million was being held by the title company and gave the auditors the address where they could send the confirmation. Before giving the auditors the address, however, one of the general partners had flown to Alaska and rented a mailbox from a Mailboxes Etc. that used a street number rather than a post office box as the address. Then when the confirmation had been sent, the general partner again flew to Alaska, completed the confirmation with no exceptions by signing a fictitious name and then sent it back to the auditors. This $3.2 million escrow and confirmation fraud would not have been discovered if the lien search and follow-up investigation hadn't taken place.*

In this case, the lien searches, the bank confirmations that revealed the loans, and the fictitious confirmation from the escrow company are all forms of documentary evidence. Once the fictitious confirmation from the escrow company and the bank loan documents were in hand, it was easy to extract a confession from the perpetrators. Unfortunately, the CPA firm that audited the partnerships was sued by the limited partners who tried to recover the losses they had incurred. Because the auditors had performed an excellent GAAS audit and because they were the ones who had actually detected the fraud, they were able to settle the case for a relatively small amount of money.

## Concealment Investigative Methods

In the previous chapter we discussed surveillance and covert operations, invigilation, and physical evidence, including the searching of computers and social engineering, all of which are theft investigation methods. Concealment investigative methods, on the other hand, deal with manipulating and searching documentary evidence, such as purchase invoices, sales invoices, credit memos, deposit slips, checks, receiving reports, bills of lading, leases, titles, sales receipts, money orders, cashier's checks, or insurance policies.

### Aspects of Documentary Evidence

Most concealment-based investigative techniques involve ways to gather documents that have been manipulated or altered. When faced with a choice between an eyewitness and a good document as evidence, most fraud experts would choose the document. Unlike witnesses, documents do not forget, they cannot be cross-examined or confused by attorneys, they cannot commit perjury, and they never tell inconsistent stories on two different occasions. Documents contain extremely valuable information for conducting fraud examinations. For example, in addition to possible fingerprints, the information on the front and back of a canceled check (which is a document) as shown in Figure 8-1.

If you were investigating a kickback or a forgery scheme, a check would direct you to the teller who processed the transaction and who may remember valuable information about the suspect. In addition, a check allows an investigator to complete a paper trail of the entire transaction.

Because documents make up a significant amount of the evidence in most fraud cases, investigators must understand the legal and administrative aspects of handling them. Specifically, investigators must understand the following aspects of documentary evidence:

- Chain of custody of documents
- Marking of evidence
- Organization of documentary evidence
- Rules concerning original versus copies of documents

#### CHAIN OF CUSTODY

From the time documentary evidence is received, its chain of custody must be maintained in order for it to be accepted by the courts. Basically, the chain of custody means that a record must be kept of when a document is received and what has happened to it since its receipt. Careful records must be maintained anytime the document leaves the care, custody, or control of the examiner. Contesting attorneys will make every attempt to introduce the possibility that the document has been altered or tampered with. A memorandum should be written that describes when the document came into the hands of the examiner, and subsequent memoranda should be written whenever the status of the document changes.

#### MARKING THE EVIDENCE

When documentary evidence is received, it should be uniquely marked so that it can be later identified. A transparent envelope should be used to store it, with the date received and the initials of the examiner written on the outside. A copy of the document should be made, and the original document should be stored in the envelope in a secure place. Copies of the document should be used during the investigation

# Figure 8-1 Information on a Check

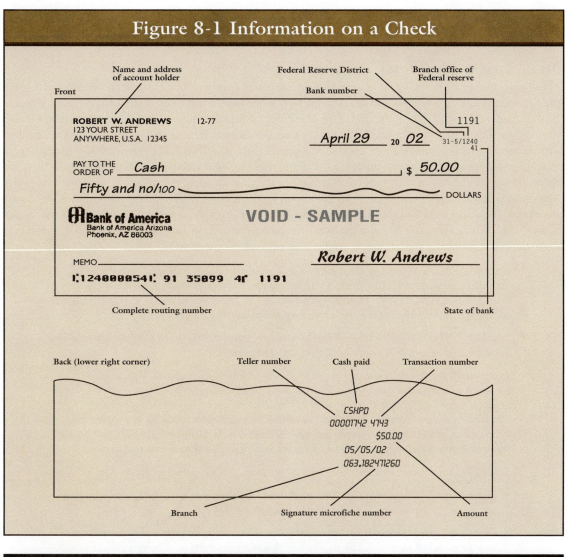

| Information About the Maker and the Maker's Bank | Information About the Bank That Processes the Check |
|---|---|
| 1. Name and address of the account holder | 1. Branch number where processed |
| 2. Bank number of the maker's bank, including: | 2. Teller who processed the transaction |
|   a. City and state of bank | 3. Sequence number of the transaction |
|   b. Bank name | 4. Information about the nature of the transaction, including: |
| 3. Bank routing number of the maker's bank including: |   a. Whether the check was cashed |
|   a. Federal Reserve District |   b. Whether the check was deposited |
|   b. Branch office of Federal Reserve |   c. Whether the check represented a payment |
|   c. State of the maker's bank | 5. Account number of the person who presented the check |
| 4. Maker's account number | 6. Date of transaction |
| 5. Check number | 7. Amount of transaction |
| 6. Amount processed | |

and trial and should be kept in the same file where the original is kept. During the trial, the original can be removed from safekeeping and used.

## ORGANIZATION OF THE EVIDENCE

Fraud cases can create tremendous amounts of documentary evidence. For example, in one case, 100 people worked full-time for more than a year to input key words into a computer so that the documents could be called up on demand during the trial. This case involved literally millions of documents. In the Lincoln Savings and Loan Association case, the judge created a document depository containing millions of documents, from which attorneys, FBI agents, and others were able to access evidence while preparing for trial. It is not uncommon today, especially in large cases, to have electronic files of all depositions and other testimony that allows pdf files of all exhibits to be coordinated electronically with the testimony. These kinds of databases are searchable by key word, by witness, by topic, and by other means. Although hard copies of documents and records are still used, they are rarely used without having electronic copies as well. The FBI has one of the most sophisticated and advanced document examination laboratories in the world. The following is an example of the kind of work they can do.

*Recently, FBI headquarters got a call from a field case agent who said he'd seized a warehouse with thousands of boxes of financial records related to a criminal investigation. He said, "We need to analyze the material for prosecution, but it will take years to go through it all. Any ideas how to speed up the process?"*

*Absolutely! This is a job for the FBI's Document Conversion Lab, or DocLab, started in 2002 as part of a new Records Management Division.*

*Just exactly what is the DocLab? A team of FBI technicians, based in Washington, who scan and digitize hard copy files and photographs using state-of-the-art technology. So far, DocLab has scanned more than 9.5 million images (single pieces of paper), formatting many of those images into readable text and uploading them into an FBI electronic application. Once digitized, the information is easily and rapidly exchanged between Bureau field offices, joint task forces, and FBI Headquarters.*

*Is the DocLab really such a big deal? Yes, more than you might think because it:*

- *Saves incredible amounts of time and space. In the above case, FBI agents walked away with a warehouse full of records ... on seven CDs.*

- *Increases search capabilities exponentially. Those millions of pieces of paper can now be searched electronically in seconds, drawing connections between people, places, and events — within and across cases — in new and important ways.*

- *Enables information-sharing far and wide. The CDs from the warehouse of financial records, for example, were copied and shared with the FBI case agent on the spot. And once uploaded into the electronic application, the files were instantaneously key word searchable throughout the FBI.*

*[Although the FBI has been] digitizing records for years, the importance of digitization grew after 9/11. Investigative priorities in the post-9/11 world of complex, voluminous, and international evidence call for focus and absolute efficiency. DocLab has dedicated trained professionals, working around the clock, who can respond quickly to urgent needs and major cases around the world. Here are just a few examples of what DocLab has done:*

- *Traveled to Afghanistan and Iraq to help scan critical counterterrorism documents;*

- *Digitized more than 20,000 pages of records from the D.C. sniper case, enabling investigators to farm out leads quickly and prepare for the massive court cases;*

- *Took more than three million paper records in poor condition and quickly scanned them for a significant counterintelligence case; and*

- *Helped Indianapolis prosecutors meet an urgent court deadline in a major health care fraud investigation.[1]*

This kind of digitization has become quite common in both civil and criminal cases. Although maybe not quite as sophisticated as the FBI, literally hundreds of organizations make it their major business purpose to digitize and make searchable documentary evidence.

Because of the possibility of a large volume of documents, a consistent organization scheme must be used. Fraud experts disagree about what the organization scheme should be. Some say that documents should be organized by witnesses, some argue for chronological organization, and others argue for organization by transaction. Whichever method is used, a database should be maintained that includes (1) dates of documents, (2) sources of documents, (3) the dates on which documents were obtained, (4) brief descriptions of document contents, (5) subjects of documents, and (6) an identifying or Bates number. (*Bates numbers* are used by attorneys involved in litigation to track all documents). As an illustration of how Bates numbering works, assume that XYZ auditors are being sued by the ABC Corporation's shareholders. Further assume that the XYZ auditors from two different offices—New York and New Jersey—worked on the case. Most likely, the 5,000 documents provided (either by subpoena, court order, or voluntarily) by XYZ will be numbered XYZ-NY 1000001–1005000. The documents provided by ABC Corporation will be labeled ABC 0000001–00100000, and so on. This way, the source of the document is known and the number provides a unique identifier that can always be tracked.

## ORIGINAL DOCUMENTS VERSUS PHOTOCOPIES

Original documents are always preferable to photocopies as evidence. In fact, depending upon the jurisdiction, usually only four situations permit the introduction of photocopies, which are considered secondary evidence in a court of law. In these four situations, the court must have proof that an original document existed and that the secondary evidence copy is a genuine copy of the original.

1. The original document has been lost or destroyed without the intent or fault of the party seeking to introduce the secondary evidence.

2. The original document is in the possession of an adverse party who fails to produce it after a written notice to do so, or when the party in possession is outside the jurisdiction of the subpoena power of the court.

3. The document or record is in the custody of a public office.

4. The original documents are too voluminous to permit careful examination, and a summary of their contents is acceptable.

Many frauds have been allowed to be perpetrated and to go undetected because auditors and others were satisfied with photocopies rather than original documents. In the ZZZZ Best case, one of the principals was said to be a master of the copy machine. According to one source, "He could play the copy machine as well as Horowitz could play the piano." (This quote comes from the video: "Cooking the Books" made by the Association of Certified Fraud Examiners) Any time photocopies are used, especially when originals would be normal, investigators must be suspicious.

## Obtaining Documentary Evidence

Most concealment investigative procedures involve accessing and accumulating documentary evidence. In the remainder of this chapter, we identify several ways to obtain such evidence. Examiners who have computer, statistics, or accounting backgrounds usually have an advantage in investigating documentary evidence.

One way to obtain documentary evidence is by chance or accident or through tips. Once in a while, auditors and others come across documents that provide evidence of fraudulent activities. Sometimes these documents are recognized by blatant alterations or forgeries. At other times, informants bring them to an organization's attention. In either case, such instances should be considered luck. In the following paragraphs, we describe other, more reliable ways of obtaining documentary evidence.

## AUDITS

Auditors conduct seven types of tests, each of which yields a form of evidence.

1. Tests of mechanical accuracy (recalculations)
2. Analytical tests (tests of reasonableness)
3. Documentation
4. Confirmations
5. Observations
6. Physical examinations
7. Inquiries

Because gathering documentation is a normal part of their work, auditors quite often can gather documentary evidence as part of an investigation without arousing suspicion. Auditors can use manual or computer procedures to gather documentary evidence.

To understand how audit procedures can provide documentary evidence, refer back to the limited partnerships case at the beginning of the chapter. In this case, the auditor sent confirmations to banks that had placed liens on property the partnerships owned. The confirmations were returned from the bank with the amounts of the loans, the dates they were taken out, and the remaining unpaid balance. Further inquiry of the financial institutions, with the aid of subpoenas, revealed copies of the loan origination documents with signatures of the borrowers and other information. Once these original loan documents were available, it was relatively easy to prove the fraud.

As another example of how documentary evidence can be helpful, consider again the fraud at Elgin Aircraft, which described in Chapter 5. The defense auditor recognized several symptoms at Elgin, including (1) the limousine (a lifestyle symptom), (2) never missing a day's work (a behavioral symptom), and (3) not verifying claims with employees (a control weakness). He decided to investigate, suspecting that the manager of the claims department was committing some kind of fraud. Reasoning that the easiest way for the manager to commit the fraud was by setting up phony doctors and billing the company for fictitious claims, the auditor decided to gather documentary evidence in the form of checks paid to various doctors to ascertain whether the doctors and claims were legitimate.

The auditor knew it would be impossible to determine conclusively whether fraud was being perpetrated without looking at every check. He also realized that, without proof of fraud, his suspicions did not justify personally examining the total population of all 6,000 checks, which were numbered 2000 through 8000. Faced with the desire to examine the checks but with limited time, the auditor realized he had three alternatives. He could audit the checks by selecting a few of them to look at, he could draw a random sample and use statistical sampling techniques to examine the checks, or he could use a computer and examine certain attributes of all checks.

If the auditor chose the first alternative and analyzed in detail, say, 40 of the checks, he could conclude that the manager was committing fraud if one or more of the selected checks had been made out to a fictitious doctor or doctors. However, if his sample of 40 checks did not include payments to fictitious doctors, the only conclusion he could draw was that there was no fraud in his sample of 40. Without drawing a random sample and using proper sampling procedures, no conclusions could be made about the total population. If he happened to find fraud, he would have succeeded. If he did not find fraud, either he was looking at the wrong sample or there was no fraud.

## DISCOVERY SAMPLING

A better approach to auditing documentary evidence in some situations is to use a form of statistical sampling called *discovery sampling*. Using discovery (statistical) sampling allows an auditor to generalize and make inferences from the sample to the population, as shown in Figure 8-2.

Discovery sampling is the easiest of all statistical sampling variations to understand. Basically, if an auditor can read a table, he or she can conduct discovery sampling. Discovery sampling deals with the probability of discovering at least one error in a given sample size if the population error rate is a certain percentage. A type of attribute sampling, which is based on normal probability theory, discovery sampling is sometimes referred to as stop-and-go sampling. Its use involves two steps: (1) drawing a random sample,

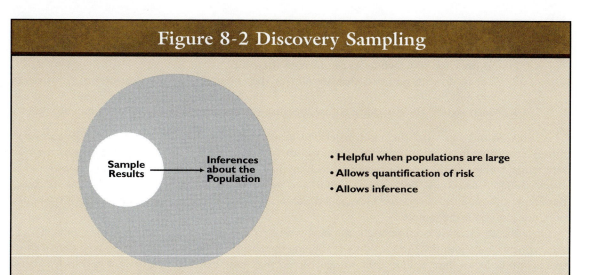

# Figure 8-2 Discovery Sampling

Sample Results → Inferences about the Population

- **Helpful when populations are large**
- **Allows quantification of risk**
- **Allows inference**

and (2) using a table to draw inferences about the population from the sample. For example, assume that the defense auditor wanted to use discovery sampling to examine checks payable to doctors. First, he would use a random number generator or a random number table to select the checks to be examined. A sample list of random numbers is shown in Table 8-1.

## Table 8-1 Partial Table of Random Numbers

| Item | (1) | (2) | (3) | (4) | (5) | (6) | (7) | (8) |
|------|------|------|------|------|------|------|------|------|
| 1000 | 37039 | 97547 | 64673 | 31546 | 99314 | 66854 | 97855 | 99965 |
| 1001 | 25145 | 84834 | 23009 | 51584 | 66754 | 77785 | 52357 | 25532 |
| 1002 | 98433 | 54725 | 18864 | 65866 | 76918 | 78825 | 58210 | 76835 |
| 1003 | 97965 | 68548 | 81545 | 82933 | 93545 | 85959 | 63282 | 61454 |
| 1004 | 78049 | 67830 | 14624 | 17563 | 25697 | 07734 | 48243 | 94318 |
| 1005 | 50203 | 25658 | 91478 | 08509 | 23308 | 48130 | 65047 | 77873 |
| 1006 | 40059 | 67825 | 18934 | 64998 | 49807 | 71126 | 77818 | 56893 |
| 1007 | 84350 | 67241 | 54031 | 34535 | 04093 | 35062 | 58163 | 14205 |
| 1008 | 30954 | 51637 | 91500 | 48722 | 60988 | 60029 | 60873 | 37423 |
| 1009 | 86723 | 36464 | 98305 | 08009 | 00666 | 29255 | 18514 | 49158 |
| 1010 | 50188 | 22554 | 86160 | 92250 | 14021 | 65859 | 16237 | 72296 |
| 1011 | 50014 | 00463 | 13906 | 35936 | 71761 | 95755 | 87002 | 71667 |
| 1012 | 66023 | 21428 | 14742 | 94874 | 23308 | 58533 | 26507 | 11208 |
| 1013 | 04458 | 61862 | 63119 | 09541 | 01715 | 87901 | 91260 | 03079 |
| 1014 | 57510 | 36314 | 30452 | 09712 | 37714 | 95482 | 30507 | 68475 |
| 1015 | 43373 | 58939 | 95848 | 28288 | 60341 | 52174 | 11879 | 18115 |
| 1016 | 61500 | 12763 | 64433 | 02268 | 57905 | 72347 | 49498 | 21871 |
| 1017 | 78938 | 71312 | 99705 | 71546 | 42274 | 23915 | 38405 | 18779 |
| 1018 | 64257 | 93218 | 35793 | 43671 | 64055 | 88729 | 11168 | 60260 |
| 1019 | 56864 | 21554 | 70445 | 24841 | 04779 | 56774 | 96129 | 73594 |
| 1020 | 35314 | 29631 | 06937 | 54545 | 04470 | 75463 | 77112 | 77126 |
| 1021 | 40704 | 48823 | 65963 | 39659 | 12717 | 56201 | 22811 | 24863 |
| 1022 | 07318 | 44623 | 02843 | 33299 | 59872 | 86774 | 06926 | 12672 |
| 1023 | 94550 | 23299 | 45557 | 07923 | 75126 | 00808 | 01312 | 46689 |
| 1024 | 34348 | 81191 | 21027 | 77087 | 10909 | 03676 | 97723 | 34469 |
| 1025 | 92277 | 57115 | 50789 | 68111 | 75305 | 53289 | 39751 | 45760 |
| 1026 | 56093 | 58302 | 52236 | 64756 | 50273 | 61566 | 61962 | 93280 |
| 1027 | 16623 | 17849 | 96701 | 94971 | 94758 | 08845 | 32260 | 59823 |
| 1028 | 50848 | 93982 | 66451 | 32143 | 05441 | 10399 | 17775 | 74169 |
| 1029 | 48006 | 58200 | 58367 | 66577 | 68583 | 21108 | 41361 | 20732 |
| 1030 | 56640 | 27890 | 28825 | 96509 | 21363 | 53657 | 60119 | 75385 |

In using a random number table to select the checks to examine, an auditor must make four decisions:

1. Where to start in the table when selecting check numbers
2. The direction in which to move through the table
3. What to do with numbers that are outside the range, in this case, that do not fall between 2000 and 8000
4. Which four of the five digits to use, because the checks are all four-digit numbers

Assume, in this case, that the auditor decided to start with the top left number (37039), to move through the table from left to right and from top to bottom, to skip numbers that fell outside the relevant range, and to use the first four digits of each number. The checks selected for examination would be checks 3703, 6467, 3154, 6685, 2514, 2300, and so forth. (How many to select is discussed later.) Randomly choosing the checks to be examined allows the auditor to make inferences about the population, not just about the sample.

Once the checks have been selected, the next step is to use a discovery sampling table, Table 8-2, to draw conclusions about the checks. When examining the checks in the sample, if the auditor finds a check to a fictitious doctor, he would be 100 percent certain that fraud exists. If he does not find such a check, he would still have to examine all 6,000 checks to be absolutely certain that no fraud occurred. If he samples anything less than 100 percent of the checks and does not find fraud, discovery sampling allows him to decide how much risk he is willing to assume. In other words, discovery sampling allows the auditor to quantify risk. Using Table 8-2, if the auditor samples 300 checks and finds none made out to fictitious doctors, he would be 95 percent confident that the true population fraud rate did not exceed 1 percent, 78 percent confident that no more than 0.5 percent of the checks were fraudulent, and so forth. The entire table is based on the assumption that no fictitious checks are found. (Again, if the auditor finds even one fictitious doctor, he would be 100 percent certain that fraud exists.)

## Table 8-2 Discovery Sampling Table

| Sample Size | Probability (percentage) of including at least one error in the sample | | | | | | | |
| | Rate of Occurrence in the Population (Percent) | | | | | | | |
| | 0.01 | 0.05 | 0.1 | 0.2 | 0.3 | 0.5 | 1 | 2 |
|---|---|---|---|---|---|---|---|---|
| 50 | | 2 | 5 | 9 | 14 | 22 | 39 | 64 |
| 60 | 1 | 3 | 6 | 11 | 16 | 26 | 45 | 70 |
| 70 | 1 | 3 | 7 | 13 | 19 | 30 | 51 | 76 |
| 80 | 1 | 4 | 8 | 15 | 21 | 33 | 55 | 80 |
| 90 | 1 | 4 | 9 | 16 | 24 | 36 | 60 | 84 |
| 100 | 1 | 5 | 10 | 18 | 26 | 39 | 63 | 87 |
| 120 | 1 | 6 | 11 | 21 | 30 | 45 | 70 | 91 |
| 140 | 1 | 7 | 13 | 24 | 34 | 50 | 76 | 94 |
| 160 | 2 | 8 | 15 | 27 | 38 | 55 | 80 | 96 |
| 200 | 2 | 10 | 18 | 33 | 45 | 63 | 87 | 98 |
| 240 | 2 | 11 | 21 | 38 | 51 | 70 | 91 | 99 |
| 300 | 3 | 14 | 26 | 45 | 59 | 78 | 95 | 99+ |
| 340 | 3 | 16 | 29 | 49 | 64 | 82 | 97 | 99+ |
| 400 | 4 | 18 | 33 | 55 | 70 | 87 | 98 | 99+ |
| 460 | 5 | 21 | 37 | 60 | 75 | 90 | 99 | 99+ |
| 500 | 5 | 22 | 39 | 63 | 78 | 92 | 99 | 99+ |
| 800 | 8 | 33 | 55 | 80 | 91 | 98 | 99+ | 99+ |
| 1,000 | 10 | 39 | 63 | 86 | 95 | 99 | 99+ | 99+ |
| 1,500 | 14 | 53 | 78 | 95 | 99 | 99+ | 99+ | 99+ |
| 2,500 | 22 | 71 | 92 | 99 | 99+ | 99+ | 99+ | 99+ |

The more confident the auditor wants to be and the less risk of not identifying fraudulent checks the auditor wants to assume, the larger the sample size that must be examined. Population size seems to make little difference in sample size, unless the sample becomes a significant part of the population (usually greater than 10 percent), and then the confidence level is higher and the risk lower than indicated in the table.

Even with discovery sampling, auditors can never be certain that fraud does not exist in a population of checks. Discovery sampling does allow inferences to be made about the problem, but it does not eliminate the possibility that the sample will not be representative of the population (sampling risk), and the possibility that the auditor will examine a fraudulent check and not recognize it (nonsampling risk). Using discovery sampling, auditors can quantify both risk and samples until they have sufficient evidence that fraud does not likely exist.

**Documentation of Discovery Sampling.** The investigator should document the method used for determining sample size (i.e., document the specified population error rate and confidence level) and the method used for selecting the sample. For instance, the source of the random number table should be documented by recording the name of the book or computer program from which the table was taken and the rules used for determining the starting point and moving through the table. Such documentation may be important if the investigator expands the sample later, if another person later reviews the sampling plan, or if the procedure later becomes evidence in court.

**Evaluation of Errors.** If the investigator finds errors using discovery sampling, he or she must determine whether the errors were unintentional or are indicative of fraud. For example, in the preceding paragraphs, finding checks made to fictitious vendors was predetermined to be indicative of fraud. However, errors in amounts of checks might be due to unintentional mathematical or typing errors or could be intentional overpayments in a fraud kickback scheme. Such evaluation can be aided if the definition of what will constitute an error indicative of fraud is made beforehand.

**Consideration of Sampling Risk.** The investigator should be aware of the sampling and nonsampling risks associated with discovery sampling. Sampling risk is the risk that the sample was not representative of the population. To reduce sampling risk, the investigator can increase the sample size or use a random number table or generator to select the items to be examined.

**Consideration of Nonsampling Risk.** The investigator should also consider nonsampling risk, which is the risk that a finding will be misinterpreted. For instance, the investigator might not recognize that an examined item contained an error, might misjudge an error as unintentional instead of intentional, or might fail to recognize that a document had been forged. Nonsampling risk cannot be quantified but can be reduced by careful planning, performance, and evaluation of the sampling procedure.

## USING TECHNOLOGY

An alternative to discovery sampling, which allows all checks to be examined, is to use technology, as we discussed in Chapter 5. Using this approach, the auditor selects a variable of interest, such as addresses of payees, checks mailed to post office boxes, or payments made to certain doctors, and then runs a query of all checks. If the auditor identifies variables that signal fraud, this approach can be effective in determining whether fraud exists. If the wrong variables are selected, it doesn't matter that all checks are reviewed; the fraud will not be discovered.

Even though using computers to find fraud can be extremely powerful, the technique requires skill in connecting to corporate databases, selecting the appropriate data, and analyzing effectively. The appendix to Chapter 6 details many of the skills required for this type of analysis.

As discussed in the previous section, sampling risk is the risk that a sample is not representative. Sampling is a staple activity during audits because it is consistent with the goals of most audits. If the financial information of a company were represented with a haystack, the purpose of an audit is to ensure the overall haystack is materially representative. Extending this analogy, is sampling consistent with the goals of fraud examination? Fraud can occur in a small number of transactions. Unlike audits, fraud examination looks for the *needle* in the haystack. Sampling poses significant risk to fraud examiners because fraudulent transactions may not be included in the sample. If the sampling rate is 5 percent, there is a 95 percent chance the fraud will not be included in the sample!

In the Elgin Aircraft case, the claims payment manager embezzled more than $12 million over a five-year period by making payments to 22 fictitious doctors. The payments were sent to two common addresses: The address of a business in a nearby city that was owned by the manager's husband and a post office box that the manager rented. Either discovery sampling or a computer search could have detected the fraud. Using discovery sampling, the auditor would have selected checks and then confirmed whether the doctors being paid were legitimate. Legitimacy could have been determined by examining the doctor's listings in telephone books, confirming their medical licenses with the state licensing board, or making inquiries through medical associations. As soon as the auditor found even one fictitious doctor, sampling would have stopped, and the entire population would have been examined to determine the extent of the fraud.

Using the technology approach, the auditor would have matched addresses of doctors and found that payments to 22 doctors were being sent to two common addresses. A common method of matching fuzzy text is the *soundex algorithm*. Soundex is a method of representing words by the way they sound rather than by the way they are spelled. For example, "123 Simple Way" and "423 Sample Street" both generate soundex values of "S514," meaning they are quite similar to one another. The soundex algorithm can be adjusted to make it more sensitive or less sensitive to differences in names.

After applying the Soundex or another fuzzy matching algorithm, the auditor may have found the common addresses. Checking out the addresses, he would have found that one was the business owned by the manager's husband and the other was her post office box.

With discovery sampling, the risk of not catching the fraud is choosing a sample that is not representative of the population (sampling risk) and examining fraudulent checks but not recognizing them as being fraudulent (nonsampling risk). With technology, the risk is not selecting the right variables to query.

Computer searches are valuable audit tools in fraud investigations. For example, a fraud examiner who suspected procurement fraud might make computer searches for or comparisons of the following items:

- Timing of bids
- Pattern of bids
- Dates of disposal with reorders of goods
- Amount of work by a given vendor
- Pattern of hiring new vendors
- Vendors with post office boxes as addresses
- Number of sole-source contracts
- Price changes in purchased items
- Company employees with vendor offices
- Vendors with Dun & Bradstreet
- Vendor addresses with company use
- Number of rush orders

Similar computer searches can gather documentary evidence relating to any kind of fraud. Using the computer to investigate fraud may well be the most promising of all investigative procedures for the future.

## HARD-TO-GET DOCUMENTARY EVIDENCE

Some documentary evidence, although valuable, is extremely difficult to obtain. The three most common examples are private bank records, tax returns, and brokerage records. Post-9/11 legislation has made it somewhat easier to access these records, but only three ways are permissible to obtain such documentary evidence: (1) by subpoena, (2) by search warrant, or (3) by voluntary consent. *Subpoenas duces tecum* are orders issued by a court or a grand jury to produce documents. Failure to honor such a subpoena is punishable by law. Because only agents of the grand jury or the court (usually law enforcement officers) can obtain documents by subpoena, a need to obtain a subpoena is one reason to coordinate fraud investigations with law enforcement officials.

Figure 8-3 contains an example of a subpoena, taken from the Internet:

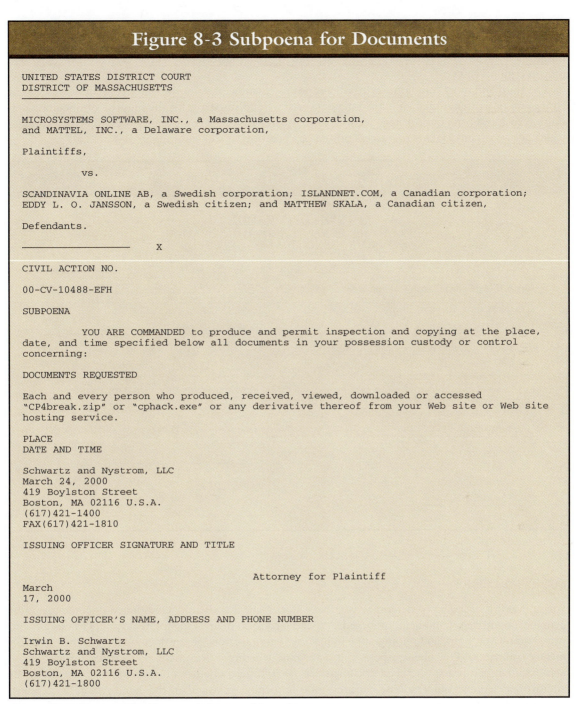

## Figure 8-3 Subpoena for Documents

```
UNITED STATES DISTRICT COURT
DISTRICT OF MASSACHUSETTS
―――――――――――――

MICROSYSTEMS SOFTWARE, INC., a Massachusetts corporation,
and MATTEL, INC., a Delaware corporation,

Plaintiffs,

          vs.

SCANDINAVIA ONLINE AB, a Swedish corporation; ISLANDNET.COM, a Canadian corporation;
EDDY L. O. JANSSON, a Swedish citizen; and MATTHEW SKALA, a Canadian citizen,

Defendants.

―――――――――――――    X

CIVIL ACTION NO.

00-CV-10488-EFH

SUBPOENA

        YOU ARE COMMANDED to produce and permit inspection and copying at the place,
date, and time specified below all documents in your possession custody or control
concerning:

DOCUMENTS REQUESTED

Each and every person who produced, received, viewed, downloaded or accessed
"CP4break.zip" or "cphack.exe" or any derivative thereof from your Web site or Web site
hosting service.

PLACE
DATE AND TIME

Schwartz and Nystrom, LLC
March 24, 2000
419 Boylston Street
Boston, MA 02116 U.S.A.
(617)421-1400
FAX(617)421-1810

ISSUING OFFICER SIGNATURE AND TITLE


                                     Attorney for Plaintiff
March
17, 2000

ISSUING OFFICER'S NAME, ADDRESS AND PHONE NUMBER

Irwin B. Schwartz
Schwartz and Nystrom, LLC
419 Boylston Street
Boston, MA 02116 U.S.A.
(617)421-1800
```

*Source: http://www.politechbot.com/cyberpatrol/cp-subpoena.txt.*

As you can see, the subpoena in Figure 8-3 was issued jointly in a civil action by two companies to provide information regarding every person who produced, received, viewed, downloaded, or accessed a certain software called "CP4break.zip" or "cphack.exe" or any derivative thereof from a Web site or Web site hosting service. Other subpoenas would look about the same; that is, they would identify who it is that is making the request for documents or information, who the request is being made of, and what exactly is being asked for. Every subpoena must be signed by a judge or court commissioner and then it is served, meaning it is delivered to the recipients, often by law enforcement officials.

A second way to obtain hard-to-get documentary evidence is to use a search warrant. A judge issues a search warrant when presented with probable cause to believe that documents have been used in committing a crime. Search warrants are executed only by law enforcement officials and are generally used only in criminal cases.

The third and most common way to obtain private documents is by voluntary consent, which can be either oral or written. Often an initial interview with a fraud suspect is for the purpose of obtaining permission to access bank or brokerage records, rather than to obtain a confession. An example of a consent, which allows a fraud examiner to access private bank records, is shown in Figure 8-4.

## Figure 8-4 Consent Form

### XYZ CORPORATION
#### CUSTOMER CONSENT AND AUTHORIZATION
#### FOR ACCESS TO FINANCIAL RECORDS

I, _____Arnold Fox McCune_____ , having read the explanation of my rights which is
            (Name of Customer)
attached to this form hereby authorize the _____XYZ Corporation Credit Union,_____
                                              (Name and Address of Financial Ins.)
to disclose these financial records: All Bank Account Records, including checking

accounts, savings accounts, and loans from 1/1/2001 to present

to Michael R. Blair and Robert W. Jacobs._____ for the following purpose(s):
_____Administrative Purposes_____

I understand that this authorization may be revoked by me in writing at any time before my records, as described above, are disclosed, and this authorization is valid for no more than three months from the date of my signature.

_____August 16, 2001_____                    *Arnold F. McCune*
                                                  (signature of customer)
                                                318 E. Birch Street

                                                Ann Harbor, MI 48159
                                                  (Address of Customer)
                                                Michael R. Blair

## Document Experts

Sometimes it is necessary to determine whether a document is authentic. Questioned documents can be genuine, counterfeit, fraudulent, or forged. A specialized form of investigation that applies forensic chemistry, microscopy, light, and photography in making determinations about documents is known as document examination. Document experts can determine whether a document was written by the person whose signature it bears; whether a document has been forged; whether a document has been altered by additives, deletions, obliterations, erasures, or photocopying; whether the handwriting is genuine; whether the entire document was printed on the same machine; whether a document was printed on the date it bears or before or after; whether two or more documents are significantly different or substantially the same; and whether pages have been substituted in a document.

Table 8-3 lists the most commonly encountered questions related to disputed documents or documents of unknown origin. Document experts can usually answer all these questions. For example, in answering questions about handwriting, examiners might look at the characteristics listed in the table.

To become a skilled examiner of questioned documents, one must acquire extensive and specialized training. Though most fraud investigators are not trained document examiners, it is important that they understand two important elements relating to document examination: (1) when to have a document examined by an expert, and (2) the responsibility of the investigator with respect to questioned

## Table 8-3 Questions About Disputed Documents

---

*Handwriting:*

1. Is the signature genuine?
2. Is the continued writing genuine?
3. Was the writing disguised?
4. Who did any unknown writing?
5. Can any hand printing that exists, if any, be identified?

6. Can any handwritten numerals, if any, be identified?
7. Which was written first, the signature or the writing above it?
8. Can the forger be identified?
9. Is the handwriting or signature consistent with the date of the document?

---

*Printing:*

1. What make and model of printer was used? During what years was the particular make and model used?
2. Can the individual printer that was used be identified?
3. Was the printing done before or after any handwriting and/or signatures?
4. Was the printing done on the date of the document or later?
5. Who did the actual printing?

6. Was the printing on the document all done at one time, or was some of it added at a later time? How much was added later?
7. Were copies made using the original document?
8. Are the copies genuine?
9. Can the printer or the document be identified from a carbon tape?

---

*Alterations and additions:*

1. Was the document altered in any way or added to at a later time? Were pages added, parts torn or cut off, purposely wrinkled or stained, etc.?
2. What original date or matter was altered or added to?
3. When was the alteration or addition made?

4. Who made the alteration or addition?
5. Has the photograph on an ID card or other ID document been removed and replaced with another?

---

*Age:*

1. Is the age of the document in accordance with its date?
2. How old are the paper, the printing, the ink, the seal, etc.?

3. Is there evidence of the manner or location in which the document was kept?

---

*Copies:*

1. Are the photocopies or photostatic reproductions copies of other documents?
2. What type of copy machine was used? What brand?
3. Can the individual copier be identified?
4. In what year was the particular make and model used? Produced?

5. Was any portion of the copy not on the original document? Was it pasted up?
6. Is there any indication that pages are missing on the copies that were part of the original?
7. Can the copy be traced to and identified as the particular original document that was its source?

---

*Other:*

1. Can machine-printed matter be identified?
2. Can the check-writer, the adding machine, the addressograph machine, or other machine be identified?
3. Was the envelope resealed?
4. Can the stapler, glue, pin, clip, or other fastener be identified?

5. Is the printed document genuine or counterfeit? If counterfeit, can the original document used as a reproduction source be determined.
6. What processes were used to print the counterfeit document?
7. Could the printing source or counterfeiter be identified if located?

*continued*

## Table 8-3 Questions About Disputed Documents (continued)

*Characteristics of handwriting:*

1. The basic movement of the handwriting—clockwise, counterclockwise, and straight-line—indicating direction, curvature, shapes, and slopes of the writing motions.
2. Slant—forward, backward, or in between.
3. The manner in which letters with loops are curved, and the size, shape, and proportion of the loops.
4. Peculiarities in the approach strokes and the upward strokes in the first letter of a word and in capital letters.
5. Characteristic initial and terminal strokes; their length and their angle in relation to letters and words.
6. Gaps between letters in specific letter combinations.
7. The manner in which the capital letters are formed, and the additional hooks or flourishes some writers place at the start or end of these letters.
8. Relative smoothness, tremor, or hesitation in the writing. Some writing flows smoothly and is free of hesitation. Other writing shows hesitation in the formation of some letters or defective line quality in the writing as a whole.
9. The manner in which the writer varies pressure in certain pen strokes, and variations in the weight and width of stroke lines.
10. The proportion and alignment of letters; the length or height and size of capital letters compared with lower case letters.
11. The manner in which the letter t is crossed, and the height and slant of the crossing—near the top of the t or lower down, straight or at an angle, with a flourish or plain; whether words ending in t are crossed.
12. The location of the dot over the letter i and its relationship to the location of the letter itself.
13. Types of ending strokes in words ending in the letters y, g, and s.
14. Open or closed letter style, as seen in such letters as a and o, and in letters that combine upward or downward strokes with loops, such as b, d, o, and g. Are the circles in these letters open or closed, broad or narrow?
15. Separation of letters within a word (e.g., separating a t from the remainder of the word, or separating a whole syllable from the rest of the word).
16. Characteristics of the portions of letters that appear above and/or below the line, such as f, g, and y.
17. Relative alignment of all letters; the uniformity and spacing of letters, words, and lines.
18. Alignment of lines.
19. Use and positioning of punctuation.
20. Indications that the writing instrument was lifted off the writing material between words and sentences.

documents. If one or more of the following warning signs exist, a document should be submitted for examination:

1. Abrasions or chemical pen or pencil erasures
2. Alterations or substitutions
3. Disguised or unnatural writings
4. Use of two or more different colors of ink
5. Charred, mutilated, or torn pages
6. Pencil or carbon marks along the writing lines
7. Existence of lines made during photocopying
8. Signs of inconsistency or disruption in the continuity of the content
9. Any suspicious appearance or unusual form

In dealing with questioned documents, the fraud investigator is responsible for taking the following steps:

- Collecting, protecting, identifying, and preserving the questioned document in as good a condition as possible
- Collecting and being able to prove to the document examiner the origins of adequate comparison specimens
- Submitting both the questioned and the comparison documents to the examiner

Two well-known organizations of document experts can offer help in fraud investigations. The first is the FBI Laboratory Division, Document Section:

*The Document Section, FBI Laboratory Division, provides expert forensic assistance and examinations of physical evidence. These services are available to all Federal agencies, U.S. Attorneys, and the U.S. Military in connection with both criminal and civil matters. These services are available to all duly constituted state, county, municipal, and other non-federal law enforcement agencies in the United States in connection with criminal matters. All expenses for these services, including provision of expert witnesses to testify to the results of their examinations in judicial proceedings and the travel expenses of these experts, are borne by the FBI.*

*Examinations of questioned documents include the full range of traditional examinations and comparisons, including, but not limited to, the following: handwriting and signatures, hand printing, typewriting, altered and obliterated documents, charred or burned paper, writing materials, photocopies, and many others.[2]*

The second organization of document experts is a private group, the American Board of Forensic Document Examiners, Inc. (ABFDE).[3] A description of the ABFDE's background, functions, and purpose follows:

*The need to identify forensic scientists qualified to provide essential professional services for the nation's judicial and executive branches of government as well as the community in general has been long recognized. In response to this professional mandate, the American Board of Forensic Document Examiners, Inc., was organized in 1977 to provide, in the interest of the public and the advancement of the science, a program of certification in forensic document examination. In purpose, function, and organization, the ABFDE is thus analogous to the certifying board[s] in various other scientific fields.*

*The objective of the Board is to establish, enhance, and maintain, as necessary, standards of qualification for those who practice forensic document examination and to certify as qualified specialists those voluntary applicants who comply with the requirements of the Board. In this way, the Board aims to make available to the judicial system, and other public, a practical and equitable system for readily identifying those persons professing to be specialists in forensic document examination who possess the requisite qualifications and competence.*

*Certification is based upon the candidate's personal and professional record of education and training, experience, and achievement, as well as on the results of a formal examination.*

*The Board is a non-profit organization in the District of Columbia. Its initial sponsors are the American Academy of Forensic Sciences and the American Society of Questioned Document Examiners. The Board is composed of officers and other directors who serve staggered terms and are elected from among nominees of designated nominating organizations or serve at-large.*

With the Internet, it is not difficult to find a qualified questioned document examiner. Searching such key words as "questioned document examiner" or "questioned document examination" will reveal numerous Web sites of questioned document examiners. Experienced investigators discount questionable or scientifically unproven methods and use what they know works best: thoroughness and dogged tenacity in pursuit of the truth. They also make sure that any technique they use is sound and fair. For example, if a question arises regarding the authenticity of a document or handwriting sample, they seek out a Qualified Documents Examiner who holds a degree in the physical sciences and has undergone many years of laboratory experience under the supervision of an experienced examiner. Use of a Qualified Document Examiner as opposed to graphologist is almost always recommended. Graphologists usually obtain their designation through a home study course, whereas a Qualified Document Examiner will hold a degree and has undergone many years of laboratory experience.

## SUMMARY OF INVESTIGATIVE TECHNIQUES

Concealment investigative techniques usually focus on obtaining documentary evidence. Documents often make up a significant and reliable amount of the evidence in fraud cases. In this chapter, we identified the legal and administrative issues and described various ways in which documentary evidence can be accumulated and examined.

## KEY TERMS

**Chain of Custody:** Keeping an accurate record of when a document is received and what has happened to it since its receipt.

**Discovery Sampling:** A form of sampling that deals with the probability of discovering at least one occurrence in a given sample.

**Document Examiner:** A person who applies forensic chemistry, microscopy, light and other tools and approaches to make determinations about the authenticity of documents.

**Nonsampling Risk:** The risk that sample results will be misinterpreted by the examiner.

**Sampling Risk:** The risk that a sample will not be representative of a population.

**Subpoena (Subpoena duces tecum):** An order issued by a court or grand jury to produce documents and or appears in a court or deposition.

## QUESTIONS AND CASES

### DISCUSSION QUESTIONS

1. What are some of the most common concealment investigative techniques?

2. What is the value of documents when conducting a fraud investigation?

3. Why is it important to obtain documentary evidence?

4. How can discovery sampling help in obtaining documentary evidence?

5. What are different ways in which investigators can obtain hard-to-get documentary evidence?

### TRUE/FALSE

1. Photocopies are always preferable to original documents as evidence.

2. There is no difference between forensic document experts and graphologists.

3. Discovery sampling is probably the most difficult of all statistical sampling variations to understand.

4. As long as a sample is selected randomly, it will always be representative of the population as a whole.

5. Even if photocopies of original documents are allowed to be introduced as evidence in a court of law, they are still considered secondary evidence.

6. A cancelled check typically shows the account number of the person who presented the check, the teller who processed the check, and the sequence number of the transaction.

7. Random number tables are ineffective and should not be used when selecting random samples from a population.

8. Using a computer can be an effective approach for determining whether fraud exists because the auditor can look at entire populations.

9. Bates numbers are identifying numbers used by attorneys involved in litigation to track all documents.

# MULTIPLE CHOICE

1. In a fraud investigation, documents usually:
   a. Contain extremely valuable information.
   b. Are rarely used in court.
   c. Are not reliable sources of information.
   d. Are only valuable in obtaining a confession.

2. Chain of custody refers to:
   a. Marking on a document so it can later be identified.
   b. A record of when a document is received and what has happened to it since its receipt.
   c. Databases used in trials to assist lawyers.
   d. The way in which courts are organized.

3. Marking documentary evidence is important to ensure that:
   a. Documents are legal.
   b. Databases can be created with valuable information.
   c. Documents can be identified later.
   d. The original can be used during an investigation.

4. Discovery sampling:
   a. Is a type of variables sampling.
   b. Is one of the more difficult statistical sampling methods to understand.
   c. Is never used in conducting a fraud examination.
   d. Deals with the probability of discovering at least one error in a given sample size if the population error is a certain percentage.

5. Documentary evidence such as private tax returns can usually only be obtained by:
   a. Subpoena.
   b. Search warrant.
   c. Voluntary consent.
   d. All of the above.

6. Which of the following is true regarding document experts?
   a. They can usually determine whether a document was written by the person whose signature the document bears.
   b. They can usually determine whether a document has been forged.
   c. They can usually determine whether the date the document bears is the date the document was written.
   d. All of the above.

7. Which of the following is a benefit of statistical sampling?
   a. It allows auditors to be certain that fraud does exist in a population.
   b. It is helpful when populations are small.
   c. It allows quantification of risk.
   d. It prevents inferences about a population.

8. When is a photocopy *not* acceptable as evidence in a court of law?
   a. When the original document has been lost or destroyed without the intent or fault of the party seeking to introduce the copied document as secondary evidence.
   b. When the original document has been lost by the fraud examiner.
   c. When the document or record is in the custody of a public office.
   d. When the original documents are too voluminous to permit careful examination.

9. Which of the following methods of gathering documents is based primarily on luck?
   a. Documents discovered during audits
   b. Hard-to-get private documents that are subpoenaed
   c. Documents discovered through searching public sources
   d. Documents provided by tipsters

10. Which of the following is true of graphologists?
    a. They can only perform their work in laboratory settings.
    b. Their work is the same as that of forensic document experts.
    c. They study handwriting as a way to interpret and identify personalities.
    d. They are required to be members of the ABFDE organization.

11. What can a fraud examiner conclude if one or more instances of fraud are found in a sample taken from a population?
    a. It indicates a slight risk that fraud exists in the population.
    b. The population contains fraud.
    c. The sample may not have been randomly selected, and thus no conclusions can be drawn.
    d. The sample is most likely not representative of the population as a whole.

12. What can a fraud examiner conclude if his or her tests confirm that no instances of fraud are present in a sample taken from a population?
    a. It indicates virtually no risk that fraud exists in the population.
    b. The population contains no fraud.
    c. No fraud is present in that particular sample.
    d. The sample is most likely not representative of the population as a whole.

13. How are most frauds concealed?
    a. By shredding source documents
    b. By converting to a paperless office without paper transactions
    c. By creating fictitious documents or altering source documents
    d. By firing employees who will not go along with the fraud

## SHORT CASES

**Case 1.** The management of AAAA Company observed that the company's cash outflows have been increasing much more rapidly than its inflows. Management cannot understand the change; from their perspective it has been "business as usual." Management asks you, a fraud expert, to help them understand what is going on.

You decide that the best place to start your investigation is to take a sample of cancelled checks and verify that both the controller and another manager signed them—a procedure required by company policy. Check numbers for the period range from 100 to 800.

Using the random numbers in Table 8-1, follow these instructions to select a random sample of 15 checks to examine:

- Start from the bottom left of the table.

- Move through the table from left to right and from bottom to top.

- Skip the numbers outside of the relevant range.

- Use the middle three digits of each number.

**Case 2.** Assume that you have selected a random sample of 15 checks from a population of 800 checks. The checks you selected are the following numbers: 664, 789, 650, 136, 365, 538, 800, 657, 110, 136, 398, 645, 214, 544, and 777. Based on this sample, what conclusions can you make in each of the following situations?

1. You determine that check #365 was not properly signed and was paid to a fictitious vendor.

2. You determine that no fraud exists in the sample of 15 checks you evaluated.

**Case 3.** As lead accountant for a small company, you notice that inventory purchases from a certain vendor increased dramatically over the past few months, while purchases from all other vendors decreased. You suspect that something may not be right.

Which method(s) would you use to investigate your suspicions?

**Case 4.** A bank manager's responsibility was making loans. Auditors discovered that several loans he made over a five-year period had not been repaid. A fraud investigation revealed that the manager had been receiving kickbacks from risky clients in exchange for extending loans to them. His loans had cost the bank millions of dollars in uncollectible loans. You have been asked to determine the amount of kickbacks your loan officer has taken.

1. What type of records would you search to find information about the manager's assets?

2. Which records would be the most helpful in this case? Why?

**Case 5.** Enron, the largest corporation to file for Chapter 11 bankruptcy at that time, was number 7 on the *Fortune* 500 list of the largest companies in the United States as ranked by revenues at the time of its bankruptcy. It was alleged that Enron executives were involved in questionable accounting and financial statement fraud, the disclosure of which led to the downward spiral in Enron's stock price and the financial ruin of thousands of employees and investors. In addition to Enron's internal accounting problems, it is alleged that its auditor, a Big 5 CPA firm, instructed employees to destroy documents related to its work for Enron.

Based on your understanding regarding a fraud examiner's responsibilities regarding documents, what should the audit firm personnel have done with the documents if they suspected that fraud had occurred?

**Case 6.** Marlin Company has suspected something "fishy" for several months. It noticed that its profits have been slowly decreasing, at the same time that revenues increased. After consulting with you, a fraud expert, the company has decided to investigate the purchasing patterns of its three purchasing agents—Curly, Larry, and Moe. You decide that a good method for investigation into the matter is examining a random sample of purchase invoices and verifying their accuracy and validity. Curly's invoices are numbered 0000 through 0999, Larry's are 1000 through 1999, and Moe's are 2000 through 2999.

When you approach Curly, Larry, and Moe, they seem somewhat defensive. They begin to harass one another, blaming each other for the mess they are involved in. Moe even twitches their noses and slaps their heads. Curly attempts to retaliate by poking Moe in the eye, but missed and hit Larry instead.

When the three were done, the CFO, Mr. Rutin-Tutin, exclaimed, "Would you three stooges quit fooling around and produce the invoices immediately?!"

The three shuffled off to their offices, grumbling all along the way. They returned a couple of hours later with photocopies of their invoices. When Mr. Rutin-Tutin asked where the original invoices were, they explained that they always copy and destroy the originals for easier storing purposes. Rather annoyed and fed up with the three morons, Mr. Rutin-Tutin hands you the stacks of photocopied invoices and tells you to do your thing.

What is wrong with this picture? Are you suspicious of a fraud here? What is a possible first step in verifying the invoices?

**Case 7.** John Doe, a fraud examiner, has been hired by ABC Corporation to investigate a shortage of cash, which management thinks is being caused by fraudulent behavior. John Doe could spend his time and money pursuing witnesses to the crime or collecting documents that would confirm fraudulent activities. As with most fraud examiners, he chooses to collect supporting documents instead of pursuing witnesses. Explain why most fraud examiners prefer documents over witnesses, and then describe elements of good document care.

## INTERNET ASSIGNMENT

Today many data analysis tools are available to provide assistance to fraud examiners when searching for possible fraudulent activities within a company. Visit the Association of Certified Fraud Examiners' Web site (http://www.cfenet.com) and list some of the computer-aided data analysis tools and services available to fraud examiners.

## DEBATE

An excerpt from the Fourth Amendment reads: "The right of the people to be secure in their persons, houses, papers, and effects, against unreasonable searches and seizures, shall not be violated, and no Warrants shall issue, but upon probable cause, supported by Oath or affirmation, and particularly describing the place to be searched, and the persons or things to be seized."

Suspecting a Mr. Dayley of running an illegal gambling and loan sharking operation, the FBI obtained a federal search warrant. The FBI entered the residence of Mr. Dayley and searched through various records. Suspecting most of the records were contained on a personal computer, the FBI began attempting to access the computer's various files.

Unable to access the needed files because of password barriers, the FBI installed a system known as a Key Logger System, or KLS. This system was able to determine the keystrokes made on a computer and thus allowed the FBI to discover the password needed to enter the incriminating files. The discovery led to the gathering of evidence linking Mr. Dayley to the suspected illegal operation.

Were Mr. Dayley's Fourth Amendment rights violated?

## END NOTES

1. http://www.fbi.gov/page2/march04/doclab033004.htm.

2. Based on a true case from http://lawlibrary.rutgers.edu/fed/html/scarfo2.html-1.html.

# CHAPTER 9

# CONVERSION INVESTIGATION METHODS

## LEARNING OBJECTIVES

After studying this chapter, you should be able to:

1. Explain why finding out how perpetrators convert and spend their stolen funds is important.

2. Understand how federal, state, and local public records can assist in following the financial "tracks" of suspected perpetrators.

3. Access information via the Internet to assist in the investigation of a suspected fraud perpetrator.

4. Perform net worth calculations on suspected fraud perpetrators and understand how net worth calculations are effective in court and in obtaining confessions.

*Phar-Mor, a dry goods retailer based in Youngstown, Ohio, was founded in 1982 by Mickey Monus.[1] Within 10 years, Phar-Mor was operating in nearly every state, with more than 300 stores. The retailer's business strategy was to sell household products and prescription drugs at prices lower than other discount stores. Phar-Mor's prices were so low and its expansion so rapid that even Wal-Mart, the king of discount prices, was nervous.*

*Unfortunately, what appeared to be one of the fastest growing companies in the United States was committing massive fraud. In reality, the company never made a legitimate profit. Investigators eventually determined that Phar-Mor overstated revenues and profits by more than $500 million. Mickey Monus personally pocketed more than $500,000.*

*Monus loved the good life and being where the action was. He diverted $10 million from revenues to prop up the National Basketball Association (the defunct minor-league basketball venture) and personally assembled the All-American Girls (a professional cheerleading squad). His stolen money was spent at expensive bars, playing golf at expensive country clubs, paying off his credit card balances, and adding rooms to his house. Monus bought an expensive engagement ring for his fiancée, and at their poolside wedding at the Ritz-Carlton Hotel, his bride wore an 18-karat gold mesh dress worth $500,000. Monus's spend-a-holic personality exhibited itself in countless ways. Many were the times that he would walk into the office at 3:00 in the afternoon and say, "Let's go to Vegas"—and he meant right then! Once there, a limo would whisk him to Caesar's Palace, where a suite awaited him 7 days a week, 24 hours a day. Monus routinely gave employees $4,000 to gamble with. As one employee said, "He was at home in the 'world of big bets and make-believe.'" To Monus, life was truly a game.[2]*

The Phar-Mor fraud is not the only one whose perpetrators enjoyed the good life. In another case, a perpetrator who confessed to embezzling $3.2 million was asked in her deposition the following question:

> *How would you describe your lifestyle during the period when the fraud was being perpetrated?*

Her response:

> *Extravagant. I drove expensive, very nice cars. We had an Audi 5000 Quattro, a Maserati Spider convertible, a Jeep Cherokee, and a Rolls- Royce. We bought expensive paintings, art, and glasswork. We held expensive parties, serving steak and lobster. We bought a condominium for my parents. We took cruises and other expensive vacations. And I wore expensive clothes, fur coats, diamonds, and gold jewelry.*

The lifestyles of Mickey Monus and this embezzler were extreme, but they demonstrate a common theme: Rarely do perpetrators save what they steal. Although most perpetrators begin their thefts because of a perceived critical need (the $3.2 million perpetrator initially stole to repay a debt consolidation loan), they frequently continue to embezzle after their immediate need is met. The money usually goes to improve their lifestyles. An important focus in investigations, therefore, involves determining how perpetrators "convert" or spend their stolen funds. As we discussed previously, conversion is the third element of the fraud triangle. Certain frauds, such as kickback schemes, do not generate fraudulent company records; investigating the theft and concealment elements of some frauds is, for practical purposes, impossible. Accordingly, these frauds are most easily detected and investigated by focusing on lifestyle changes and other conversion attempts.

Most investigations of conversion involve searching public records and other sources to trace purchases of assets, payments of liabilities, and changes in lifestyle and net worth. When people enter into financial transactions, such as buying assets, they leave tracks or "financial footprints." Trained investigators who know how to follow, study, and interpret these tracks often find valuable evidence that supports allegations of fraud.

## Conversion Searches

Conversion searches are performed for two reasons: first, to determine the extent of embezzlement and, second, to gather evidence that can be used in interrogations to obtain a confession. Effective interviewers can often get suspects to admit that their only income is earned income early in an interview. Then, by introducing evidence of a lifestyle and associated expenditures that cannot be supported by the earned income, interviewers make it difficult for the suspect to explain the source of the unknown income. Cornered suspects sometimes break down and confess.

To become proficient at conversion investigations, fraud examiners need to understand that (1) federal, state, and local agencies and other organizations maintain information that can be accessed in searches; (2) private and Internet-based sources of information are available; and (3) the net worth method of analyzing spending information is especially helpful in determining probable amounts of embezzled funds.

In addition, several private organizations, such as credit reporting agencies and companies that maintain computer databases, as well as Internet sources, provide valuable information about a person's lifestyle and spending habits.

The chart in Figure 9-1 provides a breakdown of the information sources relevant to investigators.

Investigative activities can be time intensive because of the significant amount of locations to search. Careful planning and execution of your investigative tasks are key to an efficient, effective search. The following Web sites provide overview information on how to investigate and conduct searches:

> ***How to Investigate.com:*** *http://www.howtoinvestigate.com/* This site provides information on how to conduct an investigation.

> ***Public Records Information Sources:*** *http://www.ahhapeoplefinder.com/* Public Records Information Sources gives information about credit bureaus, business reports, government agencies, state and federal records, and the directory industry.

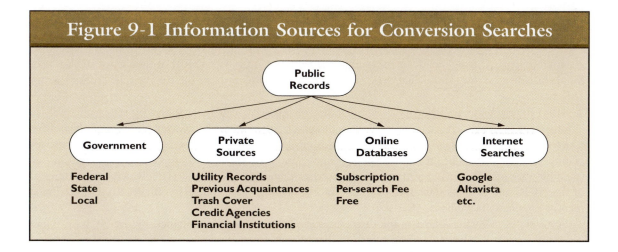

Figure 9-1 Information Sources for Conversion Searches

*Investigative Resource Center: http://www.factfind.com/* The Investigative Resource Center provides information on public and open source records and corporate records.

*Legal Resource Center: http://www.crimelynx.com/* The Legal Resource Center lists numerous government links, criminal justice statistics, record searches, and other valuable information.

*Private Investigator http://www.geocities.com/Athens/7374/links.html* This Web site offers information on various databases, postal address references, investigative organizations, and credit reporting.

## Government Sources of Information

Many federal, state, and local agencies maintain public records in accordance with various laws. Much of this information can be accessed by anyone who requests it, but some of it is protected under privacy laws that prevent disclosure to the public. Federal records are generally not as useful as state and local records in fraud investigations, but they are helpful in certain situations. Because of the bureaucracies involved, accessing federal records can be time-consuming and costly.

### Federal Sources of Information

Most federal agencies maintain information that can be helpful in investigations of fraud. Several of these agencies are described in this section.

#### DEPARTMENT OF DEFENSE

The Department of Defense maintains records on all military personnel, both active and inactive. Military information is maintained by branch of service. This department also contains information on individuals who may be a threat to national security. The department regularly shares information with other federal agencies, such as the Federal Bureau of Investigation (FBI) and Central Intelligence Agency (CIA).

Military records are not confidential and provide valuable information that can help you trace a person's whereabouts through changing addresses. Military records are also helpful in searching for hidden assets, because individuals often buy property and other assets using previous addresses. The Web site of the Department of Defense is http://www.defenselink.mil.

#### DEPARTMENT OF JUSTICE

The Department of Justice is the federal agency charged with enforcing federal criminal and civil laws. It maintains records related to the detection, prosecution, and rehabilitation of offenders. The Department of Justice includes U.S. Attorneys, U.S. Marshals, and the FBI. The Drug Enforcement Administration

(DEA) is the federal agency of the Department of Justice charged with enforcing laws against narcotics trafficking.

The FBI is the principal investigative agency of the Department of Justice. Criminal matters not assigned to other U.S. agencies are assigned to the FBI. For example, the FBI normally investigates bank fraud, organized crime, and illegal drug trade. The FBI is also responsible for national security within U.S. borders.

The FBI maintains several databases and other records that can be accessed by state and local law enforcement agencies. The major database maintained by the FBI is the *National Crime Information Center (NCIC)*. The NCIC contains information on stolen vehicles, license plates, securities, boats, and planes; stolen and missing firearms; missing persons; and individuals who are currently wanted on outstanding warrants. The FBI also maintains the *Interstate Identification Index* (III), which is an outgrowth of the NCIC and benefits state and local law enforcement agencies. The III contains arrest and criminal records on a nationwide basis.

Some states maintain databases for their states similar to the one maintained by the NCIC. To gain access to all such databases, you must present identifying information, such as your birth date or Social Security number. These databases are not generally available to private investigators. A need to obtain access to these databases is a good reason to involve local law enforcement in a fraud investigation. The Web site of the U.S. Department of Justice is http://www.usdoj.gov.

## Bureau of Prisons

This agency operates the nationwide system of federal prisons, correctional institutions, and community treatment facilities. It maintains detailed records on persons who have been incarcerated in the various federal facilities. Because fraud perpetrators are often repeat offenders, information on previous incarcerations often provides important evidence. The Web site of the U.S. Bureau of Prisons is http://www.bop.gov.

## Internal Revenue Service

The IRS enforces all internal revenue laws, except those dealing with alcohol, firearms, tobacco, and explosives, which are handled by the Bureau of Alcohol, Tobacco, and Firearms. IRS records are not available to the public, so access to its databases normally requires the involvement of law enforcement officials. The Web site of the Internal Revenue Service is http://www.irs.gov.

## Secret Service

The Secret Service is responsible for protecting the President of the United States and other federal dignitaries. It also deals with counterfeiting, theft of government checks, interstate credit card violations, and some computer crimes. The Web site of the Secret Service is http://www.ustreas.gov/usss.

## Postal Service

The Postal Service is a quasi-governmental organization that has responsibility for the U.S. mail and for protecting citizens from loss through theft that involves the mail system. *Postal inspectors* are some of the best and most helpful federal investigators. They handle major fraud cases involving the use of mail, and they work for the prosecution of offenders who violate postal laws. Postal inspectors share jurisdiction with other federal, state, and local agencies.

Postal inspectors can be helpful in investigations of employee fraud, investment scams, or management frauds. Perpetrating a fraud in the United States is difficult without using the mail system. For example, bribes and kickbacks and false advertisements are often made through the mail, and stolen checks and funds are often deposited in banks by sending them through the mail. Because the use of mail is so common in frauds, the federal mail statutes are the workhorse statutes in federal crimes. The Web site of the Postal Service is http://www.usps.gov.

## CENTRAL INTELLIGENCE AGENCY

The CIA is responsible to the President of the United States. It investigates security matters outside the United States, whereas the FBI has jurisdiction for security within U.S. borders. The CIA can provide useful information when cases involve international issues such as money laundering in the Cayman Islands or other jurisdictions. The Web site of the Central Intelligence Agency is http://www.cia.gov.

## SOCIAL SECURITY ADMINISTRATION

The Social Security Administration (SSA) has information about individuals' Social Security numbers. This agency can be helpful in identifying the area where a perpetrator was residing when a Social Security number was issued. Because every Social Security number contains information about the area (first three digits), the group (middle two digits), and the person's serial number (last four digits), Social Security information is extremely useful in fraud investigations. Once an individual's unique Social Security number is known, numerous federal, state, local, and private records can be accessed. In addition, many private sources such as credit agencies or "people finder" Web sites are significantly more useful when searched using someone's Social Security numbers. The Web site of the Social Security Administration is http://www.ssa.gov.

## OTHER FEDERAL SOURCES OF INFORMATION

Many other federal sources of information are available. The ones discussed here indicate the range and variety in the types of records available. For additional federal sources, see the U.S. Federal Government Agencies Directory at http://www.lib.lsu.edu/gov/fedgov.html or http://www.firstgov.gov/.

# State Sources of Information

State resources are often helpful in fraud investigations. Several of these are listed in this section.

## STATE ATTORNEY GENERAL

The attorney general for each state enforces all state civil and criminal laws in cooperation with local law enforcement agencies. Most state attorneys general have investigative arms (similar to the FBI for the Department of Justice), such as the State Bureau of Investigation. This agency contains records relating to individuals who have been convicted of a breach of state civil and criminal laws. The National Association of Attorneys General has a Web site at http://www.naag.org.

## BUREAU OF PRISONS

The Bureau of Prisons for each state maintains the network of state prisons and administers state corrections departments. It maintains records on all individuals who have been incarcerated in state prison systems, as well as on individuals who are on probation or parole.

## SECRETARY OF STATE

The Secretary of State maintains all types of records relating to businesses and Uniform Commercial Code (UCC) filings. Every corporation must file documents in the state in which it was chartered. These documents, which are usually maintained by the Secretary of State's office, reveal incorporators, bylaws, articles of incorporation, the registered agent, and the initial board of directors and officers. These records are public information and can be helpful in gathering information about organizations that are perpetrating fraud. They can confirm whether an organization is legally conducting business and whether its taxes have been paid. They can also provide names of partners, principal shareholders, board members, and business affiliations. This information is valuable in tracing assets, establishing conflicts of interest, identifying dummy companies, and determining changes in financial status.

Secretary of State offices also usually maintain UCC filings. These filings contain information about chattel mortgages (non–real estate transactions) and about loans to individuals or businesses on equipment, furniture, automobiles, and other personal property. UCC records can identify collateral on purchased and leased assets, the nature of the lending company, where a person banks, and whether the person has a need for money. UCC records are sometimes available in a county clerk's office (depending on the state). Much of the information maintained by a Secretary of State's office concerning businesses and UCC filings is online at the National Association of Secretaries of State at http://www.nass.org/busreg/busreg.html.

### DEPARTMENT OF MOTOR VEHICLES

Driver's license records are maintained by the Department of Motor Vehicles and are publicly available in most states. These records enable you to access a person's driving history, address, convictions for traffic violations, name, date of birth, address of birth, and photograph. Driver's license records may be a source of a person's Social Security number. In addition, driver's license numbers are used for identification in many transactions, such as those involving written checks.

### DEPARTMENT OF VITAL STATISTICS

This department maintains birth records. These records, although quite difficult to obtain, contain information about a person's date and place of birth and parents. Because many people have an affinity for the places where they grew up, local records in these areas may provide useful information. For example, a perpetrator might convert stolen money by purchasing private land or funding public projects in the area where they grew up. Birthplace areas may also contain individuals who know important information about a perpetrator.

### DEPARTMENT OF BUSINESS REGULATION

Most states have a department of business regulation or a similar agency that maintains licensing information about various professionals. Licensing information is generally maintained on accountants, attorneys, bankers, doctors, electricians, plumbers, contractors, engineers, nurses, police officers, firefighters, insurance agents, bail bondsmen, real estate agents, security guards, stockbrokers, investment bankers, teachers, servers (food handler's permit), and travel agents, among others.

Licensing information that helps you access industry guidelines also leads you to an individual's memberships, specializations, current business addresses, history of business complaints, grievances, and charges, investigations, and professional credentials.

As an example of how helpful this information can be, suppose you are investigating a fraud similar to the Elgin Aircraft example in Chapter 5, in which dummy doctors are set up. A quick check with the Department of Business Regulation in the relevant state will disclose whether the doctors being paid are legitimate.

## County and Local Records

Counties and other local agencies maintain records that are especially useful in fraud investigations. The detailed nature of these records makes them particularly valuable; however, the availability of these records varies from state to state and from county to county.

### COUNTY CLERK

County clerks maintain numerous records on local citizens, including voter registration records and marriage licenses. Marriage and voting records are always useful in fraud investigations. Voter registration records, for example, state a person's name, current address, past addresses, age, date of birth, social security number, signature, and telephone number, whether listed or unlisted. Even if a person has not voted, his or her family members (such as son, daughter, and spouse) may have voted, and thus voter registration records still provide valuable information.

Marriage records are maintained in the county clerk's office in the county of residence at the time of marriage. They often list the full legal names of the couple, their dates of birth, their Social Security numbers, their addresses at the time of marriage (and usually their parents' addresses as well), driver's license numbers, passport numbers, prior marriages, and the witnesses to those marriages. Once this information has been obtained, further searches in online and other databases are much more productive.

## COUNTY LAND OFFICE AND TAX ASSESSOR'S OFFICE

These offices contain real estate records for land located in the county. Two common methods are used to trace real estate records. First, land ownership is normally found in the County Land Office or in the office of the Recorder of Deeds. County Land Office records identify owned assets, indebtedness, mortgage holders, trustees or straw buyers, and people who knew a person before and after a sale. Second, property tax records, maintained by the County Assessor's Office, also contain property records. Property records may be indexed by address or legal description or by the owner's name, or they may be indexed by the name of the seller or the buyer. Property tax records contain information about a property's legal description and current assessed value and the taxpayer's current status. These records are helpful in identifying assets purchased and liens removed by a perpetrator.

## COUNTY SHERIFF AND OTHER OFFICERS

Offices such as that of the city police, the county constable, probation officers, and bail bondsmen contain information about criminal charges, indictment statements, pretrial information reports, conviction statements, incarceration information, and probation information.

## LOCAL COURTS

Various local courts maintain records on past law violators, including pretrial information such as personal history, employment history, personal and physical information, prior charges, divorces and property settlement agreements, personal injury lawsuits, financial claims and litigation, fraud claims and co-conspirators, bankruptcies, wills, and probates. Bankruptcy information, which can also be found at various sites online, includes the current status of bankruptcy cases, creditor lists, debts, assets, and information on character. These records can show how assets might be hidden. Information about wills and probates helps identify the assets (and sources of the assets) of perpetrators. Many perpetrators often justify their extravagant lifestyles by claiming to have inherited money. Such claims can be validated or dismissed from information contained in wills and probate.

## PERMIT DEPARTMENTS

Permit departments supply information on fire permits (hazardous chemicals), health permits (pollutants), elevator permits, and building permits. Permit-issuing departments can be helpful in identifying the nature and location of businesses, new leases, and recent construction.

# Private Sources of Information

Hundreds of sources of private information are available to those willing to search for them. Utility records (gas, electric, water, garbage, and sewer), for example, supply the names of persons billed, show whether a person lives or owns property in the service area, and identify the types of utilities a business uses.

Another way to gain financial information is through the previous acquaintances. For example, a former spouse of a suspected fraud perpetrator may have documents, including bank documents, that turn out to be key in investigations.

A surprising source of valuable financial information is *trash investigation*, also known as trash cover. "Trashing" a suspect involves looking through a person's trash for possible evidence. Note that searching trash while it is in the possession of a person is against the law. However, once the trash leaves the suspect's home, sidewalk, or fenced area, investigators can usually freely and legally search the trash. In the months of January, February, and March these searches often uncover valuable tax information. During all times of the year, it is always possible to find credit card information, bank statements, and other valuable information.

Various credit reporting companies maintain private credit records on both individuals and organizations. Reporting agencies are of two types: (1) file-based credit reporting agencies, which develop information from their credit files, and (2) public records and investigative agencies, which gather most of their information through interviews. Credit bureaus are used primarily by retail organizations.

Credit reporting companies typically maintain the following information:

- Consumer information, such as addresses, ages, family members, and incomes
- Account information, such as payment schedules, items purchased, and buying habits
- Marketing information, such as customer breakdowns by age, sex, and income levels
- Information on current and former employees

Information maintained by credit reporting agencies is governed by the Fair Credit Reporting Act of 1971. This act regulates activities of credit, insurance, and employment investigations. Under the law, a consumer-reporting agency must, on request, furnish information to an individual that is also furnished to a third party. If adverse action is to be taken against an employee as a result of third-party information, the employee must be given advance notice. The three major credit reporting agencies are:

- Experian, http://www.experian.com
- Equifax, http://www.equifax.com
- TransUnion, http://www.tuc.com

Financial institution records (including banks, brokerage, and insurance companies) are essential elements of investigations. Bank records can be obtained through a court subpoena, search warrants, a civil summons, or civil discovery. Financial institutions often sell the rights to search and retrieve records from their databases.

Until 1999, when the *Gramm-Leach-Bliley Act* was passed, investigators could only gain information from a financial institution by using false pretenses. Using false pretenses is illegal under the new act, but it does allow banks and other financial institutions to share customer information with anyone they want, including selling it to database companies. Before financial institutions can sell or disclose confidential customer information, they must provide customers the opportunity to "opt out" of information sharing, which keeps their information private. However, most people do not provide written notice to the bank denying the bank the right to sell their personal bank information (*the opting-out right*), so bank information is more readily available than ever before. Many Internet sites—for a fee—provide information such as bank account number, bank name, bank address, approximate account balance, city and state of the bank, withdrawals, deposits, savings, wire transfers, full transactions of the bank accounts, credits, collateral records, debits, transactions of loans, bankruptcies, transaction details, and outstanding loans.

## Online Databases

An increasing number of online, commercial databases provide helpful information. Databases may be subscription based, have a per-use fee, or allow unlimited free searching. Some databases overlap one another, but most contain unique information that may be useful to a case. Dialog, for example, searches 900 databases that provide information about individuals' and companies' backgrounds, employment histories, professional papers, and technical information. Many publicly available databases contain bankruptcy, court records, real estate, tax lien, UCC filing, and other important financial information. Some of the most valuable Web sites of commercial and/or public databases, along with a brief description of the type of information available on each, are listed here in alphabetical order. Please note that due to the dynamic nature of the Internet, these sites are current at publication time.

***Accurint:*** *http://www.accurint.com/* Accurint contains information about individuals from banking, human resources, government, law enforcement, legal, and media sources.

***AutoTrackXP:*** *http://www.autotrackxp.com/* AutoTrackXP, now owned by ChoicePoint, contains billions of records about individuals, including property records, bankruptcies, links to other people, and so forth.

***BizAdvantage:*** *http://www.bizadvantage.com/* This specialty database, formerly known as Brainwave, gives in-depth information such as patent, bankruptcy, UCC filings, medical updates, and business profiles.

***Black Book Online:*** *http://www.crimetime.com/online.htm* Black Book Online provides searches on bankruptcies, mail drops, corporations, real estate, businesses, death records, state records, federal records, and other valuable information.

***BRB Publications:*** *http://www.brbpublications.com* BRB Publications is a public records research library that offers access to records of more than 26,000 government agencies. It also has links to 650 state, county, city, and federal databases.

***ChoicePoint:*** *http://www.choicepointonline.com* ChoicePoint contains more than 14 billion records about individuals and businesses.

***Confi-chek Online Public Records:*** *http://www.confi-chek.com* For a fee, Confi-chek conducts background checks, asset identifications, and searches for criminal records. Information on personal real property, bankruptcy, tax liens, civil judgments, and criminal records can be obtained here.

***Data Quick:*** *http://www.dataquick.com* These databases contain property profiles, mortgage information, asset ownership information, and other valuable information.

***Dialog:*** *http://www.dialog.com/* Dialog's 900 databases contain more than 15 terabytes of high-volume information. Content areas include business, science, technology, media, news, property, law, government, and more.

***Discreet Research:*** *http://www.date411.com* Discreet Research offers an extensive line of public records, including business reports, telephone searches, preemployment information, motor vehicle records, license verifications, county criminal records, metro criminal records, state criminal records, outstanding warrants, prison records, civil records, and other valuable information.

***Dun & Bradstreet:*** *http://www.dnb.com/ (also see http://www.zapdata.com)* The Dun & Bradstreet databases contain information on more than 14 million U.S. businesses and millions of contacts for each of those businesses. Dun & Bradstreet also publishes several directories that provide background and financial information on businesses.

***EBSCO Information Systems:*** *http://www.epnet.com* This site contains many large databases that include full-text periodicals, scholarly journals, U.S. and international newspapers, reference books, and even detailed pamphlets.

***Harte-Hanks:*** *http://www.hartehanksmi.com* Harte-Hanks's databases track technology installations, business demographics, and key decision makers at more than 400,000 locations.

***IRBSearch:*** *http://www.irbsearch.com/* IRBSearch is a database that helps researchers connect individuals together. It allows searching by name, address, social security number, or phone number. Results include current and past addresses with links to possible relatives, possible associates, and neighbors along with their addresses and phone numbers.

***KnowX:*** *http://www.knowx.com* One of the most comprehensive databases available, KnowX can help you find out where a former tenant lives, what business name is being used, whether a potential employer is involved in any lawsuits, and what assets an employee has.

***LexisNexis:*** *http://www.lexis-nexis.com* LexisNexis provides access to thousands of worldwide newspapers, magazines, trade journals, industry newsletters, tax and accounting information, financial data, public records, legislation records, and data on companies and executives.

***Merlin Information Services:*** *http://www.merlindata.com/* Merlin includes public record and skiptracing databases.

*National Driver Register:* *http://www.nhtsa.dot.gov/people/perform/driver* The National Driver Register is a computerized database of information on drivers who have had their licenses revoked or suspended, or who have been convicted of serious traffic violations, such as driving while impaired by alcohol or drugs.

*NetrOnline:* *http://www.netronline.com/* NetrOnline is an information portal to official state Web sites, and tax assessors' and recorders' offices that have developed Web sites for retrieving public records. The public records include copies of deeds, parcel maps, GIS maps, tax data, ownership information and indexes, and other information.

*ProQuest:* *http://www.proquest.com* ProQuest provides access to thousands of current periodicals, as well as out-of-print and rare books, dissertations, newspapers, and other valuable information.

*PublicData*: *http://www.publicdata.com/* PublicData is an online database containing criminal, sex offender, driver's license, license plate, civil court, and voter information from most states.

*Public Record Finder:* *http://www.publicrecordfinder.com* This Web site lists more than 6,000 links to government sites that offer free searches of public records.

*Public Records:* *http://www.docusearch.com/free-links.html* Public Records is a detailed collection of 300 links to databases containing public information.

*SearchSystems*: *http://www.searchsystems.net/* SearchSystems claims to be the largest collection of free public records databases on the Internet.

*SEC's Edgar Database:* *http://www.sec.gov/edgar.shtml* This database is useful for investigating companies. The Web site offers free access to financial information on all public companies.

*Social Security Death Index:* *http://www.ancestry.com/search/rectype/vital/ssdi/main.htm* Go to this site to access information provided by the Social Security Administration.

*US Search:* *http://www.ussearch.com* US Search offers instant people searches, background checks, and instant civil and criminal court record searches. A free online credit report is available.

*Vantage Data:* *http://www.vantagedatasolutions.com/* Vantage Data offers instant online reports, including credit reports, social security checks, criminal investigations, and eviction and rental histories.

*Webgator:* *http://www.webgator.org/* Webgator is a portal with links to hundreds of public and private search engines about people, assets, and businesses.

## Internet Search

The publicly available Internet is an increasingly valuable source of information. Although search engines such as Google, Altavista, and Yahoo! do not search internal databases like AutoTrackXP or Lexis-Nexis, they index a significant amount of the Web. Results usually include media hits, corporate Web sites, and other public sites. The fact that public search results usually contain a surprising amount of information about an individual is evidenced by the increasing use of phrases such as "I *googled* Joe Brown on the 'net' and found. . . ." As an example of the depth a search engine can provide, we discuss several advanced techniques available on Google; many of these techniques are available on other search engines as well.

   *Search by phrase:* Including words in quotation marks (e.g. *"Bill Clinton"* rather than *Bill Clinton*) forces results to have an exact phrase. An exact phrase is made up of words immediately next to each other rather than simply on the page together. This technique can be extremely useful when searching for the exact name of your perpetrator. One technique that generally provides effective results is to include the person's name in quotes followed by something specific about the person, such as a business name, city, or other information that limits results to your subject.

   *Minus search terms:* If your initial search contains a significant amount of unwanted results, filter out pages you don't want by placing a minus sign before unique terms found on the unwanted pages. For example, a search for *"Paul Allen"* alone yields many hits for the Microsoft cofounder. A search for *"Paul Allen"* *-microsoft* shows results for other Paul Allens on the Internet.

   *Domain restrictions:* Google allows a search to be targeted at a specific domain ending. For example, if your subject is likely to be found on German Web sites, search for *"Subject Name"* *site:de* will limit results to those with domain names ending in ".de." A full listing of country codes can be found at http://www.iana.org/cctld/cctld-whois.htm. Domain restrictions can also limit results to a single Web site, such as *Windows Update site:microsoft.com* to search for information on Windows Update only within Microsoft's Web site.

*Google Groups:* Google has indexed the last 20 years of the Usenet archives, a group discussion forum that predates the World Wide Web by many years. This repository is entirely separate from the regular Google search engine and the Web. If your subject has been involved in online discussions (or has been the subject of online discussions), Google Groups is the best place to search. The URL for this service is http://groups.google.com. As a side note, Google Groups can be an extremely useful source of solutions to both technical and nontechnical topics.

*Cached results:* Google provides a "cached" link following most search results that links to a cached version of the result page on Google's site. In effect, Google has cached much of the publicly accessible Web! The cached versions of pages are useful when sites are temporarily inaccessible or no longer available. A similar service, the Internet Archive (http://www.archive.org/), provides saved copies of previous versions of Web sites.

*Google News:* It is important to realize that the Google News service indexes only the last 30 days of news articles available on the Web. This difference is a significant from Lexis-Nexis, which provides a historical repository of news articles found both on and off the Web.

## The Net Worth Method

Once investigators compile information about spending and lifestyle from public records and other sources, they usually want to determine the extent of the stolen funds. The most common way to make such determinations is through net worth calculations. Essentially, the *net worth method* uses the following formula, which is based on a person's assets (things owned), liabilities (debts), living expenses, and income.

### The Net Worth Calculation

1. Assets – Liabilities = Net Worth
2. Net Worth – Prior Year's Net Worth = Net Worth Increase
3. Net Worth Increase + Living Expenses = Income
4. Income – Funds from Known Sources = Funds from Unknown Sources

From public records and other sources, investigators determine an individual's purchases of real estate, automobiles, and other assets. Such records also state whether liens have been removed, thus identifying whether loans have been paid. Combining public sources information with information collected from interviews of landscapers, furniture and automobile dealers, and other relevant parties, and with information gathered through subpoenas provides a reasonably accurate accounting of assets and liabilities.

When people have income, they either purchase additional assets, pay off liabilities, or improve their lifestyles, thus increasing living expenses. Known income subtracted from unknown income gives a reasonable estimate of unknown funds. Verifying or eliminating other sources of funds (such as inheritances, gambling winnings, and gifts) gives a good estimate of the amount of stolen funds.

The net worth method for determining amounts embezzled has gained favor among fraud investigators in recent years. The FBI regularly uses this method, as does the DEA, which uses it to determine whether suspected narcotics traffickers have income from illegal drug sales. The IRS uses it to estimate unreported income in tax fraud cases. Because only assets and reductions in liabilities that can be discovered enter into the calculation, net worth calculations tend to give a conservative estimate of stolen funds. The bad news is, embezzlers typically spend increasing amounts on food, jewelry, vacations, and other luxuries that are difficult to track and cannot be factored into net worth calculations. The good news is, because these calculations are conservative, the amounts determined to be stolen are usually readily accepted as evidence by courts. They also often facilitate obtaining confessions from suspects. An effective and often fruitful way to interrogate suspects is to present accurate information regarding their expenditures and lifestyle that they cannot justify from their income.

To illustrate the net worth method, reconsider the following example that was described in a case at the end of Chapter 2:

> *Helen Weeks worked for Bonne Consulting Group (BCG) as the executive secretary in the administrative department for nearly 10 years. Her apparent integrity and dedication to her work quickly earned her a reputation as an outstanding employee and resulted in increased responsibilities. She soon made arrangements for outside feasibility studies, maintained client files, worked with outside marketing consultants, initiated the payment process, and notified the accounting department of all openings or closings of vendor accounts. During Helen's first five years of employment, BCG subcontracted all its feasibility and marketing studies through Jackson & Co. This relationship was subsequently terminated because Jackson & Co. merged with a larger, more expensive consulting group. At the time of the termination, Helen and her supervisor selected a new firm to conduct BCG's market research. However, Helen never informed the accounting department that the Jackson & Co. account was closed. Her supervisor trusted her completely and allowed her to sign for all voucher payments less than $10,000. Helen continued to process checks made payable to Jackson's account. The accounting department continued to process the payments, and Helen distributed the payments. She opened a bank account under the name Jackson & Co. and deposited the checks in the account. She paid all her personal expenses out of this account.*

Let's say we are investigating Helen's fraud. As part of our investigation, we searched public records and other sources and accumulated the following financial information shown in Table 9-1.

## Table 9-1 Financial Data for Helen Weeks

|  | Year 1 | Year 2 | Year 3 |
|---|---|---|---|
| *Assets:* |  |  |  |
| Residence | $100,000 | $100,000 | $100,000 |
| Stocks and bonds | 30,000 | 30,000 | 42,000 |
| Automobiles | 20,000 | 20,000 | 40,000 |
| CD | 50,000 | 50,000 | 50,000 |
| Cash | 6,000 | 12,000 | 14,000 |
| *Liabilities:* |  |  |  |
| Mortgage balance | $90,000 | $50,000 | -0- |
| Auto loan | 10,000 | -0- | -0- |
| *Income:* |  |  |  |
| Salary |  | $34,000 | $36,000 |
| Other |  | 6,000 | 6,000 |
| *Expenses:* |  |  |  |
| Mortgage payments |  | $ 6,000 | $ 6,000 |
| Auto loan payments |  | 4,800 | 4,800 |
| Other living expenses |  | 20,000 | 22,000 |

With this information, we can use the net worth method to estimate how much Helen may have embezzled. These calculations are given in Table 9-2.

Based on this calculation, we determine that Helen had at least $46,800 of unknown income in year 2 and $74,800 of unknown income in year 3. This information can be used in court to obtain a criminal conviction, civil judgment, or even an order against Helen, and it can also be used to obtain a confession. A good investigator, armed with these data, may well get a confession from Helen. She would first be asked to state her income and other sources of funds. The investigator would then show that she cannot maintain her lifestyle and pay her debts without additional income. Seeing that her story and the reality conflict, Helen might confess.

## Table 9-2 Comparative Net Worth–Asset Method

|  | End Year 1 | End Year 2 | End Year 3 |
|---|---|---|---|
| **Assets:** |  |  |  |
| Residence | $100,000 | $100,000 | $100,000 |
| Stocks and bonds | 30,000 | 30,000 | 42,000 |
| Auto | 20,000 | 20,000 | 40,000 |
| CD | 50,000 | 50,000 | 50,000 |
| Cash | 6,000 | 12,000 | 14,000 |
| Total assets | $206,000 | $212,000 | $246,000 |
|  |  |  |  |
| **Liabilities:** |  |  |  |
| Mortgage balance | $90,000 | $50,000 | $ — |
| Auto loan | 10,000 | — | — |
| Total liabilities | $100,000 | $50,000 | $ — |
| Net worth | $106,000 | $162,000 | $246,000 |
| Change in net worth |  | $56,000 | $84,000 |
| Plus total expenses |  | 30,800 | 32,800 |
| Total |  | $86,800 | $116,800 |
| Less known income |  | 40,000 | 42,000 |
| Income from unknown sources |  | $46,800 | $74,800 |

## SUMMARY

In previous chapters, we covered ways to investigate theft and concealment. In this chapter, we discussed ways to investigate conversion. Essentially, conversion investigations involve two steps: (1) using publicly available sources and other sources to determine a person's spending habits and other information, and (2) calculating a person's net worth to estimate the amount of money stolen. We identified various sources of information, including (1) federal sources, (2) state sources, (3) local sources, (4) county and local records, (5) financial institution records, (6) commercial and publicly available databases, and (7) online or Internet sources.

## KEY TERMS

**Gramm-Leach-Bliley Act** Passed in 1999, this law prohibits the use of false pretenses to access the personal information of others. It allows banks and other financial institutions to share or sell customer information, unless customers proactively "opt out" and ask that their information not be shared.

**National Crime Information Center (NCIC)** The major criminal database maintained by the FBI. This database contains information on stolen vehicles, securities, boats, missing persons, and other information helpful in fraud investigations.

**Net worth method** Analytical method that estimates a suspect's unexplained income. Liabilities are subtracted from assets to give net worth, then the previous year's net worth is subtracted to find the increase in net worth. Living expenses are then added to the change in net worth to determine a person's total income, and finally known income is subtracted from total income to determine the unknown income.

**Opting-out right** Right of customers to give written notice to financial institutions that prohibits the institution from sharing or selling customer's personal information.

**Postal inspectors** Inspectors or investigators hired by the U.S. Postal Service to handle major fraud cases perpetrated through the U.S. mail system.

**Trash investigation** Searching through a person's trash for possible evidence in an investigation.

# QUESTIONS AND CASES

## DISCUSSION QUESTIONS

1. What are common ways to investigate conversion of stolen assets?

2. What are "financial footprints"?

3. Why is it important to know how perpetrators convert and spend their stolen funds?

4. What are the differences between public and private sources of information?

5. How do state, federal, and local public records assist fraud investigations?

6. How does the Internet assist in determining the net worth of suspected perpetrators?

7. Why are net worth calculations so valuable?

8. What are some of the advanced techniques available when searching for information on Google?

9. How do these advanced techniques aid in the information-gathering process?

10. When searching public records, what are the four different types of information sources available to investigators?

## TRUE/FALSE

1. Perpetrators usually save what they steal.

2. One common investigation procedure determines how perpetrators convert or spend their time.

3. Investigations of perpetrators' net worth and lifestyles help investigators know what class of society the perpetrators are from.

4. It is always necessary to involve a federal law enforcement agent in order to access federal databases.

5. The Secretary of State maintains many types of records relating to business and Uniform Commercial Code filings.

6. Counties and other local agencies that contain records are usually not useful in fraud investigations.

7. Private credit records are maintained on both individuals and organizations by various credit reporting companies.

8. Several publicly available databases provide information that can be helpful in investigations.

9. The net worth method is rarely, if ever, helpful in actual fraud investigations.

10. For various reasons, the net worth method tends to be a conservative estimate of amounts stolen.

11. Conversion is the third element of the fraud triangle.

12. The Gramm-Leach-Bliley Act of 1999 made it more difficult for officials and private citizens to access information from financial institutions.

13. Before financial institutions can sell or disclose confidential customer information, they must provide customers with the opportunity to "opt out" from information sharing.

14. Federal agencies provide better records than state or county agencies for conversion investigations.

15. When people convert stolen cash by entering into financial transactions, such as buying assets, they leave tracks that investigators can follow.

16. Private financial institutions can usually sell confidential customer information.

17. The net worth method cannot help in determining the extent of stolen funds.

18. An increase in a person's net worth plus living expenses equals the person's income.

# MULTIPLE CHOICE

1. Although most perpetrators begin their thefts because of a perceived critical need, they continue to embezzle in order to:
   a. Beat the system.
   b. Fulfill an inner desire to commit fraud.
   c. Improve their lifestyle.
   d. Achieve a higher self-esteem.

2. Evidence gathered from public records can be useful in:
   a. Identifying with the suspect.
   b. Obtaining a confession.
   c. Making the suspect feel at ease.
   d. None of the above.

3. The net worth method of analyzing financial information can help to determine:
   a. The suspect's feelings about the organization.
   b. Possible perpetrators of the fraud.
   c. The suspect's personality characteristics.
   d. The amount of embezzled funds.

4. Which of the following organizations maintain public information that can be accessed in record searches?
   a. Local agencies
   b. State agencies
   c. Federal agencies
   d. All of the above

5. How useful are local and county records in fraud investigations?
   a. Very useful
   b. Not useful
   c. Somewhat useful
   d. Aren't allowed in the investigation of fraud

6. Which of the following laws regulates activities of credit, insurance, and employment investigations?
   a. Fair Investigation Act of 1980
   b. Fair Credit Reporting Act of 1971
   c. Credit, Insurance, and Employment Investigation Act
   d. There is no governing law

7. The net worth method is effective:
   a. As evidence in court.
   b. To help obtain a confession.
   c. To conduct an interview of suspects.
   d. All of the above.

8. Conversion investigations focus on how suspects:
   a. Had opportunities to steal.
   b. Had motives to commit fraud.
   c. Spent stolen money.
   d. Committed the actual theft.

9. Which of the following are possible uses of conversion-based investigation techniques?
   a. Searching public records to trace purchases of assets and payments of liabilities
   b. Attempting to locate previous spouses' bank account records
   c. Locating significant amounts of money held by related parties
   d. All of the above

10. Most conversion investigations involve searching public records and other sources to trace:
    a. Purchases of assets.
    b. Payments of liabilities.
    c. Changes in lifestyle.
    d. Net worth.
    e. All of the above.

11. A database of criminal records maintained by the FBI is the:
    a. CIA.
    b. III.
    c. NCIC.
    d. a and c.
    e. b and c.

12. Which are usually some of the best and most helpful federal fraud investigators?
    a. Officers of the Secret Service
    b. Employees of the Bureau of Prisons
    c. Officers of the Department of Vital Statistics
    d. Postal inspectors

13. Which source could you use to access valuable financial information in a fraud investigation?
    a. Financial institutions
    b. Internet sites
    c. The former spouse of a suspected fraud perpetrator
    d. Trash
    e. All of the above

14. The net worth method is a calculation based on a person's:
    a. Assets, liabilities, equity, and living expenses.
    b. Assets, liabilities, equity, and income.
    c. Assets, liabilities, income, and living expenses.
    d. Assets, income, and living expenses.

15. The formula to calculate funds from unknown sources is:
    a. Assets – Liabilities – Prior Year's Net Worth + Living Expenses – Funds from ~~Unknown~~ Sources
    b. Assets – Liabilities – Prior Year's Net Worth – Living Expenses – Funds from ~~Unknown~~ Sources
    c. Assets – Liabilities – Prior Year's Net Worth + Living Expenses + Funds from ~~Unknown~~ Sources
    d. Assets – Liabilities – Prior Year's Net Worth – Living Expenses + Funds from ~~Unknown~~ Sources

16. The Gramm-Leach-Bliley Act allows:
    a. Banks to sell customer information.
    b. Financial institutions to share information.
    c. Customers to "opt out" and ask that their information not be shared.
    d. All of the above.

17. Each of these agencies is correctly matched with the type of information the agency provides *except*:
    a. Department of Justice: Maintains records relating to the detection, prosecution, and rehabilitation of offenders.
    b. The Secret Service: Deals with counterfeiting, theft of government checks, interstate credit card violations, and some computer crimes.
    c. State Attorney General: Maintains birth records and information about people's social security numbers.
    d. Central Intelligence Agency: Investigates security matters outside the United States.
    e. Department of Business Regulation: Maintains licensing information about various professionals.

18. Each of these statements is true about the net worth method for determining embezzled amounts *except*:
    a. The net worth method generally understates amounts stolen.
    b. Much of the information necessary for determining an individual's assets, liabilities, living expenses, and income is available through public searches.
    c. Courts are generally suspicious of dollar amounts determined by the net worth method because courts realize that the net worth method can provide only approximations of the amount stolen.
    d. The net worth method is useful for obtaining confessions from suspects during interviews or interrogations.

19. Under the net worth method, what would be the unknown income of a person who has an increase in net worth of $100,000, known income of $80,000, and a salary of $60,000?
    a. $0
    b. $10,000
    c. $20,000
    d. $40,000

20. Known income subtracted from total incomes gives a reasonable estimate of:
    a. Unknown funds.
    b. Liabilities.
    c. Living expenses.
    d. Net worth.

## SHORT CASES

**Case 1.** Given the following information, determine whether illegal income is likely. If so, determine the amount of unknown income.

**Financial Data**

| | Year 1 | Year 2 | Year 3 |
|---|---|---|---|
| *Assets:* | | | |
| Residence | $100,000 | $100,000 | $100,000 |
| Baseball cards | 15,000 | 15,000 | 25,000 |
| Automobiles | -0- | 30,000 | 50,000 |
| Paintings | 50,000 | 150,000 | 250,000 |
| Cash | 6,000 | 12,000 | 14,000 |
| | | | |
| *Liabilities:* | | | |
| Mortgage balance | $100,000 | $ 50,000 | -0- |
| Auto loan | -0- | 30,000 | -0- |
| | | | |
| *Income:* | | | |
| Salary | | $ 34,000 | $ 36,000 |
| Other | | 6,000 | 6,000 |
| | | | |
| *Expenses:* | | | |
| Mortgage payments | | $ 6,000 | $ 6,000 |
| Auto loan payments | | 4,800 | 4,800 |
| Other living expenses | | 20,000 | 20,000 |

**Case 2.** You are auditing a bank and someone provides you an anonymous tip that an employee is embezzling money from the bank. You decide to investigate the allegation.

Your interviews with other bank employees confirm that the suspected embezzler has been acting strange lately. Some employees have seen the employee crying in the bathroom and acting strange in other ways. The bank recently downsized due to poor economic growth, yet the suspect recently bought a new Lexus.

From some "helpful" hints from bank employees and through your own investigation, you discover that the mortgage taken out by the suspect three years ago for his personal home has recently been paid in full.

After calculating the suspect's net worth, you determine that he has about $249,000 income from unknown sources this year alone.

1. What are possible explanations for why the suspect is experiencing emotional changes and has had an increase in unknown income?

2. Can you conclude from these facts that the suspect has indeed been committing fraud?

**Case 3.** You receive an anonymous tip that your controller is embezzling assets from your company. You begin your investigation by interviewing several employees in the accounting department, who report no unusual behavior or sudden changes in the suspect's standard of living. One interviewee does report that the controller has gone on a number of extravagant vacations.

You perform a net worth analysis based on a search of public records, and find the following information:

|  | Year 1 | Year 2 | Year 3 |
|---|---|---|---|
| Total assets | $80,000 | $82,000 | $85,000 |
| Total liabilities | 40,000 | 41,000 | 41,000 |
| Net worth | 40,000 | 41,000 | 44,000 |
| Change in net worth |  | 1,000 | 3,000 |
| Living expenses |  | 36,000 | 36,000 |
| Total income |  | 37,000 | 39,000 |
| Less known income | 35,000 | 35,000 | 36,000 |
| Unknown income |  | 2,000 | 3,000 |

1. Based on the evidence gathered in your search, what conclusions can you make about the controller?

2. Would you feel comfortable using the evidence above in an interview to obtain a confession? Why or why not?

3. What additional investigating could you pursue to obtain more evidence?

**Case 4.** Bill James is being investigated for embezzling more than $700,000 from ABC Capital Management, for whom Bill has worked for nearly 10 years. When coworkers noticed the new "toys" Bill was buying, they jokingly asked him to tell them his stock picks—they wanted in too! Bill told them that they better go adopt some rich relatives. "My Uncle Eddie didn't have any kids, so he left a chunk of his money to each of us nephews."

Explain how you might go about checking the validity of Bill's claim to a recent inheritance. Include in your discussion the relevant information you need about Uncle Eddie and where you could find that information.

**Case 5.** You manage a car dealership in a large city. Many of your sales employees are very successful and have purchased their own vehicles from your dealership. Your dealership finances the sale of some of these vehicles. One employee recently paid off the balances on a couple of new vehicles purchased from your dealership. You discover this information after investigating complaints from customers about this particular employee's actions. His sales are down, and customer complaints about his attitude abound. He previously worked for two other car dealers, both of which were satisfied with his performance. This employee is in charge of having used cars reconditioned by various automobile repair shops.

1. What signs of unusual behavior and lifestyle symptoms are present in this case, and what are some possible causes for them?

2. How might this employee be defrauding the company?

**Case 6.** Janet Moody is one of XZY Company's most trusted employees. She never complains about her work and rarely misses work due to illness or vacation. The company has been successful over the years, but is now having cash flow problems. Because of the recent downturn in the company, you take a closer look at all the company's financial records. When you ask Janet about the recent cash flow problems, she responds, "I don't know what is going on. I only do the reporting. Ask those who manage the company." This behavior differs from Janet's normal pleasant deportment. As you continue your investigation, you discover that the reported financial results do not match what the company is doing, but you can't determine why. You decide to investigate Janet further.

1. What are some behavior and lifestyle changes that you should look for?

2. What resources can you use to conduct your research?

**Case 7.** Using the net worth method, analyze the following financial data for potential signs of fraud or embezzlement. Do your results indicate that this person could be committing some type of fraud? If so, why do you think so? What other factors might you consider to determine whether fraud has been committed, other than the final total income from other sources (if any)? Is this scenario realistic?

|  | Year 1 | Year 2 | Year 3 | Year 4 | Year 5 |
|---|---|---|---|---|---|
| **Assets:** | | | | | |
| Residence | $200,000 | $200,000 | $275,000 | $275,000 | $275,000 |
| Automobile | 50,000 | 50,000 | 75,000 | 75,000 | 90,000 |
| Stocks and bonds | 75,000 | 75,000 | 100,000 | 100,000 | 125,000 |
| Cash | 15,000 | 16,500 | 18,150 | 19,965 | 21,962 |
| **Liabilities:** | | | | | |
| Mortgage balance | $175,000 | $ 50,000 | $125,000 | $107,000 | $ 40,000 |
| Auto loan balance | 40,000 | 20,000 | 35,000 | 25,000 | 10,000 |
| **Income:** | | | | | |
| Salary | | $100,000 | $107,000 | $125,000 | $133,750 |
| Other | | 10,000 | 10,000 | 10,000 | 10,000 |
| **Expenses:** | | | | | |
| Mortgage loan payments | | $ 12,000 | $ 18,000 | $ 18,000 | $ 18,000 |
| Auto loan payments | | 7,000 | 10,000 | 10,000 | 13,000 |
| Other living expenses | | 30,000 | 33,000 | 36,300 | 39,930 |

**Case 8.** The following financial data were collected during a fraud investigation:

|  | Year 1 | Year 2 | Year 3 |
|---|---|---|---|
| **Assets:** | | | |
| Residence | $280,000 | $280,000 | $280,000 |
| Automobile | 18,000 | 45,000 | 45,000 |
| CD | 5,000 | 15,000 | 15,000 |
| Cash | 8,000 | 8,000 | 2,000 |
| Stock portfolio | 3,500 | 15,000 | 15,000 |
| Boat | | 15,000 | 15,000 |
| **Liabilities:** | | | |
| Mortgage | $200,000 | $180,000 | $100,000 |
| Auto loan | 12,000 | 30,000 | |
| Other loan | | 18,000 | |
| **Income:** | | | |
| Salary | $ 55,000 | $ 90,000 | $130,000 |
| Investment | 800 | 800 | 800 |
| **Expenses:** | | | |
| Mortgage expense | $ 18,000 | $ 18,000 | $ 18,000 |
| Auto expense | 5,000 | 9,000 | 9,000 |
| Living expenses | 20,000 | 20,000 | 20,000 |

1. Without calculating the amount of unknown income, indicate possible red flags or trends you notice in these numbers.

2. Now calculate the amount of income and unknown income, using the numbers given. Does it appear that a possible fraud exists? What other explanations are possible for the unknown income?

**Case 9.** Mr. I. M. Bezzle works in the purchasing department for Big Time Inc. During the 12 years that he has worked there, he has been a trusted employee and has sole responsibility for the company's purchasing function. He started working for the company in 1990 for $30,000 a year and now makes $100,000 a year. Fellow employees and friends noticed that his lifestyle improved substantially recently since his promotion to purchasing manager. Based on an anonymous tip, the CEO asks you to look into the situation.

What steps would you take to investigate the possibility of fraud here?

**Case 10.** Tom works for XYZ Company and is suspected of embezzling funds from the company. By searching databases on the Internet, talking with his ex-wife, and searching through his trash, you gather the following information:

| | |
|---|---|
| Assets | $120,000 |
| Liabilities | 70,000 |
| Living expenses | 50,000 |
| Known income | 60,000 |
| Prior year's net worth | 10,000 |

1. Use these data to figure out Tom's income from unknown sources by performing a net worth calculation.

2. How can this information be used to motivate Tom to confess that he has stolen from XYZ Company?

**Case 11.** Sarah Welch was hired 15 years ago by Produce-R-Us, an importer of rare and exotic fruits. Produce-R-Us was started by an immigrant family 20 years ago and has grown to a national company with sales of $10 million annually. Although the business has grown, the family-owned business strives to maintain a "family atmosphere" and stress trust. Because of Sarah's honesty and hard work, the manager quickly promoted her, and she now signs checks for amounts under $5,000 and also has responsibilities for accounts payable. Now, however, the owners are suspicious of Sarah's recent lifestyle changes and have hired you to determine whether Sarah is embezzling from the company. Public records reveal the following:

| | Year 1 | Year 2 | Year 3 |
|---|---|---|---|
| *Assets:* | | | |
| Personal residence | $100,000 | $100,000 | $100,000 |
| Automobiles | 20,000 | 40,000 | 90,000 |
| Stocks and bonds | 30,000 | 30,000 | 30,000 |
| Boat | | 30,000 | 30,000 |
| CDs | 25,000 | 25,000 | 50,000 |
| *Liabilities:* | | | |
| Mortgage balance | $ 90,000 | $ 40,000 | |
| Auto loan | 10,000 | 5,000 | |
| *Income:* | | | |
| Salary | $ 37,000 | $ 40,000 | $ 42,000 |
| Other | 4,000 | 4,000 | 4,000 |
| *Expenses:* | | | |
| Mortgage payments | $ 6,000 | $ 6,000 | $ 6,000 |
| Auto loan payments | 2,000 | 2,500 | 2,500 |
| Other living expenses | 15,000 | 15,000 | 20,000 |

Perform a net worth calculation, using these data. (Ignore interest in your calculations.)

**Case 12.** After searching public records and other sources, you accumulate the following financial information for John Dough:

| | Year 1 | Year 2 | Year 3 |
|---|---|---|---|
| *Assets:* | | | |
| Residence | $150,000 | $150,000 | $150,000 |
| Residence #2 | | | 85,000 |
| Stocks and bonds | 10,000 | 20,000 | 35,000 |
| Automobiles | 18,000 | 35,000 | 35,000 |
| Boat | | 22,000 | 22,000 |
| CD | 8,000 | 27,000 | 50,000 |
| Cash | 3,500 | 7,500 | 18,000 |
| *Liabilities:* | | | |
| Mortgage balance #1 | $ 84,000 | $ 42,000 | $ 15,000 |
| Mortgage balance #2 | | | 85,000 |
| Auto loans | 12,000 | 38,000 | |
| Boat loan | | 22,000 | 5,000 |
| *Income:* | | | |
| Salary | | $ 49,000 | $ 55,000 |
| Interest/other | | 5,000 | 7,000 |
| *Expenses:* | | | |
| Mortgage payments | | $ 15,000 | $ 26,000 |
| Auto loan payments | | 6,000 | 6,000 |
| Boat loan payments | | 3,500 | 5,000 |
| Other living expenses | | 22,000 | 31,000 |

Given this financial information, determine whether there is a likelihood of illegal income. If so, determine the amount.

## EXTENSIVE CASES

**Extensive Case 1.** Mark is a young business student at the University of Georgia, who works part-time as a financial advisor at a local credit union. Mark has been married about two years. Mark's wife is currently taking care of their newborn son, while Mark finishes up school. Mark is well liked by all those who know him. In fact, those who know Mark would describe him as outgoing, funny, and very intelligent.

At the credit union, Mark's primary responsibility is to set up new accounts, make initial loan interviews, and work as a teller. While at work, Mark always appears to be working hard, and rarely misses work (even for vacations). Often times, Mark is the first one to volunteer to stay late and look over accounts or help clean up.

Over the last four months, Mark's credit union supervisor noticed Mark make many interesting purchases. Four months ago, Mark purchased a big screen television and frequently invites coworkers to watch movies at his home. One month ago, Mark bought three new wool suits, which he frequently wears to work. Two months ago, Mark traded in his old Geo Prism for a new Jeep Grand Cherokee (with many additional features). When asked where Mark was getting the money for these purchases, Mark humorously responds, "I guess people are right, when you die, you can't take it all with you. However, it sure was nice they left it with me," alluding to the fact that a wealthy grandmother had recently passed away and left Mark (her favorite grandson) a significant inheritance.

Also, recently the supervisor heard some of the new customers complaining that their balances are off by $20, $30, and even $50.

1. What fraud symptoms are present in this scenario?

2. Is it possible to know from the information given that Mark is committing fraud at the credit union?

3. What is one reasonable action the supervisor could do if he or she suspected Mark as a fraud suspect?

Assuming that the credit union decides to investigate further, calculate Mark's net worth and income from other sources.

**Financial Data for Mark**

| | Month 1 | Month 2 | Month 3 |
|---|---|---|---|
| *Assets:* | | | |
| 1992 Geo Prism | $1,000 | — | — |
| 2004 Jeep Grand Cherokee | — | $45,000 | $45,000 |
| Savings | 3,000 | 6,000 | 7,000 |
| Checking | 600 | 800 | 500 |
| CD | 2,000 | 2,000 | 2,000 |
| Laptop | 2,500 | 2,500 | 2,500 |
| Television | — | — | $1,000 |
| *Liabilities:* | | | |
| Auto loan | — | $45,000 | $45,000 |
| *Income:* | | | |
| Salary | $1,000 | $ 1,000 | $ 1,000 |
| Other | 300 | 300 | 300 |
| *Expenses:* | | | |
| Rent payments | $ 700 | $ 700 | $ 700 |
| Small expenditures | 130 | 130 | 130 |
| Auto loan payments | — | 600 | 600 |
| Other living expenses | 400 | 700 | 800 |

**Extensive Case 2.** Use the following financial data to prepare a comparative net worth assessment.

| | Year 1 | Year 2 | Year 3 |
|---|---|---|---|
| *Assets:* | | | |
| Residence | $50,000 | $50,000 | $200,000 |
| Stocks and bonds | 10,000 | 10,000 | 10,000 |
| Automobiles | 15,000 | 15,000 | 40,000 |
| Cash | 5,000 | 8,000 | 20,000 |
| *Liabilities:* | | | |
| Mortgage balance | $40,000 | $30,000 | $ 0 |
| Auto loan | 8,000 | 5,000 | 0 |
| Student loans | 10,000 | 8,000 | 0 |
| *Income:* | | | |
| Salary | $30,000 | $35,000 | $ 40,000 |
| Other | 0 | 1,000 | 1,000 |
| *Expenses:* | | | |
| Mortgage payments | $ 5,000 | $ 5,000 | $ 0 |
| Car payments | 1,000 | 5,000 | 2,500 |
| Student loan payments | 1,000 | 1,000 | 500 |
| Other living expenses | 15,000 | 15,000 | 20,000 |
| Total living expenses | $22,000 | $26,000 | $ 23,000 |

**Extensive Case 3.** Steve (Slick) Willy (age 45) just got out of jail. As a reformed citizen on parole, Slick decides to go into business for himself. He starts a collections company to help companies collect debts. The terms of his parole stipulate that he pay restitution payments to the federal government of $400 a month, or 10% of his income, whichever is greater. As his parole officer, you notice that after a year out of jail, Slick makes some interesting purchases. First, he buys a new Jaguar that he drives to parole meetings. Second, he moves into an expensive neighborhood on the north side of town and takes a cruise to Jamaica with his 18-year-old girlfriend. Yet, he has never been late making his $400 monthly payments to the federal government. After obtaining a subpoena for his bank records, you notice that he has

only $1,000 in his account. About this time, you receive a call from a man who is making payments to Slick's collection company. He states that Slick is threatening to break his legs and hurt his family if he doesn't pay Slick's company. The man says Slick demands the checks be made out to a woman, not a company.

This complaint convinces you to investigate Mr. Willy and his girlfriend. A search of UCC filings in the county shows that Slick's girlfriend owns three cars costing $90,000, a $250,000 house, and a company called Tak'In It From You. You check her bank account and see that more than $50,000 is moving through the account each month. You decide to dig through Slick and his girlfriend's trash a few times each month. In these searches, you find evidence that support the following: three car payments totaling $1,000 per month; a $1,500 monthly mortgage payment; a credit card balance of $6,000, with $100 monthly payments; a balance of $12,000 owed to Home Shopping Network, with $500 monthly payments; $400 food payments during the past two weeks; and a $3,500 payment to Jamaican cruise lines. After searching the girlfriend's trash, you talk to her neighbors, friends, and coworkers and determine that she and Slick spend between $1,500 and $2,000 a month on miscellaneous items and trips. One neighbor tells you that Slick just gave his girlfriend a two-carat diamond ring. Slick's girlfriend works as a waitress at a small restaurant and makes only $15,000 a year.

Use this information to prepare a net worth analysis of Slick's girlfriend. (Ignore interest in your calculations.)

**Extensive Case 4.** Homegrown Gardens, LLP, is a $10 million nursery and garden retailer in Colorado. Homegrown employs about 20 full-time and seasonal employees. The majority of the plants and nursery stock Homegrown sells comes from Monromio Nurseries, a wholesaler based in Oregon. Monromio is recognized throughout the West for the quality of the plants it grows and sells. Homegrown is generally happy to pay the premium prices that Monromio's plants command, because they pass the extra costs on to their customers, who value the high-quality plants they sell. However, Barry Greenstem, one of Homegrown's managing partners, is visibly upset after speaking with the owners of other nurseries at a recent trade show in Atlanta. Although Monromio has increased their prices across the board, Monromio's price hike to Homegrown is larger than the average. Barry suspects that Betty Stevenson, Homegrown's assistant manager in charge of purchasing nursery stock, may be accepting kickbacks from Monromio in return for allowing higher purchase prices. Betty and her husband, Mike, purchased a new SUV, a houseboat, and several ATVs last year and moved into a new, larger house this year. Barry knows Betty's salary isn't high enough to support the new lifestyle and he doubts that Mike's job as a city employee would provide large enough raises to justify the new "toys." Barry hires you to perform a net worth investigation of Betty and Mike to determine the amount of any unknown income. Your search of public and private records reveals the following information:

| | Two Years Ago | Last Year | This Year |
|---|---|---|---|
| *Assets:* | | | |
| Personal residence | $70,000 | $70,000 | $200,000 |
| Automobiles | 15,000 | 45,000 | 45,000 |
| Houseboat | | 30,000 | 30,000 |
| ATVs | | 12,000 | 12,000 |
| *Liabilities:* | | | |
| Mortgage balance | $35,000 | $30,500 | $100,000 |
| Auto loan | 2,500 | | |
| Loan on houseboat | | 15,000 | 11,000 |
| *Income:* | | | |
| Betty's salary | $25,000 | $25,500 | $ 26,000 |
| Mike's salary | 35,000 | 36,000 | 37,000 |
| *Expenses:* | | | |
| Mortgage payments | $ 4,500 | $ 4,500 | $ 13,000 |
| Auto payments | 1,800 | 1,800 | |
| Houseboat payments | | 2,400 | 2,400 |
| Other living expenses | 15,000 | 17,000 | 15,000 |

Using this information, calculate the amount of income from unknown sources, if any, using the net worth method. (Ignore interest in your calculations.)

## INTERNET ASSIGNMENTS

1. The Postal Service site contains a great deal of information on detecting mail fraud and the investigation efforts of the Postal Service.
   a. Access the U.S. Postal Service Web site at http://www.usps.gov. Find the site entitled "US Postal Inspection Service." (*Hint:* Use the keyword search at http://www.usps.gov; search for "fraud" or other similar words.) Review and become familiar with the fraud services provided by the Postal Inspection Service.
   b. Give a brief overview of the Postal Inspection Service.
   c. What does the Postal Inspection Service recommend in order to protect you against phony "one-shot" credit card offers?
   d. Name five characteristics of telemarketing fraud schemes.

2. An increasingly common way to commit fraud is to use the Internet. The Department of Justice now devotes an entire page on its Web site to Internet fraud. Visit the site at http://www.usdoj.gov/criminal/fraud/Internet.htm and identify three types of Internet fraud.

3. Go to http://www.howtoinvestigate.com/information.htm. Read the section entitled *Information Record Sources: local records, county records, state records, federal records, and national records.*
   a. Records are collected and maintained at three levels by government and private organizations. Name these three levels.
   b. Credit bureaus gather credit data about individuals from a vast network of retailers, businesses, and financial institutions. In exchange for these data, they provide credit information to all their members. List three giant commercial credit bureaus.
   c. What are open records? What rights do you have to use them?
   d. What are semi-open records? Give examples.
   e. What are closed records?

4. Go to http://www.howtoinvestigate.com/busback.htm. Read the section entitled *Business Background Investigations.*
   a. What does a complete business investigation include?
   b. Suppose you hire someone to perform some work on your house. Who do you call to find out whether the contractor is licensed to conduct business in your area?

## DEBATES

1. You are performing an audit of a small Internet start-up company that recently went public. During the audit, you frequently converse with the employees, with whom you have a comfortable relationship. In one conversation, an employee mentions the strange behavior of a coworker.

   Apparently, this employee comes to work very early and stays late. He is stressed at work and very irritable. Although many of the company's founders are enjoying the economic fruits of the IPO, this person did not own any stock in the company at the time of the IPO and thus did not earn much money when the company went public. Nevertheless, this person drives a new Porsche Boxter.

   Your debate topic: Is evidence sufficient to determine whether this employee is committing fraud?

2. This chapter discussed techniques for conversion investigations that involve searching public records to identify changes in lifestyle and the net worth of alleged fraud perpetrators. You recently became a Certified Fraud Examiner and joined a local fraud examination firm. Your manager explains how he prefers to work with private sources of information and not involve local law enforcement agencies in the conversion investigation stage of his cases. You disagree and feel that local law enforcement can be an excellent resource.

   Pair up with someone in your class. One of you take the position of the manager and the other take the position of the new CFE. Discuss the advantages and disadvantages of involving law enforcement agencies in your fraud investigations.

## END NOTES

1. Most of the facts for the Phar-Mor vignette were taken from the video, "How to Steal 500 Million." *Frontline* by PBS Video. Copyright © PBS 1992. Some facts were taken from an article in *The Wall Street Journal.* (See Gabriela Stern, "Chicanery at Phar-Mor Ran Deep, Close Look at Discounter Shows," *The Wall Street Journal,* January 20, 1994, p. 1.)

2. Mark F. Murray, "When a Client Is a Liability," *Journal of Accountancy*, September 1992, pp. 54–58.

# CHAPTER 10

# INQUIRY METHODS AND FRAUD REPORTS[1]

## LEARNING OBJECTIVES

**After studying this chapter you should be able to:**

1.  Describe the different types of honesty testing.
2.  Understand the interviewing process.
3.  Plan and conduct an interview.
4.  Understand the nature of admission-seeking interviews.
5.  Describe the different deceptions and lies used by perpetrators.
6.  Prepare a fraud report.

*Don Restiman was purchasing manager for Emerald Enterprises. During a four-year period, he accepted more than $400,000 in bribes from one of Emerald's suppliers by having the supplier hire and pay his daughter, Jane, as a supposed "salesperson." Jane deposited her "paycheck" into an account she shared with her father. They used the money to buy real estate, automobiles, and other valuables. Fraud was suspected in the purchasing department for several reasons, which included increased amounts of purchases from the vendor, unnecessary purchases, purchases of goods at increased prices, and prices significantly higher than those of competitors.*

*Two skilled investigators interrogated Jane. They asked her about the specifics of her "job." As the interview proceeded, it became obvious through both verbal and nonverbal cues that she was lying. She was unable to answer such simple questions as, "Where are the company's headquarters located?" "What is the address and telephone number of your office?" "What companies do you sell to?" and "Who are your closest coworkers?"*

*After several obvious lies, her attorney asked if he and his client could step outside the room for a few moments. Her attorney convinced Jane that she was perjuring herself. When they returned, Jane confessed that she was lying about being employed at Emerald. In the presence of her attorney, she signed a prepared written confession that made prosecution of her father easier.*

In this chapter, we conclude our discussion of investigation methods by discussing how to query people (witnesses or suspects), through interviews and various types of honesty testing.

## Honesty Testing

The most common inquiry method (and the most common of all investigation techniques) is the interview. However, at least three other methods can also solicit information about a person's honesty: (1) pencil-and-paper tests, (2) graphology, and (3) voice stress analysis and polygraphs.

### Pencil-and-Paper Test

Pencil-and-paper honesty tests are objective tests that elicit information about a person's honesty and personal code of ethics. They are used more frequently as employee screening devices than as tools to determine whether someone has committed a crime. Pencil-and-paper tests are considered to be between 50 and 90 percent accurate. Some of the more common ones are the Reid Report, the Personnel Selection Inventory, and the Stanton Survey. They use questions such as:

True/False    1. It is natural for most people to be a little dishonest.
True/False    2. People who are dishonest should be sent to prison.

Answers to these and similar questions create a profile of a person's personal code of conduct, on which his or her risk to a business can be assessed. According to the developers of these tests, one of their advantages is that the results can be tabulated by a computer in a matter of minutes, making them ideal for applicant screening or initial identification of possible suspects. These kinds of tests are now used by a large number of retailers in the United States.

### Graphology

Graphology is the study of handwriting for the purpose of character analysis. Its use has increased substantially in past years. Graphology is used in fields in which employee integrity is important, such as banking, manufacturing, and insurance. About 350 graphologists currently work as consultants to U.S. businesses. Note, however, that many fraud investigators are skeptical about the reliability of graphology.

### Voice Stress Analysis and Polygraphs

Voice stress analysis determines whether a person is lying or telling the truth by using a mechanical device connected to the person. Polygraphs are more complicated than voice stress analyzers in that they attempt to assess stress, and hence lying, by measuring key physical responses. The theory is that people feel guilty when they lie or are dishonest. The guilt feelings produce stress, which results in changes in behavior. Polygraphs measure pulse rate, blood pressure, galvanic skin response, and respiration. Like voice stress analyzers, polygraphs sometimes lead to incorrect decisions because they frighten innocent people. In addition, they rarely detect psychopathic liars, who feel no stress when they lie because they do not have a conscience.

The Employee Polygraph Protection Act passed a number of years ago has made the use of polygraphs more difficult. Although polygraphs are still legal, investigators must meet 11 conditions in order to use them—one of which is that investigators must inform suspects that they don't have to take the test if they don't want to.

Polygraphs and voice stress analyzers are only as good as the experts who administer them. In the hands of inexperienced administrators, they can be dangerous. Most experts agree that individuals who pass polygraph examinations are probably innocent, but that failure does not necessarily imply certain guilt.

# Interviewing—An Overview

Interviewing is by far the most common technique used to investigate and resolve fraud. An *interview* is a question-and-answer session designed to elicit information. It differs from ordinary conversation in that it is structured (not free-form) and has a purpose. It is the systematic questioning of individuals who have knowledge of events, people, and evidence of a case under investigation. Good interviewers quickly zero in on suspects and can usually get admissions from guilty parties. Interviews also help obtain (1) information that establishes the essential elements of the crime, (2) leads for developing cases and gathering other evidence, (3) the cooperation of victims and witnesses, and (4) information on the personal backgrounds and motives of witnesses. Interviews are conducted with victims, complainants, contacts, informants, clients or customers, suspects, expert witnesses, police officers, clerks, janitors, coworkers, supervisors, disgruntled spouses or friends, vendors and former vendors, and anyone who might be helpful in the investigation. Interviews are categorized into three types: (1) friendly, (2) neutral, and (3) hostile. Each type is handled differently.

The friendly interviewee goes above and beyond what is normally expected in order to be (or at least appear to be) helpful. Although friendly witnesses can be helpful, experienced investigators take care to determine their motives. In some cases, the motive truly is a sincere desire to help. However, possible motives also include a desire to get even with the suspect or to direct attention away from the interviewee as a suspect.

Neutral interviewees have nothing to gain or lose from the interview. They have no hidden motives or agendas, and they are usually the most objective and helpful of all interviewees.

Hostile interviewees are the most difficult to interview. They are often associated in some way with the suspect or the crime. Friendly and neutral interviewees can be questioned at any time, and appointments can be made in advance, but hostile interviewees should generally be questioned without prior notice. Surprise interviews provide hostile interviewees with less time to prepare defenses.

## Characteristics of a Good Interview

Good interviews share common characteristics. Interviews should be of sufficient length and depth to uncover relevant facts. Most interviewers tend to get too little, rather than too much, information. A good interview focuses on pertinent information and quickly steers talk away from irrelevant information. Extraneous or useless facts unnecessarily complicate the gathering and analysis of information. Interviews should end on a positive note.

Interviews should be conducted as closely as possible to the event in question. With the passage of time, memories of potential witnesses and respondents become faulty, and critical details can be lost or forgotten. Good interviews are objective. They endeavor to gather information in a fair and impartial manner.

## Characteristics of a Good Interviewer

Good interviewers share certain characteristics. Above all, they are "people persons" and interact well with others. Successful interviewers are people with whom others are willing to share information. Good interviewers do not interrupt respondents unnecessarily. Volunteered information, as opposed to responses to specific questions, is often pertinent information. Good interviewers display interest in the subject and in what is being said.

The person being interviewed (also called the respondent, interviewee, witness, suspect, or target) must understand that interviewers are attempting to obtain only the relevant facts and are not "out to get" someone. Interviewers can best accomplish this goal by phrasing questions in a nonaccusatory manner. Little is accomplished when interviewers are formal, ostentatious, or attempt to impress respondents with their authority. Information gathering is best accomplished by interviewing in an informal and low-key manner.

If respondents perceive that interviewers are biased, or are attempting to confirm foregone conclusions, respondents are less likely to cooperate. Accordingly, interviewers should make every effort to demonstrate a lack of bias.

Professionalism in the interview often involves a state of mind and a commitment to excellence. Interviewers should be on time, be professionally attired, and be fair in all dealings with respondents. It is vital that interviewers not appear to be a threat, but rather as people who put others at ease. If respondents perceive that they are the target of an inquiry, they will be less likely to cooperate.

## Understanding Reaction to Crisis

Fraud, like death or serious injury, is a crisis. People in crisis have a predictable sequence of reactions. Interviewers who understand these reactions are much more effective than interviewers who do not. The sequence of reactions is as follows:

1. Denial
2. Anger
3. Rationalization or bargaining
4. Depression
5. Acceptance

Denial functions as a buffer after people receive unexpected or shocking news. It allows people who are affected by or connected with the fraud to collect themselves and to mobilize other, less radical defenses. Denial screens out the reality of the situation. Some studies show that carefully balanced psychological and physiological systems must be maintained for people to function normally.[2] To avoid sudden and severe disruption of this psychological equilibrium, which can destroy or incapacitate a person, the most immediate recourse is denial, which is a strategy to maintain the status quo. Because people in denial refuse to acknowledge the stress at either the cognitive or the emotional level, they do not initiate behavioral changes that help them adjust to the new reality.

Denial takes many forms: People appear temporarily stunned or dazed; they refuse to accept the information given; they insist that there is some mistake; or they do not comprehend what has been said. Denial acts as a "shock absorber" to reduce the impact of sudden trauma. Denial of fraud gives perpetrators time to alter, destroy, or conceal valuable documents and records. It also creates delays, which can mean that witnesses disappear or become confused, and that valuable documentary evidence is lost. When denial cannot be maintained any longer, feelings of anger, rage, and resentment follow.

The anger stage is difficult to cope with, because anger is usually directed in every direction and it is also projected onto the environment—at times, even randomly. Anger arises because attempts to return to the old psychological status quo fail and are met with frustration. Suspects direct their anger at friends, relatives, and coworkers. Sometimes suspects direct their anger inward, which can result in feelings of guilt, but not always. Suspects are not the only ones to feel anger, however. Managers and other employees become hostile to auditors and investigators—perceive them as cruel or unfeeling, a reaction not unlike that of the ancient Greeks who murdered messengers bearing evil tidings.

The anger stage is a dangerous time to resolve frauds. While angry, managers and others can insult, harm, slander, or libel suspects and may terminate them without due cause. The result can be lawsuits—for slander, libel, assault, battery, or wrongful termination. An angry manager of a fast-food restaurant who believed an employee was stealing had the police handcuff the employee and drag him out of the store in front of customers. The employee, who was later found innocent, sued and won $250,000 in damages. In other situations, victims' angry reactions allowed criminals to get legal settlements larger than the amounts they stole.

People in the rationalization stage attempt to justify the dishonest act or to minimize the crime. During this stage, managers believe they understand why the crime was committed and often feel that the perpetrator's motivation was almost justifiable. Managers may feel during this period that the perpetrator is not really a bad person, that a mistake was made, and that perhaps he or she should be given one more chance. Interviews during this stage are often not objective and can be detrimental to attempts to uncover the truth, or harmful to future prosecution efforts. Rationalization leads to failure to prosecute, easy penalties, and weak testimonies. Rationalization is the last attempt of the affected group to return to the former psychologically steady state.

As attempts to resolve the problem fail, hope diminishes. Managers are faced with the emotional burden of the truth. As trauma emerges, symptoms of depression appear: people are sad, and many withdraw or lose interest in the environment. Like the stages of denial, anger, and rationalization, depression is a normal part of the coping process necessary for eventual psychological readjustment. In this stage, managers no longer deny or rationalize the dishonest act. Their anger is replaced by a sense of loss and disappointment—or sometimes embarrassment that the fraud happened on "their watch." During this stage, managers and others often become withdrawn and uncooperative. They may be unwilling to volunteer information or to assist with the investigation. Interviews conducted during this stage are often less useful than those held later. Thus, it is crucial to take the state of mind of potential witnesses into consideration during interviews.

Individuals experience different behaviors as they attempt to adjust to "life after fraud." A small fraud with minimal impact may only have a small psychological impact on individuals, whereas larger frauds with significant ramifications (such as embarrassment, loss of clients, public exposure, or job jeopardy) often have larger psychological impacts. Individuals can cycle through the emotions of denial, anger, rationalization, and depression a number of times. Some people fluctuate between two phases as they strive to reach a new psychological equilibrium.

Eventually, people reach a state in which they no longer experience depression or anger; rather, they have a realistic understanding of what happened. Acceptance is not a happy state; it is an acknowledgment of what happened and a desire to resolve the issue and move on. This phase is often precipitated by a knowledge of the facts surrounding the fraud, including a knowledge of the motivations of the perpetrator. It is during this phase that interviews are most useful and witnesses most cooperative.

To demonstrate how these reactions play out during fraud investigations, consider the following fraud, which we discussed in Chapter 5. The case involved a supervisor in the shipping department of a wholesale-retail distribution center warehouse facility stealing more than $5,000. The supervisor was responsible for overall operations of the warehouse and was also accountable for a cash fund used to give change (usually amounts between $25 and $500) to customers who came to the warehouse to pick up COD orders. The established procedures called for the supervisor to issue the customer a cash receipt, which was recorded in a will-call delivery logbook. The file containing details on the customer order was eventually matched with cash receipts by accounting personnel, and the transaction closed.

Over approximately one year, the supervisor stole small amounts of money. He concealed the fraud by submitting credit memos (with statements such as "billed to the wrong account," "to correct billing adjustment," and "miscellaneous") to clear the accounts receivable file. Per the procedures, the accounts were matched with the credit memo, and the transactions closed. A second signature was not needed on credit memos, and accounting personnel asked no questions about the supervisor's credit memos. At first, the supervisor submitted only two or three fraudulent credit memos a week, totaling approximately $100. After a few months, however, the amount increased to approximately $300 per week. To give the appearance of randomness, and to keep the accounting personnel from becoming suspicious, the supervisor intermixed comparatively large credit memo amounts with smaller ones.

The fraud surfaced when the supervisor accidentally credited the wrong customer's account for a cash transaction. By coincidence, the supervisor was on vacation when the error surfaced and was thus unable to cover his tracks when accounting personnel queried the transaction. Because of his absence, the accounts receivable clerk questioned the manager of the warehouse, who investigated the problem. The manager scrutinized cash receipts and determined that the potential for fraud existed.

## Stage 1. Denial

Because of the possibility of fraud, the general manager and the warehouse manager started their own investigation of the warehouse cash fund. Sensing a serious problem, they decided to wait until the supervisor returned from vacation before taking further action. Both managers were anxious and somewhat irritable as they waited for the supervisor to return. Each manager later said that his work performance was adversely affected by the shock and their preoccupation with the problem. Both managers rationalized that the supervisor could probably explain the error; after all, he had been with the firm for three years and they considered him a model employee.

Later, after the close of the investigation, both managers admitted that they tried to deny that the falsified credit memos represented intentional fraud. Because of their denial, they didn't take advantage of readily available evidence during the suspected employee's absence.

Company procedure required managers to contact either corporate security or the internal audit department if a fraud was suspected. However, because they trusted the supervisor, both managers convinced themselves that there was no possibility of fraud—that the whole thing was a mistake. When the supervisor returned from vacation, the managers asked him to discuss the situation. Still in the denial stage, the managers simply asked the supervisor to explain his handling of the cash fund. The supervisor—now thrown into his own first stage of crisis, denial—told them that he didn't know what they were talking about. Had he offered some explanation, the managers, who were still denying fraud, probably would have been satisfied and terminated their investigation.

But the supervisor denied the existence of the credit memos, and the managers knew this claim to be untrue, so they sent the supervisor back to work and also decided to investigate further. From an investigative standpoint, sending the supervisor back to his job was a risky action. He was again in control of the original credit memos and cash transaction logs and could have easily destroyed evidence. Simply "losing" the records would have concealed the fraud and jeopardized the investigation. At this point, the warehouse managers requested the assistance of internal audit to review the matter further. A full week passed before assistance was made available.

## Stage 2. Anger

During this week's waiting period, both managers decided that fraud had indeed been committed. They discussed their feelings and decided to confront the employee. This time they vowed they would get answers. Clearly, both managers had progressed from denial to anger. Without additional information that a full investigation could have provided, the managers confronted the supervisor and demanded an explanation. This time, the supervisor said nothing. Irate, the managers fired him on the spot, without additional explanation. Firings like this jeopardize investigations and companies in several ways. First, if fraud has not been committed, the company may be subjected to litigation and sued for wrongful dismissal, slander, or libel. Second, harsh treatment jeopardizes further cooperation by the perpetrator. In this case, the basis for the termination was the several falsified credit memorandums (totaling between $300 and $400) located by the managers.

The audit that followed revealed more than 100 falsified credit memos and losses totaling more than $5,000. The managers were surprised at the extent of the fraud. Their accusing the supervisor of fraud well before they could clearly demonstrate his guilt made the corporation vulnerable to litigation and potential liability.

## Stage 3. Rationalization and Bargaining

After the supervisor was summarily terminated, the general manager worried that both he and the warehouse manager had acted too quickly; perhaps they should have given him one more chance. They soon realized their actions opened the company to liability. Although rehiring the supervisor was contrary to company policy, the general manager still felt he could "save" this "valued" employee.

Through these rationalizations, the general manager was trying to come to terms with the fact that a trusted friend and employee committed a fraud against the firm. He was "bargaining"—that is, trying to change the facts in some way that gave an acceptable explanation, although none existed.

## Stage 4. Depression

After bargaining came depression; both the general manager and the warehouse manager grew less irritated and became much more withdrawn. Feelings of depression enveloped both individuals as they realized the scope of the situation. Their depression was reinforced by comments and reactions from other warehouse employees, as details of the fraud emerged. Interestingly enough, during this period neither manager discussed his feelings with the other. Rather, they kept their feelings to themselves, apparently because they felt that the employee had suffered enough and that the case should be closed.

## Stage 5. Acceptance

The investigation conducted by corporate security and internal audit revealed the following facts:

- The supervisor had a substance abuse problem involving cocaine and alcohol. As a result of his confrontation with management, he was considering rehabilitation.
- The supervisor convinced himself that he was simply borrowing the money. He rationalized that he had every intention of repaying the money borrowed, but he was also caught up in the machinations of the fraud and expressed surprise that in less than one year he defrauded the company of more than $5,000.
- The supervisor informed security personnel that he had spent almost his entire life savings on cocaine and had lost his family in the process. Losing his job was the last straw.
- In discussions with local management, investigators learned that several managers and employees had noticed a change in the supervisor's behavior over the previous several months. The changes, which no one acted on, included frequent mood swings; frequent tardiness and absenteeism; and a preoccupation with impressing other employees by taking them out to lunch, during which the supervisor chattered relentlessly.

Once these facts were known, both managers accepted the fraud as a reality and felt that they were back in control of the situation. Their desire at that point was to resolve the situation and get back to normal.

This fraud is typical of the reactions of innocent bystanders in a fraud. Interviewers who recognize and understand these reactions, who tailor their questions and interview approaches to the reaction stages their interviewees are in, and who can nudge interviewees to the acceptance stage will have much more successful interviews.

# Planning an Interview

When you conduct interviews, follow a plan or outline to make sure that you meet your objectives. Proper planning allows you to get the most from the interview and to minimize the time spent. Such planning involves ascertaining in advance as many facts as possible about the offense and the interviewee, and establishing a location and time for the interview that are conducive to success.

To obtain facts about the offense and the interviewee, review relevant documents to gather as much other information as possible about the following factors:

*The offense*

- Legal nature of the offense
- Date, time, and place of occurrence
- Manner in which the crime appears to have been committed
- Possible motives
- All available evidence

*The interviewee*

- Personal background information—age, education, marital status, etc.
- Attitude toward investigation
- Any physical or mental conditions, such as alcohol or drug use

It is usually best (except with hostile interviewees) to conduct interviews at the interviewee's office or workplace, so that interviewees can access necessary papers, books, and other evidence. In addition, such locations are generally more convenient for interviewees. The interview room should be one where distractions from colleagues and telephones are nonexistent or minimal.

With friendly or neutral interviewees, set up an appointment and allow sufficient (even excess) time for the interview. When you set up the appointment, identify information that the interviewee will need. Wherever possible, interview only one person at a time.

## The Interviewer's Demeanor

Take special pains to be efficient, courteous, polite, and careful with the language you use during interviews. Here are some suggestions:

- Sit fairly close to the interviewee with no desk or furniture between you. Don't walk around the room; stay seated.
- Do not talk down to the person. (Don't assume the person is less intelligent than you.)
- Be sensitive to the personal concerns of the witness, especially with regard to such matters as sex, race, religion, and ethnic background.
- Be businesslike. Conduct the interview in a professional manner. Be friendly but not social. Remember that you seek the truth; you are not trying to get a confession or a conviction.
- Avoid being authoritarian; do not dominate the interview.
- Be sympathetic and respectful. (If appropriate, tell the witness that anyone under similar conditions or circumstances might do the same thing.)
- Give careful thought to your language. Don't use technical jargon.
- Thank the witness for taking the time and trouble to cooperate.
- Keep pencil and paper out of sight during the interview.
- End every cooperative interview by expressing your sincere appreciation.

## The Language of Interviews

Language is important in interviews. Successful interviewers adhere to specific guidelines:

- Use short questions, confined to one topic, which can be clearly and easily understood.
- Ask questions that require narrative answers; whenever possible, avoid eliciting yes and no answers.
- Avoid questions that suggest part of the answer (called leading questions).
- Require witnesses to give the factual basis for any conclusions they state.
- Prevent witnesses from aimlessly wandering. Require direct responses.
- Don't let witnesses lead you away from the topic. Don't let them confuse the issue or leave basic questions unanswered.
- At any given point, concentrate more on the answer you are hearing than on the next question you plan to ask.
- Clearly understand each answer before you continue.
- Maintain full control of the interview.
- Point out some, but not all, of the circumstantial evidence.

## Question Typology

Interviewers ask five types of questions: introductory, informational, assessment, closing, and admission-seeking. In routine interviews, where your objective is to gather information from neutral or friendly witnesses, only three of the five types are normally asked: introductory, informational, and closing questions. If you have reasonable cause to believe the respondent is not being truthful, then ask assessment questions. Finally, if you decide with reasonable cause that the respondent is responsible for misdeeds, admission-seeking questions can be posed.

*Introductory Questions.* Interviewers use introductory questions for two purposes: to start the interview, and to get the respondent to verbally agree to cooperate. This process follows a step-by-step procedure in which you briefly state the purpose for the contact, then pose a question designed to get the respondent to agree to talk further.

*Informational Questions.* Once the proper format for the interview is set, interviewers turn to the fact-gathering portion. Three types of questions are asked: open, closed, and leading. (We discuss these in more detail later in the chapter.) Each question type is used in a logical sequence in order to maximize the development of information. If you have reason to believe that the respondent is being untruthful, then pose assessment questions. Otherwise, bring the interview to a logical close.

*Closing Questions.* In routine interviews, certain questions are asked at closing in order to reconfirm the facts, obtain previously undiscovered information, seek new evidence, and maintain goodwill. These three questions should always be asked in closing: (1) Do you know anyone else I should talk to? (2) Is there anything I have forgotten to ask that you believe would be relevant? And (3) if I need to talk to you again, would that be all right?

*Assessment Questions.* If interviewers have reason to believe the respondent is being deceptive, certain types of hypothetical, nonaccusatory questions are posed. By observing the verbal and nonverbal responses of the respondent to these questions, you can assess the respondent's credibility with some degree of accuracy. Your assessment will form the basis of your decision about whether to pose admission-seeking questions to obtain a legal admission of wrongdoing.

*Admission-Seeking Questions.* Admission-seeking interviews are reserved for individuals whose culpability is reasonably certain. Admission-seeking questions are posed in an exact order designed to (1) clear an innocent person or (2) encourage a culpable person to confess. These questions must not violate the rights and privileges of the person being interviewed.

## Elements of Conversation

Because interviews are essentially structured conversations, it is helpful to understand the basic elements of effective communication. Whenever two or more human beings converse, several types of communication occur—either one at a time or in combination.

*Expression.* A common function of conversation is self-expression in which one or more of the conversationalists express ideas, feelings, attitudes, or moods. The illusion of an audience is central to personal expression. The urge for spontaneous expression can be a vital asset in interviewing, and it should be encouraged in respondents. It can be directed by interviewers toward information-gathering objectives. A common error made by novice interviewers is yielding to the temptation to impress respondents with their knowledge of the subject of the interview. In doing so, interviewers risk making respondents feel threatened, resulting in respondents giving guarded responses rather than expressing their feelings frankly. Experienced interviewers have the discipline to control their own responses.

*Persuasion.* Persuasion and expression differ in that persuasion endeavors to convince the other person. At times, persuasion can be effective in interviews; it is mostly used to convince respondents of the legitimacy of the interview.

*Therapy.* Making people feel good about themselves is often a function of effective communication. In our conversations with friends, we frequently express ideas and feelings to relieve emotional tension. This release, called *catharsis,* is encouraged in psychiatric interviews. Sometimes the information sought in an interview is closely related to the respondent's inner conflicts and tensions. For example, people embezzling money typically feel guilty. Skillful interviewers know the therapeutic implication of releasing such feelings in their attempts to develop information.

*Ritual.* Some aspects of conversation are ritualistic; that is, they are cultural expressions that have no significance other than to provide security in interpersonal relations. Examples include "Good morning!" and "How are you today?" It behooves you to learn to detect ritualistic answers by respondents, and to avoid giving them yourself. Be aware of the danger of engaging in ritualistic conversation; you don't want to confuse the results with valid information.

*Information Exchange.* Information exchange is the central purpose of interviews. The word *exchange* reminds us that the flow of information in interviews goes both ways. Interviewers are often so focused on the information they wish to obtain that they fail to properly exchange information with respondents. Although you should measure the details carefully, don't be "cagey." This tactic rarely works. Two basic problems occur in the exchange of information. One, the information sought by interviewers is not of equal importance to respondents. And second, communication barriers often exist between people of diverse backgrounds. These barriers are also common between strangers.

## Inhibitors of Communication

To be an effective interviewer, you must understand that certain matters inhibit communication and others facilitate it. It is your task to minimize inhibitors and maximize facilitators. An *inhibitor* is any sociopsychological barrier that impedes the flow of relevant information by making respondents unable or unwilling to provide information. Carefully examine the following eight inhibitors to communication. The first four make respondents unwilling to cooperate; the last four make them unable to give information, even though they may be willing to do so.

*Competing Demands for Time.* Respondents may hesitate to begin an interview because of other demands on their time. They are not necessarily placing a negative value on being interviewed, but are instead weighing the value of being interviewed against doing something else. Successful interviewers convince respondents that the interview is a good use of their time.

*Threatened Egos.* Respondents in some cases withhold information because of a perceived threat to their self-esteem. Three broad responses to ego threats include repression, disapproval, and loss of status.

- *Repression.* The strongest response to a threatened ego is repression. Respondents not only refuse to admit information, but they also refuse to admit the information inwardly. They are being honest when they answer that they don't know; they have truly "forgotten" (repressed) it. Embezzlers, for example, repress their memory of the act because it does not conform to their moral code.
- *Disapproval.* A less intense but more common response to threatened egos is found when respondents possess information but hesitate to admit it because they anticipate disapproval from the interviewer. If respondents are made to feel that the interviewer will not condemn them, they may welcome the opportunity to divulge information. A generally accepting and sympathetic attitude toward respondents goes a long way toward eliciting candid responses.
- *Loss of status.* Sometimes respondents fear losing status if the information provided becomes public. This threat can sometimes be overcome by assuring them that the information will be handled confidentially.

*Etiquette.* The etiquette barrier operates when an answer to a question contains information that the respondent perceives as inappropriate. Answering candidly would be considered in poor taste or evidence of a lack of proper etiquette. For example, men feel uncomfortable discussing certain topics in front of women, and vice versa, in the same way that students do not tell teachers, and doctors do not tell patients certain things. The desire to avoid embarrassing, shocking, or threatening answers is distinct from the fear of exposing oneself. Often, the negative effects of the etiquette barrier can be forestalled by selecting the appropriate interviewer and setting for the interview.

*Trauma.* Trauma denotes an acutely unpleasant feeling associated with crisis experiences. The unpleasant feeling is often brought to the surface when the respondent is reporting the experience. Trauma is common when talking to victims, and can usually be overcome by sensitive handling of the issue.

*Forgetting.* A frequent inhibitor to communication is the respondent's inability to recall certain types of information. This issue is not a problem if the objectives of the interview deal only with current attitudes, beliefs, or expectations. The natural fading of memory over time makes it easier for the ego defense system to reconstruct a person's own image of the past by omission, addition, or distortion.

The memory problem is a much more frequent obstacle than interviewers generally expect. Even the most simple and obvious facts cannot always be elicited. Three factors contribute to an individual's recollection of an event.

- The vividness of an individual's recall relates to the event's original emotional impact, its meaningfulness at the time, and the degree to which the person's ego is involved.
- The amount of time that has elapsed since the event affects recollection.
- The nature of the interview situation, including the interviewer's techniques and tactics influence a person's ability to recall.

Knowledge of these factors will help you anticipate where problems may arise. And certain techniques (discussed later) will help you overcome many memory problems.

*Chronological Confusion.* Chronological confusion is commonly encountered in interviews that seek case history information. This term refers to the respondent's tendency to confuse the order of events, which occurs in two ways: First, two or more events are correctly recalled, but the respondent is unsure of the sequence. Or, only one event is recalled, and it is incorrectly assumed to have been true at an earlier point.

*Inferential Confusion.* This term denotes confusion and inaccuracies that result from errors of inference. These errors fall into two categories: induction and deduction. In *induction,* the respondent is asked to convert concrete experiences into a higher level of generalization. In *deduction,* the respondent is asked to give concrete examples of certain categories of experience.

*Unconscious Behavior.* Often, interview objectives call for information about a person's unconscious behavior. The three types of unconscious behavior are (1) *custom* or *habit;* (2) *circular reaction* (the immediate, unwitting response of one person to the subliminal, nonverbal clues of another, which arises under special circumstances); and (3) *acute emotional crisis* (where the behavior does not follow a habitual pattern and where it does not result from a reaction to others).

## Facilitators of Communication

*Facilitators of communication* are those sociopsychological forces that make conversations, including interviews, easier to accomplish. Facilitators require a basic understanding of what motivates people.

*Fulfilling Expectations.* An important force in social interaction is our tendency to communicate, verbally or nonverbally, our expectations to the other person. The other person then tends to respond, consciously or unconsciously, to our expectations. This manifestation of the human tendency to conform to the group and to the anticipations of higher-status persons is an attempt to achieve security.

In the interview setting, interviewers routinely communicate expectations to respondents. Strive to transmit both your general expectation of cooperation, as well as a more specific expectation that the respondent will answer the questions truthfully. Clearly distinguish between asking for information and expecting it. The former is mainly verbal communication; the latter is accomplished through nonverbal behavior.

*Recognition.* We all need the recognition and the esteem of others. Social interaction often depends on an exchange of social goods. People "perform" in exchange for recognition and other social rewards. The need for recognition can be fulfilled by attention from people outside a person's social circle. Skillful and insightful interviewers take advantage of every opportunity to give respondents sincere recognition.

*Altruistic Appeals.* Some people need to identify with a "higher" value or cause beyond their immediate self-interest. This need sometimes takes the form of identifying with the objectives of the larger group. Altruistic deeds usually increase self-esteem whether or not the deeds are made public. This element distinguishes altruism from publicity. Altruism is of major importance in motivating many respondents. Interviewers who understand their respondent's value system can use strategy and techniques that appeal to altruism.

*Sympathetic Understanding.* We all need the sympathetic response of others. We like to share our joys, fears, successes, and failures. Our need for understanding differs from our need for recognition, which requires success and increased status. Interviewers who reflect a sympathetic attitude and who know how to direct that attitude toward the objectives of their interview find their percentages of success much higher than those who lack such abilities.

*New Experience.* Some people welcome new experiences. Although variety is not everybody's spice of life, escape from dreary routine is sought by almost everyone. Sometimes respondents are motivated by curiosity regarding the interviewer. Experienced interviewers consider this factor when deciding what to say about themselves. Do not assume that just because an interview is a new experience it will satisfy the respondent's needs. Aspects of the respondent's perception of the new experience can also be ego-threatening. Respondents may be anxious about the impression they leave with interviewers. This apprehensiveness can often be detected at the beginning of the interview. Once these fears are dispelled, respondents frequently find interviews a new and interesting experience.

*Catharsis.* We obtain release from unpleasant emotional tensions by talking about the source of these tensions. We often feel better after we talk about something that upsets us. Although we are all familiar with our own experiences with catharsis, we don't always perceive this need in others. After respondents confess, they may indicate that they feel much better about themselves. The need for sympathetic understanding and the need for catharsis are related, but they are not the same thing. Interviewers who do not have time to listen to what they consider inconsequential egocentric talk often find respondents unwilling to share important information.

*Need for Meaning.* Another trait common to all of us is our need for meaning. Every society has a set of assumptions, values, explanations, and myths that serves to create order in the society. Our need for meaning is related to cognitive dissonance, the psychological tension we feel when we are aware of inconsistent facts, assumptions, and interpretations. This tension is painful, and reducing it is rewarding. In cases where the interview topic deals directly with information that disturbs a person's need for meaning, respondents are often strongly motivated to talk it through, if they are convinced of the interviewer's interest.

*Extrinsic Rewards.* This term refers to rewards that motivate the respondent (other than those gained directly from being involved in the interview). Extrinsic rewards are helpful insofar as respondents see the interview as a means to an end. Various extrinsic rewards can come into play in interview situations, including money, job advancement, and retention of privileges. Remember that what is extrinsic to you as interviewer may not be extrinsic to respondents. Sensitive interviewers recognize what extrinsic rewards, if any, respondents receive from being interviewed.

## Mechanics of the Interview

### Introductory Questions

One of the most difficult aspects of interviews is getting started. Indeed, the introduction is often the hardest part. In many instances, interviewers and respondents have not met before. Interviewers have a tall order: Meet the person, state a reason for the interview, establish necessary rapport, and get the information. The introduction is accomplished through questions as opposed to statements. Questions allow you to assess the respondent's feedback,which is an important aspect of the introduction. If the respondent is reluctant to be interviewed, that fact will come out through the introductory questions. They are designed to meet the following objectives.

*Provide the Introduction.* Obviously, you must introduce yourself as the interview commences. You should generally indicate your name and company; avoid titles. Although not always the case, the more informal the interview, generally the more relaxed is the respondent.

*Establish Rapport. Webster's* defines *rapport* as a "relation marked by harmony, conformity, accord, or affinity." In other words, establish some common ground before you begin your questioning. This task is usually accomplished by spending a few minutes in "small talk." This aspect, however, should not be overdone. Most people are aware that the interviewer is not there to chit-chat.

*Establish the Interview Theme.* State the purpose of your interview in some way prior to the commencement of serious questioning. Otherwise, the respondent may be confused, threatened, or overly cautious. Stating the purpose of the interview is known as "establishing the interview theme."

*Observe Reactions.* You need to become skilled in interpreting the respondent's reactions to questions. Social scientists say that more than half the communication between individuals is nonverbal. You must, therefore, observe systematically (though in an offhand, unobtrusive manner) the various responses respondents give during interviews.

Systematic ways can be used to observe reactions. First, pose nonsensitive questions as you establish rapport. During this phase, find some common ground so that you can "connect" with the respondent. As you establish rapport through normal conversation, observe the respondent's reactions. This assessment is your baseline for observing later behavior—when you ask more sensitive questions. If the respondent's verbal and nonverbal behavior is inconsistent from one type of question to another, you can then attempt to determine why.

***Develop the Interview Theme.*** The interview theme may relate only indirectly to the actual purpose of the interview. The goal of the theme is to get the respondent to "buy in" to assisting in the interview. Generally, the most effective interview theme is that help is being sought. Nearly all of us get satisfaction from helping others.

In most interviews, it is best to treat respondents in such a manner that they feel important about helping. During this phase of the interview, respondents must not feel threatened in any way. An effective approach is the "Columbo-style" (although perhaps not so rumpled), in which at least two thoughts go through the mind of Columbo's subjects: (1) He is no threat to me; and (2) he really needs my help. In the following examples, assume you are introducing yourself.

| *WRONG* | *RIGHT* |
|---|---|
| *Interviewer:* | *Interviewer:* |
| "I am _____ _____, a Certified Fraud Examiner with the store's fraud examination unit. I am investigating a case of suspected fraud, and you may know something about it. How long have you worked here at the company?" | "I'm _____ _____. I work here at the company. Have we met before?" |
|  | *Respondent:* |
|  | "I don't think so." |
|  | *Interviewer:* |
|  | "I am working on an assignment and I need your help. Do you have a few minutes I can spend with you now?" |

## Methodology

Respondents must perceive that they have something in common with you as interviewer, and should be made to feel good about the situation. This rapport is best achieved when respondents perceive you as open and friendly.

***Make Physical Contact.*** One way to promote respondents' perception of your being open and friendly is to shake hands at the beginning of the interview. Making physical contact helps break down psychological barriers to communication. (*Caution:* Do not invade the respondent's personal space, which can make people uncomfortable.)

Use body language to create the impression of trust during the interview: Gesture openly with your arms, clasp your hands together, and lean forward to indicate interest. You can also establish rapport verbally by using soft words, agreeing with the respondent, and avoiding negative terms.

***Establish the Purpose of the Interview.*** The purpose of your interview must be established. Obviously, when you make official contact with respondents, some reason must be given. The reason or purpose of your interview should be general and not specific. The specific purpose will be stated later. The general purpose for the interview should be one that is logical for respondents to accept and easy for you to explain. Normally, the more general, the better.

| *Example:* |  |
|---|---|
| *Interviewer:* | OR |
| "I'm working on a matter and I need your help."   OR | "I'm compiling information on our purchasing procedures." |
| "I'm reviewing procedures here at the company." |  |

***Don't Interview More Than One Person at a Time.*** One basic rule—question only one person at a time. The testimony of one respondent will invariably influence the testimony of another. Few hard and fast rules apply in interviewing, but this rule is one of them.

*Conduct the Interview in Private.* Another basic rule—conduct interviews under conditions of privacy. Interviews are best conducted out of the sight and sound of friends, relatives, or fellow employees. People are reluctant to furnish information within the hearing of others.

*Ask Nonsensitive Questions.* Sensitive questions should be scrupulously avoided until well into the interview. And then ask such questions *only* after careful deliberation and planning. During the introductory phase, avoid emotionally charged words of all types. Such words often put people on the defensive, and they are then reluctant to answer and even less likely to cooperate.

**Nonsensitive Words**

| **Instead of** | *Use* |
|---|---|
| Investigation | *Inquiry* |
| Audit | *Review* |
| Interview | *Ask a few questions* |
| Embezzle/steal/theft | *Shortage or paperwork problems* |

*Get a Commitment for Assistance.* Failure to get a commitment from the respondent to assist you is a common mistake made even by experienced interviewers. This step is critical and sets the tone for the entire interview. A commitment of assistance requires positive action on the part of the respondent. Remaining silent or simply nodding the head is generally not sufficient.

Ask for the commitment before the interview commences, and encourage respondents to voice that "yes" aloud. If you encounter silence the first time, repeat the question in a slightly different way until respondents verbalize commitment.

---

**Example:**

*Interviewer:*
"I'm _____ _____ with the company. I'm reviewing our sales returns and allowances. Do you have a few minutes?"

*Respondent:*
"Yes."

*Interviewer:*
"I'm gathering some information on certain company procedures. Maybe you can help me?"

*Respondent:*
(No response.)

*Interviewer:*
"Could I get you to help me, if you can?"

*Respondent:*
"Yes. What's this about?"

---

*Establish a Transitional Statement.* At this point, you have a commitment for assistance and must now describe in more detail the purpose of the interview. This description is made with a transitional statement that provides a legitimate basis for your inquiry, and explains to respondents how they fit into the inquiry. You can usually accomplish this task using a broad, rather than a narrow, description. Note that employees in the same company will frequently assume that your request for assistance is legitimate. After describing the basic nature of the inquiry with the transitional statement, seek a second commitment for assistance.

---

*Example:*

*Interviewer:*
"I'm gathering some information about the sales return function and how it's supposed to work. It would be very helpful if I could start by asking you to basically tell me about your job. Okay?"

---

When interviewing complete strangers, you may have to give particulars about how the respondent's assistance is needed. This explanation can take one or more of the following methods:

---

***Example:***

*Interviewer:*

"It's pretty routine, really. As I say, I work for _____ and I've been asked to gather information about some of their procedures. I thought it might be helpful to talk to you. Okay?"

OR

"It's pretty routine. I've been asked by the company to gather information on some of their procedures. I thought you might be able to help by answering a few questions. Okay?"

OR

"It's pretty routine, really. I've been asked by your company to gather some information, and they suggested I could contact you. Okay?"

---

***Seek Continuous Agreement.*** Throughout the process—from the introduction to the close—attempt to phrase questions that can be answered "yes." People find it easier to reply in the affirmative than the negative:

---

***Example:***

*Interviewer:*

"Okay?"

"Can you help me?"

"That's okay, isn't it?"

---

***Do Not Invade Body Space.*** During the introductory part of the interview, you should generally remain at a distance of four to six feet. Do not invade the respondent's personal zone (closer than about three feet), because it will make many respondents uncomfortable.

Set up the interview in such a way that you can see the person's movement from head to toe. You don't want to interview someone who is sitting behind his or her desk.

## Informational Questions

*Informational questions* are nonconfrontational, nonthreatening, and are asked for information-gathering purposes. The great majority of questions fall into this category. Applications include:

- Interviews to gain an understanding of accounting control systems
- Interviews concerning documents
- Gathering information regarding business operations or systems
- Preemployment interviews

Informational questions seek to elicit unbiased factual information. Good interviewers are alert to inconsistency in facts or behavior. Informational questions—as well as others—fall into several general categories: open, closed, leading, double-negative, complex, and attitude.

***Open Questions.*** Open questions are worded in a way that makes it difficult to answer yes or no. Typical open questions call for a monologue response, and can be answered in several different ways. During the informational phase of the interview, you should endeavor to ask primarily open questions. This type of question stimulates conversation. Informational questions are open-ended questions and force more lengthy responses. Here is an open-ended question:

> *Do me a favor and just sort of explain what the purpose of a three-parter is—how it gets filled out—these kinds of things.*

Here are a few other examples:

| *Interviewer:*<br>"Please tell me about your job."<br>"Please tell me about the operation of your department." | "What do you think about this problem?"<br>"Please describe the procedures to me." |

*Closed Questions.* Closed questions require a precise answer—usually yes or no. Closed questions also deal with specifics, such as amounts, dates, and times. As far as possible, avoid closed questions in the informational part of the interview. They are used extensively in closing questions, described later. Examples include:

| *Interviewer:* "Do you work here?" | "What day of the week did it happen?" |

*Leading Questions.* Leading questions contain the answer as a part of the question. Most commonly, they are used to confirm already known facts. Although leading questions are usually discouraged in court proceedings, they can be effective in interviews. Here is a leading question:

> *All right, so you started here in November of 1988—after working for Panasonic—
> to the best of your recollection?*

*Double-Negative Questions.* Questions or statements that contain double negatives are confusing and often suggest an answer opposite to the correct one. Do not use them. Here is an example:

| *Interviewer:*<br>"Didn't you suspect that something wasn't right?" |

*Complex Questions.* Complex questions and statements are not easily understood, cover more than one subject or topic, require more than one answer, or require a complicated answer. Simply put, avoid them—here is an example:

| *Interviewer:*<br>"What are your duties here, and how long have you been employed?" |

*Attitude Questions.* Your attitude is conveyed not only by the structure of your questions and statements, but also by the manner in which you ask them. When you wish to establish a friendly mood, employ questions such as these:

| *Interviewer:*<br>"How are you doing this morning?" | "Do you like sports?" |

It is always a good idea, however, to ask a question to which you know beforehand that the answer will be yes.

## Question Sequence

As a general rule, questioning should proceed from the general to the specific; that is, seek general information before you seek details. A variation is to "reach backward" with questions by beginning with known information and working toward unknown areas. An efficient way to reach backward is to recount the known information and then frame the next question as a logical continuation of the facts previously related. Figures and numbers are critical in accounting and fraud-related matters; unfortunately, witnesses aren't always able to recall specific amounts. You can jog the respondent's memory by comparing unknown items with items of known quantity:

---

*Interviewer:*
"Was the amount of money involved more than last year's figure?"

---

*Controlled-Answer Techniques. Controlled-answer techniques* or statements are used to stimulate a desired answer or impression. These techniques direct the interview toward a specific point. For example, it may be possible to get a person to admit knowledge of a matter by phrasing the question thus: *"I understand you were present when the internal controls were developed, so would you please describe how they were constructed?"* This phrasing provides a stronger incentive for the respondent to admit knowledge than does *"Were you present when the internal controls were developed?"*

To stimulate the person to agree to talk or to provide information, you can use an example such as, *"Because you're not involved in this matter, I'm sure you wouldn't mind discussing it with me."* This statement provides a stronger incentive to cooperate than *"Do you have any objections to telling me what you know?"* Avoid negative constructions, such as, *"I don't guess you would mind answering a few questions."*

*Free Narratives.* The *free narrative* is an orderly, continuous account of an event or incident, given with or without prompting. It is used to quickly summarize what is known about a matter. Be sure to explicitly designate the occurrence that you wish to discuss. Sometimes respondents must be controlled to prevent unnecessary digression. Otherwise, use a minimum of interruptions, and do not stop the narrative without good reason. Respondents will sometimes provide valuable clues when talking about things that are only partially related to the matter under inquiry.

## Informational Question Techniques

The following suggestions improve the quality of interviews during the information-gathering phase:

- Begin by asking questions that are not likely to cause respondents to become defensive or hostile.
- Ask questions in a manner that develops the facts in the order of their occurrence, or in some other systematic order.
- Ask only one question at a time, and frame the question so that only one answer is required.
- Ask straightforward and frank questions; generally avoid shrewd approaches.
- Give respondents ample time to answer; do not rush.
- Try to help respondents remember, but do not suggest answers; be careful not to imply any particular answer by facial expressions, gestures, methods of asking questions, or types of questions asked.
- Repeat or rephrase questions, if necessary, to get the desired facts.
- Be sure you understand the answers, and if they are not perfectly clear, have respondents interpret them at that time instead of saving further explanation for later.
- Give respondents an opportunity to qualify their answers.
- Separate facts from inferences.
- Have respondents give comparisons by percentages, fractions, estimates of time and distance, and other such comparisons to ascertain accuracy.

- Get all of the facts; almost every respondent can give you information beyond what was initially provided.
- After respondents give a narrative account, ask questions about the items discussed.
- Upon concluding the direct questioning, summarize the facts and have respondents verify that these conclusions are correct.

## Note-Taking

As stated previously, note-taking is problematic during interviews. That said, interviewers will frequently need to take some notes. If this need arises, start each interview on a separate sheet of paper. This procedure is especially helpful should documents from a particular interview be subpoenaed. Do not try to write down all the information you are given during an interview, only the pertinent facts. Taking too many notes makes the interview process cumbersome and can inhibit respondents. If a quote is particularly relevant, try to write it down verbatim. Enclose all direct quotations in quotation marks. Do not slow down the interview process for note-taking. Instead, jot down key words or phrases, then go back over the details at the end of the interview. In general, it is better to err on the side of taking too few notes rather than too many.

If a record of an interview is necessary, taping the interview is a desirable alternative to extensive notes. While permission to tape an interview must usually be received from the interviewee, the tape recorder does not normally distract after the interview begins.

*Maintain Eye Contact.* Maintain eye contact with respondents in a normal way during note-taking. Just as eye contact personalizes other human communication, it also creates a more comfortable environment and facilitates the flow of information during interviews.

*Opinions.* Avoid making notes regarding your overall opinions or impressions of a witness. Such notes can cause problems with your credibility if they are later produced in court. Be careful not to show excitement when note-taking. During interviews of targets and adverse witnesses, take notes in a manner that does not indicate the significance of the information; that is, never allow note-taking to "telegraph" your emotions.

*Writing Down Questions.* Whenever possible, do not write down a list of interview questions. Let the interview flow freely. Inadvertently allowing respondents to read a written list of questions gives them an opportunity to fabricate answers. Writing down key points you want to discuss is appropriate, however.

*Documenting Results.* Document the results of the interview as soon as possible after its conclusion—preferably immediately afterward. If this procedure is followed, you will not have to take copious notes during the interview. Law enforcement officials are generally required to maintain notes. In the private sector, the notes can usually be destroyed once a memorandum has been prepared summarizing the interview. Check with your lawyer when in doubt.

## Observing Respondent Reactions

Interviewers must be knowledgeable about behavior during interviews. Most nonverbal clues fall within one of four categories: proxemics, chronemics, kinetics, or paralinguistics.

### Proxemics

*Proxemic communication* is the use of interpersonal space to convey meaning. The relationship between interviewer and respondent is both a cause and an effect of proxemic behavior. If the distance between interviewer and respondent is greater, they both tend to watch each other's eyes for clues to meaning.

It is therefore important that the conversation occur at an acceptable distance. Correct conversational distances vary from one culture to another. In the Middle East, the distance is quite short; in Latin America, equals of the same sex carry on a conversation at a much closer distance than in North America. Often, as the subject matter of the interview changes, interviewers can note the changes in the proxemic behavior of respondents. If respondents are free to back away, they might do so when the topic becomes unpleasant or sensitive.

## CHRONEMICS

*Chronemic communication* refers to the use of time in interpersonal relationships to convey meaning, attitudes, and desires. For example, respondents who are late in keeping appointments may convey a lack of interest in the interview or may wish to avoid it.

The most important chronemic technique used by interviewers is in their timing of questions. Effective interviewers control the length of pauses and the rate of their speech. This tactic is called *pacing*. Interviewers can also control the length of time after respondents finish a sentence before they pose another question, which is called the *silent probe*.

Pacing is one of the principal nonverbal ways to set an appropriate mood. Tense interviewers often communicate anxiety by a rapid-fire rate of speech, which in turn can increase anxiety in respondents. To establish the more thoughtful, deliberative mood that stimulates free association, interviewers strive to set a relaxed, deliberate pace.

## KINETICS

*Kinetic communication* has to do with how body movements convey meaning. Even though posture, hands, and feet all communicate meaning, interviewers tend to focus attention on the face and are more accurate in their judgments of others if they can see facial movements and expressions. When you concentrate on facial expressions, your primary interest is eye contact. Eye contact primarily communicates the desire to make or avoid communication. People who feel shame normally drop their eyes to avoid returning glances. This reaction not only avoids seeing the disapproval, but also conceals personal shame and confusion.

## PARALINGUISTICS

*Paralinguistic communication* involves the use of volume, pitch, and voice quality to convey meaning. One basic difference between written and verbal communication is that oral speech gives the full range of nonverbal cues. For example, a no answer may not really mean no; it depends on how the "no" is said.

# Theme Development

All questions should be nonaccusatory during the information-seeking phase. Nothing closes up the lines of communication in interviews like accusatory questions. Therefore, be sure to formulate your questions in a way that does not elicit strong emotional reactions. Move from nonsensitive to sensitive. If respondents start to become uncomfortable with the questioning, go on to a different area and return to the sensitive question later, but from a different vantage point.

Some people do not volunteer information; they must be asked. You must not be reluctant to ask sensitive questions after you have established the proper basis. If you pose the question with confidence and show that you expect an answer, respondents are much more likely to furnish the requested information. If you are apologetic or lack confidence in the question, respondents are much less likely to answer.

# Transition Methodology

Once the introduction has been completed, you need a transition into the body of the interview. This transition is usually accomplished by asking respondents an easy question about themselves or their duties—for example:

> *Can you tell me what it is you do as far as quality control?*

## BEGIN WITH BACKGROUND QUESTIONS

Assuming that respondents do not have a problem answering the transitional question, you should then ask a series of easy, open questions designed to get them to talk about themselves.

> **Example:**
>
> *Interviewer:*
> "What is your exact title?"
> "What do your responsibilities involve?"
> "How long have you been assigned here?"
>
> "What do you like best about your job?"
> "What do you like least about your job?"
> "What would you eventually like to do for the company?"

## OBSERVE VERBAL AND NONVERBAL BEHAVIOR

During the period when respondents talk about themselves, discreetly observe their verbal and nonverbal behavior. These types of behavior will be discussed later in the chapter.

## ASK NONLEADING (OPEN) QUESTIONS

Open questioning techniques are used almost exclusively in the informational phase of interviews. The questions should seek information in a nonaccusatory way. Remember, the most effective questions are constructed as a subtle command.

> **Example:**
>
> *Interviewer:*
> "Please tell me about _____."
> "Please tell me about your current job procedures."
> "Please tell me what paperwork you are responsible for."
> "Please explain the chain of command in your department."
>
> "Please tell me what procedures are in effect to prevent errors in the paperwork."
> "Please explain what you understand to be the system of checks and balances (or internal controls) in your department."
> "Please explain where you see areas that need to be improved in the system of checks and balances in your department."

Once respondents answer open questions, you can go back and review the facts in greater detail. If the answers are inconsistent, try to clarify them. But do not challenge the honesty or integrity of respondents at this point.

## APPROACH SENSITIVE QUESTIONS CAREFULLY

Words such as "routine questions" play down the significance of the inquiry. It is important for information-gathering purposes that you do not react excessively to respondents' statements. In the following example, the interviewer is talking to a potential witness, and has decided to bring up the sensitive topic of a possible defalcation within the company. Several initial approaches could be used.

> **Example:**
>
> *Interviewer:*
> "Part of my job is to prevent and uncover waste, fraud, and abuse. You understand that, don't you?"
>      OR
>
> "Please tell me where you think the company is wasting assets or money."
>      OR
> "Where do you think the company is vulnerable to someone here abusing his or her position?"

## Dealing with Resistance

It is always possible that respondents will refuse a request for an interview. When respondent and interviewer have no connection, studies show that as many as 65 percent of the respondents will refuse an interview if contacted first by telephone. In contrast, one study concluded that only a third of respondents are reluctant to be interviewed when contacted in person.[3] The more unpleasant the topic, the more likely respondents are to refuse.

Inexperienced interviewers sometimes perceive resistance when there is none. As a result, interviewers frequently become defensive. You must overcome such feelings to complete the interview. Here are some examples of resistance you will encounter and how to try to overcome it.

*"I'm Too Busy."* When you contact a respondent without a previous appointment, the respondent may be too busy at the moment to cooperate. "I'm too busy" is also used to disguise the real source of the person's resistance, which may be lethargy, ego threat, or dislike of talking to strangers. Such objections can be overcome if you stress the following:

- The interview will be short.
- You are already there.
- The project is important.
- The interview will not be difficult.
- You need help.

*"I Don't Know Anything About It."* You will sometimes get this response immediately after stating the purpose of the interview. This resistance is typically softened by accepting the statement, and then returning with a question. For example, if the respondent says, "I don't know anything," a typical response would be:

| *Example:* | |
|---|---|
| *Interviewer:* <br> "I see. What do your duties involve, then?" | OR <br> "Well, that was one of the things I wanted to find out. Do you know about internal controls, then?" |

*"I Don't Remember."* This expression is not always one of resistance. Instead, it can also express modesty, tentativeness, or caution. One of the best ways to respond here is to simply remain silent while the person deliberates. He or she is saying, in effect, "Give me a moment to think." If this approach is not successful, you can then counter by posing a narrower question.

| *Example:* | |
|---|---|
| *Interviewer:* <br> "I understand you may not remember the entire transaction. Do you remember if it was over $10,000?" | OR <br> "It's okay if you don't remember the details. Do you remember how it made you react at the time?" |

*"What Do You Mean by That?"* When respondents ask this question, they may be signaling mild resistance. That is, they are attempting to shift the attention from themselves to you. They may also be stalling for time while they deliberate. Alternatively, they really may not understand your question. The best approach here is to treat the question as a simple request for clarification. Do not become defensive; to do so generally escalates the resistance.

## Difficult People

Interviewers invariably encounter a few difficult people. Here are five commonsense steps to take with such individuals.

*Don't React.* Sometimes respondents give interviewers a "hard time" for no apparent reason. In reality, people may refuse to cooperate for a multitude of reasons. The three natural reactions for interviewers who are verbally assailed by respondents are to strike back, give in, or terminate the interview. *Don't do them.* These tactics are not satisfactory; they do not lead to productive interviews. Instead, you should consciously ensure that you do not react to respondents' anger with hostility.

*Disarm the Person.* A common mistake is to try to reason with unreceptive people. Don't! Try instead to disarm them. Your best tactic is surprise. Stonewalling respondents *expect* you to apply pressure; attacking respondents *expect* you to resist. Disarming them surprises them—so simply listen, acknowledge the point, and agree wherever you can.

*Change Tactics.* In some situations, changing tactics is the only viable option to reduce hostility. It means recasting what respondents say in a form that directs attention back to the problem and to both your interests. In this case, you would ask respondents what they would do to solve the problem.

*Make It Easy to Say "Yes."* In negotiating with difficult people, interviewers usually make a statement and attempt to get respondents to agree with it. A better choice is to agree with one of *their* statements and go from there. It is also better to break statements into smaller ones that are harder to disagree with. This approach helps the difficult person save face.

*Make it Hard to Say "No."* You can make it difficult to say no by asking reality-based (what-if) questions. These questions get respondents to think of the consequences of not agreeing.

| | |
|---|---|
| *Example:* | |
| *Interviewer:* "What do you think will happen if we don't agree? | "What do you think I will have to do from here?" |
| | "What will you do?" |

## Volatile Interviews

*Volatile interviews* have the potential to elicit strong emotional reactions in respondents. Volatile interviews typically involve close friends and relatives of suspects, co-conspirators, and similar individuals.

The personalities of those involved in volatile interviews vary. Some individuals resent *all* authority figures; fraud examiners and law enforcement officers are authority figures.

### PHYSICAL SYMPTOMS

In volatile interviews, respondents typically react first—they don't think first. And they are frequently openly hostile to interviewers. People with high emotions often have dry mouths, so they tend to lick their lips and swallow more frequently than normal. Throat clearing is another audible sign of emotion. Restlessness shows in fidgeting, shifting in the chair, and foot-tapping. Persons under emotional stress frequently perspire more heavily.

Under stress, our complexion sometimes changes. We look red or flushed, or appear paler than normal. During stress, our heart beats more frequently; keen observers can actually see the carotid artery pulsate. (The carotid artery is the large artery on each side of the neck.) If in normal situations we maintain eye contact, we are probably under stress when we avoid eye contact. Note, however, that these symptoms are not present in all emotional situations.

### OTHER CONSIDERATIONS

It is best to use two interviewers in potentially volatile situations—based on the idea of strength in numbers. Additionally, two interviewers serve as corroborating witnesses in the event the interview takes a turn for the worse. Although you will still need to obtain information regarding who, what, why, when, where, and how, the order of the questioning varies from other types of interviews.

Use surprise in potentially volatile interviews. In many instances, volatile respondents are unaware that they are going to be questioned, and will therefore be off guard. If you don't use surprise, you run the risk of the respondent not showing up, bringing a witness, or being present with coworkers or even counsel. In these interviews, ask questions out of sequence. This approach keeps volatile respondents from knowing exactly the nature of the inquiry, and where it is leading. Although you will endeavor to obtain information regarding who, what, why, when, where, and how, ask your questions out of order. This technique is especially important in situations where respondents are attempting to protect themselves.

Hypothetical questions are less threatening and are therefore ideally suited for potentially volatile interviews. For example, suppose you are interviewing a suspect's boyfriend about his knowledge of her activities. Asking *"Did she do it?"* is a direct question. Instead, pose it as a hypothetical: *"Is there any reason why she would have done it?"*

## OVERCOMING OBJECTIONS

Volatile witnesses voice numerous objections to being interviewed. Here are some of the most common objections (along with suggested responses):

---

*Example:*

*Respondent:*
"I don't want to be involved."

*Interviewer:*
Point out that you would not be there, asking questions, if the respondent were not involved. Tell them that you are saving them trouble by discussing the matter "informally." (Do *not* say "off the record" —this phrase can cause legal problems with the information.)

*Respondent:*
"Why should I talk to you?"

*Interviewer:*
Say that you are trying to clear up a problem, and that the respondent's assistance is important.

*Respondent:*
"You can't prove that!"

*Interviewer:*
Tell the person that you are not trying to prove or disprove; you are simply gathering information.

*Respondent:*
"You can't make me talk!"

*Interviewer:*
Tell the person that you are not trying to make them do anything; you are trying to resolve a problem, and would deeply appreciate help.

---

# Assessment Questions

*Assessment questions* seek to establish the credibility of the respondent. They are used only when interviewers decide previous statements by respondents are inconsistent because of possible deception.

Once respondents answer all relevant questions about the event, and you have reason to believe they are being deceptive, establish a theme to justify additional questions. This theme can ordinarily be put forth by saying, *"I have a few additional questions."* Do not indicate in any way that these questions are for a purpose other than seeking information.

## NORMING OR CALIBRATING

*Norming or calibrating* is the process of observing behavior before critical questions are asked, as opposed to doing so during the questioning. Norming should be a routine part of all interviews. People with truthful attitudes answer questions one way; those with untruthful attitudes generally answer them differently. Assessment questions ask for agreement on matters that are against the principles of most honest people. In other words, dishonest people are likely to agree with many of the statements, while honest people won't.

Assessment questions are designed primarily to get verbal or nonverbal reactions from respondents. Interviewers then carefully assess their reactions. Suggestions for observing the verbal and physical behavior of respondents include the following:

- Use your senses of touch, sight, and hearing to establish a norm.
- Do not stare or call attention to the person's behavior.
- Be aware of the respondent's entire body.
- Observe the timing and consistency of behavior.
- Note clusters of behaviors.

On the basis of respondents' reactions to the assessment questions, interviewers then consider all the verbal and nonverbal responses together (not in isolation) to decide whether to proceed to the admission-seeking phase of the interview. Don't rely too heavily on the results of the assessment questioning.

## The Physiology of Deception

It is said that everyone lies and that we do so for one of two reasons: to receive rewards or to avoid punishment. In most people, lying produces stress. Our body attempts to relieve this stress (even in practiced liars) through verbal and nonverbal reactions.

Conclusions concerning behavior must be tempered by a number of factors. The physical environment in which the interview is conducted can affect behavior. If respondents are comfortable, fewer behavior quirks may be exhibited. The more intelligent the respondent, the more reliable the verbal and nonverbal clues. If the respondent is biased toward the interviewer, or vice versa, it will affect behavior. Stress-produced behaviors range from subtle to obvious.

Persons who are mentally unstable or who are under the influence of drugs will usually be unsuitable to interview. Because professional pathological liars are often familiar with interview techniques, they are less likely to furnish observable behavioral clues. Behavior cues of juveniles are generally unreliable. Carefully note racial, ethnic, and economic factors. Some cultures, for example, discourage looking directly at someone. Cultures use specific body languages that can be (and often are) misinterpreted by people from other cultures.

### Verbal Clues

Verbal clues are those relating to wordings, expressions, and responses to specific questions. They are also numerous; here are a few examples.

*Changes in Speech Patterns.* During deception, people often speed up or slow down their speech, or speak louder. They may change voice pitch; as we become tense, our vocal chords constrict. People also tend to cough or clear their throats during deception.

*Repetition of the Question.* Liars frequently repeat questions to gain more time to think of answers. Deceptive individuals will say, *"What was that again?"* or use similar language.

*Comments Regarding Interview.* Deceptive people often complain about the physical environment of the interview room, such as *"It's cold in here."* They also sometimes ask how much longer the interview will take.

*Selective Memory.* Deceptive people often have a fine memory for insignificant events, but when it comes to the important facts, they "just can't seem to remember."

*Making Excuses.* Dishonest people frequently make excuses about things that look bad for them, such as *"I'm always nervous; don't pay any attention to that."* Or they might say, *"Everybody does it."*

*Oaths.* On frequent occasions, dishonest people will add what they believe to be credibility to their lies by use of emphasis. That is, they use such expressions as *"I swear to God,"* or *"Honestly,"* or *"Frankly,"* or *"To tell the truth."*

*Character Testimony.* Liars often request that interviewers *"Check with my wife,"* or *"Talk to my minister."* This statement is made to add credibility to the false statement.

***Answering with a Question.*** Rather than deny the allegations outright, liars frequently answer with questions like *"Why would I do something like that?"* As a variation, deceptive people sometimes question the interview procedure by asking, *"Why are you picking on me?"*

***Overuse of Respect.*** Some deceptive people go out of their way to be respectful and friendly. When accused of wrongdoing, it is unnatural for a person to react in a friendly and respectful manner.

***Increasingly Weaker Denials.*** When honest people are accused of something they haven't done, they often become angry or forceful in their denial. The more they are accused, the more forceful their denial. Dishonest people, on the other hand, tend to "deny weakly." Upon repeated accusations, dishonest people's denials become weaker, to the point where they finally become silent.

***Specific Denials.*** Dishonest people are more likely to be specific in their denials. An honest person offers a simple and resounding *"no,"* whereas dishonest people "qualify" the denial: *"No, I did not steal $15,000 from the Company on June 27."* Other qualified denial phrases include, *"To the best of my memory,"* and *"As far as I recall,"* or similar language.

***Fewer Emotionally Charged Words.*** Liars often avoid emotionally provocative terms such as "steal," "lie," and "crime." Instead, they prefer "soft" words such as "borrow," and "it" (referring to the deed in question).

***Refusal to Implicate Other Suspects.*** Both honest respondents and liars have a natural reluctance to name others involved in misdeeds. However, liars frequently continue to refuse to implicate possible suspects, no matter how much pressure is applied by interviewers. Why? Because doing so narrows the circle of suspicion.

***Tolerance for Shady Conduct.*** Dishonest people typically have tolerant attitudes toward miscreant conduct. For example, if interviewers in a theft case ask, *"What should happen to this person when he is caught?"* honest people will usually say, *"They should be fired/prosecuted."* Dishonest people, on the other hand, are much more likely to reply, *"How should I know?"* or *"Maybe he is a good employee who got into problems. Perhaps he should be given a second chance."*

***Reluctance to Terminate Interview.*** Dishonest people are generally more reluctant to terminate interviews. They want to convince interviewers that they are not responsible, so that the investigation will not continue. Honest people generally have no such reluctance.

***Feigned Unconcern.*** Dishonest people often try to appear casual and unconcerned and frequently adopt an unnatural slouching posture. Additionally, they may react to questions with nervous or false laughter or feeble attempts at humor. Honest people typically are concerned about being suspected of wrongdoing, and treat the interviewer's questions seriously.

## Nonverbal Clues

Nonverbal clues to deception include various body movements and postures accompanying the verbal reply. Here are a few:

***Full Body Motions.*** When asked sensitive or emotional questions, dishonest people typically change posture completely—as if moving away from the interviewer. Honest people frequently lean forward toward the interviewer when questions are serious.

***Anatomical Physical Responses.*** Anatomical physical responses are our body's involuntary reactions to fright, such as increased heart rate, shallow or labored breathing, or excessive perspiration. These reactions are typical of dishonest persons accused of wrongdoing.

***Illustrators.*** "Illustrators" are motions made primarily with hands to demonstrate points when talking. During nonthreatening questions, illustrators are done at one rate. During threatening questions, illustrators may increase or decrease.

***Hands Over the Mouth.*** Frequently, dishonest people cover their mouths with their hand or fingers during deception. This reaction goes back to childhood, when many children cover their mouths when telling a lie. It is done subconsciously to "conceal" the statement.

***Manipulators.*** "Manipulators" are motions such as picking lint from clothing, playing with objects such as pencils, or holding one's hands while talking. Manipulators are displacement activities to reduce nervousness.

*Fleeing Positions.* During the interview, dishonest people often posture themselves in a "fleeing position." That is, the head and trunk may face the interviewer, but the feet and lower portion of the body point toward the door. This position indicates an unconscious effort to flee.

*Crossing the Arms.* Crossing one's arms over the middle zones of the body is a classic defensive reaction to difficult or uncomfortable questions. A variation is crossing the feet under the chair and locking them. These crossing motions occur mostly when being deceptive.

*Reaction to Evidence.* Although they try to appear outwardly unconcerned, guilty people have a keen interest in implicating evidence. Therefore, dishonest people often look at documents presented by interviewers, attempt to be casual about observing them, and then shove them away, as if wanting nothing to do with the evidence.

*Lip Movements.* Genuine smiles usually involve the whole mouth; false ones are confined to the upper half. In deception, people tend to smirk rather than to smile. Most actions that interrupt the flow of speech are stress-related. Examples include:

- Closing the mouth tightly
- Pursing lips
- Covering the mouth with the hand
- Lip and tongue biting
- Licking the lips
- Chewing on objects

## Methodology of Assessment Questions

If, based on all factors, you doubt the honesty of respondents, you can ask the following assessment questions. Note that these questions build from least sensitive to most sensitive. The initial questions seek agreement. Obviously, not all questions are asked in all situations.

In the following example, an interviewer is investigating missing funds. During a routine interview of one employee, the respondent makes several factually incorrect statements. The examiner then decides to ask a series of assessment questions and observe the answers. Here is how the interviewer starts the questioning:

---

### ASSESSMENT QUESTION 1:

*Interviewer:*
"The company is particularly concerned about fraud and abuse. There are some new laws in effect that will cost the company millions if abuses go on and we don't try to find them. Do you know which law I'm talking about?"

*Explanation:*
Most individuals do not know about the laws concerning corporate sentencing guidelines, and will therefore answer "no." The purpose of this question is to get the respondent to understand the serious nature of fraud and abuse.

### ASSESSMENT QUESTION 2:

*Interviewer:*
"Congress recently passed a law that allows for the levy of fines against companies that don't try to clean their own houses. Besides, when people take things from the company, it can cost a lot of money, so you can understand why the company's concerned, can't you?"

*Explanation:*
The majority of persons will say "yes" to this question. In the event of a no answer, you should explain the issue fully and, thereafter, attempt to get the respondent's agreement. If that agreement is not forthcoming, you should assess why not.

### ASSESSMENT QUESTION 3:

*Interviewer:*
"Of course, they are not talking about a loyal employee who gets in a bind. They're talking more about someone who is dishonest. But a lot of times, it's average people who get involved in taking something from the company. Do you know the kind of person we're talking about?"

*Explanation:*
Most people read the newspapers and are at least generally familiar with the problem of fraud and abuse. Agreement by the respondent is expected to this question.

## ASSESSMENT QUESTION 4:

*Interviewer:*
"Most of these people aren't criminals at all. A lot of times, they're just trying to save their jobs or just trying to get by because the company is so cheap that it won't pay people what they're worth. Do you know what I mean?"

*Explanation:*
Although both honest and dishonest people will probably answer yes to this question, honest people are less likely to accept the premise that these people are not wrongdoers. Many honest people will reply, *"Yes, I understand, but that doesn't justify stealing."*

## ASSESSMENT QUESTION 5:

*Interviewer:*
"Why do you think someone around here might be justified in taking company property?"

*Explanation:*
Because fraud perpetrators frequently justify their acts, dishonest people are more likely than honest ones to attempt a justification such as, *"Everyone does it,"* or *"The company should treat people better if they don't want them to steal."* Honest people, on the other hand, are much more likely to say, *"There is no justification for stealing from the company. It is dishonest."*

## ASSESSMENT QUESTION 6:

*Interviewer:*
"How do you think we should deal with someone who got in a bind and did something wrong in the eyes of the company?"

*Explanation:*
Similar to other questions in this series, honest people want to "throw the book" at the miscreant. Culpable individuals typically say, *"How should I know? It's not up to me,"* or, *"If they were a good employee, maybe we should give them another chance."*

## ASSESSMENT QUESTION 7:

*Interviewer:*
"Do you think someone in your department might have taken something from the company because that person thought he or she was justified?"

*Explanation:*
Most people—honest and dishonest—answer no to this question. However, the culpable person will more likely say yes without elaborating. Honest people, if answering yes, usually provide details.

## ASSESSMENT QUESTION 8:

*Interviewer:*
"Have you ever felt yourself—even though you didn't go through with it—justified in taking advantage of your position?"

*Explanation:*
Again, most people, both honest and dishonest, will answer no. However, dishonest people are more likely to acknowledge having at least "thought" of doing it.

## ASSESSMENT QUESTION 9:

*Interviewer:*
"Who in your department do you feel would think they were justified in doing something against the company?"

*Explanation:*
Dishonest people usually don't answer this question, saying instead that, *"I guess anyone could have a justification if they wanted to."* Honest people may name names—albeit reluctantly.

## ASSESSMENT QUESTION 10:

*Interviewer:*
"Do you believe that most people will tell their manager if they believed a colleague was doing something wrong, like committing fraud against the company?"

*Explanation:*
Honest people have a sense of integrity and are much more likely to report misdeeds. Dishonest people are more likely to say no. When pressed for an explanation, they typically

say, *"No, nothing would be done about it, and they wouldn't believe me anyhow."*

### ASSESSMENT QUESTION 11:

*Interviewer:*
"Is there any reason why someone who works with you would say they thought you might feel justified in doing something wrong?"

*Explanation:*
This question is designed to place the thought in the mind of a wrongdoer that someone has named him or her as a suspect. Honest people typically say no. Dishonest people are more likely to try to explain by saying something like, *"I know there are people around here who don't like me."*

### ASSESSMENT QUESTION 12:

*Interviewer:*
"What would concern you most if you did something wrong and it was found out?"

*Explanation:*
Dishonest people are likely to say something like, *"I wouldn't want to go to jail."* Honest people often reject the notion by saying, *"I'm not concerned at all, because I haven't done anything."* If an honest person does explain, it is usually along the lines of disappointing friends or family; dishonest people often mention punitive measures.

## Closing Questions

Closing the interview on a positive note is a must in informational interviews. Closings serve several purposes. First, it is not unusual for interviewers to misunderstand or misinterpret statements of respondents. Therefore, interviewers should go over key facts to make certain they are accurate. The closing questions phase also seeks to obtain facts previously unknown. It provides respondents further opportunity to say whatever they want about the matter at hand. When you wind down an interview, be sure to do so positively so that you can call the person back and so that they will not feel that you represent a threat when you want to talk to them the second time.

If appropriate, ask whether they know of any other documents or witnesses that would be helpful to the case. Do not promise confidentiality; instead, say, *"I'll keep your name as quiet as possible."*

People being interviewed often do not volunteer additional information regarding other witnesses or evidence. The theme, therefore, is to provide respondents opportunities to furnish further relevant facts or opinions. At the conclusion, attempt to determine which facts provided by the respondent are the most relevant. Do not go over all the information a second time.

### CLOSING QUESTION 1:

*Interviewer:*
"I want to make sure I have my information straight. Let me take a minute and summarize what we've discussed."

*Tip:*
Go over each of the key facts in summary form. The questions should be closed, so that the witness can respond either yes or no.

### CLOSING QUESTION 2:

*Interviewer:*
"You have known her for eight years, correct?"

OR
"You knew she had some financial problems, is that right?"

OR
"You suspect—but don't know for sure—that she paid a lot of past due bills recently. Is that correct?"

*Tip:*
On absolutely vital facts provided by the respondent, add *"Are you sure?"*

### CLOSING QUESTION 3:

*Interviewer:*
"Are you sure?"

*Tip:*
To obtain additional facts, ask respondents they would like to say anything else. This question gives the correct impression that you are interested in all relevant information, regardless of which side it favors. Try to actively involve respondents in helping solve the case—*"If you were trying to resolve this issue, what would you do?"* This technique is sometimes called "playing detective." Another excellent closing question is, *"Is there anything that I haven't asked you that you think would be worth[while] me asking you, that might be necessary in trying to figure this out?"*

*Tip:*
Ask respondents whether they have been treated fairly. It is especially helpful to ask this question when respondents have not been cooperative, or at the conclusion of an admission-seeking interview. Ask the question as if it were perfunctory. Ask if the respondent has anything else to say. It gives the respondent one final time to make a statement. Also ask if you can call with any additional questions. It leaves the door open to additional cooperation.

*Tip:*
Leave the respondent a business card or a telephone number. Invite the respondent to call about anything relevant. In some cases, try to obtain a commitment that the respondent will not discuss the matter. This step is not recommended with adverse or hostile respondents—it gives them ideas. Here is an example of the proper approach.

### CLOSING QUESTION 4:

*Interviewer:*
"In situations like this one, people's reputations can suffer because of rumor and innuendo. We don't want that to happen and neither do you. Therefore, I'd like your cooperation. Can I count on you not to discuss this until all the facts are out?"

*Tip:*
Shake hands with respondents, and thank them for their time and information.

## Admission-Seeking Questions

Interviewers should ask accusatory or *admission-seeking questions* only when a reasonable probability exists that the respondent has committed the act in question. An assessment of culpability can be based on verbal and nonverbal responses to interview questions, as well as documents, physical evidence, and other interviews and evidence.

A transitional theme is necessary when you proceed from assessment to admission-seeking questions. The purpose of this theme is to suggest to miscreants that they have been caught. In ideal circumstances, you would leave the room for a few minutes, to "check on something." If you have incriminating documents, place copies of them in a folder and bring them back to the room. If no documents exist, you might even fill the file folder with blank paper. When you return to the room, place the file folder on the desk, and ask,

*Example:*

*Interviewer:*
"Is there something that you would like to tell me about _____?"

OR
"Is there any reason why someone would say that you _____?"

Hand the documents to the respondent and ask for "comments." Do not introduce the evidence or explain it. In many cases, the miscreant will admit to incriminating conduct on the spot. If not, proceed.

## Purpose of Questions

Admission-seeking questions have at least two purposes. The first purpose is to distinguish innocent persons from guilty ones. Culpable individuals frequently confess during the admission-seeking phase of interviews, while innocent people do not do so unless threats or coercion are used. In some instances, the only way to differentiate the culpable from the innocent is to seek an admission of guilt.

The second purpose is to obtain a valid confession. Confessions, under the law, must be voluntarily obtained. The importance of a valid and binding confession to wrongdoing cannot be overstated. Finally, the confessor should be asked to sign a written statement acknowledging the facts. Although oral confessions are as legally as binding as written ones, written statements have greater credibility. They also discourage miscreants from later recanting.

## Preparation

Schedule interviews when you can control the situation. Normally do not conduct them on the suspect's "turf"; they are also best conducted by surprise.

*Interview Room.* The location should establish a sense of privacy. The door should be closed but not locked, with no physical barriers that prevent the target from leaving. This precaution avoids allegations of "custodial interrogation"—that you held someone against his or her will.

Keep distractions to a minimum. Ideally, no photographs, windows, or other objects should be present to distract attention. Place chairs about six feet apart, and do not permit the accused to sit behind a desk. As stated, this arrangement prevents establishing a psychological barrier the accused can "hide behind." Notes taken during the interview should be done in a way that does not reveal their significance.

*Presence of Outsiders.* Do not suggest to the accused that he or she have counsel present. Of course, this right cannot be denied. If counsel is present, you should have an understanding that he or she is an observer only; attorneys should not ask questions or object. Other than the accused and two examiners, no other observers are usually permitted in admission-seeking interviews. If the accused is a union member, a union representative may have the right to attend. However, this situation can present legal problems because it "broadcasts" the allegation to a third party. It is difficult to obtain a confession with witnesses present. Examiners should therefore consider whether the case can be proven without a confession. If so, they may choose to omit the admission-seeking interview altogether.

*Miranda Warnings.* Private investigators are not required to give Miranda warnings. Police are required to use them only if an arrest is imminent following the interview. Confessions are generally admissible in court if (1) they are obtained voluntarily, and (2) interviewers have a reasonable belief that the confession is true. Always check with counsel.

## Theme Development

People rarely confess voluntarily. However, they tend to confess when they perceive that the benefits of confession outweigh the penalties. Good interviewers, through the application of sophisticated techniques, can often convince respondents that a confession is in their best interest.

People generally will not confess if they believe that doubt remains in the mind of the accuser as to their guilt. Thus, you must convey absolute confidence in the admission-seeking accusation—even if not fully convinced. Make the accusation as a statement of fact. Accusatory questions do not ask, *"Did you do it?"* They ask, *"Why did you do it?"* Here are examples of an accusatory question:

> *Is this the first time that you have taken from the company?*
> *Is this the first time you have created an overdraft?*

Innocent people generally do not accept this question's premise. People confessing need adequate time to come to terms with their guilt; obtaining admissions and confessions takes patience. Therefore, admission-seeking interviews should be done only with sufficient privacy and when time is not a factor. Do not express disgust, outrage, or moral condemnation about the confessor's actions. To do so goes against the basic strategy in obtaining confessions, which can be summed up as *maximize sympathy and minimize the perception of moral wrongdoing.*

Offer a morally acceptable reason for the confessor's behavior. Do not convey to accused that they are "bad people." Guilty people almost never confess under such conditions. Be firm, but also project compassion, understanding, and sympathy. Endeavor to keep the confessor from voicing a denial. Once the accused denies the act, overcoming that position will be difficult.

It is generally considered legal to accuse innocent people of misdeeds they did not commit *as long as* the following holds:

- The accuser has reasonable suspicion or predication to believe the accused has committed an offense.
- The accusation is made under conditions of privacy.
- The accuser does not take any action likely to make an innocent person confess.
- The accusation is conducted under reasonable conditions.

But ALWAYS check with counsel.

## Steps in the Admission-Seeking Interview

Effective admission-seeking interviews proceed in an orderly fashion. What follows is generally accepted as most likely to succeed in obtaining confessions. That said, the order always depends on the circumstances.

*Accuse Directly.* The accusation should not be a question, but a statement. Avoid emotionally charged words such as *steal*, *fraud*, and *crime* in your accusations. Phrase the accusation so that the accused is psychologically "trapped," with no way out.

| *Direct Accusations* | |
|---|---|
| **WRONG** | **RIGHT** |
| "We have reason to believe that you . . ." OR "We think (suspect) you may have . . ." | "Our investigation has clearly established that you: <br>• made a false entry (*avoid* "fraud"). <br>• took company assets without permission (*avoid using* "theft," "embezzlement," *or* "stealing"). <br>• took money from a vendor (*avoid* "bribe" *or* "kickback"). <br>• have not told the complete truth (*avoid* "lie" *or* "fraud"). <br>  OR <br>"We have been conducting an investigation into _____, and you are clearly the only person we have not been able to eliminate as being responsible." |

*Observe Reaction.* When accused of wrongdoing, some miscreants react with silence. If the accused does deny culpability, these denials are often weak. They may almost mumble their denial. It is common for culpable individuals to avoid outright denials. Rather, they give reasons why they could not have committed the act in question. Innocent people will sometimes react with genuine shock at being accused. It is not at all unusual for an innocent person, wrongfully accused, to react with anger. As opposed to guilty people, innocent people strongly deny carrying out the act or acts in question.

*Repeat Accusation.* If the accused does not strenuously object to the accusation, repeat it with the same degree of conviction and strength.

*Interrupt Denials.* Both truthful and untruthful people will normally object to the accusation and attempt denial. It is important in instances where you are convinced of the individual's guilt that the denial be interrupted. Innocent people are unlikely to allow you to succeed in stopping their denial.

It is important to emphasize that both the innocent and culpable will make outright denials if forced to do so. Accordingly, interviewers should not solicit a denial at this stage of the admission-seeking interview.

---

*Interrupting Denials*
**WRONG**
"Did you do this?"
    OR
"Are you the responsible person?"

**RIGHT**
"Why did you do this?"

---

*Delays.* Delaying tactics are effective ways to stop or interrupt denials. Do not argue with the accused, but rather attempt to delay the outright denial.

---

*Example:*

*Interviewer:*
"I hear what you are saying, but let me finish first. Then you can talk."

---

Innocent people will usually not "hold on" or let you continue to develop this theme.

*Interruptions.* Occasionally, you may have to interrupt the accused's attempted denials repeatedly. Because this stage is crucial, be prepared to increase the tone of your interruptions to the point where you say, *"If you keep interrupting, I am going to have to terminate this conversation."* Guilty individuals find this type of statement threatening, because they want to know the extent of incriminating evidence in your possession, and your terminating the interview blocks this possibility.

*Reasoning.* If the preceding techniques are unsuccessful, you may attempt to reason with the accused, and employ some of the tactics normally used for refuting alibis (discussed later). In this situation, you present the accused with some of the evidence that implicates them. Do not disclose *all* the facts, but rather only small portions here and there.

*Establish Rationalization.* Once the accusation has been made, repeated, and the denials stopped, it is time to establish a morally acceptable rationalization that allows suspects to square their misdeeds with their conscience. This theme need not be related to the underlying causes of the misconduct. It is common and acceptable for suspects to explain away the moral consequences of the action by seizing on any plausible explanation other than being a "bad person."

If the accused do not seem to relate to one theme, continue on others until one seems to fit. Then develop that theme fully. Note that the theme explains away the moral—but not the legal—consequences of the misdeed. Interviewers are cautioned *not* to make any statements that would lead suspects to believe they will be excused from legal liability by cooperating. Interviewers must strike a balance between being in control of the interview and appearing compassionate and understanding. Again, no matter the conduct the accused has supposedly committed, never express shock, outrage, or condemnation.

*Unfair Treatment.* Probably the most common rationalization for criminal activity in general (and fraud in particular) is in fraudsters' attempts to achieve equity. Studies show that counterproductive employee behavior—including stealing—is motivated primarily by job dissatisfaction. Employees and others feel that "striking back" is important to their self-esteem. Sensitive interviewers capitalize on these feelings by suggesting to suspects that they are victims.

---

**Example:**

*Interviewer:*

"I feel like I know what makes you tick. And I know it isn't like you to do something like this without a reason. You've worked hard here to get a good reputation. I don't think the company has paid you what you're really worth. And that's the way you feel too, isn't it?"

OR

"I've seen situations like this before. And I think the company brought this on themselves. If you had been fairly treated, this wouldn't have happened, don't you agree?"

---

***Inadequate Recognition.*** Some employees feel that their efforts have gone completely without notice. As with similar themes, interviewers strive to be empathetic.

---

**Example:**

*Interviewer:*

"I've found out a few things about you. It looks to me that you've given a lot more to this

company than they recognize. Isn't that right?"

---

***Financial Problems.*** Internal criminals, especially executives and upper management, frequently engage in fraud to conceal their true financial condition—either personal or business.

***Aberration of Conduct.*** Many miscreants believe their conduct constitutes an aberration in their lives, and that it does not represent their true character. You can establish this theme using the following statements:

---

**Example:**

*Interviewer:*

"I know this is totally out of character for you. I know that this would never have happened if something wasn't going on in your life. Isn't that right?"

OR

"You've worked hard all your life to get a good reputation. I don't believe you would normally do something like this; it just doesn't fit. You must have felt forced into it. You felt forced, didn't you?"

---

***Family Problems.*** Some people commit fraud because of family problems—financial woes caused by divorce, an unfaithful spouse, or demanding children. Men especially—who may be socially conditioned to tie their masculinity to earning power—sometimes hold the notion that wealth garners respect. For their part, women often commit white-collar crime in response to the needs of their husbands and children. Skillful interviewers convert this motive to their advantage using one of the following approaches:

---

**Example:**

*Interviewer:*

"I know you've had some family problems. I know your recent divorce has been difficult for you. And I know how it is when these problems occur. You would have never done this if it hadn't been for family problems, isn't that right?"

OR

"Someone in your position and with your ethics just doesn't do things like this without a reason. And I think that reason has to do with trying to make the best possible life for your family. I know it would be difficult for me to admit to my family that we're not as well off as we were last year. And that's why you did this, isn't it?"

---

*Accuser's Actions.* Don't disclose the accuser's identity if it is not already known. But in cases where the accuser's identity is known to the suspects, it is sometimes helpful to blame the accuser for the problem. The accuser can be a colleague, manager, auditor, fraud examiner, or any similar person, or the problem can be blamed on the company.

---

*Example:*

*Interviewer:*

"You know what these auditors are like. They are hired to turn over every stone. I wonder how they would look if we put *them* under a microscope. Compared to other things that are going on, what you've done isn't that bad. Right?"

OR

"I really blame a large part of this on the company. If some of the things that went on around this company were known, it would make what you've done seem pretty small in comparison, wouldn't it?"

---

*Stress, Drugs, Alcohol.* Employees sometimes turn to drugs or alcohol to reduce stress. In some instances, the stress itself leads to aberrant behavior. The following rationalizations can work in these situations:

---

*Example:*

*Interviewer:*

"I know what you've done isn't really you. Inside, you've been in a lot of turmoil. A lot of people drink too much when they have problems. I have been through periods like that myself. And when things build up inside, it sometimes makes all of us do things we shouldn't. That's what happened here, isn't it?"

OR

"You're one of the most respected men in this company. I know you have been under tremendous pressure to succeed. Too much pressure, really. There is only so much any of us can take. That's behind what has happened here, isn't it?"

---

*Revenge.* Similar to other themes, revenge can also be effectively developed as a motive. In this technique, you attempt to blame the offense on suspects' feelings that they must "get back" at someone or something.

---

*Example:*

*Interviewer:*

"What has happened is out of character for you. I think you were trying to get back at your supervisor for the time he passed you over for a raise. I would probably feel the same. That's what happened, isn't it?"

OR

"Everyone around here knows that the board has not supported you in your efforts to turn this company around. I would understand if you said to yourself, 'I'll show them.' Isn't that what happened?"

---

*Depersonalizing the Victim.* In cases involving employee theft, an effective technique is to depersonalize the victim. Suspects are better able to cope with the moral dilemma of their actions if the victim is a faceless corporation or agency.

| **Example:** | OR |
|---|---|
| *Interviewer:* | "It's not like what you've done has really hurt one person. Maybe you thought of it this way: 'At most, I've cost each shareholder a few cents.' Isn't that the way it was?" |
| "It isn't like you took something from a friend or neighbor. I can see how you could say, 'Well, this would be okay to do as long as it was against the company, and not my coworkers.' Isn't that right?" | |

**Minor Moral Infraction.** In many cases, interviewers can reduce the accused's perception of the moral seriousness of the matter. To state again for emphasis, the moral aspect is *not* to be confused with the legal seriousness of the act. Successful fraud examiners and interviewers avoid making statements that can be construed as relieving the accused of their legal responsibility. For example, do not state: *"It is not a big deal, legally. It's just a technical violation."* Instead, play down the moral side. One effective way is through comparisons.

| **Example:** | OR |
|---|---|
| *Interviewer:* | "Everything is relative. What you've done doesn't even come close to some of the other things that have happened. You're not Ivan Boesky, right?" |
| "This problem we have doesn't mean you're 'Jack the Ripper.' When you compare what you've done to things other people do, this situation seems pretty insignificant, doesn't it?" | OR |
| | "I could see myself in your place. I probably would have done the same thing." |

**Altruism.** The moral seriousness of the matter can in many cases be deflected by claiming the action was for the benefit of others, especially if accused view themselves as caring people.

| **Example:** | OR |
|---|---|
| *Interviewer:* | "You have a big responsibility in this company. A lot of people depend on you for their jobs. I just know you did this because you thought you were doing the right thing for the company, didn't you?" |
| "I know you didn't do this for yourself. I have looked into this matter carefully, and I think you did this to help someone, didn't you?" | |

**Genuine Need.** In a very small number of cases, fraud is predicated by genuine need. For example, the accused may be paying for the medical care of sick parents or a child. Or some other financial disaster has befallen the miscreant. In these situations, the following statements can be effective:

| **Example:** | OR |
|---|---|
| *Interviewer:* | "You're like everyone else: you have to put food on the table. But in your position, it is very difficult to ask for help. You genuinely needed to do this to survive, didn't you?" |
| "I don't know many people who've had so many bad things happen all at once. I can see where you thought this was pretty much a matter of life or death, right?" | |

## Refute Alibis

Even if suspects are presented with an appropriate rationalization, they often continue to deny culpability. When interviewers succeed in stopping the denials, the accused will then normally turn to various reasons why they could not have committed the act in question. The purpose here is to convince the accused of the weight of the evidence against them. Miscreants usually have a keen interest in material that implicates them. Alibis can be generally refuted using one of the following methods.

*Display Physical Evidence.* Guilty people frequently overestimate the amount of physical evidence in the interviewer's possession. You want to reinforce this notion in the way you lay out the evidence. Therefore, display the physical evidence—usually documents in fraud matters—one piece at a time, in reverse order of importance. In this way, suspects do not immediately comprehend the full extent of the evidence. When they no longer deny culpability, stop displaying evidence.

Each time a document or piece of evidence is laid out, you should note its significance. During this phase, the accused are still trying to come to grips with being caught. Interviewers therefore expect that suspects will attempt to explain their way out of the situation. Like denials, it's best to stop the alibis and other falsehoods before they are fully articulated. Once alibis are shown to be false, you can return to the theme being developed.

*Discuss Witnesses.* Discussing the testimony of witnesses is another way to refute alibis. The objective here is to give enough information about what other people will say without providing too much information. Ideally, your statement creates the impression in suspects' minds that many people are in a position to contradict their story.

Interviewers are again cautioned about furnishing too much information so that suspects can identify witnesses. This places witnesses in a difficult position, and suspects may contact witnesses in an effort to influence testimony. Suspects sometimes take reprisals against potential witnesses, although only rarely.

---

*Example:*

*Respondent:*

"I couldn't possibly have done this. It would require the approval of a supervisor."

*Interviewer:*

"In normal situations it would. The problem is that your statement doesn't hold up. There are several people who will tell a completely different story. I can understand how you would want me to believe that. But you're only worsening the situation by making these statements. If you will help me on this, you'll also be helping yourself. Understand?"

---

*Discuss Deceptions.* The final technique is to discuss the accused's deceptions. The idea here is to appeal to their logic, not to scold or degrade. This technique is sometimes your only option if physical evidence is lacking. As with other interview situations, avoid the word *lying*.

*Present Alternatives.* After suspects' alibis have been refuted, they normally become quiet and withdrawn. Some people in this situation may cry. If so, comfort them. Do not discourage them from showing emotion. At this stage, suspects are deliberating about confessing. Interviewers at this point should present an alternative question to the accused. This question forces them to make one of two choices. One alternative allows the accused a morally acceptable reason for the misdeed; the other paints the accused in a negative light. Regardless of which answer suspects choose, they are acknowledging guilt.

---

*Example:*

*Interviewer:*

"Did you plan this deliberately, or did it just happen?"

    OR

"Did you just want extra money, or did you do this because you had financial problems?"

OR

"Did you just get greedy, or did you do this because of the way the company has treated you?"

---

*Benchmark Admission.* Either way suspects answer the alternative question—either yes or no—they have made a culpable statement, or *benchmark admission*. Once the benchmark admission is made, miscreants have made a subconscious decision to confess. The preceding questions are structured so that the negative alternative is presented first, followed by the positive one. In this way, suspects only have to nod or say "yes" for the benchmark admission to be made. They commonly answer in the negative.

| | |
|---|---|
| *Example:*<br>*Respondent:*<br>"I didn't do it deliberately."<br>　OR<br>"I didn't do it just because I wanted extra money." | OR<br>"No, I'm not just greedy." |

In the cases where suspects answer the alternative question in the negative, you should press further for a positive admission.

| | |
|---|---|
| *Example:*<br>*Interviewer:*<br>"Then it just happened on the spur of the moment?"<br>　OR<br>"Then you did it to take care of your financial problems?" | OR<br>"Then you did it because of the way you've been treated here?" |

Should the accused still not respond to the alternative question with the benchmark admission, repeat the questions, or variations thereof, until the benchmark admission is made. It is important that you get a response that is tantamount to a commitment to confess. Because only a commitment is sought at this point, the questions for the benchmark admission are constructed as leading questions. These questions can be answered yes or no; they do not require explanation. Explanations will come later.

*Reinforce Rationalization.* Once the benchmark admission is made, it is time to reinforce the confessor's decision. Then you can make the transition to the verbal confession, where the details of the offense are obtained. Reinforcing the rationalization developed earlier helps confessors feel comfortable, believing that you do not look down on them.

*Verbal Confession.* The transition to the verbal confession is made when suspects furnish the first detailed information about the offense. Thereafter, it is your job to probe gently for additional details—preferably including those that would be known only to the miscreant. As with any interview, three general approaches are used to obtain the details: chronologically, by transaction, or by event. The approach you take is governed by the circumstances of the case.

During the admission-seeking interview, it is best to first confirm the general details of the offense. For example, you will want the accused's estimates of the amounts involved, other parties to the offense, and the location of physical evidence. After these basic facts are confirmed, you can return to the specifics, in chronological order. It is imperative that you obtain an early admission that the accused knew that the conduct in question was wrong. This admission confirms the essential element of intent.

Because of the psychology underlying confessions, most confessors lie about one or more aspects of the offense, even as they confirm their overall guilt. When this happens during the verbal confession, make a mental note of the discrepancy and proceed as if you have accepted the falsehood as truthful. That is, save such discrepancies until the accused provides all other relevant facts. If the discrepancies are material to the offense, then you should either resolve them at the end of the verbal confession or wait and correct them in the written confession. If not material, such information can be omitted from the written confession.

The following items of information should be obtained during the verbal confession:

***The Accused Knew the Conduct Was Wrong.*** As stated, intent is required in all matters involving fraud. Not only must confessors have committed the act, they must have *intended* to commit it. This information can be developed as follows:

---

***Example:***

*Interviewer:*
"Now that you've decided to help yourself, I can help you too. I need to ask you some ques- | tions to get this cleared up. As I understand it, you did this, and you knew it was wrong, but you didn't really mean to hurt the company, is that right?"

---

***Facts Known Only to Confessor.*** Once intent is confirmed, questioning turns to those facts known only to the confessors. These facts include—at a minimum—their estimates of the number of instances of wrongful conduct as well as the total amount of money involved. The questions should not be phrased so that they can answer yes or no.

***Estimate of Number of Instances/Amounts.*** In fraud matters especially, it is common for suspects to underestimate the amount of funds involved, as well as the number of instances, probably because of our natural tendency to block out unpleasant matters. Take their figures with a grain of salt. If their response is "*I don't know,*" start high with the amounts and gradually come down.

---

***Example:***

*Interviewer:*
"How many times do you think this happened?"

*Respondent:*
"I don't have any idea."

*Interviewer:*
"Was it as many as 100 times?"

*Respondent:*
"No way!"

*Interviewer:*
"How about 75 times?"

*Respondent:*
"That's still too high. Probably not more than two or three times."

*Interviewer:*
"Are you pretty sure?" (If respondents' estimates are too low, gently get them to acknowledge a higher figure. But do not challenge the accused by calling them liars.)

*Respondent:*
"Maybe three times, but certainly not more than that."

---

## Motive for the Fraud

Motive is an important element in establishing the crime. The motive may be the same as the theme you developed earlier—or it may not. The most common response is "*I don't know.*" You should probe for additional information, but if it is not forthcoming, then attribute the motive to the theme you developed earlier. The motive should be established along these lines:

---

***Example:***

*Interviewer:*
"We have discussed what led you to do this. But I need to hear it in your words. Why do you think you did this?"

---

***When the Fraud Commenced.*** Interviewers need to find the approximate date and time that the fraud started. This information is usually developed by questions similar to the following:

| | |
|---|---|
| ***Example:*** | *Respondent:* |
| *Interviewer:* | "Around the middle of January of last year." |
| "I am sure you remember the first time this happened." | *Interviewer:* |
| *Respondent:* | "I admire you for having the courage to talk about this. You're doing the right thing. Tell me in detail about the first time." |
| "Yes." | |
| *Interviewer:* | |
| "Tell me about it." | |

***When/If Fraud Was Terminated.*** When the crime is fraud, especially internal fraud, the offenses are usually continuous; that is, miscreants seldom stop before they are discovered. If appropriate, interviewers should seek the date the offense terminated. The question is typically phrased as follows:

---

***Example:***

*Interviewer:*
"When was the last time you did this?"

---

## Others Involved

Most frauds are solo ventures—committed without accomplices. Rather than ask if anyone else was "involved," phrase the question something like this:

---

*Interviewer:*
"Who else knew about this besides you?"

---

By asking who else "knew," you are in effect not only asking for the names of possible conspirators, but also about others who knew what was going on but failed to report it. This question asks for specifics—not *"did someone else know?"* but rather *"who else knew?"*

## Physical Evidence

Physical evidence—regardless of how limited it may be—should be obtained from perpetrators/confessors. In many instances, illicit income from fraud is deposited directly in their bank accounts. Interviewers typically want to ask confessors to surrender their banking records voluntarily for review. Ask for either (1) a separate written authorization, or (2) language to be added to the confession noting the voluntary surrender of banking information. The first evidence is preferable.

If other relevant records can be obtained only with the confessor's consent, seek permission to review them during the oral confession. In some instances, it may be advisable to delay this step until you obtain the written confession.

| | |
|---|---|
| ***Example:*** | *Interviewer:* |
| *Interviewer:* | "Well, I just need to document the facts and clear up any remaining questions. |
| "As a part of wrapping up the details, I will be needing your banking records (or other physical evidence). You understand that, don't you?" | |
| *Respondent:* | You have decided to tell the complete story, including your side of it. I just want to make sure the facts are accurate and fair to you. We |
| "No, I don't." | |

want to make sure you're not blamed for something someone else did. And I want to report that you cooperated fully and wanted to do the right thing, okay?" (Avoid the use of the word *evidence* or references to higher tribunals, e.g., *courts* or *prosecutors*.)

*Respondent:*
"Okay."

*Interviewer:*
"Where do you keep your bank accounts?" (If the interviewer knows of at least one bank where the confessor does business, the question should be phrased: "Where do you do business besides First National Bank?")

*Respondent:*
"Just First National."

*Interviewer:*
"I'll need to get your okay to get the records from the bank if we need them. Where do you keep the original records?" (Do not ask their permission to look at the records; simply tell them the records are needed. Let them object if they have a problem with this request.)

**Disposition of Proceeds.** If it has not come out earlier, find out what happened to any illicit income derived from the misdeeds. Typically, the money has long since been used for frivolous or ostentatious purposes. It is important, however, that confessors see their actions in a more positive light; you should therefore avoid comments or questions relating to "high living."

*Example:*

*Interviewer:*
"What happened to the money?" (Let the accused explain; do not suggest an answer unless they do not respond.)

**Location of Assets.** In appropriate situations, you will want to find out if any residual assets remain that confessors can use to reduce losses. Rather than ask them *"Is there anything left?"* the question should be phrased as *"What's left?"*

*Example:*

*Interviewer:*
"What do you have left from all of this?"

*Respondent:*
"Not much. I used most of the money to cover my bills and financial obligations. A little money and a car that is paid for is all I have."

*Interviewer:*
"Well, whatever it is, this whole thing will look a lot better if you volunteered to return what you could, don't you agree?"

## Specifics of Each Offense

Once the major hurdles are overcome, interviewers then return to the specifics of each offense. Generally, you start with the first instance and work through chronologically in a logical fashion. Because these questions are information-seeking, they should be openly phrased so that the answer is independent of the question. It is best to seek the independent recollections of confessors first before you display physical evidence. If they cannot independently recall, use the documents to refresh their memory. It is generally best to resolve all issues for each instance before proceeding to the next. To determine the specifics of the offense, you usually ask specific questions:

---

**Example:**

*Interviewer:*
"Who has knowledge of this transaction?"
"What does this document mean?"
"When did this transaction occur?"

"Where did the proceeds of the transaction go?"
"Why was the transaction done?"
"How was the transaction covered up?"

---

Never promise immunity from prosecution. Confessors cannot be given immunity from prosecution by interviewers. The reason to refrain from such promises is simple: These promises can be interpreted as a way to unfairly extract statements that perpetrators would not have otherwise given.

## Signed Statements

Verbal confessions should be reduced to short and concise written statements. Rarely should they exceed two or three handwritten pages. Interviewers prepare the statements (often in advance of the admission-seeking interview) and present them to the confessors for their signature. If a prepared confession needs to be changed, the changes can be added in ink, with everyone present initialing the changes. Such endorsed changes often lend credibility that the signed statements are legitimate and were voluntarily given.

The following points should be covered in every signed statement:

***Voluntariness of Confessions.*** Getting written admissions is difficult. Law that governs confessions requires that they be completely voluntary. This point should be set forth specifically in the statement.

***Intent.*** There is no such thing as an accidental fraud or crime. Both require, as key elements of proof, that fraudsters knew the conduct was wrong and intended to commit the act. This admission is best accomplished using precise language. The statement should clearly and explicitly describe the act—for example, *"I wrongfully took assets that weren't mine from the company"* versus *"I borrowed money from the company without telling anyone."*

As a general rule, emotionally charged words, such as *lie* and *steal*, should be avoided, because confessors often balk at signing statements that use these words. Here are some suggested wordings:

| Instead of | Use |
| --- | --- |
| Lie | *I knew the statement/action was untrue.* |
| Steal | *Wrongfully took the property of _____ for my own benefit.* |
| Embezzle | *Wrongfully took _____'s property, which had been entrusted to me, and used it for my own benefit.* |
| Fraud | *I knowingly told _____ an untrue statement and he/she/they relied on it.* |

***Approximate Dates of Offense.*** Unless the exact dates of the offense are known, the words *approximately* or *about* must precede any stated dates. If confessors are unsure about the dates, include language to that effect.

***Approximate Amounts of Losses.*** Include the approximate losses, making sure they are labeled as such. It is satisfactory to state a range (*"probably not less than $____ or more than $____"*).

***Approximate Number of Instances.*** Ranges are also satisfactory for the number of instances. This number is important because it helps establish intent by showing a pattern of activity.

***Willingness to Cooperate.*** When confessors perceive that the statement's language portrays them in a more favorable light, they have an easier time signing the statement. Confessors also convert this natural tendency to be seen favorably into cooperation and a willingness to make amends.

---

**Example:**
"I am willing to cooperate in helping undo what I have done. I promise that I will try to repay whatever damages I caused by my actions."

---

*Excuse Clause.* Mention the confessor's moral excuse in the statement. This clause helps the accused believe they are being portrayed in the most favorable light. Make sure that the excuse clause wording does not diminish legal responsibility.

| *Example:* | |
|---|---|
| **WRONG:** | **RIGHT:** |
| "I didn't mean to do this." (implies lack of intent) | "I wouldn't have done this if it had not been for pressing financial problems. I didn't mean to hurt anyone." |

*Confessor* **Must** *Read Statement.* Confessors must acknowledge that they read the statement and they should then initial every page in the statement. It may be advisable to insert intentional errors in the statement so that confessors will notice them as they read it. The errors are then crossed out, the correct information inserted, and the confessor asked to initial the changes. Whether this step is advisable depends on the likelihood that the confessor will attempt to retract the statement or claim it was not read.

*Truthfulness of Statement.* The written statement should state specifically that it is true. This wording gives it added weight in ensuing litigation. However, the language should also allow for mistakes—for example:

| *Example:* |
|---|
| "This statement is true and complete to the best of my current recollection." |

## Key Points in Signed Statements

No legal requirement demands that statements must be in the handwriting or wording of declarants. Because examiners usually know how to draft valid statements, letting confessors draft the statement is generally not a good idea. A statement's wording should be precise. Declarants should read and sign the statement without undue delay. Do not ask confessors to sign the statement; instead, direct them—*"Please sign here."* Although not legally required, it is a good idea to have two people witness the signing of a statement.

*No more than one written statement should be prepared for each offense.* If facts are inadvertently omitted, they can later be added to the original statement as an addendum. For legal purposes, prepare separate statements for unrelated offenses. This rule applies because the target may be tried more than once (once for each offense). Preserve all notes taken during admission-seeking interviews, especially those concerning confessions. Access to pertinent notes aids in cross-examinations regarding the validity of signed statements. Stenographic notes, if any, should also be preserved. Once a confession is obtained, substantiate it through additional investigation, if necessary. A sample signed statement is included in Appendix A at the end of this chapter.

## The Fraud Report

Interrogation of suspect(s) is usually the final stage of investigation (although circumstances may dictate an alternative sequencing of investigation methods). Once the investigation is completed, a fraud report is prepared. This report includes all findings, conclusions, recommendations, and corrective actions taken. The report indicates all pertinent facts uncovered relative to the who, what, where, when, how, and why of the fraud. It also includes recommendations for control improvements that will minimize the exposure to similar occurrences in the future. It should not contain recommendations for disciplinary or legal action against anyone suspected of fraudulent or illegal activity, even when the investigation provides tenable evidence of probable culpability or complicity.

Particular care should be exercised to ensure that the general tone of the fraud report is neither accusatory nor conclusive as to guilt. Even when a confession of culpability or complicity is obtained during a fraud investigation, such confessions may not be considered valid or consequential evidence of guilt of fraud until a court of law decides, even if management has already taken disciplinary action on the basis of the confession. Reports that refer to a confession obtained in the course of the investigation should state merely that admission of the alleged or suspected events was obtained—not that guilt was acknowledged. Attention to language is crucial here to ensure that subjective, inflammatory, libelous, or other prejudicial connotations are absent. To be objective, factual, unbiased, and free from distortion, reports should refer to "alleged" irregularities, activity, conduct, and so forth. Accordingly, the activities investigated and reported should be described as "purported" or "alleged" to have occurred. When findings support the allegations, couch reports in language such as the following:

- The investigation disclosed the existence of reasonably credible evidence to support the allegation.
- The investigation concludes with a rebuttal presumption that the allegations or suspicions are tenable.
- The investigation concludes with plausible evidence in support of the allegation.

Appendix B at the end of this chapter details an investigation of an employee fraud and an appropriate fraud report. This completed report covers the investigation of Ivan Ben Steelin, a real estate purchasing representative who worked for Resort and Properties Inc. Ivan accepted kickbacks from Red Hot Real Estate, and he also inflated real estate prices as part of the scheme.

The fraud investigation documented by the report involved all four types of investigation procedures. The investigation was predicated on an anonymous tip received in a letter addressed to the company president. The investigation began with a review of the suspect's personnel records. It included one procedure to investigate the theft (surveillance of the suspects at a local restaurant) and several procedures to investigate the concealment (including computer searches of company databases; calculations of total purchase transactions by each real estate buyer; and determinations of the number of real estate agencies used, average price per acre paid, and the number of purchase transactions made with each vendor). The report documents the public records searches and net worth conversion. Searches were made of voter registration and marriage records, the secretary of state's records, as well as the real estate and contracting office records at the county level. Query procedures involved neutral interviews with the company's personnel manager, a home builder, and a company secretary, as well as a friendly interview with another real estate buyer and a hostile interview with the real estate agent who was suspected of making illegal payments to Ivan Ben Steelin. The interrogation of Ivan Ben Steelin (in order to gain access to his bank records) led to a signed confession. The investigation concluded with a signed confession statement and calculation of real estate overpayments (losses) by the company.

The report exemplifies the types of procedures and documentation that fraud investigations often include. We encourage you to read it carefully.

# SUMMARY

Interviewing is the most common investigation technique. Here, we have only touched the surface of this complex topic. If you are serious about pursuing fraud investigation as a career, become an excellent interviewer. Read several books on the subject, and take advantage of the excellent training that is available. Many frauds are solved, and many confessions and restitutions are obtained because of good interviewing skills. Fraud investigations often fail because of mistakes made during interviews. Counseling courses are another excellent way to develop listening and observation skills.

In this chapter, we discussed interviewing etiquette, interview techniques, types of interviews, types of questions to ask and how to ask them, and ways to elicit confessions. When conducting admission-seeking interviews, your purpose is to get a confession or to exonerate (if innocent). In these types of interviews, almost always an invisible wall stands between the interviewer and the interviewee: the interviewee does not want to confess; the interviewer seeks a confession. Good interviewers find ways to break down this invisible wall. They use techniques such as those discussed in this chapter to (1) minimize the crime in the mind of the interviewee, and (2) maximize the sympathy for the interviewee.

Wherever possible, fraud investigations should conclude with a signed confession of guilt from the perpetrator or perpetrators, and with an accurate calculation of the extent of the theft and losses. The confession and the loss calculation, as well as the fraud investigation techniques used, must be carefully documented so that civil, criminal, and other actions can be supported.

# QUESTIONS AND CASES

## DISCUSSION QUESTIONS

1. What are the three types of honesty testing?

2. What is an interview?

3. What are the five reactions of interviewees?

4. What are the five general types of questions that an interviewer can ask?

5. What are some of the different elements of communication?

6. What is an inhibitor of communication?

7. What are facilitators of communication?

8. What are informational questions?

9. What is meant by the "question sequence"?

10. What is a volatile interview?

11. What is the purpose of assessment questions?

12. What is norming or calibrating?

## TRUE/FALSE

1. Paper-and-pencil honesty tests are most frequently used to determine whether someone has committed a crime.

2. Failure to pass a polygraph test means certain guilt.

3. Interviews during the rationalization stage are often not objective and can be harmful to the potential prosecution efforts.

4. The general tone of a fraud report should be neither accusatory nor conclusive as to guilt, even if the suspect has confessed his or her involvement in the crime.

5. An interviewer should usually be sympathetic and respectful during an interview.

6. Confrontational interviews should always be conducted even if no evidence can be obtained from the suspect.

7. Telling a significant lie and getting away with it during an interview is usually difficult if the interviewer is well trained.

8. If a suspect continually repeats questions, it could be a verbal cue that he or she is lying.

9. The fraud report should include recommendations for disciplinary action.

10. The interview should always take place at the interviewee's place of work.

## MULTIPLE CHOICE

1. Which of the following is *not* a method of honesty testing?
   - a. Graphology
   - b. Voice stress analysis
   - c. Body language test
   - d. Pencil-and-paper test

   *page 268*

2. Interviews should be conducted with:
   - a. Suspects.
   - b. Coworkers.
   - c. Clients.
   - d. All of the above.

   *page 269*

3. Persons in the rationalization stage of reaction to a fraud:
   - a. Make great interviewees because they want to punish the suspect.
   - b. Want to give the suspect one more chance.
   - c. Believe without a doubt that the suspect is guilty.
   - d. Have no sympathy for the suspect.

   *page 270*

4. Planning for interviews should *not* involve:
   - a. Judging the guilt of the suspect based on available documents.
   - b. Establishing a location and time for the interview.
   - c. Ascertaining in advance as many facts as possible about the offense.
   - d. Understanding the attitude of the interviewee.

   *page 273*

5. Confrontational interviews should usually be conducted when:
   - a. Police decide that the suspect is guilty.
   - b. The examiner is starting the investigation.
   - c. All other investigative procedures have been completed.
   - d. The investigation is taking too long.

6. Which of the following is an inquiry technique that should be used by interviewers?
   - a. Use short questions, confined to one topic.
   - b. Maintain full control of the interview.
   - c. Point out some, but not all, of the circumstantial evidence.
   - d. All of the above.

   *page 274*

7. Which of the following honesty testing techniques deals with the study of handwriting for the purpose of character analysis?
   - a. Polygraph
   - b. Graphology
   - c. Pencil-and-paper test
   - d. Voice stress
   - e. None of the above

   *page 268*

8. Which of the following traits do polygraphs *not* measure when testing for stress?
   - a. Pulse rate
   - b. Blood pressure
   - c. Galvanic skin response
   - d. Respiration
   - e. Body temperature

   *page 268*

9. Interviewing is:
   - a. The systematic questioning of individuals who have knowledge of events, people, and evidence involved in a case under investigation.
   - b. The process of answering questions from an interviewer for the purpose of finding a job.
   - c. By far the most common technique used in investigating and resolving fraud.
   - d. a and c.
   - e. None of the above.

   *page 269*

10. Which of the following is the typical sequence of reactions to a crisis?
    - a. Anger, denial, rationalization, depression, acceptance
    - b. Rationalization, denial, anger, depression, acceptance
    - c. Denial, anger, rationalization, depression, acceptance
    - d. Depression, denial, anger, rationalization, acceptance
    - e. None of the above

    *page 270*

11. Which of the following reactions frequently involves appearing temporarily stunned, insisting there is some mistake, or not comprehending what has been said?
    - a. Anger
    - b. Denial
    - c. Rationalization
    - d. Depression
    - e. Acceptance

    *page 270*

12. Which of the following is a characteristic of a good interview?
    - a. Most interviews reveal too much information, so the interviewer should make the interview as concise as possible.
    - b. The interviewer should announce any bias at the outset, because the interviewee will cooperate better if the interviewee knows the type of information the interviewer is seeking.
    - c. Friendly interviewees appear helpful, but they may have hidden motives and may provide bad information.
    - d. It is important to schedule interviews ahead of time, especially if you are planning to interview a potentially hostile interviewee.

13. Each of the following is a clue that an interviewee is dishonest *except*:
    a. Upon repeated accusations, a dishonest person's denials become more vehement.
    b. In order to add credibility to false statements, liars request that the interviewers obtain character testimony from other people.
    c. Liars often refuse to implicate possible suspects—or, in other words, honest people are more wiling to name others involved in misdeeds.
    d. Dishonest people frequently cover their mouths with their hands or fingers during deception.

14. Which of the following is something that an interviewee might do or feel while in the denial phase?
    a. Insult, harm, or slander
    b. Attempt to justify the act
    c. Become sad, withdraw, or lose interest
    d. Not understand what has been said

15. Which of the following is not a good thing to do during an interview?
    a. Conduct the interview in private.
    b. Establish the purpose of the interview.
    c. Interview more than one person at once.
    d. Be careful not to invade an interviewee's body space.

## SHORT CASES

**Case 1.** Jim has been a faithful employee of Daddy's Denture, Inc. (DD's), for four years. He has held various positions where he handles receipts, credit memos, and other accounting records. Along with recently added responsibility, Jim discovered more opportunity to commit fraud.

Over the past three months, Jim figured out that he can create fictitious vendors and write checks from DD's to these fictitious vendors and deposit the checks in a new bank account he opened under a false name. Jim put this plan into action and has so far stolen $7,000 from DD's.

One day, Jim had to call in sick. A coworker, Judd, assumed Jim responsibilities for the day. As he reconciled cashed checks, Judd noticed Jim endorsed many of them himself. Judd doesn't believe what he sees. In fact, he leaves the reconciling for Jim to finish when he returns to work.

When Jim returns to work, everything seems normal at first. However, it eventually dawns on Judd that he caught Jim in the act of stealing. Judd becomes angry and confronts Jim. When Judd mentions the endorsements, Jim is dumfounded and denies being dishonest. After Judd leaves, Jim gets angry, thinking, "What right did he have to take over my duties?" and "I'll be fired for sure!!"

Back in his office, Judd continues to think about Jim's dishonesty. He decides that Jim is just human, and that he let himself slip this once. Judd decides he should let the issue pass and just hope that Jim realizes his gig is up. Judd believes Jim is a basically good guy and will probably reconcile his misdoings and return to honest ways. Later that night, Judd feels sad knowing that his good friend, Jim, has done such a bad thing.

Meanwhile, Jim decides he shouldn't be angry with Judd. He is, after all, only doing what he's been told to do by his superiors. Jim feels horrible about what he has done, not to mention the fact that he got caught. He decides to fess up and let his boss know what he has been doing before he gets into any more trouble.

Name the five reactions to crises and briefly describe how both Jim and Judd proceed through each phase.

**Case 2.** Your father-in-law owns a medium-sized air-conditioning company in Meza, Arizona. Because of the heat in Arizona, the company has done rather well and the business is continually growing. Your father-in-law received tips from other employees that one of the technical repairmen, named Damon, is disgruntled and has been padding his paycheck through different internal frauds against the company. Your father-in-law noticed that while things seem to be running more efficiently, the company has not been more profitable and so you have been helping him for the last month run secret audits as part of the internal investigation. Through your investigation you have discovered that Damon has stolen $50,000 over the last three years through the following methods.

1. Damon regularly uses the company gas card to fill up his personal pickup truck and his family's mini-van.

2. Damon takes A/C units from inventory and sells them at cost to people he knows.

3. Damon sells auxiliary A/C parts, but pockets the money from the sale without including the sale on the invoice.

4. Damon will often go home from a job on Fridays after lunch, but claims on his weekly reports that he worked until 5 p.m.

Think of how you would confront Damon. You have known him for two years and already have a working relationship. Specifically what types of questions would you ask while you are talking with him? The evidence you gathered in your investigation would support your decision to fire Damon; however, a written confession would help your court case if you decide to charge Damon for damages.

**Case 3.** Daffy Duck, the purchasing manager for ACME Corporation, is under suspicion for committing fraud. Management believes Daffy is accepting kickbacks and bribes from various vendors. As the company's fraud expert, you are investigating this possible fraud and are preparing to interview Daffy. You suspect that Daffy will be defensive and possibly hostile when interviewed.

1. What investigation procedures should be completed before your admission-seeking interview with Daffy?

2. If you find evidence that proves Daffy is committing fraud at ACME, what might Daffy's initial reaction be when confronted? What other emotions or reactions might you expect from Daffy? How do you know?

**Case 4.** An accountant for a small business is suspected of writing checks to "dummy" vendors and collecting the money himself. After a thorough investigation of the company, you determine that the company does not require authorization for vendor payments. In an interview with the suspect, you ask him if any controls are in place that could prevent someone from writing fraudulent checks. He quickly responds in the affirmative.

What type of questions could you ask next?

**Case 5.** Mike Trujillo has been involved in a serious relationship with his high school sweetheart, Bonny, for five years; they have even discussed marriage. One day, Bonny told Mike that she was seeing another man. "Mike, I love you, but I'm not in love with you." Over the course of the next few months, Mike had a bumpy ride emotionally. Initially, he simply couldn't believe it. He frequently caught himself thinking about Bonny as if they were still together. After a few days, Mike became bitter. He cut up all her pictures except for one. He hung that one on a dartboard and threw darts at it for hours. As his bitterness subsided, he looked for reasons why the breakup was actually beneficial. He told himself it was a blessing, that he wouldn't have to support Bonny's rich tastes anymore, that things were turning out for the best. However, during the next six months, Mike just couldn't get excited about dating other women. He made himself go on dates, but he never really liked any of the women he dated. He felt empty and didn't know how to fill the void in his heart. But after a few months, Mike did bounce back and started to take an interest in dating. Within four months he found Amy, the girl of his dreams, and they got married about a year later.

1. What reactions do most people have to crises and how did Mike display these reactions?

2. How does Mike's experience relate to fraud examination?

**Case 6.** You manage a division that recently discovered a suspected fraud involving accounts receivable. For the past week, you and the internal auditors have been collecting documents, gathering information, and quietly interviewing personnel. It is now time to interview the suspect, who is your accounts receivable manager. She has access both to cash receipts and the accounts receivable ledger and has allegedly stolen $4,000 over the last year by writing off small accounts as uncollectible.

Pair up with another student in your class. One of you take the part of the interviewer and one that of the suspect. Develop a brief outline on how you will conduct your interview. Remember that your task as interviewer is to remain in control of the interview, but at the same time be sympathetic and understanding. If deemed appropriate, prepare a short, written confession statement like the example given in the chapter. Swap roles after the first interview and apply what you learned in it in a second interview.

**Case 7.** You are an internal auditor at BBB Company. An employee of BBB has phoned in an anonymous tip that a fellow worker, Jane X., might be embezzling money. Jane has been a trusted employee of the company for 13 years; she quickly moved through the ranks of the company because of her exemplary record and she is now Vice President in Charge of Treasury. Your internal audit team has done thorough audits of her department for years and has found its control environment to be exceptional. In addition, she is a good friend of the CEO and CFO. They have tremendous confidence in her abilities and honesty, and she is being groomed to succeed the current CFO when he retires.

The person making the anonymous tip claims to have noticed large fluctuations in certain financial statement accounts. Accompanying these fluctuations are unexplainable debits and credits that were all entered by Jane. The person also alleges that Jane's behavior has been erratic. She is usually kind and patient, but recently she has flown off the handle for no discernible reason. She insists on balancing certain accounts by herself because she claims that they are too critical to trust with anyone else. Finally, the informant feels like Jane's lifestyle as a single mother is well above what her salary would support.

Investigating allegations against such a trusted person in the company will cause considerable disruption. If you investigate, you will have to proceed carefully, especially since you have only the word of one employee who could have ulterior motives.

1. Describe the steps you would take to investigate this suspected embezzlement.

2. As a first step in your investigation, would you interview Jane about the problem? Why or why not?

3. How would you conduct Jane's admission-seeking interview in order to be most effective?

**Case 8.** You have been talking with your best friend, John, for the past couple of weeks about a crisis in his company. He just learned that his boss has been embezzling money for the past six months. The day he learns about the alleged fraud, he calls to tell you the news. In the telephone conversation, John tells you how much he respects his boss and that his boss is his mentor. You note that his voice seems distant and he doesn't respond well to your questions. Later that week, you meet John for lunch. His demeanor is completely changed since you last spoke with him. After a few drinks, John can't stop bad-mouthing his boss. John also makes a few insulting comments about you. You decide to leave him alone for a few days until he feels better.

A week later you again meet John for lunch. The subject of the fraud comes up, and John's attitude is again considerably changed. Instead of being angry, he compares his boss's life to his own. You think it a bit odd when John says, "I completely understand why he did it. His family life was suffering, his job was in jeopardy, and his mom just died. Given the same circumstances, I might have done the same thing." You finish lunch and go your separate ways. Later that week, John calls you again. This time, he tells you that he could have prevented the fraud. He feels embarrassed that it happened right before his eyes.

A week later you ask John if there are any new developments in the investigation. He tells you that he is helping with the investigation by providing all the facts he knows and his observations over the last few months. Now all John wants is to move on.

Identify John's reactions to the fraud, and explain each stage in detail.

**Case 9.** As a result of the system audit performed at Deming Medical corporate offices, it was discovered that Paula, one of the payroll supervisors, had system access rights to transaction codes used by the HR staff. It was consequently determined that Paula took advantage of the situation and created a fake employee to whom she was issuing a paycheck every two weeks; only the checks went to Paula's banking account. Andrew Jacobsen, an investigator working on the case, did an extensive research, details of which led him to believe Paula was embezzling. Andrew is about to go in for a final interview with Paula. Paula had been interviewed before and denied she was involved in the embezzling scheme. What interviewing tactics should Andrew use to have Paula admit she was stealing from Deming and how would he know whether she tells him the truth?

**Case 10.** While auditing the accounts payable of a large clothing manufacture, you discover that four of the company's vendors have checks sent to a postal office (PO) box. After further investigation, you discover that one box is registered under the same name as the CFO's son, and another is registered under the same name as his daughter—ages 3 and 5, respectively. Finding this highly suspicious, you begin questioning the employees who work directly with the CFO to determine whether fraud is occurring in this case. After searching through the documentation of vendor transactions, the investigation leads you to suspect that the CFO is sending checks to the PO box of fictitious vendors to be collected and then deposited in his own account.

Over two weeks, you and your engagement team compile a large body of evidence implicating the CFO in the fraud. After this evidence has been gathered, you ask him to come to your office for questioning. Upon his arrival, and without wasting any time, you present all the evidence against him and ask him about his involvement in stealing money from the company. The responses you receive are defensive and antagonistic. The CFO says that he has heard that your engagement team has been "snooping" around the office, protests his innocence, and threatens to file suit against you for slander and libel if you pursue this absurd investigation that is trying to label him a criminal. Not expecting this reaction, and being frustrated that the interview is not going as you intended, you say that you have had enough for one day and cut the interview short.

1. What steps need to be taken before interviewing a person you suspect of committing fraud in a company?

2. What are some effective methods that could have helped in dealing with an interview subject you are seeking an admission from?

## EXTENSIVE CASES

**Extensive Case 1.** A small group of dockworkers in Long Beach, California, working for Meade Industries, an international shipping company, was being investigated concerning its involvement in a theft operation. The theft itself was a rather simple operation. The longshoremen unloading foreign-made products acted in collusion with their supervisors in order to steal certain items that they marked as "missing" or "damaged due to shipping" on official invoices. They later sold the items on the black market and split the money between the conspirators. The fraud was discovered when Longstreet Enterprises' Asian subsidiary contacted Meade about an unusual number of microwaves that were lost during shipment from Korea to Long Beach. Sherman, the newest member of Meade's security team, decided to simultaneously interview Lee and Jackson, two dockworkers, concerning their involvement in the fraud.

Never having actually met Sherman, Lee and Jackson were simply instructed to wait in the "interrogation" room in the security shop. Lee and Jackson arrived promptly at 8:00 a.m., dressed in their work clothes, and were seated. Via the intercom, they were told not to leave until Sherman gave them explicit permission to do so. Sherman did not enter the room until 9:30. Sherman was escorted into the room by a burly security guard carrying a nightstick.

Lee, annoyed at Sherman's tardiness, blurted out, "Hey, man, we gots to get back to work. I ain't getting paid for time off the dock."

Sherman made no reply. He only paced the room for what seemed an eternity to Jackson. Finally, Sherman moved deliberately and directly over to a chair on Lee and Jackson's side of the table. Sherman pulled his chair within inches of the two men being interrogated and straddled the chair so that the back of the chair supported his arms.

"Mr. Lee, do you know what they did with pirates in pre-colonial Virginia?" asked Sherman. Lee shrugged a little bit and was struggling for an answer when Sherman beat him to the punch, "They were executed in the gallows and then their bodies were hung in iron cages on the shores of the bay as an example to would-be thieves and pirates. Not a pretty picture is it Mr. Lee?" Lee was at a visible loss for words.

Pulling two pens and two pieces of paper from his coat pocket and slamming them onto the table, Sherman raised his voice and said, "Now let's cut through the crap, you dockies are guilty as hell. We've got a paper trail a mile long to prove it along with surveillance tapes and written confessions from Hill and Grant. Do yourselves a favor and write out your confessions. If you don't I might just have to leave you here with Bruno and if you physically assault him and he beats you silly, well then it'll be your word against his, comprende? Oh, yeah, you'll still be under investigation for grand theft."

1. Name at least three mistakes that Sherman made in interviewing Lee and Jackson.

2. The chapter identifies some of the characteristics of a good interview. In what ways could Sherman have changed the interview?

3. What were some of the threats made and claims that Sherman could not prove? Is it ever acceptable to make a threat that involves physical violence?

4. The book identifies specific locations where interviews should take place. Is the "interrogation room" one of these places? Where should have Sherman met with Lee and Jackson?

**Extensive Case 2.** It is early Monday morning, and Brian is preparing to conduct his first interview as a fraud examiner. He is to meet with Sue, a laborer in the factory his firm is investigating. She is neither a suspect nor thought to be connected with the fraud. Her name simply came up in another investigator's interviews as someone who might be able to provide additional insight. They have arranged to meet at Brian's office, so he is simply awaiting her arrival.

"Hello," he hears someone say through his partially open door. "I'm Sue."

"Come in," he replies, remaining seated behind his large oak desk. She enters and takes the empty seat across the desk from Brian. "Let me get right to the point," are his next words. "Are you aware of any reasonably credible or plausible evidence that the allegations of embezzlement at your place of employment are tenable?"

After a brief pause and a look of concern on Sue's face, Brian asks, "Do you know what embezzlement means?"

"Yes," replies Sue.

"Okay, then, do you know anyone who has embezzled from your employer?"

"No."

Sue becomes nervous as she sees Brian begin to take notes on a pad. He continues, "Specifically, have you seen Ralph perpetrating fraud?"

"No."

"Are you sure? You know that this is a big deal," he says as he stands and begins to pace around the room. "I can't imagine why anyone would steal from his own company, but he deserves to be caught if he has. It's wrong and bad, and only a horrible person would do something like this."

"I'm sure."

"Have you embezzled?"

"No," Sue states again.

"Well, then, I don't see any reason to continue. Goodbye."

Sue stands, excuses herself, and leaves the room.

What are some of the things Brian did wrong during this interview?

**Extensive Case 3.** James began working for NewCo nearly 20 years ago, eventually moving up to the position of facility and maintenance supervisor. During the past 20 years, NewCo experienced significant growth in which James played a major part in the expansion plans. Because of his great service and abilities, James earned great respect in the company. Although helpful to the company, James was forced to leave the company because of severe health problems.

Earl was called in to replace James. The sudden departure of James kept him from working with James and learning the proper policies and procedures James had put into place before he left. The lack of training created a problem for Earl, who was faced with finishing the projects James had started. The major project James left was a construction project where the price had already been determined but no work had begun. Unfortunately, Earl could not find any contractor information, nor could he find any of the contacts James had worked with.

As Earl continued to search, he realized he was in more trouble than he though because no records were available for any of the work James had performed. The lack of information forced Earl to bid the contract out to a new contractor. When Earl received the new bid and presented it to management, they were surprised to find that the new price was 30 percent less than the original bid.

Management believed the new bid price was wrong and questioned Earl to ensure he had included all of the requirements for the project. Once they determined he had, they began to ask more questions. As they looked around and reviewed some of James's previous activities,

they realized that he was no longer bidding out projects but rather giving them to specific contractors. When reviewing these contractors they found that they had no information for the contractors on file. They didn't have any addresses, phone numbers, or even tax ID numbers for payments. All they had was a name, and from that information they cut a check and James delivered the checks personally.

Based on this new information they began to question other employees about James's activities. They found that others considered him secretive and that he refused to allow anyone to work with him on his projects. Others told management that James had also recently become violent and erratic with many of the employees. Because of the number of red flags, management called you in to investigate James's previous activities.

1. Who would you interview first and why?

2. What type of information would you look for?

3. How would you approach each of the different individuals?

4. Do to James's frail condition, how would you approach the interview process and investigation?

## INTERNET ASSIGNMENTS

1. Go to the site http:/www.fbi.gov/publications/leb/1996/oct964.txt and read the article about statement analysis, which discusses interviewing and how to know whether a person is lying. This article examines the case of Susan Smith, who killed her two sons by strapping them into the car and pushing the car in to the river. The article uses the mother's statements to discuss four components of statement analysis that can help investigators known when a person is lying.

   Outline the four components of statement analysis and give a short definition of each.

2. Find a Web site about interviewing techniques. Summarize what you find.

3. Many Internet sites contain honesty tests for screening applicants or existing employees. Most of these charge a fee for their services, but they do provide an easy, quick way to test employees. At the Web site queendom.com, you can access many free tests. In the relationship tab are several honesty tests. Look for honesty tests at http://www.queendom.com/tests/minitests/fx/honesty.html. Although this test is mainly for relationships, it is free and gives you an idea of what kind of questions are asked and what information can be derived from the answers.

   Take the test and obtain the results. Analyze the questions and try to determine why they are being asked. Do you think this test is accurate? Why or why not?

## DEBATES

1. The Employee Polygraph Protection Act passed by Congress made it difficult to use polygraphs in fraud investigations. Currently, 11 conditions must be met in order for polygraph tests to be used. Assume you are members of Congress debating the use of polygraphs. Discuss both sides of the issue and make *your* recommendation. Would you make it easier or harder to obtain permission to use a polygraph?

2. You and another fraud examiner are debating whether it is ethical to "lie" during an admission-seeking interview (such as claiming to have compelling evidence of guilt when you don't) to get a confession. You believe it is okay to lie. Your coworker believes it is unethical to be deceptive. Who is correct?

## END NOTES

1. We would like to thank the Association of Certified Fraud Examiners and Chairman Joseph Wells, in particular, for allowing us to use their interview material in this book. Much of this chapter was taken from their self-study course on interviewing, *Beyond the Numbers: Professional Interview Techniques* (Austin, TX), 1998.

2. See, for example, the works of Elizabeth Kübler Ross, such as *On Death and Dying*, which stresses that we are all operating at a psychological-steady state, and that crises knock us off that equilibrium (http://www.elisabethkublerross.com/).

3. *Beyond the Numbers: Professional Interview Techniques*, p. 38.

# APPENDIX A

## SAMPLE SIGNED STATEMENT

December 14, 20XX
Edison, New Jersey

I, Dominique Santana, furnish the following free and voluntary statement to Scott Barefoot of Major Electronics, Inc. No threats or promises of any kind have been used to induce this statement.

I am a cashier at Major Electronics, Inc. Part of my duties include processing and posting cash payments, sales, returns, and allowances, as well as handling cash. Commencing in early 2001 and continuing through the current time, I have taken about $7,000 in cash from the company, knowing the cash was not mine.

I took the company's money by creating fictitious merchandise returns, forging the signature of my manager, and posting the fictitious return to the computer. I then took out the resulting cash from the register. Later, I split the money with my boyfriend, Jerry Garza, who works here in the store. He knew what I was doing and helped me several times by signing a three-part return slip as if the merchandise had been returned when it had not. Most of the time, this scheme involved my own account. I bought televisions and other merchandise using my employee discount. I then sold them to outsiders for cash. Afterward, I prepared a document showing the television was returned when it was not.

Other than my boyfriend, Jerry, no one in the store knew what I was doing. I am aware my conduct is illegal and violates the policies of Major Electronics, Inc. I participated in this scheme because I have had severe financial problems and my mother has been ill. I am truly sorry for my conduct, and promise to repay all losses. Some of the company's cash was deposited in my personal account, number 436-9241-7881 at the First National Bank, Edison, New Jersey. I hereby grant Scott Barefoot or representatives from Major Electronics permission to examine the account and to obtain copies of statements, checks, and deposits from First National Bank for the period January 1, 1992, to the present.

I have read this statement consisting of this page. I now sign my name below because this statement is true and correct to the best of my knowledge.

_____          _____
Signature:                                Witness:

_____          _____
Date                                      Date

# AN EXAMPLE FRAUD REPORT

To demonstrate how frauds can be investigated and the type of report to prepare to document investigative procedures, we present a completed fraud report of the investigation of "Ivan Ben Steelin," a real estate purchasing representative who worked for "Silver Summit Real Estate." Ivan accepted kickbacks from a company we'll call "Red Hot Real Estate" and inflated real estate prices.

The fraud investigation documented in the report involves all four types of investigative procedures. The investigation is predicated on an anonymous tip received in a letter addressed to the company president. The investigation begins with a review of the suspect's personnel records. It includes one theft investigative procedure—surveillance of the suspects at a local restaurant. Several concealment-based investigative procedures are used, including computer searches of company databases, calculations of total purchase transactions by each real estate buyer, and determinations of the number of real estate agencies used, the average price paid per acre, and the number of purchase transactions made with each vendor. The report documents public records searches and net worth conversion investigative procedures. Searches were made of voter registration and marriage records, the secretary of state's records, and real estate and contracting office records at the county level. Query investigation procedures involved neutral interviews with the company's personnel manager, a home builder, and a company secretary, as well as a friendly interview with another real estate buyer and a hostile interview with the real estate agent who was suspected of making illegal payments to Ivan Ben Steelin. An interrogation of Ivan Ben Steelin in order to gain access to his bank records leads to a signed confession. The investigation concludes with the obtaining of a signed confession statement and the calculation of real estate overpayments (losses) by the company.

Although not perfect, the report does provide an excellent example of the investigative procedures and documentation that should be pursued in fraud investigations. We encourage you to read it carefully.

INVESTIGATIVE REPORT
ON IVAN BEN STEELIN

# Silver Summit Real Estate

**Internal Audit (or Corporate Security)**
Special Cases File
030369

## Silver Summit Real Estate
Internal Audit Special Cases File
(IASCF) 030369

Regarding
Ivan Ben Steelin

### FILE INDEX

## Silver Summit Real Estate

To:       IASCF 030369
From:     Scott R. Bulloch
Date:     January 2, 2002
Re:       Ivan Ben Steelin
Subject:  Unsigned letter regarding Ivan Ben Steelin

On December 28, 2001, Vic Tumms, president and CEO of Silver Summit Real Estate, received an unsigned letter. The letter, dated December 27, 2001, referred to Ivan Ben Steelin. The letter, presented on page 2, is self-explanatory.

On December 30, 2001, the letter and its contents were discussed in a meeting at which Scott R. Bulloch (Silver Summit Real Estate's internal auditor), Vic Tumms, and Sue U. Buttz (Silver Summit Real Estate's legal counsel) were present.

Predicated on the contents of the letter, an investigation was commissioned by Sue U. Buttz, and was set to commence on January 1, 2002.

The original letter was initialed by Scott R. Bulloch and is maintained as evidence in IASCF 030369.

1

## Silver Summit Real Estate

December 27, 2001

Mr. Vic Tumms
President
Silver Summit Real Estate
5511 Vero Beach Road
Denver, Colorado 84057

Dear Mr. Tumms:

I believe you should investigate the relationship between Ivan Ben Steelin, the real estate acquisition manager, and Red Hot Real Estate. I believe we paid significantly more than fair market value for the 200 acres we purchased in the river bottom, as well as for several other properties.

Sincerely,


A Concerned Associate


1-1-2001

2

## Silver Summit Real Estate

To:        IASCF 030369
From:      Scott R. Bulloch
Date:      January 3, 2002
Re:        Ivan Ben Steelin
Subject:   Interview with Rebecca Monson

*Synopsis*

Rebecca Monson, personnel manager of Silver Summit Real Estate, advised on January 2, 2002, that Ivan Ben Steelin had been employed at Silver Summit Real Estate since January 7, 1994. Steelin's salary in 2001 was $45,000, and his supervisor was RaNae Workman, vice president of external affairs.

*Details*

Rebecca Monson, personnel manager of Silver Summit Real Estate, was interviewed at her office, 5511 Vero Beach Road, Denver, Colorado, telephone (999) 555-3463, on January 2, 2002. Rebecca was advised of the identity of the interviewers, Scott R. Bulloch and Sue U. Buttz, and provided the following information. Rebecca was advised that the nature of the inquiry was an "internal query of misconduct," as per the company's code of conduct.

The personnel records reflect that Ivan Ben Steelin, white male, date of birth August 5, 1964, social security 999-06-2828, residing at 1156 North Ocean Boulevard, Denver, Colorado, telephone (999) 225-1161, had been employed at Silver Summit Real Estate since January 7, 1994. According to the records, Steelin was married and had four children.

Steelin's initial salary was $38,000 per year, and he was an investment analyst in the external affairs department. Steelin was enlisted in the management training program on his hire date. His supervisor after he became an investment analyst was Mickey Sheraton, vice president of external affairs.

On January 1, 1996, Steelin was promoted to a purchasing representative position, still in the external affairs department. Steelin's salary was $45,000 per year, as reflected by the 2001 salary file.

RaNae Workman became vice president of external affairs in August of 1997 and was Ivan's immediate supervisor.

According to the records, prior to his employment with Silver Summit Real Estate, Ivan Ben Steelin was employed by Rockwell Laboratories in St. Louis, Missouri. His reason for leaving Rockwell Laboratories, as stated on the personnel information card, was that he wanted to be closer to his family in Colorado.

No background investigation was conducted by the company prior to hiring Steelin at Silver Summit Real Estate.

First National, Second National, Third National, and Fourth National Banks called in February 1997 to confirm Steelin's employment with Silver Summit Real Estate. The personnel department enters the nature of the inquiry in the personnel database each time an outside party asks about employees. No other parties have requested information about Steelin since February 1997.

The original personnel information card and a copy of outside party inquiries (consisting of two pages), were obtained from Rebecca Monson and initialed and dated by Scott R. Bulloch. They are maintained in IASCF 030369. Copies were left with Rebecca Monson.

Rebecca Monson was advised to keep the interview and its issues confidential.

## Personnel Information Card

Hire date: January 7, 1994                Social Security Number: 999-06-2828
Name: Steelin, Ivan Ben                   Birth date: August 5, 1964

Address at time of hire:
   1156 North Ocean Boulevard
   Denver, CO 80234

Emergency Contact:
   James Clintock                       Relation: Father-in-law
   1145 North 8000 West                 (999) 555-7974
   Denver, CO 80231

Previous Employers
_____

Rockwell Laboratories                     Position: Sales agent
66 Market Street                          Supervisor: Jeff Cole, Sales Manager
St. Louis, MO 63101                       Dates: 1988-1993

Reason for leaving: Would like to be closer to family in Colorado.

Ethics University                         Position: Mail courier
Denver, CO 80223                          Supervisor: Joseph Starks, Mail Manager
                                          Dates: 1985-1988

Reason for leaving: Graduated from Ethics University and accepted a position in St. Louis.


Reason for leaving:

Other pertinent information

*Ivan Ben Steelin*                        1-7-1994
_____
Signature                                 Date


Administrative Use Only
Background Check: No
Other: None


sb
1-2-2002

5

Outside Party Inquiries
Print date: January 3, 2002
Employee: Ivan Ben Steelin
File: 528062828

| Date | Party | Contact | Purpose |
|------|-------|---------|---------|
| 2/2/97 | First National Bank | Loan department | Confirm employment |
| 2/4/97 | Second National Bank | None given | Confirm employment |
| 2/12/97 | Third National Bank | Loan department | Confirm employment |
| 2/16/97 | Fourth National Bank | Credit department | Confirm employment |

sb
1-2-2002

### Silver Summit Real Estate

To:      IASCF 030369
From:    Scott R. Bulloch
Date:    January 4, 2002
Re:      Ivan Ben Steelin
Subject: Search of voter registration and marriage license records

*Voter Registration*
Voter registration records were examined on January 4, 2002, to confirm the information about Ivan Ben Steelin maintained by Silver Summit Real Estate's personnel department. The registration records substantiated that Steelin's address was 1156 North Ocean Boulevard, Denver, Colorado, 80234. Social security number, phone number, and date of birth were the same as maintained by the personnel department at Silver Summit Real Estate.

*Marriage License*
The marriage license of Mr. Steelin was inspected on January 4, 2002, at the Moore County Clerk's office. Ivan Ben Steelin was married to Clara Clintock on July 1, 1985. The records indicated that no previous marriages existed for either Mr. or Mrs. Steelin. The marriage license of Steelin revealed that his wife's parents, James and Jennifer Clintock, live at 1145 North 8000 West, Denver, Colorado, 80231—the address of Ivan Steelin at the time he was hired by Silver Summit Real Estate.

7

## Silver Summit Real Estate

To:       IASCF 030369
From:     Scott R. Bulloch
Date:     January 5, 2002
Re:       Ivan Ben Steelin
Subject:  Search of records at the Colorado secretary of state's office

The office of the secretary of state was visited on January 5, 2002, to survey:

- Business license records
- The UCC Records

### Business License Records

It could not be determined whether Steelin had ever sought a business license in the state of Colorado. A computer search on Prentice Hall's national database did not provide information that would substantiate that Steelin had held a business license in any other state in the United States.

### Uniform Commercial Code Records

The UCC records for Ivan Ben Steelin, 999-06-2828, 1156 North Ocean Boulevard, Denver, Colorado, reported the following information:

- Steelin made an acquisition of a boat at Ron's Boats, 25000 North State Street, Denver, Colorado, on November 12, 1998. The record reflected that a loan was not secured against the acquisition, though the cost of the boat was $23,000.
- On May 1, 1998, a purchase was made at Lund Furniture, 1400 West 1200 North, Denver, Colorado. The record reflects that the purchase, secured on store credit, cost a total of $9,425, with the acquisition items being the collateral for the credit. The purchase items consisted of:
    One (1) 44-inch Mitsubishi television set.
    One (1) Samsung home entertainment center.
    One (1) Broyhill bedroom set.
- On July 1, 1999, two automobiles were leased from Quickie Auto Imports, 1400 South State Street, Denver, Colorado, 80233.
    Auto 1: Audi 100, four-wheel-drive, VIN AUDI1234567891014.
    Auto 2: Subaru Legacy wagon, VIN SUBA1234567892024.
    The bargain purchase price, pending the end of the lease, was $45,000 less the cumulative lease payments of $1,150 per month.

8

- Cellular Three Telephone, 2200 Martin Parkway, Denver, Colorado, sold merchandise to Ivan Steelin on July 13, 1999. The record does not reflect that the acquisition was collateralized, though the cost was $2,000.
- Roger Tones Motors, 1275 South University Avenue, Denver, Colorado, sold one automobile to Ivan Ben Steelin on December 19, 2000. The automobile was partially paid for through a dealer loan, with the automobile being the collateral. The auto was a 2000 Volkswagen Passat Turbo touring sedan, VIN VW987654321123459. The purchase price was $26,497, and the amount of the loan was $10,000.
- On June 28, 2001, Bullard Jewelers Company, 1100 North University Avenue, sold merchandise on credit to Ivan Ben Steelin. The collateral to the purchase was the acquired merchandise, with the credit being extended by US Jewelers Credit Corporation of Denver, Colorado. The total cost of the acquisition was $8,200, with $4,000 being the credit amount. The description of the items identified:

  One (1) ring with 1.24 carat diamonds.
  Two (2) earrings, each with a 1.5 carat diamond.

# Silver Summit Real Estate

To:       IASCF 030369
From:     Scott R. Bulloch
Date:     January 7, 2002
Re:       Ivan Ben Steelin
Subject:  Search of real estate records

On January 7, 2002, the Moore County Land Office and the Moore County Tax Assessor's Office were visited to determine Ivan Ben Steelin's real estate holdings and their respective values.

### County Land Office

The property records of Moore County, Colorado, indicate that Ivan Ben Steelin's real estate holdings consist of:

- 1.1 acres of improved property located at 1156 North Ocean Boulevard, Denver, Colorado, 80234.

As cited by the County Land Office records, Steelin acquired the property on April 4, 1997, from Red Hot Real Estate. The records maintain that the property, consisting of 1.1 acres of land and one single-family dwelling, is indebted to Fourth National Bank. The amount of the indebtedness was not available from these records.

### County Tax Assessor's Office

The Moore County Tax Assessor's office records show a total tax base on the improved property, 1156 North Ocean Boulevard, Denver, Colorado, held by Ivan Ben Steelin, to be $275,000. The legal description of the property is as follows:

- 1.1 acres of property, with sewer and water.
- 4,100-square-foot single-family dwelling, built from building permit 19883000, issued on May 1, 1997.

The status of the tax payments, as reflected in the records, is that Steelin is current for his annual assessment.

10

## Silver Summit Real Estate

To:       IASCF 030369
From:     Scott R. Bulloch
Date:     January 8, 2002
Re:       Ivan Ben Steelin
Subject:  Search of records at the Moore County Contracting Office

On January 8, 2002, building permit 19883000 was examined at the Moore County Contracting Office.

The permit revealed the following information:

- The permit was issued to Ivan Ben Steelin on May 1, 1997.
- The designated licensed contractor on the building permit was Well's Custom Homes.
- The permit was for a single-family dwelling to be constructed at 1156 North Ocean Boulevard, Denver, Colorado, 80234.

The records accompanying the permit revealed that the dwelling passed code requirements and was available to be occupied on October 28, 1997.

11

## Silver Summit Real Estate

To:       IASCF 030369
From:     Scott R. Bulloch
Date:     January 8, 2002
Re:       Ivan Ben Steelin
Subject:  Interview with Jack Wells, owner of Wells Custom Homes

### Synopsis

Jack Wells, owner of Wells Custom Homes, telephone (999) 222-1212, was interviewed over the phone on January 8, 2002. Wells revealed that the charge for building Ivan Ben Steelin's home at 1156 North Ocean Boulevard, Denver, Colorado, was $240,000.

### Details

Jack Wells, owner of Wells Custom Homes, was interviewed over the phone on January 8, 2002. Wells was advised of the identity of the caller, Scott R. Bulloch, but not of the nature of the inquiry or of Scott R. Bulloch's position.

Wells stated that custom home construction is charged to clients on a square-foot basis. He stated that the average charge is $60 to $75 per square foot.

Wells remembered building a home for Ivan Ben Steelin. He stated that Steelin's home had been one of the first built by Wells Custom Homes. He revealed that the charge to Ivan Ben Steelin was $240,000.

Wells stated that payment had been received through a construction loan at Fourth National Bank, and that full payment had been received upon the house's passing the code requirements.

12

## Silver Summit Real Estate

To:      IASCF 030369
From:    Scott R. Bulloch
Date:    January 9, 2002
Re:      Ivan Ben Steelin
Subject: Net worth analysis of Ivan Ben Steelin

*Synopsis*
On January 9, 2002, Scott R. Bulloch and Sue U. Buttz performed a net worth analysis of Ivan Ben Steelin. The analysis revealed, conservatively, that Mr. Steelin may have had estimated income from unknown sources of $17,000, $22,000, $34,000, and $23,000 in the years 1998, 1999, 2000, and 2001, respectively.

*Details*
On January 9, 2002, Scott R. Bulloch and Sue U. Buttz performed a net worth analysis of Ivan Ben Steelin. Conservative estimates and interpolations were made with regard to Mr. Steelin's assets and liabilities. The estimates and interpolations were derived from information acquired through public records, interviews, and personnel records maintained by Silver Summit Real Estate.

The net worth analysis indicated that Mr. Steelin may have had unknown sources of income in the amounts of $17,000, $22,000, $34,000, and $23,000, in the years, 1998, 1999, 2000, and 2001, respectively.

Attached is the worksheet that details the process of determining the above-stated figures. The worksheet consists of one page; it was initialed by Scott R. Bulloch and is maintained in IASCF 030369.

13

*Net Worth Analysis*

|  | 1998 | 1999 | 2000 | 2001 |
|---|---|---|---|---|
| Assets: | | | | |
| Home | $275,000 | $275,000 | $275,000 | $275,000 |
| Cars | 5,000 | 45,000 | 70,000 | 70,000 |
| Boats | 23,000 | 23,000 | 23,000 | 23,000 |
| Furniture and other | 10,000 | 20,000 | 20,000 | 28,000 |
| Total assets | $313,000 | $363,000 | $388,000 | $396,000 |
| | | | | |
| *Liabilities:* | | | | |
| Home | $240,000 | $240,000 | $240,000 | $240,000 |
| Cars | 0 | 45,000 | 55,000 | 55,000 |
| Boats | 0 | 0 | 0 | 0 |
| Furniture and other | 10,000 | 10,000* | 10,000 | 14,000 |
| Total liabilities | $250,000 | $295,000 | $305,000 | $309,000 |
| | | | | |
| Net worth | $ 63,000 | $ 68,000 | $ 83,000 | $ 87,000 |
| Net worth increase | $ 10,000* | $  5,000 | $ 15,000 | $  4,000 |
| | | | | |
| *Living expenses:* | | | | |
| Mortgage | $ 24,000 | $ 24,000 | $ 24,000 | $ 24,000 |
| Food, etc. | 15,000 | 15,000 | 15,000 | 15,000 |
| Cars | 0 | 12,000 | 15,000 | 15,000 |
| Total living expenses | $ 39,000 | $ 51,000 | $ 54,000 | $ 54,000 |
| | | | | |
| Income | $ 49,000 | $ 56,000 | $ 69,000 | $ 58,000 |
| Known sources of income (net of taxes) | 32,000 | 34,000 | 35,000 | 35,000 |
| Funds from unknown sources | $ 17,000 | $ 22,000 | $ 34,000 | $ 23,000 |

*Determined from 1997 figures, which are not provided.

sb
1-9-2002

14

## Silver Summit Real Estate

To:       IASCF 030369
From:    Scott R. Bulloch
Date:    January 11, 2002
Re:       Ivan Ben Steelin
Subject: Average prices per acre paid by Silver Summit Real Estate

*Synopsis*

The records of the external affairs department were analyzed to track the average prices that each of the purchasing representatives has negotiated per acre of real estate purchased. Ivan Ben Steelin's average price is 23 to 42 percent higher than the average prices of the other three purchasing representatives.

*Details*

Four real estate purchasing representatives are employed by Silver Summit Real Estate. Each of the representatives is assigned purchasing tasks by the vice president of external affairs. The purchasing representative then initiates contacts and proceeds to fulfill their respective purchasing assignments.

The assignments are distributed equally among the four representatives. The records show that each representative executed the same number of real estate transactions as his or her counterpart representatives in the years 1998, 1999, 2000, and 2001.

A real estate purchasing project, for example (project 033189), to acquire 55 acres at 2000 North 8000 West, Boulder, Colorado, in 1989, revealed the following information:

- The 55-acre lot was owned by three different parties.
- Each of the three properties was listed by three different agencies, Red Hot Real Estate, Johnson Real Estate, and Monarch Real Estate, respectively.
- Steelin negotiated with Red Hot Real Estate, Peter Principle with Johnson Real Estate, and B.J. Integrity with Monarch Real Estate.
- Peter Principle's purchase of 21 acres cost $12,000, B.J. Integrity's purchase of 20.5 acres cost $10,500, and Steelin's purchase of 13.5 acres cost $10,000.

Data were gathered from purchase agreements, according to the purchasing representative, to determine the average price per acre of the real estate purchased. The data compilations revealed that Steelin's purchases were 23 to 42 percent higher than the purchases of the other purchasing representatives.

Attached (one page) are the data compilations extracted from the records of the external affairs department, as they pertain to the average prices per acre of real estate purchased. Scott R. Bulloch initialed and dated the document, and it is maintained in IASCF 030369.

15

*Average Prices Paid per Acre of Real Estate Purchased by*
*Silver Summit Real Estate*

| Purchasing Representative | 1998 | 1999 | 2000 | 2001 |
|---|---|---|---|---|
| Abraham Honest | 515 | 535 | 543 | 576 |
| B.J. Integrity | 507 | 532 | 571 | 561 |
| Peter Principle | 555 | 567 | 581 | 592 |
| Ivan Ben Steelin | 678 | 775 | 898 | 988 |

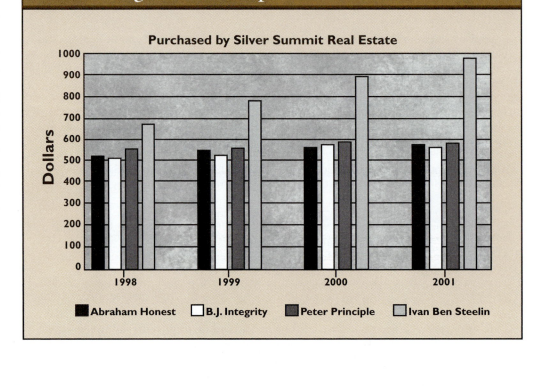

sb
1-11-2002

16

## Silver Summit Real Estate

To:       IASCF 030369
From:   Scott R. Bulloch
Date:   January 13, 2002
Re:      Ivan Ben Steelin
Subject: Computer queries on Steelin's transactions with real estate agencies

### *Synopsis*

Silver Summit Real Estate conducts real estate transactions through approved agencies that have listed the desired acquisition properties. Steelin has executed over 50 percent of his purchase transactions since January 1, 1998, through Red Hot Real Estate.

### *Details*

Computer queries on the external affairs database were executed on January 13, 2002, to determine the extent of Steelin's relations with Red Hot Real Estate.

First, the number of total transactions per purchasing representative was queried. It was revealed that each purchasing representative has performed 165 purchasing arrangements since January 1, 1998.

Eleven real estate agencies have been utilized since January 1, 1998. The agencies, all located in Moore County, Colorado, are employed based on their listing of properties, which Silver Summer Real Estate seeks to acquire. If a property is not listed, the purchasing representatives are instructed, as per external affairs department policy, to rotate their dealings among the eleven agencies. The policy states "that by rotating among the approved agencies, equity is cultivated, which will encourage the agencies to offer competitive prices."

Since January 1, 1998, each of the four purchasing representatives has dealt with all the approved agencies. Steelin put 86 transactions through Red Hot Real Estate during the period in question, January 1, 1998, through December 31, 2001. Fifty-two percent of Steelin's transactions were made through Red Hot Real Estate.

The query regarding the distribution of purchasing transactions (one page) and charts extracted (two pages) were printed, initialed, and dated by Scott R. Bulloch. The three pages are maintained in IASCF 030369.

17

*External Affairs Database*
*Distribution of Purchasing Transactions*

*January 13, 2002*
*User: Scott R. Bulloch*
*Dates searched: January 1, 1998, to December 31, 2001*

| Real Estate Agency | Abraham Honest | B.J. Integrity | Peter Principle | Ivan Ben Steelin |
|---|---|---|---|---|
| Red Hot | 17 | 10 | 17 | 86 |
| Johnson | 16 | 11 | 12 | 8 |
| Monarch | 19 | 18 | 13 | 9 |
| Rich | 10 | 15 | 17 | 7 |
| Martin | 7 | 15 | 18 | 8 |
| Labrum | 21 | 19 | 11 | 7 |
| Peterson | 16 | 10 | 20 | 7 |
| Century 46 | 22 | 20 | 14 | 9 |
| Littleton | 15 | 13 | 16 | 6 |
| Selberg | 10 | 15 | 16 | 6 |
| Baker | 12 | 19 | 9 | 8 |
| Total | 165 | 165 | 165 | 165 |

sb
1-13-2002

18

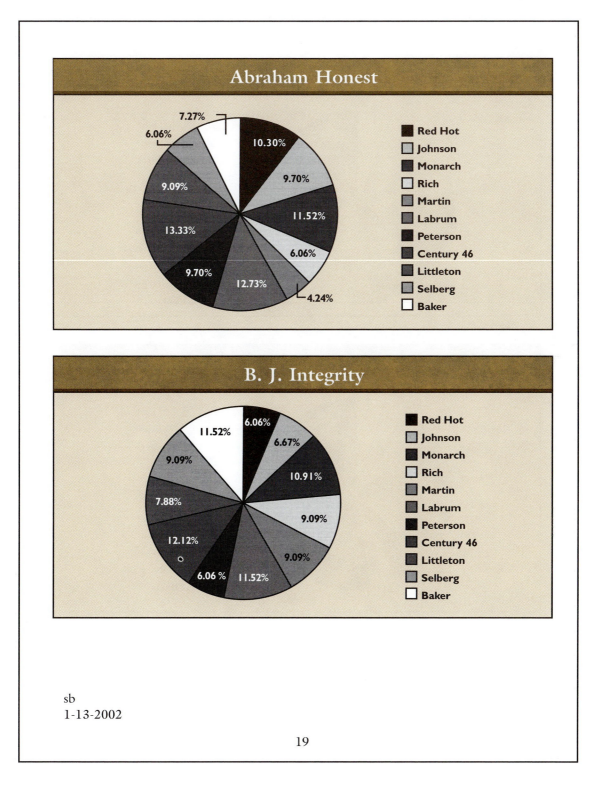

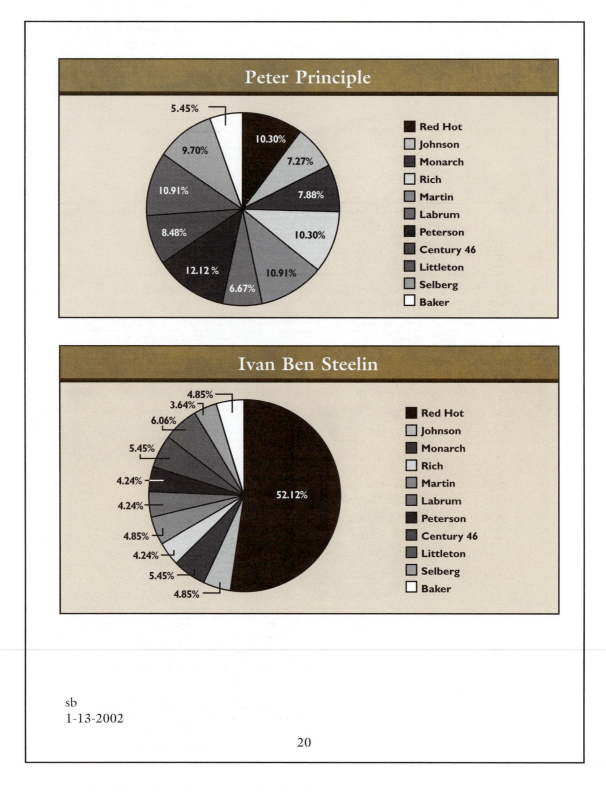

sb
1-13-2002

# Silver Summit Real Estate

To: IASCF 030369
From: Scott R. Bulloch
Date: January 20, 2002
Re: Ivan Ben Steelin
Subject: Interview with Peter Principle

*Synopsis*

Peter Principle, a purchasing representative at Silver Summit Real Estate, stated that he believes that Ivan Ben Steelin conducts his Red Hot Real Estate transactions through Richey Rich, a broker at Red Hot Real Estate.

*Details*

Peter Principle, a purchasing representative at Silver Summit Real Estate, was interviewed in his office, 5511 Vero Beach Road, Denver, Colorado, telephone (999) 555-3463, on January 20, 2002. After being advised of the interviewer, Scott R. Bulloch, and the nature of the inquiry as an investigation of misconduct, Mr. Principle provided the following information regarding Ivan Ben Steelin:

Mr. Principle stated that Red Hot Real Estate is a very aggressive agency. In particular, Mr. Principle believed that one broker, Richey Rich, was the most aggressive broker that he had dealt with.

Mr. Principle stated that Richey Rich used to call him (Principle) to solicit deals. Principle became a purchasing representative in January of 1994. Mr. Principle cited that Rich became a bother at first, but after Mr. Principle worked for six months as a purchasing representative, Mr. Rich quit calling him (Principle).

Mr. Principle believes that Ivan Ben Steelin works very closely with Richey Rich. He stated that he overheard a conversation between Rich and Steelin, in Steelin's office, in which Steelin conveyed that he'd "send business his [Rich's] way."

Mr. Principle does not know of another broker at Red Hot Real Estate whom Ivan Ben Steelin has dealt with.

# Silver Summit Real Estate

To:       IASCF 030369
From:     Scott R. Bulloch
Date:     January 22, 2002
Re:       Ivan Ben Steelin
Subject:  Interview with Michelle Wang

*Synopsis*

Michelle Wang, a secretary at Silver Summit Real Estate in the external affairs department, advised that Ivan Ben Steelin had an appointment scheduled for 3:30 PM with Richey Rich on January 22, 2002, at the Burnt Oven Pizza Restaurant.

*Details*

Michelle Wang, a secretary at Silver Summit Real Estate in the external affairs department, was interviewed at her office, 5511 Vero Beach Road, Denver, Colorado, telephone (999)-555-3463, on the morning of January 22, 2002. Ms. Wang was informed of the nature of the inquiry and of the identity of the interviewer, Scott R. Bulloch. Ms. Wang provided the following information:

Ms. Wang is responsible for answering all incoming calls at the external affairs department. If the desired party is out or unavailable, Ms. Wang records a message on carbon-copied message slips.

Ms. Wang stated that she answered several calls a week from Richey Rich for Ivan Ben Steelin. On January 21, 2002, Ms. Wang documented a message telling Mr. Steelin to meet Richey Rich at the Burnt Oven Pizza Restaurant at 3:30 PM on January 22, 2002.

The duplicate copy of the message (one page) was obtained from Ms. Wang, was initialed and dated by Scott R. Bulloch, and is maintained in IASCF 030369.

22

**External Affairs Department**

To:    Ivan                              Date:  1/21/2002
From:  Richey Rich                       Time:  10:15 AM
Of:    Red Hot Real Estate

  _X_   Called                  _____  Call Back at _____

_____  Stopped by

**Message:** Meet me at 3:30 PM on January 22—Burnt Oven Pizza Restaurant.

sb
1-22-2002

23

# Silver Summit Real Estate

To:       IASCF 030369
From:     Scott R. Bulloch
Date:     January 22, 2002
Re:       Ivan Ben Steelin
Subject:  Surveillance at Burnt Oven Pizza Restaurant

*Synopsis*

Ivan Ben Steelin had pizza and drinks with Richey Rich at the Burnt Oven Pizza Restaurant, 2750 East 1800 South, Denver, Colorado, on January 22, 2002. Steelin and Rich met from 3:30 PM to 4:45 PM. Steelin picked up the ticket of $14.50 and tipped the waiter a balance of a $20 bill. Rich gave Steelin a piece of paper before they left.

*Details*

During an interview, Michelle Wang, a secretary at Silver Summit Real Estate, advised of an appointment between Ivan Ben Steelin and Richey Rich. Ms. Wang provided a duplicate of a phone message slip regarding the appointment scheduled for 3:30 PM on January 22, 2002, at the Burnt Oven Pizza Restaurant.

According to the information provided, physical surveillance was established at the Burnt Oven Pizza Restaurant at 3:15 PM on January 22, and was terminated at 4:53 PM on the same date.

During the surveillance, Steelin and a white male, later identified as Richey Rich, had pizza and drinks. Steelin and Rich were observed writing in leather-like ring binders as they carried on a discussion.

After they consumed their provisions, Steelin put a $20 bill on the collection plate. As Steelin and Rich stood to leave, Rich was observed giving a piece of paper to Steelin, which Steelin placed in his left outside coat pocket.

The attached surveillance log furnished additional details. The surveillance log (one page) was initialed and dated by Scott R. Bulloch and is maintained in IASCF 030369.

January 22, 2002
Surveillance at the Burnt Oven Pizza Restaurant
Surveillance conducted by Scott R. Bulloch

| | |
|---|---|
| 3:15 PM | Established surveillance at the Burnt Oven Pizza Restaurant. |
| 3:25 PM | Ivan Ben Steelin arrives at the restaurant. |
| 3:33 PM | White male arrives and sits with Steelin. |
| 3:40 PM | Steelin and white male place orders with waiter. |
| 3:45 PM | Steelin and white male remove zipper ring binders from their briefcases, open them, and are observed writing in them as discussion takes place. |
| 3:48 PM | Waiter refills glasses with clear fluid. |
| 4:05 PM | Two pizzas are delivered to the table of Steelin and white male, and glasses are refilled with clear fluid. |
| 4:30 PM | Waiter takes plates and tableware from table of Steelin and white male, refills glasses, and leaves a collection plate. |
| 4:40 PM | Steelin and white male replace their zipper binders in their respective briefcases. |
| 4:42 PM | Steelin places a form of currency on the collection plate. |
| 4:45 PM | Steelin and white male stand up, white male hands Steelin a paper, and Steelin places the paper in his left outside coat pocket. |
| 4:45 PM | Steelin and white male shake hands and leave the restaurant. |
| 4:49 PM | Waiter, identified as Martin Lucky, states that the currency was a $20 bill and that the charge for the meal was $14.50. Lucky intends to keep the change as a tip. He advises that the white male is Richey Rich and that Rich is a frequent customer of the restaurant. |
| 4:53 PM | Surveillance terminated. |

sb
1-22-2002

25

## Silver Summit Real Estate

To:       IASCF 030369
From:     Scott R. Bulloch
Date:     January 28, 2002
Re:       Ivan Ben Steelin
Subject:  Interview with Richey Rich

### Synopsis
Richey Rich, a real estate broker with Red Hot Real Estate, advised that he has conducted a few transactions with Ivan Ben Steelin. Rich denied having had any inappropriate relations with Ivan Ben Steelin. Rich denied having ever had meals with Ivan Ben Steelin at the Burnt Oven Pizza Restaurant.

### Details
Richey Rich, a real estate broker with Red Hot Real Estate, was interviewed at his office, 3000 South Canyon Road, Denver, Colorado, on January 28, 2002. After being advised of the identity of the interviewer (Scott R. Bulloch) and the nature of the inquiry as an investigation of misconduct, Rich provided the following information:

"Red Hot Real Estate has done business with Silver Summit Real Estate for more than five years. Rich had conducted real estate transactions through all four of the purchasing representatives at Silver Summit Real Estate: Steelin, Honest, Integrity, and Principle."

Rich stated that he has conducted only a few transactions through Ivan Ben Steelin, because Steelin is "too demanding."

Richey Rich advised that not at any time have he and Steelin met for lunch at the Burnt Oven Pizza Restaurant, nor at any other restaurant.

Rich flatly denied furnishing bribes, kickbacks, or any other form of gratuities to Ivan Ben Steelin, or to any other purchasing representative at Silver Summit Real Estate. Rich stated that he suspects that other, unnamed agencies are furnishing gratuities to the purchasing representatives of Silver Summit Real Estate.

26

## Silver Summit Real Estate

To:        IASCF 030369
From:      Scott R. Bulloch
Date:      January 28, 2002
Re:        Ivan Ben Steelin
Subject:   Interview with Ivan Ben Steelin

Ivan Ben Steelin was interviewed at his office, 5511 Vero Beach Road, Denver, Colorado, telephone (999)-425-3463, on January 28, 2002. Steelin was advised that the interviewers were Scott R. Bulloch and Sue U. Buttz, and that an investigation was under way concerning an improper broker relationship.

Steelin was informed that the intent of the inquiry was to obtain a voluntary consent to examine his bank account records. Steelin stated that such a consent agreement was not necessary, and that he wished to meet in private at that time to discuss his predicament.

Ivan Ben Steelin was advised of his rights in regard to self-incrimination, and he executed an advice-of-rights form, a copy of which is attached. Steelin agreed to a videotaping of the interview that followed.

Steelin stated that family pressure to succeed and to measure up to his in-laws' expectations had led to his accepting payments from Richey Rich of Red Hot Real Estate. Steelin provided the attached free and voluntarily signed statement (two pages) regarding his association with Richey Rich, following the interview.

27

# Silver Summit Real Estate

## ADVICE OF RIGHTS*

Place:  Silver Summit Real Estate, 5511 Vero Beach Road, Denver, Colorado
Date:  January 28, 2002
Time:  11:30 AM

Before we ask you any questions, you must understand your rights.

You have the right to remain silent.

Anything you say can be used against you in court.

You have the right to talk to a lawyer for advice before we ask you any questions and to have a lawyer with you during questioning.

If you cannot afford a lawyer, one will be appointed for you before any questioning, if you wish.

If you decide to answer questions now without a lawyer present, you will still have the right to stop answering at any time. You also have the right to stop answering at any time until you talk to a lawyer.

## WAIVER OF RIGHTS

I have read this statement of my rights and I understand what my rights are. I am willing to make a statement and answer questions. I do not want a lawyer at this time. I understand and know what I am doing. No promises or threats have been made to me and no pressure or coercion of any kind has been used against me.

Signed: *Ivan Ben Steelin* 1-28-2002

Witness: *Scott R. Bulloch*

Witness: *Sue U. Buttz*

Time: 11:30 AM

*Private citizens are not required to give Miranda warnings. However, many prosecutors prefer that they be given.

28

## Silver Summit Real Estate

Denver, Colorado
January 28, 2002

I, Ivan Ben Steelin, furnish the following free and voluntary statement to Scott R. Bulloch and Sue U. Buttz, who have identified themselves to me as internal auditor and legal counsel, respectively, for Silver Summit Real Estate. No threats or promises of any kind have been used to induce this statement.

I have been advised that an internal inquiry has been and is being conducted to determine whether or not I have accepted any unlawful gratuities and violated the Silver Summit Real Estate code of conduct in my position as a purchasing representative for Silver Summit Real Estate. I have also been advised that I am the sole target of this internal inquiry; that the allegations could constitute a criminal act; and that I have a right to an attorney, should I choose.

I have been employed at Silver Summit Real Estate since January 7, 1994, and since January 1, 1996, have been a purchasing representative in the external affairs department, in Denver, Colorado.

I freely admit that I have accepted gratuities and other considerations from Richey Rich, real estate broker at Red Hot Real Estate, Denver, Colorado. The total amount of monies I have received is approximately $115,000 since January 1997. I have also received property, valued at approximately $35,000, from Richey Rich, on which property my personal residence was constructed.

Rich paid me the monies and provided the properties to ensure that I would continue to purchase real estate from Red Hot Real Estate. I was aware at the time I began taking money from Rich that such conduct was illegal and violated the Silver Summit Real Estate code of conduct. I committed these acts because of the financial pressure I felt to live up to others' expectations. I am sorry for my conduct, and I would like to begin to make reparations.

No one else at Silver Summit Real Estate was involved, nor did anyone else have knowledge of my activities.

29

I have read the above statement, consisting of this typewritten page and one other typewritten page. I have initialed the other page and now sign my name because this statement is true and correct to the best of my knowledge and belief.

*Ivan Ben Steelin*                    1-28-2002
Ivan Ben Steelin

*Scott R. Bulloch*
Scott R. Bulloch                      January 28, 2002

*Sue U. Buttz*
Sue U. Buttz                          January 28, 2002

# Silver Summit Real Estate

To:       IASCF 030369
From:     Scott R. Bulloch
Date:     February 13, 2002
Re:       Ivan Ben Steelin
Subject:  Estimated overpayment to Red Hot Real Estate

*Synopsis*

Computations indicate that the estimated loss to Silver Summit Real Estate for the years 1997 through 2001 due to overpayment to Red Hot Real Estate is approximately $436,568.

*Details*

On February 13, 2002, estimates were prepared concerning possible overpayment to Red Hot Real Estate as a result of activities conducted between Ivan Ben Steelin and Richey Rich.

Data on four of the eleven agencies that Silver Summit Real Estate conducts transactions with were extracted from the external affairs database. The data were extrapolated to determine the average prices paid per acre of real estate purchased through each of the four agencies.

The average cost computation was then applied to the acreage purchased from Red Hot Real Estate to determine an approximate overpayment to that agency over the last five years.

The total of the losses, as reflected on the attached one-page worksheet, is approximately $436,568 for the years 1997 through 2001.

31

### Average Cost per Acre

|            | 1997     | 1998     | 1999     | 2000     | 2001     |
|------------|----------|----------|----------|----------|----------|
| Johnson    | $505.00  | $525.00  | $545.00  | $565.00  | $576.00  |
| Labrum     | 508.00   | 520.00   | 541.00   | 560.00   | 573.00   |
| Century 46 | 503.00   | 530.00   | 548.00   | 568.00   | 581.00   |
| Monarch    | 510.00   | 524.00   | 545.00   | 567.00   | 575.00   |
| Average cost | $506.50 | $524.75 | $544.75 | $565.00 | $576.25 |

### Ivan Ben Steelin's Transactions with Red Hot Real Estate

|                          | 1997         | 1998         | 1999         | 2000         | 2001         |
|--------------------------|--------------|--------------|--------------|--------------|--------------|
| Cost paid to Red Hot     | $130,500.00  | $176,280.00  | $240,250.00  | $332,260.00  | $414,960.00  |
| Acreage received         | 200          | 260          | 310          | 370          | 420          |
| Average cost             | $652.50      | $678.00      | $775.00      | $898.00      | $988.00      |
| Expected cost for acreage | $101,200.00 | $136,435.00  | $168,872.50  | $209,050.00  | $242,025.00  |
| Estimated overpayment    | $29,200.00   | $39,845.00   | $71,377.50   | $123,210.00  | $172,935.00  |

Total loss = approximately $436,568

32

# PART FIVE

## MANAGEMENT FRAUD

357

# CHAPTER 11

# FINANCIAL STATEMENT FRAUD

## LEARNING OBJECTIVES

After studying this chapter, you should be able to:

1. Understand the role that financial statements play in U.S. businesses.

2. Describe the nature of financial statement fraud.

3. Become familiar with financial statement fraud statistics.

4. See how financial statement frauds occur and are concealed.

5. Understand the framework for detecting financial statement fraud.

6. Identify financial statement fraud exposures.

7. Explain how information regarding a company's management and directors, nature of organization, operating characteristics, relationship with others, and financial results can help assess the likelihood of financial statement fraud.

*Rite Aid Corporation opened its first store in September 1962 as Thrift D Discount Center in Scranton, Pennsylvania. From the start, the company grew rapidly through acquisitions and the opening of new stores, expanding to five northeastern states by 1965. It was officially named Rite Aid Corporation in 1968, the same year it made its first public offering and started trading on the American Stock Exchange. In 1970, Rite Aid moved to the New York Stock Exchange. Today, it is one of the nation's leading drugstore chains employing approximately 72,000 people in 28 states and the District of Columbia. Rite Aid currently operates approximately 3,400 stores, reporting total sales of $16.5 billion in 2004.*

*On June 21, 2002, the Securities and Exchange Commission filed accounting fraud charges against several former senior executives of Rite Aid Corp. The U.S. Attorney for the Middle District of Pennsylvania simultaneously announced related criminal charges. The SEC's complaint charged former CEO Martin Grass, former CFO Frank Bergonzi, and former Vice Chairman Franklin Brown with conducting a wide-ranging accounting fraud scheme. The complaint alleged that Rite Aid overstated its income in every quarter from May 1997 to May 1999, by massive*

*amounts. When the wrongdoing was ultimately discovered, Rite Aid was forced to restate its pretax income by $2.3 billion and net income by $1.6 billion, the largest restatement ever recorded. The complaint also charged that Grass caused Rite Aid to fail to disclose several related-party transactions, in which Grass sought to enrich himself at the expense of Rite Aid's shareholders. Finally, the Commission alleged that Grass fabricated Finance Committee minutes for a meeting that never occurred, in connection with a corporate loan transaction.*

*Wayne M. Carlin, Regional Director of the Commission's Northeast Regional Office, stated: "The charges against Rite Aid's executives reveal a disturbing picture of dishonesty and misconduct at the highest level of a major corporation. Rite Aid's former senior management employed an extensive bag of tricks to manipulate the company's reported earnings and defraud its investors. At the same time, former CEO Martin Grass concealed his use of company assets to line his own pockets. When the house of cards teetered on the edge of collapse, Grass fabricated corporate records in a vain effort to forestall the inevitable."*

*The Commission's complaint alleged the following:*

### Accounting Fraud Charges

- As a result of the fraudulent accounting practices, Rite Aid inflated its reported pretax income by the following amounts:

| | |
|---|---|
| 1Q98 | 38% |
| 2Q98 | 66% |
| 3Q98 | 16% |
| FY98 | 9% |
| 1Q99 | 71% |
| 2Q99 | 5,533% |
| 3Q99 | 94% |
| FY99 | Percentage not mathematically calculable—reported pretax income of $199.6 million, when actual results were loss of $14.7 million |
| 1Q00 | 54% |

The schemes that Rite Aid used to inflate its profits included the following:

- **Upcharges**—Rite Aid systematically inflated the deductions it took against amounts owed to vendors for damaged and outdated products. For vendors who did not require the unusable products to be returned to them, Rite Aid applied an arbitrary multiplier to the proper deduction amount, which resulted in overcharging its vendors by amounts that ranged from 35% to 50%. These practices, which Rite Aid did not disclose to the vendors, resulted in overstatements of Rite Aid's reported pretax income of $8 million in FY 1998 and $28 million in FY 1999.

- **Stock Appreciation Rights (SARs**—Rite Aid failed to record an accrued expense for stock appreciation rights it had granted to employees, in a program that gave the recipients the right to receive cash or stock in amounts tied to increases in the market price of Rite Aid stock. Rite Aid should have accrued an expense of $22 million in FY 1998 and $33 million in FY 1999 for these obligations

- **Reversals of Actual Expense**—In certain quarters, Bergonzi directed that Rite Aid's accounting staff reverse amounts that had been recorded for various expenses incurred and already paid. These reversals were completely unjustified and, in each instance, were put back on the books in the subsequent quarter, thus moving the expenses to a period other than that in which they had actually been paid. The effect was to overstate Rite Aid's income during the period in which the expenses were actually incurred. For example, Bergonzi directed entries of this nature which caused Rite Aid's pretax income for the second quarter of FY 1998 to be overstated by $9 million.

- **"Gross Profit" Entries**—Bergonzi directed Rite Aid's accounting staff to make improper adjusting entries to reduce cost of goods sold and accounts payable in every quarter from the first quarter of FY 1997 through the first quarter of FY 2000 (but not at year end, when the financial statements would be audited). These entries had no substantiation, and were intended purely to manipulate Rite Aid's reported earnings. For example, as a result of these entries alone, Rite Aid overstated pretax income by $100 million in the second quarter of FY 1999.

- **Undisclosed Markdowns**—Rite Aid overstated its FY 1999 net income by overcharging vendors for undisclosed markdowns on those vendors' products. The vendors did not agree to share in the cost of markdowns at the retail level, and Rite Aid misled the vendors into believing that these deductions—taken in February 1999—were for damaged and outdated products. As a result, Rite Aid overstated its FY 1999 pretax income by $30 million.

- **Vendor Rebates**—On the last day of FY 1999, Bergonzi directed that Rite Aid record entries to reduce accounts payable and cost of goods sold by $42 million, to reflect rebates purportedly due from two vendors. On March 11, 1999—nearly two weeks after the close of the fiscal year—Bergonzi directed that the books be reopened to record an additional $33 million in credits. All of these entries were improper, as Rite Aid had not earned the credits at the time they were recorded and had no legal right to receive them. Moreover, due to Rite Aid's pass-through obligations in agreements with its own customers, Rite Aid would have been obligated to pass $42 million out of the $75 million through to third parties. The $75 million in inflated income resulting from these false entries represented 37% of Rite Aid's reported pretax income for FY 1999.

- **Litigation Settlement**—In the fourth quarter of FY 1999, Grass, Bergonzi, and Brown caused Rite Aid to recognize $17 million from a litigation settlement. Recognition was improper, as the settlement was not in fact consummated in legally binding form during the relevant period.

- **"Dead Deal" Expense**—Rite Aid routinely incurred expenses for legal services, title searches, architectural drawings, and other items relating to sites considered but later rejected for new stores. Rite Aid capitalized these costs at the time they were incurred. Rite Aid subsequently determined not to construct new stores at certain of these sites. Under Generally Accepted Accounting Principles, Rite Aid should have written off the pertinent "dead deal" expenses at the time that it decided not to build on each specific site. Such writeoffs would have reduced reported income in the relevant periods. Instead, Rite Aid continued to carry these items on its balance sheet as assets. By the end of FY 1999, the accumulated dead deal expenses totaled $10.6 million.

- **"Will-Call" Payables**—Rite Aid often received payment from insurance carriers for prescription orders that were phoned in by customers but never picked up from the store. Rite Aid recorded a "will-call" payable that represented the total amount of these payments received from insurance carriers, that Rite Aid would be obligated to return to the carriers. In the fourth quarter of FY 1999, Rite Aid improperly reversed this $6.6 million payable. When Rite Aid's general counsel learned of this reversal, he directed that the payable be reinstated. Bergonzi acquiesced in the reinstatement, but then secretly directed that other improper offsetting entries be made which had the same effect as reversing the payable.

- **Inventory Shrink**—When the physical inventory count was less than the inventory carried on Rite Aid's books, Rite Aid wrote down its book inventory to reflect this "shrink" (i.e., reduction presumed due to physical loss or theft). In FY 1999, Rite Aid failed to record $8.8 million in shrink. In addition, also in FY 1999, Rite Aid improperly reduced its accrued shrink expense (for stores where a physical inventory was not conducted), producing an improper increase to income of $5 million.

### Related-Party Transactions with Grass

- Grass caused Rite Aid to fail to disclose his personal interest in three properties that Rite Aid leased as store locations. Rite Aid was obligated to disclose these interests as related-party transactions. Even after press reports in early 1999 prompted Rite Aid to issue corrective disclosure regarding these matters, Grass continued to conceal and misrepresent the facts, which caused Rite Aid's corrective disclosures to be false.

- Grass never disclosed an additional series of transactions, in which he funneled $2.6 million from Rite Aid to a partnership controlled by Grass and a relative. The partnership used $1.8 million of these funds to purchase an 83-acre site intended for a new headquarters for Rite Aid. Rite Aid subsequently paid over $1 million in costs related to this site even though it was owned by the partnership, and not by Rite Aid. After press reports raised questions about this site, Grass transferred $2.9 million back to Rite Aid from a personal bank account, but continued to conceal the series of transactions from Rite Aid's Board.

### Fabrication of Minutes by Grass

- In September 1999, when Rite Aid was in perilous financial condition, and in order to obtain a bank line of credit to keep the company afloat, Grass caused minutes to be prepared for a meeting of Rite Aid's Finance Committee, stating that the Committee had authorized the pledge of Rite Aid's stock in PCS Health Systems Inc. as collateral. Grass signed these minutes even though he knew that no such meeting occurred and the pledge was not authorized.1

On May 27, 2004 CEO Grass was sentenced to eight years in prison for his role

Rite Aid is an example of a company whose financial statements were misstated in a variety of ways. In the next three chapters, we will discuss these and other ways to manipulate the financial statements.

## The Problem of Financial Statement Fraud

America's capital markets are the envy of the world. The efficiency, liquidity, and resiliency of the markets stand second to none. **Financial statements** prepared by organizations play an important role in keeping America's markets efficient. They provide meaningful disclosures of where a company has been, where it is currently, and where it is going. Most financial statements are prepared with integrity and present a fair representation of the financial position of the organization issuing them. These financial statements are based upon generally accepted accounting principles, or GAAP, which guide how transactions are to be accounted for. Even though accounting principles do allow flexibility, standards of objectivity, integrity, and judgment must always prevail.

Unfortunately, financial statements are sometimes prepared in ways that misrepresent the financial position and financial results of an organization. The misstatement of financial statements can result from manipulating, falsifying, or altering accounting records. Misleading financial statements cause serious problems in the market and the economy. They often result in large losses by investors, lack of trust in the market and accounting systems, and litigation and embarrassment for individuals and organizations associated with **financial statement fraud**.

## Financial Statement Problems in Recent Years

During the years 2000–2002, numerous revelations of corporate wrongdoing in the United States, including financial statement fraud, created a crisis of confidence in our capital market system. Before we focus exclusively on financial statement fraud, we include an overview of the various abuses that occurred so you will understand the reasons behind the crisis of confidence in corporate America. Some of the most notable of these abuses that led to a $15 trillion dollar decline in the aggregate market value of all public company stock included the following:

- **Misstated financial statements and "cooking the books":** Examples included Qwest, Enron, Global Crossing, WorldCom, and Xerox, among others. Some of these frauds involved 20 or more people helping to create fictitious financial results and mislead the public. Although not all related to fraud, the number of financial statement restatements were 323 in 2003, 330 in 2002, 270 in 2001, and 233 in 2000.
- **Inappropriate executive loans and corporate looting:** Examples included John Rigas (Adelphia), Dennis Kozlowski (Tyco), and Bernie Ebbers (WorldCom).
- **Insider trading scandals:** The most notable example was Martha Stewart and Sam Waksal, both of whom have been convicted for selling ImClone stock.
- **Initial public offering (IPO) favoritism, including spinning and laddering** (spinning involves giving IPO opportunities to those who arrange quid pro quo opportunities, and laddering involves giving IPO opportunities to those who promise to buy additional shares as prices increase): Examples included Bernie Ebbers of WorldCom and Jeff Skilling of Enron.
- **Excessive CEO retirement perks:** Companies including Delta, PepsiCo, AOL Time Warner, Ford, GE, and IBM were highly criticized for endowing huge, costly perks and benefits, such as expensive consulting contracts, use of corporate planes, executive apartments, and maids to retiring executives.
- **Exorbitant compensation (both cash and stock) for executives:** Many executives, including Bernie Ebbers of WorldCom and Richard Grasso of the NYSE received huge cash and equity-based compensation that has since been determined excessive.
- **Loans for trading fees and other quid pro quo transactions:** Financial institutions such as Citibank and JP Morgan Chase, for example, provided favorable loans to companies such as Enron in return for the opportunity to make hundreds of millions of dollars in derivatives transactions and other fees.
- **Bankruptcies and excessive debt:** Because of the abuses described in this list and other similar problems, seven of the United States' ten largest corporate bankruptcies in history occurred in 2001 and 2002. These seven bankruptcies were WorldCom (largest ever at $101.9 billion), Enron (second largest ever at $63.4 billion), Global Crossing (fifth largest ever at $25.5 billion), Adelphia (six largest ever at $24.4 billion), United Airlines (seventh largest at $22.7 billion), PG&E (eighth largest at $21.5 billion), and Kmart (tenth largest at $17 billion.) Four of these seven included some kind of fraud.
- **Massive fraud by employees:** Although not in the news nearly as much as financial statement frauds, a large increase in fraud against organizations occurred with some of these frauds being as high as $2 to $3 billion dollars.

## Why These Problems Occurred

Each of the problems discussed here represents an ethical compromise. The explanations of why people commit fraud considered thus far in this book apply to financial statement fraud and these other problems as well.

Recall that three elements come together to motivate all frauds: (1) a perceived pressure, (2) a perceived opportunity, and (3) some way to rationalize the fraud as acceptable and consistent with one's personal code of ethics. Whether the dishonest act involves fraud against a company, such as employee embezzlement, as already discussed, or fraud on behalf of a company, such as financial statement fraud that we will now discuss, these three elements are always present. Figure 11-1 is a review of the fraud triangle, which we discussed earlier in the book.

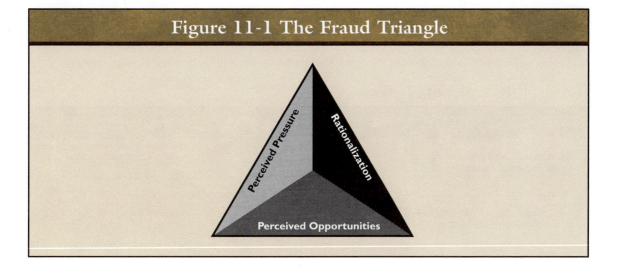

## Figure 11-1 The Fraud Triangle

Every fraud perpetrator faces some kind of *perceived pressure*. Examples of perceived financial pressures that can motivate financial statement fraud are financial losses, failure to meet Wall Street's earnings expectations, or the inability to compete with other companies.

Fraud perpetrators must also have a *perceived opportunity* or they will not commit fraud. Even with intense perceived pressures, executives who believe they will be caught and punished rarely commit fraud. On the other hand, executives who believe they have an opportunity (to commit or conceal fraud) often give in to perceived pressures. Perceived opportunities to commit management fraud include such factors as a weak board of directors or inadequate internal controls and the ability to obfuscate the fraud behind complex transactions or related-party structures.

Finally, fraud perpetrators must have some way to *rationalize* their actions as acceptable. For corporate executives, rationalizations to commit fraud might include thoughts such as "we need to keep the stock price high," "all companies use aggressive accounting practices," "it is for the good of the company," or "the problem is temporary and will be offset by future positive results."

The fraud triangle provides insights into why recent ethical compromises occurred. We believe nine factors came together to create what we call the *perfect fraud storm*. In explaining this perfect storm, we will use examples from recent frauds.

The first element of the perfect storm was the masking of many existing problems and unethical actions by the good economy of the 1990s and early 2000s. During this time, most businesses appeared to be highly profitable, including many new dot-com companies that were testing new (and many times unprofitable) business models. The economy was booming, and investment was high. In this period of perceived success, people made nonsensical investment and other decisions. The advent of "investing over the Internet" for a few dollars per trade brought many new, inexperienced people to the stock market. History has now shown that several of the frauds revealed since 2002 were actually being committed during the boom years but that the apparent booming economy hid the fraudulent behavior. The HealthSouth fraud, for example, began in 1986 and wasn't caught until 2003.

The booming economy also caused executives to believe that their companies were more successful than they were and that their companies' successes were primarily a result of good management. Academic researchers have found that extended periods of prosperity can reduce a firm's motivation to comprehend the causes of success, raising the likelihood of faulty attributions. In other words, during boom periods, many firms do not correctly ascribe the reasons behind their successes. Management usually takes credit for good company performance. When company performance degrades, boards often expect results similar to those in the past without new management styles or actions. When management does not correctly understand past reasons for success, they incorrectly think past methods will continue to work. Once methods that worked in the past only because of external factors fail, some CEOs may feel increased pressure. In some cases, this pressure contributed to fraudulent financial reporting and other dishonest acts.

The second element of the perfect fraud storm was the moral decay that has been occurring in the United States and the world in recent years. Whatever measure of integrity one uses, dishonesty appears to be increasing. For example, a number of researchers found that cheating in school, one measure of dishonesty, increased substantially in recent years. Table 11-1 summarizes some of these studies about cheating.

## Table 11-1 Studies of Honesty

| Ethical Measure | Year | % | Year | % | Study Authors |
|---|---|---|---|---|---|
| High school students who said they had cheated on an exam in last 12 mos. | 1996 | 64 | 1998 | 70 | Josephson Institute of Ethics |
| Middle school students who said they had cheated on an exam in 12 mos. | 1996 | ?? | 1998 | 54 | Josephson Institute of Ethics |
| College students across the nation admitting to cheating in high school | 1940s | 20% | Now | 75%–98% | Stephen Davis, psychology professor at Emporia State University |
| High school students admitting to cheating on exam in last year | 1992 | 61% | 2002 | 74% | Josephson Institute of Ethics (survey of 12,000 students) |
| High School students who cheated in past 12 months | 2000 | 71% | 2002 | 74% | Josephson Institute of Ethics |
| Students who had stolen | 2000 | 35% | 2002 | 38% | Josephson Institute of Ethics |
| Willing to lie to get a job | 2000 | 28% | 2002 | 39% | Josephson Institute of Ethics |
| Number of students self-reporting instances of unpermitted collaboration at nine medium to large state universities | 1963 | 11% | 1993 | 49% | Donald L. McCabe of Rutgers University |
| Percentage of American high school students who judged cheating to be "common" among their peers | 1940s | 20% | 1997 | 88% | *Who's Who Among American High School Students* (survey of 3,210 "high achievers" in 1997) |
| Number of high school students who admitted using a cheat sheet on a test | 1969 | 34% | 1989 | 68% | Fred Schab of the University of Georgia |
| Students who admitting to letting others copy their work | 1969 | 58% | 1989 | 98% | Fred Schab of the University of Georgia |

The third element of the perfect fraud storm was misplaced executive incentives. Executives of most fraudulent companies were endowed with hundreds of millions of dollars in stock options or restricted stock that made it far more important to keep the stock price rising than to report financial results accurately. In many cases, this stock-based compensation far exceeded executives' salary-based compensation. For example, in 1997, Bernie Ebbers, the CEO of WorldCom, had a cash-based salary of $935,000. Yet, during that same period, he was able to exercise hundreds of thousands of stock options, making millions in profits and received corporate loans totaling $409 million for purchase of stock and other purposes.[1] The attention of many CEOs shifted from managing the firm to managing the stock price. At the cost of countless billions of dollars, managing the stock price all too often turned into fraudulently managing the financials.

The fourth element of the perfect storm, and one closely related to the third element, was the often unachievable expectations of Wall Street analysts that targeted only short-term behavior. Company boards and management, generally lacking alternative performance metrics, used comparisons with the stock price of "similar" firms and attainment of analyst expectations as important de facto performance measures. These stock-based incentives compounded the pressure induced by the analyst expectations. Each quarter, the analysts, often coached by companies themselves, forecasted what each company's earnings per share (EPS) would be. The forecasts alone drove price movements of the shares, imbedding the expectations in the price of a company's stock. Executives knew that the penalty for missing the "street's" estimate was severe—even falling short of expectations by a small amount would drop the company's stock price by a considerable amount. Consider the following example of one of the frauds that occurred recently. For this company, the "street" made the following EPS estimates for three consecutive quarters:[2]

| Firm | 1st Quarter | 2nd Quarter | 3rd Quarter |
|------|-------------|-------------|-------------|
| Morgan Stanley | $0.17 | $0.23 | |
| Smith Barney | 0.17 | 0.21 | 0.23 |
| Robertson Stephens | 0.17 | 0.25 | 0.24 |
| Cowen & Co. | 0.18 | 0.21 | |
| Alex Brown | 0.18 | 0.25 | |
| Paine Webber | 0.21 | 0.28 | |
| Goldman Sachs | 0.17 | | |
| Furman Selz | 0.17 | 0.21 | 0.23 |
| Hambrecht & Quist | 0.17 | 0.21 | 0.23 |

Based on these estimates, the consensus estimate was that the company would have EPS of $0.17 in the first quarter, $0.22 in the second quarter, and $0.23 in the third quarter. As has now been shown, the company's actual earnings during the three quarters were $0.08, $0.13, and $0.16 respectively. In order to not miss the Wall Street estimates, management committed a fraud of $62 million or $.09 per share in the first quarter, a fraud of $.09 in the second quarter and a fraud of $0.07 in the third quarter.

The complaint in this case read (in part) as follows:

> *The goal of this scheme was to ensure that [the company] always met Wall Street's growing earnings expectations for the company. [The company's] management knew that meeting or exceeding these estimates was a key factor for the stock price of all publicly traded companies and therefore set out to ensure that the company met Wall Street's targets every quarter regardless of the company's actual earnings. During the period 1998 to 1999 alone, management improperly inflated the company's operating income by more than $500 million before taxes, which represents more than one-third of the total operating income reported by [the company].*

The fifth element in the perfect storm was the large amounts of debt and leverage each of these fraudulent companies had. This debt placed tremendous financial pressure on executives not only to have high earnings to offset high interest costs but also to report high earnings to meet debt and other covenants. For example, during 2000, Enron's derivates-related liabilities increased from $1.8 billion to $10.5 billion. Similarly, WorldCom had more than $100 billion in debt when it filed history's largest bankruptcy. During 2002 alone, 186 public companies, including WorldCom, Enron, Adelphia, and Global Crossing, with $368 billion in debt filed for bankruptcy in the United States.[3]

The sixth element of the perfect storm was the nature of U.S. accounting rules. In contrast to accounting practices in other countries such as the United Kingdom and Australia, U.S. generally accepted accounting principles (GAAP) are much more rule-based than principles-based.[4] One perspective on having rules-based standards is that if a client chooses a particular questionable method of accounting that is not specifically prohibited by GAAP, it is difficult for auditors or others to argue that the client can't use that method of accounting. The existing general principles already contained within GAAP notwithstanding, when auditors and other advisors sought to create competitive advantages by identifying and exploiting possible loopholes, it became harder to make a convincing case that a particular accounting treatment is prohibited when it "isn't against the rules." Professional judgment lapsed as the general principles already contained within GAAP and SEC regulations were ignored or minimized. The result was that rather than deferring to existing, more general rules, specific rules (or the lack of specific rules) were exploited for new, often complex financial arrangements, as justification to decide what was or was not an acceptable accounting practice.

As an example, consider the case of Enron. Even if Arthur Andersen had argued that Enron's special-purpose entities (SPEs) weren't appropriate, it would have been impossible for them to make the case that they were against any specific rules. Some have suggested that one of the reasons it took so long to get plea bargains or indictments in the Enron case was because it wasn't immediately clear whether GAAP or any laws had actually been broken.

A seventh element of the perfect fraud storm was the opportunistic behavior of some CPA firms. In some cases, accounting firms used audits as loss leaders to establish relationships with companies so they could sell more lucrative consulting services. The rapid growth of the consulting practices of the "Big 5" accounting firms, which was much higher than the growth of other consulting firms, attested to the fact that it is much easier to sell consulting services to existing audit clients than to new clients. In many cases, audit fees were much smaller than consulting fees for the same clients, and accounting firms felt little conflict between independence and opportunities for increased profits. In particular, these alternative services allowed some auditors to lose their focus and become business advisors rather than auditors. This tendency was especially true of Arthur Andersen, which had spent considerable energy building its consulting practice, only to see that practice split off into a separate firm. Privately, several Andersen partners admitted that the surviving Andersen firm and some of its partners vowed to "out consult" the firm that separated from them and became preoccupied with that goal.

The eighth element of the perfect storm was greed by executives, investment banks, commercial banks, and investors. Each of these groups benefited from the strong economy, the high level of lucrative transactions, and the apparently high profits of companies. None of them wanted to accept bad news. As a result, they sometimes ignored negative news and entered into bad transactions.[5] For example, in the Enron case, various commercial and investment banks made hundreds of millions from Enron's lucrative investment banking transactions, on top of the tens of millions in loan interest and fees. None of these firms alerted investors about derivatives or other underwriting problems at Enron. Similarly, in October 2001, after several executives abandoned Enron and negative news about Enron was reaching the public, 16 of 17 security analysts covering Enron still rated the company a "strong buy" or "buy."[6] Enron's outside law firms were also making high profits from Enron's transactions. These firms also failed to correct or disclose any problems related to the derivatives and special-purpose entities, but in fact helped draft the requisite associated legal documentation. Finally, the three major credit rating agencies, Moody's, Standard & Poor's, and Fitch/IBC—who all received substantial fees from Enron— also did nothing to alert investors of pending problems. Amazingly, just weeks prior to Enron's bankruptcy filing—after most of the negative news was out and Enron's stock was trading at $3 per share—all three agencies still gave investment grade ratings to Enron's debt.[7]

Finally, the ninth element of the perfect storm was three types of educator failures. First, educators had not provided sufficient ethics training to students. By not forcing students to face realistic ethical dilemmas in the classroom, graduates were ill-equipped to deal with the real ethical dilemmas they faced in the business world. In one allegedly fraudulent scheme, for example, participants included virtually the entire senior management of the company, including but not limited to its former chairman and chief executive officer, its former president, two former chief financial officers, and various other senior accounting and business personnel. In total, it is likely that more than 20 individuals were involved in the earnings overstatement schemes. Such a large number of participants points to a generally failed ethical compass for this group. Consider another case of a chief accountant. A CFO instructed the chief accountant to increase earnings by an amount somewhat over $100 million. The chief accountant was skeptical about the purpose of these instructions but did not challenge them. Instead, the chief accountant followed directions and allegedly created a spreadsheet containing seven pages of improper journal entries—105 in total—that he determined were necessary to carry out the CFO's instructions. Such fraud was not unusual. In many of the cases, the individuals involved had no prior records of dishonesty—and yet when they were asked to participate in fraudulent accounting, they did so quietly and of their free will.

A second educator failure was not teaching students about fraud. In the experience of one professor who taught a fraud course to business students for several years, he felt that most business school graduates would not recognize a fraud if it hit them between the eyes. The large majority of business students don't understand the elements of fraud, perceived pressures and opportunities, the process of rationalization, or red flags that indicate the possible presence of dishonest behavior. When they do see something that doesn't look right, their first reaction is to deny a colleague could be committing dishonest acts.

A third educator failure is the way we have taught accountants and business students in the past. Effective accounting education must focus less on teaching content as an end unto itself and instead use content as a context for helping students develop analytical skills. In too many cases, accountants applied what they thought was appropriate content knowledge to unstructured or different situations, only to find out later that the underlying issues were different than they had thought and that they totally missed the major risks inherent in the circumstances.

Because of these financial statement and other problems that caused such a decline in the market value of stocks and a loss of investor confidence, a number of new laws and corporate governance changes have been implemented by the SEC, PCAOB, NYSE, NASDAQ, FASB, and others. We review these changes in the appendix to this chapter.

## Nature of Financial Statement Fraud

Financial statement fraud, like other types of fraud, involves intentional deceit and attempted concealment. Financial statement fraud may be concealed through falsified documentation, including forgery. Financial statement fraud may also be concealed through collusion among management, employees, or third parties. Unfortunately, like other fraud, financial statement fraud is rarely seen. Rather, fraud symptoms, indicators, or red flags are usually observed. Because what appear to be symptoms can be caused by other legitimate factors, the presence of fraud symptoms does not always indicate the existence of fraud. For example, a document may be missing, a general ledger may be out of balance, or an analytical relationship may not make sense. However, these conditions may be the result of circumstances other than fraud. Documents may have been legitimately lost, the general ledger may be out of balance because of an unintentional accounting error, and unexpected analytical relationships may be the result of unrecognized changes in underlying economic factors. Caution should be used even when reports of alleged fraud are received, because the person providing the tip or complaint may be mistaken or may be motivated to make false allegations.

Fraud symptoms cannot easily be ranked in order of importance or combined into effective predictive models. The significance of red flags varies widely. Some factors will be present when no fraud exists; alternatively, only a smaller number of symptoms may exist when fraud is occurring. Many times, even when fraud is suspected, it can be difficult to prove. Without a confession, obviously forged documents, or a number of repeated similar fraudulent acts (so fraud can be inferred from a pattern), convicting someone of fraud is difficult. Because of the difficulty of detecting and proving fraud, investigators must exercise extreme care when performing fraud examinations, quantifying fraud, or performing other types of fraud-related engagements.

**Financial Statement Fraud Statistics.** How much financial statement fraud occurs is difficult to know. One way to measure it is to look at some of the **SEC enforcement releases** (Accounting and Auditing Enforcement Releases—AAERs). One or more enforcement release is usually issued when financial statement fraud occurs at a company that has publicly traded stock.

At least three studies examined AAERs. One of the first and most comprehensive was the Report of the National Commission on Fraudulent Financial Reporting, issued by the National Commission on Fraudulent Financial Reporting, known as the **Treadway Commission**. The Treadway Commission report found that even though financial statement frauds occur infrequently, they are extremely costly. The Treadway Commission studied frauds that occurred during a 10-year period ending in 1987.[8] This study examined 119 SEC Enforcement actions that occurred during the period 1981 through 1986.

In 1999, the **Committee of Sponsoring Organizations (COSO)** released another study of fraudulent financial statement frauds that occurred during the period 1987–1997.[9] This study found that approximately 300 financial statement frauds were the subject of SEC enforcement releases during the period. A random sample of 204 of these frauds revealed the following:

1. The average financial statement fraud period extended 23.7 months, and the frequency of fraudulent acts was consistent during the period.

2. The most common methods used to perpetrate financial statement frauds were improper revenue recognition, the overstatement of assets, and the understatement of expenses. With respect to revenue frauds, recording fictitious revenues was the most common way of perpetrating fraud, and recording revenues prematurely was the second most common way of perpetrating revenue fraud. With respect to overstating assets, overstating existing assets was most common; recording fictitious assets or assets not owned was second most common; and capitalizing items that should be expensed was the third most common. Other common types of financial statement frauds included misappropriation of assets (large enough to render the financial statements misleading) and inappropriate disclosure.

3. The assets most often misstated were accounts receivable, inventory, property, plant, and equipment, loans/notes receivable, cash, investments, patents, and natural resources.

4. The mean cumulative financial statement misstatement was $25 million, while the median cumulative misstatement was $4.1 million. The mean was disproportionally increased by several notably large frauds. The mean largest single year or quarter misstatement of net income was $9.9 million.

5. The chief executive officer (CEO) was the person who was the perpetrator of the fraud in 72 percent of the cases. Other positions (in descending order of frequency) were chief financial officer (CFO), controller, chief operating officer, other vice presidents, board of director members, lower-level personnel, and others. In 29 percent of the cases, the external auditor was named in an AAER. In these cases, the auditor was charged with either violating Rule 10(b)5 of the 1934 Securities Exchange Act or with aiding and abetting others in a violation of Rule 10(b)5.

6. In 55 percent of the fraud cases, the last audit report prior to the fraud was an unqualified audit opinion. In 24 percent of the cases, the last audit opinion contained going concern, litigation, or other uncertainties. In 17 percent of the cases, the opinion had modifications or qualifications due to a change in accounting principle or a change in auditors, and 4 percent of the cases involved other qualifications, such as a scope limitation.

7. The mean total assets of companies involved in fraudulent reporting of their financial statements were $532 million; the mean revenues, $232 million; and the mean shareholders' equity, $86 million. The medians were much lower, with $16 million in assets, $13 million in revenues, and $5 million in shareholders' equity.

8. Industries with the most frauds were the computer hardware/software industry with 12 percent of the frauds; other manufacturers with 12 percent; financial service providers with 11 percent; health care and health products with 9 percent; and retailers/wholesalers and other service providers with 7 percent each. Other industries with 3 percent or more were mining/oil and gas, telecommunications, insurance, and real estate.

9. Seventy-eight percent of the fraudulent companies were listed on the NASDAQ or other over-the-counter markets, 15 percent of the companies' stocks were traded on the New York Stock Exchange, and 7 percent were traded on the American Stock Exchange.

10. Severe consequences were usually associated with companies having fraudulent financial statements. Thirty-six percent of the companies either filed for Chapter 11 bankruptcy, were described as "defunct" in the AAERs, or were taken over by a state or federal regulator after the fraud occurred. An additional 15 percent sold a large portion of their assets, merged with another company, or had a new controlling shareholder following the occurrence of the financial statement fraud. Twenty-one percent of the companies had their stock delisted from the national stock exchange where the stock was traded. Twenty-four percent of the companies were sued or settled with shareholders or bondholders, generally as part of a class action lawsuit filed subsequent to the disclosure of the fraud.

11. Most companies either had no audit committee or had an audit committee that met less than twice per year. Even though most of the companies (75%) ostensibly had an audit

committee typically composed of outside directors, the committees generally met only annually.

12. Boards of directors were dominated by insiders and "grey" directors with significant equity ownership and apparently little experience serving as directors of other companies. Approximately 60 percent of the directors were insiders or grey directors (i.e., outsiders with special ties to the company or management). Collectively, the directors and officers owned nearly one-third of the companies' stock. Nearly 40 percent of the boards had no directors who served as outside or grey directors on another company's boards.

13. Family relationships between directors and officers were fairly common, as were individuals who apparently had significant power. In nearly 40 percent of the companies, the proxy provided evidence of family relationships between the directors and officers. The founder was on the board, or the original CEO/president was still in place in nearly one-half of the companies. More than 20 percent of the companies showed evidence of officers holding incompatible job functions (e.g., CEO and CFO).

14. Some companies committing financial statement fraud were experiencing net losses or were close to break-even positions in periods prior to the fraud. Pressures of financial strain or distress may have provided incentives for fraudulent activities for some companies. The lowest quartile of companies indicates that they were in a net loss position, and the median company had net income of only $175,000 in the year preceding the first year of the fraud period. Some companies were experiencing downward trends in net income in periods preceding the first fraud period, while other companies were experiencing upward trends in net income. Thus, the subsequent frauds may have been designed to reverse downward spirals for some companies and to preserve upward trends for other companies.

15. All sizes of audit firms were associated with companies committing financial statement frauds. Fifty-six percent of the sample fraud companies were audited by what was then a Big Eight or Big Six auditor during the fraud period, and 44 percent were audited by non-Big Eight or Big Six auditors.

16. Financial statement fraud occasionally implicated the external auditor. Auditors were named in 56 of the 195 fraud cases where AAERs explicitly named individuals. They were named for either alleged involvement in the fraud (30 of 56 cases) or for negligent auditing (26 of 56 cases). Most of the auditors explicitly named in an AAER (46 of 56) were non-Big Eight or Big Six auditors.

17. Some companies changed auditors during the fraud period. Just over 25 percent of the companies changed auditors during the time frame beginning with the last clean financial statement period and ending with the last fraud financial statement period. A majority of the auditor changes occurred during the fraud period (e.g., two auditors were associated with the fraud period) and involved changes from one non-Big 8 or Big 6 auditor to another non-Big 8 or Big 6 auditor.

18. Consequences associated with financial statement fraud were severe for the individuals allegedly involved. Individual senior executives were subject to class action legal suits and SEC actions that resulted in financial penalties for the executives personally. A significant number of individuals were terminated or forced to resign from their executive positions. However, relatively few individuals explicitly admitted guilt or eventually served prison sentences.

The third study is the report of the study that the Sarbanes-Oxley Act directed the Securities and Exchange Commission to do under Section 704 of the act.[10] The requirement was that the SEC study all of its enforcement actions filed during the period July 31, 1997, through July 30, 2002, that were based on improper financial reporting, fraud, audit failure, or auditor independence violations. Over the study period, the SEC filed 515 enforcement actions for financial reporting and disclosure violation involving 164 different entities. The number of actions in the five-year study was as follows:

| | |
|---|---|
| Year 1 | 91 |
| Year 2 | 60 |
| Year 3 | 110 |
| Year 4 | 105 |
| Year 5 | 149 |

Like the previous studies, the study found that the SEC brought the greatest number of actions in the area of improper revenue recognition, including fraudulent reporting of fictitious sales, improper timing of revenue recognition, and improper valuation of revenue. The second highest category involved improper expense recognition, including improper capitalization or deferral of expenses, improper use of reserves, and other understatement of expenses. The other categories were improper accounting for business combinations, inadequate Management's Discussion and Analysis disclosure, and improper use of off-balance sheet arrangements.

Like the previous studies, this study also found that CEOs, presidents, and CFOs were the members of management most often implicated in the frauds, followed by board chairs, chief operating officers, chief accounting officers, and vice presidents of finance. In 18 of the cases, the SEC also brought charges against auditing firms and individual auditors.

These findings are consistent with a study conducted in the United Kingdom by the Auditing Practices Board (APB) of England. Their study also found that the majority of financial statement frauds are committed by company management. They found that financial statement frauds involve no actual theft and are unlikely to be detected by statutory auditors. Of the fraud cases the APB reviewed, 14 affected the company accounts financially, and in all 14 cases, senior management played a key role. Sixty-five percent of the cases involved misstatement of financial data to boost share prices or disguise losses.[11]

**An Example of Financial Statement Fraud.** Although the percentage of fraudulent financial statements is relatively small, the damage caused by even one fraudulent set of financial statements is staggering. Consider, for example, the Phar-Mor fraud. In this case, the COO, Michael "Mickey" Monus, was sentenced to 19 years and seven months in prison. The fraud resulted in more than $1 billion in losses and the bankruptcy of the 28th largest private company in the United States. Phar-Mor's former auditors, a Big 5 firm, faced claims of more than $1 billion (which it settled for significantly less.)

The Phar-Mor fraud is a good example of how financial statement fraud occurs. Mickey Monus opened the first Phar-Mor store in 1982. It sold a variety of household products and prescription drugs at prices substantially lower than other discount stores. The key to the low prices was supposed to be "power buying," a phrase Monus used to describe his strategy of loading up on products when suppliers were offering rock-bottom prices. When he started Phar-Mor, Monus was president of Tamco, a family-held distributing company that had recently been acquired by the Pittsburgh-based Giant Eagle grocery store chain. In 1984, David Shapira, president of Giant Eagle, funded the expansion of Phar-Mor with $4 million from Giant Eagle. Shapira then became the CEO of Phar-Mor, and Monus was named president and COO. By the end of 1985, Phar-Mor had 15 stores. By 1992, a decade after the first store opened, 310 stores had been opened in 32 states, posting sales of more than $3 billion.

Phar-Mor's prices were so low that competitors wondered how it could sell products so cheap and still make a profit. It appeared to be on its way to becoming the next Wal-Mart. In fact, Sam Walton once stated that the only company he feared in the expansion of Wal-Mart was Phar-Mor. After five or six years, however, Phar-Mor began losing money. Unwilling to allow these shortfalls to damage Phar-Mor's appearance of success, Monus and his team began to engage in creative accounting, which resulted in Phar-Mor never reporting losses in its financial statements. Federal fraud examiners discerned five years later that the reported pretax income for fiscal 1989 was overstated by $350,000, and that the year 1987 was the last year that Phar-Mor actually made a profit.

Relying upon these erroneous financial statements, investors saw Phar-Mor as an opportunity to cash in on the retailing craze. Among the big investors were Westinghouse Credit Corp., Sears Roebuck & Co., mall developer Edward J. de Bartolo, and the prestigious Lazard Freres & Co. Prosecutors stated that banks and investors put $1.14 billion into the company, based on the fictitious financial statements.

To hide Phar-Mor's cash flow problems, attract investors, and make the company look profitable, Michael Monus and his subordinate, Patrick Finn, altered the inventory accounts to understate the cost of goods sold and overstate income. In addition to the financial statement fraud, internal investigations by the company estimated embezzlement in excess of $10 million. Most of the stolen funds were used to support Michael Monus's now-defunct World Basketball League. Michael Monus and Patrick Finn used three different methods of income statement fraud, including account manipulation, overstatement of inventory, and accounting rules manipulation.

In 1985 and 1986, well before the large fraud began, Michael Monus was directing Patrick Finn to understate certain expenses that came in over budget and overstate those expenses that came in under budget, making operations look efficient. Although the net effect of these first manipulations evened out, the accounting information was not accurate. Finn later suggested that this seemingly harmless request by Monus was an important precursor to the later extensive fraud.

Finn also increased Phar-Mor's actual gross profit margin of 14.2 percent to about 16.5 percent by inflating inventory accounts. The company hired an independent firm to count inventory in its stores. After the third-party inventory counters submitted a report detailing amount and retail value for a store's inventory, Phar-Mor's accountants would prepare what they called a "compilation packet." The packet calculated the amount of inventory at cost, and journal entries were then prepared. Based on the compilation, the accountants would credit inventory to properly report the sales activity, but rather than record a debit to Cost of Goods Sold, they debited so-called "bucket" accounts. To avoid auditor scrutiny, the bucket accounts were emptied at the end of each fiscal year by allocating the balance to individual stores as inventory. Because the related cost of goods sold was understated, Phar-Mor made it appear as if it were selling merchandise at higher margins. Because the cost of sales was understated, net income was overstated.

Phar-Mor would regularly pressure vendors for large, up-front payments in exchange for not selling competitors' products in their stores. These payments were called "exclusivity payments," and some vendors paid up to $25 million for these rights. Monus would use this money to cover the hidden losses and pay suppliers. Instead of deferring revenue from these exclusivity payments over the life of the vendor's contracts—consistent with generally accepted accounting principles—Monus and Finn would recognize all the revenue up front. As a result of this practice, Phar-Mor was able to report impressive results in the short run.

## Motivations for Financial Statement Fraud

Motivations to issue fraudulent financial statements vary from case to case. As indicated previously in the "perfect storm" analysis, sometimes the motivation is to support a high stock price or a bond or stock offering. At other times, the motivation is to increase the company's stock price. In some companies that issued fraudulent financial statements, top executives owned large amounts of company stock, and a decrease in the stock price would have significantly decreased their own personal net worth.

Sometimes, division managers overstate financial results to meet company expectations. Many times, pressure on management is high, and when faced with failure or cheating, some managers will turn to cheating. In the Phar-Mor case, Micky Monus wanted his company to grow quickly, so he lowered prices on 300 "price sensitive" items. Prices were cut so much that items were sold below cost, making each sale result in a loss. The strategy helped Phar-Mor win new customers and open dozens of new stores each year. However, the strategy resulted in huge loses for the company, and rather than admitting that the company was facing losses, Mickey Monus hid the losses and made Phar-Mor appear profitable. Although the motivations for financial statement fraud differ, the results are always the same—adverse consequences for the company, its principals, and its investors.

# A Framework for Detecting Financial Statement Fraud

Identifying fraud exposures is one of the most difficult steps in detecting financial statement fraud. Correctly identifying exposures means that you must clearly understand the operations and nature of the organization you are studying as well as the nature of the industry and its competitors. Investigators must have a good understanding of the organization's management and what motivates them. Investigators must understand how the company is organized. Investigators need to be aware of relationships the company has with other parties and the influence that each of those parties has on the client and its officers.

Fraudulent financial statements are rarely detected by analyzing the financial statements alone. Rather, financial statement fraud is usually detected when the information in the financial statements is compared with the real-world referents those numbers are supposed to represent, and the context in which management is operating and being motivated. Fraud is often detected by focusing on the changes in reported assets, liabilities, revenues, and expenses from period to period or by comparing company performance to industry norms. In the ZZZZ Best fraud case, for example, each period's financial statements looked correct. Only when the change in assets and revenues from period to period were examined and when assets and revenues reported in the financial statements were compared with actual building restoration projects was it determined that the financial statements were incorrect.

The exposure rectangle shown in Figure 11-2 is useful in identifying management fraud exposures. The first corner of the rectangle is the management and directors of the company. On the second corner are relationships the company has with other entities. On the third corner is the nature of the organization you are examining and the industry that organization operates in, and on the fourth corner are the financial results and operating characteristics of the organization.

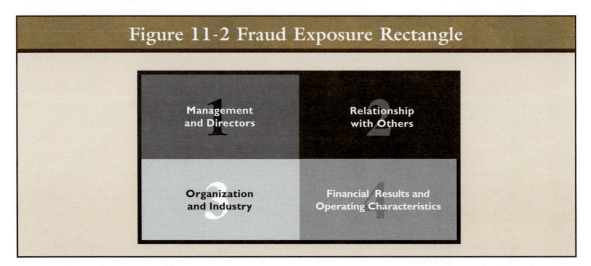

Figure 11-2 Fraud Exposure Rectangle

1 — Management and Directors
2 — Relationship with Others
3 — Organization and Industry
4 — Financial Results and Operating Characteristics

Although CPAs and others have traditionally focused almost entirely on the financial statements and results of operations to perform GAAS audits and detect financial statement fraud, each of these four areas present fraud exposures that must be examined. We now examine each of these four areas individually.

## Management and the Board of Directors

As shown in the statistics presented previously, top management is almost always involved when financial statement fraud occurs. Unlike embezzlement and misappropriation, financial statement fraud is usually committed by the highest individuals in an organization, and most often on behalf of the organization as opposed to against the organization. Because management is usually involved, management and the directors must be investigated to determine their exposure to and motivation for committing fraud. Fraud is not committed by financial statements; rather, it is perpetrated by management or other top officers or directors. In detecting financial statement fraud, gaining an understanding of management and what motivates it is at least as important as understanding the financial statements. In particular, three aspects of management should be investigated:

1. Managements' backgrounds
2. Managements' motivations
3. Managements' influence in making decisions for the organization

With respect to backgrounds, fraud investigators should understand what kinds of organizations and situations that management and directors have been associated with in the past. With today's World Wide Web, it is easy to conduct simple searches on individuals. One easy way is to type the individual's name in Google or another search engine and conduct a quick search. The search engine will quickly list all the references to the person's name, including past proxy statements and any **10-K** (the corporate report filed with the SEC) of companies the person has been affiliated with, newspaper articles about the person, and so forth. And, if that is not sufficient, it doesn't cost a lot to hire a private investigator or even use investigative services on the Web to do a search. (Search techniques were discussed in an earlier chapter.)

An example of the importance of understanding management's background is the Lincoln Savings and Loan fraud. Before perpetrating the Lincoln Savings and Loan fraud, Charles Keating was sanctioned by the **Securities and Exchange Commission (SEC)** for his involvement in a financial institution fraud problem in Cincinnati, Ohio, and, in fact, had signed a consent decree with the SEC that he would never again be involved in the management of another financial institution.

Another example where knowledge of management's background would have been helpful was Comparator Systems, the Los Angeles–based fingerprint company accused of securities fraud in 1996. CEO Robert Reed Rogers grew up in Chicago, majored in chemistry in college, and became a college lecturer in business and economics. He worked short stints at the consulting firm of McKinsey & Co. and Litton Industries. In information sent to investors, he boasted of many accomplishments, describing himself as founder and president of various companies developing products or processes. Missing from Rogers's biographical sketches is the fact that, in the mid-1970s, he was president of Newport International Metals. Newport was involved in the speculative rage of the period—precious metals. The company claimed to have the "exclusive right" to a certain mining process for producing jewelry. The company received $50,000 in securities from investors John and Herta Minar of New York to serve as collateral to secure start-up funds. Newport projected first-year revenue of $1.2 million. In 1976, Newport was cited by the state of California for unlawful sale of securities and was ordered to stop. The Minars sued and won a judgment for $50,000. In 1977, a bench warrant was issued for Rogers's arrest for failure to appear in court in connection with a lawsuit filed by investors in Westcliff International, of which Rogers was president. In 1977, as general partner of Intermedico Community Health Care, Rogers and three others borrowed $25,000 from Torrance, California, lawyer William MacCabe. Three years later, MacCabe won a court judgment worth $31,000. Certainly, Rogers had a tainted background that would have been important information to investors and others associated with Comparator Systems.

What motivates directors and management is also important to know. Are their personal worths tied up in the organization? Are they under pressure to deliver unrealistic results? Is their compensation primarily performance-based? Do they have a habit of guiding Wall Street to higher and higher expectations? Have they grown through acquisitions or internally? Are there debt covenants or other financial measures that must be met? Is management's job at risk? These questions are examples of what must be asked and answered in order to properly understand management's motivations. Many financial statement frauds have been perpetrated because management needed to report positive or high income to support stock prices, or needed to show positive earnings for a public stock or debt offering, or needed to report profits to meet regulatory or loan restrictions.

Finally, management's ability to influence decisions for the organization is important to understand because perpetrating fraud is much easier when one or two individuals have primary decision-making power than when an organization has a more democratic leadership. Most people who commit management fraud are first-time offenders, and being dishonest the first time is difficult for them. For two individuals to simultaneously be dishonest is more difficult, and for three people to simultaneously be dishonest, it is even more difficult. When decision-making ability is spread among several individuals, or when the board of directors takes an active role in the organization, fraud is much more difficult to perpetrate. Most financial statement frauds do not occur in large, historically profitable organizations. Rather, they occur in smaller organizations where one or two individuals have almost total decision-making ability, in companies that experience unbelievably rapid growth, or where the board of directors and audit committee do not take an active (something that is much harder to do now with the new corporate governance standards described in the appendix to this chapter. An active board of directors or audit committee that gets involved in the major decisions of the organization can do much to deter management fraud. In fact, it is for this reason that NASDAQ and NYSE corporate governance standards require that the majority of board members be independent and that some of the key committees, such as audit and compensation, be comprised entirely of independent directors.

Once management decides that it will commit fraud, the particular schemes used are often determined by the nature of the business's operations. Although we usually focus on the schemes and the financial results of those schemes, remember that the decision to commit fraud in the first place was made by management or other officers. Some of the key questions that must be asked about management and the directors are as follows:

### Understanding Management and Director Backgrounds

1. Have any of the key executives or board members been associated with other organizations in the past, and what was the nature of those organizations and relationships?
2. Were key members of management promoted from within the organization or recruited from the outside?
3. Have any key members of management had past regulatory or legal problems, either personally or with organizations they have been associated with?
4. Have significant changes occurred in the makeup of management or the board of directors?
5. Has turnover of management or board members been high?
6. Do any members of management or the board have criminal backgrounds?
7. Are any other issues related to the backgrounds of key members of management and the board of directors?
8. Are most board members independent?
9. Is the board chair separate from the CEO?
10. Does the company have independent audit, compensation, and nominating committees?

### Understanding What Motivates Management and the Board of Directors

1. Is the personal worth of any of the key executives tied up in the organization?
2. Is management under pressure to meet earnings or other financial expectations or does management commit to analysts, creditors, and others to achieve what appear to be unduly aggressive forecasts?
3. Is management's compensation primarily performance-based (bonuses, stock options, etc.)?
4. Is management obligated to meeting significant debt covenants or other financial restrictions?
5. Is the job security of any key members of management at serious risk?
6. Is the organization's reported financial performance decreasing?
7. Does management show an excessive interest in maintaining or increasing the entity's stock price?
8. Does management have an incentive to use inappropriate means to minimize reported earnings for tax reasons?
9. Are any other significant issues related to the motivations of management and board members?

### Understanding the Degree of Influence of Key Members of Management and the Board of Directors

1. Who are the key members of management and the board of directors who have the most influence?
2. Do one or two key people have dominant influence in the organization?
3. Is the management style of the organization more autocratic or democratic?
4. Is the organization's management centralized or decentralized?
5. Does management use ineffective means of communicating and supporting the entity's values or ethics, or do they communicate inappropriate values or ethics?
6. Does management fail to correct known reportable conditions in internal control on a timely basis?
7. Does management set unduly aggressive financial targets and expenditures for operating personnel?
8. Does management have too much involvement in or influence over the selection of accounting principles or the determination of significant estimates?
9. Are any other significant issues related to the degree of influence of key members of management and the board of directors?

## Relationships with Others

Financial statement fraud is often perpetrated with the help of other real or fictitious organizations. Enron's fraud was primarily conducted through what is known as special-purpose entities (SPEs), or business interests formed solely in order to accomplish some specific task or tasks. SPEs were not of themselves illegal, but were subject to regulatory measures that designated which SPEs are part of the larger company and which are truly independent entities not controlled by a parent. An SPE was considered independent if it met the following two criteria: (1) independent third-party investors made a substantive capital investment, generally at least 3 percent of the SPE's assets; and (2) the third-party investment is genuinely at risk. Enron was obligated to consolidate the assets and liabilities of entities not meeting these requirements. The SEC's complaint alleges that certain of Enron's SPEs should have been consolidated onto Enron's balance sheet. Further, Fastow, Kopper, and others used their simultaneous influence over Enron's business operations and the SPEs as a means to secretly and unlawfully generate millions of dollars for themselves and others.

Fastow's manipulation of SPEs was widespread. Following are two examples.

In 1997, Enron decided to sell its interest in a California windmill farm. In order for the farm to qualify for beneficial regulatory treatment, Enron, as an electric utilities holding company, had to decrease its ownership to below 50 percent. Enron, however, did not want to lose control of the profitable wind farm. Instead, Fastow created a special-purpose entity (known as RADR) and recruited "Friends of Enron" (actually friends of Kopper) as outside investors. These investors lacked sufficient funds, however, so Fastow made a personal loan of $419,000 to fund the purchase of the wind farm. RADR became immensely profitable. Fastow's loan was repaid with $62,000 interest, and Kopper arranged for yearly "gifts" of $10,000 each (keeping the gifts beneath the limit of taxable income) to members of Fastow's family. Because the RADR third-party investment was funded by Fastow, and because Fastow and Kopper clearly controlled RADR's operations, the entity should have been consolidated with Enron's financial statements.

In 1993, Enron created an entity called JEDI. Because of a substantial contribution by an independent investor, the California Public Employees' Retirement System (CalPERS), Enron was justified in not consolidating JEDI onto its books. However, in 1997, as CalPERS wanted to sell its portion of JEDI, rather than consider other independent investors, Fastow arranged for the creation of Chewco, a special-purpose entity that would buy out CalPERS. Chewco, and thus JEDI, was not eligible for the off-the-books status it was given. First, Chewco was not independent. Although Fastow abandoned the idea to be Chewco's independent investor (on Jeff Skilling's advice that Enron would be forced to disclose Fastow's participation), he substituted Kopper, himself an Enron executive who was essentially controlled by Fastow. Second, Chewco's investment in JEDI was not "genuinely at risk." It was funded through two $190 million bank loans, both of which were *guaranteed* by Enron. As with RADR, Fastow directed Kopper to continue to his gift payments, including a $54,000 payment to Fastow's wife for performing administrative duties for Chewco.

Lincoln Savings and Loan was another company that used relationships to commit fraud. In Lincoln's case, it structured sham transactions with certain straw buyers to make its negative performance appear profitable. A real estate limited partnership that committed financial statement fraud structured fraudulent transactions with bankers to hide mortgages on many of their real estate properties. Relationships with related parties are problematic because they often allow for other than arm's-length transactions. The management of ESM Government Securities, for example, hid a $400 million financial statement fraud by creating a large receivable from a nonconsolidated related entity.

Although relationships with all parties should be examined to determine whether they present management fraud opportunities or exposures, relationships with financial institutions, related organizations and individuals, external auditors, lawyers, investors, and regulators should always be carefully considered. Relationships with financial institutions and bondholders are also important because they provide an indication of the extent to which the company is leveraged. Examples of the kinds of questions that should be asked about debt relationships include the following:

- Is the company highly leveraged, and with which financial institutions?
- What assets of the organization are pledged as collateral?
- Is there debt or other restrictive covenants that must be met?
- Do the banking relationships appear normal, or are there strange relationships with financial institutions, such as using institutions in unusual geographical locations?
- Are there relationships between the officers of the financial institutions and your client organization?

The real estate partnership referred to earlier involved a Wisconsin company taking out unauthorized loans from a bank located in another state, where it had no business purpose. The bank was used because the CEO of the client company had a relationship with the bank president, who later falsified an audit confirmation sent by the bank to the auditors. The loans were discovered when the auditors performed a lien search on properties owned. Because the bank president denied the existence of the loans, liabilities were significantly understated on the balance sheet.

Relationships with related organizations and individuals (related parties) should be examined because structuring non-arm's-length and often unrealistic transactions with related organizations and individuals is one of the easiest ways to perpetrate financial statement fraud. These kinds of relationships are usually identified by examining large or unusual transactions, often occurring at strategic times (such as at the end of a period) to make the financial statements look better. The kinds of relationships and events that should be examined include the following:

- Large transactions that result in revenues or income for the organization
- Sales or purchases of assets between related entities
- Transactions that result in goodwill or other intangible assets being recognized in the financial statements
- Transactions that generate nonoperating, rather than operating, income
- Loans or other financing transactions between related entities
- Any transaction that appears to be unusual or questionable for the organization, especially transactions that are unrealistically large

The relationship between a company and its auditors is important to analyze for several reasons. Any change in auditor probably happened for a good reason. Auditing firms do not easily give up clients, and the termination of an auditor-auditee relationship is most often caused by failure of the client to pay, an auditor-auditee disagreement, suspected fraud or other problems found by the auditor, or the auditee believing the auditor's fees are too high. Although some of these reasons, such as high fees, may not signal a potential fraud problem, auditor-auditee disagreements, failure to pay an audit fee, and suspected problems can all be reasons that suggest a financial statement fraud problem. The fact that an auditor was dismissed or resigned, together with the difficulty of a first-year auditor to discover financial statement fraud, is cause for concern any time an auditor change occurs.

On occasion, one auditing firm determines to accept more risk or handle risks different from other auditing firms. Many have argued that Laventhol & Harwath, which failed in the late 1980s, was such a firm. Others argue that Arthur Andersen's failure can be attributed to the risk posture they took with their audit clients and their preoccupation with cross-selling consulting services to audit clients. Certainly, Arthur Andersen had its share of high-profile audit failures including Sunbeam, Waste Management, Enron, WorldCom, Qwest, and others. In examining a company for possible financial statement fraud, it is important to know who its auditor is and how long that relationship has existed.

Relationships with lawyers pose even greater risks than relationships with auditors. Auditors are supposed to be independent and must resign if they suspect that financial results may not be appropriate, but lawyers are usually advocates for their clients, and will often follow and support their clients until it is obvious that fraud has occurred. In addition, lawyers usually have information about a client's legal difficulties, regulatory problems, and other significant occurrences. Like auditors, lawyers rarely give up a profitable client unless something is obviously wrong. Thus, a change in legal firms without an obvious reason is often a cause for concern. And, unlike changing auditors, where a 8-K must be filed for public companies, changing lawyers involves no such reporting requirement.

Relationships with investors are important because financial statement fraud is often motivated by a debt or equity offering to investors. In addition, knowledge of the number and kinds of investors (public vs. private company, major exchange vs. small exchange, institutional vs. individual, etc.) can often provide an indication of the degree of pressure and public scrutiny upon the management of the company and its financial performance. If an organization is publicly held, investor groups or investment analysts usually follow the company closely and often can provide information or indications that something is wrong with the company. For example, "short" investors are always looking for bad news about an organization that will make its stock go down. If they suspect that something is not right, they will often contact management or even the auditors (or press) to vent their concerns. Investor groups often focus on information different from that used by auditors, and sometimes the fraud symptoms are more obvious to them than they are to auditors, especially auditors who focus only on the financial statements. Short sellers have sometimes been the ones who have disclosed financial statement frauds. By focusing on bad news, they were the first ones to put the bad news together to determine fraud was occurring in many instances. With Enron, for example, the first one to come forward with negative information about the company was Jim Chanos, who runs Kynikos Associates, a highly regarded firm specializing in short selling who stated publicly in early 2001 that "no one could explain how Enron actually made money." He noted that Enron had completed transactions with related parties that "were run by a senior officer of Enron" and assumed it was a conflict of interest. (Enron wouldn't answer questions about LJM and other partnerships.) Then in its March 5, 2001, issue, *Fortune* magazine ran a story about Enron that stated: "To skeptics, the lack of clarity raises a red flag about Enron's pricey stock . . . the inability to get behind the numbers combined with ever higher expectations for the company may increase the chance of a nasty surprise. Enron is an earnings-at-risk story." Unfortunately, investors kept ignoring this bad news until late in 2001 when a misguided earnings release led skeptics to start selling the stock. The company declared bankruptcy in late 2001.

Finally, understanding the client's relationship with regulators is important. If the company you are examining is a publicly held client, you need to know whether the Securities and Exchange Commission (SEC) has ever issued an enforcement release against them. For example, in its report pursuant to Section 704 of the Sarbanes-Oxley Act, the SEC stated that during the five-year period July 31, 1997, to July 30, 2002, it had filed 515 enforcement actions involving 869 named parties, 164 entities, and 705 individuals. You also need to know whether all annual, quarterly, and other reports have been filed on a timely basis. If they are in a regulated industry, such as banking, you need to know what their relationship is with appropriate regulatory bodies such as the FDIC, Federal Reserve, and Office of the Controller of the Currency. Are any problematic issues related to those bodies? Whether the organization owes any back taxes to the federal or state government or to other taxing districts is important to know. Because of the recourse and sanctions available to taxing authorities, organizations usually do not fall behind on their payments unless something is wrong or the organization is having serious cash flow problems. The following are some of the questions that should be asked about a company's relationships with others:

### Relationships with Financial Institutions

1. What financial institutions does the organization have significant relationships with?
2. Is the organization highly leveraged through bank or other loans?
3. Do any loan or debt covenants or restrictions pose significant problems for the organization?
4. Do the banking relationships appear normal or are any unusual attributes present with the relationships (strange geographical locations, too many banks, etc.)?
5. Do members of management or the board have personal or other close relationships with officers of any of the major banks used by the company?
6. Have any significant changes occurred in the financial institutions used by the company? If so, why?
7. Are any significant bank accounts or subsidiary or branch operations located in tax-haven jurisdictions for which business justification is apparent?
8. Have critical assets of the company been pledged as collateral on risky loans?
9. Are there any other questionable financial institution relationships?

### Relationships with Related Parties

1. Are any significant related-party transactions not in the ordinary course of business or with related entities not audited or audited by another firm?
2. Are large or unusual transactions made at or near the end of a period that significantly improve the reported financial performance of the company?
3. Are significant receivables or payables occurring between related entities?
4. Has a significant amount of the organization's revenues or income been derived from related-party transactions?
5. Is a significant part of the company's income or revenues derived from one or two large transactions?
6. Are any other related-party relationships questionable?
7. Have relationships with other entities resulted in the reporting of significant amounts of nonoperating income?

### Relationships with Auditors

1. Have frequent disputes occurred with the current or predecessor auditors on accounting, auditing, or reporting matters?
2. Has management placed unreasonable demands on the auditor, including unreasonable time constraints?
3. Has the company placed formal or informal restrictions on the auditor that inappropriately limit his or her access to people or information or his or her ability to communicate effectively with the board of directors or the audit committee?
4. Does domineering management behavior characterize the dealings with the auditor, especially any attempts to influence the scope of the auditor's work?
5. Has an auditor change occurred, and if so, for what reason?
6. Are any other relationships with the auditor questionable?

### Relationships with Lawyers

1. Has the company been involved in significant litigation concerning matters that could severely and adversely affect the company's financial results?
2. Has any attempt been made to hide litigation from the auditors or others?
3. Has any change occurred in outside counsels, and if so, for what reasons?
4. Are any other lawyer relationships questionable?

### Relationships with Investors

1. Is the organization in the process of issuing an initial or secondary public debt or equity offering?
2. Are any investor-related lawsuits pending or ongoing?
3. Are any relationships with investment bankers, stock analysts, or others problematic or questionable?
4. Has significant "short selling" of the company's stock occurred, and for what reasons?
5. Are any investor relationships questionable?

### Relationships with Regulatory Bodies

1. Does management display a significant disregard for regulatory authorities?
2. Has there been a history of securities law violations or claims against the entity or its senior management alleging fraud or violations of securities laws?
3. Have any 8-Ks been filed with the SEC, and if so, for what reasons?
4. Could any new accounting, statutory, or regulatory requirements impair the financial stability or profitability of the entity?
5. Are significant tax disputes with the IRS or other taxing authorities pending?
6. Is the company current on paying its payroll taxes and other payroll-related expenses, and is the company current on paying other liabilities?
7. Are any other relationships with regulatory bodies questionable?
8. Are there SEC investigations of any of the company's 10-K, 10-Q or other filings?

## Organization and Industry

Financial statement fraud is sometimes masked by creating an organizational structure that makes it easy to hide fraud. This situation was certainly the case with Enron and all of its nonconsolidated special-purpose entities (SPEs) (now called variable interest entities by the FASB.) Another example was Lincoln Savings and Loan, which was a subsidiary of American National, a holding company that had more than 50 other subsidiaries and related companies. Lincoln Savings and Loan had several subsidiaries, some with no apparent business purpose. A significant part of the fraud was to structure supposedly "profitable" transactions near the end of each quarter by selling land to straw buyers. To entice the buyers to participate, the perpetrators often made the down payment themselves by having Lincoln Savings and Loan simultaneously loan the straw buyers the same amount (or more) of money that they needed to make the down payments on the land. The simultaneous loan and purchase transactions were not easily identifiable because Lincoln Savings and Loan would sell the land and have another related entity make the loan. What was really happening was the creation of a complex organizational structure that had no apparent business purpose. The complexity of the organization was used as a smoke screen to hide illicit transactions.

In one transaction known as the RA Homes transaction, for example, on September 30, Lincoln Savings and Loan supposedly sold 1,300 acres known as the Continental Ranch to RA Homes for $25 million, receiving a down payment of $5 million and a note receivable for $20 million (in real estate transactions such as this, FAS 66 requires at least a 20% down payment in order to record the transaction on an accrual basis, thus recognizing profit.) On the transaction, Lincoln recognized a gain on the sale of several million dollars. However, on September 25, five days before the supposed sale, another subsidiary of Lincoln loaned RA Homes $3 million and on November 12, a different subsidiary loaned RA Homes another $2 million. Given these transactions, who made the down payment? It was obvious to the jury that Lincoln Savings and Loan itself made the down payment and that the complicated organization structure was used to hide the real nature of the transaction.

The same was true of ESM. In that case, related organizations were established to make it look like receivables were due to the company when, in fact, the related organizations were not audited and could not have paid even a small portion of the amount they supposedly owed.

The attributes of an organization that suggest potential fraud exposures include such things as an unduly complex organizational structure, an organization without an internal audit department, a board of directors or audit committee with no or few outside members, an organization where one or a small group of individuals control related entities, an organization that has off-shore affiliates with no apparent business purpose, an organization that made numerous acquisitions and recognized large merger-related charges, or an organization that is new. Investigators must understand who the owners of an organization are. Sometimes silent or hidden owners are using the organization for illegal or other questionable activities.

The COSO-sponsored study of the attributes of firms committing financial statement fraud concluded the following:

> The relatively small size of fraud companies suggests that the inability or even unwillingness to implement cost-effective internal controls may be a factor affecting the likelihood of financial statement fraud (e.g., override of controls is easier). Smaller companies may be unable or unwilling to employ senior executives with sufficient financial reporting knowledge and experience.

> The concentration of fraud among companies with under $50 million in revenues and with generally weak audit committees highlights the importance of rigorous audit committee practices even for smaller organizations. In particular, the number of audit committee meetings per year and the financial expertise of the audit committee members may deserve closer attention.

> Investors should be aware of the possible complications arising from family relationships and from individuals (founders, CEO/board chairs, etc.) who hold significant power or incompatible job functions.

The industry of the organization must also be carefully examined. Some industries are much more risky than others. For example, in the 1980s, the savings and loan (S&L) industry was extremely risky, to the extent that some auditing firms wouldn't have an S&L client. Recently, technology companies, especially dot-com and Internet companies with new and unproven business models have been extremely risky. With any company, however, the organization's performance relative to that of similar organizations in the same industry should be examined. The kinds of questions that should be asked in order to understand the exposure to management fraud are provided here.

1. Does the company have an overly complex organizational structure involving numerous or unusual legal entities, managerial lines of authority, or contractual arrangements without apparent business purpose?
2. Is a legitimate business purpose apparent for each separate entity of the business?
3. Is the board of directors comprised primarily of officers of the company or other related individuals?
4. Is the board of directors passive or active and independent?
5. Is the audit committee comprised primarily of insiders or outsiders?
6. Is the audit committee passive or active and independent?
7. Does the organization have an independent or active internal audit department?
8. Does the organization have offshore activities without any apparent business purpose?
9. Is the organization a new entity without a proven history?
10. Have significant recent changes occurred in the nature of the organization?
11. Is monitoring of significant controls adequate?
12. Are the accounting and information technology staff and organization effective?
13. Is the degree of competition or market saturation high, accompanied by declining margins?
14. Is the client in a declining industry with increasing business failures and significant declines in customer demand?
15. Are changes in the industry rapid, such as high vulnerability to quickly changing technology or product obsolescence?
16. Is the performance of the company similar or contrary to other firms in the industry?
17. Are any other significant issues related to organization and industry?

## Financial Results and Operating Characteristics

Much can be learned about exposure to financial statement fraud by closely examining management and the board of directors, relationships with others, and the nature of the organization. Looking at those three elements is always a good idea, but usually involves the same procedures for all kinds of financial statement frauds, whether the accounts manipulated are revenue accounts, asset accounts, liabilities, expenses, or equities. The kinds of exposures identified by the financial statements and operating characteristics of the organization differ from fraud scheme to fraud scheme. In examining financial statements to assess fraud exposures, a nontraditional approach to the financial statements must be taken.

Fraud symptoms most often exhibit themselves through changes in the financial statements. For example, financial statements that contain large changes in account balances from period to period are more likely to contain fraud than financial statements that exhibit only small, incremental changes in account balances. A sudden, dramatic increase in receivables, for example, is often a signal that something is wrong. In addition to changes in financial statement balances and amounts, understanding what the footnotes are really saying is important. Many times, the footnotes strongly hint that fraud is occurring; but what is contained in the footnotes is not clearly understood by auditors and others.

In assessing fraud exposure through financial statements and operating characteristics, the balances and amounts must be compared with those of similar organizations in the same industry, and the real-world referents to the financial statement amounts must be determined. If, for example, an organization's financial statements report that the company has $2 million of inventory, then the inventory has to be located somewhere, and, depending on the type of inventory it is, it should require a certain amount of space to store it, lift forks and other equipment to move and ship it, and people to manage it. Are the financial statement numbers realistic, given the actual inventory that is on hand?

Using financial relationships to assess fraud exposures requires that you know the nature of the client's business, the kinds of accounts that should be included, the kinds of fraud that could occur in the organization, and the kinds of symptoms those frauds would generate. For example, the major activities of a manufacturing company could probably be subdivided into sales and collections, acquisition and payment, financing, payroll, and inventory and warehousing. Breaking an organization down into various activities or cycles such as these and then, for each cycle, identifying the major functions that are performed, the major risks inherent in each function, the kinds of abuse and fraud that could occur, and the kinds of symptoms those frauds would generate may be helpful. An examiner can then use proactive detection techniques to determine whether a likelihood of fraud exists in those cycles. Some of the critical questions that must be asked about financial statement relationships and operating results are the following:

1. Are unrealistic changes or increases present in financial statement account balances?
2. Are the account balances realistic given the nature, age, and size of the company?
3. Do actual physical assets exist in the amounts and values indicated on the financial statements?
4. Have significant changes occurred in the nature of the organization's revenues or expenses?
5. Do one or a few large transactions account for a significant portion of any account balance or amount?
6. Are significant transactions made near the end of the period that positively impact results of operations, especially transactions that are unusual or highly complex or that pose "substance over form" questions?
7. Do financial results appear consistent on a quarter-by-quarter or month-by-month basis, or are unrealistic amounts occurring in a subperiod?
8. Does the entity show an inability to generate cash flows from operations while reporting earnings and earnings growth?
9. Is significant pressure felt to obtain additional capital necessary to stay competitive, considering the financial position of the entity—including the need for funds to finance major research and development or capital expenditures?
10. Are reported assets, liabilities, revenues, or expenses based on significant estimates that involve unusually subjective judgments or uncertainties or that are subject to potential significant change in the near term in a manner that may have a financially disruptive effect on the entity (i.e., ultimate collectibility of receivables, timing of revenue recognition, realizability of financial instruments based on the highly subjective valuation of collateral or difficult-to-assess repayment sources, or significant deferral of costs)?
11. Does growth or profitability appear unusually rapid, especially compared with that of other companies in the same industry?
12. Is the organization highly vulnerable to changes in interest rates?
13. Are unrealistically aggressive sales or profitability incentive programs in place?
14. Is a threat of imminent bankruptcy, foreclosure, or hostile takeover present?
15. Are adverse consequences on significant pending transactions possible, such as a business combination or contract award, if poor financial results are reported?
16. Has management personally guaranteed significant debts of the entity when its financial position is poor or deteriorating?
17. Does the firm continuously operate on a "crisis" basis or without a careful budgeting and planning process?
18. Does the organization have difficulty collecting receivables or have other cash flow problems?
19. Is the organization dependent on one or two key products or services, especially products or services that can become quickly obsolete or where other organizations have the ability to adapt more quickly to market swings?
20. Do the footnotes contain information about difficult-to-understand issues?
21. Are adequate disclosures made in the footnotes?
22. Are financial results or operating characteristics accompanied by questionable or suspicious factors?

## SUMMARY

In this chapter, we covered the first steps in detecting financial statement fraud: identifying fraud exposures. We discussed four different exposure areas that must be examined: (1) management and directors, (2) relationships with others, (3) organization and industry, and (4) financial results and operating characteristics. Fraud schemes are often chosen by perpetrators more often because of their "ease to commit and conceal" than by any other factor. Even though we discussed the exposures that often motivate fraud, most fraud symptoms, especially those relating to financial results and operating characteristics, are scheme-specific. In the next two chapters, we will discuss understatement of liability frauds, overstatement of asset frauds, and inadequate disclosure of frauds. For each of these various types of fraud schemes, we will discuss scheme-specific fraud exposures, symptoms that indicate that fraud may be occurring, steps and analyzes that can be taken to search for fraud symptoms, and ways to follow up on symptoms observed to determine whether they relate to fraud or are occurring because of some other reason.

## KEY TERMS

**10-K** Annual report filed by publicly traded companies to the SEC.

**10-Q** Quarterly report filed by publicly-traded companies to the SEC.

**Committee of Sponsoring Organizations (COSO)** An organization made up of representatives from major accounting organizations and concerned about internal controls and financial statement fraud.

**Financial statement fraud** The intentional misstatement of financial statements through omission of critical facts or disclosures, misstatement of amounts, or misapplication of accepted accounting principles.

**Financial statements** Financial reports that summarize the profitability and cash flows of an entity for a specific period and the financial position of the entity as of a specific date.

**SEC enforcement release** A public document released by the SEC when a company commits financial statement fraud or other perceived inappropriate activities.

**Securities and Exchange Commission (SEC)** Governmental organization with responsibility for regulating stock trading and the financial statements and reports of public companies.

**Treadway Commission** The National Commission on Fraudulent Financial Reporting that made recommendations related to financial statement fraud and other matters in 1987.

## QUESTIONS AND CASES

### DISCUSSION QUESTIONS

1. What were the schemes that Rite Aid used to inflate its profits?

2. What were some of the most notable abuses relating to financial statements that occurred between 2000–2002?

3. This chapter identifies nine factors that led to the *perfect fraud storm*. Explain how these factors helped create and foster the ethical compromises that occurred between 2000 and 2002.

4. Why are financial statements important to the effective operation of capital markets?

5. What is financial statement fraud?

6. Who usually commits financial statement fraud?

7. Why are CEOs perpetrators of financial statement fraud?

8. What are common ways in which financial statement frauds are concealed?

9. How can an active audit committee help to deter financial statement fraud in an organization?

10. What are some common motivations of financial statement fraud?

11. What are the four different exposure areas that must be examined while detecting financial statement fraud?

12. What are some of the ways financial statement fraud exposures can be identified?

13. Why must management and the board of directors be investigated when searching for financial statement fraud exposures?

14. Why must relationships with others be examined when searching for financial statement fraud exposures?

15. When looking for financial statement fraud, why is it important to analyze the relationship between a company and its auditors?

## TRUE / FALSE

1. Unlike other types of fraud, financial statement fraud is usually not concealed and is therefore relatively easy to spot.

2. Fraud symptoms, or red flags, can be caused by fraud or by legitimate factors.

3. Without a confession, forged documents, or repeated fraudulent acts that establish a pattern of dishonesty, convicting someone of fraud is often difficult.

4. According to the 1999 COSO study of fraudulent financial reporting, the most common method used to perpetrate financial statement fraud includes overstating of liabilities.

5. According to the 1999 COSO study, most companies that committed financial statement fraud had no audit committee or had an audit committee that met less than twice per year.

6. Michael "Mickey" Monus and Patrick Finn of Phar-Mor used three methods of income statement fraud, including account manipulation, overstatement of inventory, and accounting rules manipulations.

7. In identifying management fraud exposures, it is useful to think of the fraud exposure triangle, which includes (1) management and directors, (2) organizations and industry, and (3) relationships with others.

8. Financial statement fraud is usually committed by entry-level accountants against an organization.

9. In searching for financial statement fraud, the three aspects of directors and management that should be known are (1) their backgrounds, (2) their motivations, and (3) their influence in making decisions for the organization.

10. An organization's relationship with other organizations and individuals is of no interest to a fraud examiner.

11. Recording fictitious revenues is one of the most common ways of perpetrating financial statement fraud.

12. Most often, the controller or chief financial officer (CFO) of a corporation is the perpetrator of financial statement fraud because of his or her knowledge of accounting and unlimited access to accounts.

13. Financial statement fraud, like other types of fraud, is most often committed against an organization instead of on behalf of the organization.

14. Most people who commit management fraud are repeat offenders.

15. Most financial statement frauds occur in large, historically profitable organizations.

## MULTIPLE CHOICE

1. Financial statement fraud is usually committed by:
   a. Executives.
   b. Managers.
   c. Stockholders.
   d. Outsiders.
   e. a and b.

2. Which officer in a company is most likely to be the perpetrator of financial statement fraud?
   a. Chief financial officer (CFO)
   b. Controller
   c. Chief operating officer (COO)
   d. Chief executive officer (CEO)

3. When looking for financial statement fraud, auditors should look for indicators of fraud by:
   a. Examining the financial statements.
   b. Evaluating changes in financial statements.
   c. Examining relationships the company has with other parties.
   d. Examining operating characteristics of the company.
   e. All of the above.
   f. None of the above because auditors don't have a responsibility to find financial statement fraud.

4. The three aspects of management that a fraud examiner needs to be aware of include all of the following *except*:
   a. Their backgrounds.
   b. Their motivations.
   c. Their religious convictions.
   d. Their influence in making decisions for the organization.

5. Which of the following is least likely to be considered a financial reporting fraud symptom or red flag?
   a. Grey directors
   b. Family relationships between directors or officers
   c. Large increases in accounts receivable with no increase in sales
   d. Size of the firm

6. Many indicators of fraud are circumstantial; that is, they can be caused by nonfraud factors. This fact can make convicting someone of fraud difficult. Which of the following types of evidence would be most helpful in proving that someone committed fraud?
   a. Missing documentation
   b. A general ledger that is out of balance
   c. Analytical relationships that don't make sense
   d. A repeated pattern of similar fraudulent acts

7. In the Phar-Mor fraud case, several different methods were used for manipulating the financial statements. These included all of the following *except*:
   a. Funneling losses into unaudited subsidiaries.
   b. Overstating inventory.
   c. Recognizing revenue that should have been deferred.
   d. Manipulating accounts.

8. Most financial statement frauds occur in smaller organizations with simple management structures, rather than in large, historically profitable organizations, because:
   a. It is impossible to implement good internal controls in a small organization.
   b. Smaller organizations do not have investors.
   c. Management fraud is more difficult to commit when a more formal organizational structure of management is in place.
   d. People in large organizations are more honest.

9. Management fraud is usually committed on behalf of the organization rather than against it. Which of the following would *not* be a motivation of fraud on behalf of an organization?
   a. CEO needs a new car
   b. A highly competitive industry
   c. Pressure to meet expected earnings
   d. Restructure of debt covenants that can't be met

10. All of the following are indicators of financial statement fraud *except*:
   a. Unusually rapid growth of profitability
   b. Threat of a hostile takeover
   c. Dependence on one or two products
   d. Large amounts of available cash

## SHORT CASES

**Case 1.** An electronics company that produced circuit boards for personal computers was formed in a small southern town. The three founders had previously worked together for another electronics company and decided to start this new company. They ended up as senior officers and members of the board of directors in the newly formed company. One became the chairman and CEO, the second one became the company's president and COO, and the last became the controller and treasurer. Two of the three founders owned together approximately 10.7 percent of the company's common stock. The board of directors had a total of seven members, and they met together about four times a year, receiving an annual retainer of $4,500 plus a fee of $800 for each meeting attended. Their new company was well received by the townspeople, who were excited about attracting the new start-up company. The city showed its enthusiasm by providing the new company with an empty building, and the local bank provided an attractive credit arrangement for the company. In turn, the company appointed the bank's president to serve as a member of its board of directors. Two years later, the company began committing financial statement fraud, which went on for about three years. The three founders were the fraud perpetrators. Their fraud involved overstating inventory, understating the cost of goods sold, overstating the gross margin, and overstating net income.

Identify the fraud exposures present in this case.

**Case 2.** As you can see from the chart in Figure 11-3, Microsoft would experience high losses if all employees were paid in cash rather than stock. However, it was able to show a profit by granting excessive amounts of stock options, thus allowing it to understate costs and overstate earnings. However, Microsoft's press releases imply that it took a tax deduction for stock option wages of between $2.5 to $4 billion, and none of this amount was charged to earnings.

## Figure 11-3 Microsoft's Earnings and Wages Data

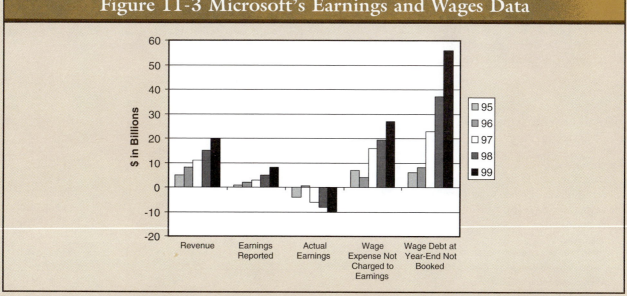

What do you think the reaction to Microsoft's stock price would be if the public suddenly realized that the company lost $10 billion in 1999, rather than earning the reported $7.8 billion? Is this financial statement fraud?

**Case 3.** ABC Company manufactures and sells software packages to small businesses. The company has enjoyed great success since it began business in 1998. Last year, the firm doubled its revenues, and its management is now looking closely at going public by making an initial public offering (IPO) next September. Senior management has been putting a lot of effort into further increasing sales by offering the company's sales representatives a generous commission as an incentive to increase their selling efforts.

The CEO, CFO, and the COO of the company have been in business together for 20 years. Two of them were high school "buddies," and the other joined the threesome in college. They still interact socially with one another, and their respective wives are also close.

In completing a background check on the company, you find that the company has a positive relationship with private investors, who are excited about the proposed IPO next September. One of the investors did inform you, however, that the company changed auditors last year because of a dispute the CEO had with the audit partner regarding some "strict revenue recognition rule."

The company has a board of directors and audit committee that meets twice a year to discuss how the business is doing. The board has decided to meet four times over the next year, because it may be necessary to discuss issues regarding the upcoming IPO. The board seems to speak highly of management and compensates them generously with stock options for their "good work."

What are some red flags that indicate that financial statement fraud may be occurring?

**Case 4.** Compare and contrast financial statement fraud with embezzlement and misappropriation, especially with respect to who usually commits the fraud. Also contrast the different kinds of fraud with respect to who benefits from the fraud.

**Case 5.** For each of the following red flags, identify which fraud exposure the risk falls under: (1) management and directors, (2) relationships with others, (3) organization and industry, or (4) financial results and operating characteristics.

a. The personal worth of directors is tied up in the organization.

b. The company has a complex organizational structure.

c. The audit committee rarely holds a meeting.

d. The company recently switched to a new law firm.

e. Although sales appear to be increasing, the cost of goods sold and inventory levels remain constant.

f. The company is about to go through a debt offering.

g. A background check indicates that the new controller has been fired from five previous jobs.

# EXTENSIVE CASES

**Extensive Case 1.** You are a fraud investigator who has been hired to detect financial statement fraud for the Chipmunk Company. You have been provided with the following financial statements, and you are now beginning your analysis of those statements.

**THE CHIPMUNK COMPANY**
**Balance Sheet**
**December 31, 2005, and 2004**

| ASSETS | 2005 | 2004 |
|---|---|---|
| Current assets | | |
| Cash | $ 1,320,096 | $ 1,089,978 |
| Accounts receivable: net (Notes 2 and 5) | 1,646,046 | 1,285,593 |
| Inventories (Notes 1(a), 3, and 5) | 15,524,349 | 12,356,400 |
| Prepaid expenses | 17,720 | 15,826 |
| Deposits | 7,916 | 5,484 |
| Total current assets | $16,516,127 | $14,753,281 |
| Property, plant, and equipment (Notes 1(b) and 4) | | |
| At cost, less accumulated depreciation | 596,517 | 612,480 |
| TOTAL ASSETS | $17,112,644 | $15,365,761 |
| | | |
| LIABILITIES | | |
| Current liabilities | | |
| Notes payable—Bank (Note 5) | $ 5,100,000 | $ 4,250,000 |
| Accounts payable | 1,750,831 | 1,403,247 |
| Accrued liabilities | 257,800 | 217,003 |
| Federal income taxes payable | 35,284 | 45,990 |
| Current portion of long-term debt (Note 6) | 5,642 | 5,642 |
| Total current liabilities | $ 7,149,557 | $ 5,921,882 |
| Long-term liabilities | | |
| Long-term debt (Note 6) | 409,824 | 415,466 |
| TOTAL LIABILITIES | $ 7,559,381 | $ 6,337,348 |
| | | |
| STOCKHOLDERS' EQUITY | | |
| Common stock (Note 7) | $      10,000 | $      10,000 |
| Additional paid-in capital | 2,500,000 | 2,500,000 |
| Retained earnings | 7,043,263 | 6,518,413 |
| Total stockholders' equity | $ 9,553,263 | $ 9,028,413 |
| TOTAL LIABILITIES AND STOCKHOLDERS' EQUITY | $17,112,644 | $15,365,761 |

**THE CHIPMUNK COMPANY**
**Statement of Income and Retained Earnings**
**For the years ended December 31, 2005, and 2004**

|  | 2005 | 2004 |
|---|---:|---:|
| Sales | $26,456,647 | $22,889,060 |
| Sales returns and allowances | 37,557 | 27,740 |
| Net sales | $26,419,090 | $22,861,320 |
| Cost of sales | 19,133,299 | 16,530,114 |
| Gross profit | $ 7,285,791 | $ 6,331,206 |
|  |  |  |
| **EXPENSES** |  |  |
| Accounting | $    48,253 | $    46,750 |
| Advertising | 28,624 | 27,947 |
| Depreciation | 46,415 | 46,578 |
| Bad debts | 148,252 | 162,344 |
| Business publications | 1,231 | 872 |
| Cleaning services | 15,817 | 12,809 |
| Fuel | 64,161 | 53,566 |
| Garbage collection | 4,870 | 4,674 |
| Insurance | 16,415 | 16,303 |
| Interest | 427,362 | 364,312 |
| Legal | 69,752 | 29,914 |
| Licensing and certification fees | 33,580 | 27,142 |
| Linen service | 3,044 | 1,939 |
| Medical benefits | 4,178 | 4,624 |
| Miscellaneous | 47,739 | 16,631 |
| Office supplies | 26,390 | 23,289 |
| Payroll benefits | 569,110 | 461,214 |
| Pension expense | 40,770 | 37,263 |
| Postage and courier | 8,623 | 20,962 |
| Property taxes | 3,978 | 27,947 |
| Rent | 158,526 | 120,000 |
| Repairs and maintenance | 51,316 | 26,439 |
| Salaries and wages | 4,310,281 | 3,970,092 |
| Security | 96,980 | 100,098 |
| Telephone | 5,707 | 7,092 |
| Travel and entertainment | 21,633 | 16,303 |
| Utilities | 63,329 | 41,919 |
| Total Expenses | $6,316,336 | $5,669,023 |
| Net income before income tax | $   969,455 | $   662,183 |
| Income tax expense | 344,605 | 239,406 |
| NET INCOME | $   624,850 | $   422,777 |
| Retained earnings at beginning of year | 6,518,413 | 6,195,636 |
| Less: Dividends | 100,000 | 100,000 |
| Retained earnings at end of year | $7,043,263 | $6,518,413 |

As part of your analysis, you are required to:

1. Calculate the 2005 and 2004 liquidity and equity ratios identified in the following table. Also calculate the change and the percentage change for the ratios and complete the table. (Formulas are given to shorten the time spent on the assignment).

2. Analyze the Chipmunk Company's ratios for both years and compare the figures with the given industry ratios. Based on the ratios identified, where do you think fraud may have occurred?

Ratio Analysis
December 31, 2005

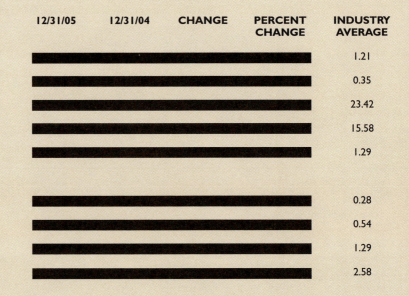

| LIQUIDITY RATIOS: | 12/31/05 | 12/31/04 | CHANGE | PERCENT CHANGE | INDUSTRY AVERAGE |
|---|---|---|---|---|---|
| Current ratio [current assets/current liabilities] | | | | | 1.21 |
| Quick ratio [(current assets − inventory)/current liabilities] | | | | | 0.35 |
| Sales/Receivables [net sales/net ending receivables] | | | | | 23.42 |
| Number of days sales in A/R [net ending receivables/(net sales/365)] | | | | | 15.58 |
| Inventory turnover [cost of sales/average inventory] | | | | | 1.29 |
| **EQUITY POSITION RATIOS:** | | | | | |
| Owners' equity/total assets [total stockholders' equity/total assets] | | | | | 0.28 |
| Long-term assets/owners' equity [net long-term assets/total stockholder equity] | | | | | 0.54 |
| Current liabilities/owners' equity [current liabilities/total stockholder equity] | | | | | 1.29 |
| Total liabilities/owners' equity [total liabilities/total stockholder equity] | | | | | 2.58 |

**Extensive Case 2.** In April 1997, Bre-X Minerals, a Canadian company, was supposedly one of the most valuable companies in the world. Bre-X had reported the largest gold deposits ever discovered. It was hailed as the mining find of the century. The gold mine, located on a remote island in the East Kalimantan Province of Indonesia, supposedly had so much gold that the actual price of gold on the open market dropped significantly due to the anticipation of an increased gold supply. Within a few months, thousands of Canadians—big-time investors, pension and mutual funds, and many small investors, including hardware store owners and factory workers—got caught up in Bre-X fever. The company's stock price shot from pennies to more than $250 per share before a 10-for-1 stock split was announced. Thousands of investors believed they were on the verge of becoming millionaires.

The story took a sudden turn for the worse when Michael de Guzman, Bre-X's chief geologist and one of only a handful of company insiders entrusted with the mine's core samples, apparently committed suicide by jumping out the back of a helicopter.

The following is a description of the Bre-X Gold Scandal,

*The search for a jungle El Dorado is over; the search for culprits in an astounding gold mine fraud has begun. Investigators opened investigations into how Bre-X Minerals, a tiny exploration company from Alberta, Canada, managed to convince countless experts and investors that a tract of land in Borneo contained the biggest gold find of the century.*

*After two years as a stock market superstar, Bre-X was suddenly a pariah after an independent consulting company* reported that the Busang site was worthless. It said thousands of seemingly promising crushed rock core samples collected by Bre-X had been doctored with gold from elsewhere in a scam "without precedent in the history of mining."

*Partners in the Indonesian project promptly jumped ship. The Indonesian government, which held a 10 percent stake, vowed to punish whoever was responsible. New Orleans-based Freeport-McMoRan Copper & Gold—which first cast doubts on Busang's value—said it was withdrawing from its planned partnership with Bre-X.*

*The company that reported the fraud, Strathcona Mineral Services, did not attempt to fix blame for the tampering, but offered to assist in subsequent investigations. Industry analysts said it seemed clear that some senior Bre-X personnel were involved, but there was no consensus whether the culprits were Canadian-based executives, geologists in the field, or both.*

*Mining analysts say only a small amount of gold—perhaps a few pounds—would have been enough to doctor the Bre-X samples to make them appear that the Busang mine was a world-class gold deposit.*

*Bre-X's president, David Walsh, who launched the Busang project from his Calgary basement while bankrupt in 1993, expressed shock at the evidence of tampering and said his company would conduct its own investigation.*

*Walsh, 51, sold off some of his Bre-X shares last year, along with other senior company officials, who together reaped more than $56 million in profits. They have been targeted by at least eight class-action lawsuits in Canada and the United States, alleging that Bre-X executives misled shareholders about Busang's potential while selling off some of their own shares.*

1. Assume you are a financial analyst who works for a major brokerage company that is heavily invested in Bre-X Minerals.
   a. In what ways would investigating *management and directors* help determine the value of Bre-X's gold prospects?
   b. In what ways would investigating the *company's relationships with other entities* help determine the value of Bre-X's gold prospects?
   c. In what ways would investigating *the organization and its industry* help determine the value of Bre-X's gold prospects?
   d. In what ways would investigating the *financial results and operating characteristics* help determine the value of Bre-X's gold prospects?

2. How was the gold industry and Canadian stock markets affected by this fraud?

3. Some of the aspects of the *perfect fraud storm* that were discussed in the chapter were also present in the Bre-X scandal. Which elements were common to both the *perfect fraud storm* and the Bre-X scandal?

4. What were some of the perpetrators motivations to commit fraud?

### INTERNET ASSIGNMENTS

1. The Internet is a great place to find additional information about financial statement fraud. Using your favorite Internet search engine, try various word combinations to see what you can find about financial statement fraud. For example, type in the search window "financial statement fraud" and check out some of the results. What did you find that interested you? Now go to the following Web address: http://www.findarticles.com/p/articles/mi_m0HYW/is_2_83/ai_97999958.

   Here you will find an article about fraud in financial statement audits. What are some of the key points of the article? What did you learn after reading this article?

2. As we discussed in this chapter, the motivation of upper management can be an indicator of possible financial statement fraud. Another indicator of financial statement fraud is related-party transactions. Go to the Web site http://www.cnn.com/2002/LAW/02/03/enron/index.html and read the article on Enron. Briefly explain how this article illustrates that management motivation and related-party transactions are indicators of this fraud.

### DEBATES

1. Some people believe that the audit industry has fallen out of touch with the realities of business. They believe that accounting standards were developed for a manufacturing environment and are not fitted for our modern needs. As a result, they contend that financial statements have turned into a game in which all companies try to match earnings forecasts set by financial analysts. Are these statements true, or do you think that they are too cynical?

2. One of the most controversial topics to affect the accounting profession has been that of earnings management. Companies have been trying to manage their earnings to match analysts' projections. Even though the accounting literature doesn't give accounting professionals a clear definition of earnings management, many people have been critical of companies for trying to manage earnings, saying that most managed financial statements are fraudulent.

   As a class or individually, analyze the pros and cons of earnings management and try to decide whether earnings management is the same as financial statement fraud.

## END NOTES

1. http://www.sec.gov/news/press/2002-92.htm.

2. http://www.usatoday.com/money/companies/management/2002-12-23-ceo-loans_x.htm.

3. The data relating to this case are real but proprietary. Because litigation is still ongoing, the source and name of the company have not been revealed.

4. http://www.bizjournals.com/portland/stories/2002/12/30/daily17.html.

5. In 2003, the SEC acknowledged that U.S. GAAP may be too "rule-based" and wrote a position paper arguing for more "principles-based" or "objectives-based" accounting standards.

6. A *Fortune* article (March 5, 2001) included the following warning about Enron: "To skeptics, the lack of clarity raises a red flag about Enron's pricey stock . . . the inability to get behind the numbers combined with ever higher expectations for the company may increase the chance of a nasty surprise. Enron is an earnings-at-risk story...." (http://www.fortune.com/fortune/print/0,15935,369278,00.html) Even with this bad news, firms kept investing heavily in Enron and partnering or facilitating Enron's risky transactions

7. http://fitzgerald.senate.gov/legislation/stkanalyst/analystmain.htm.

8. http://www.cdfa.net/cdfa/press.nsf/pages/275.

9. Fraudulent Financial Reporting 1987–1997, "An Analysis of U.S. Public Companies, 1999," Research Commissioned by the Committee of Sponsoring Organization of the Treadway Commission.

10. http://www.sec.gov/news/studies/sox704report.pdf (accessed on June 5, 2004).

11. *Internal Auditor*, February 1999, p. 15.

12. For example, with increased independence of board members, CEOs whose performance is questionable are more likely to be dismissed. This tendency is different from what it was in the past. Boeker (1992), for example, found that, historically, organizations with below-average performance and powerful chief executives failed to dismiss the chief executive. In the majority of cases, the boards were willing to take other actions to improve success, but were not willing to dismiss the CEO.

# *Appendix*

## Recent Laws and Corporate Governance Changes Including the Sarbanes-Oxley Act

As described in the chapter, the period 2001–2003 marked the discovery of some of the largest financial statement frauds in U.S. history and some of the most significant legislation regarding the auditing profession and corporate governance since the SEC acts passed in 1933–1934. These events followed a prosperous decade that saw the NASDAQ grow 10 percent per year during 1987–1995; and then from an index of 1,291 on January 1, 1997, to 5,049 on March 10, 2000, for a 391 percent increase in three years. The Dow Jones Industrial Average, while not quite so dramatic, rose from 6,448 on January 1, 1997, to a high of 11,723 on January 14, 2000, for an increase of 81 percent in three years. Much of this growth came from individual investors who found they could invest on the Internet by paying only small fees ($8 to $10 per trade).

The revelation of the first financial statement frauds, including Enron and WorldCom, caused near panic in the market. The NASDAQ fell from its high of 5,049 on March 10 to 1,114 on October 9, 2002, leaving it at only 22 percent of its peak value. Similarly, the Dow Jones Industrial Average (NYSE) fell from its high of 11,723 on January 15, 2000, to a low of 7,286 on October 9, 2002, leaving it at only 62 percent of its previous value. The total decline in worldwide stock markets was $15 trillion. These sharp declines meant that nearly everyone's 401(k) and other retirement plans and personal wealth suffered tremendous losses.

Worse yet, several well-known companies declared bankruptcy. Table 11A-1 shows the 10 largest bankruptcies in U.S. history and reveals that 6 of the 10 occurred in 2002 and 4 of the 10 (WorldCom, Enron, Global Crossing, and Adelphia) were companies rocked with huge financial statement frauds and other problems.

## Table 11A-1  10 Largest U.S. Bankruptcies

| Company | Assets (billions) | When Filed |
| --- | --- | --- |
| 1. WorldCom | $101.9 | July 2002 |
| 2. Enron | $63.4 | December 2001 |
| 3. Texaco | $35.9 | April 1987 |
| 4. Financial Corp of America | $33.9 | September 1988 |
| 5. Global Crossing | $25.5 | January 2002 |
| 6. Adelphia | $24.4 | June 2002 |
| 7. United Airlines | $22.7 | December 2002 |
| 8. PG&E | $21.5 | June 2002 |
| 9. MCorp. | $20.2 | March 1989 |
| 10. Kmart | $17.0 | January 2002 |

# The Sarbanes-Oxley Act

Because of the pressure brought by constituents, Congress was quick to act. On July 30, 2002, President Bush signed into law the Sarbanes-Oxley Act of 2002 that had been quickly passed by both the House and the Senate. The law was intended to bolster public confidence in our nation's capital markets and impose new duties and significant penalties for noncompliance on public companies and their executives, directors, auditors, attorneys, and securities analysts.

The Sarbanes-Oxley Act is comprised of 11 separate sections or titles. You can read the full text of the act on several Web sites, but the highlights of each section are discussed here.

## Title I: Public Company Accounting Oversight Board

One of the concerns of legislators was that the auditing profession was self-regulating and set its own standards and that this regulation had fallen short of what it should have been. As a result, this part of the act established a five-member Public Company Accounting Oversight Board (PCAOB), with general oversight by the SEC, to do the following:

- Oversee the audit of public companies
- Establish audit reporting standards and rules
- Inspect, investigate, and enforce compliance on the part of registered public accounting firms and those associated with the firms

Title I requires public accounting firms that participate in any audit report with respect to any public company to register with the PCOAB. It also directs the PCAOB to establish (or modify) the auditing and related attestation standards, quality control, and the ethics standards used by registered public accounting firms to prepare and issue audit reports. It requires auditing standards to include (among other things): (1) a seven-year retention period for audit work papers, (2) a second-partner review and approval of audit opinions, (3) an evaluation of whether internal control structure and procedures include records that accurately reflect transactions and disposition of assets, (4) that receipts and expenditures of public companies are made only with authorization of senior management and directors, and (5) that auditors provide a description of both material weaknesses in internal controls and of material noncompliance.

Title I also mandated continuing inspections of public accounting firms for compliance on an annual basis for firms that provide audit reports for more than 100 issuers and at least every three years for firms that provide audit reports for 100 or fewer issuers. Based on these inspections, it empowered the Board to impose disciplinary or remedial sanctions upon registered accounting firms and their associates for intentional conduct or repeated instances of negligent conduct. It also directed the SEC to report to Congress on adoption of a principles-based accounting system by the U.S. financial reporting system and funded the Board through fees collected from issuers.

With the passing of this act, control over auditing firms and auditing standards shifted from the Auditing Standards Board of the American Institute of Certified Public Accountants (AICPA) to this new quasi-governmental organization called the PCAOB. Some people argue that this part of the law relegates the AICPA to a trade organization.

## Title II: Auditor Independence

Another concern of legislators was that the work of independent auditors of public companies had been compromised by some of the other types of consulting they had been doing for their audit clients. As a result, the next section of the Sarbanes-Oxley Act prohibits an auditor from performing specified nonaudit services contemporaneously with an audit. In addition, it specifies that public company audit committees must approve allowed activities for nonaudit services that are not expressly forbidden by the act.

The prohibited activities include the following:

- Bookkeeping services
- Financial information systems design and implementation
- Appraisal or valuation services
- Actuarial services
- Internal audit outsourcing
- Management functions or human resources
- Broker or dealer, investment advisor, or investment banking

- Legal services and expert services
- Any other service that the board determines is impermissible

In addition, this section of the act prohibits an audit partner from being the lead or reviewing auditor on the same public company for more than five consecutive years (auditor rotation). It requires that auditors report to the audit committee each of the following:

- Critical accounting policies and practices used in the audit
- Alternative treatments and their ramifications within GAAP
- Material written communications between the auditor and senior management of the issuer
- Activities prohibited under Sarbanes-Oxley (Change in wording is okay)

Title II places a one-year prohibition on auditors performing audit services if the issuer's senior executives had been employed by that auditor and had participated in the audit of the issuer during the one-year period preceding the audit initiation date and encourages state regulatory authorities to make independent determinations on the standards for supervising nonregistered public accounting firms and consider the size and nature of their clients' businesses audit.

## Title III: Corporate Responsibility

The first two titles of the act were directed at auditors of public companies, but the next section targets public companies themselves and especially their board of directors and its committees. Specifically, this part of the act includes the following provisions:

- Requires each member of a public company's audit committee to be a member of the board of directors and be independent (no other compensatory fees or affiliations with the issuer)
- Confers upon the audit committee responsibility for appointment, compensation, and oversight of any registered public accounting firm employed to perform audit services
- Gives audit committees authority to hire independent counsel and other advisors and requires issuers to fund them
- Instructs the SEC to promulgate rules requiring the CEO and CFO to certify that the financial statements provided in periodic financial reports:
  - Do not contain untrue statements or material omissions
  - Present fairly in all material respects the financial conditions and results of operations
- Establishes that the CEO and CFO are responsible for internal controls designed to ensure that they receive material information regarding the issuer and consolidated subsidiaries and that the internal controls have been reviewed for their effectiveness within 90 days prior to the report and makes them identify any significant changes to the internal controls

Title III also deals with abuses and penalties for abuses for executives who violate the Sarbanes-Oxley Act. Specifically, it makes it unlawful for corporate personnel to exert improper influence upon an audit for the purpose of rendering financial statements materially misleading. It requires that the CEO and CFO forfeit certain bonuses and compensation received if the company is required to make an accounting restatement due to the material noncompliance of an issuer. It amends the Securities and Exchange Act of 1933 to prohibit a violator of certain SEC rules from serving as an officer or director if the person's conduct demonstrates unfitness to serve (the previous rule required "substantial unfitness"). It provides a ban on trading by directors and executive officers in a public company's stock during pension fund blackout periods It imposes obligations on attorneys appearing before the SEC to report violations of securities laws and breaches of fiduciary duty by a public company or its agents to the chief legal counsel or CEO of the company, and it allows civil penalties to be added to a disgorgement fund for the benefit of victims of securities violations.

## Title IV: Enhanced Financial Disclosures

Another concern addressed by the act was that another cause of the problems that had occurred was that public company financial statements did not disclose certain kinds of problematic transactions properly and that management and directors didn't act as ethically as they should have. As a result, Title IV:

- Requires financial reports filed with the SEC to reflect all material correcting adjustments that have been identified.
- Requires disclosure of all material off-balance sheet transactions and relationships that may have a material effect upon the financial status of an issue.
- Prohibits personal loans extended by a corporation to its executives and directors with some exceptions.
- Requires senior management, directors, and principal stockholders to disclose changes in securities ownership or securities-based swap agreements within two business days (formerly 10 days after the close of the calendar month).
- Requires that annual reports include an internal control report stating that management is responsible for the internal control structure and procedures for financial reporting and that they have assessed the effectiveness of the internal controls for the previous fiscal year. This Section 404 request is probably the most expensive and debated part of the Act. As a result of this requirement, most companies have spent millions of dollars documenting and testing their controls.
- Requires issuers to disclose whether they have adopted a code of ethics for their senior financial officers and whether their audit committees consist of at least one member who is a financial expert.
- Mandates regular, systematic SEC review of periodic disclosures by issuers, including review of an issuer's financial statement.

## Title V: Analyst Conflicts of Interest

In addition to concern over auditors, board members, management, and financial statements, legislators were also concerned that certain other professionals (investment bankers and financial institutions) also contributed to the problems. Accordingly, this section of the act:

- Restricts the ability of investment bankers to pre-approve research reports.
- Ensures that research analysts in investment banking firms are not supervised by persons involved in investment banking activities.
- Prevents retaliation against analysts by employers in return for writing negative reports. Establishes blackout periods for brokers or dealers participating in a public offering during which they may not distribute reports related to such offering.
- Enhances structural separation in registered brokers or dealers between analyst and investment banking activities.
- Requires specific conflict of interest disclosures by research analysts making public appearances and by brokers or dealers in research reports including:
  - Whether the analyst holds securities in the public company that is the subject of the appearance or report
  - Whether any compensation was received by the analyst, or broker or dealer, from the company that was the subject of the appearance or report
  - Whether a public company that is the subject of an appearance or report is, or during the prior one-year period was, a client of the broker or dealer
  - Whether the analyst received compensation with respect to a research report, based upon banking revenues of the registered broker or dealer.

## Title VI: Commission Resources and Authority

Title VI of the act gave the SEC more budget and more power to be effective in its role of overseeing public companies in the United States. Specifically, this part:

- Authorized a 77.21 percent increase over the appropriations for FY 2002 including money for pay parity, information and technology, security enhancements, and recovery and mitigation activities related to the September 11 terrorist attacks.
- Provided $98 million to hire no less than 200 additional qualified professionals to provide improved oversight of auditors and audit services.

- Authorized the SEC to censure persons appearing or practicing before the Commission if it finds, among other things, a person to have engaged in unethical or improper professional conduct.
- Authorized federal courts to prohibit persons from participating in penny stock offerings if the persons are the subject of proceedings instituted for alleged violations of securities laws.
- Expanded the scope of the SEC's disciplinary authority by allowing it to consider orders of state securities commissions when deciding whether to limit the activities, functions, or operations of brokers or dealers.

## Title VII: Studies and Reports

This section of the Sarbanes-Oxley Act specified that certain reports and studies should be made, including the following:

- A study of the factors leading to the consolidation of public accounting firms and its impact on capital formation and securities markets
- A study of the role of credit rating agencies in the securities markets
- A study of the number of securities professionals practicing before the Commission who have aided and abetted federal securities violations but have not been penalized as a primary violator
- A study of SEC enforcement actions it has taken regarding violations of reporting requirements and restatements of financial statements (as referred to earlier in the chapter)
- A study by the GAO on whether investment banks and financial advisors assisted public companies in earnings manipulation and obfuscation of financial conditions

## Title VIII: Corporate and Criminal Fraud Accountability

Title VIII was the part of the Sarbanes-Oxley Act that imposed criminal penalties upon violators, extended the statute of limitations for financial crimes and provided protection for whistle-blowers in fraud cases. Specifically, this part of the act:

- Imposed criminal penalties for knowingly destroying, altering, concealing, or falsifying records with intent to obstruct or influence either a federal investigation or a matter in bankruptcy and for failure of an auditor to maintain for a five-year period all audit or review work papers pertaining to an issuer of securities (penalty: 10 years in prison).
- Made nondischargeable in bankruptcy certain debts incurred in violation of securities fraud laws.
- Extended the statute of limitations to permit a private right of action for a securities fraud violation to not later than two years after its discovery or five years after the date of the violation.
- Provided whistle-blower protection to prohibit a publicly traded company from retaliating against an employee because of any lawful act by the employee to assist in an investigation of fraud or other conduct by federal regulators, Congress, or supervisors, or to file or participate in a proceeding relating to fraud against shareholders.
- Subjected to fine or imprisonment (up to 25 years) any person who knowingly defrauds shareholders of publicly traded companies.

## Title IX: White-Collar Crime Penalty Enhancements

Because of concern that corporate executives and directors who engage in unlawful conduct were not being penalized sufficiently, this part of the act increased penalties for mail and wire fraud from 5 to 20 years in prison. It also increased penalties for violations of the Employee Retirement Income Security Act of 1974 (up to $500,000 and 10 years in prison) and established criminal liability for failure of corporate officers to certify financial reports, including maximum imprisonment of 10 years for knowing that the periodic report does not comply with the act or for 20 years for willfully certifying a statement knowing it does not comply with this act.

## Title X: Corporate Tax Returns

This title expressed the sense of the Senate that the federal income tax return of a corporation should be signed by its chief executive officer.

## Title XI: Corporate Fraud Accountability

This final title of the act amended federal criminal law to establish a maximum 20-year prison term for tampering with a record or otherwise impeding an official proceeding. It authorized the SEC to seek a temporary injunction to freeze extraordinary payments earmarked for designated persons or corporate staff under investigation for possible violations of federal securities law. It also authorizes the SEC to prohibit a violator of rules governing manipulative, deceptive devices, and fraudulent interstate transactions, from serving as officer or director of a publicly traded corporation if the person's conduct demonstrates unfitness to serve, and it increased penalties for violations of the Securities Exchange Act of 1934 to up to $25 million dollars and up to 20 years in prison.

# How the SEC Enacted the Sarbanes-Oxley Act

Following the Sarbanes-Oxley Act, the SEC passed a number of statutes and laws as directed by the legislation. The Table 11A-2 summarizes some of the releases relating to Sarbanes-Oxley Act requirements.

## Table 11A-2  SEC Statutes Related to the Sarbanes-Oxley Act

| Date of Issuance | Nature of Release |
|---|---|
| January 22, 2003 | Conditions for Use of Non-GAAP Measures |
| January 23, 2003 | Disclosures required by Sec. 406 and 407 |
| January 24, 2003 | Retention of Audit Records |
| March 26, 2003 | Auditor Independence & Disclosure of Fees |
| January 27, 2003 | Disclosure of Off-Balance Sheet Arrangements (Sec. 401(a)) |
| January 27, 2003 | Management Certifications and Disclosures of Financial Expert and Code of Ethics (Sec. 406 & 407) |
| January 28, 2003 | Auditor Independence & Prohibited Services (Sec. 208) |
| January 29, 2003 | Standards for the Conduct of Attorneys (Sec. 307) |
| January 31, 2003 | Proxy Voting Rules |
| February 24, 2004 | Management's Report on Internal Control over Financial Reporting and Certification |
| March 16, 2004 | Additional Form 8-K disclosure requirements and acceleration of filing date |
| March 26, 2003 | Auditor Independence & Disclosure of Fees |
| March 26, 2003 | Financial Experts & Codes of Ethics (Sec. 406 and 407) |
| March 27, 2003 | Non-GAAP Financial Measures and Insider Trades during Blackout Periods |
| April 9, 2003 | Standards related to Audit Committees (Independence, control of audit, etc.) |
| April 14, 2004 | Disclosure Regarding Market Timing and Selective Disclosure of Portfolio Holdings |
| May 20, 2003 | Improper Influence on Conduct of Auditors (Sec. 303) |
| June 5, 2003 | Management's Reports on I/C (Sec. 404) |
| June 8, 2003 | Management's Reports on Internal Control Over Financial Reporting and Certification |
| November 10, 2003 | Purchases of Certain Equity Securities by the Issuer and Others |
| November 24, 2003 | Disclosure regarding Nominating Committee Functions and Communications Between Security Holders and Boards of Directors |

## The Public Company Accounting Oversight Board (PCAOB)

Once the PCAOB was up and running, it wasted no time in carrying out its mandate. With its authorized budget of $68 million per year, within weeks, it required that auditing firms of public companies register with the Board. It hired inspectors to carry out inspections of the audits of public companies. It hired a new audit director (Douglas Carmichael) and created a board to issue auditing standards. It established offices in several cities around the United States.

It established its mission to oversee the auditors of public companies in order to protect the interests of investors and further the public interest in the preparation of informative, fair, and independent audit reports. It issued its first auditing standard that articulates management's responsibilities for evaluating and documenting the effectiveness of internal controls over financial reporting, identifies the kinds of deficiencies that can exist, states the consequences of having deficiencies, and identifies how deficiencies must be communicated.

# Subsequent Changes Made by the Stock Exchanges

In response to the high-profile corporate failures, the SEC requested that the NYSE and NASDAQ review their listing standards with an emphasis on all matters of corporate governance. Based on that request, both NYSE and NASDAQ conducted extensive reviews of their listing standards for corporate governance and filed corporate governance reform proposals with the SEC in 2002. In April 2003, the SEC issued Rule 10A-3 that directed all stock exchanges to prohibit listing of any security of an issuer that is not in compliance with the audit committee requirements specified in Rule 10A-3. On November 4, 2003, the SEC approved, with certain modifications, the corporate governance reforms proposed by NYSE and NASDAQ. What follows is an overview of the changes that they made.

## NASDAQ Corporate Governance Changes

NASDAQ focused almost entirely upon boards of directors and executives in making governance reforms. Specifically, NASDAQ addressed the following issues:

- Independence of majority of board members
- Separate meetings of independent board members
- Compensation of officers
- Nomination of directors
- Audit committee charter and responsibilities
- Audit committee composition
- Code of business conduct and ethics
- Public announcement of going-concern qualifications
- Related-party transactions
- Notification of noncompliance

NASDAQ corporate governance reforms mandate that a majority of the board of director members are required to be independent along with a disclosure in an annual proxy (or in the 10-K if proxy is not filed) about the directors, which the board has determined to be independent under the NASD rules. In defining what constitutes an independent director, NASDAQ's rules state that a director is not independent under the following circumstances:

- The director is an officer or employee of the company or its subsidiaries.
- The director has a relationship, which in the opinion of the company's board would interfere with the director.
- Any director who is or has at any time in the last three years been employed by the company or by any parent or subsidiary of the company.
- The director accepts or has a family member who accepts any payments from the company in excess of $60,000 during the current fiscal year or any of the past three fiscal years. Payments made directly to or for the benefit of the director or a family member of the

director or political contributions to the campaign of a director or a family member of the director would be covered by this provision.

- The director is a family member of an individual who is or at any time during the past three years was employed by the company or its parent or any of its subsidiaries of the company as an executive officer.
- The director is or has a family member who is employed as an executive officer of another entity during the past three years where any of the executive officers of the listed company serve on the compensation committee of such entity.
- The director is or has a family member who is a partner in or a controlling shareholder or an executive officer of any organization in which the company or from which the company received payments for property or services in the current year or any of the past three fiscal years that exceed 5 percent of the recipient's consolidated gross revenues for that year or $200,000, whichever is more.
- The director is or has a family member who is an executive officer of a charitable organization, if the company makes payments to the charity in excess of the greater of 5 percent of the charity's revenues or $200,000.
- The director is or has a family member who is a current partner of the company's outside auditor.
- The director was a partner or employee of the company's outside auditor **and** worked on the company's audit at any time in the past three years.

Under new governance standards, independent directors are required to have regularly scheduled meetings at which only independent directors are present (thus excluding all members of management). To eliminate sweetheart deals, the compensation of the CEO and all other officers must be determined or recommended to the full board for determination by a majority of the independent directors or a compensation committee comprised solely of independent directors.

In addition, director nominees should be either selected or nominated for selection by a majority of independent directors or by a nominations committee comprised solely of nomination directors. NASDAQ changes also require each issuer to certify in writing it has adopted a formal written charter or board resolution addressing the nomination process.

- A written charter for the audit committee of the issuer must provide the following:
- The committee's purpose of overseeing the accounting and financial reporting processes and audits of the financial statements
- Specific audit committee responsibilities and authority including the means by which the audit committee carries out those responsibilities
- Outside auditor's accountability to the committee
- The committee's responsibility to ensure the independence of the outside auditor
- Audit committee consist of at least three members
- Each audit committee member is required to be:
  - Independent under the NASD rules
  - Independent under Rule 10A-3 issued by the SEC
  - Someone who has not participated in the preparation of the financial statements of the company or any current subsidiary of the company at any time during the last three years

Existing NASD rules already required that each audit committee member should be able to read and understand fundamental financial statements. This requirement did not change. However, under the new NASDAQ governance rules, one audit committee member must have past employment experience in finance and accounting, requisite professional certification in accounting or any other comparable experience or background that results in the individual's financial sophistication, including being or having been a CEO, CFO, or other senior officer with financial oversight responsibilities. Audit committee members are also prohibited from receiving any payment from the company other than the payment for board or committee services and are also prohibited from serving the audit committee in the event they are deemed to be an affiliated person of the company or any subsidiary.

Under the new NASDAQ requirements, each listed company must have a publicly available code of conduct that is applicable to all directors, officers and employees. The code of conduct must comply with "code of ethics" as set forth in Section 406(c) of the Sarbanes-Oxley Act and must provide for an enforcement mechanism that ensures the following:

- Prompt and consistent enforcement of the code
- Protection for persons reporting questionable behavior
- Clear and objective standards for compliance

Finally, each listed company that receives an audit opinion that contains a going-concern qualification must make a public announcement through the news media disclosing the receipt of such qualification within seven calendar days following the filing with the SEC of the documents that contained such an audit opinion. In addition, the audit committee of each issuer must conduct an appropriate review of all related-party transactions for potential conflicts of interest on an ongoing basis and make sure that all such transaction have been approved

## NYSE Corporate Governance Changes

Changes made by the NYSE were quite similar to those made by NASDAQ. Specifically, the NYSE addressed the following broad categories of the proposed standards:

- Independence of majority of board members
- Separate meetings of independent board members
- Nomination/Corporate governance committee
- Corporate governance guidelines
- Compensation committee
- Audit committee charter and responsibilities
- Audit committee composition
- Internal audit function
- Code of business conduct and ethics
- CEO certification
- Public reprimand letter

Like NASDAQ, NYSE governance changes require that a majority of the directors be independent. Under NYSE standards, no director qualifies as an independent director unless the board affirmatively determines that the director has no material relationships with the company. Like NASDAQ, the NYSE now requires disclosure in annual proxy (or in the 10-K if a proxy is not filed), the basis of the conclusion that the particular directors have been deemed to be independent. If an issuer fails to meet this requirement due to vacancy or due to any director ceasing to be independent due to circumstances beyond their reasonable control, the issuer must regain compliance by the earlier of the next annual meeting or one year from the date of occurrence.

- Under NYSE guidelines, independence of a director is impaired under the following circumstances:
- The director is an employee or whose immediate family member is an executive officer of the company would not be independent until three years after the termination of that employment.
- The director receives or whose immediate family member receives more than $100,000 per year in direct compensation from the listed company would not be independent until three years after he or she ceases to receive more than $100,000 per year.
- The director is affiliated or employed by, or whose immediate family member is employed in any professional capacity by a present or former internal or external auditor of the company would not be independent until three years after the end of the affiliation or the employment or auditing relationship.
- The director is affiliated with or employed or whose immediate family member is affiliated or employed as an executive officer of another company where any of the listed company's present executives serve on that company's compensation committee would not be independent until three years after the end of such service or employment relationship.

- The director is an executive officer or an employee or whose immediate family member is an executive officer of a company that makes payments to or receives payments from the listed company for property or services in an amount which, in any single fiscal year, exceeds the greater of $1 million or 2 percent of such other company's consolidated gross revenues would not be independent until three years after falling below that threshold.
- Immediate family member includes a person's spouse, parents, children, siblings, mothers- and fathers-in-law, sons- and daughters-in-law, brothers- and sisters-in-law, and anyone (other than domestic employees) who shares such person's home.
- Nonmanagement directors are required to have regularly scheduled executive meetings at which only nonmanagement directors would be present.

NYSE-listed companies are required to disclose a method to interested parties to communicate directly with the presiding director of such executive sessions or with the nonmanagement directors as a group. Each listed company must have a nominating/corporate governance committee comprising solely of independent directors.

- Like NASDAQ-listed companies, audit committees must have written charters that should address at a minimum the following:
- The committee's purpose and responsibilities
- An annual performance evaluation of the nominating/governance committee
- The committee would be required to identify members qualified to become board members consistent with the criteria approved by the board.

Each NYSE-listed company must adopt and disclose corporate governance guidelines that specify director qualification standards, director responsibilities, director access to management and as necessary and appropriate to independent advisors, director compensation, director orientation and continuing education, management succession, and annual performance evaluation of the board.

These corporate governance guidelines and charters of the most important board committees must be disclosed on the company's Web site

With respect to committees, each listed company must have a compensation committee composed solely of independent directors and that has a written charter that addresses at least the following issues:

- The committee's purpose and responsibilities
- An annual performance evaluation of the compensation committee

The committee would be required to produce a compensation report on executive compensation for inclusion in the company's annual proxy. In addition, the committee, together with the other independent directors, would determine and approve the CEO's compensation.

Listed companies must also have an audit committee that has a written charter that provides the following:

- The committee's purpose
- Annual performance evaluation of the audit committee
- Duties and responsibilities of the audit committee
- Duties and responsibilities of the audit committee as defined in the charter should include at a minimum:
  - Those provisions set out in Rule 10A-3 of SEC
  - Responsibility to annually obtain and review a report by the independent auditor
  - Discussion of the company's annual audited financial statements and quarterly financial statements with management and the independent auditor
  - Discussion of the company's earnings press releases, as well as financial information and earnings guidance provided to analysts and rating agencies
  - Discussion of policies with respect to risk assessment and risk management
  - Meet separately, periodically with management, with internal auditors and with independent auditors
  - Review with independent auditors any audit problems or difficulties and management's response
  - Set clear hiring policies for employees or former employees of independent auditors

The audit committee, which must have at least three members, must report regularly to the full board. In addition, each audit committee member is required to be:

- Independent under the NYSE rules
- Independent under Rule 10A-3 issued by the SEC
- Someone who has not participated in the preparation of the financial statements of the company or any current subsidiary of the company at any time during the last three years
- Financially literate, as such qualification is interpreted by the board in its business judgment or must become financially literate within a reasonable period of time after his or her appointment to the committee

At least one member of the committee would be required to have accounting or related financial management expertise, because the company's board interprets such qualification in its business judgment. One of the biggest differences between audit committees of NYSE-listed companies from NASDAQ-listed companies is that if an audit committee member simultaneously serves on the audit committee of more than three public companies, and the listed company does not limit the number of audit committees on which its audit committee members may serve, each board is required to determine whether such simultaneous service would impair the ability of such member to effectively serve on the listed company's audit committee. Additionally, any such determination must be disclosed in an annual proxy statement or in the annual report on Form 10-K in case the company does not file a proxy statement.

Another major difference is that NYSE governance requires each listed company have an internal audit function to provide management and the audit committee with ongoing assessments of the company's risk management processes and system of internal control. Under the guidelines, companies may choose to outsource this function to a third-party service provider other than its independent auditor but it must have the function.

Like NASDAQ, each listed company must adopt and disclose a code of business conduct and ethics that is applicable to all directors, officers, and employees. The code of conduct must be available on the company's Web site and any waiver of the code of conduct for officers and directors must be promptly disclosed. The code of conduct must provide the following elements:

- Conflicts of interest
- Corporate opportunities
- Confidentiality of information
- Fair dealing
- Protection and proper use of company assets
- Compliance with laws, rules, and regulations
- Encouraging the reporting of any illegal or unethical behavior
- Compliance standards
- Procedures to facilitate effective operation of the code

The CEO of each listed company must certify to the NYSE each year that he or she is not aware of any violation by the company of the NYSE's corporate listing standards. This certification would be required to be disclosed in the company's annual report on Form 10-K. Additionally, the CEO of each listed company would be required to promptly notify in writing to NYSE after any executive officer becomes aware of any material noncompliance with the applicable provisions of the new requirements.

The governance changes authorize the NYSE to issue a public reprimand letter to any listed company that violates NYSE governance requirements.

## Has Recent Legislation Fixed the Problem?

To determine whether recent legislation has remedied the problem and will prevent future frauds, it is important to align the three elements of the fraud triangle with remedies that have been instituted. Table 11A-3 attempts to do that.

## Table 11A-3  Remedies Enacted Through Recent Legislation

| Element of the Fraud Triangle | Element of the Perfect Fraud Storm | Remedy That Addresses This Factor |
|---|---|---|
| Perceived Pressures | 1. Misplaced executive incentives<br>2. Unrealistic Wall Street expectations<br>3. Large amounts of debt<br>4. Greed | Recent legislation and corporate governance changes have not addressed perceived pressures. Significant stock-based compensation is still being given to executives. No decrease has occurred in EPS forecasts and the size of penalties when those forecasts are not met. Companies have taken on more, not less debt.* And, no evidence indicates that executives are less motivated by greed than before the frauds. |
| Perceived Opportunities | 5. Good economy was masking many problems<br>6. Behavior of CPA firms<br>7. Rules-based accounting standards<br>8. Educator failures | Most of the legislative and governance changes have been targeted at reducing opportunities to commit fraud. The requirement that board members be more independent from management is intended to eliminate or decrease the opportunities of management to commit fraud. Other actions that are intended to decrease opportunities** are minimum sentencing guidelines, requiring executives to sign off on the accuracy of financial statements, holding management responsible for good controls, installing a whistle-blower system, inspecting auditors so that they increase the thoroughness of their audits, etc. |
| Rationalization | 9. Moral decay in society | The one legislative action that addresses this fraud element is requiring all companies to have an executive code of conduct. However, with decreasing integrity in society, it is doubtful that requiring a code of conduct will eliminate rationalizations. |

*One of the most common activities on Wall Street since the discovery of the corporate frauds has been the issuance of convertible debt by corporations. The convertibles market has been extremely hot and has resulted in significantly more debt for many companies. Unfortunately, convertible debt creates the same kinds of stock manipulation pressures (to have the stock price increase to the premium amount at which the debt can be called and converted to equity).

** Opportunity encompasses not only the ability to commit a fraud but also the opportunity to conceal the fraud (and not be caught) and to experience no serious punishment if caught.

As we described earlier in the book, fraud is like fire in that three elements come together to create fire: (1) heat, (2) fuel, and (3) oxygen. The more intense or pure one element, say oxygen, the less heat and fuel are required. The same is true with fraud. The more of one element you have, say pressures, the less of the other elements (i.e., opportunities and rationalizations) it takes to commit fraud. To the extent recent legislative and governance actions have reduced fraud opportunities, the more perceived pressure and rationalization it will take to commit financial statement fraud in the future. Eliminating opportunities will make it much more difficult for executives to argue that their personal interests will be best served by fraudulent reporting.[1] Legislative and governance changes make it harder to commit fraud, harder to conceal fraud, and impose greater penalties for those who behave dishonestly. Only when perceived pressures and the ability to rationalize increase to the point where they more than offset the decreased opportunities, will future frauds occur. Our prediction, therefore, less corporate fraud will occur in the United States in the future, but not all of it will be eliminated. The increased pressures and rationalizations that will now be necessary will generate fraud symptoms that are more egregious than those of the past. For individuals who understand fraud, these egregious fraud symptoms will be more observable than ever before, which should make fraud easier to detect.

# END NOTES

1. National Commission on Fraudulent Financial Reporting (NCFFR), Report of the National Commission on Fraudulent Financial Reporting (New York: AICPA, 1987).

# CHAPTER 12

# REVENUE- AND INVENTORY-RELATED FINANCIAL STATEMENT FRAUDS[1]

## LEARNING OBJECTIVES

After studying this chapter, you should be able to:

1. Identify revenue-related financial statement fraud schemes.
2. Understand revenue-related financial statement fraud schemes.
3. Identify ways to proactively search for revenue-related financial statement fraud schemes.
4. Understand the importance of, and ways to follow up on, revenue-related fraud symptoms.
5. Identify inventory and cost of goods sold financial statement fraud schemes.
6. Understand inventory and cost of goods sold financial statement fraud symptoms.
7. Identify ways to search for inventory and cost of goods sold financial statement fraud symptoms.
8. Understand the importance of, and ways to follow up on, inventory and cost of goods sold fraud symptoms.

*You've probably never heard of Cendant Corporation, but you are probably familiar with some of the companies it owns, such as Days Inn, Ramada Inn, Avis Car Rental, and real-estate brokerage Century 21. Cendant Corporation was formed in 1997 when CUC International Inc. merged with HFS Inc. Combining the resources of both companies was intended to create one of the world's largest and most powerful hotel, car rental, reservation, and real-estate companies. But Cendant's hopes for a successful company quickly turned upside down when HFS Inc. learned that CUC International had inflated its income and earnings to make it appear to be a growing, highly profitable, and successful enterprise. What started as a small fraud in 1983 quickly grew to a large fraud. From 1995 to 1997, the pretax operating income of CUC International was inflated by more than $500 million. Many executives of CUC International were fired and prosecuted.*

*In 1999, Cendant Corporation agreed to pay $2.8 billion to settle a shareholder lawsuit. The attorneys for the plaintiffs were awarded $262 million in fees. On April 16, 1998, when the fraud was publicly announced, Cendant's stock dropped 46 percent, making the paper value of the company drop by $14.4 billion in one day. Today, Cendant is a diversified global provider of business consumer service. They have largely overcome the fraud that cost them time, negative public exposure, and more than $2.8 billion. With headquarters in New York City, the company has approximately 60,000 employees and operates in more than 100 countries.[2]*

*You've probably also heard of Sunbeam, the maker of home appliances. Sunbeam Corporation began developing home appliances in 1910. Over the years, Sunbeam made some of the nation's best home appliances, such as the electric iron and the pop-up toaster. In July 1996, "Chainsaw Al" Dunlap became CEO and chairman of Sunbeam. "Chainsaw Al" repeatedly promised to produce a rapid turnaround in Sunbeam's financial performance. At the end of 1996, "Chainsaw Al" was unable to produce a rapid turnaround in Sunbeam's financial performance. Desperate, "Chainsaw Al" turned to a "laundry list of fraudulent techniques" to improve the company's financial performance. "Chainsaw Al" began creating "cookie jar" reserves. These reserves increased Sunbeam's reported loss for 1996, but were then used to inflate income in 1997, thus giving the picture of a rapid turnaround. In 1997, "Chainsaw Al" caused the company to recognize revenues for sales that did not meet applicable accounting rules. As a result, at least $60 million of Sunbeam's record-setting $189 million reported earnings in 1997 came from accounting fraud. In early 1998, "Chainsaw Al" took even more desperate measures to conceal the company's mounting financial problems. He again recognized revenue for sales that did not meet the applicable accounting rules. He also caused Sunbeam to engage in the acceleration of sales revenue from a later period and deleted certain corporate records to conceal pending returns of merchandise.[3]*

# Revenue-Related Fraud

By far, the most common accounts manipulated when perpetrating financial statement fraud are revenues and receivables. The COSO-sponsored study discussed in the previous chapter found that more than half of all financial statement frauds involved revenues or accounts receivable accounts. The COSO study also found that recording fictitious revenues was the most common way to manipulate revenue accounts, and that recording revenues prematurely was the second most common type of revenue-related financial statement fraud. Other studies have found similar results. In fact, because of the frequency of revenue-related financial statement frauds, the AICPA published "Audit Issues in Revenue Recognition" on its Web site (http://www.aicpa.org) in January 1999. This publication contained authoritative and nonauthoritative auditing guidance to help financial statement auditors identify and respond to warning signals of improper revenue recognition. It focuses on issues related to the sale of goods and services in the ordinary course of business. The publication also discusses management's responsibility to report revenues accurately and selected accounting standards applicable to **revenue recognition**. Several other AICPA activities also address "earnings management" and "financial statement fraud" practices that threaten the integrity of the financial reporting process.

Revenue-related financial statement frauds are prevalent for two reasons. First, in many cases, acceptable alternatives are available for recognizing revenue, and these alternatives can be interpreted and applied in situation-specific ways. Just as organizations are different, the kinds of revenues they generate are different, and these different types of revenues need different recognition and reporting methods and criteria. A company that collects cash before delivering goods or performing a service, such as a franchiser, for example, needs to recognize revenue differently than a company that collects cash after the delivery of goods or the performance of a service, such as a manufacturing firm. A company that has long-term, construction-type contracts needs different revenue recognition criteria than a company whose revenue is based on small, discrete performance acts. In many cases, it is difficult to identify the most significant performance or earnings event that should control the timing of revenue recognition.

Consider, for example, a company that explores, refines, and distributes oil. When should that company recognize revenue from its oil? When it discovers the oil in the ground (for which there is a ready market and a determinable price), when it refines the crude oil or condensate into products such as jet and diesel fuel, when it distributes the oil to its service stations for resale, or when it actually sells the refined oil to customers? Similarly, consider a company that performs human clinical trials on new drugs produced by pharmaceutical companies to determine whether the drugs should be approved by the Food and Drug Administration for sale and distribution to the public. Suppose a contract with a pharmaceutical company states that the drug will be tested on 100 patients over a period of six months, and each patient will be observed and tested weekly. Further assume that the testing company is to be paid $100 per patient visit for a total of $2,600 (26 visits) per patient and a total contract amount of $260,000 ($2,600 per patient × 100 patients). Because the pharmaceutical company does not want to be billed every time a patient is tested, it specifies that the testing company can submit bills for payment only when certain "billing milestones" have been reached, such as 25 patient visits, 50 patient visits, 75 patient visits, and 100 patient visits. In this case, when should the revenues be recognized—at the time the patient visits take place, at the time bills can be submitted to the pharmaceutical company, when all visits have taken place, or at some other time?

These difficult issues require significant judgment. In these and many other similar situations, both conservative and liberal ways can be applied to revenue recognition criteria. Even financial reporting experts do not always agree when an organization has had sufficient performance to recognize revenue and what the major revenue-recognition criteria should be. In numerous cases, these and other difficult revenue-recognition issues have been debated and have been at the heart of financial statement fraud lawsuits. Specifically, in both of these cases, the companies started out using liberal ways of recognizing revenues and when those weren't sufficient, managements starting committing fraud. In the oil company case, the fraud involved recognizing oil sales on fictitious ships that were supposedly sailing the oceans and recognizing other types of fictitious revenues. In the medical testing case, using mechanical whiteout, contracts with drug companies were altered so that instead of stating that the testing company would get $100 per patient, for example, the contracts were changed to read $400 per patient.

These differences in revenue recognition and performance criteria across organizations make it difficult to develop absolute revenue recognition rules that can be applied in every or even most cases. Indeed, in many situations significant judgment must be exercised to determine when and how much revenue to recognize. This subjectivity provides opportunities for financial statement manipulation by managers who want to "cook the books."

The second reason why revenue-related frauds are so common is because it is so easy to manipulate net income using revenue and receivable accounts. In the video "Cooking the Books," produced by the Association of Certified Fraud Examiners, Barry Minkow, mastermind of the ZZZZ Best Fraud, states, "Receivables are a wonderful thing. You create a receivable and you have revenue." When you have revenue, you have income. The easiest way to increase reported net income is to add a little revenue and a few more receivables. In addition, revenues and receivables can be manipulated in several simple ways. For example, an organization can create additional revenues by simply holding its books open for a time after the end of the period and including revenues in the current period that should be recognized in the next period. This type of revenue fraud is often referred to as early recognition of revenues or abusing the cutoff. Revenues can also be recognized earlier than they should in cases of long-term construction-type contracts where revenues recognized depend upon the percentage of completion of a project. Secondly, a company can create fictitious documentation, sales, or customers to make it appear that sales were higher than they actually were for the period. Alternatively, contracts upon which revenue recognition is based can be altered or forged. Or, in the most egregious cases, topside journal entries that create revenues and receivables without underlying documentation can be created.

One of the most egregious revenue-related frauds in recent years was that committed by Qwest International. Qwest, a Denver-based company, is the dominant local telephone company in 14 states. It was founded in 1995 and became a public company in 1997. In 2001, it had 57,000 employees and reported revenues of $18 billion. In 2001, it had 30 million customers who made 600 million e-mails and 240 million telephone calls per day on its 190,000 miles of telephone network. During the years 1999, 2000, and 2001, it overstated revenues by $2 to $4 billion. In 2000 and 2001 alone, it wrote off revenue of $2.2 billion. When the fraud was discovered, the price of the company's stock dropped by 89 percent. Four former executives at the company were indicted on 12 charges related to corporate accounting fraud: Grant Graham, the former chief financial officer of Qwest's Global Business Unit; Thomas Hall, former senior vice president of the Government and Educational Solutions Group within Qwest's Global Business Unit; John Walker, a former vice president in the Government and Educational Solutions Group; and Bryan Treadway, a former assistant controller at Qwest. Qwest's revenue fraud schemes included the following:

- Swapping with other telecom firms the rights to use fiber-optic strands for no legitimate business reason, and immediate booking of revenues to meet Wall Street's earnings expectations. Using this method, known as "round-tripping," the company recognized gains of $3 billion in revenue from selling and swapping. Many of these secret swap deals that boosted revenues were with other telecom companies that also revealed major revenue-related frauds, including Global Crossing ($720 million in swap revenues from deals with Qwest), Enron, Flag, and Cable&Wireless.
- Improperly recognizing revenue from "bill and hold" transactions and falsifying documents to hide the fraud. One notable "bill and hold" transaction was with the Arizona School Facilities Board in the third quarter of 2000.
- Selling equipment at twice the normal price and then offering a discount on service contracts. Because the profit on the sales could be recognized earlier than the revenue on the service contracts, the company booked at an 80 percent profit margin more than $100 million in revenues. This method became known as illegally "splitting transactions."
- Changing the publication dates on telephone directors to artificially boost revenue in 2000 and 2001, a practice that became known as "Dex shuffling."
- Although not a revenue-related fraud, suspending the depreciation expense on 570,000 rural access lines as part of a planned $1.8 billion sale.

Of these fraud schemes, the round-tripping or swapping was the biggest. Roughly $1.5 billion of $2.2 billion in revenue written off in 2000 and 2001 came from swaps or sales of fiber-optic rights, while equipment sales accounted for only several hundred million dollars.

The fraud was discovered by a combination of reports from Morgan Stanley telecom analysts, anonymous tips, and direct complaints from disgruntled employees of Global Crossing and Qwest, SEC informal and formal investigations, a U.S. Department of Justice criminal investigation, a Qwest four-member audit committee internal probe, and a Qwest internal investigation ordered by Qwest's new CEO.

## Identifying Revenue-Related Exposures

In addition to the factors identified previously that provide fraud exposures, specific revenue-related exposures must be considered. These exposures are the various fraud schemes that can be used to misstate the financial statements. One of the best ways to understand how revenue-related financial statement frauds can be perpetrated is to understand first the various kinds of revenue transactions that exist. Probably the best way to understand revenue-related transactions is to analyze and diagram the various transactions between an organization and its customers, analyzing the accounts that are involved in each transaction, and trying to determine how misstatement could occur in each transaction. In the case of revenues, these transactions in a typical company might be diagrammed in Figure 12-1.

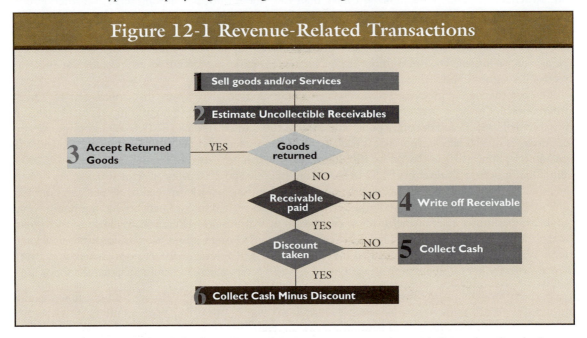

**Figure 12-1 Revenue-Related Transactions**

Once the revenue transactions are diagrammed, a good way to understand the various fraud schemes that can be used to manipulate the financial statements is to correlate the accounts involved in each transaction with the kinds of manipulations that can occur. The numbers provided in the diagram to identify the transactions can be used to prepare a table such as the one shown in Table 12-1:

## Table 12-1  Transaction Types Used in Various Fraud Schemes

| Transaction | Accounts Involved | Fraud Schemes |
|---|---|---|
| 1. Sell goods and/or services to customers | Accounts receivable and Revenues (e.g., sales revenue) | 1. Record fictitious sales (related-parties, sham sales, bill-and-hold sales, sales with conditions or side letters, consignment sales, etc.)<br>2. Recognize revenues too early (improper cut-off, holding books open after close of a reporting period, percentage of completion, etc.)<br>3. Overstate real sales (improper valuation of revenue, alter contracts, inflate amounts, etc.) |

## Table 12-1  Transaction Types Used in Various Fraud Schemes (Continued)

| Transaction | Accounts Involved | Fraud Schemes |
|---|---|---|
| 2. Estimate uncollectible receivables | Bad debt expense and Allowance for doubtful accounts | 4. Understate allowance for doubtful accounts, thus overstating receivables |
| 3. Accept returned goods from customers | Sales returns and Accounts receivable | 5. Not record returned goods from customers<br>6. Record returned goods after the end of the period |
| 4. Write off uncollectible receivables in a later period | Allowance for doubtful accounts and Accounts receivable | 7. Don't write off uncollectible receivables<br>8. Write off receivables as uncollectible in a later period |
| 5. Collect cash after discount period | Cash and Accounts receivable | 9. Record bank transfers as cash received from customers<br>10. Manipulate cash received from related parties<br>11. Record fictitious cash entries such as debiting cash and crediting receivables |
| 6. Collect cash within discount period | Cash, Sales discounts, and Accounts receivable | 12. Not record discounts given to customers |

As you probably noticed, all 12 of these fraud schemes result in overstated revenues and thus overstated net income. Of course, it would also be possible to understate revenues and net income by committing fraud in the opposite direction. Such frauds are extremely rare and usually occur only when a company wants to manage or smooth income or understate net income in order to pay lower income taxes.

Once the various types of fraud schemes (exposures) have been identified, scheme-specific symptoms can be identified, proactive auditing or investigation can take place, and symptoms observed can be followed up to determine whether fraud actually exists.

## Identifying Revenue-Related Fraud Symptoms

Unlike murder or bank robbery, fraud is rarely observed. Instead, only symptoms, indicators, or red flags are observed. To detect fraud, you must be able to identify something as being a symptom or red flag. As you learned earlier in this book, fraud symptoms (for all types of fraud) can be divided into six categories:

1. **Analytical Symptoms**. These events, transactions, or characteristics are unusual—too big, too small, wrong time, wrong person, etc. They are the unexpected or unexplained, or things out of the ordinary or that you would not expect.

2. **Accounting or Documentary Systems**. These discrepancies in the records involve missing documents, photocopies where originals should exist, ledgers that don't balance, or similar aspects.

3. **Lifestyle Symptoms.** When people steal, they spend their ill-gotten gains. You rarely find perpetrators who save what they steal. Once the critical need is met that motivated the fraud, perpetrators start to improve their lifestyle. Although management fraud in smaller companies and other types of misappropriation are often motivated by lifestyle symptoms, these types of symptoms are usually not a factor in financial statement fraud in large organizations.

4. **Control Symptoms**. These breakdowns in the control environment, accounting system, or internal control activities or procedures are often so egregious that they hint that a management override is taking place. Examples are an override or lack of segregation of duties when segregation should exist, a weak or missing audit committee, etc.

5. **Behavioral and Verbal Symptoms**. Most fraud perpetrators are first-time offenders. When they commit fraud, they feel guilty; this guilt creates stress. Fraud perpetrators change their behavior to cope with this stress or to hide fraud symptoms. These changes in behavior, together with verbal responses, are often excellent fraud symptoms.

6. **Tips and Complaints**. The last category of fraud symptoms is tips or complaints from employees, spouses, vendors, customers, and others. Although no tip should be ignored, the providing of a tip that fraud is occurring does not automatically mean that fraud is taking place. Fraud tips and complaints may be motivated by nonfactors, such as revenge, attention seeking, or other reasons.

It is important to know that in detecting fraud, symptoms or red flags are only symptoms or red flags in context. For example, management and the external auditor could see the same thing and, because of their background, it could legitimately be a symptom to one party but not the other. Take, for example, the case where management knows from other transactions that they cannot trust the CFO because he has lied to them about various issues. The auditor may have no knowledge about management's distrust of the CFO. Thus, if both the auditor and other members of management see revenue that should be recognized in a later year recognized in an earlier year, for example, it could very well represent a red flag for management but not for the auditor. The auditor, whose standards tell him or her to neither assume guilt or innocence of the CFO, could interpret the problem as an unintentional error while management, who already questions the integrity of the CFO, would more likely consider the problem as a fraud.

With revenue-related financial statement frauds, some of the most common symptoms in each of these six categories are as follows:

### Analytical Symptoms

1. Reported revenue or sales account balances that appear too high.
2. Reported sales discounts account balances that appear too low.
3. Reported sales returns account balances that appear too low.
4. Reported **bad debt expense** account balances that appear too low.
5. Reported accounts receivable account balances that appear too high or are increasing too fast.
6. Reported **allowance for doubtful accounts** account balances that appear too low.
7. Too little cash collected from the revenues that are being reported.
8. Unusual entries made at the end of the accounting period that increase revenues.
9. Rapid changes in the mix or types of revenues.
10. Changes in relationships between costs and revenues.
11. Changes in relationships between cash and receivables.
12. Changes in relationships between any two revenue-related accounts.
13. Major new, unknown customers.

### Accounting or Documentary Symptoms

1. Revenue-related transactions not recorded in a complete or timely manner or improperly recorded as to amount, accounting period, classification, or entity policy.
2. Unsupported or unauthorized revenue-related balances or transactions.
3. Last-minute revenue adjustments by the entity that significantly improve financial results.
4. Missing documents in the revenue cycle.
5. Unavailability of other than photocopied documents to support revenue transactions, when documents in original form are supposed to exist.
6. Significant unexplained items on bank and other reconciliations.
7. Revenue-related ledgers (sales, cash receipts, etc.) that do not balance.
8. Unusual discrepancies between the entity's revenue-related records and corroborating evidence (such as accounts receivable confirmation replies).

### Control Symptoms

1. Management override of significant internal control activities related to the revenue cycle.
2. New, unusual, or large customers that appear not to have gone through the customer-approval process.

### Behavioral or Verbal Symptoms

1. Inconsistent, vague, or implausible responses from management or employees arising from revenue inquiries or analytical procedures.
2. Denied access to facilities, employees, records, customers, vendors, or others from whom revenue-related audit evidence might be sought.
3. Undue time pressures imposed by management to resolve contentious or complex revenue-related issues.
4. Unusual delays by the entity in providing revenue-related, requested information.
5. Untrue responses by management to queries made by auditors.
6. Suspicious behavior by or responses from members of management when asked about revenue-related transactions or accounts.

### Lifestyle Symptoms

1. Major sales of company stock during blackout periods.
2. Significant bonuses tied to meeting earnings forecasts.
3. Executives' personal net worth tied up in company stock.

### Tips and Complaints

1. Tips or complaints that revenue-related fraud (any of the schemes discussed) might be occurring, either from the company whistle-blower system or in other ways.
2. Revenue frauds disclosed at companies with which this company does significant amounts of business (e.g., Qwest and Global Crossing-type relationships).

Obviously, the preceding list is not exhaustive, but it is indicative of the kinds of revenue related symptoms that can be observed.

## Actively Looking for Revenue-Related Fraud Symptoms

For financial statement fraud to be detected, fraud symptoms must be observed and recognized. In some of the most famous financial statement fraud cases, symptoms should have been readily observable, but were not recognized by auditors and others. In fact, in some cases symptoms are observed and even inquired about, but alternative explanations from management are accepted. For example, in the HealthSouth financial statement fraud case that was discovered in 2003, a congressional committee now says regulators and auditors were warned (received red flags) of accounting problems at HealthSouth as early as 1998. A *New York Post* article by Jenny Anderson stated the following:

> *"We now have evidence that five years ago warnings were given to HealthSouth's corporate watchdogs their outside auditor, and perhaps even the SEC about the accounting shenanigans at the company. Yet no one appears to have listened," said a statement from Committee on Energy and Commerce Chairman Billy Tauzin (R.-La.) and Oversight and Investigations Subcommittee Chairman James Greenwood (R.-Pa.). They are investigating the matter.*
>
> *Chairman Tauzin was referring to a memo dated Nov. 11, 1998, from a "Fleeced Shareholder" that asked various detailed questions such as, "How can the HealthSouth outpatient clinics treat patients without pre-certification, book the revenue, and carry it after being denied payment?" Apparently, when the memo was received in 1998, the audit partner called the CFO and general counsel to inquire about the issues but nothing further happened. As a follow-up to the fraud, on March 19, 2003, the SEC filed a civil lawsuit claiming HealthSouth chairman Richard Scrushy had committed massive accounting fraud and overstated earnings by $1.4 billion. Since then the Justice Department has reached plea agreements with five ex-CFOs and six other employees.*[4]

Auditors and examiners can find fraud symptoms in two ways: either they wait until they "likely discover symptoms by chance," or they "proactively search for symptoms." For years, auditors and accountants relied primarily on chance (a tip, anomalies from a sample taken, stumbling on fraud evidence, etc.)

to discover symptoms. Because of developments in technology and lessons learned from fraud research, we now have tools and knowledge available to proactively search for fraud symptoms. The specific way you actively search for symptoms depends upon the kinds of symptoms you are looking for.

## Actively Searching for Revenue-Related Analytical Symptoms

In a previous chapter, we discussed using technology to proactively search for financial statement fraud. Analytical symptoms relating to revenue accounts involve those accounts being too high or too low, increasing too fast or not fast enough, or other abnormal relationships. But, when proactively searching for analytical symptoms, the question is "too high, too low, or unusual relative to what?" To determine whether analytical symptoms exist, a point of reference, an expectation, or some reasonable balance or relationship to which recorded amounts can be compared is necessary. The most practical ways to look for analytical symptoms are to focus on changes and comparisons within and from the financial statements. The specific analysis that are conducted usually include the following:

1. Analyzing financial balances and relationships within financial statements
2. Comparing financial statement amounts or relationships with other things

The two common ways to perform within-statement analysis are the following:

1. Looking for unusual changes in revenue-related account *balances* from period to period (looking at trends)
2. Looking for unusual changes in revenue-related *relationships* from period to period

Two types of analysis also can be performed where financial statement amounts and relationships are compared to other information:

1. Comparing financial results and trends of the company with those of similar firms in the same industry or with industry averages
2. Comparing recorded amounts in the financial statements with assets or the real-world referents they are supposed to represent.

The chart in Table 12-2 summarizes these approaches.

## Table 12-2  Types of Financial Statement Analysis

| Analyzing Financial Balances and Relationships *within* Financial Statements | Look for unusual changes in revenues and accounts receivable *balances* from period to period (trends). | Look for unusual changes in revenue-cycle-account *relationships* from period to period. |
| --- | --- | --- |
| Comparing Financial Statement Amounts or Relationships *with* Nonfinancial Statement Information | Compare financial results and trends of the company with those of *similar firms* in the same industry. | Compare recorded amounts in the financial statements with nonfinancial statement amounts. |

**Focusing on Changes in Recorded Account Balances (Amounts) from Period to Period.** Recorded amounts from one period can be compared to recorded amounts in another period in three ways. The first and least effective method is to focus on and calculate changes in the actual financial statement *numbers* themselves. It is often difficult, however, to assess the magnitude or significance of changes in account balances looking only at raw data, especially when the numbers are large.

The second method, and one where it is much easier to recognize analytical symptoms, is to use a process described earlier in Chapter 5, called horizontal analysis. Horizontal analysis is a method whereby you examine percentage changes in account balances from period to period. The calculation of percentage change is made by dividing the difference between period 2 and period 1's account balance by period 1's account balances. Thus, for example, if an organization had an accounts receivable balance of $100,000 in period 1 and $130,000 in period 2, horizontal analysis would reveal a percentage change of 30 percent, calculated as follows:

$$\frac{\$130{,}000 - \$100{,}000}{\$100{,}000} = 30\%$$

The third way to examine changes from period to period is to study the statement of cash flows. Perhaps you are wondering why we perform horizontal analysis only on the income statement and balance sheet, but not on the statement of cash flows. The reason is because horizontal analysis converts income statements and balance sheets to "change" statements, and the statement of cash flows is already a "change statement." Every number on the statement of cash flows represents the change in account balances from one period to the next. On the statement of cash flows, the changes in accounts receivable, inventory, accounts payable, and other accounts appear on the statement itself. Studying the statement of cash flows is like looking at the differences in raw numbers on the balance sheet and income statement from one period to the next, except that the calculations have already been made for you. When searching for fraud, examining the statement of cash flows is as effective as comparing actual changes in account balances. It is probably easier than recalculating the differences between two successive financial statements for selected accounts, but it is usually much less effective than using horizontal analysis.

**Focusing on Changes in Revenue-Related Relationships.** Examining changes in financial statement relationships from period to period is one of the best ways to discover analytical fraud symptoms. Changes in relationships from period to period can be examined in two primary ways. The first is to focus on changes in various revenue-related ratios from period to period. (Ratios, as you will recall, are summary calculations of significant relationships in the financial statements.) Examining revenue-related ratios provides an efficient method of focusing on relationship symptoms within the financial statements. The most common ratios used to discover revenue-related analytical fraud symptoms are the following:

> **Gross Profit (Margin) Ratio**: This ratio is calculated by dividing gross profit (margin) by net sales. Gross profit (margin), which is calculated by subtracting cost of goods sold from net sales, is a measure of markup percentage. The **gross profit (margin) ratio** provides a measure of the markup as a percentage of sales. If someone is perpetrating revenue-related fraud by overstating sales (revenues), understating sales discounts or sales returns, overstating sales by recording fictitious sales, or recognizing next period's sales this period, this ratio will increase. (The ratio will also increase if management understates the cost of goods sold by overstating inventory, understating purchases, or by using other means.) When a company's gross profit percentage increases dramatically, something inappropriate may be going on, and that something could be fraud.

> **Sales Return Percentage:** This ratio provides a measure of the percentage of sales that are being returned by customers. It is calculated by dividing **sales returns** by total sales. When the **sales return percentage ratio** gets too high, it is a signal that too many goods are being returned. When the ratio becomes too low, it is a signal that fraud or other problems could be occurring. One of the main methods perpetrators used to commit the Miniscribe fraud was to understate sales returns. In fact, the fraud became so egregious that at one time bricks were being boxed and shipped as software, with revenues being recognized at the time of shipment. When the bricks were returned by customers, they were stored in a separate location and not recorded as sales returns, allowing revenues and income to be overstated.

> **Sales Discount Percentage:** This ratio is similar to the sales return percentage and is calculated by dividing sales discounts by gross sales. It provides a measure of the percentage of sales discounts taken by customers. A ratio that suddenly decreases may mean that customers are taking longer to pay (and not taking the discounts), or, in the case of fraud, it may mean that the discounts are not being recorded in the accounting records.

> **Accounts Receivable Turnover: Accounts receivable turnover** is one of the most widely used ratios to analyze revenues and is calculated by dividing sales by accounts receivable. Historically, this ratio has been used to examine the efficiency with which receivables are being collected. This ratio is also an excellent analytical tool for identifying fraud symptoms. One of the easiest ways to perpetrate revenue-related frauds is to record fictitious receivables and revenues. Unless the ratio is equal to 1, adding the same amount to the numerator

(net sales) and denominator (accounts receivable) will change the ratio. If the ratio generally exceeds 1, recording fictitious sales will decrease the ratio. If the ratio is generally less than 1, recording fictitious sales will increase the ratio. Only in rare cases will the recording of significant amounts of fictitious revenues and receivables not affect this ratio. Sudden changes in this ratio usually signal that fraud may be occurring.

**Number of Days in Receivables:** This ratio provides the same information as the accounts receivable turnover ratio. It is calculated by dividing 365 by the accounts receivable turnover. The advantage of the **number of days in receivables ratio** is that it identifies how fast or how slowly receivables are being collected in number of days, which is easy to understand. Adding fictitious receivables will generally increase the number of days it takes to collect receivables, because none of the fictitious receivables will be collected.

**Allowance for Uncollectible Accounts as a Percentage of Receivables:** This ratio, which is calculated by dividing the allowance for uncollectible accounts by total accounts receivable, provides a measure of the percentage of receivables that are expected to be uncollectible. A common way to overstate receivables (and hence net income) is to not record bad accounts receivable as uncollectible. In one famous fraud, for example, this percentage decreased from 4 percent to less than one-half percent before the fraud was discovered.

**Asset Turnover Ratio:** This ratio, calculated by dividing total sales by average total assets, provides a measure of how many times an organization "turned over" its assets or the amount of sales revenue generated with each dollar of assets owned by the company. When a company records fictitious revenues, this ratio increases. And, as is the case with all other ratios, unusually large increases in this ratio might indicate that some kind of revenue-related fraud is occurring. You should recognize, however, that this ratio is usually not as sensitive to receivable and revenue frauds as are the ratios already discussed.

**Working Capital Turnover Ratio:** The working capital turnover ratio is calculated by dividing sales by average working capital (current asset – current liabilities) for a period. This ratio indicates the amount of working capital used in generating sales for the period. Significant increases in this ratio could be a symptom that some kind of revenue-related fraud is occurring. As with asset turnover, this ratio is not as sensitive as the previous ratios in highlighting revenue-related frauds.

**Operating Performance Margin Ratio:** This ratio is calculated by dividing net income by total sales. It provides a measure of the profit margin of a company. Often, when revenue-related frauds occur, fictitious revenues are added without adding any additional expenses. These types of fictitious entries have the effect of increasing revenues and net income by the same or similar amounts (except for the tax effect). The result of adding fictitious revenues without additional expenses is a dramatic increase in this ratio.

**Earnings per Share:** This is commonly used ratio measures the profitability of an organization. It is calculated by dividing net income by the number of shares of stock outstanding. A dramatic increase in this ratio could be a signal that some kind of fraud is occurring, but is not necessarily indicative of revenue-related fraud. Again, it is one of the least sensitive ratios in helping to detect revenue-related financial statement fraud.

When using ratios to discover financial statement fraud symptoms, remember that the size or direction of the ratio is usually not important; rather, the changes (and speed of changes) in the ratios are what signal possible fraud.

The second way to focus on financial statement relationships as fraud symptoms is to convert the financial statements to **common-size financial statements** (percentages) and perform vertical analysis, a method that was also discussed in Chapter 5. Just as horizontal analysis is the most effective way to search for analytical fraud symptoms relating to changes in account balances, vertical analysis is generally the most effective way to identify changes in financial statement relationships that must be investigated. With ratios, you generally focus on only one or two financial statement relationships at a time. If that relationship turns out to be the best indicator of fraud, you may identify a fraud symptom. On the other hand, with vertical analysis, you can simultaneously view the relationships between all numbers on the balance sheet or income statement.

The difficulty in using ratios, horizontal analysis, vertical analysis, or any other tool to recognize analytical fraud symptoms is knowing when a change in an account balance or relationship is significant enough to signal possible fraud. Experience with and knowledge about a company, its history, these analytical tools, and other firms in the same industry are obviously helpful. Generally, the more dramatic the change, the higher the likelihood that something unusual (possibly fraud) is occurring. You should never conclude on the basis of analytical evidence alone, however, that the management of a company is perpetrating fraud. At best, analytical tools merely identify potential problem areas or "circumstantial evidence" that needs further analysis and investigation.

**Comparing Financial Statement Information with That of Other Companies.** One of the best ways to detect financial statement fraud is to compare the performance of the company you are examining with the performance of other, similar companies in the industry. Performance that runs counter to the performance of other firms in the same industry often signals fraud or other problems. For example, in the Equity Funding fraud, the financial statements showed a highly profitable and growing insurance company at a time when the rest of the insurance industry was struggling and significantly less profitable. Economic and industry-wide factors usually affect similar firms in similar ways. Comparisons with other firms can be made using horizontal or vertical analysis, ratio analysis, changes reported in the statement of cash flows, or changes in the financial statement numbers themselves. Common-sizing the financial statements are usually helpful when making interfirm comparisons. Common-size comparisons between companies in the same industry can quickly draw attention to, and thus encourage the investigation of, variations in financial performance. Working with percentages is usually much easier than comparing raw financial statement data.

**Comparing Financial Statement Amounts with the Assets They Are Supposed to Represent.** Comparing recorded amounts in the financial statements with real-world assets, while an excellent way to detect fraud, is not as useful for detecting revenue-related frauds as it is for detecting cash, inventory, and physical asset frauds. Generally, real-world, nonmonetary assets cannot be examined with revenues. The notable exception, of course, is a company that earns revenue constructing assets such as buildings, bridges, and highways and recognizes revenue on the percentage-of-completion method. In those cases, the constructed assets should be examined to determine whether the revenue recognized is reasonable, given the degree of completion of the projects.

## Actively Searching for Control Symptoms

The importance of identifying control weaknesses as possible fraud symptoms has already been discussed in this book. However, two control-related points need mentioning with respect to revenue-related frauds. First, accountants and financial statement auditors are accustomed to accepting a limited number of control exceptions when assessing the adequacy of a system of internal controls. This approach is used because they view control breakdowns or weaknesses as something that needs to be fixed "in the future." As a fraud examiner, what you must remember is that most frauds are motivated by something called the fraud triangle as discussed previously and shown in Figure 12-2.

When an organization is experiencing pressures and management rationalizes that the pressures are only short-term and will correct themselves in the future, all that is needed to commit financial statement fraud is some kind of perceived opportunity. Usually, these perceived opportunities exhibit themselves in the form of a control weakness, a control breakdown, or the overriding of key controls. For that reason, fraud examiners and investigators usually consider a control breakdown not only as something that must be fixed "in the future," but something that must be examined to see whether it has been "abused in the past." In fact, one of the most common ways frauds are detected is by investigating control weaknesses or overrides to see if abuses occurred.

The second control factor that deserves special attention is that, with financial statement fraud, the control environment, rather than specific control activities or procedures is often weak. In many cases of financial statement fraud, the audit committee or board of director is weak or inactive, the internal audit department is weak or inactive, and usually only one or two executives have controlling power in the

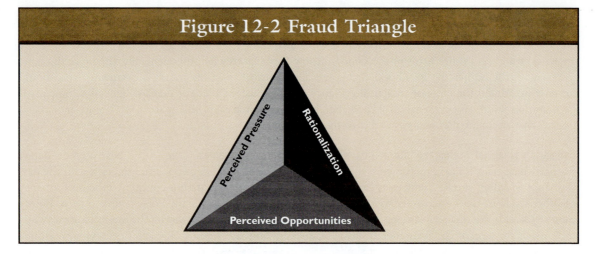

## Figure 12-2 Fraud Triangle

organization. Although this problem should have been fixed by the Sarbanes-Oxley Act, new SEC rules, and new stock exchange governance requirements that were described in the appendix to the Chapter 11, instances where boards, audit committees, and executives don't behave as they should or even as they are designed on organizational charts still an issue. External auditors are now supposed to assess the quality of a firm's control environment. It would be helpful to obtain evidence from them about how effective the control environment is when trying to detect or investigate fraud.

## Actively Searching for Behavioral or Verbal and Lifestyle Symptoms

Lifestyle symptoms are much more helpful when trying to detect employee fraud than financial statement frauds because most financial statement frauds do not benefit the perpetrators directly. Rather, they make the organization look better than it really is. The perpetrators benefit only indirectly—through a higher stock price, not defaulting on a restrictive agreement, and so on. (They often benefit indirectly by, for example, being able to exercise stock options at a higher price because the financial results were overstated.) The same is not true of behavioral and verbal symptoms, however. In fact, one fraud detection tool that is often underused by fraud examiners and financial statement auditors is making verbal inquiries and personal observations. In fact, SAS 99 requires that external auditors make inquiries of management and others regarding fraud. Those who wrote SAS 99 believe that these inquiries should be required because most often it is through inquiries that fraudulent activity can be identified. Under SAS 99, financial statement auditors are now be required to make inquiries of the following individuals or groups about possible fraudulent activity or red flags: (1) management, (2) audit committee members, (3) internal audit personnel, and (4) other employees.

Management of an organization (or others) usually has difficulty committing fraud without feeling guilty and without others knowing about the fraud. In fact, to perpetrate financial statement fraud, it is usually necessary to involve other people such as accountants and subsidiary personnel. Fraud examiners and auditors should learn to ask key fraud-related questions, such as:

- Have you seen anything that indicates that something isn't right or that could be considered a red flag of fraud?
- Have you been asked to make any accounting entries that you consider to be unusual or about which you had questions regarding their propriety?
- "Is there anything suspicious I should be aware of in this company?"
- Have there been any attempts to manage earnings?
- Do any unusual operating or nonoperating income items concern you?
- "What is your explanation of why revenues (or returns, discounts, bad debts, allowances, etc.) increased or decreased so dramatically?"

- "Should I pay particular attention to any specific individuals in the organization, or units in the organization?"
- "What part of this organization, or which individuals, keep you awake worrying at night?"
- Are there any accountants or executives in the company whose integrity and/or motivation you question?
- Is any executive or top-level accountant in the organization ever referred to by a name that implies a cover-up or blaming others ("slick," "Teflon," "conniving," "managing numbers," etc.)?

With many frauds, individuals with questions about propriety of transactions or activities may be looking for a way out of the fraud, or looking for someone to talk to, but they do not because no one asks them. You would think these individuals would voice their concerns through a company whistle-blowing system. However, until they are asked specifically about something they don't want to lie about, they often don't come forward. Certainly, financial statement auditors must become much better in communicating with audit clients and their personnel, and not relying so much on the financial statements themselves. Liberal communication with a manager who is committing financial statement fraud will often reveal inconsistencies in responses that can help you understand that everything is not the way it is being presented. Lying consistently takes significant work and a good memory, and a good auditor or fraud examiner can often detect inconsistencies. Certainly, financial statement auditors and even fraud examiners cannot be expected to catch all lying. They are not trained to do so. However, the likelihood of catching lying is much greater when examiners communicate directly and liberally with their clients.

Finally, with respect to behavioral symptoms, remember that committing fraud, especially for first-time offenders, creates stress. The perpetrators must find a way to cope with that stress, and they usually do so by changing their behavior. Although financial statement auditors and fraud examiners may not be familiar enough with the management of a company to recognize changes in behavior, others within the organization are. In these situations, asking questions of lots of people will often reveal that something is not right.

## Actively Searching for Tips and Complaints Symptoms

The best way to search for tips and complaints of revenue-related fraud or any fraud is to institute an ombudsman, hotline, or other type of system whereby people can call with tips and complaints. (As described earlier in this book, having such a whistle-blower system and not retaliating against whistle-blowers is now a requirement in the United States for all public companies.) Certainly, instituting whistle-blowing systems to gather information about clients is difficult for financial statement auditors and fraud examiners. However, even if not a public company, they should strongly encourage their clients to implement such a system. In most organizations, some individuals have knowledge or suspicions that fraud is occurring but are afraid to come forward because of the following reasons:

- They don't know who to tell or how to come forward.
- They don't want to wrongly accuse someone.
- They are afraid of "whistle-blower" repercussions.
- They only have suspicions rather than actual knowledge.

Whistle-blowing systems are effective in obtaining information from these types of individuals. If a company already has a hotline, financial statement auditors and fraud examiners can review hotline records and transcripts to see what kind of information has been collected. Any tips or complaints about top management or other key personnel or about fraud related to the financial statements, controls, legal requirements, or fraud should be pursued vigorously. In addition, other complaints should also be reviewed from the perspective that whistle-blowers don't want to inform directly about a suspected fraud but rather about tangential activities of the suspect so he or she will be scrutinized carefully.

## Following Up on Revenue-Related Fraud Symptoms as an Investigator

As a fraud investigator, the presence of fraud symptoms provides predication or "reason to believe that fraud may be occurring." When predication exists, and if conditions warrant, an investigation should take place. In this case, various investigative procedures help to determine whether fraud is actually occurring and, if so, the extent of that fraud. The specific investigative procedures used, and the order in which they are used, depends on the kind of fraud suspected and the ease of collecting evidence. The investigation section of this book provided information about how to investigate all types of fraud, including revenue-related frauds.

# Inventory and Cost of Goods Sold Frauds

Another common type of financial statement fraud is the manipulation of inventory and **cost of goods sold** accounts. Several high-profile financial statement frauds have involved the overstatement of inventory. Phar-Mor, for example, significantly overstated the value of its inventory, and then moved inventory back and forth between stores, so that it could be counted multiple times.

A recent example of inventory fraud was Rite Aid Corporation. Although Rite Aid committed several different types of fraud, one of the most prevalent was overstating net income by managing the value of its inventory. Specifically, senior management allegedly failed to record millions in shrinkage of its physical inventory due to loss or theft. The CFO also made adjusting journal entries to lower the cost of goods sold.

Historically, inventory frauds have been such a significant problem that a few years ago the *Wall Street Journal* featured a front-page article titled "Inventory Chicanery Tempts More Firms, Fools More Auditors."[3] To understand why inventory and cost of goods sold frauds are so common, you should understand how inventory accounts affect the income statement. The calculations on a typical income statement are as follows in Table 12-3:

### Table 12-3　Effects of Inventory Overstatement on the Income Statement

| Income Statement | When Inventory Is Overstated, Then: |
| --- | --- |
| -Gross Revenues (Sales) | Are not Affected |
| -Sales Returns | Are not Affected |
| -Sales Discounts | Are not Affected |
| **Net Revenues (Sales)** | Are not Affected |
| -Cost of Goods Sold | Is Understated |
| **Gross Margin** | Is Overstated |
| -Expenses | Are not Affected |
| **Net Income** | Is Overstated |

From these calculations, you can see that if inventory is overstated, cost of goods sold is understated, and gross margin and net income are overstated by an equal amount (less the tax effect). To better understand the effect of cost of goods sold on inventory, consider how cost of goods sold is calculated as shown in Table 12-4.

## Table 12-4 Cost of Goods Sold Calculation

| | Period 1, Overstatement of Inventory | Period 2 |
|---|---|---|
| Beginning Inventory | Not Affected | Overstated |
| +Purchases of Inventory | Not Affected | Not Affected |
| -Returns of Inventory to Vendor | Not Affected | Not Affected |
| -Purchase Discounts on Inventory Purchases | Not Affected | Not Affected |
| = Goods Available for Sale | Not Affected | Overstated |
| -Ending Inventory | Overstated | Not Affected |
| =Cost of Goods Sold | Understated | Overstated |

This calculation shows that the overstatement of ending inventory in period one has an effect on cost of goods sold in both periods one and two. It also shows that cost of goods sold can be understated, either by understating purchases or overstating inventory. It can also be understated by overstating purchase returns or purchase discounts. Of these alternatives, overstating the end-of-period inventory tends to be the most common fraud because it not only increases net income, but it also increases recorded assets and makes the balance sheet look better. The chart in Table 12-4 also illustrates why overstating inventory is a fraud that is difficult to maintain without getting caught. In the first period, when ending inventory is overstated, cost of goods sold is understated, making gross margin and net income overstated. However, that overstated ending inventory becomes the beginning inventory in period 2, meaning that if further overstatements of ending inventory aren't made, then cost of goods sold in period 2 will be overstated and gross margin and net income will be understated. This offsetting effect from one period to the next makes it necessary for perpetrators who want to continue committing fraud (they all do—one-time perpetrators are rare) to overstate ending inventory in period 2 by an even larger amount in order to both offset the effect of having an overstated beginning inventory and wanting to commit additional fraud. Perpetrators who are smart should commit other types of financial statement fraud other than overstating inventory because of the compounding effect from period to period.

## Identifying Inventory and Cost of Goods Sold Exposures

To understand inventory-related financial statement frauds, we will follow the same process we used to discuss revenue-related frauds. That is, we first identify financial statement fraud exposures. Then we discuss inventory-related fraud symptoms. Third, we consider ways to actively search for fraud symptoms. Finally, we cover ways to follow up on symptoms observed to discover inventory/cost of goods sold financial statement frauds.

As with revenue-related frauds, one of the best ways to identify financial statement fraud exposures is to diagram the various kinds of inventory-related transactions that can occur in an organization. For many companies, that diagram might appear as it does in Figure 12-3.

As you can see from the flowchart in Figure 12-3, nine different transactions and accounts are involved in accounting for inventories and cost of goods sold. Table 12-5 shows the accounts involved in each of these transactions and the kinds of fraud that could occur to determine fraud exposures or the various ways in which inventory or cost of goods sold frauds can be perpetrated. For purposes of illustration, we will assume a perpetual inventory system. (The effect on cost of goods sold and the types of possible fraud schemes used are the same under either the perpetual or periodic inventory methods.)

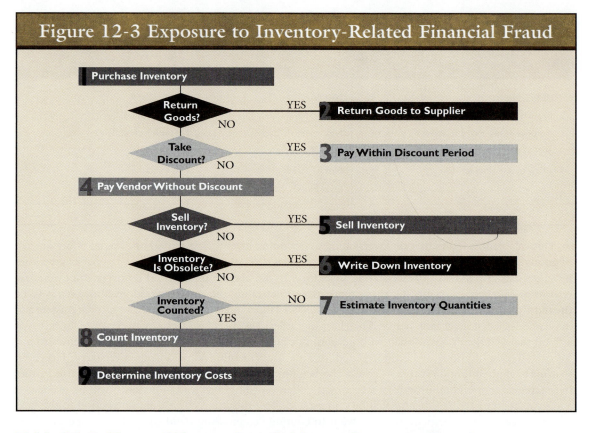

## Figure 12-3 Exposure to Inventory-Related Financial Fraud

## Table 12-5  Types of Transactions Subject to Inventory Fraud

| Transaction | Accounts Involved | Fraud Schemes |
|---|---|---|
| Purchase inventory | Inventory, Accounts payable | • Underrecord purchases<br>• Record purchases late (cut-off problem)<br>• Not record purchases |
| Return merchandise to supplier | Accounts payable, Inventory | • Overstate returns<br>• Record returns in an earlier period (cut-off problem) |
| Pay vendor within discount period | Accounts payable, Inventory, Cash | • Overstate discounts<br>• Not reduce inventory cost |
| Pay vendor, without discount | Account payable, Cash | (considered later in this chapter) |
| Inventory is sold; cost of goods sold is recognized | Cost of goods sold, Inventory | • Record too low an amount for cost of goods sold<br>• Not record cost of goods sold nor reduce inventory |
| Inventory becomes obsolete and is written down | Loss on write-down of inventory, Inventory | Not write off or write down obsolete inventory |
| Inventory quantities are estimated | Inventory shrinkage, Inventory | Overestimate inventory (use incorrect ratios, etc.) |
| Inventory quantities are counted | Inventory shrinkage, Inventory | • Overcount inventory (double counting, etc.)<br>• Capitalize as inventory costs that should be expensed |
| Inventory cost is determined | Inventory, Cost of goods sold | • Incorrect costs are used<br>• Incorrect extensions are made<br>• Record fictitious inventory |

As you can see, by focusing on the various transactions and inventory counts, we have identified 16 fraud schemes that can be used to overstate inventory and understate cost of goods sold. Obviously, some of these fraud schemes are much more common than others, but all can be used to manipulate inventory and cost of goods sold on the financial statements. And, as was the case with revenues, all of these fraud schemes have the effect of increasing net income. (Obviously, although much more rare, it would also be possible to commit inventory fraud by understating inventory and net income if, for example, a company wanted to decrease the amount of income taxes it paid to the government.)

As stated earlier, inventory overstatement frauds present a much more difficult challenge to perpetrators than do revenue frauds. With revenue-related frauds, reported revenues are overstated in the current period, and accounts receivable are overstated on the balance sheet. However, a compounding effect does not occur in the subsequent period. With inventory frauds, however, the "overstated ending inventory" of one period becomes the "overstated beginning inventory" of the next period and causes net income to be understated in the second period. Thus, if a dishonest management wanted to continue the fraud and overstate net income in a second period (and most frauds are multiple-period frauds), it would have to perpetrate a fraud of an equivalent magnitude just to offset the overstated beginning inventory, and then commit an additional fraud if it again wanted to overstate inventory to increase net income. The results are larger misstatements of inventory, and a fraud that is much easier to detect. Fortunately, most financial statement frauds are perpetrated because of desperation, and a dishonest management generally worries only about how income can be overstated in the current period, with no thought of the problems it creates for itself in subsequent periods.

## Identifying Symptoms of Inventory and Cost of Goods Sold Fraud

Once again, we will use the six categories of fraud symptoms to discuss inventory and cost of goods sold frauds. Some of the most common symptoms with these types of fraud are listed here. Rather than discuss them in detail as we did for revenue-related frauds, we will simply list them by category.

### Analytical Symptoms

- Reported inventory balances that appear too high or are increasing too fast.
- Reported cost of goods sold balances that appear too low or are decreasing too fast.
- Reported purchase returns that appear too high or are increasing too rapidly.
- Reported purchase discounts that appear too high or are increasing too rapidly.
- Reported purchases that appear too low for inventory levels.
- Capitalized inventory that looks as if it should be expensed.

### Accounting or Documentary Symptoms

- Inventory or cost of goods sold transactions that are not recorded in a complete or timely manner or improperly recorded as to amount, accounting period, classification, or entity.
- Unsupported or unauthorized inventory or cost of goods sold-related transactions.
- End-of-period inventory or cost of goods sold adjustments that significantly change the entity's financial results.
- Missing documents related to inventory or cost of goods sold.
- Unavailability of other than photocopied documents to support inventory or cost of goods sold transactions when original documents should exist.
- Cost of goods sold-related accounting records (purchases, sales, cash payments, etc.) that do not balance.
- Unusual discrepancies between the entity's inventory or cost of goods sold records and corroborating evidence (such as inventory counts).
- Differences between inventory counts and inventory records, especially systematic differences.
- Differences between receiving reports and inventory actually received.
- Differences between purchase orders, purchase invoices, receiving records, and inventory records.

- Purchases from suppliers not approved on vendor lists.
- Missing inventory when performing inventory counts.
- Duplicate purchase orders or invoice numbers.
- Vendors not listed in Dun & Bradstreet or telephone directories.

### Control Symptoms

- Management override of significant internal control activities related to purchases, inventory, or cost of goods sold.
- New or unusual vendors that appear not to have gone through the regular vendor-approval process.
- Weaknesses in the inventory counting process.

### Behavioral or Verbal Symptoms

- Inconsistent, vague, or implausible responses from management or employees arising from inventory, purchase, or cost of goods sold-related inquiries or analytical procedures.
- Denied access to facilities, employees, records, customers, vendors, or others from whom inventory or cost of goods sold-related evidence might be sought.
- Undue time pressures imposed by management to resolve contentious or complex inventory or cost of goods sold-related issues.
- Unusual delays by the entity in providing requested inventory or cost of goods sold related information.
- Untrue, inconsistent, or questionable responses by management to inventory, cost of goods sold, or other queries made by auditors.
- Suspicious behavior or responses from members of management when asked about inventory or cost of goods sold-related transactions, vendors, obsolescence, or accounts.

### Lifestyle Symptoms

- As with revenue-related frauds, lifestyle symptoms are often not relevant to financial statement frauds involving large organizations. In smaller companies, however, where officers can benefit personally from higher stock prices or from obtaining bank loans, they can be relevant symptoms.

### Tips and Complaints

- Tips or complaints that come in through the whistle-blowing system or through other means may suggest that inventory, purchase, or cost of goods sold fraud (any of the schemes discussed earlier) might be occurring.

Obviously these lists are not exhaustive. Rather, they represent some of the more common inventory and cost of goods sold-related fraud symptoms that can be observed.

## Actively Searching for Inventory-Related Control Symptoms

Because inventory frauds, like revenue-related frauds, are so easy to perpetrate, a good control environment and control procedures should be in place. Recall that the COSO study of financial statement fraud found that most companies committing financial statement fraud were relatively small, had "inactive" audit committees, had boards of directors that were dominated by insiders and "grey" directors with significant equity ownership and little experience serving as directors of other companies, and had family relationships among directors or officers. The relatively small size of fraudulent companies suggests that the inability or even unwillingness to implement cost-effective controls is probably a factor affecting the likelihood of financial statement fraud. (It is in these types of environment that the override of controls is easier.)

As a result, controls over inventory must be examined closely. Remember that the lack of a key control provides a fraud opportunity that completes the fraud triangle. With respect to inventory, purchases, and cost of goods sold, we are primarily concerned with the controls over the purchasing process (purchase requisitions, purchase orders, etc.), receiving (receiving reports, physical control, etc.), recording of liabilities (vendor's invoice, debit memos, etc.), cash disbursements (checks, etc.), storage, processing, and shipping of inventory, transferring the cost of inventory sold, accurately tracking inventory costs (especially in manufacturing firms), and physically observing inventory. In each case, we want to make sure that recorded inventory represents goods actually received or manufactured, existing acquisition transactions are actually recorded, transaction amounts are accurate, transactions are properly classified, transactions are recorded in the proper periods, and transactions are included in the proper financial statement accounts. Where inventory controls are weak or easily overridden, a missing control or an observance of an override represents a fraud symptom, not just a control weakness. As such, it should be pursued with the same vigilance as any other fraud symptom.

## Actively Searching for Behavioral or Verbal and Lifestyle Symptoms

As with other financial statement frauds, lifestyle symptoms are usually not effective in helping you find inventory-related financial statement fraud because financial statement fraud usually does not benefit the perpetrators directly. However, searching for behavioral and verbal symptoms can be fruitful. Often, recorded inventory amounts are subject to management's intent. For example, if management plans to, and believes it can, sell existing inventory, it will not write inventory amounts off as obsolete. Usually, the best evidence relating to management's intent is management inquiry. Where possible, these inquiries should be corroborated, but such corroborations sometimes are not possible. With inventory, it is important that financial statement auditors and fraud examiners ask many questions relative to the nature, age, salability, and other characteristics of inventory as well as inventory levels (increases or decreases), significant changes in vendors, and so on. The best way to determine whether management is lying is to identify inconsistencies between what you observe (e.g., analytical and documentary symptoms) and what management is telling you.

## Actively Searching for Tips and Complaints Symptoms

Tip and complaint symptoms are fruitful areas for detecting inventory-related frauds. In most cases, because of its physical characteristics, inventory must be brought into a firm, handled within the firm, and shipped when sold. All this movement means that people must be involved in managing and handling the physical flow of inventory. Usually, these individuals do not understand the nature of audits or forensic examinations, nor the kinds of fraud that could be occurring. As an example of the value of asking questions and getting tips, consider the case of a staff auditor for what was formerly a Big 6 CPA firm that was auditing the inventory of a sprinkler pipe manufacturer. As he observed the inventory, some of it looked old and not salable. However, when he asked the CFO and CEO about the inventory, they stated that it was fine and would be sold in the normal course of business. Being curious, however, he brought a sack lunch the next day and ate in the inventory warehouse with the warehouse workers. After discussing with them his background, telling them he was a small town country boy and talking about sports, he asked them to tell him how the various types of pipe were used. They were forthright in telling him that most of the pipe on hand would never be sold because it was "useless." His firm ended up insisting that the client write down the pipe inventory by several million dollars. Talking to those who actually handle the inventory will often reveal information that is helpful, especially when you ask the right questions.

In addition to individuals who handle the inventory, it is often helpful to communicate directly with vendors to determine their relationships with the company. Although you shouldn't intrude in the company's business and ruin its relationships with vendors, you can often learn valuable information about inventory costs, amounts of purchases, and other factors by speaking with those from whom inventory is purchased. Similarly, talking with large customers and assessing inventory quality and product returns will often provide evidence about whether bricks are being shipped as software or whether inventory is overvalued.

The important point to remember is that even though most companies today have a whistle-blower system, you must still actively look for tips. As we stated earlier, individuals often suspect that something wrong is going on, but are afraid to come forward or are just not asked. And, as was the case with revenue-related fraud, if the company has a whistle-blower system, you should review its records to see whether any calls have come in about inventory-related suspicions.

## Proactively Looking for Inventory and Cost of Goods Sold-Related Fraud Symptoms

As with revenue-related frauds, for inventory and cost of goods sold financial statement frauds to be detected, fraud symptoms must be observed and recognized. Take the MiniScribe Corporation financial statement fraud, for example. MiniScribe's management, with the assistance of other officers and employees, engaged in a series of fraudulent activities that overstated inventory and materially inflated the reported net income. Because management used the inventory account to overstate inventory (and inventory errors offset in subsequent periods, resulting in the need to misstate larger and larger amounts), the fraud grew rapidly. In the first year, the inventory overstatement was $4.5 million. In the second year, the overstatement was $22 million. And, in the third year (two quarters only), the overstatement was $31.8 million. To understand the kinds of symptoms that were available, understanding how management perpetrated the fraud is necessary. In the first year, senior managers from MiniScribe broke into the auditors' files to find inventory lists that designated which items in inventory had been test-counted. With this information, the officers then inflated the values of the inventory items that had not been counted by the auditors. In the second year, with the need to misstate inventory by a much larger amount, management used three different approaches:

1. Created fictitious "inventory in transit" amounts.
2. Recorded a transfer of $9 million in nonexistent inventory from MiniScribe's U.S. books to the books of MiniScribe's Far East subsidiaries.
3. Received raw materials into inventory just prior to the end of the fiscal year without recording the corresponding accounts payable liability.

In the third year, management resorted to even more egregious ways to overstate inventory. As an example of its desperate attempts to misstate inventory, it shipped boxes of bricks labeled as disk drives to two MiniScribe distributors and recorded the shipments as consigned inventory. Management even created a computer program called "Cook Book" to generate fictitious inventory numbers. It also accumulated scrap that had been written off the company's books, repackaged it, and added it to the accounting records as inventory. Employees of the company even prepared false inventory tickets to increase recorded inventory.

In the first year, the fraud would probably have been difficult to detect. When members of management break into auditors' files, steal information, and forge computer records that are not test-counted by auditors, the fraud has little chance of being caught. Maybe management's behavior or responses to auditors' inquiries will change and possibly someone will provide a tip, but not many accounting, documentary, or control symptoms can alert an auditor that fraud is occurring in such a situation. Also, because the fraud in that first year was only $4.5 million, the analytical symptoms were not too significant.

In the second year, as the fraud grew to $22 million and took on different forms, more and more symptoms must have become apparent. For example, the huge increase in the inventory balance had to have been an analytical symptom. Why did inventory increase so fast and why did the relationships between inventory, sales, and cost of goods sold stay the same? What about the large in-transit inventory amounts, especially at year-end? Together with the $9 million transfer of inventory from the U.S. parent's books to an Asian subsidiary's books, these two transactions should have raised concerns. Certainly, inventory that is listed as an asset without recording the corresponding purchases creates an accounting symptom. With these kinds of suspicious year-end transactions, inquiries of management should increase, providing auditors and fraud examiners with an opportunity to observe the consistency of management's behavior and verbal responses. In the second year, some overriding of key controls and maybe even a tip or two had to appear as more and more people became knowledgeable about the fraud.

In the third year, when boxes of bricks were being shipped, consigned inventory increased, and a new fraudulent computer program was written, more and more symptoms had to surface. Returns of merchandise (bricks) and customer complaints had to be increasing, more and more employees had to be involved (thus, a higher probability of a tip or complaint), and false inventory tickets and the reclassification of obsolete inventory as good inventory had to be present.

## Searching for Inventory and Cost of Goods Sold Analytical Symptoms

As with all other types of fraud, inventory and cost of goods sold fraud symptoms can be found in one of two ways:

1. Wait until you "happen on to them by chance."
2. Proactively search for them.

The specific way you search for symptoms depends upon the kinds of symptoms you are looking for. Remember that analytical symptoms relate to accounts or relationships being too high or too low or exhibiting unusual characteristics. Also remember that to determine whether accounts are too high or too low or unusual, you must have a point of reference—an expectation or some basis against which recorded amounts can be compared. As was the case with revenue-related fraud symptoms, the most practical way to look for analytical symptoms is to focus on changes and comparisons within and from the financial statements. Table 12-6 summarizes the methods we previously discussed, but focuses only on inventory.

### Table 12-6 Analyzing Financial Statements for Inventory Fraud

| Analyzing Financial Balances and Relationships *Within* Financial Statements | Look for unusual changes in inventory and cost of goods sold account *balances* from period to period. | Look for unusual changes in inventory and cost of goods sold *relationships* from period to period. |
|---|---|---|
| *Comparing* Financial Statement Amounts or Relationships with Nonfinancial Statement Information | Compare financial results and trends of the company with those of *similar firms* in the same industry. | Compare recorded amounts in the financial statements with nonfinancial statement amounts. |

**Focusing on Changes in Recorded Balances from Period to Period.** Recall from our discussion of revenue-related frauds the three ways to focus on changes in recorded balances from period to period. The first and usually least effective method is to focus on the changes in the actual financial statement *numbers*. Because financial statement inventory and cost of goods sold numbers are often large, it is often difficult, examining the numbers alone, to assess the magnitude of changes or to distinguish significant from insignificant changes. A second, similar method is to study the statement of cash flows. This statement identifies changes in account balances from one period to the next. The advantage of focusing on the statement of cash flows is that the "change" numbers have already been calculated.

Probably the best way to examine changes in account balances from period to period is to use horizontal analysis. As you will recall, horizontal analysis allows you to examine percentage changes in account balances from period to period. Even though performing horizontal analysis on all balance sheet and income statement accounts is usually best because you usually don't know what kind of fraud you are looking for, inventory and cost of goods sold frauds will usually reveal themselves with unusual changes in the inventory account on the balance sheet and the cost of goods sold numbers on the income statements. Generally, fraud is suggested when inventory increases are too high to be realistic, a monotonic increase occurs in inventory balances from period to period, or cost of goods sold increases do not mirror the increases in either sales or in inventory. However, any change that appears to be unusual or unrealistic can be an analytical financial statement fraud symptom. When looking for all these symptoms, remember that it isn't the change itself that signals that something may not be right but the pace of the change. The faster and more dramatic the pace of change in these accounts, the more likely it is that fraud could be occurring.

**Focusing on Changes in Relationships from Period to Period.** As with revenue-related financial statement frauds, two primary methods can be used to focus on changes in relationships from period to period. The first is to examine ratio changes from one period to the next. The second is to convert the financial statements to common-size statements and use vertical analysis to examine the percentage changes from period to period. The most helpful ratios used to examine inventory and cost of goods sold relationships are as follows:

> **Gross Profit (Margin) Ratio:** This ratio is calculated by dividing gross profit (margin) by sales. The reason it is helpful in identifying inventory frauds is when a company overstates its inventory balance, cost of goods sold is usually understated. The result is an increase in the gross profit (margin) ratio. Thus, a significant increase in the gross profit ratio can signal either a revenue- or inventory-related fraud.

> **Inventory Turnover:** This ratio, which is computed by dividing cost of goods sold by the average inventory, is useful in determining whether inventory is overstated or cost of goods sold is understated. Generally, overstating inventory has the effect of decreasing this ratio because the denominator is increased. Similarly, understating cost of goods sold will also decrease this ratio.

> **Number of Days' Sales in Inventory**: This ratio, which measures the average time it takes to sell inventory, is computed by dividing the number of days in a period by the inventory turnover ratio. Thus, if cost of goods sold is $500, average inventory is $200, with 365 days in a year, the inventory turnover ratio is 2.5 ($500/$200), and the number of days' sales in inventory is 146 (365/2.5). It means that the company "turns" or sells its inventory, on average, every 146 days. When a company overstates inventory, the inventory turnover ratio tends to decrease, and the number of days' sales in inventory increases. For example, if the company overstated inventory by $100 or reported $300 in inventory, the inventory turnover ratio would be 1.67 ($500/$300), and the number of day's sales in inventory would be approximately 219 days (365/1.67).

Four other ratios can also be helpful in detecting inventory and cost of goods sold-related frauds. Even though they are usually not as sensitive as the three ratios already discussed, asset turnover, working capital turnover, operating performance ratio, and earnings per share can sometimes be helpful in identifying inventory-related financial statement frauds. The **asset turnover ratio**, calculated by dividing net sales by average total assets, provides a measure of how many times an organization "turned over" its assets. This ratio is most helpful in detecting fraud when inventory comprises a large percentage of the total assets of an organization. The **working capital turnover** ratio, as you will recall, is calculated by dividing net sales by average working capital (current assets – current liabilities) for a period. When inventory is overstated, the denominator of this ratio increases, causing the overall ratio to decrease. Again, this ratio is most helpful in detecting financial statement fraud when inventory comprises a major portion of current assets. The **operating performance ratio** is calculated by dividing net income by net sales. It provides a measure of the profit margin of a company. When inventory is overstated or cost of goods sold is understated, net income is artificially increased causing this ratio to increase. Finally, **earnings per share**, the most commonly used ratio, measures the profitability of an organization. When net income is overstated, earnings per share increase. When earnings increase dramatically, the cause should be investigated, with the result sometimes being overstated inventory or understated cost of goods sold.

Remember that when using ratios to discover financial statement fraud symptoms, an absolutely large or small ratio does not mean much. Rather, the *change* in the ratios from period to period is what is of interest.

The second way to focus on financial statement relationships is to convert the financial statements to common-size statements and perform vertical analysis. If inventory as a percentage of total assets or as a percentage of sales keeps increasing, or if cost of goods sold as a percentage of net sales keeps decreasing, there could be fraud. Consider, for example, the financial statement fraud at Crazy Eddie Inc. At one point, Crazy Eddie Inc. was one of the hottest names in consumer electronics. What began in 1970 as a single store selling TVs, stereos, and other electronic products mushroomed into an empire with so many stores that *The New Yorker* magazine once ran a cartoon in which all roads led to Crazy Eddie. The piercing slogan "C-r-r-r-azy Eddie! His Prices are ins-a-a-a-ne!" blurted incessantly on radio and TV stations and brought customers in droves. At one point, Crazy Eddie stock traded for as much as $43.25 per share.

In the end, however, the company was under court-protected bankruptcy because of its much-publicized inventory problems. As much as $65 million in inventory was suddenly and inexplicably missing or phantom. When new management took over the company in a desperate rescue attempt, the $65 million inventory write-off more than erased all the earnings the company had ever reported. It seems that during the inventory counts, company officers had drafted phony inventory count sheets and improperly included merchandise, so that the reported ending inventory and net income would be higher. The resulting artificially high profits and stock price allowed its founder, Eddie Antar, to rake in $68.4 million from stock sales.

The fictitious inventory that was added increased substantially inventory balances from period to period, increased gross profit margin, decreased the inventory turnover ratio, increased the number of days' sales in inventory, and were quite obvious in the percentage changes using vertical and horizontal analysis. Indeed, Crazy Eddie Inc. was rich in analytical symptoms for anyone who looked for them.

### Comparing Financial Statement Information with That of Other Companies.

Maintaining large amounts of inventory is quite expensive, especially if the inventory is large, bulky, heavy, or requires special handling. Because inventory handling and warehouse costs, as well as the financing costs, are extremely expensive, most companies today are taking extreme steps to decrease the amount of inventory they have on hand. Dell Computer, for example, keeps little, if any, inventory and only purchases its inventory just-in-time to make computers ordered by its customers. Investors often see large amounts of inventory as "management ineptitude" or "lack of efficiency in operations." Therefore, in most cases, when a company's reported inventory balance increases, you should ask why. Increasing amounts of inventory are especially questionable when other companies against which a company competes are not increasing their inventory balances. Increased inventories can represent poor management decisions, fraud, or increased sales expectations, which if not realized, can cause significant losses for the company. Economic and industry-wide factors usually affect similar firms in similar ways. Financial results that are inconsistent with those of other similar firms quite often signal a problem. The comparisons can be made using horizontal or vertical analysis, ratio analysis, changes reported in the statement of cash flows, or mere changes in the financial statement numbers themselves.

In comparing inventory balances and trends with other similar companies, the type of inventory a company has should be considered. Increasing inventory balances in rapidly changing industries (such as the computer or software industries), in industries with high amounts of spoilage or obsolescence (such as groceries), or in industries that normally would not have high inventory balances raise even more serious questions. When inventory balances are increasing, either by themselves or in relation to other numbers, you should always ask yourself why or what it is about this company that makes it different from other similar firms. If a ready answer is not forthcoming, you may have a fraud on your hands.

### Comparing Financial Statement Amounts with Assets They Are Supposed to Represent or with Nonfinancial Statement Factors.

Comparing recorded amounts in the financial statements with the assets they are supposed to represent is an excellent way to detect inventory-related financial statement frauds. In the Laribee case cited in an earlier chapter, the inventory represented by the financial statement amounts "would have required three times the capacity of the buildings" the company had to store it. In another case, the auditors of a company were suspicious of the inventory amounts reported on the financial statements. Their observation of inventory had revealed no serious shortages, and yet it seemed dramatically overstated. Why would the company's inventory increase fivefold in one year? Suspecting that something was awry, the auditors decided to look at the physical attributes of the actual inventory that was supposed to be owned by their client. Their investigation revealed that the sheet metal inventory was grossly overstated. Management had falsified the inventory by preparing fictitious records. Company management had prepared inventory tags and delivered them to the auditors. The auditors had verified the amount of inventory shown on the tags and had deposited them in a box in the conference room they used during the audit. At night, a manager had then added spurious tags to the box. The manager had also substituted new inventory reconciliation lists to conform with the total of the valid and spurious tags.

The magnitude of the fraud was discovered when the auditors performed volume tests on the inventory. First, they converted the purported $30 million of sheet metal stock into cubic feet. Then they determined the volume of the warehouse that was supposed to contain the inventory. At best, it could have contained one-half the reported amount—it was far too small to house the total. Next, they examined the inventory tags and found that some rolls of sheet metal were supposed to weigh 50,000 pounds. However, none of the forklifts that were supposed to move the inventory could lift more than 3,000 pounds. Finally, the auditors verified the reported inventory purchases and found purchase records supporting an inventory of about 30 million pounds. Yet, the reported amount was 60 million pounds. Faced with this evidence, management admitted that it had grossly overstated the value of the inventory to show increased profits. Management had previously forecast increased earnings, and without the overstatement, earnings would have fallen far short of target.

## SUMMARY

Revenue and inventory frauds are closely related, because revenues are generated by selling inventory. Inventory, by its nature, generally has unique physical characteristics. Identifying these physical characteristics and making sure the numbers reported on the financial statements match these characteristics (volume, weight, etc.) is a good way to make sure the reported amount of inventory is realistic.

## KEY TERMS

**Accounts receivable turnover** Sales divided by average accounts receivable; a measure of the efficiency with which receivables are being collected.

**Allowance for doubtful accounts** A contra-asset (receivable) account representing the amount of receivables that are estimated to be uncollectible.

**Allowance for uncollectible assets as a percentage of receivables** Allowance for doubtful accounts divided by accounts receivable; a measure of the percentage of receivables estimated to be uncollectible.

**Asset turnover ratio** Total sales divided by average total assets; a measure of the amount of sales revenue generated with each dollar of assets.

**Bad debt expense** An expense representing receivables or revenues that are presumed not to be collectible.

**Common-size financial statements** Financial statements that have been converted to percentages.

**Cost of goods sold** The cost of goods sold to customers; calculated by subtracting ending inventory from the sum of beginning inventory plus purchases.

**Earnings per share** Net income divided by the number of shares of stock outstanding; a measure of profitability.

**Gross profit (margin) ratio** Gross profit (margin) divided by net sales; a measure of markup.

**Number of days in receivable ratio** 365 (number of days in a year) divided by accounts receivable turnover; a measure of how long it takes to collect receivables.

**Operating performance ratio** Net Income divided by Total Sales; a measure of the percentage of revenues that become profits.

**Revenue recognition** Determining that revenues have been earned and are collectible and thus should be reported on the income statement.

**Sales return percentage ratio** Sales returns divided by total sales; a measure of the percentage of sales being returned by customers.

**Sales returns (sales returns and allowances)** Sold merchandise that is returned by customers or damaged, or other sold merchandise for which credit is given.

**Working capital turnover ratio** Sales divided by average working capital; a measure of the amount of working capital used to generate revenues.

# QUESTIONS AND CASES

## DISCUSSION QUESTIONS

1. What are some common revenue-related financial statement fraud schemes?

2. What are some possible ways to proactively search for revenue-related financial statement fraud schemes?

3. Why is it important to follow up on revenue-related fraud symptoms?

4. What are some of the most common inventory-related financial statement fraud schemes?

5. What are some of the ways to proactively search for inventory financial statement fraud schemes?

6. What are common-size financial statements?

7. Why do you suspect that revenue-related financial statement fraud schemes are the most common and that inventory-related fraud schemes are also common?

8. What is the effect on net income of not recording sales returns?

9. What is the effect on net income of overstating ending inventory?

10. How can comparing financial statement amounts with actual assets help determine whether fraud is present?

## TRUE/FALSE

1. Understated revenues and understated net income are among the most common types of financial statement fraud.

2. Two of the reasons revenue-related financial statement fraud is so prevalent are because revenue recognition can be highly subjective and because revenue is so easily manipulated.

3. Performing a horizontal analysis of the statement of cash flows is an excellent way to proactively search for revenue-related financial statement fraud.

4. The most common accounts manipulated when perpetrating financial statement fraud are revenues and accounts receivable.

5. An increase in gross margin and an increase in number of days' sales in inventory could be an indication of inflated inventory fraud.

6. A sales discounts amount that appears too low could be a fraud symptom.

7. Comparing financial results and trends of a company with those of similar firms is an ineffective way to look for fraud symptoms.

8. Focusing on changes in financial statements from period to period can help identify analytical fraud symptoms.

9. Controls over inventory should be closely examined when searching for fraud symptoms.

10. The gross profit (margin) ratio is calculated by dividing gross profit by cost of goods sold.

## MULTIPLE CHOICE

1. The most common accounts manipulated when perpetrating financial statement fraud are:
   a. An expense.
   b. Inventory.
   c. Revenue.
   d. Accounts Payable.

2. Why would a company want to understate net income?
   a. To increase profits
   b. To increase stock price
   c. To gain consumer confidence
   d. To pay less in taxes

3. Reported revenue and sales account balances that appear too high are examples of:
   a. Analytical symptoms.
   b. Documentary symptoms.
   c. Lifestyle symptoms.
   d. Verbal symptoms.

4. Horizontal analysis is a method that:
   a. Examines financial statement numbers from period to period.
   b. Examines percent changes in account balances from period to period.
   c. Examines transactions from period to period.
   d. None of the above.

5. Adding fictitious receivables will usually result in a(n):
   a. Sales return percentage that remains constant.
   b. Increased sales discount percentage.
   c. Increase in accounts receivable turnover.
   d. Increase in the number of days in receivables.

6. Comparing recorded amounts in the financial statements with real-world assets they are supposed to represent would be most effective in detecting:
   a. Cash and inventory fraud.
   b. Accounts payable fraud.
   c. Revenue-related fraud.
   d. Accounts receivable fraud.

7. Lifestyle symptoms are most effective with:
   a. Revenue-related financial statement frauds.
   b. Inventory-related financial statement frauds.
   c. Employee frauds.
   d. Accounts payable financial statement frauds.

8. Which of the following is not an inventory-related documentary symptom?
   a. Duplicate purchase orders
   b. Missing inventory during inventory counts
   c. Excess inventory tags
   d. Inventory sub-ledgers that don't balance with the inventory general ledger account

9. When looking for inventory fraud, it is important to ask which of the following questions?
   a. What is the nature of inventory?
   b. What is the age of inventory?
   c. What is the salability of inventory?
   d. All are important questions to ask.

10. Which of the following ratios would *not* generally be used to look for inventory and cost of goods sold-related frauds?
    a. Accounts payable turnover
    b. Gross profit margin
    c. Inventory turnover
    d. Number of days' sales in inventory

11. In order to analyze financial statements for fraud, an auditor or fraud examiner should consider:
    a. Only the types of accounts that should be included in the financial statements.
    b. Only the types of fraud the company is susceptible to.
    c. Only the nature of the company's business and industry.
    d. The auditor should consider all of the above.

12. Last minute revenue adjustments, unsupported balance sheet amounts, and improperly recorded revenues are examples of:
    a. Analytical symptoms.
    b. Documentary symptoms.
    c. Control symptoms.
    d. Perceptional symptoms.

13. Accounts that can be manipulated in revenue fraud include all the following *except*:
    a. Accounts receivable.
    b. Bad debt expense.
    c. Inventory.
    d. Sales discounts.

14. Which financial ratio is *not* useful in detecting revenue-related fraud?
    a. Gross profit margin ratio
    b. Account receivable turnover ratio
    c. Asset turnover ratio
    d. Debt to equity ratio

15. The asset turnover ratio measures:
    a. The average time an asset is used by the company.
    b. The average useful life of capital assets.
    c. Sales that are generated with each dollar of the assets.
    d. Assets that are purchased with each dollar of sales.

16. The most common way to overstate revenues is to:
    a. Record revenues prematurely.
    b. Abuse the cut-off line for recording revenues.
    c. Create fictitious revenues.
    d. None of the above.

17. Which of the following is a possible scheme for manipulating revenue when returned goods are accepted from customers?
    a. Understate allowance for doubtful accounts (thus overstating receivables)
    b. Record bank transfers when cash is received from customers
    c. Write off uncollectible receivables in a later period
    d. Avoid recording of returned goods from customers

18. All of the following ratios are useful in detecting large revenue fraud *except*:
    a. Gross profit margin.
    b. Current ratio.
    c. Number of days' sales in inventory.
    d. Accounts receivable turnover.

19. Each of the following illicit revenue transactions is correctly linked with the financial statement accounts involved *except*:
    a. Recognize revenues too early – Accounts receivable, revenue.
    b. Understate allowance for doubtful accounts – Bad debt expense, allowance for doubtful accounts.
    c. Don't write off uncollectible receivables – Sales returns, sales discounts.
    d. Don't record discounts given to customers – Cash, sales discounts, accounts receivable.

e. Record returned goods after the end of the period – Sales returns, accounts receivable.

20. Identify which ratio is correctly linked to the information that the ratio could reveal about the company's potential for revenue fraud.
    a. Gross profit margin: This ratio will increase if management overstates inventory.
    b. Sales return percentage: A sudden decrease in this ratio can mean that customer discounts are not being recorded in the accounting records.
    c. Allowance for uncollectible accounts as a percent of receivables: When a company records fictitious receivables, this ratio increases.
    d. Operating profit margin: A dramatic decrease in this ratio could indicate fraud.

## SHORT CASES

**Case 1.** During the audit of a major client, you notice that revenues have increased dramatically from the third to the fourth quarter and especially over the previous periods of last year. You've received tips alleging that the company is overstating its revenues. What steps would you take to examine the legitimacy of management's assertions regarding its reported revenue?

**Case 2.** Thomas is the CEO of a business that just went public. He is feeling intense pressure for the business to succeed because all of his relatives invested heavily in his company. Since going public, sales have been flat, and Thomas is worried about not meeting analysts' and even relatives' expectations. Which financial statement accounts might Thomas attempt to manipulate in order to meet analysts projected earnings?

**Case 3.** The following information is provided for Technoworld, a company specializing in providing Internet technology assistance for clients:

|  | 2002 | 2003 | 2004 | 2005 |
|---|---|---|---|---|
| Cash | $1,000 | $1,200 | $1,400 | $1,500 |
| Accounts Receivable | 250 | 375 | 600 | 900 |
| Inventory | 600 | 700 | 825 | 975 |
| PP&E (net) | 1,500 | 1,700 | 1,800 | 1,950 |
| Notes Receivable | 500 | 500 | 500 | 500 |
| Total Assets | $3,850 | $4,475 | $5,125 | $5,825 |
| | | | | |
| Accounts Payable | $700 | $900 | $1,000 | $1,100 |
| Other Current Liabilities | 200 | 300 | 350 | 425 |
| Notes Payable | 1,200 | 1,400 | 1,500 | 1,750 |
| Total Liabilities | $2,100 | $2,600 | $2,850 | $3,275 |
| | | | | |
| Stock Outstanding | $1,000 | $1,000 | $1,000 | $1,000 |
| Retained Earnings | 750 | 875 | 1,275 | 1,550 |
| Total Shareholders' Equity | $1,750 | $1,875 | $2,275 | $2,550 |
| Total Liabilities and Shareholders' Equity | $3,850 | $4,475 | $5,125 | $5,825 |

Perform a horizontal analysis of this balance sheet and identify any accounts that may be questionable. Take into account technology industry trends when performing the analysis.

For Cases 4 and 5, use the following information.

*Five-Year Financial Data for Company AAA*

|  | Year 1 | Year 2 | Year 3 | Year 4 | Year 5 |
|---|---|---|---|---|---|
| Sales | $100,000.00 | $105,000.00 | $110,250.00 | $137,812.50 | $206,718.75 |
| COGS | 75,000.00 | 78,750.00 | 82,687.50 | 66,150.00 | 59,535.00 |
| Margin | 25,000.00 | 26,250.00 | 27,562.50 | 71,662.50 | 147,183.75 |

**Case 4.** Perform horizontal analysis of the data to indicate any potential red flags regarding possible overstatement of sales.

**Case 5.** Perform vertical analysis of the data to indicate any potential red flags regarding possible understatement of the cost of goods sold (COGS).

**Case 6.** Fraud investigators found that 70 percent of the nearly $160 million in sales booked by an Asian subsidiary of a European company between September 1999 and June 2000 were fictitious. In an effort to earn rich bonuses tied to sales targets, the Asian subsidiary's managers used highly sophisticated schemes to fool auditors. One especially egregious method involved funneling bank loans through third parties to make it look as though customers had paid, when in fact they hadn't.

In a lawsuit filed by the company's auditors, it was alleged that former executives "deliberately" provided "false or incomplete information" to the auditors and conspired to obstruct the firm's audits. To fool the auditors, the subsidiary used two types of schemes. The first involved factoring unpaid receivables to banks to obtain cash up front. Side letters that were concealed from the auditors gave the banks the right to take the money back if they couldn't collect from the company's customers. Hence, the factoring agreements amounted to little more than loans.

The second, more creative, scheme was used after the auditors questioned why the company wasn't collecting more of its overdue bills from customers. It turns out the subsidiary told many customers to transfer their contracts to third parties. The third parties then took out bank loans, for which the company provided collateral, and then "paid" the overdue bills to the company using the borrowed money. The result was that the company was paying itself. When the contracts were later canceled, the company paid "penalties" to the customers and the third parties to compensate them "for the inconvenience of dealing with the auditors."

The investigators also found that the bulk of the company's sales came from contracts signed at the end of quarters, so managers could meet ambitious quarterly sales targets and receive multimillion-dollar bonuses. For example, 90 percent of the revenue recorded by the subsidiary in the second quarter of 2000 was booked in several deals signed in the final nine days of the quarter. But the company was forced to subsequently cancel 70 percent of those contracts because the customers—most of them tiny start-ups—didn't have the means to pay.

List revenue-related fraud symptoms and schemes used in this case. Briefly discuss how actively searching and understanding revenue-related fraud symptoms could have led to discovering the fraud by the company's auditors.

**Case 7.** Toolsito is a medium-sized company that buys copper rod and plastic materials to produce insulated copper wiring. Toolsito operates out of a single building of about 500,000 square feet that includes office space (3%), production area (57%), shipping and receiving (15%), and finished goods and raw materials inventory warehousing (25%). You have gathered the following data about the company's inventories and performance, and now you are ready to conduct an analysis on these numbers to discover possible fraud symptoms.

|  | 2005 | 2004 |
|---|---|---|
| Finished Goods Inventory | $1,654,500 | $1,175,500 |
| (Approx. 300 million ft. – 2005) | | |
| (Years are fine) | | |
| Copper Rod Inventory | $2,625,000 | $1,650,000 |
| (Approx. 5.9 million lbs. – 2005) | | |
| Plastics Inventory | $224,500 | $182,000 |
| (Approx. 1.1 million lbs. – 2005) | | |
| Accounts Payable (for Inv. Purchases) | $450,000 | $425,000 |
| Days Purchases in A/P | 43.6 days | 44.2 days |
| Days Sales in Receivables | 56.3 days | 48.4 days |
| Market Price of Insulated Wire (per foot) | $0.008 | $0.009 |
| Market Price of Copper Rod (per lb.) | $0.480 | $0.480 |
| Market Price of Plastics (per lb.) | $0.120 | $0.190 |

How would you go about looking for red flags? Determine whether you think red flags of possible fraud are present in 2005.

**Case 8.** Decide whether each situation is a symptom of revenue fraud. Then explain (a) why the situation is or is not a symptom, and (b) if it is a symptom, how it would be found using computer queries or traditional methods.

Y / N        Sales discounts appear too high.

Y / N        Accounts receivable increases as a percentage of revenues.

Y / N        Bad debt allowance increases by the same percentage as accounts receivable.

Y / N        Sales returns increase.

Y / N        Large percent of revenues are recorded in the fourth quarter.

Y / N        Unexplained reconciling items appear on the bank statement.

**Case 9.** Your auditing firm just landed a new client: a large software company managed by two brothers who together own 15 percent of the stock. You learn that the company fired its last auditor. You also notice that the company is involved in a lot of off-book business ventures. Identify the possible symptoms of fraud and which aspect of the fraud exposure rectangle each symptom corresponds to.

**Case 10.** After graduating from college with your MBA, you decide to take your Grandma's secret cinnamon roll recipe and open up a bakery. You grew up devouring your Grandma's rolls, and you have convinced her to give you the secret. You are confident that your bakery will be the next big hit in the fast-food business.

You take out a business loan for the maximum amount your bank will give you, hire several employees, and open a beautiful store that is designed to look like your Grandma's home. After eight months of hard work and diligence, you are crushed when you realized that your store manager has been stealing from you. One of your recent hires tell you that during her last shift the manager, Stephanie, voided a sale of 2 dozen cinnamon rolls, stamped the receipt as a return, and pocketed the money. Stephanie warned the new hire not to say anything and told her she deserved the money because she didn't get paid enough. Encouraged by your open door policy, the employee confides in you.

1. Identify what symptoms this fraud will generate. In addition, identify how this fraud will directly affect your revenue and inventory accounts.

2. Explain the steps you should take to search for each symptom you identified in the previous question. In particular, describe the computer queries and transactions that should be searched to find this fraud.

3. After you have identified several of the symptoms, do you have enough evidence to prove that she is guilty? What other evidence is required or useful in this case?

4. Besides searching for symptoms of the fraud, what other investigative steps can be taken to elicit a confession or otherwise prove the fraud?

5. What steps could have been taken to prevent this fraud from occurring in the first place?

**Case 11.** Sue is a customer account representative for ABC company. She recently acquired several new accounts when a previous representative, Dan, took an early retirement. Sue reviewed each of Dan's accounts to help familiarize her with his clients and understand how she can better serve each one's individual needs. As she was reviewing the client list, she found a major customer she had never heard of before. Surprised that she had not yet done business with the company, she called them to introduce herself as the new representative.

When Sue placed the call, she found that the reported number had been disconnected. Thinking that the customer may have done business with them in the past and have moved on, she reviewed the account transactions and found that the most recent transaction had taken place the week prior. During her review, she also noticed the latest transaction was for an unusually large amount for ABC.

As Sue pursued her curiosity, she went to other employees to find out more about the company. In her questioning, she found that none of the employees had ever heard of the customer. Once she had run out of other avenues, Sue decided to contact the controller to find out whether he could provide any additional information. When Sue opened the company directory, she was amazed when she recognized his home address: it was the same address as the mystery customer!

1. What are some of the possible scenarios for why the addresses match?

2. What other symptoms would be present in each of the scenarios you identified in the previous question?

3. What are the implications of the address match if the company is private? If the company was publicly traded?

4. Assuming the company was preparing for an IPO, who should Sue contact and what should she say?

5. If Sue believes these revenues are fictitious, what should her next course of action be?

**Case 12.** Pablo is studying financial statements to decide which companies he should invest in. Pablo identifies Jawanna Corp. as having abnormally high financial ratios compared with other companies in its industry. Skeptical, he examines the footnotes of the financial statements further for indications that the company might be deceiving investors.

Name and explain four common symptoms that fraudulent companies try to hide in the disclosures to the financial statements.

**Case 13.** Financial statements are the end product of the accounting cycle and are used by investors to make informed decisions. These financial statements can be analyzed to help determine whether any fraudulent activities are occurring in the company. As you know, the balance sheet, income statement, and statement of cash flows are the three primary financial statements.

List and briefly describe some of the ways these three financial statements can help detect fraud.

**Case 14.** Although financial statement fraud can be committed in many different ways and by people in different positions, history shows that the majority of financial statement fraud is committed by people in upper management who have added pressures as well as more opportunities to commit fraud. Using the Internet, research the following individuals and match each individual with the position they held within their company and the financial statement fraud they were associated with.

| People | Positions |
|---|---|
| 1. Kenneth Lay | A. Firm attorney |
| 2. David Duncan | B. CFO |
| 3. Jeff Skilling | C. Audit partner |
| 4. Andrew Fastow | D. Founding as well as last CEO |
| 5. Michael Odom | E. CEO only six months |
| 6. Michael Kopper | F. Assistant to Fastow |
| 7. Nancy Temple | G. Risk management partner |

**Case 15.** Home Safety, Inc.'s management has been trying for months to acquire one of its largest competitors in the home security industry—Lock-It-Up Company. Before agreeing to the acquisition, Home Safety's board of directors wanted Lock-It-Up's books to be audited. They asked your firm to perform the audit and due diligence, and specifically that you examine the owner's family and roles in the company.

**Lock-It-Up Company**

Lock-It-Up is a large, local home security business that has been in the area for a long time. They have held a large market share for several years, and they receive many referrals from present users of their home security systems. They own five large locations in the area from which they perform business and are an optimal takeover target.

**Internal Environment**

- *Management style:* The owner of the business, Jeff Lester, has taken a hands-off approach to managing his business. He frequently takes extended vacations with his family and rarely examines the books of his business. He is happy with his level of income and is not concerned with the future, believing that his company will always be profitable.

- *Executives:* Several of the owner's relatives hold high positions in the company. The owner's brother, Chucky "Gambling Genius" Lester, is the chief accountant and answers only to his brother, Jeff. He is majority owner of a local amateur sports team, which has struggled to sell tickets and is facing bankruptcy.

- *Employees:* The company takes advantage of the cheap labor at the large, local university. Each summer, it hires hundreds of students to sell its products door-to-door. Successful students from previous years train the new students, and expectations and motivations are high. The temporary labor force is paid subminimum wage but can earn significant commissions on sales. Last year, some of the students earn more than $80,000 in commissions in just four months of summer sales, with some receiving quota rewards such as cruises and new cars.

- *Internal controls:* In order to facilitate quicker purchases and obtain deals from vendors, Jeff left Chucky a stack of blank, presigned checks. Anyone

in the purchasing department has access to these checks and can use them as needed.

1. As the auditor, list the concerns you have that may suggest fraud is occurring in the company.

2. What controls would you suggest the company put in place to prevent potential fraud from occurring for each of the concerns you listed in previous question?

3. Would you feel comfortable signing off on Home Safety's financial statements if they were to acquire Lock-It-Up this year? Why or why not?

4. What are some factors in the auditor-client relationship that can make it more difficult for the auditor to detect fraud?

## EXTENSIVE CASE

Enron Corporation began as a small natural gas distributor and over the course of 15 years grew to become the seventh largest company in the United States. Soon after the federal deregulation of natural gas pipelines in 1985, Enron was born by the merging of Houston Natural Gas and InterNorth, a Nebraska pipeline company. Initially, Enron was merely involved in the distribution of gas, but it later became a market maker in facilitating the buying and selling of futures of natural gas, electricity, broadband, and other products. However, Enron's continuous growth eventually came to an end as a complicated financial statement fraud and multiple scandals sent Enron through a downward spiral to bankruptcy.

During the 1980s several major national energy corporations began lobbying Washington to deregulate the energy business. Their claim was that the extra competition resulting from a deregulated market would benefit both businesses and consumers. Consequently, the national government began to lift controls on who was allowed to produce energy and how it was marketed and sold. But, as competition in the energy market increased, gas and energy prices began to fluctuate greatly. Over time, Enron incurred massive debts and no longer had exclusive rights to its pipelines. It needed some new and innovative business strategies.

Kenneth Lay, chairman and CEO, hired the consulting firm McKinsey & Company to assist in developing a new plan to help Enron get back on its feet. Jeffrey Skilling, a young McKinsey consultant who had a background in banking and asset and liability management, was assigned to work with Enron. He recommended that Enron create a "Gas Bank" to buy and sell gas. Skilling, who later became chief executive at Enron, recognized

that Enron could capitalize on the fluctuating gas prices by acting as an intermediary and creating a futures market for buyers and sellers of gas; it would buy and sell gas to be used tomorrow at a stable price today.

Although brilliantly successful in theory, Skilling's gas bank idea faced a major problem. The natural gas producers who agreed to supply Enron's gas bank desperately needed cash and required cash as payment for their products. But, Enron also had insufficient cash levels. Therefore, management decided to team up with banks and other financial institutions, establishing partnerships that would provide the cash needed to complete the transactions with Enron's suppliers. Under the direction of Andrew Fastow, a newly hired financial genius, Enron also created several special-purpose entities (SPEs), which served as the vehicles through which money was funneled from the banks to the gas suppliers, thus keeping these transactions off Enron's books. As Enron's business became more and more complicated, its vulnerability to fraud and eventual disaster also grew. Initially, the newly formed partnerships and SPEs worked to Enron's advantage. But, in the end, it was the creation of these SPEs that culminated in Enron's death.

Within just a few years of instituting its gas bank and the complicated financing system, Enron grew rapidly, controlling a large part of the U.S. energy market. At one point, it controlled as much as a quarter of all of the nation's gas business. It also began expanding to create markets for other types of products including electricity, crude oil, coal, plastics, weather derivatives, and broadband. In addition, Enron continued to expand its trading business and with the introduction of Enron Online in the late 1990s it became one of the largest trading companies on Wall Street, at one time generating 90 percent of its income through trades. Enron soon had more contracts than any of its competitors and, with market dominance, could predict future prices with great accuracy, thereby guaranteeing superior profits.

To continue enhanced growth and dominance Enron began hiring the "best and brightest" traders. But, Enron was just as quick in firing its employees as it was in hiring new ones. Management created the Performance Review Committee (PRC), which became known as the harshest employee ranking system in the country. Its method of evaluating employee performance was nicknamed "rank and yank" by Enron employees. Every six months employees were ranked on a scale of 1-to-5. Those ranked in the lowest category (1) were immediately "yanked" (fired) from their position and replaced by new recruits. Surprisingly, during each employee review, management required that at least 15% of all the employees ranked were given a 1 and therefore yanked from their position and income. The employees ranked with a 2 or 3 were also given notice that they were liable to be released in the near future. These ruthless performance reviews created fierce internal competition between fellow employees who faced a strict ultimatum; perform or be replaced. Furthermore, it created a work environment where employees were unable to express opinions or valid concerns for fear of a low-ranking score by their superiors.

With so much pressure to succeed and maintain its position as the global energy market leader, Enron began to jeopardize its integrity by committing fraud. The SPEs, which originally were used for good business purposes, were now used illegally to hide bad investments, poor-performing assets, and debt; to manipulate cash flows; and eventually, to report more than $1 billion of false income. The following are examples of how specific SPEs were used fraudulently.

**Chewco:** In 1993, Enron and the California Public Employees Retirement System (CalPERS) formed a 50/50 partnership called Joint Energy Development Investments Limited (JEDI). In 1997, Enron's Andrew Fastow established the Chewco SPE, which was designed to repurchase CalPERS share of equity in JEDI at a large profit. However, Chewco crossed the bounds of legality in two ways.

First, it broke the 3 percent equity rule, which allowed corporations such as Enron to "not consolidate" if outsiders contributed even 3 percent of the capital, but the other 97 percent could come from the company. When Chewco bought out JEDI, however, half of the $11.4 million that bought the 3 percent equity involved cash collateral provided by Enron—meaning that only 1.5 percent was owned by outsiders. Therefore, the debts and losses incurred at Chewco were not listed where they

belonged, on Enron's financial reports, but remained only on Chewco's separate financial records.

Secondly, because Fastow was an Enron officer, he was, therefore, unauthorized to personally run Chewco without direct approval from Enron's board of directors and public disclosure with the SEC. In an effort to secretly bypass these restrictions, Fastow appointed one of his subordinates, Michael Kopper, to run Chewco, under Fastow's close supervision and influence. Fastow continually applied pressure to Kopper to prevent Enron from getting the best possible deals from Chewco and therefore giving Michael Kopper huge profits.

Chewco was eventually forced to consolidate its financial statements with Enron. By doing so, however, it caused large losses on Enron's balance sheet and other financial statements. The Chewco SPE accounted for 80 percent (approximately $400 million) of all of Enron's SPE restatements. Moreover, Chewco set the stage for Andrew Fastow as he continued to expand his personal profiting SPE empire.

**LJM 1 & 2:** The LJM SPEs (LJM1 and LJM2) were two organizations sponsored by Enron that also participated heavily in fraudulent deal making. LJM1 and its successor, LJM2, were similar to the Chewco SPE in that they also broke the two important rules set forth by the SEC. First, although less than 3 percent of the SPE equity was owned by outside investors, LJM's books were kept separate from Enron's. An error in judgment by Arthur Andersen allowed LJM's financial statements to go unconsolidated. Furthermore, Andrew Fastow (now CFO at Enron) was appointed to personally oversee all operations at LJM. Without the governing controls in place, fraud became inevitable.

LJM1 was first created by Fastow as a result of a deal Enron made with a high-speed Internet service provider called Rhythms NetConnections. In March 1998 Enron purchased $10 million worth of shares in Rhythms and agreed to hold the shares until the end of 1999, when it was authorized to sell those shares. Rhythms released its first IPO in April 1999 and Enron's share of Rhythms stock immediately jumped to a net worth of $300 million.

Fearing that the value of the stock might drop again before they could sell it, Enron searched for an investor from whom it would purchase a put option (i.e., insurance against a falling stock price). However, because Enron had such a large share and because Rhythms was such a risky company, Enron could not find an investor at the price Enron was seeking. So, with the approval of the board of directors and a waiver of Enron's Code of Conduct, Fastow created LJM1, which used Enron stock as its capital to sell the Rhythms stock put options to Enron. In effect, Enron was insuring itself against a plummeting Rhythms stock price. But, because Enron was basically insuring itself and paying Fastow and his subordinates millions of dollars to run the deal, Enron really had no insurance. With all of its actions independent of Enron's financial records, LJM1 was able to provide a hedge against a profitable investment.

LJM2 was the sequel to LJM1 and is infamous for its involvement in its four major deals known as the Raptors. The Raptors were deals made between Enron and LJM2 which enable Enron to hide losses from Enron's unprofitable investments. In total the LJM2 hid approximately $1.1 billion worth of losses from Enron's balance sheet.

LJM1 and LJM2 were used by Enron to alter its actual financial statements and by Fastow for personal profits. Enron's books took a hard hit when LJM finally consolidated its financial statements, a $100 million SPE restatement. In the end, Fastow pocketed millions of dollars from his involvement with the LJM SPEs.

Through complicated accounting schemes, Enron was able to fool the public for a time into thinking that its profits were continually growing. The energy giant cooked its books by hiding significant liabilities and losses from bad investments and poor assets, by not recognizing declines in the value of its aging assets, by reporting more than $1 billion of false income, and by manipulating its cash flows, often during fourth quarters. However, as soon as the public became aware of Enron's fraudulent acts, both investors and the company suffered. As investor confidence in Enron dropped because of its fraudulent deal making, so did Enron's stock price. In just one year Enron stock plummeted from a high of about $95 per share to below $1 per share. The decrease in equity made it impossible for Enron to cover its expenses and liabilities and it was forced to declare bankruptcy on December 2, 2001. Enron had been reduced from a company claiming almost $62 billion worth of assets to nearly nothing.

**Questions:**

1. What important internal controls were ignored when LJM1 was created?

2. How might Enron's harsh Performance Review Committee (PRC) have aided company executives in committing the fraud?

3. The fraud at Enron is one of many major financial statement frauds that occurred in recent years (Qwest, Global Crossing, WorldCom, etc.). What are some factors that could explain why the falsifying of financial statements is occurring so frequently? List four factors.

4. Suppose you are a certified fraud examiner but enjoy investing in the stock market as an additional source of income. Upon research of Enron's stock, you notice that although its stock has a history of strong growth and a seemingly promising future, Enron's financial reports are unclear and, frankly, confusing. In fact, you can't even explain how Enron is making money. Could this lack of clarity in its financial reporting serve as a red flag in alerting you to the possibility of fraud at Enron? Why or why not?

5. How could the auditors, Arthur Andersen in this case, have performed their audits and not caught the Enron fraud? Is it possible for a financial statement auditor to form a GAAS-compliant audit and not catch major financial statement fraud? How would GAAS auditing need to change to guarantee that all frauds are caught?

## INTERNET ASSIGNMENTS

1. Horizontal and vertical analysis are effective ways to search for analytical fraud symptoms. Search the Internet for the annual report of a company of your choice. Perform both a horizontal and vertical analysis for the assets portion of the balance sheet. You may find it helpful to use Excel or similar spreadsheet software.

2. Go to the IBM company Web site (http://www.ibm.com) and download the most recent financial statements. In the notes to the financial statements, read the significant accounting policies concerning revenue and inventory. Do the policies seem legitimate? What concerns might you have? Then, go to the financial statements and do a year-to-year comparison of the three accounts. Were the changes as expected? Is anything unusual? Does IBM explain any unusual fluctuations in the notes?

# DEBATE

Mendoza is considering investing in IBM. However, he is captivated by IBM's growth at an average of 27 percent per year since 1994. IBM had made a remarkable change from a struggling company to a leading company in the personal computer market. Mendoza has asked for your advice as to whether the growth is genuine. He suspects there might have been some fraudulent or unethical actions taken by IBM to increase its income.

After a brief look at the recent history and performance of IBM, you decide to look more closely at the financial statements. As you review the financial statements, you begin to have some concerns about the true nature of IBM's growth. Certain accounting procedures cause doubts as to whether the growth came from IBM's core business operations or from carefully planned accounting adjustments that seem to be unethical. As you proceed in your investigations, you pay particular attention to the following areas:

*Pensions:* IBM changed its pension plan to a cash balance plan. The returns of this plan exceeded the amount recognized as an expense. Accounting rules require the company to add the excess returns to earnings, but the gains cannot be spent on anything other than pension benefits. IBM increased its earnings per share by making this adjustment.

*Stock Repurchases:* Since 1995, IBM spent a lot of money making stock repurchases. A stock repurchase may be beneficial to a company by increasing earnings per share, because earnings will be spread across fewer shareholders.

You conclude that the financial statements were in accordance with GAAP, and you are confident that all accounting rules were followed. However, you have to explain to Mendoza whether the behavior was ethical. What would you tell him?

# END NOTES

1   The Sarbanes-Oxley Act required in Section 704 that the SEC study enforcement actions over the five years (July 31, 1997, to July 30, 2002) preceding its enactment in order to identify areas of issuer financial reporting that are most susceptible to fraud, inappropriate manipulation, or inappropriate earnings management. This study provided many great examples of financial statement fraud that have been used in this and the next chapter.

2.  Daniel Wise, "Cendant Lawyers Get Record $262 Million in Securities Fraud Case," *New York Law Journal* (August 22, 2000).

3.  "Inventory Chicanery Tempts More Firms, Fools More Auditors," *Wall Street Journal* (December 14, 1992), p.1.

4.  http://www.yourlawyer.com/practice/news.htm?story_id=5966&topic=HealthSouth%20%20Fraud (accessed on June 9, 2004).

# CHAPTER 13

# LIABILITY, ASSET, AND INADEQUATE DISCLOSURE FRAUDS

## LEARNING OBJECTIVES

After studying this chapter, you should be able to:

1. Identify fraudulent schemes that understate liabilities.
2. Understand the understatement of liabilities fraud.
3. Identify fraudulent schemes that overstate assets.
4. Understand the overstatement of assets fraud.
5. Identify fraudulent schemes that inadequately disclose financial statement information.
6. Understand the inadequate disclosure fraud.

*Waste Management, Inc., is the leading provider of comprehensive waste and environmental services in North America. Headquartered in Houston, the company's network of operations includes 429 collection operations, 366 transfer stations, 289 active landfill disposal sites, 17 waste-to-energy plants, 138 recycling plants, and 85 beneficial-use landfill gas projects. Waste Management provides services to nearly 21 million residential, industrial, municipal, and commercial customers. A few years ago, Waste Management allegedly improperly inflated its operating income and other measures of performance by deferring the recognition of current period operating expenses into the future by netting one-time gains against current and prior period misstatements and current period operating expenses. Senior management increased operating income by understating operating expenses—making repeated fourth quarter adjustments to improperly reduce depreciation expense on its equipment cumulatively from the beginning of the year, using a non-GAAP method of capitalizing interest on landfill development costs, failing to accrue properly for*

*its tax and self-insurance expenses, improperly using purchase accounting to increase its environmental remediation reserves (liabilities), improperly charging operating expenses to the environmental remediation reserves, and failing to write-off permitting and project costs on impaired or abandoned landfills. These frauds were huge—causing the company, in 1998, to restate its 1992–1997 earnings by $1.7 billion, the largest restatement in corporate history (March 26, 2002) up until that time.*

The revenue- and inventory-related frauds discussed in Chapter 12 are certainly the most common financial statement frauds. However, several other types of financial statement frauds include understating liabilities and improper expense recognition, overstating assets, using cookie jar reserves, improper use of merger reserves, and inadequate disclosure. In this chapter, we deal with the following three types of financial statement fraud: (1) understating liabilities, (2) overstating assets, and (3) inadequate disclosure.

# Understatement of Liabilities Fraud

We begin by reviewing an example of understating liabilities already referred to in a previous chapter. A number of years ago, one of the Big 5 CPA firms was being sued for not detecting a financial statement fraud in its GAAS audits. The company misstating its financial statements was involved in a series of real estate limited partnerships organized under a state's Uniform Limited Partnership Act. The largest of those partnerships—and the one with the most fraud—had more than 5,000 limited partners and two general partners. The partnerships were engaged in the business of acquiring, owning, and operating commercial real estate, consisting solely of new and existing convenience real properties leased on a triple net basis to and operated by franchisers or franchisees of national and regional retail chains under long-term **leases**.[1] The convenience retail business lessees consisted primarily of restaurants (fast-food, family style, and casual theme, such as Wendy's, Hardees, Peso's Country Kitchen, Applebee's, Popeye's, Arby's, and Village Inns), but also included Blockbuster Video stores and childcare centers. Investments by limited partners were used to purchase or construct and fully pay for properties. None of the properties had mortgages.

The two general partners also had significant real estate investments of their own and needed money to support these cash-strapped, personal investments. They saw the equity in the partnership's fully paid commercial properties as a great source of cash. Accordingly, they approached a bank in another state (where they did not think the loans would be discovered) and borrowed millions of dollars against the equity in the limited partnership's assets, thus incurring significant amounts of debt for the partnership.

Fortunately, the auditors were concerned that the "triple net" nature of the leases meant that the partnership had significant risk, because the failure by a lessee to pay local property taxes or utilities, for example, could encumber the properties with liens. As a result, to determine whether all the lessees were current on their obligations, the auditors performed lien searches on all properties. What they found surprised them considerably. Their lien searches revealed a number of liens against Arizona and Texas properties by a Kansas bank. Because the partnership had no business in Kansas, the liens drew significant attention from the auditors. The auditors first approached management and asked about the liens. They were told that the liens were recorded as part of a lending arrangement with the bank that was never completed and should have been released. To corroborate the explanations of management, the auditors sent a confirmation to the Kansas bank. The confirmation letter read as follows:

> *In connection with the audit of the [named] partnership for the year ending December 31, 1995, our auditors became aware of several mortgage liens held by your bank on properties located in Arizona and Texas. These liens were recorded as part of a lending arrangement with your bank which was not completed. Because the liens have not been released, our auditors would like confirmation from you on the enclosed form as to the balance of loans or other liabilities outstanding to your bank from the [named] partnership at December 31, 1995. If such balance was zero at that date, please so state.*
>
> *Your prompt response will be appreciated. Please fax a copy of your response to the attention of [named auditor] at [telephone number] and also return the enclosed form in the envelope provided. Thank you for your attention to this matter.*

In response, the auditors received both a fax and an original letter dated April 12, 1996, from the executive vice president of the bank. That letter read as follows:

> *In response to [name of signer] letter of January 24, 1996, regarding your audit of [named partnership], please be advised as follows: (1) [named partnership] has no debt or obligation outstanding to the bank, and (2) the bank's attorneys are in the process of releasing the collateral liens, since it is the bank's understanding that the borrower does not intend to utilize its existing line of credit arrangements.*

Like the real auditors in this case, at this point you might have been content with your belief that this partnership had no unrecorded liabilities and that the line of credit had never really been used. Unfortunately, that assumption was wrong. You should read the letters one more time. The first letter specifies December 31, 1995, as the date on which the auditors wanted to know whether liabilities existed, the response letter from the bank does not specify any date, except that the letter was dated April 12. In reality, it had significant liabilities on December 31, 1995, that continued until April 11, 1996, at which time they were removed. On April 12, the bank could truthfully say it held no unrecorded liabilities; but on April 13, 1996, new liabilities were recorded. In other words, no liabilities happened on only one day—April 12. The bank's president and executive vice president had been coerced by the partnership's general partners to remove the liabilities for one day and respond to the auditors; they were acting in collusion with the general partners to mislead the auditors. Although this incident was not the only financial statement fraud perpetrated by the general partners, it was the largest. These unrecorded liabilities, which could never be paid off, resulted in significant adverse consequences for the limited partnership.

These kinds of **understatement of liability frauds** are difficult for auditors to detect. In fact, all financial statement frauds can be thought of as being on a continuum of "easy to detect and should probably have been detected by auditors" to "difficult to detect and could probably not have been detected by any auditor performing a GAAS audit." The factors that make frauds difficult to detect are such factors as:

- Collusion by insiders or outsiders, as was the case with the bank executives
- Forgery, which GAAS auditors are not trained to detect
- A complex audit trail or fraud that is mainly revealed on internal reports that are not reviewed as part of a financial statement audit
- Lying by management and other key people
- A fraud that takes the form of normal-type transactions of the company—in other words, it is not unusual
- Silence by individuals who knew or should have known about the fraud
- Off-book nature of the fraud, meaning that no records on the company's books are fraudulent, such as the fraud discussed previously
- The existence of misleading documentation
- Frauds that are small, relative to financial statement balances, or large frauds that are broken up into small amounts and scattered throughout subsidiaries
- Frauds that use odd-numbered, normal looking transactions rather than rounded amounts
- Frauds in which management hides the fraud and even prepares fraudulent documentation when asked for evidence
- Fraud committed by individuals who have never been involved in fraud before

Before we discuss how to identify understatement of liability fraud, it is important to note that in some major frauds the perpetrators manipulated liabilities in more complicated ways than just understating or hiding them.

One way to manipulate liabilities is to improperly use **restructuring** and other liability reserves. Recording a reserve on a company's books, whether for a merger, restructuring, environmental cleanup, litigation, or for other reasons, usually involves recognizing an expense and a related liability or contra-asset. In establishing reserves, companies should comply with GAAP by recording reserves only where a liability exists. Once a reserve is established, payments made by the company properly related to the reserve are offset against the reserve and not reported as an expense in the current period. Unfortunately, reserves have been improperly used by companies to manage earnings. These companies typically create excess reserves (by initially overaccruing a liability) in one accounting period and then reducing the excess reserve in later accounting periods. The reversal of the reserve creates net income that can be used to meet earnings shortfalls. These kinds of overstated reserves are sometimes referred to as "cookie jar" reserves because they can be put in the "jar"/books and then taken out and "eaten"/used when needed.

Xerox Corporation, Sunbeam Corporation, and W.R. Grace Co., all major corporations, were charged by the SEC for using cookie jar reserves to manipulate income. Basically, they recorded extra liabilities (such as recording income as deferred income) when results were better than expected (or when a loss, restructuring, lawsuit, merger, or other event already occurred anyway and "taking a big bath would be perceived by investors as no worse than a little bath") and then reversed those liabilities into income when better results were needed. (In some cases, they were able to report the creation of the reserves as nonoperating expenses and the reversal of the liability to income as operating income.) Thus, they overstated liabilities in one period and then understated them in subsequent periods. Xerox allegedly manipulated its reserves in order to meet market earnings expectations. Specifically, the SEC alleged that during the periods 1997 through 2000, Xerox maintained $396 million in cookie jar reserves, which it periodically released into earnings to artificially improve its operating results. Sunbeam created cookie jar reserves in 1996 to increase its reported loss, and reversed those excess reserves into income during 1997 to artificially inflate earnings. W.R. Grace & Co recorded liabilities, through the deferral of income, in order to build cookie jar reserves and then later used the reserves to meet earnings estimates.

## Identifying Understatement of Liability Fraud Exposures

As with revenue and inventory frauds, the easiest way to identify understatement of liability fraud exposures is to identify the various kinds of transactions that involve liabilities and can be understated. In identifying these transactions, you should accurately specify the type of organization you are dealing with, because different kinds of companies have different types of liabilities and liability-fraud exposures. Table 13-1 lists the six primary types of transactions that can create liabilities for a typical retail or wholesale company. Analyzing the accounts involved in these transactions, we can identify at least 19 different ways (some are similar) in which liabilities can be understated and the financial statements misstated.

## Table 13-1 Liability Transactions

| Transaction | Accounts Involved | Fraud Schemes |
|---|---|---|
| 1. Purchase inventory | Inventory, Accounts payable | 1. Record payables in subsequent period.<br>2. Don't record purchases.<br>3. Overstate purchase returns and purchase discounts.<br>4. Record payments made in later periods as being paid in earlier periods.<br>5. Fraudulent recording of payments (e.g., kiting). |
| 2. Incur payroll and other accrued liabilities | Payroll tax expense, Salary expense, Various expenses, Salaries payable, Payroll taxes payable, Various accrued liabilities | 6. Not record accrued liabilities.<br>7. Record accruals in later period. |
| 3. Sell products purchased | Accounts receivable, Sales revenue, Unearned revenue | 8. Record unearned revenues as earned revenues (or vice versa if you're trying to build cookie jar reserve. |
| 4. Sell service products, repay deposits, or repurchase something in the future (future commitments) | Warranty (service) expense, Warranty or service liability | 9. Not record warranty (service) liabilities.<br>10. Underrecord liabilities.<br>11. Record deposits as revenues.<br>12. Not record repurchase agreements and commitments. |
| 5. Borrow money | Cash, Notes payable, Mortgages payable, etc. | 13. Borrow from related parties at less than arm's-length transactions.<br>14. Don't record liabilities.<br>15. Borrow against equities in assets.<br>16. Write off liabilities as forgiven.<br>17. Claim liabilities as personal debt rather than as debt of the entity. |
| 6. Incur contingent liabilities | Loss from contingencies, Losses payable | 18. Don't record contingent liabilities that are probable.<br>19. Record contingent liabilities at amounts too low. |

**Understating Accounts Payable.** The first category of fraud schemes involves various kinds of cut-off problems related to the purchase of inventory. Even though minor cut-off problems probably occur in many companies, large financial statement misstatements can result from committing this type of fraud. In one case, for example, the auditors actually discovered a $28 million unrecorded liability for inventory purchased before year-end. It was not recorded as a liability or discovered because management committing the fraud altered purchasing records, bank statements, and correspondence with vendors to make it look like the inventory was paid for before year-end. Another example was the Sirena Apparel Group, Inc. The SEC alleged that the company's CEO and CFO materially overstated Sirena's revenue and earnings by instructing personnel to hold open the March 1999 fiscal quarter until Sirena had reached its sales target for that period but not to record purchases after the end of the period. Thus, not only did Sirena's management commit a revenue fraud, but by not recording purchases during the extended days they were recording revenues, they had no corresponding cost of goods sold and purchase-related liabilities.

Understating liabilities related to the purchase of inventory merely means that we are looking at the other side of the transactions we considered in Chapter 12. When accounts payable-related liabilities are understated, purchases and inventory are often understated as well, or the ledgers do not balance. In the case of ZZZZ Best, Barry Minkow and his colleagues would actually use interbank transfers or kites to make it appear as if liabilities had been paid (as cash received when creating receivables). Accounts payable can be understated by a combination of (1) not recording purchases or recording the purchases after the end of the year, (2) overstating purchase returns or purchase discounts, (3) making it appear as if liabilities have been paid off or forgiven when they have not (like ZZZZ Best did or by predating a payment made in a subsequent period to make it appear as if it had been paid during the current period). Whatever the method used, understating accounts payable and other purchase-related liabilities is a common way to misstate the financial statements. Also, if a purchase is not recorded but the inventory is counted and included in the ending inventory amount for a period, net income is overstated by exactly the amount of the understatement (less tax effects).

**Understating Accrued Liabilities.** Accrued liabilities that should be recorded at the end of an accounting period but are not can often add up to millions of dollars. Some of the common **accrued liabilities** are salaries payable, payroll taxes payable, rent payable, utilities payable, interest payable, and so forth. When these liabilities are not recorded or are understated, net income is usually overstated because the other (debit) side of an accrual entry is usually to an expense account. These types of financial statement frauds tend to be rather small, and they are easy to perpetrate and can result in misstated financial statements. For example, one company experienced a $2.1 million understatement of payroll taxes payable and a $1 million understatement of accrued salaries. In another fraud, the CFO failed to pay or recognize as liabilities various property and payroll taxes. Instead, he deposited the money in his own bank accounts. This nearly $10 million fraud was discovered when a state complained to the company that it had not been making payroll tax deposits. Although this particular fraud is more of an employee fraud than a financial statement fraud, it was large enough in this company to result in materially misstated financial statements.

**Recognizing Unearned Revenue (Liability) as Earned Revenue.** The third category of liabilities that can be understated (or overstated in the case of cookie jar reserves) is **unearned revenues**. Sometimes, cash is received prior to the performance of a service or the shipment of goods. Or a company may be in the business of requiring tenants or others to make deposits that can be intentionally recorded as revenue. When someone pays in advance of the performance of a service or the sale of a product, the entry recorded should recognize the cash received and a liability for the future service or product. Later, when the service is performed or the product is shipped, the liability should be eliminated and revenue should be recognized. A company that collects cash in advance and wants to understate liabilities can merely record revenues at the time cash is received, rather than later when the service is performed. Recognizing revenues instead of recording a liability has a positive effect on the reported financial statements, both because it understates liabilities and overstates revenues and net income, making the company look better. Similarly, if a company collects deposits that may have to be returned in the future and recognizes them as revenues, they are overstating revenues and understating liabilities. In one case, a company recorded $3 million of customer deposits as revenues, overstating net income by the full $3 million. The important point to remember about deferred revenue liabilities is that revenues should almost always be recorded as earned when the service is performed or the product is shipped. By manipulating the timing of revenue recognition, a company can easily either understate or overstate deferred revenue liabilities. To understand the motivation for these types of frauds, remember that stock prices are affected by both risk and return. A company that can report smoothly growing earnings may not have a higher cumulative return than a company whose earnings go up and down but its perceived risk will be much lower. As a result its stock price will be considerably higher. This motivation to smooth earnings or meet Wall Street's earnings forecasts has been the motivation for many frauds.

**Not Recording or Underrecording Future Obligations.** The fourth category, underrecording warranty or service obligations, is also a type of fraud that is easy to perpetrate and results in overstated net income and understated liabilities. For example, every time a large automobile manufacturer sells a car, it provides some kind of warranty agreement, such as three-year, 36,000-mile bumper-to-bumper coverage. According to the matching rule, the expense (and liability) that will be incurred to service these warranties must be recorded in the same period in which the automobiles are sold. A company can understate this warranty or service liability by not recording any liability or by recording an amount that is too low. Consider, for example, the case of a health spa chain, or any other company for that matter, that offers a money-back guarantee if you are not satisfied after 30 days. If revenue is recorded at the time customers enroll to be members, and an adequate expense is not estimated and recorded for customers who will demand their money back, liabilities can be significantly understated.

As an example, in the Lincoln Savings and Loan case, revenue was recognized on land sale transactions, even though hidden promises were made to buyers that Lincoln would buy the property back in two years at a higher price. According to Statement of Financial Accounting Standards No. 66, "Accounting for Sales of Real Estate," revenue should not have been recognized on these kinds of transactions. Similarly, in the ESM case, significant repurchase commitments were recorded, but were offset by fictitious receivables from an affiliated company that was not audited. In reality, the affiliated company had no assets, and the reported receivable was just a ruse to hide the fact that liabilities exceeded assets by approximately $400 million. The relevant financial statement footnote from the ESM fraud that explains these liabilities was as follows:

> *The Company entered into repurchase [liability] and resale [receivable] agreements with customers whereby specific securities are sold or purchased for short durations of time. These agreements cover securities, the rights to which are usually acquired through similar purchase/resale agreements. The company has agreements with an affiliated company for securities purchased under agreements to resell [receivables, meaning the company will get cash when it resells the securities] amounting to approximately $1,308,199,000 and securities sold under agreement to repurchase [liabilities] amounting to approximately $944,356,000 at December 31, 1983.*

The financial statements that were accompanied by this footnote reported that the total amount of repurchase and resell agreements were equal on the balance sheet. (This anomaly needed explanation itself. In how many financial statements are total receivables exactly equal to total liabilities for three consecutive years, as in this case?) Thus, when you combined the balance sheet numbers with this footnote, you could see that a net receivable from an affiliate was $363,843,000 ($1,308,199,000 – $944,356,000), and a net liability to third parties was the same amount. This net obligation (liability) to repurchase securities was being camouflaged by a fictitious receivable from a related entity.

Whether the obligation in the future is to service or provide warranty on a product, to repay a deposit, or to repurchase securities, the result is the same—understated liabilities. Cash must be spent or returned, service must be performed, or a product must be delivered at a future date.

## Not Recording or Underrecording Various Types of Debt

The limited partnership scenario discussed at the beginning of this chapter illustrated one way to understate debt—unauthorized borrowing against the equity in a company's assets. Other ways to underrecord these types of liabilities include the following:

- Either not reporting or underrecording debt to related parties
- Borrowing but not disclosing debt incurred on existing lines of credit.
- Not recording loans incurred
- Claiming that existing debt has been forgiven by creditors
- Claiming that debt on the company's books is personal debt of the owners or principals, rather than debt of the business

Consider the case of General Electrodynamics Corporation (GEC), for example. GEC manufactured hydraulic scales. In 1983, GEC was facing a probable fiscal-year loss of $5,307. Members of the company's management wrote off a $118,106 debt, an outstanding loan that began with a major supplier, recognizing the write-off as revenue. The company justified the revenue classification by claiming that the debt had been forgiven. The transaction converted the loss to a positive bottom-line profit of $112,853. Even though the debt had neither been forgiven by the supplier nor paid by the company, the managers wrote it off anyway. Auditors were neither able to confirm the transaction nor support it through alternative audit procedures. GEC's financial statements did discuss the (fraudulent) entry in their **footnotes** to the financial statements, and the auditors issued an unqualified opinion. When the fraud was discovered, the two managers defended their actions, stating "the vendor could not demand payment," because it never pressured GEC for the balance, and it continued to do business with GEC.

**Omission of Contingent Liabilities.** Statement of Financial Accounting Standards No. 5, "Accounting for Contingencies," requires contingent liabilities to be recorded as liabilities on the balance sheet if the likelihood of loss or payment is "probable." If likelihood of loss is reasonably possible, the **contingent liability** should be disclosed in the footnotes to the financial statements. If the probability of payment is "remote," no mention of the liability needs to be made in the financial statements. Contingent liabilities can be used to fraudulently misstate financial statements by underestimating the probability of occurrence and not recording or disclosing contingent liabilities in the financial statements. As an example, consider the case of Pfizer, Inc., a pharmaceutical company. In a civil case, plaintiffs alleged that Pfizer failed to disclose material information concerning the Shiley heart valve. This material information included the results of at least one product liability suit that Pfizer lost. Four years earlier, Pfizer reportedly knew that the Shiley heart valve was problematic, and it took the valve off the market. However, by that time, approximately 60,000 valves had been implanted. As of the date of the complaint, 389 fractures of the valve had been reported, and the FDA reported that 248 deaths had been attributed to failed Shiley values. Moreover, Pfizer maintained that surgery to replace the implanted valves would be more risky than leaving them in. Pfizer did not record a contingent liability for this potential liability.

## Detecting Understatement of Liability Fraud Symptoms

In discussing how liability-related frauds can be detected, we will only consider accounting/documentary and analytical symptoms because they are the most productive. As was the case with inventory and revenue frauds, we will not cover control symptoms in detail because they are adequately covered in other texts and standards. Lifestyle symptoms will also not be covered, except to note that in the case where principals use company assets to benefit themselves personally, the principals' lifestyles can exhibit symptoms of fraud. Behavior and tip symptoms for understatement of liability frauds are no different from other types of financial statement fraud and so will not be discussed further. Remember, however, that inconsistent, vague, or implausible responses or behavior by or from management or employees can represent fraud symptoms.

**Analytical Symptoms.** Analytical symptoms related to accounts payable understatements usually relate to reported balances that appear too low. They also include purchase or cost of goods sold numbers that appear too low, or purchase returns or purchase discounts that appear too high. Analytical symptoms related to unearned revenues involve reported payroll, payroll tax, rent, interest, utility, or other accrued liabilities that appear too low. Sometimes, income that is too "smooth" can also signal a fraud. Determination of whether these balances are "too low" is made by comparing the recorded amounts to balances in past periods, relationships with other accounts, and comparisons with balances in other related companies. Analytical symptoms for premature recognition of unearned revenues involve unearned liability account balances that appear too low and revenue accounts that appear too high. Significant judgment is needed, in most cases, to determine whether revenues are being recognized before they are earned, including examining terms of contracts, sales agreements, and other revenue-related documentation. Analytical symptoms for the under- or nonrecording of service warranties or other future commitments include balances in such accounts as warranty, repurchases, or deposits that appear too low. In many cases, the assessment about whether they are too low can be made by comparing them with other accounts (e.g., comparing warranties with sales). Analytical symptoms for unrecorded notes and mortgages payable include unreasonable relationships between interest expense and recorded liabilities, significant decreases in recorded debt, significant purchases of assets with no recorded debt, and recorded amounts of notes payable, mortgages payable, lease liabilities, **pension** liabilities, and other debts that appear to be too low. Finally, analytical symptoms are usually not particularly helpful in discovering contingent liabilities that should be recorded, because it is difficult to determine whether a contingent liability should be recorded and, if so, how much. Frequently, past amounts to make comparisons with or ways to identify an expectation against which the amount of a contingent liability should be recorded do not exist.

**Accounting or Documentary Symptoms.** Documentary symptoms involve such things as invoices being received but no liability recorded; large purchases recorded at the beginning of a period; large payments made in subsequent periods, backdated to the current period; the presence of receiving reports with no recorded liability; amounts listed on vendor statements but no recorded liability; and errors in cut-off tests. Documentary symptoms that relate to all kinds of understatement of liability fraud include the following:

- Photocopied purchase-related records where originals should exist
- Unusual discrepancies between the entity's records and confirmation replies
- Transactions not recorded in a complete or timely manner or improperly recorded as to amount
- Accounting period, classification, or entity policy; unsupported or unauthorized balances or transactions
- Last-minute adjustments by the entity that significantly affect financial results
- Missing documents; significant unexplained items on reconciliations
- Denied access to records, facilities, certain employees, customers, vendors, or others from whom audit evidence might be sought

Documentary symptoms can also relate to specific accounts. With payroll, for example, documentary symptoms might include employees with no withholdings, lack of payments to governmental entities, no accruals at year-end, payroll tax rates that are too low, fewer employees paid than are listed on the payroll records, and **capitalization** of employee wages as start-up or other deferred costs when they should be expensed. Documentary symptoms for understatement of interest might include, for example, existence of notes payable with no interest expense, bank confirmations indicating the existence of notes not recorded by the company, and interest expense deducted on tax returns but not recorded on the financial statements. Documentary symptoms include inconsistencies between revenue recognition criteria and timing specified in contracts and sales agreements, the method and timing with which revenues are recognized, large re-classification entries near the end of a period that result in increased revenues and lower liabilities, differences between confirmation balances and the amounts of revenue recognized by the company, lack of shipping documentation for recorded revenues, revenues recognized before customers are billed, and inconsistencies in the timing or method of recording liabilities.

Documentary symptoms related to the under- or nonrecording of service or other future obligations take the form of differences between the amount expensed as warranty or service costs and the amount that should have been expensed, based on sales contracts or sales agreements, differences between the way deposits are treated and the way they should be treated, differences in confirmations of **repurchase agreements**, deposit or other confirmed amounts and balances reported on the financial statements, and differences between what contracts say should be recorded as a liability and what the company is doing. Documentary symptoms for under- or nonrecording of liabilities include liabilities listed on bank confirmations but not recorded by the company, presence of unrecorded liens, differences between contract amounts and loans recorded, presence of interest expense with no recorded debt, writing off liabilities without payment of cash, significant purchases of assets without a comparable decrease in cash or increase in liabilities, and significant repayment of debt immediately prior to year-end, with new borrowing immediately after year-end.

Documentary symptoms provide the best opportunity to find contingent liabilities that should be recorded. Symptoms of possible underrecording include identification of lawsuits by attorneys, payments to attorneys without acknowledged litigation, mention of litigation in corporate minutes, correspondence with governmental agencies, such as the Environmental Protection Agency, or the Securities and Exchange Commission, significant payments to plaintiffs and others, filing of an 8-K with the SEC, withdrawal or issuance of an other-than-clean audit opinion by predecessor auditors, or correspondence from previous auditors, banks, regulators, or others.

## Proactively Searching for Symptoms Related to the Underreporting of Liabilities

In the limited partnership fraud discussed at the beginning of this chapter, the auditors found liens indicating that loans existed on properties for which there were not supposed to be any loans. Although dishonest bankers misled them, the auditors discovered the liens only because they were concerned that, under a triple-net lease arrangement, some lessees might be putting partnership properties at risk by not paying property taxes, utilities, and other expenses. In this case, a symptom of fraud was discovered by accident. Rather than wait for such accidents, proactively searching for fraud symptoms is much more effective.

As you will recall, proactive searching for analytical symptoms means that we are looking for accounts that appear too high or too low or that are unusual in some other way. As you learned in Chapter 12 in determining whether accounts are too high or too low, we look for changes and comparisons. Table 12-2 provided in Chapter 12 focused on understatement of liability schemes; it is reprinted here as Table 13-2.

### Table 13-2 Types of Financial Statement Analysis

| **Analyzing Financial Balances and Relationships Within Financial Statements** | Look for unusual changes in liability *balances* from period to period (trends) by (1) focusing on changes in the actual financial statement numbers, (2) studying the statement of cash flows, and (3) using horizontal analysis. | Look for unusual changes in *liability relationships* from period to period by (1) computing relevant ratios and examining changes in the ratios from period to period, and (2) using vertical analysis. |
| --- | --- | --- |
| **Comparing Financial Statement Amounts or Relationships with Nonfinancial Statement Information** | Compare financial results and trends of the company with those of similar firms in the same industry. | Compare recorded amounts in the financial statements with nonfinancial statement amounts. |

**Focusing on Changes in Recorded Balances from Period to Period.** When looking for liability balances that are too low, you must focus on all reported liabilities and liabilities that may not have been recorded. As noted in Table 13-2, you can focus on the changes in liability account balances by looking for changes in the actual numbers, by studying the statement of cash flows (which looks at actual change numbers but may not separately list every liability account), or by using horizontal analysis, which is our preferred method. In using these three methods to focus on changes in liability balances, you should compare balances over several years and pay special attention to liabilities that have been eliminated, significant changes in the write-down of long-term liabilities, accruals and service liabilities that have not been recorded or are recorded at significantly lower balances than in previous periods, and contingent liabilities that have been disclosed in the footnotes but may need to be recorded as liabilities in the financial statements. Using horizontal analysis, you can quickly examine the percentage changes in the liability accounts and determine if they are unusual. For example, an expert who was retained as a witness in the ESM fraud case performed a horizontal analysis on ESM's balance sheets and income statements. What he found was liability (and other) account balances that were changing by 400 percent, 1,700 percent, 250 percent, and so forth, which are large changes, especially in accounts that had large balances. His conclusion was that someone was manipulating the financial statements because the changes were too large to be believable. As it turned out, it was management that was manipulating the financial statements and plugging in numbers to make them balance.

When looking for changes in account balances, remember that every liability account is a candidate for fraud. Therefore, in analyzing the results of your horizontal analysis, you should look at each liability, consider the most common types of fraud exposures (those discussed in the first part of this chapter), and then look to see whether the kinds of changes are suggestive of that type of fraud. For example, if long-term notes payable changes from $2.1 million to $1.1 million and back to $2.1 million in three consecutive years, you might be concerned about year 2, especially considering the possibility that liabilities were paid off to be immediately restored after the end of the year. Similarly, if service or **warranty liabilities** decreased from $3.2 million to $2.2 million to $1.7 million at the same time total sales were increasing, you would probably be concerned that warranty liabilities were being significantly understated. Analytical symptoms only make sense when you follow the analytical process:

1. Ask what kind of fraud could be occurring.
2. Identify what symptoms those frauds would generate.
3. Determine whether those symptoms are being observed.
4. Follow up to determine whether what was observed is a symptom of fraud or an abnormality that is being caused by something else.

**Focusing on Changes in Relationships from Period to Period.** Focusing on changes in relationships to identify analytical fraud symptoms is one of the best ways to detect understatement of liability financial statement frauds. Some of the ratios that are most revealing in detecting liability fraud are listed in Table 13-3.

The second way to focus on financial statement relationships is to prepare common-size financial statements and perform vertical analysis. Using this approach, you compute each liability as a percent of total assets (or total liabilities and stockholders' equity) and then focus on the change in these percentages. In conducting this analysis, remember that large financial statement balances generally do not change much, while small liability balances may change significantly and be normal. Ask yourself why every major change is occurring, and whether you think it is unusual, given other changes in the financial statements. For example, purchasing significant amounts of fixed assets and not incurring additional long-term debt may be unusual, especially if the company does not have a large cash balance. Similarly, liabilities decreasing but interest expense increasing, or vice versa, would be rare.

**Comparing Financial Statement Information with That of Other Companies.** Generally, comparing a company's liability balances with those of other companies is not as useful as comparing revenues, accounts receivable, inventory, and other balances. A company can finance its operations in three different ways:

- Earnings
- Borrowing
- Owner (stockholder) investments

The amount of each of these financing methods used is usually a matter of management philosophy rather than industry norm. For example, in the computer industry, Hewlett-Packard (HP) has had little debt and financed its operations mostly from owner investments and earnings, while Texas Instruments has traditionally financed its business mostly through borrowing. The relationships between interest expense and debt, the amount of warranty expense as a percentage of sales, and other similar relationships can be compared across firms, however. You would probably be concerned if a company's warranty expense and liability were only 1 percent of sales, when all other companies in the same industry recorded warranty expense of 3 percent of sales.

## Table 13-3 Some Ratios Used in Detecting Fraud

| Type of Liability Fraud | Ratios to Examine |
|---|---|
| Underrecording accounts payable | 1. Acid-test ratio (quick assets/current liabilities)<br>2. Current ratio (current assets/current liabilities)<br>3. Accounts payable/Purchases<br>4. Accounts payable/Cost of goods sold<br>5. Accounts payable/Total liabilities<br>6. Accounts payable/Inventory<br><br>All of these ratios should be examined over time and changes observed. All the ratios focus on the reasonableness of the accounts payable balance relative to related account balances. Increases in the first two ratios and decreases in the last four ratios are most indicative of fraud. |
| Underrecording accrued liabilities, including salaries, payroll taxes, interest, and rent | 7. Various accruals/Number of days to accrue compared with same ratio in previous years<br>8. Various accruals/Related expenses<br><br>The amount to be accrued depends upon the length of time between the end of the accounting year and the last time expenses were recorded. You would probably be concerned about any lack of accruals or significant decreases in these ratios from previous years on a per-day basis. With certain accruals, you can examine the relationship between various expenses (e.g., payroll tax expense/salary expense) to see whether enough payroll taxes have been recorded. |
| Underrecording of unearned revenues (a liability) | 9. Unearned revenue/Revenue<br><br>It is difficult to find good ratios to search for unrecorded, unearned revenues. Generally to determine whether revenues have been recognized as earned when they are, in fact, unearned, you need to examine actual contracts and sales agreements to determine what services have to be performed or what products provided. |
| Underrecording of service (warranty) liabilities and other liabilities to perform something in the future (e.g., repurchase securities, repay deposits, etc.) | 10. Warranty expense/Sales<br><br>The amount of warranty or service expense and liability should relate directly with sales volume. Ratios that reveal that deposit, repurchase agreements, or other similar liabilities are understated are more difficult to find. |
| Underrecording of various liabilities (notes, mortgages, leases, pensions, etc.) | 11. Interest expense/Notes payable<br>12. Long-term debt/Stockholders' equity<br>13. Various types of debt/Total assets<br>14. Total liabilities/Total assets<br>15. Pension expense/Salary expense<br>16. Lease expense/Total fixed assets<br><br>In thinking about the kinds of ratios to examine, you need to focus on each individual liability on the balance sheet. The question you should always ask is "What should this liability balance relate to, and has that relationship changed over time? If so, why?" |
| Not recording contingent liabilities | Generally, no ratios reveal contingent liabilities that should be recorded have been recorded. Generally, you will have to look for documentary symptoms to find unrecorded or undisclosed contingent liabilities. |

**Comparing Financial Statement Amounts with Assets They Are Supposed to Represent or with Nonfinancial Statement Factors.** Because most liabilities do not represent specific assets, comparing liability balances with nonfinancial statement amounts is usually difficult. The notable exception, of course, is mortgage liabilities, which are loans that are secured with specific assets. You can examine assets on which **mortgages** are incurred. Eliminating a mortgage payable or finding no mortgages on new buildings (when the company practice is to mortgage all buildings) are fraud symptoms that should be investigated.

**Actively Searching for Accounting and Documentary Symptoms.** Documentary symptoms can be helpful in detecting understatement of liability financial statement frauds. The specific documentary symptoms you search for vary according to the liability that is understated. Table 13-4 summarizes some of the most common kinds of documentary symptoms by type of liability. In most cases, queries can be designed, using either commercial packages, such as ACL, or tailored queries, to search for these symptoms.

## Table 13-4 Documentary Symptoms of Fraud

| Types of Liability Understatement | Symptoms to Actively Search For |
|---|---|
| Accounts Payable | 1. Payments made in subsequent period for liabilities that existed at the balance sheet date and were not recorded.<br>2. More inventory counted than identified through purchasing and inventory records.<br>3. Receiving reports near the end of a period, without corresponding purchase invoices.<br>4. Amounts listed on vendor statements not recorded as purchases.<br>5. Differences on confirmations not easily reconciled with purchase records.<br>6. Discrepancies in cut-off tests. |
| Accrued Liabilities | 7. 1099s with no withholdings, where withholdings should exist.<br>8. Employees with no withholdings.<br>9. Vendor statements (utilities, etc.) where no liability is recorded.<br>10. Loans with no interest.<br>11. Leased buildings with no rent or lease expense. |
| Unearned Revenues | 12. Reclassification entries near the end of the period that increase earned revenues and decrease unearned revenues.<br>13. Differences between customer confirmations and company records about how much revenue has been earned. |
| Service (Warranty) Liabilities, Deposits, Repurchase Agreements—Obligations to Perform Services, Deliver Products, or Return Money in the Future | 14. Inconsistencies in customer agreements or contracts and recording of expenses.<br>15. Differences in customer confirmations regarding client obligations (e.g., repurchase agreements, etc.).<br>16. Warranty payments that exceed warranty liabilities.<br>17. Deposits recognized as revenues. |
| Liabilities to Pay Money (Notes Payable, Mortgage Payable, Pension Liabilities, Lease Liabilities, etc.) | 18. Liens on properties that are supposed to be paid for.<br>19. Approval of loans by board of directors but not listed as liabilities.<br>20. Loans listed by banks on bank confirmations but not recorded by company.<br>21. Lack of pension accrual.<br>22. Lease payments with no lease liability.<br>23. Conservative assumptions used to calculate pension liability.<br>24. Unusually large credits on bank statements. |
| Contingent Liabilities | 25. Discussion of contingent liabilities in board minutes.<br>26. Contingencies discussed in footnotes.<br>27. Significant payments to lawyers.<br>28. Lawsuits brought to your attention for the first time in attorney letters.<br>29. Letters from regulators, such as OSHA, EPA, SEC, etc. |

Because of the many different types of liabilities and so many different ways in which they can be understated, following up on symptoms observed is important. Companies that are in trouble have a strong motivation to understate liabilities. Sometimes the understatements are small, but sometimes they are large (e.g., $350 million in the ESM case).

Because understated liabilities may involve only one or two omitted transactions, unusual revelations, such as surprise liens, surprise loan contracts, written-off debt, and surprise debt on bank confirmations, must be followed up carefully. In many cases, management will offer alternative explanations, such as the lien or contract is a mistake, it is personal debt, or it is a line of credit never activated. With respect to liabilities, you make sure that management's explanations are true, and support the explanations with corroborating evidence to the extent deemed necessary under the circumstances.

Before leaving understatement of liability fraud, it is important to note that finding understated liabilities is one of the most difficult frauds to find. In some cases, the understated liabilities are with accounts, vendors, or lenders with whom the company has no other business or has a reported zero balance at the time. Searching for unrecorded liabilities by examining board minutes, examining bank and vendor confirmations, and even letters from attorneys is sometimes fruitful. And, anytime any evidence (such as a tip) emerges that indicates a liability might exist, it should be vigorously pursued. In many ways, finding unrecorded liability frauds is the same as finding off-book frauds. No evidence of the fraud exists in the books of the company. Asset or revenue frauds, on the other hand, are often easier to detect because they involve reported assets that can be examined.

# Overstatement of Asset Fraud

Assets can be overstated in many ways, which means the **overstatement of asset fraud** can occur in many ways. Impaired assets whose value has deteriorated may not be written down or off as they should be; expenditures that should be expensed could be capitalized as assets; assets could not be properly depreciated or amortized; or reported asset values may be too high for other reasons. Most nonfinancial assets are typically carried on the books at historical cost, less accumulated depreciation. Asset-value should be written down, and a corresponding expense or loss recorded if the asset is impaired. GAAP includes different impairment standards for different types of assets. If the permanently impaired asset values are not written down, the company's expenses or losses will be understated and net income overstated.

As an example of failure to record asset impairment, consider the case of New Jersey Resources Corporation (NJR). NJR, an energy company, allegedly failed to recognize an impairment of the carrying value of its oil and gas properties resulting in an overstatement of the company's net income by $6.3 million. And, as already discussed, Waste Management used a non-GAAP method of capitalizing interest on landfill development costs (thus recognizing assets that should have been expenses) and made repeated fourth quarter adjustments to improperly reduce depreciation expenses on its equipment cumulatively from the beginning of the year, thus overstating its landfills and other assets.

## Identifying Asset Overstatement Fraud

Most organizations have several different types of assets on their balance sheets. The Waste Management was an alleged example of the overstatement of tangible assets. As was the case with liabilities, different assets can be overstated in different ways. Figure 13-1 identifies the five most common types of assets that are overstated.

**Improper Capitalization of Costs as Assets That Should Be Expensed in the Current Period.** Even though most financial statement frauds occur in smaller, less-established companies, CPAs must also be alert to the symptoms of financial statement fraud when auditing large, well-established companies. Many of these companies are not very old, and, in many cases, are not very profitable. In trying to make their financial statements look better, a way to overstate assets is to capitalize as **intangible assets** such things as start-up or preoperation costs, advertising costs, research and development, marketing costs, and certain salaries and other initial costs. Managements of these companies often argue that they are in the start-up

# Figure 13-1 Common Types of Asset Overstatement

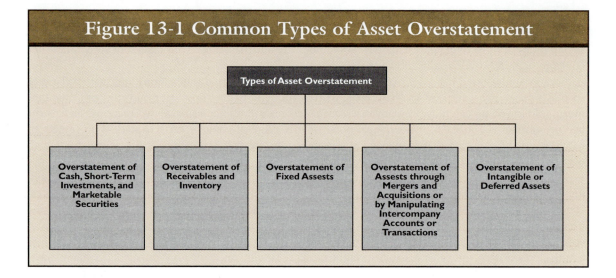

Types of Asset Overstatement

| Overstatement of Cash, Short-Term Investments, and Marketable Securities | Overstatement of Receivables and Inventory | Overstatement of Fixed Assets | Overstatement of Assests through Mergers and Acquisitions or by Manipulating Intercompany Accounts or Transactions | Overstatement of Intangible or Deferred Assets |

or development phase and therefore these costs must be capitalized as deferred charges and written off against profitable operations in the future. In some cases, these deferred charges are justified; in other cases, they are clearly fraudulent. The question of whether these types of costs should be capitalized is usually one of whether the costs are being incurred to generate future revenues and whether sufficient future revenues are likely to be generated, against which the costs can be written off. Consider the following cases where litigation or SEC action took place.[2]

Computer Science Corporation (CSC) developed and sold computer-related services known as proprietary systems, one of which is known as "Computicket" (CT). Marx, an investor, availed himself of financial data of CSC. That financial data explained CSC's policy regarding capitalizing development expenses. The policy, in part, stated that CSC would initially capitalize development expenses rather than treat them as charges against current income. When a system (such as CT) became fully operational (defined as generating revenue in excess of expenses), CSC would begin to amortize the capitalized expenses over a specified period of time, presumably over the revenue-generating time period. At one point, CSC had approximately $6.8 million in capitalized costs for CT. In a registration statement filed with the SEC, CSC stated that it expected to begin amortizing CT's capitalized expenses later.

From its inception, CT had not met internal projections for market capture. CT supposedly experienced problems getting equipment installed, and it had been running deficits of $500,000 per month. In addition, CT lost one of its major contracts. Moreover, CSC had attempted, without success, to sell CT proprietary packages to various prospects for differing amounts. In October and November, CSC had gone so far as to discuss the abandonment of CT. The inference was clear: the likelihood of CT's commercial success became progressively more doubtful with the passage of time.

Marx sued CSC for violations of SEC Rule 10b-5. The court in *Marx v. Computer Sciences Corporation*, 507 F.2d. 485, stated that the failure to disclose facts indicating that CT was in serious financial trouble was an omission "to state a material fact necessary, in order to make the statements not misleading."

Another case of improperly capitalizing costs as assets is Livent, Inc. The SEC charged Livent, a theatrical entertainment company, with fraudulently capitalizing preproduction costs by transferring them to fixed asset (rather than expense) accounts. The SEC alleged that Livent also deferred expenses by transferring expenses from current productions to shows that had not yet opened or that had longer amortization periods, thus leaving them on the books as assets when they should have been written off.

In most cases, the fraudulent capitalization of deferred charges that should be expensed does not occur all at once. Rather, it starts with the recording of some deferred charges that are appropriate or, at worst, questionable, and then progresses to where management is capitalizing costs that could not even remotely be considered worthy of being capitalized. Many times, capitalizing deferred charges, like other types of financial statement fraud, is like starting down a slippery slope—it is hard to stop, especially if the organization needs profits, and the further down the slope you get, the easier it is to justify capitalizing costs that are not appropriate.

Capitalizing costs that should be expensed has the effect of increasing net income by the same amount of the capitalized costs, because expenses that should be deducted from revenues are not deducted until the future periods in which they are amortized. In many cases, these illicit capitalized costs are not written off for many years into the future.

We conclude our discussion in this section by considering the most prominent example of a company improperly capitalizing expenditures—WorldCom. In its amended complaint against WorldCom, the SEC alleged that WorldCom overstated the income reported in its financial statements by approximately $9 billion. One way that WorldCom allegedly accomplished this overstatement was to reduce improperly its operating expenses by recharacterizing certain expenses as capital assets. Specifically, senior officials at the company directed accounting managers to transfer certain "line costs" and "computer costs" (which should have been reported as current operating expenses) to its capital asset accounts. This transfer caused the company to materially understate expenses and overstate net income, which allowed the company to report earnings that were in line with analysts' estimates.

**Inflated Assets Through Mergers and Acquisitions (or Restructuring) or by Manipulating Intercompany Accounts or Transactions.** In several financial statement fraud cases, companies involved in **mergers** or **acquisitions** overstated their assets (or overstated their liabilities by creating cookie jar reserves as discussed earlier), either by inappropriately using market values instead of book values, by having the wrong entity act as the purchaser of the other entity, through improperly allocating book values to assets (e.g., assigning higher book values to assets that will be amortized or depreciated over longer periods or not depreciated at all, and lower values to assets that will be amortized or depreciated over shorter periods), or through other means. In fact, Warren Buffet, chairman of Berkshire Hathaway and world famous investor, included the following comments in his March 1999 letter to his company's shareholders:

> *Many managements purposefully work at manipulating numbers and deceiving investors when it comes to mergers and big restructurings…. During mergers, major auditing firms sometimes point out the possibilities for a little accounting magic (or a lot). (http://www.berkshirehathaway.com/1998ar/1998final.html)*

As an example of financial statement fraud associated with a merger, consider the case of Malibu Capital Corporation.

> *For at least three and a half years, Lehman, Lucchesi & Walker (LLW) served as the auditors for Malibu Capital Corporation. Malibu subsequently merged with Colstar Petroleum Corporation. Prior to the combination with Colstar, Malibu supposedly had no business purpose other than to merge with or acquire one or a small number of private companies. LLW gave Malibu an unqualified opinion on the financial statements. These statements identified Colstar as the "acquired corporation." The combination was treated as a "purchase" of Colstar by Malibu, and Colstar's primary asset was adjusted up from $11,055 to $1,342,600.*
>
> *Under generally accepted accounting principles, the combination should have been treated as a "reverse purchase" with Colstar as the "acquiring corporation" with no adjustment to Colstar's assets. As a result of the improper accounting treatment, Malibu allegedly overstated its assets 102 times.*

In this case, the asset was written up by having the wrong entity act as the purchaser. In another case, Chester Holdings Ltd., assets were overstated a mergers by overstating the fair value of the assets. The SEC alleged that officers and directors of Chester Holdings overstated the value of consideration paid for five acquisitions of assets and businesses and overstated the value of assets acquired in the company's financial statements. For example, the officers claimed that the company acquired a knitting company for $14 million in stock when the fair value of the assets was worth no more than $4.9 million. This case shows that in any instances of a revaluation of assets or a merger of two companies, the values used may not be appropriate, especially when the companies merging are related parties, when companies are struggling, or when they have a strong incentive to report profits.

In addition to merger-related problems, fraud is sometimes perpetrated by manipulating intercompany accounts or transactions. As an example, consider the AFCO fraud, which involved the manipulation of intercompany transactions to make the company appear more profitable than it really was.

*AFCO started as a medical-dental equipment leasing business. One owner was a former insurance salesman, and the other was two years out of law school. The company was mildly successful during its first two years. Several new branches were formed, including a land development company. The land development company purchased 1,000 acres of undeveloped property in Sardine Canyon in northern Utah and began to develop an "old English" family resort called Sherwood Hills. The resort was intended to include summer and winter sports, making it a year-round enterprise. Although it was reasonably popular in the summer, the heavy winter snows and poor accessibility made it an unappealing winter resort. To raise money for additional development and marketing efforts, limited partnerships were sold, mostly to physicians and dentists.*

*Other AFCO projects included a shopping center, apartment complexes, a medical center, and a 700-acre site in West Jordan, Utah. This development, known as Glenmoor Village, was touted as Utah's biggest real estate development. It was to include 1,400 homes in a totally planned community, an 18-hole golf course, and equestrian facilities.*

*As with Sherwood Hills, development of Glenmoor Village was extremely expensive. Maintenance of a positive cash flow depended on lot sales, but sales were slow because the area lacked essential services, such as roads and utilities. AFCO had borrowed heavily to make these investments, but only 400 of the 1,400 lots were sold. Residents complained that promised improvements were never made.*

*Because of severe cash shortages and an inability to obtain additional bank financing, AFCO turned to middle-class homeowners to fund the company. The company's salespeople would contact friends, acquaintances, and referrals and would offer them opportunities to invest. Using elaborate flip charts and relying on the reputation of other investors, salespeople persuaded homeowners to allow the company to borrow on the equity in their homes. If homeowners would allow a second mortgage, AFCO would service the second mortgage and pay the homeowner an additional 10 percent on the money used. Because second mortgage rates were approximately 20 percent, AFCO was, in effect, offering nearly 30 percent for the money. AFCO was very accommodating: if a homeowner did not want the return in cash, it would lease a BMW or a Mercedes for the homeowner and service the lease.*

*Although the investment sounded legitimate, returns to be made to homeowners were based on inflated financial statements and empty promises. The investment was nothing more than another Ponzi scheme. Early investors were paid the 10 percent returns from subsequent investments, and the second mortgage payments were never paid. The assistant U.S. attorney in the district of Utah called the president of AFCO "one of the most ruthless swindlers seen in these parts in years." He sweet-talked about 650 people, many of them business people, into investing some $70 million in his schemes. He later declared bankruptcy, foreclosing his investors' chances of getting their money back.*

In getting people to invest in AFCO, owners of the company used fraudulently prepared financial statements to make the company look better than it really was. The financial statements used by the company and restated as they should have been are shown in Figure 13-2:

## Figure 13-2 AFCO Financial Statements

**AFCO**
**Balance Sheet, Statement of Income, and Retained Earnings**

| | Originally Issued | Restated |
|---|---|---|
| **Assets** | | |
| Current assets: | | |
| Cash | $ 1,299 | $ 1,299 |
| Current portion of contract receivable | 276,084 | 0 |
| Interest receivable | 124,197 | 0 |
| Total current assets | 401,580 | 1,299 |
| Contact receivable long-term portion | $ 8,373,916 | 0 |
| Investment property: | | |
| Real estate Jackson Village (at market) | $ 10,832,480 | |
| Real estate Mountainland Hills | 1,800,000 | ? |
| | $ 12,623,480 | ? |
| Total assets | $ 21,398,480 | $ 1,299+? |
| | | |
| **Liabilities and stockholders' equity** | | |
| Current liabilities: | | |
| Accounts payable to related parties | $ 27,000 | $ 27,000 |
| Accrued Interest | 176,965 | 176,965 |
| Current portion of long-term debt | 902,944 | 902,944 |
| Total current liabilities | $ 1,106,909 | $ 1,106,909 |
| Long-term debt less current portion | $ 12,781,668 | $ 12,781,688 |
| Deferred income taxes | $ 3,041,729 | $ 3,041,729 |
| Contingencies | | |
| Stockholders' equity: | | |
| Common stock, par value $1.00, authorized 50,000 shares; issued and outstanding, 1,000 shares | $ 1,000 | $ 1,000 |
| Appraisal increase | 1,663,606 | 0 |
| Retained earnings | 2,804,044 | ? |
| | $ 4,468,650 | |
| | $ 21,398,976 | |
| | | |
| Gain on sales of Mountain Hills | $ 4,887,000 | 0 |
| Interest income | 324,197 | 0 |
| Total income | $ 5,211,197 | |
| Interest expense | $ 627,796 | $ 627,796 |
| General and administrative expenses | 27,190 | 27,190 |
| | $ 654,986 | $ 654,986 |
| Income before income taxes | $ 4,556,211 | $ (654,986) |
| Provision for federal and state income taxes | 2,258,855 | 0 |
| Net income | $ 2,297,356 | $ (654,986) |

In this case, the outside CPA firm issued an adverse opinion because some of the assets on AFCO's financial statements had been stated at fair market value instead of at cost and because a large portion of AFCO's assets were comprised of a receivable and interest due from the sale of property to a related party. Because of the related-party nature of the sale, the CPA firm could not determine whether the transaction was arm's-length.

In AFCO's case, the adverse opinion was a significant warning signal that something was wrong. As it turned out, the sale of land to the related company, the income from this sale, the receivable arising from that transaction, and the interest on the receivable were all misstatements that resulted from a phantom transaction. When the phantom sale and its impacts were subtracted from AFCO's balance sheet, all that remained was $1,299 in cash and some real estate whose cost financial statement readers could not evaluate because it was recorded at market value. Total assets were far less than the $21 million represented by the company.

**Overstatement of Fixed Assets (Property, Plant, and Equipment).** Fixed assets can be overstated in many ways. Some of the most common are leaving worthless or expired assets on the books (not writing them off), underreporting depreciation expense (e.g., Waste Management), overstating residual values, recording fixed assets at inflated values (sometimes through sham or related-party purchases), or just fabricating fixed assets to record on the financial statements. One company, for example, recorded assets on its balance sheet at their "estimated fair market value" when, in fact, the assets had been fully depreciated in prior years. In another case, the management of a company recorded a large asset called "refunds forthcoming" for worker's compensation reimbursements, for which they had no assurance that they would ever be reimbursed. In still another case, a health provider collected large sums of overpayments by customers and classified the overpayments as assets, even though they were legally obligated to return the overpayments.

Sometimes these asset overstatements become quite significant. The March 17, 1999, issue of *The Wall Street Journal*, for example, carried an article titled "Audit Showing Baby Bells Can't Locate $5 Billion in Gear Could Spur Rate Cuts." This article described how the Baby Bell companies (e.g., Bell Atlantic Corp., SBC Communications, Inc., Nynex Telephone Company, Southern Bell Telephone, and Bell South) could not locate $5 billion in telecommunications and other equipment that they were carrying on their balance sheets as assets. Whether these companies committed fraud is a question that would have to be investigated, but the article reported how a Federal Communications Commission (FCC) audit of these companies could not find nearly one-tenth of the equipment it surveyed and was recommending that the assets be written off.

As an example of overstatement of asset fraud, consider the following case example:

> One of the major types of frauds perpetrated by Lincoln Savings and Loan involved purchasing property at inflated amounts and then reselling the property at even higher amounts to "straw buyers." This "land flipping" resulted in overstated assets on the balance sheet and unrealistically high profits when the land was "sold." Many of these kinds of transactions took place at Lincoln, and most of them happened on or near the end of quarters so that reported quarterly income would be positive. One was the "Continental Ranch" transaction. In this case, Lincoln purchased land at arguably inflated prices and recorded the asset on its financial statements. Then, on September 30, 1986, when Lincoln was desperate for profits, it sold 1,300 acres of the ranch to R.A. Homes (a straw buyer) for $25 million, including $5 million in cash and a $20 million note receivable. What was not easily detectable by the auditors and others was that a related entity loaned R.A. Homes $3 million on September 25, 1986, and another $2 million on November 12, 1986. In essence, Lincoln "paid the down payment to itself." This transaction, like so many others in the company, had the intermediate effect of allowing inflated land values to be reported on the balance sheet, and the end effect of reporting high profits on the transaction and overstated accounts receivable.

A final way to overstate fixed assets is to underrecord depreciation expense. This type of underrecording can be done by using asset lives that are too long, allocating too much cost in a basket purchase of land and building to land that is not depreciated, using salvage values that are too high, failing to make the accrual entries for depreciation, or reversing the accrual entries as Waste Management did.

**Cash and Short-Term Investment (Including Marketable Securities) Fraud.** In several famous cases, **marketable securities** were materially overstated, but it is generally quite hard to overstate cash because cash balances can be easily confirmed with banks and other financial institutions. Sometimes cash that is restricted and can't be spent is shown as unrestricted on the balance sheet. (In most cases, restricted cash should be shown as a long-term asset.) What is more common with respect to cash is to have employees or vendors steal cash of a significant enough magnitude to result in misstated financial statements without management's knowledge. For example, consider the following four cases: a reasonably small thrift institution where a vice president embezzled several million dollars over a period of 16 years; a small, five-branch bank where a proof operator embezzled $7 million over 8 years; General Motors, where one car dealer embezzled $436 million; and a large international financial institution where a rogue trader lost $2.8

billion of his company's cash. These large cash thefts resulted in financial statement fraud of a different type than we have been discussing in this book—financial statement misstatement without management's knowledge.

Compared to cash, management can usually overstate marketable securities more easily, especially securities that are not widely traded. What many people do not realize is that the term *publicly traded* means more than just companies whose securities are traded on the New York Stock Exchange, the American Stock Exchange, and NASDAQ. Many smaller, over-the-counter stocks are traded only rarely and are not actively listed by even over-the-counter stock exchanges, but whose stock prices are circulated among brokers by such means as "pink sheets." These pink sheets are distributed daily to brokers and listing dealers who might be willing to buy and sell through other methods. Putting a market value on many of these securities is often difficult (and placing a market value on securities that are not publicly traded is even more difficult), and once in a while, dishonest management will materially overstate the security's value. As an example, one well-known fraud case involving sham transactions between the company and related parties, materially overvalued securities listed as current assets on the balance sheet. Another case involved a minority investment in another company that was being carried at several million dollars when, in fact, the company invested in had a negative stockholders' equity and had losses of several million dollar in each of the preceding five years. The securities should have been written off because the investment was basically worthless.

Another way both assets and liabilities can be manipulated is to either keep liabilities off the balance sheet or transfer troubled assets off the balance sheet in an SPE or other entity and record an investment or receivable from that entity. In many cases, this method is what Enron used. Using off-balance sheet special-purpose entities (SPEs), it hid both hid liabilities and structured transactions to hide or record false profits on the sale of worthless assets. The SEC alleged that members of Enron's management engaged in a complex scheme to create an appearance that certain entities that they funded and controlled were independent of the company, allowing the company to incorrectly move its interest in these companies off its balance sheet. The SEC alleged that these entities were designed to improve the company's financial results, and to misappropriate millions of dollars represented by undisclosed fees and other illegal profits.

Another large case involving only off-balance sheet assets was PNC Financial Services Group, Inc. This case was the SEC's first enforcement action resulting from a company's accounting for and disclosure of off-balance sheet arrangements involving SPEs in its filings and press releases. The SEC found that, in violation of GAAP, PNC transferred from its financial statements approximately $762 million of volatile, troubled or underperforming loans (assets for a financial institution) and venture capital assets to three SPEs created by a third-party financial institution in the second, third, and fourth quarters of 2001, which results in material overstatements of PNC's earnings, among other things. The SEC's order stated that PNC should have consolidated those SPEs into its financial statements because it retained the risks and rewards of ownership.

Finally, a well-known case of off balance-sheet loans was Adelphia Corporation. The SEC alleged that Adelphia failed to record more than $2.3 billion in bank debt by deliberately shifting those liabilities onto books of Adelphia's off-balance sheet, unconsolidated affiliates. Adelphia's senior management disguised the liabilities by creating sham transactions backed by fictitious documents that gave the false impression that Adelphia had actually repaid the notes.

**Overstatement of Accounts Receivable (Not Related to Revenue Recognition) or Inventory (Not Related to Cost of Goods Sold).** In Chapter 12, we discussed the inflation of accounts receivable in conjunction with the recording of fictitious revenues and the overstatement of inventory in conjunction with the understatement of cost of goods sold. Sometimes, however, accounts receivable or inventory can be overstated in an attempt to overstate assets and cover thefts of cash rather than to overstate reported income. That was the case with ESM, where management had stolen approximately $350 million and covered the theft by creating a fictitious receivable from a related entity. In the Phar-Mor case, one of the reasons inventory was overstated was to offset cash that Micky Monus had taken out of the business to support his now-defunct World Basketball League.

**Summary of Overstatement of Asset Fraud Exposures.** Let's now summarize the various types of asset overstatement fraud schemes discussed thus far. Although certainly not exhaustive, Table 13-5 identifies some of the most common methods used.

## Table 13-5 Frauds Involving Overstatement of Assets

| Kind of Asset Overstatement | Accounts Involved | Fraud Schemes |
|---|---|---|
| Improper capitalization of costs as assets that should be expensed | Various deferred charge and intangible assets accounts | 1. Inappropriately capitalizing as assets various kinds of start-up costs, marketing costs, salaries, research and development costs, and other such expenditures. |
| Inflating assets through mergers, acquisitions, and restructuring or through manipulation of intercompany accounts and transactions | Can be any asset | 2. Using market values rather than book values to record assets. <br> 3. Having the wrong entity be the "purchaser." <br> 4. Allocating costs among assets in inappropriate ways. <br> 5. Recording fictitious assets or inflating the value of assets in intercompany accounts or transactions. |
| Overstating fixed assets | Land, buildings, equipment, leasehold improvements, and so forth | 6. Sham purchases and sales of assets with "straw buyers." <br> 7. Overstating asset costs with related parties. <br> 8. Not recording depreciation. <br> 9. Collusion with outside parties to overstate assets (e.g., allocating inventory costs to fixed assets). |
| Misstating cash and marketable securities | Cash, marketable securities, and other short-term assets | 10. Misstating marketable securities with the aid of related parties. <br> 11. Misappropriation of cash resulting in misstated financial statements without management's knowledge. |
| Overstating accounts receivable or inventory to hide thefts of cash by management | Accounts receivable, inventory | 12. Covering thefts of cash or other assets by overstating receivables or inventory. |

## Identifying and Actively Searching for Asset Overstatement Fraud Symptoms

In many ways, the methods used to discover overstated assets are quite similar to those used to detect understated liabilities. That is, often just one or two large fictitious accounting entries, rather than a series of smaller entries, result in asset overstatement. In some ways, however, asset overstatements are often easier to detect than other types of financial statement fraud because the overstated assets are always included on the balance sheet, whereas understated liabilities are not on the financial statement. Fraud investigators can start their detection process by examining the assets that make up the reported amounts, determining whether they really exist and whether they are listed in the appropriate amounts and periods.

In the following paragraphs, we organize our discussion of asset overstatement fraud according to the five types of asset overstatement discussed earlier. Because the various types of asset overstatements are quite different, we discuss both the relevant symptoms and how to actively search for those symptoms. Although this approach is different from the method used in previous sections, it is more efficient, given the differing nature of the assets involved. Once again, we will not separately discuss control, lifestyle, behavioral, or tips and complaint symptoms for each category of asset overstatement because, for the most part, they are not unique to asset overstatement schemes. Rather, we will discuss separately only analytical and documentary symptoms and then discuss other symptoms where appropriate. As is always the case, this emphasis does not mean that these other types of symptoms are not important. In fact, in some cases, they are the best type of fraud symptoms. However, they are generally more generic and can be symptomatic of many different types of fraud, not just asset overstatement.

**Inappropriately Capitalizing Costs as Assets That Should Be Expensed.** Before discussing specific analytical and documentary symptoms related to inappropriately capitalizing costs as assets, we will discuss some general characteristics of these types of assets. In identifying symptoms, the first thing you must ask is whether these types of deferred charges exist on the balance sheet. In many companies, they do not. When they do exist, you should always consider them candidates for fraud and then convince yourself that their capitalization is appropriate, rather than assuming that they are appropriate and then determining whether they are fraudulent. This more skeptical approach is often justified because of the "intangible" nature of these assets and the ease with which they can be abused. Questions you should ask include the following:

1. Do the deferred charges have future benefits that are specifically identifiable?
2. Is it likely that the company will earn sufficient future revenues and profits against which the costs can be specifically written off, and if so, when?
3. Are the deferred charges the types that could be acceptable under GAAP (in most cases, for example, research and development costs are not) and are capitalized by other similar companies?
4. Are the incentives strong for management to manage earnings or "find profits" in this company?
5. Are the deferred charges or intangible assets properly valued? What is the basis of the evaluations?

**Analytical Fraud Symptoms.** In most cases, analytical symptoms relate to the size of the deferred charges on the balance sheet relative to prior periods and to other similar companies or whether the same types of assets exist at all at other companies. You should be concerned, for example, if deferred charges make up a major portion of a company's total assets. Other analytical symptoms might include the size of various deferred charges (e.g., advertising costs) compared to the amount of advertising or other expenses on the income statement. You would probably be less concerned with a company that capitalizes only a small part of its advertising costs than you would with a company that capitalizes all of its advertising costs.

As stated earlier, the four kinds of analysis that can be used in searching for analytical fraud symptoms are:

1. Comparing changes and trends in financial statement account balances.
2. Comparing changes and trends in financial statement relationships.
3. Comparing financial statement balances with nonfinancial statement information or things, such as the assets they represent.
4. Comparing financial statement balances and policies with those used by other similar companies.

In thinking about which of these kinds of analysis would be most helpful in determining whether costs have been improperly capitalized, nonfinancial statement "things" can probably be associated with only a few deferred charge financial statement numbers. The one notable exception is, of course, if a company is making acquisitions of additional entities or entering new ventures, you might expect additional capitalization of deferred charges. So you could look to determine whether any significant events have occurred for which it would make sense to capitalize certain kinds of expenditures. When looking at trends in account balances, you would probably be quite concerned, for example, if the amount of deferred charges increased substantially without the occurrence of significant events that might trigger such capitalization. In addition, you would normally expect more capitalization in the early years of a business's life than in later years, and so it would be unusual for the balance in the deferred charge accounts to increase as the company became more mature. If anything, you would expect that the amortization of such costs would cause the deferred charge balances to decrease.

Examining changes in account balances may provide limited information, but you would almost always want to examine changes in the deferred charge financial statement relationships from period to period. You would probably also want to compare the financial statement amounts and capitalization policies with those of other, similar companies. Some of the most appropriate financial statement relationships on which to focus are the following:

- Total deferred charges/Total assets
- Total deferred charges/Total intangible assets
- Deferred charge write-offs (amortization)/Deferred charge balance

Through examining these and other similar ratios over time, you could quickly determine whether deferred charges are increasing as a percentage of total assets or total intangible assets, and what percentage of deferred charges are being written off or amortized each year.

One of the best ways to detect inappropriate capitalization of costs is by making comparisons with other, similar companies. If your client is the only firm that is capitalizing certain kinds of expenditures as deferred charges, you should probably be skeptical of the practice. If a company is capitalizing certain costs while other, similar firms are expensing them in the current period, you should ask yourself, "What is unique about my client that makes capitalizing more appropriate for them than for the other companies?" If you cannot arrive at a clear, defensible answer to that question, you should probably recognize that your client's reported income is inflated over the income of other similar firms.

**Accounting or Documentary Symptoms.** As was the case with other types of frauds, documentary symptoms are of two types: (1) general symptoms that could relate to all asset overstatement schemes, or most financial statement fraud schemes for that matter, and (2) documentary symptoms that relate to improper capitalization of costs as assets that should be expensed in the current period. Some of the general asset overstatement symptoms will be presented here, and then not repeated for other asset overstatement schemes:

- Asset-related transactions not recorded in a complete or timely manner or improperly recorded as to amount, accounting period, classification, or entity policy
- Unsupported or unauthorized asset-related balances or transactions
- Last-minute asset adjustments that significantly improve financial results
- Missing documents related to assets
- Unavailability of other than photocopied documents to support asset transactions when documents in original form are supposed to exist
- Asset-related ledgers that do not balance
- Unusual discrepancies between the entity's asset-related records and corroborating evidence or management explanations

Documentary symptoms specifically related to capitalization of costs as assets that should be expensed might include invoices from related parties that could misstate the nature of expenses, year-end reclassifications or journal entries that reduce recorded expenses and increase recorded deferred charges, and differences between the way costs are described on invoices and the way they are recorded in the accounting records.

In many cases, examining the kinds of exposures and motivations may reveal an incentive to overstate assets, which may be more important than searching for specific documentary or analytical symptoms. For example, management is more likely to stretch what they consider to be appropriate accounting when strong management incentives to show profits are present, when the organization is new or is in an industry where capitalization may or may not be appropriate, or where financial results and operating characteristics could potentially motivate misstatement. In one case, for example, a firm capitalized significant amounts of costs as assets, while other firms in the same industry expensed similar expenditures. After lengthy litigation, it was determined that the capitalization was improper and that the company should have been using the same accounting methods as its competitors.

**Overstating Assets Through Mergers, Acquisitions, or Restructurings or Manipulating Intercompany Accounts or Transactions.** As was the case with improper capitalization, understanding the general context of a merger or an intercompany transaction may be more important in determining whether fraud exists than trying to identify specific analytical or documentary symptoms. For example, when you are concerned about overstatement of assets through a merger, you should ask yourself if the accounts used by the merged companies are appropriate; if the way the merger was recorded is appropriate, given the nature of the companies involved; if the after-merger book values are higher or lower than the pre-merger amounts and, if so, why; what motivated the merger; and whether the appropriate company was the purchaser or the company purchased. Again, with mergers, acquisitions, and restructurings, understanding management and its motivations, the nature of the companies involved, whether the merged companies were related parties, and what financial results or operating characteristics could have motivated the merger are important. For example, several companies, including Cendant and Kimberly-Clark, supposedly entered into mergers in order to create huge merger reserves that could be later reversed into income to create better post-merger reported results. The SEC accused Kimberly-Clark of improperly accounting for merger-related restructuring reserves. The company took a $1.44 billion charge in relation to an acquisition. Periodic reevaluations of its reserve balance determined that the original estimate for certain of its merger-related reserves was too high. Instead of reducing the reserve as required by GAAP, the company reallocated excess amounts to other merger-related programs or to new programs. The company also allegedly released into earnings certain amounts of its merger-related reserves without adequate support. Good fraud detection efforts require that examiners always look at how reserve accruals were subsequently used. Were they used in the way they were established to be used? If not, were excess reserves handled according to GAAP?

**Analytical Fraud Symptoms.** Analytical fraud symptoms are usually not especially helpful in determining asset overstatements related to mergers or restructurings. With analytical symptoms, you are comparing trends and changes. When a merger or other change in the form of a business entity occurs, you have a new, reformatted entity that has no history. As a result, you usually cannot look for either changes in financial statement account balances or financial statement relationships. The one exception that may be helpful sometimes is to compare various asset ratios for the individual companies prior to the merger and the combined company after the merger. By looking at such asset ratios as total intangible assets divided by total assets, total fixed assets divided by total assets, and total current assets divided by total assets, you can quickly get an idea of how the structure of the companies has changed. You would probably be concerned, for example, if total intangible assets as a percentage of total assets increased from an average of 10 percent in the two previous companies to 40 percent of total assets in the combined company, especially if the transaction were handled as a business combination (pooling) rather than a purchase.

Comparing the recorded post-merger assets with the actual assets they are supposed to represent is often helpful. If reported asset values increased substantially, for example, you should check to see that the assets are not listed on the balance sheet at amounts that exceed their fair market values. Generally, when mergers occur, finding similar companies against which the financial statement balances of your company can be compared is difficult.

**Accounting or Documentary Symptoms.** When a merger occurs, one of the first steps should be to make sure that the accounting methods used were appropriate and consistent with accounting standards. After that, you can examine the specific merger or intercompany transactions to make sure that both the types of transactions and the amounts make sense. If, for example, a merger or intercompany transaction was between related parties, you should probably make sure that the amounts used (such as market values of assets) are appropriate. Finding inconsistencies between appraised and recorded amounts for assets is an excellent documentary fraud symptom. Similarly, if more of the post-merger assets have longer amortization or depreciation periods than the assets of previous companies, you should probably examine them more closely. In one company, for example, the post-merger asset values were significantly inflated over the same assets in the pre-merger companies. Upon further analysis, investigators determined that the lesser-known merged company did not really exist. It was a fabricated company set up to make the financial statements look better "through a merger."

### Overstatement of Fixed Assets (Property, Plant, and Equipment).

Overstated fixed assets generally get on the financial statements in one of three ways:

1. Inflated amounts are recorded in non-arm's-length purchase transactions.
2. Assets are not written down to their appropriate book, market, or residual values because insufficient depreciation is recorded, they are obsolete, or their values are otherwise impaired.
3. Assets that simply do not exist are fictitiously recorded in financial statement accounts.

In the Penn Central fraud case, railroad cars that had been abandoned in old mine shafts for many years were still being carried on the balance sheet at significant book values. These "assets" had been abandoned and could not have been recovered even if the company had wanted to, because in many cases, the railroad tracks that led to the mineshafts had been removed, and the railroad ties had been sold to landscaping companies. Similarly, in another case, an oil company reported significant amounts for several fixed assets, including a refinery that was no longer in use and oil reserves that were in the ground.

### Analytical Symptoms.

All four types of analysis can be performed to determine whether fixed assets are overstated. Horizontal analysis, analysis of the statement of cash flows, or comparisons of account balances from period to period can be used to determine how much individual fixed asset account balances have changed. Unrealistically large changes in land, property, equipment, or other fixed asset account balances could indicate that fraud is occurring. Fixed asset relationships can also be examined by computing ratios such as the following:

- Total fixed assets/Total assets
- Individual fixed asset account balances/Total fixed assets
- Total fixed assets/Long-term debt
- Depreciation expense for various categories of assets/Assets being depreciated
- Accumulated depreciation/Depreciable assets (per asset category)

The first two ratios provide evidence about whether fixed asset balances are reasonable relative to other asset balances. The third ratio identifies the relationship between debt and fixed assets, providing a measure of solvency. If fixed assets increase significantly while long-term debt does not, a fraud problem may exist, especially if evidence that cash, marketable securities, or other assets used to purchase the fixed assets is not present. The last two ratios examine whether fixed assets are being adequately depreciated.

Vertical analysis over several periods can also be used to determine the percentage changes in financial statement balances and relationships over time. You might be concerned, for example, if fixed assets increased from 50 percent of total assets to 70 percent of total assets at a time when the revenues of the company had not increased much.

Because fixed assets have tangible existence, you can compare the financial statement balances with the actual assets to determine whether the recorded amounts represent assets that actually exist and are recorded in approximately the appropriate amounts. Even though you may not know how much complicated or company-specific assets should cost or be valued on the books, many different types of analysis can be made. For example, if you were concerned about a retail company such as Sears or Wal-Mart, you could compute total assets on a per-store basis and see how that amount changed over time. You would not expect too much of a per-store change, unless the companies started building larger superstores, for example. You can also ask questions, such as "Does it make sense that this type of company would have these types of assets, would have assets in these locations, or would have increased assets so much without significant changes in the structure of the company?"

Finally, comparing total fixed assets or fixed assets as a percentage of total assets with other similar companies is always helpful in determining whether a company's recorded asset totals are reasonable. For example, suppose that you compared two automobile manufacturing companies. If one had $50 of fixed assets for every $1 of sales while the other had $100 of fixed assets for every $1 of sales, you should ask "Why?" Perhaps the first company is that much more efficient, the second company has just spent millions renovating its manufacturing facilities, the second company's fixed assets are newer and less depreciated, or the second company is overstating its assets and committing fraud—all are alternatives that you should consider. Another analytical test that is often helpful is to determine the percentage of a class of asset costs that are being depreciated each year (a measure of depreciable life). If one company depreciates its assets over 10 years while another similar company used 20-year asset lives, you should probably ask why.

**Accounting or Documentary Symptoms.** Overstating fixed assets by recording inflated amounts usually occurs with transactions between related parties. Therefore, determining whether large purchases of fixed assets are arm's-length transactions or are purchases from related entities is important. If the vendor or provider of the assets is a related party, you need to determine why the company bought the assets from that entity and whether the amounts recorded are reasonable. You should ask the following types of questions:

- Were there appraisals of purchased fixed assets?
- Were the purchase transactions recorded near the end of the year?
- Did the transaction(s) involve exchanges of assets or a purchase of assets?
- Are the assets purchased the kinds of assets this company would normally purchase, or are they tangential to the business?
- Are there inconsistencies in the documentation for the transactions?
- Are the assets recorded on the books of your client at the same or lower amounts than they were on the seller's books?

**Overstatement of Cash and Short-Term Investments (Including Marketable Securities).** As stated earlier, the management of a company usually has difficulty overstating cash by an amount significant enough to materially impact the financial statements. Two reasons explain why. First, corroborating recorded amounts of cash is usually quite easy by confirming bank and financial institution balances. If cash frauds are going to be concealed on bank confirmations, they usually require the collusive efforts of outsiders, which is quite rare. Second, the amount of cash that a company has is usually small relative to the amounts of receivables, inventory, or fixed assets. What does happen quite often, though, is that an employee, customer, or someone else steals enough cash from a company to materially and adversely affect the financial statements.

**Analytical Symptoms.** For both cash and marketable securities, it is usually helpful to perform all four types of analysis. Recorded amounts of individual categories of cash and marketable securities can be examined over time to detect any unrealistic changes. Usually, if marketable securities increase, then cash should decrease by a similar amount, because the cash was probably used to purchase the marketable securities (unless debt was used or some other asset was traded for the securities). Various types of relationships can also be examined over time, using overhead analysis or the following ratios. These ratios help you understand whether the relationship between cash and marketable securities is reasonable in relation to total current assets or total assets.

- Current ratio: Current assets/Current liabilities
- Quick ratio: Current assets (inventory and prepaids)/Current liabilities
- Current assets/Total assets
- Marketable securities/Total current assets
- Cash/Total current assets

Because cash balances can be confirmed, recorded amounts of cash can usually be compared with non-financial statement information or assets. Banks provide an independent verification that the recorded amounts are appropriate. With marketable securities, you can confirm the market values and amounts with brokers or by checking the financial pages of newspapers. Comparing cash and marketable security balances with those of similar companies is usually not helpful. Even similar companies often have significantly different amounts of cash and marketable securities because they have different plans and different spending patterns. In determining whether recorded amounts of cash and marketable securities are reasonable, you should always ask questions such as, "Does it makes sense for the company to have the amount of cash or marketable securities it has?" If the balances are high, the reason for the large balances should be plausible because, in many cases, having large amounts of cash on hand does not make sense.

**Accounting or Documentary Symptoms.** The best accounting symptoms for discovering cash or marketable security over- or understatements are usually differences between recorded amounts and amounts confirmed with banks, brokers, and other independent parties. You might also be concerned if it makes sense for the company to have physical possession of marketable security certificates and they do not; or if they should have bank statements or bank reconciliations and they do not; or if they have bank statements that cannot be reconciled. You would also be concerned if banks used by the company are off-shore, are in other locations, or have other specific characteristics that do not make business sense. These, together with the more generic documentary symptoms discussed earlier, can help you determine whether financial statement fraud is occurring.

**Overstatement of Receivables or Inventory (Not Revenue- or Cost of Goods Sold-Related).** Almost always, when accounts receivable are overstated, revenues are overstated. Similarly, when inventory is overstated, the cost of goods sold is usually understated. Once in a while, however, inventory or accounts receivable (or other assets) are overstated to conceal large thefts of cash or other assets. As stated earlier, much of the Phar-Mor inventory overstatement was used to conceal large thefts of cash by Micky Monus. Similarly, accounts receivable were overstated by about $350 million in the ESM case to hide the fact that the three principals had embezzled approximately $350 million from customers.

# Inadequate Disclosure Fraud

The final type of financial statement fraud we will discuss is inadequate disclosure fraud.

   **Inadequate disclosure fraud** involves the issuance of fraudulent or misleading statements or press releases without financial statement line-item effects. That is, somewhere in its annual report or through press releases or other media, management makes statements that are wrong but do not impact the numbers in the financial statements. Disclosure fraud can also include statements that should have been, but were not, made by management (misleading because of what is not said—fraud by omission).

   As as example, the SEC recently alleged that a private manager of elementary and secondary public schools, Edison Schools Inc., failed to disclose significant information regarding its business operations. The SEC alleged that Edison failed to disclose that a substantial portion of its reported revenues consisted of payments that never reached Edison. These funds were instead expended by school districts (Edison's clients) to pay teacher salaries and other costs of operating schools that were managed by Edison. The SEC did not find that Edison's revenue recognition practices contravened GAAP or that earnings were misstated. However, the SEC nonetheless found that Edison committed violations by failing to provide accurate disclosure in the MD&A section in their filings. The MD&A section is supposed to discuss the company's financial conditions and results of operations to enhance investor understanding of financial statements. During the period 1997 to 2002, the SEC had 43 of these types of enforcement matters.

   Because no financial statement impact occurs with inadequate disclosure fraud, it does not make sense that analytical symptoms would be present, where either you are examining trends and changes in financial statement balances or relationships or you are comparing financial statement balances with nonfinancial statement factors or with financial statement balances of other companies. Documentary symptoms may be present, depending on the type of nonfinancial statement misstatement.

   Because of the different nature of disclosure frauds, we will first categorize disclosure frauds and then introduce you to some disclosure frauds in each category. From these examples, we identify the kinds of symptoms that are available for detecting disclosure frauds. Because misleading disclosures can relate to anything, disclosure symptoms generally vary from fraud to fraud. As a result, drawing symptom generalizations is difficult.

One thing you should remember is that fraud exposures are relevant to disclosure-type frauds. Managements of companies rarely make willful misstatements if they have no significant pressures or opportunities to do so. Therefore, when you observe management, the organizational structure, the relationships with other parties, or operating characteristic exposures, you should increase your level of skepticism, not only about the numbers in the financial statements, but also about the disclosures and representations that are being made by management throughout the annual report or in other information.

## Kinds of Disclosure Fraud

Disclosure frauds can be easily categorized into three different groups:

1. Overall misrepresentations about the nature of the company or its products, usually made through news reports, interviews, annual reports, and elsewhere.
2. Misrepresentations in the Management Discussions and Analysis (MD&A), such as Edison Schools Inc., or in other nonfinancial statement sections of annual reports, 10-Ks, 10-Qs, and other reports.
3. Misrepresentations and omissions in the footnotes to the financial statements, such as the failure to disclose related-party transactions.

**Misrepresentations About the Overall Nature of the Company or Its Products.** Quite often, the business press reports on a company or organization that has completely misrepresented what it is about or makes misleading claims about the nature of its products. The following two companies are examples of this type of fraud.

They called it the "dog-and-pony" show. A "prospect" would be brought to Comparator Systems, a tiny Los Angeles-based company that, in June 1996, was accused of securities fraud by the Securities and Exchange Commission. On a table would be a small machine, a fingerprint identification device that Comparator says could help the world stop imposters and make investors who bought its penny-priced shares rich. Imagine, a technology that would one day let businesses and governments quickly and affordably verify that people are who they claim to be. Robert Reed Rogers, the chairman and CEO, would practice the art of telepathically "beaming" confidence. The company's small band of employees, who might not have been paid in months, would wear their most respectable outfits. Then Comparator executives would demonstrate the technology, sometimes using a machine that the SEC says was stolen from Scottish inventors. These demonstrations were part of one of the largest stock market scandals of the 1990s. The SEC says Comparator was telling a convincing story about a phony product, and turning that story into money through stock sales.

Comparator is a story of how a company snagged investors from Middle America and the hallowed halls of Harvard to rising business districts in Malaysia. It is also a tale of how a company with allegedly worthless assets, a product it did not own, a 29-person payroll it had not met for 11 of 13 years, and a stock market value of $40 million became worth $1 billion in three days of frenzied stock trading in May 1996 on the NASDAQ stock market. The stock of this virtually unknown company was the most active ever on NASDAQ, rising from 6 cents a share to $2 a share in three days. Its stock accounted for one-fourth of the NASDAQ trading volume during those three days. In the end, it turned out that Comparator was an imposter—the same kind of imposter its "technology" was supposed to detect.

In 1997, Bre-X Minerals, which we discussed in Chapter 11, became the center of a Canadian fraud investigation. Bre-X claimed that it discovered as much as 71 million ounces of gold, worth $21 billion, in Indonesian Borneo. The hype surrounding Bre-X transformed the tiny Calgary, Alberta-based firm over three years into a company with a $4.5 billion market value. The stock's run-up transformed its executives into millionaires. The "gold discovery" now appears to have been faked by adding outside gold to samples taken from the Busang site in Borneo. Industry experts say that it would have been almost impossible for the scam to exist and management not to know about it, given the extent of the fraud. Bre-X's stock was traded in Toronto and Montreal and on NASDAQ in the United States. The stock's price plummeted 80 percent in one day when the fraud was discovered. After the discovery, Bre-X said that the company was pulling out of the Busang project.

Comparator and Bre-X are examples of companies that misrepresented themselves or their products. Apparently, Comparator never had a state-of-the-art fingerprinting machine that could distinguish imposters from real people. Nor did Bre-X have a mine in Borneo containing 71 million ounces of gold. Yet, combined, these companies cost investors hundreds of millions of dollars and had an aggregate market value of nearly $6 billion. These companies are certainly not alone. Many others have claimed to be something they were not. These types of misrepresentations are the worst types of disclosure fraud, because they are "imposters." They are no different from a person who enters a bank, claims to be a certain bank customer, and withdraws money from that customer's account using fictitious or stolen identification.

**Misrepresentations in Management Discussions and Other Nonfinancial Information in Financial Reports.** In recent years, a company's annual report has become as much a public relations document as it is a report of financial condition and operations. Most annual reports include various statements by management, including management's "discussion and analysis," historical performance charts, announcements of new products and strategic directions, and plans and goals for the future. Sometimes, management's statements included in the annual report contain false disclosures and outright lies. Other times, management fails to make disclosures that are necessary to help investors and creditors understand what is really going on. Consider, for example, the following company:

> *E.F. Hutton Group, Inc., allegedly developed a cash management system for moving customer funds received by Hutton branch offices through bank accounts maintained at regional offices and ultimately to Hutton's corporate bank accounts located in New York City and Los Angeles. The system required the branch offices to calculate the daily net activity in their branch accounts, and then to remove from the accounts all funds in excess of the required compensating balances. On certain days, the branches were alleged to have overdrafted their bank accounts to offset excess collected on other days. If, on the day after a branch overdrafted its bank account, insufficient funds were collected from customers to cover the overdraft, or if a delay occurred in the check clearing process, the branch was to deposit a "branch reimbursement check" in the branch bank account to make up the difference. Branch reimbursement checks were drawn on zero balance checking accounts that were funded at the end of each day. Certain members of the senior management of Hutton supposedly encouraged greater use of the draw- down procedures, which increased the interest income and reduced the interest expense of Hutton. Net interest income was significant in Hutton's financial statements. Hutton allegedly failed to disclose in its management discussion and analysis that the increased use of the overdrafting practices was a material cause of the significant increase in net interest income. The complaint also alleged that Hutton's management discussion and analysis failed to disclose that the reduced use of the bank overdrafting practices the next year was a material cause of the significant decrease in Hutton's net interest income that year.*

In Hutton's case, the company materially changed the nature of its operations, making as much money from using bank floats and kiting as from selling securities. In this case, the management discussion and analysis section of the annual report should have described these events. As you can see from this example, fraudulent financial reporting can occur as much from failure to disclose as it can from disclosing misleading information.

**Misleading Footnote Disclosures.** The third type of disclosure fraud involves misleading footnote disclosures or the omission of key or required disclosures. A company's footnotes should provide relevant disclosures necessary to help investors and creditors understand the financial statements and make investment and credit decisions. Sometimes, disclosures that should be made in the footnotes are missing, and other times the disclosures that are included are misleading. Many of these misleading disclosures affect financial statement balances, but some do not. In this section, we will focus only on those that have no financial statement impact.

Probably the most frequent type of footnote disclosure fraud is not disclosing transactions with related parties. Auditors and others are required by both GAAP and GAAS to look closely at related-party transactions, and often management believes it can avoid such scrutiny if it does not reveal that related parties exist.

A recent example of failing to disclose related-party transactions was Adelphia Corporation. The SEC alleged that Adelphia engaged in numerous undisclosed related-party transactions with board members, executive officers and entities they controlled. These transactions resulted in the channeling of company funds and stock into entitties controlled by senior management, the payment for timber rights that reverted to senior management, the construction of a golf course on land owned or controlled by senior management, and the payment of personal loans. The SEC alleged that Adelphia failed to disclose the existence of these transactions or misrepresented their terms in its financial statements. More than $300 million of company funds were diverted to senior management without adequate disclosure to investors. On June 25, 2002, Adelphia and certain of its subsidiaries filed for bankruptcy. The executive officers were also handcuffed and hauled off to jail. At the time of writing of this book, the criminal trial for the Rigas family members, the executives of the company, was going on.

Rite Aid was another company that failed to disclose related-party transactions. At Rite Aid, the CEO sought to enrich himself at the expense of shareholders by failing to disclose both his personal interest in leased property for Rite Aid store locations and several transactions where he funneled $2.6 million from Rite Aid to a partnership that he and a relative controlled.

Other frequent types of disclosure fraud include the following:

- Failing to disclose contingent liabilities that are reasonably possible or probable and that would create a loss for the company
- Failing to disclose contractual obligations, including restrictions on specific assets or liabilities
- Incorrectly disclosing contingent gains that are probably not going to occur
- Failing to disclose information regarding loans to creditors
- Inadequately disclosing significant accounting policies
- Inadequately disclosing information about market value declines of assets, including marketable securities
- Inadequately disclosing information about pension or other long-term liabilities
- Lack of disclosure of significant events

Of course, to be fraud, the lack of disclosure or misleading disclosures must be intentional. As an example of this type of fraud, consider the case of Centennial Savings and Loan.

> *Centennial Savings and Loan began in the mid-1970s with about $18 million in assets. The company eventually increased those assets to a supposed $408 million before the fraud was discovered. In 1985, examiners began to discover discrepancies within the company's financial statements. In January 1986, the FBI began to investigate Centennial. Among other illegal acts and fraud, Centennial had conspired with executives of other savings and loans to create loans for former Centennial officials. These loans violated federal regulations that prevent thrifts from making more than $100,000 in unsecured loans to affiliated persons. Executives of Centennial also received and paid kickbacks to help these loans go through. In addition, the company was involved in suspicious joint ventures with other savings and loans that were highly speculative. They also engaged in various real estate deals that significantly overstated asset values. None of this information was ever disclosed in the footnotes to the financial statements. The related-party nature of the loans to former Centennial officers was never disclosed (probably because the loans were illegal). Also, the related-party transactions of the questionable joint ventures with other savings and loans were not disclosed.*

In this case, financial statement fraud involved not disclosing related-party transactions, among other things. In other fraud cases, disclosures about asset impairment, contingent liabilities, and significant events were either missing or misleading. Sometimes, as was the case with the ESM footnote disclosure discussed earlier, information about fraud that is occurring is actually provided in the footnotes, but is concealed in a way so that most readers would not detect it.

## Detecting Inadequate Disclosure Fraud

Detecting inadequate disclosure fraud is not as easy as detecting the other types of fraud. In fact, without a tip or complaint, it is difficult to know that disclosure fraud is occurring. It is usually easier to detect inadequate disclosure fraud that involves misleading disclosures than it is to detect disclosure fraud that involves missing disclosures. Also, the kinds of symptoms you look for are different, depending upon the kind of disclosure fraud you are concerned about. With overall misrepresentation of a company or its products, it is necessary to look for symptoms related to the nature of the company, its assets and organization, its management, and its operating characteristics. With disclosure fraud relating to the nonfinancial statement part of annual reports or in the footnotes to the financial statements, you look for different kinds of symptoms. In the two sections that follow, we discuss symptoms related first to overall misrepresentation and then to footnote and annual report disclosure-type fraud.

## Symptoms Related to Overall Misrepresentation About the Company or Its Assets

Taking a broad view, the kinds of symptoms you look for to find frauds such as those of Comparator and Bre-X are similar to the kinds of symptoms you search for when looking for investment scams and Ponzi schemes. As another example, recall the AFCO case discussed previously.

   To help you discover whether companies like AFCO, Comparator, or Bre-X are fraudulent, you will want to understand the client's financial situation, financial goals and objectives, and risk tolerance. You will also want to look out for companies that have unrealistically large growth in assets, revenues, or profits, companies that have a short history, involve unknown management, or have other characteristics that would make their performance or representations look suspicious. In addition, the following list of questions should prove useful in helping you identify whether a company and its products are legitimate:

- Does the company's performance make sense when compared with the performance of other similar companies?
- Is the company cash poor? Is it desperate for investors to put money into it immediately?
- Does the success of the company depend on a special tax loophole or tax avoidance scheme?
- Is there anything that cannot be fully disclosed because it is one of the company's unique reasons for success?
- Is the business new in town?
- What is the background of the principals? Where do they come from, and what were their operations in previous locations?
- Have any of the principals been involved in bankruptcy or scandals before?
- Are the appraisal figures and financial claims provided by the company's representatives true?
- Does the company's success depend on kickbacks, complicated marketing schemes, special concessions to those who have money, or unwritten deals that cannot be talked about because of domestic or foreign laws?
- Are the company's financial reports audited? If so, for how many years? What type of audit opinion did they receive?
- Does the company's success depend on someone's "unique expertise" (such as an uncanny ability to predict commodity prices or unusually good salesmanship) for financial success?
- What would happen if one person's special skills were removed from the company?
- Is the company making guaranteed promises? Can the promises be verified?
- Does the company's success depend on high financial leverage?
- Would investors be liable if the company's debts were not paid?
- Are the principals in the business living "high on the hog," even though the business is relatively new?
- Is the company's stock listed on a national exchange? If so, which one, and what has been its history on that exchange?
- What is the nature of the company and its board of directors? Does the company have an audit committee or internal auditors?
- Is the company's success based on a recent announcement of a major success or discovery? If so, have independent sources confirmed the truthfulness of the announcements?

In the Comparator case, for example, Comparator compiled bad debts in approximately 27 cases, owing $478,554 in principal and accrued interest from final court judgments, according to the company's last 10-K report to the SEC. Another eight cases, worth $300,000, were in dispute. The company's bad debts included rent owed for three different Los Angeles area offices. The company used stock to pay veterinarian, dental, and legal bills. The CEO, Robert Reed Rogers, distributed shares of stock like water. Rogers, himself, was past president of several companies that had previous brushes with the law. In one, his company claimed to have "exclusive right" to certain mining processes for producing jewelry. In another, a bench warrant was issued for his arrest for failure to appear in court in connection with a lawsuit filed by investors. As the general partner of a health care company, Rogers and his partners were sued and had judgments against them. Comparator was also late with, and did not make, some filings to the SEC. In fact, dealers stopped trading Comparator stock, and the company was dropped from newspaper stock listings and from the public's eyes for a while. One investor who looked at the company called the company's balance sheet "puff" and "inflated," because it included worthless patents and other assets.

Another example of misrepresentation came to light when a professor received a call from a fellow professor at another university, who asked him about a company his university was investing in. The professor making the call was suspicious, because the company was making claims that if his university and other universities and not-for-profit groups invested their endowments in the company, they would double their endowments in a year or less. The company had a wealthy investor who would match the amount the university invested. The more this faculty member described the company, the more it sounded like a classic Ponzi scheme. After listening for about 30 minutes, the professor who called concluded by stating that "I do not know whether this company is fraudulent. However, I have always believed if something crawled like a snake, looked like a snake, and acted like a snake, it was probably a snake." He told the caller that the company had all the characteristics of a "snake," or an investment scam. The calling professor investigated the company and discovered the now famous "New Era" fraud.

## Disclosure Fraud Related to Financial Reports and Financial Statement Footnotes

Several fraud examination techniques can be used to detect inadequate disclosures. First, you should look for inconsistencies between disclosures and information in the financial statements and other information available. Second, you should make inquiries of management and other personnel concerning related-party transactions, contingent liabilities, and contractual obligations. These inquiries should be made at several levels of management and be done separately and judiciously. Inquiries should also be made about different accounting policies that management is aware of. Even though some of these inquiries may be routine or involve basic questions, differences in responses could tip you off that management is engaging in fraudulent activities.

Another way to identify inadequate disclosures, especially concerning related parties, is to review the company's files and records with the SEC and other regulatory agencies concerning names of officers and directors who occupy management or directorship positions in other companies. It would be possible, given the number and kinds of databases available today, to search for common ownership and directorship interests. If you suspect something may be awry, you can use databases such as Lexis-Nexis to perform background searches on key individuals. Other good places to look for inadequate disclosures is in the board of directors minutes, correspondence and invoices from attorneys, confirmations with banks and others, contracts, loan agreements, loan guarantees, leases, correspondence from taxing and regulatory authorities, pension plan documents, sales agreements, and any type of legal document.

In many cases of disclosure fraud, financial statement auditors have actually "had their hands on the fraud" but did not recognize it for what it was. To detect disclosure fraud and all types of financial statement fraud, auditors and others realize that such things as inconsistencies between financial statements and other information, for example, represent a fraud symptom and not just a mistake or an error that someone made. If something does not look right, is not consistent with GAAP, or has other characteristics that make you uncomfortable, you should not be satisfied with management explaining away the problem. Detecting fraud requires you to look beyond transactions, documents, and other information and ask yourself what possible explanations exist for its occurrence or for it being reported or represented the way it is.

These days acquiring answers to questions you have about business relationships, management backgrounds, and other information from publicly available sources is not difficult. If something looks suspicious or questionable, look for ways to research the issue or gather independent evidence, rather than just accept management representations. If members of management will commit financial statement fraud, they will certainly lie to you.

# Other Types of Financial Statement Fraud

Obviously, we have not covered all types of financial statement fraud. We covered those types that are most common. Before we conclude this final chapter on financial statement fraud, we introduce you to some of the less common types of financial statement frauds.

## Inappropriate Accounting for Nonmonetary Transactions

Most business transactions involve exchanges of cash or other monetary assets or incurrence of liabilities for goods or services. The amount of monetary assets exchanged or liabilities incurred generally provides an objective basis for measuring the cost of nonmonetary assets or services received by an enterprise as well as for measuring gain or loss on nonmonetary assets transferred from an enterprise. Exchanges that involve little or no monetary assets or liabilities are referred to as nonmonetary transactions. In general, under GAAP, accounting for nonmonetary transactions should be based on the fair value of the assets (or services) involved, which is the same basis as that used in monetary transactions.

An example of this type of fraud was Critical Path, Inc. The SEC found that Critical Path improperly reported as revenue several transactions, the largest of which was a barter transaction. In this transaction, a software company agreed to buy out a periodic royalty obligation for $2.8 million and buy another $240,000 of software, in exchange for Critical Path's agreement to buy approximately $4 million of software services from the software company. The SEC alleged that Critical Path recorded a $3.09 million sale to the software company improperly as revenue for the third quarter. The company failed to establish the fair value of either the software it received from, or the software it sent to, the software company. Furthermore, the SEC found that Critical Path did not ensure that the value ascribed to the software Critical Path received reasonably reflected its expected use of the software as required under GAAP. The company restated its financial statements to correct this problem.

## Inappropriate Accounting for Roundtrip Transactions

During the past few years, the SEC has brought enforcement actions against companies that engaged in improper accounting through the use of "roundtrip transactions." These transactions involved simultaneous prearranged sales transactions often of the same product in order to create a false impression of business activity and revenue. The SEC had 19 of these types of enforcement actions during the five-year period 1997–2002. An example was Homestore.com Inc. where the SEC charged three former executives of Homestore with arranging fraudulent roundtrip transactions for the sole purpose of artificially inflating Homestore's revenues in order to exceed Wall Street analysts' expectations. The essence of these transactions was a circular flow of money by which Homestore recognized its own cash as revenue. Specifically, the Commission alleged that Homestore paid inflated sums to various vendors for services or products; in turn, the vendors used these funds to buy advertising from two media companies. The media companies then bought advertising from Homestore either on their own behalf or as agents for other advertisers. Homestore recorded the funds it received from the media companies as revenue in its financial statements, in violation of GAAP. Global Crossing and WorldCom also engaged in these types of transactions.

## Improper Accounting for Foreign Payments in Violation of the Foreign Corrupt Practices Act (FCPA)

The FCPA was passed in 1977 to combat corrupt business practices such as bribery. Some FCPA cases (which are also frauds) also involve the improper accounting by companies for payments to foreign government officials. BellSouth and IBM were two companies that had such transactions. The SEC alleged that BellSouth violated the FCPA by authorizing payments to local officials through their subsidiaries in Venezuela and Nicaragua. Senior management at BellSouth's Venezuelan subsidiary allegedly authorized more than $10 million in payments to six offshore companies, which were improperly recorded as bona fide services. In addition, the SEC alleged that management at the Nicaraguan subsidiary authorized payments, recorded as "consulting services," to the wife of a Nicaraguan legislator who presided over a hearing that allowed BellSouth to increase its ownership interest in its Nicaraguan subsidiary.

IBM had a $250 million contract to integrate and modernize the computer system of a commercial bank owned by the Argentine government. IBM-Argentina allegedly entered into a subcontract with an Argentine corporation for $22 million, which funneled approximately $4.5 million of these funds to several directors of the government-owned commercial bank. IBM recorded the expenses as third-party subcontractor expenses. IBM-Argentina's former senior management overrode IBM's procurement and contracting procedures and hid the details from financial personnel. Management provided the procurement department with fabricated documentation and stated inaccurate and incomplete reasons for hiring the Argentine corporation.

## Improper Use of Non-GAAP Financial Measures

When improperly used, non-GAAP financial measures that include or exclude unusual expenses or gains may provide a misleading financial picture. The SEC recently issued a cautionary release on non-GAAP financial measures and brought two antifraud enforcement actions in this area. The two enforcement actions involved Trump Hotels and Casino Resorts, Inc., and Ashford.com, Inc. The SEC alleged that Trump Hotels issued a press release announcing positive results for its third quarter earnings using a pro forma net income figure that differed from net income calculated in conformity with GAAP. Although the release expressly stated the results excluded a one-time charge, it failed to disclose the inclusion of a one-time gain of $17.2 million. The release created a misleading impression that the company had exceeded earnings expectations when actual net earnings were lower than the same quarter of the previous year and the company had in fact failed to meet analysts' expectations.

Ashford misstated its pro forma results by improperly deferring $1.5 million in expenses under a contract with Amazon.com. The SEC also alleged that Ashford.com incorrectly classified certain marketing expense as depreciation and amortization expenses that materially understated the company's true marketing expenses. In addition, because Ashford allegedly excluded depreciation and amortization from its non-GAAP financial results, Ashford's expense misclassification improved its non-GAAP financial results. In its year-end 10-K, the company reclassified the expenses in question.

## Improper Use of Off-Balance Sheet Arrangements

Off-balance sheet arrangements often are used to provide financing, liquidity, market, or credit risk support or to engaged in leasing, hedging, or research and development services. A common use of off-balance sheet arrangements is to allocate risks among third parties. Off-balance sheet arrangements may involve the use of complex structures, including structured finance or special-purpose entities (SPEs—now called variable interest entities by the FASB), to facilitate a company's transfer of, or access to, assets. In many cases, the transferor of assets has some contingent liability or continuing involvement with the transferred assets. Depending on the nature of the obligations and the related accounting treatment under GAAP, the company's financial statements may not fully reflect the company's obligations with respect to the SPE or its arrangements. Transactions with SPEs commonly are structured so that the company that establishes or sponsors the SPE and engages in transactions with it is not required to consolidate the SPE into its financial statements under GAAP.

Four examples of companies that improperly used off-balance sheet arrangements were the PNC Financial Services Group, Inc., Adelphia Communications Corporation, Dynegy Inc., and Enron. Because Enron is such a famous case, here we will discuss only Enron and in a little more detail than normal.

Enron's fraud was primarily conducted through what is known as special-purpose entities (SPEs), or business interest(s) formed solely in order to accomplish some specific task or tasks. SPEs are not of themselves illegal, but are subject to regulatory measures that designate which SPEs are part of the larger company and which are truly independent entities not controlled by a parent. An SPE is considered independent if it meets the following two criteria: (1) independent third-party investors made a substantive capital investment, generally at least three percent of the SPE's assets; and (2) the third-party investment is genuinely at risk. Enron was obligated to consolidate the assets and liabilities of entities not meeting these requirements. The SEC's complaint alleged that certain of Enron's SPEs should have been consolidated onto Enron's balance sheet. Further, Fastow, Kopper, and others used their simultaneous influence over Enron's business operations and the SPEs as a means to secretly and unlawfully generate millions of dollars for themselves and others.

Fastow's manipulation of SPEs was widespread. Following are two examples.

- In 1997, Enron decided to sell its interest in a California windmill farm. In order for the farm to qualify for beneficial regulatory treatment, Enron, as an electric utilities holding company, had to decrease its ownership to below 50 percent. Enron, however, did not want to lose control of the profitable wind farm. Instead, Fastow created a special-purpose entity (known as RADR) and recruited "Friends of Enron" (actually friends of Kopper) as outside investors. These investors lacked sufficient funds, however, so Fastow made a personal loan of $419,000 to fund the purchase of the wind farm. RADR became immensely profitable. Fastow's loan was repaid with $62,000 interest, and Kopper arranged for yearly "gifts" of $10,000 each (keeping the gifts beneath the limit of taxable income) to members of Fastow's family. Because the RADR third-party investment was funded by Fastow, and because Fastow and Kopper clearly controlled RADR's operations, the entity should have been consolidated with Enron's financial statements.

- In 1993, Enron created an entity called JEDI. Because of a substantial contribution by an independent investor, the California Public Employees Retirement System (CalPERS), Enron was justified in not consolidating JEDI onto its books. However, in 1997, when CalPERS wanted to sell its portion of JEDI, rather than consider other independent investors, Fastow arranged for the creation of Chewco, a special-purpose entity that would buy out CalPERS. Chewco, and thus JEDI, was not eligible for the off-the-book status it was given. First, Chewco was not independent. Although Fastow abandoned the idea to be Chewco's independent investor (on Jeff Skilling's advice that Enron would be forced to disclose Fastow's participation), he substituted Kopper, himself an Enron executive who was essentially controlled by Fastow. Second, Chewco's investment in JEDI was not "genuinely at risk." It was funded through two $190 million bank loans, both of which were guaranteed by Enron. As with RADR, Fastow directed Kopper to make gift payments, including a $54,000 payment to Fastow's wife for performing administrative duties for Chewco.

# SUMMARY

Looking for fraud is like hiking in a forest. Perpetrators of fraud, like animals in the forest that stand camouflaged and motionless as they try to conceal themselves and their frauds. Many people can usually walk right by a deer or an elk in the forest and not see the animal unless they are looking for movement, changes in color or shadows, or changes in shapes, or the animal is pointed out to them. Likewise, to discover fraud, a person must look for analytical symptoms (movements), accounting or documentary symptoms (changes in color), behavioral and lifestyle symptoms (changes in shapes), control symptoms (changes in shadows), and tips and complaints (the evidence that is pointed out).

# KEY TERMS

**Accrued liability** Liabilities arising from end-of-period adjustments, not from specific transactions.

**Acquisition** The purchase of something, such as the purchase of one company by another company.

**Capitalization** Recording expenditures as assets rather than as expenses. (For example, start-up costs of a company that are "capitalized" are recorded as assets and amortized.)

**Contingent liability** A possible liability. If the likelihood of payment is "probable," the contingent liability must be reported as a liability on the financial statements; if likelihood of payment is reasonably possible, it must be disclosed in the footnotes to the financial statements; if likelihood of payment is remote, no mention of the possible liability needs to be made.

**Deferred charge (asset):** An expenditure that has been capitalized to be expensed in the future.

**Fixed assets** The property, plant, and equipment assets of an organization.

**Footnotes** The accompanying information to a company's financial statements that provides interpretive guidance to the financial statements or includes related information that must be disclosed.

**Inadequate disclosure fraud** The issuance of fraudulent or misleading statements or press releases without financial statement line-item effect or the lack of appropriate disclosures that should have been but were not made by management.

**Intangible asset** An asset that has no tangible existence (e.g., goodwill).

**Lease** An obligation to make periodic payments over a specified period for use or "rent" of an asset; does not involve ownership of the asset.

**Marketable securities** Short-term stocks, bonds, and other noncash assets; sometimes called short-term investments.

**Mergers** The combining of two organizations into one business entity.

**Mortgage** Long-term loan secured by property, such as a home mortgage.

**Overstatement of asset fraud** Financial statement fraud involving recording assets at amounts higher than they should be.

**Pension** Post-retirement cash benefits paid to former employees.

**Repurchase agreement** An agreement to buy back something previously sold.

**Restructuring** The reevaluation of a company's assets because of impairment of value or for other reasons. Restructured companies usually have lower amounts of assets and look quite different than before the restructuring.

**Understatement of liability fraud** Financial statement fraud that involves understating liabilities or amounts owed to others.

**Unearned revenues** Amounts that have been received from customers but for which performance of a service or sale of a product has not yet been made.

**Warranty liabilities** An obligation to perform service and repair items sold within a specific period of time or use after sale.

# QUESTIONS AND CASES

## DISCUSSION QUESTIONS

1. Why is understatement of liability fraud difficult to discover?

2. List four methods used to perform analytical analysis to search for financial statement fraud symptoms. Give an example of each method as it applies to searching for symptoms related to underreporting of liabilities.

3. Explain what is meant by "cut-off problems" as they relate to accounts payable.

4. Why might liabilities be understated if proper adjusting entries are not made at the end of an accounting period?

5. What is the difference between unearned revenue and earned revenue?

6. If a contingent liability is only a possible liability, why might not disclosing contingent liabilities constitute financial statement fraud?

7. Explain why improper capitalization of amounts spent could result in financial statement fraud and overstatement of assets.

8. Is cash an asset that is frequently overstated when committing financial statement fraud? Why or why not?

9. In what ways could financial statement fraud result from a merger?

10. If all financial statement amounts are presented appropriately, could financial statement fraud still be occurring?

## TRUE/FALSE

1. Fraud auditors should usually be concerned with liabilities being overstated as well as understated.

2. Confirmations with vendors are an effective way to discover unrecorded liabilities.

3. Accrued liabilities are an important account to look at when searching for fraud because it is easy to understate liabilities in these accounts.

4. Symptoms of unrecorded contingent liabilities can be found by performing analytical procedures on certain financial statement ratios.

5. Some misleading footnotes have no effect on the financial statement balances.

6. Understatement of liability fraud is usually more difficult to find than overstatement of asset fraud.

7. When searching for unrecorded liabilities, investigating vendors with zero balances would be just as important as investigating vendors with large balances.

8. Assets most often improperly capitalized are fixed assets.

9. Financial statement fraud involving footnote disclosures can be either frauds of omission or frauds of commission.

10. A company that claims to be something it is not in a 10-K report is committing a kind of financial statement fraud.

## MULTIPLE CHOICE

1. Which of the following are primary types of transactions that can create liabilities for a company?
   a. Purchasing inventory
   b. Borrowing money
   c. Selling purchased goods
   d. Leasing assets
   e. All of the above

2. When accounts payable-related liabilities are understated, purchases and inventory are often _____, or the financial statements don't balance.
   a. Overstated
   b. Understated
   c. Correctly stated
   d. It is impossible to tell.

3. Recognizing something as a revenue instead of as a liability has a positive effect on the reported financial statements because:
   a. It understates liabilities.
   b. It overstates revenues
   c. It overstates net income.
   d. It overstates assets.
   e. All of the above.
   f. a, b, and c are correct. — P.443

4. The most common fraud involving car companies and the warranties they offer would most likely be:
   a. Understating accrued liabilities.
   b. Recognizing unearned revenue.
   c. Not recording or underrecording future obligations. — P.444
   d. Not recording or underrecording various types of debt.

5. FAS 5 requires contingent liabilities to be recorded as liabilities on the balance sheet if the likelihood of loss or payment is:
   a. Remote.
   b. Reasonably possible.
   c. Probable. — P.445
   d. Not determinable.

6. Analytical symptoms of accounts payable fraud usually relate to reported accounts payable balances that appear:
   a. Too low. — P.445
   b. Too high.
   c. Too perfect.
   d. Unchanged.

7. Proactively searching for analytical symptoms related to financial statement fraud means that we are looking for accounts that appear:
   a. Too low.
   b. Too high.
   c. Unusual.
   d. Could be any of the above. — P.447

8. When focusing on changes, you should consider changes from period to period in:
   a. Recorded balances.
   b. Relationships between balances.
   c. Balances of other nonsimilar companies.
   d. Both a and b. — P.447
   e. All of the above.

9. Overstating cash is usually difficult because:
   a. Cash balances can be easily confirmed with banks and other financial institutions. — P.456
   b. Cash is hard to steal.
   c. Cash is normally not a fraudulent account.
   d. Cash is usually a small asset.

10. Inadequate disclosure fraud usually involves:
    a. Statements in the footnotes that are wrong but do not impact the financial statement.
    b. Disclosures that should have been made in the footnotes, but were not.
    c. Both a and b. — P.464
    d. Neither a or b.

11. When examining whether a company has under-recorded accounts payable, each of the following ratios is helpful *except*:
    a. Acid-test ratio.
    b. Accounts payable/Purchases.
    c. Accounts payable/Cost of goods sold.
    d. Unearned revenue/Accounts payable. — P.449
    e. Current ratio.

12. Each of the following assets is correctly linked with how it can be overstated *except*:
    a. Inventory can be overstated by improperly capitalizing these assets.
    b. Marketable securities can be overstated because they are not widely traded, and it is difficult to assign an accurate value to the securities.
    c. Fixed assets can be overstated by leaving expired assets on the books.
    d. Assets can be inflated in mergers, acquisitions, and restructurings by having the wrong entity act as the asset's purchases.

13. Which of the following factors does not make fraud more difficult to detect?
    a. Collusion with outsiders
    b. Forgery, which GAAS auditors are not routinely trained to detect
    c. Off-book frauds in which no records on the company's books are fraudulent
    d. All of the above make fraud more difficult to detect

14. A form 1099 with missing withholdings (where they should be reported) may be a fraud symptom for which liability account?
    a. Accounts payable
    b. Unearned revenues
    c. Contingent liabilities
    d. Accrued liabilities

15. In liability fraud, liabilities are most often:
    a. Understated.
    b. Overstated.
    c. Recorded as assets.
    d. Recorded as expenses.

16. Which of the following is usually the hardest fraud to detect?
    P.441
    a. Liability fraud
    b. Revenue fraud
    c. Asset fraud
    d. Disclosure fraud

17. You observe that a company's current ratio is dramatically increasing. This change may indicate fraud in that:
    a. Contingent liabilities are not recorded. — P.450
    b. Accounts payable is understated.
    c. Expenses have been inappropriately capitalized as assets.
    d. Fixed assets are overstated.

18. Of the following, which is the most difficult account for management to intentionally misstate?
    a. Income taxes payable
    b. Cash —
    c. Securities
    d. Prepaid expenses

## SHORT CASES

**Case 1.** John is the manager of a small computer sales and support chain. He has stores located throughout the state of California and is in strong competition with all of the major computer providers within that state. John's company is known for providing quick support and friendly service. In the process of selling goods to customers, John's company will often offer deals that include free service or low-priced service for the products being purchased. John's competitors offer the same types of deals to their customers, but because of the small mobile size of John's company, he is better able to provide quick service to his customers. John is the president of his company and has raised funding through issuing stock. He has not used external loan funding much in the past. John has approximately 50 stores located in California, and is in the process of obtaining business locations outside of the state. John's main goal is to be successful in the computer business because of the quick customer service his company provides. He believes his company will be able to charge higher prices because people will be willing to pay the initial higher price on computer components for the added customer service on the back end.

John has managers in all of the different stores who report directly to him. They do not communicate regularly with other store managers on inventory issues or customer service representative availabilities. John found much success in the past because of the customer service he has been able to provide. In recent years, the competition has become more successful in duplicating his activities or in providing low-maintenance products. John's company has provided financial statements on a yearly basis so investors can follow the company's success. With the growing success of competitors, John has found it more difficult to be successful. During the past year, John's company recorded significant revenues from sales that will require warranty service over the next few years. However, John's reported warranty expenses stayed the same. In addition, the reported inventory levels remained approximately the same as in previous years. No additional financing or loans were recorded on the financial statements, even though assets continued to grow. Revenue was the only financial statement amount that changed dramatically.

What are possible fraud symptoms in this case? What could look like fraud but be explained by industry trends?

**Case 2.** Enron is a large energy trading company that allegedly committed massive fraud. Their primary method of "committing fraud" was to record liabilities in related partnerships (SPEs) that were not consolidated or combined with Enron's financial statements. Company executives have maintained that they did not know about these massive off-balance sheet liabilities, which have been estimated to be several billion dollars.

As a fraud investigator, how would you go about finding the existence of these liabilities and partnerships?

**Case 3.** Qwest is the dominant local telephone company in 14 states and the owner of an international fiber-optic network. In 2002, the company was investigated by the SEC for not including certain expense items related to its merger with U.S. West, among other issues. Why would the SEC be concerned if Qwest had not included certain expense items in a merger?

**Case 4.** Until its demise, Arthur Andersen was recognized as one of the most respected CPA firms in the world. Arthur Andersen, as did other large CPA firms, operated as a limited liability corporation or LLC. At the time that its involvement as Enron's auditor was making news every day, an article in *The Wall Street Journal* stated that it wasn't clear whether the LLC form of organization was going to offer Andersen's partners protection from creditors' lawsuits or whether creditors would be able to take the personal assets of Andersen's partners. Assume that Andersen has 2,000 partners and that creditor claims in the Enron case total $50 billion.

If Arthur Andersen was a corporation, how would you expect creditor litigation to be reported in the financial statements? Would failure to report the litigation constitute financial statement fraud?

**Case 5.** In its 2001 annual report, investors of Adelphia Communications were startled to find a footnote to the financial statements that reported that the company had guaranteed as much as $2.7 billion in loans to a private entity owned by CEO John Rigas and his family. As a result of the footnote, Adelphia lost more than 50 percent of its market value in a little more than a week. Explain why you think the market value of Adelphia fell so dramatically with the footnote disclosure that the company had guaranteed loans to an entity owned by the company's CEO and his family.

**Case 6.** The officers of an oil refiner, trader, and hedger based in New York City were arrested by the FBI for committing massive financial statement fraud. The executives used many schemes to perpetuate the fraud, one of which was to hide a $30 million accounts payable from the auditors and show it as a payable arising in the following year. To conceal the fraud, they altered purchasing records, using white-out, and provided only photocopies of the records to the auditors. The Big 4 firm that audited this company was later sued for audit negligence in not finding this fraud. In your opinion, were the auditors negligent for accepting photocopies of purchasing records and not detecting this accounts payable understatement?

**Case 7.** What follows are the comparative balance sheets and statements of income for XYZ Company for the years 2004–2006.

CONSOLIDATED BALANCE SHEETS — XYZ Company

| | 2006 | 2005 | 2004 |
|---|---|---|---|
| *Assets* | | | |
| Current assets | | | |
| Cash and cash equivalents | $ 1,542 | $ 851 | $ 317 |
| Receivables | 5,602 | 4,115 | 3,329 |
| Inventories | 1,524 | 1,112 | 900 |
| Deferred income taxes | 851 | 302 | 456 |
| Total current assets | $ 9,519 | $ 6,380 | $ 5,002 |
| Land | 22,547 | 15,239 | 12,045 |
| Buildings | 10,982 | 8,475 | 7,698 |
| Machinery | 6,233 | 5,008 | 3,511 |
| Accumulated depreciation | (396) | (305) | (235) |
| Total Assets | $48,885 | $34,797 | $28,021 |
| | | | |
| *Liabilities and Stockholders' Equity* | | | |
| Current liabilities | | | |
| Accounts payable | $ 5,603 | $ 4,112 | $ 4,758 |
| Taxes payable | 786 | 543 | 235 |
| Total current liabilities | $ 6,389 | $ 4,655 | $ 4,993 |
| Long-term debt | 16,987 | 16,115 | 19,546 |
| Deferred income taxes | 845 | 562 | 354 |
| *Stockholders' Equity* | | | |
| Common stock | 22,220 | 12,764 | 2,907 |
| Retained earnings | 2,444 | 701 | 221 |
| Total liabilities and stockholders' equity | $48,885 | $34,797 | $28,021 |

CONSOLIDATED STATEMENTS OF INCOME — XYZ Company

| | 2006 | 2005 | 2004 |
|---|---|---|---|
| Revenues | $26,534 | $22,473 | $18,739 |
| Cost of goods sold | 18,201 | 18,161 | 15,406 |
| Gross margin | $ 8,333 | $ 4,312 | $ 3,333 |
| Operating expenses | 5,428 | 3,512 | 2,965 |
| Operating income before taxes | $ 2,905 | $ 800 | $ 368 |
| Income taxes | 1,162 | 320 | 147 |
| Net Income | $ 1,743 | $ 480 | $ 221 |

Calculate all ratios needed to determine if XYZ is possibly under-reporting accounts payable. If you detect possible fraud, explain why you think it might exist.

**Case 8.** During the audit of a manufacturing client, you are instructed to do vertical and horizontal financial statement analysis. In your analysis, you notice little increase in the client's overall long-term liabilities. However, you remember that a note was extended to the client by a bank in the region, and you cannot find where the note is reflected on the financial statements. When you ask the controller about the loan, he claims that the debt has been forgiven by the regional bank, but upon further investigation, he cannot provide you with corroborating evidence to support his claim.

Claiming that creditors have forgiven existing debt is one way to understate liabilities. Describe several other ways a company might try to understate liabilities.

**Case 9.** ABC Technologies, Inc., designs, manufactures, and markets an extensive line of PC cards. The company sells its PC cards primarily to original equipment manufactures (OEMs) for industrial and commercial applications in a market with intense competition. In fact, many OEM companies ran into financial difficulty in 2005 because of fierce competition. The following is part of the company's financial statements for 2004 and 2005.

1.  Determine the red flags that exist in the following statements. Describe the scenarios that might contain these symptoms.

2.  Based upon the red flags and scenarios you identified, determine what types of financial statement fraud the company may be involved in. (*Hint*: Pay careful attention to Cost of Goods Sold, Sales, and Allowance for Doubtful Accounts.)

ABC Technologies, Inc.
Consolidated Balance Sheet (Partial)—Unaudited

| | Dec. 31, 2005 | Dec. 31, 2004 |
|---|---|---|
| Assets | | |
| *Current Assets:* | | |
| Cash and cash equivalents | $ 6,181,520 | $ 970,446 |
| Available-for-sales securities | 4,932,763 | ———— |
| Accounts Receivable, net of allowance for doubtful accounts of $148,300 and $139,200 at Dec. 31, 2005, and 2004, respectively | 12,592,231 | 3,9323,170 |
| Inventories | 18,229,317 | 8,609,492 |
| Other current assets | 18,229,317 | 8,609,492 |
| Total Current Assets | $60,165,148 | $22,121,600 |

ABC Technologies, Inc.
Consolidated Income Statement (Partial)
Year ended Dec. 31—Unaudited

| | 2005 | 2004 | 2003 |
|---|---|---|---|
| Sales | 37,847,681 | 12,445,015 | 8,213,236 |
| Cost of Goods Sold | 15,895,741 | 6,832,927 | 4,523,186 |
| Gross Margin | 21,951,940 | 5,612,088 | 3,690,050 |

**Case 10.** On the morning of April 20, 2002, Stephen Lowber, chief financial officer of Cutter and Buck, Inc., slowly arose from his bed, walked across the bedroom floor, and gazed out the window. It was a surprisingly clear, sunny day in Seattle, Washington. Despite the beauty of the day, the expression on Lowber's face was not positive. Cutter and Buck, a company that designs and markets upscale sportswear and outerwear, had enjoyed financial success. It recently announced revenue of $54.6 million for the fourth quarter and $152.5 million for the entire fiscal year. Cutter and Buck also announced it was rated as the hottest golf apparel band from 1997 to 2001 by *Gold World Business* magazine, a leading golf trade publication. Despite the success and positive publicity of his company, Lowber was haunted internally because he knew it was a shell full of fraud.

Cutter and Buck Inc. had been encountering declining sales as it approached the end of its fiscal year ended April 30, 2000. In the final days of April, the company negotiated deals with three distributors under which Cutter and Buck would ship them a total of $5.7 million in products. The distributors were assured they had no obligation to pay for any of the goods until customers located by Cutter and Buck paid the distributors.

At the end of 2000, Lowber learned that these three distributors were operating as Cutter and Buck's warehouses. Rather than restate and correct the company's financial statements, Lowber concealed the transactions from Cutter and Buck's independent auditors and board of directors by arranging for distributors to return $3.8 million in unsold inventory in early 2001. The returns were accounted for as a reduction in sales during fiscal year 2001. Additionally, Lowber instructed personnel to override the recorded business lines instead of the business line under which those sales were originally recorded in order to hide the magnitude of the returns.

As a result of these fraudulent transactions, Cutter and Buck's management overstated true fourth quarter and annual revenue of fiscal year 2000 by 12 percent and 4% percent, respectively.[3]

1. What were the main types of financial statement fraud committed at Cutter and Buck? Do these types of fraud occur often?

2. What should have been the appropriate accounting treatments?

3. The three parts of the fraud triangle are pressure, opportunity, and rationalization. List some of the pressures that may have led to this fraud.

**Case 11.** In November 2001, Wehav Funds, a profitable engineering firm, signed a loan guarantee as a third party for No Certainty Company, a newly formed organization focused on pharmaceutical research and development. Because Wehav Funds was a reputed and successful company, the loan was processed and approved by the National Bank at the end of November 2001.

Due to the nature of the pharmaceutical industry, No Certainty projects are considered inherently risk. The company is currently awaiting FDA approval of a miracle drug that, according to marketing research, has the potential to generate millions of dollars of revenue per year. If the drug is not approved, No Certainty will not have the financial resources to continue business. The loan guarantee by Wehav Funds will come into effect, and Wehav Funds have to front the full amount of the loan.

The end of the fiscal year is approaching, and as the auditors, you must decide how Wehav Funds must account for this loan guarantee in their financial statements.

Under what circumstances must you record a contingent liability on the balance sheet? When must it be disclosed in the notes?

What do you feel is the appropriate accounting treatment for the No Certainty transaction with Wehav Funds? Would your "fraud radar" go off if the company refused to record this item in the financial statements?

**Case 12.** David Sutherland, a partner and fraud examiner in Rachin Cohen & Holtz LLP was driving to a client when he heard a CNN announcement that LucidCom, a newly emerged provider of network infrastructure and connectivity products, reported strong fourth-quarter earnings and announced a 14 percent jump in the company's stock. David quickly picked up his cell phone and dialed a number of his friend who recently was laid off from Netledger, a company Lucidcom acquired just a few months prior.

David made a few other calls, and in a matter of weeks, he learned that Netledger had assets that were practically worthless to LucidCom and that those assets were reported as goodwill instead of written down after acquisition. He knew that those assets would slowly be amortized as depreciation of goodwill. For David, this change in the allocation of the purchase price represented a big red flag. When a company acquires another company, it is common to assign part of the revenue to assets and part to goodwill. The assets are recorded at fair market value and the remainder of the cost is assigned to goodwill. If worthless assets are moved to goodwill instead of written down, the company can slowly amortize the cost of those assets as depreciation of goodwill instead of recording those costs as an expense the current period.

What David questioned was whether LucidCom was being honest about the disclosures and causes of growth. Were the earnings impressive because of the company's productivity and sound business strategy or because LucidCom took advantage of an acquisition and toyed with financial reports. What type of fraud is represented in this case? Can you think of ways this type of fraud can be prevented?

**Case 13.** You keep looking over the financial statement to see where your analysis is going wrong, but you can't see any problems—it just looks like inventory is getting larger and larger, but you know that you haven't seen growth in the actual levels of inventory that the financials seem to be indicating. You just finished a comprehensive audit of all the physical controls of inventory so you doubt inventory is being stolen. Everything else in the financials seems to look fine. In fact, they seem to indicate that the company is improving in profitability.

1. What might be a valid reason for the increase in inventory cost?

2. Assuming that fraud is being committed, how could a fraud perpetrator commit this type of fraud?

3. What could be done to prevent this type of fraud?

## EXTENSIVE CASES

**Extensive Case 1.** On March 26, 2002, the Securities and Exchange Commission charged six Waste Management executive officers for the perpetration of a five-year financial fraud. The following is an article summarizing the SEC's complaint against these officers.

*The complaint names Waste Management's former most senior officers: Dean L. Buntrock, Waste Management's founder, chairman of the board of directors, and chief executive officer during most of the relevant period; Phillip B. Rooney, president and chief operating officer, director, and CEO for a portion of the relevant period; James E. Koenig, executive vice president and chief financial officer; Thomas C. Hau, vice president, corporate controller, and chief accounting officer; Herbert Getz, senior vice president, general counsel, and secretary; and Bruce D. Tobecksen, vice president of finance.*

*According to the complaint, the defendants violated, and aided and abetted violations of, antifraud, reporting, and record-keeping provisions of the federal securities laws. The Commission is seeking injunctions prohibiting future violations, disgorgement of defendants' ill-gotten gains, civil money penalties, and officer and director bars against all defendants.*

*The complaint alleges that defendants fraudulently manipulated the company's financial results to meet predetermined earnings targets. The company's revenues were not growing fast enough to meet these targets, so defendants instead resorted to improperly eliminating and deferring current period expenses to inflate earnings. They employed a multitude of improper accounting practices to achieve this objective. Among other things, the complaint charges that defendants:*

- *Avoided depreciation expenses on their garbage trucks by both assigning unsupported and inflated salvage values and extending their useful lives,*

- *Assigned arbitrary salvage values to other assets that previously had no salvage value,*

- *Failed to record expenses for decreases in the value of landfills as they were filled with waste,*

- *Refused to record expenses necessary to write off the costs of unsuccessful and abandoned landfill development projects,*

- *Established inflated environmental reserves (liabilities) in connection with acquisitions so that the excess reserves could be used to avoid recording unrelated operating expenses,*

- *Improperly capitalized a variety of expenses, and*

- *Failed to establish sufficient reserves (liabilities) to pay for income taxes and other expenses.*

*Defendants' improper accounting practices were centralized at corporate headquarters, according to the complaint. Each year, Buntrock, Rooney, and others prepared an annual budget in which they set earnings targets for the upcoming year. During the year, they monitored the company's actual operating results and compared them to the quarterly targets set in the budget, the complaint says. To reduce expenses and inflate earnings artificially, defendants then primarily used "top-level adjustments" to conform the company's actual results to the predetermined earnings targets, according to the complaint. The inflated earnings of prior periods then became the floor for future manipulations. The consequences, however, created what Hau referred to as a "one-off" problem. To sustain the scheme, earnings fraudulently achieved in one period had to be replaced in the next.*

*Defendants allegedly concealed their scheme in a variety of ways. They are charged with making false and misleading statements about the company's accounting practices, financial condition, and future prospects in filings with the Commission, reports to shareholders, and press releases. They also are charged with using accounting manipulations known as "netting" and "geography" to make reported results appear better than they actually* were and avoid public scrutiny. Defendants allegedly used netting to eliminate approximately $490 million in current period operating expenses and accumulated prior period accounting misstatements by offsetting them against unrelated one-time gains on the sale or exchange of assets. They are charged with using geography entries to move tens of millions of dollars between various line items on the company's income statement to, in Koenig's words, "make the financials look the way we want to show them."

Defendants were allegedly aided in their fraud by the company's long-time auditor, Arthur Andersen LLP, which repeatedly issued unqualified audit reports on the company's materially false and misleading annual financial statements. At the outset of the fraud, management capped Andersen's audit fees and advised the Andersen engagement partner that the firm could earn additional fees through "special work." Andersen nevertheless identified the company's improper accounting practices and quantified much of the impact of those practices on the company's financial statements. Andersen annually presented company management with what it called Proposed Adjusting Journal Entries (PAJEs) to correct errors that understated expenses and overstated earnings in the company's financial statements.

Management consistently refused to make the adjustments called for by the PAJEs, according to the complaint. Instead, defendants secretly entered into an agreement with Andersen fraudulently to write off the accumulated errors over periods of up to ten years and to change the underlying accounting practices, but to do so only in future periods, the complaint charges. The signed, four-page agreement, known as the Summary of Action Steps (attached to the Commission's complaint), identified improper accounting practices that went to the core of the company's operations and prescribed 32 "must do" steps for the company to follow to change those practices. The Action Steps thus constituted an agreement between the company and its outside auditor to cover up past frauds by committing additional frauds in the future, the complaint charges.

Defendants could not even comply with the Action Steps agreement, according to the complaint. Writing off the errors and changing the underlying accounting practices as prescribed in the agreement would have prevented the company from meeting earnings targets and defendants from enriching themselves, the complaint says.

Defendants' scheme eventually unraveled. In mid-July 1997, a new CEO ordered a review of the company's accounting practices. That review ultimately led to the restatement of the company's financial statements for 1992 through the third quarter of 1997. When the company filed its restated financial statements in February 1998, the company acknowledged that it had misstated its pre-tax earnings by approximately $1.7 billion. At the time, the restatement was the largest in corporate history.

As news of the company's overstatement of earnings became public, Waste Management's shareholders (other than the defendants who sold company stock and thus avoided losses) lost more than $6 billion in the market value of their investments when the stock price plummeted by more than 33%. (http://www.sec.gov/news/headlines/wastemgmt6.htm)

**Questions:**

1. The U.S. Securities and Exchange Commission is often called the "watchdog" of corporate America. How does it assist in preventing fraud?

2. According to the summary, why did the Waste Management executives commit the fraud?

3. You are an ambitious manager in the sales department of a company and have just received the upcoming year's targeted earnings report. You are concerned that top management has set revenue targets for your division that are practically unreachable. However, anticipating a promotion to vice president of sales if your division maintains good performance, you are determined to reach management's goal. What actions would you take to satisfy management's expectations and still maintain your integrity?

**Extensive Case 2.** WorldCom Corporation began as a small company in the 1980s and, under the direction of CEO and cofounder Bernie Ebbers, it quickly grew to become one of the largest telecommunications companies in the world. Ebbers's success resulted in his theory that survival in the telecommunications industry would come only through company growth and expansion. Therefore, during the next two decades WorldCom grew through acquisitions, purchasing more than 60 different firms in the later half of the 1990s alone. In 1997 WorldCom acquired MCI in a transaction that cost the company roughly $37 billion, and it would have purchased Sprint if it had not been prevented by federal antitrust regulations.

In less than two decades WorldCom had grown from a small telephone company to a corporate giant, controlling about half of the U.S. internet traffic and handling at least half of the e-mail traffic throughout the world. The value of WorldCom stock followed the company's growth, eventually reaching more than $60 per share. However, corporate scandal and falsified financial statements soon led the company down the dreaded spiral until, in 2002, it filed for the largest Chapter 11 bankruptcy in U.S. history. In 1998, WorldCom experienced a sudden and unexpected halt in its formerly increasing revenues. WorldCom's stock immediately took a hit. As its stock continued to drop, WorldCom became unable to reach Wall Street expectations, and in a desperate effort to maintain investor confidence, the company resorted to dishonesty.

WorldCom had established a large reserve account, which was initially maintained to cover the liabilities of companies it purchased. However, when revenues from operations continued to decrease, the company decided to use these reserve funds to boost its numbers. In total, WorldCom illegally converted $3.8 billion of reserve funds into revenues from operations.

However, these fictitious revenues were not enough to help WorldCom meet its expected level of revenue. So, in December 2000, CFO Scott Sullivan ordered accountants at the company's Texas division to reclassify many of the company's expenses. Members of the accounting staff were to reclassify operating expenses (an income statement account) as capital expenses (a long-term asset account). For example, lease expenses and computer expenses would become lease assets and computer assets.

This reclassification of expenses did two things. First, by greatly decreasing operating expenses on its income statement, WorldCom increased its net income. Secondly, by converting operating expenses into capital assets, the company increased its long-term asset account. The idea was that a huge increase in both retained earnings (from an increase in net income) and assets would inevitably lead to an increase in the value of WorldCom and its stock. Overall, nearly $3.85 billion of operating expenses were misclassified as capital assets.

Other fraudulent activity dug the company's fraud deeper and deeper until the schemes were eventually detected and investigated by the company's own internal audit department and the SEC. In the end, it was discovered that more than $11 billion dollars had been defrauded from a company that was soon forced to file the largest Chapter 11 bankruptcy ever recorded. As a result of the fraud, thousands of employees lost not only their jobs, but also their entire retirement savings. The fraud cost investors billions of dollars as the company quickly went from a multibillion dollar franchise to bankrupt. Several company executives were indicted on counts of conspiracy and security fraud. The main perpetrator, Scott Sullivan (CFO), received a sentence requiring him to pay as much as $25 million in fines and serve up to 65 years in prison. Other executives received similar sentences. In essence, the WorldCom fraud left those involved in the company with nearly nothing. It proved a prominent example of the age-old adage "Cheaters never prosper."

**Questions:**

1.  Suppose you are an accountant for pre-fraud WorldCom. You have just been instructed by the CFO to alter specific company accounts in order to boost the company's numbers before fourth quarter disclosures. You know the actions are unethical, but you fear that refusing to comply with executive orders may result in punishment and possible termination of your job. What would you do?

2.  Although it usually doesn't involve physically stealing money, financial statement fraud is commonly considered the most expensive type of fraud. Why is this true?

3.  The Sarbanes-Oxley Act of 2002 has, in many ways, changed the role of financial statement auditors. In addition to ensuring financial statement accuracy, independent auditors are now required to review a company's internal controls and report their assessments in the company's annual report. How might these new policies help prevent financial statement fraud from occurring?

## INTERNET ASSIGNMENT

Enron founder and former chairman and CEO Kenneth Lay was finally indicted in July 2004 for his role in the Enron scandals. The SEC's complaint against Lay, ironically, seemed to corroborate Lay's protests that he had nothing to do with the manipulation of Enron's books. The complaint, however, did heavily accuse Lay, in concert with Jeffrey Skilling and Richard Causey, of disclosure fraud. Review the SEC's complaint at http://www.sec.gov/litigation/complaints/comp18776.pdf, beginning with paragraph 59, and answer the following questions:

1.  The SEC complaint accuses the defendants of disseminating false and misleading statements through which seven forums?
2.  How many separate incidents does the SEC complaint identify with Causey, Skilling, and Lay making false and misleading statements?
3.  How many false or misleading reports does the SEC accuse the defendants of causing to be filed with the SEC?
4.  Using the SEC's online EDGAR Database, look up the last false and misleading Form 8-K dated November 9, 2001. Form 8-K is supposed to

report significant events that are of interest to public investors; summarize the significant events reported by this particular 8-K (reflected by the six bullet points at the beginning of the document).

## DEBATE

The following article appeared in a local newspaper after the Enron Fraud was disclosed:

Off-Balance-Sheet Land Is Where Death Spirals Lurk

*Enron's crash has shown that very scary liabilities can hide in a set of books.*

*Pay no attention to those liabilities behind the curtain.*

*That is the message corporate America has sent to investors in recent years as executives have shunted billions of dollars in new and existing financial obligations off their books and into the nether world known as "off the balance sheet."*

*When the stock market roared, investors were only too happy to believe that what they didn't know about their company's true financial picture couldn't hurt them. But now, in a crestfallen market reverberating with shock waves from the Enron collapse, shareholders are realizing that just because an obligation is absent from a company's balance sheet does not mean that it can't come back to bite them.*

*What occurred at the Enron Corporation, at considerable distance from the assets and liabilities on its balance sheet, may of course prove an anomaly. The company, now in bankruptcy but once the world's dominant energy trader, was an aggressive user of*

*partnerships separated from the parent but for which the parent's shareholders remained on the hook. Perhaps worse, it also committed the ultimate sin of omission—it failed to disclose the extent of its contingent liabilities related to those partnerships. Under U.S. federal securities laws, those details should probably have been listed in at least the footnotes to the company's financial statements.*

*In itself, off-balance-sheet financing is no vice. Companies can use it in perfectly legitimate ways that carry little risk to shareholders. The trouble is, while more companies are relying on off-balance-sheet methods to finance their operations, investors are usually unaware until it is too late that a company with a clean balance sheet may be loaded with debt.*

*Critics contend that one intent of these structures is to try to move debt off the radar screen so that companies appear less financially leveraged than they actually are. As a result, if investors take the financial statements at face value and not delve very deeply into these off-balance-sheet arrangements, the financial statements can be misunderstood. (http://pages.stern.nyu.edu/~adamodar/New_Home_Page/articles/isthisdebt.htm)*

Is it ethical to keep the types of liabilities discussed in this article off the balance sheet, or is this a type of financial statement fraud?

## END NOTES

1. http://www.securitiessleuth.com/roguesgallery/chainsaw_al_5_17_01.htm.

2. A triple-net lease means that the lessee is responsible for paying property taxes, maintenance, insurance, and utilities. Most of the leases were for periods of 14 years or more.

3. Securities and Exchange Commission at http://www.sec.gov/news/press/2003-93.htm, and Cutter and Buck at http://www.cutterbuck.com/

4. Thanks to Jack C. Robertson of the University of Texas for allowing us to use this and a few other examples from his book, Fraud Examination for Managers and Auditors (Austin, TX: Viesca Books, 1997).

# PART SIX

## OTHER TYPES OF FRAUD

# CHAPTER 14

# CONSUMER FRAUD

## LEARNING OBJECTIVES

After studying this chapter, you should be able to:

1. Understand the seriousness of consumer fraud.
2. Define what consumer fraud is.
3. Classify the various types of consumer fraud.
4. Know how to prevent consumer fraud.
5. Understand identity theft.
6. Describe foreign-advance fee scams.
7. Recognize work-at-home fraud schemes.
8. Identify telemarketing fraud.
9. Understand the various investment scams.

*Jacob, an 18 year-old senior in high school, had the misfortune of being educated firsthand about identity theft.[1] While he was attending an after-school club, his car was broken into in the school parking lot. To his misfortune, his wallet and stereo were stolen, and his car was vandalized. Jacob called the police and filed a report. After a few days, Jacob had fixed the car, been reissued a new drivers license, and had returned to what he believed to be normal life. However, the worst was yet to come. Three days later, he realized his bank account balance of $1,800 had been drained, and within a few months, Jacob was receiving bogus credit card bills. After a careful investigation, Jacob realized that he had not only been robbed of his wallet and money, but his identity had been stolen. By the time Jacob reported to the credit card companies that his identity had been stolen and cards were being issued in his name, his credit rating had been ruined. As part of the investigation, Jacob asked his mother to call the FBI to report the fraud. When Jacob's mother notified the local FBI office of the fraud, they told her that this excuse was common among teenagers to justify their spending habits and a way for teenagers to get their parents to give them more money for drugs, music, or other teenage "necessities." The FBI told Jacob's mother to get a report of the expenses from the credit card agency and then look around Jacob's room to find those objects that had been purchased. Jacob's mother did as the FBI asked, but to her relief, found none of the objects listed. Finally, after several more calls to the FBI, the FBI finally decided to investigate and file a report. Upon further investigation, it was determined that Jacob's identity truly had been stolen. However, it would take years to clean up his credit report, bills, and other problems created by the theft.*

## Frauds Against Individuals

With advances in technology, consumer fraud is on the increase. **Consumer fraud** is described as any fraud that takes place against an individual. For example, consumer frauds can involve telephone fraud, magazine fraud, sweepstakes fraud, foreign money offers (such as Nigerian money scams), counterfeit drugs, Internet services, Internet auctions, identity theft, and bogus multilevel marketing schemes.

Up to this point in the book, we looked employee or occupational fraud, management fraud, vendor fraud, and customer fraud. However, our discussion of consumer fraud has been limited. Although we briefly discussed investment fraud, which is a form of consumer fraud, we have not discussed the different types of consumer frauds. This chapter will focus on consumer fraud and how to protect ourselves and our families from its negative consequences. The topics discussed thus far in the book will be used daily by those who pursue employment in government, accounting, corporations, law, universities, hospitals, or technology corporations; however, the contents of this chapter should affect and help every individual, regardless of future occupation. This chapter may well be the most important material you study throughout your college career. The best defense against consumer fraud is education. The purpose of this chapter is to educate you about consumer fraud, how it occurs, and how to protect yourself.

## Identity Theft

According to the Federal Trade Commission, identity theft is the largest type of consumer fraud, affecting thousands of people every day. More than 42 percent of the frauds reported to the Federal Trade Commission (FTC) over the last few years involved some type of identity theft.[2] **Identity theft** describes those circumstances when someone uses another person's name, address, Social Security number, bank or credit card account number, or other identifying information to commit fraud or other crimes.

Unfortunately, personal data such as bank account and credit card numbers, Social Security numbers, telephone calling card numbers, and other valuable information can be used by others to profit at your expense. Some of the most detrimental consequences of identity theft aren't the actual losses of money, but rather the loss of credit, reputation, and erroneous information that is incredibly difficult to restore. If a fraudster takes steps to ensure that bills for the falsely obtained credit cards, or bank statements showing the unauthorized withdrawals, are sent to an address other than the victim's, the victim may not become aware of what is happening until the criminal has already inflicted substantial damage on the victim's assets, credit, and reputation. Indeed, as with most fraud, the most important way to fight identity theft is to prevent it from happening in the first place. Once identity theft has occurred, it is difficult, expensive, and time consuming to investigate and resolve.

Identity fraud, like all fraud, can be explained by the fraud triangle of pressure, opportunity, and rationalization. Many times those whom we trust are in the best position to defraud us. Some consumer fraud victims trusted their neighbors to get the mail while they were away. Other victims innocently trusted their dinner servers while they were out to eat to run their credit card. Still other victims simply trusted a baby sitter while they were out.

Some identity thefts completely ruined an individual's life. For example, one criminal incurred more than $100,000 of credit card debt, bought homes, handguns, motorcycles, and obtained a federal loan—all in the victim's name. What's more, the perpetrator then called the victim and taunted him stating that he had stolen the individual's identity—and that there was nothing he could do about it. After the perpetrator was finally caught, the victim and his wife spent nearly four years and $15,000 of their own time and money to try to restore their credit and reputation that had been ruined. The perpetrator served a brief sentence for making a false claim while buying a firearm, but never had to make restitution to the victim for the harm he had caused.[3]

### How Fraudsters Convert Personal Information to Financial Gain

Once fraudsters access personal information, they use that information to their financial benefit. Some common activities of perpetrators are listed here:

- *Perpetrators buy large-ticket items, such as computers or televisions.* Using a fake credit/debit card, a fraudster will usually buy items that are quite expensive and can easily be sold on the black market. Fraudsters will spend the stolen money quickly, usually on drugs or other vices.

- *Perpetrators take out car, home, or other loans.* Once a fraudster has gained confidence in the identity theft (through other successful small purchases), he or she often takes out a loan using the victim's identity. The most common type of loan is an automobile loan. Because automobiles can easily be traced (using the license plates or vehicle identification number), the car is usually quickly sold so that it cannot be traced to the fraudster.

- *Perpetrators establish phone or wireless service in victim's name.* Fraudsters often set up a phone or wireless service in the victim's name. This activity allows fraudsters to more easily convince banks, businesses, and others that they really are the person they claim to be. Fraudsters will also use telephones as a form of communication to buy or sell drugs, gain information to steal more identities, begin telemarketing schemes, or support other fraud schemes.

- *Perpetrators use counterfeit checks or debit cards.* Using debit cards or counterfeit checks, fraudsters will drain victim's bank accounts. As discussed later in the chapter, one of the biggest risks of debit cards is the lack of insurance to cover fraudulent transactions. This factor makes it extremely important that consumers only have a reasonable amount of cash in their checking or debit account. That way, if a fraudster should drain a victim's checking account, the loss will be minimal.

- *Perpetrators open a new bank account.* Fraudsters will use victim's personal information to open a new checking account under their name. Using the checks received from the new account, they will write checks that will not only cause problems of bounced checks, but in the process, destroy the person's name and credit.

- *Perpetrators file for bankruptcy under the victim's name.* Fraudsters sometimes file for bankruptcy under a victim's name. Such filings keep victims from knowing that their identity has been stolen. In the process, victim's credit report and reputation are damaged, a problem that takes years to repair.

- *Perpetrators report victims' names to police in lieu of their own.* Fraudsters have been known to use victims' names and identities to keep their own records from being blemished. Furthermore, if a fraudster does have a criminal record, he or she might use a victim's name to purchase guns or other difficult-to-obtain items. If a fraudster does have an encounter with the police and uses a victim's identity, many times, the fraudster will be released because the victim has no previous criminal record. However, if the fraudster is summoned to court and does not appear, a warrant for the victim's arrest may be issued. Again, it may take years to clear a victim's name and reputation from federal, state, local, and business records.

- *Perpetrators open new credit card accounts.* Fraudsters will often open new credit card accounts enabling them to spend money in a victim's name with no immediate consequences. It is one of the easiest ways for perpetrators to defraud victims once their identity has been stolen.

- *Perpetrators change victim's mailing addresses.* Fraudsters often change the mailing address on a victim's credit card accounts. This tactic prevents the victim from even knowing a problem exists and enables the fraudster to continue using the credit card and identity. Because the perpetrators, not the victim will be receiving the billing statements, fraudsters can continue their schemes for increased lengths of time.[4]

## The Process of Identity Theft

Perpetrators of identity theft follow a common pattern after they steal a victim's identity. To help you understand this process, we created the *identity theft cycle*. Although some fraudsters perpetrate their frauds in slightly different ways, most generally follow the pattern illustrated in Figure 14-1.

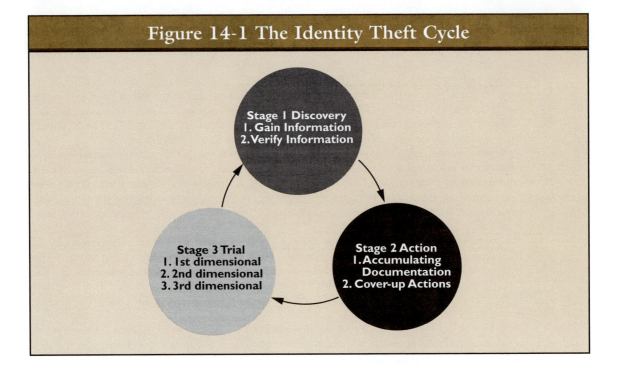

## Figure 14-1 The Identity Theft Cycle

**Stage 1: Discovery.** The discovery stage involves two phases: information gathering and information verification. It is the first step in the identity theft cycle because all other actions the perpetrator takes depend upon the accuracy and effectiveness of the discovery stage. A powerful discovery stage will constitute a solid foundation for the perpetrator to commit identity theft. The smarter the perpetrator, the better the discovery foundation will be. If a perpetrator has a weak foundation, the evidence gathered will be less likely to support a high-quality identity theft, which minimizes the victim's overall financial losses.

During the *information gathering phase*, fraudsters do all they can to gather a victim's information. Examples of discovery techniques include any information-gathering technique such as trash searches, searching someone's home or computer, stealing mail, phishing, or any other means whereby a perpetrator gathers information about a victim.

During the *information verification phase*, a fraudster uses any means to verify the information that is already gathered. Examples include telephone scams (where the perpetrator will call the victim and act as a representative of a business to verify the information gathered) and trash searches (when another means was used to gather the original information). Although some fraudsters may not initially go through the information verification process, they will eventually use some information verification procedures at some point during the scam.

**Stage 2: Action.** The action stage, the second phase of the identity theft cycle, involves two phases: accumulating documentation and covering up actions.

*Accumulating documentation* refers to the process that the perpetrator uses to obtain the needed tools to defraud the victim. For example, using the information already obtained, the perpetrator may apply for a bogus credit card, fake checking account, or driver's license in the victim's name. Although the perpetrator has not actually stolen any funds from the perpetrator, he or she has now accumulated the necessary tools to do so. Any action taken by the perpetrator to acquire tools that will later be used to provide financial benefit using the victim's identity fall into this category.

*Covering up actions* involve any actions that are used to cover the financial footprints that are left throughout the identity theft process. For example, in this stage, a fraudster might change the physical address or e-mail of the victim so the perpetrator receives the statements rather than the victim when credit card statements are sent by the financial institution. These cover-up actions allow the perpetrator to continue the fraud for a longer period of time without being noticed.

**Stage 3: Trial.** The trial stage involves any part of the identity theft process that gives the perpetrator financial benefits. It occurs in three phases: 1st dimensional actions, 2nd dimensional actions, and 3rd dimensional actions. The trial stage is considered to be the most critical stage of the identity theft cycle because it is when the fraudster's work starts to pay off.

The first actions fraudsters use to test the effectiveness of their fraud schemes are referred to as *1st dimensional actions*. For example, a fraudster might go to a gas station and use a stolen credit card to actually determine whether the card really works. If the card works, the fraudster gains confidence in the theft and moves on to bigger scams. However, if the card does not work, the fraudster faces no immediate threat of consequences and can quickly discard the card without facing anyone.

The actions taken by a fraudster once the initial trial has been successful are called *2nd dimensional actions*. These actions usually involve face-to-face interactions with others. For example, if the card used at the gas station was successful, the fraudster will move on to bigger items. The perpetrator may go to the mall and buy shoes, stereo equipment, or other large-ticket items. Any actions used to benefit the perpetrator after the initial testing period are considered to be 2nd dimensional actions.

Finally, *3rd dimensional actions* are used after the perpetrator has considerable confidence in the identity theft. For example, a fraudster may establish telephone accounts, open new bank accounts, take out an auto loan, or perform other actions that significantly benefit the perpetrator. These 3rd dimensional actions are the most risky for a fraudster. The likelihood of a fraudster being caught during 3rd dimensional actions is greater than at any other period in the identity theft.

Once a fraudster has been involved in 3rd dimensional actions he or she will usually go back to the discovery stage and begin to con a new victim. The process then starts again.

## Stealing a Victim's Identity

Stealing a victim's identity isn't as difficult as it may seem. Fraudsters use numerous ways to get the information required to commit identity theft. Some of the more common types of information-gathering techniques used by identity fraudsters are listed here:

1. Fraudsters gain personal information by posing as a legitimate employee, government official, or representative of any organization.

2. Fraudsters rummage through consumers' trash. Pre-approved credit cards, tax information, any receipts containing credit card numbers, Social Security receipts, or financial records are valuable sources of information for any fraudster.

3. Fraudsters skim victims' credit cards for information when they pay their bills. **Skimming** is a process in which fraudsters use an information storage device to gain access to valuable information when your credit card is processed.

4. Fraudsters gather information from businesses by stealing information from their employer, hacking into organizations' computers, or bribing/conning an employee who has access to confidential records.

5. Fraudsters steal wallets or purses to gain confidential information or identification. Valuable information is contained in almost every wallet.

6. Fraudsters sneak into victims' homes and steal their information.

7. Fraudsters steal mail, which can include bank information, checks, credit card information, tax information, or pre-approved credit cards.

8. Fraudsters complete a "change of address form" at the local post office and have victims' mail delivered to a P.O. box or other address of the fraudster's convenience.

9. Fraudsters engage in **shoulder surfing** where they watch consumers from a nearby location as consumers give credit card or other valuable information over the phone.[5]

10. In recent years, fraudsters have begun to use the Internet to steal important information, through a technique known as phishing. **Phishing** is a high-tech scam that uses spam or pop-up messages to deceive consumers into disclosing credit card numbers, bank account information, Social Security number, passwords, or other sensitive information. **Phishers** (fraudsters who engage in phishing) will send e-mail or pop-up message claiming to be from legitimate businesses or organizations with whom consumers deal (e.g., Internet services providers, banks, online payment services, or even government agencies). The message will usually say that the victim needs to "update" or "validate" his or her account. The message then directs the victim to some Web site that looks like a legitimate organization site. The purpose of this site is to trick the victim into divulging personal information.[6]

## Minimizing the Risk

An individual can avoid or minimize vulnerability to identity theft in a number of ways. The harder it is for a fraudster to access personal information, the less likely a fraudster is to try and defraud someone. Consumers need to take proactive means to protect and minimize these risks. Here are some of the most effective ways:

- *Guard your mail from theft.* When away from home, have the U.S. Postal Service hold your personal mail. Consumers can call 1-800-275-8777 for this service. It is also beneficial to deposit outgoing mail at post office collection boxes or at a local post office, rather than in an unsecured mailbox outside your home.
- *Opt out of pre-approved credit cards.* One of the most common and easiest ways for a fraudster to commit identity theft is to simply fill out the pre-approved credit card applications consumers receive via the mail and send them in. Although many individuals destroy pre-approved credit cards, this approach only protects consumers from having fraudsters go through their trash. Fraudsters still have the opportunity to open a victim's mail box and steal pre-approved credit card applications even before victims are aware they have arrived. What most consumers don't know is that they have the opportunity to opt out of pre-approved credit card offers. Consumers can call 1-888-5-OPTOUT (1-888-567-8688) to have their name removed from direct marketing lists. Consumers will need to provide their Social Security number in order for credit bureaus to identify consumer's files and remove them from their lists. Even after opting out consumers may still receive some credit offers because some companies use different lists from those of the credit bureaus. Another option available to consumers is to contact the individual credit bureaus. Consumers should write directly to the direct marketing association at both of the following addresses to opt out of any pre-approved offers.

Direct Marketing Association
**Mail Preference Service**
PO Box 9008
Farmingdale, NY 11735

Direct Marketing Association
**Telephone Preference Service**
PO Box 9014
Farmingdale, NY 11735

Individuals should include all pertinent information, including full name, current address, and current telephone number. The credit bureaus' contact information is listed here.

### Equifax Opt Out
Options
Equifax Inc
PO Box 740123
Atlanta, GA  30374-0123

### TransUnion Opt Out
TransUnion LLC
Name Removal Option
PO Box 97328
Jackson, MS 39288

### Experian Opt Out
1-800-353-0809

- *Guard Social Security cards and numbers.* An individual's Social Security number is valuable information for any fraudster. With knowledge of someone's Social Security number, fraudsters can open all kinds of new accounts in the victim's name. Therefore, consumers should always keep their Social Security card in a safe place. If individuals are living with roommates, it is even more important that they safeguard this information. Although a roommate may never steal an individual's information, a friend, brother, or sister of a roommate may. Remember, it is those we trust who have the greatest opportunity to commit fraud. Many schools will actually use student's Social Security numbers as a form of recognition for test taking or for gaining access to the school's Intranet. It is important to change this number as quickly as possible. Many computers automatically remember passwords so users do not have to enter them again. It is important to make sure these numbers are not easily accessible. Many states give the option to have citizens Social Security numbers printed on their driver's license; however, it is never required. If an individual's driver's license contains a Social Security number, that person should get a new driver's license as soon as possible.
- *Safeguard all personal information.* Safeguarding personal information is important for every individual. Consumers who have roommates, employ outside help to clean or perform other domestic services, or are having outside people in their house for any reason need to be particularly careful. One certified fraud examiner recommends that individuals put their most important documents in an empty ice cream container in their freezer. It is his belief that if someone does come in an individual's house, it is probably the last place they will look. For the normal consumer, however, a locked safe may be sufficient.
- *Guard trash from theft.* Consumers need to tear or shred receipts, insurance information, credit applications, doctor's bills, checks and bank statements, old credit cards, and any credit offers they receive in the mail, as well as any other source of personal information. Remember all consumers can opt out of prescreened credit card offers by calling 1-888-567-8688. Buying a shredder is one of the wisest purchases individuals can make.
- *Protect wallet and other valuables.* Consumers should carry their wallet in their front pocket and never leave it in their car or any other place where it can be stolen. It is important for consumers to always be aware of the location of their wallet and its contents. Individuals should only carry identification information and credit and debit cards that they regularly use in their wallet. Many individuals loose track of the number of credit cards they have. Consumers should limit themselves to only two or three credit cards and keep the 24-hour emergency telephone numbers of all credit cards they possess in their cell phone's address book. That way, if credit cards are ever stolen the victim can quickly call the issuing credit card company and put a block on all transactions. Although debit cards help consumers stay out of debt, most do not have fraud protection insurance. On the other hand, nearly all credit cards now come with fraud protection insurance. Before getting debit or credit cards, consumers should realize the risks that are involved with each and try to minimize those risks to protect themselves.

- *Protect passwords.* Individuals should use passwords on credit card, bank, and telephone accounts that are not easily determinable or available. Consumers should avoid using their birthday, their mother's maiden name, their spouse's name, the last four digits of their phone number, a series of consecutive numbers such as 1-2-3-4, or anything else that is predictable. Many organizations will use a default password when opening new accounts. Consumers need to make sure they change these default passwords as quickly as possible. Many individuals use the same password for all accounts. Although this approach does make it easier for individuals to remember their passwords, it makes it extremely easy for a fraudster to gain access to all of the victim's accounts once the fraudster has gained access to one account. For example, a fraudster who works for a bank may have access to your bank password. If the password is the same for all other transactions, the fraudster will now have unlimited access to all of a victim's information and financial accounts. Therefore, consumers should not use the same password for different accounts and should change their password periodically.

- *Protect your home.* It is important that consumers protect their house from fraudsters. Some fraudsters have been known to actually break into a home and not steal a single physical object. The victims may not even know someone has been inside their home. The perpetrator will steal all information that is needed to easily commit identity theft and then leave. In order to prevent this from happening, it is important to lock all doors, preferably with deadbolt or double locks, and lock all windows. It is a good idea to have an alarm system. If an alarm system is too expensive, it is sometimes possible to get an alarm system sticker, sign, or box and set it outside an individual's house. Its presence will make fraudsters believe that the house has a security system when it does not. If consumers have an automatic garage door with a code box to open the garage door, they need to pay particular attention that others are not watching when they press the numbers on the code box. Fraudsters will wait for hours to watch someone enter the code box numbers so that they have an easy access into the victim's home. This method is not only an easy way to break into someone's home, but it is an easy way for a fraudster to break into the home and then leave without anybody knowing they were even there. It is important to periodically change the password to the code box. On a typical code box, it is easy to determine which numbers are used in the password by noticing that the 3 or 4 numbers used in the password contain more wear and tear than the numbers that are not used in the password. By changing the password periodically, individuals can prevent a fraudster from knowing which numbers are contained in their password. Finally, if consumers have baby monitors in the house, they should make sure that they are not being monitored by neighbors or anybody else. Much like on the movie *Signs*, by M. Night Shyamalan and starring Mel Gibson, baby monitors actually do pick up frequencies of other baby monitors. Fraudsters have actually been known to listen to phone calls and intercept valuable personal information because someone has been talking on the phone in a room with a baby monitor.

- *Protect personal computers.* Remember that legitimate companies rarely ask for confidential information via e-mail. If an individual has a question about his or her account, that person should call the company using a phone number known to be legitimate. If consumers get an e-mail or pop-up message that asks for personal or financial information, they should make sure that they do not reply or click on the link in the message. Fraudsters are even using cookies and spyware software to gather personal and confidential information from consumers' hard drives.

  E-mail is not a secure way to send personal information. If a consumer needs to send information over the Web, it is important to make sure that it is encrypted and that the Web site is genuine. Secure Web sites will have an icon on the browser's status bar that shows the site to be secure. If a Web site begins with "https:," it is more secure than a Web site that only starts with "http:"—the "s" means that the site is secure.

  When using credit cards to do anything online, consumers need to make sure that they check the credit card statements and bank account statements as soon as possible. Remember that if a statement is late by even a couple days, consumers should contact their bank or credit card company and check the billing addresses and account balances. Its lateness could be a red flag that something isn't right.

Even though nearly all banks now use the Internet for automatic payments and other purposes, Internet transactions are still not completely secure. One CEO of a large regional bank recently confessed confidentially that even though his bank did not feel that it was completely safe to conduct online banking, they felt that it was necessary to keep up with all the other banks who were now using online banking.

It is important to not open any attachments or download any files from e-mail that consumers receive unless they know who has sent them and their purposes in sending them. Use antivirus software and keep it up-to-date. Many phishing e-mails contain software that can harm computers and trace activities while consumers are on the Internet. Most antivirus software packages watch incoming communications for bad files. A firewall is an effective way to block communications from unauthorized sources. Broadband connections are especially vulnerable, and caution should be used when using broadband connections. If a consumer feels that he or she has received fraudulent e-mails or encountered other suspicious activities, she or he should e-mail it, without opening the attachments, to http://www.ftc.gov for the FTC's inspection.

- *Take advantage of the Gramm-Leach-Bliley Act.* Everyone in America who has an account with a credit union, savings and loan, bank, insurance agency, investment account, or mortgage company will have their private information sold to marketing companies, company affiliates, or other third parties. Under the Gramm-Leach-Bliley Act, financial institutions have the *right* to share personal information for a profit. Have you ever wondered why you get more advertisements for clothing than your roommate? Or perhaps, your roommate gets more pre-approved credit card applications that you do. Part of the reason is because banks, credit unions, and financial institutions actually sell your information to marketing groups. These groups know how much money consumers spend on clothes, food, gas, and travel for any given year. These marketing agencies then market to consumers in a way that is most effective. The **Gramm-Leach-Bliley Act** makes it possible, via the Internet, to determine how much money is in anyone's bank account, how much a mortgage is, and any other personal information.

  The Gramm-Leach-Bliley Act also gives individuals the right to opt out of having their information sold. The problem is that many individuals are unaware that they have this option. The majority of individuals aren't even aware that their information is being sold, used, and circulated through various marketing and other agencies. To prevent identity theft and protect confidentiality, every individual should go to their financial institutions and opt out of having their information shared.[7]

## Prosecution of Identity Theft

When people commit identity theft, they can be prosecuted criminally or civilly or both. To succeed in criminal or civil prosecution, it is usually necessary to show that the perpetrator acted with **intent** to defraud the victim. Showing intent is best accomplished by gathering appropriate evidential matter. Appropriate **evidential matter** consists of the underlying data and all corroborating information available. With most identity thefts, once evidential matter is obtained, such as proof that a credit card, auto loan, or any large-ticket item was purchased with a fake identity, it is relatively easy to prove intent.

In Chapter 1, we stated that criminal law is that branch of law that deals with offenses of a public nature. Criminal laws generally deal with offenses against society as a whole. They are prosecuted either federally or by a state for violating a statute that prohibits some type of activity. Every state as well as the federal government has statutes prohibiting identity thefts in their various forms. Table 14-1 lists some of the more common identity fraud federal statues that every fraud examiner should be aware of.

## Table 14-1 Common Identity Fraud Statutes

| Statute | Title and Code | Description |
|---|---|---|
| Identity Theft and Assumption Deterrence Act | Title 18, U.S. Code § 1028 | This act is one of the most direct and effective statutes against identity theft. This act was passed as a result of many identity thefts that resulted in little or no fines or forms of punishment. |
| Gramm-Leach-Bliley Act | Title 15 U.S. Code § 6801-6809 | Passed in 1999, this law prohibits the use of false pretenses to access the personal information of others. (Before this time it was actually legal to call up the bank and act as someone else to gain their confidential personal information.) |
| Health Information Portability and Accountability Act of 1996 | Standards for Privacy of Individually Identifiable Health Information, Final Rule—45 CFT Parts 160 and 165 | This law finally came into effect on April 14, 2001. It protects the privacy and confidentiality of patient information. |
| Drivers Privacy Protection Act of 1994 | Title 18 U.S. Code §2721 | This act ensures that personal information obtained by departments of motor vehicles is not disclosed. |
| Family Educational Rights and Privacy Act of 1974 | Title 20 U.S. Code § 1232 | This act makes it illegal for any agency that receives federal funding to disclose any educational or personal information of any individual. |
| Fair Credit Reporting Act | Title 15 U.S. Code § 1681 | This act gives exact procedures for correcting mistakes on credit reports. It also requires that credit reports can only be obtained for legitimate business needs. |
| Electronic Fund Transfer Act | Title 15 U.S. Code § 1693 | This act provides some consumer protection for all fraudulent transactions that involve using a credit card or other electronic means to debit or credit an account. |
| Fair Debt Collection Practices Act | Title 15 U.S. Code § 1692 | This act protects consumers from unfair or deceptive practices used by debt collectors to collect overdue bills that a creditor has forwarded for collection. |
| Fair Credit Billing Act | Title 15 U.S. Code, Chapter 41 | This act limits consumers' liability for fraudulent credit card charges. |

Usually, when perpetrators are convicted, they serve jail sentences or pay fines. Before perpetrators are convicted, however, they must be proven guilty "beyond a reasonable doubt." Also, juries must rule unanimously on guilt for the perpetrator to be convicted.[8]

## After Identity Theft Occurs

Chances are that at some time in the future, you or someone you know will become a victim of identity theft. If you are unfortunate enough to become a victim of identity theft, it is important to act quickly to minimize the damages. A small amount of time, such as a couple of days, can make a big difference when identity theft has taken place.

Victims of identity theft should immediately contact the Federal Trade Commission. The Federal Trade Commission is available online at http://www.ftc.gov, or by telephone at 1-877-ID THEFT (877-438-4338). The Federal Trade Commission has the responsibility to work with those people who believe they have been victims of identity theft. The Federal Trade Commission will not only provide victims with valuable materials, but will also help contact enforcement agencies and credit reporting agencies to minimize damages.

Although the Federal Trade Commission is the primary agency responsible for helping victims of identity theft, a few other agencies are helpful for identity theft victims as well. The local FBI or U.S. Secret Service agencies in a victim's area can help report and investigate different types of identity theft. If a victim believes that some or part of his or her mail has been redirected, the local Postal Inspection Service can help fix the mail as well as identify whether the perpetrator has used mail as a tool to help commit the fraud. If a victim suspects that the perpetrator may have used improper identification information and caused tax violations, victims should call the Internal Revenue Service at 1-800-829-0433. If a victim believes that his or her Social Security number has been used fraudulently, he or she should call the Social Security Administration at 1-800-269-0271.

Because a victim's reputation and credit report are directly affected by identity theft, it is important to contact the principal credit reporting agencies: Trans Union, Equifax, and Experian. Due to the gravity of identity theft, all three principal credit reporting agencies have developed fraud units to help victims of identity theft. These fraud units can be called at the following numbers: 1-800-680-7289 (Trans Union), 1-800-525-6285 (Equifax), and 1-800-397-3742 (Experian).

Many identity thefts involve fraudulent checks. Therefore, victims of identity theft should contact all major check verification companies. If victims have had checks stolen or bank accounts set up in their name, check verification companies can help restore credit as well as clear up financial debts. If a victim is aware of a particular merchant that has received a stolen check, the victim should identify the verification company that merchant uses and contact them. Some of the more popular of the many check verification companies are listed here:

| | |
|---|---|
| Equifax | 1-800-437-5120 |
| CheckRite | 1-800-766-2748 |
| National Processing Company | 1-800-526-5380 |
| SCAN | 1-800-262-7771 |
| TeleCheck | 1-800-710-9898 |
| CrossCheck | 1-800-552-1900 |
| ChexSystems | 1-800-428-9623 |

In addition to these agencies, identity theft victims should contact all creditors with whom their name or identifying data have been fraudulently used. Victims should also contact financial institutions that they believe may contain fraudulent accounts in their name. Victims will probably need to change personal identification numbers (PINs), bank accounts cards, checks, and any other personal identifying data.[9]

# Other Forms of Consumer Fraud

## Foreign Advance-Fee Scams

**Foreign advance-fee scams** have been around for years; however, with the advent of the Internet, they have recently become widespread and common. Unfortunately, many individuals have become victim to this form of consumer fraud. We now discuss some of the more common types of foreign advance-fee scams.

**Nigerian money offers** are a form of foreign advance-fee scams where individuals from Nigeria or another underdeveloped country contact victims through e-mail, fax, or telephone and offer the victim millions of dollars. The catch is that in order to transfer the victim these monies, it is necessary to provide name and bank account numbers, including routing numbers and other information. The fraudster then uses this information to drain the victim's account. Figure 14-2 gives an example of a typical Nigerian money offer received via e-mail.

## Figure 14-2 E-Mail of Nigerian Money Offer Fraud

Subject:　PLS ASSIST A WIDOW
Date:　　Fri, 06 Aug 2004 14:38:44 +0200
From:　　maryam_abacha13@virgilio.it
To:　　　xxxxxxxxxxxxxxxxxxxxxxxxxxx


DEAR Sir, Madam.


I am Hajia Maryam Abacha, Widow of the Late Gen. Sani Abacha former Nigerian Military Head of State who died as a result of cardiac arrest. The name of your company appeared in one of our directories as one of the companies my Late Husband wanted to do business with before he died. I therefore decided to contact you in confidence so that I can be able to move out the sum of US $35,750,000.00 (Thirty Five Million Seven Hundred and Fifty Thousand U.S Dollars) which was secretly defaced and sealed in big metal box for security reasons in your account.

I personally therefore appeal to you for your urgent assistance to move this money into your country where I believe it will be safe since I cannot leave the country due to the restriction of movement imposed on me and members of my family by the Nigerian Government. You can contact me or my family lawyer.

Upon the receipt of your acceptance to assist me, my lawyer shall arrange with you for a face-to-face meeting outside Nigeria in order to liaise with him towards the effective completion of this transaction. However, arrangement has been put in place to move this money out of the country in batches in a secret vault through a diplomatic security company to any European Country as soon as you indicate your interest.

I also want you to be assured that all necessary arrangement for the hitch-free of this transaction has been concluded. Conclusively, I have decided to offer you 25% of the total sum 5% will be for whatever expenses that will be incurred, while 70% is to be used in buying shares in your company subsequent to our free movement by the Nigerian Government.


Please reply.
Best regards,
HAJIA M ABACHA

Notice that this letter contains several characteristics that are common to almost all fraudulent money offers. The first characteristic of this e-mail is the promise of money. The e-mail states that for your minimal help you will receive "25 percent of $35,750,000" or about $9,375,000 plus "5 percent of $35,750,000" or about $1,875,000 for any expenses incurred. Receiving just over $11 million for helping someone sounds like a pretty good deal to most people. However, remember if something sounds too good to be true—it usually is. The second characteristic of this fraudulent e-mail is that the letter asks for help. In order to obtain victims' personal information, the perpetrator will deceive (con) the victim into believing that he or she really is needed for one reason or another. Usually the perpetrator will describe it as a "once-in-a-lifetime" opportunity. Third, the perpetrator will try to build a relationship of confidence with the victim. The perpetrator will use different means to elicit the victim's sympathy. In the example in Figure 14-2, the perpetrator relates the death of her husband so that the victim will further sympathize with the perpetrator. Fourth, as with most of these requests, this letter states the need for "urgent assistance." Nearly all fraudulent money offers ask that the victim respond immediately and confidentially. Fifth, this e-mail makes the victim feel as though he or she is the only person to receive this "special" opportunity. However, literally thousands of people are getting this exact same e-mail daily. Sixth, this e-mail states that it is necessary to meet "for a face-to-face meeting outside Nigeria." This request is again to instill confidence. Meetings such as these never take place or, if they do, victims never know the true identity of the perpetrator or reason for the meeting. Victims who have tried to attend such meetings have been kidnapped, robbed, and even killed. It is almost always dangerous to meet anybody that you have met online. Seventh, the perpetrator of this letter claims to "be the widow of the Late Gen. Sani Abacha former Nigerian Military Head of State who died as a result of cardiac arrest." Nearly all fraudulent money offers will claim to have strong ties to high-ranking foreign officials.

Many fraudulent money offers will also send official-looking documents. These documents are always forgeries; yet, to many victims they add credibility to the perpetrators' claims. Often, fraudulent money offers will also ask victims to send their bank account number to show that the victim is willing to accept the offer. Other offers will ask victims to pay large "fees" to process the transaction. Once a victim responds to the e-mail, or has been deceived one time, the perpetrator will continue to have the victim pay transaction fees—each time telling the victim that this one is the last fee required.

Although Nigerian money offers are the most common type of foreign advance-fee scams, several other foreign-advance fee scams are becoming more and more popular. One of these scams is a clearinghouse scam. A **clearinghouse scam** involves a victim receiving a letter that falsely claims the writer represents a foreign bank. This foreign bank is supposedly acting as a clearinghouse for venture capital in a certain country. The fraudulent company will try to get victims to invest into foreign venture capital companies for high returns. To give the impression that they are legitimate, the perpetrators will set up bank accounts in the United States. When the victims transfer money into the domestic account, the perpetrators quickly transfer the money overseas where it will never be seen again. Some clearinghouse scams will actually give back a portion of the original investments in the form of dividends. However, such transfers are made only to give the victim more confidence in the scam so that the victim will invest additional money. Eventually the money is transferred and lost.

Another type of foreign advance-fee scam is the **purchase of real estate scam**. This scam usually takes the form of someone trying to sell a piece of real estate or other property to the victim. Perpetrators will see advertisements for land (or other assets) being sold and send possible victims letters offering to purchase the property on behalf of a foreign concern. The victims are defrauded when they agree to pay "up-front fees" to a "special broker." Once paid, the victim will never hear from the perpetrator again.

**Sale of crude oil at below-market price fraud** is another type of foreign advance-fee scam. In this scam, the victim receives an offer to purchase crude oil at a price well below market price. However, in order to receive these "below market prices," it is necessary to pay special registration and licensing fees. Once the victim pays these fees, the seller disappears.

Finally, **disbursement of money from wills** is a foreign advance-fee scam that is becoming ever more popular. In this scam, perpetrators con charities, universities, not-for-profit organizations, and religious groups. These organizations will receive a letter from a mysterious "benefactor" interested in contributing a large sum of money. However, to get the money, the charity is required to pay inheritance taxes or government fees. Once these taxes and fees are paid, the victims are unable to contact the benefactor.

All of these schemes have common elements. They all come from an unknown party who claims to have access to large sums of money or assets. The perpetrators are always willing to transfer that money or other assets to the victims, but only after money or information is extracted from the victims. The perpetrators are not well-known businesses (even though they sometimes represent that they are) and they usually assert some urgency to participate. The best advice we can give to avoid being a victim to these types of schemes is simple: "If it looks like a snake, crawls like a snake and acts like a snake, it probably is a snake."[10]

A final point about these types of scams. An investigator friend forwarded a mailing that was sent to various perpetrators of foreign-advance fee scams. The letter was an advertisement for a conference, which was to be held at a five-star hotel in Africa. The topic of the conference: "Ways to Improve the Collectibility and Success of Foreign-Advance Fee Scams." Isn't it interesting that those who would deceive others would have a conference at an expensive hotel to trade secrets on how to be more successful at deception?

## Work at Home Schemes

Nearly everyone has seen the advertisements that read, "I work at home and love it—work part time and earn $1,000–$5,000 a week." Although not all work at home schemes are illegal or fraudulent, many of them are.

You can find people marketing fraudulent work-at-home schemes on the telephone, in chat rooms, on the Internet, through telephone polls, as banners or advertisements on automobiles, through the use of fliers, on message boards, in classified ads, and though all other types of communication media. According to one report, con artists pitching work-at-home schemes rake in approximately $427 billion a year.[11] Here are some of the more common work-at-home schemes.

**Multilevel Marketing.** Just about everyone has been approached at some time or another to join a **multilevel marketing (MLM) organization**. When structured correctly and with honest people, multilevel marketing is a well-established, legitimate form of business. In most multilevel marketing programs, company representatives act as sellers of real products such as facial crèmes, health aids, detergents, and food supplements. These individuals are independent distributors of a legitimate business. In order to increase the distribution process, representatives of these organizations recruit friends, family members, and others to join them in selling the products. Generally, distributors make money both on what they sell personally and what those whom they have recruited sell.

However, one of the most common work-at-home schemes is the fraudulent manipulation of legitimate multilevel marketing organizations. Among the many variations of fraudulent MLMs, one kind of fraudulent multilevel marketing organization is also called a pyramid or **Ponzi scheme**. Instead of selling real, legitimate products, they have only illusionary products and profits. As stated previously in this book, one of the most famous frauds of all time was a pyramid scheme perpetrated by Carlo "Charles" Ponzi. Because Charles Ponzi's scam was one of the first large-scale frauds of the twentieth century, pyramid schemes and many fraudulent MLMs have been dubbed "Ponzi schemes." Ponzi MLMs can look just like nonfraudulent MLMs. However, Ponzi MLMs tend to focus their efforts on the recruiting of new members instead of the selling of legitimate products. In the beginning of a pyramid scheme, the investments of subsequent investors are used to pay promised returns to earlier investors. These seemingly real returns excite early investors who then spread the "good news" about the investment to their friends and relations. Sooner or later, however, the scheme either becomes too big and too exposed or subsequent investors dry up. With no new money to make the scheme look like it is working the entire organization usually collapses leaving only a few people at the top of the pyramid who have actually made money—those at bottom always lose their investment (Figure 14-3).

So how do consumers tell the difference between a legitimate MLM and fraudulent MLM, including Ponzi schemes? Usually investors can tell the difference by the focus of the marketing. If the focus is on recruitment, instead of products, the MLM may be fraudulent. As stated, fraudulent **pyramid schemes** make their money by getting new people to invest in the company, which in turns pays dividends to those who have already invested. **Headhunter fees**, which are fees paid as commission for signing additional recruiters, signal one type of problem. It is illegal for MLM distributors to receive a commission simply for signing up new distributors—a product must be part of the distribution process. When investing in an MLM, investors should avoid MLMs that include headhunter fees. Some MLMs are organized much

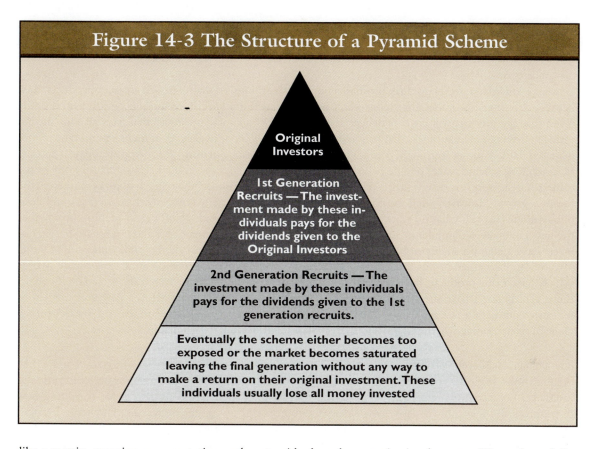

Figure 14-3 The Structure of a Pyramid Scheme

**Original Investors**

**1st Generation Recruits — The investment made by these individuals pays for the dividends given to the Original Investors**

**2nd Generation Recruits — The investment made by these individuals pays for the dividends given to the 1st generation recruits.**

**Eventually the scheme either becomes too exposed or the market becomes saturated leaving the final generation without any way to make a return on their original investment. These individuals usually lose all money invested**

like a matrix, meaning representatives only get paid when the organization becomes "X number of distributors deep" or "Y number of distributors wide." This requirement, too, can be a red flag that the organization's focus is on recruitment instead of marketing products.[12]

**Front loading** is a related, fraudulent process whereby even representatives of legitimate MLMs are required to buy large, expensive amounts of inventory. These types of companies often require distributors to buy the goods because because of a lack of any legitimate demand from other people for the goods. It is only the promise of making large windfalls that motivate the purchase of unusually overpriced goods or services. In these cases, when the organization collapses, individuals are unable to sell their inventory, and are left with substantial financial losses.

Investors should avoid paying money or signing contracts in any high pressure situation. It is always wise as an investor to take sufficient time to contemplate the business opportunity so you can understand all aspects of the investment. Many fraudulent organizations will pressure individuals to pay money during special **opportunity meetings**. Perpetrators know that if they can't hook a possible victim during an opportunity meeting, they probably won't. A fraudster's success is determined by how good he or she can manipulate victims' emotions. Most consumer fraud perpetrators have great people skills. They understand people, and they understand how to get what they want. It is usually the honest, innocent, and gullible who are especially susceptible to consumer fraud. For this reason, the uneducated and elderly, as well as those who don't understand the language or who are dependent on others are especially vulnerable.

Individuals should be skeptical of business opportunities that make any promises that seem to good to be true. For example, many businesses promise unusually high returns with little or no hard work. If these promises were really true, the perpetrators certainly wouldn't need another consumer's help. Successful, legitimate MLMs require considerable amounts of work. Any business that promises the contrary should raise a red flag. One of the biggest marketing campaigns of illegal MLMs is the promise that investors will always make money from their future downline (distributors under them) growth. However, this claim is not only a sign of the focus on recruitment—instead of the focus being on product sales—but it is also a sign that the business is trying to use emotional excitement to lure investors. No one can guarantee that investor's downlines will grow. It is the individual investor's hard work and effort that will determine downline growth.[13]

**Snake oil plans** are plans that promise enormous earnings or claim to sell miracle products. Just because a business promises that its product will do something special or unique does not necessarily mean that the product will actually deliver as promised. No "miracle product" that fixes all ailments has yet been invented. Any business that promises its product will fix or heal every ailment should raise immediate red flags. Another warning signal is a business that promises a **ground floor opportunity**. This classic marketing scheme makes people believe that they will make money simply because they are one of the earliest investors in this new venture. These consumers are guaranteed that they will make money as the business grows. However, what most investors don't realize is that any company that offers ground floor opportunities probably has no track record and history. Furthermore it is difficult to determine whether the new company is fraudulent. Businesses whose opportunities are greater for those who are the first to invest have a high possibility of being fraudulent. Legitimate MLMs provide the same opportunity for all investors to earn equal profits, regardless of placement in the organizational pyramid. Legitimate MLMs usually have many products, have been around for many years, and have proven track records. Of course, these MLMs don't have the attractiveness of high-risk, possibly fraudulent MLMs. Any investor who is seriously considering investing in a MLM should contact the Better Business Bureau and State Attorney General to determine whether complaints have been made against the company.[14]

**International Multilevel Marketing Schemes.** Some countries have outlawed all types of pyramid and MLM organizations, regardless of whether the company has valid products. The reason these countries outlawed multilevel organizations is because they believe that all plans that pay commission for recruiting new distributors will inevitably collapse when new distributors can no longer be recruited. When a pyramid collapses, it leaves thousands of people with no savings or income causing instability within a country. Such collapses have even caused economies to fail. In the early 1990s, Albania, a former communist state, had a free economy for the first time. Everyone was starting capitalism from scratch and on an equal economic basis. Few people had property or contacts. Soon after, however, people began using politics as a means to gain financially. Those who were politicians could open or close doors and were the first to take advantage of new opportunities. Many individuals learned that through crime they could improve their lives—or so it seemed. Criminals started to gain power and money. The politicians needed that money to stay in power. The people were not educated and had no experience with capitalism. Albania soon became an economic matrix, where anything was legal. Many individuals were kidnapped by gangsters. Thousands of people left the country. The only way the new "free" economy could survive was through crime. Most people within the country did not pay taxes. Countries, such as the United States, who applauded the country when it abandoned communism, watched the country turn from a free economy to a criminalistic economy. The economy soon became engulfed with fraudulent multilevel marketing schemes. Individuals began to put the little money they had into these fraudulent pyramid schemes. The recruiters for the schemes promised investors that they would get ahead financially and even become rich. Instead of working and investing, many citizens of Albania grew lazy and waited for their money to come to them, which is what had been promised. The Albanian government allowed the schemes to continue. The multilevel marketing schemes became so common that instigators of the schemes became celebrities. These owners were invited to political and social parties. They were accepted and legitimized. One fraudulent organization even sponsored an Italian race car team. MLMs became a fever, and even the most educated Albanian citizens were soon investing in them. Unfortunately, in 1997, these schemes collapsed, causing angry Albanians to ransack their own state. Albania was thrown into complete economic confusion. The economy was destroyed. To this day, the effects of the pyramid schemes and MLMs are still negatively affecting Albania.[15]

**Chain Letters, Mail Stuffing, Product Testing, and Craft Assembly.** Fraudsters have found numerous ways to con victims out of small amounts of money. Chain letters, mail stuffing, product testing, and craft assembly are all common methods.

**Chain letter scams** usually begin when a gullible consumer sees an advertisement stating something like the following, "Make copies of this letter and send them to people whose names we will provide. All you have to do is send us $10 for our mailing list and labels. Look at the chart below and see how you will automatically receive thousands of dollars in return!!!" However, the only people who benefit from chain letters are the mysterious few at the top of the chain who constantly change names, addresses, and post office boxes. They sometimes attempt to intimidate consumers by threatening bad luck, trying to impress, or by describing themselves as successful professionals who know all about nonexistent sections of alleged legal codes. Any such chain letter program is illegal and a scam. In essence, it is an MLM without a product.

In **mail stuffing scams,** consumers respond to an advertisement that promises income simply for stuffing envelopes. When answering such ads, consumers don't receive envelopes for stuffing, but instead get promotional material asking for cash in exchange for details on money-making plans. The details usually turn out to be instructions on how to go into the business of placing the same kind of ad the advertiser ran in the first place. Pursuing the envelope ad plan may require spending several hundred dollars more for advertising, postage, envelopes, and printing. This system feeds on continuous recruitment of people to offer the same plan. The variations on this type of scheme all require the customer to spend money on advertising and materials.

**Product testing fraud** usually begins when consumers receive brochures featuring different products. The brochures usually request that consumers review the products presented and send their commentaries to the supplier for review. The brochure promises that participants, in addition to payments for services rendered, will be able to keep the products reviewed. It typically requires some sort of enrollment fee ranging from $10 to $25 dollars. Those who respond to these advertisements usually never receive any information after the fees are paid. On the other hand, those who are enrolled and request products for testing may end up paying hundreds of dollars in postage and handling for items worth far less than the fees.

In **craft assembly scams,** perpetrators promise high pay for working on different projects. These projects can include anything from wooden calendars, to paper towel holders, to hair clips, and even holiday decorations. Victims are usually required to purchase costly materials, equipment, and training. The victims are usually required to sign a contract that obligates the victim to purchase more material and equipment than is needed. Usually the perpetrator will promise to pay the investor for the goods he or she produces. However, in the end, the perpetrators will almost always refuse to pay the investor for the work rendered, declaring that the work does "not meet standards." Unfortunately, no work is ever "up to standard," leaving consumers with overpriced equipment and supplies, and no income. In order for the consumers to sell their goods, they must find their own customers.

## Bogus Mystery Shopping Scams

Fraudsters take advantage of many consumers through a scheme known as a **mystery shopping scam**. During this bogus scam, perpetrators promise victims a job that involves strolling through stores, enjoying the displays, shopping for merchandise, and then filing reports on the experiences they have had. Fraudsters promise victims compensation ranging from $10–$40 an hour, plus the opportunity to keep all products evaluated. Although some mystery shopper's advertisements are legitimate, the majority are not. Usually victims are conned out of $19.95, $29.95, or $49.95. For this fee, or "application charge," consumers are promised supplies with a list of places and companies that may hire mystery shoppers. Usually, however, this list is a simple collection of department store addresses and contact information. Other scams require that consumers buy merchandise from a particular Web site. The employer promises, after the evaluation to refund all cost including expenses. However, after the item is purchased the employer will always find a reason not to issue a refund. Because teenagers and college students are constantly looking for supplemental income, they are especially vulnerable to this type of fraud. Figure 14-4 provides examples of three mystery shopping letters. These letters were received by a college student in March and April of 2004. The second and third letters are the letters that were received by this same student after inquiring about the initial proposal.

## Figure 14-4  Mystery Shopping Letters

**Letter received March 15, 2004**

Dear Student,

I would like to bring to your attention a special part-time job opportunity. If you wish to increase your budget by spending only a few hours a week working as a mystery shopper, please consider this offer.

The mystery shoppers are people, who pretend to be regular customers, so they can secretly evaluate various companies' products and customer services. On average, most of the mystery shoppers earn from $150 to $400 per week. In addition, they shop at different stores, eat at the best restaurants, and see the newest movies for free.

All their expenses are covered by the company that hires them. The best part is that as a secret shopper you can get free goods and have all your transportation costs covered.

The job we offer you has a very flexible working time. You can easily combine your daily responsibilities with your work as a mystery shopper; because you can choose only the assignments you like and work at a convenient time for you!

If you are interested, please reply to this e-mail and I will send you more information on how you can start.

Best regards,
Mike Monroe

**After initially inquiring about the offer, the following letter was received March 16, 2004.**

Hello (student's name),

Thank you for your reply and interest in being a Mystery Shopper! You will be working for the companies who need your evaluation services. We are an agent that brings you a database of information in which you can find all the companies that are looking to hire Mystery Shoppers. Our staff is contacting, testing, and researching such companies to bring you only the best of them—the serious ones. We give you only approved ones with direct links to their application forms and exclusive help if you have any questions. Today, we are running an exclusive special—$29.95 for a lifetime membership.

## Figure 14-4  Mystery Shopping Letters (continued)

You can obtain more information by visiting our Web site at:

Please look through the FAQs and if you still have questions I will be more than happy to answer you.

Looking forward to working with you.

Best regards,
Mike Monroe

**After not responding to the second letter, the following letter was received two weeks later on April 2, 2004.**

I would like to inform you of the special promotion we are running today. It is a limited offer and you can sign up for a lifetime account for only $14.99 (regular membership costs $30). You have shown interest in our program but maybe the sign-up fee was too much for you—this is your chance to get access to our database for a half price!
The Web address for the promotion is:

http://www.(address of fraudulent Web site).com

Simply click on the link or Copy & Paste in your browser. Sign up today! Do not miss this limited time offer of only $14.99 for a Permanent Membership.

—-

Best wishes,
Mike Monroe

Notice that when the victim did not respond to the second e-mail, the perpetrator quickly sent out another e-mail offering an even lower price. This tactic is typical of any type of consumer fraud. Perpetrators will ask for a certain amount of money and if the victim is unwilling to commit that much money, the price will quickly be lowered. The letter is also appealing to the perpetrator's target group—teenagers and college students. By offering a flexible schedule, great compensation, and the opportunity to eat the best restaurants, the perpetrator is appealing to just about every teenager and college student in the country. The truth, however, is that mystery shopping is not nearly as glamorous as it sounds. Normally mystery shopping is done by merchandise managers who are familiar with suppliers, prices, products, and other trades of the industry. Furthermore, real mystery shoppers have years of experience in the industry. Therefore, whenever a teenager or college student receives this type of offer, he or she can almost always be assured that it is some type of a scam.

## Telemarketing Fraud

"Really it's the truth," replied the confident voice on the other end of the telephone. "Normally, I don't make these kinds of calls. I've got a whole staff to do that. I have 15 years of experience in the business, I'm currently in charge of a large staff, I have over 600 clients, and manage over $60 million for those clients. I don't even need this account—but I want it—this is a great opportunity for you."

This script is typical of the kind of messages used throughout the United States by **telemarketing fraud** artists. Fraudsters set up giant rooms (referred to as boiler rooms) in rented offices where they train salespeople to find and defraud victims. These professional fraudsters move from city to city using different names. Calling people in other cities and states in an effort to hinder law enforcement, these con artists swindle victims out of money. Gathering complied lists from magazine subscriptions, they identify investors believed to be good targets. New recruits are given scripts and receive specialized training to counter every possible objection. These recruits hook victims through promises of no-risk investments, secrets tips, and incredible rates of returns.

The North American Securities Administrators Association, an association of state investment regulators, estimates that unwary investors lose about $1 million every hour to investment fraud promoted over the telephone. Throughout the last two decades the telephone has become a major tool used to defraud innocent victims. The opportunity to speak with a person directly makes telemarketing fraud more effective than Internet or mail-based approaches. Furthermore, the lack of face-to-face contact gives fraudster's added schemes and opportunities to commit fraud. Offenders can act as corporate or government employees without the victim's knowledge. Younger perpetrators can impersonate middle-age authority figures in order to add credibility with older victims. Fraudsters can call anywhere, anytime, making it possible to focus in on more likely victims.

In August 2004, when Hurricane Charley swept through Florida and destroyed countless homes, thousands of people applied for government grants to help cover the cost of damage. Fraudsters used this opportunity to their advantage and committed fraud in two ways. First, fraudsters began calling Florida hurricane victims and telling them that in order to process their government grants they would need their bank account number and other personal information. As if the victims of the hurricane had not been through enough, they quickly saw their bank accounts drained. Second, fraudsters would call hurricane victims and tell them that in order to process their government grant they needed to pay up-front fees. Fraudsters had the victims send these fees to P.O. boxes, where the fraudsters quietly took the money and vanished.

**Scams That Prey on the Elderly.** As with all consumer frauds, those who are most susceptible are usually the uneducated and the elderly. However, the elderly are more susceptible to telemarketing fraud than almost any other type of fraud. Fraudsters target the elderly for several reasons: First, many older individuals are extremely lonely, and fraudsters use this loneliness to build a relationship of trust. Second, when elderly people are conned out of money, they rarely tell family and friends or even report the incident. The elderly are usually extremely embarrassed that they have been a victim of fraud. They are also scared that if they report the fraud, family members may deem them unable to take care of themselves and take away their financial responsibility and independence. Third, the elderly are extremely trusting; many do not believe that someone would actually take advantage of them. Once defrauded, these gullible victims often go into a state of denial. Fourth, because fraudsters are able to build such strong ties between themselves and the victim, fraudsters will con elderly victims out of money seven or even eight times before the victim refuses to pay more money. Remember, these fraudsters are masters of manipulation. They focus on manipulating human traits such as greed, fear, excitement, and gullibility.

Because the elderly are susceptible and reluctant to report fraud, it is important that family and friends of elderly exercise special caution. If you personally know someone in your family who appears to have been defrauded by a telemarketer, it is important to avoid confronting that person directly. Many parent-child relationships have been strained and even irreparably damaged because children have approached the issue in a confrontational or threatening manner. Fraudsters will even manipulate victims' emotions to believe that they are more concerned about the victim's welfare than the victim's own family is, convincing the victim that his or her family is greedy and wants their money. When approaching a possible victim of telemarketing fraud, it is important to avoid words such as *defrauded, victimized, duped, swindled,* or any other word that the victim can possibly interpret as confrontational or judgmental. Family members should approach the matter indirectly and patiently. Usually, if the victim of fraud is approached in a sensitive and respectful way, the person's dignity will not be offended. As with all fraud, the most effective way to combat telemarketing fraud is through prevention. Education is the best form of prevention. Therefore, it is a good idea to educate parents, grandparents, or anyone else you believe might be susceptible to telemarketing fraud. Remember, because fraudsters need the voluntary participation of the victim, possible victims can defend against the fraud artist by just saying "no" or hanging up the telephone.

**Safeguards Against Telemarketing Fraud.** You have no legitimate reason to give Social Security, credit card, or other information over the telephone unless you initiate the call. If anyone ever asks for Social Security numbers or personal information, it should send a red flag that something isn't right. Fraudsters sometimes even act as government officials or other representatives to get this vital information.

It is always risky to provide credit card or bank account information over the telephone when making purchases. Consumers should only provide this information when they are actually purchasing something and have initiated the transaction. Even if the company is completely legitimate, consumers run the risk that the salesperson or representative who enters a consumer's information may capture the victim's credit card number, expiration date, and verification number and use the information later to commit fraud.

A telemarketer who won't take no for an answer should also send a red flag that something isn't right. Legitimate companies will send detailed information about a product or service. They will give consumers time to make informed decisions. They don't pressure individuals into buying something now. Language such as "This special offer will no longer be available after today," or "We only have a few products left in stock—hurry and buy now" are also signals of a fraudulent transaction.

Magazine sweepstakes and prize-winning scams are often perpetrated via the telephone. Fraudulent companies usually require individuals to buy something or pay a fee in order to claim a prize. However, it is illegal for a company to require consumers to buy something or pay a fee in order to claim a prize. Therefore, if a proposal or contest requires up-front cost it is probably fraudulent. Buying something should not improve chances of winning a sweepstakes or other contest. If so, the contest is illegal.

In the last decade, it has become extremely common for fraudsters to deceive individuals who have been victims of fraud, telling them that for an up-front fee, they can recover their lost money. This tactic is just another way for perpetrators to get more money from a gullible victim. If an individual receives a telephone call from someone who claims to be from the FBI, Department of Justice, or any other government agency and insists that the individual send money, it is almost certain the call is coming from a fraudster. It is illegal for any federal law enforcement agent to ask for "fees" or "taxes." The FBI and Department of Justice receive funding from Congress through the appropriations process. They do not receive money from any other source. If someone calls representing a government organization, consumers should write down their name and telephone number, and then call their local FBI office to verify validity.

Remember, telemarketers will use any language they can to deceive possible victims. They are professionals and make money through manipulating victims' emotions. Consumers should never believe any promise of easy money. If someone promises money with little or no work, loans or credit cards with bad credit, or any type of money-making investments with no risk, it should signal that something is not right.

When entering into transactions over the telephone, it is critical that individuals know who they are dealing with. If someone claims to be from a certain company or organization, consumers should verify that claim by calling a legitimate phone number of the organization they are dealing with before giving out any personal information. If the company or organization is unfamiliar, individuals should check it out with the Better Business Bureau or a state consumer protection agency group. However, even if the organization being dealt with is not identified as a fraudulent organization, it still could be. To avoid detection, fraudsters start up new companies every few months. As a result, the fact that no one has made a complaint with the Better Business Bureau doesn't mean that the organization is legitimate.[17]

**Avoid Sales Calls.** To minimize risk to telemarketing fraud, avoid getting on marketing or calling list by choosing to register with the National Do Not Call Registry. This free service is provided by the Federal government. Consumers can register either by phone or via the Internet. The National Do Not Call Registry's phone number is 1-866-290-4326 or 1-888-322-1222. Individuals can also register online at http://www.donotcall.gov. Once consumers register on the Do Not Call Registry, companies can still call if a consumer has inquired about a product, submitted an application, or made payments on or purchased an item within the last 18 months. Registration expires every five years; therefore consumers must reregister. The registry does not track number changes or disconnections. Therefore, if a consumer receives a new number or is disconnected, it is necessary to reregister. When signing up for a service, buying a product, or communicating with an organization, individuals will often sign a contract that gives an organization permission to contact them or give their information to marketing agencies. Therefore, it is important to read all contracts, order forms, and other correspondence before signing any document. Marketing agencies update their own records with the National Do Not Call Registry every three months. As a result, some agencies don't stop calling individuals for a while after they register with the Do Not Call Registry. If telemarketers ignore the fact that an individual's number is on the Do Not Call Registry, they can be liable for up to $11,000 in civil lawsuits. Some agencies, such as not-for-profit groups, charities, political organizations, and survey groups are still allowed to call consumers. However, if these organizations use professional organizations to raise funds, they must honor requests not to call again.

**Telemarketing Fraud Involves Large and Small Transactions.** Telemarketing frauds can involve large or small transactions. Large transactions usually involve some type of investment scam, while smaller transactions usually involve sweepstakes, bogus fees, or magazine subscriptions. Large transaction frauds provide much more benefit for the perpetrator; however, they require considerably more effort and are more risky for the perpetrator. We have seen investment scams as large as $50,000–$100,000 per victim. Smaller transactions usually involve amounts anywhere from $10 or $20 to a few hundred dollars. The smaller the transaction, the easier it is for fraudsters to deceive victims. Once a perpetrator has had success with a victim, the perpetrator will continue to call that victim using other fraud schemes. Telemarketing fraudsters are innovative and come up with new ways and means to defraud consumers every day.

## Investment Scams

**Investment fraud** is any fraud that is related to stocks, bonds, commodities, limited partnerships, real estate, or other types of investments. In investment fraud, perpetrators usually make fraudulent promises or misstatements of fact to induce people to make investments. Investment frauds are often set up as Ponzi schemes. Investments frauds can occur within or outside business organizations. An example of investment fraud in a business was the loans made by General Motors Acceptance Corporation (GMAC) to a Long Island, New York, automobile dealer.

> *John McNamara, a wealthy car dealer, conned $436 million from GMAC. He first set up a company, Kay Industries, to produce invoices showing he was buying vans. The vans didn't exist. Then he sent inventories to GMAC to get a 30-day loan, worth about $25,000, for each van. Over seven years, he got $6.3 billion in loans, and he used most of the money to pay off old loans. He paid back a total of $5.8 billion over the seven years. He pocketed $436 million—about 7 percent of the total loans—and invested it in real estate, gold mines, oil businesses, and commodities brokerages.*

While GMAC thought it was loaning money to a legitimate car dealer, what it was really doing was investing in a classic Ponzi scheme (a scheme in which early investments are repaid with subsequent investments). The only difference between this investment scam and one that is perpetrated outside an organization was that this investment scheme had only one investor, GMAC.

An example of an investment scam that took place outside a business organization and involved numerous investors was the AFCO fraud.

*AFCO, based in Salt Lake City, Utah, started as a medical-dental equipment leasing business. One owner was a former insurance salesman, and the other was two years out of law school. The company was mildly successful during its first two years. Several new branches were formed, including a land development company. The land development company purchased 1,000 acres of underdeveloped property in Sardine Canyon in northern Utah and began to develop an "Old English" family resort called Sherwood Hills. The resort was intended to include summer and winter sports, making it a year-round enterprise. Although it was reasonably popular in the summer, the heavy winter snows and poor accessibility made it an unappealing winter resort. To raise money for additional development and marketing efforts, limited partnerships were sold, mostly to physicians and dentist.*

*Other AFCO projects included a shopping center, apartment complexes, a medical center, and a 700-acre site in West Jordan, Utah. This development was known as Glenmoor Village and was touted as Utah's biggest real estate development. It was to include 1,400 homes in a totally planned community, an 18-hole golf course, and equestrian facilities.*

*As with Sherwood Hills, development of Glenmoor Village was extremely expensive. Maintenance of a positive cash flow depended on lot sales, but sales were slow because the area lacked essential services such as roads and utilities. AFCO had borrowed heavily to make these investments, but only 400 of the 1,400 lots were sold. Residents complained that promised improvements were never made.*

*Because of severe cash shortages and an inability to obtain additional bank financing, AFCO turned to middle-class homeowners to fund the company. The company's salespeople would contact friends, acquaintances, and referrals, and would offer them opportunities to invest. Using elaborate flipcharts and relying on the reputation of other investors, salespeople persuaded homeowners to allow the company to borrow on the equity of these investors' homes. If homeowners would allow a second mortgage, AFCO would service the second mortgage and pay the homeowner an additional 10 percent on the money used. Because second mortgage rates were approximately 20 percent, AFCO was, in effect, offering nearly 30 percent for the money. AFCO was very accommodating: if a homeowner didn't want the return in cash, it would lease a BMW or a Mercedes for the homeowner and service the lease.*

Even though the investment sounded legitimate, returns to be paid to homeowners were based on inflated financial statements and empty promises. The investment was nothing more than a twist on a traditional Ponzi scheme. Early investors were paid the 10 percent returns from subsequent investments, and the second mortgage payments were never paid. The assistant U.S. attorney in the district of Utah called the president of AFCO, "one of the most ruthless swindlers seen in these parts." The president of AFCO sweet-talked about 650 people, many of them business professionals, into investing some $70 million in his schemes. He later declared bankruptcy, foreclosing investors' chances of getting their money back.

Numerous red flags or fraud symptoms signal potential investment fraud. Anyone considering investing money or other assets in any organization, real or fictitious, should watch for the following symptoms, which have been associated with investment scams:

- Unreasonable promised rates of return
- Investments that do not make sound business sense
- Pressure to get in early on the investment
- Use of a special tax loophole or a tax avoidance scheme
- A business that is new in town and does not offer an adequate history of where its principals came from and what its operations were in previous locations
- A business with a history of bankruptcy or scandals
- Appraisal figures or financial claims that have not been soundly verified
- Project dependency on kickbacks, complicating marketing schemes, special concessions to people who have money, or unwritten deals that can't be talked about because of domestic or foreign laws

- Unaudited financial reports or adverse opinions given on financial reports
- Investments that assume continued inflation or appreciation in predicting attractive rates of return that are unrealistic over time
- Investment success that is dependent on someone's "unique expertise" (e.g., an uncanny ability to predict commodity prices or unusually good salesmanship) for financial success
- Representation of the emotional desirability of holding an investment as its principal attraction
- Insufficient verification or guarantee of an investment
- Dependency on high financial leverage for success
- Investor liability for debts that are not paid
- Luxurious lifestyles of principals, even though the business is relatively new
- An investment that is not suitable for your risk tolerance
- Pressure to put all your savings into a particular investment
- Inability to pull out or liquidate the investment
- Inducements that make investors feel sorry for the principals or put in additional money to help them overcome temporary problems

## SUMMARY

In this chapter we discussed several types of consumer fraud. The many types of consumer fraud all have one characteristic in common that is different from other types of fraud—they take advantage of individuals. Consumers lose billions of dollars every year to consumer fraud. As discussed, the uneducated, elderly, gullible, and trusting are the most susceptible to consumer fraud. Consumer fraud artists are excellent manipulators of emotion. They feed on the ability to successfully manipulate victims' emotions. The best way to prevent consumer fraud from happening is through education and taking proactive measures to protect yourself.

## ADDITIONAL NOTE TO STUDENTS AND INSTRUCTORS

Because of the severity of consumer fraud, the U.S. government has invested substantial time and resources to battle consumer fraud in its various forms. As a result of this investment, the Federal Trade Commission has made available, free of charge, many additional resources that are especially helpful while studying this chapter. For example, at http://www.ftc.gov/bcp/conline/edcams/telemarketing/listentoafraud.htm, individuals can listen to actual FBI recordings of telemarketing fraud. The Federal Trade Commission also makes available numerous free CDs and other materials that give additional information on the topics discussed in this chapter. Students can also view what an actual complaint form looks like and learn how to fill one out.

## KEY TERMS

**Chain letter scam** Fraudsters promise to pay victims to make copies of a letter and send them to consumers. In order to get the letter the victims must pay an advance fee.

**Clearinghouse scam** Involves a victim receiving a letter that falsely claims the writer represents a foreign bank. This foreign bank falsely acts as a clearinghouse for venture capital in a certain country.

**Consumer fraud** Any fraud that takes place against a consumer or individual.

**Craft assembly scams** Perpetrators falsely promise high pay for working on different projects. Victims are usually required to purchase costly materials, equipment, and training.

**Disbursement of money from wills** Organizations receive letters from mysterious "benefactors" interested in contributing a large sum of money. However, to get the money, the charity is required to pay inheritance taxes or government fees.

**Evidential matter** The underlying data and all corroborating information available about a fraud.

**Foreign advance-fee scam** Any scam in which the perpetrator claims to be a foreigner, and the victim is required to pay "up-front" fees or taxes in order to receive a substantial amount of money.

**Front loading** A fraudulent process whereby representatives of legitimate or fraudulent MLMs are required to buy large, expensive amounts of inventory.

**Gramm-Leach-Bliley Act** Passed in 1999, this law prohibits the use of false pretenses to access personal information of others. It does allow banks and other financial institutions to share or sell customer information, unless customers proactively opt out and ask that their information not be shared.

**Ground floor opportunity** A classic marketing scheme that makes people believe that they will make money simply because they are one of the earliest investors in a new venture.

**Headhunter fees** Fees paid as commission for signing additional recruiters of multilevel marketing organizations.

**Identity theft** A term used to describe those circumstances when someone uses another person's name, address, Social Security number, bank or credit card account number, or other identifying information to commit fraud or other crimes.

**Intent** Knowingly and purposefully engaging in deceitful activities for the purpose of taking advantage.

**Investment fraud** Any fraud related to stocks, bonds, commodities, limited partnerships, real estate, or other types of investments.

**Mail stuffing scam** A scam that promises income simply for stuffing envelopes. Victims are required to pay considerable up-front cost for information about the opportunity.

**Multilevel marketing (MLM) organization** A well-established, legitimate form of business. In most multilevel marketing programs, company representatives act as sellers of real products. These individuals are independent distributors of a legitimate business.

**Mystery shopping scams** Perpetrators falsely promise victims a job that involves shopping for merchandise and filing reports on the experiences for substantial compensation.

**Nigerian money offers** A form of foreign advance-fee scams in which individuals from Nigeria or another underdeveloped country contact victims and offer millions of dollars.

**Opportunity meeting** A high-pressure meeting in which fraudsters influence individuals to invest money in fraudulent organizations.

**Phishers** Fraudsters who engage in phishing.

**Phishing** A high-tech scam that uses spam or pop-up messages to deceive consumers into disclosing credit card numbers, bank account information, Social Security number, passwords, or other sensitive information.

**Ponzi schemes** Name given for a variety of fraudulent multilevel marketing organizations and pyramid schemes.

**Product testing fraud** Falsely promising to consumers the opportunity to review products and send their commentaries to suppliers for substantial income. Victims are required to pay enrollment fees ranging from $10 to $25.

**Pyramid schemes** A manipulated multilevel marketing organization where fraudsters—instead of selling real, legitimate products—sell only illusionary products and profits. Investments of subsequent investors are used to pay the promised returns of earlier investors.

**Sale of crude oil at below-market price fraud** Involves a victim receiving a letter that falsely offers the opportunity to purchase crude oil at prices well below market price.

**Shoulder surfing** A process in which criminals watch consumers from a nearby location as they give credit card or other valuable information over the phone.

**Skimming** A process in which fraudsters use information storage devices to gain access to valuable information from victims' credit cards.

**Snake oil plans** Plans that promise enormous earnings or claim to sell miracle products.

**Telemarketing fraud** Any fraud in which the perpetrator communicates with the victim via telephone.

# QUESTIONS AND CASES

## DISCUSSION QUESTIONS

1. Why is it important to study consumer fraud?

2. What is identity theft?

3. What are some methods perpetrators use to steal a person's identity?

4. What are some proactive steps that consumers can take to minimize risk of identity theft?

5. What are some examples of foreign advance-fee scams?

6. What is a Nigerian money offer?

7. What is the difference between a fraudulent multilevel marketing organization and a legitimate multilevel marketing organization?

8. How does consumer fraud affect entire countries' economies?

9. Why are the elderly and uneducated so susceptible to fraud?

10. What are investment scams?

## TRUE/FALSE

1. Identity theft is the most common consumer fraud.

2. Identity theft can result in an individual's loss of credit.

3. The best way to prevent a fraudster from establishing a pre-approved credit card in your name is to destroy all credit card applications as soon as you receive them.

4. Keeping your wallet in your front pocket will help prevent it from being lost or stolen.

5. The Gramm-Leach-Bliley Act states that it is illegal for organizations to share your personal information with any other party or individual.

6. In a clearinghouse scam, the perpetrator tries to convince you that you have won some prize if you will only claim it; as a result of your claiming the prize, you are usually obligating yourself to buy something or invest something.

7. Illegal multilevel marketing companies almost always focus their efforts on recruiting new members rather than on the selling legitimate products.

8. Elderly people are more susceptible to chain letters scams than any other type of fraud.

9. The larger the amount requested by a fraudulent telemarketer, the easier it is for him or her to deceive victims.

10. By federal law, no organization or company can sell individuals' personal information without the express written consent of those individuals.

11. Once an identity theft victim has reported a fraud to the Federal Trade Commission, the FTC will help a victim contact the FBI, Secret Service, and local police to coordinate an investigation.

12. The National Processing Company was given authority by the FTC to preregister consumers for the National Do-Not-Call Registry.

13. Pyramid organizations eventually fail, causing all but a few of the investors to lose their investments.

14. Congress outlawed pyramid organizations in the United States in 1934.

## MULTIPLE CHOICE

1. Phishing is the method of:
   a. Using e-mail or other Internet applications to deceive people into disclosing valuable personal information.
   b. Convincing a person to divulge personal information over the telephone.
   c. Hacking into another's computer files to access personal information.
   d. Hiring a con artist to steal personal information from a person.

2. Multilevel marketing companies:
   a. Are illegal.
   b. Increase their distribution process by recruiting additional company sales representatives.
   c. Can legally pay commission to representatives for simply signing up new recruits.
   d. Require little time and effort to be successful.

3. In order to protect yourself from identity theft, you should:
   a. Only give out your Social Security number when purchasing a product online or over the telephone.
   b. Always shred or tear receipts, credit car offers, doctor's bills, insurance information, or any other documents that contain sensitive personal information.
   c. Leave your wallet at home or in the car.
   d. Maintain the same password for every personal account.
   e. All the above.

4. The Gramm-Leach-Bliley Act gives you the right to:
   a. Periodically change your Social Security number to avoid identity theft.
   b. Receive a yearly stipend to cover the losses incurred as a victim of identity fraud.
   c. Claim your high credit report although an identity fraudster has damaged it severely.
   d. Sue the perpetrator for more money than you were defrauded out of.
   e. Opt out of having your personal information sold to organizations.

5. If you become a victim of identity theft you should first:
   a. Wait to see where the perpetrator is spending your money; then, using this information, plan an investigation with the local FBI organization.
   b. Contact friends and neighbors to inquire whether they have any useful information about the perpetrator.
   c. Contact the Federal Trade Commission for assistance and advice. = P. 454
   d. None of the above.

6. Which is a common characteristic of fraudulent money offer letters?
   a. The letter will ask for help, convincing the victim that his or her assistance is desperately needed.
   b. Through the letter, the perpetrator will try to build a relationship of trust with the victim.
   c. The letter promises the victim a large amount of money for little or no effort on the victim's part.
   d. The letter will make the victim feel that he or she is the only person receiving the "once in a lifetime" offer.
   e. All the above. P. 456

7. Which of the following is the most common reason that elderly people are so susceptible to telemarketing fraud?
   a. The elderly are often financially in need.
   b. The elderly have an excess amount of cash to invest.
   c. The elderly are often lonely and enjoy talking to friendly callers. — P. 504
   d. None of the above.

8. Consumers should provide credit card numbers or bank account information over the telephone only when:
   a. They initiated the call and are purchasing a legitimate product. —
   b. They are asked to give the information.
   c. The entity receiving this information is a legitimate company.
   d. They feel confident that the receiving entity will protect such information.
   e. By doing so, they qualify to receive certain financial benefits.

9. What is the best defense against consumer fraud?
   a. The National Do-Not-Call Registry
   b. Credit card insurance
   c. Education
   d. The Federal Trade Commission (FTC)

10. What does "https" stand for?
    a. Hypertext transfer point (secure)
    b. Hypertext transfer point (site)
    c. Hypertext transfer protocol (system) —
    d. Hypertext transfer protocol (sign)
    e. Hypertext transfer protocol (secure)

11. Which federal statute requires that credit reports can only be obtained for legitimate business needs?
    a. Title 15 U.S. Code § 1692
    b. Final Rule—45 CFT Parts 160 and 165
    c. Title 15 U.S. Code, Chapter 41
    d. Title 15 U.S. Code § 1681 — P. 454

12. Which of the following is *not* listed in the chapter as a common characteristic of Nigerian money offer letters?
    a. The promise of money to lure victims
    b. Urgency to invest quickly
    c. Picture of perpetrator to assure victims — 497
    d. Strong ties to high-ranking foreign officials to lure victims

## SHORT CASES

**Case 1.** In 2003, the FTC conducted a survey on the frequency and types of identity thefts perpetrated in the United States. The survey's results are available online at http://www.ftc.gov/os/2003/09/synovatereport.pdf. From each of the six main sections in the report, choose and report on two statistics of interest (twelve total). Your report should list the statistic, the page number in the report, and one or two paragraphs detailing why you find that statistic interesting, important, or applicable to what you have learned in this chapter.

**Case 2.** The following paragraph from the FTC's pamphlet "When Bad Things Happen to Your Good Name" describes the headaches for identity theft victims trying to restore their credit. "Unlike victims of other crimes, who generally are treated with respect and sympathy, identity theft victims often find themselves having to prove that they're victims, too—not deadbeats trying to get out of paying bad debts. So how do you go about proving something you didn't do? Getting the right documents and getting them to the right people is key."

Throughout this course, you learned the importance of fraud examiners keeping accurate, detailed records. In this respect, identity theft victims become detectives who need evidence to prove somebody beside themselves is responsible for the accounts, debts, and misdeeds committed in their name. Unfortunately, victims often don't have documents to prove their innocence.

To help victims begin the process of proving innocence, the FTC and others developed an ID Theft Affidavit. An affidavit is a document with some legal status when signed in the presence of a witness or notary. Look up the affidavit at http://www.ftc.gov/bcp/conline/pubs/credit/affidavit.pdf. Fill out the affidavit using the example of Jacob at the beginning of this chapter. Be as detailed as possible—be creative when asked for pertinent information that wasn't provided as part of the example (dates, etc.). Turn in the completed affidavit, along with your answers to these questions:

1. T/F All companies are required to accept the affidavit as a valid legal document.

2. T/F This affidavit is designed for both existing accounts fraudulently used and new accounts fraudulently opened.

3. To what organizations might a victim send a completed affidavit?

4. To what organizations should victims *not* send an affidavit?

**Case 3.** Following the directions discussed in this chapter, write to the direct marketing association and the three credit bureaus and request to opt out of pre-approved credit card mailings. Turn in a copy of the letter to your professor.

**Case 4.** On September 24, 2003, Miguel Carcamo was going through his mail. For some reason, Miguel had not yet received his bank statement, which he usually received at the beginning of each month. Although he was concerned, he took no action and decided not to worry about it. After all, was it his fault that the bank was a little behind? Two weeks later, Miguel got a mysterious call from a creditor claiming that he needed to pay an overdue balance on his Visa Card. Miguel, frustrated to receive such a call in the middle of dinner with his family, told the person that he must be mistaken and that he had paid his bill already this month. Before the caller was able to ask any more questions, Miguel hung up the phone. On October 15, 2003, Miguel tried to use his credit card. Unfortunately, the card didn't work because of insufficient funds. Upset and embarrassed, Miguel called his bank to inquire about the card. The bank had already closed for the day; however, Miguel left a message explaining what had happened. On October 16, 2003, Miguel's bank called regarding the message he had left the night before. The caller stated that Miguel had not only maxed out the credit limit on his Visa Card but had also maxed out on the increased credit limit he had recently applied for. Miguel stated that he had not applied for an increased credit limit.

It took several days, but after an investigation, Miguel discovered that he had been a victim of identity theft. Fortunately, besides his bank account being drained for a few thousand dollars, he had had only two fraudulent credit cards issued in his name. Both his bank statement and the new credit card statements were sent to a P.O. box.

1. What were some of the obvious red flags of identity theft that Miguel should have noticed?

2. When Miguel noticed the red flags, how could he have minimized his losses?

3. Now that Miguel has been a victim of identity theft, what are some of the steps he should do to repair the damage to his reputation, credit, and finances?

**Case 5.** Jenny Lanstrom regularly visits her grandfather, Mike Lanstrom every Thursday night. Jenny's grandfather has been a widower for the past six years. Jenny's grandfather is intelligent, is a decorated veteran of World War II, and over the years has been active in community service. Because Mike Lanstrom practiced as a family doctor for 46 years, he is a respected member of the community. For the last several months, Jenny has noticed something different about her grandfather. Lately, he has been agitated and upset.

One Thursday night, Mike told Jenny about products he had been buying over the phone. As Jenny investigated further, she realized that her grandfather had bought several products from a vendor by the name of Products for Life. Although the transactions were not large, the total amount had already added up to several hundred dollars. The next day, Jenny decided to research the company Products for Life on the Internet. Surprisingly, Jenny was unable to find any information about the company. Jenny became extremely worried that someone was taking advantage of her grandfather.

1. What should Jenny do? Do you believe she should confront her grandfather about the possibility of fraud? If so, how should she approach him?

2. Jenny realizes she should avoid certain words and phrases when talking to her grandfather about fraud. What are these words and phrases?

3. Why are elderly so susceptible to fraud?

4. In what ways do fraudsters manipulate elderly victims' emotions?

**Case 6.** Go to the Florida Attorney General's Consumer Fraud Web site:

http://myfloridalegal.com/pages.nsf/
4492d797dc0bd92f85256cb80055fb97/
81bf89afaf04dbeb85256cc6006ff6bf

Pick a transaction that you will likely be involved in from the list on the page. Read about that transaction, including tips for consumers. Write a one-page paper describing the potential fraud schemes that occur with your transaction. Include the red flags that show up, and detail the preventative measures one should take.

### EXTENSIVE CASE

The following is an example of a foreign-advance fee money scam. Read the letter and respond to the questions that follow.

——— Original Message ———

**Subject:** Fruitful Transaction
**Date:** Tue, 27 Jul 2004 17:12:55 -0700 (PDT)
**From:** Gardiah Mfana <inquiriesgm4@yahoo.com>
**Reply-To:** inquiriesgm5@yahoo.com
**To:** steve_albrecht@byu.edu

Gardiah Mfana
#45 Pine Way, I Close,
Sandton-Johannesburg,
South Africa.

Dear Sir,

In order to transfer from a Bank some amount of money, I have the courage to look for a reliable and honest person who will be capable for this important business believing that you will never let me down either now or in the future.

I am Gardiah Mfana, a consulting auditor of prime banks here in South Africa. On June 6, 2000, an American Mining Consultant/Contractor with the South African Mining Corporation, Mr. Gregory A. Williams made a numbered time (fixed) deposit for twelve calendar months, value US $50,200,000.00 in an account. On maturity, the bank sent a routine notification to his forwarding address but got no reply.

After a month, the bank sent another reminder and finally his contract employers, the South African Mining Corporation, wrote to inform the bank that Mr. Gregory A. Williams died from an automobile accident, that he died without making a will, and all attempts by the American Embassy to trace his next of kin was fruitless.

I therefore, made further investigation and discovered that Mr. Gregory A. Williams in fact was an immigrant from Jamaica and only recently obtained American citizenship. He did not declare any kin or relations in all his official documents, including his Bank deposit paper work. This money, total US $50,200,000.00, is still sitting in my bank as a dormant account. No one will ever come forward to claim it, and according to South African banking policy, after 5 years, the money will revert to the ownership of the South African Government if the account owner is certified dead. This is the situation, and my proposal is that I am looking for a foreigner who will stand in as the next of kin to Mr. Gregory A. Williams, and a Bank Account abroad will then facilitate the transfer of this money to the beneficiary/next of kin. This is simple, all you have to do is to immediately send me a bank account anywhere in the world for me to arrange the proper money transfer paperwork. This money (total USD $50.2M) will then be paid into this Account for us to share in the ratio of 70% for me, 25% for you and 5% for expenses that might come up during transfer process. There is no risk at all, and all the paper work for this transaction will be done by me using my position and connection in the banks in South Africa.

This business transaction is guaranteed. If you are interested, please reply immediately, sending the following details:

1 Your Full Name/Address

2 Your Private Telephone/fax Number.

3 Your full bank account details, where these funds will be transferred into, a new/an empty account can serve.

Please observe the utmost confidentiality, and rest assured that this transaction would be most profitable for both of us because I shall require your assistance to invest my share in your country. You have to note that you must send me a private fax number where I will be sending you documents in case I cannot e-mail it to you.

I look forward to your earliest reply.

Yours,

Gardiah Mfana.

## Questions:

1. Do you think Gardiah Mfana is an actual person?

2. Do you believe that his proposition is real? Why or why not?

3. List and explain at least three elements of fraud that are present in this letter.

4. What characteristics found in this fraud are similar to the characteristics found in all types of Nigerian money offers?

5. Why do you think so many people become victim to this type of fraud?

6. What can you do to protect yourself from becoming a victim of consumer fraud?

## INTERNET ASSIGNMENT

Using the Internet, go to the FTC's consumer telemarketing Web site found at http://www.ftc.gov/bcp/menu-tmark.htm. This Web site lists dozens of actual telemarketing scams that have been reported by citizens throughout the country. Browse through these reports and write a one-paragraph summary of three of them. Be sure to include the following:

1. How the scam was perpetrated?

2. What were some of the common characteristics of each of the scams?

3. What was the dollar amount lost to the victim?

4. What other interesting facts did you notice?

## DEBATE

In this chapter we discussed the Gramm-Leach-Bliley Act, which gives credit unions, savings and loans, banks, insurance agencies, mortgage companies, and other financial institutions the right to sell customer information to marketing companies, affiliates, and others. Some individuals believe that this activity is ethical since customers have the right to opt out of having their information sold and because by law these organizations have the right to make additional income through selling customers' information. On the other hand, some individuals believe that these organizations do not educate customers and unfairly keep them ignorant to the use of their information.

Split the class into small groups. Have the groups discuss the following.

1. Is the Gramm-Leach-Bliley Act ethical? Why or why not?

2. Do organizations have a responsibility to educate customers about the Gramm-Leach-Bliley Act? Why or why not?

3. Just because something is legal, is it ethical? Why or why not?

## END NOTES

1. This story is true; however, the names have been changed to protect the individual.

2. http://www.ftc.gov/opa/2002/01/idtheft.htm (accessed August 9, 2004).

3. http://www.usdoj.gov/criminal/fraud/idtheft.html (accessed August 14, 2004).

4. http://www.consumer.gov/idtheft/ (accessed August 18, 2004).

5. http://www.usdoj.gov/criminal/fraud/idtheft.html (accessed August 10, 2004).

6. http://www.ftc.gov/bcp/conline/pubs/alerts/phishingalrt.htm (accessed August 13, 2004).

7. http://www.usdoj.gov/criminal/fraud/idtheft.html#What%20Can%20I%20Do%20About%20Identity%20Theft (accessed August 19, 2004).

8. http://www.identitytheft911.com/education/lawsandregulations.htm (accessed August 20, 2004).

9. http://www.privacyrights.org/fs/fs17a.htm (accessed August 22, 2004).

10. For more information about foreign advance-fee scams, see Joseph Wells, "There are Many Variations of These Con Games,"Journal of Accountancy,  April, 2004.

11. http://www.aarp.org/money/consumerprotection/scams/Articles/a2002-10-02-FraudsWorkatHome.html (accessed August 13, 2004).

12. http://www.usdoj.gov/fraud.htm (accessed August 14, 2004).

13. http://www.stopspam.org/faqs/mlm_vs_pyr.html (accessed August 16, 2004).

14. http://www.fraud.org/tips/telemarketing/pyramid.htm (accessed August 22, 2004).

15. Thomas L. Friedman, The Lexus and the Olive Tree (New York: Anchor Books, 2000), pp. 156–157.

16. http://www.usdoj.gov/criminal/fraud/telemarketing/ (accessed August 19, 2004).

17. http://www.ftc.gov/bcp/conline/edcams/telemarketing/ (accessed August 20, 2004).

# CHAPTER 15

# FRAUD AGAINST ORGANIZATIONS

## LEARNING OBJECTIVES

After studying this chapter, you should be able to:

1. Recognize the various ways in which employees, vendors, and customers can steal assets.
2. Describe the nature of thefts of cash through larceny, skimming, and fraudulent disbursements.
3. Explain the nature of thefts of inventory and other assets.
4. Understand the nature of bribery.

*David Miller began work selling insurance in Wheeling, West Virginia. After 10 months, he was fired for stealing $200. After an assortment of odd jobs, he moved to Ohio and worked as an accountant for a local baker. Miller was caught embezzling funds and paid back the $1,000 he had stolen. After the $1,000 was paid back, he was dismissed but not reported to authorities.*

*Miller then returned to Wheeling and went to work for Wheeling Bronze, Inc., a bronze-casting maker. In December 1971, the president of Wheeling Bronze discovered that several returned checks were missing, along with a $30,000 cash shortfall. After an extensive search, workers uncovered a number of canceled checks with forged signatures. Miller was questioned, and he confessed to the scheme. He was given the choice of paying back the stolen amount or going to jail. Miller's parents took out a mortgage on their home to pay back the stolen money. No charges were ever filed.*

*Several months later, Miller found a job in Pennsylvania working for Robinson Pipe Cleaning. When Miller was caught embezzling funds, he again avoided prosecution by promising to repay the $20,000 he had stolen. In 1974, Crest Industries hired Miller as an accountant. Miller proved to be the ideal employee and was quickly promoted to the position of office manager. He was dedicated, worked long hours, and did outstanding work. Soon after his promotion, he purchased a new home, a new car, and a new wardrobe. In 1976, Miller's world unraveled again when Crest's auditors discovered that $31,000 was missing. Once again Miller made a tearful confession and a promise to repay all money stolen. Miller confessed that he had written several checks to himself and had then recorded*

*payments to vendors on the copies of the checks. To cover his tracks, he altered the company's monthly bank statements. He used the money he had stolen to finance his lifestyle and to repay Wheeling Bronze and Robinson Pipe Cleaning.*

*Miller claimed that he had never before embezzled funds. He showed a great deal of remorse—so much that Crest even hired a lawyer for him. He gave Crest a lien on his house, and he was quietly dismissed. Because the president of Crest did not want the publicity to harm Miller's wife and three children, Crest never pressed charges against him.*

*Miller next took a job as an accountant in Steubenville, Ohio, with Rustcraft Broadcasting Company, a chain of radio and TV stations. Associated Communications acquired Rustcraft in 1979, and Miller moved to Pittsburgh to become Associated's new controller. Miller immediately began dipping into Associated's accounts. Over a six-year period, he embezzled approximately $1.36 million, $445,000 of that in the same year he was promoted to CFO. Miller used various methods to embezzle the money. One approach to circumvent the need for two signatures on every check was to ask another executive who was leaving on vacation to sign several checks "just in case" the company needed additional cash while he was gone. Miller used most of these checks to siphon funds off to his personal accounts. While working at Associated, Miller was able to lead a very comfortable lifestyle. He bought a new house and several expensive cars. He bought vacation property and a very expensive wardrobe.*

*Miller's lifestyle came crashing down while he was on vacation. A bank officer called to inquire about a check written to Mr. Miller. An investigation ensued, and Miller confessed to embezzling funds. As part of the out-of-court settlement with Miller, Associated Communications received most of Miller's personal property. After leaving Associated, Miller was hired by a former colleague. Miller underwent therapy and believed he had resolved his problem with compulsive embezzlement.*

*When interviewed about his past activities, Miller said that he felt his problem with theft was an illness, just like alcoholism or compulsive gambling. The illness was driven by a subconscious need to be admired and liked by others. He thought that by spending money others would like him. Miller stated "that once he got started, he couldn't stop.[1]*

In Part Four of this book, we discussed the investigation of fraud. In Part Five, we discussed financial statement frauds. In this chapter, we cover employee, customer, and vendor fraud against organizations. In Chapter 16, we discuss frauds associated with bankruptcies, divorce, and taxes. In studying these chapters, you should recognize that there are many other types of frauds. Fraud perpetrators are creative, and new schemes are developed every day. Our approach in this section is to introduce you to some of the most common types of fraud and whet your appetite for fraud study, so that you will want to study other types of frauds on your own.

## Fraud Statistics

In this chapter, we draw heavily (with permission) from Joe Wells's works, including his book, *Occupational Fraud and Abuse*. This book contains by far the best taxonomy of the various types of fraud.[2]

In 1993, under Joe Wells's direction, the Association of Certified Fraud Examiners (ACFE) began a major research project studying approximately 2,600 different frauds reported by more than 2,000 Certified Fraud Examiners. That study, which was published in 1996, provided many interesting findings about fraud, one of which was the classification of occupational fraud and abuse into three main categories: (1) asset misappropriation, (2) corruption, and (3) fraudulent financial statements. In 2002, the ACFE published an update of that study based on an analysis of an additional 663 occupational fraud cases. From the three main categories of fraud identified in the studies, 44 separate fraud schemes were identified and classified. Because financial statement frauds were covered in Chapters 11–13, we will focus in this chapter on misappropriation and corruption.

Statistics about fraud against organizations that were revealed in the ACFE's first fraud research study can be found in Table 15-1.

### Table 15-1 Summary of ACFE's Fraud Statistics

- Fifty-eight percent of the frauds against organizations are perpetrated by employees, 30 percent by management, and 12 percent by owners.

- The median loss from frauds perpetrated by employees was $60,000; by managers was $250,000; and by owners was $1,000,000.

- The median loss from frauds perpetrated by males was $185,000; the median loss from frauds committed by females was $48,000.

## Table 15-1 Summary of ACFE's Fraud Statistics (continued)

- Median fraud losses increased with age:
  - Less than 25 years old           $ 12,000
  - 26–30 years old                  50,000
  - 31–35 years old                  54,000
  - 36–40 years old                  100,000
  - 41–50 years old                  196,000
  - 51–60 years old                  280,000
  - Over 60 years old               346,000

- Median fraud losses differed by marital status:
  - Married (72% of all perpetrators)      $150,000
  - Divorced (8% of all perpetrators)       80,000
  - Single (11% of all perpetrators)        54,000
  - Separated (9% of all perpetrators)     50,000

- Median fraud losses also varied by level of education:
  - High school (42% of all perpetrators)     $ 50,000
  - College (45% of all perpetrators)        200,000
  - Post-graduate (13% of all perpetrators)   275,000

- Median fraud losses also varied by size of victim organization:
  - 1–100 employees                $120,000
  - 101–1,000 employees            100,000
  - 1,001–10,000 employees        80,000
  - Over 10,000 employees         126,000

The highlights of the 2002 study follow:
- An extrapolation from the study mans that total losses of approximately $600 billion per year occur in the United States, or about $4,500 per employee, as a result of occupational fraud.
- More than half of the frauds studied caused losses of at least $100,000 and nearly one in six caused losses in excess of $1 million.
- Asset misappropriations accounted for 80 percent of all frauds. Cash is the targeted asset 90 percent of the time. Corruption schemes accounted for 13 percent of all occupational frauds and cause more than $500,000 per loss, on average. Fraudulent financial statements are the most costly of all frauds and, although only 7 percent of all frauds are of this type, the average amount of such frauds is $4.25 million.
- The average scheme in the 2002 study lasted 18 months before it was detected.
- The most common method for detecting the frauds was by a tip from an employee, customer, vendor, or anonymous source. The second most common method was by accident.
- Organizations with fraud hotlines cut their fraud losses by approximately 50 percent per scheme. Internal audits, external audits, and background checks also significantly reduce fraud losses.
- The typical perpetrator is a first-time offender. Only 7 percent of occupational fraudsters in the 2002 study had prior convictions for fraud-related offenses.
- Small businesses were the most vulnerable to occupational fraud and abuse. The average scheme in a small business causes $127,500 in losses. The average scheme in the largest companies costs $97,000.

# Asset Misappropriations

Employees, vendors, and customers of organizations have three opportunities to steal assets: (1) they can steal *receipts* of cash and other assets as they are coming into an organization; (2) they can steal cash and other assets that are *on hand*; or (3) they can commit *disbursement fraud* by having the organization pay for something it shouldn't pay for or pay too much for something it purchases. With each of these three types of fraud, the perpetrators can act alone or they can work in collusion with others. The diagram in Figure 15-1 outlines the misappropriation possibilities:

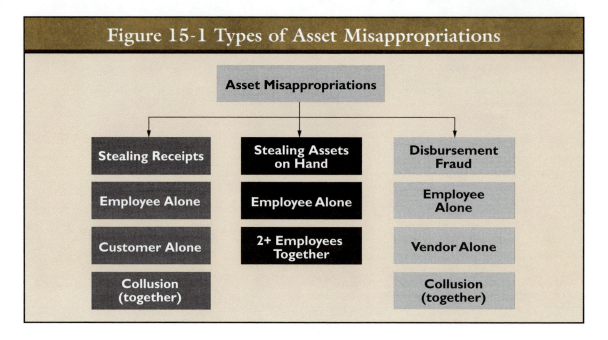

## Figure 15-1 Types of Asset Misappropriations

The fraud taxonomy developed by Joe Wells is more complicated and detailed than the one shown in Figure 15-1. Based on the 2,600 frauds studied, he divides asset misappropriations into two major categories: (1) thefts of cash and (2) thefts of inventory and other assets. He further subdivides thefts of cash into three subgroups: (1) larceny (intentionally taking away an employer's cash without the consent and against the will of the employer), (2) skimming (the removal of cash from a victim entity prior to its entry in an accounting system), and (3) fraudulent disbursements. Similarly, he divides the misappropriation of assets other than cash, including inventory, into two groups: (1) misuse and (2) larceny. We will discuss the misappropriation of assets according to his classification scheme.

## Theft of Cash Through Larceny

With larceny, cash is stolen by employees or others after it has already been recorded in the company's accounting system. As a result, larceny schemes are easier to detect than skimming schemes and are far less common. In its fraud study, the ACFE found that cash larceny accounted for only about 3 percent of all frauds, and that the median loss was only $22,000 per incident, third lowest among all types of fraud.

Cash larcenies can take place in any circumstance in which an employee has access to cash. Common larceny schemes involve the theft of cash or currency on hand (e.g., in a cash register or cash box) or from bank deposits. Cash larcenies are most successful when they involve relatively small amounts over extended periods of time. With such thefts, businesses often write the small missing amounts off as "shorts" or "miscounts," rather than as thefts. For example, in one bank, the annual cash shortages by tellers exceed $3 million per year. Some of this teller shortage may be caused by miscounting, and certainly customers are more likely to inform a teller when he or she gives them too little cash than when the teller gives them too much cash. However, a significant portion of the shortage is probably caused by larceny.

## Theft of Cash Through Skimming

An example of skimming is the fraud perpetrated by Marvin Culpepper. Marvin was the business manager at Muffler's Incorporated. Two of his responsibilities were to collect cash from customers and open all incoming mail. He was also responsible for making daily bank deposits. At Muffler's Incorporated, customers paid for their automobile repairs in one of three ways: (1) by check, (2) with cash, or (3) with a credit card. Over a period of six years, Marvin skimmed approximately half of the receipts from customers who paid by cash. He concealed his thefts by never recording the work as being done. Never once did he skim money from customers who paid by check or credit card because those types of thefts would have been much harder to conceal. In total, Marvin stole more $600,000 from Muffler's Incorporated.

Marvin's theft illustrates the most basic skimming scheme—taking money from the sale of goods or services but making no record of the sale. Another example of this type of skimming is the ice cream store cashier who sells two-scoop ice cream cones to customers and either does not enter the sales into the cash register or enters the sales as single-scoop sales.

More complicated skimming schemes occur when employees understate sales and collections by recording false or larger-than-reality sales discounts, misappropriate customer payments and write off the receivable as "uncollectible," embezzle a first customer's payment and then credit that customer's account when a second customer pays (a delayed recognition of payment, called lapping), or work together with customers to allow them to pay later than required or less than required. As an example of this latter type of fraud, consider the $2.2 million fraud experienced by a *Fortune* 500 company. This fraud was perpetrated when an employee who was responsible for making receivable collections from customers gave a high-volume customer extra time to pay receivables without reporting them as delinquent. As a result of this fraud, the dishonest customer was able to invest cash that should have been used to pay the accounts payable in short-term securities prior to payment, thus earning interest exceeding $2 million. The money was then split with the accounts receivable manager, who worked for the victim company. This fraud had elements of both skimming and corruption.

## Cash Theft Through Fraudulent Disbursements

The research studies of the ACFE found that fraudulent disbursements comprised by far the highest percentage of asset misappropriations. In fact, based on the number of cases studied, fraudulent disbursements represented 67 percent of all cases, more than double the total of skimming (28.9% of all misappropriations) and larceny (4.1% of all cases.)

The ACFE divides fraudulent disbursements into six major types: (1) check tampering, (2) register disbursement schemes, (3) billing schemes, (4) expense schemes, (5) payroll schemes, and (6) others. In terms of frequency and amount of losses, billing schemes are the largest, as shown in Table 15-2.

## Table 15-2 Types of Disbursements Fraud

| Type of Fraud | Percent of Cases | Percent of Losses |
|---|---|---|
| Billing schemes | 33.3% | 51.6% |
| Check tampering | 24.5 | 13.2 |
| Payroll schemes | 16.5 | 10.7 |
| Expense schemes | 14.9 | 4.0 |
| Other fraudulent disbursements | 8.1 | 0.1 |
| Register disbursement schemes | 2.7 | 20.4 |

**Check Tampering.** Check tampering is a type of fraudulent disbursement scheme in which an employee either (1) prepares a fraudulent check for his or her own benefit, or (2) intercepts a check intended for a third party and converts the check to his or her own benefit. Check tampering is unique among the disbursement frauds because it is the one group of schemes in which the perpetrator physically prepares the fraudulent check. In most fraudulent disbursement schemes, the culprit generates a payment to himself or herself by submitting some false document to the victim company, such as an invoice or a timecard. The false document represents a claim for payment and causes the victim company to issue a check, which the perpetrator then converts. These frauds essentially amount to trickery: the perpetrator fools the company into handing over its money. Check-tampering schemes are fundamentally different. With check tampering, the fraud perpetrator takes physical control of a check and makes it payable to himself or herself by either forging the maker (signing the check), forging endorsements, or altering payees.

**Register Disbursement Schemes.** Register disbursement schemes are among the least costly of all disbursement schemes, averaging only $22,500 per incident. Two basic fraudulent schemes take place at the register: false refunds and false voids. With false refunds, a fraud perpetrator processes a transaction as if a customer were returning merchandise, even though no actual return takes place. The fraud perpetrator then takes money from the cash register in the amount of the false return. Because the register tape shows that a merchandise return has been made, it appears that the disbursement is legitimate. The concealment problem for perpetrators is that, with false refunds, a debit is made to the inventory system showing that merchandise has been returned. Because no inventory was returned, the recorded inventory amount is overstated and an inventory count may reveal the "missing" inventory. A similar but more difficult fraud to detect is the overstating of refunds. In these cases, merchandise is actually returned, but the value of the return is overstated. For example, assume that a customer returned merchandise costing $10. The dishonest employee may record the return as $15, give the customer $10, and pocket $5.

Fictitious voids are similar to refund schemes in that they generate a disbursement from the cash register. When a sale is voided on a register, a copy of the customer's receipt is usually attached to a void slip, along with the signature or initials of a manager that indicates that the transaction has been approved. To process a false void, the cashier usually keeps the customer's receipt at the time of sale and then rings in a voided sale after the customer has left. Whatever money the customer paid for the item is removed from the register as though it was being returned to the customer. The copy of the customer's receipt is attached to the voided slip to verify the authenticity of the transaction. Unfortunately for the perpetrator, voided sales create the same kind of concealment problems that false returns do—that is, someone might discover that inventory that was supposed to have been returned is missing.

**Billing Schemes.** Both check tampering and register disbursement schemes require perpetrators to physically take cash or checks from their employers. With billing schemes, the perpetrator does not have to undergo the risk of taking company cash or merchandise. In a billing scheme, the perpetrator submits or alters an invoice that causes the employer to willingly issue a check or make other types of payments. Though the support for the payment is fraudulent, the disbursement itself is facially valid. Billing schemes are extremely common and quite expensive. The median cost of billing schemes in the ACFE study was $250,000, by far the highest of all asset misappropriation classifications. Because the majority of most businesses' disbursements are made in the purchasing cycle, larger thefts can be hidden through false billing schemes than through other kinds of fraudulent disbursements. Employees who utilize billing schemes are just going where the money is.

The three most common types of billing schemes are (1) setting up dummy companies (shell companies) to submit invoices to the victim organization, (2) altering or double-paying nonaccomplice vendor's statements, and (3) making personal purchases with company funds. Dummy or shell companies are fictitious entities created for the sole purpose of committing fraud. Many times, they are nothing more than a fabricated name and a post office box that an employee uses to collect disbursements from false billings. However, since the checks received will be made out in the name of the shell company, the perpetrator will normally also set up a bank account in the new company's name, listing himself as an authorized signer on the account.

Rather than using shell companies as vessels for overbilling schemes, some employees generate fraudulent disbursements by using the invoice of nonaccomplice vendors. For example, perpetrators using this scheme may double-pay an invoice. By intentionally paying some bills twice, then requesting the recipients to return one of the checks, the perpetrator keeps the returned check. Another related scheme is to intentionally pay the wrong vendor and then ask for the payment to be returned. Or, a dishonest employee might intentionally overpay a legitimate vendor, asking for a return of the overpayment portion.

The final common billing scheme is making personal purchases with company funds. The purchases may be for perpetrators themselves or for their businesses, their families, or others.

**Expense Schemes.** Expense and payroll schemes are similar to billing schemes. The perpetrators of these frauds produce false documentation that causes the victim company to unknowingly make a fraudulent disbursement. With expense and payroll schemes, the false documentation includes items like timecards, sales orders, and expense reports. Expense schemes involve overbilling the company for travel and other related business expenses, such as business lunches, hotel bills, and air travel.

Four common types of expense disbursement schemes are (1) mischaracterizing expenses, (2) overstating expenses, (3) submitting fictitious expenses, and (4) submitting the same expenses multiple times. The first type of fraud involves mischaracterizing a personal expense to make it look like a business expense. For example, personal travel might be claimed as a business trip, a personal lunch as a business lunch, or a personal magazine subscription as a company subscription. Overstating expenses usually involves doctoring a receipt or other supporting documentation to reflect a higher cost than what was actually paid. The employee may use eradicating fluid, a ball point pen, or some other method to change the price reflected on the receipt. If the company does not require original documents as support, the perpetrator generally attaches a copy of the receipt to his expense report. In some cases, such as taxi receipts, the perpetrator actually completes the receipt himself, writing in an amount higher than was actually spent.

Fictitious expense schemes usually involve creating bogus support documents, such as false receipts. The emergence of personal computers and graphics programs has made it possible to easily create realistic-looking counterfeit receipts. Alternatively, perpetrators committing this type of fraud sometimes obtain blank receipts from vendors or printers, and then fill them out and submit them. The least common of the expense schemes is the submission of multiple reimbursements for the same expense.

**Payroll Schemes.** Even though payroll schemes are common examples of fraud, in reality they account for only a small percentage of all frauds—1.9 percent of the total losses in the ACFE studies. Payroll fraud schemes fall into four major categories: (1) ghost employees, (2) falsified hours and salary, (3) commission schemes, and (4) false workers' compensation claims. Of all payroll fraud schemes, ghost employee schemes tend to generate the largest losses. According to the ACFE, their average loss of $275,000 per occurrence is high and costly to organizations. Ghost employee frauds involve putting someone on the payroll (or keeping a former employee on the payroll) who does not actually work for the victim company. Through the falsification of personnel or payroll records, fraud perpetrators cause paychecks to be generated to a ghost. These paychecks are then cashed by the fraud perpetrators or their accomplices.

For ghost-employee fraud schemes to work, four things must happen: (1) the ghost must be added to the payroll, (2) timekeeping and wage rate information must be collected, (3) a paycheck must be issued to the ghost (unless direct deposits are used), and (4) the check must be delivered to the perpetrator or an accomplice. By far the most common method of misappropriating funds from payroll is the overpayment of wages, accounting for 55.4 percent of all payroll frauds. For hourly employees, the size of a paycheck is based on two essential factors: the number of hours worked and the rate of pay. Therefore, for hourly employees to fraudulently increase the size of their paychecks, they must either falsify the number of hours worked or change the wage rate. Because salaried employees do not receive compensation based on their time at work, in most cases these employees generate fraudulent wages by increasing their rates of pay.

Commissions are a form of compensation calculated as a percentage of the amount of transactions a salesperson or other employee generates. This unique form of compensation is not based on hours worked or a set yearly salary, but rather on an employee's revenue output. A commissioned employee's wages are a percentage based on the amount of sales the employee generates. Thus, an employee on commission can fraudulently increase pay by (1) falsifying the amount of sales made, or (2) increasing the rate of commission. The most common method of committing commission-based payroll fraud is to falsify the amount of sales made in one of three ways: (1) creating fictitious sales, (2) falsifying the value of sales made by altering prices listed on sales documents, or (3) overstating sales by claiming sales made by another employee or in another period.

Some commission payment plans are structured in ways that almost encourage fraud. Take, for example, a graduated commission scheme, such as one that pays 5 percent if a salesperson generates revenue of less than $100,000, 7 percent if the salesperson generates revenues of between $100,000 and $200,000, and 10 percent if sales exceed $200,000. Working under this system, sales agents have a strong incentive to generate revenues exceeding $200,000 so they can earn a 10 percent commission on all sales. Thus, total sales that fall just short of $200,000 prompt a strong incentive to create "additional revenues" that will help the salesperson qualify for the higher commission rate.

**Other Fraudulent Disbursements.** Workers' compensation is not a payroll account, but rather an insurance expense. Nevertheless, it is essentially an employee benefit, entitling persons injured on the job to compensation while they heal. By far the most common way to commit workers' compensation fraud is to fake an injury and collect payments from the victim company's insurance carrier. In some cases, the employee colludes with a doctor, who processes bogus claims for unnecessary medical treatments and then splits the payments for those fictitious treatments with the "injured" employee.

The primary victim of a workers' compensation scheme is not the employer, but rather the insurance carrier for the employer. The insurance carrier pays for the fraudulent medical bills and the unnecessary absences of the perpetrator. Nevertheless, employers are also victims of these crimes because bogus claims can result in higher premiums for the company in the future.

Before we move on to theft of assets other than cash, it is important to know that in the past few years, even some executives of corporations have allegedly looted their companies of huge amounts of cash, usually through disbursement frauds. The two most famous of these types of frauds, sometimes referred to as corporate looting, were Dennis Kozlowski, chief executive; Mark Belnick, chief corporate counsel; and Mark Swartz, chief financial officer, of Tyco International Ltd. (Tyco), and John Rigas and his sons of Adelphia Corporation (Adelphia.)

The Tyco case is a looting case. It involved egregious, self-serving, and clandestine misconduct by the three most senior executives at Tyco. From at least 1996 until June of 2002, Dennis Kozlowski and Mark H. Swartz allegedly took hundreds of millions of dollars in secret, unauthorized, and improper low-interest or interest-free loans and compensation from Tyco. Kozlowski and Swartz concealed these transactions from Tyco's shareholders. Kozlowski and Swartz later pocketed tens of millions of dollars by causing Tyco to forgive repayment of many of their improper loans. They also concealed these transactions from Tyco's shareholders. In addition, Kozlowski and Swartz engaged in numerous highly profitable related-party transactions with Tyco and awarded themselves lavish perquisites—without disclosing either the transactions or perquisites to Tyco shareholders. At the same time that Kozlowski and Swartz engaged in their massive covert defalcation of corporate funds, Kozlowski regularly assured investors that at Tyco "nothing was hidden behind the scenes," that Tyco's disclosures were "exceptional" and that Tyco's management "prided itself on having sharp focus with creating shareholder value." Similarly, Swartz regularly assured investors that "Tyco's disclosure practice remains second to none." Belnick, the chief counsel, also defrauded Tyco shareholders of millions of dollars through egregious self-dealing transactions. From 1998 into early 2002, Belnick received approximately $14,000,000 in interest-free loans from Tyco to buy and renovate a $4,000,000 apartment on Central Park West and to buy and renovate a $10,000,000 ski chalet in Park City, Utah. The original loans and the forgiveness of the loans were hidden from the compensation committee of the board of directors.

Kozlowski, Swartz, and Belnick also spent lavishly on themselves. One of the most egregious expenditures involved Kozlowski throwing a party for his second wife, Karen, paid for with company funds. The party was held on the island of Sardinia in the Mediterranean Sea and cost approximately $2 million (or $70,000 per person), including paying travel costs for the guests. The planning memo for the party, with certain obscene parts deleted was as follows:

*Guests arrive at the club starting at 7:15 p.m. Two gladiators are standing next to the door, one opens the door, the other helps the guests. We have a lion or horse with a chariot for the shock value. We have gladiators standing guard every couple feet. The guests come into the pool area, the band is playing, and they are dressed in elegant chic. There is a big ice sculpture of Dennis with lots of shellfish and caviar at his feet. The waiters are dressed in linen with fig wreathes on their heads. There is a full bar with fabulous linens. The pool has floating candles and flowers. We have rented fig trees with tiny lights everywhere. At 8:30, the waiters instruct that dinner is served. The tables have incredible linens with chalices as wineglasses. The band continues to play light music through dinner. After dinner, they kick it up a bit. We start the show of pictures on the screen, great background music in sync with the slides. At the end, Elvis is on the screen wishing Karen a Happy Birthday and apologizing that he could not make it. It starts to fade and Elvis is on stage and starts singing happy birthday with the Swingdogs. A huge cake is brought out. The cake explodes. Elvis kicks it in full throttle. At 11:30, the light show starts. People are displayed on the mountain, fireworks are coming from both ends of the golf course in sync with music. Swingdogs start up and the night is young.[3]*

Like Tyco, the Adelphia fraud was also a case of corporate looting (as well as financial statement manipulation to cover the frauds.) Because of their actions, both the Securities and Exchange Commission and Federal Government prosecutors filed charges against Adelphia founder John J. Rigas; his three sons, Timothy J. Rigas, Michael J. Rigas, and James P. Rigas; and two senior executives at Adelphia, James R. Brown, and Michael C. Mulcahey.

In addition to manipulating financial statements, the conspirators were charged with rampant self-dealing, including the undisclosed use of corporate funds for Rigas family stock purchases, the purchase of timber rights to land in Pennsylvania, the construction of a golf club for $12.8 million, paying off personal margin loans and other Rigas family debts, and purchase luxury condominiums in Colorado, Mexico, and New York City for the Rigas family.

## Theft of Inventory and Other Assets

A person can misappropriate company assets other than cash in one of two ways. The asset can be misused (or "borrowed"), or it can be stolen. Simple misuse is obviously the less egregious of the two types of fraud. Assets that are misused but not stolen typically include company vehicles, company supplies, computers, and other office equipment. These assets are also used by some employees to conduct personal work on company time. In many instances, these side businesses are of the same nature as the employer's business, so the employee is essentially competing with the employer and using the employer's equipment to do it.

Although the misuse of company property might be a problem, the theft of company property is a much greater concern. Losses from inventory theft, for example, can run into the millions of dollars. The means employed to steal company property range from simple larceny—walking off with company property—to more complicated schemes involving the falsification of company documents and records. Larceny usually involves taking inventory or other assets from the company premises, without attempting to conceal it in the books and records or "justify" its absence. Most noncash larceny schemes are not complicated. They are typically committed by employees (such as warehouse personnel, inventory clerks, and shipping clerks) who have access to inventory and other assets.

Another common type of noncash asset theft is the use of asset requisitions and other forms that allow assets to be moved from one location in a company to another location. Often, fraud perpetrators use internal documents to gain access to merchandise that they otherwise might not be able to handle without raising suspicion. Transfer documents allow fraud perpetrators to move assets from one location to another and then take the merchandise for themselves. The most basic scheme occurs when an employee requisitions materials to complete a work-related project and then steals the materials. In more extreme cases, a fraud perpetrator might completely fabricate a project that necessitates the use of certain assets that he or she intends to steal.

A third type of noncash asset theft involves the use of the purchasing and receiving functions of a company. If assets are purchased by employees for personal use, that is a purchasing scheme fraud. On the other hand, if assets were intentionally purchased by the company but simply misappropriated by a fraud perpetrator, a noncash asset fraud has been committed. In this case, the perpetrator's company is deprived not only of the cash it paid for the merchandise, but also the merchandise itself. In addition, because the organization doesn't have as much inventory on hand as it thinks it has, stock-outs and unhappy customers often result.

# Corruption

All the schemes discussed thus far in this chapter fall into the broad category called asset misappropriation. A second major type of occupational abuse or fraud committed against organizations is corruption. Corruption is one of the oldest white-collar crimes. The tradition of "paying off" public officials or company insiders for preferential treatment is rooted in the crudest business systems developed.

Corruption can be broken down into the following four scheme types: (1) bribery schemes, (2) conflicts of interest schemes, (3) economic extortion schemes, and (4) illegal gratuity schemes. By far the largest of these is bribery which accounts for 89.2 percent of all corruption losses, compared to 9 percent for conflicts of interest schemes, 1.6 percent for economic extortion schemes and 0.2 percent for illegal gratuity schemes. Although bribery schemes are not as common as some types of fraud, their median loss is by far the highest of any of the fraud schemes discussed in this chapter—more than $500,000 per incident.

## Bribery

Bribery involves the offering, giving, receiving, or soliciting anything of value to influence an official act. The term *official act* means that traditional bribery statutes only proscribe payments made to influence the decisions of government agents or employees. Certainly one of the most infamous cases of bribery in early history was that of Judas Iscariot, the disciple who betrayed Jesus Christ. Judas was paid 30 pieces of silver by the chief priests and elders of Jerusalem to disclose the location of Jesus so that he could be captured and executed. Another example of bribery was the scandal that rocked Washington, D.C., in the early 1920s. The paper trail of corruption led back to the White House Cabinet and nearly implicated then-President Warren G. Harding. Known as the Teapot Dome Scandal, the incident surrounded several key members of Harding's staff, who mishandled the leasing of naval oil reserve lands.

Many occupational fraud schemes involve commercial bribery, which is similar to the traditional definition of bribery, except that something of value is offered to influence a business decision rather than an official act of government. In a commercial bribery scheme, payment is received by an employee without the employer's consent. In other words, commercial bribery cases deal with the acceptance of under-the-table payments in return for the exercise of influence over a business transaction.

Bribery schemes generally fall into two broad categories: kickbacks and bid-rigging schemes. Kickbacks are undisclosed payments made by vendors to employees of purchasing companies. The purpose of a kickback is usually to enlist the corrupt employee in an overbilling scheme. Sometimes vendors pay kickbacks simply to get extra business from the purchasing company. Unfortunately, once kickbacks are paid by vendors, the control of purchasing transactions usually transfers from the buyer to the vendor. When the vendor is in control of the purchasing transactions, more goods are usually bought at higher prices, and the quality of goods purchased can deteriorate substantially.

Earlier we described the kickback scheme that resulted in Pinkerton's buying approximately $11 million of unneeded guard uniforms at increased prices and lower quality. In a common type of kickback scheme, a vendor submits a fraudulent or inflated invoice to the victim company, and the employee of that company helps make sure that payment is made on the false invoice. For this type of assistance, the employee receives some form of payment from the vendor. That payment, or kickback, can take the form of cash, reduced prices for goods purchased, the hiring of a relative, the promise of subsequent employment, or some other form. Kickback schemes almost always attack the purchasing function of the victim company.

Bid-rigging schemes occur when an employee fraudulently assists a vendor in winning a contract through the competitive bidding process. This process, in which several suppliers or contractors are vying for contracts in what can be a cutthroat environment, can be tailor-made for bribery. Any advantage one vendor can gain over competitors in this arena is extremely valuable. The benefit of "inside influence" can insure that a vendor will win a sought-after contract. Many vendors are willing to pay for this influence. The way competitive bidding is rigged depends largely upon the level of influence of the corrupt employee. The more power a person has over the bidding process, the more likely the person can influence the selection of a supplier. Therefore, employees involved in bid-rigging schemes, like those in kickback schemes, tend to have a good measure of influence over or access to the bidding process. Potential targets for accepting bribes include buyers, contracting officials, engineers and technical representatives, quality or product assurance representatives, subcontractor liaison employees, or anyone else with authority over the awarding of contracts.

## Conflicts of Interest

A conflict of interest occurs when an employee, manager, or executive has an undisclosed economic or personal interest in a transaction that adversely affects the company. As with other corruption schemes, conflicts of interest involve the exertion of an employee's influence to the detriment of the company. Conflicts usually involve self-dealing by an employee. In some cases, the employee's act benefits a friend or relative, even though the employee receives no personal financial benefit from the transaction.

To be classified as a conflict of interest scheme, the employee's interest in a transaction must be undisclosed. The essential element in a conflict case is that the fraud perpetrator takes advantage of his or her employer: the victim company is unaware that its employee has divided loyalties. If an employer knows of the employee's interest in a business deal or negotiation, conflict of interest is eliminated, even in arrangements favorable to the employee.

Most conflict schemes fall into one of two categories: (1) purchase schemes, or (2) sales schemes. The most common type of purchasing scheme involves the employee (or a friend or relative of the employee) having some kind of ownership or employment interest in the vendor that submits the invoice. The bill must originate from a real company in which the fraud perpetrator has an economic or personal interest, and the perpetrator's interest in the company must be undisclosed to the victim company.

The most common sales scheme involves an employee with a hidden interest having the victim company sell its goods or services below fair market value. This type of fraud results in a lower profit margin or even a loss on the sale. As an example, a few years ago one of the largest paper and pulp companies in the United States discovered a major fraud being perpetrated by some of its employees. To get wood for making paper, the company both owned its own forests and purchased lumber from others. One of the vendors providing lumber to the company turned out to be a group of its own employees who were cutting timber on the company's own forest reserves and then selling the timber back to the company. In this case, the company was losing twice—once by paying for lumber it already owned, and then by having less of its own timber to harvest.

Some of the most egregious cases of conflict-of-interest frauds were the mutual fund frauds that took place recently in the United States. Since the beginning of the mutual fund industry in the 1920s, mutual funds have been thought of as a relatively safe investment vehicle. Mutual funds were sold as a limited risk investment that was, in the words of the great poet Bob Dylan, "always safe" and, thus, represented as a "shelter from the storm."[4] However recent revelations showed America's $7 trillion mutual fund industry to be rife with self-dealing, conflicts of interest, illegality, and impropriety. Not only were funds preferentially allowing select investors to unlawfully trade in exchange for higher fees and other forms of profit, but fund insiders, including the most senior executives and founders of certain funds, engaged in the same unlawful trading conduct for their own personal gains.

Most of the mutual fund frauds involved basic schemes in which mutual fund companies allowed certain preferred clients to make illegal trades, including rapid in-and-out trades and well as trades based upon information not yet reflected in the price of the mutual fund's assets. The unlawful trading schemes engaged in by mutual funds involved two practices known as "market timing" and "late trading." These manipulative practices were possible because of the way in which mutual funds are valued. Specifically, mutual funds in the United States are valued once a day, at 4:00 p.m. Eastern Time (ET) following the close of the financial markets in New York. The price, known as the net asset value (NAV), reflects the closing prices of the securities that comprise a particular fund's portfolio plus the value of any uninvested cash that the fund manager maintains for the fund. Thus, although the shares of a mutual fund are bought and sold all day long, the price at which the shares trade does not change during the course of the day. Orders placed any time up to 4:00 p.m. are priced at that day's NAV, and orders placed after 4:01 p.m. are priced at the next day's NAV. This practice, known as "forward pricing," has been required by law since 1968.

Illegal market timing is an investment technique that involves short-term "in and out" trading of mutual fund shares. According to a Stanford University study, market timing may have caused losses to long-term mutual fund investors of approximately $5 billion each year.[5] Rapid trading is antithetical to the premise that mutual funds are long-term investments meant for buy-and-hold investors. In-and-out trading capitalizes on the fact that a mutual fund's price does not reflect the fair value of the assets held by the fund. A typical example of market timing involves a U.S. mutual fund that holds Japanese shares. Because of the time zone difference, the Japanese market may close at 2:00 a.m. ET in the United States. If the U.S. mutual fund manager uses the closing prices of the Japanese shares in his or her fund to arrive at an NAV at 4:00 p.m. in New York, the manager is relying on market information that is fourteen hours old. If positive market moves occurred during the New York trading day, which is a reliable indicator that the Japanese market will rise when it later opens, the fund's stale NAV will not reflect the expected price change and, thus, will be artificially low. The NAV does not reflect the time-current market value of the stocks held by the mutual fund. Thus, a trader who buys the Japanese fund at the "stale" price is virtually assured of a profit that can be realized the next day by selling at the higher NAV. Because of the artificial difference between the NAV and fair value has long been recognized, mutual funds represented to their investors that they imposed policies to prevent investors from profiting from the stale pricing by rapidly trading in and out of the funds. Most mutual fund prospectuses represent to investors that the funds monitor, prohibit, and prevent rapid trading because it is detrimental to long-term investors. Despite their representations to the contrary, mutual funds, as well as their investment advisers, permitted such trading for their own profit. The resulting harm, known as "dilution," caused by the transfer of wealth from long-term investors to market timers, came dollar-for-dollar at the expense of long-term investors' profits.

Late trading, an even worse fraudulent practice, allowed selected investors to purchase mutual funds after 4:00 p.m., using that day's NAV, rather than the next day's NAV, as required under the law. It has been likened to betting today on yesterday's horse races. Because a fund's NAV is calculated after the markets close at 4:00 p.m. ET, orders to buy, sell, or exchange mutual fund shares placed before 4:00 p.m. ET on a given day receive that day's NAV. Orders placed after 4:00 p.m. ET are supposed to be priced at the follow day's NAV. This pricing mechanism was legislated in order to place all investors on a level playing field whereby no investor can benefit from after-hours information in making investment decisions. Certain mutual funds, however, allowed select customers to capitalize on positive earnings news by agreeing to sell them mutual fund shares at the prior trading day's NAV. In essence, these select investors were allowed to immediately reap the benefit of the stock's upward movement the following day due to information learned after 4:00 p.m. ET. In contrast, all other investors who purchased after 4:00 p.m. ET were required to pay the next day's NAV. Again, any money made in this manner comes out of the value of the mutual fund and, therefore, on a dollar-for-dollar basis, the pockets of its investors. Mutual funds presumably allowed this type of trading to happen in exchange for the hedge funds' business in other areas. This egregious late trading was not limited to a few isolated cases but rather was rampant throughout the industry.

Examples of violators were Putnam Investments and Pilgrim, Baxter & Associates. Putnam was the fifth largest fund firm in the United States with $263 billion in assets. In Putnam's case, four investment fund managers engaged in market timing trades and personally made large windfalls. Two other fund managers made market timing trades in funds they didn't manage and also made huge windfalls. It turns out that Putnam discovered the problem as early as 2000, but took no disciplinary action. As a result, the SEC charged Putnam and the managers with civil securities fraud. Putnam also faces 16 class-action lawsuits and, when the problems were discovered, Putnam's investors withdrew more than 10 percent of the fund's assets. Harold Baxter of Pilgrim supposedly gave nonpublic portfolio information to a friend, who in turn gave that information to clients who conducted rapid trades in Pilgrim's PBHG family of funds. Supposedly, Gary Pilgrim made millions in profits from short-term trading. Based on allegations of illegal market timing and late-trading, the following mutual funds now have investigations or civil suits against them: Massachusetts Financial Services Co. (MFS), Strong Financial, Invesco Funds Group, Federated Investors, Securities Trust Co, Pilgrim, Baxter & Associates, Putnam Investments, Fred Alger Management, Bank One, Prudential Securities, Alliance Capital Management, Bank of America, Janus Capital Group, and Canary Capital Partners.

## Economic Extortion and Illegal Gratuities

Compared to bribery and conflicts of interests, economic extortion and illegal gratuities occur relatively infrequently and are usually quite small. Economic extortion is basically the flipside of a bribery scheme. Instead of a vendor offering a payment to an employee to influence a decision, the employee demands a payment from a vendor in order to make a decision in that vendor's favor. In any situation where an employee might accept bribes to favor a particular company or person, the situation could be reversed to a point where the employee extorts money from a potential purchaser or supplier. Illegal gratuities are also similar to bribery schemes, except it is not necessarily an intent to influence a particular business decision but rather to reward someone for making a favorable decision. Illegal gratuities are made after deals are approved.

## SUMMARY

Employees, vendors, and customers can commit fraud against an organization. The classification scheme used in this chapter was developed by Joe Wells, chairman and CEO of the Association of Certified Fraud Examiners. It isn't the only fraud taxonomy available, but it is detailed and based on an empirical study of more than 2,600 frauds. The graphic in Figure 15-2 is a taxonomy of the misappropriation and corruption schemes described in this chapter.

Organizations that understand the kinds of frauds that can occur can personalize this taxonomy to their individual organizations and determine where their risks are greatest. Once these risks are identified, they can take proactive steps to reduce or eliminate the risks and audit for frauds that may be occurring.

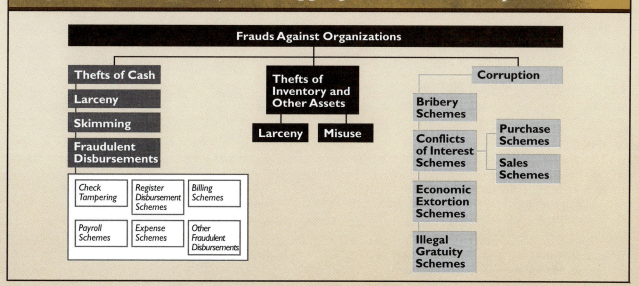

Figure 15-2 Taxonomy of Misappropriation and Corruption Frauds

# KEY TERMS

**Bid-rigging Schemes:** Frauds involving employees assisting vendors in winning contracts  by providing them some kind of unfair advantage.

**Billing Schemes:** Stealing cash by submitting a false or altered invoice so that payment is made by an organization.

**Bribery:** Offering, giving, receiving, or soliciting anything of value to influence an official act.

**Check Tampering:** Stealing cash by preparing fraudulent checks or intercepting checks made payable to others.

**Conflicts of Interest:** Fraud in which employees, managers or executives put their personal interest above the company's interest, usually resulting in an adverse affect on the organization.

**Corruption:** "Paying off" or "bribing" public or company officials in order to receive preferential treatment.

**Disbursement Fraud:** Fraud perpetrated by having an organization pay for something it shouldn't or paying too much for something it should pay for.

**Economic Extortion:** Demanding payment from a vendor in order to make a decision in the vendor's favor; opposite of bribery.

**Expense Schemes:** Recording a fictitious expense and having the organization pay for it; examples are travel reimbursement schemes, fictitious payroll, etc.

**Illegal Gratuities:** Payments made to reward a favorable decision—payment is made after the deal is approved.

**Larceny:** Stealing cash after it has been recorded in an organization's accounting records; an example is stealing petty cash.

**Misappropriation:** Another name for frauds committed against an organization.

**Register Disbursement Schemes:** Using a register to steal cash from an organization; examples include false refunds and false voids.

**Skimming:** Embezzling a portion of the cash receipts of an organization.

# QUESTIONS AND CASES

## DISCUSSION QUESTIONS

1. What are the three types of fraud against organizations that employees, vendors, and customers use to steal an organization's assets?

2. Describe what is meant by theft of cash through larceny.

3. Describe what is meant by theft of cash through skimming.

4. How does the ACFE categorize fraudulent disbursements?

5. What is meant by check tampering?

6. What is a register disbursement scheme?

7. What is meant by a billing scheme?

8. What are expense fraud schemes?

9. How do executives illegally loot their companies to receive large financial benefits?

10. What are payroll disbursement fraud schemes?

11. What is meant by the term corruption?

12. What is meant by the term bribery?

13. Briefly describe how the use of databases could help in detecting kickback fraud schemes.

14. When does a conflict of interest occur? Give an example.

## TRUE/FALSE

1. At the present time, approximately 25,000 members make up the Association of Certified Fraud Examiners.

2. Employee frauds constitute a greater percentage of all frauds and have greater median losses than do management and owner frauds combined.

3. Statistics show that fraud losses are directly proportional to age and inversely proportional to education.

4. Larceny, skimming, and misuse are all subdivisions of theft of cash.

5. Skimming schemes are far less common than larceny schemes.

6. Billing schemes have by far the highest median costs per incident of all frauds.

7. Kickback schemes always involve the purchasing function of the victim company.

8. Bribery is one of the four types of corruption.

9. Commercial bribery is different from traditional bribery, in that the offer made in commercial bribery is to influence an official act of government, and traditional briberies never involve government officials.

10. Failure to account for missing inventory that was supposed to have been returned is a problem found in voided sales frauds.

11. Asset misappropriations are divided into two categories: theft of cash and theft of inventory.

12. Larceny is the stealing of cash by employees before the cash has been recorded in the company's accounting system.

13. Understating sales and stealing cash is an example of skimming.

14. The two basic fraudulent register disbursement schemes are false refunds and false voids.

15. Ghost employee schemes usually generate the largest losses among the payroll disbursement fraud schemes.

16. Corruption is divided into four fraud scheme types: (1) bribery, (2) conflict of interest, (3) economic extortion, and (4) illegal services.

17. Kickbacks are undisclosed payments made by employees of purchasing companies to vendors.

18. Compared to bribery and conflicts of interest, economic extortion fraud schemes occur relatively infrequently.

19. Illegal gratuities are made before deals are approved but after payment has been accepted.

## MULTIPLE CHOICE

1. Most frauds against organizations are perpetrated by:
   a. Employees. — P.518
   b. Owners.
   c. Vendors.
   d. A collusion of two of the above.

2. What are three types of asset misappropriation?
   a. Stealing receipts, purchasing fraud, and disbursement fraud
   b. Stealing receipts, purchasing fraud, and stealing assets on hand
   c. Stealing receipts, disbursement fraud, and stealing assets on hand — P.519
   d. Stealing receipts, disbursement fraud, and purchasing fraud

3. Out of all the types of frauds discussed in this chapter, which type is perpetrated least often?
   a. Skimming schemes
   b. Larceny — P.520
   c. Check schemes
   d. Payroll

4. Which of the following is *not* one of the most common billing schemes?
   a. Setting up dummy companies to submit invoices to the victim organization
   b. Changing the quantity or price on an invoice to favor a customer — P.522

   c. Altering or double-paying nonaccomplice vendor's statements
   d. Making personal purchases with company funds

5. The most affected party in a workers' compensation fraud case is which of the following?
   a. Employer
   b. Employer's insurance carrier — P.524
   c. Other employees
   d. Government

6. Which of the following is a major difference between larceny and skimming?
   a. Larceny is committed before the cash is entered into the accounting system, while skimming is committed after the cash is entered into the system.
   b. Larceny is committed after the cash is entered into the accounting system, while skimming is committed before the cash is entered into the system. —
   c. Larceny involves fraudulent disbursements of cash, while skimming involves fraudulent receipts of cash.
   d. Larceny involves fraudulent receipts of cash, while skimming involves fraudulent disbursements of cash.

7. Which of the following types of disbursement frauds occur least frequently?
   a. Expense tampering
   b. Payroll schemes
   c. Register disbursement schemes — P. 521
   d. Billing schemes

8. Which of the following results in the highest loss per case?
   a. Expense tampering
   b. Payroll schemes
   c. Register disbursement schemes
   d. Billing schemes — P. 522

9. Which of the following is not considered a misappropriation of assets?
   a. Payroll disbursement schemes
   b. Kickbacks
   c. Expense schemes
   d. Skimming

10. Which of the following is not true of billing schemes?
    a. The perpetrator takes physical possession of his or her employer's cash.
    b. The perpetrator often sets up a dummy company.
    c. It is one of the most commonly committed disbursement schemes.
    d. It usually involves dealing with the victim organization's purchasing department.

## SHORT CASES

**Case 1.** Regina finally landed her dream job at Abercroanie & Fetch. After just a couple of days on the job, we find out why. Often, when people return merchandise, Regina will ring up on the register that they returned something of more value than it was really worth. She then pockets the extra cash and gives the customer the amount due. Regina finds this method effective because people really are returning something, so inventories and the register totals won't be out of balance at the end of the day.

1. What type of fraud is Regina committing?

2. How could her employer detect this kind of fraud?

**Case 2.** In a Las Vegas casino, an employee discovered a flaw in the accounting system. The accounts payable clerk discovered that he was able to change the names of vendors in the computer system to his name. He would create false invoices and create a check for the false invoice. The name on the check would be changed to the name of the employee. After the check was printed, the name in the system could then be changed back to the appropriate vendor. The check register would show only the name of the vendor. The fraudulent employee had authorization to sign checks under $1,000. By writing small checks, he was able to defraud the company of $10,000. This fraud was caught by accident. An employee of another department was looking through the vendor list on her computer after the fraudulent employee had changed the vendor name to his name. A few entries later, the vendor name changed again. She wondered how this switch could occur and asked her supervisor. Soon after, the fraudulent employee was caught.

1. What kind of fraud is being committed?

2. What percent of frauds are of this type?

3. How could this fraud have been prevented?

**Case 3.** You work as the assistant to the controller of a small, privately owned company. Part of your job is to create weekly reports of the company's inventories. For the past several months, you have been excluding from your report a room full of damaged and obsolete inventory. Although these assets would usually have little or no market value, one of the owners recently found an interested buyer who wants to purchase the goods for scrap material at a deep discount. Even with this discount, the sales price of these items will be approximately $50,000.

The company has been experiencing severe financial difficulties. Today, in fact, the owners filed for bankruptcy. The controller has asked you to create one last inventory report, reminding you to ignore the damaged/obsolete inventory like usual. When you ask him about the interested buyer, he says that the owner found the buyer only by a stroke of luck, and that the goods really are worthless, so you should record them as such.

1. What should you do?

2. What issues are involved?

**Case 4.** Ed Neilson is the purchasing agent for Style, nationwide high-fashion women's online stores. He joined the company after graduating from college five years ago. Over the years, Ed developed close relationships with one of the company's vendor's owners—Sarah

Love. Sarah owns a small manufacturing line, designing exclusive French fashion clothes and accessories. After dating for seven months, Ed and Sarah became engaged four months ago. Sarah's fashions have historically sold well in the Style chain, but with the recent decline in the retail industry, high-fashion, high-cost-item sales have decreased substantially. Ed believes that this trend is just short term and thus decides to help his fiancé by guaranteeing $50,000 monthly purchases from Sarah's line.

Is Ed involved in a fraud scheme? Explain your answer.

**Case 5.** Conduct a survey of managers or owners of at least 10 local businesses. Ask whether, to the best of the manager or owner's knowledge, the organization has ever been a victim of fraud. In each case determine the following:

1. Whether the perpetrators were employees, management, owners, or customers

2. The dollar amounts of the fraud

3. The gender, age, marital status, and education level of the perpetrator

4. The size of the company by number of employees

Put together a list similar to the one in Table 15-1. In a paragraph or two, compare and contrast the results of your mini-survey to those of the ACFE's comprehensive study.

**Case 6.** Read the article "The Case of the Pilfering Purchasing Manager" by Joseph Wells (*Journal of Accountancy*, May 2004, p. 80; available at http://www.aicpa.org/pubs/jofa/joaiss.htm), and answer the following questions:

1. What internal control deficiencies allowed Bruce to commit fraud without being detected?

2. What three ways does Joseph Wells suggest could have prevented this fraud?

3. Who is Chris Rosetti's employer and what two certifications does he hold?

4. How much money did Bruce receive from the $350,000 of frauds he perpetrated? Why do you think he was willing to commit fraud for this limited sum?

5. What tips does Joseph Wells give to fraud investigators? What general category do kickback frauds belong to?

6. List the red flags for detecting kickback frauds.

**Case 7.** Read the article "When Good Workers Go Bad" by Karen E. Klein (BusinessWeek Online, May 29, 2001; available at http://www.businessweek.com/smallbiz/content/may2001/sb20010529_956.htm).

1. What nine suggestions are given to prevent employee fraud?

2. Refer back to the article at the beginning of the chapter about David Miller. Which principle did each of his employers fail to implement?

**Case 8.** Employee Theft Anonymous (ETA) is "a workplace theft prevention program." Its primary function is to open avenues for employees to report theft and fraud anonymously, either over the phone or online. On its Web site, ETA hosts an 11-question questionnaire that tests visitors' knowledge regarding employee theft. Answers are at the bottom of the page. Take the quiz (be honest and don't look at the answers), print the quiz with your answers, and then check your answers. Give yourself a score (out of 11), and turn in the quiz to your teacher. This assignment will not be graded on your score, but on completion. The quiz is available at http://www.etheft.com/thequestionnaire1.html.

**Case 9.** Ken was the only accountant for a small-town land development company. He was terminated when the company fell on hard times. One year later, when the owner of the company was reviewing the payments received from a land-owner for development cost, he discovered that they were three payments behind for a total of $60,000. He contacted the land owner who showed him the check stubs and the cancelled checks. After further research he found that the account in which the checks were deposited belonged to Ken, his former accountant.

1. What type of fraud did Ken commit?

2. What actions should be taken against Ken?

3. How could this fraud have been prevented?

**Case 10.** Jill recently began working at a local florist. In addition to creating floral arrangements, Jill spends a good deal of her time talking to customers and ringing up sales. Over time she identifies a weakness in the procedures for ringing up voids. No approval is necessary to void a sale and the void slip collects little information about the sale. After Jill completes a sale and the customer leaves, she sometimes voids the sale and pockets the cash. The floral shop doesn't miss the lost inventory because they have a high inventory turnover ratio and high loses due to flowers losing their bloom.

1. What type of fraud is Jill committing?

2. What could the florist do to prevent this type of fraud from occurring?

**Case 11.** Hospital administrator Ronald Thomas was recently convicted for fraud he committed against his employer, White Cross Hospital System.[6] Over a period of six years, he allegedly made payments to a dummy company for maintenance charges while simultaneously running a scheme with maintenance contractors where he either paid them for work never performed or overpaid them for work. The skyscraper where Thomas worked was only 10 years old. Maintenance charges rose from $5.2 million in 1994 to $16.4 million in 2000. It was worth noting that the judge on the case questioned whether White Cross Hospital System deserved less than full restitution for failing to notice the problem. However, it was determined that federal law on restitution does not allow such charges, so Ronald Thomas will be making monthly payments toward the alleged $8 million he stole until he makes full restitution after leaving prison. He was able to quickly repay $3.2 million of the theft with assets recovered by the government, including two homes and a nice yacht. Not bad for a man who was supposed to be making $90,000 per year.

1. What specific types of fraud did Ronald Thomas commit?

2. The judge was concerned that the hospital should have taken some kind of responsibility for not detecting the fraud. What could the hospital have done to prevent or detect the fraud earlier?

**Case 12.** Steve Stevenson thought the whole deal seemed fishy but he didn't know why. He had noticed that the contracts for custodial work for the schools in the district had almost all been going to the same custodial company, Johnson Cleaning, and they seemed to just barely manage to be the lowest bid on each of the bids they had won. He was especially concerned because now they were charging more than they had contracted for and the budget for custodial work was starting to be stretched. Something seemed fishy, but he didn't want to jump to any conclusions. John Johnson, who also worked for the district, handled the bid process. Steve thought that he might go and ask if he knew anything about what was going on. He should have some ideas since his cousin owned Johnson Cleaning.

What might be an explanation for what Steve has noticed?

**Case 13.** Hank just loves his new job as a sales clerk at the local classy department store named Fashion's My Style®. It's a great way for him to earn a few dollars while attending high school. Not only does his job pay quite well, but his job allows Hank to receive discounts on all his clothes. Because Fashion's My Style is the coolest place to shop, Hank sees many of his friends while he is working. He's found that, in addition to enhancing his social standing with his friends, he can supplement his income by selling items to friends at a price far below

market level. Hank does this by taking additional markdowns and discounts off at the register. For making these "discounts," his friends pay him a portion of the savings as well as allow him to come to all the parties.

1. What type of fraud is Hank committing?

2. How could the company find out that this fraud is occurring?

**Case 14.** Match the following terms with their corresponding definitions:

Billing scheme
Asset misappropriation
Check tampering
Disbursement fraud
Expense scheme
Investment scam
Illegal gratuities
Lapping
Payroll fraud scheme
Skimming

1. Scheme in which perpetrators produce false documents to claim false expenses.

2. Fraud that involves stealing one customer's payment and then crediting that customer's account when a subsequent customer pays.

3. Scheme in which employees prepare fraudulent checks on their own behalf or intercept checks intended for a third party and convert the checks for their own benefit.

4. Submission of a false or altered invoice that causes an employer to willingly issue a check.

5. Using the payroll function to commit fraud, such as creating ghost employees or overpaying wages.

6. A reward given to someone for making a favorable decision.

7. Theft that is committed by stealing receipts, stealing assets on hand, or by committing some type of disbursement fraud.

8. Removal of cash from a victim organization prior to its entry in an accounting system.

9. Having an organization pay for something it shouldn't pay for or pay too much for something it purchases.

10. Scheme in which perpetrators deceive individuals into putting their money into a false investment.

## EXTENSIVE CASES

**Extensive Case 1.** In 1987, Bill Eaves worked in the purchasing department of Marion County. In 1990, Eaves was promoted to assistant county administrative officer for personnel. Five years later, Eaves was promoted to county administrative officer—the county's top executive. At the time of this promotion, he hired James Hart from Billings County to replace him as the county's human resources administrator. In 1999, Eaves retired as county administrative officer, but he continued to manage the county as a contract employee, while the county searched for his successor. At that time, Hart was selected to replace Eaves as county administrative officer.

Following his retirement, Eaves asked Bell Waste Systems Company if he could buy them out of their contract to operate some of the county's landfills, because he believed the landfills could turn a profit if operated privately. Bell Company turned down Eaves offer, but hired Eaves as a consultant to help it develop and pitch a proposal to take over the operation of all the county's landfills. Eaves asked Hart for help. Hart promised to help Bell Company win county business in exchange for thousands of dollars in cash or in-kind payments from Eaves. Eaves accepted this exchange.

Eaves signed a consulting agreement with Bell Company, which ultimately paid him $4.6 million. Under the agreement, Bell Company promised to pay Eaves $1 million if the county allows Bell to operate the county landfill system and $50,000 per month if the amount of garbage dumped at county landfills exceeds 850,000 tons a year, and the county issued municipal bonds to finance landfill closure and postclosure maintenance.

Hart headed the county board of supervisors and approved a contract with Bell to operate all the county's landfills worth more than $20 million a year. Bell started work on the contract. Hart, his friends, and other county officials were given free lodging, meals, fishing, and golf in Cabo San Lucas, the costs of which were covered by Eaves. In addition, Hart signed a promissory note for $90,000 he received from Eaves.

Hernandez Trucking started paying kickbacks to Robert Max, vice president of Bell Company, equaling about $2 per truckload of dirt delivered to county landfills to cover garbage. Max received approximately $256,000, which he shared with Eaves and Hart.

In January 2001, Eaves, Hart, and Max were under investigation by the FBI because of a tip from one county official. They were among numerous people to testify in front of a special grand jury convened to investigate a failed trash project and political corruption in the county.

Identify the type of fraud being committed and explain your reasons for choosing that particular type.

**Extensive Case 2.** Boris Yuroslavsev, an immigrant from the Ukraine, is a hotel owner in Las Vegas. Since his arrival in the United States during the 1960s, Boris built a successful and popular hotel. Until recently, the hotel averaged $20 million in total revenue per year. Lately though, rumors claim that Boris's hotel, the *Russian Roulette*, may be suffering unusual losses.

Recently, a number of Boris's key staff quit, complaining about low wages and nonexistent benefits. In fact, the hotel's main attraction, its popular restaurant chef Alec Klarinko, quit as well as the hotel's headlining performer.

While Boris focused on coming up with a new compensation policy, he hired CPA Tony Slinko to look into the hotel's diminishing cash flows. The first thing Tony did was head for the kitchen to partake of the award-winning food. The new chef, Jim Smoot, wasn't what Tony expected. First of all, he wasn't Russian, as most of the employees seemed to be, and second he refused to talk about why he had come to the *Russian Roulette* when so many wanted to leave.

After his visit to the kitchen, Tony began sifting through the accounting documentation looking for possible fraud symptoms. Tony reasoned that if employees felt like they weren't being compensated accordingly, they may be apt to defraud the hotel.

**Questions:**

1. Could Tony be right? Are employees defrauding the company or has the *Russian Roulette* finally bit the bullet?

2. What are possible fraud activities associated with declining cash flows?

## INTERNET ASSIGNMENTS

1. Visit the Association of Certified Fraud Examiners at http://www.cfenet.com//about/josephtwells.asp and read a short introduction on Joseph T. Wells.

    1. What is Mr. Wells's background? What major aspects of his background would be crucial to his success as a CFE?

    2. What books has Mr. Wells written?

    3. What organizations or groups is Mr. Wells currently a member of?

2. Visit http://www.securitymanagement.com/library/000714.html. Once you have logged onto the site, read the article "A Fistful of Dollars," written by Joseph T. Wells.

1. According to Mr. Wells, who is most likely to steal from a company?

2. When Mr. Wells speaks of internal fraud deterrence in his article, what are the three areas he suggests a company should focus on in order to more successfully deter fraud within their organization? Which areas of focus do you think would be the most effective in deterring fraud?

3. What is the fourth suggestion given to companies by Mr. Wells to help deter and also detect fraud within their organizations? Do you think this approach is a cost-beneficial way to deal with fraud within a company?

## DEBATE

Look at the various fraud statistics in Table 15-1. Determine the characteristics of the person most likely to perpetrate a large fraud. Then, debate your decision over a person with these characteristics and give the reasons why such a person is more likely to be a fraud perpetrator than a person with different characteristics.

## END NOTES

1. Bryan Burrough, "David L. Miller Stole from His Employer and Isn't in Prison," *Wall Street Journal* (September 19, 1986), p. 1.

2. After working for the FBI, Joe Wells started Wells & Associates, a group of consulting criminologists concentrating on white-collar crime prevention, detection, and education. That venture led to the formation of the Association of Certified Fraud Examiners, a professional organization of fraud professionals that now has approximately 25,000 members. Since its inception, Joe Wells has been chairman of the board of directors and CEO. His book was published by the Obsidian Publishing Company, Inc. in 1997 (800 West Avenue, Austin, TX 78701).

3. http://www.usatoday.com/money/industries/manufacturing/2003-10-27-tyco_x.htm

4. Much of this discussion was taken from Berstein Litowitz Berger & Grossman LLP, *Institutional Investor* Advocate, 5 (Fourth Quarter 2003).

5. http://www.fool.com/News/mft/2003/mft03091208.htm (accessed on May 1, 2004).

6. Ideas in the case taken from a true case discussed in article, "Legal Issues: Former Blue Cross official sentenced to prison for $14.1 million billing scheme," *Health and Medicine Week*, December 1, 2003, p. 544.

CHAPTER 16

# BANKRUPTCY, DIVORCE, AND TAX FRAUD

## LEARNING OBJECTIVES

After studying this chapter, you should be able to:

1. Explain why fraud is so prevalent in bankruptcy, tax and divorce cases.
2. Describe the nature of bankruptcy and gain a familiarity with bankruptcy codes.
3. Understand civil and criminal bankruptcy fraud statutes.
4. Identify the participants involved in the bankruptcy process.
5. Recognize different bankruptcy and divorce fraud schemes.
6. Understand how perpetrators fraudulently conceal and transfer assets and income in bankruptcies and divorces.
7. Define tax fraud and be familiar with common tax fraud schemes.

*Robert Brennan, a former penny-stock tycoon, was convicted in April 2001 of bankruptcy fraud. Jurors found Brennan guilty of hiding $4.5 million in assets from the federal government before he filed for bankruptcy in 1995.*

*The legal proceedings spanned six weeks, including 19 days of testimony and arguments that exposed federal jurors to high-stakes action at the Mirage hotel-casino in Las Vegas and the complexities of international finance. Brennan was known in Las Vegas because of his ties to the now-imploded El Rancho hotel-casino on the Strip. A Brennan company, International Thoroughbred Breeders, at one point proposed to redevelop the dilapidated property into a new casino resort, but those plans never materialized.*

*The case alleged that Brennan continued to live a lavish lifestyle, despite being millions of dollars in debt. Testimony came from or references were made to a soap-opera star whom Brennan dated, a Catholic Cardinal whom Brennan knew, international arms traders, and former football coach Bill Parcells, who posted assets for Brennan's bond.*

*Brennan, 57, was convicted on 7 of 13 counts. The jury was convinced he had hidden money offshore, and that he cashed in casino chips without reporting them just three weeks after he filed for bankruptcy protection.*

*Brennan was acquitted on charges that cash was delivered to him in a handoff in a London hotel. He was found guilty of spending $100,000 on private flights around the world, but innocent of illegally spending $60,000 on a yacht cruise.*

*Brennan filed for bankruptcy protection just before he was due to pay millions to compensate First Jersey investors whom U.S. District Judge Richard Owen in Manhattan determined had been cheated. That judgment, won by the Securities and Exchange Commission, was more than $78 million.*

*That ruling led to a series of legal setbacks for Brennan, who is now barred from the securities industry after regulators found he continued to use high-pressure "boiler room" tactics to sell stocks.[1]*

The occurrence of **bankruptcy**—the legal process that either allows a debtor to work out an orderly plan to settle debts or liquidate assets and distribute them to creditors—is on the increase. Bankruptcy fraud, like the one just described, is a growing problem in the United States. Entering false financial information on bankruptcy petitions and schedules occurs in an estimated 70 percent of the bankruptcy cases. The same is true of divorce and tax fraud cases. Although actual statistics aren't available, most divorces involving significant amounts of assets include allegations of fraud. The reason that fraud is so common in bankruptcies, divorces, and paying taxes is because, in all three situations, assets are being taken away from someone or some organization and given to someone else. In bankruptcy cases, the assets taken are given to creditors. In divorces, assets taken are given to spouses and attorneys representing spouses. In tax cases, assets taken away are claimed by the government. To keep assets from being taken, individuals often attempt to fraudulently hide or transfer assets so that they can't be known or discovered. Transfers of assets to offshore bank accounts, relatives, friends, and other hiding places are all too common in bankruptcy, divorce, and when paying taxes.

Both bankruptcy and divorce fraud can be criminal or civil matters. Criminal divorce and bankruptcy frauds are often investigated by the FBI or other law enforcement agencies. Civil bankruptcy and divorce frauds may be investigated by trustees, examiners, creditors, and creditors' committees appointed by the bankruptcy or divorce courts. Tax fraud cases are usually criminal matters.

CPAs and other fraud examiners can play an important role in both investigating and testifying in bankruptcy and divorce fraud cases and in testifying in tax fraud cases. The Criminal Investigation Division of the Internal Revenue Service usually investigates tax fraud cases.

Roles that fraud examiners can assume in divorce and bankruptcy cases include the following:

- Serve as an examiner or trustee in bankruptcy cases.
- Serve on creditors' committees or represent creditors' committees by investigating the debtor's financial affairs and preparing investigation reports in bankruptcy cases.
- Assist the U.S. Department of Justice, the Office of the United States Trustee, panel trustees, and others by preparing detailed reports of investigation findings in bankruptcy cases.
- Assist in recovering assets for creditors in both divorce and bankruptcy cases.
- Serve as private investigators to find hidden assets or examine lifestyles of divorce or bankruptcy participants.

Several different types of bankruptcy and divorce frauds are noteworthy:

- *Bankruptcy or divorce resulting from fraud.* When fraudulent activity results in too few assets remaining to pay creditor and investor claims, an entity will generally file bankruptcy. Similarly, when one marriage partner discovers that his or her marital partner has committed fraud, he or she often seeks divorce to salvage a reputation or because of a lack of trust in the partner. The fraudulent activity can involve hiding assets from others, stealing money or other assets, or misrepresenting business dealings by committing investment scams or financial statement fraud.
- *Bankruptcy and divorce used to perpetrate fraud.* During bankruptcy and divorce, an automatic stay is often granted during which creditors or marital partners are prohibited from taking any action against the debtor or marriage partner. Some debtors and marital partners use this period to perpetrate fraud. For example, they may fraudulently transfer assets to other related organizations or individuals.
- *Bankruptcy and divorce used to conceal fraud.* This type of fraud generally results in the books and records of the debtor or marital partner being destroyed, inaccurate, or hard to locate.

When a fraud examiner is engaged to investigate a "bankruptcy or divorce resulting from fraud," the focus is on the fraudulent activity occurring before the bankruptcy filing or divorce. Such fraud may be any of the types of fraud already discussed in this book.

This chapter focuses on the remaining two types of bankruptcy fraud (bankruptcy used to perpetrate fraud and bankruptcy used to conceal fraud) and on divorce and tax fraud. We discuss tax fraud first. We next discuss fraud associated with divorce. Finally, we discuss bankruptcy fraud. In considering bankruptcy fraud, we provide an overview of the Bankruptcy Code and the various types of bankruptcy. We also discuss civil and criminal bankruptcy and fraud statutes and an overview of the activities of the key participants in the bankruptcy and divorce process (that is, the bankruptcy court, U.S. Trustee, court-appointed or panel trustees, examiner, debtor, creditors, and adjusters). In the last two sections of the chapter we will discuss a common type of bankruptcy fraud—bust-outs and the concealment of assets or income and fraudulent transfers of assets, which are common in both divorce and bankruptcy.

# Tax Fraud

**Tax fraud** can be committed against any governmental or other organization that collects taxes, including the federal government, state governments, local governments, or other taxing authorities. The types of tax fraud committed against all of these organizations are similar. In this book, we will confine our discussions to tax fraud committed against the U.S. government and its tax-collecting agency, the Internal Revenue Service (IRS). The IRS, a branch of the Department of Treasury, deals directly with more Americans than any other institution, public or private. In 2003, the IRS collected nearly $2 trillion in revenue and processed more than 222 million tax returns. It cost taxpayers 48 cents for each $100 collected by the IRS.

The tax system in the United States depends on voluntary compliance, which means that each of us is responsible for filing a tax return when required, and for determining and paying the correct amount of tax. Fortunately, the vast majority of Americans recognize their legal responsibility, and properly report and pay their tax obligations. Unfortunately, some Americans are not as honest and intentionally pay no tax at all or underpay their taxes. This intentional underpaying of taxes is tax fraud. You should recognize that tax fraud is different from trying to follow complex tax rules and underpaying taxes or even being aggressive in taking advantage of legal tax minimization strategies. Americans should pay the least amount of tax they legally owe. Tax fraud, such as not reporting income that should be taxed or deliberately overstating (without basis) tax deductions and exemptions, is wrong and illegal.

If the IRS suspects that you are underpaying your taxes or if you are selected for a random audit, your return will be audited by an IRS tax compliance auditor. If the audit reveals that you have underpaid your taxes, the auditor can either assess you civil fines and penalties or worse, refer your case to the IRS's criminal investigation division.

Auditors are trained to look for tax fraud—a willful act done with the intent to defraud the IRS—which includes the area of tax underpayment beyond honest mistakes. Using a false Social Security number, keeping two sets of financial books, hiding income or claiming a blind spouse as a dependent when you are single are all examples of tax fraud. Even though tax auditors are trained to look for fraud, however, they do not routinely suspect it. They know the tax law is complex and expect to find a few errors in every tax return. They will give you the benefit of the doubt most of the time and not go after you for tax fraud.

## Fraud and the Criminal Investigation Division

A careless mistake on your tax return might tack on a 20 percent penalty to your tax bill. Although not good, this penalty is much less than the one for tax fraud, which is 75 percent. The line between negligence and fraud is not always clear, even to the IRS and the courts. The arm of the IRS that investigates tax fraud is known as Criminal Investigation, or CI. CI is directed at the portion of U.S. taxpayers who willfully and intentionally violate their known legal duty of voluntarily filing income tax returns or paying the correct amount of income, employment, or excise taxes. These individuals pose a serious threat to tax administration and the U.S. economy.

The Criminal Investigation's fraud work encompasses a wide variety of cases involving tax and money laundering crimes. CI investigations involve a broad spectrum of individuals and industries from all facets of the economy, from small business owners to self-employed to large corporations.

The mission of CI is to serve the American public by investigating potential criminal violations of the Internal Revenue Code and related financial crimes in a manner that fosters confidence in the tax system and compliance with the law. IRS CI special agents combine accounting skills with law enforcement skills to investigate financial crimes. Special agents are trained to "follow the money." No matter what the source, all income earned, both legal and illegal, has the potential of becoming involved in crimes that fall within the investigative jurisdiction of the IRS Criminal Investigation. Because of the expertise required to conduct complex financial investigations, IRS special agents are among the best financial investigators for the federal government.

The specific laws under which tax fraud perpetrators are charged can be found in Table 16-1.

## Table 16-1 Tax Laws Against Fraud Perpetrators

| Law | Nature of Law | Description and Punishment |
|-----|---------------|---------------------------|
| Title 26 USC § 7201 | Attempt to evade or defeat tax | Any person who willfully attempts to evade or defeat any tax imposed by this title or the payment thereof shall, in addition to other penalties provided by law, be guilty of a felony and, upon conviction thereof:<br>• Shall be imprisoned not more than 5 years<br>• Or fined not more than $250,000 for individuals ($500,000 for corporations)<br>• Or both, together with the costs of prosecution |
| Title 26 USC § 7202 | Willful failure to collect or pay over tax | Any person required under this title to collect, account for, and pay over any tax imposed by this title who willfully fails to collect or truthfully account for and pay over such tax shall, in addition to penalties provide by the law, be guilty of a felony:<br>• Shall be imprisoned not more than 5 years<br>• Or fined not more than $250,000 for individuals ($500,000 for corporations)<br>• Or both , together with the costs of prosecution |
| Title 26 USC § 7203 | Willful failure to file return, supply information, or pay tax | Any person required under this title to pay any estimated tax or tax, or required by this title or by regulations made under authority thereof to make a return, keep any records, or supply any information, who willfully fails to pay such estimated tax or tax, make such return, keep such records, or supply such information, at the time or times required by law or regulations, shall, in addition to other penalties provided by law, be guilty of a misdemeanor and, upon conviction thereof:<br>• Shall be imprisoned not more than 1 years<br>• Or fined not more than $100,000 for individuals ($200,000 for corporations)<br>• Or both, together with cost of prosecution |
| Title 26 USC § 7206(1) | Fraud and false statements | Any person who . . . (1) Declaration under penalties of perjury - Willfully makes and subscribes any return, statement, or other document, which contains or is verified by a written declaration that is made under the penalties of perjury, and which he does not believe to be true and correct as to every material matter; shall be guilty of a felony and, upon conviction thereof:<br>• Shall be imprisoned not more than 3 years<br>• Or fined not more than $250,000 for individuals ($500,000 for corporations)<br>• Or both, together with cost of prosecution |
| Title 26 USC § 7206(2) | Fraud and false statements | Any person who . . . (2) Aid or assistance—Willfully aids or assists in, or procures, counsels, or advises the preparation or presentation under, or in connection with any matter arising under, the Internal Revenue laws, of a return, affidavit, claim, or other document, which is fraudulent or is false as to any material matter, whether or not such falsity or fraud is with the knowledge or consent of the person authorized or required to present such return, affidavit, claim, or document; shall be guilty of a felony and, upon conviction thereof:<br>• Shall be imprisoned not more than 3 years<br>• Or fined not more than $250,000 for individuals ($500,000 for corporations)<br>• Or both, together with cost of prosecution |
| Title 26 USC § 7212(A) | Attempts to interfere with administration of Internal Revenue laws | Whoever corruptly or by force endeavors to intimidate or impede any officer or employee of the United States acting in an official capacity under this title, or in any other way corruptly or by force obstructs or impedes, or endeavors to obstruct or impede, the due administration of this title, upon conviction:<br>• Shall be imprisoned not more than 3 years<br>• Or fined not more than $250,000 for individuals ($500,000 for corporations)<br>• Or both |
| Title 18 USC § 371 | Conspiracy to commit offense or to defraud the United States | If two or more persons conspire either to commit any offense against the United States, or to defraud the United States, or any agency thereof in any manner or for any purpose, and one or more of such persons do any act to effect the object of the conspiracy, each:<br>• Shall be imprisoned not more than 5 years<br>• Or fined not more than $250,000 for individuals ($500,000 for corporations)<br>• Or both |

Table 16-2 summarizes the tax fraud investigation activity of CI over three recent years.

## Table 16-2 IRS Criminal Investigations Activity, 2001–2003

| | FY 2003 | FY 2002 | FY 2001 |
|---|---|---|---|
| Investigations Initiated | 1,814 | 1,810 | 1,392 |
| Prosecution Recommendations | 974 | 837 | 789 |
| Indictments/Informations | 770 | 758 | 805 |
| Sentenced | 672 | 809 | 781 |
| Incarceration Rate | 79.8% | 75.4% | 80.4% |
| Average Months to Serve | 28 | 24 | 23 |

As examples of the kinds of tax fraud investigated by CI, consider the following five cases.

### Former IRS Employee Sentenced on Fraud and Tax Evasion Charges

On June 3, 2004, in Minneapolis, Minnesota, Sandra Jean Valencia was sentenced to 33 months in prison, followed by three years supervised release and ordered to pay $605,203 in restitution. Valencia pleaded guilty to mail fraud, wire fraud, and tax evasion. Appointed by her grandmother to take care of her financial affairs, Valencia admitted in court that she used her position under the power of attorney and as trustee from 1997 through 2000 to transfer the vast majority of her grandmother's assets to herself. Valencia depleted her grandmother's stock holdings, sold 76 acres of her farmland and her household belongings, and emptied her bank accounts. Valencia also deposited approximately $41,000 of her grandmother's life insurance proceeds into her own bank account. Valencia admitted to evading income taxes for calendar years 1997 through 2000.

### Three Employees Who Defrauded Pitney Bowes Sentenced to Federal Prison

On May 28, 2004, in New Haven, Connecticut, Raymond J. Wisnieski, Otto Guhl, Jr., and Robert J. Wilson were sentenced after previously pleading guilty to a two-count information charging involvement in a scheme of mail fraud and with filing a false U.S. personal income tax return. Wisnieski was sentenced to 37 months in prison, Guhl received 21 months of in prison, and Wilson was sentenced to 18 months in prison. All three were also sentenced to three years of supervised release and a fine of $5,000. Wisnieski, an assistant controller of the Accounting, Tax and Disbursement Services Department of Mailing Systems Finance, a division of Pitney Bowes, arranged for false entries to be made to the accounting records at Pitney Bowes to the benefit of himself, Guhl, and Wilson. Guhl and Wilson worked under Wisnieski in the same department. The false entries suggested that Pitney Bowes had withheld from the defendants' income significantly more federal and state income taxes than, in fact, had been withheld. As part of the scheme, the defendants would tell Pitney Bowes that the withholding amounts were mistakenly overstated and have Pitney Bowes refund to them a portion of the monies that the company's accounting system suggested had been withheld.

Because the defendants would not typically seek payment from Pitney Bowes for the entire overstated withholding amount, Pitney Bowes would still forward to the IRS, at the required time, the taxes that allegedly had been withheld from each defendant's salary. Thereafter, the defendants would file their yearly federal personal income tax returns. Because the withholding payments made by Pitney Bowes to the IRS far exceeded the taxes due on the defendants' actual salary, the defendants would each year receive a substantial refund. During the scheme, the tax returns filed by the defendants were materially false because they did not include as income the money the defendants had stolen from Pitney Bowes as a result of their scheme.

During the scheme, Wisnieski unlawfully obtained $492,972 from Pitney Bowes and failed to pay $112,287 in federal income taxes. Guhl unlawfully obtained $351,496 from Pitney Bowes and failed to pay $78,703 in federal income taxes. Wilson unlawfully obtained $177,200 from Pitney Bowes and failed to pay $37,036 in federal income taxes.

**Sister and Brother Convicted in International Money Laundering Criminal Enterprise Case**
On May 28, 2004, in Seattle, Washington, Nghiem Nu-Doan Truong and her brother, Tung Quoc Truong, were convicted of conspiracy to engage in money laundering and immediately sentenced to four years' imprisonment and three years' imprisonment, respectively. After their imprisonment, both defendants were sentenced to serve three years of supervised release. Also, a preliminary order of forfeiture was entered into court authorizing the criminal forfeiture of more than $1 million in cash and real property seized from Nghiem Nu-Doan Truong and My-A, Inc. According to court documents, the Truongs operated a lucrative money transfer business under the name of My-A, Inc., which opened it doors in mid-2001 to the Vietnamese community in Seattle. My-A, Inc. expanded to include more than 20 branch offices and subagents in at least 13 other states. During 2002 and 2003, the Truongs transferred more than $11 million of funds derived from marijuana trafficking by using various bank accounts to conceal and disguise the nature, location, source, and ownership of the funds belonging to, or intended for, Cong Chinh Dinh and Andy Hoang by intentionally failing to document the transfer of currency, falsifying business records; structuring currency deposits; failing to prepare required currency transaction reports for domestic and international movement of funds; sending currency interstate by air delivery rather than wire transferring funds through banks; not paying taxes on money laundering profits, and transporting and smuggling of currency through the use of money couriers from a place in the United States into Canada.

**Doctor Sentenced to 41 Months in Prison for Tax Evasion**
On May 30, 2003, in Athens, Georgia, Dr. Bradford G. Brown was sentenced to serve 41 months in federal prison for tax evasion. At trial, the government introduced evidence that Brown, during the 1994 and 1995 tax years, evaded income taxes on more than $1.2 million of income by failing to deposit all of his medical receipts into his business account. Instead, he deposited income into bank accounts that he never disclosed to his accountant, thus breaching their explicit agreement that all of his income would be deposited into his business bank account for purposes of computing his income. Brown's scheme included the 1996–2001 tax years when he delinquently filed tax returns for these years that included a total tax liability in excess of $1 million while only being credited by the Internal Revenue Service with paying $4,192 of his total tax liability for the 1994–2001 tax years. In addition to his prison sentence, Brown was ordered to pay a $40,000 fine and make restitution to the IRS in excess of $3 million.

**Woman Sentenced for Tax Fraud Relating to Her Embezzlement of More Than $3 Million**
On May 8, 2003, in Charleston, West Virginia, Patricia Griffith was sentenced to 27 months in prison and fined $6,000 for income tax evasion. Griffith, who pled guilty this past January, admitted she embezzled in excess of $3 million from 1990 through 1999 from Kanawha Valley Radiologists, Inc. Griffith failed to report to the IRS the money she embezzled. (Yes, stolen money is taxable!) In particular, in the 1997 tax year, the tax year for which she was charged, Griffith failed to report more than $400,000 of monies she embezzled resulting in a tax liability of $120,000 for that year alone. Griffith was ordered by the Court to work with the IRS with respect to restitution for the 1997 tax year.

Some of the most common tax fraud schemes are:

- Deliberately underreporting or omitting income
- Overstating the amount of deductions
- Keeping two sets of books
- Making false entries in books and records
- Claiming personal expenses as business expenses
- Claiming false deductions
- Hiding or transferring assets or income
- Illegal money laundering schemes

The most common of these tax fraud schemes is deliberately underreporting income. Among individuals, a government study found the bulk of the underreporting of income was done by self-employed restaurateurs, clothing store owners, and car dealers. Telemarketers and salespeople came in next, followed by doctors, accountants, and hairdressers.

Self-employed taxpayers who overdeduct business-related expenses—such as car expenses—came in a far distant second among tax fraud criminals. The IRS has concluded that only 6.8% of deductions are overstated or fictitious.

Just how much tax fraud occurs in the United States? According to one source in a recent year, 2,472 Americans were convicted of tax crimes—0.0022 percent of all taxpayers. This number is small, especially considering that the IRS estimates that 17 percent of all taxpayers are not complying with the tax laws in some way or another.[2] According to the IRS, individual taxpayers commit 75 percent of the tax fraud—mostly middle-income earners. Corporations do most of the rest.

## CI Investigative Careers

Like the FBI, working for IRS Criminal Investigation (CI) means you are a government employee and are part of a network of local, state, and federal law enforcement agencies. The IRS works closely with the Department of Justice, U.S. Attorneys, the FBI, U.S. Customs, the Drug Enforcement Administration, U.S. Postal Inspection Service, Inspectors General of all federal agencies, and U.S. Marshals Service. Many federal agencies rely on CI to unravel criminal activities by following the financial trail, which ultimately leads to violation of the tax laws and numerous other related financial crimes or other federal offenses. It is not unusual for a tax fraud investigation to uncover motives for other serious crimes such as corruption, embezzlement, extortion, or even murder.

To work as an entry-level CI special agent, you must be a U.S. citizen and not be older than 37 years of age. You must have completed a four-year course of study or bachelor's degree in any field of study that included or was supplemented by at least 15 semester hours in accounting, plus an additional 9 semester hours from among the following or closely related fields: finance, economics, business law, tax law, or money and banking, or you must have a combination of education and experience that together meet the total qualification requirements, such as being a CPA. Individuals with more education or experience can be hired into more advanced positions in CI.

## Divorce Fraud

More than 1 million **divorce** cases are filed annually in this country, for the purpose of dissolving a marriage relationship. Most people who choose to get married do so with splendid, even idealistic, intentions. As a minimum, they intend to stay together "till death do us part" and love and nurture each other throughout the marriage. For many and enormously complex reasons, however, approximately 50 percent of all marriages fail. Whatever the underlying reasons, dissolving such a relationship is, in most cases, a serious matter that can often result in disastrous effects on all involved.

Having worked together to construct a lifestyle, with long-range plans and sincere effort, the decision to tear it apart, to declare that the good intentions have irreconcilably failed, and to change to a distinctly different lifestyle evokes emotions of all kinds, and often at a fever pitch. If children are involved, the complexity and alternatives become magnified even more.

Amicable breakups are not common. Instead, divorce wars often ensue. In some cases, an amicable breakup is drastically changed once the legal system becomes involved. Our justice system is adversarial—a battle by definition. Divorce attorneys can ethically only serve one party of a divorce, and their job is to advocate for that one person. Pit two divorce attorneys against each other, each trying to achieve the best results for their client, and even amicable couples can quickly find themselves in a legal war against each other. Divorce pits husband against wife, mother against father, and hostility escalates into the ultimate war, the trial. Add in the formality of court proceedings, and the original participants often find that their relationship and their intentions no longer resemble anything recognizable.

Either during or after a divorce, many a spouse feels cheated by the marriage dissolution proceedings. In particular, the economically dependent spouse may begin to question whether the planned or actual settlement is a good one and whether the other spouse may be holding or may have held back vital information about the existence or value of marital assets.

It should not be surprising, therefore, that much of the debate in divorce proceedings and a great deal of postjudgment divorce motions are filed seeking to set aside or reopen the decree. The basis for these disagreements and motions are often fraud on the part of the other spouse. Several steps must be taken to prove fraud in a divorce. As in all frauds, the party attempting to prove divorce fraud must show (1) that a false representation, usually one of fact, was made by the other party; (2) that the defendant's knowledge or belief that the representation was false or was made with reckless indifference to the truth; and (3) that the defendant showed an intent to induce the plaintiff to act or refrain from acting in a certain way. Most divorce fraud litigation results from two factors: (1) the plaintiff spouse alleges that the defendant hid assets from the divorce court so they would not have to be shared or taken away, or (2) that the values assigned to assets were unrealistically low, thus resulting in an unfair divorce settlement.

The predication, detection, and investigation approaches for divorce fraud are no different from those discussed in previous chapters. It is important to understand, however, that individuals sometimes go to great length to hide assets. We will discuss some of the ways assets are concealed as we discuss bankruptcy in this chapter. After all, as stated previously, the kind of frauds committed in both cases are similar; that is, they are committed to hide or protect assets.

# Bankruptcy Fraud

Even though most readers of this book are probably quite familiar with divorce, many are not familiar with how bankruptcy works. Thus, we will spend most of our time in this chapter discussing bankruptcy. However, because the motivation for and schemes used to commit fraud are often similar in both circumstances, everything we discuss in this section is applicable to divorce fraud.

Bankruptcy frauds, such as the one described at the beginning of the chapter, represent an ever-growing problem in the United States. The bankruptcy system, an arm of the U.S. District Court, is a critical component of the U.S. government because of the impact bankruptcy filings have on the national and local economies. Abuse of the system, such as fraud, by an individual filing for bankruptcy (debtor) or a professional within the system undermines the integrity of the system as a whole. Through abuse and corruption of the system, the effectiveness of the rehabilitation process, the system's primary function for the debtor, is reduced.

Monies defrauded from a bankruptcy never reach the pockets of deserving creditors and investors. As bankruptcy frauds occur more frequently, creditors and investors lose faith that their interests will be protected. This loss of faith can have a ripple effect in the economy through the tightening of credit, the raising of interest rates, and subsequent economic reactions.

The number of bankruptcies and associated bankruptcy frauds increased every year over the last five years. The increase in the number of petitions filed with the **bankruptcy court** resulted in a corresponding increase in administrative activity and a lessening of the available time and resources to enforce policy, procedures, and to detect fraud by the bankruptcy court infrastructure.

Over the past decade, professionals involved in the bankruptcy system have seen a decrease in the stigma attached to an individual or corporation filing for bankruptcy. Bankruptcy relief is now more widely accepted than ever before. Along with this perceived elimination of the shame, the changing economic climate in the United States contributed to a significant rise in bankruptcy filings over the past decade.

The vast majority of bankruptcies filed in the United States come in the form of complete liquidations. An analysis of current FBI bankruptcy fraud investigations reveals that the most common fraud scheme utilized in fraudulent bankruptcy filings, like divorce, involves the concealment of a debtor's assets. The concealment of assets encompasses approximately 70 percent of bankruptcy fraud. Concealment prevents these assets from being liquidated and transferred to creditors to extinguish debts.

Even though concealing assets from the bankruptcy court is a fairly self-explanatory fraud scheme, it can be accomplished in a variety of ways. A business or an individual can conceal assets. For example, an individual in Chapter 7 bankruptcy listed his assets as being well below his liabilities. Although this situation should be typical in most bankruptcy filings, the eventual outcome was not. After the debtor's bankruptcy was dismissed, the debtor continued living an extravagant lifestyle. The debtors were reported by their neighbors, who claimed that the debtors concealed several assets from the bankruptcy court, including boats, Rolex watches, and country club memberships. An investigation determined the debtors did not list these assets on their bankruptcy schedules in hopes of avoiding total liquidation of their assets.

In the case of a business filing for bankruptcy protection, concealment of assets typically occurs on a larger scale. For example, a business owner placed his company in Chapter 11 bankruptcy because the company was facing a severe cash shortage. However, just prior to filing for bankruptcy, the business owner transferred large sums of cash and other company assets to family members as well as outside business interests controlled by the owner. The debtor's objective was to protect these assets from sale or liquidation.

Bankruptcy fraud also involves schemes to include petition mills, multiple filing, false statements, trustee fraud, attorney fraud, forged filings, embezzlement, credit card fraud, and bust-outs. After the concealment-of-assets fraud schemes, petition mills and multiple filings are the most prominent bankruptcy fraud schemes.

Petition mill fraud schemes are becoming increasingly popular in large cities with poor or immigrant populations. The scheme revolves around keeping an individual from being evicted from his or her dwelling, usually a person who is renting versus owning. Typically, when an individual is experiencing financial troubles, the first "creditor" to contact the distressed individual is his or her landlord. In order to avoid eviction as well as the high cost of a lawyer, the individual answers an advertisement in the newspaper or responds to a billboard or poster intentionally posted in targeted neighborhoods. The advertisement explains how a "typing service" will help them keep their homes or apartments if faced with eviction. Unbeknownst to the individual, the service files a bankruptcy on the individual's behalf. The service charges an exorbitant fee for this service and drags the process out for several months, leading the individual to believe that the company is providing them a great service. In reality, the service is stripping the individual of any savings they might have and prolonging the inevitable eviction.

Two ways of perpetrating the multiple filing fraud schemes are the most popular:

1. Filing for bankruptcy in different states by utilizing true personal identifiers
2. Using false names or Social Security numbers to file in the same or different states (Typically, a debtor who files several bankruptcies in two or more states lists nearly identical assets and liabilities in each filing. The debtor becomes discharged from the debts and, in the process, makes off with several of the assets left off a particular petition. If the debtor fears being caught, then the debtor simply travels to another state and files for another bankruptcy.)

## The Bankruptcy Code

When people or organizations are unable to pay their debts and have more liabilities than assets, they can file a bankruptcy petition with the courts. The filing of a bankruptcy petition initiates a legal process under the jurisdiction of the U.S. District Court that automatically refers the petition to the bankruptcy court. Bankruptcies have several purposes, including giving a debtor relief from creditor collection and foreclosure actions and protecting creditors from unfair collection efforts by other creditors. A bankruptcy filing allows the debtor to work out an orderly plan to settle debts or liquidates assets and distributes the proceeds to creditors in a way that treats creditors equitably. The filing of a bankruptcy petition creates a separate entity, an "estate," which consists of the property or income of the debtor that will be used to settle the debts and over which the bankruptcy court has control.

Title 11 of the U.S. Code is referred to as the **Bankruptcy Code**. The Code is a federal statute that governs the bankruptcy process. The Code provides for several types of bankruptcy. Chapters 1, 3, and 5 contain general provisions that apply to all bankruptcies. Chapters 7, 11, and 13 apply to specific types of bankruptcy.

Chapters 7 and 11 may be used by corporations or individuals. Under Chapter 7, the bankruptcy is a complete liquidation or "shutting down of the business," and all assets are liquidated and used to pay creditors, usually for some percentage of actual debts owed. In contrast, under Chapter 11, the creditors are told to "back off" or to give the bankrupt entity some space or breathing room and time until it can reorganize its operational and financial affairs, settle its debts, and continue to operate in a reorganized fashion. Chapter 13 bankruptcies are reorganizations (similar to Chapter 11) that can be used by individuals meeting certain tests (individuals with regular income and with debts of $1 million or less). Debtors make regular payments to creditors over a specified number of years under Chapter 13. If reorganization doesn't work in Chapters 11 or 13 bankruptcies, judges often order a complete adjudication or Chapter 7 bankruptcy.

In Chapter 11, if the bankruptcy court confirms a plan for reorganization (or liquidation) in corporate cases or a discharge in individual cases, it becomes legally binding on the debtor and creditors. Only obligations provided for in the reorganized plan remain; and these obligations are settled in the amount, time, and manner provided for in the plan. If assets are liquidated, the proceeds are distributed to creditors in the order of priority specified in the Bankruptcy Code. For example, secured creditors usually are paid before unsecured creditors.

## Civil and Criminal Bankruptcy Fraud Statutes

Criminal bankruptcy fraud cases are generally prosecuted by the U.S. Attorney's office in the applicable U.S. District Court. In criminal cases, the government must prove its case beyond a reasonable doubt. Convictions may result in jail sentences or other criminal penalties.

Some of the more relevant sections of the bankruptcy code relating to criminal fraud include the following:

1. Concealment of Assets, False Oaths and Claims, and Bribery (18 USC 152). This section makes it a crime for a person to "knowingly and fraudulently" do any of the following:

   - Conceal property of a debtor's estate from creditors or from the bankruptcy trustee, custodian, or other officer of the court charged with custody of the property.
   - Make a false oath or account in a bankruptcy case.
   - Make a false declaration, certification, verification, or statement under penalty of perjury, such as intentionally omitting property, debt, or income from an Official Form required in a bankruptcy case. The court may infer fraudulent intent from the existence of an unexplained false statement unless the debtor can prove that the false statement was an unintentional honest mistake.
   - Present a false proof of claim against the debtor's estate. A proof of claim is a document filed with the bankruptcy court by a creditor stating the nature and amount of the claim against the debtor. The debt settlement plan takes into account "allowed" claims; that is, claims that the bankruptcy court accepts as valid claims. A creditor would be the likely perpetrator of this crime.
   - Receive a "material amount of property" from a debtor after the filing of a bankruptcy petition, with the "intent to defeat the provisions" of the Bankruptcy Code.
   - "Give, offer, receive, or attempt to obtain money or property, remuneration, compensation, reward, advantage or promise thereof for acting or forbearing to act" in a bankruptcy case.
   - In a personal capacity or as an agent or officer of a person or corporation, transfer or conceal his or the other person's or corporation's property, in contemplation of a bankruptcy case involving himself or the other person or corporation, or with the "intent to defeat the provisions" of the Bankruptcy Code.
   - In contemplation of a bankruptcy filing, or after such a filing, "conceal, destroy, mutilate, falsify, or make a false entry in any recorded information (including books, documents, records, and papers)" relating to the debtor's "property or financial affairs."
   - After a bankruptcy filing, "withhold any recorded information (including books, documents, records, and papers)" relating to the debtor's "property or financial affairs" from a custodian, trustee, or other officer of the court.

   Obviously, this statute is intended to target fraudulent acts by someone filing bankruptcy. You should also note that even though criminal statues related to divorce aren't as specific as these related to bankruptcy, these same kinds of offenses in divorce cases are often "prosecutable" in criminal court.

2. Embezzlement Against the Debtor's Estate (18 USC 153). This section applies to bankruptcy trustees, custodians, attorneys, or other court officers, and to anyone engaged by a court officer to perform a service for a debtor's estate. The statute makes it a crime for such persons to "knowingly and fraudulently appropriate to [their] own use, embezzle, spend, or transfer" any property, or to hide or destroy any document, belonging to the debtor's estate. This section of the code is intended to punish those who abuse their appointment to assist in the orderly transfer of assets in a bankruptcy. As an example of someone who was prosecuted under this section of the code, a court-appointed trustee was convicted of stealing $15 million from a debtor's assets before the remaining assets were distributed to creditors. Similarly, many divorce lawyers who were hired to assist in wealthy divorce cases have been prosecuted for misappropriating assets of the divorced couple.

3. Adverse Interest and Conduct of Officers (18 USC 154). This section prohibits a custodian, trustee, marshal, or other court officer from knowingly:

   - Purchasing, directly or indirectly, any property of the debtor's estate of which the person is an officer in a bankruptcy case.
   - Refusing to permit a reasonable opportunity for the inspection by parties in interest of the documents and accounts relating to the affairs of the estate in the person's charge when directed by the court to do so.
   - Refusing to permit a reasonable opportunity for the inspection by the U.S. Trustee of the documents and accounts relating to the affairs of the estate in the person's charge.

   This section of the code targets conflicts of interest by those appointed or hired to equitably dissolve assets in bankruptcy cases. For example, this section makes it an offense for court-appointed individuals to purchase property of a debtor for fear that an unreasonably low price will be paid.

4. Bankruptcy Fraud. This section makes it a crime to do any of the following to execute or conceal a fraud scheme:

   a. File a bankruptcy petition.
   b. File a document in a bankruptcy proceeding.
   c. Make a false or fraudulent representation, claim, or promise with respect to a bankruptcy proceeding, either before or after the bankruptcy petition is filed.

This section is the "catch-all" section that prohibits every other type of fraud associated with bankruptcies.

## Civil Bankruptcy Statutes

As you already learned in this course, the purpose of criminal laws is to "right a wrong" or send someone to jail or have them pay fines, but the purpose of civil laws is to seek monetary remedies or recover stolen funds.

Bankruptcy cases can involve civil proceedings conducted in the U.S. Bankruptcy Court. Plaintiffs may seek remedies when they are damaged by inappropriate conduct, for example, in a fraudulent transfer matter. The plaintiff (who is usually a trustee) need only demonstrate a preponderance of evidence (or sometimes clear and convincing evidence) that the defendant (normally the debtor or a related party) is liable for civil remedies. The specific remedies that may be sought depend on the charges involved. The following are some of the most pertinent sections of the Bankruptcy Code that provide civil remedies for bankruptcy fraud.

1. Offenses Leading to Revocation of Debt Discharge in Chapter 11 and Chapter 13 Cases. Section 1144 of the Bankruptcy Code provides for the revocation of a Chapter 11 reorganization plan and for the revocation of debt forgiveness or discharge in a Chapter 11 bankruptcy if the plan's approval was obtained through fraudulent means. Similarly, Code Section 1328(e) provides for the revocation of debt forgiveness or discharge in a Chapter 13

case if the discharge was obtained through fraud actions. Sections 1144 and 1328(e) are not specific as to what constitutes fraud for their purposes, but include any intentional deceit or criminal action discussed previously in this text. As an example of the kind of fraud targeted by this section, if a debtor lied about (usually by understating) the amount of his or her assets in order to get debts forgiven, the forgiveness or discharge of the debts could be revoked.

2. Fraudulent Transfers. Section 548 of the Bankruptcy Code defines a fraudulent transfer as a transfer made, or obligation incurred, *within one year before the bankruptcy petition's filing date* that was:

   a. Made with the actual intent to hinder, delay, or defraud creditors, for example, by giving debtor property to relatives with the intent of placing it beyond the reach of creditors, or
   b. Made for less than reasonably equivalent value if:

      1. The debtor was insolvent or became insolvent as a result of the transfer, or
      2. The debtor's capital remaining after the transfer was unreasonably small (for instance, the debtor was constantly behind in paying bills after the transfer), or
      3. The debtor intended to, or believed it would, incur debts it would be unable to repay when they matured.

This statute is one of the real workhorses of the Bankruptcy Code because hiding assets or trading or selling them at amounts below market value to relatives or friends (often involving kickbacks) is probably the most common type of fraud committed in both bankruptcy and divorce cases.

## Participants in the Bankruptcy Process

It is important for fraud investigators to understand the roles of key participants in the bankruptcy process. The parties discussed in this section are:

- Bankruptcy court
- U.S. Trustee
- Court-appointed trustee or panel
- Examiner
- Debtor
- Creditors
- Adjusters (operations or field agents)

### BANKRUPTCY COURT

Bankruptcy petitions are filed with the U.S. Bankruptcy Clerk's Office. All bankruptcy petitions are subject to U.S. District Court jurisdiction, but are automatically referred to the U.S. Bankruptcy Court for supervision. Bankruptcy judges hear cases involving debtors' and creditors' rights, approve reorganization plans, award professional fees, and conduct hearings and trials to resolve disputes. A divorce court would play a similar role in divorce hearings.

### U.S. TRUSTEE

The Office of the U.S. Trustee is an agency in the Department of Justice that is responsible for the following functions:

- Administering bankruptcy cases
- Appointing trustees, examiners, and Chapter 11 committees
- Overseeing and monitoring trustees
- Reviewing employees and fee applications
- Appearing in court on matters of interest to the debtor's estate and creditors

A U.S. Trustee or Assistant Trustee heads each of the 21 regions in the United States. Each regional office of the Office of the U.S. Trustee may have the following staff:

- *Staff attorneys.* Staff attorneys review fee applications, motions to appoint trustees and examiners, motions to convert or dismiss a case, and other pleadings. They also represent the U.S. Trustee as a party in interest.
- *Bankruptcy analysts.* These analysts review operating reports and other financial information and oversee the debtor's case to assure compliance with the Bankruptcy Code and to protect the estate's assets.
- *Special investigative units (SIUs).* Some regions have SIUs that investigate criminal complaints in bankruptcy cases.

## COURT-APPOINTED OR PANEL TRUSTEE

Court-appointed or panel **trustees** are usually individuals or firms, such as accountants or lawyers, who identify and collect a debtor's assets and then allocate those assets to creditors in an orderly manner. The duties of a court-appointed or panel trustee in Chapter 7 cases, as set forth in 11 USC 704, are as follows:

a. Collect and liquidate the property of the debtor's estate and close the estate as quickly as is compatible with the best interests of the involved parties.
b. Account for all property received.
c. Ensure that the debtor files the statement of intention to retain or surrender property as specified in 11 USC 521 (2)(B).
d. Investigate the financial affairs of the debtor.
e. If necessary, examine proofs of claims and object to improper claims.
f. If appropriate, oppose the discharge of the debtor.
g. Furnish information about the estate and its administration when requested by a party in interest, unless the court orders otherwise.
h. If the business of the debtor is authorized to be operated, file with the court, the U.S. Trustee, and any applicable tax-collecting governmental unit, periodic reports and summaries of the operation of the business, including a statement of receipts and disbursements and such other information as the U.S. Trustee or the court requires.
i. Make a final report and file a final account of the administration of the estate with the court and with the U.S. Trustee.

In Chapter 11 cases, the court-appointed or panel trustee's duties, as set forth in 11 USC 1106, are as follows:

a. Perform the duties of the trustee specified in items b., e., g., h., and i. of the preceding paragraph.
b. If the debtor has not done so, file the list, schedule, and statement required under 11 USC 521 (1).
c. Except to the extent that the court orders otherwise, investigate the acts, conduct, assets, liabilities, and financial condition of the debtor, the operation of the debtor's business and the desirability of the continuance of that business, and any other matter relevant to the case or to the formulation of a plan.
d. As soon as practical:

1) File a statement of any investigation conducted under item c. of this paragraph, including any fact ascertained pertaining to fraud, dishonesty, incompetence, misconduct, mismanagement, or irregularity in the management of the affairs of the debtor, or to a cause of action available to the estate.
2) Transmit a copy or a summary of any such statement to any creditors' committee or equity security holders' committee, to any indenture trustee, and to such other entity as the court designates.

e. As soon as practical, file a reorganization plan under 11 USC 1121, file a report of why the trustee will not file a plan, or recommend conversion of the case to a case under Chapters 7, 12, or 13 or dismissal of the case.

f. For any year for which the debtor has not filed a tax return required by law, furnish, without personal liability, such information as may be required by the governmental unit with which such tax return was to be filed, in light of the condition of the debtor's books and records and the availability of such information.

g. After confirmation of a plan, file such reports as are necessary or as the court orders.

Bankruptcy trustees often hear allegations of fraud by the debtor or its principals. In Chapter 11 cases, alleged fraud is generally the reason the court appoints a trustee. The trustee's authority to investigate fraud involves investigating the affairs of the debtor in Chapter 7 bankruptcies and (a) investigating the acts, conduct, assets, liabilities, and financial condition of the debtor, the operation of the debtor's business and the desirability of the continuance of such business and (b) filing a statement of investigation conducted in the case of a Chapter 11 bankruptcy. If the trustee conducts an investigation and decides that sufficient evidence of bankruptcy fraud exists, a report on the results of the investigation should be filed with the U.S. Attorney.

The trustee has significant powers to gather information in an investigation. A trustee, in effect, assumes the role of the debtor with all the rights thereto. Thus, the trustee can obtain information from the debtor's attorneys and accountants. The trustee can even break the attorney-client privilege because the trustee becomes the client. The trustee can also obtain access to the debtor's records that are in the hands of the criminal authorities.

### EXAMINERS

An examiner (usually some type of fraud examiner or investigator) is generally appointed by a bankruptcy judge in a Chapter 11 proceeding to investigate allegations of fraud or misconduct by the debtor or its principals. The examiner's role is to investigate and report the results of the investigation to the court and other interested parties as soon as possible. Examiners can subpoena records and depose witnesses. Generally, they cannot operate businesses, make business decisions, or propose reorganization plans. However, the court may expand an examiner's role to perform some functions of trustees or debtors-in-possession.

### DEBTORS

A **debtor** is the person or entity who is the subject of a Chapter 11 filing. A debtor in an involuntary, or forced, bankruptcy proceeding is called an *alleged debtor*.

The debtor's primary goal in a bankruptcy proceeding is to settle its obligations as favorably to its interest as possible. Bankruptcy fraud by individual debtors often results from concealing assets or making false statements on Office Forms. Bankruptcy fraud by business debtors often results from inflating debt and underreporting assets.

### CREDITORS

A **creditor** is defined as one who holds a valid claim against a debtor. The Bankruptcy Code allows committees to represent classes of creditors. In Chapter 11 cases, creditors committees have the power to investigate the acts, conduct, and financial condition of a debtor and any other matters relevant to the case.

### ADJUSTERS

Adjusters are also called operations or field agents. Adjusters assist the trustee by performing such duties as securing business facilities and assets, locating assets of the debtor's estate, locating business records, opening new bank accounts, investigating asset thefts, and arranging asset sales.

## Participants in Divorce Cases

Divorce laws and statutes are much simpler than those related to bankruptcy. Divorce actions are usually initiated by a disgruntled spouse who believes he or she has been wronged or injured in some way. The parties involved are usually the husband and wife, attorneys for both sides, and a divorce court. When allegations of fraud, such as hiding or illegally transferring assets arise, the attorneys for the party alleging fraud usually hire investigators to try to locate such hidden assets. Investigative techniques such as surveillance, public records searches, and even subpoenas of private records are most often used. Evidence discovered by hired investigators is then presented to the divorce court by the appropriate attorney to obtain the most favorable divorce settlements possible. Most divorce fraud cases are civil, but when evidence of egregious fraudulent acts by one marital partner has been shown, law enforcement officials are often involved in investigations and criminal charges can be filed.

## Fraud Investigator's Relationship to Participants in Bankruptcy Proceedings

Code Section 327(a) allows trustees to employ, with the court's approval, attorneys, accountants, or other professionals to represent or assist the trustee. Also, Code Section 1103 allows a creditors' committee to employ, with the court's approval, attorneys, accountants, or their agents to perform services for the committee. Although the Code does not specifically authorize it, bankruptcy courts have typically allowed examiners to employ CFEs and even CPAs and other professionals. Fraud examiners and accountants may be used to conduct fraud investigations as well as provide consulting and other financial services.

Before professionals can be compensated from estate funds, they must be employed under Code Section 327. The court must approve the employment of those professionals. Code Section 330 sets forth the conditions regarding compensation of professionals and lists specific requirements relating to retention.

A creditor may engage a CPE, CPA, or other professional independently from the court to investigate allegations of bankruptcy fraud. In such cases, the creditor usually compensates the investigator directly without court approval. Under certain conditions the creditor may apply to the court to have the costs of the investigation paid by the state if they result in criminal prosecution.

The retention of a fraud examiner or investigator in a bankruptcy proceeding must be approved by the bankruptcy judge. This approval is required whenever the investigator is paid by the debtor's estate, whether the investigator is engaged by the debtor, trustee, debtor-in-possession, creditors' committee, or stockholders. However, in the rare cases that an investigator provides services to and is directly paid by an individual creditor or stockholder, these requirements do not apply.

When a fraud investigator is retained, an affidavit of a proposed investigator (see sample affidavit in Appendix A) is prepared. The affidavit is addressed to the court and is submitted by the attorney for the person who engaged the investigator (such as the trustee, examiner, or creditors' committee) as part of the application for retention. The affidavit is a legal document that is sworn under oath (under penalties of perjury) and must be notarized. The exact content and extent of detail required in an affidavit varies by jurisdiction.

A description of the proposed services is generally included and is particularly important. U.S. Trustees require the services of professionals to be categorized and have developed broad categories of service. One such category is litigation consulting, which includes fraud examination or forensic accounting. Fraud investigation services would be included in this category. Another category is asset analysis and recovery, which would be relevant in hiring someone to search for possible fraudulent transfers.

The description of services should be reasonably detailed, but the extent of detail required depends on the preferences of the bankruptcy judge. In considering the request for compensation, the judge will compare actual services rendered to proposed services in the application and order for retention. Judges often disallow compensation for services that were not authorized.

Once the services of a fraud investigator are approved, an application for retention (see sample application in Appendix B) is usually prepared by the attorney for the person engaging the investigator, based primarily on information in the affidavit and discussions with the investigator.

Once the application for retention is approved, the judge issues an order authorizing the services. The investigator generally should verify that the order is signed before beginning work.

# Bankruptcy and Divorce Fraud Schemes— The Planned Bankruptcy (Bust-Out)

The two most common bankruptcy fraud schemes are the planned bankruptcy, or bust-out, and the fraudulent concealment of assets during, or in contemplation of, a bankruptcy. This latter scheme is also the most common type of fraud in divorce cases.

A **bust-out** may take several forms, but all essentially involve intentionally obtaining loans or purchasing inventory on a credit basis and concealing, or absconding with, the proceeds from the loan or sale of the inventory or with the inventory itself before the creditors are paid. Insolvency is declared and bankruptcy is filed, but the creditors find that no assets left from which they can be paid. If the scam works, the perpetrators retain the loan or sales proceeds or the inventory but escape liability for the unpaid debt. Government statistics estimate that losses to creditors from bust-outs amount to $1 billion a year.

A bust-out may involve setting up a new company or using an established company. In the first type of bust-out, the fraud perpetrators set up a new company and operate it legitimately for a while in order to establish credibility (a reputation for honesty) and a credit rating with banks (that provide loans) or suppliers (who sell goods on credit). The new company may purposely take a name similar to that of an existing, well-known, and reputable company in order to trick unwary lenders and suppliers into thinking they are dealing with the well-known company or with a subsidiary or affiliate of a well-known company. The scam company may also submit intentionally misstated financial statements to suppliers or creditors to inflate its financial position and profitability.

In the second type of bust-out, the perpetrators quietly buy an established company that already has a good reputation and credit rating and take over its management. Credit-rating agencies are usually not aware of the ownership and management change. The perpetrators then rely on the established credit rating to get credit from suppliers and loans from banks.

In either type of bust-out, the perpetrators buy large amounts of inventory on credit from numerous suppliers. The perpetrators may also obtain bank loans on the basis of the credit rating. At first, the perpetrators pay the suppliers promptly in order to build up their credit rating, creating incentives for suppliers to extend higher amounts of credit. The cash with which to pay the suppliers is obtained from the loans or from selling the goods at deep discounts through co-conspirators in other markets. (The merchandise usually is of a type that can be sold quickly at cost.) The perpetrators buy larger and larger amounts of inventory on credit and eventually stop paying the suppliers. They stockpile the inventory and either conceal it for later sale in another location or secretly liquidate it at bargain prices. If the perpetrators obtained bank loans, they siphon off some or all of the proceeds into accounts of hidden "shell" corporations.

The perpetrators then either claim insolvency and file for bankruptcy or simply close up shop without filing bankruptcy and abscond with the sales and bank loan proceeds. The company will appear to be insolvent because the sales of inventory at bargain or liquidation prices reduced profits and cash flow, and the siphoning off of the sales proceeds reduced assets and cash, while the liabilities to lenders and suppliers remain. If the perpetrators flee without filing for bankruptcy, the unpaid lenders and suppliers may file an involuntary bankruptcy petition against the company. In either case, however, the lenders and suppliers find few or no assets left in the company with which to pay off the company debts.

In a bust-out, usually the intent at the start is to make a company insolvent and perhaps also to eventually file bankruptcy as part of the scheme to defraud creditors. If the perpetrators do not file a bankruptcy petition, they cannot be charged with bankruptcy fraud. Almost all bust-out schemes usually involve concealing assets—either sales or loan proceeds or inventory.

A bust-out can be hard to detect. If a company claims insolvency and files for bankruptcy, it can be difficult for creditors to detect that the insolvency was the result of actions deliberately taken for the purpose of perpetrating fraud. Indicators of a bust-out include the following:

- A company's only listed address and phone number are a post office box and an answering service. (Investigators should be aware that post office boxes can appear as street addresses.)
- A new company is owned and managed by persons from another state or is vague about its ownership or type of business.

- A sudden change is made in a company's management, especially if the change is made without public notice.
- Credit references either cannot be verified or seem too eager to provide favorable references. (These references may be phony or collusive.)
- The size of orders placed on credit and the credit balances with suppliers suddenly and dramatically increase.
- The inventory is suddenly depleted, without explanation.
- "Customers" have a history of buying goods at unreasonable discounts.

# Fraudulent Concealment of Assets or Income in Bankruptcies or Divorces

Although bust-outs are unique to bankruptcy, fraudulent concealment of assets or income is a common type of fraud in both bankruptcy and divorce. This section discusses what constitutes the debtor's or divorcee's estate (i.e., what assets and income might be concealed), methods of concealing these assets or income, and procedures to investigate possible concealments.

## The Debtor's or Divorcee's Estate

When a company or individual (including an individual who owns an unincorporated business) files for bankruptcy under Chapters 7, 11, or 13 of the Bankruptcy Code, or an individual files or is involved in a divorce, an estate is created. This estate consists of the property (or income, in some cases) of the debtor or divorcee, which will be used to settle debts and over which the bankruptcy or divorce court has control. In a **Chapter 7 bankruptcy**, all the estate assets are liquidated and the proceeds are used to settle debts. In **Chapters 11 or 13 bankruptcies**, some of the estate's assets may be liquidated or turned over to creditors in settlement of debt, but most estate assets normally are not liquidated or turned over to creditors because the purpose of Chapters 11 and 13 bankruptcies is to allow the individual or organization to retain assets and to settle debts from future income. In a divorce case, the estate or assets of the married couple are usually divided between the two marital partners after the debts of the couple are paid.

Generally, the debtor's estate or divorce partner's assets consist of all property as of the date the bankruptcy or divorce petition was filed and the postpetition proceeds or earnings from such property. For example, an estate would include a building owned as of the petition date and the rent earned from the building during the postpetition period. Or, as another example, an estate would include postpetition collections of accounts receivable that existed as of the petition date.

## Bankruptcy Statutes Concerning Concealment of Assets

Title 18, Section 152, of the U.S. Code makes it a crime to knowingly and fraudulently conceal property of a debtor's estate or falsify any documents, records, or statements during, or in contemplation of, a bankruptcy. As previously discussed, the Bankruptcy Code provides for revocation of debt forgiveness or discharge obtained through fraud, including (the authors believe) concealment of assets or intentional misstatement of records or statements filed in the case. Even if the debtor is not convicted of criminal or civil fraud, any concealed assets or income that are located can be brought back into the estate to be used to settle debts.

## Means of Concealing Assets or Income

As previously noted, fraudulent concealment of assets or income is one of the most common types of bankruptcy and divorce frauds. The following are some ways in which assets or income may be fraudulently concealed:

1. Cash received in payment of receivables may be diverted to another entity, usually to a related party.

2. Inventory may be shipped to an off-site location or sold to a related party, fence, or other co-conspirator at a steeply discounted price.

3. Assets or income may be shifted to another entity controlled by the debtor or a divorced party. The transfer may be accomplished through means such as changing the title to assets, depositing amounts into accounts of other individuals or companies, and paying bogus or padded fees and expenses.

4. Sales may not be reported in the debtor company's books; instead the sales proceeds are diverted.

5. Payments may be made to fictitious individuals or vendors and the amounts diverted to the debtor or to a divorced party. Also, payments to conspiring vendors or individuals may be padded, or purchase discounts may not be recorded, and the overpayment diverted to the debtor or a marriage partner.

6. Income from controlled organizations may be intentionally understated by overstating expenses. Also, a debtor company may pay excessive compensation to owners.

7. The debtor's personal expenses may be paid by the company and mischaracterized as business expenses.

8. The debtor's or divorced partner's books and records or other financial information may be damaged or hidden.

9. Interests in partnerships, corporations, lawsuit proceeds, or other assets may not be disclosed.

## Indicators of Possible Asset or Income Concealment

Some indicators of possible asset or income concealment include the following:

1. Transfers of property or large payments to related parties or individuals, such as insiders, shareholders, or relatives

2. Frequent and unusual transfers between bank accounts, particularly between business and personal accounts

3. Transactions frequently made in cash but normally are made on account (sales, purchases, etc.)

4. Unusually large and unexplainable payments to particular vendors

5. Unusual or rapid reductions in assets

6. Increases in operating losses that are not explained by the economic factors the company or individual faced

7. Inconsistencies between financial statements or tax returns and the Official Forms filed for the bankruptcy or records filed in divorce cases

8. Travel to off-shore tax havens or locations that allow secret bank accounts

9. Missing, inaccurate, or damaged records

## Fraudulent Transfers

Section 548 of the Bankruptcy Code defines a fraudulent transfer as a transfer made, or obligation incurred, within one year before the bankruptcy petition's filing date that was:

a. Made with the actual intent to hinder, delay, or defraud creditors, for example, by giving debtor property to relatives with the intent of placing it beyond the reach of creditors, *or*

b. Made for less than the reasonably equivalent value if:

1) The debtor was insolvent or became insolvent as a result of the transfer (insolvency for this purpose is defined beginning in Paragraph 906.5), *or*

2) The debtor's capital remaining after the transfer was unreasonably small (for instance, the debtor was constantly behind in paying bills after the transfer), *or*

3) The debtor intended to, or believed it would, incur debts it would be unable to repay when they matured.

Part (a) of the definition constitutes actual fraud, for which fraudulent intent must be shown. Part (b) constitutes constructive fraud, for which intent to defraud need not be shown, as long as one of the conditions in part (b) is met. The one-year cutoff date applies to either type of fraudulent transfer. However, a longer cutoff period may apply if state statutes are applied in the bankruptcy case.

The preceding paragraph indicates that a fraudulent transfer may be made with or without actual intent to defraud creditors. The statutes discussed in Section 901 generally apply when actual intent to defraud creditors is proved. Also, the bankruptcy court can avoid (cancel) the transfer and bring the property back into the estate for use to settle debts.

The Bankruptcy Code also contains provisions that apply when a transfer meets the Code's definition of constructive fraud, even if the transfer cannot be shown to involve actual intent to defraud creditors. The bankruptcy court can avoid constructively fraudulent transfers and bring the assets back into the estate for use to settle debts.

## Civil Liability for False Accusations

An important issue for fraud investigators in both bankruptcy and divorce cases is the risk of civil liability for false accusations. Debtors and divorced partners often have little to lose by challenging the investigator on every word of his or her report. In this situation, the investigator may be placed on the defensive by the debtor's or divorcee's aggressive attacks. The investigator should be careful to ensure that all findings and conclusions in any report provided are properly supported with evidence. Unsupported conclusions could expose the investigator to charges of false accusations, which could result in costly civil liability.

## KEY TERMS

**Bankruptcy** A legal process that either allows a debtor to work out an orderly plan to settle debts or liquidate assets and distribute them to creditors.

**Bankruptcy Code** Title 11 of the United States code—the federal statute that governs the bankruptcy process.

**Bankruptcy court** The federal court that supervises all bankruptcy proceedings.

**Bust-out.** A planned bankruptcy.

**Chapter 7 bankruptcy** Complete liquidation or "shutting down of a business" and distribution of any proceeds to creditors.

**Chapter 11 bankruptcy** Bankruptcy that allows the bankrupt entity time to reorganize its operational and

financial affairs, settle its debts, and continue to operate in a reorganized fashion.

**Creditor** A person or entity owed money by a debtor.

**Debtor** A person or entity declaring bankruptcy.

**Divorce** The legal separation of two married partners resulting in the dissolution of their marriage.

**Tax fraud** Willfully and intentionally violating the known legal duty of voluntarily filing income tax returns and paying the correct amount of income, employment, or excise taxes.

**Trustee** Individual or firm who collects a debtor's assets and distributes them to creditors.

## QUESTIONS AND CASES

### DISCUSSION QUESTIONS

1. Why is fraud so prevalent in bankruptcy and divorce cases?

2. What is bankruptcy? What are the most common types of bankruptcy?

3. What are some of the more relevant sections of the bankruptcy code related to fraud?

4. What is tax fraud?

5. When a bankruptcy takes place, who are the major participants involved?

6. What are some of the most common bankruptcy fraud schemes?

7. What are some of the most common divorce fraud schemes?

8. What are some of the most common tax fraud schemes?

9. What are some of the most common ways fraud perpetrators conceal and transfer assets or income during bankruptcy and divorces?

10. What is a court-appointed or panel trustee?

11. What is an affidavit of proposed investigator?

12. Who usually initiates the filing of an application for retention of investigator?

13. Why should fraud investigators involved in bankruptcy or divorce cases be careful about what they put in their reports?

14. What is the Criminal Investigation Division of the IRS?

15. Is it necessary to report illegal income (such as fraud gains) on income tax returns?

## TRUE/FALSE

1. Civil bankruptcy cases are usually investigated by the FBI and other law enforcement agencies.

2. A person acting as an officer in a bankruptcy case is prohibited from purchasing any property of the debtor's estate.

3. Fraudulent transfers can occur up to two years before the debtor files for bankruptcy.

4. Bust-out schemes usually involve the concealment of assets, sales proceeds, and inventory.

5. Debtors in bankruptcy cases have the power to sue investigators over false accusations.

6. Chapter 11 bankruptcies represent complete liquidation or shutting down of a business.

7. A *debtor* is the person or entity who is subject to a bankruptcy filing.

8. Most divorce-related fraud cases are civil rather than criminal.

9. The retention of a fraud investigator in a bankruptcy case must always be approved by the bankruptcy court's judge.

10. A "planned bankruptcy" is usually referred to as a bust-out.

11. The U.S. tax system is based on voluntary compliance.

12. Americans should pay the least amount of taxes they legally owe.

13. The U.S. Department of Treasury is branch of the Internal Revenue Service.

14. Tax fraud can be committed against state, federal, or local governments.

15. To work as an entry-level Criminal Investigation special agent you must be at least 29 years of age.

## MULTIPLE CHOICE

1. Which of the following describes a Chapter 13 bankruptcy?
   a. All assets are liquidated and used to pay creditors.
   b. Reorganizations can be used by individuals with debts less than a million dollars.
   c. Entity is given time to reorganize its financial affairs, settle debts, and continue operations.
   d. Debtors receive all their payments up front from liquidated assets.

2. Which of the following is *not* a more relevant section of the bankruptcy code relating to fraud?
   a. Concealment, false oaths, and bribery
   b. Embezzlement against the debtor's estate
   c. Illegal liquidation of assets and processes to settle debts
   d. Adverse interest and conduct of officers

3. Bankruptcy courts do *not* have which of the following responsibilities?
   a. Appointing trustees, examiners, and committees
   b. Supervising bankruptcy petitions
   c. Approving reorganization plans
   d. Conducting hearings and trials to resolve disputes

4. Which of the following is *not* a characteristic of an affidavit of proposed investigator?
   a. Content and extent of detail required does not vary by jurisdiction.
   b. Is prepared when a fraud investigator is retained.
   c. Legal document is sworn under oath and must be notarized.
   d. Addressed to the court and is submitted by an attorney for the person who engaged the investigator.

5. Which of the following is the least likely symptom of a possible bust-out?
   a. Company's only listed address is a post office box
   b. Dramatic increase in size of credit orders
   c. Public notice of change in management
   d. Sudden decrease in inventory

6. Which of the following is the major reason why there is so much divorce fraud?
   a. Assets are being taken away from one divorce partner and are given to another.
   b. Divorce proceedings usually take a long time.
   c. States make divorces difficult.
   d. Children usually get most assets in divorce cases.

7. Which of the following investigative methods would most likely be used more in divorce cases than in bankruptcy cases?
   a. Surveillance
   b. Public records searches
   c. Subpoena of private records
   d. Interviews

8. The retention of a fraud investigator in a bankruptcy proceeding must be approved by the bankruptcy judge unless:
   a. The debtor's estate pays the investigator.
   b. The trustee pays the investigator.
   c. The creditors' committee pays the investigator.
   d. An individual creditor or shareholder pays the investigator.

9. Which of the following is *not* an indicator of a possible bust-out?
   a. An address that is a post office box
   b. New ownership of a company
   c. Slow buildup of inventory
   d. Dramatic increase in the size of credit orders

10. Which of the following is an indicator of possible hiding of assets in a divorce?
    a. Assets transferred to an off-site location
    b. Changing the title to assets
    c. Payments made to fictitious individuals
    d. All of the above are possible indicators of hiding assets

11. Which of the following is not a way that individuals can commit tax fraud?
    a. Overstating the amount of deductions
    b. Keeping two sets of books
    c. Paying the least amount of taxes the individual owes
    d. Making false entries in books and records

12. The Criminal Investigation Division's:
    a. Chief responsibility is to detect taxpayers who willfully and intentionally violate their known legal duty of voluntarily filing income tax.
    b. Chief responsibility is checking the accuracy of tax returns.
    c. Chief responsibility is to detect fraud in public corporations tax fillings.
    d. Chief responsibility is to detect fraud in U.S. citizens tax filings.

13. Which of the following is not an example of tax fraud?
    a. Using a false Social Security number
    b. Keeping two sets of financial books
    c. Reporting information regarding passive income
    d. Claiming a blind spouse as a dependent when you are single

14. If an audit reveals that an individual has underpaid his or her taxes, the auditor:
    a. Can assess civil fines.
    b. Can assess penalties.
    c. Can refer the case to the Criminal Investigation Division.
    d. Must refer the case to the federal courts for further investigation.

15. To work as an entry-level CI special agent:
    a. You must be a U.S. citizen.
    b. You must not be older than 43 years of age.
    c. You must have completed a four-year course of study or bachelor's degree.
    d. You must have received training in accounting or a closely related field.

## ■ SHORT CASES

**Case 1.** Willy and Buck Forsythe are brothers who often engage in shady business deals and regularly swindle honest people out of their money. Willy and Buck decided to take their business to a new level. A small hardware store in town has a good reputation for honesty and friendly service. With the large amounts of money accumulated from other schemes, Willy and Buck decide to buy the hardware store. They make the owner an offer he can't refuse, and they are soon in the hardware business.

As new managers of the store, Willy and Buck make some changes. They begin to order bigger shipments from suppliers, paying them off promptly, using money acquired through loans. They sell off a lot of these shipments at cost to their unruly friend, Billy the Kid. As orders get larger and payments remain prompt, the suppliers are willing to extend more and more credit to the hardware store. Also, because it appears that business is good, the bank is willing to lend more money.

Things are going just as planned for Willy and Buck. When they have a lot of money on loan from the bank, and they have just sold huge amounts of inventory to Billy that they had purchased on credit, they file for bankruptcy. The suppliers and the bank are perplexed, but upon investigation, they find that Willy and Buck really don't have the money to pay them back nor the inventory to liquidate in order to pay them. Willy and Buck have successfully "sold" their inventory or hidden their cash in other bank accounts, so it appears they don't have the means to pay back their creditors.

What kind of scheme are Willy and Buck involved in, and how could the bank and the suppliers have detected it sooner?

**Case 2.** A small credit union asks you to help them investigate an alleged fraud in a bankruptcy case. They want you to start right away because they are worried that the debtor will destroy evidence vital to their case. They have not received permission from the judge involved in the case to contract you; but they tell you that if you find fraud, you will have no problem with the judge.

What should your response be to this arrangement?

**Case 3.** You are hired as a fraud auditor to examine the assets of a company that recently filed Chapter 11 bankruptcy. The company manufactures and sells circuit boards for children's computerized toys. You have access to its financial statements and warehouses. The company is a closely held corporation. Some suggestions indicate that the company is fraudulently concealing assets.

Give three red flags that you would look for to indicate fraudulent asset concealment.

**Case 4.** Colleen Philbrock just turned twenty-two and her hard work finally started to pay off. Six months earlier Colleen graduated from the state university with a master's degree in accounting (MAcc). Colleen graduated with honors and was one of the youngest in her class. Unlike most of the intellectuals she had studied with throughout her career, Colleen was extremely social and had great communication skills. After graduation she took a job with a well-known regional accounting firm. The firm specialized in assisting companies with their technology problems. Colleen knew that the connections and knowledge she would gain working for the firm would be beneficial throughout her career. Now, six months after graduation, she has a full-time job offer with one of the firm's strongest clients.

Within a few days on her new job, Colleen adapted to her new environment and to her new responsibilities of running the entire accounting department along with two other recent graduates. However, it wasn't long until Colleen began to notice that something wasn't right. After a few weeks, Colleen realized that the firm's executives were participating in illegal transactions.

Importing expensive technological products from China, the company executives were selling the products under the table to contacts unknown to Colleen. Once the firm received the products at the shipping dock, the executives' "personal employees" marked the products and took them to a separate location. The entire operation was done with little paperwork. The money made from the special products received special attention. Colleen was told to report this inflow of cash in an account called "personal executive consulting services." This categorization allowed the executives to personally use the money at their convenience.

1. Does Colleen have a responsibility to report the fraud?

2. If so, to whom should she report the fraud?

3. Assuming that the fraud has been continuing for several years, what would be the tax ramifications to the executives of not reporting earnings on their tax returns?

4. Even though the money is from illegal sources, are the executives required to report the income on their yearly tax returns?

5. Earlier in the book we discussed the net worth method. How do you think the net worth method can help prosecutors determine the extent of company executives' illegal income?

**Case 5.** Trek, Inc., experienced two bad financial years, resulting in too few assets remaining to pay creditors in full. Trek wants to file for bankruptcy. What are its options and which one would be best for Trek, Inc.?

**Case 6.** Suppose you work with the Criminal Investigation Division of the IRS. You were recently assigned a case that involves a $3, million tax evasion scandal. The Internal Revenue Service discovered the case when they were performing a routine audit. Because the IRS believed that the case involved fraud, the IRS agent referred the case to the Criminal Investigation Division who in turn referred the case to you. After investigating the case, you determine that the case involves significant fraud. Before prosecuting the case further you want to review the specific laws under which fraud perpetrators are charged.

1. Identify the specific laws under which tax fraud perpetrators are charged.

2. Explain how each of these laws relates to tax fraud.

3. In prosecuting fraud, are some of the laws more applicable than others? Are all of the laws you listed broken when tax fraud occurs? Why or why not?

**Case 7.** In the fall of 2001, Enron, the eighth largest corporation in the United States, declared bankruptcy unexpectedly and investors lost approximately $60 billion.

From your reading about this famous case, did Enron's bankruptcy involve fraud? If so, what type?

**Case 8.** Your best friend, Sue, always wanted to be an FBI agent for the U.S. government. However, because of the recent restructured changes in the FBI (due to the increased terrorism threat), Sue is uncertain whether she wants to pursue an FBI career. She feels that the FBI does not provide as much career security as she once thought that it did. Sue is excellent with numbers, taxes, law, and communication. After reading the chapter and learning about the Criminal Investigation Division of the IRS, you are excited to tell Sue about it.

1. Explain the purpose and mission of the Criminal Investigation Division.

2. Explain what other governmental agencies the Criminal Investigation Division works with.

3. Explain the requirement for an entry-level Criminal Investigation special agent.

**Case 9.** John Dewey is the husband of Mary Dewey. He is also the CEO of a large public relations firm. Mary recently filed for divorce, alleging mental brutality, and is asking for half of John's and the couple's assets. In the six months prior to being served for divorce, John has taken business trips to the Cayman Islands, Switzerland, Hong Kong, and Barbados. These were the first business-related trips John had ever taken to these locations. When John's and the couple's assets were identified during the divorce proceedings, Mary was surprised to learn that John's and his company's net worth totaled only $50,000, and that her half would only be $25,000. She was disappointed because, up until the divorce, John had been giving her $200,000 per year to spend.

What kind of fraud is most likely in this case?

**Case 10.** As mentioned in the chapter, lawyers, creditors, and trustees can often be involved in bankruptcy fraud. Read the letter at http://www.clr.org/Safford6c04.html. It was written by a debtor to the U.S. Attorney's office.

List the individuals the debtor accuses, these individuals' roles in the bankruptcy proceedings, and the fraudulent behavior the debtor accuses them of.

**Case 11.** Look up the U.S. Trustee Program's 2002 Annual Report.

1. How is a trustee defined (p. 1)?

2. What are the functions of the trustee program (p. 1)?

3. The program routinely hires bankruptcy analysts of what two certifications (p. 3)?

4. What initiative did the program launch in 2001 (p. 7)? For what purpose?

5. What specific actions can the program take under this initiative?

6. According to the report, what other crimes is bankruptcy fraud often connected with (p. 21)?

7. The Trustee Program refers criminal cases to the district attorney's office. The report separates these referrals into six categories. List the categories and provide a one-sentence description of each type of scheme.

8. List the 10 duties of a U.S. Trustee (p. 31).

**Case 12.** Attorney Joel Steinberg of Alexandria, Virginia, pleaded guilty to wire fraud in the Eastern District of Virginia, based on his actions of embezzling from a client in Chapter 13 bankruptcy. Steinberg embezzled more than $22,000 intended for payment to the client's mortgage holders under the Chapter 13 plan. Evidence of the embezzlement came to light when the debtor client complained to the Chapter 13 trustee, who notified the Alexandria office. After investigating, the U.S. Trustee filed a civil complaint against Steinberg seeking disgorgement of all fees paid by the debtor, an accounting of all monies received, a surcharge for all late fees and penalties levied against the debtor by his mortgage companies, and disbarment from practice before the bankruptcy court. During discovery, which included subpoenaing Steinberg's trust account records, further misconduct was discovered in unrelated cases. The allegations in the U.S. Trustee's civil complaint formed the basis of his criminal indictment. Before the criminal trial, Steinberg agreed to disbarment for at least five years.

Which section of the bankruptcy code makes Steinberg's activities illegal?

**Case 13.** After a jury trial, Charles H. Barber and his parents, Charles M. and Helen J. Barber, of Minerva, New York, were found guilty on charges of theft of public funds, wire fraud, bankruptcy fraud, and money laundering conspiracy. The charges arose from the Barbers' schemes to defraud and their use of bankruptcy proceedings to further those schemes. Both father and son were convicted of concealing assets from the bankruptcy trustee and creditors and making false statements under penalty of perjury. The father was also found guilty of transferring approximately $489,000 from his brokerage account to an account in the Bahamas in contemplation of bankruptcy, and the mother was found to have engaged in bankruptcy fraud by receiving property in her name to defeat the bankruptcy laws. The Albany office assisted in the investigation and preparation for the bankruptcy aspects of the trial.

If the father was to be prosecuted criminally, what fact would have to hold regarding his transfer of money?

**Case 14.** BBB Company successfully manufactured quality electronics products for the past 20 years. It is a publicly traded company with 1 million shares outstanding. During the past three years, the company has fallen on hard times. Profit margins in the electronics manufacturing industry have been squeezed due to competition in Japan. For most of the company's history, research and development (R&D) costs have been a substantial portion of expenses. However, in the last three years, they have not had any R&D expenses. This fact may have led to the decline in perception of quality, for which customers expressed concern.

Suppliers have also been complaining that BBB Company bought increasing amounts of inventory on credit and pressured them to loosen credit terms. However, the company showed decreasing inventory over the last three years as sales declined. Recently, the company CFO talked the local bank into increasing BBB's credit limit, and the company used its entire line of credit. The CFO convinced the bankers that the current downturn in sales was temporary and that the company had a new product line that would be lucrative.

With all its financial pressures, the company recently decided to file for bankruptcy. It cannot cover the interest payments on loans, nor can it meet its growing accounts payable balance. As creditors begin to seek monetary recovery through assets, they discover little inventory and extraordinarily high expenses in the current year. Also, some cash (from loans) disappeared without leaving a paper trail.

1. What evidence indicates that the company has been planning to declare bankruptcy? If so, for how many years?

2. If this bankruptcy was fraudulently planned and assets disappeared, will BBB Company still be allowed to declare bankruptcy?

**Case 15.** Abbott Insurance Company (AIC) was based in Florida. Because the company was experiencing financial problems, the state's regulatory board required the company to either find an infusion of capital or declare bankruptcy. The officers were successful in finding a group of investors who purchased 90 percent of the company for $4 million. Unfortunately, once in control, the new owners started offering single-premium annuities with higher-than-market interest rates. They used the money received from selling the annuities to fund mortgages for their friends. Because most mortgages were bad, the company declared bankruptcy. Subsequent investigation revealed that the new owners had fraudulently stolen nearly $200 million from the company.

What kind of investigation in this bankruptcy case most likely disclosed the fraudulent acts of the new owners?

**Case 16.** Liz Clayton, supermodel and wife of Andrew Dyce, better known as Flash, lead guitarist and vocalist for the popular heavy metal band Flash Metal, is filing for divorce. Each cited that their careers kept them separated from each other and that they have drifted apart from each other over the 12 years they have been married. The divorce settlement went quickly and both sides were pleased. Little did Liz know that Flash had been concealing assets from her over the past year. Liz didn't know much about Flash Metal, including who the current and past members were. Over the 20 years that Flash Metal has been a group, musicians have come and gone with only one original person still in the band, Flash.

When the marriage started to get rocky, Flash decided to hide some of the assets from Liz just in case of divorce. Over the past six months while Flash Metal was on their record-breaking world tour, Flash would take his concert profits and make a check out to a past band member to hide his income from Liz. After the divorce was settled, the checks were voided and Flash was successful in hiding $1.2 million from his unsuspecting wife.

What could Liz have done to avoid being swindled by her ex-husband?

**Case 17.** Bill and Sue were college students when they met each other in the library and began dating. After a few short months, they decided to get married. After a time, both Bill and Sue discovered the relationship was not what they had planned. Bill did not like Sue's candles and stuffed animals with which Sue insisted on filling the house, and Sue did not care for Bill's habit of spending all his money on the lottery. So, after a few failed attempts at reconciling the matter, both concluded that divorce would be best. Each agreed to split their assets 50-50.

Due to Sue's displeasure in seeing lottery tickets cluttering the house, Bill kept most of the tickets inside his desk on campus. A few months before the divorce, one of Bill's lottery tickets hit the jackpot, giving him a little under $1 million. Instead of depositing the money into the couple's joint account, he hid it by creating a different bank account. Bill never brought up the news to Sue, and the court did not find out about the money during the court proceedings.

1. What type of fraud did Bill commit?

2. What can Sue do about this situation?

**Case 18.** John and Sally have recently been having serious marital problems. They are seeing a counselor in order to "save their marriage." During the past several months John has been selling their recreational assets including an expensive boat, snowmobiles, four-wheelers, and a cabin in the beautiful Smoky Mountains. John has been selling all these toys to his friend Sam for extremely low prices. Sally believes his story that he is selling them because they are hard up for money and that he is putting the money into their savings account, she does not know who has been purchasing the assets. She is shocked during the divorce to find out how little money is in the savings account. Where had it all gone? She never paid much attention to the finances and had trusted John completely.

1. What kind of scheme are John and Sam involved in?

2. How could Sally verify that the assets were actually sold?

3. What are some possible motives for John to sell the recreational assets at extremely low prices?

## ■ EXTENSIVE CASE

Hotel worker Danny Ruiz was living with his wife and four children in a cramped New York apartment when he saw a television ad promising the family a way out. "Why rent when you can own your own home?" Pennsylvania builder Gene Percudani asked. The company even offered to pay his rent for a year, while he saved for a down payment. So the Ruiz family fled the city for the Pocono Mountains, where they bought a three-bedroom Cape Cod in 1999 for $171,000. However, when they tried to refinance less than two years later, the home was valued at just $125,000. "I just about flipped," said Mr. Ruiz. Later his Mrs. Ruiz remarked about her husband saying, "He went nuts."

Gene Percudani, a 51 year-old native of Queens, New York, built a thriving homebuilding business in this market, running folksy television ads offering New Yorkers new homes in Pennsylvania. If they joined Percudani's program, called "Why Rent," homeowners would find financing through another of his companies, Chapel Creek Mortgage, which brokered loans from J.P. Morgan Chase and the company's Chase Manhattan Mortgage unit.

For years, the "Why Rent" program appealed to workers with modest salaries such as Eberht Rios, a truck driver for UPS. The Rios bought a home in Pocono for $140,000. This year, when he tried to refinance, he was told the home was valued at only $100,000. One local appraiser, Dominick Stranieri, signed off on most of the "Why Rent" deals that state officials now say were overpriced, including the homes for the Rios and the Ruiz families. Percudani's firm picked Stranieri as his appraiser because of his quick work and low fee of $250, instead of the typical $300 to $400. In exchange for a steady stream of work, Mr. Stranieri accepted without question valuations from Mr. Percudani's company.

Other common methods of creating revenues include investors and others buying distressed properties and then, using inflated appraisals, selling them for a big profit. In order to secure the efforts of a "dirty appraiser," those involved with the fraud would pay up to $1,500 under the table on top of the appraiser's standard fee of $400.

Another unique twist to the plot is that few of the people involved in making mortgage loans these days have a long-term interest in them. Traditionally, bankers had made loans directly and held them, giving the lenders a strong incentive to find fair appraisals to protect their interest. Today, however, many appraisers are picked by independent mortgage brokers, who are paid per transaction and have little stake in the long-term health of the loans. Many lenders have also lost a long-term interest in their loans, because they sell them off to investors. Appraisers increasingly fear that if they don't go along with higher valuations sought by brokers, their business will dry up.

Think a county appraiser would do a lot better than a private practitioner? Joel Marcus, a New York-based attorney recently had his property valued at $2.2 million by a county appraiser, up from $2 million the previous year, which means a $7,200 jump in his property-tax bill. Based on recent home sales in his neighborhood, Mr. Marcus believes his property is valued at between $1.7 million and $1.8 million, causing Marcus to appeal the appraisal.

Although, a good appraisal required hours of legwork, visiting a property to check its condition, and coming up with at least three comparable sales, Percudani says he isn't surprised that later appraisals, or even different appraisals made at the same time, could result in different values. "Appraisals are opinions," he says. "Value, like beauty, is in the eye of the beholder." Stranieri and Percudani deny any wrongdoing and say they operated independently and that any home that declined in value did so because of a weak economy. "It's like buying a stock," Mr. Percudani says in an interview "The value goes up. The value goes down."

**Questions:**

1. How is an opportunity created to commit appraisal fraud? Does the appraiser act alone or is collusion routinely involved?

2. How is appraisal fraud detected? Is intent to deceive easily proven in appraisal fraud?

3. What pressures or perceived pressures can motivate appraisers to make faulty valuations?

4. How do appraisers rationalize their fraudulent behavior?

5. What pressures would cause a county to fraudulently inflate property values?

6. What controls would help to prevent appraisal fraud?

7. What natural controls exist to prevent homeowners from the desire to "massage the value" of their homes? (*Hint*: Think about a homeowner's motivation.)

## INTERNET ASSIGNMENTS

1. Visit the IRS's bankruptcy site at: http://www.irs.gov/irs/article/0,,id=117520,00. html and answer the following questions:

    1. What percentage of bankruptcy petitions does the IRS estimate contain some kind of fraud?

    2. What are the major goals of the IRS's Criminal Investigation Division's bankruptcy fraud program?

    3. Read two or three examples of bankruptcy fraud and be prepared to discuss them in class.

2. The Internet contains many resources to learn more about bankruptcy and bankruptcy fraud. Many firms and professionals that participate in bankruptcy and fraud investigation proceedings maintain Web sites on the Internet. One such Web site is maintained by William G. Hays & Associates, Inc., at http://www.wghaysinc.com/. Go to the site and find the link to Bankruptcy and Receiver Services. List 10 ways in which the company or its president have been involved with the U.S. Department of Justice in bankruptcy proceedings.

## END NOTES

1. Sun Staff and Wire Reports, "Vegas Casino Figure Jailed after Bankruptcy Fraud Conviction," Las Vegas Sun (April 17, 2001).

2. http://www.nolo.com/lawcenter/ency/ article.cfm/ObjectID/95D63E16-B8B3-4824-94C8E27B6809F3F1/catID/7E3077AD-3EC9-4C89-818260239E41F3D4.

# APPENDIX A

## AFFIDAVIT OF PROPOSED INVESTIGATOR

**UNITED STATES BANKRUPTCY COURT**
**WESTERN DISTRICT OF TEXAS**

|  |  |
|---|---|
| In the Matter<br><br>of<br><br><br>**ARCHIBALD, WALL & CO.**<br><br><br><br>Debtor. | No. X5-30870-BKC-RAM<br><br>AFFIDAVIT FOR RETENTION<br><br>AS INVESTIGATOR<br><br>FOR THE EXAMINER |

STATE OF TEXAS              )

                           ) **SS:**

COUNTY OF SAGE             )

MARY JONES, being duly sworn, deposes and says:

1.     THAT I am a Certified Fraud Examiner (CFE) or Certified Public Accountant (CPA), licensed under the laws of the State of Texas and a member of the firm of Jones, Sally, and Doo, LLP with offices at 950 N. Beacon Street, Monroe, Texas 77034.

2.     THAT neither deponent nor any member of deponent's firm is related to or has any business association with the debtor, the examiner, or the official Creditors' Committee except that our firm may have been retained in other matters in which some of the aforementioned persons may have been parties.

3.     THAT deponent's firm maintains offices in Monroe, Texas. Total personnel numbers approximately 45 of whom nine are partners. Applicant has been known for many years for its expertise in accounting practice as related to the field of bankruptcy and fraud investigation, and has frequently been requested to serve in such matters by the legal, financial and business community.

4.     THAT deponent has surveyed the books and records of the debtor and is familiar with the matter and is familiar with the work to be done. That work is contemplated to be the following:

     a.   Review of incorporation documents and other documents of the Debtor related to the formation and operation of the Debtor and consideration of whether they indicate that two separate entities were one entity.

     b.   Investigation of the circumstances of the Debtor's obtaining of bank loans, including review of bank loan applications and related documents and financial statements submitted in obtaining the loans, and interviews of bank officials about the loan applications.

c.    Tracing of the disposition of loan proceeds and transfers of certain assets.

d.    Investigation of the Debtor's accounts receivable collection effort, including analysis of accounts receivable history, write-offs, setoffs, and collections, and review of the collectibility of account balances.

e.    Interviews of current or former principals of the Debtor with respect to the foregoing matters.

f.    Provision of litigation consulting services and expert witness testimony if necessary and requested by examiner.

g.    Performance of other services as requested by the examiner consistent with professional standards to aid the examiner in its investigation of the debtor.

5.    THAT in addition to the foregoing, the firms of JONES, SALLY, & DOO, LLP may be required to attend before the Bankruptcy Court with respect to the acts and conduct of the Debtor.

6.    THAT the cost of the foregoing services is based on the following current hourly rates:

| | |
|---|---|
| Partner | $250 per hour |
| Senior | $100 per hour |
| Paraprofessional | $ 30 per hour |

7.     ACTUAL and necessary out-of-pocket expenses will be incurred in connection with the rendition of these services. These will be billed separately in addition to the above.

WHEREFORE, your deponent respectfully requests that an Order be entered authorizing the retention of JONES, SALLY & DOO, LLP to perform the above mentioned services.

_____

MARY JONES

Sworn to before me this

10th day of May 2003

_____

NOTARY PUBLIC

# APPENDIX B

## APPLICATION FOR RETENTION OF INVESTIGATOR

Phillip Gallagher, Esq.

GALLAGHER, JOHNSON & SMITH

P.O. Box 75609

Sage, Texas 76031


ATTORNEYS FOR GEORGE SMITH, EXAMINER


IN THE UNITED STATES BANKRUPTCY COURT

FOR THE WESTERN DISTRICT OF TEXAS


IN RE:                                §

                                      §

ARCHIBALD, WALL & CO., PA    §    CASE NO. X5-30870-BKC-RAM

                                      §

DEBTOR.                         §

## APPLICATION FOR AUTHORITY TO

## EMPLOY INVESTIGATOR FOR THE EXAMINER

TO THE HONORABLE Linda Alright, U.S. BANKRUPTCY JUDGE:

COMES NOW, George Smith, the Court-appointed Examiner herein ("Examiner"), by and through his counsel, and files this his Application for Authority to Employ Investigator for the Examiner ("Application"), and in support thereof would respectfully show this Court as follows:

1.     On March 15, 2003, Archibald, Wall & Co., PA ("Debtor") filed its voluntary petition under Chapter 11 of the Bankruptcy Code ("Code"), 11 U.S.C. §§ 101, *et seq.*, thereby commencing the above-captioned bankruptcy case. Thereafter, on May 5, 2003, George Smith was appointed the Examiner of the Debtor's estate and continues to act in that capacity.

2.     Your Examiner requests authority to employ the firm of Jones, Sally, & Doo, LLP (the "Firm").

3.     Your Examiner has selected the Firm for the reason that it has had considerable experience in matters of this nature and he believes that the Firm is well qualified to provide him with investigation services in his capacity as Examiner.

4.     The professional services, which the Firm is anticipated to render, include: (a) to provide the Examiner with litigation consulting and forensic accounting services in connection with allegations of bank fraud and bankruptcy fraud by current or former principals of the Debtor; (b) to provide financial analysis in connection with the write-

offs and collectibility of accounts receivable balances of the Debtor estate; (c) to investigate the disposition and transfers of certain loan proceeds and assets for possible fraudulent transfers; (d) to provide evidence for determining whether there is cause for the appointment of a trustee; and (e) to perform all other investigation services for your Examiner which may be, or become, necessary herein.

5.    As evidenced by the Affidavit of Proposed Investigator . . . and to the best of your Examiner's knowledge, the Firm has no relationship that would raise a possible disqualification or conflict of interest. Consequently, the employment of the Firm is in compliance with § 327 of the Code.

6.    Your Examiner believes that the employment of the Firm would be in the best interest of this estate by providing your Examiner with the necessary and beneficial services set forth in paragraph four (4) above.

WHEREFORE, PREMISES CONSIDERED, your Examiner respectfully requests that this Court enter an Order authorizing him to employ Jones, Sally, & Doo, LLP as Investigator of the Examiner in this bankruptcy proceeding; and for such other and further relief to which he may be justly entitled.

Respectfully submitted,

GALLAGHER, JOHNSON & SMITH

By:_____

Phillip Gallagher, Esq.

# CHAPTER 17

# FRAUD IN E-COMMERCE[1]

## LEARNING OBJECTIVES

After studying this chapter, you should be able to:

1. Understand e-commerce fraud risk.
2. Take measures to prevent fraud in e-commerce.
3. Detect e-business fraud.

*James, Vijay, and Em became good friends through their groupwork in MBA school, and after graduation they decided to start an Internet business together. After careful research, they started an online store selling all types of antispam software. Sales were slow for the first year, and the business was going under. Vijay, a marketing major, contacted Google, Yahoo!, and several other search engines and purchased advertisements that showed up on results pages when certain search terms were entered by users.*

*Initially, the program went well. During the first few weeks, their advertisement campaign generated a 1 to 2 percent click-through rate (CTR), meaning that 1 to 2 percent of users clicked on their advertisement link when it was presented in Google or Yahoo's search results pages. Vijay knew that businesses using CTR campaigns must pay a few dollars or cents for each click-through. More clicks result in more cost. However, Vijay felt this cost was more than offset in the resulting purchases of antispam software on their site.*

*Imagine Vijay's surprise when he returned from an extended vacation and found that his campaign statistics had jumped from 1 to 2 percent to an abnormal 35 to 40 percent CTR! At first he was elated, but then he realized something must be amiss. Overall sales had not changed, and Web site traffic had remained relatively stable.*

*Vijay had been a victim of click-through fraud. Although names have been changed, this fraud occurred with several large search engines. Click-through fraud occurs when a competitor or an adverse individual repetitively clicks advertisements with no intention of purchasing products or services at the advertising site. Advanced implementations of this fraud use custom scripts and robots to quickly generate enormous costs through clicks. These robots can impersonate different IP addresses, network segments, and browsers and fool search engines into thinking each click is unique. Click-through frauds can cost businesses tens or hundreds of thousands of dollars in advertising dollars if they are allowed to continue over time.[2]*

In recent years, the technology revolution provided perpetrators with new ways to commit and conceal fraud and to convert the ill-gotten gains. Consider Internet and electronic business (e-business) transactions. Essentially, **e-business** uses information technology and electronic communication networks to exchange business information and to conduct paperless transactions. Compared to other inventions, the Internet is truly revolutionary. It took radio more than 35 years and television 15 years to reach 60 million people. In contrast, the World Wide Web reached over 90 million people in just three years. Internet traffic doubles every 100 days.[3] In 1999, an estimated 200–275 million people used the Internet, and the year 2005 may see 800 million to 1 billion users. When Jack Welch (former CEO of General Electric) was asked where the Internet ranks in priority in his company, he responded that "it's numbers 1, 2, 3 and 4."[4] According to the U.S. Census Bureau, first-quarter retail e-commerce sales for 2003 were $12 billion, a 26 percent increase from the first quarter of 2002.

In this chapter, we discuss unique aspects of e-business fraud, risks specific to e-business, and how to prevent electronic fraud. We discuss e-business fraud detection briefly, but do not discuss fraud investigation because the methods used to investigate e-business fraud are the same as for other frauds. Remember that e-businesses conduct regular transactions (e.g., purchasing and selling products and services); only their medium of exchange is different. Once you understand the risks inherent in this new area of fraud, you will know where to target your detection efforts.

# Fraud Risks in E-Commerce

Although fraud can occur in any environment, several aspects of e-business environments present unique risks. These characteristics of the New Economy, which is basically Internet-driven, create pressures and opportunities specific to e-commerce fraud. Just like other frauds, these new frauds are perpetrated when pressures, opportunities, and rationalizations come together. E-commerce elements that create increased or unique risks are listed in Table 17-1.

## Table 17-1 Elements of Fraud Risk in E-Commerce

| Pressures |
| --- |
| • Dramatic growth, creating tremendous cash flow needs |
| • Merger or acquisition activity, increasing pressures to "improve the reported financial results" |
| • Borrowing or issuing stock, additional pressures to "cook the books" |
| • New products that require intensive and expensive marketing and for which an existing market does not yet exist |
| • Unproven or flawed business models with tremendous cash flow pressures |

| Opportunities |
| --- |
| • New and innovative technologies for which security developments often lag transaction developments |
| • Complex information systems that make installing controls difficult |
| • The transfer of large amounts of information, a factor that poses theft and identity risks such as illegal monitoring and unauthorized access |
| • Removal of personal contact, which allows for easier impersonation or falsified identity |
| • Lack of "brick-and-mortar" and other physical facilities that facilitate falsifying Web sites and business transactions |
| • Inability to distinguish large or established companies from new or smaller companies, making it easy to deceive customers by falsifying identity and business descriptions |
| • Electronic transfer of funds, allowing large frauds to be committed more easily |
| • Compromised privacy, resulting in easier theft by using stolen or falsified information |

| Increased Propensity to Rationalize |
| --- |
| • The perceived distance that decreases the personal contact between customer and supplier |
| • Transactions between anonymous or unknown buyers and sellers that prevents parties from seeing who they are hurting |
| • New Economy thinking that sees traditional methods of accounting as no longer applicable |

# E-Commerce Risks Inside Organizations

Many of the most serious e-commerce fraud risks are found within organizations. Once perpetrators are within firewalls and security checks, it is much easier to infiltrate systems, steal money and information, and cause damage. Inside perpetrators know the control environment, understand security mechanisms, and find ways to bypass security. One of the most serious problems is abuse of power that has been granted to users. For example, programmers and technical support personnel usually have full, superuser access to the systems they create and administer. Often, removal of programmer access is overlooked when systems go into production, allowing them free and unlimited access to corporate data years into the future.

The theft of money is often the primary goal in traditional fraud. In the electronic environment, however, **data theft** presents an even larger concern. For example, stolen personal information about customers can be sold or misused, and individuals can be blackmailed. The theft of electronic data is thus a concern for both businesses and consumers. Information technology (IT) managers and assurance providers therefore need to be aware of the critical points in e-business infrastructures at which data can be stolen.

Even if a perpetrator does not have personal access to needed systems, he or she can hijack others' passwords to achieve access. **Passwords** can be the Achilles' heel of many systems because password selection is left to the end user and cannot be fully controlled. Mothers' maiden names, kids' birthdays, favorite locations, and other personal information used to generate passwords can be guessed by perpetrators when fraud is internal and employees know each other personally. Even when corporate policies require periodic password changing, many users circumvent the intent by adding a sequential number or other character to the end of their old passwords. It is common to find a few employees who write their passwords down on sticky notes placed in their desk drawers or even on their computer monitors. In addition, in a world with increasing numbers of passwords, secret PINs, and account numbers to remember, many users reuse the same password from internal systems to Internet sites and from e-mail clients to application logins. If a perpetrator can discover a user's password in a relatively unprotected system, that password is likely useful in more secure systems.

Unencrypted communications between users often pose a threat that most employees do not appreciate. For example, although encrypted e-mail access has been available for decades, most users still check their mail using unencrypted POP, IMAP, or other protocols. Because most e-mail clients log in and check for new mail every few minutes, perpetrators have significant opportunities to sniff passwords and infiltrate systems. E-mail text is also not regularly encrypted, even if a user is using an encrypted connection to his or her server. Unless the e-mail text itself has been encrypted using S/MIME or PGP, the e-mail transfers in plain text between servers. Recently, the increasing use of instant messaging provides perpetrators a new method of gathering information. Instant messaging is not normally encrypted, and most clients store conversations locally on users' computers. **Sniffing** is the viewing of information that passes along a network line, and it is a common method of gathering information from unencrypted communications. Sniffing is easily done on most networks with downloadable applications such as ethereal and tcpdump.

Even though firewalls, spam filters, and virus applications protect organizations from external attack, employee laptops often present risks that are difficult to manage. For example, each time managers go on business trips, they connect their laptops to unprotected environments in hotel and other business networks. Home DSL and cable networks are similarly risky. On these networks, computers are exposed to viruses and hackers from which they are normally protected at work. In addition, information on stolen laptops can provide significant opportunities for perpetrators. Finally, when employees return from trips or home and plug their laptops back into the corporate network, they bypass firewalls and controls. Viruses, trojans, and worms are able to enter protected areas because employees physically walk laptops from unprotected networks to protected networks.

Recently, the advent of USB key drives and portable external hard drives pose security threats. These devices are wonderful steps forward from the days of unreliable floppy disks. However, their ubiquitous nature and large capacities allow them to quickly download significant amounts of information from internal networks. These devices, including camera phones and iPod-like music players, have been banned at many military installations because of the potential threat they pose. For example, when iPods first hit the market, a common tactic by customers at CompUSA stores was to connect an iPod to a display computer and quickly steal software like Microsoft Office. Because of the iPod's speedy firewire connection, stealing hundreds of megabytes of data could be done within just a few minutes.

Vandalism is always a risk with internal systems. From sophisticated denial-of-service attempts on local machines to deletion of files to physical damage, vandalism is an easy way for employees to harm internal systems. Vandalism can be obvious, or it can be very difficult to find—hiding for weeks or months before its effects are discovered.

## E-Commerce Risks Outside Organizations

In February 2003, the BBC reported an all-too-familiar story. Visa and MasterCard admitted that a hacker breached the security system of a company that processed cards on behalf of merchants. More than 5 million card numbers, including personal information of cardholders, were stolen. Because Visa and MasterCard credit cards are issued by many different financial institutions, reissuance of cards presented a major logistical problem.[5] The broker who was hacked into suffered a significant loss because of the break in. Stories such as this one are common in the news today; a simple Google search provides countless stories of stolen accounts and card numbers.

The Internet provides a rich medium for external hackers to gain access to personal systems. Hackers are relatively protected because they cross international boundaries and are mostly anonymous. Tracking and prosecution are often difficult. When successful investigation and prosecution do occur, sentences are typically light and do little to deter would-be attackers. For example, Jeffrey Lee Parson, a 19-year-old who unleashed part of the MSBlast worm attack, received 18–37 months in prison. Jan de Wit, author of the Anna Kournikova virus, received 150 hours of community service in The Netherlands. In the mid-1990s, hackers broke into a new server installation that had not yet been secured. While the owner was helping at Boy Scout camp, the hackers took control of his Linux workstation and installed a robot to search for bootlegged movies. When he arrived home, he tracked the hackers to a mid-East European country. If the bootlegged movies were investigated, detectives would be led to the author's computer rather than the hackers' location. His computer (along with hundreds of other computers around the world) not only provided a robot army to locate movies, but also provided protection from detection.

Computer viruses must be taken seriously in today's e-commerce environment. Viruses come in three varieties. True viruses attach themselves to existing programs on a computer. Viruses were rampant during the 1980s and 1990s. Today's largest threat comes from Internet worms, self-contained programs that spread via direct transfer, e-mail, or other mechanisms. Compared with the old days of difficult assembly language viruses, today's worms are extremely easy to write and distribute because they are usually written in Visual Basic (a relatively simple language) and spread via social mechanisms—by getting users to click on them! Where it took a sophisticated hacker in previous years, today's worms can be written by intermediate users. Finally, a trojan horse is a program that claims to do something useful, but also contains hidden behavior. The ubiquitous nature of some programs, like Windows, Microsoft Outlook, and Internet Explorer, provides an ample hostbed through which viruses, worms, and trojans can spread. In addition, many of the users of these programs are less experienced online users and are more susceptible to social tricks.

Spyware has become a difficult online problem in recent years. Spyware, similar to a trojan horse, installs monitoring software in addition to regular software a user downloads or buys. For example, peer-to-peer music sharing networks are some of the worst spyware offenders. Many of these programs install monitors that send online user behaviors to companies that turn a profit on the personal information they collect. More targeted spyware can lift information from internal directories and files and send it to external entities.

Phishing is a common method hackers use to extract personal or corporate information from employees. Phishers send e-mail or pop-up messages to users asking for personal information in inventive ways. For example, a hacker might send an e-mail impersonating technical support to company employees. If even 1 percent of the employees respond back with their password or other information, the hacker may be able to access a company's internal networks and open future back doors before preventative steps can be taken. False Web sites are another method of tricking users into providing personal information. A scam that recently hit PayPal involved e-mail being sent to many customers with a link to a PayPal-like site. Users who clicked the link were presented with a login page that impersonated PayPal's regular login screen. Their attempt to login with their usernames and passwords inadvertently sent their login information to the false site. Users were then redirected back to the regular PayPal login screen where they tried to login once again. Most users never even knew they had been at an imposter site on the first try.

**Spoofing** changes the information in e-mail headers or IP addresses. Perpetrators hide their identities by simply changing the information in the header, thus allowing unauthorized access. Because e-mail was one of the first online technologies, few security measures were placed into its protocols. E-mail headers are created by e-mail clients, and as such, are extremely easy to forge. You have probably received an e-mail that says it is from a friend, but the friend never actually sent it. This e-mail probably had a forged *From:* field.

**Falsified identity** is a major source of risk in e-business. For an electronic transaction to take place, each party to the transaction needs to be confident that the claimed identity of the other party is authentic. These threats are less of a concern in traditional electronic data interchange (EDI) settings because traditional EDI uses relatively limited access points, dedicated lines, and established value-added network providers as intermediaries. But authenticity is a significant concern for transactions conducted through electronic channels in e-business.

Database query (SQL) injections and cross-site scripting (CSS) present risks that many sites are not designed to handle. In a SQL injection, hackers send a database command after regular data in an online submission form. Because most back-end systems simply relay commands from forms to databases, the SQL injection is executed by the corporate database. This command might insert an unauthorized record giving a hacker access, or it might simply drop tables with common names (such as the users table, customers table, etc.). Cross-site scripting is a method of injecting Javascript and other browser commands to Web sites. When these commands are interpreted by users' browsers, unauthorized behavior occurs. Common examples are redirection of users to a false Web site and hijacking of user cookie IDs for unauthorized access.

Like traditional businesses that accept checks or credit cards, e-businesses must also verify customer identity. When customers have falsified their identities, businesses lose money on fraudulent requests for products or services.

As noted in Chapter 16, one of the most common frauds in traditional business is the bust-out—the planned bankruptcy. In its simplest form, perpetrators set up a business, buy inventory on credit, sell it for low prices, and then run off with the money before the bills are paid. Bust-outs are especially problematic in e-business. Instead of renting a brick-and-mortar store, the perpetrators merely establish (at significantly less cost) a false Web site. The false Web site may grab confidential information or conduct fraudulent transactions. False Web sites look like the site of a real bank or an online broker or retailer and collect identification and credit card numbers from unsuspecting customers. Alternatively, perpetrators use false Web sites to conduct business transactions that they never intend to pay for.

Another sneaky method of electronic-based fraud is **Web-visit hijacking**. E-mail messages and Web visits can be hijacked because subtle differences in Internet host names often go unnoticed by Internet users. For example, "computer.com" and "computer.org" are two completely different host names that can be easily confused. If the two names are owned by different entities, one site could mimic the other and trick users into thinking they are dealing with the original Web site or e-mail address.

Fraud risks in e-commerce systems are significant. While traditional methods of fraud, such as bribery and kickbacks, are understood by many people, most employees do not fully appreciate the risks and methodologies that online fraud perpetrators take. Fortunately, managers and users are becoming increasingly educated on e-commerce fraud. For example, most business users and students now know they should not click on e-mail attachments from unknown senders. However, due to the rapidly changing tactics of perpetrators and new opportunities presented by changing protocols and technology, e-commerce fraud is likely to remain a problem in the future.

# Preventing Fraud in E-Commerce

Preventing fraud in every business setting involves reducing or eliminating the elements that motivate fraud: pressure, opportunity, and rationalization. In e-business settings, reducing pressures and eliminating rationalizations has thus far proved difficult. The lack of personal contact makes it hard to know what pressures exist or what rationalizations perpetrators are using. Therefore, the best businesses can hope for is to avoid conducting transactions with firms that are experiencing high pressures or have dishonest managers.

One of the greatest fallacies of e-commerce security is a prevention measure known as security through obscurity. **Security through obscurity** is the tactic of keeping security holes, encryption algorithms, and processes secret in an effort to confuse attackers. Many managers are lured into a false sense of security when they feel that entry into their system is convoluted enough to discourage attackers. Rather than employing robust security measures, companies that employ security through obscurity play the odds by hoping that attackers will not figure out how their security works. Experience shows that obscurity only heightens the challenge to a hacker—making him or her more interested in getting in! The early computer industry of the 1970s and 1980s is littered with failed attempts at hidden algorithms and obscure security. For example, try searching the Internet for password crackers for older programs like WordPerfect or Microsoft Excel. Because these programs didn't use robust encryption, password crackers abound.

In contrast to obscurity, true security is found when algorithms and processes are made public and stand the test of time. For example, the triple-DES and AES encryption algorithms have been public for many years, and yet they are still generally considered secure because they seem to be mathematically sound. As far as we know, neither algorithm has been broken. Virtual private networks (VPNs), SSL, and other security measures based upon these algorithms are always more secure than algorithms based upon private, untested methods. Of course, we are not suggesting that companies publish their security measures on their Web site home page, but rather that security measures be based on time-tested methods that have withstood public scrutiny.

## The Control Environment   VIRUS - PC CILLIN / SPYSWARE

One of the best ways to prevent fraud in e-business settings is to focus on reducing opportunities, usually through the implementation of appropriate internal controls. In traditional businesses, internal controls involve five different elements: (1) the control environment, (2) risk assessment, (3) control activities or procedures, (4) information and communication, and (5) monitoring. In e-businesses, the first three elements are far more relevant and important in preventing fraud than the last two. Therefore, we limit our discussion to control environment, risk assessment, and control activities.

The essence of effectively controlled organizations lies in the attitude of their management. If top management believes that control is important, others in an organization will respond by conscientiously observing established controls. On the other hand, if it is clear to employees that management is only giving lip service to the idea of controls, rather than meaningful support, the organization's control objectives will almost certainly not be achieved, and fraud is a more likely occurrence. Because controls are so important, firms endeavoring to prevent e-business fraud must do everything possible to establish and observe good controls. Another key strategy is understanding the controls in place in the companies with whom the organization conducts its electronic business.

As noted in earlier chapters, the following are the most important components of the control environment:

- *Integrity and Ethical Values.* An organization's culture of integrity and ethics is the product of what its standards are and how they are communicated and reinforced in the firm. This culture includes management's actions to remove or reduce incentives and temptations that might prompt personnel to engage in fraud. It also includes the communication of organizational values and behavioral standards to personnel through policy statements and codes of conduct and by example. A good question to ask about companies that engage in electronic business is whether they have a formal code of conduct and whether it is available to be examined.

- **Board of Directors and Audit Committee Participation.** An effective board of directors is independent of management, and its members carefully scrutinize management's activities. The board delegates responsibility for internal control to management, but they undertake regular, independent assessments of management-established internal controls. In addition, the presence of an active and objective board often discourages management from overriding existing controls. A study of financial statement frauds during the period 1987 to 1997 revealed that a weak or ineffective board was one of the most common elements in firms that issued fraudulent financial statements.[6]

- **Management's Philosophy and Operating Style.** Management provides clear signals to employees about the importance of internal controls. For example, does management take significant risks, or are they risk-averse? Are profit plans and budget data set as "best possible" plans or "most likely" targets? Can management be described as "fat and bureaucratic," "lean and mean," dominated by one or a few individuals, or is it just right? Understanding these and similar aspects of management's philosophy and operating styles provides a sense of management's attitude about internal controls and fraud.

- **Human Resources Policies and Practices.** The most important aspect of internal control is personnel. If employees are competent and trustworthy, other controls can be absent and reliable transactions will still result. Honest, efficient people are able to perform at a high level, even when few other controls support them. However, dishonest people can reduce to shambles a system with numerous controls in place.

## Risk Assessment

Risk assessment identifies the risks of doing business with e-business partners. A key part of the assessment focuses on the control environment of those organizations. Another part identifies key risks in the electronic exchange of information and money, so that control procedures tailored to the special challenges that these exchanges present can be installed—procedures that counter the risk of data theft, sniffing, unauthorized access to passwords, falsified identity, spoofing, customer impersonation, false Web sites, and e-mail or Web site hijacking.

Many different security firms focus on risk assessment. These firms specialize in trying to gain access to networks and secure information, and they report their findings directly to management. Normally, a security audit includes an investigation into technology, processes, controls, and other factors at a client. The Robert Redford movie *Hackers* highlighted a firm doing just this type of work.

## Preventing Fraud Through Control Activities

As you learned earlier in this textbook, control activities are the policies and procedures that ensure that necessary actions are taken to address risks and frauds. As you also learned, control activities generally fall into the following five types:

1. Adequate separation of duties
2. Proper authorization of transactions and activities
3. Adequate documents and records
4. Physical control over assets and records
5. Independent checks on performance

Although all of these activities can be used to prevent fraud in many forms in traditional organizations and transactions, they are not as effective in e-businesses.

### ADEQUATE SEPARATION OF DUTIES

In e-business, this control is useful for making sure that individuals who authorize transactions are different from those who actually execute them. Probably the most common frauds in purchasing and sales transactions are kickbacks and bribery. Kickbacks occur where one individual becomes too close to suppliers or customers. Adequate segregation of duties prevents bribery because employees don't have complete control of transactions.

## PROPER AUTHORIZATION OF TRANSACTIONS AND ACTIVITIES

Proper authorization is another key control in e-business. The most common authorization controls are passwords, firewalls, digital signatures and certificates, and biometrics. Every transaction must be properly authorized.

- *Passwords.* Passwords are a vital part of the security of any electronic system, but they are also an Achilles' heel. Why? Because they involve people. Compromising passwords allows unauthorized transactions to be made. To prevent fraud, organizations should have clearly communicated policies regarding selecting, changing, and disclosing passwords. In an electronic environment, no other control can better prevent fraud than the wise use of passwords.
- *Digital Signatures and Certificates.* Just as signatures on paper documents serve as authorization or verification, digital signatures reassure users that transactions are valid. **Digital signatures and certificates** thus prevent falsified identity and impersonation and as such are increasingly important.
- *Biometrics.* One of the most promising areas of technology and systems security is **biometrics**—the use of unique features of the human body to create secure access controls. Because each of us possesses unique biological characteristics (e.g., iris and retina patterns, fingerprints, voice tones, facial structures, and writing styles), scientists are developing specialized security devices that have the potential to be highly accurate in authenticating identity. Access and permission to execute a transaction is granted or denied, based on how similar the subsequent reading is to the reference template.

## ADEQUATE DOCUMENTS AND RECORDS

Documents and records (sales invoices, purchase orders, subsidiary records, sales journals, employee time cards, and even checks) are the physical objects by which transactions are entered and summarized.

In e-business, most documents are electronic. This lack of hard-copy documentation, the very essence of e-business, creates new opportunities for fraud. Documents and records typically are detective controls, not preventive controls. They are the audit trail and enable auditors and fraud examiners to investigate suspected wrongdoing. Although most computer systems create records of transactions that can be accessed or reconstructed, smart perpetrators figure out how to remove evidence of transactions from servers and computers.

Because many of the traditional document controls aren't available in e-commerce, controls must be put in place. The primary electronic transaction and document control is encryption, which protects confidential and sensitive information (such as checks or purchase or sales transactions) from being sniffed or stolen.[7] Public-key encryption allows information to be sent in encrypted format over unsecured networks such as the Internet, and is widely used to protect data and ensure privacy. In public-key arrangements, communicating parties have two keys, one that is made public and another that is held private. These keys are inversely related: If one key is used to "lock" a message, the other must be used to "unlock" it. Thus, a message locked by a public key can be read only by the party holding the private key. Similarly, a message that can be unlocked by a particular public key can have originated only from the party holding the corresponding private key. Public-key encryption is thus used for privacy (by locking a message with the intended recipient's public key) and for authenticity (by locking a message with the originator's private key).

## PHYSICAL CONTROL OVER ASSETS AND RECORDS

When records—electronic or paper—are not adequately protected, they can be stolen, damaged, or lost. Highly computerized companies need to go to special lengths to protect computer equipment, programs, and data files.

Three categories of controls protect IT equipment, programs, and data files from fraud. As with other types of assets, physical controls are used to protect computer facilities. Examples are locks on doors to the computer room and terminals and adequate and safe storage space for software and data files. In addition to software-based security, the software and hardware that comprise the IT infrastructure must be physically secure. Remember that authorized personnel who can access computers and servers can also execute unauthorized transactions or steal sensitive information. Sometimes physical infrastructure is so sensitive and critical to e-business operations that the system is placed in an isolated location with only high-level security access.

## INDEPENDENT CHECKS ON PERFORMANCE

As with traditional business, a key control component in e-business is the careful and continuous review of the other four components—the independent checks and internal verification. The need for independent checks arises because internal controls change over time. Personnel forget or fail to follow procedures, or become careless—*unless* someone observes and evaluates their performance. The likelihood of fraudulent transactions goes up when controls break down.

Independent checks are particularly important in preventing fraud in e-business. Organizations should always conduct checks on their e-business partners. These checks can range from simple Dun & Bradstreet reviews to full-fledged investigations of the firm and its officers. A quick search of Lexis-Nexis and other financial databases or the Internet often reveals business partners' problems the organization should be aware of before they conduct electronic business.

Electronic fraud, especially that perpetrated by smaller companies, is often committed by individuals high in the organization, and quite often on behalf of the organization as opposed to against the organization. Because management is often involved, management and the directors or business partners must be investigated to determine their exposure to, and motivation for, committing fraud. To prevent fraud, gaining an understanding of the management or the organization's business partners and what motivates them is important. In particular, three items—(1) backgrounds, (2) motivations, and (3) decision-making influence—must be examined. What organizations and situations have management and directors been associated with in the past? What really drives and motivates the organization's leaders? Is their personal worth tied up in the organization? Are they under pressure to deliver unrealistic results? Is their compensation primarily performance-based? Do they have debt covenants or other financial pressures that must be met? Management's ability to influence decisions is important to understand because perpetrating fraud when only one or two individuals have primary decision-making power is much easier.

# Detecting E-Business Fraud

In Chapter 6, we introduced proactive fraud detection in which the types of fraud that can occur are identified and then technology and other activities are used to look for fraud symptoms. That is, fraud examiners (1) endeavor to understand the business or operations of the organization, (2) identify what frauds can occur in the operation, (3) determine the symptoms that the most likely frauds would generate, (4) use databases and information systems to search for those symptoms, and (5) follow up on the symptoms to determine whether they are being caused by actual fraud or by other factors.

This method of fraud detection works well in detecting e-business fraud. One of the best techniques for implementing this type of fraud detection is to use technology to catch technology fraud. Many of the hacker tools were actually written to troubleshoot security measures and catch perpetrators rather than to hack into systems. It is extremely important that fraud investigators who specialize in e-commerce understand the tools and methods that perpetrators use. Knowledge of Web servers, e-mail clients and servers, and intrusion programs such as nmap, airsnort, and ethereal is critical to catching perpetrators and securing systems. Fraud investigators who want to specialize in e-commerce fraud should take several information systems or computer science networking and security courses. Because most of today's corporate servers and the Internet infrastructure are Unix-based, knowledge of Unix is imperative. Most clients' applications are Windows-based, which makes knowledge of the security strengths and weaknesses in Windows essential.

Computer scripts, written in any number of languages, can monitor logs and systems for potential break-ins. An assortment of different intrusion detection systems (IDS) can be purchased on the market today. Careful use and monitoring of these systems should be done at every organization.

The appendix to Chapter 6 provides an introduction to detecting fraud in e-commerce systems and corporate databases. Planting automated queries in electronic purchasing records to examine changes in the percentage of goods purchased from different vendors by individual buyer, price changes, the number of returns (indicating lower quality), and comparisons of these factors with other vendors is easy. These variables can even be analyzed on a combined basis; for example, the system might look for increased purchases from the vendor whose prices are increasing the fastest. Computer systems can be programmed to provide information when changes exceed a certain amount. For example, price changes of a certain percentage within a certain period might be queried.

The advantage of e-business transactions is that information about the transactions is captured in databases that can be analyzed in numerous ways. These data make fraud detection easier than ever before. The most difficult aspect of detecting e-business fraud is correctly specifying the types of frauds that can occur and the symptoms they will generate. Also, symptoms are only circumstantial evidence at best. Perfectly legitimate explanations may indicate why factors appear to be symptoms, but are not fraud. Just as e-business transactions make fraud easier to commit, they also make it much easier to detect.

As discussed earlier in this chapter, a rigorous, time-tested process for security should be used. Security through obscurity should never be an option. Standards-based systems such as virtual private networks, firewalls, public and private key infrastructure, SSL encryption, and other means should be employed and monitored at all times.

In addition to technical measures, social preventions and detections are important. Regular audits of user behavior on the system should be done by watching how users interact with their systems. Employees need to be trained on what e-commerce fraud looks like so they can spot problems. For example, in the autobiographical book *The Cuckoos Egg*, Clifford Stoll discovered an international spy using his systems for entrance into U.S. military systems. Stoll's investigation started with a mere 75-cent discrepancy in system audit logs. Thus, users need to be trained that even though computer anomalies may not look significant, they can often signal deeper problems. Just as employee tip lines can provide information in traditional fraud cases, tips can be useful in electronic fraud if employees understand what to look for.

## SUMMARY

Electronic fraud is a significant problem that is increasing both in frequency of occurrence and in amount. Because personal contact is limited in e-business settings and because defrauding people is easier when perpetrators can't see the personal hurt they are causing, fraud risks are higher than in other settings. Because of the ease of perpetrating electronic fraud, organizations must have proactive fraud prevention and detection efforts in place. Fraud prevention, of course, is the most cost-effective element in a proactive strategy.

Organizations and individuals that install proactive prevention measures find that those measures pay big dividends. Passwords, firewalls, digital signatures and certificates, and biometrics are prevention measures designed specifically to protect electronic transactions.

Even though electronic fraud provides significant new opportunities for perpetrators and cannot be totally eliminated, the very nature of e-commerce provides the perfect audit trail for prevention and detection.

## KEY TERMS

**Biometrics** Using unique features of the human body (e.g., retinal scans) to create secure access controls.

**Data theft** The stealing of data or personal information through such means as sniffing, spoofing, and customer impersonation.

**Digital signatures and certificates** A signature sent over the Internet.

**E-business** The use of information technology and electronic communication networks to exchange business information and conduct transactions in electronic, paperless form.

**Falsified identity (customer impersonation)** Pretending to be someone you're not—a major problem in e-business transactions.

**Passwords** Secret codes or names that allow users to access networks and other computer systems.

**Security through obscurity** Reliance upon secrecy of design, implementation, or holes to provide security rather than the use of time-tested methods that have withstood public scrutiny.

**Sniffing** Illegal or unauthorized viewing of information as it passes along a network communication channel.

**Spoofing** Changing the information in an e-mail header or an IP address to hide identities.

**Web-visit hijacking** Mimicking another, similarly named Web site in order to trick or confuse e-mail and e-business users into sending information to a business other than the intended one.

## QUESTIONS AND CASES

### DISCUSSION QUESTIONS

1. In what ways do e-business transactions pose heightened fraud risks?

2. What are some common ways e-business fraud is perpetrated?

3. How can the authenticity of a party to an e-business transaction be verified?

4. What is sniffing?

5. Why is spoofing a significant risk in e-business?

6. What is a password?

7. Why does biometrics offer significant promise as a way to authenticate e-business transactions?

8. Is the deductive, five-step detection approach relevant to e-business fraud detection?

9. Why can it be dangerous to provide credit card information over the Internet?

10. Can e-business fraud risks ever be completely eliminated?

11. What methods of security through obscurity does your school employ? How do these methods increase security? How do they decrease security?

### TRUE/FALSE

1. Fraud risks are higher when the entity with whom you are transacting business cannot be seen.

2. Data theft is a bigger problem in e-business transactions than money theft.

3. Sniffing changes e-mail headers or IP addresses.

4. Falsified identity and customer impersonation are the same thing.

5. In many e-business sales, password protection is the only barrier to unauthorized access.

6. Customer impersonation is similar to a bust-out fraud.

7. Segregation of duties is an important control in preventing e-business fraud.

8. Digital signatures use human features to create secure access controls.

9. Biometrics is a form of authorization control.

10. It is often easier to analyze e-business transaction data than data from other types of transactions because information is captured in databases that can be manipulated.

### MULTIPLE CHOICE

1. Which of the following is *not* a fraud risk unique to e-business transactions?
   a. Innovative technologies where security lags process development
   b. Selling new products
   c. Complex information systems
   d. Removal of personal contact

2. E-business transactions make it easier to commit which type of fraud?
   a. Kickbacks
   b. Customer impersonation
   c. Setting up dummy companies
   d. Stealing petty cash

3.  Which of the following is *not* an element of a company's control environment?
    a.  Audit committee participation
    b.  Management's philosophy
    c.  Hiring policies
    d.  Independent checks

4.  Which of the following is *not* an internal control activity or procedure?
    a.  Physical safeguards
    b.  Segregation of duties
    c.  Internal auditors
    d.  Documents and records

5.  Which of the following fraud risks involves changing IP addresses?
    a.  Spoofing   — P.577
    b.  Sniffing
    c.  False Web sites
    d.  Customer impersonation

6.  Which of the following fraud risks involves viewing information as it passes along network channels?
    a.  Sniffing
    b.  Spoofing
    c.  False Web sites
    d.  Web-visit hijacking —

7.  Using a subtly different Internet host name to mimic another business is known as:
    a.  Spoofing. —
    b.  Sniffing.
    c.  Web-visit hijacking.
    d.  Falsified identity.

8.  Passwords and biometrics are both:
    a.  Authorization controls. — P580
    b.  Independent check controls.
    c.  Physical controls.
    d.  Document controls.

9.  Which of the following human features is generally *not* used in biometrics?
    a.  Fingerprints
    b.  Voice tones
    c.  Retina patterns
    d.  Weight — P580

10. Which of the following types of controls is *not* used to protect IT processing equipment?
    a.  Physical controls
    b.  Authorization controls
    c.  Independent checks or references
    d.  Documents and records — P579

## SHORT CASES

**Case 1.** Your company, ImSecure Inc., is a security investigation firm. You have been contacted by Darling Company, a producer of cardstock for greeting card companies such as Hallmike and Birthday Wishes Company. Darling currently requires orders to be placed several weeks in advance of the delivery date. Orders come in through traditional channels (account reps, paper forms, etc.). Hallmike, Darling's largest client, now requires Darling to use e-commerce for order transmission and payment. Because of this new change, Darling is considering moving all of its clients to electronic data interchange (EDI) for orders and payments.

Detail the new opportunities that e-commerce solutions such as EDI present for internal and external perpetrators to defraud Darling Company.

**Case 2.** Search the Internet for a recent story about information being stolen from a company. Examples include stolen credit card numbers, personal information, and proprietary secrets. Summarize the article in two or three paragraphs. Detail several measures that could have prevented or detected this fraud earlier.

**Case 3.** Dan Jones is the new CIO of Ricochet Systems, an Internet securities broker. After assessing the e-commerce risks in his company, he determines that passwords are a weak link that needs additional protecting.

However, he is unsure as to what the requirements for a robust password are. At your monthly golf outing, Dan asks you—knowing your background in computer forensics—what checks and policies should be in place on passwords in his company. How often should passwords be changed? What requirements should be enforced on passwords chosen by employees (length, dictionary words, etc.)? What alternatives to passwords might Dan investigate? You tell Dan you'll send him a detailed e-mail message answering these questions when you get back to work. Write this message giving Dan advice for his password policies.

**Case 4.** What is a virtual private network (VPN)? How do VPNs provide security within organizations? What is IPSEC? Is it considered secure? What other protocols exist for VPNs? Are they considered secure?

**Case 5.** Your company, ABC Reading, writes unique OpenGL-based reading software for grade schoolers. ABC employs about 30 sales representatives who interact with school districts around the nation to sell and support your software. ABC has given each sales representative a powerful laptop to demonstrate your 3-D software to principals and district representatives. Because of the nature of their jobs, sales reps are constantly connecting their laptops to school and hotel networks during the day and to your corporate network via VPN. You are worried about viruses and worms entering your corporate network through one of their laptops. What protections and preventions would you take to ensure against this risk?

**Case 6.** As the new intern for the summer, you have been asked to investigate two methods of e-mail encryption: S/MIME and Pretty Good Privacy (PGP). Compare and contrast the two systems. Why do two standards exist? Which standard do you think your employer should use? Why?

*Optional activity:* Set up S/MIME or PGP-based plug-ins in student e-mail clients. Use the activity to learn how to get/create a public/private key pair and encrypt mail.

**Case 7.** A number of security/intrusion detection firms exist in the market. Research one of these firms and report on its services, costs, and benefits. Would you hire such a firm for a start-up company? Would you hire one for an established, small company? Would you hire one for a *Fortune* 1000 company? Why?

**Case 8.** (If allowed by your school's policy) Download and install a network sniffer application such as ethereal or tcpdump. Sniff the traffic on your local network for 10 minutes and report on your experience. What did you find? Why do these applications exist? How does their existence and distribution affect worldwide hacking and detection of hackers?

**Case 9.** Where have you seen security through obscurity employed (other than a key under the doormat at home)? Did it work? How did it make the situation more or less secure? What more robust methods could be used to provide security?

**Case 10.** The fifth annual survey of e-commerce fraud conducted by CyberSource Corporation in 2003 supports many of the ideas stated in this chapter. Go to http://www.cybersource.com/fraudreport/ and read the report. Then answer the following questions.

1. What percent of revenue do merchants expect to lose to fraud?

2. How much does this percentage translate to (in dollars) for the entire U.S. economy?

3. What indirect costs are associated with e-commerce fraud?

4. According to CyberSource vice president Perry Dembner, what is the best way to solve the problem of e-commerce fraud?

5. What is the difference in the fraud rate between international and domestic orders for merchants who take both?

6. Besides manual review, what are some other methods merchants use to decrease the risks of fraud, particularly credit card fraud?

**Case 11.** Identify a local company that conducts e-commerce, preferably one with whom you have previously done business or are otherwise familiar with. Research the company and become knowledgeable in its basic operations and services. Contact the company and inform them you are interested in learning more about doing business with them over the Internet, but that you are concerned about the security of online transactions. Inquire as to how the company guarantees the security of their site and consumers' personal information. Ask the company whether they have a formal code of conduct and, if so, whether it is available to be examined

In essay format, describe your conversation with the company's representative, explain the security measures the company uses, and comment on the company's code of conduct. Conclude your essay by stating whether and why you would be comfortable engaging in online transactions with this company.

**Case 12.** Conduct a random survey of at least 30 people. From the survey responses, draw out several conclusions about attitudes of consumers' toward e-commerce. Write a brief essay summarizing your conclusions. Attach to it any spreadsheets or charts used in your analysis. The survey should include, but not necessarily be limited to, the following questions:

1. How often do you purchase products or services over the Internet?

   *Never / Two to three times a year / At least once a month / Several times a month*
   a. If "never," why?
   b. Name two or three companies from whom you purchase products online.
   c. What steps do you take to check the security of the sites and the legitimacy of the companies from whom you make online purchases?

2. How often do you pay your bills over the Internet?

   *Never / Two to three times a year / At least once a month / Several times a month*
   a. If "never," why?
   b. Name two or three companies with whom you make online payments?
   c. What steps do you take to check the security of the sites and the legitimacy of the companies with whom you pay bills online?

3. How often do you view or manipulate banking and credit card information over the Internet?

   *Never / Two to three times a year / At least once a month / Several times a month*
   a. If "never," why?
   b. What is the name of your bank or credit card provider that provides your financial information online?

c. What steps do you take to check the security of the sites and the legitimacy of the companies with whom access online financial information?

4. How often do you double-check your bank and credit card statements for accuracy?

   *Never / Sometimes / Every month*

5. How comfortable are you with submitting your Social Security number over the Internet?

   *Extremely uncomfortable / Uncomfortable / Neutral / Comfortable / Extremely comfortable*

6. How comfortable are you submitting your credit card number over the Internet?

   *Extremely uncomfortable / Uncomfortable / Neutral / Comfortable / Extremely comfortable*

7. How regularly do you run spyware removal programs on your personal computers?

   *Never / Once a year / Several times a year / At least monthly*

8. What is your age?

**Case 13.** Together with other students from your class, identify a small, local company that does e-business and whose owner or manager is willing to talk with you about its operations. With your professor's approval, meet with the company manager and explain to him or her that you are studying fraud examination and would like to discuss with the company's vulnerability to fraud. Follow the steps to proactive fraud examination:

1. Endeavor to understand the business or operation of the organization.

2. Identify what frauds can occur in the operation.

3. Determine the symptoms that the most likely frauds would generate.

4. Propose several queries that might identify those symptoms.

5. Propose methods to follow up any revelations of those symptoms.

The interview with the owner or manager should only last 30–40 minutes and should cover steps 1, 2, and 3. After the interview, brainstorm steps 4 and 5 as a group. Write a 500-word essay that includes your responses to each step. Before the interview, offer to submit a copy of the completed essay to the owner or manager.

**Case 14.** Two years ago, your best friend Scott Adams started a home business selling custom made chairs and tables. His original designs quickly became popular, and he began selling in large quantities. To take advantage of the upcoming holiday season, Scott decided to begin selling over the Internet. He contacted a Web page designer, and he is now ready to go live with the site. Although he is familiar with the gist of Internet retailing, Scott is concerned about the possibility of fraud involving false online purchases where perpetrators impersonate customers and make orders. Knowing about your background in fraud examination, he comes to you and asks how to prevent and detect fraud in his new venture.

1. List three fraud schemes Scott should be concerned about.

2. Identify the steps Scott should take to detect and prevent each scheme.

## END NOTES

1. "Preventing and Detecting Fraud in Electronic Commerce Systems," *The E-Business Handbook* (Boca Raton, FL: St. Lucie Press, 2002) , pp. 315–338,

2. http://www.vnunet.com/News/106245.

3. This discussion was taken from Steven M. Glover, Stephen W. Liddle, and Douglas F. Prawitt, *E-Business: Principles and Strategies for Accountants* (Upper Saddle River, NJ: Prentice Hall, 2001).

4. Naanette Brynes and Paul C. Judge, "Internet Anxiety," *Business Week,* June 28, 1999.

5. *E-Business: Principles and Strategies for Accountants,* op. cit., p. 1.

6. http://news.bbc.co.uk/1/hi/business/2774477.stm.

7. M. S. Beasley, J. V. Carcello, and D. R. Hermanson, *Fraudulent Financial Reporting: 1987–1997: An Analysis of U.S. Public Companies,* Committee of Sponsoring Organizations (COSO), 1999.

8. Encryption is the conversion of data into a form called a ciphertext, which cannot be easily understood by unauthorized people. Decryption is the process of converting encrypted data back into its original form, so it can be understood.

# PART SEVEN

## RESOLUTION OF FRAUD

# CHAPTER 18

# LEGAL FOLLOW-UP

## LEARNING OBJECTIVES

After studying this chapter, you should be able to:

•     Identify aspects of the court system.

•     Understand the civil litigation process.

•     Understand the criminal litigation process.

•     Describe the nature of an expert witness.

**FBI and IRS Raid Offices of Slatkin**

*Federal regulators pounced on EarthLink co-founder, Reed. E. Slatkin, raiding his offices and persuading a federal judge to freeze his bank and brokerage accounts to prevent him from hiding investors' money or destroying documents.*

*The actions turn what had been a civil matter—with investors accusing Slatkin of running a 16-year Ponzi scheme—into a criminal investigation.*

*Moreover, documents filed Friday revealed several Hollywood names on Slatkin's list of investors. At 8 a.m., agents from the FBI and Internal Revenue Service began hauling boxes of documents from the converted garage of Slatkin's former home in the Santa Barbara suburb of Goleta, which since the early 1990s has housed his stock-trading and money management businesses. Regulators also took documents from the Santa Fe, N.M., office of Slatkin's bookkeeper.*

*At the same time, the Securities and Exchange Commission asked a U.S. district judge for the Central District of California to freeze Slatkin's assets, claiming that he had been operating a fraudulent investment scheme since 1986. The request was granted.*

*Slatkin's attorney, Brian Sun, said his client was "fully cooperating" with the investigations. Slatkin, through his attorneys, provided computer passwords and a computer hard drive to investigators at the scene, Sun said.*

*The SEC said Slatkin provided investigators with investor account statements and year-end summaries showing he had invested in a wide variety of large- and small-company stocks.*

*The SEC said its investigation of Slatkin's bank and brokerage records showed Slatkin used part of a $10 million deposit made by one investor to make payments to other investors.*[1]

When a fraud occurs, investigators or victim organizations and individuals must decide what actions to take against the perpetrators. Actions that can be pursued range from doing nothing to merely transferring or punishing the perpetrator to termination and pursuing various legal remedies. Obviously, such activities should not be pursued until an investigation has been completed and the identity of the perpetrator is known, along with some sense of the schemes used, the amounts taken, and other important facts of the case. In this chapter, we discuss various legal remedies that are available. We begin by discussing the state and federal court system in the United States. We then discuss civil and criminal fraud trials and the various elements of the trial with which fraud examiners should be familiar.

## The Court System

To understand the kinds of legal answers that are available in the United States, you must have some knowledge of how the federal and state courts operate. The court organization in the U.S. justice system is the combination of separate interlocking courts. The state courts throughout the United States can handle nearly every type of case. Only the U.S. Constitution, the state's constitution, and the state's laws govern state courts. The state or local courts handle most legal cases in the United States.

The state and local courts generally handle fraud cases. **Federal courts** handle only those cases over which the U.S. Constitution or federal laws give them authority. The federal courts hear fraud cases that involve federal laws or include several states.

### State Courts

Although state court organizations differ from state to state, the diagram in Figure 18-1 shows how the state courts are generally organized.

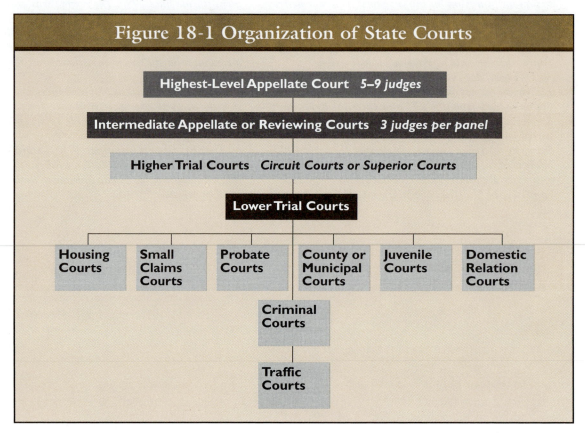

### Figure 18-1 Organization of State Courts

Highest-Level Appellate Court   *5–9 judges*

Intermediate Appellate or Reviewing Courts   *3 judges per panel*

Higher Trial Courts   *Circuit Courts or Superior Courts*

Lower Trial Courts

Housing Courts | Small Claims Courts | Probate Courts | County or Municipal Courts | Juvenile Courts | Domestic Relation Courts

Criminal Courts

Traffic Courts

The **lower-level trial courts** try misdemeanors (small crimes) and preliminaries (pretrial issues) for felony and civil cases that are below a determined dollar amount, usually below $10,000. Several different types of lower trial courts include housing courts that hear housing and landlord-tenant issues, small claims courts where individuals can inexpensively bring small actions against others, probate courts where the assets of deceased persons are distributed, and so forth. All lower trial courts are courts where actions are judged initially.

The **higher-level trial courts**, also courts where initial actions are heard, try felony and civil cases that are above a determined dollar amount, usually above $10,000. The distinguishing factors between the lower and higher trial courts are the amounts of the crimes and the seriousness of the crimes.

Plaintiffs or defendants who are not satisfied with the outcomes of lower or higher trial courts can appeal court decisions to appellate or reviewing courts. Usually, the first level of review is conducted by the **appellate courts**. If these courts can satisfy plaintiffs and defendants, no further appeals are made.

The last level of appeals at the state level is the highest-level appellate courts. These courts review decisions made by the lower appellate courts, and their decisions are final.

## Federal Courts

Figure 18-2 shows how the federal courts are organized. The federal courts are established to enforce federal laws and statutes. They include **bankruptcy courts** to adjudicate bankruptcy proceedings and **tax courts** to hear tax cases. For example, although bankruptcy fraud cases are usually tried in bankruptcy courts and tax fraud cases are tried in tax courts, most fraud cases involving federal laws or statutes (such as mail fraud, violations of the Racketeer Influenced and Corrupt Organizations (RICO) Act, banking, and securities regulations) are tried in one of the U.S. district courts. These courts try criminal and civil cases under federal laws.

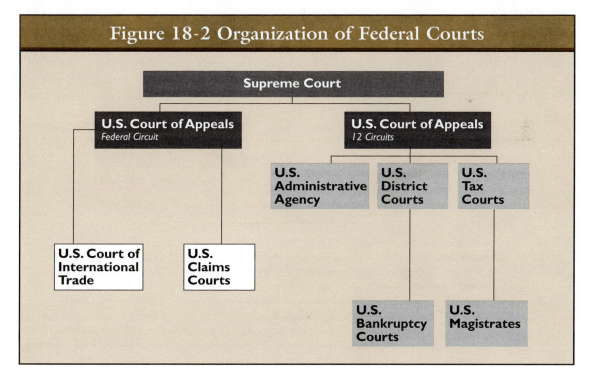

**Figure 18-2 Organization of Federal Courts**

If defendants or plaintiffs are not satisfied with judgments rendered in district courts, they can appeal the findings in one of the 12 circuit courts of appeal. The final court of appeal is the U.S. Supreme Court, which reviews decisions made by the appellate courts.

As an example of how appeal courts work, consider the following:

> *In 1994, a jury in Anchorage, Alaska, ordered Exxon Corporation to pay $5 billion to thousands of commercial fisherman and property owners for damages done in 1989 when the Exxon Valdez ship spilled 11 million gallons of oil in Alaska's Prince William Sound. Plaintiffs had alleged that the black "goo" that was spread across 1,500 miles of shoreline had reduced property values and damaged fishing and hunting grounds. When Exxon appealed the findings, the three-judge panel of the 9th U.S. circuit court of appeals said that some damages were justified, but that $5 billion was excessive. The appeals court ordered the lower court to determine a lesser amount of damages.[2]*

## Civil and Criminal Fraud Trials

When individuals commit fraud, they can be prosecuted criminally, civilly, or both. Once sufficient evidence is obtained, through a fraud investigation, the defrauded company must decide whether to pursue the case criminally, civilly, or both, or to take no action at all. Many times, a defrauded company will not pursue a case in criminal or civil court in order to avoid additional expenses and negative public exposure. Rather, it merely fires the perpetrator or files a claim with a bonding company. (Sometimes it is the bonding company that pursues legal actions against the perpetrators.)

When the defrauded company pursues civil remedies in court, the case is most often settled before it goes to trial. Even in criminal cases, plea bargains entered into with the perpetrators avoid lengthy and costly trials.

As we discussed in Chapter 1, **criminal law** is that branch of law that deals with offenses of a public nature. Criminal laws generally deal with offenses against society as a whole. They are prosecuted either federally or by the state for violating a statute that prohibits some type of activity. Every state and the

---

Just what is fidelity bonding? In a perfect world, employee fraud would never happen. Unfortunately, it does. To protect themselves, companies often purchase **fidelity bonding** coverage on their employees. Basically, in this insurance contract available through insurance companies, an agency guarantees payment to an employer looking for protection in the event of unforeseen financial loss through the dishonest actions of an employee.

How important is bonding? It is estimated that one-third of all bankruptcies are caused by employee theft.

Companies can apply for three basic types of fidelity bonds. Of course, the more specialized the coverage is, the more the company pays.

1. *Name Schedule Fidelity Bond*
   The company designates a set amount of coverage for a list of employees that it provides to the insurance company. Each time the company hires a new employee, it contacts the insurance company to have that person added to the list if the company wants that person covered. Collection under this coverage hinges on absolute proof that an employee did in fact steal from the company.
2. *Blanket Position Bond*
   Under this type of bond, the employer specifies coverage for a position rather than the individual. Each employee of a business is covered, and new employees are added automatically. Coverage is offered for each employee up to the maximum established in the insurance policy. Blanket position bonds don't require proof of the individual's responsibility for the theft.
3. *Primary Commercial Blanket Bond*
   Like the blanket position bond, this bond covers each employee in the company. This type of coverage does not accommodate each employee, but rather treats the employees as one unit. In other words, it does not matter whether one or five people were involved in the crime, the company will be able to claim the same amount.

federal government have statutes prohibiting a wide variety of fraudulent and corrupt practices. Usually, when perpetrators are convicted criminally, they serve jail sentences or pay fines. They are also required to make restitution payments to victims. Before a perpetrator is convicted criminally, he or she must be proven guilty "beyond a reasonable doubt." Juries must rule unanimously on guilt for the perpetrator to be convicted.

**Civil law** is the body of law that provides remedies for violations of private rights. Civil law deals with rights and duties between individuals. Civil claims begin when one party files a complaint against another, usually for the purpose of gaining financial restitution. The purpose of a civil lawsuit is to compensate for harm done to another individual or organization. Unlike criminal cases, the jury in civil cases need not consist of 12 jurors, but may have as few as 6 jurors. The verdict of the jury need not be unanimous. Civil cases are often heard by judges instead of juries. To be successful, the plaintiff in a civil case must only prove his or her case by the "preponderance of the evidence." In other words, the evidence supporting the plaintiff must only be slightly more than any evidence supporting the defendant. In both civil and criminal proceedings, the parties may call expert witnesses to give their opinion on matters thought to be too technical for the jurors or judge to understand. Fraud examiners and accountants are often used as experts in fraud cases to compute and testify to the amount of damages, the nature of the fraud, and whether the parties were negligent in their actions and committed fraud.

## Overview of the Civil Litigation Process

During the civil litigation process, cases go through common stages. Certain courts, such as divorce courts or bankruptcy courts, may have different procedures that we do not discuss in this book. Every civil case involves four basic stages:

1. Investigation and pleadings
2. Discovery
3. Motion practice and negotiation
4. Trial and appeal

Most fraud cases follow these four stages, although in some cases the stages may overlap. For example, investigation may occur during motion practice.

### Investigation and Pleadings

The civil litigation process usually begins when a client in a case of suspected fraud approaches an attorney. Before the attorney is notified, the investigator should have gathered important evidence about the facts of the case, such as how the fraud occurred, the amount of the fraud, the accused perpetrator, and so forth.

For litigation to begin, it is necessary for the plaintiff to file an initial pleading. The **initial pleading,** or **complaint,** explains the alleged violation of the law and the monetary expenses or damages sought in the case. The response to the claim is called a motion or answer. The **motion** is usually an objection to the plaintiff's complaint that points out defects of the case and asks for a specific remedy. The **remedy** may include dismissal of all or part of the original complaint. The **answer** is the response to the complaint that denies or admits various allegations. Sometimes, a defendant in a civil case will file a counterclaim, such as sex, race, or age discrimination or invasion of privacy rights. For example, the defendant may claim that he lost his job because of sex discrimination in order to divert the jury's attention away from the fraud.

### Discovery

**Discovery** is the legal process by which each party's attorneys try to find all information about the other side's case before the trial begins. Because discovery can be time-consuming and expensive, this stage can by the most difficult part of litigation. Attorneys obtain information about the other side's case by filing motions for the production of documents, filing interrogatories, filing requests for admissions, obtaining subpoenas, and taking depositions of both parties and nonparties to the litigation.

**Production Requests.** A production request is a means of securing documents in the other party's possession that are relevant to the issues of the case. These documents can be bank statements, property titles, stock holdings, accounting records, and other important information relevant to the case. Attorneys may request documents to establish that the opposing party has no documents or to avoid appearance of documents presented at trial that have not been previously reviewed. The production request should be specific, containing the facts of the case and defensible in court if necessary. Fraud investigators can provide significant assistance in preparing a production request because of their knowledge of the case. Fraud investigators can also assist in evaluating whether documents produced by the opposing side satisfy requests. Document requests are typically made at the beginning of discovery to allow attorneys time to review all relevant documents before eliciting testimony of witnesses or consultants. After both parties have received responses and if the responses contain no objections, the counsels of both parties arrange to exchange documents at a time and place convenient for all parties.

**Interrogatories.** An **interrogatory** is a series of written questions that specifically identify information needed from the opposing party. Fraud investigators can often provide important interrogatory service by suggesting relevant questions to ask the other side. Fraud investigators can draft responses to questions received and ensure that answers are consistent with the presentation to be made at trial. Normally, responses to interrogatories must be made within 30 days. If answers are not given in a timely fashion, the court may issue an order demanding that all questions be answered and may charge the noncomplying party with fees and costs incurred by the other party in obtaining the order. Interrogatories usually ask questions about personnel, documents, and the nature of the organization, although any questions can be asked. Often responses to interrogatories will include statements such as "the request is unduly burdensome" or "the infraction is unavailable."

**Requests for Admission.** A **request for admission** asks the opposing party to admit designated facts relevant to litigation. These facts may relate to authenticity of documents or precise facts about certain issues. For example, a request for admission may ask the opposing party to admit that the company was incorporated in a particular state during a specific period. Request for admissions must be answered within a certain time period. If answers are not given in a timely fashion, the court may issue an order demanding that all questions be answered and may charge the noncomplying party with fees and costs incurred by the other party.

**Subpoenas.** A **subpoena** is a written order in the name of the court, requiring a witness to submit to a deposition, give testimony at trial, or report to an administrative body. A *subpoena duces tecum* requires the recipient to produce documents pertinent to the case. The court clerk or an attorney as an officer of the court may issue subpoenas. Subpoenas are often the only method of ensuring production of information or documents from witnesses who are not parties to a lawsuit. For example, a subpoena could be used to require a brokerage house to produce records pertaining to the opposing party's account. Subpoenas are sometimes used to obtain documents to compare with documents produced by the opposing party. If the witness believes that the defendant has altered a bank statement sent as part of a document request, a copy of the defendant's bank statement might be subpoenaed from the bank, and documents supporting the transactions may be vouched to the statement to establish the completeness of information.

**Depositions.** A **deposition** is testimony taken before trial begins. Judges usually are not present at depositions. The conditions are usually less formal than in a courtroom, but the rules and regulations of court apply. The opposing side's attorney takes fact and expert witness dispositions.

A deposition is a powerful tool in the hands of a skilled attorney. He or she can see how the witness reacts to questioning. If the witness is not prepared for the deposition, the attorney may be able to obtain admissions or errors not possible at trial. The attorney may also get a witness to commit to a particular position at deposition that can prevent him or her from suddenly recalling a favorable matter at trial.

The individual being deposed is under oath, and a court reporter records the questions and answers and later transcribes the notes. The witness generally is given an opportunity to approve the written transcript and make any necessary corrections. Deposition transcripts may be read to the court at trial for a variety of reasons. One of these reasons is to impeach or question the accuracy of the trial testimony of the witness. For example, if the witness gives seemingly contradictory evidence at deposition and trial, the transcript may be read to convince the jury to give the witness's testimony little weight. In some cases, the deposition will be videotaped and the tape will be shown at trial.

Fraud investigators may assist the client's attorney by preparing questions to ask opposing witnesses during depositions. Fraud investigators can sometimes attend the depositions of other witnesses. Although only attorneys can ask questions during depositions, the fraud investigator can communicate with the client's attorney during breaks or by using written notes. Attending the depositions of opposing experts may be especially helpful for fraud investigators. Their depositions may reveal information and opinions that are not accurately reflected in the expert's written report or work papers. A fraud investigator's technical knowledge of the areas of testimony can help ensure that the deposition reveals all of the opposing expert's opinions and the methodologies and supporting information used in reaching those opinions. In many ways, being deposed is much more difficult than testifying in court. Expert witnesses, for example, are questioned by the other side's attorneys but not by their own. Good witnesses realize that it is best to be good "defensive" witnesses in depositions and good "offensive" witnesses in court.

**Motion Practice and Negotiation.** At various stages during discovery, the opposing parties may seek rulings from the trial judge on a variety of questions. For example, a defendant may file a motion for summary judgment before a case even goes to trial. In a **motion for summary judgment**, counsel requests the court to rule that all or a part of the claim should be dismissed because no genuine issue of a material fact is present. At times during discovery, the witness may be requested to execute an affidavit on a relevant fact in support of a motion. An **affidavit** is a written declaration given under oath.

## Settlement Negotiations

Either of the parties may negotiate a **settlement** at any time during the litigation. If a settlement is reached, the case is usually resolved. However, settlement discussions and negotiations cannot usually be introduced at trial. Fraud investigators can be useful during settlement negotiations because they can assist in resolving differences between the two parties. Most large civil cases are ultimately settled rather than going to trial.

## Trial and Appeal

If the case is not closed by motion practice or settlement, it goes to trial. Before the trial begins, attorneys for both sides generally will meet with the judge and agree to certain ground rules regarding the scope of the litigation, what documents will be admitted, and how long the trial will last. In most jurisdictions, the litigating parties have the right to demand a jury trial, and in most cases, a jury trial will be held. Usually when one side prefers a jury, the other side wants a judge, or vice versa. If either party wants a jury, a jury trial will usually be held.

A fraud investigator's testimony is intended to aid the jury in understanding the technical issues involved. In addition to providing trial testimony, fraud investigators often assist in developing questions that will be asked of the opposing side's expert or fact witnesses during cross-examination by the client's attorney.

In jury trials, the judge determines issues of the law. At the conclusion of the trial, the judge will *charge the jury*. In this charge, the judge provides instructions to the jury on the law to be applied in reaching its verdict. After the jury returns a verdict, parties have a limited period in which they may file motions to have the verdict set aside in whole or in part or to have the judge grant a new trial. If these motions are overruled, a judgment will be entered, and both parties will have a specified time to appeal.

An appeal usually relates to matters of law and not to facts of the case. It is a request to a higher court to overturn the verdict or order a retrial due to some legal defect during the trial. For example, an appeal may be based on the contention that some inappropriate evidence was admitted during the trial or that the trial judge wrongfully instructed the jury on one or more legal issues.

# Overview of the Criminal Litigation Process

The litigation process in criminal cases differs significantly from civil cases because the criminal justice system includes more protections for the rights of the defendant. These protections arise primarily from three amendments to the U.S. Constitution—the Fourth Amendment, the Fifth Amendment, and the Sixth Amendment. Each stage of criminal litigation is also governed by rules established by the jurisdiction in which the case is tried. The Federal Rules of Evidence and Federal Rules of Criminal Procedures are applicable in providing testimony in federal courts. Many state courts follow the federal rules with little modification. The common stages through which criminal cases progress are discussed in the following paragraphs.

## Filing Criminal Charges

After the investigator believes he or she has obtained enough evidence to prosecute a defendant, the defrauded party determines whether to pursue criminal charges. If the decision is made to pursue criminal charges, the victim of the fraud contacts the district attorney for the county in which the fraud was perpetrated. The district attorney coordinates with the local police in the preparation of an arrest **warrant** or summons. If the case involves a federal crime, notice is also sent to the U.S. Attorney's Office.

## Arresting and Charging the Defendant

Representatives of the government do not have unlimited power to search or arrest citizens. Instead, they must comply with the requirements of the U.S. Constitution, including the Fourth and Fifth Amendments.

**The Fourth Amendment.** The **Fourth Amendment** protects defendants against unreasonable searches and seizures by the government. It requires that probable cause exist before a defendant is arrested or searched. Probable cause is the level of evidence required for a reasonable person to believe that a crime has been committed and the accused committed it. The level of evidence necessary to show probable cause is less than certainty, but more than speculation or suspicion. Evidence seized without meeting this requirement can be excluded from trial. Searches at the place of business by employers or investigators hired by employers generally are not subject to this amendment, unless they were carried out in a prejudicial or careless manner. In fraud trials, documents seized by the employer are frequently turned over to the government. The government can generally use these documents as evidence even though a search warrant was not issued to obtain the evidence. However, if the defendant's attorney can show that the fraud investigator was really an agent of the district attorney when gathering the information, and therefore was subject to the rules against unreasonable searches and seizures, the government may not be able to use some of the evidence gathered by the fraud investigator.

**The Fifth Amendment.** The **Fifth Amendment** provides defendants the following protections:

- Requires an indictment of a grand jury before a defendant is held for a capital crime (one where the death penalty or other certain punishments are possible).
- Precludes a person from being tried twice for the same crime.
- Gives the defendant the right to refuse to incriminate himself or herself—often referred to as "pleading the fifth."

- Requires the state to apply due process of law.
- Forbids the state from taking a private party's property without just compensation.

As we stated earlier, agents of the government must have probable cause before they can arrest the accused. Arrest for a crime occurs in three ways:

1. Arrest without a warrant by a private citizen or police officer who observes a crime being committed.
2. Arrest after a warrant has been issued (obtaining a warrant requires a preliminary showing of probable cause).
3. Arrest after an indictment by the grand jury. (The purpose of the grand jury is to determine whether probable cause exists; grand jury indictments are generally used in fraud cases.)

## Preliminary Hearings

If the accused is arrested based on a warrant, the arrest will be followed by either a preliminary hearing or a grand jury proceeding depending on whether the defendant's attorney or prosecutor reaches a judge first. The purpose of a **preliminary hearing** is to determine whether "probable cause" exists to charge the defendant with a crime—not to establish his or her guilt or innocence. Although preliminary hearings are held before judges, hearsay and illegally obtained evidence can be heard. The defendant is represented by an attorney who can cross-examine the prosecution's witnesses. The defendant attempts to demonstrate that the prosecution does not have enough evidence to show probable cause. Without enough evidence to show probable cause, charges are dismissed and the defendant is released. However, this dismissal of charges does not preclude the government from instituting a later prosecution for the same offense, once it has gathered better evidence.

## Grand Jury

Because a preliminary hearing is an opportunity for the defendant to obtain discovery of the prosecution's case without disclosing its evidence, the prosecution generally prefers to obtain a grand jury indictment. Once the defendant is indicted by a grand jury, probable cause is satisfied and a preliminary hearing is not held. The defense, however, may file a motion to obtain most, if not all, of the factual information they could have obtained during a preliminary hearing.

A **grand jury** is a body of 16 to 23 people, selected from the community, who are sworn as jurors and deliberate in secret. Grand jurors listen to evidence presented by witnesses and prosecutors. A grand jury also has the right to subpoena witnesses and documents and can issue contempt orders, fines, or jail terms to enforce the subpoena. A grand jury can consider any evidence, even that which would not be admissible at trial. Defendants do not have a right to be notified that a grand jury is considering evidence against them. Nor are they allowed to review the evidence, confront their accusers, or present evidence in their defense. Defendants who appear before a grand jury cannot be accompanied by their attorneys. However, defendants can periodically leave the grand jury room to discuss their cases with counsel. Defendants appearing before grand juries retain the right against self-incrimination. At least 12 grand jurors must agree for an indictment to be issued. An indictment is not a conviction. At trial, the defendant will have the Sixth Amendment protections denied during the grand jury process.

The **Sixth Amendment** protections relate only to trials. This amendment provides the defendant with the following rights:

- Receive a speedy and public trial.
- Be heard by an impartial jury.
- Have a trial held in the state and district in which the crime was committed.
- Be informed of the accusation.
- Confront witnesses against him.
- Compel witnesses to attend the trial.
- Be represented by legal counsel.

## Arraignment

Generally, in a fraud trial, the grand jury will hear evidence of wrongdoing before the defendant is in custody. Once the defendant is indicted, he or she will receive a summons to attend an arraignment that includes the time and place to appear. Alternatively, the defendant may be arrested and brought to the arraignment. At the **arraignment**, the charges against the defendant are read. The defendant may plead guilty, not guilty, or **nolo contendere** (the defendant does not contest the charges but does not admit guilt). If the defendant pleads not guilty, a trial may be held and bail will be set. If the defendant pleads guilty or nolo contendere, sentencing will follow.

## Discovery

Pretrial discovery in criminal trials differs significantly from that in civil trials. Depositions are allowed only in exceptional circumstances (such as the illness or anticipated death of a witness). According to Rule 16 of the Federal Rules of Criminal Procedure, upon request the defendant may obtain the following:

a. Copies of all relevant statements made by the defendant that are in the government's possession
b. A copy of the defendant's prior criminal record
c. All documents, items, test results, written reports of expert witnesses, or other evidence the government intends to introduce at trial or that are necessary to the defense
d. Copies of all prior statements made by witnesses relevant to the information about which they have testified

If the defendant requests the prosecution to produce any or all of the items listed in item (c), the defendant must provide the same items to the prosecution. However, defendants are not required to disclose information that is self-incriminatory—only information expected to be introduced as evidence at trial.

## Pretrial Motions

Before a criminal trial, the defendant can file motions with the court. This process is similar to that in civil trials. Two motions that are frequently made include the following:

- A request that the charges be dismissed as a matter of law
- A request to suppress certain evidence because it was illegally obtained

## Trial and Appeal

Civil fraud trials in state courts are sometimes held before criminal trials. The prosecutor may choose not to investigate until the defrauded company finds evidence of fraud. In these cases, the defrauded party's attorney notifies the District Attorney of the investigation. The District Attorney may wait to indict the defendant until enough evidence has been obtained in the defrauded party's investigation to show probable cause, and might use that evidence in the criminal trial. Federal criminal trials are generally held first. Having a civil trial first can benefit the prosecution because the defendant may make admissions during the civil trial that can be used in the criminal trial. Also, in civil trials, the defrauded party may have greater access to the documents of the defendant during discovery. If the defendant does not present requested documents during a civil trial, he or she can be held in contempt of court and fined.

**Burden of Proof.** Defendants in criminal trials are considered innocent until proven guilty. A unanimous jury decision may not be required in a civil case, but in most jurisdictions, a jury's decision in a criminal trial must be unanimous. The burden of proof necessary to find a defendant guilty in a criminal trial is also significantly greater than the level needed to prove civil liability. Civil actions require that the "preponderance of the evidence" (usually interpreted to mean more than 50%) support one side of the action. In a criminal case, the guilt of the accused must be established "beyond a reasonable doubt."

**Appeal.** After the jury has returned a verdict, the defendant may file motions to have the verdict set aside. If that is unsuccessful, the defendant may appeal the verdict. An appeal is a request to a higher court to overturn the verdict or order a retrial due to some legal defect in the trial proceedings.

# Being an Expert Witness

Because fraud examiners and accountants are often retained as expert witnesses in both civil and criminal cases, we conclude this chapter by discussing the role of expert witnesses and guidelines that will help you be an effective expert witness.

Most witnesses in a fraud trial are fact or character witnesses. The exception is the **expert witness** who can offer opinions—based on experience, education, or training—about the fraud. The process of qualifying an expert witness to testify is known as **voir dire**. The judge rules on whether an expert witness is qualified to provide evidence on a matter before the court.

Once qualified, an expert witness can testify about the nature of the fraud, the damages suffered in the fraud, the negligence of the victim in allowing the fraud to happen, standards (such as accounting standards) that were violated, and other aspects related to the fraud.

Expert witnesses usually study the facts of the case during the discovery stage of the trial. To prepare, they usually read fact witness depositions, study relevant documents and other materials related to the case, and make sure they understand all the authoritative literature related to the issues of the case. Often, the expert is required or asked to prepare a report that sets out his or her opinions.

After the fact discovery period ends, experts are usually deposed by the attorneys on the other side of the case. The deposition is probably the most stressful part of the case because, except for a few clarifying questions at the end, the opposition's attorneys ask the questions. Those attorneys have several goals during the deposition of the expert: (1) to understand what the expert's opinions are, (2) to understand the credentials and experience of the expert, (3) to identify evidence that can either impeach the expert or be used against his or her testimony during the trial, and (4) to obtain an assessment of how difficult the expert will be in the case.

During the deposition, a good expert will take a defensive posture—answering only the questions that are asked in the most abbreviated way possible. Good experts never volunteer anything beyond what is asked, and they should always listen carefully to the questions to make sure they hear exactly what is being asked. Before answering, experts should pause to give the attorneys for their side of the case an opportunity to object to the question on the basis of relevance, foundation, or other reasonable objection. At times, experts are even instructed by their attorneys to not answer specific questions. Expert witnesses should never forget that their opinions are only as good as their reputation and integrity. They should never sell their opinions to the highest bidder, but rather should give their honest opinions at all times.

Following the deposition, experts work with the attorneys representing their side of the case to prepare for the trial. During this period, experts will decide how to best present their opinions to the judge or jury. Usually graphics and other visuals are helpful in conveying, in simple terms, complex fraud issues.

During the trial, the expert witness first encounters direct examination by the attorneys representing his or her side of the case. At the beginning of direct examination, the attorney asking the questions will usually cover the qualifications of the expert, so that the judge or jury hearing the case can establish in their minds how well qualified the expert is. Once the expert's qualifications are established, the attorney then asks questions that, when answered honestly, will support the case he or she is trying to make. Following direct examination, the expert is cross-examined by the attorneys representing the other side of the case.

Articles coaching individuals how to be expert witnesses are plentiful in the literature, but nothing substitutes for good preparation. No matter how extensive the personal qualifications of an expert, the witness's credibility is weakened by being unprepared or not being familiar with the facts of the case. Most experts agree that, once prepared, the do's and don'ts listed for the various situations in Tables 18-1, 18-2, and 18-3 should be followed when testifying as an expert.

## Table 18-1 Do's and Don'ts at Deposition or Trial

1. Do listen carefully and concentrate on each question.
2. Do think about the question and digest it before attempting to respond; don't give snap answers.
3. Don't try to guess or bluff your way through an answer. If you do not know the answer to a question or do not understand the question, say so.
4. Do restrict your answer to the question asked; don't editorialize your answer or volunteer information.
5. Don't respond to statements or observations, only to questions.
6. Do answer questions convincingly; don't repeatedly attempt to hedge your answers or be overcautious.
7. Don't memorize answers to questions you expect to be asked; do phrase your response in your own words
8. Do answer questions honestly; don't attempt to figure out what the best answer to each question might be.
9. Do speak out the answer to each question. Body language, such as hand signals or nods, cannot be recorded by the stenographer.
10. Do be cautious before answering any hypothetical question and make sure you understand the assumptions, and then spell them out as part of your answer.
11. Do try to "read messages" intended by objections to questions by the lawyer with whom you are working. His or her objection may be designed to caution you about some risk or problem with the question.
12. Don't hesitate to take the time necessary to review exhibits put before you before responding to any questions based on them.
13. Do explain all assumptions on which your conclusions are based and do be prepared for opposing counsel to attack them.

## Table 18-2 Additional Do's and Don'ts at Trial

1. Do be mindful that your personal characteristics and professionalism may influence the jury as much as or even more than the substantive content of you testimony.
2. Do be yourself; jurors are apt to sense when you are not being natural.
3. Do your best to appear authoritative, credible, businesslike, serious, assertive, polite, self-confident, sincere, candid, fair, and spontaneous.
4. Don't appear pompous, aggressive, insincere, or unfair..
5. Do remember that you are independent—avoid bias or unnecessary advocacy of the client's position.
6. Do focus on the lawyer asking the questions, but remember to look at and direct your answers to the jury as well. Don't overlook the reactions of the jurors to your answers; do try to be responsive to their nonverbal signals.
7. Do correct any errors you make as soon as you can.
8. Do tailor your answers to the jury's educational level and do your best to speak in plain English; don't use technical terms that lay people will not understand.
9. Don't bore the jury; try to speak with clarity and feeling and avoid long, overly detailed answers.
10. Don't hesitate to raise your voice; pause or use some other natural gesture to emphasize an important point.
11. Do speak just loud enough and just fast enough to be comfortably understood by the jury.
12. Don't bring notes, work papers, or other material to the witness stand unless counsel for your side approves.
13. Don't try to play lawyer while on the stand. Your job is to answer the questions honestly and responsively; counsel for your side will take care of the legal matters.
14. Don't look to counsel for your side or the judge or anyone else to bail you out if a question stumps you or you otherwise get yourself into a hole.

## Table 18-3 Do's and Don'ts in Cross-Examination

1. Don't lose your temper or become angry or antagonistic; do recognize that it is opposing counsel's job to attempt to discredit you.
2. Don't be concerned if opposing counsel scores points, which is entirely to be expected when your side relinquishes the offensive to the other side; all you can do is try to keep the damage to a minimum.
3. Don't quibble unduly or become argumentative with opposing counsel.
4. Don't respond evasively or ambiguously to questions, no matter how difficult they may be.
5. Do be extra careful if opposing counsel takes on a friendly air, which may be a tactic designed solely to catch you off guard.
6. Don't become hostile if opposing counsel tries to bully you. Jurors are likely to respect you for not becoming unduly perturbed and to sympathize with you if you get "beat up."
7. Do resist responding with simple yes or no answers that may be misleading without some qualification or explanation. Either provide the qualification or explanation directly by responding "yes, but" or "no, but" or request the opportunity to do so.
8. Do your best to recognize signals, such as careless answers, that indicate you may be getting tired or losing your competitive edge. It is advisable in such a situation to indicate the need for a break.
9. Don't allow opposing counsel to entice you into answering questions that concern matters outside of your area of expertise.
10. Do maintain the position you took in your direct testimony.
11. Don't allow opposing counsel to con you into an advocacy role; unduly taking your client's side can cause you to lose your independence in the eyes of the jury.

# KEY TERMS

**Affidavit** A written statement or declaration given under oath.

**Appellate court** A review court in which participants in lower court cases can have their cases reviewed or retried if they are unhappy with the outcome.

**Arraignment** A court hearing at which the charges against the defendant are read and the defendants given the opportunity to plead guilty, not guilty, or nolo contendere.

**Bankruptcy court** A federal court that hears only bankruptcy cases.

**Civil law** That body of law that provides remedies for violation of the rights and duties between individuals.

**Complaint** A request filed by a plaintiff asking for civil proceedings against someone, usually to seek damages.

**Criminal law** The branch of law that deals with offenses of a public nature or against society.

**Deposition** Sworn testimony taken before a trial begins at which the opposing side's attorneys ask questions of witnesses.

**Discovery** The legal process by which each party's attorneys try to find all possible information about the other side's case before a trial begins.

**Expert witness** A trial witness who can offer opinions based upon unique experience, education, or training about a specific matter,

**Federal court** Court established by the federal government to enforce federal laws and statutes.

**Fidelity bonding** Insurance coverage purchased by employers to provide reimbursement for amounts stolen by employees.

**Fifth Amendment** Provision of the U.S. Constitution giving defendants certain protections, including (1) an indictment by a grand jury before being held for a capital crime, and (2) not being tried twice for the same crime.

**Fourth Amendment** Provision of the U.S. Constitution that protects defendants against unreasonable searches and seizures by the government.

**Grand jury** A body of 16–23 individuals who deliberate in secret to decide whether sufficient evidence exists to charge someone in a preliminary hearing.

**Higher-level trial court** A state court that tries felony (larger crimes) and civil cases above a predetermined amount monetary damage amount.

**Initial pleading** A complaint filed by a plaintiff to request legal proceedings against someone.

**Interrogatory** A series of written questions that specifically identify information needed from the opposing party.

**Lower-level trial court** A state court that tries misdemeanors (small crimes) and pretrial issues.

**Motion** The response to a complaint or pleading by the defendant. Sometimes *motion* refers to any request made to the judge for a ruling in a case by either party.

**Motion for summary judgment** A request to the judge to dismiss a claim or part of a claim because no genuine issue of material fact is present.

**Nolo contendere** A plea by a defendant that does not contest the charges but does not admit guilt.

**Preliminary hearing** A pretrial hearing to determine whether probable cause supports charging the defendant with a crime.

**Remedy:** Judgment asked for in civil cases that would right a private wrong.

**Request for admission** A request that the opposing party admit designated facts as relevant to litigation.

**Settlement** A negotiated pretrial agreement between the parties to resolve a legal dispute.

**Sixth Amendment** Provision of the U.S. Constitution ensuring trial-related protections for defendants, such as the right to a speedy trial and the right to be heard by an impartial jury.

**Subpoena** A written order in the name of the court, requiring a witness to submit to a deposition, give testimony at trial, or report to an administrative body.

**Tax court** A federal court that hears only tax cases.

**Voir dire** The legal process of qualifying an expert witness.

**Warrant** An order issued by a judge to arrest someone.

# QUESTIONS AND CASES

## DISCUSSION QUESTIONS

1. How are state courts organized?

2. How are federal courts organized?

3. What is the difference between civil and criminal fraud trials?

4. What steps are involved in the civil litigation process?

5. What is an interrogatory?

6. What is a deposition?

7. Why are depositions a powerful tool in obtaining information?

8. What steps are involved in the criminal litigation process?

9. What is discovery?

10. How are fraud examiners used as expert witnesses?

11. What are some of the do's and don'ts of being an expert witness?

12. What types of fraud-related things can an expert witness testify about?

13. During deposition, what posture should an expert witness display?

## TRUE/FALSE

1. Most fraud cases are tried in federal courts.

2. Civil cases must consist of a jury of at least six jurors.

3. The prosecution usually prefers to present evidence at a grand jury because the accused does not have the right to hear the evidence.

4. If, during a preliminary hearing, sufficient evidence is not available to show probable cause, the defendant can still be prosecuted at a later time when more evidence is available.

5. The burden of proof necessary to prove a defendant is guilty in a criminal trial is significantly greater than in a civil trial.

6. To be successful, the plaintiff in a civil case must prove his or her case beyond a reasonable doubt.

7. Investigation is the legal process by which each party's attorneys try to find all information about the other side's case before the trial begins.

8. An interrogatory is a series of written questions that specifically identifies information needed from the opposing party.

9. A request for confession asks the opposing party to admit designated facts relevant to litigation.

10. The parties in a civil case may negotiate a settlement during any stage of litigation.

11. The federal courts will only hear cases that involve federal law, more than one state, or a federal statute.

12. The defendant can choose to have his or her case tried in either a state lower court or a state higher court.

13. An individual committing fraud can be prosecuted either criminally or civilly, but not both.

14. A deposition is a testimony taken before the trial begins in a situation that is usually less formal than a courtroom, but in which the court rules and regulations still apply.

## MULTIPLE CHOICE

1. To be convicted in a criminal case, the standard of evidence is:
   a. Beyond a shadow of a doubt.
   b. Beyond a reasonable doubt.
   c. Preponderance of evidence.
   d. All of the above.

2. Most court cases are decided in state courts, except when:
   a. Federal laws are in question.
   b. The case involves several states.
   c. The amount exceeds $100,000.
   d. Both a and b.

3. Which of the following rights is *not* provided by the Fifth Amendment?
   a. Individuals are protected from double jeopardy (being tried twice for the same crime).
   b. States cannot seize private property without just compensations.
   c. Individuals have the right to refuse to incriminate themselves.
   d. Miranda rights must be read upon arrest.

4. During a trial or deposition, expert witnesses should:
   a. Respond aggressively.
   b. Bring notes and work papers to cite.
   c. Answer questions convincingly, without hedging the answers.
   d. Memorize well-crafted responses to say what sounds effective.

5. During cross-examination, expert witnesses should:
   a. Address areas outside of their areas of expertise.
   b. Appreciate opposing council when they act very friendly.
   c. Respond evasively and ambiguously to tough questions.
   d. Maintain the same positions taken during direct testimony.

6. When deposing an expert witness, the opposing attorneys try to achieve all of the following goals *except*:
   a. Understanding the expert's opinion.
   b. Understanding the expert's credentials.
   c. Seeking admission of guilt.
   d. Obtaining an assessment of how difficult the expert will be in the case.

7. Having a civil trial before a criminal trial has the following benefits:
   a. Defendant may make admissions during civil trial that can be used in criminal trial.
   b. Greater access to documents of the defendant.
   c. Defendant is not guaranteed the right to an attorney.
   d. Both a and b.

8. Which of the following is *not* one of the common stages of a criminal case?
   a. Filing a criminal charge
   b. Filing a complaint
   c. Discovery
   d. Trial and appeal

9. In a civil trial, settlements may be negotiated:
   a. At any time during the litigation.
   b. After arraignment.
   c. At no time once negotiation begins.
   d. Only after judge orders negotiation between parties.

10. Which of the following actions can fraud victims pursue after sufficient evidence is obtained?
    a. Prosecute in a criminal court
    b. Pursue civil litigation
    c. Take no action at all
    d. All of the above

## SHORT CASES

**Case 1.** Mr. Bill is the sole proprietor of a small play-dough production company. Over the last few months, he noticed revenues dropping and started wondering what is going on. After giving it much thought, he realizes that his accountant has been cooking the books and stealing money from him, at least it seems to be the case. Mr. Bill is pretty upset and immediately runs down to the local courthouse and files a complaint against his accountant. Too anxious to wait for the legal process to continue, Mr. Bill decides to go to his accountant's personal residence and search for evidence of fraud. To his delight, he finds some papers that document his accountant's illegal activities.

Mr. Bill hurries to the office, where he confronts his accountant and shows him all of the papers he found at his house, informing him that a complaint has been filed. His accountant, Mr. Pringles, calmly laughs and walks away, apparently not affected at all by what Mr. Bill has told him.

Explain why Mr. Pringles is not worried in the least about Mr. Bill's discovery.

**Case 2.** In April 1994, a Wall Street bond trader turned on the television and saw a news report accusing him of committing a large securities scam. This trader learned that his employer had accused him of creating $300 million of phony profits and, as a result, getting bogus bonuses of $8 million. He claimed he was innocent, and it took about three years for him to prove his innocence. In the months that followed the accusations, he was investigated by the Securities and Exchange Commission, the National Association of Securities Dealers, and the Justice Department. In 1997, this bond trader was cleared of all major charges brought against him.

1. Assume that you are the employer. What type of legal action would you seek against this bond trader? Why?

2. What type of court would your case more likely be assigned to? Why?

**Case 3.** In June 2000, the Securities and Exchange Commission brought civil charges against seven top executives of Cendant Company. The SEC alleged that these officials had, among other things, inflated income by more than $100 million through improper use of company reserves. These proceedings were a result of a long-standing investigation by the SEC of financial fraud that started back in the 1980s.

In your opinion, how far along is this case? Why?

**Case 4.** Briefly research a recent publicized fraud to become familiar with the major facts involved. Identify ways that a fraud investigator could add value in the (1) investigation, (2) legal follow-up, and (3) implementation of controls to prevent similar problems from happening in the future.

**Case 5.** When O.J. Simpson was tried for the murder of his wife, Nicole Simpson, he was ruled not guilty in the criminal court hearings. However, when Nicole Simpson's family sued Simpson civilly, he was ordered to compensate Nicole's family several million dollars. How could that be?

**Case 6.** You are a manager for a large department store. It has recently come to light that a receiving clerk has been stealing merchandise. About $5,000 has been stolen. The clerk has stopped his stealing, and the faulty internal control weaknesses that were determined to have allowed the fraud have been fixed. No action has been taken yet to punish the perpetrator, who still works at his same job. The clerk happens to be the nephew of one of the other managers, who, while he understands that his nephew's behavior was unacceptable, would like to keep the theft relatively quiet.

What action, if any, should be taken against the receiving clerk in this situation? What consequences will probably result from that action?

**Case 7.** Recently, the Supreme Court declined to hear a securities fraud case pitting disgruntled investors against former Cendant Corp. executives. The justices, acting without comment, turned away an appeal by former Cendant chairman Walter Forbes and vice chairman Christopher McLeod of a ruling on how to establish whether a fraud is made "in connection with" a securities offering.

The executives argued that the June 2000 ruling by the U.S. Third Circuit Court of Appeals is so broad that it could unleash a flood of securities fraud lawsuits. . . . The ruling stems from a lawsuit in which a New Jersey district court dismissed securities fraud claims against Cendant and former top executives there. Investors appealed that ruling to the federal appeals court. The appellate court sent the case back to the district court for further review, prompting the former executives to appeal to the Supreme Court.

The case revolves around allegedly misleading statements about Cendant's financial health in conjunction with a proposed 1998 merger with American Bankers

Insurance Group, Inc., which promised American Bankers shareholders $67 per share in cash or Cendant stock. . . .

Disgruntled investors said they relied on Cendant's upbeat assessment of its finances, and "lost enormous sums of money" when American Bankers Insurance stock fell from nearly $65 to $35.50 when the merger was terminated. A New Jersey district court rejected the claims, saying connections between any misrepresentations by Cendant and the investors' purchases of American Bankers Insurance Group shares were too tenuous to be deemed to be "in connections with 'those purchases.'"

1. Why were the securities fraud claims against Cendant ultimately dismissed?

2. What was the appeals process followed by the prosecuting investors? Does this process resemble what you learned in the chapter?

3. Do you think the Supreme Court's decision was valid? Do you think they should have at least heard the case? Why or why not?

**Case 8.** Answer the following questions:

1. After being named as a defendant in a corporate fraud case, the XYZ accounting firm was found guilty of negligence and fined $25 billion. As a partner for the firm, what would you recommend as the next course of action?

2. As part of the preparations for a large financial statement fraud case, you issue a production request to see the other party's bank statements. When the statements are provided to you, some of them are only photocopies. The opposing party claims that the originals were accidentally destroyed. What could you do in this situation?

**Case 9.** You are involved as an expert witness in a case of alleged fraud by top management against the corporation. Supposedly, working in collusion, top management defrauded the company of $5 million over two years. The allegations suggest that the fraud involved stealing $5 million and then concealing the fraud by overstating expense accounts and manipulating balance sheet accounts.

Following the initial discovery of this alleged fraud, shareholders of the company brought a lawsuit against top management. The prosecuting attorney for the shareholders has retained you to assist as an expert witness in this case. The case has already moved into the discovery phase.

What will your role likely be as an expert witness? At what point in the process will you be most involved? What might you do to assist the prosecution as much as possible?

**Case 10.** Bobby Jones, an accountant for ABC Corporation, is suspected of committing fraud. Some information already gathered about the fraud points to Bobby Jones as the most likely perpetrator. In his scheme, Bobby supposedly stole more than $5 million over the past three years. Due to the magnitude of the fraud, and to set an example in the company, ABC decides to prosecute Bobby both civilly and criminally.

Describe what will happen to Bobby Jones during the civil litigation, including the stages of civil litigation that he and ABC will go through.

**Case 11.** John was recently convicted by a jury of committing fraud against his employer. After the trial, it was revealed that some key evidence against John used in trial was obtained through his employer's records and John's workstation computer. Before searching John's computer, the investigators did not have any evidence or idea that John was involved in the fraud. In fact, they stumbled on the fraud by accident. John is convinced that he has grounds for appeal. He believes the evidence found on his work computer is inadmissible because the investigators did not have probable cause to search his computer.

Is John right that he could appeal the guilty verdict? Were his rights violated?

**Case 12** The FBI is on the trail of a drug supplier in Pineville, USA. The Feds believe that the supplier works at OHS Manufacturing, the employer of 75 percent of the Pineville citizens. The FBI asks OHS Manufacturing to assist in the investigation of one of OHS's employees. Specifically, the FBI asks one of OHS's managers to search the employee's locker and give the FBI any illegal drugs found.

Do you believe this action could be a possible violation of the Fourth Amendment? Why or why not?

**Case 13.** Mr. Oaks has worked as the CEO of Turley Bank for the last three years. This past year, the outside auditor discovered some fraudulent loan activity in which Mr. Oaks was circumventing internal controls to lend money to friends and family. After a thorough investigation, the board of trustees concluded that Mr. Oaks had committed more than $10 million in loan fraud. Mr. Oaks denied any wrongdoing. Now, the board is contemplating pursuing a civil case against Mr. Oaks, seeking repayment of the $10 million.

1. What are some reasons why Turley Bank would not pursue a civil case against Mr. Oaks?

2. If Turley Bank decides to pursue a civil case against Mr. Oaks, what are some reasons why the bank would settle out of court before the actual trial?

3. If Turley Bank decides to pursue a civil case against Mr. Oaks, what are some reasons why Mr. Oaks would settle out of court before the actual trial?

**Case 14.** To help understand the material discussed in the chapter, do the following:

1. Give at least three characteristics of a grand jury.

2. Without looking at the list in the chapter, list at least three do's and don'ts that an expert witness should keep in mind during cross-examination.

3. During the discovery stage of a civil litigation process, several methods of obtaining information may be used. One of these methods is by taking depositions.
   a. What are depositions?
   b. Why are depositions a powerful tool in obtaining evidence?
   c. What are the other three stages of civil litigation that cases usually go through in addition to discovery?

---

**■  EXTENSIVE CASE**

John Rigas (founder and CEO of Adelphia Communications Corp.) was an extraordinary man. Throughout his professional career he was honored for his entrepreneurial achievements and his humanitarian service. Among other awards, he received three honorable doctorate degrees from distinguished universities, was named Entrepreneur of the Year by Rensselaer Polytechnic Institute (his college alma mater), and was inducted into the Cable Television Hall of Fame by *Broadcasting and Cable* magazine. He worked hard to acquired wealth and status. But a $2.3 billion financial fraud eventually cost Rigas everything.

Rigas and his company, Adelphia Communications, started out small. With $72,000 of borrowed money, he

began his business career in 1950 by purchasing a movie theatre in Coudersport, Pennsylvania. Two years later, he overdrew his bank account to buy the town cable franchise with $300 of his own money. Through risky debt-financing, Rigas continued to acquire assets until, in 1972, he and his brother created Adelphia Communications Corporation. The company grew quickly, eventually becoming the sixth largest cable company in the world with over 5.6 million subscribers.

From its inception, Adelphia had always been a family business, owned and operated by the Rigas clan. During the 1990s, the company was run by John Rigas, his three sons, and his son-in-law. Altogether, the members of the Rigas family occupied a majority five of the nine seats on

Adelphia's board of directors and held the following positions:

John Rigas, CEO and chairman of the board (father)

Tim Rigas, CFO and board member (son)

Michael Rigas, Executive vice president and board member (son)

James Rigas, Executive vice president and board member (son)

Peter Venetis, board member (son-in-law)

This family dominance in the company was maintained through stock voting manipulation. The company issued two types of stock: Class A stock, which held one vote each, and Class B stock, which held ten votes each. When shares of stock were issued, however, the Rigas family kept all Class B shares to themselves, giving them a majority ruling when company voting occurred.

With a majority presence on the board of directors and an effectual influence among voting shareholders, the Rigases were able to control virtually every financial decision made by the company. However, exclusive power led to corruption and fraud. The family established a cash management system, an enormous account of commingled revenues from Adelphia Communications Corp., other Rigas entities, and loan proceeds. Although funds from this account were used throughout all the separate entities, none of their financial statements were ever consolidated.

The family began to dip into the cash management account, using these funds to finance their extravagant lifestyle and to hide their crimes. The company paid $4 million to buy personal shares of Adelphia stock for the family. It paid for Tim Rigas's $700,000 membership at the Golf Club at Briar's Creek in South Carolina. With company funds, the family bought three private jets, maintained several vacation homes (in Cancun, Beaver Creek Hilton Head, and Manhattan), and began construction of a private world-class golf course. In addition, Adelphia financed, with $3 million, the production of Ellen Rigas's (John Rigas's daughter) movie *Song Catcher*. John Rigas was honored for his large charitable contributions. But these contributions also likely came from company proceeds.

In the end, the family racked up approximately $2.3 billion in fraudulent off-balance sheet loans. The company manipulated its financial statements to conceal the amount of debt it was accumulating. False transactions and phony companies were created to inflate Adelphia's earnings and to hide its debt. When the family fraud was eventually caught, it resulted in a SEC investigation, a Chapter 11 bankruptcy filing, and multiple indictments and heavy sentences. The perpetrators (namely John Rigas and his sons) were charged with the following counts:

Violation of the RICO Act

Breach of fiduciary duties

Waste of corporate assets

Abuse of control

Breach of contract

Unjust enrichment

Fraudulent conveyance

Conversion of corporate assets

Until he was convicted of serious fraud, everybody loved John Rigas. He was trusted and respected in the small town of Coudersport and famous for his charitable contributions and ability to make friends. He had become a role model for others to follow. With a movie theatre and a $300 cable tower he had built one of the biggest empires in the history of cable television. From small beginnings, he became a multimillion dollar family man who stressed good American values. But his goodness only masked the real John Rigas, and in the end it was his greed and deceit that ultimately cost him and his family everything.

**Questions:**

1. The fraud triangle is made of perceived pressure, perceived opportunity, and rationalization. How do you think John Rigas rationalized his dishonest use of company assets?

2. How else do people rationalize fraudulent behavior?

3. How would owning and operating a family business create temptations and opportunities to commit fraud?

4. Based upon the facts of the case, do you think this case will be prosecuted criminally, civilly, or both? Explain your answer.

5. Suppose you were an expert witness in this case, what would be some of the facts that you would pay special attention to?

## INTERNET ASSIGNMENT

Refer back to the first page of this chapter. On it is an excerpt from an *Los Angeles Times* article about Reed Slatkin's fraud. The article insinuates that the FBI and IRS's raiding of Slatkin's office marked the beginning of the government's investigation of Slatkin's financial activities. In fact, Slatkin was under investigation for at least four years prior to the raid, and nearly a year and half previous to it, the SEC had already conducted a series of depositions featuring, among others, Reed Slatkin as a witness. Transcripts of two of these frauds are available online. Open http://slatkinfraud.com/depo_jan.htm (Depo 1) and http://slatkinfraud.com/depo_feb.htm (Depo 2). All page numbers refer to Depo 1 except as individually noted.

1. *Page 1.* Where was this deposition conducted?

2. *Page 1.* Name the three individuals representing the SEC.

3. Based on the chapter's explanation of depositions, do you think these three are lawyers or SEC investigators (fraud examiners)?

4. *Page 1-11.* Using the explanation of *discovery* in the chapter, what is meant by "The above-entitled matter came on for hearing at 10:12 a.m., *pursuant to notice*"? (italics added). (Also, see page 6-23 to page 7-7.)

5. *Page 2.* Another vital aspect of deposition is subpoena duces tecum, a written order that commands an individual or organization to produce case-related documents that will often be used as evidence in the deposition or trial and are usually called *exhibits*. What two exhibits are presented in this deposition?

6. *Depo 2, Page 2.* Compare the number of exhibits used in Depo 1 to the number used in Depo 2. By the nature of the exhibits listed for Depo 2, why do you think the SEC employed so many more exhibits in the second part of the deposition than the first?

7. *Pages 7-9 to 10-13.* Quickly read over this discussion. Using the explanation of *subpoenas* in the chapter, why are the examiners so particular in their questions regarding the subpoenaed documents?

8. *Page 3.* According to Mr. Dunbar, what is the purpose of this deposition, or "investigation"?

9. *Depo 1, Pages 52-16 to 55-14; Depo 2, Pages 214-3 to 215-4.* Quickly read over these discussions. Referring also to the chapter, describe briefly the role of Mr. Boltz, Mr. Slatkin's attorney.

10. *Pages 134-14 to 137-17.* Quickly read over this discussion. Keeping in mind that Mr. Slatkin handled investments for hundreds of "friends" but was not a registered investment advisor, and paying particular attention to Mr. Boltz's "promptings" in this section, for what reason does Mr. Boltz apparently believe his client is under investigation?

11. *Page 142-2 to 144-25.* Throughout the deposition, both Mr. Slatkin and his interrogators reference NAA Financial, a Swiss institution housing most of Slatkin's "friends' money." On a scale of one to ten, how confident is Mr. Boltz concerning NAA Financial?
    a. When asked how he can be certain that NAA Financial is "good for the money," how does he respond?
    b. Is Mr. Boltz's method of verification legitimate?
    c. Has he personally made contact?
    d. Who is Mitchell Axiall?

13. Now go to http://www.sec.gov/litigation/litreleases/lr17796.htm. This SEC litigation release identifies Daniel Jacobs as a co-conspirator in Slatkin's effort to deceive the SEC. Pay close attention to the bulleted section.
    a. What do you learn about NAA Financial?
    b. Who is Michel (Mitchell) Axiall?

## DEBATE

1. Sam's Electronics Universe discovered and investigated a kickback fraud perpetrated by its purchasing agent. The fraud lasted eight months and cost the company $2 million in excess inventory purchases. The perpetrator personally benefited by receiving kickbacks of $780,000. Your boss wants to seek restitution of what the company has lost, but is worried about the ramifications of a trial and how it might hurt your company's image in the market. She is trying to decide whether she should pursue remedies through a civil trial, or turn the case over to the district attorney to prosecute the perpetrator criminally. Pair up with somebody and choose sides. Discuss the pros and cons of each approach of legal follow-up to fraud.

2. Daren has been retained as an expert witness in a recent fraud case by the defendants. He will be providing information concerning the defendant's activities, explaining why the defendant's activities are in accordance with GAAP and normal business practice. Throughout the litigation process, Daren

has been completely honest with the attorneys in his deposition and any other correspondence. Daren believes that the activities of the defendant have been in accordance with GAAP. The case continues and is brought to trial. A few days before Daren is called to testify in the trial, he discovers some new

documents and information, which could possibly represent fraudulent behavior by the defendant.

What ethical issues does Daren face in the light of this new information he has received? What concerns should Daren have? What are some possible actions Daren could take?

## END NOTES

1.  Liz Pulliam Weston: "Money Talk, FBI and IRS Raid Offices of Slatkin," *Los Angeles Times*, May 12, 2001.

2.  *USA Today*, November 8, 2001, p. 6A.

3.  http://library.lp.findlaw.com/articles/file/00343/006898/title/Subject/topic/Securities%20Law_Fraud/filename/securitieslaw_2_5593

# *APPENDIX*

# FINANCIAL STATEMENT FRAUD STANDARDS

This textbook contains three chapters on financial statement fraud. Because of the high costs associated with financial statement fraud, regulators have paid much attention over the years to this problem. Such scrutiny has resulted in both auditing standards as well as influential reports issued by organizations and parties interested in the fair presentation of financial statements. In this appendix, we review the professional standards and reports that have been issued related to financial statement fraud in order to provide you with the necessary historical background to understand issues related to fraudulent financial statements. Standards and reports are presented chronologically.

## Auditors' Responsibility to Detect Financial Statement Fraud: A Brief History

During the early part of this century, there was universal agreement, even among auditors, that the detection of fraud was one of the primary purposes for conducting an audit of financial statements. Indeed, as noted in a best-selling auditing textbook by Carmichael and Willingham (1971), detecting fraud is deeply rooted in the historical role of auditors, dating back to the early sixteenth century. As late as the 1930s, most auditors emphasized that one of the primary purposes of an audit was detection of fraud. Mautz and Sharaf (1961) stated, "Until recently there was substantial acceptance of the idea that an independent audit had as one of its principal purposes the detection and prevention of fraud and other irregularities."[1] An early edition of Montgomery (the first auditing text) listed three objectives of the audit:

1. The detection of fraud,
2. The detection of technical errors, and
3. The detection of errors in principle.

By the late 1930s, a visible change occurred in the auditing profession's willingness to accept responsibility for fraud detection as a purpose for auditing financial statements. This revolutionary change culminated in the issuance of Statement on Auditing Procedure (SAP) No. 1, *Extensions of Auditing Procedure*. SAP No. 1 contained the following statement:

> *The ordinary examination incident to the issuance of financial statements, accompanied by a report and opinion of an independent certified public accountant, is not designed to discover all defalcations, because that is not its primary objective, although discovery of defalcation frequently results. . . . To exhaust the possibility of all cases of dishonesty or fraud, the independent auditor would have to examine in detail all transactions. This would entail a prohibitive cost to the great majority of business enterprises—a cost which would pass all bounds of reasonable expectation of benefit or safeguard there from, and place an undue burden on industry.*

Since SAP No. 1 was issued, the profession has struggled to refine and articulate its position on detecting fraud and to establish standards capable of convincing users that auditors should have only a limited role in detecting fraud. During the late 1950s, SAP No. 1, as well as the profession, endured vigorous attacks, and pressure mounted for the AICPA to reconsider its official position as stated in SAP No. 1. The AICPA responded in 1960 by issuing a new standard, SAP No. 30, *Responsibilities and Functions of the Independent Auditor in the Examination of Financial Statements*. Many accounting professionals viewed SAP No. 30 as unresponsive to user concerns because it added no new responsibility to detect fraud. Specifically, SAP No. 30 stated an auditor's responsibility to detect irregularities as follows:

> *The ordinary examination incident to the expression of an opinion on financial statements is not primarily or specifically designed, and cannot be relied upon, to disclose defalcations and other similar irregularities, although their discovery may result. Similarly, although the discovery of deliberate misrepresentations by management is usually more closely associated with the objective of the ordinary examination, such examination cannot be relied upon to assure its discovery.*

Although the standard did stress that an auditor was obliged to "be aware of the possibility that fraud may exist," it also clarified that an auditor held no responsibility beyond the minimum duty to design tests that would detect fraud.

Although the courts appeared to hold auditors responsible for failure to detect fraud, it took the Equity Funding case and its associated scrutiny of the profession to determine that SAP No. 30 was inadequate.

The Committee on Auditor's Responsibility (Cohen Commission), comprised largely of non-AICPA members, reached a different conclusion, however. The Cohen Commission issued a report in 1978 that highlighted the widening gap between auditor performance and financial statement user expectations. The Cohen report primarily targeted the development of conclusions and recommendations regarding appropriate responsibilities of independent auditors, including the auditor's responsibility for the detection of fraudulent financial reporting. According to the Cohen Commission, the auditor:

> . . . *has a duty to search for fraud, and should be expected to detect those frauds that the examination would normally uncover.*

The commission went on to say that

> . . . *users of financial statements should have a right to assume that audited financial information is not unreliable because of fraud. . . . An audit should be designed to provide reasonable assurance that the financial statements are not affected by material fraud.*

SAS No. 16, *The Independent Auditor's Responsibility for the Detection of Errors or Irregularities,* was issued in 1977, admitting some obligation to search for fraud in the normal course of a GAAS audit. According to SAS No. 16:

> *The independent auditor's objective in making an examination of financial statements in accordance with (GAAS) is to form an opinion on whether the financial statements present fairly financial position, results of operations, and the changes in financial position in conformity with (GAAP). . . . Consequently, under (GAAS), the independent auditor has the responsibility, within the inherent limitations of the auditing process . . . to plan his examination to search for (material) errors and irregularities.*

Although SAS No. 16 required auditors to "search for" fraud, it did not require them to "detect" fraud. Even after SAS No. 16 was issued, auditors remained unwilling to accept or acknowledge a substantial responsibility for detecting fraud. SAS No. 16 contained similar "defensive and qualifying" language that was included in SAP No. 1 and SAP No. 30: phrases such as "inherent limitations of the auditing process" and "unless the auditor's examination reveals evidentiary matter to the contrary, his reliance on the truthfulness of certain representations and the genuineness of records and documents obtained during the examination was reasonable" allowed auditors to justify the unwillingness to detect fraud.

## Report of the National Commission on Fraudulent Financial Reporting

In October 1987, the National Commission on Fraudulent Financial Reporting (Treadway Commission) issued a landmark report in response to concerns about fraudulent financial reporting. This report helped refocus the business community on the problem of fraudulent financial reporting. Considered an update to the Cohen report, the Treadway study of incidents of financial statement fraud also focused on a broader range of parties playing a vital role in the financial reporting process. The report included 49 extensive recommendations embracing the roles of top management and boards of directors of public companies, independent public accountants and the public accounting profession, the SEC and other regulatory and law enforcement bodies, and the academic community. The Treadway Commission identified numerous causal factors that can lead to financial statement fraud.

Although the Treadway report is not covered in detail in this book, it is strongly recommended that you become familiar with its contents. The report highlights many of the problems that lead to financial statement fraud and provides a basis for activity by organizations such as the AICPA and others. Since the issuance of the Treadway report, there have been many efforts to build upon the commission's findings—that is, to minimize incidents of fraudulent financial reporting. These efforts have primarily focused on the roles that auditors, managers, boards of directors, and audit committees play in the financial statement process.

## Efforts Related to the Role of Auditors—SAS No. 53

Soon after the issuance of the Treadway report, the AICPA's Auditing Standards Board (ASB) issued Statement on Auditing Standards No. 53, *The Auditor's Responsibility to Detect and Report Errors and Irregularities*. The ASB issued SAS No. 53 to strengthen the auditor's responsibility related to the detection of instances of material fraudulent financial reporting. SAS No. 53 modified the auditor's responsibility to require the auditor to "design the audit to provide reasonable assurance of detecting errors and irregularities." SAS No. 53 was designed to narrow the expectation gap between the assurances auditors provide and what financial statement users expect regarding the detection of fraudulent financial reporting. SAS No. 53 required the auditor to provide reasonable assurance that material irregularities would be detected, which extended the auditor's responsibility beyond what was required by SAS No. 16.

## Public Oversight Board's 1993 Special Report

Subsequent to the issuance of SAS No. 53, the Public Oversight Board of the AICPA SEC Practice Section (the POB) issued a Special Report entitled *In the Public Interest: Issues Confronting the Accounting Profession*. The report was issued primarily in response to continuing signs of failing public confidence in public accountants and auditors, particularly the widespread belief that auditors have a responsibility for detecting management fraud, which many viewed auditors as not meeting. Based on the POB's belief that the integrity and reliability of audited financial statements are critical to the U.S. economy, the Special Report contained specific recommendations for improving and strengthening the accounting profession's performance by enhancing its capacity and willingness to detect fraud and improve the financial reporting process. It also called for improved guidance beyond that in SAS No. 53 to assist auditors in assessing the likelihood of fraud, a strengthening of the process to ensure auditor independence and professionalism, and changes in the corporate governance process. The POB was especially interested in enhancing the auditing profession's potential for detecting management fraud.

## AICPA Board of Director's 1993 Report

Also in 1993, the AICPA's Board of Directors issued its report, *Meeting the Financial Reporting Needs of the Future: A Public Commitment for the Public Accounting Profession*. In that report, the AICPA Board of Directors expressed its determination to keep the U.S. financial reporting system the best in the world, supporting the recommendations and initiatives of others to assist auditors in the detection of material misstatements in financial statements resulting from fraud, and encouraged every participant in the financial reporting process—management, their advisors, regulators, and independent auditors—to share in this responsibility.

## AICPA SEC Practice Section Initiatives

Soon after the issuance of the POB's Special Report and the AICPA's Board of Directors' report, the AICPA undertook efforts related to improving the integrity of the financial reporting process, particularly through improved detection of fraudulent financial reporting. The AICPA's SEC Practice Section formed a Professional Issues Task Force that has published guidance about emerging or unresolved practice issues that surface through litigation analysis, peer review, or internal inspection. The SEC Practice

Section also amended membership requirements to require that concurring partners provide assurance that those consulting on accounting and auditing matters are aware of all relevant facts and circumstances related to the consultation issue and to the auditee, to ensure that the conclusion reached is an appropriate one. The AICPA SEC Practice Section also created the Detection and Prevention of Fraud Task Force. That task force issued a document in 1994 entitled *Client Acceptance and Continuance Procedures for Audit Clients.*[2] That document emphasized that understanding the components of engagement risk is critical to deciding whether to accept new clients, continue old ones, and in any event to manage the "audit risk" that accompanies those decisions.

## Panel on Audit Effectiveness

At the request of the chairman of the SEC, the Public Oversight Board appointed a panel of eight members, charging it to thoroughly examine the current audit model. The panel made recommendations that it believed would result in more effective audits that would improve the reliability of financial statements, enhance their credibility, contribute to investors' confidence in the profession, and improve the efficiency of the capital markets. One of the panel's recommendations was because "audit firms may have reduced the scope of their audits and level of testing and because the auditing profession may not have kept pace with a rapidly changing environment, the profession needs to address vigorously the issue of fraudulent financial reporting, including fraud in the form of illegitimate earnings management." They recommended that the auditing standards should create a "forensic-type" fieldwork phase on all audits. They suggested that this work should be based on the possibility of dishonesty and collusion, overriding of controls, and falsification of documents. Auditors would be required during this phase, in some cases on a surprise basis, to perform substantive tests directed at the possibility of fraud. The panel's recommendations also call for auditors to examine non-standard entries, and to analyze certain opening financial statement balances to assess, with the benefit of hindsight, how certain accounting estimates and judgments or other matters were resolved. The intent of the panel's recommendations was twofold: to enhance the likelihood that auditors will be able to detect material fraud, and to establish implicitly a deterrent to fraud by positing a greater threat to its successful concealment.[3]

## SAS No. 82

In 1997, the AICPA responded to various calls for improved auditing guidance related to the detection of material misstatements due to fraudulent financial reporting by issuing SAS No. 82, *Consideration of Fraud in a Financial Statement Audit.* SAS 82 was written to help reduce the "expectation gap" that exists between financial statement auditors and users of financial statements. It was determined that SAS 82 would only be successful in narrowing the expectation gap if, as a result of applying the standard, (1) auditors detect more fraud sooner (that is, the standard bolsters the actual fraud detection performance of auditors), or (2) the standard is successful in convincing financial statement users that auditors should not be held responsible for detecting all financial statement fraud. Although many people were optimistic about the standard accomplishing the first of these possibilities, few believe that the second result will ever happen.

Although SAS 82 was a giant step forward, it did not narrow the expectations gap as much as hoped and it has now been replaced by SAS 99.

SAS 82 was an auditing standard that clarified the fraud detection responsibilities of certified public accountants (CPAs) and provided guidance to those who performed financial statement audits. Like all other standards, SAS 82 offered instructions on how the ten generally accepted auditing standards (GAAS) should be interpreted and followed. SAS 82 primarily provided guidance on how financial statement auditors should consider the possibility of fraud when:

- Exercising due professional care (general auditing standard No. 3)
- Planning an audit (fieldwork standard No. 1)
- Evaluating internal controls (fieldwork standard No. 2), and
- Gathering sufficient, competent evidentiary matter to support the audit opinion (fieldwork standard No. 3)

SAS 82 was much more comprehensive than the preceding fraud-related auditing standards. Although it did not change the overall responsibilities of GAAS auditors to provide "reasonable assurance that material misstatement of the financial statement does not exist," it more explicitly identified what auditors must do to try to discover such fraud. The following are the key provisions of the standard that were intended to remove the "fuzziness" that existed with previous standards, and that attempted to help auditors better detect material financial statement misstatement caused by fraud.

1. SAS 82 was the first-ever auditing standard that solely addresses fraud. Previous standards addressed "errors" and irregularities" together.
2. SAS 82 was the first GAAS auditing standard to use the term *fraud*. Previous standards used the more nebulous term *irregularity* when referring to fraud.
3. SAS 82 made it clear that the auditor's responsibilities with respect to fraud extend throughout the entire audit and do not end when the planning phase is finished. Previous standards were not clear regarding post-planning responsibilities.
4. SAS 82 required GAAS auditors to document how they assessed the risk of fraud in their audits. Previous fraud standards did not require specific documentation. There was a general feeling among SAS 82 task force members that requiring documentation would, in many cases, drive behavior that is consistent with the standard.
5. SAS 82 required GAAS auditors to document how they responded to the risks of fraud they discovered when conducting their audits. Previous standards hardly mentioned how risks of fraud should be documented, evaluated, or addressed.
6. SAS 82 emphasized the need for "professional skepticism" in dealing with clients.
7. SAS 82 provided specific guidance to auditors about the kind of risks they must consider (more than 30 different examples of risk factors are presented), and how observed risk factors should be considered and addressed.
8. SAS 82 required GAAS auditors to ask management specifically about the risks of fraud, what they perceive to be the company's greatest fraud exposures, and whether they have knowledge of fraud that has been perpetrated on or within the company.

## Statement on Auditing Standards No. 99: Considerations of Fraud in a Financial Statement Audit

Statement on Auditing Standards (SAS) 99 establishes standards and provided guidance to auditors in fulfilling their responsibility as it relates to fraud in an audit of financial statements conducted in accordance with generally accepted auditing standards (GAAS). SAS 99 does not change the auditor's responsibility to plan and perform the audit to obtain reasonable assurance about whether the financial statements are free of material misstatement, whether caused by error or fraud. However, SAS 99 does establish standards and provide guidance to auditors in fulfilling that responsibility, as it relates to fraud. The following is an overview of the content of SAS 99:

**Description and characteristics of fraud.** This section of the statement describes fraud and its characteristics, including the aspects of fraud particularly relevant to an audit of financial statements.

**Discussion among engagement personnel regarding the risks of material misstatement due to fraud.** This section requires, as part of planning the audit, that there be a discussion among the audit team members to consider the susceptibility of the entity to material misstatement due to fraud and to reinforce the importance of adopting an appropriate mindset of professional skepticism.

**Obtaining the information needed to identify the risks of material misstatement due to fraud.** This section requires the auditor to gather the information necessary to identify the risks of material misstatement due to fraud, by the following:

1. Making inquiries of management and others within the entity.
2. Considering the results of the analytical procedures performed in planning the audit. (The statement also requires that the auditor perform analytical procedures relating to revenue.)
3. Considering fraud risk factors.
4. Considering certain other information.

**Identifying risks that may result in a material misstatement due to fraud.** This section requires the auditor to use the information gathered above to identify risks that may result in a material misstatement due to fraud.

**Assessing the identified risks after taking into account an evaluation of the entity's programs and controls.** This section requires the auditor to evaluate the entity's programs and controls that address the identified risks of material misstatement due to fraud, and to assess the risks taking into account this evaluation.

**Responding to the results of the assessment.** This section requires the auditor to respond to the results of the risk assessment. This response may include the following:

1. A response to identified risks that has an overall effect on how the audit is conducted; that is, a response involving more general considerations apart from the specific procedures otherwise planned.
2. A response to identified risk that involves the nature, timing, and extent of the auditing procedures to be performed.
3. A response involving the performance of certain procedures to further address the risk of material misstatement due to fraud involving management override of controls.

**Evaluating audit test results.** This section requires the auditor's assessment of the risk of material misstatement due to fraud to be ongoing throughout the audit and the auditor evaluate at the completion of the audit whether the accumulated results of auditing procedures and other observations affect the assessment. It also requires the auditor to consider whether identified misstatements may be indicative of fraud and, if so, directs the auditor to evaluate their implications.

**Communicating about fraud to management, the audit committee, and others.** This section provides guidance regarding the auditor's communications about fraud to management, the audit committee, and others.

**Documenting the auditor's consideration of fraud.** This section describes related documentation requirements.

## The Roles of Management, Boards of Directors, and Audit Committees

Although auditors play a vital role in the detection of instances of material fraudulent financial reporting, the Treadway Commission's 1987 report noted that the prevention and early detection of fraudulent financial reporting must start with the entity that prepares the financial statements. Every fraudulent financial statement for which the auditor has been held responsible was prepared by executives who intentionally misstated financial information to deceive not only shareholders, investors, and creditors, but the auditor as well. Thus, the Treadway report contains several recommendations for public companies, particularly addressing responsibilities of top management, the board of directors, and audit committees. The Treadway report calls for all public companies to maintain internal controls that provide reasonable assurance that fraudulent financial reporting will be prevented or subjected to early detection. The Treadway Commission specifically calls for the development of additional, integrated guidance on internal controls.

## COSO's 1992 Report

In 1992, COSO issued *Internal Control—Integrated Framework* in response to calls for better internal control systems to help senior executives better control the enterprises they run. In addition to noting that internal controls can help an entity achieve its performance and profitability targets and prevent the loss of resources, COSO's report also notes that internal control can significantly help an entity ensure reliable financial reporting. Specifically, the COSO report:

- Provides a high-level overview of the internal control framework directed to the chief executive and other senior officers, board members, legislators, and regulators.
- Defines internal control, describe its components, and provide criteria against which managements, boards of directors, and others can assess their internal control systems.
- Provides guidance to those entities that report publicly on internal control over the preparation of their published statements.
- Contains materials that might be useful in conducting an evaluation of internal controls.

## Audit Committee Requirements of Major U.S. Stock Exchanges

Often, boards of directors of companies assign responsibility for oversight of the financial reporting process to an audit committee, comprised of a subgroup of the board. In the United States, all three major securities markets—the New York Stock Exchange (NYSE), American Stock Exchange (AMEX), and National Association of Securities Dealer's Automated Quotation System (NASDAQ)—have requirements addressing audit committee composition. The NYSE requires, and the AMEX recommends, that listed companies have audit committees made up entirely of outside directors.[4] NASDAQ requires only that a majority of the audit committee consist of outside directors for companies trading on the National Market System; however, companies trading as a NASDAQ Small-Cap Issue are not required to maintain a minimum number of outside directors on their audit committees. These audit committee requirements were generally in place by the time the Treadway report was issued. However, other regulatory actions were undertaken in the 1990s related to the corporate governance process. For example, the Federal Deposit Insurance Corporation implemented new audit committee composition requirements mandating the inclusion of independent directors who, for certain large depository institutions, must include individuals with banking experience.[5]

## Public Oversight Board's Advisory Panel Report

In 1994, the POB issued a report entitled *Strengthening the Professionalism of the Independent Auditor.* This report encouraged boards of directors to play an active role in the financial reporting process and for the auditing profession to look to the board of directors—the shareholders' representative—as its client. The Advisory Panel urged the POB, the SEC, and others to encourage adoption of proposals such as increasing the representation of outsiders on the board and reducing board size to strengthen the independence of boards of directors and their accountability to shareholders. In addition to strengthening the role of the board of directors in the oversight of management, the Advisory Panel recommended that audit committees should expect auditors to be more forthcoming in communicating first with the audit committee and then with the full board to provide the auditor's perspective on the company's operations, as well as the company's financial reporting policies and practices.

## Public Oversight Board's 1995 Report

The POB stated in their 1995 publication, *Directors, Management, and Auditors: Allies in Protecting Shareholder Interests,* that practices followed by well-governed corporations should foster an environment where the independent auditor, management, audit committee, and board of directors play interactive and timely roles in the financial reporting process.

After the Enron "debacle," there was significant controversy about the accounting profession and its regulation and oversight. Because of the criticism of the Public Oversight Board, it went out of business effective March 31, 2002.[6]

## The Independence Standards Board

To strengthen the role of the auditor as an independent assurer of credible financial information and a major source of information for the audit committee and board, the accounting profession and the SEC agreed in 1997 to establish a new private sector body—the Independence Standards Board—to set independence rules and guidance for auditors of public companies. The Independence Standards Board did not make a significant difference in the profession.

## Sarbanes-Oxley Act of 2002

All of the efforts described thus far have helped focus attention on and reduce the number of incidences of fraudulent financial reporting. However, none of them have had the impact that the Sarbanes-Oxley Act of 2002 had. SarBox as it is unofficially called, completely changed the corporate landscape with respect to fraud prevention, detection and investigation. Sarbanes-Oxley significantly increased the responsibility of auditors, boards of directors, audit committees, management and others. It was the most significant securities legislation since the SEC Acts of 1933 and 1934 that established the SEC and required SEC reporting.

Since we discussed Sarbanes-Oxley in detail in Appendix A in Chapter 11, we will not discuss it here. You should recognize its significance, however. Anyone interested in preventing, detecting, or investigating fraud or in working in a public company environment should be familiar with its contents.

## END NOTES

1. Marx, R. K., and H. A. Sharaf, "The Philosophy of Auditing," American Accounting Association, 1961.

2. http://www.aicpa.org/members/div/secps/lit/practice/943.htm

3. The Panel on Audit Effectiveness: Report and Recommendations, August 31, 2000, c/o The Public Oversight Board, One Station Place, Stamford, CT 06902. This report can be found at http://www.probauditpanel.org.

4. http://www.sec.gov/rules/sro/ny9939o.htm

5. This information can be accessed at the Federal Deposit Insurance Corporation web site at http://www.fdic.gov/regulations/laws/rules/2000-8500.html. Section D: Audit Committees.

6. http://www.smartpros.com/x33441.xml

# BIBLIOGRAPHY

Albrecht, Conan C., "Proactively Detecting Fraud," *Financial Post,* July 2001, pp. 13-15.

———, "Root Out Financial Deception," *Journal of Accountancy,* April 2002, pp. 30-36.

Albrecht, Conan C., Chad O. Albrecht, and Timothy Williams, "Conducting Ethical Investigations," *Security Management,* forthcoming.

Albrecht, Conan C., and J. Gregory Dunn, "Can Auditors Detect Fraud?" *Journal of Forensic Accounting,* Volume II, Number 1, January-June 2001, pp. 1-12.

———, "Conducting a Pro-Active Fraud Audit: A Case Study," *Journal of Forensic Accounting,* Volume II, No. 2, December 2001, pp. 203-219.

Albrecht, W. Steve, Conan C. Albrecht, and Chad O. Albrecht, "Fraud and Corporate Executives: Agency, Stewardship and Broken Trust," *Journal of Forensic Accounting,* Volume V, Number 1, January-June 2004, pp. 109-130.

Albrecht, W. Steve, M. B. Romney, D. J. Cherrington, I. R. Payne, and A. J. Roe, 1982, *How to Detect and Prevent Business Fraud,* Englewood Cliffs, NJ: Prentice-Hall.

Albrecht, W. Steve, and M. B. Romney, 1986, "Red-flagging Management Fraud: A Validation," *Advances in Accounting* 3: 323–333.

Albrecht, W. Steve, and J. J. Willingham, 1993, "An Evaluation of SAS No. 53: The Auditor's Responsibility to Detect and Report Errors and Irregularities," *The Expectation Gap Standards: Progress, Implementation Issues, Research Opportunities,* New York: AICPA.

Albrecht, W. Steve, G. W. Wernz, and T. L. Williams, 1995, *Fraud: Bringing Light to the Dark Side of Business,* New York, New York: Irwin Professional Publishing, pp. 56–59 and 118–119.

Albrecht, W. Steve, K. R. Howe, and M. B. Romney, 1982, *Detecting Fraud: The Internal Auditor's Perspective,* Maitland, FL: The Institute of Internal Auditors Research Foundation.

American Institute of Certified Public Accountants (AICPA). 1988. *Consideration of Fraud in a Financial Statement Audit.* Statement on Auditing Standards No 53. New York: AICPA.

———, 1997. *Consideration of Fraud in a Financial Statement Audit.* Statement on Auditing Standards No. 81. New York: AICPA.

———, 2002. *Consideration of Fraud in a Financial Statement Audit.* Statement on Auditing Standards No. 99, New York: AICPA.

Ashton, R. E., and A. Wright, 1989, "Identifying Audit Adjustments with Attention-Directing Procedures," *The Accounting Review,* Vol. LXIV, No. 4 (October): 710–728.

Association of Certified Fraud Examiners, 1995, *Report to the Nation: Occupational Fraud and Abuse,* Austin, Texas.

Beasley, M. S., J. V. Carcello, and D. R. Hermanson, 1999, *Fraudulent Financial Reporting: 1987–1997: An Analysis of U.S. Public Companies,* Committee of Sponsoring Organizations (COSO).

Bell, T. B., and J. V. Carcello, 1998, "Assessing the Likelihood of Fraudulent Financial Reporting," Working paper, Montvale, NJ: KPMG.

Bonner, S. E., Z. V. Palmrose, and S. M. Young, 1998, "Fraud Type and Auditor Litigation: An Analysis of SEC Accounting and Auditing Enforcement Releases," *The Accounting Review* 73 (October): 503–532.

Cressy, D. R., 1953, *Other People's Money: The Social Psychology of Embezzlement,* New York: Free Press.

Deshmukh, A., K. E. Karim, and P. H. Siegel, 1998, "An Analysis of the Efficiency and Effectiveness of Auditing to Detect Management Fraud: A Signal Detection Theory Approach," *International Journal of Auditing:* 127–138.

DeZoort, F. T., and T. A. Lee, 1998, "The Impact of SAS No. 82 on Perceptions of External Auditor Responsibility for Fraud Detection," *International Journal of Auditing:* 167–182.

Eining, M. M., and P. B. Dorr, 1991, "The Impact of Expert System Usage on Experiential Learning in an Audit Setting," *Journal of Information Systems* (Spring): 1–16.

Eining, M. M., D. R. Jones, and J. K. Loebbecke, 1997, "Reliance on Decision Aids: An Examination of Management Fraud," *Auditing: A Journal of Practice and Theory* 16 (Fall): 1–19.

Elliott, R. K., and J. J. Willingham, Jr., 1980, *Management Fraud: Detection and Deterrence,* New York: Petrocelli Books, Inc.

Erickson, M., B. W. Mayhew, and W. L. Felix, 2000. Why do audits fail? Evidence from Lincoln Savings and Loan, *Journal of Accounting Research* (Spring): 165-194.

Geis, G., 1982, *On White-Collar Crime,* Lexington, MA: Lexington Books.

Geis, G., and R. F. Meier, 1977, *White-Collar Crime: Offenses in Business, Politics, and the Professions,* Revised Edition, New York: The Free Press.

Glover, S.M., D. F. Prawitt, J.J. Schultz, Jr., and M. F. Zimbelman. 2003. A comparison of audit planning decisions in response to increased fraud risk: Before and after SAS No. 82. *Auditing: A Journal of Practice & Theory* (September): 237-251.

Green, B. P., and J. H. Choi, 1997, "Assessing the Risk of Management Fraud Through Neural Network Technology," *Auditing: A Journal of Practice and Theory* 16 (Spring): 14–28.

Guy, D. M., and J. M. Mancino, 1998, *Consideration of Fraud in a Financial Statement Audit: What Every CPA Should Know About SAS No. 82,* A 4-hour CPE course, New York, New York: AICPA, pp. 4-7.

Hackenbrack, K., 1993, "The Effects of Experience with Different Sized Clients on Auditor Evaluations of Fraudulent Financial Reporting Indicators," *Auditing: A Journal of Practice and Theory* 12 (Spring): pp. 99–110.

Hollinger, R. C., 1989, *Dishonesty in the Workplace: A Manager's Guide to Preventing Employee Theft,* Park Ridge, IL: London House Press.

Hylas, R. E., and R. H. Ashton, "Audit Detection of Financial Statement Errors," *The Accounting Review,* Vol. LVII, No. 4 (October): 751–765.

Knapp, C.Z., and M.C. Knapp, 2001. The effects of experience and explicit fraud risk assessment in detecting fraud with analytical procedures. *Accounting, Organizations and Society* 26: 25-37.

Loebbecke, J. K., and J. J. Willingham, Jr., 1988, "Review of SEC Accounting and Auditing Enforcement Releases," Working paper, University of Utah.

Loebbecke, J. K., M. M. Eining, and J. J. Willingham, Jr., 1989, "Auditors' Experience with Material Irregularities: Frequency, Nature, and Detect-Ability," *Auditing: A Journal of Practice and Theory* 9 (Fall): 1–28.

Merchant, K. A., 1987, *Fraudulent and Questionable Financial Reporting: A Corporate Perspective,* Morristown, NJ: Financial Executives Research Foundation.

Nieschwietz, R.J., J.J. Schultz, Jr. And M.F. Zimbelman. 2000. Empirical research on external auditors' detection of financial statement fraud, *Journal of Accounting Literature* 19: 190-246.

Palmrose, Z. V., 1987, "Litigation and Independent Auditors: The Role of Business Failures and Management Fraud," *Auditing: A Journal of Practice and Theory* 6 (Spring): 90–103.

Pincus, K. V., 1989, "The Efficacy of a Red Flags Questionnaire for Assessing the Possibility of Fraud," *Accounting, Organizations, and Society* 14: 153–163.

Romney, M. B., W. Steve Albrecht, and D. J. Cherrington, March 1980, "Red-flagging the White-Collar Criminal," *Management Accounting,* pp. 51–57.

Summers, S. L., and J. T. Sweeney, 1998, "Fraudulently Misstated Financial Statements and Insider Trading: An Empirical Analysis," *The Accounting Review* 73 (January): 131–146.

Sutherland, E. H., 1949, *White-Collar Crime,* New York: Dryden Press.

Zimbelman, M. F., 1997, "The Effects of SAS No. 82 on Auditors' Attention to Fraud Risk Factors and Audit Planning," *Journal of Accounting Research* 35 (Supplement): 75–97.

# GLOSSARY

## A

**Accounting and Auditing Enforcement Release (AAER)** Public document released by the SEC when a company commits financial statement fraud or other inappropriate activities.

**Accounting anomalies** Inaccurate or questionable source documents, accounting records, correspondence or other records; can be either electronic or paper and can be formal or informal records.

**Accounting cycle** Procedures for analyzing, recording, classifying, summarizing, and reporting the transactions of a business.

**Accounting system** Policies and procedures for recording economic transactions in an organized manner.

**Accounts receivable turnover ratio** The rate at which a company collects its receivables; computed by dividing sales by average accounts receivable.

**Accounts receivable turnover** Sales divided by average accounts receivable; a measure of the efficiency with which receivables are being collected.

**Accrued liability** Liabilities arising from end-of-period adjustments, not from specific transactions.

**Acquisition** The purchase of something, such as the purchase of one company by another company.

**Affidavit** Written statement or declaration given under oath.

**Allowance for doubtful accounts** A contra-asset (receivable) account representing the amount of receivables that are estimated to be uncollectible.

**Allowance for uncollectible assets as a percentage of receivables** Allowance for doubtful accounts divided by accounts receivable; a measure of the percentage of receivables estimated to be uncollectible.

**Analytical anomalies** Relationships, procedures, or events that do not make sense; anything unusual or unexpected.

**Appellate Court** Review court to which participants in lower court cases can have their cases reviewed or retried if they are unhappy with the outcome.

**Arraignment** Court hearing where charges against the defendant are read. At the arraignment, the defendants may plead guilty, not guilty, or nolo contendere.

**Asset fraud** Financial statement fraud in which assets are recorded at higher amounts than they should be.

**Asset misappropriations** Theft that is committed by stealing receipts, stealing assets on hand, or by committing some type of disbursement fraud.

**Asset turnover** Total sales divided by average total assets; a measure of the amount of sales revenue generated with each dollar of assets.

**Asset turnover ratio** Total sales divided by average total assets; a measure of the amount of sales revenue generated with each dollar of assets.

**Association of Certified Fraud Examiners (ACFE)** An international organization, based in Austin, Texas, dedicated to fighting fraud and white-collar crime.

**Audit command language (ACL)** Popular commercial data-mining software; helps investigators detect fraud.

**Audit trail** Documents and records that can be used to trace transactions.

**Autocratic management** Management conducted by a few key people who do not accept advice or participation from other employees.

## B

**Bad debt expense** An expense representing receivables and/or revenues that are presumed not to be collectible.

**Balance sheet** Financial statement that reports a company's assets, liabilities, and owners' equity as of a particular date.

**Bankruptcy** A legal process that either allows a debtor to work out an orderly plan to settle debts or to liquidate a debtor's assets and distribute them to creditors.

**Bankruptcy Code** Title 11 of the U.S. Code—the federal statute that governs the bankruptcy process.

**Bankruptcy Courts** Federal courts that hear only bankruptcy cases.

**Benford's law** Mathematical algorithm that accurately predicts that, for many data sets, the first digit of each group of numbers in a random sample will begin with a 1 more than a 2, a 2 more than a 3, a 3 more than a 4, and so on; predicts the percentage of time each digit will appear in a sequence of numbers.

**Bid-rigging scheme** Collusive fraud wherein an employee helps a vendor illegally obtain a contract that was supposed to involve competitive bidding.

**Billing scheme** Submission of a false or altered invoice that causes an employer to willingly issue a check.

**Biometrics** Using unique features of the human body (for example, retinal scans) to create secure access controls.

**Bribery** The offering, giving, receiving, or soliciting anything of value to influence an official act.

**Bust-out** A planned bankruptcy.

## C

**Capitalization** Recording expenditures as assets rather than as expenses. (For example, start-up costs that are "capitalized" are recorded as assets and amortized.)

**Chain letter scam** Fraudsters promise to pay victims to make copies of a letter and send them to consumers. In order to get the letter the victims must pay an advance fee.

**Chain of custody** Maintaining detailed records about documents from the time they are received in the investigation process until the trial is completed. Helps to substantiate that documents have not been altered or manipulated since coming into the investigator's hands.

**Chapter 11 bankruptcy** Bankruptcy that allows the bankrupt entity time to reorganize its operational and financial affairs, settle its debts, and continue to operate in a reorganized fashion.

**Chapter 7 bankruptcy** Complete liquidation or "shutting down of a business" and distribution of any proceeds to creditors.

**Check tampering** Scheme in which dishonest employees (1) prepare fraudulent checks for their own benefit, or (2) intercept checks intended for a third party and convert the checks for their own benefit.

**Civil law** Body of law that provides remedies for violation of private rights—deals with rights and duties between individuals.

**Clearinghouse scam** Involves a victim receiving a letter that falsely claims the writer represents a foreign bank. This foreign bank falsely acts as a clearinghouse for venture capital in a certain country.

**Code of conduct** A written statement that conveys expectations about what is and is not appropriate in an organization.

**Collusion** Fraud perpetrated by two or more employees or others, each of whose job responsibilities is necessary to complete the fraud.

**Commercial data-mining software** Commercial software packages that use query techniques to detect patterns and anomalies in data that may suggest fraud.

**Committee of Sponsoring Organizations (COSO)** Organization made up of representatives from major accounting firms that focus on internal controls and financial statement fraud.

**Common-size financial statements** Financial statements that have been converted to percentages.

**Complaint** Request filed by a plaintiff to request civil proceedings against someone—usually to seek damages.

**Concealment** Efforts taken to hide a fraud from being discovered.

**Concealment investigative methods** Investigating a fraud by focusing on the cover-up efforts, such as the manipulation of source documents.

**Conflicts of Interest** Fraud in which employees, managers or executives put their personal interest above the company's interest, usually resulting in an adverse affect on the organization.

**Consumer fraud** Any fraud that takes place against a consumer or individual.

**Contingent liability** A possible liability. If the likelihood of payment is "probable," the contingent liability must be reported as a liability on the financial statements; if likelihood of payment is reasonably possible, it must be disclosed in the footnotes to the financial statements; if likelihood of payment is remote, no mention of the possible liability needs to be made.

**Control activities or procedures** Specific error-checking routines performed by company personnel.

**Control environment** The actions, policies, and procedures that reflect the overall attitudes of top management, the directors, and the owners about control and its importance to the entity.

**Conversion** The spending of stolen assets by perpetrators.

**Corruption** Dishonesty that involves the following schemes: (1) bribery, (2) conflicts of interest, (3) economic extortion, and (4) illegal gratuities.

**Cost of goods sold** The cost of goods sold to customers; calculated by subtracting ending inventory from the sum of beginning inventory plus purchases.

**Covert operations** Placing an agent in an undercover role in order to observe the suspect.

**Craft assembly scams** Perpetrators falsely promise high pay for working on different projects. Victims are usually required to purchase costly materials, equipment, and training.

**Creditor** A person or entity owed money by a debtor.

**Criminal law** Branch of law that deals with offenses of a public nature or against society.

**Current ratio** Measure of the liquidity of a business; equal to current assets divided by current liabilities.

**Customer fraud** Customers not paying for goods purchased, getting something for nothing, or deceiving organizations into giving them something they should not have.

## D

**Data theft** Theft of data or personal information through such means as sniffing, spoofing, and customer impersonation.

**Database** Set of interrelated, centrally controlled data files that are stored with as little redundancy as possible. A database consolidates many records previously stored in separate files into a common pool of data and serves a variety of users and data processing applications.

**Debtor** A person or entity declaring bankruptcy.

**Debt-to-equity ratio** The number of dollars of borrowed funds for every dollar invested by owners; computed as total liabilities divided by total equity.

**Deductive fraud detection** Determining the types of frauds that can occur and then using query techniques and other methods to determine if those frauds may actually exist.

**Deferred asset** Expenditure that has been capitalized to be expensed in the future.

**Deposition** Sworn testimony taken before a trial begins. At depositions, the opposing side's attorneys ask questions of witnesses.

**Digital signatures and certificates** A signature sent over the Internet.

**Disbursement fraud** Having an organization pay for something it shouldn't pay for or pay too much for something it purchases.

**Disbursement of money from wills** Organizations receive letters from mysterious "benefactors" interested in contributing a large sum of money. However, to get the money, the charity is required to pay inheritance taxes or government fees.

**Disclosure fraud** The issuance of fraudulent or misleading statements or press releases without financial statement line-item effect or the lack of appropriate disclosures that should have been, but were not, made by management.

**Discovery sampling** Sampling used in fraud detection that assumes a zero expected error rate. The methodology allows an auditor to determine confidence levels and make inferences from the sample to the population.

**Discovery** Legal process by which each party's attorneys try to find all information about the other side's case before a trial begins.

**Divorce** The legal separation of two married partners resulting in the dissolution of their marriage.

**Document examiner** Specialized investigator who applies forensic chemistry, microscopy, photography, and other scientific methods to determine whether documents or other evidence are genuine, forged, counterfeit, or fraudulent.

**Documentary evidence** Evidence gathered from paper, documents, computer records, and other written, printed, or electronic sources.

**Documents and records** Documentation of all transactions in order to create an audit trail.

**Dummy or shell company** Fictitious entity created for the sole purpose of committing fraud; usually involves an employee making fraudulent payments to the dummy company.

## E

**Earnings per share** Net income divided by the number of shares of stock outstanding; a measure of profitability.

**E-Business** The use of information technology and electronic communication networks to exchange business information and conduct transactions in electronic, paperless form.

**Economic Extortion** Demanding payment from a vendor in order to make a decision in the vendor's favor; opposite of bribery.

**Economic extortion scheme** Involves an employee demanding payment from a vendor in order to make or influence a decision in that vendor's favor.

**Electronic surveillance** Using video, e-mail, wire-tapping, and so on to watch fraud suspects.

**Elements of fraud** The theft act, concealment, and conversion that are present in every fraud.

**Embezzlement** Theft or fraudulent appropriation of money through deception; often used interchangeably with the term fraud.

**Employee Assistance Programs (EAPs)** Programs that help employees deal with problems such as substance abuse, gambling, money management and debt, health, family, and other pressures.

**Employee embezzlement** Employees deceiving their employers by taking company assets.

**Evidence square** A categorization of fraud investigative procedures that includes testimonial evidence, documentary evidence, physical evidence, and personal observation.

**Evidential matter** The underlying data and all corroborating information available about a fraud.

**Expense scheme** Scheme in which perpetrators produce false documents to claim false expenses.

**Expense Schemes** Recording a fictitious expense and having the organization pay for it; examples are travel reimbursement schemes, fictitious payroll, etc.

**Expert witness** Trial witness who can offer opinions about a matter, based on unique experience, education, or training.

## F

**Falsified identity (customer impersonation)** Pretending to be someone you're not—a major problem in e-business transactions.

**Federal Courts** Courts established by the federal government to enforce federal laws and statutes.

**Fidelity bonding** Insurance coverage purchased by employers to provide reimbursement for amounts stolen by employees.

**Fifth Amendment to the U.S. Constitution** Provides defendants certain protections, including (1) an indictment by a grand jury before being held for a capital crime, and (2) not being tried twice for the same crime.

**Financial statement fraud** Intentional misstatement of financial statements by omitting critical facts or disclosures, misstating amounts, or misapplying GAAP.

**Financial statements** Financial reports such as the balance sheet, income statement, and statement of cash flows that summarize the profitability and cash flows of an entity for a specific period and the financial position of the entity as of a specific date.

**Fixed assets** Property, plant, and equipment assets of an organization.

**Fixed point surveillance** Watching a fraud suspect from a fixed point, such as a restaurant, office, or other set location.

**Footnotes** Information that accompanies a company's financial statements and that provides interpretive guidance to the financial statements or includes related information that must be disclosed.

**Foreign advance-fee scam** Any scam in which the perpetrator claims to be a foreigner, and the victim is required to pay "up-front" fees or taxes in order to receive a substantial amount of money.

**Fourth Amendment to the U.S. Constitution** Protects defendants against unreasonable searches and seizures by the government.

**Fraud** "A generic term that embraces all the multi-farious means which human ingenuity can devise, which are resorted to by one individual, to get an advantage over another by false representations. No definite and invariable rule can be laid down as a general proposition in defining fraud, as it includes surprise, trickery, cunning and unfair ways by which another is cheated. The only boundaries defining it are those which limit human knavery."

**Fraud detection** The activity of searching for or finding indicators that suggest that fraud may be occurring, finding predication of fraud.

**Fraud investigation** Following up on fraud predication to determine if fraud is or has occurred and, if so, by whom, for how much, in what ways, and where. The process of gathering evidence to either confirm or reject the fraud predication.

**Fraud prevention** All efforts and means extended to deter fraud from occurring; involves eliminating perceived pressures, perceived opportunities and/or rationalizations; any action that discourages or diminishes the likelihood that fraud will occur

**Front loading** A fraudulent process whereby representatives of legitimate or fraudulent MLMs are required to buy large, expensive amounts of inventory.

## G

**Gramm-Leach Bliley Act** Passed in 1999, this law prohibits the use of false pretenses to access the personal information of others. It does allow banks and other financial institutions to share or sell customer information, unless customers proactively "opt out" and asks that their information not be shared.

**Grand jury** Body of 4 to 23 individuals who deliberate in secret to decide whether there is sufficient evidence to charge someone in a preliminary hearing.

**Gross profit margin** Gross profit margin divided by net sales; a measure of markup.

**Ground floor opportunity** A classic marketing scheme that makes people believe that they will make money simply because they are one of the earliest investors in a new venture.

## H

**Headhunter fees** Fees paid as commission for recruiting someone to fill a position; often paid in multi-level marketing organizations.

**Higher trial courts** State courts that try felony (larger crimes) and civil cases above a predetermined amount.

**Horizontal analysis** Tool that determines the percentage change in balance sheet and income statement numbers from one period to the next.

## I

**Identity theft** A term used to describe those circumstances when someone uses another person's name, address, Social Security number, bank or credit card account number, or other identifying information to commit fraud or other crimes.

**Illegal gratuities** Similar to bribery, except that there is no intent to influence a particular business decision, but rather to reward someone for making a favorable decision.

**Inadequate disclosure fraud** The issuance of fraudulent or misleading statements or press releases without financial statement line-item effect or the lack of appropriate disclosures that should have been but were not made by management.

**Income statement** Financial statement that reports the amount of net income earned by a company during a specified period.

**Independent checks** Procedures for verifying and monitoring other controls.

**Inductive fraud detection** Proactively searching for fraud by identifying anomalies or unusual or unexpected patterns and/or relationships, without determining in advance the kinds of fraud you are looking for.

**Inherent risks** A business's susceptibility to fraud, errors and other problems, assuming that appropriate controls are not in place.

**Initial pleading** Complaint filed by a plaintiff to request legal proceedings against someone.

**Intangible asset** An asset that has no tangible existence (for example, goodwill).

**Intent** Knowingly and purposefully engaging in deceitful activities for the purpose of taking advantage.

**Internal control structure** Specific policies and procedures designed to provide management with reasonable assurance that the goals and objectives it believes important to the entity will be met.

**Internal control weakness** Weakness in the control environment, accounting system, or the control activities or procedures.

**Interrogatory** A series of written questions that specifically identify information needed from the opposing party.

**Inventory turnover ratio** Measure of the efficiency with which inventory is managed; computed by dividing cost of goods sold by average inventory for a period.

**Investment fraud** Any fraud related to stocks, bonds, commodities, limited partnerships, real estate, or other types of investments.

**Investment scams** The selling of fraudulent and worthless investments to unsuspecting investors.

**Invigilation** Imposing strict temporary controls on an activity so that, during the observation period, fraud is virtually impossible. Involves keeping detailed records before, during, and after the invigilation period and comparing suspicious activity during the three periods to obtain evidence about whether fraud is occurring.

## J

**Jurisdiction** The limit or territory over which an organization has authority.

## K

**Kickback fraud** Fraud perpetrated by an employee and the employee's vendor or customer. Usually involves the employee buying goods or services from the vendor at an overstated price or giving the customer a lower-than-normal price, and in return the vendor or customer pays the employee a "kickback."

**Kiting** Fraud that conceals cash shortages by (1) transferring funds from one bank to another and (2) recording the receipt on or before the balance sheet date and the disbursement after the balance sheet date.

## L

**Labeling** A term used by moral development researchers to imply teaching and training.

**Lapping** Fraud that involves stealing one customer's payment and then crediting that customer's account when a subsequent customer pays.

**Larceny** Intentionally taking an employer's cash or other assets without the consent and against the will of the employer, after it has been recorded in the company's accounting system.

**Lease** Obligation to make periodic payments over a specified period for use or "rent" of an asset; does not involve ownership of the asset.

**Liability frauds** Financial statement fraud in which liabilities (amounts owed to others) are understated.

**Lien** Claim on property for the satisfaction of just debt.

**Lower trial courts** State courts that try misdemeanors (small crimes) and pretrial issues.

## M

**Mail stuffing scam** A scam that promises income simply for stuffing envelopes. Victims are required to pay considerable up-front cost for information about the opportunity.

**Management fraud** Deception perpetrated by an organization's top management through the manipulation of financial statement amounts or disclosures.

**Marketable securities** Stocks, bonds, and other non-cash assets; sometimes called short-term investments.

**Marking the evidence** Placing unique identification tags or descriptions on documents when they are received, so that they can be identified during the investigation and trial process.

**Merger** Combining of two organizations into one business entity.

**Misappropriation** Another name for frauds committed against an organization.

**Miscellaneous fraud** Deception that doesn't fall into any of the other five categories of fraud.

**Mobile observation** Another term for tailing.

**Modeling** Setting an example.

**Mortgage** Long-term loan secured by property, such as a home mortgage.

**Motion** Response to a complaint or pleading by the defendant. Sometimes "motion" refers to any request made to the judge for a ruling in a case by either party.

**Motion for dismissal** Request to the judge to dismiss a claim because there is no genuine issue of a material fact.

**Moving surveillance** Another term for tailing; involves following suspects wherever they go (within limits) and observing or recording their activities.

**Multilevel marketing (MLM) organization** A form of business in which company representatives build networks of individuals under them to sell products or market services and then get commissions for each sale made by their network. MLM's can be legitimate or illegitimate, depending on whether products are involved and whether marketing practices are ethical.

**Mystery shopping scams** Perpetrators falsely promise victims a job that involves shopping for merchandise and filing reports on the experiences for substantial compensation.

## N

**National Crime Information Center (NCIC)** The major criminal database maintained by the FBI. This database contains information on stolen vehicles, securities, boats, missing persons, and other information helpful in fraud investigations.

**Net income** An overall measure of the performance of a company; equal to revenues minus expenses for the period.

**Net worth method** Analytical method that estimates a suspect's unexplained income. Liabilities are subtracted from assets to give net worth, then the previous year's net worth is subtracted to find the increase in net worth. Living expenses are then added to the change in net worth to determine a person's total income, and finally known income is subtracted from total income to determine the unknown income.

**Nigerian money offers** A form of foreign advance-fee scams in which individuals from Nigeria or another underdeveloped country contact victims and offer millions of dollars.

**Nolo contendere** Plea by a defendant that does not contest the charges but does not admit guilt.

**Nonsampling risk** Risk that a sample will be examined and the characteristics of the sample will be misinterpreted.

**Number of days in receivables** 365 (number of days in a year) divided by accounts receivable turnover; a measure of how long it takes to collect receivables.

## O

**Operating performance ratio** Net income divided by total sales; a measure of the percentage of revenues that become profits.

**Opportunity meeting** A high-pressure meeting in which fraudsters influence individuals to invest money in fraudulent organizations.

**Opting-out right** Right of customers to give written notice to financial institutions that prohibits the institution from sharing or selling customer's personal information.

**Overstatement of asset fraud** Financial statement fraud involving recording assets at amounts higher than they should be.

## P

**Participative management** Management style that expects everyone in the organization to take ownership and responsibility for their conduct and responsibilities and that allows input into decisions.

**Passwords** Secret codes or names that allow users to access networks and other computer systems.

**Payroll fraud scheme** Using the payroll function to commit fraud, such as creating ghost employees or overpaying wages.

**Pension** Postretirement cash benefits paid to former employees.

**Perceived opportunity** A situation where people believe they have a favorable or promising combination of circumstances to commit fraud and not be detected.

**Perceived pressure** A situation where people perceive they have a need to commit fraud; a constraining influence on the will or mind, as a moral force.

**Perpetrator** A person who has committed a fraud.

**Personal observation evidence** Evidence that is sensed (seen, heard, felt, etc.) by investigators.

**Phishers** Fraudsters who engage in phishing.

**Phishing** A high-tech scam that uses spam or pop-up messages to deceive consumers into disclosing credit card numbers, bank account information, Social Security number, passwords, or other sensitive information.

**Physical evidence** Evidence of a tangible nature—includes fingerprints, tire marks, weapons, stolen property, identification numbers or marks on stolen objects, and so on—that can be used in an investigation to provide information about a fraud or other crime.

**Physical safeguards** Vaults, fences, locks, and so on that protect assets from theft.

**Ponzi schemes** Name given for a variety of fraudulent multilevel marketing organizations and pyramid schemes.

**Population** Collection of all units with similar characteristics from which samples are drawn.

**Postal inspectors** Inspectors or investigators hired by the U.S. Postal Service to handle major fraud cases that are perpetrated through the U.S. mail system.

**Predication** Circumstances that, taken as a whole, would lead a reasonable, prudent professional to believe that a fraud has occurred, is occurring, or will occur.

**Preliminary hearing** Pretrial hearing to determine whether there is "probable cause" to charge the defendant with a crime.

**Product testing fraud** Falsely promising to consumers the opportunity to review products and send their commentaries to suppliers for substantial income. Victims are required to pay enrollment fees ranging from $10 to $25.

**Profit margin** Measure of the profit generated from each dollar of revenue; calculated by dividing net income by revenue. Also known as return on sales, profit margin percentage, profit margin ratio, operating performance ratio.

**Psychopath** A person with a personality disorder, especially one manifested in aggressively antisocial behavior.

**Pyramid schemes** A manipulated multilevel marketing organization where fraudsters—instead of selling real, legitimate products—sell only illusionary products and profits. Investments of subsequent investors are used to pay the promised returns of earlier investors.

## Q

**Quick (acid-test) ratio** Measure of a firm's ability to meet current liabilities, computed by dividing net quick assets (all current assets, except inventories and prepaid expenses) by current liabilities.

## R

**Rationalization** Self-satisfying but incorrect reasons for one's behavior.

**Register disbursement scheme** Scheme that involves false refunds or false voids.

**Remedy** Judgments asked for in civil cases (what it would take to right a private wrong).

**Repurchase agreements** Agreement to buy back something previously sold.

**Request for admission** Request that the opposing party admit designated facts relevant to litigation.

**Restructuring** Reevaluation of a company's assets because of impairment of value or for other reasons. Restructured companies usually have lower amounts of assets and look quite different than before the restructuring.

**Return on equity** Measure of the profit earned per dollar of investment; computed by dividing net income by equity.

**Revenue recognition** Determining that revenues have been earned and are collectible and thus should be reported on the income statement.

**Revenue** Increases in a company's resources from the sale of goods or services.

**Risk assessment** The identification, analysis, and management of risk, such as the risk associated with the possibility of fraud.

## S

**Sale of crude oil at below-market price fraud** Involves a victim receiving a letter that falsely offers the opportunity to purchase crude oil at prices well below market price.

**Sales return percentage (ratio)** Sales returns divided by total sales; a measure of the percentage of sales being returned by customers.

**Sales returns (sales returns and allowances)** Sold merchandise that is returned by customers and/or damaged, or other sold merchandise for which credit is given.

**Sample** Portion of the population that is examined in order to draw inferences about the population.

**Sampling risk** Risk that a sample is not representative of the population.

**Sarbanes-Oxley** U.S. legislation passed in 2002 whose goal is to minimize the occurrence of fraud and increase the penalties for perpetrators when it occurs.

**Search warrant** Order issued by a judge that gives the investigator consent to search a suspect's personal information, such as bank records, tax returns, or their premises.

**SEC enforcement release** A public document released by the SEC when a company commits financial statement fraud or other perceived inappropriate activities.

**Securities and Exchange Commission (SEC)** Government body responsible for regulating stock trading and the financial statements and reports of public companies.

**Security through obscurity** Reliance upon secrecy of design, implementation, or holes to provide security rather than the use of time-tested methods that have withstood public scrutiny.

**Segregation of duties** Division of tasks into two parts, so one person does not have complete control of the task.

**Settlement** Negotiated pretrial agreement between the parties to resolve a legal dispute.

**Shoulder surfing** A process in which criminals watch consumers from a nearby location as they give credit card or other valuable information over the phone.

**Sixth Amendment to the U.S. Constitution** Provides trial-related protections to defendants, such as the right to a speedy trial and the right to be heard by an impartial jury.

**Skimming** Removal of cash from a victim organization prior to its entry in an accounting system.

**Snake oil plans** Plans that promise enormous earnings or claim to sell miracle products.

**Sniffing** Illegal or unauthorized viewing of information as it passes along a network communication channel.

**Spoofing** Changing the information in an e-mail header or an IP address used to hide identities.

**Statement of cash flows** Financial statement that reports an entity's cash inflows (receipts) and outflows (payments) during an accounting period.

**Static surveillance** Another term for fixed-point surveillance.

**Stationary surveillance** Locating a scene to be observed, anticipating the actions that are most likely to occur at the scene, and keeping detailed notes on tape or film on all activities involving the suspect.

**Statistical analysis** The use of statistics and number patterns to discover relationships in certain data, such as Benford's law.

**Statute** A law or regulation; a law enacted by the legislative branch of a government.

**Subpoena (subpoena duces tecum)** Order issued by a court or a grand jury to produce documents or requiring a witness to submit to a deposition, give testimony at trial, or report to an administrative body.

**Surveillance** Investigation technique that relies on the senses, especially hearing and seeing.

**System of authorizations** A system of limits on who can and cannot perform certain functions.

## T

**Tailing** Secretly following a fraud suspect in an attempt to gain additional information; another name for moving surveillance.

**Tax courts** Federal courts that hear only tax cases.

**Tax fraud** Willfully and intentionally violating the legal duty of voluntarily filing income tax returns and/or paying the correct amount of income, employment, or excise taxes.

**10-K** Annual report filed by publicly traded companies to the SEC.

**10-Q** Quarterly report filed by publicly traded companies to the SEC.

**Telemarketing fraud** Any fraud in which the perpetrator communicates with the victim via telephone.

**Testimonial evidence** Evidence based on querying techniques, such as interviewing, interrogation, and honesty testing.

**Theft act** The commission of a fraud.

**Theft Act Investigation** Fraud investigation methods that focus on the fraudulent transfer of assets; includes surveillance, invigilation, seizing computers and examing physical evidence.

**Theft investigation methods** Investigation methods that focus on the actual transfer of assets from the victim to the perpetrator; helps determine how the theft was committed and often includes methods such as surveillance and covert operations, invigilation, and the obtaining of physical evidence.

**Trash investigation** Searching through a person's trash for possible evidence in an investigation.

**Treadway Commission** National Commission on Fraudulent Financial Reporting that made recommendations on financial statement fraud and other matters in 1987.

**Trustee** Individual or firm who collects a debtor's assets and distributes them to creditors.

## U

**Understatement of liability fraud** Financial statement fraud that involves understating liabilities or amounts owed to others.

**Unearned revenues** Amounts that have been received from customers but for which performance of a service or sale of a product has not yet been made.

## V

**Vendor fraud** An overcharge for purchased goods, the shipment of inferior goods, or the nonshipment of goods even though payment is made.

**Vertical analysis** Tool that converts financial statement numbers to percentages so that they are easy to understand and analyze.

**Victim** The person or organization deceived by the perpetrator.

**Voir dire** Legal process of qualifying an expert witness.

**Vulnerability chart** Tool that coordinates the various elements of a fraud investigation to help identify possible suspects.

## W

**Warrant** Order issued by a judge to arrest someone.

**Warranty liabilities** Obligation to perform service and repair items sold within a specific period of time and/or use after sale.

**Web-visit hijacking** Mimicking another, similarly named web site in order to trick or confuse e-mail and e-business users into sending information to a business other than the intended one.

**Whistle-blower system** A response mechanism that makes it easy for employees and others to report questionable activities. (Also called hotlines.)

**Working capital turnover ratio** Sales divided by average working capital; a measure of the amount of working capital used to generate revenues.

# INDEX

## E

## G

## H